The Sporting Life
TRAINERS REVIEW
Flat Season 1994

Compiled by
John Bigley, Colin Havercroft and Michael Frost

Published 1994 by The Sporting Life
One Canada Square, Canary Wharf, London E14 5AP

© 1994 The Sporting Life

ISBN 0 901091 75 8

Editorial and Production by Martin Pickering Bloodstock Services
Cover designed by P. W. Reprosharp Ltd, London EC1
Cover printed by Robert Pearce & Co Ltd, Orpington, Kent
Text printed by Bath Press Ltd, Bath and London

Cover picture
Collage of Leading Trainers: *Left to right: Peter Chapple-Hyam, Mark Prescott, David Loder, Roger Charlton, Mark Johnston, Michael Bell, Reg Akehurst, Henry Cecil, Julie Cecil, William Haggas, Lynda Ramsden and Mick Channon.*
(Photographs: Ray Wright)

CONTENTS

TRAINER SECTION

MRS V ACONLEY (Westow, North Yorks)

	No. of Horses	Races Run	1st	2nd	3rd	Unpl	Per cent	£1 Level Stake
2-y-o	3	5	0	0	1	4	-	- 5.00
3-y-o	3	17	0	2	1	14	-	- 17.00
4-y-o+	10	37	1	2	0	34	2.7	- 29.00
Totals	16	59	1	4	2	52	1.7	- 51.00

Jan	Feb	Mar	Apr	May	Jun	Jul	Aug	Sep	Oct/Nov
0-7	0-4	0-2	0-5	0-6	1-8	0-11	0-7	0-7	0-2

Winning Jockey	W-R	£1 Level Stake	Winning Course	W-R	£1 Level Stake
L Dettori	1-3	+ 5.00	Pontefract	1-8	0.00

Winning Horse	Age	Races Run	1st	2nd	3rd	Unpl	Win £
Eightandahalf	5	4	1	0	0	3	3,028

Favourites	0-1		Total winning prize-money	£3,028

1993 Form	6-56	10.7%	- 18.00	1991 Form	1-32	3.1%	- 23.00
1992 Form	0-51			1990 Form	0-2		

J AKEHURST (Upper Lambourn, Berks)

	No. of Horses	Races Run	1st	2nd	3rd	Unpl	Per cent	£1 Level Stake
2-y-o	5	19	1	0	2	16	5.3	+ 7.00
3-y-o	3	22	2	2	0	18	9.1	- 6.50
4-y-o+	3	18	2	0	2	14	11.1	+ 2.00
Totals	11	59	5	2	4	48	8.5	+ 2.50

Jan	Feb	Mar	Apr	May	Jun	Jul	Aug	Sep	Oct/Nov
0-0	0-0	0-0	0-2	0-8	0-4	2-10	1-14	2-12	0-9

Winning Jockeys	W-R	£1 Level Stake		W-R	£1 Level Stake
G Carter	3-14	+ 14.00	S Sanders	1-3	+ 23.00
L Dettori	1-2	+ 5.50			

Winning Courses					
Haydock	1-1	+ 4.00	Salisbury	1-7	+ 8.00
Goodwood	1-2	+ 24.00	Sandown	1-10	- 2.50
Brighton	1-3	+ 5.00			

Winning Horses	Age	Races Run	1st	2nd	3rd	Unpl	Win £
Lord Oberon	6	14	2	0	2	10	6,256
Hi-Aud	2	6	1	0	1	4	4,338
Thatcherella	3	9	1	1	0	7	3,649
Admiralella	3	10	1	1	0	8	2,381

Favourites	1-3	33.3%	+ 2.00	Total winning prize-money			£16,624

1993 Form	3-73	4.1%	- 58.12	1991 Form	13-95	13.7%	+ 35.63
1992 Form	6-87	6.9%	- 53.50	1990 Form	4-31	12.9%	- 10.62

R AKEHURST (Epsom, Surrey)

	No. of Horses	Races Run	1st	2nd	3rd	Unpl	Per cent	£1 Level Stake
2-y-o	10	31	2	3	5	21	6.5	- 22.75
3-y-o	16	84	5	3	8	68	6.0	- 36.00
4-y-o+	49	254	41	35	25	153	16.1	+ 54.74
Totals	75	369	48	41	38	242	13.0	- 4.01

BY MONTH

2-y-o	W-R	Per cent	£1 Level Stake	3-y-o	W-R	Per cent	£1 Level Stake
January	0-0	-	0.00	January	0-0	-	0.00
February	0-0	-	0.00	February	0-0	-	0.00
March	0-0	-	0.00	March	0-1	-	- 1.00
April	0-0	-	0.00	April	0-8	-	- 8.00
May	0-1	-	- 1.00	May	2-15	13.3	- 1.00
June	0-1	-	- 1.00	June	0-10	-	- 10.00
July	0-3	-	- 3.00	July	1-13	7.7	- 2.00
August	1-5	20.0	- 0.50	August	0-15	-	- 15.00
September	1-9	11.1	- 5.25	September	0-9	-	- 9.00
Oct/Nov	0-12	-	- 12.00	Oct/Nov	2-13	15.4	+ 10.00

4-y-o+	W-R	Per cent	£1 Level Stake	Totals	W-R	Per cent	£1 Level Stake
January	1-9	11.1	+ 17.00	January	1-9	11.1	+ 17.00
February	0-2	-	- 2.00	February	0-2	-	- 2.00
March	0-3	-	- 3.00	March	0-4	-	- 4.00
April	4-26	15.4	+ 6.00	April	4-34	11.8	- 2.00
May	5-33	15.2	+ 3.00	May	7-49	14.3	+ 1.00
June	8-36	22.2	+ 32.40	June	8-47	17.0	+ 21.40
July	9-38	23.7	+ 26.46	July	10-54	18.5	+ 21.46
August	7-35	20.0	+ 4.13	August	8-55	14.5	- 11.37
September	2-34	5.9	- 21.75	September	3-52	5.8	- 36.00
Oct/Nov	5-38	13.2	- 7.50	Oct/Nov	7-63	11.1	- 9.50

DISTANCE

2-y-o	W-R	Per cent	£1 Level Stake	3-y-o	W-R	Per cent	£1 Level Stake
5f-6f	1-14	7.1	- 9.50	5f-6f	1-25	4.0	- 10.00
7f-8f	1-17	5.9	- 13.25	7f-8f	2-43	4.7	- 24.00
9f-13f	0-0	-	0.00	9f-13f	1-10	10.0	- 4.00
14f+	0-0	-	0.00	14f+	1-6	16.7	+ 2.00

4-y-o+	W-R	Per cent	£1 Level Stake	Totals	W-R	Per cent	£1 Level Stake
5f-6f	3-23	13.0	- 2.00	5f-6f	5-62	8.1	- 21.50
7f-8f	8-80	10.0	+ 14.75	7f-8f	11-140	7.9	- 22.50
9f-13f	18-97	18.6	+ 28.16	9f-13f	19-107	17.8	+ 24.16
14f+	12-54	22.2	+ 13.83	14f+	13-60	21.7	+ 15.83

TYPE OF RACE

Non-Handicaps	W-R	Per cent	£1 Level Stake	Handicaps	W-R	Per cent	£1 Level Stake
2-y-o	2-26	7.7	- 17.75	2-y-o	0-4	-	- 4.00
3-y-o	1-27	3.7	- 19.00	3-y-o	4-51	7.8	- 11.00
4-y-o+	5-33	15.2	+ 15.50	4-y-o+	29-185	15.7	+ 39.21
Selling	0-10	-	- 10.00	Selling	2-9	22.2	- 3.62
Apprentice	0-3	-	- 3.00	Apprentice	3-17	17.6	+ 4.90
Amat/Ladies	1-1	100.0	+ 1.75	Amat/Ladies	1-3	33.3	+ 3.00
Totals	9-100	9.0	- 32.50	Totals	39-269	14.5	+ 28.49

COURSE GRADE

	W-R	Per cent	£1 Level Stake
Group 1	20-184	10.9	- 5.27
Group 2	13-70	18.6	- 1.37
Group 3	9-58	15.5	+ 11.75
Group 4	6-57	10.5	- 9.12

FIRST TIME OUT

	W-R	Per cent	£1 Level Stake
2-y-o	0-7	-	- 7.00
3-y-o	1-13	7.7	- 5.00
4-y-o+	4-44	9.1	- 24.50
Totals	5-64	7.8	- 36.50

JOCKEYS RIDING

	W-R	Per cent	£1 Level Stake		W-R	Per cent	£1 Level Stake
T Quinn	14-109	12.8	- 25.79	G Bardwell	1-4	25.0	+ 0.50
A Munro	7-25	28.0	+ 48.38	D Holland	1-5	20.0	+ 2.50
S Sanders	6-46	13.0	+ 21.15	Pat Eddery	1-7	14.3	- 1.00
A Clark	4-26	15.4	- 2.50	C Rutter	1-7	14.3	- 4.00
G Carter	3-9	33.3	+ 11.50	Paul Eddery	1-8	12.5	+ 18.00
J Quinn	3-30	10.0	- 9.50	R Perham	1-8	12.5	0.00
Mr T McCarthy	2-3	66.7	+ 5.75	A McGlone	1-8	12.5	- 2.00
J Weaver	1-3	33.3	+ 1.50	R Moogan	1-11	9.1	- 8.50

Akehurst R

D Harrison	0-11	N Adams	0-2	Mr P Taiano	0-1
J Reid	0-11	R Hughes	0-2	N Carlisle	0-1
F Norton	0-8	A Tucker	0-1	P Robinson	0-1
L Dettori	0-7	A Whelan	0-1	R Cochrane	0-1
L Carter	0-4	D Wright	0-1	S Whitworth	0-1
M Baird	0-2	J Fortune	0-1	Stephen Davies	0-1
M J Kinane	0-2	J Tate	0-1		

COURSE RECORD

	Total W-R	Non-Handicaps 2-y-o	Non-Handicaps 3-y-o+	Handicaps 2-y-o	Handicaps 3-y-o+	Per cent	£1 Level Stake
Brighton	6-26	0-2	1-7	0-0	5-17	23.1	+ 4.13
Lingfield	6-29	0-4	2-8	0-1	4-16	20.7	+ 5.75
Ascot	5-15	0-0	0-2	0-0	5-13	33.3	+ 45.83
Sandown	4-28	0-0	0-1	0-0	4-27	14.3	- 4.50
Nottingham	3-10	0-1	1-3	0-0	2-6	30.0	+ 15.50
Leicester	3-14	0-3	0-2	0-0	3-9	21.4	+ 17.50
Epsom	3-17	0-0	0-2	0-0	3-15	17.6	+ 19.40
Folkestone	3-28	0-3	0-9	0-0	3-16	10.7	- 14.12
Newmarket	3-37	1-5	0-3	0-1	2-28	8.1	- 15.50
Bath	2-14	0-0	0-2	0-0	2-12	14.3	- 7.25
Lingfield (AW)	2-16	0-0	1-6	0-0	1-10	12.5	+ 13.00
Haydock	1-1	0-0	1-1	0-0	0-0	100.0	+ 8.00
Chepstow	1-5	0-1	0-2	0-0	1-2	20.0	+ 1.00
York	1-5	0-0	0-0	0-0	1-5	20.0	+ 10.00
Warwick	1-12	0-1	0-2	0-0	1-9	8.3	- 7.00
Doncaster	1-13	0-1	0-4	0-1	1-7	7.7	- 9.00
Salisbury	1-13	1-3	0-3	0-0	0-7	7.7	- 9.25
Goodwood	1-23	0-0	1-5	0-0	0-18	4.3	- 20.50
Kempton	1-23	0-1	0-7	0-0	1-15	4.3	- 17.00

Newbury	0-20	Beverley	0-2	Newcastle	0-1
Windsor	0-10	Ayr	0-1	Redcar	0-1
Yarmouth	0-3	Chester	0-1	Wolverhampton (AW)	0-1

WINNING HORSES

	Age	Races Run	1st	2nd	3rd	Unpl	Win £
Face North	6	6	2	1	0	3	73,821
Knowth	5	7	1	3	0	3	46,182
Urgent Request	4	5	2	2	0	1	33,854
Admiral's Well	4	7	2	2	0	3	23,378
Astrac	3	8	2	1	2	3	19,728
Special Risk	4	12	4	5	1	2	14,040
Aljazzaf	4	4	1	0	1	2	11,208
Dancing Sensation	7	11	2	1	1	7	10,323
Ibsen	6	9	3	1	2	3	9,689
Quantity Surveyor	5	12	3	1	1	7	9,117
Samah	4	10	1	0	3	6	8,870
Exhibit Air	4	5	3	0	0	2	8,490

4

Faugeron	5	8	1	1	0	6	8,480
Pharamineux	8	6	2	1	0	3	8,315
Domulla	4	6	2	0	1	3	8,142
Shujan	5	5	1	1	0	3	7,960
Reimei	5	6	2	1	1	2	7,307
Island Blade	5	10	1	2	1	6	7,100
Proton	4	6	2	2	2	0	6,431
Another Fiddle	4	6	1	0	1	4	4,659
Te Amo	2	5	1	1	0	3	3,978
Noble Kingdom	2	4	1	0	2	1	3,807
Top Pet	4	12	1	1	3	7	3,699
Well Arranged	3	1	1	0	0	0	3,633
Michaelmas Park	3	6	1	0	0	5	3,444
Fay's Song	6	8	1	2	0	5	3,314
Wildfire	3	9	1	0	0	8	3,254
Sarazar	5	5	1	1	1	2	3,006
Long Furlong	6	8	1	1	2	4	2,760
Valiant Words	7	2	1	0	0	1	2,743

WINNING OWNERS

	Races Won	Value £		Races Won	Value £
Normandy Developments London	3	82,301	I Goldsmith	2	7,307
Ruelles Partners	1	46,182	The Lime St Racing Syndicate	1	7,100
S Aitken	3	42,724	Fernray Ltd	2	6,984
A D Spence	5	32,495	William Alexander	1	4,659
C J Titcomb	2	19,728	The Fairy Story Partnership	1	3,807
Tony Alper Garages Ltd	5	14,921	Mrs A Valentine	1	3,699
M E Lee Partnership	4	14,040	Mrs Anne-Marie Hamilton	1	3,633
R N C Lynch	1	11,208	Miss Maureen Stopher	1	3,444
Chelgate Public Relations Ltd	2	10,323	S Harper	1	3,314
S Kay	3	9,689	R F Kilby	1	3,254
K R Snellings	2	8,315	Paul Lau	1	2,760
A W Boon	2	8,142	B Smith	1	2,743
Sir Eric Parker	1	7,960			

Favourites	14-65	21.5%	- 11.99	Total winning prize-money			£360,730
Longest winning sequence			3	Average SP of winner			6.6/1
Longest losing sequence			34	Return on stakes invested			-1.1%
1993 Form	48-300	16.0%	+ 15.76	1991 Form	42-301	14.0%	+ 27.04
1992 Form	30-270	11.1%	- 39.79	1990 Form	34-344	9.9%	-129.61

C N ALLEN (Newmarket)

	No. of Horses	Races Run	1st	2nd	3rd	Unpl	Per cent	£1 Level Stake
2-y-o	6	23	1	0	0	22	4.3	- 19.75
3-y-o	8	77	10	9	5	53	13.0	- 28.87
4-y-o+	4	25	3	2	2	18	12.0	+ 33.00
Totals	18	125	14	11	7	93	11.2	- 15.62

BY MONTH

2-y-o	W-R	Per cent	£1 Level Stake	3-y-o	W-R	Per cent	£1 Level Stake
January	0-0	-	0.00	January	3-11	27.3	+ 3.50
February	0-0	-	0.00	February	0-12	-	- 12.00
March	0-0	-	0.00	March	1-5	20.0	- 2.25
April	0-1	-	- 1.00	April	1-8	12.5	- 2.00
May	0-0	-	0.00	May	1-9	11.1	- 6.37
June	0-1	-	- 1.00	June	2-12	16.7	- 3.75
July	0-6	-	- 6.00	July	1-9	11.1	- 5.00
August	0-8	-	- 8.00	August	0-0	-	0.00
September	1-4	25.0	- 0.75	September	1-4	25.0	+ 6.00
Oct/Nov	0-3	-	- 3.00	Oct/Nov	0-7	-	- 7.00

4-y-o+	W-R	Per cent	£1 Level Stake	Totals	W-R	Per cent	£1 Level Stake
January	0-1	-	- 1.00	January	3-12	25.0	+ 2.50
February	0-0	-	0.00	February	0-12	-	- 12.00
March	1-1	100.0	+ 33.00	March	2-6	33.3	+ 30.75
April	0-0	-	0.00	April	1-9	11.1	- 3.00
May	0-4	-	- 4.00	May	1-13	7.7	- 10.37
June	0-5	-	- 5.00	June	2-18	11.1	- 9.75
July	1-4	25.0	+ 9.00	July	2-19	10.5	- 2.00
August	0-6	-	- 6.00	August	0-14	-	- 14.00
September	1-2	50.0	+ 9.00	September	3-10	30.0	+ 14.25
Oct/Nov	0-2	-	- 2.00	Oct/Nov	0-12	-	- 12.00

DISTANCE

2-y-o	W-R	Per cent	£1 Level Stake	3-y-o	W-R	Per cent	£1 Level Stake
5f-6f	1-15	6.7	- 11.75	5f-6f	0-9	-	- 9.00
7f-8f	0-8	-	- 8.00	7f-8f	3-21	14.3	- 1.00
9f-13f	0-0	-	0.00	9f-13f	7-46	15.2	- 17.87
14f+	0-0	-	0.00	14f+	0-1	-	- 1.00

4-y-o+	W-R	Per cent	£1 Level Stake	Totals	W-R	Per cent	£1 Level Stake
5f-6f	0-0	-	0.00	5f-6f	1-24	4.2	- 20.75
7f-8f	1-16	6.3	- 3.00	7f-8f	4-45	8.9	- 12.00
9f-13f	2-8	25.0	+ 37.00	9f-13f	9-54	16.7	+ 19.13
14f+	0-1	-	- 1.00	14f+	0-2	-	- 2.00

TYPE OF RACE

Non-Handicaps	W-R	Per cent	£1 Level Stake	Handicaps	W-R	Per cent	£1 Level Stake
2-y-o	1-11	9.1	- 7.75	2-y-o	0-3	-	- 3.00
3-y-o	5-33	15.2	- 14.87	3-y-o	4-36	11.1	- 16.00
4-y-o+	0-1	-	- 1.00	4-y-o+	3-13	23.1	+ 45.00
Selling	0-12	-	- 12.00	Selling	1-10	10.0	0.00
Apprentice	0-0	-	0.00	Apprentice	0-5	-	- 5.00
Amat/Ladies	0-0	-	0.00	Amat/Ladies	0-1	-	- 1.00
Totals	6-57	10.5	- 35.62	Totals	8-68	11.8	+ 20.00

COURSE GRADE

	W-R	Per cent	£1 Level Stake
Group 1	2-21	9.5	- 6.25
Group 2	1-19	5.3	- 14.50
Group 3	3-25	12.0	+ 1.25
Group 4	8-60	13.3	+ 3.88

FIRST TIME OUT

	W-R	Per cent	£1 Level Stake
2-y-o	0-4	-	- 4.00
3-y-o	0-8	-	- 8.00
4-y-o+	2-4	50.0	+ 41.00
Totals	2-16	12.5	+ 29.00

JOCKEYS RIDING

	W-R	Per cent	£1 Level Stake		W-R	Per cent	£1 Level Stake
G Bardwell	4-27	14.8	- 7.25	T Ives	1-5	20.0	- 1.00
E Guest	3-29	10.3	+ 18.50	J Quinn	1-5	20.0	+ 8.00
L Dettori	2-6	33.3	+ 0.38	N Carlisle	1-6	16.7	+ 5.00
G Hind	2-15	13.3	- 7.25				

F Savage	0-7	M Roberts	0-2	G Duffield	0-1
M Baird	0-3	P Robinson	0-2	G Forster	0-1
A Mackay	0-2	W Carson	0-2	J Weaver	0-1
E Johnson	0-2	A Garth	0-1	Miss R Lowes	0-1
J Carroll	0-2	D Wright	0-1	R Still	0-1
Karen Markham	0-2	G Carter	0-1		

COURSE RECORD

	Total W-R	Non-Handicaps 2-y-o	Non-Handicaps 3-y-o+	Handicaps 2-y-o	Handicaps 3-y-o+	Per cent	£1 Level Stake
Wolverhampton (AW)	3-22	0-3	2-10	0-0	1-9	13.6	- 8.25
Warwick	2-7	0-0	1-3	0-1	1-3	28.6	+ 1.63
Yarmouth	2-10	1-2	0-2	0-0	1-6	20.0	+ 6.25
Lingfield (AW)	2-12	0-0	0-3	0-0	2-9	16.7	+ 25.50
Haydock	1-1	0-0	0-0	0-0	1-1	100.0	+ 10.00
Bath	1-2	0-0	0-0	0-0	1-2	50.0	+ 8.00
Redcar	1-7	0-0	1-3	0-0	0-4	14.3	- 2.50
Southwell (AW)	1-9	0-0	0-5	0-0	1-4	11.1	- 5.00
Newmarket	1-10	0-3	1-2	0-2	0-3	10.0	- 6.25

Brighton	0-7	Pontefract	0-2	Doncaster	0-1
Folkestone	0-6	Ripon	0-2	Goodwood	0-1
Beverley	0-3	Sandown	0-2	Kempton	0-1
Leicester	0-3	Windsor	0-2	Newcastle	0-1
Ayr	0-2	Ascot	0-1	Salisbury	0-1
Edinburgh	0-2	Carlisle	0-1	York	0-1
Lingfield	0-2	Catterick	0-1		
Nottingham	0-2	Chepstow	0-1		

WINNING HORSES

	Age	Races Run	1st	2nd	3rd	Unpl	Win £
Mr Devious	3	21	4	4	3	10	11,247
Lone Risk	3	16	4	3	1	8	10,488
Mathal	5	3	1	0	0	2	5,995
Magication	4	16	1	1	2	12	3,468
Caspian Gold	3	5	1	0	0	4	2,847
Miss Mercy	2	6	1	0	0	5	2,831
Priscilla Rose	3	12	1	2	1	8	2,688
Bassio	5	1	1	0	0	0	2,005

WINNING OWNERS

	Races Won	Value £		Races Won	Value £
Theobalds Stud	7	18,759	B Homewood	1	2,976
Jeff Lewis	3	9,146	M Venus	1	2,688
Four Js Syndicate	1	5,995	Mrs Shirley Darby	1	2,005

Favourites	2-12	16.7%	- 6.00	Total winning prize-money	£41,569

Longest winning sequence	2	Average SP of winner	6.8/1
Longest losing sequence	20	Return on stakes invested	-12.5%

1993 Form	4-81	4.9%	- 42.50	1991 Form	15-184	8.2%	- 76.97
1992 Form	7-118	5.9%	- 58.37	1990 Form	19-269	7.1%	-119.09

E J ALSTON (Preston, Lancs)

	No. of Horses	Races Run	1st	2nd	3rd	Unpl	Per cent	£1 Level Stake
2-y-o	4	17	1	1	1	14	5.9	- 9.00
3-y-o	10	75	6	10	9	50	8.0	- 6.50
4-y-o+	26	190	13	18	17	142	6.8	- 51.95
Totals	40	282	20	29	27	206	7.1	- 67.45

BY MONTH

2-y-o	W-R	Per cent	£1 Level Stake	3-y-o	W-R	Per cent	£1 Level Stake
January	0-0	-	0.00	January	0-3	-	- 3.00
February	0-0	-	0.00	February	0-4	-	- 4.00
March	0-1	-	- 1.00	March	0-3	-	- 3.00
April	0-1	-	- 1.00	April	2-10	20.0	+ 6.50
May	0-1	-	- 1.00	May	1-8	12.5	+ 1.00
June	0-0	-	0.00	June	1-14	7.1	- 9.00
July	0-5	-	- 5.00	July	0-12	-	- 12.00
August	0-3	-	- 3.00	August	1-8	12.5	+ 13.00
September	0-3	-	- 3.00	September	1-7	14.3	+ 10.00
Oct/Nov	1-3	33.3	+ 5.00	Oct/Nov	0-6	-	- 6.00

4-y-o+	W-R	Per cent	£1 Level Stake	Totals	W-R	Per cent	£1 Level Stake
January	2-16	12.5	- 5.25	January	2-19	10.5	- 8.25
February	1-13	7.7	- 9.25	February	1-17	5.9	- 13.25
March	1-14	7.1	- 3.00	March	1-18	5.6	- 7.00
April	2-14	14.3	+ 4.25	April	4-25	16.0	+ 9.75
May	0-17	-	- 17.00	May	1-26	3.8	- 17.00
June	2-31	6.5	+ 2.80	June	3-45	6.7	- 6.20
July	1-27	3.7	- 22.50	July	1-44	2.3	- 39.50
August	1-20	5.0	- 13.00	August	2-31	6.5	- 3.00
September	1-18	5.6	- 7.00	September	2-28	7.1	0.00
Oct/Nov	2-20	10.0	+ 18.00	Oct/Nov	3-29	10.3	+ 17.00

DISTANCE

2-y-o	W-R	Per cent	£1 Level Stake	3-y-o	W-R	Per cent	£1 Level Stake
5f-6f	1-16	6.3	- 8.00	5f-6f	5-25	20.0	+ 26.50
7f-8f	0-1	-	- 1.00	7f-8f	0-30	-	- 30.00
9f-13f	0-0	-	0.00	9f-13f	1-17	5.9	0.00
14f+	0-0	-	0.00	14f+	0-3	-	- 3.00

4-y-o+	W-R	Per cent	£1 Level Stake	Totals	W-R	Per cent	£1 Level Stake
5f-6f	3-55	5.5	- 33.75	5f-6f	9-96	9.4	- 15.25
7f-8f	4-64	6.3	+ 3.00	7f-8f	4-95	4.2	- 28.00
9f-13f	4-55	7.3	- 20.20	9f-13f	5-72	6.9	- 20.20
14f+	2-16	12.5	- 1.00	14f+	2-19	10.5	- 4.00

TYPE OF RACE

Non-Handicaps	W-R	Per cent	£1 Level Stake	Handicaps	W-R	Per cent	£1 Level Stake
2-y-o	1-14	7.1	- 6.00	2-y-o	0-3	-	- 3.00
3-y-o	2-23	8.7	+ 7.00	3-y-o	4-46	8.7	- 7.50
4-y-o+	1-45	2.2	- 41.75	4-y-o+	12-126	9.5	+ 8.80
Selling	0-10	-	- 10.00	Selling	0-4	-	- 4.00
Apprentice	0-1	-	- 1.00	Apprentice	0-10	-	- 10.00
Amat/Ladies	0-0	-	0.00	Amat/Ladies	0-0	-	0.00
Totals	4-93	4.3	- 51.75	Totals	16-189	8.5	- 15.70

9

COURSE GRADE

	W-R	Per cent	£1 Level Stake
Group 1	5-87	5.7	+ 4.80
Group 2	5-50	10.0	- 3.50
Group 3	7-53	13.2	+ 8.75
Group 4	3-92	3.3	- 77.50

FIRST TIME OUT

	W-R	Per cent	£1 Level Stake
2-y-o	0-3	–	- 3.00
3-y-o	0-8	–	- 8.00
4-y-o+	1-26	3.8	- 11.00
Totals	1-37	2.7	- 22.00

JOCKEYS RIDING

	W-R	Per cent	£1 Level Stake		W-R	Per cent	£1 Level Stake
J Quinn	8-49	16.3	+ 46.00	D Harrison	1-3	33.3	+ 23.00
K Fallon	5-53	9.4	- 4.95	D Holland	1-4	25.0	+ 3.00
N Carlisle	2-13	15.4	- 3.50	A Mackay	1-5	20.0	+ 12.00
J Fortune	2-27	7.4	- 15.00				

S Knott	0-52	M Hills	0-2	G Bardwell	0-1	
M Fenton	0-10	P Fessey	0-2	G Carter	0-1	
J Weaver	0-7	S Bethley	0-2	J Carroll	0-1	
N Varley	0-6	S Lanigan	0-2	J Reid	0-1	
C Teague	0-4	S Maloney	0-2	J Stack	0-1	
P Robinson	0-4	T Williams	0-2	J Williams	0-1	
S Wood	0-4	A Clark	0-1	M Roberts	0-1	
D Moffatt	0-3	A McGlone	0-1	N Adams	0-1	
D Wright	0-3	C Asmussen	0-1	R Hills	0-1	
D Griffiths	0-2	Claire Balding	0-1	R Hughes	0-1	
F Norton	0-2	D Biggs	0-1	R Perham	0-1	
G Duffield	0-2	D McKeown	0-1			

COURSE RECORD

	Total W-R	Non-Handicaps 2-y-o	3-y-o+	Handicaps 2-y-o	3-y-o+	Per cent	£1 Level Stake
Pontefract	3-12	1-1	0-3	0-1	2-7	25.0	+ 3.50
Hamilton	3-30	0-2	2-8	0-0	1-20	10.0	+ 1.25
Wolverhampton (AW)	3-40	0-0	0-16	0-0	3-24	7.5	- 25.50
Newcastle	2-8	0-1	1-2	0-0	1-5	25.0	+ 31.00
Ripon	2-14	0-1	0-3	0-0	2-10	14.3	+ 12.00
Chester	2-19	0-2	0-3	0-0	2-14	10.5	- 3.00
Beverley	1-4	0-0	0-1	0-0	1-3	25.0	+ 11.00
Thirsk	1-7	0-0	0-0	0-0	1-7	14.3	- 2.50
Newmarket	1-8	0-0	0-2	0-0	1-6	12.5	+ 26.00
York	1-8	0-0	0-0	0-0	1-8	12.5	- 0.20
Ayr	1-23	0-2	0-3	0-0	1-18	4.3	- 12.00

Haydock	0-29	Catterick	0-9	Newbury	0-2
Southwell (AW)	0-15	Warwick	0-7	Nottingham	0-2
Edinburgh	0-11	Doncaster	0-6	Chepstow	0-1
Carlisle	0-10	Leicester	0-4		
Redcar	0-10	Sandown	0-3		

WINNING HORSES

	Age	Races Run	1st	2nd	3rd	Unpl	Win £
Whittle Woods Girl	3	15	5	1	5	4	42,936
Chinour	6	10	1	2	0	7	28,920
No Comebacks	6	14	2	0	5	7	15,046
Marowins	5	14	3	2	2	7	12,461
Kummel King	6	11	1	3	2	5	7,895
Ambuscade	8	8	2	0	1	5	7,763
Gondo	7	18	1	3	0	14	7,460
Cronk's Courage	8	11	2	0	0	9	6,495
Persian Soldier	7	5	1	0	2	2	5,117
Marble	3	10	1	0	1	8	3,002
Rymer's Rascal	2	7	1	1	0	5	2,642

WINNING OWNERS

	Races Won	Value £		Races Won	Value £
John Jackson	5	42,936	Mrs Helen O'Brien	1	7,460
Frank McKevitt	1	28,920	Mrs S Y Alston	2	6,495
Lionel Snowden	2	15,046	Norman Firth	1	5,117
Whitehills Racing Syndicate	3	12,461	George M Thomson	1	3,002
David Hall	1	7,895	Brian Chambers	1	2,642
Mrs Lynne Firth	2	7,763			

Favourites	6-15	40.0%	+ 14.30	Total winning prize-money	£139,735
Longest winning sequence			2	Average SP of winner	9.7/1
Longest losing sequence			51	Return on stakes invested	-23.9%
1993 Form	20-190	10.5%	- 3.57	1991 Form 12-111 10.8%	+ 6.50
1992 Form	14-190	7.4%	- 78.00	1990 Form 6-82 7.3%	- 15.50

D W P ARBUTHNOT (Compton, Berks)

	No. of Horses	Races Run	1st	2nd	3rd	Unpl	Per cent	£1 Level Stake
2-y-o	8	45	5	2	5	33	11.1	- 2.50
3-y-o	5	31	3	3	2	23	9.7	- 12.50
4-y-o+	10	86	7	9	13	57	8.1	- 27.37
Totals	23	162	15	14	20	113	9.3	- 42.37

BY MONTH

2-y-o	W–R	Per cent	£1 Level Stake	3-y-o	W–R	Per cent	£1 Level Stake
January	0-0	-	0.00	January	0-0	-	0.00
February	0-0	-	0.00	February	0-0	-	0.00
March	0-0	-	0.00	March	0-0	-	0.00
April	0-0	-	0.00	April	1-2	50.0	+ 4.00
May	0-4	-	- 4.00	May	0-7	-	- 7.00
June	2-7	28.6	+ 5.00	June	1-7	14.3	+ 2.00
July	1-5	20.0	+ 3.50	July	1-4	25.0	- 0.50
August	1-10	10.0	- 5.00	August	0-1	-	- 1.00
September	0-8	-	- 8.00	September	0-6	-	- 6.00
Oct/Nov	1-11	9.1	+ 6.00	Oct/Nov	0-4	-	- 4.00

4-y-o+	W–R	Per cent	£1 Level Stake	Totals	W–R	Per cent	£1 Level Stake
January	1-6	16.7	- 1.50	January	1-6	16.7	- 1.50
February	1-7	14.3	- 4.37	February	1-7	14.3	- 4.37
March	0-3	-	- 3.00	March	0-3	-	- 3.00
April	0-5	-	- 5.00	April	1-7	14.3	- 1.00
May	0-7	-	- 7.00	May	0-18	-	- 18.00
June	3-13	23.1	+ 16.50	June	6-27	22.2	+ 23.50
July	1-13	7.7	- 8.00	July	3-22	13.6	- 5.00
August	1-11	9.1	+ 6.00	August	2-22	9.1	0.00
September	0-10	-	- 10.00	September	0-24	-	- 24.00
Oct/Nov	0-11	-	- 11.00	Oct/Nov	1-26	3.8	- 9.00

DISTANCE

2-y-o	W–R	Per cent	£1 Level Stake	3-y-o	W–R	Per cent	£1 Level Stake
5f-6f	2-28	7.1	- 12.50	5f-6f	0-8	-	- 8.00
7f-8f	3-17	17.6	+ 10.00	7f-8f	0-7	-	- 7.00
9f-13f	0-0	-	0.00	9f-13f	3-15	20.0	+ 3.50
14f+	0-0	-	0.00	14f+	0-1	-	- 1.00

4-y-o+	W–R	Per cent	£1 Level Stake	Totals	W–R	Per cent	£1 Level Stake
5f-6f	2-26	7.7	- 3.00	5f-6f	4-62	6.5	- 23.50
7f-8f	0-25	-	- 25.00	7f-8f	3-49	6.1	- 22.00
9f-13f	4-26	15.4	- 7.37	9f-13f	7-41	17.1	- 3.87
14f+	1-9	11.1	+ 8.00	14f+	1-10	10.0	+ 7.00

TYPE OF RACE

Non-Handicaps	W–R	Per cent	£1 Level Stake	Handicaps	W–R	Per cent	£1 Level Stake
2-y-o	2-25	8.0	- 11.50	2-y-o	1-13	7.7	+ 4.00
3-y-o	1-9	11.1	- 5.50	3-y-o	2-21	9.5	- 6.00
4-y-o+	0-14	-	- 14.00	4-y-o+	5-58	8.6	- 10.87
Selling	2-5	40.0	+ 7.00	Selling	0-4	-	- 4.00
Apprentice	0-0	-	0.00	Apprentice	0-1	-	- 1.00
Amat/Ladies	0-0	-	0.00	Amat/Ladies	2-12	16.7	- 0.50
Totals	5-53	9.4	- 24.00	Totals	10-109	9.2	- 18.37

COURSE GRADE

	W-R	Per cent	£1 Level Stake
Group 1	2-74	2.7	- 40.00
Group 2	3-15	20.0	0.00
Group 3	3-40	7.5	- 18.00
Group 4	7-33	21.2	+ 15.63

FIRST TIME OUT

	W-R	Per cent	£1 Level Stake
2-y-o	1-8	12.5	+ 0.50
3-y-o	0-4	–	- 4.00
4-y-o+	2-10	20.0	+ 7.50
Totals	3-22	13.6	+ 4.00

JOCKEYS RIDING

	W-R	Per cent	£1 Level Stake		W-R	Per cent	£1 Level Stake
B Thomson	3-16	18.8	+ 4.50	J Williams	2-16	12.5	- 8.87
T Quinn	3-25	12.0	+ 2.00	J Weaver	1-5	20.0	+ 12.00
B Doyle	2-8	25.0	+ 12.50	A Munro	1-7	14.3	+ 3.00
Mrs D Arbuthnot	2-14	14.3	- 2.50	R Price	1-23	4.3	- 17.00

G Bardwell	0-6	M Birch	0-2	N Varley	0-1
M Tebbutt	0-6	M Fenton	0-2	Pat Eddery	0-1
J Quinn	0-4	A Garth	0-1	R Cochrane	0-1
M Roberts	0-3	D Harrison	0-1	R Hills	0-1
W Woods	0-3	F Norton	0-1	S Whitworth	0-1
C N Adamson	0-2	J D Smith	0-1	W Newnes	0-1
D Wright	0-2	J Reid	0-1	W R Swinburn	0-1
J Tate	0-2	J Stack	0-1		
L Dettori	0-2	M Hills	0-1		

COURSE RECORD

	Total W-R	Non-Handicaps 2-y-o	Non-Handicaps 3-y-o+	Handicaps 2-y-o	Handicaps 3-y-o+	Per cent	£1 Level Stake
Folkestone	4-7	1-3	0-0	0-0	3-4	57.1	+ 29.50
Brighton	2-5	1-1	1-2	0-0	0-2	40.0	+ 3.50
Ripon	1-2	0-0	0-1	0-0	1-1	50.0	+ 4.50
Pontefract	1-4	0-0	0-0	0-1	1-3	25.0	+ 6.00
Windsor	1-4	1-1	0-3	0-0	0-0	25.0	+ 3.00
Warwick	1-5	1-2	0-1	0-1	0-1	20.0	0.00
Ascot	1-6	0-0	0-0	1-1	0-5	16.7	+ 11.00
Southwell (AW)	1-6	0-0	0-3	0-0	1-3	16.7	- 1.50
Chepstow	1-8	0-3	0-0	0-2	1-3	12.5	- 3.00
Sandown	1-8	0-1	0-1	0-0	1-6	12.5	+ 9.00
Wolverhampton (AW)	1-8	0-1	0-2	0-0	1-5	12.5	- 5.37

Newbury	0-15	Lingfield (AW)	0-6	Beverley	0-3
Goodwood	0-11	Epsom	0-5	Newcastle	0-2
Newmarket	0-11	Haydock	0-5	Salisbury	0-2
Bath	0-9	Lingfield	0-5	Catterick	0-1
Kempton	0-7	Doncaster	0-4	Chester	0-1
Leicester	0-7	Nottingham	0-4	Yarmouth	0-1

WINNING HORSES

	Age	Races Run	1st	2nd	3rd	Unpl	Win £
Melasus	2	4	2	0	0	2	13,440
Love Legend	9	22	1	2	4	15	7,635
Keen Vision	6	9	2	2	2	3	6,724
Holy Wanderer	5	4	2	1	0	1	6,608
Jemima Puddleduck	3	10	2	0	1	7	6,115
Dark Eyed Lady	4	8	1	1	0	6	4,540
John Lee Hooker	2	5	1	1	0	3	3,570
Tom's Birthday	2	6	1	0	1	4	2,553
Strat's Legacy	7	12	1	1	1	9	2,423
Fabulous Princess	3	6	1	0	0	5	2,386
Never So Rite	2	7	1	0	1	5	2,174

WINNING OWNERS

	Races Won	Value £		Races Won	Value £
Mrs A Haynes	2	13,440	Stephen Crown	2	4,939
George S Thompson	1	7,635	Mrs M Gutkin	1	4,540
C D Osborne	2	6,724	Christopher Wright	1	3,570
Mrs J A Leek	2	6,608	Jack Blumenow	1	2,423
Mrs B J Lee	2	6,115	J S Gutkin	1	2,174

Favourites	3-13	23.1%	- 0.37	Total winning prize-money	£58,169
Longest winning sequence			2	Average SP of winner	7.0/1
Longest losing sequence			35	Return on stakes invested	-26.2%
1993 Form	19-129	14.7%	+ 33.75	1991 Form	12-155	7.7%	- 56.57
1992 Form	12-171	7.0%	- 52.25	1990 Form	20-147	13.6%	+ 59.75

R W ARMSTRONG (Newmarket)

	No. of Horses	Races Run	1st	2nd	3rd	Unpl	Per cent	£1 Level Stake
2-y-o	16	40	5	7	4	24	12.5	0.00
3-y-o	19	119	15	8	7	89	12.6	+ 13.21
4-y-o+	6	28	3	3	5	17	10.7	+ 48.33
Totals	41	187	23	18	16	130	12.3	+ 61.54

BY MONTH

2-y-o	W-R	Per cent	£1 Level Stake	3-y-o	W-R	Per cent	£1 Level Stake
January	0-0	-	0.00	January	0-1	-	- 1.00
February	0-0	-	0.00	February	0-1	-	- 1.00
March	0-0	-	0.00	March	1-2	50.0	+ 0.50
April	0-0	-	0.00	April	1-16	6.3	- 10.00
May	0-0	-	0.00	May	3-10	30.0	+ 40.50
June	0-1	-	- 1.00	June	4-21	19.0	+ 3.48
July	2-9	22.2	+ 9.00	July	2-23	8.7	- 12.77
August	0-6	-	- 6.00	August	0-9	-	- 9.00
September	1-12	8.3	- 4.50	September	3-17	17.6	+ 15.50
Oct/Nov	2-12	16.7	+ 2.50	Oct/Nov	1-19	5.3	- 13.00

4-y-o+	W-R	Per cent	£1 Level Stake	Totals	W-R	Per cent	£1 Level Stake
January	1-4	25.0	+ 0.33	January	1-5	20.0	- 0.67
February	0-0	-	0.00	February	0-1	-	- 1.00
March	0-3	-	- 3.00	March	1-5	20.0	- 2.50
April	0-4	-	- 4.00	April	1-20	5.0	- 14.00
May	0-2	-	- 2.00	May	3-12	25.0	+ 38.50
June	0-5	-	- 5.00	June	4-27	14.8	- 2.52
July	1-4	25.0	+ 1.00	July	5-36	13.9	- 2.77
August	0-2	-	- 2.00	August	0-17	-	- 17.00
September	1-4	25.0	+ 63.00	September	5-33	15.2	+ 74.00
Oct/Nov	0-0	-	0.00	Oct/Nov	3-31	9.7	- 10.50

DISTANCE

2-y-o	W-R	Per cent	£1 Level Stake	3-y-o	W-R	Per cent	£1 Level Stake
5f-6f	3-18	16.7	+ 6.50	5f-6f	1-22	4.5	- 7.00
7f-8f	2-22	9.1	- 6.50	7f-8f	14-73	19.2	+ 44.21
9f-13f	0-0	-	0.00	9f-13f	0-23	-	- 23.00
14f+	0-0	-	0.00	14f+	0-1	-	- 1.00

4-y-o+	W-R	Per cent	£1 Level Stake	Totals	W-R	Per cent	£1 Level Stake
5f-6f	0-0	-	0.00	5f-6f	4-40	10.0	- 0.50
7f-8f	2-16	12.5	+ 56.00	7f-8f	18-111	16.2	+ 93.71
9f-13f	1-11	9.1	- 6.67	9f-13f	1-34	2.9	- 29.67
14f+	0-1	-	- 1.00	14f+	0-2	-	- 2.00

TYPE OF RACE

Non-Handicaps	W-R	Per cent	£1 Level Stake	Handicaps	W-R	Per cent	£1 Level Stake
2-y-o	5-38	13.2	+ 2.00	2-y-o	0-2	-	- 2.00
3-y-o	8-52	15.4	- 7.29	3-y-o	7-67	10.4	+ 20.50
4-y-o+	2-12	16.7	+ 60.00	4-y-o+	1-16	6.3	- 11.67
Selling	0-0	-	0.00	Selling	0-0	-	0.00
Apprentice	0-0	-	0.00	Apprentice	0-0	-	0.00
Amat/Ladies	0-0	-	0.00	Amat/Ladies	0-0	-	0.00
Totals	15-102	14.7	+ 54.71	Totals	8-85	9.4	+ 6.83

Armstrong R W

COURSE GRADE					FIRST TIME OUT			
	W-R	Per cent	£1 Level Stake			W-R	Per cent	£1 Level Stake
Group 1	14-99	14.1	+ 80.23	2-y-o		2-16	12.5	+ 5.50
Group 2	2-29	6.9	- 10.00	3-y-o		3-19	15.8	+ 2.23
Group 3	6-37	16.2	+ 8.98	4-y-o+		1-6	16.7	- 1.67
Group 4	1-22	4.5	- 17.67					
				Totals		6-41	14.6	+ 6.06

JOCKEYS RIDING

	W-R	Per cent	£1 Level Stake			W-R	Per cent	£1 Level Stake
R Price	12-91	13.2	+ 35.25	J Reid		1-1	100.0	+ 7.50
R Hills	3-18	16.7	+ 55.73	L Dettori		1-6	16.7	- 1.67
W Carson	3-45	6.7	- 21.00	Pat Eddery		1-7	14.3	+ 0.50
W R Swinburn	2-6	33.3	- 1.77					

M Hills	0-3	B Raymond	0-1	J Weaver			0-1
M Roberts	0-2	G Bardwell	0-1	M Baird			0-1
W Woods	0-2	J Fanning	0-1	S Raymont			0-1

COURSE RECORD

	Total W-R	Non-Handicaps 2-y-o	3-y-o+	Handicaps 2-y-o	3-y-o+	Per cent	£1 Level Stake
Doncaster	6-13	2-3	3-7	0-0	1-3	46.2	+ 19.23
Ascot	2-11	1-2	1-5	0-0	0-4	18.2	+ 59.00
Goodwood	2-12	0-3	1-2	0-0	1-7	16.7	+ 10.50
Yarmouth	2-13	1-5	1-4	0-0	0-4	15.4	- 3.77
Beverley	1-1	0-0	1-1	0-0	0-0	100.0	+ 1.25
Newcastle	1-2	0-0	1-1	0-0	0-1	50.0	+ 3.00
Windsor	1-4	0-1	0-0	0-0	1-3	25.0	+ 13.00
Nottingham	1-5	0-2	1-1	0-0	0-2	20.0	+ 5.00
Haydock	1-6	0-0	0-2	0-0	1-4	16.7	+ 20.00
Ripon	1-6	0-0	1-3	0-0	0-3	16.7	+ 7.00
Thirsk	1-6	0-1	0-3	0-0	1-2	16.7	0.00
Lingfield (AW)	1-9	0-0	0-2	0-0	1-7	11.1	- 4.67
Leicester	1-12	0-3	0-3	0-0	1-6	8.3	- 4.50
Sandown	1-14	0-1	0-5	0-0	1-8	7.1	- 5.50
Newmarket	1-28	1-8	0-10	0-0	0-10	3.6	- 13.00

Brighton	0-8	Southwell (AW)	0-4	Chester	0-1
Lingfield	0-7	Newbury	0-3	Salisbury	0-1
Folkestone	0-6	Pontefract	0-2	Warwick	0-1
York	0-5	Wolverhampton (AW)	0-2		
Kempton	0-4	Ayr	0-1		

WINNING HORSES

	Age	Races Run	1st	2nd	3rd	Unpl	Win £
Maroof	4	5	1	2	0	2	190,006
Dance Turn	3	4	2	0	0	2	30,839
Tajannub	2	4	2	0	1	1	27,984
Gabr	4	4	1	0	2	1	22,200
Mur Taasha	3	11	3	1	1	6	19,427
Ishtiyak	3	9	1	0	0	8	15,240
Benfleet	3	9	2	1	0	6	9,341
Danish Heights	3	5	2	1	0	2	7,935
Mokaafi	3	8	1	1	1	5	6,755
Shefoog	2	2	1	1	0	0	4,829
Tira Heights	2	4	1	0	0	3	4,724
Scenic Heights	2	1	1	0	0	0	4,609
Masnad	3	2	1	1	0	0	4,548
Asalib	3	8	1	0	0	7	3,926
Murayah	3	4	1	0	0	3	3,292
Jari	3	4	1	0	0	3	3,089
Able Choice	4	10	1	1	1	7	2,951

WINNING OWNERS

	Races Won	Value £		Races Won	Value £
Hamdan Al-Maktoum	13	296,466	C G Donovan	2	9,341
George Ward	2	30,839	Ahmed Al Shafar	1	4,829
George Tong	4	17,267	Dr Cornel Li	1	2,951

Favourites	5-22	22.7%	- 7.04	Total winning prize-money	£361,693

Longest winning sequence		2	Average SP of winner	9.8/1
Longest losing sequence		34	Return on stakes invested	32.9%

1993 Form	28-156	17.9%	+ 58.00	1991 Form	10-114	8.8%	- 28.89
1992 Form	15-152	9.9%	- 5.75	1990 Form	26-155	16.8%	- 24.88

J R ARNOLD (Upper Lambourn, Berks)

	No. of Horses	Races Run	1st	2nd	3rd	Unpl	Per cent	£1 Level Stake
2-y-o	9	31	2	1	1	27	6.5	- 11.67
3-y-o	1	4	0	0	0	4	-	- 4.00
4-y-o+	3	7	0	0	0	7	-	- 7.00
Totals	13	42	2	1	1	38	4.8	- 22.67

Jan	Feb	Mar	Apr	May	Jun	Jul	Aug	Sep	Oct/Nov
0-2	0-0	0-0	0-3	0-2	0-6	1-3	1-12	0-7	0-7

17

Winning Jockeys	W-R	£1 Level Stake				W-R	£1 Level Stake
R Hills	1-6	- 1.67	B Thomson			1-12	+ 3.00

Winning Courses							
Thirsk	1-1	+ 3.33	Doncaster			1-2	+ 13.00

Winning Horses	Age	Races Run	1st	2nd	3rd	Unpl	Win £
Rupiana	2	5	1	0	0	4	3,520
Chaldon Herring	2	5	1	0	0	4	3,224

Favourites	1-1	100.0%	+ 3.33	Total winning prize-money	£6,743

1993 Form	1-4	25.0%	+ 5.00

MRS S M AUSTIN (Malton, North Yorks)

	No. of Horses	Races Run	1st	2nd	3rd	Unpl	Per cent	£1 Level Stake
2-y-o	1	4	0	0	0	4	-	- 4.00
3-y-o	0	0	0	0	0	0	-	0.00
4-y-o+	5	18	3	0	3	12	16.7	+ 13.50
Totals	6	22	3	0	3	16	13.6	+ 9.50

Jan	Feb	Mar	Apr	May	Jun	Jul	Aug	Sep	Oct/Nov
0-0	0-1	0-1	0-3	0-4	1-4	2-5	0-2	0-1	0-1

Winning Jockey	W-R	£1 Level Stake		W-R	£1 Level Stake
J Marshall	3-17	+ 14.50			

Winning Courses					
Beverley	2-6	+ 14.50	Pontefract	1-4	+ 7.00

Winning Horse	Age	Races Run	1st	2nd	3rd	Unpl	Win £
Sea-Ayr	4	12	3	0	3	6	9,178

Favourites	0-1		Total winning prize-money	£9,178

1993 Form	0-10	1991 Form	0-15
1992 Form	0-2	1990 Form	0-11

A BAILEY (Tarporley, Cheshire)

	No. of Horses	Races Run	1st	2nd	3rd	Unpl	Per cent	£1 Level Stake
2-y-o	7	22	2	0	2	18	9.1	- 2.50
3-y-o	13	67	2	2	4	59	3.0	- 54.00
4-y-o+	21	126	22	5	7	92	17.5	+ 12.80
Totals	41	215	26	7	13	169	12.1	- 43.70

BY MONTH

2-y-o	W-R	Per cent	£1 Level Stake	3-y-o	W-R	Per cent	£1 Level Stake
January	0-0	-	0.00	January	1-9	11.1	- 5.00
February	0-0	-	0.00	February	0-5	-	- 5.00
March	0-0	-	0.00	March	0-5	-	- 5.00
April	0-0	-	0.00	April	0-1	-	- 1.00
May	0-2	-	- 2.00	May	0-11	-	- 11.00
June	0-0	-	0.00	June	0-3	-	- 3.00
July	0-2	-	- 2.00	July	0-6	-	- 6.00
August	0-3	-	- 3.00	August	0-8	-	- 8.00
September	1-7	14.3	- 0.50	September	1-8	12.5	+ 1.00
Oct/Nov	1-8	12.5	+ 5.00	Oct/Nov	0-11	-	- 11.00

4-y-o+	W-R	Per cent	£1 Level Stake	Totals	W-R	Per cent	£1 Level Stake
January	3-10	30.0	+ 23.50	January	4-19	21.1	+ 18.50
February	1-7	14.3	- 2.00	February	1-12	8.3	- 7.00
March	0-11	-	- 11.00	March	0-16	-	- 16.00
April	2-12	16.7	+ 10.00	April	2-13	15.4	+ 9.00
May	1-17	5.9	- 12.50	May	1-30	3.3	- 25.50
June	3-14	21.4	- 0.75	June	3-17	17.6	- 3.75
July	7-25	28.0	+ 6.30	July	7-33	21.2	- 1.70
August	2-8	25.0	+ 1.75	August	2-19	10.5	- 9.25
September	1-11	9.1	- 2.00	September	3-26	11.5	- 1.50
Oct/Nov	2-11	18.2	- 0.50	Oct/Nov	3-30	10.0	- 6.50

DISTANCE

2-y-o	W-R	Per cent	£1 Level Stake	3-y-o	W-R	Per cent	£1 Level Stake
5f-6f	2-11	18.2	+ 8.50	5f-6f	0-17	-	- 17.00
7f-8f	0-11	-	- 11.00	7f-8f	2-35	5.7	- 22.00
9f-13f	0-0	-	0.00	9f-13f	0-14	-	- 14.00
14f+	0-0	-	0.00	14f+	0-1	-	- 1.00

4-y-o+	W-R	Per cent	£1 Level Stake	Totals	W-R	Per cent	£1 Level Stake
5f-6f	8-39	20.5	+ 13.75	5f-6f	10-67	14.9	+ 5.25
7f-8f	6-44	13.6	- 14.70	7f-8f	8-90	8.9	- 47.70
9f-13f	8-39	20.5	+ 17.75	9f-13f	8-53	15.1	+ 3.75
14f+	0-4	-	- 4.00	14f+	0-5	-	- 5.00

Bailey A

TYPE OF RACE

Non-Handicaps	W-R	Per cent	£1 Level Stake	Handicaps	W-R	Per cent	£1 Level Stake
2-y-o	1-15	6.7	- 2.00	2-y-o	0-2	-	- 2.00
3-y-o	0-23	-	- 23.00	3-y-o	2-36	5.6	- 23.00
4-y-o+	4-18	22.2	- 5.95	4-y-o+	14-85	16.5	+ 8.50
Selling	1-10	10.0	- 3.50	Selling	2-7	28.6	+ 2.00
Apprentice	1-1	100.0	+ 20.00	Apprentice	1-14	7.1	- 10.75
Amat/Ladies	0-0	-	0.00	Amat/Ladies	0-4	-	- 4.00
Totals	7-67	10.4	- 14.45	Totals	19-148	12.8	- 29.25

COURSE GRADE

	W-R	Per cent	£1 Level Stake
Group 1	7-75	9.3	- 20.00
Group 2	3-35	8.6	- 22.25
Group 3	4-26	15.4	- 3.00
Group 4	12-79	15.2	+ 1.55

FIRST TIME OUT

	W-R	Per cent	£1 Level Stake
2-y-o	0-7	-	- 7.00
3-y-o	1-9	11.1	- 5.00
4-y-o+	3-16	18.8	+ 14.50
Totals	4-32	12.5	+ 2.50

JOCKEYS RIDING

	W-R	Per cent	£1 Level Stake		W-R	Per cent	£1 Level Stake
D Wright	10-78	12.8	- 11.20	Richard Edwards	1-1	100.0	+ 2.25
A Mackay	4-54	7.4	- 33.25	K Darley	1-2	50.0	+ 4.50
L Piggott	3-8	37.5	+ 6.00	J Fortune	1-5	20.0	- 0.50
F Norton	3-9	33.3	+ 12.50	W Hawksley	1-10	10.0	+ 11.00
S Whitworth	2-16	12.5	- 3.00				

Angela Gallimore	0-5	Dale Gibson	0-1	M Hills	0-1
L Dettori	0-5	G Bardwell	0-1	Paul Eddery	0-1
Miss E Gatehouse	0-4	G Carter	0-1	S Drowne	0-1
W Newnes	0-3	G Milligan	0-1	T Williams	0-1
B Russell	0-2	J Quinn	0-1	V Halliday	0-1
M Baird	0-2	J Williams	0-1		

COURSE RECORD

	Total W-R	Non-Handicaps 2-y-o	3-y-o+	Handicaps 2-y-o	3-y-o+	Per cent	£1 Level Stake
Wolverhampton (AW)	8-50	1-3	3-18	0-0	4-29	16.0	- 6.45
Hamilton	3-13	0-0	0-2	0-0	3-11	23.1	+ 5.50
Ayr	3-24	1-2	0-4	0-0	2-18	12.5	- 6.50
Chester	3-27	0-5	0-4	0-0	3-18	11.1	- 14.25
Southwell (AW)	2-2	0-0	1-1	0-0	1-1	100.0	+ 6.50
Haydock	2-25	0-4	0-2	0-1	2-18	8.0	- 5.50
Sandown	1-1	0-0	0-0	0-0	1-1	100.0	+ 8.00
Edinburgh	1-2	0-0	0-0	0-0	1-2	50.0	+ 5.50
Kempton	1-3	0-0	0-1	0-0	1-2	33.3	+ 6.00
Nottingham	1-4	0-0	0-1	0-0	1-3	25.0	+ 0.50
Lingfield (AW)	1-10	0-0	1-5	0-0	0-5	10.0	+ 11.00

Doncaster	0-9	Warwick	0-4	Bath	0-1
Catterick	0-7	Goodwood	0-3	Newbury	0-1
Leicester	0-7	Lingfield	0-2	Pontefract	0-1
Carlisle	0-4	Redcar	0-2	York	0-1
Newcastle	0-4	Ripon	0-2		
Newmarket	0-4	Thirsk	0-2		

WINNING HORSES

	Age	Races Run	1st	2nd	3rd	Unpl	Win £
Bold Street	4	12	4	1	0	7	20,160
Pickles	6	15	5	0	0	10	18,009
Everset	6	13	5	1	2	5	14,519
Veloce	6	18	2	0	3	13	6,596
Spring Flyer	4	4	2	0	0	2	5,998
Mentalasanythin	5	8	1	0	1	6	4,013
Crystal Loop	2	5	1	0	1	3	3,766
Lady Broker	4	2	1	0	0	1	3,582
David James' Girl	2	3	1	0	0	2	3,566
Vanessa Rose	3	11	1	0	1	9	3,418
Maz	3	6	1	0	0	5	2,977
Tommy Tempest	5	9	1	1	0	7	2,716
Rave-On-Hadley	4	11	1	1	0	9	2,669

WINNING OWNERS

	Races Won	Value £		Races Won	Value £
Codan Trust Co Ltd	6	26,158	Roy Matthews	1	3,766
Denis Gallagher	5	18,009	Esprit De Corps Racing	1	3,582
A Bailey	5	13,752	David James Racing Services	1	3,566
Gordon Mytton	2	7,161	P J McGuirl	1	2,716
Maximo Gonzalez	2	6,596	K Higson	1	2,669
Mrs M O'Donnell	1	4,013			

Favourites	10-29	34.5%	+ 8.05	Total winning prize-money			£91,987
Longest winning sequence			2	Average SP of winner			5.6/1
Longest losing sequence			25	Return on stakes invested			-20.3%
1993 Form	24-270	8.9%	-113.96	1991 Form	11-95	11.6%	- 32.87
1992 Form	16-180	8.9%	- 57.58	1990 Form	10-180	5.6%	- 88.09

R J BAKER (Tiverton, Devon)

	No. of Horses	Races Run	1st	2nd	3rd	Unpl	Per cent	£1 Level Stake
2-y-o	6	10	0	0	0	10	-	- 10.00
3-y-o	7	28	0	0	3	25	-	- 28.00
4-y-o+	8	45	1	3	4	37	2.2	- 32.00
Totals	21	83	1	3	7	72	1.2	- 70.00

Jan	Feb	Mar	Apr	May	Jun	Jul	Aug	Sep	Oct/Nov
0-3	0-3	0-0	0-5	0-10	0-15	1-13	0-8	0-14	0-12

	W-R	£1 Level Stake		W-R	£1 Level Stake
Winning Jockey			Winning Course		
W Ryan	1-3	+ 10.00	Chester	1-4	+ 9.00

	Age	Races Run	1st	2nd	3rd	Unpl	Win £
Winning Horse							
Star Player	8	14	1	2	2	9	8,656

Favourites	0-0		Total winning prize-money	£8,656

1993 Form	2-74	2.7%	- 63.00	1992 Form	2-40	5.0%	- 3.00

G B BALDING (Andover, Hants)

	No. of Horses	Races Run	1st	2nd	3rd	Unpl	Per cent	£1 Level Stake
2-y-o	0	0	0	0	0	0	-	0.00
3-y-o	10	49	5	3	2	39	10.2	+ 1.75
4-y-o+	10	61	4	1	2	54	6.6	- 14.50
Totals	20	110	9	4	4	93	8.2	- 12.75

Jan	Feb	Mar	Apr	May	Jun	Jul	Aug	Sep	Oct/Nov
0-1	0-0	1-5	1-15	1-16	0-14	1-16	0-13	2-15	3-15

	W-R	£1 Level Stake		W-R	£1 Level Stake
Winning Jockeys					
S Drowne	2-2	+ 21.75	Iona Wands	1-4	+ 1.50
J Williams	2-49	- 37.00	A Clark	1-4	+ 11.00
J Reid	1-1	+ 8.00	N Varley	1-5	+ 12.00
M Wigham	1-1	+ 14.00			
Winning Courses					
Warwick	3-9	+ 13.75	Folkestone	1-4	+ 13.00
Newbury	2-7	+ 29.00	Sandown	1-5	+ 4.00
Haydock	1-1	+ 6.00	Kempton	1-12	- 6.50

Winning Horses	Age	Races Run	1st	2nd	3rd	Unpl	Win £
Brave Tornado	3	5	2	0	0	3	6,972
Matching Green	5	5	2	0	0	3	6,706
Major Bugler	5	1	1	0	0	0	6,223
The French Friar	3	6	1	1	0	4	4,236
Dakota Girl	3	8	1	0	1	6	3,548
Bryan Robson	3	6	1	0	0	5	3,166
Lady Lacey	7	17	1	1	1	14	2,931

Favourites	3-8	37.5%	+ 7.25	Total winning prize-money			£33,781

1993 Form	7-81	8.6%	- 12.90	1991 Form	18-247	7.3%	- 67.47
1992 Form	15-196	7.7%	- 75.79	1990 Form	18-188	9.6%	- 8.59

I A BALDING (Kingsclere, Berks)

	No. of Horses	Races Run	1st	2nd	3rd	Unpl	Per cent	£1 Level Stake
2-y-o	32	84	5	9	5	65	6.0	- 58.25
3-y-o	28	174	31	25	15	103	17.8	+ 3.89
4-y-o+	17	127	15	10	6	96	11.8	- 38.35
Totals	77	385	51	44	26	264	13.2	- 92.71

BY MONTH

2-y-o	W-R	Per cent	£1 Level Stake	3-y-o	W-R	Per cent	£1 Level Stake
Mar/Apr	0-0	-	0.00	Mar/Apr	1-16	6.3	- 10.25
May	0-5	-	- 5.00	May	7-34	20.6	+ 12.92
June	0-2	-	- 2.00	June	8-36	22.2	+ 6.37
July	0-7	-	- 7.00	July	8-31	25.8	+ 4.60
August	0-12	-	- 12.00	August	5-25	20.0	- 1.75
September	2-29	6.9	- 19.25	September	2-22	9.1	+ 4.00
Oct/Nov	3-29	10.3	- 13.00	Oct/Nov	0-10	-	- 10.00

4-y-o+	W-R	Per cent	£1 Level Stake	Totals	W-R	Per cent	£1 Level Stake
Mar/Apr	2-15	13.3	- 6.50	Mar/Apr	3-31	9.7	- 16.75
May	1-21	4.8	- 19.56	May	8-60	13.3	- 11.64
June	6-25	24.0	+ 18.30	June	14-63	22.2	+ 22.67
July	3-25	12.0	- 16.09	July	11-63	17.5	- 18.49
August	0-16	-	- 16.00	August	5-53	9.4	- 29.75
September	3-17	17.6	+ 8.50	September	7-68	10.3	- 6.75
Oct/Nov	0-8	-	- 8.00	Oct/Nov	3-47	6.4	- 31.00

23

DISTANCE

2-y-o	W-R	Per cent	£1 Level Stake	3-y-o	W-R	Per cent	£1 Level Stake
5f-6f	2-33	6.1	- 26.25	5f-6f	12-34	35.3	+ 22.52
7f-8f	3-48	6.3	- 29.00	7f-8f	10-69	14.5	- 6.92
9f-13f	0-3	-	- 3.00	9f-13f	8-65	12.3	- 11.71
14f+	0-0	-	0.00	14f+	1-6	16.7	0.00

4-y-o+	W-R	Per cent	£1 Level Stake	Totals	W-R	Per cent	£1 Level Stake
5f-6f	5-15	33.3	- 1.35	5f-6f	19-82	23.2	- 5.08
7f-8f	3-52	5.8	- 28.50	7f-8f	16-169	9.5	- 64.42
9f-13f	4-41	9.8	- 11.00	9f-13f	12-109	11.0	- 25.71
14f+	3-19	15.8	+ 2.50	14f+	4-25	16.0	+ 2.50

TYPE OF RACE

Non-Handicaps	W-R	Per cent	£1 Level Stake	Handicaps	W-R	Per cent	£1 Level Stake
2-y-o	5-75	6.7	- 49.25	2-y-o	0-9	-	- 9.00
3-y-o	10-83	12.0	- 32.83	3-y-o	18-79	22.8	+ 37.68
4-y-o+	6-21	28.6	- 4.35	4-y-o+	6-94	6.4	- 41.00
Selling	0-0	-	0.00	Selling	0-0	-	0.00
Apprentice	2-4	50.0	+ 3.29	Apprentice	1-11	9.1	- 7.25
Amat/Ladies	0-0	-	0.00	Amat/Ladies	3-9	33.3	+ 10.00
Totals	23-183	12.6	- 83.14	Totals	28-202	13.9	- 9.57

COURSE GRADE

	W-R	Per cent	£1 Level Stake
Group 1	24-223	10.8	- 66.35
Group 2	6-59	10.2	- 24.25
Group 3	18-86	20.9	+ 7.89
Group 4	3-17	17.6	- 10.00

FIRST TIME OUT

	W-R	Per cent	£1 Level Stake
2-y-o	2-32	6.3	- 15.00
3-y-o	1-28	3.6	- 24.25
4-y-o+	2-17	11.8	- 7.50
Totals	5-77	6.5	- 46.75

JOCKEYS RIDING

	W-R	Per cent	£1 Level Stake		W-R	Per cent	£1 Level Stake
L Dettori	23-125	18.4	- 3.00	J Weaver	1-3	33.3	+ 1.00
R Cochrane	9-65	13.8	- 1.00	Paul Eddery	1-4	25.0	+ 0.50
D Griffiths	4-26	15.4	- 5.71	T Ives	1-7	14.3	- 4.00
Mr A Balding	3-8	37.5	+ 11.00	K Darley	1-8	12.5	- 4.00
W Ryan	3-16	18.8	+ 6.50	M J Dwyer	1-9	11.1	- 5.25
M Hills	3-37	8.1	- 19.75	S O'Gorman	1-40	2.5	- 32.00

T Quinn	0-9	W Carson	0-2	M Perrett	0-1
Pat Eddery	0-4	A Munro	0-1	M Roberts	0-1
B Raymond	0-2	Aimee Cook	0-1	Mr A Holdsworth	0-1
C Asmussen	0-2	C Scudder	0-1	R Hills	0-1
G Carter	0-2	F Norton	0-1	W Newnes	0-1
G Hind	0-2	J Reid	0-1	W R Swinburn	0-1
M J Kinane	0-2	L Piggott	0-1		

COURSE RECORD

	Total W-R	Non-Handicaps 2-y-o	3-y-o+	Handicaps 2-y-o	3-y-o+	Per cent	£1 Level Stake
Bath	7-28	1-6	2-9	0-1	4-12	25.0	+ 5.00
Goodwood	5-28	0-7	2-7	0-0	3-14	17.9	+ 4.41
Windsor	3-11	0-0	1-7	0-0	2-4	27.3	+ 2.10
Haydock	3-12	0-2	0-1	0-0	3-9	25.0	+ 3.50
Kempton	3-16	1-3	1-5	0-1	1-7	18.8	+ 9.50
Sandown	3-20	0-3	1-3	0-0	2-14	15.0	- 7.56
Doncaster	3-22	1-6	1-4	0-3	1-9	13.6	- 3.50
Ascot	3-26	0-2	1-4	0-1	2-19	11.5	- 0.70
Leicester	2-8	0-2	1-2	0-0	1-4	25.0	- 0.50
Beverley	2-9	0-1	0-2	0-0	2-6	22.2	- 1.00
Nottingham	2-9	0-2	1-2	0-1	1-4	22.2	+ 9.00
Pontefract	2-13	0-3	1-5	0-0	1-5	15.4	+ 1.29
Newmarket	2-28	0-5	2-8	0-1	0-14	7.1	- 14.50
Salisbury	2-28	0-11	0-8	0-0	2-9	7.1	- 12.00
Newbury	2-44	0-12	1-13	0-0	1-19	4.5	- 30.50
Wolverhampton (AW)	1-1	0-0	1-1	0-0	0-0	100.0	+ 1.00
Catterick	1-3	1-3	0-0	0-0	0-0	33.3	0.00
Lingfield	1-5	0-0	1-3	0-0	0-2	20.0	- 1.75
Ripon	1-5	0-1	1-2	0-0	0-2	20.0	- 1.00
Brighton	1-7	0-0	0-2	0-0	1-5	14.3	0.00
Chester	1-7	0-0	0-1	0-0	1-6	14.3	- 2.50
Warwick	1-7	1-2	0-2	0-1	0-2	14.3	- 5.00

York	0-19	Thirsk	0-7	Folkestone	0-6
Chepstow	0-8	Epsom	0-6	Newcastle	0-2

WINNING HORSES

	Age	Races Run	1st	2nd	3rd	Unpl	Win £
Lochsong	6	6	4	0	0	2	149,025
Blue Siren	3	7	2	2	1	2	29,878
Jayannpee	3	12	5	1	0	6	25,715
Master Charlie	4	7	1	0	0	6	25,050
Robin Lake	3	13	6	1	0	6	22,274
Palana	3	5	1	0	0	4	13,186
Hill Of Dreams	4	14	3	1	1	9	10,639
Pay Homage	6	11	1	0	0	10	10,575
Brandon Court	3	10	2	3	1	4	9,722
Clouded Elegance	4	10	2	0	0	8	9,469

Farnham	3	12	3	1	2	6	9,313
Poker Chip	4	9	1	1	2	5	7,927
Winged Victory (Ire)	4	12	1	1	0	10	7,602
Golden Arrow	3	8	1	3	0	4	7,555
Moccasin Run	3	4	1	0	1	2	6,648
Brandon Prince	6	12	1	0	0	11	5,572
Stiletto Blade	2	3	1	1	0	1	4,881
Grey Shot	2	1	1	0	0	0	4,794
Spinning	7	7	1	2	0	4	4,673
Hunters' Heaven	3	11	1	1	0	9	4,435
Rory Creek	3	6	1	1	1	3	4,264
Dashing Water	2	3	1	0	1	1	4,163
Blair Castle	3	6	1	0	0	5	3,904
Overbrook	2	5	1	1	1	2	3,658
Most Thoughtful	2	3	1	0	0	2	3,553
Sight'n Sound	3	7	1	1	2	3	3,136
Dancing Heights	3	4	1	0	1	2	3,093
Java Shrine	3	9	1	1	0	7	3,030
Red Valerian	3	6	1	2	0	3	2,908
Memory's Gold	3	8	1	1	1	5	2,681
Mountain Ballet	3	4	1	0	1	2	2,249
Lochbelle	3	6	1	1	1	3	2,223

WINNING OWNERS

	Races Won	Value £		Races Won	Value £
J C Smith	12	206,026	Robert Hitchins	3	9,313
George Strawbridge	9	46,372	Highflyers	1	3,904
Paul Mellon	9	40,615	Sir William Purves	1	3,658
J Paniccia	5	25,715	The Cromhall Stud Partnership	1	3,553
David R Watson	1	25,050	R Leah	1	3,093
R P B Michaelson	3	15,294	Mrs Duncan Allen	1	2,908
Miss A V Hill	1	10,575	The Queen	1	2,249
M E Wates	2	9,469			

Favourites	26-69	37.7%	+ 17.79	Total winning prize-money			£407,795

Longest winning sequence			2
Longest losing sequence			21

Average SP of winner			4.7/1
Return on stakes invested			-24.1%

1993 Form	50-342	14.6%	- 62.80	1991 Form	53-362	14.6%	- 50.22
1992 Form	36-316	11.4%	- 42.11	1990 Form	48-375	12.8%	- 41.74

J E BANKS (Newmarket)

	No. of Horses	Races Run	1st	2nd	3rd	Unpl	Per cent	£1 Level Stake
2-y-o	7	18	3	1	0	14	16.7	+ 35.50
3-y-o	6	23	2	1	1	19	8.7	- 13.75
4-y-o+	5	22	2	2	1	17	9.1	+ 5.00
Totals	18	63	7	4	2	50	11.1	+ 26.75

Jan	Feb	Mar	Apr	May	Jun	Jul	Aug	Sep	Oct/Nov
0-0	1-2	1-2	1-7	0-4	0-9	1-10	0-8	0-8	3-13

Winning Jockeys	W-R	£1 Level Stake		W-R	£1 Level Stake
K Rutter	2-3	+ 24.00	J Quinn	2-33	- 18.75
A Mackay	2-4	+ 38.50	J Weaver	1-1	+ 5.00

Winning Courses					
Pontefract	2-4	+ 7.75	Southwell (AW)	1-3	+ 23.00
Lingfield (AW)	1-1	0.00	Warwick	1-5	+ 29.00
Nottingham	1-2	+ 4.00	Yarmouth	1-11	0.00

Winning Horses	Age	Races Run	1st	2nd	3rd	Unpl	Win £
Traikey	2	1	1	0	0	0	5,250
Moody	2	1	1	0	0	0	3,721
Lesley's Fashion	3	4	1	0	0	3	2,898
Irish Senor	3	8	1	0	0	7	2,840
Yaakum	5	3	1	0	0	2	2,557
Bottles	7	7	1	2	0	4	2,243
Failte Ro	2	2	1	0	0	1	844

Favourites	1-3	33.3%	+ 0.25	Total winning prize-money		£20,351

1993 Form	7-46	15.2%	+ 18.33	1991 Form	3-61	4.9%	- 27.00
1992 Form	4-52	7.7%	- 31.75				

MRS P A BARKER (Wetherby, West Yorks)

	No. of Horses	Races Run	1st	2nd	3rd	Unpl	Per cent	£1 Level Stake
2-y-o	0	0	0	0	0	0	-	0.00
3-y-o	0	0	0	0	0	0	-	0.00
4-y-o+	4	10	1	1	0	8	10.0	+ 3.00
Totals	4	10	1	1	0	8	10.0	+ 3.00

Jan	Feb	Mar	Apr	May	Jun	Jul	Aug	Sep	Oct/Nov
0-0	0-2	0-1	0-0	1-2	0-2	0-2	0-1	0-0	0-0

Winning Jockey	W-R	£1 Level Stake	Winning Course	W-R	£1 Level Stake
J Lowe	1-2	+ 11.00	Carlisle	1-1	+ 12.00

Winning Horse	Age	Races Run	1st	2nd	3rd	Unpl	Win £
Dance On Sixpence	6	4	1	1	0	2	3,287

Favourites	0-0		Total winning prize-money	£3,287

1993 Form	1-30	3.3%	- 22.50	1991 Form	1-23	4.3%	+ 3.00
1992 Form	0-15			1990 Form	0-30		

W L BARKER (Richmond, North Yorks)

	No. of Horses	Races Run	1st	2nd	3rd	Unpl	Per cent	£1 Level Stake
2-y-o	1	4	0	0	0	4	-	- 4.00
3-y-o	2	14	1	2	2	9	7.1	- 5.00
4-y-o+	11	57	1	5	6	45	1.8	- 31.00
Totals	14	75	2	7	8	58	2.7	- 40.00

Jan	Feb	Mar	Apr	May	Jun	Jul	Aug	Sep	Oct/Nov
0-4	0-2	0-2	0-13	0-11	2-14	0-11	0-12	0-6	0-0

Winning Jockey	W-R	£1 Level Stake		W-R	£1 Level Stake
D Moffatt	2-5	+ 30.00			

Winning Courses					
Beverley	1-9	+ 17.00	Catterick	1-11	- 2.00

Winning Horses	Age	Races Run	1st	2nd	3rd	Unpl	Win £
Henry Will	10	9	1	0	1	7	4,510
Lochon	3	10	1	2	2	5	2,951

Favourites	0-1		Total winning prize-money	£7,461

1993 Form	1-52	1.9%	- 39.00	1991 Form	0-7
1992 Form	1-35	2.9%	- 23.00		

D H BARONS (Kingsbridge, Devon)

	No. of Horses	Races Run	1st	2nd	3rd	Unpl	Per cent	£1 Level Stake
2-y-o	0	0	0	0	0	0	-	0.00
3-y-o	1	5	1	0	2	2	20.0	+ 4.00
4-y-o+	0	0	0	0	0	0	-	0.00
Totals	1	5	1	0	2	2	20.0	+ 4.00

Jan	Feb	Mar	Apr	May	Jun	Jul	Aug	Sep	Oct/Nov
0-0	0-0	0-0	0-2	1-3	0-0	0-0	0-0	0-0	0-0

Winning Jockey	W-R	£1 Level Stake	Winning Course		W-R	£1 Level Stake
J Williams	1-1	+ 8.00	Leicester		1-1	+ 8.00

Winning Horse	Age	Races Run	1st	2nd	3rd	Unpl	Win £
Northern Bailiwick	3	5	1	0	2	2	3,834

Favourites	0-0		Total winning prize-money	£3,834

1993 Form	0-0		1991 Form	0-0
1992 Form	0-0		1990 Form	0-1

R E BARR (Middlesborough, Co Durham)

	No. of Horses	Races Run	1st	2nd	3rd	Unpl	Per cent	£1 Level Stake
2-y-o	0	0	0	0	0	0	-	0.00
3-y-o	0	0	0	0	0	0	-	0.00
4-y-o+	2	25	2	2	3	18	8.0	- 8.50
Totals	2	25	2	2	3	18	8.0	- 8.50

Jan	Feb	Mar	Apr	May	Jun	Jul	Aug	Sep	Oct/Nov
0-0	0-0	0-1	0-4	0-6	1-4	1-4	0-4	0-2	0-0

Winning Jockey	W-R	£1 Level Stake			W-R	£1 Level Stake
S Webster	2-8	+ 8.50				

Winning Courses						
Edinburgh	1-8	- 2.50	Redcar		1-10	+ 1.00

Winning Horse	Age	Races Run	1st	2nd	3rd	Unpl	Win £
Thatched	4	15	2	2	3	8	6,207

Favourites	0-2		Total winning prize-money	£6,207

1993 Form	0-10		1991 Form	0-11
1992 Form	0-21			

T D BARRON (Thirsk, North Yorks)

	No. of Horses	Races Run	1st	2nd	3rd	Unpl	Per cent	£1 Level Stake
2-y-o	8	29	5	5	4	15	17.2	- 6.25
3-y-o	9	52	10	4	5	33	19.2	+ 27.75
4-y-o+	19	151	22	21	15	93	14.6	+ 21.50
Totals	36	232	37	30	24	141	15.9	+ 43.00

BY MONTH

2-y-o	W-R	Per cent	£1 Level Stake	3-y-o	W-R	Per cent	£1 Level Stake
January	0-0	-	0.00	January	0-4	-	- 4.00
February	0-0	-	0.00	February	0-3	-	- 3.00
March	0-0	-	0.00	March	0-2	-	- 2.00
April	1-2	50.0	+ 1.50	April	0-1	-	- 1.00
May	0-3	-	- 3.00	May	3-10	30.0	+ 6.75
June	1-1	100.0	+ 2.50	June	2-9	22.2	+ 8.00
July	0-4	-	- 4.00	July	2-8	25.0	+ 11.00
August	0-8	-	- 8.00	August	1-8	12.5	- 3.00
September	2-5	40.0	+ 6.75	September	1-5	20.0	+ 10.00
Oct/Nov	1-6	16.7	- 2.00	Oct/Nov	1-2	50.0	+ 5.00

4-y-o+	W-R	Per cent	£1 Level Stake	Totals	W-R	Per cent	£1 Level Stake
January	1-12	8.3	- 8.50	January	1-16	6.3	- 12.50
February	3-14	21.4	+ 15.75	February	3-17	17.6	+ 12.75
March	4-15	26.7	+ 2.75	March	4-17	23.5	+ 0.75
April	2-16	12.5	- 5.00	April	3-19	15.8	- 4.50
May	2-17	11.8	- 8.50	May	5-30	16.7	- 4.75
June	1-10	10.0	+ 1.00	June	4-20	20.0	+ 11.50
July	4-24	16.7	+ 15.00	July	6-36	16.7	+ 22.00
August	0-18	-	- 18.00	August	1-34	2.9	- 29.00
September	1-12	8.3	- 5.00	September	4-22	18.2	+ 11.75
Oct/Nov	4-13	30.8	+ 32.00	Oct/Nov	6-21	28.6	+ 35.00

DISTANCE

2-y-o	W-R	Per cent	£1 Level Stake	3-y-o	W-R	Per cent	£1 Level Stake
5f-6f	3-17	17.6	- 6.00	5f-6f	2-10	20.0	+ 4.00
7f-8f	2-12	16.7	- 0.25	7f-8f	3-26	11.5	- 0.50
9f-13f	0-0	-	0.00	9f-13f	5-16	31.3	+ 24.25
14f+	0-0	-	0.00	14f+	0-0	-	0.00

4-y-o+	W-R	Per cent	£1 Level Stake	Totals	W-R	Per cent	£1 Level Stake
5f-6f	9-40	22.5	+ 49.25	5f-6f	14-67	20.9	+ 47.25
7f-8f	8-76	10.5	- 25.50	7f-8f	13-114	11.4	- 26.25
9f-13f	5-31	16.1	+ 1.75	9f-13f	10-47	21.3	+ 26.00
14f+	0-4	-	- 4.00	14f+	0-4	-	- 4.00

TYPE OF RACE

Non-Handicaps	W–R	Per cent	£1 Level Stake	Handicaps	W–R	Per cent	£1 Level Stake
2-y-o	4-20	20.0	– 5.25	2-y-o	1-8	12.5	0.00
3-y-o	2-12	16.7	+ 0.25	3-y-o	7-33	21.2	+ 19.50
4-y-o+	2-25	8.0	– 14.50	4-y-o+	16-102	15.7	+ 23.50
Selling	1-9	11.1	– 5.50	Selling	1-7	14.3	+ 3.00
Apprentice	0-0	–	0.00	Apprentice	3-13	23.1	+ 25.00
Amat/Ladies	0-0	–	0.00	Amat/Ladies	0-3	–	– 3.00
Totals	9-66	13.6	– 25.00	Totals	28-166	16.9	+ 68.00

COURSE GRADE

	W–R	Per cent	£1 Level Stake
Group 1	12-54	22.2	+ 50.00
Group 2	4-58	6.9	– 30.25
Group 3	4-32	12.5	– 4.00
Group 4	17-88	19.3	+ 27.25

FIRST TIME OUT

	W–R	Per cent	£1 Level Stake
2-y-o	1-7	14.3	– 3.50
3-y-o	1-9	11.1	0.00
4-y-o+	1-19	5.3	– 6.00
Totals	3-35	8.6	– 9.50

JOCKEYS RIDING

	W–R	Per cent	£1 Level Stake		W–R	Per cent	£1 Level Stake
J Fortune	17-111	15.3	+ 3.25	G Mitchell	1-1	100.0	+ 14.00
K Darley	7-23	30.4	+ 22.25	J Carroll	1-2	50.0	+ 4.00
W Carson	2-3	66.7	+ 17.00	Mrs A Dennis	1-3	33.3	+ 7.00
N Varley	2-9	22.2	+ 7.00	L Charnock	1-4	25.0	+ 1.50
Kimberley Hart	2-11	18.2	+ 12.00	D Harrison	1-5	20.0	+ 8.00
B Raymond	1-1	100.0	+ 2.50	Paul Eddery	1-8	12.5	– 4.50

J Fanning	0-15	G Hind	0-2	M Birch	0-1
V Halliday	0-6	J Quinn	0-2	M J Kinane	0-1
W Ryan	0-4	Mrs A Farrell	0-2	N Connorton	0-1
Jenny Benson	0-3	S Maloney	0-2	T Quinn	0-1
L Dettori	0-3	A Whelan	0-1	W Woods	0-1
A Mackay	0-2	C Hawksley	0-1		
D Moffatt	0-2	J Lowe	0-1		

COURSE RECORD

	Total W–R	Non-Handicaps 2-y-o	3-y-o+	Handicaps 2-y-o	3-y-o+	Per cent	£1 Level Stake
Wolverhampton (AW)	7-29	0-0	1-8	0-0	6-21	24.1	+ 27.75
York	4-11	0-0	0-0	0-1	4-10	36.4	+ 31.00
Southwell (AW)	4-28	0-0	1-10	0-1	3-17	14.3	+ 4.00
Newcastle	3-10	0-0	0-1	0-1	3-8	30.0	+ 5.00
Edinburgh	3-13	0-0	2-5	0-1	1-7	23.1	– 1.75
Thirsk	3-18	1-3	0-4	0-0	2-11	16.7	+ 0.75
Ayr	2-11	1-3	0-3	0-0	1-5	18.2	– 1.00

31

Barron T D

Folkestone	1-1	1-1	0-0	0-0	0-0	100.0	+ 3.00
Goodwood	1-1	0-0	0-0	0-0	1-1	100.0	+ 16.00
Haydock	1-1	0-0	0-0	0-0	1-1	100.0	+ 10.00
Hamilton	1-3	1-1	0-0	0-0	0-2	33.3	+ 0.50
Pontefract	1-7	0-0	0-0	0-0	1-7	14.3	+ 1.00
Lingfield (AW)	1-7	0-0	0-3	0-0	1-4	14.3	- 3.75
Catterick	1-8	0-1	0-1	1-1	0-5	12.5	0.00
Nottingham	1-8	0-0	0-2	0-0	1-6	12.5	+ 3.00
Beverley	1-10	0-1	0-0	0-1	1-8	10.0	- 4.50
Doncaster	1-14	0-2	1-1	0-1	0-10	7.1	- 5.00
Redcar	1-23	0-4	0-3	0-0	1-16	4.3	- 14.00

Ripon	0-14	Leicester	0-2	Newbury	0-1
Newmarket	0-4	Ascot	0-1	Warwick	0-1
Chepstow	0-2	Carlisle	0-1		
Chester	0-2	Lingfield	0-1		

WINNING HORSES

	Age	Races Run	1st	2nd	3rd	Unpl	Win £
For The Present	4	8	1	1	3	3	48,250
Saddlehome	5	9	5	1	0	3	32,126
Tread The Boards	3	13	4	1	3	5	15,761
Allinson's Mate	6	19	3	2	3	11	11,036
Old Comrades	7	15	3	1	3	8	9,576
Brackenthwaite	4	7	2	0	0	5	9,438
Dream Carrier	6	16	3	3	1	9	8,308
Musical Season	2	7	2	2	2	1	7,087
Palo Blanco	3	8	2	1	1	4	6,508
Ashover	4	15	2	3	1	9	6,340
Prizefighter	3	6	2	0	0	4	5,838
Slades Hill	7	9	1	1	0	7	3,469
Chaldon Herring	2	5	1	0	1	3	3,392
Touch Above	8	9	1	1	2	5	3,207
Icanspell	3	9	1	0	0	8	3,024
Striffolino	2	2	1	0	0	1	2,941
Superpride	2	3	1	1	1	0	2,563
The Lone Dancer	3	5	1	2	1	1	2,349
Across The Bay	7	20	1	6	2	11	2,274

WINNING OWNERS

	Races Won	Value £		Races Won	Value £
Mrs J Hazell	2	51,457	J G Brown	2	6,508
Kevin Shaw	3	21,081	Timothy Cox	2	6,340
Geoffrey Martin	4	15,761	B T R B Owners Group (1990)	1	3,469
P D Savill	4	12,924	Dave Scott	1	3,392
Stephen Woodall	4	11,332	Lady Burnham	1	2,941
W H Clarke	2	11,045	Mrs Muriel Ward	1	2,563
Peter Jones	3	11,036	Mrs A M Jeffrey	1	2,349
P J Dennis	3	9,576	W Dixon	1	2,274
Alex Gorrie	2	9,438			

Favourites	10-28	35.7%	+ 15.00	Total winning prize-money		£183,486

Longest winning sequence			4	Average SP of winner		6.4/1
Longest losing sequence			29	Return on stakes invested		18.5%

1993 Form	26-270	9.6%	-111.92	1991 Form	39-331	11.8%	- 75.22
1992 Form	41-345	11.9%	- 48.70	1990 Form	58-337	17.2%	- 42.83

R BASTIMAN (Wetherby, West Yorks)

	No. of Horses	Races Run	1st	2nd	3rd	Unpl	Per cent	£1 Level Stake
2-y-o	0	0	0	0	0	0	-	0.00
3-y-o	2	6	0	0	0	6	-	- 6.00
4-y-o+	8	59	8	2	6	43	13.6	- 10.27
Totals	10	65	8	2	6	49	12.3	- 16.27

Jan	Feb	Mar	Apr	May	Jun	Jul	Aug	Sep	Oct/Nov
3-4	1-3	1-5	0-8	0-6	1-5	0-4	1-3	0-12	1-15

Winning Jockeys	W-R	£1 Level Stake			W-R	£1 Level Stake
H Bastiman	6-39	- 16.27	A Culhane		1-4	+ 11.00
L Charnock	1-3	+ 8.00				

Winning Courses						
Wolverhampton (AW)	3-9	+ 2.13	Southwell (AW)		1-5	- 0.50
Ripon	1-2	+ 13.00	Hamilton		1-6	+ 5.00
Beverley	1-4	- 1.90	Pontefract		1-7	- 2.00

Winning Horses	Age	Races Run	1st	2nd	3rd	Unpl	Win £
Hillzah	6	13	4	1	1	7	13,260
Super Rocky	5	8	1	0	2	5	3,720
Deputy Tim	11	8	1	0	1	6	3,184
First Option	4	8	1	0	1	6	2,672
Golden Torque	7	2	1	0	0	1	2,243

Favourites	3-9	33.3%	+ 2.60	Total winning prize-money		£25,079

1993 Form	9-107	8.4%	+ 21.50	1991 Form	14-127	11.0%	+ 4.25
1992 Form	10-127	7.9%	- 37.67	1990 Form	12-119	10.1%	- 8.25

B BEASLEY (Hambleton, North Yorks)

	No. of Horses	Races Run	1st	2nd	3rd	Unpl	Per cent	£1 Level Stake
2-y-o	3	10	0	0	0	10	–	- 10.00
3-y-o	2	14	1	0	2	11	7.1	- 8.00
4-y-o+	11	88	8	10	7	63	9.1	- 15.50
Totals	16	112	9	10	9	84	8.0	- 33.50

Jan	Feb	Mar	Apr	May	Jun	Jul	Aug	Sep	Oct/Nov
1-3	1-5	1-5	0-7	0-13	3-11	0-13	1-21	2-18	0-16

Winning Jockeys	W-R	£1 Level Stake		W-R	£1 Level Stake
K Darley	3-7	+ 18.00	A Munro	1-6	+ 9.00
J Carroll	1-3	+ 2.50	A Culhane	1-7	+ 1.00
T Quinn	1-4	+ 2.00	J Tate	1-22	- 12.00
J Williams	1-5	+ 4.00			

Winning Courses					
Lingfield (AW)	2-6	+ 9.00	Edinburgh	1-6	+ 2.00
Epsom	1-1	+ 14.00	Redcar	1-8	+ 5.00
Newcastle	1-3	+ 5.00	Southwell (AW)	1-11	- 1.00
Doncaster	1-4	0.00	Hamilton	1-14	- 8.50

Winning Horses	Age	Races Run	1st	2nd	3rd	Unpl	Win £
Misteropogigo	4	6	3	1	2	0	38,383
Mustn't Grumble	4	14	3	1	3	7	10,933
Four Of Spades	3	12	1	0	2	9	2,534
Super Benz	8	16	1	3	0	12	2,511
Gemikosix	4	5	1	0	1	3	2,358

Favourites	1-7	14.3%	- 3.00	Total winning prize-money		£56,719

1993 Form	8-115	7.0%	- 53.00	1992 Form	14-152	9.2%	- 32.02

M BELL (Newmarket)

	No. of Horses	Races Run	1st	2nd	3rd	Unpl	Per cent	£1 Level Stake
2-y-o	36	142	27	14	17	84	19.0	- 49.98
3-y-o	28	178	17	13	21	127	9.6	- 55.37
4-y-o+	9	62	11	6	4	41	17.7	+ 7.86
Totals	73	382	55	33	42	252	14.4	- 97.49

BY MONTH

2-y-o	W-R	Per cent	£1 Level Stake	3-y-o	W-R	Per cent	£1 Level Stake
January	0-0	-	0.00	January	0-2	-	- 2.00
February	0-0	-	0.00	February	1-1	100.0	+ 5.00
March	1-3	33.3	+ 4.00	March	3-10	30.0	+ 1.80
April	4-8	50.0	+ 7.75	April	2-22	9.1	- 5.00
May	5-17	29.4	- 4.89	May	3-27	11.1	- 10.67
June	1-17	5.9	- 14.25	June	2-32	6.3	- 6.50
July	8-25	32.0	- 3.65	July	2-34	5.9	- 17.50
August	4-21	19.0	- 9.44	August	1-24	4.2	- 19.50
September	1-27	3.7	- 21.50	September	3-19	15.8	+ 6.00
Oct/Nov	3-24	12.5	- 8.00	Oct/Nov	0-7	-	- 7.00

4-y-o+	W-R	Per cent	£1 Level Stake	Totals	W-R	Per cent	£1 Level Stake
January	0-0	-	0.00	January	0-2	-	- 2.00
February	0-0	-	0.00	February	1-1	100.0	+ 5.00
March	1-6	16.7	- 1.50	March	5-19	26.3	+ 4.30
April	1-9	11.1	- 6.50	April	7-39	17.9	- 3.75
May	1-11	9.1	+ 10.00	May	9-55	16.4	- 5.56
June	3-11	27.3	+ 1.63	June	6-60	10.0	- 19.12
July	3-11	27.3	+ 8.13	July	13-70	18.6	- 13.02
August	1-6	16.7	- 3.90	August	6-51	11.8	- 32.84
September	0-5	-	- 5.00	September	4-51	7.8	- 20.50
Oct/Nov	1-3	33.3	+ 5.00	Oct/Nov	4-34	11.8	- 10.00

DISTANCE

2-y-o	W-R	Per cent	£1 Level Stake	3-y-o	W-R	Per cent	£1 Level Stake
5f-6f	21-84	25.0	- 21.11	5f-6f	2-32	6.3	- 22.70
7f-8f	6-54	11.1	- 24.87	7f-8f	10-64	15.6	+ 15.33
9f-13f	0-4	-	- 4.00	9f-13f	4-68	5.9	- 41.00
14f+	0-0	-	0.00	14f+	1-14	7.1	- 7.00

4-y-o+	W-R	Per cent	£1 Level Stake	Totals	W-R	Per cent	£1 Level Stake
5f-6f	6-23	26.1	+ 19.63	5f-6f	29-139	20.9	- 24.18
7f-8f	2-15	13.3	- 2.90	7f-8f	18-133	13.5	- 12.44
9f-13f	3-19	15.8	- 3.87	9f-13f	7-91	7.7	- 48.87
14f+	0-5	-	- 5.00	14f+	1-19	5.3	- 12.00

TYPE OF RACE

Non-Handicaps	W-R	Per cent	£1 Level Stake	Handicaps	W-R	Per cent	£1 Level Stake
2-y-o	26-111	23.4	- 23.98	2-y-o	0-22	-	- 22.00
3-y-o	7-65	10.8	- 34.87	3-y-o	10-106	9.4	- 13.50
4-y-o+	6-22	27.3	+ 9.10	4-y-o+	5-36	13.9	+ 2.76
Selling	1-7	14.3	- 2.00	Selling	0-6	-	- 6.00
Apprentice	0-0	-	0.00	Apprentice	0-4	-	- 4.00
Amat/Ladies	0-0	-	0.00	Amat/Ladies	0-3	-	- 3.00
Totals	40-205	19.5	- 51.75	Totals	15-177	8.5	- 45.74

Bell M

<table>
<tr><th colspan="4">COURSE GRADE</th><th colspan="4">FIRST TIME OUT</th></tr>
<tr><th></th><th>W-R</th><th>Per cent</th><th>£1 Level Stake</th><th></th><th>W-R</th><th>Per cent</th><th>£1 Level Stake</th></tr>
<tr><td>Group 1</td><td>22-169</td><td>13.0</td><td>- 17.68</td><td>2-y-o</td><td>5-35</td><td>14.3</td><td>- 9.42</td></tr>
<tr><td>Group 2</td><td>6-47</td><td>12.8</td><td>- 29.80</td><td>3-y-o</td><td>3-28</td><td>10.7</td><td>- 10.50</td></tr>
<tr><td>Group 3</td><td>14-101</td><td>13.9</td><td>- 36.34</td><td>4-y-o+</td><td>2-9</td><td>22.2</td><td>- 2.00</td></tr>
<tr><td>Group 4</td><td>13-65</td><td>20.0</td><td>- 13.67</td><td></td><td></td><td></td><td></td></tr>
<tr><td></td><td></td><td></td><td></td><td>Totals</td><td>10-72</td><td>13.9</td><td>- 21.92</td></tr>
</table>

JOCKEYS RIDING

<table>
<tr><th></th><th>W-R</th><th>Per cent</th><th>£1 Level Stake</th><th></th><th>W-R</th><th>Per cent</th><th>£1 Level Stake</th></tr>
<tr><td>M Fenton</td><td>28-197</td><td>14.2</td><td>- 73.31</td><td>M J Kinane</td><td>1-2</td><td>50.0</td><td>+ 11.00</td></tr>
<tr><td>M Hills</td><td>16-76</td><td>21.1</td><td>+ 1.19</td><td>D Harrison</td><td>1-2</td><td>50.0</td><td>+ 1.50</td></tr>
<tr><td>J Reid</td><td>2-2</td><td>100.0</td><td>+ 10.63</td><td>G Faulkner</td><td>1-3</td><td>33.3</td><td>+ 14.00</td></tr>
<tr><td>P Robinson</td><td>2-6</td><td>33.3</td><td>+ 4.50</td><td>D Biggs</td><td>1-4</td><td>25.0</td><td>+ 9.00</td></tr>
<tr><td>J Fanning</td><td>2-12</td><td>16.7</td><td>- 0.50</td><td>L Dettori</td><td>1-5</td><td>20.0</td><td>- 2.50</td></tr>
</table>

<table>
<tr><td>R Mullen</td><td>0-10</td><td>Dale Gibson</td><td>0-2</td><td>F Norton</td><td>0-1</td></tr>
<tr><td>G Duffield</td><td>0-6</td><td>J Carroll</td><td>0-2</td><td>K Darley</td><td>0-1</td></tr>
<tr><td>T Quinn</td><td>0-5</td><td>L Charnock</td><td>0-2</td><td>K Fallon</td><td>0-1</td></tr>
<tr><td>W Carson</td><td>0-5</td><td>Pat Eddery</td><td>0-2</td><td>K Rutter</td><td>0-1</td></tr>
<tr><td>G Bardwell</td><td>0-4</td><td>Paul Eddery</td><td>0-2</td><td>L Piggott</td><td>0-1</td></tr>
<tr><td>D Moffatt</td><td>0-3</td><td>R Hills</td><td>0-2</td><td>Miss A Harwood</td><td>0-1</td></tr>
<tr><td>J Weaver</td><td>0-3</td><td>B Doyle</td><td>0-1</td><td>Miss C Preston</td><td>0-1</td></tr>
<tr><td>M Baird</td><td>0-3</td><td>C Dwyer</td><td>0-1</td><td>Mr T Cuff</td><td>0-1</td></tr>
<tr><td>A Clark</td><td>0-2</td><td>C Hodgson</td><td>0-1</td><td>N Carlisle</td><td>0-1</td></tr>
<tr><td>A Mackay</td><td>0-2</td><td>C N Adamson</td><td>0-1</td><td>N Kennedy</td><td>0-1</td></tr>
<tr><td>A Munro</td><td>0-2</td><td>D McCabe</td><td>0-1</td><td>P Tulk</td><td>0-1</td></tr>
</table>

COURSE RECORD

<table>
<tr><th></th><th>Total W-R</th><th colspan="2">Non-Handicaps</th><th colspan="2">Handicaps</th><th>Per cent</th><th>£1 Level Stake</th></tr>
<tr><th></th><th></th><th>2-y-o</th><th>3-y-o+</th><th>2-y-o</th><th>3-y-o+</th><th></th><th></th></tr>
<tr><td>Warwick</td><td>5-12</td><td>2-4</td><td>3-5</td><td>0-0</td><td>0-3</td><td>41.7</td><td>+ 9.53</td></tr>
<tr><td>Newmarket</td><td>5-71</td><td>2-24</td><td>1-19</td><td>0-4</td><td>2-24</td><td>7.0</td><td>- 38.90</td></tr>
<tr><td>Beverley</td><td>4-12</td><td>3-4</td><td>0-2</td><td>0-2</td><td>1-4</td><td>33.3</td><td>- 0.17</td></tr>
<tr><td>Yarmouth</td><td>4-17</td><td>3-6</td><td>0-0</td><td>0-2</td><td>1-9</td><td>23.5</td><td>+ 6.75</td></tr>
<tr><td>Goodwood</td><td>3-9</td><td>1-3</td><td>1-1</td><td>0-0</td><td>1-5</td><td>33.3</td><td>+ 16.00</td></tr>
<tr><td>York</td><td>3-9</td><td>1-2</td><td>0-1</td><td>0-1</td><td>2-5</td><td>33.3</td><td>+ 24.50</td></tr>
<tr><td>Folkestone</td><td>3-16</td><td>1-3</td><td>1-5</td><td>0-1</td><td>1-7</td><td>18.8</td><td>- 6.00</td></tr>
<tr><td>Nottingham</td><td>3-20</td><td>2-7</td><td>0-3</td><td>0-1</td><td>1-9</td><td>15.0</td><td>- 6.67</td></tr>
<tr><td>Newcastle</td><td>2-6</td><td>1-1</td><td>0-2</td><td>0-0</td><td>1-3</td><td>33.3</td><td>- 0.49</td></tr>
<tr><td>Newbury</td><td>2-12</td><td>1-5</td><td>1-3</td><td>0-1</td><td>0-3</td><td>16.7</td><td>+ 1.50</td></tr>
<tr><td>Sandown</td><td>2-12</td><td>1-3</td><td>1-3</td><td>0-2</td><td>0-4</td><td>16.7</td><td>- 6.70</td></tr>
<tr><td>Southwell (AW)</td><td>2-16</td><td>0-3</td><td>1-5</td><td>0-0</td><td>1-8</td><td>12.5</td><td>- 5.00</td></tr>
<tr><td>Salisbury</td><td>1-1</td><td>1-1</td><td>0-0</td><td>0-0</td><td>0-0</td><td>100.0</td><td>+ 2.25</td></tr>
<tr><td>Thirsk</td><td>1-1</td><td>1-1</td><td>0-0</td><td>0-0</td><td>0-0</td><td>100.0</td><td>+ 1.25</td></tr>
<tr><td>Edinburgh</td><td>1-3</td><td>0-0</td><td>0-1</td><td>0-0</td><td>1-2</td><td>33.3</td><td>+ 1.50</td></tr>
<tr><td>Haydock</td><td>1-4</td><td>1-1</td><td>0-0</td><td>0-0</td><td>0-3</td><td>25.0</td><td>- 2.09</td></tr>
<tr><td>Hamilton</td><td>1-5</td><td>0-1</td><td>1-3</td><td>0-1</td><td>0-0</td><td>20.0</td><td>+ 1.00</td></tr>
<tr><td>Lingfield (AW)</td><td>1-5</td><td>0-0</td><td>0-1</td><td>0-1</td><td>1-3</td><td>20.0</td><td>- 2.50</td></tr>
</table>

Epsom	1-6	0-1	0-1	0-0	1-4	16.7	+ 15.00
Catterick	1-8	0-2	1-2	0-1	0-3	12.5	- 6.20
Redcar	1-8	0-3	1-2	0-0	0-3	12.5	- 6.00
Kempton	1-9	0-2	0-1	0-0	1-6	11.1	- 5.00
Ripon	1-9	1-5	0-0	0-0	0-4	11.1	- 3.00
Pontefract	1-10	1-3	0-2	0-1	0-4	10.0	- 7.25
Lingfield	1-12	1-3	0-3	0-1	0-5	8.3	- 9.50
Brighton	1-14	1-2	0-7	0-1	0-4	7.1	- 12.80
Doncaster	1-14	0-3	1-3	0-1	0-7	7.1	- 9.50
Ascot	1-15	1-7	0-2	0-0	0-6	6.7	- 10.00
Leicester	1-21	1-9	0-4	0-1	0-7	4.8	- 14.00

Windsor	0-11	Bath	0-3	Chepstow	0-2
Wolverhampton (AW)	0-5	Ayr	0-2	Chester	0-2

WINNING HORSES

	Age	Races Run	1st	2nd	3rd	Unpl	Win £
Princely Hush	2	7	4	1	0	2	44,896
Hoh Magic	2	5	3	0	1	1	36,051
Roger The Butler	4	11	3	1	0	7	26,932
Persian Brave	4	7	2	2	2	1	26,738
Germane	2	5	1	1	3	0	19,014
Orange Place	3	6	2	0	0	4	17,406
Princess Oberon	4	12	3	0	1	8	14,966
Locorotondo	3	8	3	0	2	3	13,408
Allez Cyrano	3	8	2	0	1	5	12,859
Persian Affair	3	10	3	0	1	6	12,716
Blockade	5	8	2	1	0	5	11,592
Cim Bom Bom	2	7	3	0	0	4	11,035
Thick As Thieves	2	8	4	2	0	2	10,553
Endless Wave	2	8	2	0	1	5	8,203
Puck's Castle	2	4	1	1	1	1	5,110
Smart Guest	2	7	1	1	2	3	4,408
Flying Girl	2	5	1	0	0	4	3,785
Presently	3	5	1	0	0	4	3,753
Bay Queen	4	6	1	1	0	4	3,590
Maralinga	2	4	1	0	1	2	3,580
Lancer	2	2	1	0	1	0	3,530
Hinton Rock	2	4	1	1	1	1	3,266
King Curan	3	5	1	0	0	4	3,141
Easy D'Or	3	9	1	0	1	7	3,028
Prism	2	3	1	1	0	1	2,979
Prima Cominna	2	3	1	0	1	1	2,964
Cyrus The Great	2	6	1	0	0	5	2,898
A Million To One	2	4	1	1	0	2	2,791
Double-D	3	6	1	0	0	5	2,766
Indian Dreamer	3	9	1	1	0	7	2,669
Red Dancer	3	11	1	3	3	4	2,381
Joyrider	3	7	1	1	0	5	2,249

WINNING OWNERS

	Races Won	Value £		Races Won	Value £
P A Philipps	4	44,896	Mrs E A Harris	1	3,785
R P B Michaelson	5	41,704	Mrs Anne Yearley	1	3,753
D F Allport	2	32,329	Hoh Supply Limited	1	3,723
M B Hawtin	3	26,932	B J Warren	1	3,590
E D Kessly	1	19,014	D K R & Mrs J B Oliver	1	3,580
Archer Van & Truck Hire Ltd	2	17,406	Sir Thomas Pilkington	1	3,266
The P 1 Partnership	3	13,408	Baron F C Oppenheim	1	3,028
J L C Pearce	2	12,859	H R H Prince Fahd Salman	1	2,979
Mrs G Rowland-Clark	3	12,716	Mrs B Long	1	2,964
A M Warrender	2	11,592	W J P Jackson	1	2,898
Yucel Birol	3	11,035	Million In Mind Partnership (3)	1	2,791
Christopher Wright	4	10,553	Miss Sarah Chidgey	1	2,766
Mrs Monica Caine	2	8,203	R B Holt	1	2,669
Billy Maguire	2	6,670	Lawster Partnership	1	2,381
Sheikh Mohammed	1	5,110	Lady D'Avigdor-Goldsmid	1	2,249
Mrs D Weatherby	1	4,408			

Favourites	26-68	38.2%	- 3.57	Total winning prize-money		£325,254
Longest winning sequence			2	Average SP of winner		4.2/1
Longest losing sequence			26	Return on stakes invested		-25.5%
1993 Form	42-364	11.5%	- 83.14	1991 Form	43-278	15.5% + 9.14
1992 Form	39-327	11.9%	-120.01	1990 Form	21-200	10.5% - 17.64

C J BENSTEAD (Epsom, Surrey)

	No. of Horses	Races Run	1st	2nd	3rd	Unpl	Per cent	£1 Level Stake
2-y-o	7	29	2	1	1	25	6.9	- 10.50
3-y-o	5	30	3	3	3	21	10.0	- 17.77
4-y-o+	2	23	3	1	0	19	13.0	+ 14.00
Totals	14	82	8	5	4	65	9.8	- 14.27

Jan	Feb	Mar	Apr	May	Jun	Jul	Aug	Sep	Oct/Nov
0-0	0-0	1-2	0-7	1-6	2-11	1-12	3-17	0-13	0-14

Winning Jockeys	W-R	£1 Level Stake		W-R	£1 Level Stake
T Williams	2-12	+ 20.00	B Rouse	1-9	0.00
M Wigham	1-1	+ 8.50	P Robinson	1-10	- 5.00
W Carson	1-7	- 5.27	J Williams	1-13	- 8.00
J Lowe	1-8	- 2.50			

Winning Courses					
Lingfield (AW)	2-4	+ 28.00	Folkestone	1-5	+ 4.00
Bath	1-3	+ 2.00	Lingfield	1-6	+ 3.50
Yarmouth	1-3	+ 2.50	Newbury	1-7	- 2.00
Brighton	1-4	- 2.27			

Winning Horses	Age	Races Run	1st	2nd	3rd	Unpl	Win £
Tarthooth	3	8	2	1	1	4	7,051
Zinbaq	8	12	2	0	0	10	5,958
Deevee	5	11	1	1	0	9	3,728
Muchtarak	2	3	1	1	0	1	3,659
Tanbih	3	9	1	2	1	5	2,811
Sally Weld	2	9	1	0	1	7	2,720

Favourites	2-4	50.0%	+ 2.73	Total winning prize-money			£25,928

1993 Form	9-91	9.9%	- 50.29	1991 Form	5-99	5.1%	- 62.00
1992 Form	9-124	7.3%	- 31.25	1990 Form	6-161	3.7%	-124.00

W BENTLEY (Middleham, North Yorks)

	No. of Horses	Races Run	1st	2nd	3rd	Unpl	Per cent	£1 Level Stake
2-y-o	4	25	1	2	0	22	4.0	+ 9.00
3-y-o	2	3	0	0	0	3	–	- 3.00
4-y-o+	4	25	4	2	2	17	16.0	+ 12.88
Totals	10	53	5	4	2	42	9.4	+ 18.88

Jan	Feb	Mar	Apr	May	Jun	Jul	Aug	Sep	Oct/Nov
0-0	0-0	0-1	0-3	0-8	2-10	2-9	0-8	0-8	1-6

Winning Jockeys	W-R	£1 Level Stake		W-R	£1 Level Stake
R Lappin	3-15	+ 1.88	J Lowe	1-5	+ 29.00
J Carroll	1-1	+ 20.00			

Winning Courses					
Hamilton	4-6	+ 31.88	Newcastle	1-4	+ 30.00

Winning Horses	Age	Races Run	1st	2nd	3rd	Unpl	Win £
Sir Arthur Hobbs	7	11	4	2	1	4	11,882
Our Bairn	2	5	1	0	0	4	3,160

Favourites	2-3	66.7%	+ 3.88	Total winning prize-money		£15,042

1993 Form	1-25	4.0%	- 21.00	1991 Form	0-22		
1992 Form	0-12			1990 Form	1-53	1.9%	- 44.00

J BERRY (Cockerham, Lancs)

	No. of Horses	Races Run	1st	2nd	3rd	Unpl	Per cent	£1 Level Stake
2-y-o	73	409	60	48	55	246	14.7	-134.91
3-y-o	31	216	30	24	27	135	13.9	- 64.31
4-y-o+	30	286	33	39	24	190	11.5	- 71.84
Totals	134	911	123	111	106	571	13.5	-271.06

BY MONTH

2-y-o	W-R	Per cent	£1 Level Stake	3-y-o	W-R	Per cent	£1 Level Stake
January	0-0	-	0.00	January	0-8	-	- 8.00
February	0-0	-	0.00	February	2-10	20.0	- 3.50
March	4-10	40.0	+ 1.16	March	1-8	12.5	+ 3.00
April	8-29	27.6	+ 10.00	April	1-27	3.7	- 20.00
May	15-59	25.4	+ 22.88	May	3-26	11.5	- 11.17
June	9-61	14.8	- 21.85	June	9-32	28.1	+ 1.29
July	12-76	15.8	- 32.65	July	6-35	17.1	- 13.18
August	4-67	6.0	- 48.45	August	4-28	14.3	- 2.75
September	6-70	8.6	- 47.00	September	2-28	7.1	- 6.50
Oct/Nov	2-37	5.4	- 19.00	Oct/Nov	2-14	14.3	- 3.50

4-y-o+	W-R	Per cent	£1 Level Stake	Totals	W-R	Per cent	£1 Level Stake
January	1-14	7.1	- 1.00	January	1-22	4.5	- 9.00
February	2-11	18.2	+ 2.00	February	4-21	19.0	- 1.50
March	3-22	13.6	- 7.75	March	8-40	20.0	- 3.59
April	6-33	18.2	- 10.22	April	15-89	16.9	- 20.22
May	8-52	15.4	+ 12.75	May	26-137	19.0	+ 24.46
June	5-40	12.5	- 11.12	June	23-133	17.3	- 31.68
July	3-36	8.3	- 23.00	July	21-147	14.3	- 68.83
August	2-35	5.7	- 25.00	August	10-130	7.7	- 76.20
September	2-26	7.7	- 12.50	September	10-124	8.1	- 66.00
Oct/Nov	1-17	5.9	+ 4.00	Oct/Nov	5-68	7.4	- 18.50

DISTANCE

2-y-o	W-R	Per cent	£1 Level Stake	3-y-o	W-R	Per cent	£1 Level Stake
5f-6f	56-350	16.0	-101.69	5f-6f	22-146	15.1	- 48.67
7f-8f	4-59	6.8	- 33.22	7f-8f	3-41	7.3	- 24.17
9f-13f	0-0	-	0.00	9f-13f	5-26	19.2	+ 11.53
14f+	0-0	-	0.00	14f+	0-3	-	- 3.00

4-y-o+	W-R	Per cent	£1 Level Stake	Totals	W-R	Per cent	£1 Level Stake
5f-6f	26-216	12.0	- 38.09	5f-6f	104-712	14.6	-188.45
7f-8f	6-62	9.7	- 31.75	7f-8f	13-162	8.0	- 89.14
9f-13f	0-5	-	- 5.00	9f-13f	5-31	16.1	+ 6.53
14f+	1-3	33.3	+ 3.00	14f+	1-6	16.7	0.00

TYPE OF RACE

Non-Handicaps	W-R	Per cent	£1 Level Stake	Handicaps	W-R	Per cent	£1 Level Stake
2-y-o	48-281	17.1	- 62.79	2-y-o	3-67	4.5	- 58.70
3-y-o	14-92	15.2	- 30.00	3-y-o	8-94	8.5	- 52.13
4-y-o+	14-88	15.9	- 25.17	4-y-o+	16-178	9.0	- 38.50
Selling	13-70	18.6	- 7.29	Selling	3-19	15.8	+ 3.28
Apprentice	0-5	-	- 5.00	Apprentice	4-12	33.3	+ 10.24
Amat/Ladies	0-0	-	0.00	Amat/Ladies	0-5	-	- 5.00
Totals	89-536	16.6	-130.25	Totals	34-375	9.1	-140.81

COURSE GRADE

	W-R	Per cent	£1 Level Stake
Group 1	34-309	11.0	-103.80
Group 2	19-138	13.8	- 28.62
Group 3	24-186	12.9	- 52.62
Group 4	46-278	16.5	- 86.02

FIRST TIME OUT

	W-R	Per cent	£1 Level Stake
2-y-o	14-73	19.2	- 13.01
3-y-o	0-26	-	- 26.00
4-y-o+	4-29	13.8	- 6.75
Totals	18-128	14.1	- 45.76

JOCKEYS RIDING

	W-R	Per cent	£1 Level Stake		W-R	Per cent	£1 Level Stake
J Carroll	59-389	15.2	- 83.78	L Piggott	2-10	20.0	- 2.00
G Carter	20-154	13.0	- 48.93	S D Williams	2-26	7.7	- 16.00
J Fortune	6-21	28.6	+ 7.45	Le Tollboll	1-2	50.0	+ 1.25
P Roberts	5-64	7.8	- 48.95	A Mackay	1-4	25.0	0.00
K Darley	4-27	14.8	- 11.50	W Carson	1-5	20.0	- 1.75
P Fessey	4-29	13.8	- 8.76	A Munro	1-5	20.0	+ 1.00
Ruth Coulter	3-9	33.3	+ 13.20	M Birch	1-5	20.0	+ 1.00
G Hind	3-9	33.3	+ 0.88	T Quinn	1-11	9.1	+ 6.00
G Duffield	3-12	25.0	+ 6.00	N Carlisle	1-14	7.1	- 6.00
L Dettori	2-5	40.0	+ 6.50	D McKeown	1-17	5.9	- 4.00
J Williams	2-8	25.0	+ 2.33				

L Charnock	0-30	Emma O'Gorman	0-3	W Ryan	0-2
G Bardwell	0-5	Miss I D W Jones	0-3	C Rutter	0-1
J Weaver	0-4	Mr D Parker	0-3	F Lynch	0-1
N Adams	0-4	D Holland	0-2	J Lowe	0-1
Pat Eddery	0-4	F Norton	0-2	K Fallon	0-1
Paul Eddery	0-4	M Hills	0-2	S Whitworth	0-1
A Clark	0-3	P Robinson	0-2	W Newnes	0-1
Dale Gibson	0-3	T Ives	0-2	W Woods	0-1

COURSE RECORD

	Total W-R	Non-Handicaps 2-y-o	3-y-o+	Handicaps 2-y-o	3-y-o+	Per cent	£1 Level Stake
Wolverhampton (AW)	15-77	4-16	7-28	0-2	4-31	19.5	- 12.40
Hamilton	9-59	4-23	3-13	0-2	2-21	15.3	+ 0.13
Newcastle	8-44	5-15	2-10	0-4	1-15	18.2	- 4.55
Edinburgh	7-37	3-19	1-6	0-3	3-9	18.9	- 8.06
Catterick	7-48	2-16	1-12	2-7	2-13	14.6	- 17.47
Southwell (AW)	6-49	2-13	1-19	0-3	3-14	12.2	- 22.25
Ayr	6-50	3-17	1-7	0-3	2-23	12.0	- 23.13
Lingfield	5-16	5-11	0-3	0-0	0-2	31.3	+ 15.08
Warwick	5-21	3-8	2-8	0-2	0-3	23.8	+ 3.41
Redcar	5-26	3-13	1-5	0-3	1-5	19.2	+ 8.50
Ripon	5-35	3-18	0-1	0-2	2-14	14.3	- 9.20
Bath	4-15	2-8	1-1	0-0	1-6	26.7	+ 0.25
Pontefract	4-24	1-11	2-5	0-3	1-5	16.7	- 2.00
Doncaster	4-35	2-11	1-7	0-3	1-14	11.4	+ 5.50
Folkestone	3-4	2-2	1-1	0-1	0-0	75.0	+ 4.50
Sandown	3-12	0-2	3-7	0-2	0-1	25.0	+ 0.38
Epsom	3-13	2-5	0-0	0-0	1-8	23.1	+ 5.00
Carlisle	3-24	1-9	2-9	0-0	0-6	12.5	- 15.75
Chester	3-30	1-9	0-3	1-3	1-15	10.0	- 14.75
Beverley	3-32	3-20	0-6	0-4	0-2	9.4	- 23.00
Chepstow	2-7	1-3	0-1	0-1	1-2	28.6	+ 10.50
Ascot	2-17	1-8	0-3	0-0	1-6	11.8	- 2.50
Goodwood	2-23	1-5	1-5	0-5	0-8	8.7	- 16.75
Leicester	2-24	1-9	1-7	0-4	0-4	8.3	- 13.50
Newmarket	2-30	1-7	0-8	0-3	1-12	6.7	- 6.50
Haydock	2-45	0-12	1-6	0-7	1-20	4.4	- 30.00
Newbury	1-13	1-4	0-2	0-2	0-5	7.7	- 8.00
Thirsk	1-23	0-11	0-3	0-2	1-7	4.3	- 20.25
York	1-23	0-5	0-6	0-2	1-10	4.3	- 19.25

Nottingham	0-20	Kempton		0-4	Yarmouth	0-2
Lingfield (AW)	0-18	Windsor		0-3		
Brighton	0-6	Salisbury		0-2		

WINNING HORSES

	Age	Races Run	1st	2nd	3rd	Unpl	Win £
Mind Games	2	6	3	1	0	2	33,825
Limerick Belle	2	7	3	1	1	2	20,759
Very Dicey	6	19	6	3	2	8	18,859
Stephensons Rocket	3	11	4	1	1	5	16,220
Two Moves In Front	4	13	3	0	0	10	15,078
Lago Di Varano	2	10	3	2	0	5	15,032
Up And At 'Em	4	9	1	0	0	8	14,265
Noor El Houdah	2	13	5	1	1	6	14,115
Gorinsky	6	12	1	2	1	8	13,302
Lucky Parkes	4	9	3	4	0	2	12,816
Amron	7	9	1	1	0	7	10,868
Dom One	2	8	3	0	2	3	10,517
Mister Bloy	3	14	4	1	2	7	10,439

Monkey Adel	2	12	3	2	2	5	10,231
Nagnagnag	2	6	2	3	0	1	10,141
Wali	4	10	3	1	3	3	9,897
Another Episode	5	16	3	3	1	9	9,741
Fairy Fay	2	8	4	2	0	2	9,351
Best Kept Secret	3	15	3	2	3	7	8,594
Frisky Miss	3	14	3	4	3	4	8,492
Sunday Mail Lass	2	7	3	0	1	3	8,232
T O O Mamma's	3	16	3	2	0	11	8,097
Palacegate Jo	3	10	3	2	1	4	8,000
Laurel Delight	4	4	1	1	0	2	7,460
Question Ali	2	8	2	2	0	4	7,423
Margaret's Gift	4	8	1	0	0	7	7,393
El Yasaf	6	3	1	1	0	1	7,336
Willrack Farrier	2	6	2	0	0	4	6,815
Ansellady	3	8	2	1	1	4	6,026
Palacegate Touch	4	12	1	1	1	9	5,796
Ansellman	4	11	1	0	0	10	5,481
Monkey Wench	3	12	2	1	2	7	5,469
Jimmy The Skunk	3	7	2	1	2	2	5,034
Annie Fay	2	8	2	2	2	2	5,000
We're Joken	2	8	2	1	1	4	4,847
Cee-Jay-Ay	7	20	1	4	1	14	4,638
Sweet Cheap Pet	2	15	2	2	5	6	4,537
Palacegate Jack	3	9	1	0	2	6	4,203
Press The Bell	4	12	1	2	1	8	4,175
Swan At Whalley	2	3	1	0	0	2	4,065
Lloc	2	9	1	1	3	4	3,785
Curie Express	2	8	1	0	1	6	3,692
Breakfast Creek	2	7	1	2	2	2	3,598
Local Heroine	4	12	1	1	1	9	3,534
Most Uppity	2	5	1	0	0	4	3,521
Persian Fayre	2	8	1	0	1	6	3,379
Blackpool Festival	2	8	1	1	2	4	3,365
Master M-E-N	2	11	1	2	0	8	3,292
Satisfied Prince	2	7	1	1	1	4	3,290
Sound The Trumpet	2	8	1	2	3	2	3,026
Champagne Ateaster	3	12	1	2	1	8	3,002
Sunday Mail Too	2	6	1	1	2	2	2,888
Best Of All	2	3	1	1	0	1	2,853
Silver Thatching	2	10	1	2	1	6	2,768
Mr M-E-N	3	13	1	1	1	10	2,750
River Garnock	2	2	1	0	0	1	2,739
Daily Starshine	2	9	1	0	2	6	2,661
Bonnifer	5	4	1	0	1	2	2,624
Curie Crusader	3	3	1	0	0	2	2,512
Clan Scotia	2	7	1	1	1	4	2,485
Lady Quinta	2	8	1	1	1	5	2,456
Wendy's Way	2	9	1	1	2	5	2,431
Lady Pui	2	5	1	0	0	4	2,422
Drumdonna	4	12	1	1	3	7	2,390
Farndale	7	18	1	2	2	13	2,381
Six For Luck	2	3	1	0	0	2	2,349
Tannerrun	2	4	1	0	0	3	2,249
Different Times	4	8	1	1	1	5	2,198

WINNING OWNERS

	Races Won	Value £		Races Won	Value £
Robert Hughes (Shropshire)	3	33,825	J Naughton	1	7,336
Palacegate Corporation Ltd	8	27,741	Pitpersons	2	6,815
J David Abell	9	22,412	Manchester Evening News Ltd	2	6,042
Robert Aird	5	20,670	Mrs A E Robertson	2	5,469
John Stephenson & Sons Ltd	4	16,220	J K M Oliver	2	4,847
J Berry	5	15,288	Mrs Norma Peebles	2	4,639
Norman Jackson	3	15,032	Richard Jinks	1	4,638
Mrs A Hughes	1	14,265	Sam Berry	2	4,537
Basheer Kielany	5	14,115	Sydney Mason	1	4,175
Bernard Hathaway	4	13,807	H H Barlow	1	4,065
William Robertson	1	13,302	Lord Mostyn	1	3,785
Joseph Heler	3	12,816	Express Marie Curie Racing Club	1	3,692
Godolphin	1	12,407	Mrs M J Dandy	1	3,598
Ansells Of Watford	3	11,507	Mrs L J Meylan	1	3,534
Scottish Daily Record & Sunday Mail	4	11,120	The Sussex Stud Limited	1	3,521
Roy Peebles	1	10,868	Murray Grubb	1	3,379
The Monkey Racing Club Ltd	3	10,231	Blackpool Gazette & Herald Ltd	1	3,365
Sir Clement Freud	2	10,141	J E Marsden	1	3,002
Dab Hand Racing	3	9,897	Mohammed Obaid Al Maktoum	1	2,880
Manny Bernstein (Racing) Ltd	3	8,594	Twenty Four Carat Racing	1	2,768
Mrs Margaret Sinanan	3	8,492	Express Newspapers Plc	1	2,661
Joint Venture Racing	3	8,464	L Browne	1	2,624
Thomas Doherty	2	8,352	Scotia Racing Club	1	2,485
Roland A Black	3	8,097	J A Corbett	1	2,456
H B Hughes	3	7,559	Miss Wendy Jones	1	2,431
Laurel (Leisure) Ltd	1	7,460	John Hulme	1	2,422
T & M A Bibby	2	7,423	William Burns	1	2,349
Mrs T G Holdcroft	1	7,393	Daniel Comerford	1	2,198

Favourites	49-139	35.3%	+ 2.70	
Longest winning sequence			3	
Longest losing sequence			38	
1993 Form	133-815	16.3%	- 84.19	
1992 Form	107-800	13.4%	-164.48	

Total winning prize-money		£473,209
Average SP of winner		4.2/1
Return on stakes invested		-29.8%
1991 Form	143-837	17.1% -184.88
1990 Form	127-807	15.7% -158.61

J D BETHELL (Middleham, North Yorks)

	No. of Horses	Races Run	1st	2nd	3rd	Unpl	Per cent	£1 Level Stake
2-y-o	7	31	3	3	3	22	9.7	+ 5.33
3-y-o	11	64	0	10	6	48	-	- 64.00
4-y-o+	9	76	7	7	10	52	9.2	+ 16.00
Totals	27	171	10	20	19	122	5.8	- 42.67

BY MONTH

2-y-o	W-R	Per cent	£1 Level Stake	3-y-o	W-R	Per cent	£1 Level Stake
January	0-0	-	0.00	January	0-0	-	0.00
February	0-0	-	0.00	February	0-1	-	- 1.00
March	0-0	-	0.00	March	0-1	-	- 1.00
April	0-3	-	- 3.00	April	0-8	-	- 8.00
May	0-3	-	- 3.00	May	0-9	-	- 9.00
June	0-4	-	- 4.00	June	0-12	-	- 12.00
July	0-3	-	- 3.00	July	0-14	-	- 14.00
August	1-4	25.0	+ 11.00	August	0-6	-	- 6.00
September	1-6	16.7	- 1.67	September	0-7	-	- 7.00
Oct/Nov	1-8	12.5	+ 9.00	Oct/Nov	0-6	-	- 6.00

4-y-o+	W-R	Per cent	£1 Level Stake	Totals	W-R	Per cent	£1 Level Stake
January	0-1	-	- 1.00	January	0-1	-	- 1.00
February	0-0	-	0.00	February	0-1	-	- 1.00
March	0-1	-	- 1.00	March	0-2	-	- 2.00
April	0-4	-	- 4.00	April	0-15	-	- 15.00
May	1-10	10.0	- 6.50	May	1-22	4.5	- 18.50
June	1-11	9.1	+ 23.00	June	1-27	3.7	+ 7.00
July	2-13	15.4	+ 1.50	July	2-30	6.7	- 15.50
August	1-12	8.3	- 4.00	August	2-22	9.1	+ 1.00
September	1-12	8.3	+ 3.00	September	2-25	8.0	- 5.67
Oct/Nov	1-12	8.3	+ 5.00	Oct/Nov	2-26	7.7	+ 8.00

DISTANCE

2-y-o	W-R	Per cent	£1 Level Stake	3-y-o	W-R	Per cent	£1 Level Stake
5f-6f	1-23	4.3	- 8.00	5f-6f	0-22	-	- 22.00
7f-8f	2-8	25.0	+ 13.33	7f-8f	0-17	-	- 17.00
9f-13f	0-0	-	0.00	9f-13f	0-17	-	- 17.00
14f+	0-0	-	0.00	14f+	0-8	-	- 8.00

4-y-o+	W-R	Per cent	£1 Level Stake	Totals	W-R	Per cent	£1 Level Stake
5f-6f	0-8	-	- 8.00	5f-6f	1-53	1.9	- 38.00
7f-8f	3-36	8.3	- 5.50	7f-8f	5-61	8.2	- 9.17
9f-13f	4-24	16.7	+ 37.50	9f-13f	4-41	9.8	+ 20.50
14f+	0-8	-	- 8.00	14f+	0-16	-	- 16.00

TYPE OF RACE

Non-Handicaps	W-R	Per cent	£1 Level Stake	Handicaps	W-R	Per cent	£1 Level Stake
2-y-o	1-20	5.0	- 15.67	2-y-o	1-9	11.1	+ 8.00
3-y-o	0-24	-	- 24.00	3-y-o	0-38	-	- 38.00
4-y-o+	0-8	-	- 8.00	4-y-o+	6-65	9.2	- 7.00
Selling	1-3	33.3	+ 12.00	Selling	0-2	-	- 2.00
Apprentice	0-1	-	- 1.00	Apprentice	1-1	100.0	+ 33.00
Amat/Ladies	0-0	-	0.00	Amat/Ladies	0-0	-	0.00
Totals	2-56	3.6	- 36.67	Totals	8-115	7.0	- 6.00

45

Bethell J D

<table>
<tr><td colspan="5" align="center">**COURSE GRADE**</td><td colspan="5" align="center">**FIRST TIME OUT**</td></tr>
<tr><td></td><td>W-R</td><td>Per cent</td><td>£1 Level Stake</td><td></td><td></td><td>W-R</td><td>Per cent</td><td>£1 Level Stake</td></tr>
<tr><td>Group 1</td><td>4-70</td><td>5.7</td><td>- 25.50</td><td>2-y-o</td><td></td><td>0-6</td><td>-</td><td>- 6.00</td></tr>
<tr><td>Group 2</td><td>3-35</td><td>8.6</td><td>- 7.67</td><td>3-y-o</td><td></td><td>0-9</td><td>-</td><td>- 9.00</td></tr>
<tr><td>Group 3</td><td>0-33</td><td>-</td><td>- 33.00</td><td>4-y-o+</td><td></td><td>0-9</td><td>-</td><td>- 9.00</td></tr>
<tr><td>Group 4</td><td>3-33</td><td>9.1</td><td>+ 23.50</td><td></td><td></td><td></td><td></td><td></td></tr>
<tr><td></td><td></td><td></td><td></td><td>Totals</td><td></td><td>0-24</td><td>-</td><td>- 24.00</td></tr>
</table>

JOCKEYS RIDING

<table>
<tr><td></td><td>W-R</td><td>Per cent</td><td>£1 Level Stake</td><td></td><td>W-R</td><td>Per cent</td><td>£1 Level Stake</td></tr>
<tr><td>B Thomson</td><td>1-1</td><td>100.0</td><td>+ 16.00</td><td>T Williams</td><td>1-6</td><td>16.7</td><td>+ 9.00</td></tr>
<tr><td>G Carter</td><td>1-2</td><td>50.0</td><td>+ 2.33</td><td>J Lowe</td><td>1-10</td><td>10.0</td><td>- 6.50</td></tr>
<tr><td>N Connorton</td><td>1-4</td><td>25.0</td><td>+ 11.00</td><td>J Marshall</td><td>1-16</td><td>6.3</td><td>+ 18.00</td></tr>
<tr><td>D Harrison</td><td>1-5</td><td>20.0</td><td>+ 4.00</td><td>J Weaver</td><td>1-16</td><td>6.3</td><td>+ 1.00</td></tr>
<tr><td>T Ives</td><td>1-6</td><td>16.7</td><td>+ 2.00</td><td>A Munro</td><td>1-19</td><td>5.3</td><td>- 13.50</td></tr>
</table>

<table>
<tr><td>W Carson</td><td>0-19</td><td>N Varley</td><td>0-2</td><td>M Fenton</td><td>0-1</td></tr>
<tr><td>R Hills</td><td>0-12</td><td>A Mackay</td><td>0-1</td><td>M Hills</td><td>0-1</td></tr>
<tr><td>J Carroll</td><td>0-10</td><td>B Raymond</td><td>0-1</td><td>M J Kinane</td><td>0-1</td></tr>
<tr><td>G Duffield</td><td>0-6</td><td>D McKeown</td><td>0-1</td><td>M Roberts</td><td>0-1</td></tr>
<tr><td>Dale Gibson</td><td>0-5</td><td>D Wright</td><td>0-1</td><td>Paul Eddery</td><td>0-1</td></tr>
<tr><td>Pat Eddery</td><td>0-4</td><td>G Hind</td><td>0-1</td><td>R Cochrane</td><td>0-1</td></tr>
<tr><td>K Darley</td><td>0-3</td><td>J Quinn</td><td>0-1</td><td>Stephen Davies</td><td>0-1</td></tr>
<tr><td>L Dettori</td><td>0-3</td><td>J Tate</td><td>0-1</td><td>V Halliday</td><td>0-1</td></tr>
<tr><td>J Fanning</td><td>0-2</td><td>Kim Tinkler</td><td>0-1</td><td>W Newnes</td><td>0-1</td></tr>
<tr><td>J Stack</td><td>0-2</td><td>M Birch</td><td>0-1</td><td></td><td></td></tr>
</table>

COURSE RECORD

<table>
<tr><td></td><td>Total W-R</td><td colspan="2">Non-Handicaps</td><td colspan="2">Handicaps</td><td>Per cent</td><td>£1 Level Stake</td></tr>
<tr><td></td><td></td><td>2-y-o</td><td>3-y-o+</td><td>2-y-o</td><td>3-y-o+</td><td></td><td></td></tr>
<tr><td>Goodwood</td><td>2-4</td><td>0-0</td><td>0-1</td><td>0-0</td><td>2-3</td><td>50.0</td><td>+ 20.00</td></tr>
<tr><td>Catterick</td><td>2-9</td><td>0-1</td><td>0-1</td><td>0-1</td><td>2-6</td><td>22.2</td><td>+ 13.50</td></tr>
<tr><td>Newcastle</td><td>2-10</td><td>0-1</td><td>0-2</td><td>1-1</td><td>1-6</td><td>20.0</td><td>+ 10.50</td></tr>
<tr><td>Chester</td><td>1-7</td><td>1-2</td><td>0-1</td><td>0-0</td><td>0-4</td><td>14.3</td><td>- 2.67</td></tr>
<tr><td>Ripon</td><td>1-7</td><td>0-1</td><td>0-0</td><td>0-0</td><td>1-6</td><td>14.3</td><td>+ 1.00</td></tr>
<tr><td>Edinburgh</td><td>1-9</td><td>0-2</td><td>0-1</td><td>0-0</td><td>1-6</td><td>11.1</td><td>+ 25.00</td></tr>
<tr><td>Redcar</td><td>1-11</td><td>1-3</td><td>0-0</td><td>0-1</td><td>0-7</td><td>9.1</td><td>+ 4.00</td></tr>
</table>

<table>
<tr><td>Ayr</td><td>0-13</td><td>Hamilton</td><td>0-5</td><td>Wolverhampton (AW)</td><td>0-3</td></tr>
<tr><td>York</td><td>0-11</td><td>Newmarket</td><td>0-5</td><td>Ascot</td><td>0-2</td></tr>
<tr><td>Doncaster</td><td>0-10</td><td>Nottingham</td><td>0-5</td><td>Chepstow</td><td>0-2</td></tr>
<tr><td>Thirsk</td><td>0-10</td><td>Carlisle</td><td>0-4</td><td>Epsom</td><td>0-2</td></tr>
<tr><td>Pontefract</td><td>0-8</td><td>Kempton</td><td>0-3</td><td>Lingfield (AW)</td><td>0-2</td></tr>
<tr><td>Haydock</td><td>0-6</td><td>Leicester</td><td>0-3</td><td>Yarmouth</td><td>0-2</td></tr>
<tr><td>Southwell (AW)</td><td>0-6</td><td>Sandown</td><td>0-3</td><td>Newbury</td><td>0-1</td></tr>
<tr><td>Beverley</td><td>0-5</td><td>Windsor</td><td>0-3</td><td></td><td></td></tr>
</table>

WINNING HORSES

	Age	Races Run	1st	2nd	3rd	Unpl	Win £
Coureur	5	10	2	0	2	6	19,560
Hunters Of Brora	4	9	1	2	0	6	7,400
Flamboro	2	10	2	1	1	6	6,890
Amin	2	2	1	0	0	1	4,580
True Precision	4	11	1	0	1	9	3,678
Double Echo	6	7	1	2	0	4	3,534
Tumbling (USA)	6	15	1	3	5	6	3,158
Warm Toes	4	9	1	0	1	7	2,300

WINNING OWNERS

	Races Won	Value £		Races Won	Value £
Robert Gibbons	4	30,118	T R Lock	1	3,678
Footballers' Racing Club	2	6,890	Mrs John Lee	1	3,534
Sheikh Amin Dahlawi	1	4,580	Mrs G Fane	1	2,300

Favourites	2-20	10.0%	- 11.00	Total winning prize-money		£51,100
Longest winning sequence			1	Average SP of winner		11.8/1
Longest losing sequence			39	Return on stakes invested		-25.0%
1993 Form	7-123	5.7%	- 49.00	1991 Form	11-156	7.1% - 21.62
1992 Form	5-112	4.5%	- 70.50	1990 Form	10-120	8.3% - 48.00

P J BEVAN (Uttoxeter, Staffs)

	No. of Horses	Races Run	1st	2nd	3rd	Unpl	Per cent	£1 Level Stake
2-y-o	2	11	0	0	0	11	-	- 11.00
3-y-o	1	2	0	0	0	2	-	- 2.00
4-y-o+	4	18	2	0	0	16	11.1	+ 10.00
Totals	7	31	2	0	0	29	6.5	- 3.00

Jan	Feb	Mar	Apr	May	Jun	Jul	Aug	Sep	Oct/Nov
0-1	0-0	0-0	0-3	0-5	1-3	0-3	0-7	0-2	1-7

Winning Jockeys	W-R	£1 Level Stake		W-R	£1 Level Stake
D Denby	1-4	+ 17.00	C Hawksley	1-18	- 11.00

Winning Courses					
Haydock	1-2	+ 19.00	Nottingham	1-3	+ 4.00

Winning Horse	Age	Races Run	1st	2nd	3rd	Unpl	Win £
My Rossini	5	9	2	0	0	7	6,161

Favourites	0-1			Total winning prize-money			£6,161

1993 Form	3-21	14.3%	+ 3.00	1991 Form	1-20	5.0%	- 15.50
1992 Form	2-16	12.5%	+ 2.00	1990 Form	0-14		

M BLANSHARD (Upper Lambourn, Berks)

	No. of Horses	Races Run	1st	2nd	3rd	Unpl	Per cent	£1 Level Stake
2-y-o	5	33	3	1	5	24	9.1	- 10.75
3-y-o	8	63	0	3	6	54	-	- 63.00
4-y-o+	6	51	2	8	4	37	3.9	- 22.00
Totals	19	147	5	12	15	115	3.4	- 95.75

Jan	Feb	Mar	Apr	May	Jun	Jul	Aug	Sep	Oct/Nov
0-2	0-0	0-3	1-15	1-18	0-24	0-25	2-23	1-28	0-9

Winning Jockeys	W-R	£1 Level Stake		W-R	£1 Level Stake
J Quinn	2-35	- 16.50	M Roberts	1-7	+ 10.00
W Ryan	1-4	- 1.25	Stephen Davies	1-10	+ 3.00

Winning Courses					
Salisbury	2-16	+ 9.00	Windsor	1-6	+ 0.50
Redcar	1-1	+ 1.75	Newbury	1-13	+ 4.00

Winning Horses	Age	Races Run	1st	2nd	3rd	Unpl	Win £
Bajan Rose	2	7	2	1	2	2	8,858
La Spezia	4	8	1	2	1	4	6,264
Sea Baron	4	15	1	4	1	9	4,143
Bowden Rose	2	9	1	0	2	6	3,883

Favourites	1-4	25.0%	- 1.25	Total winning prize-money			£23,147

1993 Form	6-122	4.9%	- 69.00	1991 Form	6-136	4.4%	- 85.00
1992 Form	8-179	4.5%	- 88.25	1990 Form	5-128	3.9%	- 76.50

M J BOLTON (Shrewton, Wilts)

	No. of Horses	Races Run	1st	2nd	3rd	Unpl	Per cent	£1 Level Stake
2-y-o	0	0	0	0	0	0	-	0.00
3-y-o	1	2	0	0	0	2	-	- 2.00
4-y-o+	2	16	2	1	2	11	12.5	+ 31.00
Totals	3	18	2	1	2	13	11.1	+ 29.00

Jan	Feb	Mar	Apr	May	Jun	Jul	Aug	Sep	Oct/Nov
0-0	0-0	0-0	0-1	1-2	0-3	1-2	0-5	0-4	0-1

Winning Jockeys	W-R	£1 Level Stake					W-R	£1 Level Stake
J Reid	1-2	+ 32.00	A McGlone				1-2	+ 11.00

Winning Courses								
Bath	1-1	+ 33.00	Epsom				1-1	+ 12.00

Winning Horses	Age	Races Run	1st	2nd	3rd	Unpl	Win £
Vanborough Lad	5	9	1	0	1	7	3,248
Rocquaine Bay	7	7	1	1	1	4	3,210

Favourites	0-0	Total winning prize-money	£6,458

1993 Form	0-23				
1992 Form	5-28	17.9%	+ 7.00		
1991 Form	1-40	2.5%	- 36.00		
1990 Form	2-34	5.9%	- 11.00		

C B B BOOTH (Flaxton, North Yorks)

	No. of Horses	Races Run	1st	2nd	3rd	Unpl	Per cent	£1 Level Stake
2-y-o	3	6	0	0	0	6	-	- 6.00
3-y-o	5	33	1	1	2	29	3.0	- 23.00
4-y-o+	4	19	1	2	0	16	5.3	- 8.00
Totals	12	58	2	3	2	51	3.4	- 37.00

Jan	Feb	Mar	Apr	May	Jun	Jul	Aug	Sep	Oct/Nov
0-3	0-0	0-0	0-5	0-10	0-10	1-5	1-8	0-8	0-9

Winning Jockeys	W-R	£1 Level Stake					W-R	£1 Level Stake
L Dettori	1-3	+ 8.00	A Culhane				1-4	+ 6.00

Winning Courses								
Beverley	1-2	+ 9.00	Redcar				1-8	+ 2.00

Winning Horses	Age	Races Run	1st	2nd	3rd	Unpl	Win £
Baliana	4	7	1	0	0	6	3,459
Bayou	3	12	1	0	0	11	2,861

Favourites	0-1	Total winning prize-money	£6,320

1993 Form	2-65	3.1%	- 48.00	1991 Form	5-59	8.5%	- 11.70
1992 Form	3-80	3.8%	- 63.75	1990 Form	4-74	5.4%	- 48.50

J R BOSLEY (Wantage, Oxon)

	No. of Horses	Races Run	1st	2nd	3rd	Unpl	Per cent	£1 Level Stake
2-y-o	0	0	0	0	0	0	-	0.00
3-y-o	3	12	0	0	0	12	-	- 12.00
4-y-o+	5	40	3	5	4	28	7.5	+ 6.50
Totals	8	52	3	5	4	40	5.8	- 5.50

Jan	Feb	Mar	Apr	May	Jun	Jul	Aug	Sep	Oct/Nov
0-3	0-2	0-1	1-3	0-6	0-11	0-10	2-6	0-7	0-3

Winning Jockeys	W-R	£1 Level Stake			W-R	£1 Level Stake
Pat Eddery	1-1	+ 6.50	Aimee Cook		1-6	+ 20.00
C Rutter	1-5	+ 8.00				

Winning Courses						
Ripon	1-2	+ 11.00	Windsor		1-4	+ 22.00
Salisbury	1-2	+ 5.50				

Winning Horses	Age	Races Run	1st	2nd	3rd	Unpl	Win £
Pusey Street Boy	7	19	1	5	1	12	3,686
Persian Bud	6	9	1	0	2	6	3,522
Windrush Boy	4	4	1	0	0	3	3,236

Favourites	0-3	Total winning prize-money	£10,444

1993 Form	3-38	7.9%	- 3.00	1991 Form	0-7
1992 Form	0-27			1990 Form	0-22

R BOSS (Newmarket)

	No. of Horses	Races Run	1st	2nd	3rd	Unpl	Per cent	£1 Level Stake
2-y-o	7	26	2	2	4	18	7.7	- 11.67
3-y-o	14	75	10	3	8	54	13.3	+ 7.50
4-y-o+	3	25	2	2	0	21	8.0	- 10.00
Totals	24	126	14	7	12	93	11.1	- 14.17

BY MONTH

2-y-o	W-R	Per cent	£1 Level Stake	3-y-o	W-R	Per cent	£1 Level Stake
January	0-0	-	0.00	January	0-0	-	0.00
February	0-0	-	0.00	February	0-1	-	- 1.00
March	0-0	-	0.00	March	1-5	20.0	+ 6.00
April	0-3	-	- 3.00	April	1-12	8.3	- 1.00
May	1-3	33.3	+ 7.00	May	1-17	5.9	- 11.00
June	0-4	-	- 4.00	June	1-13	7.7	- 10.50
July	0-5	-	- 5.00	July	3-10	30.0	+ 14.75
August	0-3	-	- 3.00	August	1-5	20.0	+ 2.00
September	0-6	-	- 6.00	September	2-6	33.3	+ 14.25
Oct/Nov	1-2	50.0	+ 2.33	Oct/Nov	0-6	-	- 6.00

4-y-o+	W-R	Per cent	£1 Level Stake	Totals	W-R	Per cent	£1 Level Stake
January	0-0	-	0.00	January	0-0	-	0.00
February	0-0	-	0.00	February	0-1	-	- 1.00
March	0-2	-	- 2.00	March	1-7	14.3	+ 4.00
April	0-1	-	- 1.00	April	1-16	6.3	- 5.00
May	1-3	33.3	+ 6.00	May	3-23	13.0	+ 2.00
June	0-5	-	- 5.00	June	1-22	4.5	- 19.50
July	1-4	25.0	+ 2.00	July	4-19	21.1	+ 11.75
August	0-7	-	- 7.00	August	1-15	6.7	- 8.00
September	0-1	-	- 1.00	September	2-13	15.4	+ 7.25
Oct/Nov	0-2	-	- 2.00	Oct/Nov	1-10	10.0	- 5.67

DISTANCE

2-y-o	W-R	Per cent	£1 Level Stake	3-y-o	W-R	Per cent	£1 Level Stake
5f-6f	2-20	10.0	- 5.67	5f-6f	2-12	16.7	+ 9.00
7f-8f	0-6	-	- 6.00	7f-8f	7-46	15.2	- 1.50
9f-13f	0-0	-	0.00	9f-13f	1-15	6.7	+ 2.00
14f+	0-0	-	0.00	14f+	0-2	-	- 2.00

4-y-o+	W-R	Per cent	£1 Level Stake	Totals	W-R	Per cent	£1 Level Stake
5f-6f	0-6	-	- 6.00	5f-6f	4-38	10.5	- 2.67
7f-8f	1-16	6.3	- 7.00	7f-8f	8-68	11.8	- 14.50
9f-13f	1-3	33.3	+ 3.00	9f-13f	2-18	11.1	+ 5.00
14f+	0-0	-	0.00	14f+	0-2	-	- 2.00

TYPE OF RACE

Non-Handicaps	W-R	Per cent	£1 Level Stake	Handicaps	W-R	Per cent	£1 Level Stake
2-y-o	2-22	9.1	- 7.67	2-y-o	0-4	-	- 4.00
3-y-o	4-32	12.5	+ 0.25	3-y-o	5-35	14.3	+ 12.00
4-y-o+	0-3	-	- 3.00	4-y-o+	2-21	9.5	- 6.00
Selling	0-3	-	- 3.00	Selling	0-3	-	- 3.00
Apprentice	0-0	-	0.00	Apprentice	0-1	-	- 1.00
Amat/Ladies	1-1	100.0	+ 2.25	Amat/Ladies	0-1	-	- 1.00
Totals	7-61	11.5	- 11.17	Totals	7-65	10.8	- 3.00

51

Boss R

<table>
<tr><th colspan="4">COURSE GRADE</th><th></th><th colspan="4">FIRST TIME OUT</th></tr>
<tr><th></th><th>W-R</th><th>Per
cent</th><th>£1 Level
Stake</th><th></th><th></th><th>W-R</th><th>Per
cent</th><th>£1 Level
Stake</th></tr>
<tr><td>Group 1</td><td>9-54</td><td>16.7</td><td>+ 30.33</td><td>2-y-o</td><td></td><td>0-7</td><td>-</td><td>- 7.00</td></tr>
<tr><td>Group 2</td><td>1-16</td><td>6.3</td><td>- 10.00</td><td>3-y-o</td><td></td><td>1-14</td><td>7.1</td><td>- 3.00</td></tr>
<tr><td>Group 3</td><td>1-33</td><td>3.0</td><td>- 27.00</td><td>4-y-o+</td><td></td><td>0-3</td><td>-</td><td>- 3.00</td></tr>
<tr><td>Group 4</td><td>3-23</td><td>13.0</td><td>- 7.50</td><td></td><td></td><td></td><td></td><td></td></tr>
<tr><td></td><td></td><td></td><td></td><td>Totals</td><td></td><td>1-24</td><td>4.2</td><td>- 13.00</td></tr>
</table>

JOCKEYS RIDING

<table>
<tr><th></th><th>W-R</th><th>Per
cent</th><th>£1 Level
Stake</th><th></th><th>W-R</th><th>Per
cent</th><th>£1 Level
Stake</th></tr>
<tr><td>W Ryan</td><td>6-24</td><td>25.0</td><td>+ 33.33</td><td>W Carson</td><td>1-6</td><td>16.7</td><td>+ 5.00</td></tr>
<tr><td>Pat Eddery</td><td>3-13</td><td>23.1</td><td>+ 11.75</td><td>J Weaver</td><td>1-9</td><td>11.1</td><td>- 6.50</td></tr>
<tr><td>Mrs M Cowdrey</td><td>1-1</td><td>100.0</td><td>+ 2.25</td><td>L Dettori</td><td>1-11</td><td>9.1</td><td>- 5.00</td></tr>
<tr><td>G Duffield</td><td>1-5</td><td>20.0</td><td>+ 2.00</td><td></td><td></td><td></td><td></td></tr>
</table>

<table>
<tr><td>M Roberts</td><td>0-16</td><td>M J Kinane</td><td>0-2</td><td>P McCabe</td><td>0-1</td></tr>
<tr><td>W Woods</td><td>0-8</td><td>Paul Eddery</td><td>0-2</td><td>R Cochrane</td><td>0-1</td></tr>
<tr><td>E Guest</td><td>0-6</td><td>J Carroll</td><td>0-1</td><td>R Hills</td><td>0-1</td></tr>
<tr><td>A McGlone</td><td>0-3</td><td>L Piggott</td><td>0-1</td><td>Stephen Davies</td><td>0-1</td></tr>
<tr><td>D Harrison</td><td>0-2</td><td>M Hills</td><td>0-1</td><td>T Ives</td><td>0-1</td></tr>
<tr><td>J Tate</td><td>0-2</td><td>M Perrett</td><td>0-1</td><td>W R Swinburn</td><td>0-1</td></tr>
<tr><td>J Williams</td><td>0-2</td><td>Miss C Clagett</td><td>0-1</td><td></td><td></td></tr>
<tr><td>M Fenton</td><td>0-2</td><td>N Carlisle</td><td>0-1</td><td></td><td></td></tr>
</table>

COURSE RECORD

<table>
<tr><th></th><th>Total
W-R</th><th colspan="2">Non-Handicaps</th><th colspan="2">Handicaps</th><th>Per
cent</th><th>£1 Level
Stake</th></tr>
<tr><th></th><th></th><th>2-y-o</th><th>3-y-o+</th><th>2-y-o</th><th>3-y-o+</th><th></th><th></th></tr>
<tr><td>Kempton</td><td>2-3</td><td>0-0</td><td>1-1</td><td>0-0</td><td>1-2</td><td>66.7</td><td>+ 17.00</td></tr>
<tr><td>Edinburgh</td><td>2-4</td><td>0-0</td><td>1-2</td><td>0-0</td><td>1-2</td><td>50.0</td><td>+ 5.50</td></tr>
<tr><td>Newmarket</td><td>2-18</td><td>1-4</td><td>1-6</td><td>0-1</td><td>0-7</td><td>11.1</td><td>- 9.92</td></tr>
<tr><td>Haydock</td><td>1-1</td><td>0-0</td><td>0-0</td><td>0-0</td><td>1-1</td><td>100.0</td><td>+ 16.00</td></tr>
<tr><td>Goodwood</td><td>1-3</td><td>0-0</td><td>1-3</td><td>0-0</td><td>0-0</td><td>33.3</td><td>+ 0.25</td></tr>
<tr><td>Sandown</td><td>1-4</td><td>1-1</td><td>0-2</td><td>0-0</td><td>0-1</td><td>25.0</td><td>+ 6.00</td></tr>
<tr><td>Thirsk</td><td>1-6</td><td>0-1</td><td>0-1</td><td>0-0</td><td>1-4</td><td>16.7</td><td>0.00</td></tr>
<tr><td>Doncaster</td><td>1-7</td><td>0-0</td><td>0-3</td><td>0-0</td><td>1-4</td><td>14.3</td><td>+ 4.00</td></tr>
<tr><td>Folkestone</td><td>1-7</td><td>0-4</td><td>0-0</td><td>0-0</td><td>1-3</td><td>14.3</td><td>- 1.00</td></tr>
<tr><td>Nottingham</td><td>1-9</td><td>0-1</td><td>0-2</td><td>0-0</td><td>1-6</td><td>11.1</td><td>- 3.00</td></tr>
<tr><td>York</td><td>1-9</td><td>0-1</td><td>1-1</td><td>0-0</td><td>0-7</td><td>11.1</td><td>+ 6.00</td></tr>
</table>

<table>
<tr><td>Pontefract</td><td>0-8</td><td>Lingfield</td><td>0-5</td><td>Epsom</td><td>0-2</td></tr>
<tr><td>Yarmouth</td><td>0-6</td><td>Ascot</td><td>0-4</td><td>Lingfield (AW)</td><td>0-2</td></tr>
<tr><td>Brighton</td><td>0-5</td><td>Windsor</td><td>0-4</td><td>Beverley</td><td>0-1</td></tr>
<tr><td>Catterick</td><td>0-5</td><td>Wolverhampton (AW)</td><td>0-4</td><td>Warwick</td><td>0-1</td></tr>
<tr><td>Leicester</td><td>0-5</td><td>Newbury</td><td>0-3</td><td></td><td></td></tr>
</table>

WINNING HORSES

	Age	Races Run	1st	2nd	3rd	Unpl	Win £
Caleman	5	9	1	0	0	8	21,398
Welsh Mist	3	8	2	1	1	4	16,061
Lady Fairfax	3	5	1	0	0	4	10,844
Don Pepe	3	10	3	0	2	5	9,769
Kindergarten Boy	3	12	2	1	2	7	7,417
Stolen Melody	2	3	1	1	0	1	5,443
Access Adventurer	3	4	1	0	0	3	3,942
Bring On The Choir	2	3	1	0	0	2	3,910
Mon Rouge	3	3	1	0	1	1	3,864
Prince Songline	4	7	1	1	0	5	2,928

WINNING OWNERS

	Races Won	Value £		Races Won	Value £
M Berger	1	21,398	Mrs June Root	2	7,417
P Asquith	3	19,924	Mrs A M Upsdell	1	5,443
Bernard Gover	2	14,754	Miss Elaine D Williams	1	3,942
Mrs Elaine Aird	3	9,769	K Sturgis	1	2,928

Favourites	4-12	33.3%	+ 1.83	Total winning prize-money		£85,573
Longest winning sequence			1	Average SP of winner		7.0/1
Longest losing sequence			19	Return on stakes invested		-11.2%
1993 Form	10-107	9.3%	- 46.25	1991 Form	18-194	9.3%	- 78.53
1992 Form	9-110	8.2%	- 55.50	1990 Form	36-230	15.7%	- 40.88

J F BOTTOMLEY (Malton, North Yorks)

	No. of Horses	Races Run	1st	2nd	3rd	Unpl	Per cent	£1 Level Stake
2-y-o	6	25	1	2	4	18	4.0	- 21.00
3-y-o	2	4	0	0	0	4	-	- 4.00
4-y-o+	4	40	4	4	4	28	10.0	- 10.90
Totals	12	69	5	6	8	50	7.2	- 35.90

Jan	Feb	Mar	Apr	May	Jun	Jul	Aug	Sep	Oct/Nov
2-5	0-7	2-4	0-2	0-6	1-7	0-16	0-6	0-8	0-8

Winning Jockeys	W-R	£1 Level Stake			W-R	£1 Level Stake
G Bardwell	2-10	+ 0.10	L Dettori		1-5	+ 3.00
M Birch	1-3	+ 1.00	N Kennedy		1-21	- 10.00

Winning Courses						
Southwell (AW)	3-19	+ 8.00	Pontefract		1-4	0.00
Lingfield (AW)	1-1	+ 1.10				

Winning Horses	Age	Races Run	1st	2nd	3rd	Unpl	Win £
Qualitair Aviator	8	7	2	0	0	5	4,986
Royal Citizen	5	10	1	2	2	5	2,691
In Good Faith	2	3	1	0	1	1	2,642
Comtec's Legend	4	15	1	1	1	12	2,243

Favourites	2-4	50.0%	+ 2.10	Total winning prize-money			£12,562

1993 Form	2-58	3.4%	- 39.00	1991 Form	4-94	4.3%	- 29.00
1992 Form	3-53	5.7%	- 19.50	1990 Form	5-108	4.6%	- 57.25

S R BOWRING (Edwinstowe, Notts)

	No. of Horses	Races Run	1st	2nd	3rd	Unpl	Per cent	£1 Level Stake
2-y-o	0	0	0	0	0	0	-	0.00
3-y-o	6	51	7	3	6	35	13.7	+ 16.50
4-y-o+	8	61	5	9	5	42	8.2	- 11.00
Totals	14	112	12	12	11	77	10.7	+ 5.50

BY MONTH

2-y-o	W-R	Per cent	£1 Level Stake	3-y-o	W-R	Per cent	£1 Level Stake
January	0-0	-	0.00	January	0-1	-	- 1.00
February	0-0	-	0.00	February	0-3	-	- 3.00
March	0-0	-	0.00	March	0-3	-	- 3.00
April	0-0	-	0.00	April	0-6	-	- 6.00
May	0-0	-	0.00	May	0-7	-	- 7.00
June	0-0	-	0.00	June	1-7	14.3	+ 2.00
July	0-0	-	0.00	July	2-6	33.3	+ 17.50
August	0-0	-	0.00	August	2-7	28.6	+ 10.00
September	0-0	-	0.00	September	1-7	14.3	- 1.00
Oct/Nov	0-0	-	0.00	Oct/Nov	1-4	25.0	+ 8.00

4-y-o+	W-R	Per cent	£1 Level Stake	Totals	W-R	Per cent	£1 Level Stake
January	0-10	-	- 10.00	January	0-11	-	- 11.00
February	0-7	-	- 7.00	February	0-10	-	- 10.00
March	0-2	-	- 2.00	March	0-5	-	- 5.00
April	0-5	-	- 5.00	April	0-11	-	- 11.00
May	1-11	9.1	- 4.00	May	1-18	5.6	- 11.00
June	0-4	-	- 4.00	June	1-11	9.1	- 2.00
July	1-3	33.3	+ 1.00	July	3-9	33.3	+ 18.50
August	1-7	14.3	+ 6.00	August	3-14	21.4	+ 16.00
September	1-6	16.7	+ 9.00	September	2-13	15.4	+ 8.00
Oct/Nov	1-6	16.7	+ 5.00	Oct/Nov	2-10	20.0	+ 13.00

DISTANCE

2-y-o	W-R	Per cent	£1 Level Stake	3-y-o	W-R	Per cent	£1 Level Stake
5f-6f	0-0	-	0.00	5f-6f	4-28	14.3	+ 16.50
7f-8f	0-0	-	0.00	7f-8f	3-20	15.0	+ 3.00
9f-13f	0-0	-	0.00	9f-13f	0-3	-	- 3.00
14f+	0-0	-	0.00	14f+	0-0	-	0.00

4-y-o+	W-R	Per cent	£1 Level Stake	Totals	W-R	Per cent	£1 Level Stake
5f-6f	3-25	12.0	+ 1.00	5f-6f	7-53	13.2	+ 17.50
7f-8f	2-18	11.1	+ 6.00	7f-8f	5-38	13.2	+ 9.00
9f-13f	0-15	-	- 15.00	9f-13f	0-18	-	- 18.00
14f+	0-3	-	- 3.00	14f+	0-3	-	- 3.00

TYPE OF RACE

Non-Handicaps	W-R	Per cent	£1 Level Stake	Handicaps	W-R	Per cent	£1 Level Stake
2-y-o	0-0	-	0.00	2-y-o	0-0	-	0.00
3-y-o	1-19	5.3	- 10.00	3-y-o	6-27	22.2	+ 31.50
4-y-o+	0-9	-	- 9.00	4-y-o+	4-44	9.1	- 5.00
Selling	0-0	-	0.00	Selling	0-6	-	- 6.00
Apprentice	0-1	-	- 1.00	Apprentice	1-5	20.0	+ 6.00
Amat/Ladies	0-0	-	0.00	Amat/Ladies	0-1	-	- 1.00
Totals	1-29	3.4	- 20.00	Totals	11-83	13.3	+ 25.50

COURSE GRADE

	W-R	Per cent	£1 Level Stake
Group 1	1-13	7.7	+ 2.00
Group 2	1-6	16.7	+ 11.00
Group 3	4-38	10.5	+ 4.00
Group 4	6-55	10.9	- 11.50

FIRST TIME OUT

	W-R	Per cent	£1 Level Stake
2-y-o	0-0	-	0.00
3-y-o	0-6	-	- 6.00
4-y-o+	0-8	-	- 8.00
Totals	0-14	-	- 14.00

JOCKEYS RIDING

	W-R	Per cent	£1 Level Stake		W-R	Per cent	£1 Level Stake
S Webster	6-19	31.6	+ 31.50	G Strange	2-29	6.9	- 11.00
S D Williams	3-21	14.3	+ 11.00	Dale Gibson	1-7	14.3	+ 10.00

J Lowe	0-7	N Varley	0-2	M Fenton	0-1
J Quinn	0-7	A Mackay	0-1	Miss R Clark	0-1
N Kennedy	0-4	D Holland	0-1	R Price	0-1
S Maloney	0-3	F Norton	0-1	S Bethley	0-1
J Weaver	0-2	G Bardwell	0-1		
J Williams	0-2	J Fanning	0-1		

COURSE RECORD

	Total W-R	Non-Handicaps 2-y-o	3-y-o+	Handicaps 2-y-o	3-y-o+	Per cent	£1 Level Stake
Southwell (AW)	6-32	0-0	1-12	0-0	5-20	18.8	+ 11.50
Leicester	2-7	0-0	0-2	0-0	2-5	28.6	+ 16.00
Ayr	1-1	0-0	0-0	0-0	1-1	100.0	+ 14.00
Thirsk	1-1	0-0	0-0	0-0	1-1	100.0	+ 16.00
Yarmouth	1-3	0-0	0-0	0-0	1-3	33.3	+ 10.00
Beverley	1-11	0-0	0-4	0-0	1-7	9.1	− 5.00

Wolverhampton (AW)	0-15	Ripon	0-4	York		0-3
Nottingham	0-10	Catterick	0-3	Carlisle		0-2
Pontefract	0-7	Newmarket	0-3	Haydock		0-2
Doncaster	0-4	Warwick	0-3	Redcar		0-1

WINNING HORSES

	Age	Races Run	1st	2nd	3rd	Unpl	Win £
Sailormaite	3	16	6	1	3	6	19,430
Broadstairs Beauty	4	15	4	3	3	5	16,059
Angelic Dancer	3	11	1	1	1	8	3,948
Sandmoor Denim	7	10	1	3	0	6	3,104

WINNING OWNERS

	Races Won	Value £		Races Won	Value £
S R Bowring	6	19,430	Mrs P A Barratt	1	3,948
Mrs Judy Hunt	4	16,059	E H Lunness	1	3,104

Favourites	2-7	28.6%	+ 3.00	Total winning prize-money	£42,540
Longest winning sequence			2	Average SP of winner	8.8/1
Longest losing sequence			50	Return on stakes invested	4.9%
1993 Form	8-107	7.5%	− 56.50	1991 Form	2-56	3.6%	− 19.00
1992 Form	9-104	8.7%	+ 24.90	1990 Form	4-78	5.1%	− 6.00

J M BRADLEY (Chepstow, Gwent)

	No. of Horses	Races Run	1st	2nd	3rd	Unpl	Per cent	£1 Level Stake
2-y-o	2	13	0	0	1	12	−	− 13.00
3-y-o	5	27	1	1	2	23	3.7	− 16.00
4-y-o+	20	104	7	7	6	84	6.7	− 25.67
Totals	27	144	8	8	9	119	5.6	− 54.67

Jan	Feb	Mar	Apr	May	Jun	Jul	Aug	Sep	Oct/Nov
0-5	0-12	0-5	0-8	1-18	3-28	2-21	0-27	0-9	2-11

Winning Jockeys	W-R	£1 Level Stake			W-R	£1 Level Stake
L Charnock	2-5	+ 24.00	Amanda Sanders		1-1	+ 16.00
R Waterfield	2-11	+ 11.00	J Weaver		1-7	- 2.67
K Rutter	2-22	- 5.00				

Winning Courses	W-R	£1 Level Stake			W-R	£1 Level Stake
Thirsk	2-5	+ 10.33	Folkestone		1-1	+ 11.00
Hamilton	2-9	+ 19.00	Edinburgh		1-7	+ 10.00
Chepstow	2-14	+ 3.00				

Winning Horses	Age	Races Run	1st	2nd	3rd	Unpl	Win £
Sooty Tern	7	15	3	2	0	10	12,396
Ballymac Girl	6	2	2	0	0	0	7,153
Mr Cube	4	20	1	0	1	18	3,106
Dots Dee	5	13	1	2	3	7	2,954
Comeonup	3	9	1	1	1	6	2,722

Favourites	1-3	33.3%	+ 1.33	Total winning prize-money			£28,330
1993 Form	6-86	7.0%	- 36.25	1991 Form	2-58	3.4%	- 26.00
1992 Form	3-85	3.5%	- 46.00	1990 Form	4-73	5.5%	- 30.50

G C BRAVERY (Newmarket)

	No. of Horses	Races Run	1st	2nd	3rd	Unpl	Per cent	£1 Level Stake
2-y-o	6	20	1	0	4	15	5.0	- 17.12
3-y-o	3	22	1	2	2	17	4.5	- 18.00
4-y-o+	2	12	1	1	0	10	8.3	- 9.00
Totals	11	54	3	3	6	42	5.6	- 44.12

Jan	Feb	Mar	Apr	May	Jun	Jul	Aug	Sep	Oct/Nov
0-2	1-2	1-6	0-7	0-5	1-6	0-13	0-2	0-7	0-4

Winning Jockeys	W-R	£1 Level Stake			W-R	£1 Level Stake
C Hawksley	1-5	- 1.00	N Carlisle		1-7	- 4.00
M Hills	1-6	- 3.12				

Winning Courses	W-R	£1 Level Stake			W-R	£1 Level Stake
Wolverhampton (AW)	2-3	+ 3.88	Southwell (AW)		1-14	- 11.00

Winning Horses	Age	Races Run	1st	2nd	3rd	Unpl	Win £
Keston Pond	4	8	1	1	0	6	3,348
Puppet Master	2	5	1	0	1	3	2,787
Cazanove's Pet	3	7	1	1	1	4	2,243

Favourites	1-2	50.0%	+ 0.88	Total winning prize-money			£8,378
1993 Form	5-77	6.5%	- 7.00	1992 Form	5-23	21.7%	+ 20.63

J J BRIDGER (Liphook, Hants)

	No. of Horses	Races Run	1st	2nd	3rd	Unpl	Per cent	£1 Level Stake
2-y-o	6	22	0	1	0	21	-	- 22.00
3-y-o	8	31	3	2	1	25	9.7	- 10.00
4-y-o+	9	37	2	4	2	29	5.4	- 17.00
Totals	23	90	5	7	3	75	5.6	- 49.00

Jan	Feb	Mar	Apr	May	Jun	Jul	Aug	Sep	Oct/Nov
1-8	2-6	0-2	0-10	2-13	0-22	0-11	0-6	0-6	0-6

Winning Jockeys	W-R	£1 Level Stake			W-R	£1 Level Stake
T Williams	3-42	- 21.00	N Varley		2-10	+ 10.00

Winning Courses					
Lingfield (AW)	3-18	+ 3.00	Lingfield	1-13	- 8.00
Goodwood	1-11	+ 4.00			

Winning Horses	Age	Races Run	1st	2nd	3rd	Unpl	Win £
Thorny Bishop	3	11	3	2	1	5	9,406
Shades Of Jade	6	10	2	0	0	8	6,585

Favourites	0-3	Total winning prize-money	£15,991

1993 Form	2-72	2.8%	- 31.00	1991 Form	0-63		
1992 Form	2-73	2.7%	- 53.37	1990 Form	2-57	3.5%	- 18.00

W M BRISBOURNE (Baschurch, Salop)

	No. of Horses	Races Run	1st	2nd	3rd	Unpl	Per cent	£1 Level Stake
2-y-o	3	4	0	0	0	4	-	- 4.00
3-y-o	6	22	2	0	1	19	9.1	+ 2.75
4-y-o+	2	12	0	0	0	12	-	- 12.00
Totals	11	38	2	0	1	35	5.3	- 13.25

Jan	Feb	Mar	Apr	May	Jun	Jul	Aug	Sep	Oct/Nov
0-0	0-0	0-0	0-4	1-5	1-7	0-3	0-7	0-4	0-8

Winning Jockey	W-R	£1 Level Stake			W-R	£1 Level Stake
A Garth	2-14	+ 10.75				

Winning Courses					
Carlisle	1-3	+ 18.00	Wolverhampton (AW)	1-4	- 0.25

Winning Horse	Age	Races Run	1st	2nd	3rd	Unpl	Win £
Hill Farm Dancer	3	6	2	0	1	3	5,439

Favourites	0-0		Total winning prize-money	£5,439

1993 Form	2-32	6.3%	- 9.00	1991 Form	0-15
1992 Form	2-27	7.4%	- 7.00		

C E BRITTAIN (Newmarket)

	No. of Horses	Races Run	1st	2nd	3rd	Unpl	Per cent	£1 Level Stake
2-y-o	31	84	5	4	6	69	6.0	- 11.50
3-y-o	40	191	16	15	22	138	8.4	- 98.55
4-y-o+	30	167	8	9	16	134	4.8	- 92.38
Totals	101	442	29	28	44	341	6.6	-202.43

BY MONTH

2-y-o	W-R	Per cent	£1 Level Stake	3-y-o	W-R	Per cent	£1 Level Stake
January	0-0	-	0.00	January	0-0	-	0.00
February	0-0	-	0.00	February	1-2	50.0	- 0.33
March	0-0	-	0.00	March	0-6	-	- 6.00
April	0-0	-	0.00	April	1-20	5.0	- 7.00
May	0-2	-	- 2.00	May	3-29	10.3	- 16.43
June	0-7	-	- 7.00	June	4-36	11.1	- 6.50
July	0-12	-	- 12.00	July	3-26	11.5	- 6.37
August	1-16	6.3	- 13.00	August	1-24	4.2	- 21.50
September	2-27	7.4	+ 1.50	September	1-27	3.7	- 22.67
Oct/Nov	2-20	10.0	+ 21.00	Oct/Nov	2-21	9.5	- 11.75

4-y-o+	W-R	Per cent	£1 Level Stake	Totals	W-R	Per cent	£1 Level Stake
January	0-2	-	- 2.00	January	0-2	-	- 2.00
February	0-5	-	- 5.00	February	1-7	14.3	- 5.33
March	0-5	-	- 5.00	March	0-11	-	- 11.00
April	0-21	-	- 21.00	April	1-41	2.4	- 28.00
May	2-23	8.7	+ 5.00	May	5-54	9.3	- 13.43
June	0-26	-	- 26.00	June	4-69	5.8	- 39.50
July	2-26	7.7	- 6.50	July	5-64	7.8	- 24.87
August	0-20	-	- 20.00	August	2-60	3.3	- 54.50
September	1-18	5.6	- 10.00	September	4-72	5.6	- 31.17
Oct/Nov	3-21	14.3	- 1.88	Oct/Nov	7-62	11.3	+ 7.37

DISTANCE

2-y-o	W-R	Per cent	£1 Level Stake	3-y-o	W-R	Per cent	£1 Level Stake
5f-6f	2-27	7.4	- 3.00	5f-6f	3-21	14.3	- 9.17
7f-8f	3-57	5.3	- 8.50	7f-8f	5-74	6.8	- 50.58
9f-13f	0-0	-	0.00	9f-13f	7-82	8.5	- 28.05
14f+	0-0	-	0.00	14f+	1-14	7.1	- 10.75

4-y-o+	W-R	Per cent	£1 Level Stake	Totals	W-R	Per cent	£1 Level Stake
5f-6f	0-6	-	- 6.00	5f-6f	5-54	9.3	- 18.17
7f-8f	1-62	1.6	- 52.00	7f-8f	9-193	4.7	-111.08
9f-13f	4-76	5.3	- 32.88	9f-13f	11-158	7.0	- 60.93
14f+	3-23	13.0	- 1.50	14f+	4-37	10.8	- 12.25

TYPE OF RACE

Non-Handicaps	W-R	Per cent	£1 Level Stake	Handicaps	W-R	Per cent	£1 Level Stake
2-y-o	2-74	2.7	- 63.50	2-y-o	3-9	33.3	+ 53.00
3-y-o	15-122	12.3	- 38.55	3-y-o	1-63	1.6	- 54.00
4-y-o+	3-42	7.1	- 25.88	4-y-o+	5-115	4.3	- 56.50
Selling	0-8	-	- 8.00	Selling	0-6	-	- 6.00
Apprentice	0-1	-	- 1.00	Apprentice	0-2	-	- 2.00
Amat/Ladies	0-0	-	0.00	Amat/Ladies	0-0	-	0.00
Totals	20-247	8.1	-136.93	Totals	9-195	4.6	- 65.50

COURSE GRADE

	W-R	Per cent	£1 Level Stake
Group 1	12-252	4.8	-153.37
Group 2	4-44	9.1	- 23.43
Group 3	8-95	8.4	- 26.30
Group 4	5-51	9.8	+ 0.67

FIRST TIME OUT

	W-R	Per cent	£1 Level Stake
2-y-o	0-31	-	- 31.00
3-y-o	4-40	10.0	- 15.33
4-y-o+	1-30	3.3	- 9.00
Totals	5-101	5.0	- 55.33

JOCKEYS RIDING

	W-R	Per cent	£1 Level Stake		W-R	Per cent	£1 Level Stake
M Roberts	20-276	7.2	-119.10				
B Doyle	8-107	7.5	- 26.83	W R Swinburn	1-12	8.3	- 9.50

G Crealock	0-24	R Cochrane	0-2	L Dettori	0-1
B Russell	0-6	A McGlone	0-1	Mrs K Miller	0-1
B Raymond	0-3	G Bardwell	0-1	P Robinson	0-1
B Thomson	0-2	J Carroll	0-1	R Street	0-1
N Imai	0-2	J Williams	0-1		

COURSE RECORD

	Total W-R	Non-Handicaps 2-y-o	3-y-o+	Handicaps 2-y-o	3-y-o+	Per cent	£1 Level Stake
Yarmouth	7-32	1-3	3-11	1-1	2-17	21.9	+ 33.45
Newmarket	6-66	0-14	5-30	0-2	1-20	9.1	- 27.37
Folkestone	3-20	0-2	0-6	1-1	2-11	15.0	+ 25.00
Southwell (AW)	2-8	0-0	2-3	0-0	0-5	25.0	- 1.33
Ascot	2-33	0-6	1-14	1-1	0-12	6.1	- 8.00
Newcastle	1-3	0-0	1-2	0-0	0-1	33.3	+ 5.00
Epsom	1-7	0-0	1-4	0-0	0-3	14.3	+ 6.00
Lingfield	1-7	0-2	1-2	0-0	0-3	14.3	- 3.75
Redcar	1-8	0-0	1-4	0-0	0-4	12.5	- 2.00
Salisbury	1-8	0-2	1-4	0-0	0-2	12.5	- 3.68
Chester	1-9	0-0	1-5	0-0	0-4	11.1	- 2.00
Nottingham	1-14	0-3	1-5	0-0	0-6	7.1	- 10.75
Newbury	1-23	1-3	0-11	0-0	0-9	4.3	- 15.50
Sandown	1-23	0-6	0-7	0-0	1-10	4.3	- 16.50

Doncaster	0-24	Goodwood	0-10	Beverley	0-4
Kempton	0-24	Lingfield (AW)	0-10	Chepstow	0-4
York	0-22	Pontefract	0-9	Ripon	0-3
Leicester	0-16	Windsor	0-9	Ayr	0-2
Haydock	0-15	Bath	0-7	Thirsk	0-2
Warwick	0-11	Brighton	0-7	Wolverhampton (AW)	0-2

WINNING HORSES

	Age	Races Run	1st	2nd	3rd	Unpl	Win £
Shambo	7	9	1	0	2	6	29,250
Rudagi	3	3	2	0	0	1	14,341
Tudor Island	5	8	2	2	1	3	10,536
Autumn Affair	2	6	1	2	1	2	10,179
Madary	3	5	2	0	1	2	9,027
Luana	3	9	2	0	3	4	8,560
Garden Of Heaven	5	4	1	0	1	2	6,972
Musetta	2	5	1	1	0	3	6,462
Needle Gun	4	4	1	0	1	2	5,299
Sieve Of Time	3	7	1	0	2	4	5,127
Bin Nashwan	2	3	1	0	0	2	4,759
Ionio	3	5	1	1	0	3	4,712
Alanees	3	6	1	2	0	3	4,653
Leopardess	3	5	1	0	1	3	4,379
Ertlon	4	10	1	0	0	9	4,240
Elpidos	2	4	1	0	0	3	3,980
Karachi	4	8	1	1	0	6	3,682
Lala Musa	3	7	1	0	2	4	3,526
Cedez Le Passage	3	7	1	1	1	4	3,524
Joy Of Freedom	4	4	1	0	0	3	3,391
Czarna	3	4	1	0	0	3	3,368
Gonolek	3	4	1	0	2	1	3,340
Mister Fire Eyes	2	7	1	0	0	6	3,184
Stompin	3	8	1	2	1	4	3,132
Papagayos	3	10	1	1	1	7	2,249

WINNING OWNERS

	Races Won	Value £		Races Won	Value £
Mrs C E Brittain	1	29,250	Mrs Sonia Rogers	1	4,379
Saeed Manana	5	28,201	Sheikh Marwan Al Maktoum	1	3,526
B H Voak	3	18,561	A J Richards	1	3,524
Ray Richards	2	13,311	James Miller	1	3,391
D Sieff	2	10,536	Ovidstown Investments Ltd	1	3,368
Mohamed Obaida	2	9,412	Sheikh Ahmed Al Maktoum	1	3,340
Hilal Salem	2	9,027	C T Olley	1	3,184
The Dowager Lady Beaverbrook	2	8,692	Parrot Racing	1	2,249
C E Brittain	2	7,922			

Favourites	7-21	33.3%	– 3.08	Total winning prize-money	£161,871
Longest winning sequence			2	Average SP of winner	7.3/1
Longest losing sequence			45	Return on stakes invested	-45.8%
1993 Form	37-453	8.2%	-137.11	1991 Form	53-545	9.7%	-121.61
1992 Form	63-599	10.5%	-157.44	1990 Form	42-507	8.3%	- 71.96

M BRITTAIN (Warthill, North Yorks)

	No. of Horses	Races Run	1st	2nd	3rd	Unpl	Per cent	£1 Level Stake
2-y-o	5	17	0	0	1	16	–	- 17.00
3-y-o	11	72	0	4	4	64	–	- 72.00
4-y-o+	12	99	11	8	7	73	11.1	+ 14.00
Totals	28	188	11	12	12	153	5.9	- 75.00

BY MONTH

2-y-o	W-R	Per cent	£1 Level Stake	3-y-o	W-R	Per cent	£1 Level Stake
January	0-0	–	0.00	January	0-0	–	0.00
February	0-0	–	0.00	February	0-1	–	- 1.00
March	0-0	–	0.00	March	0-2	–	- 2.00
April	0-4	–	- 4.00	April	0-18	–	- 18.00
May	0-3	–	- 3.00	May	0-13	–	- 13.00
June	0-2	–	- 2.00	June	0-10	–	- 10.00
July	0-2	–	- 2.00	July	0-12	–	- 12.00
August	0-2	–	- 2.00	August	0-11	–	- 11.00
September	0-3	–	- 3.00	September	0-4	–	- 4.00
Oct/Nov	0-1	–	- 1.00	Oct/Nov	0-1	–	- 1.00

4-y-o+	W-R	Per cent	£1 Level Stake	Totals	W-R	Per cent	£1 Level Stake
January	0-0	-	0.00	January	0-0	-	0.00
February	0-1	-	- 1.00	February	0-2	-	- 2.00
March	0-3	-	- 3.00	March	0-5	-	- 5.00
April	1-19	5.3	+ 7.00	April	1-41	2.4	- 15.00
May	0-13	-	- 13.00	May	0-29	-	- 29.00
June	3-13	23.1	+ 5.00	June	3-25	12.0	- 7.00
July	4-14	28.6	+ 12.50	July	4-28	14.3	- 1.50
August	1-19	5.3	- 12.50	August	1-32	3.1	- 25.50
September	1-8	12.5	+ 7.00	September	1-15	6.7	0.00
Oct/Nov	1-9	11.1	+ 12.00	Oct/Nov	1-11	9.1	+ 10.00

DISTANCE

2-y-o	W-R	Per cent	£1 Level Stake	3-y-o	W-R	Per cent	£1 Level Stake
5f-6f	0-13	-	- 13.00	5f-6f	0-20	-	- 20.00
7f-8f	0-4	-	- 4.00	7f-8f	0-36	-	- 36.00
9f-13f	0-0	-	0.00	9f-13f	0-16	-	- 16.00
14f+	0-0	-	0.00	14f+	0-0	-	0.00

4-y-o+	W-R	Per cent	£1 Level Stake	Totals	W-R	Per cent	£1 Level Stake
5f-6f	1-7	14.3	+ 19.00	5f-6f	1-40	2.5	- 14.00
7f-8f	0-9	-	- 9.00	7f-8f	0-49	-	- 49.00
9f-13f	7-51	13.7	- 6.50	9f-13f	7-67	10.4	- 22.50
14f+	3-32	9.4	+ 10.50	14f+	3-32	9.4	+ 10.50

TYPE OF RACE

Non-Handicaps	W-R	Per cent	£1 Level Stake	Handicaps	W-R	Per cent	£1 Level Stake
2-y-o	0-7	-	- 7.00	2-y-o	0-3	-	- 3.00
3-y-o	0-16	-	- 16.00	3-y-o	0-41	-	- 41.00
4-y-o+	0-3	-	- 3.00	4-y-o+	9-82	11.0	+ 17.50
Selling	0-14	-	- 14.00	Selling	2-13	15.4	+ 0.50
Apprentice	0-1	-	- 1.00	Apprentice	0-7	-	- 7.00
Amat/Ladies	0-0	-	0.00	Amat/Ladies	0-1	-	- 1.00
Totals	0-41	-	- 41.00	Totals	11-147	7.5	- 34.00

COURSE GRADE

	W-R	Per cent	£1 Level Stake
Group 1	3-36	8.3	+ 2.00
Group 2	2-38	5.3	- 25.00
Group 3	5-74	6.8	- 27.00
Group 4	1-40	2.5	- 25.00

FIRST TIME OUT

	W-R	Per cent	£1 Level Stake
2-y-o	0-4	-	- 4.00
3-y-o	0-11	-	- 11.00
4-y-o+	0-11	-	- 11.00
Totals	0-26	-	- 26.00

JOCKEYS RIDING

	W-R	Per cent	£1 Level Stake		W-R	Per cent	£1 Level Stake
J Lowe	6-122	4.9	- 72.00	G Duffield	1-3	33.3	+ 2.00
G Bardwell	2-10	20.0	+ 15.00	A Munro	1-6	16.7	+ 20.00
G Carter	1-2	50.0	+ 5.00				

	W-R			W-R			W-R
J Fanning	0-8	G Parkin	0-2	J Carroll			0-1
L Charnock	0-7	A Eddery	0-1	K Darley			0-1
J Marshall	0-5	A Garth	0-1	M Kneafsey			0-1
D Wright	0-4	A Tucker	0-1	N Varley			0-1
S Webster	0-3	D Griffiths	0-1	R Street			0-1
A Mackay	0-2	Dale Gibson	0-1	S Maloney			0-1
C Teague	0-2	G Hind	0-1				

COURSE RECORD

	Total W-R	Non-Handicaps 2-y-o	3-y-o+	Handicaps 2-y-o	3-y-o+	Per cent	£1 Level Stake
Beverley	4-27	0-4	0-6	0-1	4-16	14.8	- 6.00
Newmarket	1-2	0-0	0-0	0-0	1-2	50.0	+ 8.00
Sandown	1-2	0-0	0-0	0-0	1-2	50.0	+ 5.00
Doncaster	1-6	0-0	0-0	0-0	1-6	16.7	+ 15.00
Southwell (AW)	1-11	0-1	0-3	0-0	1-7	9.1	+ 4.00
Redcar	1-12	0-1	0-0	0-0	1-11	8.3	- 5.50
Nottingham	1-15	0-1	0-2	0-0	1-12	6.7	+ 11.00
Ripon	1-15	0-0	0-2	0-0	1-13	6.7	- 8.50

Hamilton	0-16	Thirsk	0-9	Chester	0-2
Newcastle	0-13	Ayr	0-8	Warwick	0-2
Edinburgh	0-11	Wolverhampton (AW)	0-5	Carlisle	0-1
Pontefract	0-11	Leicester	0-4	Haydock	0-1
Catterick	0-10	York	0-4	Yarmouth	0-1

WINNING HORSES

	Age	Races Run	1st	2nd	3rd	Unpl	Win £
Eire Leath-Sceal	7	24	6	0	2	16	21,994
Gold Desire	4	14	2	2	0	10	8,087
Top Prize	6	14	2	1	0	11	5,955
Nordic Brave	8	5	1	1	0	3	3,699

WINNING OWNERS

	Races Won	Value £		Races Won	Value £
Mel Brittain	9	33,780	Northgate Lodge Racing Ltd	2	5,955

Favourites	0-5		Total winning prize-money		£39,735

Longest winning sequence		1	Average SP of winner		9.3/1
Longest losing sequence		54	Return on stakes invested		-39.9%

1993 Form	9-203	4.4%	-123.00	1991 Form	21-420	5.0%	-214.25
1992 Form	7-224	3.1%	-141.00	1990 Form	27-543	5.0%	-260.59

C D BROAD (Westbury-on-Severn, Glos)

	No. of Horses	Races Run	1st	2nd	3rd	Unpl	Per cent	£1 Level Stake
2-y-o	2	6	0	0	0	6	-	- 6.00
3-y-o	4	11	0	0	0	11	-	- 11.00
4-y-o+	9	35	2	2	0	31	5.7	- 9.00
Totals	15	52	2	2	0	48	3.8	- 26.00

Jan	Feb	Mar	Apr	May	Jun	Jul	Aug	Sep	Oct/Nov
0-1	0-5	0-5	0-3	0-7	2-11	0-8	0-4	0-6	0-2

Winning Jockeys	W-R	£1 Level Stake			W-R	£1 Level Stake
J Reid	1-2	+ 7.00	V Slattery		1-3	+ 14.00

Winning Courses	W-R	£1 Level Stake			W-R	£1 Level Stake
Southwell (AW)	1-4	+ 13.00	Warwick		1-8	+ 1.00

Winning Horses	Age	Races Run	1st	2nd	3rd	Unpl	Win £
King's Shilling	7	2	1	0	0	1	2,588
Junction Twentytwo	4	7	1	0	0	6	2,070

Favourites	0-3		Total winning prize-money		£4,658

1993 Form	2-26	7.7%	- 4.00	1991 Form	1-20	5.0%	+ 14.00
1992 Form	1-34	2.9%	- 19.00				

C P E BROOKS (Upper Lambourn, Berks)

	No. of Horses	Races Run	1st	2nd	3rd	Unpl	Per cent	£1 Level Stake
2-y-o	0	0	0	0	0	0	-	0.00
3-y-o	0	0	0	0	0	0	-	0.00
4-y-o+	3	12	3	0	0	9	25.0	+ 4.00
Totals	3	12	3	0	0	9	25.0	+ 4.00

Jan	Feb	Mar	Apr	May	Jun	Jul	Aug	Sep	Oct/Nov
0-0	1-1	0-0	0-1	0-3	1-3	0-2	1-2	0-0	0-0

		£1 Level			£1 Level
Winning Jockeys	W-R	Stake		W-R	Stake
R Cochrane	2-4	+ 6.00	T Quinn	1-1	+ 5.00

		£1 Level			£1 Level
Winning Courses					
Lingfield (AW)	1-1	+ 5.00	Goodwood	1-3	+ 3.50
Bath	1-2	+ 1.50			

		Races					Win
Winning Horses	Age	Run	1st	2nd	3rd	Unpl	£
Fieldridge	5	7	2	0	0	5	7,023
Soviet Express	4	4	1	0	0	3	2,532

Favourites	1-1	100.0%	+ 2.50	Total winning prize-money	£9,555

1993 Form	1-17	5.9%	- 6.00	1991 Form	1-9	11.1%	- 4.00
1992 Form	0-1			1990 Form	0-1		

D BURCHELL (Ebbw Vale, Gwent)

	No. of	Races					Per	£1 Level
	Horses	Run	1st	2nd	3rd	Unpl	cent	Stake
2-y-o	2	3	0	0	0	3	-	- 3.00
3-y-o	4	8	0	0	1	7	-	- 8.00
4-y-o+	21	58	4	1	7	46	6.9	- 37.12
Totals	27	69	4	1	8	56	5.8	- 48.12

Jan	Feb	Mar	Apr	May	Jun	Jul	Aug	Sep	Oct/Nov
0-7	1-10	0-1	0-2	1-12	2-8	0-9	0-9	0-6	0-5

		£1 Level			£1 Level
Winning Jockeys	W-R	Stake		W-R	Stake
R Price	3-37	- 18.50	A Procter	1-3	- 0.62

		£1 Level			£1 Level
Winning Courses					
Wolverhampton (AW)	3-34	- 23.12	Chepstow	1-7	+ 3.00

		Races					Win
Winning Horses	Age	Run	1st	2nd	3rd	Unpl	£
Acrow Line	9	6	2	0	2	2	5,202
Desert Power	5	5	1	0	0	4	3,209
Broom Isle	6	5	1	0	1	3	2,847

Favourites	1-3	33.3%	- 0.62	Total winning prize-money	£11,257

1993 Form	10-65	15.4%	+ 21.80	1991 Form	4-63	6.3%	+ 29.00
1992 Form	1-48	2.1%	- 45.75	1990 Form	7-75	9.3%	- 27.50

P BURGOYNE (Upper Lambourn, Berks)

	No. of Horses	Races Run	1st	2nd	3rd	Unpl	Per cent	£1 Level Stake
2-y-o	0	0	0	0	0	0	-	0.00
3-y-o	2	2	0	0	0	2	-	- 2.00
4-y-o+	10	46	1	3	2	40	2.2	- 39.00
Totals	12	48	1	3	2	42	2.1	- 41.00

Jan	Feb	Mar	Apr	May	Jun	Jul	Aug	Sep	Oct/Nov
0-2	0-1	0-0	0-4	1-9	0-10	0-9	0-5	0-3	0-5

Winning Jockey	W-R	£1 Level Stake	Winning Course	W-R	£1 Level Stake
J Tate	1-10	- 3.00	Leicester	1-4	+ 3.00

Winning Horse	Age	Races Run	1st	2nd	3rd	Unpl	Win £
Rock The Barney	5	11	1	2	1	7	3,236

Favourites	0-3	Total winning prize-money	£3,236

1993 Form	1-38	2.6%	- 32.00	1991 Form	0-36
1992 Form	0-16			1990 Form	0-35

K R BURKE (Wantage, Oxon)

	No. of Horses	Races Run	1st	2nd	3rd	Unpl	Per cent	£1 Level Stake
2-y-o	4	11	0	0	0	11	-	- 11.00
3-y-o	6	27	3	3	4	17	11.1	+ 2.00
4-y-o+	9	43	6	5	5	27	14.0	- 13.52
Totals	19	81	9	8	9	55	11.1	- 22.52

Jan	Feb	Mar	Apr	May	Jun	Jul	Aug	Sep	Oct/Nov
0-4	4-12	0-3	1-8	0-6	1-11	2-11	0-12	1-11	0-3

Winning Jockeys	W-R	£1 Level Stake		W-R	£1 Level Stake
D Holland	3-11	- 0.77	G Carter	1-3	- 1.75
A Clark	2-6	+ 10.00	N Adams	1-10	- 8.00
J Tate	2-6	+ 23.00			

Winning Courses					
Southwell (AW)	4-13	+ 3.98	Epsom	1-3	+ 5.00
Wolverhampton (AW)	2-14	- 7.50	Windsor	1-5	+ 3.00
Ayr	1-2	+ 17.00			

Burke K R

Winning Horses	Age	Races Run	1st	2nd	3rd	Unpl	Win £
Daring Destiny	3	8	2	2	1	3	57,235
Top Shiel	6	13	4	3	1	5	10,564
Mr Bean	4	9	1	2	2	4	3,143
Roseate Lodge	8	12	1	0	1	10	2,937
Charlies Dream	3	9	1	0	1	7	2,243

Favourites	4-11	36.4%	- 2.02	Total winning prize-money			£76,122

1993 Form	7-96	7.3%	- 45.50	1991 Form	2-42	4.8%	- 17.00
1992 Form	1-38	2.6%	- 31.50	1990 Form	0-14		

P BUTLER (Lewes, East Sussex)

	No. of Horses	Races Run	1st	2nd	3rd	Unpl	Per cent	£1 Level Stake
2-y-o	1	7	0	1	0	6	-	- 7.00
3-y-o	3	21	1	1	2	17	4.8	+ 13.00
4-y-o+	6	23	0	1	1	21	-	- 23.00
Totals	10	51	1	3	3	44	2.0	- 17.00

Jan	Feb	Mar	Apr	May	Jun	Jul	Aug	Sep	Oct/Nov
0-0	0-1	0-6	0-5	1-12	0-10	0-4	0-0	0-8	0-5

Winning Jockey	W-R	£1 Level Stake	Winning Course	W-R	£1 Level Stake
M Baird	1-19	+ 15.00	Windsor	1-3	+ 31.00

Winning Horse	Age	Races Run	1st	2nd	3rd	Unpl	Win £
Little Luke	3	14	1	1	2	10	3,210

Favourites	0-1		Total winning prize-money	£3,210

1993 Form	3-62	4.8%	- 19.50	1991 Form	0-28
1992 Form	3-42	7.1%	- 15.50	1990 Form	0-11

N BYCROFT (Brandsby, North Yorks)

	No. of Horses	Races Run	1st	2nd	3rd	Unpl	Per cent	£1 Level Stake
2-y-o	7	24	1	1	1	21	4.2	- 3.00
3-y-o	9	73	1	4	3	65	1.4	- 62.00
4-y-o+	6	59	3	6	3	47	5.1	- 1.50
Totals	22	156	5	11	7	133	3.2	- 66.50

Jan	Feb	Mar	Apr	May	Jun	Jul	Aug	Sep	Oct/Nov
0-2	0-0	0-9	2-16	0-25	2-20	0-28	1-26	0-21	0-9

Winning Jockeys	W-R	£1 Level Stake			W-R	£1 Level Stake
K Fallon	1-6	+ 15.00	L Charnock		1-19	+ 15.00
N Kennedy	1-7	+ 4.00	S Maloney		1-22	- 15.50
J Fanning	1-16	+ 1.00				

Winning Courses	W-R	£1 Level Stake			W-R	£1 Level Stake
Catterick	1-9	+ 25.00	Hamilton		1-14	- 7.50
Redcar	1-11	+ 6.00	Ayr		1-18	- 7.00
Southwell (AW)	1-12	+ 9.00				

Winning Horses	Age	Races Run	1st	2nd	3rd	Unpl	Win £
Plum First	4	21	1	1	0	19	5,527
Craigie Boy	4	15	1	5	1	8	4,435
Cafe Solo	3	11	1	1	1	8	3,290
Shotley Again	4	10	1	0	1	8	3,132
Little Ginger Nut	2	4	1	0	1	2	2,249

Favourites	0-7			Total winning prize-money		£18,632
1993 Form	5-135	3.7%	- 92.17	1991 Form	6-114	5.3%	- 48.25
1992 Form	4-106	3.8%	- 66.25	1990 Form	2-169	1.2%	-141.00

T H CALDWELL (Warrington, Cheshire)

	No. of Horses	Races Run	1st	2nd	3rd	Unpl	Per cent	£1 Level Stake
2-y-o	6	22	1	2	1	18	4.5	- 18.00
3-y-o	1	4	0	0	1	3	-	- 4.00
4-y-o+	8	34	1	2	2	29	2.9	- 26.00
Totals	15	60	2	4	4	50	3.3	- 48.00

Jan	Feb	Mar	Apr	May	Jun	Jul	Aug	Sep	Oct/Nov
0-1	0-2	0-7	0-5	0-8	0-13	1-13	1-8	0-3	0-0

Winning Jockeys	W-R	£1 Level Stake			W-R	£1 Level Stake
R Hills	1-2	+ 6.00	K Darley		1-3	+ 1.00

Winning Courses	W-R	£1 Level Stake			W-R	£1 Level Stake
Ripon	1-3	+ 1.00	Haydock		1-5	+ 3.00

Winning Horses	Age	Races Run	1st	2nd	3rd	Unpl	Win £
Total Stranger	2	8	1	2	0	5	2,779
Sparky's Song	4	4	1	0	0	3	2,742

Favourites	1-2	50.0%	+ 2.00	Total winning prize-money		£5,520
1993 Form	0-23			1991 Form	0-19	
1992 Form	1-38	2.6%	+ 13.00	1990 Form	0-5	

N A CALLAGHAN (Newmarket)

	No. of Horses	Races Run	1st	2nd	3rd	Unpl	Per cent	£1 Level Stake
2-y-o	9	37	3	0	3	31	8.1	- 20.75
3-y-o	14	73	6	9	10	48	8.2	- 10.00
4-y-o+	1	1	0	0	0	1	-	- 1.00
Totals	24	111	9	9	13	80	8.1	- 31.75

Jan	Feb	Mar	Apr	May	Jun	Jul	Aug	Sep	Oct/Nov
0-7	1-1	0-2	0-7	1-20	2-19	0-14	1-17	3-15	1-9

Winning Jockeys	W-R	£1 Level Stake		W-R	£1 Level Stake
M Roberts	2-8	+ 2.25	L Carter	1-4	+ 8.00
Pat Eddery	2-18	- 5.00	B Thomson	1-5	+ 4.00
W R Swinburn	1-1	+ 7.00	D Harrison	1-9	+ 12.00
M Baird	1-3	+ 3.00			

Winning Courses					
Kempton	3-7	+ 15.00	Windsor	1-6	+ 15.00
Hamilton	1-1	+ 2.25	Lingfield (AW)	1-10	+ 2.00
Haydock	1-1	+ 7.00	Yarmouth	1-11	- 5.00
Nottingham	1-4	+ 3.00			

Winning Horses	Age	Races Run	1st	2nd	3rd	Unpl	Win £
Be Warned	3	15	2	4	3	6	9,862
Battleship Bruce	2	5	2	0	0	3	7,510
Asking For Aces	3	7	1	1	1	4	3,623
Tharwa	2	8	1	0	3	4	3,436
Prince Azzaan	3	8	1	0	0	7	2,898
Encore Senor	3	4	1	0	1	2	2,873
Aylesford	3	7	1	1	0	5	2,831

Favourites	1-14	7.1%	- 10.75	Total winning prize-money		£33,032

1993 Form	13-151	8.6%	- 88.34	1991 Form	30-265	11.3%	- 30.99
1992 Form	21-178	11.8%	- 65.03	1990 Form	31-197	15.7%	- 17.39

P CALVER (Ripon, North Yorks)

	No. of Horses	Races Run	1st	2nd	3rd	Unpl	Per cent	£1 Level Stake
2-y-o	3	12	2	0	2	8	16.7	+ 28.00
3-y-o	5	21	1	0	0	20	4.8	0.00
4-y-o+	8	73	4	5	6	58	5.5	- 43.75
Totals	16	106	7	5	8	86	6.6	- 15.75

Jan	Feb	Mar	Apr	May	Jun	Jul	Aug	Sep	Oct/Nov
0-1	0-2	0-3	0-10	4-20	1-16	0-18	0-13	1-12	1-11

Winning Jockey	W-R	£1 Level Stake		W-R	£1 Level Stake
Dale Gibson	7-29	+ 61.25			

Winning Courses					
Redcar	2-13	+ 36.00	Doncaster	1-7	- 1.00
Ayr	1-3	+ 4.00	Thirsk	1-14	- 10.50
Haydock	1-5	- 1.25	Ripon	1-16	+ 5.00

Winning Horses	Age	Races Run	1st	2nd	3rd	Unpl	Win £
Boursin	5	8	3	1	1	3	8,047
Perryston View	2	6	2	0	1	3	7,046
Somerton Boy	4	6	1	0	2	3	3,518
Kid Ory	3	6	1	0	0	5	3,210

Favourites	1-8	12.5%	- 4.50	Total winning prize-money			£21,820
1993 Form	12-100	12.0%	+ 13.83	1991 Form	8-109	7.3%	- 0.25
1992 Form	6-70	8.6%	- 18.75	1990 Form	18-131	13.7%	- 26.90

M J CAMACHO (Malton, North Yorks)

	No. of Horses	Races Run	1st	2nd	3rd	Unpl	Per cent	£1 Level Stake
2-y-o	7	23	0	4	2	17	-	- 23.00
3-y-o	9	41	2	6	2	31	4.9	- 27.00
4-y-o+	10	41	6	2	4	29	14.6	- 9.75
Totals	26	105	8	12	8	77	7.6	- 59.75

Jan	Feb	Mar	Apr	May	Jun	Jul	Aug	Sep	Oct/Nov
2-6	0-0	1-7	2-15	2-14	0-11	0-12	1-11	0-17	0-12

Winning Jockeys	W-R	£1 Level Stake		W-R	£1 Level Stake
L Charnock	7-88	- 47.25	S Webster	1-2	+ 2.50

Winning Courses					
Wolverhampton (AW)	2-5	+ 2.75	Catterick	1-6	+ 4.00
Thirsk	2-7	+ 7.50	Newcastle	1-10	- 6.00
Southwell (AW)	2-21	- 12.00			

Winning Horses	Age	Races Run	1st	2nd	3rd	Unpl	Win £
Hi Nod	4	9	1	0	1	7	15,920
Sea Devil	8	6	3	0	0	3	7,488
Blyton Lad	8	2	1	0	0	1	4,151
Noragan	3	7	1	2	0	4	3,028
El Nido	6	10	1	1	2	6	2,930
Fairey Firefly	3	4	1	1	0	2	2,306

Favourites	2-8	25.0%	0.00	Total winning prize-money			£35,822
1993 Form	12-103	11.7%	- 32.58	1991 Form	15-109	13.8%	- 11.21
1992 Form	20-113	17.7%	+ 31.76	1990 Form	20-140	14.3%	+ 63.18

B R CAMBIDGE (Bishop's Wood, Staffs)

	No. of Horses	Races Run	1st	2nd	3rd	Unpl	Per cent	£1 Level Stake
2-y-o	0	0	0	0	0	0	-	0.00
3-y-o	0	0	0	0	0	0	-	0.00
4-y-o+	4	42	2	2	3	35	4.8	- 20.00
Totals	4	42	2	2	3	35	4.8	- 20.00

Jan	Feb	Mar	Apr	May	Jun	Jul	Aug	Sep	Oct/Nov
0-2	1-3	0-3	0-3	1-8	0-5	0-7	0-7	0-3	0-1

Winning Jockeys	W-R	£1 Level Stake			W-R	£1 Level Stake
K Rutter	1-2	+ 7.00	Mrs H Noonan		1-13	0.00

Winning Courses	W-R	£1 Level Stake			W-R	£1 Level Stake
Beverley	1-5	+ 4.00	Wolverhampton (AW)		1-15	- 2.00

Winning Horses	Age	Races Run	1st	2nd	3rd	Unpl	Win £
Spice And Sugar	4	13	1	1	1	10	3,184
Breezed Well	8	13	1	0	0	12	2,950

Favourites	0-1		Total winning prize-money		£6,134

1993 Form	2-43	4.7%	- 29.50	1991 Form	4-22	18.2%	+ 17.50
1992 Form	0-26			1990 Form	2-19	10.5%	- 8.00

H CANDY (Wantage, Oxon)

	No. of Horses	Races Run	1st	2nd	3rd	Unpl	Per cent	£1 Level Stake
2-y-o	5	24	2	1	3	18	8.3	- 2.00
3-y-o	18	93	9	7	11	66	9.7	- 28.02
4-y-o+	5	19	2	1	1	15	10.5	+ 2.00
Totals	28	136	13	9	15	99	9.6	- 28.02

BY MONTH

2-y-o	W-R	Per cent	£1 Level Stake	3-y-o	W-R	Per cent	£1 Level Stake
Mar/Apr	0-0	-	0.00	Mar/Apr	0-6	-	- 6.00
May	0-0	-	0.00	May	2-14	14.3	+ 2.85
June	0-2	-	- 2.00	June	0-13	-	- 13.00
July	0-2	-	- 2.00	July	3-17	17.6	+ 9.50
August	2-7	28.6	+ 15.00	August	1-17	5.9	- 14.37
September	0-7	-	- 7.00	September	3-16	18.8	+ 3.00
Oct/Nov	0-6	-	- 6.00	Oct/Nov	0-10	-	- 10.00

4-y-o+	W-R	Per cent	£1 Level Stake	Totals	W-R	Per cent	£1 Level Stake
Mar/Apr	0-2	-	- 1.00	Mar/Apr	0-8	-	- 7.00
May	0-3	-	- 3.00	May	2-17	11.8	- 0.15
June	1-3	33.3	+ 5.00	June	1-18	5.6	- 10.00
July	0-3	-	- 3.00	July	3-22	13.6	+ 4.50
August	0-2	-	- 2.00	August	3-26	11.5	- 1.37
September	1-5	20.0	+ 8.00	September	4-28	14.3	+ 4.00
Oct/Nov	0-1	-	- 1.00	Oct/Nov	0-17	-	- 17.00

DISTANCE

2-y-o	W-R	Per cent	£1 Level Stake	3-y-o	W-R	Per cent	£1 Level Stake
5f-6f	2-10	20.0	+ 12.00	5f-6f	3-12	25.0	+ 7.50
7f-8f	0-14	-	- 14.00	7f-8f	2-35	5.7	- 12.00
9f-13f	0-0	-	0.00	9f-13f	4-41	9.8	- 18.52
14f+	0-0	-	0.00	14f+	0-5	-	- 5.00

4-y-o+	W-R	Per cent	£1 Level Stake	Totals	W-R	Per cent	£1 Level Stake
5f-6f	0-0	-	0.00	5f-6f	5-22	22.7	+ 19.50
7f-8f	1-8	12.5	0.00	7f-8f	3-57	5.3	- 26.00
9f-13f	0-5	-	- 5.00	9f-13f	4-46	8.7	- 23.52
14f+	1-6	16.7	+ 7.00	14f+	1-11	9.1	+ 2.00

TYPE OF RACE

Non-Handicaps	W-R	Per cent	£1 Level Stake	Handicaps	W-R	Per cent	£1 Level Stake
2-y-o	1-14	7.1	- 9.00	2-y-o	1-8	12.5	+ 9.00
3-y-o	6-51	11.8	- 5.15	3-y-o	3-32	9.4	- 12.87
4-y-o+	0-7	-	- 7.00	4-y-o+	2-11	18.2	+ 10.00
Selling	0-4	-	- 4.00	Selling	0-2	-	- 2.00
Apprentice	0-2	-	- 2.00	Apprentice	0-4	-	- 4.00
Amat/Ladies	0-0	-	0.00	Amat/Ladies	0-1	-	- 1.00
Totals	7-78	9.0	- 27.15	Totals	6-58	10.3	- 0.87

COURSE GRADE

	W-R	Per cent	£1 Level Stake
Group 1	3-63	4.8	- 35.00
Group 2	3-17	17.6	- 3.50
Group 3	6-49	12.2	+ 9.48
Group 4	1-7	14.3	+ 1.00

FIRST TIME OUT

	W-R	Per cent	£1 Level Stake
2-y-o	1-5	20.0	0.00
3-y-o	1-18	5.6	- 5.00
4-y-o+	1-5	20.0	+ 3.00
Totals	3-28	10.7	- 2.00

JOCKEYS RIDING

	W-R	Per cent	£1 Level Stake		W-R	Per cent	£1 Level Stake
W Newnes	12-93	12.9	+ 6.98	B Thomson	1-1	100.0	+ 7.00
S Dawson	0-17			A McGlone	0-1	J Quinn	0-1
Sarah Holland	0-11			A Munro	0-1	Mrs C Dunwoody	0-1
C Rutter	0-5			F Norton	0-1	T Quinn	0-1
M Roberts	0-2			Georgina Frost	0-1		

COURSE RECORD

	Total W-R	Non-Handicaps 2-y-o	3-y-o+	Handicaps 2-y-o	3-y-o+	Per cent	£1 Level Stake
Chepstow	3-12	0-2	2-6	0-0	1-4	25.0	+ 16.85
Lingfield	2-11	0-0	1-8	0-0	1-3	18.2	- 2.50
Windsor	2-11	0-1	1-8	1-1	0-1	18.2	+ 16.00
Yarmouth	1-1	0-0	0-0	0-0	1-1	100.0	+ 1.63
Warwick	1-4	0-0	0-2	0-1	1-1	25.0	+ 4.00
Salisbury	1-5	1-2	0-1	0-0	0-2	20.0	0.00
Kempton	1-8	0-1	0-4	0-0	1-3	12.5	+ 5.00
Newbury	1-11	0-2	1-5	0-1	0-3	9.1	- 2.00
Newmarket	1-18	0-1	1-5	0-3	0-9	5.6	- 12.00

Leicester	0-10	Bath	0-5	Ascot	0-2
Goodwood	0-8	Doncaster	0-3	Haydock	0-2
Nottingham	0-8	Epsom	0-3	Pontefract	0-2
Sandown	0-8	Folkestone	0-3	Brighton	0-1

WINNING HORSES

	Age	Races Run	1st	2nd	3rd	Unpl	Win £
Eveningperformance	3	7	3	0	1	3	20,883
Weather Break	3	4	1	0	0	3	5,285
Balance Of Power	2	9	1	0	1	7	4,932
Mnemonic	2	2	1	0	0	1	4,178
Telopea	3	5	1	0	2	2	3,835
Weaver Bird	4	5	1	0	0	4	3,655
Riparius	3	9	1	0	4	4	3,606
Exemption	3	8	1	2	1	4	3,465
Salsifis	3	8	1	0	1	6	3,443
Museum	3	7	1	2	0	4	3,330
High Five	4	6	1	0	0	5	3,236

WINNING OWNERS

	Races Won	Value £		Races Won	Value £
Mrs David Blackburn	5	29,775	T A F Frost	1	3,465
Kingstone Warren Partners	2	8,168	P A Deal	1	3,443
Girsonfield Ltd	2	8,013	H R H Prince Fahd Salman	1	3,330
Mrs Henry Candy	1	3,655			

Favourites	3-7	42.9%	+ 4.13	Total winning prize-money		£59,848

Longest winning sequence		3	Average SP of winner	7.3/1
Longest losing sequence		22	Return on stakes invested	-20.6%

1993 Form	6-127	4.7%	- 67.17	1991 Form	16-220	7.3%	- 55.00
1992 Form	21-200	10.5%	+ 11.93	1990 Form	23-189	12.2%	+ 23.20

J M CARR (Malton, North Yorks)

	No. of Horses	Races Run	1st	2nd	3rd	Unpl	Per cent	£1 Level Stake
2-y-o	5	14	0	1	1	12	-	- 14.00
3-y-o	3	9	0	1	2	6	-	- 9.00
4-y-o+	7	36	2	2	4	28	5.6	- 21.00
Totals	15	59	2	4	7	46	3.4	- 44.00

Jan	Feb	Mar	Apr	May	Jun	Jul	Aug	Sep	Oct/Nov
0-4	0-1	0-2	0-5	0-8	1-7	1-11	0-10	0-6	0-5

Winning Jockey	W-R	£1 Level Stake			W-R	£1 Level Stake
K Darley	2-8	+ 7.00				

Winning Courses						
Haydock	1-2	+ 3.00	Thirsk		1-5	+ 5.00

Winning Horse	Age	Races Run	1st	2nd	3rd	Unpl	Win £
Here Comes A Star	6	18	2	2	4	10	6,718

Favourites	1-2	50.0%	+ 3.00	Total winning prize-money	£6,718

1993 Form	5-48	10.4%	- 21.00	1992 Form	2-34	5.9%	- 22.00

H R A CECIL (Newmarket)

	No. of Horses	Races Run	1st	2nd	3rd	Unpl	Per cent	£1 Level Stake
2-y-o	45	90	26	17	12	35	28.9	- 8.35
3-y-o	51	205	47	33	26	99	22.9	+ 1.39
4-y-o+	7	29	3	4	3	19	10.3	- 21.95
Totals	103	324	76	54	41	153	23.5	- 28.91

Cecil H R A

BY MONTH

2-y-o	W-R	Per cent	£1 Level Stake		3-y-o	W-R	Per cent	£1 Level Stake
Mar/Apr	0-1	-	- 1.00		Mar/Apr	5-30	16.7	+ 4.57
May	0-0	-	0.00		May	8-36	22.2	- 11.12
June	2-9	22.2	+ 0.25		June	10-39	25.6	- 5.57
July	5-11	45.5	+ 0.58		July	7-25	28.0	+ 13.75
August	5-23	21.7	- 12.72		August	8-25	32.0	+ 12.40
September	4-16	25.0	- 5.09		September	6-30	20.0	- 9.70
Oct/Nov	10-30	33.3	+ 9.63		Oct/Nov	3-20	15.0	- 2.94

4-y-o+	W-R	Per cent	£1 Level Stake		Totals	W-R	Per cent	£1 Level Stake
Mar/Apr	1-8	12.5	- 6.20		Mar/Apr	6-39	15.4	- 2.63
May	1-6	16.7	- 3.00		May	9-42	21.4	- 14.12
June	1-4	25.0	- 1.75		June	13-52	25.0	- 7.07
July	0-5	-	- 5.00		July	12-41	29.3	+ 9.33
August	0-1	-	- 1.00		August	13-49	26.5	- 1.32
September	0-2	-	- 2.00		September	10-48	20.8	- 16.79
Oct/Nov	0-3	-	- 3.00		Oct/Nov	13-53	24.5	+ 3.69

DISTANCE

2-y-o	W-R	Per cent	£1 Level Stake		3-y-o	W-R	Per cent	£1 Level Stake
5f-6f	5-14	35.7	+ 6.57		5f-6f	2-9	22.2	- 0.50
7f-8f	20-75	26.7	- 18.25		7f-8f	11-51	21.6	- 7.23
9f-13f	1-1	100.0	+ 3.33		9f-13f	24-120	20.0	- 4.66
14f+	0-0	-	0.00		14f+	10-25	40.0	+ 13.78

4-y-o+	W-R	Per cent	£1 Level Stake		Totals	W-R	Per cent	£1 Level Stake
5f-6f	0-2	-	- 2.00		5f-6f	7-25	28.0	+ 4.07
7f-8f	0-3	-	- 3.00		7f-8f	31-129	24.0	- 28.48
9f-13f	2-10	20.0	- 5.95		9f-13f	27-131	20.6	- 7.28
14f+	1-14	7.1	- 11.00		14f+	11-39	28.2	+ 2.78

TYPE OF RACE

Non-Handicaps	W-R	Per cent	£1 Level Stake		Handicaps	W-R	Per cent	£1 Level Stake
2-y-o	26-88	29.5	- 6.35		2-y-o	0-0	-	0.00
3-y-o	41-168	24.4	+ 2.14		3-y-o	6-36	16.7	+ 0.25
4-y-o+	3-17	17.6	- 9.95		4-y-o+	0-12	-	- 12.00
Selling	0-2	-	- 2.00		Selling	0-0	-	0.00
Apprentice	0-1	-	- 1.00		Apprentice	0-0	-	0.00
Amat/Ladies	0-0	-	0.00		Amat/Ladies	0-0	-	0.00
Totals	70-276	25.4	- 17.16		Totals	6-48	12.5	- 11.75

76

COURSE GRADE

	W-R	Per cent	£1 Level Stake
Group 1	35-179	19.6	- 13.36
Group 2	10-42	23.8	- 10.30
Group 3	29-91	31.9	+ 1.68
Group 4	2-12	16.7	- 6.93

FIRST TIME OUT

	W-R	Per cent	£1 Level Stake
2-y-o	9-45	20.0	- 10.55
3-y-o	4-51	7.8	- 26.80
4-y-o+	1-7	14.3	- 4.00
Totals	14-103	13.6	- 41.35

JOCKEYS RIDING

	W-R	Per cent	£1 Level Stake		W-R	Per cent	£1 Level Stake
W Ryan	32-154	20.8	- 30.78	J Lowe	3-6	50.0	+ 7.00
Pat Eddery	17-44	38.6	+ 6.54	W R Swinburn	2-3	66.7	+ 13.00
A McGlone	15-83	18.1	- 40.17	R Cochrane	1-1	100.0	+ 1.50
M J Kinane	6-20	30.0	+ 27.00				

A Munro	0-3	C Rutter	0-1	Paul Eddery	0-1
D Lockhart	0-3	L Dettori	0-1	S Dawson	0-1
C Asmussen	0-1	M Hills	0-1	W Newnes	0-1

COURSE RECORD

	Total W-R	Non-Handicaps 2-y-o	3-y-o+	Handicaps 2-y-o	3-y-o+	Per cent	£1 Level Stake
Newmarket	9-57	4-14	4-34	0-0	1-9	15.8	+ 3.45
Pontefract	5-7	3-3	2-4	0-0	0-0	71.4	+ 6.38
Haydock	5-15	1-3	4-6	0-0	0-6	33.3	+ 9.08
Nottingham	5-15	3-9	2-6	0-0	0-0	33.3	+ 4.80
Leicester	5-19	2-10	3-9	0-0	0-0	26.3	- 1.62
York	4-21	2-4	1-13	0-0	1-4	19.0	- 7.12
Yarmouth	4-23	1-8	2-11	0-0	1-4	17.4	- 9.30
Bath	3-5	0-0	3-5	0-0	0-0	60.0	+ 3.05
Beverley	3-6	1-3	2-3	0-0	0-0	50.0	+ 0.54
Ripon	3-6	0-0	2-3	0-0	1-3	50.0	+ 3.80
Windsor	3-7	0-1	3-6	0-0	0-0	42.9	+ 5.50
Newcastle	3-10	1-3	2-3	0-0	0-4	30.0	- 4.07
Doncaster	3-12	1-2	2-10	0-0	0-0	25.0	+ 0.42
Goodwood	3-15	1-3	2-8	0-0	0-4	20.0	- 3.27
Ascot	3-17	1-2	2-13	0-0	0-2	17.6	+ 6.25
Thirsk	2-4	1-1	0-2	0-0	1-1	50.0	+ 5.00
Chester	2-8	1-2	1-5	0-0	0-1	25.0	- 3.43
Kempton	2-8	0-2	2-6	0-0	0-0	25.0	- 3.70
Sandown	2-11	0-3	1-7	0-0	1-1	18.2	- 3.50
Redcar	2-14	1-7	1-5	0-0	0-2	14.3	- 8.17
Folkestone	1-4	1-2	0-2	0-0	0-0	25.0	- 2.43
Warwick	1-4	1-1	0-3	0-0	0-0	25.0	- 0.50
Salisbury	1-6	0-1	1-4	0-0	0-1	16.7	- 3.50
Chepstow	1-9	0-3	1-5	0-0	0-1	11.1	- 7.67
Newbury	1-11	0-3	1-7	0-0	0-1	9.1	- 8.90

Brighton	0-2	Ayr	0-1	Southwell (AW)	0-1
Catterick	0-2	Epsom	0-1		
Lingfield	0-2	Lingfield (AW)	0-1		

WINNING HORSES

	Age	Races Run	1st	2nd	3rd	Unpl	Win £
King's Theatre	3	6	2	1	1	2	285,692
Kissing Cousin	3	3	2	0	0	1	132,993
Distant View	3	6	2	2	0	2	101,967
Eltish	2	5	3	1	1	0	94,281
Red Route	3	7	3	3	0	1	55,294
Coigach	3	5	2	1	0	2	37,618
Cicerao	3	4	2	0	0	2	35,999
Opera Score	3	5	2	0	2	1	26,692
State Crystal	3	4	1	2	1	0	20,860
Kalabo	2	4	2	1	0	1	18,538
Well Beloved	3	9	3	3	0	3	14,859
Electrify	3	5	3	0	1	1	13,999
Howard's End	3	6	2	3	0	1	9,764
Peter Quince	4	5	2	0	1	2	9,250
Averti (USA)	3	8	2	1	1	4	9,127
Vettori	2	2	1	0	0	1	8,627
Poltarf	3	6	2	0	1	3	8,599
Pengamon	2	4	2	0	0	2	8,404
Al Widyan	2	4	2	0	1	1	8,241
Double Dagger	3	5	2	2	0	1	7,900
Backgammon	3	7	2	0	2	3	7,522
Loxandra	3	4	1	0	0	3	7,440
Epagris	2	1	1	0	0	0	5,734
Zamalek	2	3	1	1	0	1	5,553
Evert	3	5	1	2	1	1	5,110
Peace Envoy	2	2	1	1	0	0	5,075
Moonshell	2	1	1	0	0	0	4,482
Florid	3	5	1	0	1	3	4,374
Craigmill	2	4	1	3	0	0	4,350
Private Line	2	1	1	0	0	0	4,195
Milly Ha Ha	3	6	1	1	2	2	4,150
Smuggling	3	2	1	0	0	1	4,127
Shapely	2	1	1	0	0	0	4,121
Saint Keyne	4	3	1	1	0	1	4,089
Cambrel	3	4	1	0	1	2	3,904
Stelvio	2	1	1	0	0	0	3,807
Balliol Boy	2	1	1	0	0	0	3,807
New Century	2	4	1	1	1	1	3,741
Tom Waller	3	3	1	1	0	1	3,729
Fabulous Fairy	3	4	1	0	0	3	3,713
Classic Cliche	2	2	1	1	0	0	3,692
Isle Of Pines	3	3	1	0	1	1	3,632
Touring	3	6	1	1	1	3	3,624
Thames Sword	2	3	1	1	0	1	3,617
Zahran	3	3	1	0	1	1	3,578
Homely	2	1	1	0	0	0	3,554
Neverending	2	5	1	3	1	0	3,553
Totality	3	2	1	1	0	0	3,526
Holtye	2	3	1	1	0	1	3,490
Nestos	3	8	1	1	2	4	3,332
Mistle Thrush	3	5	1	2	0	2	3,292
Al Rawda	2	3	1	1	0	1	3,165
Supreme Star	3	8	1	1	1	5	2,898

WINNING OWNERS

	Races Won	Value £		Races Won	Value £
Sheikh Mohammed	16	483,314	J Smallman	2	8,404
K Abdulla	19	273,650	S Khaled	2	6,451
Cliveden Stud	5	64,554	Mrs H G Cambanis	1	5,734
Sir David Wills	3	41,968	Buckram Oak Holdings	1	5,553
Ivan Allan	3	39,691	Lady Howard De Walden	1	4,127
Lord Howard De Walden	8	36,204	Wafic Said	1	3,807
L Marinopoulos	6	26,194	H R H Prince Fahd Salman	1	3,741
Michael Poland	1	20,860	Charles H Wacker III	1	3,729
Prince A A Faisal	4	14,984	Robert H Smith	1	3,713

Favourites	43-107	40.2%	- 7.45	Total winning prize-money		£1,046,674
Longest winning sequence			4	Average SP of winner		2.9/1
Longest losing sequence			13	Return on stakes invested		-8.9%
1993 Form	94-408	23.0%	- 17.28	1991 Form	119-381	31.2% + 17.10
1992 Form	109-383	28.5%	- 11.43	1990 Form	111-351	31.6% - 8.67

MRS J CECIL (Newmarket)

	No. of Horses	Races Run	1st	2nd	3rd	Unpl	Per cent	£1 Level Stake
2-y-o	11	26	3	2	3	18	11.5	- 8.00
3-y-o	17	70	14	4	9	43	20.0	+ 14.08
4-y-o+	10	36	6	4	5	21	16.7	+ 21.50
Totals	38	132	23	10	17	82	17.4	+ 27.58

BY MONTH

2-y-o	W-R	Per cent	£1 Level Stake	3-y-o	W-R	Per cent	£1 Level Stake
Mar/Apr	0-0	-	0.00	Mar/Apr	2-11	18.2	+ 4.00
May	0-1	-	- 1.00	May	5-17	29.4	+ 5.75
June	0-1	-	- 1.00	June	1-10	10.0	- 4.50
July	0-3	-	- 3.00	July	2-8	25.0	+ 0.08
August	0-3	-	- 3.00	August	2-6	33.3	+ 3.75
September	2-10	20.0	+ 6.00	September	0-5	-	- 5.00
Oct/Nov	1-8	12.5	- 6.00	Oct/Nov	2-13	15.4	+ 10.00

4-y-o+	W-R	Per cent	£1 Level Stake	Totals	W-R	Per cent	£1 Level Stake
Mar/Apr	1-3	33.3	+ 6.00	Mar/Apr	3-14	21.4	+ 10.00
May	3-9	33.3	+ 24.00	May	8-27	29.6	+ 28.75
June	1-7	14.3	+ 4.00	June	2-18	11.1	- 1.50
July	0-6	-	- 6.00	July	2-17	11.8	- 8.92
August	0-3	-	- 3.00	August	2-12	16.7	- 2.25
September	1-5	20.0	- 0.50	September	3-20	15.0	+ 0.50
Oct/Nov	0-3	-	- 3.00	Oct/Nov	3-24	12.5	+ 1.00

DISTANCE

2-y-o	W-R	Per cent	£1 Level Stake	3-y-o	W-R	Per cent	£1 Level Stake
5f-6f	1-7	14.3	− 5.00	5f-6f	2-10	20.0	+ 0.25
7f-8f	2-19	10.5	− 3.00	7f-8f	6-22	27.3	+ 10.08
9f-13f	0-0	−	0.00	9f-13f	6-35	17.1	+ 6.75
14f+	0-0	−	0.00	14f+	0-3	−	− 3.00

4-y-o+	W-R	Per cent	£1 Level Stake	Totals	W-R	Per cent	£1 Level Stake
5f-6f	0-5	−	− 5.00	5f-6f	3-22	13.6	− 9.75
7f-8f	2-12	16.7	+ 6.00	7f-8f	10-53	18.9	+ 13.08
9f-13f	3-11	27.3	+ 7.50	9f-13f	9-46	19.6	+ 14.25
14f+	1-8	12.5	+ 13.00	14f+	1-11	9.1	+ 10.00

TYPE OF RACE

Non-Handicaps	W-R	Per cent	£1 Level Stake	Handicaps	W-R	Per cent	£1 Level Stake
2-y-o	3-25	12.0	− 7.00	2-y-o	0-1	−	− 1.00
3-y-o	9-36	25.0	+ 6.75	3-y-o	3-31	9.7	− 12.67
4-y-o+	3-12	25.0	+ 6.50	4-y-o+	2-20	10.0	+ 8.00
Selling	0-0	−	0.00	Selling	0-0	−	0.00
Apprentice	0-0	−	0.00	Apprentice	2-2	100.0	+ 21.00
Amat/Ladies	0-0	−	0.00	Amat/Ladies	1-5	20.0	+ 6.00
Totals	15-73	20.5	+ 6.25	Totals	8-59	13.6	+ 21.33

COURSE GRADE

	W-R	Per cent	£1 Level Stake
Group 1	11-69	15.9	+ 11.75
Group 2	3-25	12.0	− 1.25
Group 3	7-27	25.9	+ 16.75
Group 4	2-11	18.2	+ 0.33

FIRST TIME OUT

	W-R	Per cent	£1 Level Stake
2-y-o	0-10	−	− 10.00
3-y-o	2-17	11.8	− 2.00
4-y-o+	4-10	40.0	+ 38.00
Totals	6-37	16.2	+ 26.00

JOCKEYS RIDING

	W-R	Per cent	£1 Level Stake		W-R	Per cent	£1 Level Stake
Paul Eddery	13-77	16.9	+ 2.58	S Mulvey	1-3	33.3	+ 7.00
P Robinson	2-3	66.7	+ 25.00	Mrs J Crossley	1-5	20.0	+ 6.00
R Hills	1-1	100.0	+ 1.75	J Carroll	1-5	20.0	+ 1.00
A Whelan	1-1	100.0	+ 12.00	B Raymond	1-6	16.7	− 2.25
W Woods	1-2	50.0	0.00	A Clark	1-13	7.7	− 9.50

G Duffield	0-2	J Stack	0-1	N Carlisle	0-1
J Tate	0-2	J Weaver	0-1	R Cochrane	0-1
L Piggott	0-2	K Darley	0-1	Stephen Davies	0-1
C Asmussen	0-1	L Dettori	0-1		
D Wright	0-1	M Tebbutt	0-1		

COURSE RECORD

	Total W-R	Non-Handicaps 2-y-o	3-y-o+	Handicaps 2-y-o	3-y-o+	Per cent	£1 Level Stake
Goodwood	4-5	0-1	3-3	0-0	1-1	80.0	+ 17.75
Doncaster	3-10	0-0	1-5	0-1	2-4	30.0	+ 27.50
Southwell (AW)	2-2	0-0	0-0	0-0	2-2	100.0	+ 9.33
Thirsk	2-3	0-0	1-1	0-0	1-2	66.7	+ 10.75
Leicester	2-4	1-3	1-1	0-0	0-0	50.0	+ 5.00
Pontefract	2-4	0-1	2-3	0-0	0-0	50.0	+ 8.75
Nottingham	1-2	0-0	1-1	0-0	0-1	50.0	+ 4.00
Haydock	1-3	0-0	0-1	0-0	1-2	33.3	+ 4.00
Ascot	1-4	0-0	1-2	0-0	0-2	25.0	+ 1.50
Lingfield	1-4	1-1	0-1	0-0	0-2	25.0	+ 6.00
Beverley	1-6	0-2	1-2	0-0	0-2	16.7	+ 3.00
Yarmouth	1-6	0-2	0-1	0-0	1-3	16.7	+ 1.00
Sandown	1-7	0-1	1-3	0-0	0-3	14.3	- 1.00
York	1-13	1-4	0-5	0-0	0-4	7.7	- 11.00

Newmarket	0-12	Carlisle	0-3	Ayr	0-1
Kempton	0-7	Chepstow	0-3	Bath	0-1
Brighton	0-5	Newcastle	0-3	Chester	0-1
Redcar	0-5	Ripon	0-3	Edinburgh	0-1
Newbury	0-4	Folkestone	0-2	Windsor	0-1
Salisbury	0-4	Warwick	0-2	Wolverhampton (AW)	0-1

WINNING HORSES

	Age	Races Run	1st	2nd	3rd	Unpl	Win £
Alderbrook	5	5	3	0	0	2	37,317
Gneiss	3	5	2	0	0	3	19,060
Mary Hinge	3	5	2	1	0	2	15,216
Rory	3	8	3	2	2	1	10,172
Gondolier	6	3	1	0	0	2	9,820
Forest Cat	2	2	1	0	0	1	5,434
Baby Loves	3	2	1	0	0	1	4,151
Cloud	2	3	1	0	0	2	4,064
Sticks And Stones	2	3	1	0	0	2	3,739
Foil Stone	3	5	1	0	1	3	3,602
Jermyn Street	3	4	1	0	1	2	3,503
Night In A Million	3	6	1	0	0	5	3,470
White Lodge	3	4	1	0	0	3	3,348
Star Jazz	3	4	1	0	0	3	3,340
Hilary Gerrard	4	5	1	0	2	2	3,173
Banana Cove	3	7	1	0	1	5	3,101
Visimotion	4	9	1	3	1	4	2,448

WINNING OWNERS

	Races Won	Value £		Races Won	Value £
E Pick	3	37,317	Arthur B Hancock III	1	4,064
Mrs J Cecil	5	25,388	Lady Howard De Walden	1	3,602
Matthew Oram	2	19,060	John Bray	1	3,503
Lord Howard De Walden	2	13,168	R W G Threlfall	1	3,470
Martin Myers	2	6,912	Southgate Racing	1	3,340
George Ward	1	5,434	Sir Thomas Pilkington	1	3,101
S S Niarchos	1	4,151	Anthony Cherry-Downes	1	2,448

Favourites	4-17	23.5%	- 3.92	Total winning prize-money	£134,956
Longest winning sequence			2	Average SP of winner	6.0/1
Longest losing sequence			17	Return on stakes invested	21.3%
1993 Form	28-206	13.6%	- 80.06	1991 Form	19-95	20.0%	- 3.45
1992 Form	30-162	18.5%	+ 75.32				

A CHAMBERLAIN (Swindon, Wilts)

	No. of Horses	Races Run	1st	2nd	3rd	Unpl	Per cent	£1 Level Stake
2-y-o	0	0	0	0	0	0	-	0.00
3-y-o	0	0	0	0	0	0	-	0.00
4-y-o+	5	21	1	2	3	15	4.8	- 4.00
Totals	5	21	1	2	3	15	4.8	- 4.00

Jan	Feb	Mar	Apr	May	Jun	Jul	Aug	Sep	Oct/Nov
0-0	0-0	0-2	0-1	0-2	0-2	0-3	1-3	0-5	0-3

Winning Jockey	W-R	£1 Level Stake	Winning Course	W-R	£1 Level Stake
J D Smith	1-6	+ 11.00	Windsor	1-3	+ 14.00

Winning Horse	Age	Races Run	1st	2nd	3rd	Unpl	Win £
Bee Beat	6	16	1	2	3	10	2,456

Favourites	0-0	Total winning prize-money	£2,456
1993 Form	0-13	1991 Form	0-25
1992 Form	0-14	1990 Form	0-17

N CHAMBERLAIN (West Auckland, Co Durham)

	No. of Horses	Races Run	1st	2nd	3rd	Unpl	Per cent	£1 Level Stake
2-y-o	1	3	0	0	0	3	-	- 3.00
3-y-o	0	0	0	0	0	0	-	0.00
4-y-o+	3	19	2	0	2	15	10.5	+ 31.00
Totals	4	22	2	0	2	18	9.1	+ 28.00

Jan	Feb	Mar	Apr	May	Jun	Jul	Aug	Sep	Oct/Nov
0-0	0-0	0-1	1-6	0-2	0-1	0-4	1-3	0-5	0-0

Winning Jockeys	W-R	£1 Level Stake			W-R	£1 Level Stake
M Fenton	1-2	+ 7.00	Miss C Metcalfe		1-7	+ 34.00

Winning Courses	W-R	£1 Level Stake			W-R	£1 Level Stake
Ayr	1-2	+ 39.00	Hamilton		1-6	+ 3.00

Winning Horses	Age	Races Run	1st	2nd	3rd	Unpl	Win £
Public Way	4	7	1	0	2	4	3,287
Gymcrak Cyrano	5	7	1	0	0	6	2,710

Favourites	0-0			Total winning prize-money		£5,997
1993 Form	1-30	3.3%	- 13.00	1991 Form	0-18	
1992 Form	1-10	10.0%	+ 16.00	1990 Form	0-14	

M R CHANNON (Upper Lambourn, Berks)

	No. of Horses	Races Run	1st	2nd	3rd	Unpl	Per cent	£1 Level Stake
2-y-o	48	290	41	24	49	176	14.1	- 69.96
3-y-o	22	170	13	21	17	119	7.6	- 83.06
4-y-o+	14	168	19	11	17	121	11.3	- 27.50
Totals	84	628	73	56	83	416	11.6	-180.52

BY MONTH

2-y-o	W-R	Per cent	£1 Level Stake	3-y-o	W-R	Per cent	£1 Level Stake
January	0-0	-	0.00	January	0-5	-	- 5.00
February	0-0	-	0.00	February	1-7	14.3	+ 6.00
March	3-8	37.5	+ 7.85	March	0-10	-	- 10.00
April	7-27	25.9	+ 9.23	April	1-19	5.3	- 15.50
May	6-33	18.2	- 6.42	May	0-20	-	- 20.00
June	8-42	19.0	- 7.62	June	3-33	9.1	- 14.00
July	6-38	15.8	- 4.50	July	4-25	16.0	- 5.34
August	4-43	9.3	- 27.00	August	3-24	12.5	+ 5.40
September	4-54	7.4	- 20.50	September	1-19	5.3	- 16.62
Oct/Nov	3-45	6.7	- 21.00	Oct/Nov	0-8	-	- 8.00

Channon M R

4-y-o+	W-R	Per cent	£1 Level Stake	Totals	W-R	Per cent	£1 Level Stake
January	0-0	-	0.00	January	0-5	-	- 5.00
February	1-2	50.0	+ 11.00	February	2-9	22.2	+ 17.00
March	5-14	35.7	+ 29.25	March	8-32	25.0	+ 27.10
April	0-23	-	- 23.00	April	8-69	11.6	- 29.27
May	4-31	12.9	- 4.25	May	10-84	11.9	- 30.67
June	5-28	17.9	+ 3.50	June	16-103	15.5	- 18.12
July	1-19	5.3	- 12.50	July	11-82	13.4	- 22.34
August	2-11	18.2	+ 1.50	August	9-78	11.5	- 20.10
September	1-20	5.0	- 13.00	September	6-93	6.5	- 50.12
Oct/Nov	0-20	-	- 20.00	Oct/Nov	3-73	4.1	- 49.00

DISTANCE

2-y-o	W-R	Per cent	£1 Level Stake	3-y-o	W-R	Per cent	£1 Level Stake
5f-6f	37-211	17.5	- 12.71	5f-6f	6-58	10.3	- 6.62
7f-8f	4-77	5.2	- 55.25	7f-8f	7-66	10.6	- 30.44
9f-13f	0-2	-	- 2.00	9f-13f	0-36	-	- 36.00
14f+	0-0	-	0.00	14f+	0-10	-	- 10.00

4-y-o+	W-R	Per cent	£1 Level Stake	Totals	W-R	Per cent	£1 Level Stake
5f-6f	2-51	3.9	- 30.50	5f-6f	45-320	14.1	- 49.83
7f-8f	16-107	15.0	+ 6.50	7f-8f	27-250	10.8	- 79.19
9f-13f	1-9	11.1	- 2.50	9f-13f	1-47	2.1	- 40.50
14f+	0-1	-	- 1.00	14f+	0-11	-	- 11.00

TYPE OF RACE

Non-Handicaps	W-R	Per cent	£1 Level Stake	Handicaps	W-R	Per cent	£1 Level Stake
2-y-o	25-184	13.6	- 57.89	2-y-o	7-57	12.3	- 1.75
3-y-o	10-86	11.6	- 27.69	3-y-o	1-49	2.0	- 36.00
4-y-o+	4-16	25.0	+ 13.00	4-y-o+	11-131	8.4	- 42.25
Selling	9-57	15.8	- 20.32	Selling	2-14	14.3	+ 4.50
Apprentice	1-6	16.7	- 2.75	Apprentice	3-19	15.8	- 0.37
Amat/Ladies	0-1	-	- 1.00	Amat/Ladies	0-8	-	- 8.00
Totals	49-350	14.0	- 96.65	Totals	24-278	8.6	- 83.87

COURSE GRADE	W-R	Per cent	£1 Level Stake	FIRST TIME OUT	W-R	Per cent	£1 Level Stake
Group 1	29-245	11.8	- 29.04	2-y-o	10-45	22.2	+ 15.85
Group 2	11-120	9.2	- 64.52	3-y-o	1-22	4.5	- 18.50
Group 3	14-138	10.1	- 75.57	4-y-o+	2-14	14.3	+ 4.00
Group 4	19-125	15.2	- 11.39	Totals	13-81	16.0	+ 1.35

84

JOCKEYS RIDING

	W-R	Per cent	£1 Level Stake		W-R	Per cent	£1 Level Stake
R Hughes	12-93	12.9	- 23.37	J Stack	2-17	11.8	- 6.50
T Quinn	9-71	12.7	- 28.77	Pat Eddery	2-19	10.5	- 9.00
R Painter	9-84	10.7	- 12.37	R Waterfield	2-20	10.0	- 7.75
K Darley	5-32	15.6	- 0.95	W Woods	2-34	5.9	- 23.75
A Munro	4-16	25.0	+ 0.20	S Whitworth	1-2	50.0	+ 3.00
C Rutter	4-22	18.2	- 8.37	Lorna Vincent	1-3	33.3	0.00
L Dettori	3-14	21.4	+ 4.33	L Piggott	1-3	33.3	- 1.47
J Weaver	3-19	15.8	- 5.50	J Reid	1-7	14.3	+ 8.00
P Robinson	2-5	40.0	+ 12.00	A Tucker	1-11	9.1	+ 2.00
G Duffield	2-6	33.3	+ 1.25	D Harrison	1-12	8.3	+ 9.00
W Carson	2-7	28.6	+ 2.00	G Bardwell	1-15	6.7	- 2.00
F Norton	2-16	12.5	+ 3.50	Paul Eddery	1-19	5.3	- 15.00

Candy Morris	0-12	B Doyle	0-2	K Fallon	0-1
G Carter	0-11	B Thomson	0-2	M Hills	0-1
J Carroll	0-5	D McKeown	0-2	M J Kinane	0-1
Miss J Winter	0-5	D Wright	0-2	M Tebbutt	0-1
B Raymond	0-4	N Varley	0-2	Mr J Durkan	0-1
N Adams	0-4	R Cochrane	0-2	S Perks	0-1
A Clark	0-3	T Williams	0-2	T Ives	0-1
M Roberts	0-3	A Ball	0-1	W Newnes	0-1
Mr Raymond White	0-3	D Holland	0-1	W Ryan	0-1
A Eddery	0-2	D Sweeney	0-1		
A Mackay	0-2	J Fortune	0-1		

COURSE RECORD

	Total W-R	Non-Handicaps 2-y-o	3-y-o+	Handicaps 2-y-o	3-y-o+	Per cent	£1 Level Stake
Newmarket	6-42	3-12	1-10	1-9	1-11	14.3	+ 0.98
Beverley	4-14	2-4	0-2	0-2	2-6	28.6	+ 2.55
Wolverhampton (AW)	4-24	1-8	0-5	1-1	2-10	16.7	+ 4.25
Doncaster	4-25	3-10	0-3	0-2	1-10	16.0	+ 10.85
Folkestone	4-27	2-14	0-4	2-3	0-6	14.8	- 9.75
Bath	4-28	3-9	1-9	0-1	0-9	14.3	- 0.75
Brighton	4-29	2-9	1-6	0-4	1-10	13.8	- 11.27
Catterick	3-14	1-6	0-3	0-1	2-4	21.4	- 1.37
York	3-14	1-5	1-4	0-0	1-5	21.4	+ 15.00
Sandown	3-17	1-9	0-0	2-4	0-4	17.6	+ 17.00
Nottingham	3-20	3-8	0-3	0-3	0-6	15.0	- 9.00
Lingfield	3-23	2-10	1-4	0-2	0-7	13.0	+ 1.50
Lingfield (AW)	3-24	0-2	3-13	0-0	0-9	12.5	+ 5.25
Goodwood	3-32	1-7	1-8	0-4	1-13	9.4	- 3.50
Ayr	2-3	1-2	1-1	0-0	0-0	66.7	+ 2.38
Redcar	2-9	1-4	0-0	0-0	1-5	22.2	- 2.00
Haydock	2-19	1-8	1-3	0-3	0-5	10.5	- 11.75
Kempton	2-21	1-3	0-6	0-3	1-9	9.5	- 8.50
Warwick	2-23	1-10	0-4	0-1	1-8	8.7	- 11.80
Newbury	2-34	0-10	0-3	1-6	1-15	5.9	- 22.50
Carlisle	1-2	0-0	1-1	0-0	0-1	50.0	- 0.47
Ripon	1-5	1-4	0-0	0-0	0-1	20.0	- 2.50

85

Southwell (AW)	1-5	0-3	0-0	0-0	1-2	20.0	+ 6.00
Edinburgh	1-6	0-3	1-2	0-0	0-1	16.7	- 3.50
Epsom	1-7	1-1	0-1	0-1	0-4	14.3	- 2.50
Hamilton	1-7	0-2	1-3	0-1	0-1	14.3	- 4.50
Yarmouth	1-7	0-2	1-2	0-1	0-2	14.3	- 4.62
Newcastle	1-12	0-4	1-3	0-0	0-5	8.3	- 7.50
Chepstow	1-18	0-7	0-3	1-2	0-6	5.6	- 15.25
Salisbury	1-39	1-15	0-8	0-0	0-16	2.6	- 35.25

Windsor	0-24	Pontefract	0-11	Leicester	0-9
Ascot	0-19	Thirsk	0-10	Chester	0-5

WINNING HORSES

		Races					Win
	Age	Run	1st	2nd	3rd	Unpl	£
Piccolo	3	8	2	1	0	5	96,844
Sumoquinn	2	8	6	0	1	1	29,515
Glowing Jade	4	12	2	0	2	8	20,716
Kelly Mac	4	25	6	2	3	14	20,632
In Love Again	2	15	4	1	2	8	16,727
Silca Blanka	2	5	2	0	0	3	15,050
Fleet Hill	2	5	2	0	2	1	13,111
Knobbleeneeze	4	15	3	3	3	6	12,053
Double Flutter	5	20	4	1	1	14	11,333
Great Deeds	3	3	1	0	1	1	10,065
Statom	2	7	2	0	1	4	7,628
Mazeeka	3	13	3	0	3	7	7,573
Sweet Trentino	3	12	2	3	0	7	7,356
Princess Sadie	2	9	2	1	1	5	7,126
Pharsical	3	12	2	1	2	7	6,728
Saint Express	4	7	1	0	1	5	6,108
Welton Arsenal	2	8	1	1	3	3	4,787
Oneineverycolour	2	9	2	4	0	3	4,665
Poly Laureon	2	11	2	2	3	4	4,417
White Lady	3	4	1	1	2	0	4,127
Super Deeds	2	3	1	1	0	1	4,064
Musica	2	2	1	0	1	0	3,923
Domicksky	6	26	1	2	0	23	3,785
Poly Amanshaa	2	14	1	2	0	11	3,659
Nordesta	2	5	1	0	1	3	3,621
Katya	2	8	1	3	0	4	3,606
Fantasy Racing	2	9	1	1	4	3	3,485
Champagne Grandy	4	16	1	1	2	12	3,407
Rigsby	2	7	1	0	2	4	3,377
Stato One	2	5	1	0	0	4	3,266
Lady Davenport	2	7	1	0	2	4	3,078
Gone To Heaven	2	3	1	0	1	1	3,052
Little Hooligan	3	18	1	3	0	14	2,898
Springborne Lad	2	2	1	0	0	1	2,803
Gibaltarik	2	2	1	0	0	1	2,611
Al Corniche	2	10	1	1	2	6	2,575
Dungeon Dancer	2	10	1	2	1	6	2,469

Monsieur Petong	3	26	1	6	5	14	2,467
Morocco	5	15	1	0	3	11	2,423
Poly Lane	2	2	1	0	0	1	2,243
Giggleswick Gossip	2	12	1	0	5	6	2,174
Scissor Ridge	2	8	1	1	0	6	2,174
Any One Line	2	7	1	0	1	5	2,070

WINNING OWNERS

	Races Won	Value £		Races Won	Value £
John Mitchell & Partners	2	96,844	Mrs Jean Keegan	2	4,665
Mick Quinn Racing & Sports Club	7	32,413	The Classicstone Partnership	2	4,539
Brian T Eastick	2	20,716	Mrs D Hanson	1	4,127
K A Dack	6	20,632	Jonathan Knight	1	3,923
W H Ponsonby	4	16,727	M J Watson	1	3,785
Aldridge Racing Ltd	2	15,050	Aston House Stud	1	3,621
S Manghnani	2	14,129	John W Mitchell	1	3,606
Anthony Andrews	3	12,053	Peter Bonar	1	3,485
John Carey	4	11,333	Grandy Girls	1	3,407
Sheet & Roll Convertors Ltd	4	10,319	Michael A Foy	1	3,377
Mrs A V Ferguson	1	9,333	T Leigh And Partners	1	3,266
M Channon	3	9,048	Noel O'Callaghan	1	3,078
Mrs N K Crook	2	7,628	P D Savill	1	3,052
Stephen Crown	3	7,573	T W Langley	1	2,611
Dollar Racing	2	7,356	A And M Racing Partners	1	2,575
J R Good	2	7,126	Martin Myers	1	2,423
R J Sunley Tice	2	6,728	B Minty	1	2,174
M G St Quinton	1	6,108	Trevor Mitchell	1	2,174
Business Forms Express	1	4,787			

Favourites	27-85	31.8% - 2.50	Total winning prize-money	£375,791
Longest winning sequence		2	Average SP of winner	5.1/1
Longest losing sequence		46	Return on stakes invested	-28.7%
1993 Form	41-415	9.9% - 64.99	1991 Form 22-235	9.4% - 55.25
1992 Form	27-303	8.9% -120.09	1990 Form 16-162	9.9% + 2.66

D W CHAPMAN (Stillington, North Yorks)

	No. of Horses	Races Run	1st	2nd	3rd	Unpl	Per cent	£1 Level Stake
2-y-o	2	11	0	0	0	11	-	- 11.00
3-y-o	8	23	0	2	0	21	-	- 23.00
4-y-o+	18	143	11	9	13	110	7.7	- 50.05
Totals	28	177	11	11	13	142	6.2	- 84.05

BY MONTH

2-y-o	W-R	Per cent	£1 Level Stake	3-y-o	W-R	Per cent	£1 Level Stake
January	0-0	-	0.00	January	0-0	-	0.00
February	0-0	-	0.00	February	0-3	-	- 3.00
March	0-0	-	0.00	March	0-4	-	- 4.00
April	0-0	-	0.00	April	0-1	-	- 1.00
May	0-2	-	- 2.00	May	0-1	-	- 1.00
June	0-2	-	- 2.00	June	0-5	-	- 5.00
July	0-1	-	- 1.00	July	0-4	-	- 4.00
August	0-4	-	- 4.00	August	0-0	-	0.00
September	0-2	-	- 2.00	September	0-2	-	- 2.00
Oct/Nov	0-0	-	0.00	Oct/Nov	0-3	-	- 3.00

4-y-o+	W-R	Per cent	£1 Level Stake	Totals	W-R	Per cent	£1 Level Stake
January	5-19	26.3	+ 43.85	January	5-19	26.3	+ 43.85
February	2-20	10.0	- 14.40	February	2-23	8.7	- 17.40
March	3-15	20.0	+ 5.50	March	3-19	15.8	+ 1.50
April	0-12	-	- 12.00	April	0-13	-	- 13.00
May	0-15	-	- 15.00	May	0-18	-	- 18.00
June	0-15	-	- 15.00	June	0-22	-	- 22.00
July	1-22	4.5	- 18.00	July	1-27	3.7	- 23.00
August	0-10	-	- 10.00	August	0-14	-	- 14.00
September	0-9	-	- 9.00	September	0-13	-	- 13.00
Oct/Nov	0-6	-	- 6.00	Oct/Nov	0-9	-	- 9.00

DISTANCE

2-y-o	W-R	Per cent	£1 Level Stake	3-y-o	W-R	Per cent	£1 Level Stake
5f-6f	0-9	-	- 9.00	5f-6f	0-17	-	- 17.00
7f-8f	0-2	-	- 2.00	7f-8f	0-6	-	- 6.00
9f-13f	0-0	-	0.00	9f-13f	0-0	-	0.00
14f+	0-0	-	0.00	14f+	0-0	-	0.00

4-y-o+	W-R	Per cent	£1 Level Stake	Totals	W-R	Per cent	£1 Level Stake
5f-6f	4-66	6.1	- 41.50	5f-6f	4-92	4.3	- 67.50
7f-8f	4-47	8.5	- 34.65	7f-8f	4-55	7.3	- 42.65
9f-13f	3-28	10.7	+ 28.10	9f-13f	3-28	10.7	+ 28.10
14f+	0-2	-	- 2.00	14f+	0-2	-	- 2.00

TYPE OF RACE

Non-Handicaps	W-R	Per cent	£1 Level Stake	Handicaps	W-R	Per cent	£1 Level Stake
2-y-o	0-6	-	- 6.00	2-y-o	0-2	-	- 2.00
3-y-o	0-9	-	- 9.00	3-y-o	0-9	-	- 9.00
4-y-o+	4-29	13.8	- 16.65	4-y-o+	3-75	4.0	- 54.50
Selling	0-10	-	- 10.00	Selling	0-7	-	- 7.00
Apprentice	2-2	100.0	+ 3.10	Apprentice	0-6	-	- 6.00
Amat/Ladies	1-6	16.7	+ 45.00	Amat/Ladies	1-16	6.3	- 12.00
Totals	7-62	11.3	+ 6.45	Totals	4-115	3.5	- 90.50

COURSE GRADE

	W-R	Per cent	£1 Level Stake
Group 1	0-14	-	- 14.00
Group 2	0-30	-	- 30.00
Group 3	0-23	-	- 23.00
Group 4	11-110	10.0	- 17.05

FIRST TIME OUT

	W-R	Per cent	£1 Level Stake
2-y-o	0-2	-	- 2.00
3-y-o	0-7	-	- 7.00
4-y-o+	2-17	11.8	- 11.40
Totals	2-26	7.7	- 20.40

JOCKEYS RIDING

	W-R	Per cent	£1 Level Stake		W-R	Per cent	£1 Level Stake
L Dettori	4-9	44.4	+ 3.35	Miss R Clark	1-12	8.3	- 8.00
L Aspell	2-6	33.3	- 0.90	M Kneafsey	1-18	5.6	+ 33.00
M Baird	2-11	18.2	+ 0.50	J Fanning	1-22	4.5	- 13.00

K Darley	0-15	J Williams	0-2	G Parkin	0-1
L Charnock	0-15	N Carlisle	0-2	J Carroll	0-1
S Wood	0-15	W Carson	0-2	J Weaver	0-1
A Culhane	0-9	W Woods	0-2	M Roberts	0-1
M Fenton	0-5	A Eddery	0-1	N Connorton	0-1
Claire Balding	0-4	A Mackay	0-1	O Pears	0-1
J Stack	0-3	D Griffiths	0-1	P McCabe	0-1
K Fallon	0-3	D McCabe	0-1	T Quinn	0-1
J Lowe	0-2	D McKeown	0-1	V Halliday	0-1
J Quinn	0-2	Dale Gibson	0-1		
J Tate	0-2	E Johnson	0-1		

COURSE RECORD

	Total W-R	Non-Handicaps 2-y-o	3-y-o+	Handicaps 2-y-o	3-y-o+	Per cent	£1 Level Stake
Southwell (AW)	8-62	0-4	7-24	0-0	1-34	12.9	+ 15.45
Lingfield (AW)	2-11	0-0	0-3	0-0	2-8	18.2	+ 0.50
Edinburgh	1-5	0-0	0-0	0-0	1-5	20.0	- 1.00

Wolverhampton (AW)	0-19	Nottingham	0-4	Newmarket	0-2
Catterick	0-10	Hamilton	0-3	York	0-2
Redcar	0-10	Lingfield	0-3	Ayr	0-1
Ripon	0-9	Newcastle	0-3	Beverley	0-1
Pontefract	0-8	Warwick	0-3	Chepstow	0-1
Thirsk	0-8	Doncaster	0-2	Epsom	0-1
Leicester	0-6	Haydock	0-2	Goodwood	0-1

WINNING HORSES

	Age	Races Run	1st	2nd	3rd	Unpl	Win £
No Submission	8	19	4	1	3	11	8,972
Kalar	5	14	2	2	0	10	4,764
Tempering	8	13	2	2	0	9	4,313

Prime Mover	6	18	1	0	1	16	3,590
Kabcast	9	7	1	1	1	4	2,671
Sporting Spirit	4	4	1	0	0	3	2,243

WINNING OWNERS

	Races Won	Value £		Races Won	Value £
T S Redman	4	8,972	Richard Berenson	2	4,313
Phillip Kneafsey	2	5,833	Mrs M M Marshall	1	2,671
E Stockdale	2	4,764			

Favourites	5-14	35.7%	– 0.05	Total winning prize-money	£26,553
Longest winning sequence			2	Average SP of winner	7.5/1
Longest losing sequence			61	Return on stakes invested	-47.5%
1993 Form	23-269	8.6%	-144.98	1991 Form 24-365 6.6% -158.10	
1992 Form	15-282	5.3%	– 79.75	1990 Form 22-415 5.3% -245.78	

M C CHAPMAN (Market Rasen, Lincs)

	No. of Horses	Races Run	1st	2nd	3rd	Unpl	Per cent	£1 Level Stake
2-y-o	0	0	0	0	0	0	–	0.00
3-y-o	4	43	4	2	1	36	9.3	+ 54.00
4-y-o+	13	63	0	1	1	61	–	– 63.00
Totals	17	106	4	3	2	97	3.8	– 9.00

Jan	Feb	Mar	Apr	May	Jun	Jul	Aug	Sep	Oct/Nov
0-13	0-5	0-3	0-8	0-15	2-21	0-4	2-15	0-11	0-11

Winning Jockeys	W-R	£1 Level Stake		W-R	£1 Level Stake
D McCabe	3-26	+ 30.00	K Fallon	1-3	+ 38.00

Winning Courses					
Pontefract	2-24	+ 32.00	Yarmouth	1-12	– 5.00
Ripon	1-2	+ 32.00			

Winning Horses	Age	Races Run	1st	2nd	3rd	Unpl	Win £
Non Vintage	3	5	1	0	0	4	4,778
Britannia Mills	3	17	1	1	0	15	3,158
Lincoln Treasure	3	8	1	0	0	7	2,532
Ozzie Jones	3	13	1	1	1	10	2,469

Favourites	0-1			Total winning prize-money	£12,937
1993 Form	10-169	5.9%	– 74.25	1991 Form 7-111 6.3% + 3.50	
1992 Form	1-79	1.3%	– 72.00	1990 Form 1-62 1.6% – 28.00	

D N CHAPPELL (West Ilsley, Berks)

	No. of Horses	Races Run	1st	2nd	3rd	Unpl	Per cent	£1 Level Stake
2-y-o	2	7	4	0	0	3	57.1	+ 6.48
3-y-o	3	10	2	0	1	7	20.0	+ 10.00
4-y-o+	1	1	0	1	0	0	–	– 1.00
Totals	6	18	6	1	1	10	33.3	+ 15.48

Jan	Feb	Mar	Apr	May	Jun	Jul	Aug	Sep	Oct/Nov
0-0	0-0	0-0	0-0	1-2	2-4	1-3	0-2	0-1	2-6

Winning Jockeys	W–R	£1 Level Stake				Winning Jockeys	W–R	£1 Level Stake
M Hills	3-4	+ 6.23				Stephen Davies	1-2	+ 1.25
M J Kinane	1-1	+ 6.00				B Thomson	1-4	+ 9.00

Winning Courses	W–R	£1 Level Stake				Winning Courses	W–R	£1 Level Stake
Ascot	1-1	+ 12.00				Newbury	1-2	+ 2.50
Goodwood	1-1	+ 2.25				Sandown	1-3	+ 4.00
Kempton	1-1	+ 3.00				Windsor	1-4	– 2.27

Winning Horses	Age	Races Run	1st	2nd	3rd	Unpl	Win £
Brief Glimpse	2	5	3	0	0	2	76,423
Cape Merino	3	2	1	0	0	1	18,491
Judge Advocate	2	2	1	0	0	1	8,090
White Shoot	3	3	1	0	0	2	4,416

Favourites	1-3	33.3%	– 1.27	Total winning prize-money	£107,420
1993 Form	1-8	12.5%	+ 26.00		

P W CHAPPLE-HYAM (Manton, Wilts)

	No. of Horses	Races Run	1st	2nd	3rd	Unpl	Per cent	£1 Level Stake
2-y-o	37	88	22	8	10	48	25.0	+ 22.14
3-y-o	28	107	15	11	13	68	14.0	– 44.72
4-y-o+	7	27	2	2	2	21	7.4	– 6.50
Totals	72	222	39	21	25	137	17.6	– 29.08

BY MONTH

2-y-o	W-R	Per cent	£1 Level Stake	3-y-o	W-R	Per cent	£1 Level Stake
January	0-0	-	0.00	January	1-1	100.0	+ 0.67
February	0-0	-	0.00	February	0-0	-	0.00
March	0-0	-	0.00	March	0-1	-	- 1.00
April	2-4	50.0	+ 1.63	April	3-23	13.0	- 12.77
May	5-8	62.5	+ 2.85	May	2-23	8.7	- 9.00
June	3-18	16.7	- 12.48	June	4-23	17.4	- 9.25
July	3-13	23.1	+ 8.33	July	0-10	-	- 10.00
August	1-10	10.0	- 7.62	August	3-10	30.0	+ 0.63
September	3-19	15.8	+ 18.20	September	1-9	11.1	- 0.50
Oct/Nov	5-16	31.3	+ 11.23	Oct/Nov	1-7	14.3	- 3.50

4-y-o+	W-R	Per cent	£1 Level Stake	Totals	W-R	Per cent	£1 Level Stake
January	0-0	-	0.00	January	1-1	100.0	+ 0.67
February	0-0	-	0.00	February	0-0	-	0.00
March	0-0	-	0.00	March	0-1	-	- 1.00
April	2-7	28.6	+ 13.50	April	7-34	20.6	+ 2.36
May	0-7	-	- 7.00	May	7-38	18.4	- 13.15
June	0-4	-	- 4.00	June	7-45	15.6	- 25.73
July	0-3	-	- 3.00	July	3-26	11.5	- 4.67
August	0-2	-	- 2.00	August	4-22	18.2	+ 8.99
September	0-4	-	- 4.00	September	4-32	12.5	+ 13.70
Oct/Nov	0-0	-	0.00	Oct/Nov	6-23	26.1	+ 7.73

DISTANCE

2-y-o	W-R	Per cent	£1 Level Stake	3-y-o	W-R	Per cent	£1 Level Stake
5f-6f	10-39	25.6	- 14.29	5f-6f	1-7	14.3	- 2.00
7f-8f	12-47	25.5	+ 38.43	7f-8f	7-43	16.3	- 20.60
9f-13f	0-2	-	- 2.00	9f-13f	6-54	11.1	- 21.75
14f+	0-0	-	0.00	14f+	1-3	33.3	- 0.37

4-y-o+	W-R	Per cent	£1 Level Stake	Totals	W-R	Per cent	£1 Level Stake
5f-6f	0-10	-	- 10.00	5f-6f	11-56	19.6	- 26.29
7f-8f	1-5	20.0	- 1.50	7f-8f	20-95	21.1	+ 16.33
9f-13f	1-11	9.1	+ 6.00	9f-13f	7-67	10.4	- 17.75
14f+	0-1	-	- 1.00	14f+	1-4	25.0	- 1.37

TYPE OF RACE

Non-Handicaps	W-R	Per cent	£1 Level Stake	Handicaps	W-R	Per cent	£1 Level Stake
2-y-o	22-84	26.2	+ 26.14	2-y-o	0-4	-	- 4.00
3-y-o	15-68	22.1	- 5.72	3-y-o	0-34	-	- 34.00
4-y-o+	1-13	7.7	+ 4.00	4-y-o+	1-11	9.1	- 7.50
Selling	0-0	-	0.00	Selling	0-0	-	0.00
Apprentice	0-1	-	- 1.00	Apprentice	0-5	-	- 5.00
Amat/Ladies	0-1	-	- 1.00	Amat/Ladies	0-1	-	- 1.00
Totals	38-167	22.8	+ 22.42	Totals	1-55	1.8	- 51.50

COURSE GRADE					**FIRST TIME OUT**		
	W-R	Per cent	£1 Level Stake			W-R	Per cent	£1 Level Stake
Group 1	24-157	15.3	- 35.03	2-y-o	15-37	40.5	+ 22.02
Group 2	5-23	21.7	+ 6.13	3-y-o	6-28	21.4	- 6.60
Group 3	5-29	17.2	0.00	4-y-o+	1-7	14.3	+ 10.00
Group 4	5-13	38.5	- 0.18				
				Totals	22-72	30.6	+ 25.42

JOCKEYS RIDING

	W-R	Per cent	£1 Level Stake			W-R	Per cent	£1 Level Stake
J Reid	24-129	18.6	- 39.07	M Hills		1-1	100.0	+ 16.00
S Whitworth	5-16	31.3	+ 18.69	W Carson		1-1	100.0	+ 1.75
R Havlin	5-29	17.2	+ 5.75	M Roberts		1-3	33.3	+ 5.50
B Thomson	2-15	13.3	- 9.70					

Kate Dovey	0-4	Mrs J Chapple-Hyam	0-2	Pat Eddery	0-1
K Darley	0-3	R Cochrane	0-2	S Harrison	0-1
C Asmussen	0-2	Aimee Cook	0-1	T Sprake	0-1
J Weaver	0-2	F Norton	0-1	W Newnes	0-1
L Dettori	0-2	J Carroll	0-1	Y Take	0-1
M J Kinane	0-2	J Quinn	0-1		

COURSE RECORD

	Total W-R	Non-Handicaps 2-y-o	Non-Handicaps 3-y-o+	Handicaps 2-y-o	Handicaps 3-y-o+	Per cent	£1 Level Stake
Newbury	11-32	8-15	3-8	0-1	0-8	34.4	+ 2.22
Chepstow	3-9	1-4	2-3	0-0	0-2	33.3	+ 14.00
Haydock	2-5	1-2	0-1	0-0	1-2	40.0	+ 0.30
Salisbury	2-6	1-3	1-3	0-0	0-0	33.3	+ 6.50
Warwick	2-7	0-1	2-4	0-0	0-2	28.6	- 1.25
Doncaster	2-14	2-6	0-4	0-0	0-4	14.3	- 3.00
Goodwood	2-20	2-9	0-6	0-1	0-4	10.0	- 4.90
Newmarket	2-28	2-9	0-12	0-1	0-6	7.1	+ 0.20
Catterick	1-1	1-1	0-0	0-0	0-0	100.0	+ 3.00
Nottingham	1-1	0-0	1-1	0-0	0-0	100.0	+ 3.50
Southwell (AW)	1-1	1-1	0-0	0-0	0-0	100.0	+ 0.40
Lingfield (AW)	1-1	0-0	1-1	0-0	0-0	100.0	+ 0.67
Kempton	1-2	0-1	1-1	0-0	0-0	50.0	+ 15.00
Lingfield	1-2	0-1	1-1	0-0	0-0	50.0	+ 0.63
Redcar	1-4	0-1	1-2	0-0	0-1	25.0	+ 1.00
Leicester	1-5	1-4	0-0	0-0	0-1	20.0	- 3.50
Ayr	1-6	1-2	0-1	0-0	0-3	16.7	- 4.38
Brighton	1-6	0-3	1-3	0-0	0-0	16.7	+ 3.00
Epsom	1-7	0-1	1-4	0-0	0-2	14.3	- 4.00
York	1-14	1-5	0-2	0-1	0-6	7.1	- 12.47
Ascot	1-26	0-9	1-14	0-0	0-3	3.8	- 21.00

Bath	0-5	Hamilton	0-2	Carlisle	0-1
Beverley	0-4	Newcastle	0-2	Sandown	0-1
Chester	0-3	Pontefract	0-2	Windsor	0-1
Edinburgh	0-2	Thirsk	0-2		

Chapple-Hyam P W

WINNING HORSES

	Age	Races Run	1st	2nd	3rd	Unpl	Win £
Painter's Row	2	2	2	0	0	0	28,643
Turtle Island	3	4	1	0	2	1	20,220
Morgana	3	5	3	1	1	0	14,168
Chaddleworth	4	5	1	0	0	4	10,618
Wootton Rivers	4	4	1	0	1	2	10,566
Flowerdrum	2	2	1	0	0	1	9,715
Close Conflict	3	3	2	0	0	1	8,720
Moon Mistress	3	3	1	1	0	1	8,208
Citadeed	2	4	2	0	0	2	7,818
Bedivere	2	6	2	0	0	4	7,713
Snowtown	2	3	1	0	1	1	7,068
Rambrino	2	4	1	0	0	3	5,756
Court Of Honour	2	2	1	0	0	1	5,409
Salt Lake	3	3	1	0	0	2	4,633
Grandinare	2	1	1	0	0	0	4,577
Spectrum	2	1	1	0	0	0	4,566
Final Appearance	2	2	1	0	0	1	4,436
Golden Nashwan	3	6	1	0	0	5	4,424
Queen's Ransom	2	2	1	1	0	0	4,225
Helmsman	2	3	1	1	1	0	4,121
Varnishing Day	2	2	1	0	0	1	4,078
Judgement Day	2	1	1	0	0	0	3,978
Myself	2	5	1	2	1	1	3,892
Ginger Tree	2	2	1	0	1	0	3,807
Rubhahunish	3	3	1	1	0	1	3,753
Golden Danehill	2	3	1	0	0	2	3,688
Triple Tie	3	5	1	0	1	3	3,606
General Monash	2	2	1	0	1	0	3,590
Missel	2	3	1	0	1	1	3,375
Star Of The Dance	3	1	1	0	0	0	3,190
Classical Rock	3	1	1	0	0	0	2,873
Flawed Logic	3	5	1	2	0	2	2,831
Astral Invasion	3	3	1	0	0	2	2,768

WINNING OWNERS

	Races Won	Value £		Races Won	Value £
R E Sangster	24	129,962	HRH Princess Michael of Kent	1	8,208
Lord Weinstock	3	33,209	Scuderia Golden Horse SRL	2	8,112
Ivan Allan	3	10,691	Sheikh Mohammed	2	7,182
Miss Patrizia Vaglica	1	10,566	M Tabor	1	4,577
Bloomsbury Stud	2	8,526			

Favourites	21-52	40.4%	- 3.79	Total winning prize-money		£221,033
Longest winning sequence			3	Average SP of winner		3.9/1
Longest losing sequence			19	Return on stakes invested		-13.1%
1993 Form	52-239	21.8%	- 50.52	1991 Form	27-112	24.1% + 20.35
1992 Form	41-245	16.7%	- 54.70			

94

R CHARLTON (Beckhampton, Wilts)

	No. of Horses	Races Run	1st	2nd	3rd	Unpl	Per cent	£1 Level Stake
2-y-o	25	77	22	16	8	31	28.6	+ 23.51
3-y-o	32	118	22	24	13	59	18.6	- 25.59
4-y-o+	7	33	4	4	4	21	12.1	- 6.77
Totals	64	228	48	44	25	111	21.1	- 8.85

BY MONTH

2-y-o	W-R	Per cent	£1 Level Stake	3-y-o	W-R	Per cent	£1 Level Stake
January	0-0	-	0.00	January	1-2	50.0	- 0.20
February	0-0	-	0.00	February	0-0	-	0.00
March	0-0	-	0.00	March	1-4	25.0	- 2.27
April	0-2	-	- 2.00	April	2-13	15.4	- 8.95
May	1-3	33.3	- 0.90	May	5-20	25.0	- 1.12
June	2-6	33.3	- 0.75	June	6-25	24.0	+ 13.93
July	2-12	16.7	- 4.75	July	3-20	15.0	- 5.90
August	6-14	42.9	+ 12.67	August	2-15	13.3	- 9.33
September	5-24	20.8	+ 12.83	September	2-14	14.3	- 6.75
Oct/Nov	6-16	37.5	+ 6.41	Oct/Nov	0-5	-	- 5.00

4-y-o+	W-R	Per cent	£1 Level Stake	Totals	W-R	Per cent	£1 Level Stake
January	0-0	-	0.00	January	1-2	50.0	- 0.20
February	0-0	-	0.00	February	0-0	-	0.00
March	1-1	100.0	+ 0.73	March	2-5	40.0	- 1.54
April	0-3	-	- 3.00	April	2-18	11.1	- 13.95
May	0-3	-	- 3.00	May	6-26	23.1	- 5.02
June	0-3	-	- 3.00	June	8-34	23.5	+ 10.18
July	1-6	16.7	+ 1.00	July	6-38	15.8	- 9.65
August	1-6	16.7	+ 6.00	August	9-35	25.7	+ 9.34
September	1-6	16.7	- 0.50	September	8-44	18.2	+ 5.58
Oct/Nov	0-5	-	- 5.00	Oct/Nov	6-26	23.1	- 3.59

DISTANCE

2-y-o	W-R	Per cent	£1 Level Stake	3-y-o	W-R	Per cent	£1 Level Stake
5f-6f	13-43	30.2	- 5.57	5f-6f	2-12	16.7	- 8.17
7f-8f	9-33	27.3	+ 30.08	7f-8f	8-39	20.5	- 1.72
9f-13f	0-1	-	- 1.00	9f-13f	11-60	18.3	- 10.37
14f+	0-0	-	0.00	14f+	1-7	14.3	- 5.33

4-y-o+	W-R	Per cent	£1 Level Stake	Totals	W-R	Per cent	£1 Level Stake
5f-6f	0-3	-	- 3.00	5f-6f	15-58	25.9	- 16.74
7f-8f	2-9	22.2	+ 10.00	7f-8f	19-81	23.5	+ 38.36
9f-13f	2-17	11.8	- 9.77	9f-13f	13-78	16.7	- 21.14
14f+	0-4	-	- 4.00	14f+	1-11	9.1	- 9.33

TYPE OF RACE

Non-Handicaps	W-R	Per cent	£1 Level Stake	Handicaps	W-R	Per cent	£1 Level Stake
2-y-o	22-73	30.1	+ 27.51	2-y-o	0-4	-	- 4.00
3-y-o	17-84	20.2	- 16.59	3-y-o	5-32	15.6	- 7.00
4-y-o+	1-11	9.1	- 5.50	4-y-o+	3-22	13.6	- 1.27
Selling	0-0	-	0.00	Selling	0-0	-	0.00
Apprentice	0-1	-	- 1.00	Apprentice	0-1	-	- 1.00
Amat/Ladies	0-0	-	0.00	Amat/Ladies	0-0	-	0.00
Totals	40-169	23.7	+ 4.42	Totals	8-59	13.6	- 13.27

COURSE GRADE

	W-R	Per cent	£1 Level Stake
Group 1	25-139	18.0	- 1.62
Group 2	6-28	21.4	- 11.10
Group 3	11-47	23.4	- 4.59
Group 4	6-14	42.9	+ 8.46

FIRST TIME OUT

	W-R	Per cent	£1 Level Stake
2-y-o	5-25	20.0	0.00
3-y-o	8-32	25.0	- 7.34
4-y-o+	2-7	28.6	+ 0.23
Totals	15-64	23.4	- 7.11

JOCKEYS RIDING

	W-R	Per cent	£1 Level Stake		W-R	Per cent	£1 Level Stake
Pat Eddery	23-92	25.0	- 2.54	J Reid	2-4	50.0	+ 0.78
T Sprake	4-23	17.4	- 0.10	J Weaver	2-4	50.0	+ 10.00
D Harrison	3-6	50.0	+ 25.00	R Cochrane	2-11	18.2	+ 0.10
L Dettori	3-9	33.3	+ 0.22	K Darley	2-11	18.2	- 6.72
S Raymont	3-25	12.0	- 9.39	Paul Eddery	1-10	10.0	- 6.00
T Quinn	2-4	50.0	+ 2.80	W Ryan	1-10	10.0	- 4.00

Rhona Gent	0-4	W R Swinburn	0-2	M Fenton	0-1
C Hodgson	0-3	B Thomson	0-1	M Hills	0-1
C Asmussen	0-2	D Holland	0-1	S Whitworth	0-1
W Carson	0-2	G Hind	0-1		

COURSE RECORD

	Total W-R	Non-Handicaps 2-y-o	3-y-o+	Handicaps 2-y-o	3-y-o+	Per cent	£1 Level Stake
Bath	6-13	2-2	3-9	0-0	1-2	46.2	+ 7.78
Kempton	6-20	3-7	2-8	0-1	1-4	30.0	+ 12.83
Newmarket	5-22	2-8	3-9	0-1	0-4	22.7	+ 18.92
Goodwood	4-16	1-4	1-5	0-0	2-7	25.0	- 4.30
Newbury	4-25	2-11	1-9	0-0	1-5	16.0	- 2.37
Chepstow	2-4	1-2	1-2	0-0	0-0	50.0	+ 4.38
Warwick	2-4	0-0	1-2	0-0	1-2	50.0	+ 9.53
Wolverhampton (AW)	2-5	1-1	1-3	0-0	0-1	40.0	- 1.67
Leicester	2-6	2-2	0-4	0-0	0-0	33.3	+ 3.75
Haydock	2-10	0-1	1-4	0-0	1-5	20.0	- 0.95

York	2-11	1-2	0-4	0-0	1-5	18.2	+	1.75
Salisbury	2-14	2-7	0-5	0-0	0-2	14.3	-	8.83
Catterick	1-1	1-1	0-0	0-0	0-0	100.0	+	2.50
Edinburgh	1-1	0-0	1-1	0-0	0-0	100.0	+	1.10
Redcar	1-1	1-1	0-0	0-0	0-0	100.0	+	1.75
Brighton	1-4	0-0	1-2	0-0	0-2	25.0	-	2.27
Chester	1-4	1-2	0-1	0-1	0-0	25.0	-	1.75
Lingfield	1-4	1-1	0-2	0-0	0-1	25.0	+	1.00
Doncaster	1-11	0-4	1-5	0-0	0-2	9.1	-	5.50
Nottingham	1-11	1-5	0-4	0-0	0-2	9.1	-	7.50
Sandown	1-11	0-1	1-8	0-0	0-2	9.1	-	9.00

Windsor	0-10	Epsom	0-2	Ripon	0-1
Ascot	0-8	Folkestone	0-2	Southwell (AW)	0-1
Newcastle	0-3	Pontefract	0-2	Yarmouth	0-1

WINNING HORSES

	Age	Races Run	1st	2nd	3rd	Unpl	Win £
Don Corleone	2	4	2	0	0	2	28,205
Everglades	6	10	2	0	0	8	17,365
Mystic Hill	3	6	2	0	1	3	16,994
Shandine	2	6	3	2	0	1	14,241
Interim	3	7	2	1	1	3	13,581
Art Of War	2	3	2	0	0	1	13,267
Wandesta	3	2	1	0	0	1	10,625
Crystal Cavern	2	2	1	0	0	1	10,372
Shonara's Way	3	6	2	0	2	2	9,081
Wavian	2	7	2	3	0	2	8,618
Titania's Way	3	6	2	1	0	3	7,877
Source Of Light	5	3	1	0	0	2	7,020
Cajun Cadet	3	6	1	2	0	3	6,862
Myrtle Quest	2	3	1	0	0	2	5,250
Didina	2	3	1	1	1	0	5,180
Fox Sparrow	4	7	1	1	3	2	4,758
King Of Naples	3	4	1	1	1	1	4,588
Forest Gazelle	3	3	1	1	0	1	4,422
Lady Writer	2	2	1	0	1	0	4,150
Spout	2	2	1	1	0	0	4,093
Athene	3	5	1	2	0	2	4,078
Nazute	2	5	1	1	1	2	4,059
Nash Terrace	2	1	1	0	0	0	3,953
Rainfest	3	2	1	0	0	1	3,950
Belfry	2	5	1	0	1	3	3,892
New Albion	3	4	1	0	0	3	3,761
Painted Desert	2	3	1	1	0	1	3,746
Maiandros	2	3	1	0	0	2	3,739
Jacob Faithful	3	3	1	0	1	1	3,692
Yenda	3	2	1	1	0	0	3,606
Rockcracker	2	6	1	1	1	3	3,592

Charlton R

Mentor	2	4	1	1	1	1	3,580
Pen Point	3	2	1	1	0	0	3,552
Chattel	2	5	1	1	2	1	3,338
Pomorie	3	6	1	0	1	4	3,216
Floral Spark	3	7	1	2	1	3	3,114
Bosky	3	2	1	0	0	1	2,686
Imprecise	3	4	1	1	1	1	2,600

WINNING OWNERS

	Races Won	Value £		Races Won	Value £
K Abdulla	16	82,900	Ippotour S A	2	7,319
Sir Philip Oppenheimer	6	43,850	Lord De La Warr,		
Wafic Said	2	28,205	Mrs M Kerr-Dineen	1	4,588
Miss Sophie Oppenheimer	2	17,365	Highclere Th'bred Racing Ltd	1	3,892
Mrs Alexandra J Chandris	4	16,957	Rupert Hambro	1	3,592
Lady Rothschild	4	13,808	Saeed Abdullah Humaid	1	3,552
Michael Pescod	2	10,921	J G Charlton	1	3,114
Miss M Sheriffe	2	10,008	Duke Of Roxburghe	1	2,600
Lord Weinstock	2	8,030			

Favourites	24-63	38.1%	- 4.81	Total winning prize-money			£260,700
Longest winning sequence			3	Average SP of winner			3.6/1
Longest losing sequence			12	Return on stakes invested			-3.9%
1993 Form	47-185	25.4%	+ 74.24	1991 Form	26-180	14.4%	- 57.48
1992 Form	43-170	25.3%	+ 61.61	1990 Form	37-159	23.3%	+ 19.55

P F I COLE (Whatcombe, Oxon)

	No. of Horses	Races Run	1st	2nd	3rd	Unpl	Per cent	£1 Level Stake
2-y-o	71	219	28	35	22	134	12.8	- 78.69
3-y-o	62	284	35	39	36	174	12.3	- 46.24
4-y-o+	18	77	5	5	11	56	6.5	- 29.00
Totals	151	580	68	79	69	364	11.7	-153.93

BY MONTH

2-y-o	W-R	Per cent	£1 Level Stake	3-y-o	W-R	Per cent	£1 Level Stake
January	0-0	-	0.00	January	1-2	50.0	0.00
February	0-0	-	0.00	February	0-0	-	0.00
March	1-1	100.0	+ 1.75	March	0-5	-	- 5.00
April	2-6	33.3	- 0.50	April	7-47	14.9	- 12.69
May	3-18	16.7	- 12.33	May	4-61	6.6	- 24.93
June	5-26	19.2	+ 9.00	June	10-53	18.9	+ 31.75
July	6-31	19.4	- 14.25	July	5-33	15.2	+ 8.00
August	3-40	7.5	- 19.00	August	6-39	15.4	- 12.87
September	3-48	6.3	- 37.26	September	1-24	4.2	- 19.50
Oct/Nov	5-49	10.2	- 6.10	Oct/Nov	1-20	5.0	- 11.00

4-y-o+	W-R	Per cent	£1 Level Stake	Totals	W-R	Per cent	£1 Level Stake
January	0-1	-	- 1.00	January	1-3	33.3	- 1.00
February	0-0	-	0.00	February	0-0	-	0.00
March	0-0	-	0.00	March	1-6	16.7	- 3.25
April	0-9	-	- 9.00	April	9-62	14.5	- 22.19
May	0-18	-	- 18.00	May	7-97	7.2	- 55.26
June	2-18	11.1	+ 2.00	June	17-97	17.5	+ 42.75
July	2-11	18.2	+ 2.00	July	13-75	17.3	- 4.25
August	1-3	33.3	+ 12.00	August	10-82	12.2	- 19.87
September	0-13	-	- 13.00	September	4-85	4.7	- 69.76
Oct/Nov	0-4	-	- 4.00	Oct/Nov	6-73	8.2	- 21.10

DISTANCE

2-y-o	W-R	Per cent	£1 Level Stake	3-y-o	W-R	Per cent	£1 Level Stake
5f-6f	16-103	15.5	- 33.93	5f-6f	5-26	19.2	+ 23.50
7f-8f	11-112	9.8	- 48.26	7f-8f	11-126	8.7	- 55.49
9f-13f	1-4	25.0	+ 3.50	9f-13f	17-122	13.9	- 23.50
14f+	0-0	-	0.00	14f+	2-10	20.0	+ 9.25

4-y-o+	W-R	Per cent	£1 Level Stake	Totals	W-R	Per cent	£1 Level Stake
5f-6f	0-2	-	- 2.00	5f-6f	21-131	16.0	- 12.43
7f-8f	1-16	6.3	- 5.00	7f-8f	23-254	9.1	-108.75
9f-13f	3-33	9.1	- 7.00	9f-13f	21-159	13.2	- 27.00
14f+	1-26	3.8	- 15.00	14f+	3-36	8.3	- 5.75

TYPE OF RACE

Non-Handicaps	W-R	Per cent	£1 Level Stake	Handicaps	W-R	Per cent	£1 Level Stake
2-y-o	24-181	13.3	- 67.19	2-y-o	2-25	8.0	- 9.00
3-y-o	23-167	13.8	- 37.45	3-y-o	11-100	11.0	+ 5.33
4-y-o+	3-33	9.1	- 11.00	4-y-o+	2-40	5.0	- 14.00
Selling	2-15	13.3	- 4.50	Selling	0-3	-	- 3.00
Apprentice	0-3	-	- 3.00	Apprentice	1-11	9.1	- 8.12
Amat/Ladies	0-1	-	- 1.00	Amat/Ladies	0-1	-	- 1.00
Totals	52-400	13.0	-124.14	Totals	16-180	8.9	- 29.79

Cole P F I

<table>
<tr><td colspan="5">COURSE GRADE</td><td colspan="4">FIRST TIME OUT</td></tr>
<tr><td></td><td>W-R</td><td>Per cent</td><td>£1 Level Stake</td><td></td><td></td><td>W-R</td><td>Per cent</td><td>£1 Level Stake</td></tr>
<tr><td>Group 1</td><td>35-309</td><td>11.3</td><td>- 80.44</td><td>2-y-o</td><td></td><td>8-71</td><td>11.3</td><td>- 40.29</td></tr>
<tr><td>Group 2</td><td>12-102</td><td>11.8</td><td>- 40.66</td><td>3-y-o</td><td></td><td>7-62</td><td>11.3</td><td>- 16.33</td></tr>
<tr><td>Group 3</td><td>18-114</td><td>15.8</td><td>+ 7.44</td><td>4-y-o+</td><td></td><td>0-18</td><td>-</td><td>- 18.00</td></tr>
<tr><td>Group 4</td><td>3-55</td><td>5.5</td><td>- 40.27</td><td></td><td></td><td></td><td></td><td></td></tr>
<tr><td></td><td></td><td></td><td></td><td>Totals</td><td></td><td>15-151</td><td>9.9</td><td>- 74.62</td></tr>
</table>

JOCKEYS RIDING

<table>
<tr><td></td><td>W-R</td><td>Per cent</td><td>£1 Level Stake</td><td></td><td>W-R</td><td>Per cent</td><td>£1 Level Stake</td></tr>
<tr><td>T Quinn</td><td>49-360</td><td>13.6</td><td>- 41.34</td><td>M Roberts</td><td>1-2</td><td>50.0</td><td>+ 2.50</td></tr>
<tr><td>C Rutter</td><td>5-52</td><td>9.6</td><td>- 22.50</td><td>R Hughes</td><td>1-3</td><td>33.3</td><td>+ 18.00</td></tr>
<tr><td>Pat Eddery</td><td>2-6</td><td>33.3</td><td>+ 6.57</td><td>R Cochrane</td><td>1-7</td><td>14.3</td><td>- 5.00</td></tr>
<tr><td>A Clark</td><td>2-12</td><td>16.7</td><td>- 8.29</td><td>A Munro</td><td>1-9</td><td>11.1</td><td>0.00</td></tr>
<tr><td>W Carson</td><td>2-12</td><td>16.7</td><td>- 1.33</td><td>Aimee Cook</td><td>1-9</td><td>11.1</td><td>- 6.12</td></tr>
<tr><td>J Weaver</td><td>1-1</td><td>100.0</td><td>+ 1.25</td><td>M Hills</td><td>1-9</td><td>11.1</td><td>- 4.00</td></tr>
<tr><td>M J Kinane</td><td>1-1</td><td>100.0</td><td>+ 3.33</td><td></td><td></td><td></td><td></td></tr>
</table>

<table>
<tr><td>T G McLaughlin</td><td>0-46</td><td>W R Swinburn</td><td>0-2</td><td>M Tebbutt</td><td>0-1</td></tr>
<tr><td>J Reid</td><td>0-6</td><td>A Mackay</td><td>0-1</td><td>Miss E Houghton</td><td>0-1</td></tr>
<tr><td>K Darley</td><td>0-4</td><td>A McGlone</td><td>0-1</td><td>Mr M Armytage</td><td>0-1</td></tr>
<tr><td>B Thomson</td><td>0-3</td><td>A Tucker</td><td>0-1</td><td>P Robinson</td><td>0-1</td></tr>
<tr><td>J Fortune</td><td>0-3</td><td>B Raymond</td><td>0-1</td><td>R Waterfield</td><td>0-1</td></tr>
<tr><td>J Quinn</td><td>0-3</td><td>D Biggs</td><td>0-1</td><td>S Drowne</td><td>0-1</td></tr>
<tr><td>L Dettori</td><td>0-3</td><td>D Toole</td><td>0-1</td><td>S Perks</td><td>0-1</td></tr>
<tr><td>D Holland</td><td>0-2</td><td>G Hind</td><td>0-1</td><td>T Sprake</td><td>0-1</td></tr>
<tr><td>G Carter</td><td>0-2</td><td>M Birch</td><td>0-1</td><td>W Ryan</td><td>0-1</td></tr>
<tr><td>J Carroll</td><td>0-2</td><td>M Fenton</td><td>0-1</td><td></td><td></td></tr>
<tr><td>Paul Eddery</td><td>0-2</td><td>M Perrett</td><td>0-1</td><td></td><td></td></tr>
</table>

COURSE RECORD

<table>
<tr><td></td><td>Total W-R</td><td colspan="2">Non-Handicaps</td><td colspan="2">Handicaps</td><td>Per cent</td><td>£1 Level Stake</td></tr>
<tr><td></td><td></td><td>2-y-o</td><td>3-y-o+</td><td>2-y-o</td><td>3-y-o+</td><td></td><td></td></tr>
<tr><td>Ascot</td><td>7-31</td><td>4-6</td><td>1-8</td><td>0-0</td><td>2-17</td><td>22.6</td><td>+ 28.50</td></tr>
<tr><td>Goodwood</td><td>7-35</td><td>2-11</td><td>2-11</td><td>0-1</td><td>3-12</td><td>20.0</td><td>+ 13.16</td></tr>
<tr><td>Nottingham</td><td>5-14</td><td>1-6</td><td>3-4</td><td>0-0</td><td>1-4</td><td>35.7</td><td>+ 27.50</td></tr>
<tr><td>Chester</td><td>5-18</td><td>2-5</td><td>2-8</td><td>1-1</td><td>0-4</td><td>27.8</td><td>- 5.15</td></tr>
<tr><td>Sandown</td><td>5-27</td><td>3-8</td><td>2-11</td><td>0-0</td><td>0-8</td><td>18.5</td><td>+ 8.70</td></tr>
<tr><td>Newmarket</td><td>5-58</td><td>2-25</td><td>2-19</td><td>0-3</td><td>1-11</td><td>8.6</td><td>- 33.75</td></tr>
<tr><td>Brighton</td><td>4-37</td><td>1-8</td><td>3-15</td><td>0-2</td><td>0-12</td><td>10.8</td><td>- 23.01</td></tr>
<tr><td>York</td><td>3-21</td><td>2-7</td><td>1-9</td><td>0-0</td><td>0-5</td><td>14.3</td><td>+ 3.00</td></tr>
<tr><td>Bath</td><td>3-23</td><td>1-6</td><td>2-12</td><td>0-0</td><td>0-5</td><td>13.0</td><td>- 1.50</td></tr>
<tr><td>Leicester</td><td>3-26</td><td>2-14</td><td>1-7</td><td>0-3</td><td>0-2</td><td>11.5</td><td>- 13.93</td></tr>
<tr><td>Windsor</td><td>2-16</td><td>0-6</td><td>1-4</td><td>0-1</td><td>1-5</td><td>12.5</td><td>- 11.21</td></tr>
<tr><td>Chepstow</td><td>2-18</td><td>1-7</td><td>0-6</td><td>0-1</td><td>1-4</td><td>11.1</td><td>+ 7.33</td></tr>
<tr><td>Lingfield</td><td>2-24</td><td>1-8</td><td>0-10</td><td>0-1</td><td>1-5</td><td>8.3</td><td>- 6.50</td></tr>
<tr><td>Kempton</td><td>2-30</td><td>1-8</td><td>1-13</td><td>0-1</td><td>0-8</td><td>6.7</td><td>- 26.85</td></tr>
<tr><td>Newbury</td><td>2-51</td><td>0-15</td><td>1-18</td><td>0-3</td><td>1-15</td><td>3.9</td><td>- 39.43</td></tr>
<tr><td>Beverley</td><td>1-3</td><td>1-3</td><td>0-0</td><td>0-0</td><td>0-0</td><td>33.3</td><td>+ 2.00</td></tr>
</table>

Pontefract	1-4	0-1	0-2	0-0	1-1	25.0	+ 5.00
Lingfield (AW)	1-4	0-0	1-3	0-1	0-0	25.0	- 2.00
Newcastle	1-5	1-2	0-1	0-0	0-2	20.0	- 3.60
Yarmouth	1-8	0-2	1-5	0-0	0-1	12.5	- 5.75
Doncaster	1-16	1-6	0-6	0-1	0-3	6.3	- 11.67
Epsom	1-16	0-5	1-5	0-0	0-6	6.3	- 10.50
Folkestone	1-16	0-7	1-6	0-1	0-2	6.3	- 14.27
Haydock	1-17	0-7	0-5	0-1	1-4	5.9	- 6.00
Warwick	1-20	0-3	0-6	1-5	0-6	5.0	- 9.00
Salisbury	1-21	0-8	0-5	0-0	1-8	4.8	- 4.00

Southwell (AW)	0-6	Catterick	0-4	Hamilton	0-2
Wolverhampton (AW)	0-5	Ayr	0-2	Redcar	0-2

WINNING HORSES

		Races					Win
	Age	Run	1st	2nd	3rd	Unpl	£
Sri Pekan	2	6	5	1	0	0	99,141
Tioman Island	4	3	1	1	1	0	33,450
Humbert's Landing	3	4	2	0	1	1	21,874
Montjoy	2	3	1	1	1	0	21,388
Brave Music	2	5	1	1	1	2	18,455
River Deep	3	7	2	0	1	4	18,131
Air Commodore	3	12	2	2	2	6	15,795
Persian Elite	3	7	3	0	0	4	15,105
Girl From Ipanema	3	3	1	1	0	1	13,680
Endless Light	3	5	2	0	0	3	10,136
Dreamer	2	6	2	0	2	2	9,768
Velvet Moon	3	6	1	0	0	5	9,681
Green Perfume	2	5	1	4	0	0	9,381
Fawlty Towers	3	6	2	1	0	3	8,758
Inzar (USA)	2	3	2	0	0	1	8,742
Alanar	2	2	2	0	0	0	8,615
Star Manager	4	8	1	0	0	7	8,595
Microlite	3	9	2	2	3	2	8,208
Darren Boy	3	6	1	0	1	4	7,773
Romios	2	7	2	0	1	4	7,284
Fiendish	2	3	1	2	0	0	6,970
Potentate	3	8	2	1	1	4	6,321
Blaaziing Joe	3	4	1	0	0	3	5,038
Salmon Ladder	2	2	1	0	1	0	5,027
Trembling	2	7	1	1	0	5	4,923
Posidonas	2	2	1	0	1	0	4,232
Gaylord	2	4	1	0	2	1	4,175
Revere	4	5	1	1	1	2	4,150
Star Master	3	2	1	0	1	0	4,085
Yet More Roses	3	8	1	1	1	5	3,980
Indigo Time	2	2	1	0	0	1	3,956
Cameron Highland	3	6	1	1	1	3	3,904
Call The Guv'Nor	5	8	1	0	1	6	3,743
Belle Ile	3	6	1	0	0	5	3,659
Elite Justice	2	5	1	1	0	3	3,614

Precede	2	3	1	1	0	1	3,578
Free Life	2	8	1	0	0	7	3,560
Santa Fan	2	3	1	0	0	2	3,536
Las Flores	3	4	1	1	0	2	3,485
Runaway Pete	4	2	1	1	0	0	3,459
Strategic Choice	3	5	1	3	0	1	3,418
Life At Sea	3	5	1	3	0	1	3,377
Omnia	3	4	1	0	1	2	3,260
Silver Hunter	3	4	1	1	2	0	3,165
Sugar Town	3	8	1	1	0	6	2,952
Lord Sky	3	2	1	0	1	0	2,888
Time Star	3	2	1	0	1	0	2,873
Calling Jamaica	2	1	1	0	0	0	2,858
Total Joy	3	7	1	1	0	5	2,799
Upper Grosvenor	3	1	1	0	0	0	2,795
Aqua Rigia	2	5	1	0	2	2	2,701

WINNING OWNERS

	Races Won	Value £		Races Won	Value £
H R H Sultan Ahmad Shah	8	139,290	D F Allport	1	7,773
H R H Prince Fahd Salman	26	122,699	C Shiacolas	2	7,284
Lord Donoughmore	2	21,874	Athos Christodoulou	1	4,232
Lord Portman	2	21,407	N W L Abbott	1	3,980
Sir George Meyrick	1	21,388	Terry Neill	1	3,956
W H Ponsonby	3	19,538	C M Budgett	1	3,659
Elite Racing Club	4	18,718	Anthony Speelman	1	3,578
M Arbib	3	17,040	Alan C Elliot	1	3,536
Christopher Wright	2	16,538	Thomas T S Liang	1	3,459
Lord Sondes	1	9,381	Stephen Crown	1	2,888
Mrs Linda Gardiner	2	9,214	Hon Piers Portman	1	2,799
Planning Consultancy Limited	2	8,208			

Favourites	24-77	31.2%	- 26.59	Total winning prize-money	£472,439
Longest winning sequence			2	Average SP of winner	5.3/1
Longest losing sequence			44	Return on stakes invested	-26.5%
1993 Form	68-491	13.8%	-133.70	1991 Form	73-392	18.6%	- 31.18
1992 Form	86-461	18.7%	- 71.61	1990 Form	53-394	13.5%	- 60.48

H J COLLINGRIDGE (Newmarket)

	No. of Horses	Races Run	1st	2nd	3rd	Unpl	Per cent	£1 Level Stake
2-y-o	6	16	0	1	1	14	-	- 16.00
3-y-o	10	60	1	3	6	50	1.7	- 47.00
4-y-o+	16	80	10	6	7	57	12.5	+ 10.00
Totals	32	156	11	10	14	121	7.1	- 53.00

BY MONTH

2-y-o	W-R	Per cent	£1 Level Stake	3-y-o	W-R	Per cent	£1 Level Stake
January	0-0	-	0.00	January	0-0	-	0.00
February	0-0	-	0.00	February	0-0	-	0.00
March	0-0	-	0.00	March	0-4	-	- 4.00
April	0-0	-	0.00	April	0-6	-	- 6.00
May	0-0	-	0.00	May	0-7	-	- 7.00
June	0-1	-	- 1.00	June	1-6	16.7	+ 7.00
July	0-0	-	0.00	July	0-12	-	- 12.00
August	0-1	-	- 1.00	August	0-8	-	- 8.00
September	0-5	-	- 5.00	September	0-6	-	- 6.00
Oct/Nov	0-9	-	- 9.00	Oct/Nov	0-11	-	- 11.00

4-y-o+	W-R	Per cent	£1 Level Stake	Totals	W-R	Per cent	£1 Level Stake
January	0-5	-	- 5.00	January	0-5	-	- 5.00
February	1-3	33.3	+ 2.00	February	1-3	33.3	+ 2.00
March	3-9	33.3	+ 30.00	March	3-13	23.1	+ 26.00
April	1-16	6.3	- 10.50	April	1-22	4.5	- 16.50
May	0-13	-	- 13.00	May	0-20	-	- 20.00
June	2-10	20.0	+ 5.50	June	3-17	17.6	+ 11.50
July	1-7	14.3	+ 0.50	July	1-19	5.3	- 11.50
August	1-10	10.0	- 2.50	August	1-19	5.3	- 11.50
September	0-3	-	- 3.00	September	0-14	-	- 14.00
Oct/Nov	1-4	25.0	+ 6.00	Oct/Nov	1-24	4.2	- 14.00

DISTANCE

2-y-o	W-R	Per cent	£1 Level Stake	3-y-o	W-R	Per cent	£1 Level Stake
5f-6f	0-6	-	- 6.00	5f-6f	0-7	-	- 7.00
7f-8f	0-6	-	- 6.00	7f-8f	1-24	4.2	- 11.00
9f-13f	0-4	-	- 4.00	9f-13f	0-26	-	- 26.00
14f+	0-0	-	0.00	14f+	0-3	-	- 3.00

4-y-o+	W-R	Per cent	£1 Level Stake	Totals	W-R	Per cent	£1 Level Stake
5f-6f	5-28	17.9	+ 8.50	5f-6f	5-41	12.2	- 4.50
7f-8f	2-18	11.1	+ 15.50	7f-8f	3-48	6.3	- 1.50
9f-13f	3-23	13.0	- 3.00	9f-13f	3-53	5.7	- 33.00
14f+	0-11	-	- 11.00	14f+	0-14	-	- 14.00

TYPE OF RACE

Non-Handicaps	W-R	Per cent	£1 Level Stake	Handicaps	W-R	Per cent	£1 Level Stake
2-y-o	0-15	-	- 15.00	2-y-o	0-1	-	- 1.00
3-y-o	0-25	-	- 25.00	3-y-o	1-28	3.6	- 15.00
4-y-o+	1-12	8.3	- 4.50	4-y-o+	9-64	14.1	+ 18.50
Selling	0-3	-	- 3.00	Selling	0-2	-	- 2.00
Apprentice	0-0	-	0.00	Apprentice	0-6	-	- 6.00
Amat/Ladies	0-0	-	0.00	Amat/Ladies	0-0	-	0.00
Totals	1-55	1.8	- 47.50	Totals	10-101	9.9	- 5.50

103

COURSE GRADE

	W-R	Per cent	£1 Level Stake		W-R	Per cent	£1 Level Stake
Group 1	2-35	5.7	- 17.50	2-y-o	0-6	-	- 6.00
Group 2	1-18	5.6	- 12.50	3-y-o	0-10	-	- 10.00
Group 3	4-56	7.1	+ 3.50	4-y-o+	2-16	12.5	+ 18.00
Group 4	4-47	8.5	- 26.50	Totals	2-32	6.3	+ 2.00

(center-right title: **FIRST TIME OUT**)

JOCKEYS RIDING

	W-R	Per cent	£1 Level Stake		W-R	Per cent	£1 Level Stake
J Quinn	4-68	5.9	- 32.50	W Woods	1-5	20.0	+ 2.50
C Dwyer	3-14	21.4	+ 2.00	V Smith	1-11	9.1	+ 15.00
M Hills	1-4	25.0	+ 9.00	C Hawksley	1-38	2.6	- 33.00

A P Colgan	0-3	F Norton	0-1	M Humphries	0-1
Dale Gibson	0-2	G Carter	0-1	S O'Gorman	0-1
G Bardwell	0-2	G Duffield	0-1	W Newnes	0-1
K Fallon	0-2	L Dettori	0-1		

COURSE RECORD

	Total W-R	Non-Handicaps 2-y-o	3-y-o+	Handicaps 2-y-o	3-y-o+	Per cent	£1 Level Stake
Southwell (AW)	3-5	0-0	0-0	0-0	3-5	60.0	+ 7.50
Windsor	3-9	0-0	1-2	0-0	2-7	33.3	+ 24.50
Newcastle	1-1	0-0	0-0	0-0	1-1	100.0	+ 9.00
Sandown	1-5	0-0	0-1	0-0	1-4	20.0	+ 2.50
Leicester	1-10	0-1	0-5	0-0	1-4	10.0	+ 16.00
Lingfield	1-10	0-2	0-2	0-0	1-6	10.0	- 4.50
Folkestone	1-19	0-2	0-7	0-0	1-10	5.3	- 11.00

Nottingham	0-13	Brighton	0-4	Catterick	0-1
Lingfield (AW)	0-11	Goodwood	0-4	Epsom	0-1
Newmarket	0-9	Kempton	0-4	Hamilton	0-1
Warwick	0-9	Edinburgh	0-2	Ripon	0-1
Yarmouth	0-9	Haydock	0-2	Thirsk	0-1
Pontefract	0-8	Salisbury	0-2	York	0-1
Doncaster	0-7	Ascot	0-1		
Beverley	0-5	Bath	0-1		

WINNING HORSES

	Age	Races Run	1st	2nd	3rd	Unpl	Win £
Moving Image	4	11	3	1	0	7	9,083
Ballyranter	5	11	2	1	4	4	7,522
Bright Paragon	5	16	2	1	2	11	6,958
Westfield Moves	6	9	2	1	1	5	5,985
Yoxall Lodge	4	4	1	0	0	3	3,611
South Eastern Fred	3	10	1	2	1	6	3,469

WINNING OWNERS

	Races Won	Value £		Races Won	Value £
Mrs Christine Rawson	3	9,083	A G Wakley	2	5,985
P J Byrnes	2	7,522	Mrs Anne Featherstone	1	3,611
D C G Cooper	2	6,958	South Eastern Electrical Plc	1	3,469

Favourites	1-10	10.0% - 7.50	Total winning prize-money		£36,629
Longest winning sequence		2	Average SP of winner		8.4/1
Longest losing sequence		47	Return on stakes invested		-34.0%
1993 Form	8-150	5.3% - 93.87	1991 Form	9-139	6.5% - 6.50
1992 Form	10-143	7.0% - 50.12	1990 Form	7-158	4.4% -100.75

D J S COSGROVE (Newmarket)

	No. of Horses	Races Run	1st	2nd	3rd	Unpl	Per cent	£1 Level Stake
2-y-o	6	24	1	1	1	21	4.2	- 18.00
3-y-o	8	39	0	7	2	30	-	- 39.00
4-y-o+	8	34	3	5	3	23	8.8	- 21.25
Totals	22	97	4	13	6	74	4.1	- 78.25

Jan	Feb	Mar	Apr	May	Jun	Jul	Aug	Sep	Oct/Nov
0-0	0-3	1-2	0-6	0-8	3-18	0-18	0-18	0-11	0-13

Winning Jockeys	W-R	£1 Level Stake		W-R	£1 Level Stake
J Lowe	2-4	+ 5.25	L Newton	1-51	- 45.00
J Weaver	1-1	+ 2.50			

Winning Courses	W-R	£1 Level Stake		W-R	£1 Level Stake
Southwell (AW)	2-4	+ 5.25	Wolverhampton (AW)	1-7	- 3.50
Pontefract	1-6	0.00			

Winning Horses	Age	Races Run	1st	2nd	3rd	Unpl	Win £
Tiger Shoot	7	7	2	2	2	1	5,749
Everset	6	3	1	1	0	1	3,210
Cats Bottom	2	7	1	1	0	5	2,768

Favourites	2-6	33.3% + 0.75	Total winning prize-money		£11,727
1993 Form	6-60	10.0% - 11.44	1992 Form	3-50	6.0% - 27.00

L G COTTRELL (Cullompton, Devon)

	No. of Horses	Races Run	1st	2nd	3rd	Unpl	Per cent	£1 Level Stake
2-y-o	5	16	2	0	0	14	12.5	+ 0.75
3-y-o	3	9	0	0	0	9	-	- 9.00
4-y-o+	8	49	4	2	8	35	8.2	- 30.70
Totals	16	74	6	2	8	58	8.1	- 38.95

Jan	Feb	Mar	Apr	May	Jun	Jul	Aug	Sep	Oct/Nov
0-2	2-2	0-2	1-7	1-12	0-6	0-7	0-7	0-13	2-16

Winning Jockeys	W-R	£1 Level Stake		W-R	£1 Level Stake
N Carlisle	4-41	- 12.25	D Holland	1-8	- 3.50
L Dettori	1-2	- 0.20			

Winning Courses	W-R	£1 Level Stake		W-R	£1 Level Stake
Lingfield (AW)	2-6	+ 0.30	Chepstow	1-3	+ 3.00
Warwick	2-11	+ 8.00	Windsor	1-6	- 2.25

Winning Horses	Age	Races Run	1st	2nd	3rd	Unpl	Win £
Montserrat	2	6	2	0	0	4	6,266
Storm Free	8	8	2	0	2	4	5,798
Sky Burst	4	8	1	0	2	5	3,591
Cape Pigeon	9	10	1	0	1	8	3,143

Favourites	1-4	25.0%	- 2.20	Total winning prize-money		£18,797

| 1993 Form | 10-87 | 11.5% | + 41.95 | 1991 Form | 10-83 | 12.0% | + 4.00 |
| 1992 Form | 8-98 | 8.2% | - 38.42 | 1990 Form | 4-125 | 3.2% | - 97.00 |

L M CUMANI (Newmarket)

	No. of Horses	Races Run	1st	2nd	3rd	Unpl	Per cent	£1 Level Stake
2-y-o	18	40	5	7	6	22	12.5	- 18.45
3-y-o	35	166	28	27	17	94	16.9	- 31.74
4-y-o+	14	63	14	14	6	29	22.2	+ 8.88
Totals	67	269	47	48	29	145	17.5	- 41.31

BY MONTH

2-y-o	W-R	Per cent	£1 Level Stake	3-y-o	W-R	Per cent	£1 Level Stake
Mar/Apr	0-0	-	0.00	Mar/Apr	2-20	10.0	- 2.75
May	0-0	-	0.00	May	7-36	19.4	- 11.87
June	0-2	-	- 2.00	June	6-28	21.4	+ 1.00
July	0-2	-	- 2.00	July	3-26	11.5	- 7.75
August	1-5	20.0	- 0.50	August	6-31	19.4	- 12.37
September	3-13	23.1	+ 2.25	September	2-15	13.3	- 9.00
Oct/Nov	1-18	5.6	- 16.20	Oct/Nov	2-10	20.0	+ 11.00

4-y-o+	W-R	Per cent	£1 Level Stake	Totals	W-R	Per cent	£1 Level Stake
Mar/Apr	1-5	20.0	- 1.00	Mar/Apr	3-25	12.0	- 3.75
May	1-5	20.0	+ 6.00	May	8-41	19.5	- 5.87
June	2-15	13.3	- 8.00	June	8-45	17.8	- 9.00
July	4-15	26.7	- 1.62	July	7-43	16.3	- 11.37
August	3-10	30.0	+ 8.25	August	10-46	21.7	- 4.62
September	1-7	14.3	+ 4.00	September	6-35	17.1	- 2.75
Oct/Nov	2-6	33.3	+ 1.25	Oct/Nov	5-34	14.7	- 3.95

DISTANCE

2-y-o	W-R	Per cent	£1 Level Stake	3-y-o	W-R	Per cent	£1 Level Stake
5f-6f	2-13	15.4	- 1.50	5f-6f	0-1	-	- 1.00
7f-8f	3-25	12.0	- 14.95	7f-8f	8-52	15.4	- 6.37
9f-13f	0-2	-	- 2.00	9f-13f	14-88	15.9	- 18.12
14f+	0-0	-	0.00	14f+	6-25	24.0	- 6.25

4-y-o+	W-R	Per cent	£1 Level Stake	Totals	W-R	Per cent	£1 Level Stake
5f-6f	0-1	-	- 1.00	5f-6f	2-15	13.3	- 3.50
7f-8f	1-11	9.1	- 7.00	7f-8f	12-88	13.6	- 28.32
9f-13f	5-32	15.6	+ 5.25	9f-13f	19-122	15.6	- 14.87
14f+	8-19	42.1	+ 11.63	14f+	14-44	31.8	+ 5.38

TYPE OF RACE

Non-Handicaps	W-R	Per cent	£1 Level Stake	Handicaps	W-R	Per cent	£1 Level Stake
2-y-o	5-38	13.2	- 16.45	2-y-o	0-2	-	- 2.00
3-y-o	12-93	12.9	- 58.37	3-y-o	14-66	21.2	+ 27.88
4-y-o+	4-26	15.4	+ 0.25	4-y-o+	9-33	27.3	+ 9.88
Selling	0-0	-	0.00	Selling	0-0	-	0.00
Apprentice	2-4	50.0	+ 1.75	Apprentice	1-5	20.0	- 2.25
Amat/Ladies	0-0	-	0.00	Amat/Ladies	0-2	-	- 2.00
Totals	23-161	14.3	- 72.82	Totals	24-108	22.2	+ 31.51

Cumani L M

<table>
<tr><th colspan="4">COURSE GRADE</th><th></th><th colspan="4">FIRST TIME OUT</th></tr>
<tr><th></th><th>W-R</th><th>Per
cent</th><th>£1 Level
Stake</th><th></th><th></th><th>W-R</th><th>Per
cent</th><th>£1 Level
Stake</th></tr>
<tr><td>Group 1</td><td>26-182</td><td>14.3</td><td>- 20.44</td><td></td><td>2-y-o</td><td>2-18</td><td>11.1</td><td>- 5.00</td></tr>
<tr><td>Group 2</td><td>11-32</td><td>34.4</td><td>+ 1.75</td><td></td><td>3-y-o</td><td>3-35</td><td>8.6</td><td>- 15.37</td></tr>
<tr><td>Group 3</td><td>8-50</td><td>16.0</td><td>- 24.00</td><td></td><td>4-y-o+</td><td>1-14</td><td>7.1</td><td>- 10.00</td></tr>
<tr><td>Group 4</td><td>2-5</td><td>40.0</td><td>+ 1.38</td><td></td><td></td><td></td><td></td><td></td></tr>
<tr><td></td><td></td><td></td><td></td><td></td><td>Totals</td><td>6-67</td><td>9.0</td><td>- 30.37</td></tr>
</table>

JOCKEYS RIDING

<table>
<tr><th></th><th>W-R</th><th>Per
cent</th><th>£1 Level
Stake</th><th></th><th>W-R</th><th>Per
cent</th><th>£1 Level
Stake</th></tr>
<tr><td>L Dettori</td><td>11-46</td><td>23.9</td><td>+ 5.75</td><td>M J Kinane</td><td>2-13</td><td>15.4</td><td>- 5.00</td></tr>
<tr><td>J Weaver</td><td>8-43</td><td>18.6</td><td>+ 10.05</td><td>J Reid</td><td>2-18</td><td>11.1</td><td>+ 7.00</td></tr>
<tr><td>K Darley</td><td>7-18</td><td>38.9</td><td>+ 4.88</td><td>R Cochrane</td><td>2-21</td><td>9.5</td><td>- 12.50</td></tr>
<tr><td>C Hodgson</td><td>6-42</td><td>14.3</td><td>- 8.12</td><td>R Hughes</td><td>1-2</td><td>50.0</td><td>+ 1.25</td></tr>
<tr><td>Pat Eddery</td><td>5-16</td><td>31.3</td><td>- 3.12</td><td>Jo Hunnam</td><td>1-4</td><td>25.0</td><td>- 2.00</td></tr>
<tr><td>G Mitchell</td><td>2-6</td><td>33.3</td><td>+ 0.50</td><td></td><td></td><td></td><td></td></tr>
</table>

<table>
<tr><td>G Carter</td><td>0-4</td><td>D Harrison</td><td>0-2</td><td>J Carroll</td><td>0-1</td></tr>
<tr><td>T Quinn</td><td>0-4</td><td>K Fallon</td><td>0-2</td><td>J Fortune</td><td>0-1</td></tr>
<tr><td>W Ryan</td><td>0-4</td><td>Mrs S Cumani</td><td>0-2</td><td>L Piggott</td><td>0-1</td></tr>
<tr><td>A Munro</td><td>0-3</td><td>B Thomson</td><td>0-1</td><td>M Denaro</td><td>0-1</td></tr>
<tr><td>M Hills</td><td>0-3</td><td>C Asmussen</td><td>0-1</td><td>R Hills</td><td>0-1</td></tr>
<tr><td>M Roberts</td><td>0-3</td><td>D Holland</td><td>0-1</td><td>W R Swinburn</td><td>0-1</td></tr>
<tr><td>O Urbina</td><td>0-3</td><td>D Moffatt</td><td>0-1</td><td></td><td></td></tr>
</table>

COURSE RECORD

<table>
<tr><th></th><th>Total
W-R</th><th colspan="2">Non-Handicaps</th><th colspan="2">Handicaps</th><th>Per
cent</th><th>£1 Level
Stake</th></tr>
<tr><th></th><th></th><th>2-y-o</th><th>3-y-o+</th><th>2-y-o</th><th>3-y-o+</th><th></th><th></th></tr>
<tr><td>Newmarket</td><td>7-62</td><td>2-21</td><td>1-22</td><td>0-1</td><td>4-18</td><td>11.3</td><td>- 20.07</td></tr>
<tr><td>Brighton</td><td>6-12</td><td>0-1</td><td>4-8</td><td>0-0</td><td>2-3</td><td>50.0</td><td>+ 7.50</td></tr>
<tr><td>Goodwood</td><td>4-17</td><td>1-2</td><td>1-7</td><td>0-0</td><td>2-8</td><td>23.5</td><td>+ 8.75</td></tr>
<tr><td>Newbury</td><td>3-12</td><td>0-0</td><td>1-7</td><td>0-0</td><td>2-5</td><td>25.0</td><td>- 2.00</td></tr>
<tr><td>Ascot</td><td>3-16</td><td>0-1</td><td>2-10</td><td>0-0</td><td>1-5</td><td>18.8</td><td>+ 9.00</td></tr>
<tr><td>Doncaster</td><td>3-19</td><td>0-2</td><td>1-7</td><td>0-1</td><td>2-9</td><td>15.8</td><td>+ 6.25</td></tr>
<tr><td>York</td><td>3-23</td><td>0-0</td><td>2-9</td><td>0-0</td><td>1-14</td><td>13.0</td><td>- 3.00</td></tr>
<tr><td>Salisbury</td><td>2-3</td><td>0-0</td><td>2-2</td><td>0-0</td><td>0-1</td><td>66.7</td><td>+ 2.25</td></tr>
<tr><td>Beverley</td><td>2-7</td><td>0-0</td><td>2-4</td><td>0-0</td><td>0-3</td><td>28.6</td><td>- 0.75</td></tr>
<tr><td>Yarmouth</td><td>2-12</td><td>0-1</td><td>0-5</td><td>0-0</td><td>2-6</td><td>16.7</td><td>- 4.00</td></tr>
<tr><td>Catterick</td><td>1-1</td><td>0-0</td><td>0-0</td><td>0-0</td><td>1-1</td><td>100.0</td><td>+ 3.00</td></tr>
<tr><td>Chepstow</td><td>1-1</td><td>0-0</td><td>0-0</td><td>0-0</td><td>1-1</td><td>100.0</td><td>+ 1.75</td></tr>
<tr><td>Hamilton</td><td>1-1</td><td>0-0</td><td>0-0</td><td>0-0</td><td>1-1</td><td>100.0</td><td>+ 1.25</td></tr>
<tr><td>Lingfield</td><td>1-1</td><td>0-0</td><td>1-1</td><td>0-0</td><td>0-0</td><td>100.0</td><td>+ 1.00</td></tr>
<tr><td>Edinburgh</td><td>1-2</td><td>0-0</td><td>0-1</td><td>0-0</td><td>1-1</td><td>50.0</td><td>+ 0.38</td></tr>
<tr><td>Newcastle</td><td>1-3</td><td>0-0</td><td>0-1</td><td>0-0</td><td>1-2</td><td>33.3</td><td>+ 3.50</td></tr>
<tr><td>Chester</td><td>1-5</td><td>0-1</td><td>1-3</td><td>0-0</td><td>0-1</td><td>20.0</td><td>- 2.50</td></tr>
<tr><td>Nottingham</td><td>1-5</td><td>0-1</td><td>0-1</td><td>0-0</td><td>1-3</td><td>20.0</td><td>- 0.50</td></tr>
<tr><td>Thirsk</td><td>1-6</td><td>1-1</td><td>0-3</td><td>0-0</td><td>0-2</td><td>16.7</td><td>- 1.50</td></tr>
<tr><td>Leicester</td><td>1-7</td><td>1-4</td><td>0-2</td><td>0-0</td><td>0-1</td><td>14.3</td><td>- 4.75</td></tr>
<tr><td>Haydock</td><td>1-10</td><td>0-1</td><td>0-4</td><td>0-0</td><td>1-5</td><td>10.0</td><td>- 5.50</td></tr>
<tr><td>Sandown</td><td>1-11</td><td>0-0</td><td>0-7</td><td>0-0</td><td>1-4</td><td>9.1</td><td>- 8.37</td></tr>
</table>

Pontefract	0-7	Windsor	0-5	Redcar	0-2
Epsom	0-6	Kempton	0-3	Folkestone	0-1
Bath	0-5	Ripon	0-3	Warwick	0-1

WINNING HORSES

	Age	Races Run	1st	2nd	3rd	Unpl	Win £
Only Royale	5	3	1	0	0	2	79,425
Midnight Legend	3	8	4	1	1	2	78,848
Barathea	4	4	1	2	0	1	56,794
Saxon Maid	3	8	3	1	0	4	36,988
Captain Jack	4	9	4	1	0	4	26,870
Spin Doctor	4	5	2	0	0	3	15,355
Noble Rose	3	2	1	1	0	0	14,490
Smart Alec	2	2	2	0	0	0	13,493
Rehlat Farah	3	7	3	0	1	3	13,467
Paonic	3	9	2	3	0	4	13,215
Lille Hammer	4	6	1	1	0	4	12,538
Old Hickory	3	8	2	0	2	4	12,483
Tree Of Life	4	7	2	2	0	3	9,980
Ptoto	3	7	2	3	0	2	9,823
Hesell Street	3	6	2	1	0	3	8,657
Daronne	3	6	2	1	0	3	8,099
Fetes Galantes	4	8	2	2	0	4	7,578
Thunderheart	3	14	2	3	3	6	6,312
Baaderah	2	5	1	1	1	2	4,768
All Time Great	2	2	1	0	0	1	4,178
Mandarina	2	2	1	0	1	0	4,093
Kettlestone	3	4	1	0	0	3	4,007
Verdigris	3	9	1	2	0	6	3,590
Leonova	3	6	1	1	2	2	3,473
Duke Of Warsaw	3	5	1	1	1	2	3,165
Caladesi	3	6	1	3	0	2	2,668
Classic Caboose	4	4	1	0	2	1	2,297

WINNING OWNERS

	Races Won	Value £		Races Won	Value £
Sheikh Mohammed	9	123,543	Sultan Mohammed	3	15,150
G Sainaghi	1	79,425	Gerald Leigh	2	13,493
Umm Qarn Racing	4	78,848	Lord Halifax	2	9,980
Lord Carnarvon	4	26,870	Paul G S Silver	2	8,657
Baron Edouard De Rothschild	4	23,588	Fittocks Stud Limited	2	6,661
Paolo Riccardi	4	23,038	Helena Springfield Ltd	1	4,178
Sheikh Ahmed Al Maktoum	4	18,235	Consultco Ltd	1	3,743
Lord De La Warr,			J Mayor	1	3,590
Michael Kerr-Dineen	2	15,355	Richard L Duchossios	1	2,297

Favourites	25-68	36.8%	+ 5.44	Total winning prize-money	£456,652

Longest winning sequence	2	Average SP of winner	3.8/1
Longest losing sequence	14	Return on stakes invested	-15.4%

1993 Form	39-277	14.1%	- 95.64	1991 Form	72-334	21.6%	- 63.91
1992 Form	54-292	18.5%	- 69.25	1990 Form	108-405	26.7%	+ 16.83

P D CUNDELL (Newbury, Berks)

	No. of Horses	Races Run	1st	2nd	3rd	Unpl	Per cent	£1 Level Stake
2-y-o	3	10	0	0	0	10	-	- 10.00
3-y-o	4	19	0	0	1	18	-	- 19.00
4-y-o+	4	42	6	1	2	33	14.3	+ 13.00
Totals	11	71	6	1	3	61	8.5	- 16.00

Jan	Feb	Mar	Apr	May	Jun	Jul	Aug	Sep	Oct/Nov
0-1	0-1	1-3	1-11	3-15	0-10	1-8	0-2	0-10	0-10

Winning Jockeys	W-R	£1 Level Stake		W-R	£1 Level Stake
D Griffiths	5-23	+ 17.00	W Newnes	1-8	+ 7.00

Winning Courses					
Warwick	2-7	+ 6.50	Newbury	1-6	+ 7.00
Lingfield	1-1	+ 4.50	Brighton	1-8	+ 7.00
Salisbury	1-3	+ 5.00			

Winning Horses	Age	Races Run	1st	2nd	3rd	Unpl	Win £
Leigh Crofter	5	13	4	1	0	8	16,281
Great Hall	5	20	1	0	2	17	3,590
Marwell Mitzi	4	6	1	0	0	5	3,106

Favourites	1-3	33.3%	+ 0.50	Total winning prize-money	£22,977

1993 Form	7-60	11.7%	+ 6.50	1991 Form	1-16	6.3%	+ 18.00
1992 Form	1-37	2.7%	- 20.00	1990 Form	0-22		

K O CUNNINGHAM-BROWN (Stockbridge, Hants)

	No. of Horses	Races Run	1st	2nd	3rd	Unpl	Per cent	£1 Level Stake
2-y-o	5	12	1	0	0	11	8.3	+ 14.00
3-y-o	3	18	1	2	0	15	5.6	- 14.50
4-y-o+	16	107	6	8	9	84	5.6	+ 59.50
Totals	24	137	8	10	9	110	5.8	+ 59.00

Jan	Feb	Mar	Apr	May	Jun	Jul	Aug	Sep	Oct/Nov
0-8	0-3	0-4	1-12	0-13	1-22	2-19	1-20	0-15	3-21

Winning Jockeys	W-R	£1 Level Stake			W-R	£1 Level Stake
C Teague	2-2	+ 21.00	L Dettori		1-6	+ 0.50
J Weaver	1-2	+ 13.00	J Quinn		1-10	+ 11.00
D Harrison	1-2	+ 24.00	B Doyle		1-24	+ 77.00
D Griffiths	1-4	- 0.50				

Winning Courses						
Newbury	2-6	+108.00	Folkestone		1-10	- 3.50
Doncaster	1-2	+ 8.00	Windsor		1-14	+ 7.00
Bath	1-6	- 2.50	Salisbury		1-21	- 6.00
Warwick	1-6	+ 20.00				

Winning Horses	Age	Races Run	1st	2nd	3rd	Unpl	Win £
Jolto	5	9	3	3	1	2	11,278
Village Green	4	19	1	0	2	16	7,939
Lees Please	2	5	1	0	0	4	3,808
Ewar Gold	4	14	1	0	0	13	3,670
Sheltered Cove	3	7	1	2	0	4	2,785
Norling	4	12	1	2	2	7	2,381

Favourites	0-8			Total winning prize-money		£31,860
1993 Form	4-173	2.3%	- 89.50	1991 Form	2-68	2.9%	- 30.00
1992 Form	18-143	12.6%	+100.33	1990 Form	4-98	4.1%	- 43.00

B J CURLEY (Newmarket)

	No. of Horses	Races Run	1st	2nd	3rd	Unpl	Per cent	£1 Level Stake
2-y-o	0	0	0	0	0	0	-	0.00
3-y-o	0	0	0	0	0	0	-	0.00
4-y-o+	1	3	1	1	0	1	33.3	+ 4.00
Totals	1	3	1	1	0	1	33.3	+ 4.00

Jan	Feb	Mar	Apr	May	Jun	Jul	Aug	Sep	Oct/Nov
0-0	0-0	0-0	0-0	0-0	1-2	0-0	0-0	0-1	0-0

Winning Jockey	W-R	£1 Level Stake	Winning Course	W-R	£1 Level Stake
M Fenton	1-1	+ 6.00	Yarmouth	1-1	+ 6.00

Winning Horse	Age	Races Run	1st	2nd	3rd	Unpl	Win £
Threshfield	8	3	1	1	0	1	2,763

Favourites	0-2			Total winning prize-money		£2,763
1993 Form	2-19	10.5%	- 6.75	1991 Form	3-27	11.1%	- 15.90
1992 Form	0-6			1990 Form	3-33	9.1%	- 17.00

C A CYZER (Horsham, West Sussex)

	No. of Horses	Races Run	1st	2nd	3rd	Unpl	Per cent	£1 Level Stake
2-y-o	8	23	3	3	0	17	13.0	- 1.80
3-y-o	18	107	10	2	12	83	9.3	- 32.25
4-y-o+	15	118	6	5	16	91	5.1	- 33.75
Totals	41	248	19	10	28	191	7.7	- 67.80

BY MONTH

2-y-o	W-R	Per cent	£1 Level Stake	3-y-o	W-R	Per cent	£1 Level Stake
January	0-0	-	0.00	January	0-0	-	0.00
February	0-0	-	0.00	February	0-0	-	0.00
March	0-1	-	- 1.00	March	0-2	-	- 2.00
April	0-0	-	0.00	April	1-13	7.7	0.00
May	0-1	-	- 1.00	May	1-11	9.1	- 8.75
June	0-1	-	- 1.00	June	3-17	17.6	+ 7.00
July	0-4	-	- 4.00	July	1-18	5.6	- 9.50
August	1-6	16.7	- 3.80	August	2-18	11.1	- 10.00
September	2-7	28.6	+ 12.00	September	1-17	5.9	- 11.00
Oct/Nov	0-3	-	- 3.00	Oct/Nov	1-11	9.1	+ 2.00

4-y-o+	W-R	Per cent	£1 Level Stake	Totals	W-R	Per cent	£1 Level Stake
January	0-0	-	0.00	January	0-0	-	0.00
February	0-0	-	0.00	February	0-0	-	0.00
March	0-1	-	- 1.00	March	0-4	-	- 4.00
April	2-10	20.0	+ 12.00	April	3-23	13.0	+ 12.00
May	1-27	3.7	+ 7.00	May	2-39	5.1	- 2.75
June	2-23	8.7	- 11.75	June	5-41	12.2	- 5.75
July	0-21	-	- 21.00	July	1-43	2.3	- 34.50
August	0-16	-	- 16.00	August	3-40	7.5	- 29.80
September	1-15	6.7	+ 2.00	September	4-39	10.3	+ 3.00
Oct/Nov	0-5	-	- 5.00	Oct/Nov	1-19	5.3	- 6.00

DISTANCE

2-y-o	W-R	Per cent	£1 Level Stake	3-y-o	W-R	Per cent	£1 Level Stake
5f-6f	2-13	15.4	+ 1.20	5f-6f	0-4	-	- 4.00
7f-8f	0-8	-	- 8.00	7f-8f	3-48	6.3	- 13.00
9f-13f	1-2	50.0	+ 5.00	9f-13f	5-48	10.4	- 15.50
14f+	0-0	-	0.00	14f+	2-7	28.6	+ 0.25

4-y-o+	W-R	Per cent	£1 Level Stake	Totals	W-R	Per cent	£1 Level Stake
5f-6f	1-22	4.5	- 11.00	5f-6f	3-39	7.7	- 13.80
7f-8f	2-29	6.9	+ 22.00	7f-8f	5-85	5.9	+ 1.00
9f-13f	1-38	2.6	- 35.75	9f-13f	7-88	8.0	- 46.25
14f+	2-29	6.9	- 9.00	14f+	4-36	11.1	- 8.75

TYPE OF RACE

Non-Handicaps	W-R	Per cent	£1 Level Stake	Handicaps	W-R	Per cent	£1 Level Stake
2-y-o	2-18	11.1	- 8.80	2-y-o	1-4	25.0	+ 8.00
3-y-o	8-67	11.9	- 5.75	3-y-o	2-31	6.5	- 17.50
4-y-o+	3-31	9.7	+ 14.25	4-y-o+	3-70	4.3	- 31.00
Selling	0-8	-	- 8.00	Selling	0-4	-	- 4.00
Apprentice	0-1	-	- 1.00	Apprentice	0-10	-	- 10.00
Amat/Ladies	0-1	-	- 1.00	Amat/Ladies	0-3	-	- 3.00
Totals	13-126	10.3	- 10.30	Totals	6-122	4.9	- 57.50

COURSE GRADE

	W-R	Per cent	£1 Level Stake
Group 1	11-124	8.9	- 41.50
Group 2	2-42	4.8	- 24.80
Group 3	1-31	3.2	- 24.00
Group 4	5-51	9.8	+ 22.50

FIRST TIME OUT

	W-R	Per cent	£1 Level Stake
2-y-o	0-8	-	- 8.00
3-y-o	2-18	11.1	+ 10.00
4-y-o+	0-15	-	- 15.00
Totals	2-41	4.9	- 13.00

JOCKEYS RIDING

	W-R	Per cent	£1 Level Stake		W-R	Per cent	£1 Level Stake
J Reid	3-6	50.0	+ 10.45	K Darley	1-2	50.0	+ 11.00
J D Smith	3-54	5.6	- 19.00	R Price	1-2	50.0	+ 11.00
N Hall	2-11	18.2	+ 2.50	T Quinn	1-3	33.3	0.00
K Fallon	2-15	13.3	0.00	R Cochrane	1-7	14.3	- 5.00
J Weaver	2-17	11.8	+ 32.00	A Clark	1-29	3.4	- 22.00
M Roberts	2-22	9.1	- 8.75				

T Williams	0-13	D McKeown	0-2	D Harrison		0-1
D Biggs	0-9	G Duffield	0-2	E Johnson		0-1
G Bardwell	0-5	J Quinn	0-2	J Fortune		0-1
G Carter	0-5	N Carlisle	0-2	J Williams		0-1
W Woods	0-5	N Gwilliams	0-2	L Dettori		0-1
Mr K Santana	0-4	W Newnes	0-2	R Hughes		0-1
P Robinson	0-4	W Ryan	0-2	S Mulvey		0-1
B Thomas	0-3	A Culhane	0-1	W Carson		0-1
J Lowe	0-3	A Mackay	0-1	Y Take		0-1
Pat Eddery	0-3	A McGlone	0-1			

COURSE RECORD

	Total W-R	Non-Handicaps 2-y-o	3-y-o+	Handicaps 2-y-o	3-y-o+	Per cent	£1 Level Stake
Newmarket	3-37	0-3	2-19	0-2	1-13	8.1	- 10.75
Southwell (AW)	2-11	0-1	2-4	0-0	0-6	18.2	+ 32.00
Sandown	2-13	0-0	1-7	0-0	1-6	15.4	0.00
Goodwood	2-19	0-2	2-12	0-0	0-5	10.5	- 3.75

Cyzer C A

Lingfield (AW)	2-21	0-0	0-4	0-0	2-17	9.5	-	7.50
Newbury	1-4	0-1	1-1	0-0	0-2	25.0	-	1.00
Bath	1-5	1-1	0-2	0-0	0-2	20.0	+	2.00
Epsom	1-5	0-0	1-4	0-0	0-1	20.0	+	2.00
Doncaster	1-7	0-1	1-3	0-0	0-3	14.3	-	1.00
Wolverhampton (AW)	1-8	0-0	0-3	0-0	1-5	12.5	+	9.00
Salisbury	1-9	0-0	1-5	0-0	0-4	11.1	+	6.00
Kempton	1-14	0-1	0-6	1-1	0-6	7.1	-	2.00
Brighton	1-19	1-3	0-8	0-0	0-8	5.3	-	16.80

Lingfield	0-13	Windsor	0-7	Haydock	0-2
Ascot	0-11	Yarmouth	0-5	Chester	0-1
Chepstow	0-9	Leicester	0-4	Nottingham	0-1
York	0-9	Warwick	0-4		
Folkestone	0-7	Newcastle	0-3		

WINNING HORSES

	Age	Races Run	1st	2nd	3rd	Unpl	Win £
Master Planner	5	14	1	0	2	11	10,273
Party Season	3	9	2	0	2	5	7,865
Pursuit Of Glory	3	8	2	0	0	6	7,489
Sally Slade	2	9	2	1	0	6	6,199
Princely Gait	3	7	2	1	0	4	5,660
Crazy Paving	3	4	1	0	0	3	5,163
Bold Resolution	6	11	1	2	0	8	5,107
Uncharted Waters	3	4	1	0	0	3	3,749
Shot At Love	3	5	1	0	0	4	3,721
Seasonal Splendour	4	7	1	1	1	4	3,664
Pillow Talk	3	12	1	0	3	8	3,606
Great Crusader	2	5	1	1	0	3	3,525
Words Of Wisdom	4	15	1	0	2	12	3,106
Hostile Invader	4	7	1	0	1	5	2,985
Dinner At Eight	4	9	1	0	0	8	2,558

WINNING OWNERS

	Races Won	Value £		Races Won	Value £
R M Cyzer	16	64,075	M J Morrison	1	3,106
Gerald Leigh	2	7,489			

Favourites	4-9	44.4%	- 0.30	Total winning prize-money		£74,670
Longest winning sequence			2	Average SP of winner		8.5/1
Longest losing sequence			29	Return on stakes invested		-27.3%
1993 Form	20-222	9.0%	- 63.74	1991 Form	20-217	9.2% - 79.48
1992 Form	27-200	13.5%	+ 81.75	1990 Form	9-165	5.5% - 70.50

D J S FFRENCH DAVIS (Upper Lambourn, Berks)

	No. of Horses	Races Run	1st	2nd	3rd	Unpl	Per cent	£1 Level Stake
2-y-o	5	17	1	2	0	14	5.9	- 6.00
3-y-o	3	18	0	2	2	14	-	- 18.00
4-y-o+	2	5	0	0	0	5	-	- 5.00
Totals	10	40	1	4	2	33	2.5	- 29.00

Jan	Feb	Mar	Apr	May	Jun	Jul	Aug	Sep	Oct/Nov
0-0	0-0	0-2	0-4	0-9	1-10	0-4	0-4	0-4	0-3

Winning Jockey	W-R	£1 Level Stake	Winning Course	W-R	£1 Level Stake
N Adams	1-22	- 11.00	Brighton	1-7	+ 4.00

Winning Horse	Age	Races Run	1st	2nd	3rd	Unpl	Win £
Jobber's Fiddle	2	9	1	1	0	7	3,115

Favourites	0-1	Total winning prize-money	£3,115

R DICKIN (Stratford-upon-Avon, Warwicks)

	No. of Horses	Races Run	1st	2nd	3rd	Unpl	Per cent	£1 Level Stake
2-y-o	1	3	0	0	0	3	-	- 3.00
3-y-o	4	14	0	0	0	14	-	- 14.00
4-y-o+	7	26	2	2	1	21	7.7	- 2.50
Totals	12	43	2	2	1	38	4.7	- 19.50

Jan	Feb	Mar	Apr	May	Jun	Jul	Aug	Sep	Oct/Nov
0-3	0-0	0-0	1-3	0-12	0-7	0-1	0-3	0-5	1-9

Winning Jockeys	W-R	£1 Level Stake		W-R	£1 Level Stake
T Quinn	1-2	+ 4.50	D Meredith	1-7	+ 10.00

Winning Courses	W-R	£1 Level Stake		W-R	£1 Level Stake
Pontefract	1-2	+ 15.00	Newmarket	1-6	+ 0.50

Winning Horses	Age	Races Run	1st	2nd	3rd	Unpl	Win £
Kadastrof	4	5	1	2	0	2	7,570
Ballasecret	6	10	1	0	0	9	4,143

Favourites	1-2	50.0%	+ 4.50	Total winning prize-money	£11,713

1993 Form	4-68	5.9%	- 16.00	1991 Form	5-46	10.9%	- 2.75
1992 Form	3-42	7.1%	+ 23.50	1990 Form	1-28	3.6%	- 2.00

M DIXON (Epsom, Surrey)

	No. of Horses	Races Run	1st	2nd	3rd	Unpl	Per cent	£1 Level Stake
2-y-o	3	9	0	0	0	9	-	- 9.00
3-y-o	4	19	0	0	0	19	-	- 19.00
4-y-o+	3	18	1	2	2	13	5.6	- 15.90
Totals	10	46	1	2	2	41	2.2	- 43.90

Jan	Feb	Mar	Apr	May	Jun	Jul	Aug	Sep	Oct/Nov
0-3	0-3	0-3	1-4	0-5	0-5	0-8	0-5	0-8	0-2

Winning Jockey		W-R	£1 Level Stake	Winning Course		W-R	£1 Level Stake
A Clark		1-17	- 14.90	Folkestone		1-5	- 2.90

Winning Horse		Age	Races Run	1st	2nd	3rd	Unpl	Win £
Princess Ermyn		5	9	1	2	1	5	3,054

Favourites	1-2	50.0%	+ 0.10	Total winning prize-money	£3,054

1993 Form	6-53	11.3%	+ 2.00	1991 Form	0-1
1992 Form	5-79	6.3%	- 20.50		

M DODS (Darlington, Co Durham)

	No. of Horses	Races Run	1st	2nd	3rd	Unpl	Per cent	£1 Level Stake
2-y-o	4	17	2	2	1	12	11.8	+ 7.75
3-y-o	7	28	2	1	2	23	7.1	- 3.00
4-y-o+	10	98	7	5	9	77	7.1	- 49.50
Totals	21	143	11	8	12	112	7.7	- 44.75

BY MONTH

2-y-o	W-R	Per cent	£1 Level Stake	3-y-o	W-R	Per cent	£1 Level Stake
January	0-0	-	0.00	January	0-2	-	- 2.00
February	0-0	-	0.00	February	0-0	-	0.00
March	0-1	-	- 1.00	March	0-2	-	- 2.00
April	1-1	100.0	+ 20.00	April	0-0	-	0.00
May	0-2	-	- 2.00	May	0-8	-	- 8.00
June	0-1	-	- 1.00	June	0-2	-	- 2.00
July	0-4	-	- 4.00	July	1-2	50.0	+ 6.00
August	1-2	50.0	+ 1.75	August	0-6	-	- 6.00
September	0-2	-	- 2.00	September	1-3	33.3	+ 14.00
Oct/Nov	0-4	-	- 4.00	Oct/Nov	0-3	-	- 3.00

4-y-o+	W-R	Per cent	£1 Level Stake	Totals	W-R	Per cent	£1 Level Stake
January	0-12	-	- 12.00	January	0-14	-	- 14.00
February	0-1	-	- 1.00	February	0-1	-	- 1.00
March	0-1	-	- 1.00	March	0-4	-	- 4.00
April	1-14	7.1	- 10.50	April	2-15	13.3	+ 9.50
May	2-20	10.0	- 1.00	May	2-30	6.7	- 11.00
June	1-18	5.6	- 14.00	June	1-21	4.8	- 17.00
July	2-13	15.4	+ 2.00	July	3-19	15.8	+ 4.00
August	1-8	12.5	- 1.00	August	2-16	12.5	- 5.25
September	0-5	-	- 5.00	September	1-10	10.0	+ 7.00
Oct/Nov	0-6	-	- 6.00	Oct/Nov	0-13	-	- 13.00

DISTANCE

2-y-o	W-R	Per cent	£1 Level Stake	3-y-o	W-R	Per cent	£1 Level Stake
5f-6f	2-15	13.3	+ 9.75	5f-6f	0-6	-	- 6.00
7f-8f	0-2	-	- 2.00	7f-8f	1-8	12.5	+ 9.00
9f-13f	0-0	-	0.00	9f-13f	1-14	7.1	- 6.00
14f+	0-0	-	0.00	14f+	0-0	-	0.00

4-y-o+	W-R	Per cent	£1 Level Stake	Totals	W-R	Per cent	£1 Level Stake
5f-6f	7-67	10.4	- 18.50	5f-6f	9-88	10.2	- 14.75
7f-8f	0-21	-	- 21.00	7f-8f	1-31	3.2	- 14.00
9f-13f	0-10	-	- 10.00	9f-13f	1-24	4.2	- 16.00
14f+	0-0	-	0.00	14f+	0-0	-	0.00

TYPE OF RACE

Non-Handicaps	W-R	Per cent	£1 Level Stake	Handicaps	W-R	Per cent	£1 Level Stake
2-y-o	2-11	18.2	+ 13.75	2-y-o	0-4	-	- 4.00
3-y-o	0-14	-	- 14.00	3-y-o	2-11	18.2	+ 14.00
4-y-o+	0-16	-	- 16.00	4-y-o+	5-62	8.1	- 26.50
Selling	1-9	11.1	- 5.00	Selling	0-4	-	- 4.00
Apprentice	0-0	-	0.00	Apprentice	1-10	10.0	- 1.00
Amat/Ladies	0-0	-	0.00	Amat/Ladies	0-2	-	- 2.00
Totals	3-50	6.0	- 21.25	Totals	8-93	8.6	- 23.50

COURSE GRADE

	W-R	Per cent	£1 Level Stake
Group 1	1-23	4.3	- 15.00
Group 2	3-38	7.9	- 6.25
Group 3	3-36	8.3	- 17.50
Group 4	4-46	8.7	- 6.00

FIRST TIME OUT

	W-R	Per cent	£1 Level Stake
2-y-o	0-4	-	- 4.00
3-y-o	0-6	-	- 6.00
4-y-o+	0-9	-	- 9.00
Totals	0-19	-	- 19.00

JOCKEYS RIDING

	W-R	Per cent	£1 Level Stake		W-R	Per cent	£1 Level Stake
J Weaver	2-11	18.2	- 0.50	N Connorton	1-7	14.3	+ 1.00
W Woods	1-1	100.0	+ 9.00	S Whitworth	1-7	14.3	0.00
B Russell	1-2	50.0	+ 7.00	J Stack	1-8	12.5	- 4.00
J Fortune	1-4	25.0	+ 13.00	S Webster	1-18	5.6	+ 3.00
W Carson	1-4	25.0	+ 4.00	Dale Gibson	1-48	2.1	- 44.25

V Halliday	0-13	G Parkin	0-1	Mr M Buckley	0-1
J Fanning	0-3	J Marshall	0-1	Mr R Hale	0-1
A Garth	0-2	K Darley	0-1	N Carlisle	0-1
D Denby	0-1	K Rutter	0-1	P Bowe	0-1
D Moffatt	0-1	M Fenton	0-1	Pat Eddery	0-1
D Wright	0-1	M Tebbutt	0-1	S Copp	0-1

COURSE RECORD

	Total W-R	Non-Handicaps 2-y-o	3-y-o+	Handicaps 2-y-o	3-y-o+	Per cent	£1 Level Stake
Carlisle	2-9	0-0	0-2	0-0	2-7	22.2	+ 10.00
Thirsk	2-9	1-3	0-0	0-0	1-6	22.2	+ 19.00
Pontefract	2-10	0-0	0-0	0-0	2-10	20.0	+ 0.50
Sandown	1-1	0-0	0-0	0-0	1-1	100.0	+ 7.00
Catterick	1-6	0-0	1-3	0-0	0-3	16.7	- 2.00
Edinburgh	1-7	0-2	0-1	0-1	1-3	14.3	+ 10.00
Redcar	1-15	1-3	0-1	0-1	0-10	6.7	- 11.25
Hamilton	1-16	0-2	0-6	0-0	1-8	6.3	- 8.00

Ripon	0-14	Ayr	0-6	Goodwood	0-1
Wolverhampton (AW)	0-12	Haydock	0-5	Newmarket	0-1
Southwell (AW)	0-10	Leicester	0-2	Nottingham	0-1
Beverley	0-7	Lingfield (AW)	0-2	York	0-1
Newcastle	0-7	Doncaster	0-1		

WINNING HORSES

	Age	Races Run	1st	2nd	3rd	Unpl	Win £
Ned's Bonanza	5	18	2	1	1	14	8,092
Blue Grit	8	12	2	0	1	9	7,262
Walworth Lady	3	8	1	1	2	4	3,248
Birchwood Sun	4	14	1	2	2	9	3,132
Barbezieux	7	7	1	0	1	5	2,899
French Grit	2	4	1	1	0	2	2,888
Red Hot Risk	2	10	1	1	1	7	2,832
Dayjuz	4	16	1	2	1	12	2,364
King Chestnut	3	5	1	0	0	4	2,316

WINNING OWNERS

	Races Won	Value £		Races Won	Value £
C Michael Wilson	3	10,150	The Smith And Allan Oils		
Ned Jones	2	8,092	Racing Club	1	2,832
Vernon Spinks	1	3,248	Three Plus One Racing	1	2,364
A G Watson	1	3,132	C Graham	1	2,316
M J K Dods	1	2,899			

Favourites	2-5	40.0%	+ 2.25	Total winning prize-money			£35,032

Longest winning sequence		1	Average SP of winner			7.9/1
Longest losing sequence		44	Return on stakes invested			-31.3%

1993 Form	5-129	3.9%	- 66.00	1991 Form	3-40	7.5%	- 26.50
1992 Form	7-69	10.1%	+ 2.55	1990 Form	0-5		

T W DONNELLY (Swadlincote, Leics)

	No. of Horses	Races Run	1st	2nd	3rd	Unpl	Per cent	£1 Level Stake
2-y-o	0	0	0	0	0	0	-	0.00
3-y-o	1	3	0	0	0	3	-	- 3.00
4-y-o+	5	27	3	3	1	20	11.1	+ 11.00
Totals	6	30	3	3	1	23	10.0	+ 8.00

Jan	Feb	Mar	Apr	May	Jun	Jul	Aug	Sep	Oct/Nov
0-0	0-0	0-2	1-3	0-3	0-7	2-6	0-5	0-1	0-3

Winning Jockeys	W-R	£1 Level Stake			W-R	£1 Level Stake
S D Williams	1-4	+ 9.00	N Connorton		1-7	+ 6.00
J Lowe	1-4	+ 8.00				

Winning Courses	W-R	£1 Level Stake			W-R	£1 Level Stake
Thirsk	1-1	+ 12.00	Hamilton		1-4	+ 9.00
Leicester	1-3	+ 9.00				

Winning Horses	Age	Races Run	1st	2nd	3rd	Unpl	Win £
Tomashenko	5	9	2	2	1	4	6,853
Cavatina	4	6	1	0	0	5	3,753

Favourites	0-0			Total winning prize-money		£10,606

1993 Form	1-15	6.7%	0.00	1991 Form	0-3
1992 Form	0-6				

S DOW (Epsom, Surrey)

	No. of Horses	Races Run	1st	2nd	3rd	Unpl	Per cent	£1 Level Stake
2-y-o	13	56	4	4	4	44	7.1	- 1.00
3-y-o	12	63	4	7	3	49	6.3	- 53.37
4-y-o+	19	108	8	12	14	74	7.4	- 35.50
Totals	44	227	16	23	21	167	7.0	- 89.87

BY MONTH

2-y-o	W-R	Per cent	£1 Level Stake	3-y-o	W-R	Per cent	£1 Level Stake
January	0-0	-	0.00	January	0-0	-	0.00
February	0-0	-	0.00	February	0-0	-	0.00
March	0-0	-	0.00	March	1-3	33.3	- 1.50
April	0-3	-	- 3.00	April	0-7	-	- 7.00
May	1-10	10.0	+ 11.00	May	0-7	-	- 7.00
June	0-8	-	- 8.00	June	2-10	20.0	- 4.62
July	1-8	12.5	+ 13.00	July	0-11	-	- 11.00
August	1-10	10.0	- 3.00	August	1-11	9.1	- 8.25
September	1-12	8.3	- 6.00	September	0-8	-	- 8.00
Oct/Nov	0-5	-	- 5.00	Oct/Nov	0-6	-	- 6.00

4-y-o+	W-R	Per cent	£1 Level Stake	Totals	W-R	Per cent	£1 Level Stake
January	0-6	-	- 6.00	January	0-6	-	- 6.00
February	0-2	-	- 2.00	February	0-2	-	- 2.00
March	0-5	-	- 5.00	March	1-8	12.5	- 6.50
April	0-9	-	- 9.00	April	0-19	-	- 19.00
May	1-10	10.0	+ 16.00	May	2-27	7.4	+ 20.00
June	1-15	6.7	- 7.50	June	3-33	9.1	- 20.12
July	2-19	10.5	- 10.25	July	3-38	7.9	- 8.25
August	3-14	21.4	+ 7.25	August	5-35	14.3	- 4.00
September	0-16	-	- 16.00	September	1-36	2.8	- 30.00
Oct/Nov	1-12	8.3	- 3.00	Oct/Nov	1-23	4.3	- 14.00

DISTANCE

2-y-o	W-R	Per cent	£1 Level Stake	3-y-o	W-R	Per cent	£1 Level Stake
5f-6f	1-39	2.6	- 18.00	5f-6f	0-16	-	- 16.00
7f-8f	3-16	18.8	+ 18.00	7f-8f	0-16	-	- 16.00
9f-13f	0-1	-	- 1.00	9f-13f	4-30	13.3	- 20.37
14f+	0-0	-	0.00	14f+	0-1	-	- 1.00

4-y-o+	W-R	Per cent	£1 Level Stake	Totals	W-R	Per cent	£1 Level Stake
5f-6f	0-13	-	- 13.00	5f-6f	1-68	1.5	- 47.00
7f-8f	4-38	10.5	- 13.50	7f-8f	7-70	10.0	- 11.50
9f-13f	2-35	5.7	- 18.50	9f-13f	6-66	9.1	- 39.87
14f+	2-22	9.1	+ 9.50	14f+	2-23	8.7	+ 8.50

TYPE OF RACE

Non-Handicaps	W-R	Per cent	£1 Level Stake	Handicaps	W-R	Per cent	£1 Level Stake
2-y-o	1-41	2.4	- 20.00	2-y-o	3-11	27.3	+ 23.00
3-y-o	1-19	5.3	- 16.62	3-y-o	3-38	7.9	- 30.75
4-y-o+	1-10	10.0	- 7.25	4-y-o+	4-78	5.1	- 27.50
Selling	0-4	-	- 4.00	Selling	1-1	100.0	+ 6.50
Apprentice	1-2	50.0	+ 0.75	Apprentice	0-7	-	- 7.00
Amat/Ladies	0-4	-	- 4.00	Amat/Ladies	1-12	8.3	- 3.00
Totals	4-80	5.0	- 51.12	Totals	12-147	8.2	- 38.75

COURSE GRADE

	W-R	Per cent	£1 Level Stake
Group 1	9-90	10.0	- 2.75
Group 2	2-50	4.0	- 44.62
Group 3	0-36	-	- 36.00
Group 4	5-51	9.8	- 6.50

FIRST TIME OUT

	W-R	Per cent	£1 Level Stake
2-y-o	1-13	7.7	+ 8.00
3-y-o	1-11	9.1	- 9.50
4-y-o+	0-19	-	- 19.00
Totals	2-43	4.7	- 20.50

JOCKEYS RIDING

	W-R	Per cent	£1 Level Stake		W-R	Per cent	£1 Level Stake
M Roberts	5-28	17.9	+ 52.50	L Dettori	1-1	100.0	+ 5.00
A Whelan	3-17	17.6	+ 1.50	J Reid	1-9	11.1	- 7.50
Stephen Davies	2-21	9.5	- 11.12	Mr T Cuff	1-15	6.7	- 6.00
W Ryan	2-28	7.1	- 19.25	T Quinn	1-21	4.8	- 18.00

G Hind	0-12	M Hills	0-4	D McKeown	0-1
F Norton	0-11	R Moogan	0-3	L Carter	0-1
D Harrison	0-7	A Munro	0-2	L Piggott	0-1
P Robinson	0-6	C Rutter	0-2	M Wigham	0-1
G Carter	0-5	J D Smith	0-2	Miss Y Haynes	0-1
N Adams	0-5	J Weaver	0-2	R Hills	0-1
Paul Eddery	0-5	K Darley	0-2	S Dawson	0-1
B Thomson	0-4	A Martinez	0-1	T Ives	0-1
G Duffield	0-4	D Biggs	0-1	W R Swinburn	0-1

COURSE RECORD

	Total W-R	Non-Handicaps 2-y-o	Non-Handicaps 3-y-o+	Handicaps 2-y-o	Handicaps 3-y-o+	Per cent	£1 Level Stake
Newbury	3-12	0-3	1-1	1-1	1-7	25.0	+ 3.75
York	2-7	0-0	0-0	1-2	1-5	28.6	+ 25.00
Lingfield (AW)	2-18	0-0	0-4	0-1	2-13	11.1	- 1.50
Goodwood	2-19	0-5	1-5	1-1	0-8	10.5	+ 4.75
Brighton	2-22	0-4	1-5	0-1	1-12	9.1	- 16.62
Folkestone	2-23	1-3	0-8	0-1	1-11	8.7	- 0.50
Warwick	1-6	0-0	0-1	0-1	1-4	16.7	- 0.50
Epsom	1-10	0-1	0-0	0-0	1-9	10.0	+ 3.00
Kempton	1-14	0-3	0-2	0-1	1-8	7.1	- 11.25

121

Lingfield	0-18	Doncaster	0-5	Haydock	0-2
Windsor	0-14	Nottingham	0-5	Southwell (AW)	0-2
Leicester	0-11	Newmarket	0-4	Catterick	0-1
Salisbury	0-10	Yarmouth	0-4	Wolverhampton (AW)	0-1
Ascot	0-7	Newcastle	0-3		
Sandown	0-7	Bath	0-2		

WINNING HORSES

		Races					Win
	Age	Run	1st	2nd	3rd	Unpl	£
Menas Gold	2	8	3	0	1	4	20,875
Young Ern	4	4	1	1	1	1	16,893
I'Lleaveittoyou	4	12	2	1	2	7	10,588
Chakalak	6	15	1	1	3	10	8,155
Roisin Clover	3	10	2	2	0	6	7,841
Sir Thomas Beecham	4	8	1	1	1	5	3,883
Beautete	3	13	1	2	2	8	3,054
Villavina	4	4	1	0	0	3	3,026
Rockville Pike	2	3	1	0	0	2	3,006
Headless Heights	5	6	1	1	1	3	2,511
Bandar Perak	3	5	1	0	0	4	1,934
Hillsdown Boy	4	2	1	0	0	1	1,841

WINNING OWNERS

	Races Won	Value £		Races Won	Value £
T R Mountain	3	20,875	D G Churston	1	3,054
M F Kentish	1	16,893	Eurostrait Ltd	1	3,026
Ray Hawthorn	2	10,588	Harold Nass	1	3,006
P F Chakko	1	8,155	Littleton Racing	1	2,511
Brightelm Racing	2	7,841	P Ang	1	1,934
Mrs Heather Chakko	1	3,883	J E Mills	1	1,841

Favourites	4-12	33.3%	- 1.87	Total winning prize-money		£83,606
Longest winning sequence			2	Average SP of winner		7.7/1
Longest losing sequence			56	Return on stakes invested		-38.9%

1993 Form	21-267	7.9%	- 58.67	1991 Form	17-213	8.0%	- 31.92
1992 Form	17-205	8.3%	- 73.62	1990 Form	5-188	2.7%	-163.54

MISS J S DOYLE (East Garston, Berks)

	No. of Horses	Races Run	1st	2nd	3rd	Unpl	Per cent	£1 Level Stake
2-y-o	2	6	0	0	1	5	-	- 6.00
3-y-o	2	8	0	0	2	6	-	- 8.00
4-y-o+	2	11	1	2	1	7	9.1	+ 2.00
Totals	6	25	1	2	4	18	4.0	- 12.00

Jan	Feb	Mar	Apr	May	Jun	Jul	Aug	Sep	Oct/Nov
0-1	0-0	0-0	0-0	0-2	0-2	0-5	0-4	0-3	1-8

Winning Jockey		W-R	£1 Level Stake	Winning Course			W-R	£1 Level Stake
J Quinn		1-2	+ 11.00	Newbury			1-5	+ 8.00

Winning Horse		Age	Races Run	1st	2nd	3rd	Unpl	Win £
Fatack		5	3	1	1	0	1	5,436

Favourites	0-0			Total winning prize-money				£5,436

1993 Form	2-32	6.3%	- 20.50	1992 Form	0-5

E DUNLOP (Newmarket)

	No. of Horses	Races Run	1st	2nd	3rd	Unpl	Per cent	£1 Level Stake
2-y-o	10	12	1	0	1	10	8.3	- 8.00
3-y-o	1	1	0	0	0	1	-	- 1.00
4-y-o+	0	0	0	0	0	0	-	0.00
Totals	11	13	1	0	1	11	7.7	- 9.00

Jan	Feb	Mar	Apr	May	Jun	Jul	Aug	Sep	Oct/Nov
0-0	0-0	0-0	0-0	0-0	0-0	0-0	0-0	0-0	1-13

Winning Jockey		W-R	£1 Level Stake	Winning Course			W-R	£1 Level Stake
W Ryan		1-3	+ 1.00	Yarmouth			1-3	+ 1.00

Winning Horse		Age	Races Run	1st	2nd	3rd	Unpl	Win £
Lynton Lad		2	2	1	0	0	1	4,832

Favourites	0-2			Total winning prize-money				£4,832

J L DUNLOP (Arundel, West Sussex)

	No. of Horses	Races Run	1st	2nd	3rd	Unpl	Per cent	£1 Level Stake
2-y-o	58	176	24	34	21	97	13.6	- 64.88
3-y-o	45	228	35	29	30	134	15.4	- 48.72
4-y-o+	20	99	23	13	6	57	23.2	+ 35.06
Totals	123	503	82	76	57	288	16.3	- 78.54

Dunlop J L

BY MONTH

2-y-o	W-R	Per cent	£1 Level Stake	3-y-o	W-R	Per cent	£1 Level Stake
Mar/Apr	0-0	-	0.00	Mar/Apr	8-46	17.4	- 14.04
May	3-12	25.0	+ 0.12	May	7-40	17.5	- 1.06
June	0-15	-	- 15.00	June	7-41	17.1	- 15.61
July	4-22	18.2	- 2.62	July	4-32	12.5	- 5.67
August	3-35	8.6	- 23.02	August	2-19	10.5	- 12.50
September	6-45	13.3	- 19.90	September	6-29	20.7	+ 11.25
Oct/Nov	8-47	17.0	- 4.46	Oct/Nov	1-21	4.8	- 12.00

4-y-o+	W-R	Per cent	£1 Level Stake	Totals	W-R	Per cent	£1 Level Stake
Mar/Apr	4-23	17.4	- 3.95	Mar/Apr	12-69	17.4	- 17.99
May	4-14	28.6	+ 5.88	May	14-66	21.2	+ 4.94
June	3-13	23.1	+ 3.63	June	10-69	14.5	- 26.98
July	3-16	18.8	- 0.50	July	11-70	15.7	- 8.79
August	3-13	23.1	+ 9.50	August	8-67	11.9	- 26.02
September	3-12	25.0	+ 9.50	September	15-86	17.4	+ 0.85
Oct/Nov	3-8	37.5	+ 12.00	Oct/Nov	12-76	15.8	- 4.46

DISTANCE

2-y-o	W-R	Per cent	£1 Level Stake	3-y-o	W-R	Per cent	£1 Level Stake
5f-6f	10-52	19.2	- 7.23	5f-6f	1-8	12.5	+ 3.00
7f-8f	13-120	10.8	- 56.40	7f-8f	14-81	17.3	+ 5.33
9f-13f	1-4	25.0	- 1.25	9f-13f	18-115	15.7	- 38.90
14f+	0-0	-	0.00	14f+	2-24	8.3	- 18.15

4-y-o+	W-R	Per cent	£1 Level Stake	Totals	W-R	Per cent	£1 Level Stake
5f-6f	1-6	16.7	+ 0.50	5f-6f	12-66	18.2	- 3.73
7f-8f	5-21	23.8	+ 9.67	7f-8f	32-222	14.4	- 41.40
9f-13f	10-43	23.3	+ 15.00	9f-13f	29-162	17.9	- 25.15
14f+	7-29	24.1	+ 9.89	14f+	9-53	17.0	- 8.26

TYPE OF RACE

Non-Handicaps	W-R	Per cent	£1 Level Stake	Handicaps	W-R	Per cent	£1 Level Stake
2-y-o	20-154	13.0	- 60.98	2-y-o	3-21	14.3	- 8.90
3-y-o	19-110	17.3	- 24.48	3-y-o	16-115	13.9	- 21.24
4-y-o+	10-33	30.3	+ 16.93	4-y-o+	14-67	20.9	+ 23.13
Selling	0-0	-	0.00	Selling	0-0	-	0.00
Apprentice	0-0	-	0.00	Apprentice	0-0	-	0.00
Amat/Ladies	0-0	-	0.00	Amat/Ladies	0-3	-	- 3.00
Totals	49-297	16.5	- 68.53	Totals	33-206	16.0	- 10.01

COURSE GRADE

	W-R	Per cent	£1 Level Stake
Group 1	46-325	14.2	- 60.82
Group 2	12-75	16.0	- 17.09
Group 3	20-88	22.7	+ 3.11
Group 4	4-15	26.7	- 3.74

FIRST TIME OUT

	W-R	Per cent	£1 Level Stake
2-y-o	5-58	8.6	- 36.25
3-y-o	7-44	15.9	- 13.04
4-y-o+	5-20	25.0	+ 8.05
Totals	17-122	13.9	- 41.24

JOCKEYS RIDING

	W-R	Per cent	£1 Level Stake		W-R	Per cent	£1 Level Stake
W Carson	34-188	18.1	- 27.34	B Thomson	3-15	20.0	- 3.74
Pat Eddery	13-42	31.0	+ 35.88	M Birch	2-3	66.7	+ 10.00
T Quinn	5-29	17.2	+ 11.50	J Weaver	2-7	28.6	+ 3.25
M Roberts	4-7	57.1	+ 24.10	K Fallon	1-2	50.0	+ 3.50
G Duffield	4-11	36.4	+ 2.41	R Hughes	1-6	16.7	- 1.00
J Reid	4-11	36.4	+ 1.48	K Darley	1-13	7.7	- 10.25
L Dettori	4-14	28.6	+ 10.00	G Carter	1-20	5.0	- 15.50
W Ryan	3-14	21.4	- 1.83				

S Whitworth	0-25	M J Kinane	0-4	G Hind	0-1
R Hills	0-22	P Robinson	0-4	J Carroll	0-1
L Piggott	0-10	A McGlone	0-3	J Fortune	0-1
Paul Eddery	0-8	R Cochrane	0-3	J Lowe	0-1
T Williams	0-7	M Hills	0-2	Mr T Cuff	0-1
W Newnes	0-7	Miss E Houghton	0-2	N Adams	0-1
B Raymond	0-5	B Rouse	0-1	Robin Gray	0-1
A Munro	0-4	C Asmussen	0-1	T Ives	0-1
J Quinn	0-4	G Bardwell	0-1		

COURSE RECORD

	Total W-R	Non-Handicaps 2-y-o	3-y-o+	Handicaps 2-y-o	3-y-o+	Per cent	£1 Level Stake
Goodwood	7-33	1-8	4-10	0-3	2-12	21.2	- 3.44
Leicester	6-25	1-15	1-3	0-1	4-6	24.0	+ 11.41
Haydock	6-26	2-4	2-6	1-1	1-15	23.1	+ 2.20
Sandown	6-31	2-6	2-9	0-0	2-16	19.4	- 1.74
Ascot	6-33	2-4	1-13	0-0	3-16	18.2	+ 13.00
Newmarket	5-68	1-26	3-23	0-4	1-15	7.4	- 30.17
Thirsk	4-11	1-3	2-6	0-0	1-2	36.4	+ 5.91
Nottingham	4-21	1-8	2-7	0-0	1-6	19.0	- 4.73
Kempton	4-25	0-8	1-8	0-0	3-9	16.0	+ 5.50
York	4-27	2-5	2-10	0-2	0-10	14.8	- 10.00
Newbury	4-36	0-14	3-12	0-1	1-9	11.1	- 18.17
Bath	3-6	0-1	1-1	0-0	2-4	50.0	+ 5.26
Windsor	3-7	0-2	1-2	0-0	2-3	42.9	+ 7.00
Warwick	3-9	0-3	1-1	1-2	1-3	33.3	- 0.49
Doncaster	3-23	1-7	0-6	1-3	1-7	13.0	+ 0.50
Salisbury	3-23	1-9	0-4	0-0	2-10	13.0	- 10.25
Beverley	2-8	0-3	0-2	0-1	2-2	25.0	+ 1.00

Dunlop J L

Pontefract	2-8	1-2	1-1	0-0	0-5	25.0	-	3.83
Brighton	2-11	1-2	0-2	0-0	1-7	18.2	-	0.50
Chester	1-3	0-0	1-2	0-0	0-1	33.3	+	0.75
Folkestone	1-4	1-2	0-1	0-0	0-1	25.0	-	1.25
Redcar	1-6	1-2	0-1	0-0	0-3	16.7	+	0.50
Ripon	1-8	1-2	0-1	0-0	0-5	12.5	-	0.50
Epsom	1-9	0-2	1-4	0-0	0-3	11.1	-	4.50

Lingfield	0-13	Newcastle	0-9	Catterick	0-2
Chepstow	0-11	Ayr	0-5	Yarmouth	0-2

WINNING HORSES

		Races				Win
	Age	Run	1st	2nd	3rd	Unpl	£
Erhaab	3	5	2	1	1	1	546,964
Aqaarid	2	2	2	0	0	0	105,405
Lavinia Fontana	5	3	1	1	0	1	72,465
Mehthaaf	3	6	2	0	1	3	59,303
My Patriarch	4	6	2	1	0	3	38,948
Bulaxie	3	4	2	0	0	2	37,750
Duke Of Eurolink	5	6	2	0	1	3	35,446
Sovinista	3	2	2	0	0	0	27,196
Luhuk	3	8	2	1	1	4	26,564
Scribe	4	2	1	0	0	1	20,400
West Buoyant	3	10	1	1	0	8	19,900
Harlestone Brook	4	8	3	2	0	3	18,453
Subya	2	7	3	2	0	2	16,215
Dawning Street	6	1	1	0	0	0	15,535
Ultimo Imperatore	3	3	1	1	0	1	13,825
Chimanimani	3	7	4	1	0	2	13,207
Eurolink Thunder	4	4	1	0	1	2	12,575
Sun Grebe	4	10	1	2	0	7	11,745
Son Of Sharp Shot	4	11	3	0	1	7	11,388
Bird Of Time	3	11	3	2	2	4	11,284
Dumaani	3	7	1	0	2	4	10,698
Ihtiram	2	7	2	1	1	3	10,353
Swallows Dream	3	6	2	2	0	2	10,205
Beauchamp Hero	4	12	1	1	1	9	9,935
Indian Light	2	3	2	1	0	0	9,145
Special Dawn	4	4	2	0	0	2	8,861
Karayib	2	7	2	3	1	1	8,217
Nwaamis	2	1	1	0	0	0	7,227
Star Tulip	2	9	2	3	2	2	6,931
Sawlajan	3	5	1	0	1	3	6,860
Khamaseen	3	4	1	1	0	2	5,360
Blackpatch Hill	5	5	1	1	1	2	4,836
Jawlaat	2	3	1	1	0	1	4,761
Visto Si Stampi	4	1	1	0	0	0	4,674
Beauchamp Jazz	2	7	1	3	1	2	4,548
Taipan	2	2	1	0	0	1	4,545
Cazzuto	3	8	1	0	1	6	4,468
Khattat	4	6	1	2	1	2	4,403

Llia	2	2	1	0	0	1	4,322
Kassab	4	3	1	1	0	1	4,271
He's A King	4	6	1	0	0	5	4,110
Noblissima	3	7	1	1	1	4	3,917
Scotsky	2	2	1	0	0	1	3,875
Bahri	2	4	1	3	0	0	3,822
Eurolink Chieftain	3	5	1	0	0	4	3,807
Be Exciting	3	7	1	0	3	3	3,753
Achares	3	6	1	1	0	4	3,692
Emerging Market	2	3	1	1	0	1	3,692
Brave Patriarch	3	4	1	0	2	1	3,688
Madurai	3	7	1	1	2	3	3,652
Muntafi	3	6	1	1	0	4	3,611
Muwafik	3	2	1	1	0	0	3,348
Iron Gent	3	5	1	1	0	3	3,290
Zuboon	3	8	1	2	3	2	3,231
Evezio Rufo	2	1	1	0	0	0	3,163
Warning Order	2	4	1	1	1	1	2,902
First Bite	2	4	1	0	0	3	2,826

WINNING OWNERS

	Races Won	Value £		Races Won	Value £
Hamdan Al-Maktoum	22	809,037	Sir Thomas Pilkington	1	11,745
Cyril Humphris	1	72,465	N C Clark	3	11,284
Eurolink Group Plc	4	51,827	Nicholas Jones	2	6,931
Windflower O'seas Holdings Inc	8	45,989	J Macdonald-Buchanan	1	4,322
J L Dunlop	10	44,615	Lady Swaythling	1	4,110
Peter S Winfield	3	42,636	Peter Wragg	1	3,875
Hesmonds Stud	2	37,750	Stonethorn Stud Farms Ltd	1	3,753
I H Stewart-Brown	2	27,196	Philip Wroughton	1	3,692
Mrs E M H Ogden White	2	24,317	Cuadra Africa	1	3,692
Prince A A Faisal	4	21,575	Angelo Macchi	1	3,290
S Khaled	1	19,900	G Mazza	1	3,163
Gerecon Italia	2	18,499	Ian Cameron	1	2,902
E Penser	2	14,483	Ettore Landi	1	2,826
Lord Swaythling	3	13,690			

Favourites	38-101	37.6%	+ 16.80		Total winning prize-money			£1,309,562
Longest winning sequence			3		Average SP of winner			4.2/1
Longest losing sequence			29		Return on stakes invested			-15.6%
1993 Form	93-536	17.4%	- 17.79		1991 Form	58-366	15.8%	- 64.77
1992 Form	75-505	14.9%	-167.24		1990 Form	78-444	17.6%	- 50.88

T DYER (Invergowrie, Dundee)

	No. of Horses	Races Run	1st	2nd	3rd	Unpl	Per cent	£1 Level Stake
2-y-o	4	8	0	0	0	8	-	- 8.00
3-y-o	1	3	0	1	1	1	-	- 3.00
4-y-o+	6	31	1	2	6	22	3.2	- 23.00
Totals	11	42	1	3	7	31	2.4	- 34.00

Jan	Feb	Mar	Apr	May	Jun	Jul	Aug	Sep	Oct/Nov
0-0	0-0	0-5	0-6	1-6	0-3	0-7	0-5	0-5	0-5

Winning Jockey	W-R	£1 Level Stake	Winning Course	W-R	£1 Level Stake
Stephen Davies	1-10	- 2.00	Doncaster	1-6	+ 2.00

Winning Horse	Age	Races Run	1st	2nd	3rd	Unpl	Win £
Tawafij	5	12	1	1	2	8	14,068

Favourites	0-4	Total winning prize-money	£14,068

1993 Form	2-11	18.2%	- 1.75

M H EASTERBY (Malton, North Yorks)

	No. of Horses	Races Run	1st	2nd	3rd	Unpl	Per cent	£1 Level Stake
2-y-o	26	162	10	12	14	126	6.2	- 102.13
3-y-o	22	143	11	12	19	101	7.7	- 66.74
4-y-o+	12	87	10	6	4	67	11.5	- 10.00
Totals	60	392	31	30	37	294	7.9	- 178.87

BY MONTH

2-y-o	W-R	Per cent	£1 Level Stake	3-y-o	W-R	Per cent	£1 Level Stake
Mar/Apr	0-11	-	- 10.00	Mar/Apr	0-19	-	- 16.00
May	3-17	17.6	- 1.00	May	2-35	5.7	- 9.00
June	0-26	-	- 26.00	June	3-25	12.0	- 8.12
July	2-38	5.3	- 26.50	July	3-27	11.1	- 15.37
August	2-30	6.7	- 19.75	August	3-27	11.1	- 5.25
September	0-29	-	- 29.00	September	0-9	-	- 9.00
Oct/Nov	3-11	27.3	+ 11.12	Oct/Nov	0-1	-	- 1.00

4-y-o+	W-R	Per cent	£1 Level Stake	Totals	W-R	Per cent	£1 Level Stake
Mar/Apr	0-13	-	- 11.00	Mar/Apr	0-43	-	- 37.00
May	4-14	28.6	+ 8.00	May	9-66	13.6	- 2.00
June	0-15	-	- 15.00	June	3-66	4.5	- 49.12
July	3-13	23.1	+ 11.00	July	8-78	10.3	- 30.87
August	2-9	22.2	+ 16.00	August	7-66	10.6	- 9.00
September	0-14	-	- 14.00	September	0-52	-	- 52.00
Oct/Nov	1-9	11.1	- 3.00	Oct/Nov	4-21	19.0	+ 7.12

DISTANCE

2-y-o	W-R	Per cent	£1 Level Stake	3-y-o	W-R	Per cent	£1 Level Stake
5f-6f	8-107	7.5	- 58.63	5f-6f	3-32	9.4	+ 0.50
7f-8f	2-53	3.8	- 41.50	7f-8f	3-63	4.8	- 49.12
9f-13f	0-2	-	- 2.00	9f-13f	5-44	11.4	- 14.12
14f+	0-0	-	0.00	14f+	0-4	-	- 4.00

4-y-o+	W-R	Per cent	£1 Level Stake	Totals	W-R	Per cent	£1 Level Stake
5f-6f	1-20	5.0	- 14.00	5f-6f	12-159	7.5	- 72.13
7f-8f	7-46	15.2	+ 14.00	7f-8f	12-162	7.4	- 76.62
9f-13f	1-14	7.1	- 8.00	9f-13f	6-60	10.0	- 24.12
14f+	1-7	14.3	- 2.00	14f+	1-11	9.1	- 6.00

TYPE OF RACE

Non-Handicaps	W-R	Per cent	£1 Level Stake	Handicaps	W-R	Per cent	£1 Level Stake
2-y-o	4-100	4.0	- 85.38	2-y-o	2-34	5.9	- 10.00
3-y-o	2-41	4.9	- 36.24	3-y-o	8-84	9.5	- 16.25
4-y-o+	0-7	-	- 7.00	4-y-o+	10-76	13.2	+ 1.00
Selling	4-31	12.9	- 9.75	Selling	1-9	11.1	- 5.25
Apprentice	0-0	-	0.00	Apprentice	0-6	-	- 6.00
Amat/Ladies	0-0	-	0.00	Amat/Ladies	0-4	-	- 4.00
Totals	10-179	5.6	-138.37	Totals	21-213	9.9	- 40.50

COURSE GRADE

	W-R	Per cent	£1 Level Stake
Group 1	12-119	10.1	- 47.50
Group 2	5-109	4.6	- 50.75
Group 3	8-88	9.1	- 47.00
Group 4	6-76	7.9	- 33.62

FIRST TIME OUT

	W-R	Per cent	£1 Level Stake
2-y-o	0-26	-	- 26.00
3-y-o	0-22	-	- 22.00
4-y-o+	0-12	-	- 12.00
Totals	0-60	-	- 60.00

JOCKEYS RIDING

	W-R	Per cent	£1 Level Stake		W-R	Per cent	£1 Level Stake
M Birch	15-176	8.5	- 79.00	K Darley	2-17	11.8	- 3.00
S Maloney	10-126	7.9	- 61.75	L Charnock	2-18	11.1	+ 11.00
J Stack	2-7	28.6	+ 1.88				

Dale Gibson	0-5	J Carroll	0-1	Mr S Swiers	0-1	
J Fanning	0-5	J Tate	0-1	Mrs A Farrell	0-1	
K Fallon	0-5	J Williams	0-1	N Connorton	0-1	
N Carlisle	0-5	M Fenton	0-1	Pat Eddery	0-1	
J Lowe	0-4	M Hills	0-1	S Copp	0-1	
J Quinn	0-3	M J Dwyer	0-1	S Lanigan	0-1	
G Hind	0-2	Mark Brown	0-1	T Lucas	0-1	
W Carson	0-2	Miss A Deniel	0-1			
D Moffatt	0-1	Mr D Parker	0-1			

COURSE RECORD

	Total W-R	Non-Handicaps 2-y-o	3-y-o+	Handicaps 2-y-o	3-y-o+	Per cent	£1 Level Stake
Beverley	7-44	1-11	0-9	0-5	6-19	15.9	- 5.75
Haydock	4-21	1-5	0-3	1-2	2-11	19.0	0.00
Newcastle	4-31	2-11	0-1	0-2	2-17	12.9	- 2.38
Ayr	3-18	0-3	1-1	0-3	2-11	16.7	- 2.62
Ripon	3-31	1-12	0-3	0-0	2-16	9.7	- 3.75
Carlisle	2-16	1-7	1-5	0-0	0-4	12.5	- 10.12
Catterick	2-36	0-12	0-7	1-5	1-12	5.6	- 11.00
Edinburgh	1-3	1-2	0-1	0-0	0-0	33.3	+ 0.50
Chester	1-6	0-1	0-0	0-1	1-4	16.7	+ 4.00
Southwell (AW)	1-17	1-9	0-3	0-1	0-4	5.9	- 9.00
Doncaster	1-25	0-6	0-3	0-4	1-12	4.0	- 18.50
Pontefract	1-25	0-8	0-3	0-4	1-10	4.0	- 22.25
Redcar	1-44	0-14	0-8	0-3	1-19	2.3	- 23.00

Thirsk	0-28	Leicester	0-3	Warwick	0-1
York	0-22	Wolverhampton (AW)	0-3	Yarmouth	0-1
Hamilton	0-8	Ascot	0-1		
Nottingham	0-7	Newmarket	0-1		

WINNING HORSES

	Age	Races Run	1st	2nd	3rd	Unpl	Win £
Sinners Reprieve	3	14	3	2	0	9	12,326
Forever Diamonds	7	6	2	0	0	4	11,533
Harpoon Louie	4	7	2	0	0	5	11,344
Cumbrian Rhapsody	4	14	2	1	1	10	9,545
Bold Angel	7	5	1	1	0	3	9,072
Golden Hello	3	7	2	0	1	4	6,285
Beneficiary	3	13	2	1	1	9	5,656
Cumbrian Waltzer	9	11	1	0	0	10	5,175
High Ranking	2	9	2	0	0	7	5,173

Winning Line	3	7	1	1	1	4	4,143
Euro Rebel	2	5	1	0	0	4	4,045
Northern Chief	4	13	1	0	0	12	3,850
Sandmoor Chambray	3	7	1	1	2	3	3,818
Thornton Gate	5	12	1	0	1	10	3,583
Super Park	2	5	1	0	1	3	3,453
Cumbrian Minstrel	2	8	1	1	1	5	3,140
Dominelle	2	10	1	1	0	8	3,136
Casual Water	3	8	1	0	0	7	2,976
Domybly	2	7	1	0	1	5	2,870
Carapelle	3	10	1	0	2	7	2,798
Instantaneous	2	4	1	0	0	3	2,782
Pocket Edition	2	11	1	2	1	7	2,724
Persistent	2	7	1	1	0	5	2,554

WINNING OWNERS

	Races Won	Value £		Races Won	Value £
Cumbrian Industrials Ltd	4	17,859	C H Stevens	1	4,045
Mrs J B Mountifield	3	12,326	R Tindall	1	3,850
Mrs J B Russell	2	11,533	Sandmoor Textiles Co Ltd	1	3,818
P D Savill	2	11,344	T H Bennett	1	3,583
A M Wragg	1	9,072	A D Bottomley	1	3,453
Reg Griffin	3	8,438	Mrs Sue Tindall	1	3,136
G E Shouler	2	6,285	G H Leatham	1	2,976
White Rose Racing	2	5,668	Mrs Anne Henson	1	2,724
Mrs Jennifer E Pallister	2	5,173	John M Pinder	1	2,554
Peter Hurst	1	4,143			

Favourites	7-35	20.0%	- 11.88	Total winning prize-money	£121,977
Longest winning sequence			2	Average SP of winner	5.9/1
Longest losing sequence			69	Return on stakes invested	-45.6%
1993 Form	43-399	10.8%	-134.42	1991 Form	58-531	10.9%	-187.51
1992 Form	38-386	9.8%	-144.69	1990 Form	61-562	10.9%	-230.30

M W EASTERBY (Sherriff Hutton, North Yorks)

	No. of Horses	Races Run	1st	2nd	3rd	Unpl	Per cent	£1 Level Stake
2-y-o	24	124	2	6	7	109	1.6	- 95.12
3-y-o	12	56	2	3	2	49	3.6	- 47.37
4-y-o+	11	54	4	3	2	45	7.4	- 26.37
Totals	47	234	8	12	11	203	3.4	-168.86

Jan	Feb	Mar	Apr	May	Jun	Jul	Aug	Sep	Oct/Nov
0-0	2-3	0-4	1-32	1-38	3-36	0-33	1-27	0-29	0-32

Winning Jockeys	W–R	£1 Level Stake		W–R	£1 Level Stake
K Darley	2–17	- 6.00	S Maloney	1–8	+ 2.00
T Lucas	2–78	- 72.49	C Munday	1–34	- 24.00
L Dettori	1–4	- 1.37	L Charnock	1–43	- 17.00

Winning Courses					
Southwell (AW)	2–26	- 18.37	Catterick	1–16	- 13.37
Sandown	1–2	+ 4.00	Ripon	1–24	- 14.00
Edinburgh	1–4	+ 22.00	Thirsk	1–29	- 26.12
Leicester	1–5	+ 5.00			

Winning Horses	Age	Races Run	1st	2nd	3rd	Unpl	Win £
Hasta La Vista	4	13	2	1	2	8	7,032
Pete Afrique	3	6	1	0	0	5	5,999
Penny Hasset	6	8	1	2	0	5	3,444
Tolls Choice	5	9	1	0	0	8	3,288
Maid O'Cannie	3	11	1	3	2	5	2,847
Able Sheriff	2	7	1	1	0	5	2,734
Stuffed	2	7	1	0	0	6	2,406

Favourites	3–14	21.4%	- 5.86	Total winning prize-money		£27,751

1993 Form	16–209	7.7%	- 98.95	1991 Form	14–258	5.4%	-182.09
1992 Form	12–150	8.0%	- 45.50	1990 Form	25–286	8.7%	- 94.71

G H EDEN (Newmarket)

	No. of Horses	Races Run	1st	2nd	3rd	Unpl	Per cent	£1 Level Stake
2-y-o	3	4	1	0	0	3	25.0	+ 5.00
3-y-o	3	24	2	4	2	16	8.3	+ 2.00
4-y-o+	5	35	0	4	2	29	-	- 35.00
Totals	11	63	3	8	4	48	4.8	- 28.00

Jan	Feb	Mar	Apr	May	Jun	Jul	Aug	Sep	Oct/Nov
1-7	0-7	0-4	0-4	1-8	1-11	0-4	0-5	0-4	0-9

Winning Jockeys	W–R	£1 Level Stake		W–R	£1 Level Stake
Stephen Davies	2–11	+ 7.00	J Weaver	1–5	+ 12.00

Winning Courses					
Catterick	1–1	+ 8.00	Lingfield (AW)	1–17	0.00
Yarmouth	1–4	+ 5.00			

Winning Horses	Age	Races Run	1st	2nd	3rd	Unpl	Win £
It Must Be Millie	3	9	2	1	0	6	6,037
Bobanlyn	2	1	1	0	0	0	2,364

Favourites	0-2		Total winning prize-money	£8,401

1993 Form	2-70	2.9%	- 64.42	1991 Form	4-70	5.7%	- 10.75
1992 Form	5-68	7.4%	- 42.00	1990 Form	2-78	2.6%	- 65.50

C R EGERTON (Chaddleworth, Berks)

	No. of Horses	Races Run	1st	2nd	3rd	Unpl	Per cent	£1 Level Stake
2-y-o	5	14	2	2	1	9	14.3	+ 17.00
3-y-o	5	15	0	1	3	11	-	- 15.00
4-y-o+	5	14	2	1	3	8	14.3	+ 2.25
Totals	15	43	4	4	7	28	9.3	+ 4.25

Jan	Feb	Mar	Apr	May	Jun	Jul	Aug	Sep	Oct/Nov
0-0	0-0	0-0	0-6	1-7	1-10	0-7	1-4	0-6	1-3

Winning Jockeys	W-R	£1 Level Stake		W-R	£1 Level Stake
A Procter	2-7	+ 9.25	M Roberts	1-2	+ 19.00
B Raymond	1-1	+ 9.00			

Winning Courses					
Brighton	1-1	+ 2.25	Ripon	1-1	+ 9.00
Leicester	1-1	+ 12.00	Yarmouth	1-1	+ 20.00

Winning Horses	Age	Races Run	1st	2nd	3rd	Unpl	Win £
Don't Forsake Me	5	7	2	0	3	2	5,105
Elite Hope	2	4	1	1	0	2	5,004
Star Of Gold	2	4	1	1	0	2	4,295

Favourites	0-2		Total winning prize-money	£14,404

1993 Form	1-12	8.3%	- 8.50

B ELLISON (Consett, Co Durham)

	No. of Horses	Races Run	1st	2nd	3rd	Unpl	Per cent	£1 Level Stake
2-y-o	2	6	0	0	0	6	-	- 6.00
3-y-o	1	6	0	0	0	6	-	- 6.00
4-y-o+	6	28	1	1	2	24	3.6	- 7.00
Totals	9	40	1	1	2	36	2.5	- 19.00

Ellison B

Jan	Feb	Mar	Apr	May	Jun	Jul	Aug	Sep	Oct/Nov
0-0	0-0	0-3	0-7	1-10	0-6	0-13	0-0	0-1	0-0

Winning Jockey	W-R	£1 Level Stake	Winning Course	W-R	£1 Level Stake
J Stack	1-11	+ 10.00	Pontefract	1-8	+ 13.00

Winning Horse	Age	Races Run	1st	2nd	3rd	Unpl	Win £
Muswell Brook	4	6	1	0	1	4	2,740

Favourites	0-0			Total winning prize-money		£2,740

1993 Form	1-56	1.8%	- 47.50	1991 Form	3-51	5.9%	- 1.50
1992 Form	4-87	4.6%	- 60.50	1990 Form	0-6		

C C ELSEY (Lambourn, Berks)

	No. of Horses	Races Run	1st	2nd	3rd	Unpl	Per cent	£1 Level Stake
2-y-o	4	9	0	0	0	9	–	- 9.00
3-y-o	5	48	2	5	6	35	4.2	- 15.50
4-y-o+	5	31	3	1	1	26	9.7	- 5.75
Totals	14	88	5	6	7	70	5.7	- 30.25

Jan	Feb	Mar	Apr	May	Jun	Jul	Aug	Sep	Oct/Nov
1-11	1-10	1-8	0-8	1-13	0-10	0-6	1-6	0-10	0-6

Winning Jockeys	W-R	£1 Level Stake		W-R	£1 Level Stake
M Tebbutt	1-1	+ 0.25	W Newnes	1-10	- 7.00
C Rutter	1-7	+ 19.00	J Quinn	1-13	- 6.50
Miss A Elsey	1-8	+ 13.00			

Winning Courses					
Lingfield (AW)	2-22	- 17.75	Chepstow	1-5	+ 16.00
Windsor	1-3	+ 23.00	Southwell (AW)	1-11	- 4.50

Winning Horses	Age	Races Run	1st	2nd	3rd	Unpl	Win £
Rapporteur	8	4	2	0	0	2	6,411
Evanro	3	12	1	1	1	9	4,078
Queens Stroller	3	14	1	3	2	8	3,558
Kissavos	8	16	1	1	0	14	2,745

Favourites	1-4	25.0%	- 2.75	Total winning prize-money		£16,791

1993 Form	14-136	10.3%	- 16.17	1991 Form	7-121	5.8%	- 70.00
1992 Form	9-110	8.2%	- 63.19	1990 Form	8-98	8.2%	- 36.27

C W C ELSEY (Malton, North Yorks)

	No. of Horses	Races Run	1st	2nd	3rd	Unpl	Per cent	£1 Level Stake
2-y-o	3	16	0	1	1	14	-	- 16.00
3-y-o	5	38	1	2	6	29	2.6	- 35.00
4-y-o+	4	24	4	2	4	14	16.7	+ 21.30
Totals	12	78	5	5	11	57	6.4	- 29.70

Jan	Feb	Mar	Apr	May	Jun	Jul	Aug	Sep	Oct/Nov
0-0	0-0	0-1	1-10	1-4	0-6	2-17	1-16	0-11	0-13

Winning Jockeys	W-R	£1 Level Stake				W-R	£1 Level Stake
Miss A Elsey	2-4	+ 4.30		G Hind		1-3	0.00
K Darley	1-3	0.00		N Kennedy		1-24	+ 10.00

Winning Courses							
Edinburgh	2-7	+ 30.00		Newbury		1-4	- 1.00
Ayr	1-4	- 1.20		Catterick		1-6	- 0.50

Winning Horses	Age	Races Run	1st	2nd	3rd	Unpl	Win £
Philgun	5	16	3	1	3	9	10,122
Linpac West	8	5	1	1	1	2	4,590
Bustle'Em	3	5	1	0	1	3	1,704

Favourites	3-3	100.0%	+ 5.80	Total winning prize-money			£16,415

1993 Form	4-95	4.2%	- 25.00	1991 Form	4-88	4.5%	- 61.00
1992 Form	9-100	9.0%	- 25.57	1990 Form	9-140	6.4%	- 77.04

D R C ELSWORTH (Whitsbury, Hants)

	No. of Horses	Races Run	1st	2nd	3rd	Unpl	Per cent	£1 Level Stake
2-y-o	9	36	1	3	5	27	2.8	- 32.25
3-y-o	20	117	6	9	13	89	5.1	- 87.99
4-y-o+	19	79	7	9	7	56	8.9	- 15.75
Totals	48	232	14	21	25	172	6.0	-135.99

Elsworth D R C

BY MONTH

2-y-o	W-R	Per cent	£1 Level Stake	3-y-o	W-R	Per cent	£1 Level Stake
January	0-0	-	0.00	January	0-0	-	0.00
February	0-0	-	0.00	February	0-0	-	0.00
March	0-0	-	0.00	March	0-0	-	0.00
April	0-1	-	- 1.00	April	0-12	-	- 12.00
May	0-6	-	- 6.00	May	1-25	4.0	- 12.00
June	0-5	-	- 5.00	June	0-18	-	- 18.00
July	1-8	12.5	- 4.25	July	4-21	19.0	- 7.99
August	0-3	-	- 3.00	August	1-14	7.1	- 11.00
September	0-6	-	- 6.00	September	0-16	-	- 16.00
Oct/Nov	0-7	-	- 7.00	Oct/Nov	0-11	-	- 11.00

4-y-o+	W-R	Per cent	£1 Level Stake	Totals	W-R	Per cent	£1 Level Stake
January	0-1	-	- 1.00	January	0-1	-	- 1.00
February	0-0	-	0.00	February	0-0	-	0.00
March	0-2	-	- 2.00	March	0-2	-	- 2.00
April	0-10	-	- 10.00	April	0-23	-	- 23.00
May	2-13	15.4	+ 8.50	May	3-44	6.8	- 9.50
June	1-12	8.3	- 4.00	June	1-35	2.9	- 27.00
July	2-11	18.2	+ 4.25	July	7-40	17.5	- 7.99
August	0-8	-	- 8.00	August	1-25	4.0	- 22.00
September	2-15	13.3	+ 3.50	September	2-37	5.4	- 18.50
Oct/Nov	0-7	-	- 7.00	Oct/Nov	0-25	-	- 25.00

DISTANCE

2-y-o	W-R	Per cent	£1 Level Stake	3-y-o	W-R	Per cent	£1 Level Stake
5f-6f	0-18	-	- 18.00	5f-6f	1-31	3.2	- 27.50
7f-8f	1-18	5.6	- 14.25	7f-8f	2-42	4.8	- 26.12
9f-13f	0-0	-	0.00	9f-13f	3-43	7.0	- 33.37
14f+	0-0	-	0.00	14f+	0-1	-	- 1.00

4-y-o+	W-R	Per cent	£1 Level Stake	Totals	W-R	Per cent	£1 Level Stake
5f-6f	0-6	-	- 6.00	5f-6f	1-55	1.8	- 51.50
7f-8f	0-13	-	- 13.00	7f-8f	3-73	4.1	- 53.37
9f-13f	4-38	10.5	+ 2.25	9f-13f	7-81	8.6	- 31.12
14f+	3-22	13.6	+ 1.00	14f+	3-23	13.0	0.00

TYPE OF RACE

Non-Handicaps	W-R	Per cent	£1 Level Stake	Handicaps	W-R	Per cent	£1 Level Stake
2-y-o	0-30	-	- 30.00	2-y-o	0-5	-	- 5.00
3-y-o	6-79	7.6	- 49.99	3-y-o	0-36	-	- 36.00
4-y-o+	1-17	5.9	- 13.50	4-y-o+	6-55	10.9	+ 4.75
Selling	1-1	100.0	+ 2.75	Selling	0-0	-	0.00
Apprentice	0-1	-	- 1.00	Apprentice	0-6	-	- 6.00
Amat/Ladies	0-0	-	0.00	Amat/Ladies	0-2	-	- 2.00
Totals	8-128	6.3	- 91.74	Totals	6-104	5.8	- 44.25

COURSE GRADE

	W-R	Per cent	£1 Level Stake
Group 1	8-154	5.2	-104.99
Group 2	3-39	7.7	- 24.00
Group 3	3-25	12.0	+ 7.00
Group 4	0-14	-	- 14.00

FIRST TIME OUT

	W-R	Per cent	£1 Level Stake
2-y-o	0-9	-	- 9.00
3-y-o	0-20	-	- 20.00
4-y-o+	0-18	-	- 18.00
Totals	0-47	-	- 47.00

JOCKEYS RIDING

	W-R	Per cent	£1 Level Stake		W-R	Per cent	£1 Level Stake
M Roberts	5-31	16.1	- 9.99	W Newnes	2-28	7.1	- 7.50
J Williams	3-51	5.9	- 19.50	L Dettori	1-5	20.0	- 1.25
T Quinn	2-16	12.5	- 0.75	B Doyle	1-32	3.1	- 28.00

R Cochrane	0-15	P Robinson	0-2	M Birch	0-1
D Harrison	0-10	R Hughes	0-2	M Fenton	0-1
B Rouse	0-9	A Mackay	0-1	M J Kinane	0-1
I Hudson	0-4	B Raymond	0-1	Mr S Swiers	0-1
Pat Eddery	0-3	C N Adamson	0-1	Mrs D Arbuthnot	0-1
W R Swinburn	0-3	D Holland	0-1	R Hills	0-1
A Procter	0-2	D Wright	0-1	S Lanigan	0-1
C Asmussen	0-2	G Bardwell	0-1	T Ives	0-1
J Reid	0-2	J Quinn	0-1		

COURSE RECORD

	Total W-R	Non-Handicaps 2-y-o	Non-Handicaps 3-y-o+	Handicaps 2-y-o	Handicaps 3-y-o+	Per cent	£1 Level Stake
Bath	3-10	0-1	2-5	0-0	1-4	30.0	+ 22.00
Kempton	2-16	0-0	1-12	0-0	1-4	12.5	+ 4.00
Newmarket	2-22	1-6	0-4	0-0	1-12	9.1	- 5.25
Salisbury	2-28	0-6	1-9	0-0	1-13	7.1	- 16.50
Epsom	1-10	0-0	1-7	0-0	0-3	10.0	- 7.12
Lingfield	1-11	0-2	1-6	0-0	0-3	9.1	- 7.50
Ascot	1-19	0-0	0-4	0-1	1-14	5.3	- 16.75
Newbury	1-25	0-6	0-8	0-1	1-10	4.0	- 20.50
Sandown	1-26	0-2	1-12	0-0	0-12	3.8	- 23.37

Goodwood	0-21	Windsor	0-6	Ayr	0-1
York	0-10	Doncaster	0-4	Beverley	0-1
Chepstow	0-7	Wolverhampton (AW)	0-4	Warwick	0-1
Folkestone	0-7	Lingfield (AW)	0-2	Yarmouth	0-1

WINNING HORSES

	Age	Races Run	1st	2nd	3rd	Unpl	Win £
Statajack	6	13	3	2	3	5	18,978
Muse	7	6	2	1	1	2	10,141
Indian Express	3	10	2	1	2	5	5,574
Lucky Lucaya	2	7	1	1	1	4	4,893
Ivor's Flutter	5	3	1	0	0	2	3,712
Towering Talent	3	6	1	0	2	3	3,692
Atours	6	2	1	0	0	1	3,553
Trade Wind	3	11	1	1	0	9	3,503
Pink Brief	3	4	1	1	1	1	3,398
Call Of The Night	3	6	1	0	0	5	3,292

WINNING OWNERS

	Races Won	Value £		Races Won	Value £
Mrs M E Slade	3	18,978	W I M Perry	1	3,712
White Horse Racing Ltd	2	10,141	J C Smith	1	3,692
Raymond Tooth	2	6,689	Oh So Rosie Partnership	1	3,553
J McGarry	2	5,574	Ray Richards	1	3,503
Lucayan Stud	1	4,893			

Favourites	5-19	26.3%	- 4.49	Total winning prize-money	£60,736
Longest winning sequence		2	Average SP of winner	5.9/1
Longest losing sequence		50	Return on stakes invested	-58.6%

1993 Form	33-275	12.0%	- 57.54	1991 Form	40-354	11.3%	- 93.91
1992 Form	32-325	9.8%	- 55.51	1990 Form	44-335	13.1%	+ 11.79

R W EMERY (Rugby, Warwicks)

	No. of Horses	Races Run	1st	2nd	3rd	Unpl	Per cent	£1 Level Stake
2-y-o	0	0	0	0	0	0	-	0.00
3-y-o	3	12	0	0	0	12	-	- 12.00
4-y-o+	8	37	1	4	4	28	2.7	- 27.00
Totals	11	49	1	4	4	40	2.0	- 39.00

Jan	Feb	Mar	Apr	May	Jun	Jul	Aug	Sep	Oct/Nov
0-0	0-0	0-5	0-6	1-9	0-3	0-11	0-8	0-0	0-7

		£1 Level			£1 Level
Winning Jockey	W-R	Stake	Winning Course	W-R	Stake
T Williams	1-21	- 11.00	Goodwood	1-1	+ 9.00

		Races				Win
Winning Horse	Age	Run	1st	2nd	3rd	Unpl	£
Scottish Park	5	11	1	1	1	8	4,078

Favourites	0-0	Total winning prize-money	£4,078

138

J ETHERINGTON (Malton, North Yorks)

	No. of Horses	Races Run	1st	2nd	3rd	Unpl	Per cent	£1 Level Stake
2-y-o	3	11	0	0	0	11	-	- 11.00
3-y-o	8	33	1	0	2	30	3.0	- 12.00
4-y-o+	3	26	2	5	3	16	7.7	- 18.25
Totals	14	70	3	5	5	57	4.3	- 41.25

Jan	Feb	Mar	Apr	May	Jun	Jul	Aug	Sep	Oct/Nov
0-0	0-0	0-0	1-6	0-11	1-9	0-14	0-8	1-9	0-13

Winning Jockeys	W-R	£1 Level Stake			W-R	£1 Level Stake
M Birch	1-4	0.00	L Charnock		1-11	+ 10.00
J Fortune	1-8	- 4.25				

Winning Courses	W-R	£1 Level Stake			W-R	£1 Level Stake
Catterick	1-7	- 3.25	Redcar		1-10	+ 11.00
Hamilton	1-8	- 4.00				

Winning Horses	Age	Races Run	1st	2nd	3rd	Unpl	Win £
Salu	5	12	1	3	3	5	3,522
Frustrated Poet	3	6	1	0	0	5	3,436
Aegaen Lady	5	5	1	0	0	4	3,005

Favourites	2-8	25.0%	- 0.25	Total winning prize-money		£9,962

1993 Form	10-128	7.8%	- 51.25	1991 Form	9-193	4.7%	- 87.71
1992 Form	15-147	10.2%	- 45.08	1990 Form	17-201	8.5%	- 98.77

J M P EUSTACE (Newmarket)

	No. of Horses	Races Run	1st	2nd	3rd	Unpl	Per cent	£1 Level Stake
2-y-o	10	27	1	3	0	23	3.7	- 25.20
3-y-o	5	22	1	0	2	19	4.5	- 15.00
4-y-o+	5	37	1	4	3	29	2.7	- 16.00
Totals	20	86	3	7	5	71	3.5	- 56.20

Jan	Feb	Mar	Apr	May	Jun	Jul	Aug	Sep	Oct/Nov
0-0	0-0	0-3	0-9	0-8	1-21	1-12	0-14	1-11	0-8

Winning Jockeys	W-R	£1 Level Stake			W-R	£1 Level Stake
R Cochrane	2-21	- 12.20	M Tebbutt		1-27	- 6.00

Winning Courses	W-R	£1 Level Stake			W-R	£1 Level Stake
Ayr	1-2	+ 19.00	Windsor		1-6	+ 1.00
Folkestone	1-3	- 1.20				

Eustace J M P

Winning Horses	Age	Races Run	1st	2nd	3rd	Unpl	Win £
Master Of Passion	5	12	1	1	1	9	12,428
Lunar Mission	3	5	1	0	1	3	4,542
Brockton Flame	2	5	1	1	0	3	2,577

Favourites	1-4	25.0%	- 2.20	Total winning prize-money		£19,546

1993 Form	6-78	7.7%	- 29.50	1991 Form	10-118	8.5%	- 59.82
1992 Form	7-91	7.7%	- 59.00	1990 Form	6-78	7.7%	- 3.00

P D EVANS (Welshpool, Powys)

	No. of Horses	Races Run	1st	2nd	3rd	Unpl	Per cent	£1 Level Stake
2-y-o	4	20	0	3	1	16	-	- 20.00
3-y-o	10	61	2	9	6	44	3.3	- 49.12
4-y-o+	17	87	7	10	8	62	8.0	- 22.75
Totals	31	168	9	22	15	122	5.4	- 91.87

Jan	Feb	Mar	Apr	May	Jun	Jul	Aug	Sep	Oct/Nov
2-17	0-18	0-10	0-23	3-23	0-20	1-10	0-23	1-9	2-15

Winning Jockeys	W-R	£1 Level Stake		W-R	£1 Level Stake
J Stack	3-8	+ 26.50	V Halliday	1-12	- 3.00
A Clark	2-22	- 11.75	D Holland	1-22	- 19.12
S Sanders	2-32	- 12.50			

Winning Courses					
Wolverhampton (AW)	3-56	- 42.87	Doncaster	1-6	+ 0.50
Kempton	1-2	+ 11.00	Edinburgh	1-6	+ 3.00
York	1-2	+ 9.00	Haydock	1-13	+ 2.00
Newmarket	1-3	+ 5.50			

Winning Horses	Age	Races Run	1st	2nd	3rd	Unpl	Win £
Master Beveled	4	19	5	4	3	7	44,369
Samson-Agonistes	8	14	2	4	2	6	5,349
Alllegsnobrain	3	19	1	2	2	14	3,132
Palacegate Jo	3	3	1	0	0	2	2,595

Favourites	2-13	15.4%	- 7.87	Total winning prize-money		£55,445

1993 Form	17-117	14.5%	+ 13.68	1991 Form	3-55	5.5%	- 22.50
1992 Form	6-87	6.9%	- 11.50	1990 Form	0-33		

J L EYRE (Hambleton, North Yorks)

	No. of Horses	Races Run	1st	2nd	3rd	Unpl	Per cent	£1 Level Stake
2-y-o	10	36	2	3	5	26	5.6	- 26.25
3-y-o	9	39	4	5	7	23	10.3	- 1.50
4-y-o+	20	121	10	16	13	82	8.3	- 15.10
Totals	39	196	16	24	25	131	8.2	- 42.85

BY MONTH

2-y-o	W-R	Per cent	£1 Level Stake	3-y-o	W-R	Per cent	£1 Level Stake
January	0-0	-	0.00	January	0-2	-	- 2.00
February	0-0	-	0.00	February	0-0	-	0.00
March	0-0	-	0.00	March	0-0	-	0.00
April	0-0	-	0.00	April	0-2	-	- 2.00
May	0-2	-	- 2.00	May	0-4	-	- 4.00
June	0-2	-	- 2.00	June	0-3	-	- 3.00
July	0-4	-	- 4.00	July	1-5	20.0	+ 2.00
August	0-8	-	- 8.00	August	2-9	22.2	+ 8.50
September	2-8	25.0	+ 1.75	September	0-7	-	- 7.00
Oct/Nov	0-12	-	- 12.00	Oct/Nov	1-7	14.3	+ 6.00

4-y-o+	W-R	Per cent	£1 Level Stake	Totals	W-R	Per cent	£1 Level Stake
January	2-6	33.3	+ 19.00	January	2-8	25.0	+ 17.00
February	0-4	-	- 4.00	February	0-4	-	- 4.00
March	0-5	-	- 5.00	March	0-5	-	- 5.00
April	0-10	-	- 10.00	April	0-12	-	- 12.00
May	1-12	8.3	+ 3.00	May	1-18	5.6	- 3.00
June	0-10	-	- 10.00	June	0-15	-	- 15.00
July	2-25	8.0	- 6.60	July	3-34	8.8	- 8.60
August	1-19	5.3	- 4.00	August	3-36	8.3	- 3.50
September	3-19	15.8	+ 5.50	September	5-34	14.7	+ 0.25
Oct/Nov	1-11	9.1	- 3.00	Oct/Nov	2-30	6.7	- 9.00

DISTANCE

2-y-o	W-R	Per cent	£1 Level Stake	3-y-o	W-R	Per cent	£1 Level Stake
5f-6f	0-18	-	- 18.00	5f-6f	0-8	-	- 8.00
7f-8f	2-17	11.8	- 7.25	7f-8f	2-19	10.5	+ 1.00
9f-13f	0-1	-	- 1.00	9f-13f	1-5	20.0	- 0.50
14f+	0-0	-	0.00	14f+	1-7	14.3	+ 6.00

4-y-o+	W-R	Per cent	£1 Level Stake	Totals	W-R	Per cent	£1 Level Stake
5f-6f	1-27	3.7	- 22.50	5f-6f	1-53	1.9	- 48.50
7f-8f	7-62	11.3	+ 23.40	7f-8f	11-98	11.2	+ 17.15
9f-13f	2-26	7.7	- 10.00	9f-13f	3-32	9.4	- 11.50
14f+	0-6	-	- 6.00	14f+	1-13	7.7	0.00

TYPE OF RACE

Non-Handicaps	W-R	Per cent	£1 Level Stake	Handicaps	W-R	Per cent	£1 Level Stake
2-y-o	1-20	5.0	- 16.75	2-y-o	1-10	10.0	- 3.50
3-y-o	1-21	4.8	- 16.50	3-y-o	2-12	16.7	+ 14.00
4-y-o+	1-15	6.7	0.00	4-y-o+	6-76	7.9	- 14.60
Selling	0-10	-	- 10.00	Selling	1-7	14.3	0.00
Apprentice	0-2	-	- 2.00	Apprentice	3-14	21.4	+ 15.50
Amat/Ladies	0-1	-	- 1.00	Amat/Ladies	0-8	-	- 8.00
Totals	3-69	4.3	- 46.25	Totals	13-127	10.2	+ 3.40

COURSE GRADE

	W-R	Per cent	£1 Level Stake
Group 1	4-49	8.2	- 8.00
Group 2	4-44	9.1	- 11.00
Group 3	4-43	9.3	- 10.25
Group 4	4-60	6.7	- 13.60

FIRST TIME OUT

	W-R	Per cent	£1 Level Stake
2-y-o	0-9	-	- 9.00
3-y-o	0-6	-	- 6.00
4-y-o+	2-15	13.3	+ 10.00
Totals	2-30	6.7	- 5.00

JOCKEYS RIDING

	W-R	Per cent	£1 Level Stake		W-R	Per cent	£1 Level Stake
J Fortune	7-33	21.2	+ 38.90	K Darley	1-6	16.7	- 2.75
D Griffiths	1-1	100.0	+ 7.00	O Pears	1-8	12.5	+ 7.00
M Humphries	1-2	50.0	+ 15.00	J Tate	1-9	11.1	- 1.00
T Williams	1-4	25.0	+ 2.50	N Varley	1-21	4.8	- 14.00
G Macdonald	1-5	20.0	- 0.50	M McAndrew	1-24	4.2	- 12.00

N Connorton	0-8	M Baird	0-2	G Hind	0-1
N Adams	0-7	M Birch	0-2	K Fallon	0-1
S Maloney	0-7	M Roberts	0-2	L Dettori	0-1
J Stack	0-4	Mr P Looker	0-2	Miss I D W Jones	0-1
N Carlisle	0-4	T Quinn	0-2	Miss M Carson	0-1
D McKeown	0-3	W Ryan	0-2	Miss P Robson	0-1
L Piggott	0-3	A Munro	0-1	Mr A Manners	0-1
Mrs C Hirst	0-3	B Raymond	0-1	Mr D Parker	0-1
F Norton	0-2	B Russell	0-1	Paul Eddery	0-1
J Carroll	0-2	C Teague	0-1	R Hughes	0-1
J Fanning	0-2	Claire Balding	0-1	Ruth Coulter	0-1
J Marshall	0-2	D Lockhart	0-1	S Webster	0-1
J Weaver	0-2	G Carter	0-1		
L Charnock	0-2	G Duffield	0-1		

COURSE RECORD

	Total W-R	Non-Handicaps 2-y-o	3-y-o+	Handicaps 2-y-o	3-y-o+	Per cent	£1 Level Stake
York	2-6	0-0	0-0	0-0	2-6	33.3	+ 15.00
Pontefract	2-17	0-2	0-3	0-1	2-11	11.8	+ 8.00
Catterick	2-19	0-3	1-4	0-2	1-10	10.5	+ 2.40
Thirsk	2-21	0-5	1-4	0-1	1-11	9.5	- 9.50
Lingfield	1-3	0-0	0-1	1-1	0-1	33.3	+ 3.50
Wolverhampton (AW)	1-7	0-0	0-3	0-0	1-4	14.3	+ 10.00
Ripon	1-9	0-0	0-3	0-0	1-6	11.1	+ 6.00
Beverley	1-10	1-3	0-0	0-0	0-7	10.0	- 6.75
Haydock	1-10	0-3	0-2	0-0	1-5	10.0	- 2.00
Hamilton	1-12	0-1	0-1	0-1	1-9	8.3	- 7.50
Southwell (AW)	1-13	0-2	0-7	0-0	1-4	7.7	- 5.00
Doncaster	1-14	0-3	0-1	0-2	1-8	7.1	- 2.00

Carlisle	0-12	Newmarket		0-5	Bath		0-1
Newcastle	0-12	Ayr		0-2	Leicester		0-1
Redcar	0-9	Chester		0-2	Lingfield (AW)		0-1
Edinburgh	0-8	Nottingham		0-2			

WINNING HORSES

	Age	Races Run	1st	2nd	3rd	Unpl	Win £
Celestial Choir	4	21	5	5	0	11	37,802
Tethys	3	6	2	1	3	0	11,769
Calder King	3	18	2	4	3	9	9,246
Eurotwist	5	4	1	0	0	3	6,888
Prince Belfort	6	16	2	2	2	10	6,290
Vishnu	4	7	1	2	0	4	3,720
Evan 'Elp Us	2	7	1	3	1	2	3,680
Saint Amigo	2	11	1	0	4	6	3,600
Shalabia	5	4	1	0	2	1	3,468

WINNING OWNERS

	Races Won	Value £		Races Won	Value £
Lowlands Racing Ltd	4	35,559	N C White	1	3,720
M Gleason	2	11,769	E J Ashton	1	3,680
Colin Barker	2	9,246	E Richmond	1	3,600
J L Eyre	1	6,888	Mrs Corrina Hirst	1	3,468
Mrs Carole Sykes	2	6,290	Jeff Slaney	1	2,243

Favourites	2-16	12.5% - 8.25	Total winning prize-money		£86,463
Longest winning sequence		2	Average SP of winner		8.6/1
Longest losing sequence		33	Return on stakes invested		-21.9%
1993 Form	5-92	5.4% - 43.50	1992 Form	1-22	4.5% - 17.50

R A FAHEY (Malton, North Yorks)

	No. of Horses	Races Run	1st	2nd	3rd	Unpl	Per cent	£1 Level Stake
2-y-o	5	21	0	1	3	17	–	– 21.00
3-y-o	2	14	2	0	0	12	14.3	+ 16.00
4-y-o+	0	0	0	0	0	0	–	0.00
Totals	7	35	2	1	3	29	5.7	– 5.00

Jan	Feb	Mar	Apr	May	Jun	Jul	Aug	Sep	Oct/Nov
0-0	0-0	0-0	0-1	0-8	1-6	1-7	0-7	0-6	0-0

Winning Jockeys	W-R	£1 Level Stake				W-R	£1 Level Stake
S D Williams	1-1	+ 8.00		Mrs L Fahey		1-3	+ 18.00

Winning Courses							
Carlisle	1-2	+ 19.00		Ayr		1-4	+ 5.00

Winning Horse	Age	Races Run	1st	2nd	3rd	Unpl	Win £
Murphy's Gold	3	12	2	0	0	10	5,869

Favourites	0-3		Total winning prize-money	£5,869

1993 Form	1-9	11.1%	+ 4.00

C W FAIRHURST (Middleham, North Yorks)

	No. of Horses	Races Run	1st	2nd	3rd	Unpl	Per cent	£1 Level Stake
2-y-o	8	41	4	4	4	29	9.8	– 16.56
3-y-o	8	61	0	5	10	46	–	– 61.00
4-y-o+	9	77	2	4	6	65	2.6	– 40.00
Totals	25	179	6	13	20	140	3.4	–117.56

Jan	Feb	Mar	Apr	May	Jun	Jul	Aug	Sep	Oct/Nov
1-8	0-4	0-11	2-12	0-25	1-28	1-31	0-23	1-23	0-14

Winning Jockeys	W-R	£1 Level Stake				W-R	£1 Level Stake
J Fanning	3-80	– 39.56		Mrs S Bosley		1-8	+ 3.00
P Robinson	2-3	+ 7.00					

Winning Courses							
Windsor	1-1	+ 4.00		Newcastle		1-10	+ 3.00
Wolverhampton (AW)	1-6	+ 20.00		Ripon		1-10	– 5.00
Edinburgh	1-9	– 7.56		Beverley		1-19	– 8.00

Winning Horses	Age	Races Run	1st	2nd	3rd	Unpl	Win £
Polly Particular	2	7	2	0	0	5	7,660
Brisas	7	9	1	0	1	7	3,028
Prudent Pet	2	7	1	0	0	6	2,914
New Heights	2	6	1	2	2	1	2,694
Larn Fort	4	16	1	1	1	13	2,600

Favourites	1-3	33.3%	-	1.56	Total winning prize-money		£18,896

1993 Form	0-5						

J R FANSHAWE (Newmarket)

	No. of Horses	Races Run	1st	2nd	3rd	Unpl	Per cent	£1 Level Stake
2-y-o	29	55	6	10	6	33	10.9	- 15.75
3-y-o	25	118	14	16	19	69	11.9	- 6.35
4-y-o+	15	76	4	15	11	46	5.3	- 54.53
Totals	69	249	24	41	36	148	9.6	- 76.63

BY MONTH

2-y-o	W-R	Per cent	£1 Level Stake	3-y-o	W-R	Per cent	£1 Level Stake
January	0-0	-	0.00	January	0-0	-	0.00
February	0-0	-	0.00	February	0-0	-	0.00
March	0-0	-	0.00	March	0-2	-	- 2.00
April	0-0	-	0.00	April	1-21	4.8	- 16.00
May	0-1	-	- 1.00	May	4-18	22.2	+ 17.33
June	0-2	-	- 2.00	June	4-24	16.7	+ 14.00
July	2-5	40.0	- 1.25	July	1-16	6.3	- 11.00
August	1-5	20.0	+ 6.00	August	1-13	7.7	- 6.50
September	1-12	8.3	+ 5.00	September	3-17	17.6	+ 4.82
Oct/Nov	2-30	6.7	- 22.50	Oct/Nov	0-7	-	- 7.00

4-y-o+	W-R	Per cent	£1 Level Stake	Totals	W-R	Per cent	£1 Level Stake
January	0-2	-	- 2.00	January	0-2	-	- 2.00
February	0-2	-	- 2.00	February	0-2	-	- 2.00
March	0-2	-	- 2.00	March	0-4	-	- 4.00
April	0-11	-	- 11.00	April	1-32	3.1	- 27.00
May	0-8	-	- 8.00	May	4-27	14.8	+ 8.33
June	1-12	8.3	- 8.00	June	5-38	13.2	+ 4.00
July	2-13	15.4	- 8.53	July	5-34	14.7	- 20.78
August	0-9	-	- 9.00	August	2-27	7.4	- 9.50
September	0-9	-	- 9.00	September	4-38	10.5	+ 0.82
Oct/Nov	1-8	12.5	+ 5.00	Oct/Nov	3-45	6.7	- 24.50

DISTANCE

2-y-o	W–R	Per cent	£1 Level Stake	3-y-o	W–R	Per cent	£1 Level Stake
5f-6f	4-14	28.6	+ 10.25	5f-6f	0-11	–	– 11.00
7f-8f	2-41	4.9	– 26.00	7f-8f	8-52	15.4	+ 11.33
9f-13f	0-0	–	0.00	9f-13f	3-47	6.4	– 12.00
14f+	0-0	–	0.00	14f+	3-8	37.5	+ 5.32

4-y-o+	W–R	Per cent	£1 Level Stake	Totals	W–R	Per cent	£1 Level Stake
5f-6f	0-11	–	– 11.00	5f-6f	4-36	11.1	– 11.75
7f-8f	0-10	–	– 10.00	7f-8f	10-103	9.7	– 24.67
9f-13f	3-41	7.3	– 20.75	9f-13f	6-88	6.8	– 32.75
14f+	1-14	7.1	– 12.78	14f+	4-22	18.2	– 7.46

TYPE OF RACE

Non-Handicaps	W–R	Per cent	£1 Level Stake	Handicaps	W–R	Per cent	£1 Level Stake
2-y-o	5-52	9.6	– 23.75	2-y-o	1-3	33.3	+ 8.00
3-y-o	7-61	11.5	+ 2.33	3-y-o	7-54	13.0	– 5.68
4-y-o+	2-32	6.3	– 27.53	4-y-o+	2-43	4.7	– 26.00
Selling	0-0	–	0.00	Selling	0-0	–	0.00
Apprentice	0-2	–	– 2.00	Apprentice	0-2	–	– 2.00
Amat/Ladies	0-0	–	0.00	Amat/Ladies	0-0	–	0.00
Totals	14-147	9.5	– 50.95	Totals	10-102	9.8	– 25.68

COURSE GRADE

	W–R	Per cent	£1 Level Stake
Group 1	9-126	7.1	– 28.68
Group 2	4-28	14.3	– 13.25
Group 3	5-64	7.8	– 24.75
Group 4	6-31	19.4	– 9.95

FIRST TIME OUT

	W–R	Per cent	£1 Level Stake
2-y-o	3-29	10.3	– 6.25
3-y-o	3-25	12.0	+ 8.00
4-y-o+	0-14	–	– 14.00
Totals	6-68	8.8	– 12.25

JOCKEYS RIDING

	W–R	Per cent	£1 Level Stake		W–R	Per cent	£1 Level Stake
W Woods	7-47	14.9	+ 3.83	J Weaver	1-2	50.0	+ 1.50
A Munro	4-17	23.5	+ 21.50	B Raymond	1-3	33.3	– 0.75
W R Swinburn	3-26	11.5	– 6.25	Pat Eddery	1-6	16.7	– 2.00
L Dettori	2-9	22.2	+ 5.32	K Fallon	1-12	8.3	– 8.00
W Ryan	2-24	8.3	– 17.78	D Harrison	1-16	6.3	– 4.00
J Reid	1-2	50.0	+ 15.00				

N Varley	0-17	C Asmussen	0-3	P Bowe	0-2
G Duffield	0-14	K Darley	0-3	C Rutter	0-1
P Robinson	0-7	G Bardwell	0-2	M Hills	0-1
R Hills	0-5	J Carroll	0-2	M J Kinane	0-1
T Quinn	0-5	L Piggott	0-2	R Hughes	0-1
G Carter	0-4	M Roberts	0-2	T Ives	0-1
J Quinn	0-4	M Tebbutt	0-2		
W Carson	0-4	N Carlisle	0-2		

COURSE RECORD

	Total W-R	Non-Handicaps 2-y-o	Non-Handicaps 3-y-o+	Handicaps 2-y-o	Handicaps 3-y-o+	Per cent	£1 Level Stake
Catterick	3-5	1-3	2-2	0-0	0-0	60.0	- 0.45
Sandown	3-16	0-3	0-2	0-0	3-11	18.8	+ 10.00
Yarmouth	3-19	0-6	2-6	0-0	1-7	15.8	0.00
Warwick	2-2	1-1	0-0	0-0	1-1	100.0	+ 9.50
Thirsk	2-6	1-2	0-3	0-0	1-1	33.3	+ 0.25
Kempton	2-14	1-1	1-6	0-0	0-7	14.3	+ 24.00
Newcastle	1-1	0-0	0-0	1-1	0-0	100.0	+ 10.00
Ripon	1-2	0-0	1-2	0-0	0-0	50.0	+ 3.00
Chepstow	1-4	0-0	1-2	0-0	0-2	25.0	- 0.75
Redcar	1-6	1-4	0-0	0-0	0-2	16.7	- 2.50
Newbury	1-7	0-2	0-3	0-0	1-2	14.3	- 2.00
Southwell (AW)	1-8	0-0	1-4	0-0	0-4	12.5	- 3.00
Doncaster	1-9	0-2	0-5	0-0	1-2	11.1	- 4.68
Windsor	1-9	0-0	1-6	0-0	0-3	11.1	+ 8.00
Newmarket	1-45	0-11	0-18	0-2	1-14	2.2	- 32.00

Leicester	0-15	Salisbury	0-6	Pontefract	0-3
Folkestone	0-11	Beverley	0-5	Hamilton	0-2
Haydock	0-11	Chester	0-5	Ayr	0-1
Goodwood	0-10	Lingfield (AW)	0-5	Bath	0-1
Ascot	0-8	York	0-4		
Nottingham	0-6	Lingfield	0-3		

WINNING HORSES

	Age	Races Run	1st	2nd	3rd	Unpl	Win £
Bold Gait	3	9	3	2	1	3	32,482
Be Mindful	2	6	2	1	2	1	10,940
Polka Dancer	4	4	1	1	0	2	9,412
Beaming	3	5	1	0	1	3	5,407
Spring Sixpence	4	7	1	0	1	5	5,361
Storm Nymph	3	6	1	0	2	3	4,993
Bishop Of Cashel	2	3	1	1	0	1	4,800
Kamchatka	3	4	1	0	0	3	4,688
Polo Kit	3	5	1	1	1	2	4,397
Deceive	2	1	1	0	0	0	4,207
Green Seed	2	2	1	0	1	0	3,921
Misbelief	4	9	1	4	1	3	3,720

Fanshawe J R

Midnight Snack	3	4	1	1	1	1	3,672
Tromond	3	5	1	1	0	3	3,672
Cap O'Rushes	3	5	1	1	1	2	3,670
Decant	3	6	1	1	2	2	3,626
Mood Swings	2	1	1	0	0	0	3,600
Karshi	4	6	1	2	1	2	3,393
Tshusick	3	5	1	1	1	2	3,266
Storey's Gate	3	8	1	1	0	6	3,052
Bonny Melody	3	6	1	2	2	1	2,243

WINNING OWNERS

	Races Won	Value £		Races Won	Value £
Mrs I Phillips	3	32,482	Mana Al Maktoum	1	3,921
Cheveley Park Stud	5	20,894	T & J Vestey	1	3,720
Dr Catherine Wills	2	10,940	T D Holland-Martin	1	3,672
S J Richmond-Watson	1	9,412	Abdullah Saeed	1	3,670
Sheikh Mohammed	2	8,289	Lord Vestey	1	3,393
Mrs Dare Wigan	1	5,407	Bottisham Heath Stud	1	3,266
C I T Racing Ltd	1	5,361	Mrs David Russell	1	3,052
Moncrisp Limited	1	4,800	Mrs Mary Watt	1	2,243

Favourites	8-35	22.9%	- 11.13	Total winning prize-money	£124,521
Longest winning sequence			3	Average SP of winner	6.2/1
Longest losing sequence			35	Return on stakes invested	-30.8%
1993 Form	34-270	12.6%	- 58.17	1991 Form	22-152	14.5%	+ 7.14
1992 Form	28-248	11.3%	- 48.70	1990 Form	18-113	15.9%	+ 58.96

P J FEILDEN (Newmarket)

	No. of Horses	Races Run	1st	2nd	3rd	Unpl	Per cent	£1 Level Stake
2-y-o	0	0	0	0	0	0	-	0.00
3-y-o	0	0	0	0	0	0	-	0.00
4-y-o+	3	22	1	1	2	18	4.5	- 17.50
Totals	3	22	1	1	2	18	4.5	- 17.50

Jan	Feb	Mar	Apr	May	Jun	Jul	Aug	Sep	Oct/Nov
1-5	0-1	0-1	0-0	0-0	0-2	0-2	0-6	0-2	0-3

		£1 Level			£1 Level
Winning Jockey	W-R	Stake	Winning Course	W-R	Stake
Miss J Feilden	1-3	+ 1.50	Lingfield (AW)	1-7	- 2.50

Winning Horse	Age	Races Run	1st	2nd	3rd	Unpl	Win £
Don't Drop Bombs	5	10	1	1	2	6	2,669

Favourites	1-4	25.0%	+ 0.50	Total winning prize-money			£2,669

1993 Form	0-33			1991 Form	5-53	9.4%	- 27.00
1992 Form	5-65	7.7%	- 35.05	1990 Form	6-60	10.0%	- 3.00

P S FELGATE (Melton Mowbray, Leics)

	No. of Horses	Races Run	1st	2nd	3rd	Unpl	Per cent	£1 Level Stake
2-y-o	0	0	0	0	0	0	-	0.00
3-y-o	2	7	0	0	0	7	-	- 7.00
4-y-o+	9	85	10	5	7	63	11.8	+ 18.50
Totals	11	92	10	5	7	70	10.9	+ 11.50

BY MONTH

2-y-o	W-R	Per cent	£1 Level Stake	3-y-o	W-R	Per cent	£1 Level Stake
January	0-0	-	0.00	January	0-0	-	0.00
February	0-0	-	0.00	February	0-0	-	0.00
March	0-0	-	0.00	March	0-0	-	0.00
April	0-0	-	0.00	April	0-0	-	0.00
May	0-0	-	0.00	May	0-0	-	0.00
June	0-0	-	0.00	June	0-0	-	0.00
July	0-0	-	0.00	July	0-0	-	0.00
August	0-0	-	0.00	August	0-3	-	- 3.00
September	0-0	-	0.00	September	0-3	-	- 3.00
Oct/Nov	0-0	-	0.00	Oct/Nov	0-1	-	- 1.00

4-y-o+	W-R	Per cent	£1 Level Stake	Totals	W-R	Per cent	£1 Level Stake
January	0-1	-	- 1.00	January	0-1	-	- 1.00
February	1-2	50.0	+ 2.50	February	1-2	50.0	+ 2.50
March	0-2	-	- 2.00	March	0-2	-	- 2.00
April	0-14	-	- 14.00	April	0-14	-	- 14.00
May	2-12	16.7	+ 3.50	May	2-12	16.7	+ 3.50
June	5-15	33.3	+ 48.50	June	5-15	33.3	+ 48.50
July	0-11	-	- 11.00	July	0-11	-	- 11.00
August	1-8	12.5	+ 3.00	August	1-11	9.1	0.00
September	1-11	9.1	- 2.00	September	1-14	7.1	- 5.00
Oct/Nov	0-9	-	- 9.00	Oct/Nov	0-10	-	- 10.00

DISTANCE

2-y-o	W-R	Per cent	£1 Level Stake	3-y-o	W-R	Per cent	£1 Level Stake
5f-6f	0-0	-	0.00	5f-6f	0-4	-	- 4.00
7f-8f	0-0	-	0.00	7f-8f	0-3	-	- 3.00
9f-13f	0-0	-	0.00	9f-13f	0-0	-	0.00
14f+	0-0	-	0.00	14f+	0-0	-	0.00

4-y-o+	W-R	Per cent	£1 Level Stake	Totals	W-R	Per cent	£1 Level Stake
5f-6f	7-50	14.0	+ 25.50	5f-6f	7-54	13.0	+ 21.50
7f-8f	2-26	7.7	- 9.00	7f-8f	2-29	6.9	- 12.00
9f-13f	0-0	-	0.00	9f-13f	0-0	-	0.00
14f+	1-9	11.1	+ 2.00	14f+	1-9	11.1	+ 2.00

TYPE OF RACE

Non-Handicaps	W-R	Per cent	£1 Level Stake	Handicaps	W-R	Per cent	£1 Level Stake
2-y-o	0-0	-	0.00	2-y-o	0-0	-	0.00
3-y-o	0-5	-	- 5.00	3-y-o	0-0	-	0.00
4-y-o+	0-14	-	- 14.00	4-y-o+	10-66	15.2	+ 37.50
Selling	0-3	-	- 3.00	Selling	0-1	-	- 1.00
Apprentice	0-0	-	0.00	Apprentice	0-3	-	- 3.00
Amat/Ladies	0-0	-	0.00	Amat/Ladies	0-0	-	0.00
Totals	0-22	-	- 22.00	Totals	10-70	14.3	+ 33.50

COURSE GRADE

	W-R	Per cent	£1 Level Stake
Group 1	2-14	14.3	+ 28.00
Group 2	1-9	11.1	+ 2.00
Group 3	3-34	8.8	- 8.00
Group 4	4-35	11.4	- 10.50

FIRST TIME OUT

	W-R	Per cent	£1 Level Stake
2-y-o	0-0	-	0.00
3-y-o	0-2	-	- 2.00
4-y-o+	0-9	-	- 9.00
Totals	0-11	-	- 11.00

JOCKEYS RIDING

	W-R	Per cent	£1 Level Stake		W-R	Per cent	£1 Level Stake
G Hind	5-38	13.2	+ 21.00	A Mackay	1-4	25.0	+ 7.00
K Darley	2-6	33.3	+ 14.00	P McCabe	1-9	11.1	0.00
N Carlisle	1-1	100.0	+ 3.50				

		W-R			W-R			W-R
J Lowe		0-7	M Roberts		0-2	D Wright		0-1
G Duffield		0-3	W Ryan		0-2	J Stack		0-1
J D Smith		0-3	D Biggs		0-1	N Kennedy		0-1
J Williams		0-3	D Griffiths		0-1	S D Williams		0-1
M Baird		0-3	D McCabe		0-1	S Perks		0-1
K Fallon		0-2	D McKeown		0-1			

COURSE RECORD

	Total W-R	Non-Handicaps 2-y-o	3-y-o+	Handicaps 2-y-o	3-y-o+	Per cent	£1 Level Stake
Wolverhampton (AW)	3-13	0-0	0-2	0-0	3-11	23.1	+ 7.00
Beverley	2-7	0-0	0-0	0-0	2-7	28.6	+ 10.00
Chester	1-3	0-0	0-1	0-0	1-2	33.3	+ 8.00
Doncaster	1-3	0-0	0-0	0-0	1-3	33.3	+ 5.00
Yarmouth	1-3	0-0	0-2	0-0	1-1	33.3	+ 6.00
Haydock	1-4	0-0	0-0	0-0	1-4	25.0	+ 30.00
Southwell (AW)	1-16	0-0	0-7	0-0	1-9	6.3	- 11.50

Leicester	0-13	Folkestone	0-2	Pontefract	0-1
Nottingham	0-10	Newcastle	0-2	Redcar	0-1
Ripon	0-3	Newmarket	0-2	Thirsk	0-1
Warwick	0-3	Catterick	0-1		
York	0-3	Lingfield	0-1		

WINNING HORSES

	Age	Races Run	1st	2nd	3rd	Unpl	Win £
Highborn	5	9	4	1	2	2	23,269
Life's A Breeze	5	12	2	1	2	7	5,714
Macs Maharanee	7	12	1	0	1	10	4,425
Glenfield Greta	6	11	1	0	1	9	3,720
Melodic Drive	4	9	1	0	0	8	3,339
Rolling The Bones	5	9	1	0	0	8	3,262

WINNING OWNERS

	Races Won	Value £		Races Won	Value £
Yorkshire Racing Club Owners	4	23,269	S M Grey	1	3,720
Paul Tacon	2	5,714	Mrs C M Stevens	1	3,339
John S Martin	1	4,425	M F Hyman	1	3,262

Favourites	1-4	25.0%	+ 0.50	Total winning prize-money	£43,729

Longest winning sequence		3	Average SP of winner	9.4/1
Longest losing sequence		21	Return on stakes invested	12.5%

1993 Form	8-93	8.6%	- 56.80	1991 Form	6-97	6.2%	- 46.37
1992 Form	10-83	12.0%	- 24.04	1990 Form	10-156	6.4%	- 79.25

M J FETHERSTON-GODLEY (East Ilsley, Berks)

	No. of Horses	Races Run	1st	2nd	3rd	Unpl	Per cent	£1 Level Stake
2-y-o	5	36	4	0	4	28	11.1	+ 6.00
3-y-o	6	49	2	8	7	32	4.1	- 39.00
4-y-o+	3	28	1	3	2	22	3.6	- 18.00
Totals	14	113	7	11	13	82	6.2	- 51.00

Jan	Feb	Mar	Apr	May	Jun	Jul	Aug	Sep	Oct/Nov
0-0	0-0	0-0	0-9	2-15	1-18	0-18	1-12	2-20	1-21

Winning Jockeys	W-R	£1 Level Stake		W-R	£1 Level Stake
Pat Eddery	2-9	+ 14.00	W R Swinburn	1-6	- 1.50
A Munro	1-4	+ 1.50	J Reid	1-6	+ 3.00
M Roberts	1-5	+ 5.00	F Norton	1-36	- 26.00

Winning Courses					
Doncaster	2-6	+ 14.00	Warwick	1-5	+ 0.50
Brighton	1-3	+ 7.00	Newmarket	1-6	+ 7.00
Chester	1-3	+ 1.50	Goodwood	1-7	+ 2.00

Winning Horses	Age	Races Run	1st	2nd	3rd	Unpl	Win £
Naked Welcome	2	9	2	0	3	4	14,325
Royal Figurine	3	11	1	1	0	9	7,096
Prince Rudolf	2	14	2	0	1	11	5,807
Macfarlane	6	11	1	1	0	9	3,840
Miriam	3	13	1	2	3	7	3,236

Favourites	0-8		Total winning prize-money	£34,304

1993 Form	7-75	9.3%	- 30.00	1991 Form	13-151	8.6%	- 74.79
1992 Form	7-98	7.1%	- 26.00	1990 Form	7-123	5.7%	- 72.59

R F FISHER (Ulverston, Cumbria)

	No. of Horses	Races Run	1st	2nd	3rd	Unpl	Per cent	£1 Level Stake
2-y-o	4	5	1	1	0	3	20.0	+ 16.00
3-y-o	5	15	0	1	0	14	-	- 15.00
4-y-o+	2	10	0	0	2	8	-	- 10.00
Totals	11	30	1	2	2	25	3.3	- 9.00

Jan	Feb	Mar	Apr	May	Jun	Jul	Aug	Sep	Oct/Nov
0-1	0-0	0-0	0-4	0-5	1-11	0-3	0-1	0-2	0-3

Winning Jockey	W-R	£1 Level Stake	Winning Course	W-R	£1 Level Stake
N Connorton	1-5	+ 16.00	Edinburgh	1-5	+ 16.00

Winning Horse	Age	Races Run	1st	2nd	3rd	Unpl	Win £
Tedburrow	2	2	1	0	0	1	2,349

Favourites	0-0		Total winning prize-money	£2,349

1993 Form	5-50	10.0%	- 13.50	1991 Form	0-3
1992 Form	0-12			1990 Form	0-6

J G FITZGERALD (Malton, North Yorks)

	No. of Horses	Races Run	1st	2nd	3rd	Unpl	Per cent	£1 Level Stake
2-y-o	6	28	0	5	4	19	-	- 28.00
3-y-o	5	16	1	1	0	14	6.3	- 11.00
4-y-o+	18	80	6	6	6	62	7.5	- 58.02
Totals	29	124	7	12	10	95	5.6	- 97.02

Jan	Feb	Mar	Apr	May	Jun	Jul	Aug	Sep	Oct/Nov
1-4	1-8	0-3	1-11	2-23	1-18	0-17	1-18	0-10	0-12

Winning Jockeys	W-R	£1 Level Stake		W-R	£1 Level Stake
K Fallon	4-41	- 25.77	L Piggott	1-2	+ 1.00
Paul Eddery	2-12	- 3.25			

Winning Courses					
Southwell (AW)	5-36	- 15.27	Ripon	1-5	- 1.75
Kempton	1-2	+ 1.00			

Winning Horses	Age	Races Run	1st	2nd	3rd	Unpl	Win £
Bold Pursuit	5	11	3	2	1	5	8,301
Heart Broken	4	13	2	1	0	10	5,881
Jamaica Bridge	4	6	1	0	0	5	3,407
Collector General	3	1	1	0	0	0	3,054

Favourites	4-9	44.4%	+ 2.73	Total winning prize-money	£20,643

1993 Form	17-167	10.2%	- 53.24	1991 Form	12-176	6.8%	- 98.25
1992 Form	8-151	5.3%	- 79.67	1990 Form	21-206	10.2%	- 24.70

R M FLOWER (Jevington, East Sussex)

	No. of Horses	Races Run	1st	2nd	3rd	Unpl	Per cent	£1 Level Stake
2-y-o	3	6	0	0	0	6	-	- 6.00
3-y-o	2	15	2	0	2	11	13.3	+ 2.00
4-y-o+	9	52	5	3	2	42	9.6	- 9.17
Totals	14	73	7	3	4	59	9.6	- 13.17

Jan	Feb	Mar	Apr	May	Jun	Jul	Aug	Sep	Oct/Nov
0-2	0-5	0-1	0-6	0-11	3-13	0-11	4-9	0-9	0-6

Winning Jockeys	W-R	£1 Level Stake		W-R	£1 Level Stake
M J Dwyer	2-2	+ 19.00	M Roberts	1-2	+ 2.33
Stephen Davies	2-4	+ 10.00	S Lanigan	1-6	+ 1.50
J Lowe	1-1	+ 12.00			

Winning Courses	W-R	£1 Level Stake		W-R	£1 Level Stake
Brighton	2-7	+ 7.00	Newmarket	1-4	+ 9.00
Redcar	1-1	+ 6.50	Yarmouth	1-9	+ 4.00
Goodwood	1-4	+ 0.33	Lingfield	1-10	- 2.00

Winning Horses	Age	Races Run	1st	2nd	3rd	Unpl	Win £
Oozlem	5	15	3	2	0	10	9,288
Fort Knox	3	13	2	0	2	9	5,805
Duckey Fuzz	6	6	1	0	2	3	5,483
Sharp Imp	4	10	1	1	0	8	3,054

Favourites	1-4	25.0%	+ 0.33	Total winning prize-money	£23,630
1993 Form	3-28	10.7%	- 7.00		

A L FORBES (Uttoxeter, Staffs)

	No. of Horses	Races Run	1st	2nd	3rd	Unpl	Per cent	£1 Level Stake
2-y-o	2	5	0	0	0	5	-	- 5.00
3-y-o	4	20	2	5	1	12	10.0	- 13.20
4-y-o+	11	42	0	4	4	34	-	- 42.00
Totals	17	67	2	9	5	51	3.0	- 60.20

Jan	Feb	Mar	Apr	May	Jun	Jul	Aug	Sep	Oct/Nov
0-10	2-10	0-10	0-6	0-8	0-7	0-2	0-4	0-7	0-3

Winning Jockey	W-R	£1 Level Stake	Winning Course	W-R	£1 Level Stake
S D Williams	2-35	- 28.20	Wolverhampton (AW)	2-25	- 18.20

Winning Horse	Age	Races Run	1st	2nd	3rd	Unpl	Win £
Killing Time	3	10	2	5	1	2	5,194

Favourites	1-3	33.3%	-	1.20	Total winning prize-money		£5,194

1993 Form   0-21

B FORSEY (Taunton, Somerset)

	No. of Horses	Races Run	1st	2nd	3rd	Unpl	Per cent	£1 Level Stake
2-y-o	0	0	0	0	0	0	-	0.00
3-y-o	0	0	0	0	0	0	-	0.00
4-y-o+	8	40	1	3	3	33	2.5	- 19.00
Totals	8	40	1	3	3	33	2.5	- 19.00

Jan	Feb	Mar	Apr	May	Jun	Jul	Aug	Sep	Oct/Nov
0-2	0-0	0-1	1-6	0-8	0-10	0-10	0-2	0-1	0-0

Winning Jockey	W-R	£1 Level Stake	Winning Course	W-R	£1 Level Stake
Miss A Purdy	1-13	+ 8.00	Ripon	1-1	+ 20.00

Winning Horse	Age	Races Run	1st	2nd	3rd	Unpl	Win £
Ripsnorter	5	6	1	2	0	3	3,314

Favourites	0-3	Total winning prize-money	£3,314

1993 Form	0-16	1991 Form	1-5	20.0%	+ 8.00
1992 Form	0-35				

D R GANDOLFO (Wantage, Oxon)

	No. of Horses	Races Run	1st	2nd	3rd	Unpl	Per cent	£1 Level Stake
2-y-o	0	0	0	0	0	0	-	0.00
3-y-o	1	2	1	0	1	0	50.0	+ 7.00
4-y-o+	0	0	0	0	0	0	-	0.00
Totals	1	2	1	0	1	0	50.0	+ 7.00

Jan	Feb	Mar	Apr	May	Jun	Jul	Aug	Sep	Oct/Nov
0-0	0-0	0-0	0-0	0-0	1-1	0-1	0-0	0-0	0-0

Winning Jockey	W-R	£1 Level Stake	Winning Course	W-R	£1 Level Stake
B Thomson	1-2	+ 7.00	Epsom	1-1	+ 8.00

Winning Horse	Age	Races Run	1st	2nd	3rd	Unpl	Win £
Moment Of Glory	3	2	1	0	1	0	2,699

Favourites	0-0		Total winning prize-money	£2,699

1993 Form	0-5	1991 Form	0-18
1992 Form	0-9	1990 Form	0-6

N A GASELEE (Upper Lambourn, Berks)

	No. of Horses	Races Run	1st	2nd	3rd	Unpl	Per cent	£1 Level Stake
2-y-o	0	0	0	0	0	0	-	0.00
3-y-o	1	1	0	0	0	1	-	- 1.00
4-y-o+	2	11	2	1	2	6	18.2	+ 16.00
Totals	3	12	2	1	2	7	16.7	+ 15.00

Jan	Feb	Mar	Apr	May	Jun	Jul	Aug	Sep	Oct/Nov
0-0	0-0	0-0	0-0	1-3	0-3	0-0	0-2	1-2	0-2

Winning Jockeys	W-R	£1 Level Stake		W-R	£1 Level Stake
L Dettori	1-1	+ 5.00	B Rouse	1-5	+ 16.00

Winning Courses					
Ayr	1-1	+ 5.00	Goodwood	1-1	+ 20.00

Winning Horse	Age	Races Run	1st	2nd	3rd	Unpl	Win £
On Air	6	8	2	1	2	3	14,706

Favourites	0-0		Total winning prize-money	£14,706

1993 Form	0-2	1991 Form	0-14
1992 Form	0-0	1990 Form	0-4

J A GLOVER (Worksop, Notts)

	No. of Horses	Races Run	1st	2nd	3rd	Unpl	Per cent	£1 Level Stake
2-y-o	5	30	4	4	3	19	13.3	- 12.62
3-y-o	7	47	1	6	3	37	2.1	- 44.90
4-y-o+	7	47	4	6	5	32	8.5	- 3.00
Totals	19	124	9	16	11	88	7.3	- 60.52

Jan	Feb	Mar	Apr	May	Jun	Jul	Aug	Sep	Oct/Nov
0-5	1-4	0-4	0-7	0-14	1-14	2-13	0-23	2-22	3-18

Winning Jockeys	W-R	£1 Level Stake			W-R	£1 Level Stake
D McKeown	3-33	- 23.77	G Carter		1-6	+ 9.00
M Birch	2-3	+ 7.25	S Richardson		1-7	+ 8.00
S D Williams	2-35	- 21.00				

Winning Courses	W-R	£1 Level Stake			W-R	£1 Level Stake
Wolverhampton (AW)	4-16	+ 14.13	Leicester		1-7	- 0.50
Beverley	1-3	+ 0.75	Southwell (AW)		1-15	- 9.00
Yarmouth	1-4	+ 11.00	Pontefract		1-16	- 13.90

Winning Horses	Age	Races Run	1st	2nd	3rd	Unpl	Win £
Arc Lamp	8	14	3	0	0	11	7,866
Clifton Fox	2	3	2	0	0	1	7,336
What A Nightmare	2	11	2	1	2	6	4,348
Fighter Squadron	5	14	1	1	1	11	3,652
Souperficial	3	12	1	1	1	9	2,658

Favourites	1-6	16.7%	- 3.90	Total winning prize-money	£25,860

1993 Form	9-133	6.8%	- 68.75	1991 Form	4-103	3.9%	- 51.00
1992 Form	25-194	12.9%	+ 2.25	1990 Form	5-84	6.0%	- 16.50

S GOLLINGS (Louth, Lincs)

	No. of Horses	Races Run	1st	2nd	3rd	Unpl	Per cent	£1 Level Stake
2-y-o	0	0	0	0	0	0	-	0.00
3-y-o	2	11	2	2	1	6	18.2	- 4.75
4-y-o+	4	17	1	1	2	13	5.9	+ 4.00
Totals	6	28	3	3	3	19	10.7	- 0.75

Jan	Feb	Mar	Apr	May	Jun	Jul	Aug	Sep	Oct/Nov
0-0	0-0	0-0	0-0	0-0	0-0	2-7	0-8	1-4	0-9

Winning Jockeys	W-R	£1 Level Stake			W-R	£1 Level Stake
J Tate	1-1	+ 2.25	Stephen Davies		1-7	- 4.00
M J Dwyer	1-1	+ 20.00				

Winning Courses	W-R	£1 Level Stake			W-R	£1 Level Stake
Sandown	1-1	+ 2.25	Yarmouth		1-2	+ 19.00
Newmarket	1-2	+ 1.00				

Winning Horses	Age	Races Run	1st	2nd	3rd	Unpl	Win £
Prizefighter	3	10	2	2	1	5	7,268
East Barns	6	11	1	1	2	7	3,184

Favourites	2-3	66.7%	+ 3.25	Total winning prize-money	£10,452

J H M GOSDEN (Newmarket)

	No. of Horses	Races Run	1st	2nd	3rd	Unpl	Per cent	£1 Level Stake
2-y-o	36	70	9	17	7	37	12.9	- 18.27
3-y-o	94	369	72	64	45	188	19.5	- 34.31
4-y-o+	22	82	12	18	13	39	14.6	- 27.92
Totals	152	521	93	99	65	264	17.9	- 80.50

BY MONTH

2-y-o	W-R	Per cent	£1 Level Stake	3-y-o	W-R	Per cent	£1 Level Stake
January	0-0	-	0.00	January	0-0	-	0.00
February	0-0	-	0.00	February	1-3	33.3	- 1.09
March	0-0	-	0.00	March	2-7	28.6	- 4.31
April	0-0	-	0.00	April	8-44	18.2	+ 1.41
May	0-1	-	- 1.00	May	13-53	24.5	+ 2.37
June	0-5	-	- 5.00	June	10-55	18.2	- 7.06
July	1-7	14.3	+ 10.00	July	14-54	25.9	+ 1.54
August	0-8	-	- 8.00	August	10-76	13.2	- 11.45
September	4-25	16.0	- 1.37	September	10-43	23.3	- 4.47
Oct/Nov	4-24	16.7	- 12.90	Oct/Nov	4-34	11.8	- 11.25

4-y-o+	W-R	Per cent	£1 Level Stake	Totals	W-R	Per cent	£1 Level Stake
January	0-0	-	0.00	January	0-0	-	0.00
February	0-0	-	0.00	February	1-3	33.3	- 1.09
March	0-2	-	- 2.00	March	2-9	22.2	- 6.31
April	4-13	30.8	+ 6.00	April	12-57	21.1	+ 7.41
May	2-12	16.7	+ 1.00	May	15-66	22.7	+ 2.37
June	2-15	13.3	- 10.67	June	12-75	16.0	- 22.73
July	1-14	7.1	- 11.50	July	16-75	21.3	+ 0.04
August	1-8	12.5	- 3.50	August	11-92	12.0	- 22.95
September	1-11	9.1	- 7.75	September	15-79	19.0	- 13.59
Oct/Nov	1-7	14.3	+ 0.50	Oct/Nov	9-65	13.8	- 23.65

DISTANCE

2-y-o	W-R	Per cent	£1 Level Stake	3-y-o	W-R	Per cent	£1 Level Stake
5f-6f	3-38	7.9	- 16.27	5f-6f	11-36	30.6	+ 0.08
7f-8f	6-32	18.8	- 2.00	7f-8f	34-191	17.8	- 24.90
9f-13f	0-0	-	0.00	9f-13f	26-132	19.7	- 1.49
14f+	0-0	-	0.00	14f+	1-10	10.0	- 8.00

4-y-o+	W-R	Per cent	£1 Level Stake	Totals	W-R	Per cent	£1 Level Stake
5f-6f	0-7	-	- 7.00	5f-6f	14-81	17.3	- 23.19
7f-8f	5-29	17.2	- 4.75	7f-8f	45-252	17.9	- 31.65
9f-13f	7-40	17.5	- 10.17	9f-13f	33-172	19.2	- 11.66
14f+	0-6	-	- 6.00	14f+	1-16	6.3	- 14.00

TYPE OF RACE

Non-Handicaps	W-R	Per cent	£1 Level Stake	Handicaps	W-R	Per cent	£1 Level Stake
2-y-o	9-68	13.2	- 16.27	2-y-o	0-2	-	- 2.00
3-y-o	52-254	20.5	- 43.49	3-y-o	20-111	18.0	+ 13.18
4-y-o+	8-52	15.4	- 13.00	4-y-o+	4-25	16.0	- 9.92
Selling	0-0	-	0.00	Selling	0-0	-	0.00
Apprentice	0-2	-	- 2.00	Apprentice	0-0	-	0.00
Amat/Ladies	0-2	-	- 2.00	Amat/Ladies	0-5	-	- 5.00
Totals	69-378	18.3	- 76.76	Totals	24-143	16.8	- 3.74

COURSE GRADE

	W-R	Per cent	£1 Level Stake
Group 1	55-336	16.4	- 73.70
Group 2	19-72	26.4	+ 23.80
Group 3	15-94	16.0	- 18.45
Group 4	4-19	21.1	- 12.15

FIRST TIME OUT

	W-R	Per cent	£1 Level Stake
2-y-o	3-36	8.3	- 3.50
3-y-o	16-92	17.4	- 14.31
4-y-o+	3-22	13.6	- 7.25
Totals	22-150	14.7	- 25.06

JOCKEYS RIDING

	W-R	Per cent	£1 Level Stake		W-R	Per cent	£1 Level Stake
L Dettori	59-271	21.8	- 4.57	B Thomson	1-2	50.0	+ 5.00
G Hind	9-70	12.9	- 23.90	D Holland	1-3	33.3	+ 12.00
J Carroll	7-36	19.4	- 15.96	P Robinson	1-3	33.3	+ 4.00
W Carson	5-14	35.7	+ 3.75	W Woods	1-4	25.0	+ 13.00
A McGlone	2-8	25.0	+ 7.00	R Cochrane	1-5	20.0	+ 1.00
Pat Eddery	2-26	7.7	- 17.25	Paul Eddery	1-6	16.7	- 3.37
D Harrison	1-1	100.0	+ 7.00	R Hills	1-6	16.7	- 4.20
A Clark	1-2	50.0	0.00				

G Carter	0-10	Mr J Durkan	0-3	W Ryan	0-2
Dale Gibson	0-9	S Raymont	0-3	D McKeown	0-1
J Quinn	0-5	W R Swinburn	0-3	J Stack	0-1
G Duffield	0-4	A Munro	0-2	M Henry	0-1
M J Kinane	0-4	B Raymond	0-2	M Hills	0-1
Mrs L Pearce	0-4	J Reid	0-2	R Havlin	0-1
J Lowe	0-3	J Weaver	0-2	S Dawson	0-1

COURSE RECORD

	Total W-R	Non-Handicaps 2-y-o	3-y-o+	Handicaps 2-y-o	3-y-o+	Per cent	£1 Level Stake
Newmarket	12-86	1-16	9-50	0-0	2-20	14.0	- 25.04
Newbury	7-24	0-3	5-16	0-0	2-5	29.2	+ 8.95
Goodwood	7-38	2-5	1-19	0-0	4-14	18.4	+ 5.20
York	6-24	0-1	5-13	0-0	1-10	25.0	+ 10.75
Doncaster	6-28	1-7	3-16	0-0	2-5	21.4	- 0.50

Gosden J H M

Chester	5-13	0-0	5-8	0-0	0-5	38.5	+	9.76
Sandown	5-29	0-3	2-17	0-0	3-9	17.2	–	3.25
Redcar	4-11	0-2	2-4	0-0	2-5	36.4	+	11.33
Ripon	4-11	0-0	2-9	0-0	2-2	36.4	+	4.12
Haydock	4-25	1-3	2-17	0-0	1-5	16.0	–	9.25
Ascot	4-41	1-4	2-17	0-1	1-19	9.8	–	30.42
Salisbury	3-10	1-2	1-6	0-0	1-2	30.0	+	20.50
Leicester	3-19	0-6	3-10	0-0	0-3	15.8	–	5.92
Yarmouth	3-25	0-3	3-17	0-0	0-5	12.0	–	12.25
Bath	2-4	0-0	1-2	0-0	1-2	50.0	+	6.80
Wolverhampton (AW)	2-7	0-0	2-5	0-0	0-2	28.6	–	4.31
Pontefract	2-9	0-1	2-6	0-0	0-2	22.2	+	3.91
Nottingham	2-11	1-4	1-4	0-1	0-2	18.2	–	0.62
Ayr	2-12	0-0	1-8	0-0	1-4	16.7	–	6.09
Lingfield	2-12	0-2	2-8	0-0	0-2	16.7	–	9.16
Windsor	2-14	0-0	1-13	0-0	1-1	14.3	–	1.00
Southwell (AW)	1-1	0-0	1-1	0-0	0-0	100.0	+	0.91
Hamilton	1-3	1-1	0-0	0-0	0-2	33.3	–	0.37
Folkestone	1-5	0-0	1-2	0-0	0-3	20.0	–	2.75
Thirsk	1-9	0-0	1-8	0-0	0-1	11.1	–	6.75
Epsom	1-10	0-0	1-6	0-0	0-4	10.0	–	7.25
Kempton	1-15	0-2	1-12	0-0	0-1	6.7	–	12.80

Brighton	0-6	Beverley	0-3	Edinburgh	0-1
Chepstow	0-6	Catterick	0-3		
Newcastle	0-4	Warwick	0-2		

WINNING HORSES

		Races					Win
	Age	Run	1st	2nd	3rd	Unpl	£
Halling	3	6	3	0	0	3	71,555
Muhtarram	5	3	1	1	1	0	66,355
Linney Head	3	3	2	0	0	1	47,858
Wainwright	5	8	3	2	1	2	44,527
Emperor Jones	4	5	1	2	0	2	44,280
Hill Hopper	3	6	4	2	0	0	37,473
Zieten	4	2	1	0	0	1	33,459
Pollen Count	5	2	2	0	0	0	26,560
Dime Time	3	12	3	1	2	6	25,496
Island Of Silver	3	7	4	2	1	0	24,891
Presenting	2	2	2	0	0	0	20,380
Mutakddim	3	6	3	1	0	2	20,241
Del Deya	4	4	1	1	0	2	19,884
Lower Egypt	4	8	2	2	2	2	18,105
Full Deposit	3	3	2	0	0	1	11,359
Diesan	3	7	1	1	2	3	10,046
Manssai	3	7	2	1	1	3	9,401
Red Earth	3	4	2	2	0	0	9,339
Nimphidia	3	5	2	2	0	1	8,807
Gleam Of Light	3	4	2	0	0	2	8,777
Winter Coat	3	7	1	2	1	3	7,685
Muktabas	2	1	1	0	0	0	7,165

P G Tips	3	5	2	2	0	1	7,114
Satin Velvet	3	4	1	1	0	2	7,067
Mystic Eagle	3	4	2	1	0	1	7,014
Wafayt	3	6	1	2	1	2	6,970
Durable	3	5	2	0	2	1	6,669
Airport	3	5	1	2	1	1	6,524
Istibshar	3	7	1	0	1	5	5,520
Solar Beam	3	2	1	0	0	1	5,299
Capias	3	5	1	1	0	3	5,068
Rainbow Mountain	3	4	1	1	0	2	4,944
Karoo Lark	3	3	1	0	1	1	4,944
Shoaq Albarr	3	3	1	1	0	1	4,860
Learmont	4	4	1	1	1	1	4,822
Assyrian	3	2	1	0	1	0	4,724
Shepton Mallet	3	1	1	0	0	0	4,654
Tegwen	3	5	1	2	0	2	4,653
Trimming	2	2	1	1	0	0	4,514
Puissant	3	3	1	0	1	1	4,450
Sudood	3	3	1	1	1	0	4,396
Pianola	3	1	1	0	0	0	4,373
Bunting	2	2	1	0	1	0	4,347
Dover Straits	3	5	1	2	0	2	4,293
Katsura	3	3	1	1	0	1	4,219
Leap For Joy	2	4	1	1	1	1	4,131
Realize	3	8	1	1	0	6	4,078
Laubali	3	4	1	0	0	3	4,007
Glanmerin	3	5	1	0	0	4	3,980
Flemensfirth	2	1	1	0	0	0	3,969
Pastel	2	5	1	2	0	2	3,835
Minstrel's Gift	3	5	1	0	1	3	3,721
New Man	2	3	1	1	0	1	3,678
Fire Worshipper	3	2	1	0	0	1	3,647
Tortuga	3	4	1	1	0	2	3,633
Lantern Hill	3	2	1	0	1	0	3,632
Clovis Point	3	7	1	3	2	1	3,590
Night Bell	3	5	1	4	0	0	3,570
Isle Of Spice	3	3	1	1	0	1	3,553
Line Out	3	4	1	0	2	1	3,469
Laila Alawi	3	5	1	0	0	4	3,466
Knight Of Poland	3	3	1	0	1	1	3,460
Quivira	3	5	1	0	1	3	3,444
Winburg	3	3	1	0	0	2	3,391
Najm Almaydaan	3	5	1	0	0	4	3,077
Aljathaab	3	5	1	0	0	4	3,042
Promise City	3	7	1	1	1	4	2,701

WINNING OWNERS

	Races Won	Value £		Races Won	Value £
Sheikh Mohammed	40	371,142	Anthony Speelman	1	7,685
Hamdan Al-Maktoum	7	103,288	R W M D'Abo	2	7,114
Sheikh Ahmed Al Maktoum	6	48,303	David J Heerensperger	2	7,014
Godolphin	4	45,210	Herbert Allen	2	6,669
Cheveley Park Stud	5	41,194	Mohammed Al Nabouda	1	4,347
K Abdulla	6	27,928	Seisuke Hata	1	4,131
C M Watt	3	25,496	Lord Hartington	1	4,078
George Strawbridge	2	20,380	Rex Norton	1	3,980
The Spinal Injuries Association	2	18,105	Mrs Rachel Hood	1	3,678
Sheikh Ahmed Bin Saeed			Saeed Manana	1	3,391
Al Maktoum	2	9,401	Sheikh Marwan Al Maktoum	1	3,042
Hesmonds Stud	2	8,576			

Favourites	46-141	32.6%	- 10.56	Total winning prize-money £774,152

Longest winning sequence			3	Average SP of winner	3.7/1
Longest losing sequence			27	Return on stakes invested	-15.4%

1993 Form	110-453	24.3%	+ 82.91	1991 Form	86-384	22.4%	- 7.12
1992 Form	113-519	21.8%	+ 7.73	1990 Form	87-354	24.6%	+ 12.87

N A GRAHAM (Newmarket)

	No. of Horses	Races Run	1st	2nd	3rd	Unpl	Per cent	£1 Level Stake
2-y-o	7	19	2	1	3	13	10.5	- 0.50
3-y-o	15	67	5	4	7	51	7.5	- 40.50
4-y-o+	6	26	1	5	5	15	3.8	- 19.00
Totals	28	112	8	10	15	79	7.1	- 60.00

Jan	Feb	Mar	Apr	May	Jun	Jul	Aug	Sep	Oct/Nov
1-7	3-6	1-4	0-10	1-20	0-19	1-14	0-10	1-11	0-11

Winning Jockeys	W-R	£1 Level Stake		W-R	£1 Level Stake
J Weaver	5-30	- 2.75	G Hind	1-1	+ 8.50
D Harrison	1-1	+ 11.00	L Dettori	1-4	- 0.75

Winning Courses	W-R	£1 Level Stake		W-R	£1 Level Stake
Lingfield (AW)	4-14	+ 3.50	Newcastle	1-1	+ 8.50
Wolverhampton (AW)	2-5	+ 11.00	Ripon	1-1	+ 8.00

Winning Horses	Age	Races Run	1st	2nd	3rd	Unpl	Win £
Wild Ace	3	7	2	0	0	5	6,144
Crumpton Hill	2	3	1	0	1	1	3,702
Top Pearl	2	5	1	0	1	3	3,216
Trinity House	3	7	1	0	0	6	3,024
Legal Artist	4	5	1	2	1	1	2,821
Tiddy Oggie	3	1	1	0	0	0	2,601
Plinth	3	10	1	1	2	6	2,355

Favourites	1-13	7.7%	- 9.50	Total winning prize-money			£23,864

1993 Form	7-84	8.3%	- 13.70	1991 Form	7-81	8.6%	- 24.56
1992 Form	6-90	6.7%	- 48.21	1990 Form	6-73	8.2%	- 38.50

B GUBBY (Bagshot, Surrey)

	No. of Horses	Races Run	1st	2nd	3rd	Unpl	Per cent	£1 Level Stake
2-y-o	4	14	0	2	1	11	-	- 14.00
3-y-o	2	9	0	0	0	9	-	- 9.00
4-y-o+	4	26	5	1	2	18	19.2	+ 14.83
Totals	10	49	5	3	3	38	10.2	- 8.17

Jan	Feb	Mar	Apr	May	Jun	Jul	Aug	Sep	Oct/Nov
1-4	0-2	0-5	0-1	1-8	1-12	1-6	1-7	0-2	0-2

Winning Jockeys	W-R	£1 Level Stake		W-R	£1 Level Stake
L Dettori	1-1	+ 5.00	Mrs M Busby	1-6	+ 5.00
Paul Eddery	1-3	+ 1.33	A Whelan	1-6	+ 7.00
T Ives	1-4	+ 2.50			

Winning Courses					
Lingfield (AW)	4-16	+ 11.83	Brighton	1-8	+ 5.00

Winning Horses	Age	Races Run	1st	2nd	3rd	Unpl	Win £
Our Eddie	5	10	3	1	1	5	8,892
Cone Lane	8	7	2	0	1	4	5,306

Favourites	0-0		Total winning prize-money	£14,198

1993 Form	1-37	2.7%	- 33.25	1991 Form	0-52		
1992 Form	2-70	2.9%	- 36.00	1990 Form	7-49	14.3%	+ 74.50

R GUEST (Newmarket)

	No. of Horses	Races Run	1st	2nd	3rd	Unpl	Per cent	£1 Level Stake
2-y-o	5	9	0	0	2	7	-	- 9.00
3-y-o	6	41	4	2	3	32	9.8	- 13.50
4-y-o+	5	25	2	6	3	14	8.0	- 8.00
Totals	16	75	6	8	8	53	8.0	- 30.50

Jan	Feb	Mar	Apr	May	Jun	Jul	Aug	Sep	Oct/Nov
0-1	1-2	0-2	0-3	0-7	2-13	2-13	0-14	1-14	0-6

Winning Jockeys	W-R	£1 Level Stake			W-R	£1 Level Stake
S Eiffert	2-10	+ 3.50	A Mackay		1-4	+ 4.00
J Weaver	1-3	+ 5.00	W Woods		1-9	- 0.50
J Carroll	1-4	+ 2.50				

Winning Courses						
Lingfield	2-3	+ 13.50	Lingfield (AW)		1-4	+ 5.00
Pontefract	1-2	+ 4.50	Wolverhampton (AW)		1-6	+ 2.00
Warwick	1-3	+ 1.50				

Winning Horses	Age	Races Run	1st	2nd	3rd	Unpl	Win £
Dia Georgy	3	11	2	2	0	7	6,288
Gallery Artist	6	12	2	4	1	5	5,516
Dom Pennion	3	4	1	0	1	2	3,926
Nice Welcome	3	5	1	0	1	3	3,540

Favourites	0-5		Total winning prize-money	£19,270

1993 Form	9-78	11.5%	- 26.92	1991 Form	5-92	5.4%	- 60.87
1992 Form	15-86	17.4%	+ 23.50	1990 Form	7-151	4.6%	-110.95

W J HAGGAS (Newmarket)

	No. of Horses	Races Run	1st	2nd	3rd	Unpl	Per cent	£1 Level Stake
2-y-o	8	22	1	3	2	16	4.5	- 17.67
3-y-o	15	93	15	18	9	51	16.1	+ 7.87
4-y-o+	5	40	6	6	5	23	15.0	+ 28.00
Totals	28	155	22	27	16	90	14.2	+ 18.20

164

BY MONTH

2-y-o	W-R	Per cent	£1 Level Stake		3-y-o	W-R	Per cent	£1 Level Stake	
January	0-0	-		0.00	January	0-6	-	-	6.00
February	0-0	-		0.00	February	1-3	33.3	+	3.50
March	0-0	-		0.00	March	0-4	-	-	4.00
April	0-1	-	-	1.00	April	7-10	70.0	+	41.87
May	0-0	-		0.00	May	2-17	11.8	-	10.37
June	0-0	-		0.00	June	2-14	14.3	-	8.38
July	0-2	-	-	2.00	July	0-12	-	-	12.00
August	0-5	-	-	5.00	August	3-10	30.0	+	20.25
September	0-6	-	-	6.00	September	0-11	-	-	11.00
Oct/Nov	1-8	12.5	-	3.67	Oct/Nov	0-6	-	-	6.00

4-y-o+	W-R	Per cent	£1 Level Stake		Totals	W-R	Per cent	£1 Level Stake	
January	0-0	-		0.00	January	0-6	-	-	6.00
February	0-0	-		0.00	February	1-3	33.3	+	3.50
March	0-0	-		0.00	March	0-4	-	-	4.00
April	1-4	25.0	+	13.00	April	8-15	53.3	+	53.87
May	1-3	33.3	+	23.00	May	3-20	15.0	+	12.63
June	1-4	25.0	-	1.00	June	3-18	16.7	-	9.38
July	1-4	25.0		0.00	July	1-18	5.6	-	14.00
August	2-9	22.2	+	9.00	August	5-24	20.8	+	24.25
September	0-7	-	-	7.00	September	0-24	-	-	24.00
Oct/Nov	0-9	-	-	9.00	Oct/Nov	1-23	4.3	-	18.67

DISTANCE

2-y-o	W-R	Per cent	£1 Level Stake		3-y-o	W-R	Per cent	£1 Level Stake	
5f-6f	0-11	-	-	11.00	5f-6f	6-19	31.6	+	32.37
7f-8f	1-10	10.0	-	5.67	7f-8f	4-33	12.1	+	2.50
9f-13f	0-1	-	-	1.00	9f-13f	4-35	11.4	-	25.00
14f+	0-0	-		0.00	14f+	1-6	16.7	-	2.00

4-y-o+	W-R	Per cent	£1 Level Stake		Totals	W-R	Per cent	£1 Level Stake	
5f-6f	2-11	18.2	+	12.00	5f-6f	8-41	19.5	+	33.37
7f-8f	2-17	11.8	-	10.00	7f-8f	7-60	11.7	-	13.17
9f-13f	2-8	25.0	+	30.00	9f-13f	6-44	13.6	+	4.00
14f+	0-4	-	-	4.00	14f+	1-10	10.0	-	6.00

TYPE OF RACE

Non-Handicaps	W-R	Per cent	£1 Level Stake		Handicaps	W-R	Per cent	£1 Level Stake	
2-y-o	1-15	6.7	-	10.67	2-y-o	0-5	-	-	5.00
3-y-o	11-51	21.6	+	7.24	3-y-o	4-35	11.4	+	7.63
4-y-o+	2-6	33.3	+	1.00	4-y-o+	4-33	12.1	+	28.00
Selling	0-2	-	-	2.00	Selling	0-2	-	-	2.00
Apprentice	0-1	-	-	1.00	Apprentice	0-4	-	-	4.00
Amat/Ladies	0-1	-	-	1.00	Amat/Ladies	0-0	-		0.00
Totals	14-76	18.4	-	6.43	Totals	8-79	10.1	+	24.63

COURSE GRADE

	W–R	Per cent	£1 Level Stake
Group 1	7-65	10.8	+ 19.00
Group 2	4-28	14.3	- 2.25
Group 3	4-26	15.4	- 4.88
Group 4	7-36	19.4	+ 6.33

FIRST TIME OUT

	W–R	Per cent	£1 Level Stake
2-y-o	0-8	-	- 8.00
3-y-o	3-14	21.4	+ 22.00
4-y-o+	3-4	75.0	+ 42.00
Totals	6-26	23.1	+ 56.00

JOCKEYS RIDING

	W–R	Per cent	£1 Level Stake		W–R	Per cent	£1 Level Stake
M Hills	10-40	25.0	+ 42.70	R Hills	2-8	25.0	+ 20.25
B Thomson	3-23	13.0	- 3.25	A Munro	1-1	100.0	+ 1.00
K Darley	2-5	40.0	+ 18.00	T Ives	1-2	50.0	- 0.38
R Cochrane	2-6	33.3	+ 6.88	W Woods	1-3	33.3	0.00

J Williams	0-8	B Rouse	0-2	D Biggs	0-1
M Tebbutt	0-5	F Norton	0-2	D Carson	0-1
W Ryan	0-5	G Carter	0-2	G Bardwell	0-1
L Dettori	0-4	G Milligan	0-2	J Tate	0-1
L Piggott	0-4	J Carroll	0-2	K Fallon	0-1
B Russell	0-3	J Quinn	0-2	K Rutter	0-1
G Duffield	0-3	M Roberts	0-2	Mrs M Haggas	0-1
J Weaver	0-3	T Quinn	0-2	S Drowne	0-1
W Carson	0-3	B Raymond	0-1	W R Swinburn	0-1
B Doyle	0-2	C Rutter	0-1		

COURSE RECORD

	Total W–R	Non-Handicaps 2-y-o	3-y-o+	Handicaps 2-y-o	3-y-o+	Per cent	£1 Level Stake
Wolverhampton (AW)	3-10	0-0	2-8	0-0	1-2	30.0	+ 1.38
Haydock	2-7	0-0	2-4	0-0	0-3	28.6	- 2.75
Leicester	2-7	0-1	1-3	0-0	1-3	28.6	+ 9.50
Ripon	2-9	0-1	0-1	0-0	2-7	22.2	+ 9.00
Chester	1-2	0-0	1-1	0-0	0-1	50.0	+ 2.00
Kempton	1-2	0-0	0-0	0-0	1-2	50.0	+ 15.00
Sandown	1-2	0-0	1-1	0-0	0-1	50.0	+ 0.25
Beverley	1-3	0-0	1-3	0-0	0-0	33.3	0.00
Catterick	1-3	0-0	1-3	0-0	0-0	33.3	+ 1.00
Folkestone	1-4	1-2	0-2	0-0	0-0	25.0	+ 0.33
Goodwood	1-4	0-1	0-1	0-0	1-2	25.0	+ 22.00
Nottingham	1-4	0-1	1-1	0-1	0-1	25.0	- 2.38
Southwell (AW)	1-4	0-1	1-2	0-0	0-1	25.0	- 2.38
Warwick	1-6	0-1	1-2	0-1	0-2	16.7	+ 15.00
Lingfield	1-8	0-2	0-2	0-0	1-4	12.5	- 4.25
York	1-11	0-0	0-2	0-0	1-9	9.1	+ 15.00
Newmarket	1-20	0-2	1-7	0-0	0-11	5.0	- 11.50

Lingfield (AW)	0-8	Thirsk	0-4	Pontefract	0-2
Yarmouth	0-8	Redcar	0-3	Chepstow	0-1
Ascot	0-5	Brighton	0-2	Edinburgh	0-1
Ayr	0-5	Doncaster	0-2	Newcastle	0-1
Newbury	0-4	Epsom	0-2	Windsor	0-1

WINNING HORSES

	Age	Races Run	1st	2nd	3rd	Unpl	Win £
Numbered Account	3	9	3	0	2	4	24,402
Patto	3	4	3	0	0	1	12,100
Gobsmacked	3	11	3	4	0	4	11,509
Neatstep	3	9	3	1	1	4	10,043
Absolute Magic	4	11	2	2	2	5	8,971
Sharaar	4	6	1	0	1	4	7,570
Rock Symphony	4	11	1	1	2	7	7,475
Miss Pin Up	5	5	1	2	0	2	4,854
River Board	4	7	1	1	0	5	3,241
Silver Tzar	2	3	1	0	0	2	2,986
Bold Jewel	3	3	1	0	2	0	2,963
Lyphard's Fable	3	10	1	3	0	6	2,951
Referential	3	11	1	3	2	5	2,665

WINNING OWNERS

	Races Won	Value £		Races Won	Value £
Highclere Th'bred Racing Ltd	3	24,402	Mrs C E Feather	1	7,475
B Haggas	6	23,609	E Baldwin	1	4,854
Cheveley Park Stud	5	15,957	Mrs M M C Clark	1	3,241
Mrs Barbara Bassett	2	8,971	P A Deal	1	2,986
Ali K Al Jafleh	1	7,570	Saeed Abdullah Humaid	1	2,665

Favourites	10-31	32.3%	- 2.63	Total winning prize-money	£101,729

Longest winning sequence	3	Average SP of winner	6.9/1
Longest losing sequence	48	Return on stakes invested	11.7%

1993 Form	13-127	10.2%	- 40.12	1991 Form	27-136	19.9%	+ 37.00
1992 Form	13-132	9.8%	- 58.49	1990 Form	21-141	14.9%	- 20.68

W W HAIGH (Malton, North Yorks)

	No. of Horses	Races Run	1st	2nd	3rd	Unpl	Per cent	£1 Level Stake
2-y-o	1	5	0	1	1	3	-	- 5.00
3-y-o	5	28	1	5	2	20	3.6	- 23.50
4-y-o+	9	53	5	8	10	30	9.4	- 18.00
Totals	15	86	6	14	13	53	7.0	- 46.50

Jan	Feb	Mar	Apr	May	Jun	Jul	Aug	Sep	Oct/Nov
0-6	1-1	1-2	0-10	0-16	0-11	2-12	2-16	0-4	0-8

Winning Jockeys	W-R	£1 Level Stake			W-R	£1 Level Stake
D McKeown	3-42	- 26.00	J Tate		1-6	- 1.50
B Raymond	1-1	+ 9.00	Dale Gibson		1-21	- 12.00

Winning Courses						
Newcastle	2-5	+ 4.50	Haydock		1-6	+ 4.00
Southwell (AW)	2-17	- 6.00	Redcar		1-11	- 2.00

Winning Horses	Age	Races Run	1st	2nd	3rd	Unpl	Win £
Solomon's Dancer	4	11	2	1	2	6	9,074
I'm A Dreamer	4	7	1	0	2	4	3,173
Mr Towser	3	10	1	5	0	4	3,028
Round By The River	5	6	1	1	2	2	2,576
Claudia Miss	7	7	1	0	1	5	2,243

Favourites	1-9	11.1%	- 6.00	Total winning prize-money		£20,093

1993 Form	11-105	10.5%	- 35.00	1991 Form	7-80	8.8%	- 48.29
1992 Form	9-100	9.0%	- 27.37	1990 Form	5-87	5.7%	- 19.00

MISS S E HALL (Middleham, North Yorks)

	No. of Horses	Races Run	1st	2nd	3rd	Unpl	Per cent	£1 Level Stake
2-y-o	9	37	2	5	4	26	5.4	- 5.50
3-y-o	7	31	5	4	3	19	16.1	- 6.00
4-y-o+	8	46	4	8	7	27	8.7	- 22.00
Totals	24	114	11	17	14	72	9.6	- 33.50

BY MONTH

2-y-o	W-R	Per cent	£1 Level Stake	3-y-o	W-R	Per cent	£1 Level Stake
January	0-0	-	0.00	January	0-0	-	0.00
February	0-0	-	0.00	February	0-0	-	0.00
March	0-0	-	0.00	March	0-0	-	0.00
April	0-1	-	- 1.00	April	1-1	100.0	+ 4.00
May	0-2	-	- 2.00	May	0-4	-	- 4.00
June	1-2	50.0	+ 24.00	June	1-6	16.7	- 2.50
July	0-5	-	- 5.00	July	0-5	-	- 5.00
August	1-12	8.3	- 6.50	August	3-10	30.0	+ 6.50
September	0-8	-	- 8.00	September	0-4	-	- 4.00
Oct/Nov	0-7	-	- 7.00	Oct/Nov	0-1	-	- 1.00

4-y-o+	W-R	Per cent	£1 Level Stake	Totals	W-R	Per cent	£1 Level Stake
January	0-0	-	0.00	January	0-0	-	0.00
February	0-0	-	0.00	February	0-0	-	0.00
March	0-2	-	- 2.00	March	0-2	-	- 2.00
April	0-2	-	- 2.00	April	1-4	25.0	+ 1.00
May	1-10	10.0	- 4.00	May	1-16	6.3	- 10.00
June	1-5	20.0	+ 2.00	June	3-13	23.1	+ 23.50
July	1-11	9.1	- 6.00	July	1-21	4.8	- 16.00
August	1-6	16.7	0.00	August	5-28	17.9	0.00
September	0-4	-	- 4.00	September	0-16	-	- 16.00
Oct/Nov	0-6	-	- 6.00	Oct/Nov	0-14	-	- 14.00

DISTANCE

2-y-o	W-R	Per cent	£1 Level Stake	3-y-o	W-R	Per cent	£1 Level Stake
5f-6f	2-27	7.4	+ 4.50	5f-6f	2-8	25.0	+ 1.50
7f-8f	0-10	-	- 10.00	7f-8f	1-7	14.3	- 2.00
9f-13f	0-0	-	0.00	9f-13f	1-11	9.1	- 4.00
14f+	0-0	-	0.00	14f+	1-5	20.0	- 1.50

4-y-o+	W-R	Per cent	£1 Level Stake	Totals	W-R	Per cent	£1 Level Stake
5f-6f	0-1	-	- 1.00	5f-6f	4-36	11.1	+ 5.00
7f-8f	3-24	12.5	- 7.00	7f-8f	4-41	9.8	- 19.00
9f-13f	1-20	5.0	- 13.00	9f-13f	2-31	6.5	- 17.00
14f+	0-1	-	- 1.00	14f+	1-6	16.7	- 2.50

TYPE OF RACE

Non-Handicaps	W-R	Per cent	£1 Level Stake	Handicaps	W-R	Per cent	£1 Level Stake
2-y-o	1-27	3.7	- 1.00	2-y-o	1-9	11.1	- 3.50
3-y-o	2-11	18.2	- 2.50	3-y-o	2-17	11.8	- 4.50
4-y-o+	0-7	-	- 7.00	4-y-o+	4-37	10.8	- 13.00
Selling	0-1	-	- 1.00	Selling	0-1	-	- 1.00
Apprentice	0-0	-	0.00	Apprentice	1-3	33.3	+ 1.00
Amat/Ladies	0-0	-	0.00	Amat/Ladies	0-1	-	- 1.00
Totals	3-46	6.5	- 11.50	Totals	8-68	11.8	- 22.00

COURSE GRADE

	W-R	Per cent	£1 Level Stake
Group 1	1-43	2.3	- 37.00
Group 2	6-43	14.0	- 9.00
Group 3	1-12	8.3	- 7.00
Group 4	3-16	18.8	+ 19.50

FIRST TIME OUT

	W-R	Per cent	£1 Level Stake
2-y-o	0-9	-	- 9.00
3-y-o	1-7	14.3	- 2.00
4-y-o+	1-8	12.5	- 2.00
Totals	2-24	8.3	- 13.00

JOCKEYS RIDING

	W-R	Per cent	£1 Level Stake		W-R	Per cent	£1 Level Stake
N Connorton	7-74	9.5	- 15.00	J Fortune	1-4	25.0	+ 1.00
S Mulvey	2-2	100.0	+ 7.50	J Stack	1-8	12.5	- 1.00

Dale Gibson	0-3	C Rutter	0-1	N Varley	0-1
G Bardwell	0-2	G Duffield	0-1	Nicola Howarth	0-1
J Lowe	0-2	J Fanning	0-1	R Cochrane	0-1
L Piggott	0-2	J Reid	0-1	Stephen Davies	0-1
M Fenton	0-2	J Tate	0-1	W Woods	0-1
S Webster	0-2	Mrs A Farrell	0-1		
A Whelan	0-1	N Kennedy	0-1		

COURSE RECORD

	Total W-R	Non-Handicaps 2-y-o	3-y-o+	Handicaps 2-y-o	3-y-o+	Per cent	£1 Level Stake
Ripon	3-23	0-8	0-6	0-0	3-9	13.0	- 6.50
Carlisle	2-3	0-0	1-1	0-0	1-2	66.7	+ 6.50
Thirsk	2-5	0-1	1-2	1-1	0-1	40.0	+ 5.50
Hamilton	1-5	0-1	0-0	0-0	1-4	20.0	0.00
Catterick	1-8	1-3	0-0	0-2	0-3	12.5	+ 18.00
Ayr	1-13	0-4	0-2	0-2	1-5	7.7	- 7.00
Redcar	1-15	0-3	0-1	0-1	1-10	6.7	- 8.00

York	0-9	Newmarket	0-4	Southwell (AW)	0-2
Newcastle	0-6	Beverley	0-3	Goodwood	0-1
Doncaster	0-5	Pontefract	0-3	Nottingham	0-1
Haydock	0-5	Edinburgh	0-2	Wolverhampton (AW)	0-1

WINNING HORSES

	Age	Races Run	1st	2nd	3rd	Unpl	Win £
Sky Music	3	5	3	0	0	2	11,435
Leif The Lucky	5	8	2	2	1	3	10,451
Corio	2	8	2	1	1	4	7,355
Silverlocks	4	8	1	1	1	5	5,345
Mam'Zelle Angot	4	8	1	3	1	3	4,435
Bowcliffe	3	4	1	0	0	3	4,068
Opus One	3	7	1	0	3	3	2,449

WINNING OWNERS

	Races Won	Value £		Races Won	Value £
Miss Betty Duxbury	5	23,151	J Hanson	1	4,068
Footballers' Racing Club	3	11,435	R Ogden	1	2,449
R Fenwick-Gibson	1	4,435			

Favourites	4-11	36.4%	+ 10.50	Total winning prize-money			£45,538
Longest winning sequence			2	Average SP of winner			6.3/1
Longest losing sequence			33	Return on stakes invested			-29.4%
1993 Form	14-93	15.1%	- 21.47	1991 Form	6-88	6.8%	- 39.17
1992 Form	9-84	10.7%	- 9.52	1990 Form	12-133	9.0%	- 46.35

M D HAMMOND (Middleham, North Yorks)

	No. of Horses	Races Run	1st	2nd	3rd	Unpl	Per cent	£1 Level Stake
2-y-o	0	0	0	0	0	0	-	0.00
3-y-o	7	19	3	0	1	15	15.8	+ 15.75
4-y-o+	21	89	9	5	8	67	10.1	- 21.75
Totals	28	108	12	5	9	82	11.1	- 6.00

BY MONTH

2-y-o	W-R	Per cent	£1 Level Stake	3-y-o	W-R	Per cent	£1 Level Stake
January	0-0	-	0.00	January	0-0	-	0.00
February	0-0	-	0.00	February	0-0	-	0.00
March	0-0	-	0.00	March	0-0	-	0.00
April	0-0	-	0.00	April	0-2	-	- 2.00
May	0-0	-	0.00	May	2-4	50.0	+ 4.75
June	0-0	-	0.00	June	1-5	20.0	+ 21.00
July	0-0	-	0.00	July	0-4	-	- 4.00
August	0-0	-	0.00	August	0-1	-	- 1.00
September	0-0	-	0.00	September	0-1	-	- 1.00
Oct/Nov	0-0	-	0.00	Oct/Nov	0-2	-	- 2.00

4-y-o+	W-R	Per cent	£1 Level Stake	Totals	W-R	Per cent	£1 Level Stake
January	0-3	-	- 3.00	January	0-3	-	- 3.00
February	0-4	-	- 4.00	February	0-4	-	- 4.00
March	0-3	-	- 3.00	March	0-3	-	- 3.00
April	1-4	25.0	+ 11.00	April	1-6	16.7	+ 9.00
May	2-17	11.8	- 2.00	May	4-21	19.0	+ 2.75
June	1-17	5.9	- 10.50	June	2-22	9.1	+ 10.50
July	4-13	30.8	+ 14.50	July	4-17	23.5	+ 10.50
August	1-11	9.1	- 7.75	August	1-12	8.3	- 8.75
September	0-11	-	- 11.00	September	0-12	-	- 12.00
Oct/Nov	0-6	-	- 6.00	Oct/Nov	0-8	-	- 8.00

DISTANCE

2-y-o	W-R	Per cent	£1 Level Stake	3-y-o	W-R	Per cent	£1 Level Stake
5f-6f	0-0	-	0.00	5f-6f	0-0	-	0.00
7f-8f	0-0	-	0.00	7f-8f	2-6	33.3	+ 2.75
9f-13f	0-0	-	0.00	9f-13f	1-9	11.1	+ 17.00
14f+	0-0	-	0.00	14f+	0-4	-	- 4.00

4-y-o+	W-R	Per cent	£1 Level Stake	Totals	W-R	Per cent	£1 Level Stake
5f-6f	4-18	22.2	+ 4.75	5f-6f	4-18	22.2	+ 4.75
7f-8f	1-21	4.8	- 14.50	7f-8f	3-27	11.1	- 11.75
9f-13f	3-35	8.6	- 2.00	9f-13f	4-44	9.1	+ 15.00
14f+	1-15	6.7	- 10.00	14f+	1-19	5.3	- 14.00

TYPE OF RACE

Non-Handicaps	W-R	Per cent	£1 Level Stake	Handicaps	W-R	Per cent	£1 Level Stake
2-y-o	0-0	-	0.00	2-y-o	0-0	-	0.00
3-y-o	1-8	12.5	+ 18.00	3-y-o	1-7	14.3	- 2.00
4-y-o+	0-9	-	- 9.00	4-y-o+	9-75	12.0	- 7.75
Selling	1-3	33.3	+ 0.75	Selling	0-1	-	- 1.00
Apprentice	0-0	-	0.00	Apprentice	0-2	-	- 2.00
Amat/Ladies	0-0	-	0.00	Amat/Ladies	0-3	-	- 3.00
Totals	2-20	10.0	+ 9.75	Totals	10-88	11.4	- 15.75

COURSE GRADE

	W-R	Per cent	£1 Level Stake
Group 1	0-17	-	- 17.00
Group 2	3-17	17.6	+ 3.25
Group 3	4-39	10.3	+ 15.75
Group 4	5-35	14.3	- 8.00

FIRST TIME OUT

	W-R	Per cent	£1 Level Stake
2-y-o	0-0	-	0.00
3-y-o	1-4	25.0	+ 22.00
4-y-o+	1-21	4.8	- 6.00
Totals	2-25	8.0	+ 16.00

JOCKEYS RIDING

	W-R	Per cent	£1 Level Stake		W-R	Per cent	£1 Level Stake
J Marshall	7-50	14.0	+ 3.25	Dale Gibson	1-7	14.3	+ 2.00
K Darley	1-3	33.3	+ 0.75	D McKeown	1-11	9.1	+ 15.00
J Carroll	1-4	25.0	+ 1.00	G Duffield	1-12	8.3	- 7.00

J Stack	0-3	L Dettori	0-1	P Robinson	0-1
J Weaver	0-3	M Hills	0-1	S Maloney	0-1
D Moffatt	0-2	Mr C Bonner	0-1	T Williams	0-1
A Ferris	0-1	Mrs A Farrell	0-1	W Carson	0-1
A Garth	0-1	Mrs D Kettlewell	0-1		
B Raymond	0-1	Mrs L Pearce	0-1		

COURSE RECORD

	Total W-R	Non-Handicaps 2-y-o	3-y-o+	Handicaps 2-y-o	3-y-o+	Per cent	£1 Level Stake
Carlisle	3-14	0-0	0-4	0-0	3-10	21.4	+ 2.50
Chester	2-2	0-0	0-0	0-0	2-2	100.0	+ 15.00
Catterick	2-5	0-0	0-1	0-0	2-4	40.0	+ 5.50
Beverley	2-12	0-0	1-1	0-0	1-11	16.7	+ 29.00
Redcar	1-7	0-0	0-0	0-0	1-7	14.3	- 3.75
Pontefract	1-9	0-0	0-1	0-0	1-8	11.1	+ 1.00
Hamilton	1-17	0-0	1-5	0-0	0-12	5.9	- 13.25

Edinburgh	0-7	York	0-4	Thirsk	0-2
Southwell (AW)	0-7	Doncaster	0-3	Wolverhampton (AW)	0-2
Ripon	0-6	Haydock	0-3	Ayr	0-1
Newmarket	0-4	Newcastle	0-2	Leicester	0-1

WINNING HORSES

	Age	Races Run	1st	2nd	3rd	Unpl	Win £
Master Ofthe House	8	8	4	0	1	3	18,993
Miss Movie World	5	7	3	0	0	4	9,431
Riva's Book	3	7	2	0	0	5	5,341
Formidable Liz	4	8	1	1	0	6	4,997
Troy's Dream	3	2	1	0	0	1	3,317
Explosive Speed	6	6	1	2	1	2	3,210

WINNING OWNERS

	Races Won	Value £		Races Won	Value £
Allerton Racing Club	4	18,993	Trevor Hemmings	3	8,657
J Johnson	4	14,428	Wetherby Racing Bureau Plc	1	3,210

Favourites	3-8	37.5%	+ 3.00	Total winning prize-money	£45,287
Longest winning sequence			1	Average SP of winner	7.5/1
Longest losing sequence			30	Return on stakes invested	-5.6%

1993 Form	11-155	7.1%	- 46.00	1991 Form	1-42	2.4%	- 31.00
1992 Form	9-58	15.5%	- 3.49	1990 Form	5-25	20.0%	+ 15.50

B HANBURY (Newmarket)

	No. of Horses	Races Run	1st	2nd	3rd	Unpl	Per cent	£1 Level Stake
2-y-o	19	57	8	7	8	34	14.0	- 13.59
3-y-o	17	108	11	15	8	74	10.2	- 52.17
4-y-o+	8	56	6	3	9	38	10.7	- 21.94
Totals	44	221	25	25	25	146	11.3	- 87.70

Hanbury B

BY MONTH

2-y-o	W-R	Per cent	£1 Level Stake	3-y-o	W-R	Per cent	£1 Level Stake
January	0-0	-	0.00	January	0-2	-	- 2.00
February	0-0	-	0.00	February	0-1	-	- 1.00
March	0-0	-	0.00	March	0-2	-	- 2.00
April	0-1	-	- 1.00	April	1-17	5.9	- 14.25
May	0-3	-	- 3.00	May	2-22	9.1	- 12.62
June	1-4	25.0	+ 2.00	June	1-18	5.6	- 13.50
July	1-9	11.1	- 5.75	July	5-19	26.3	- 1.80
August	3-14	21.4	+ 3.83	August	2-17	11.8	+ 5.00
September	2-12	16.7	0.00	September	0-9	-	- 9.00
Oct/Nov	1-14	7.1	- 9.67	Oct/Nov	0-1	-	- 1.00

4-y-o+	W-R	Per cent	£1 Level Stake	Totals	W-R	Per cent	£1 Level Stake
January	0-0	-	0.00	January	0-2	-	- 2.00
February	0-0	-	0.00	February	0-1	-	- 1.00
March	0-0	-	0.00	March	0-2	-	- 2.00
April	2-5	40.0	+ 2.21	April	3-23	13.0	- 13.04
May	0-11	-	- 11.00	May	2-36	5.6	- 26.62
June	1-10	10.0	- 6.75	June	3-32	9.4	- 18.25
July	3-11	27.3	+ 12.60	July	9-39	23.1	+ 5.05
August	0-8	-	- 8.00	August	5-39	12.8	+ 0.83
September	0-7	-	- 7.00	September	2-28	7.1	- 16.00
Oct/Nov	0-4	-	- 4.00	Oct/Nov	1-19	5.3	- 14.67

DISTANCE

2-y-o	W-R	Per cent	£1 Level Stake	3-y-o	W-R	Per cent	£1 Level Stake
5f-6f	7-36	19.4	+ 0.91	5f-6f	3-15	20.0	- 7.67
7f-8f	1-21	4.8	- 14.50	7f-8f	3-57	5.3	- 41.50
9f-13f	0-0	-	0.00	9f-13f	5-36	13.9	- 3.00
14f+	0-0	-	0.00	14f+	0-0	-	0.00

4-y-o+	W-R	Per cent	£1 Level Stake	Totals	W-R	Per cent	£1 Level Stake
5f-6f	2-4	50.0	+ 3.21	5f-6f	12-55	21.8	- 3.55
7f-8f	2-11	18.2	+ 7.25	7f-8f	6-89	6.7	- 48.75
9f-13f	2-34	5.9	- 25.40	9f-13f	7-70	10.0	- 28.40
14f+	0-7	-	- 7.00	14f+	0-7	-	- 7.00

TYPE OF RACE

Non-Handicaps	W-R	Per cent	£1 Level Stake	Handicaps	W-R	Per cent	£1 Level Stake
2-y-o	8-52	15.4	- 8.59	2-y-o	0-3	-	- 3.00
3-y-o	6-62	9.7	- 40.05	3-y-o	4-40	10.0	- 10.62
4-y-o+	3-10	30.0	+ 0.46	4-y-o+	2-43	4.7	- 21.50
Selling	0-4	-	- 4.00	Selling	1-2	50.0	+ 2.50
Apprentice	0-0	-	0.00	Apprentice	1-4	25.0	- 1.90
Amat/Ladies	0-0	-	0.00	Amat/Ladies	0-1	-	- 1.00
Totals	17-128	13.3	- 52.18	Totals	8-93	8.6	- 35.52

174

COURSE GRADE

	W-R	Per cent	£1 Level Stake
Group 1	10-115	8.7	- 45.94
Group 2	5-44	11.4	- 19.50
Group 3	7-49	14.3	- 19.22
Group 4	3-13	23.1	- 3.04

FIRST TIME OUT

	W-R	Per cent	£1 Level Stake
2-y-o	3-19	15.8	- 1.50
3-y-o	1-17	5.9	- 14.25
4-y-o+	2-8	25.0	- 1.87
Totals	6-44	13.6	- 17.62

JOCKEYS RIDING

	W-R	Per cent	£1 Level Stake		W-R	Per cent	£1 Level Stake
B Raymond	7-42	16.7	+ 1.63	M Birch	1-3	33.3	+ 3.50
W R Swinburn	6-35	17.1	- 8.66	J Weaver	1-5	20.0	- 0.67
W Ryan	3-19	15.8	- 6.92	K Darley	1-6	16.7	- 4.43
L Piggott	2-9	22.2	+ 9.25	R Cochrane	1-10	10.0	- 5.00
Pat Eddery	1-1	100.0	+ 6.00	P Bowe	1-19	5.3	- 16.90
W Woods	1-2	50.0	+ 4.50				

T Ives	0-7	N Carlisle	0-2	J Reid	0-1
J O'Dwyer	0-6	P Robinson	0-2	J Williams	0-1
R Hills	0-5	Paul Eddery	0-2	L Newton	0-1
D Holland	0-4	W Newnes	0-2	M Fenton	0-1
J Tate	0-4	A Munro	0-1	M Perrett	0-1
L Dettori	0-4	C Hodgson	0-1	M Roberts	0-1
M Hills	0-4	D Griffiths	0-1	M Tebbutt	0-1
A McGlone	0-3	G Duffield	0-1	Mr M Armytage	0-1
D McKeown	0-3	J Carroll	0-1	N Varley	0-1
J Stack	0-3	J Lowe	0-1		
W Carson	0-3	J Quinn	0-1		

COURSE RECORD

	Total W-R	Non-Handicaps 2-y-o	Non-Handicaps 3-y-o+	Handicaps 2-y-o	Handicaps 3-y-o+	Per cent	£1 Level Stake
Newmarket	4-36	1-10	2-11	0-1	1-14	11.1	- 3.67
Bath	2-3	2-2	0-0	0-0	0-1	66.7	+ 8.33
Nottingham	2-7	1-2	0-2	0-0	1-3	28.6	+ 3.50
Salisbury	2-8	1-4	0-2	0-0	1-2	25.0	+ 5.00
Lingfield (AW)	1-1	0-0	1-1	0-0	0-0	100.0	+ 1.75
Catterick	1-2	0-1	0-0	0-0	1-1	50.0	+ 0.88
Folkestone	1-2	1-1	0-0	0-0	0-1	50.0	+ 2.33
Epsom	1-4	0-1	0-1	0-0	1-2	25.0	- 1.90
Hamilton	1-4	0-1	0-2	0-0	1-1	25.0	- 0.50
Pontefract	1-4	0-0	1-3	0-0	0-1	25.0	- 1.12
Ayr	1-6	0-2	0-3	0-0	1-1	16.7	+ 0.50
Lingfield	1-7	1-3	0-2	0-0	0-2	14.3	- 2.00
Kempton	1-8	0-0	1-3	0-1	0-4	12.5	- 5.12
Thirsk	1-8	1-3	0-2	0-0	0-3	12.5	- 4.75
York	1-8	0-2	0-0	0-0	1-6	12.5	+ 9.00
Beverley	1-9	0-0	1-4	0-0	0-5	11.1	- 7.43
Haydock	1-9	0-1	1-2	0-0	0-6	11.1	- 4.00
Newbury	1-11	0-1	1-4	0-0	0-6	9.1	- 7.75
Ripon	1-11	0-3	1-4	0-0	0-4	9.1	- 7.75

Hanbury B

Sandown	0–10	Doncaster	0–5	Brighton	0–1
Yarmouth	0–10	Goodwood	0–5	Carlisle	0–1
Leicester	0–9	Warwick	0–4	Windsor	0–1
Ascot	0–7	Redcar	0–3	Wolverhampton (AW)	0–1
Chester	0–6	Chepstow	0–2		
Newcastle	0–6	Southwell (AW)	0–2		

WINNING HORSES

	Age	Races Run	1st	2nd	3rd	Unpl	Win £
En Attendant	6	6	1	0	0	5	24,075
Marsoom	3	9	2	2	0	5	19,984
Midhish	4	3	2	0	1	0	16,792
Raknah	3	10	4	2	0	4	15,436
Bsheer	3	9	2	1	0	6	8,586
Cheyenne Spirit	2	6	2	0	0	4	7,915
Green Palm Tree	2	4	1	2	1	0	4,688
Bin Ajwaad	4	4	1	0	0	3	4,287
Blue Blazer	4	13	1	2	1	9	4,054
Moments Of Fortune	2	2	1	0	0	1	3,992
Maydaan	2	2	1	0	0	1	3,899
Dance Band	2	2	1	1	0	0	3,664
Sovereign Page	5	11	1	1	3	6	3,623
Munguy	2	7	1	2	1	3	3,469
Rupan	3	7	1	1	1	4	3,216
Ramani	3	6	1	0	0	5	3,202
Bent Al Fala	2	5	1	0	2	2	2,812
Chancey Fella	3	8	1	2	1	4	2,070

WINNING OWNERS

	Races Won	Value £		Races Won	Value £
Saeed Suhail	4	25,378	Mohammed Saeed	1	4,688
Mrs B Newton	1	24,075	A Merza	1	4,287
Hilal Salem	3	22,796	McHalapar Syndicate	1	4,054
Abdullah Ali	5	17,974	Mrs Ben Hanbury	1	3,623
Jaber Abdullah	4	15,436	Juma Humaid	1	3,469
C Mauritzon	2	7,915	R R Prettie	1	2,070

Favourites	8–31	25.8%	– 6.07	Total winning prize-money			£135,765
Longest winning sequence			2	Average SP of winner			4.3/1
Longest losing sequence			35	Return on stakes invested			–39.7%
1993 Form	35–222	15.8%	– 40.37	1991 Form	36–302	11.9%	– 45.68
1992 Form	39–308	12.7%	– 64.98	1990 Form	36–274	13.1%	– 51.86

R HANNON (East Everleigh, Wilts)

	No. of Horses	Races Run	1st	2nd	3rd	Unpl	Per cent	£1 Level Stake
2-y-o	123	478	57	65	65	291	11.9	-107.66
3-y-o	77	454	41	48	46	319	9.0	-221.16
4-y-o+	30	180	13	11	17	139	7.2	- 57.24
Totals	230	1112	111	124	128	749	10.0	-386.06

BY MONTH

2-y-o	W-R	Per cent	£1 Level Stake	3-y-o	W-R	Per cent	£1 Level Stake
January	0-0	-	0.00	January	0-0	-	0.00
February	0-0	-	0.00	February	0-1	-	- 1.00
March	0-5	-	- 5.00	March	4-19	21.1	- 4.27
April	3-17	17.6	- 4.67	April	12-71	16.9	- 5.89
May	7-47	14.9	- 13.34	May	6-80	7.5	- 17.00
June	9-61	14.8	- 31.66	June	7-85	8.2	- 49.75
July	11-92	12.0	- 6.09	July	4-64	6.3	- 49.30
August	13-89	14.6	- 27.90	August	4-50	8.0	- 33.45
September	8-95	8.4	- 2.50	September	2-52	3.8	- 40.50
Oct/Nov	6-72	8.3	- 16.50	Oct/Nov	2-32	6.3	- 20.00

4-y-o+	W-R	Per cent	£1 Level Stake	Totals	W-R	Per cent	£1 Level Stake
January	1-3	33.3	+ 4.50	January	1-3	33.3	+ 4.50
February	2-5	40.0	+ 9.91	February	2-6	33.3	+ 8.91
March	0-9	-	- 9.00	March	4-33	12.1	- 18.27
April	2-26	7.7	- 9.50	April	17-114	14.9	- 20.06
May	2-33	6.1	- 17.90	May	15-160	9.4	- 48.24
June	2-25	8.0	+ 4.50	June	18-171	10.5	- 76.91
July	1-18	5.6	- 1.00	July	16-174	9.2	- 56.39
August	1-19	5.3	- 15.25	August	18-158	11.4	- 76.60
September	1-26	3.8	- 20.50	September	11-173	6.4	- 63.50
Oct/Nov	1-16	6.3	- 3.00	Oct/Nov	9-120	7.5	- 39.50

DISTANCE

2-y-o	W-R	Per cent	£1 Level Stake	3-y-o	W-R	Per cent	£1 Level Stake
5f-6f	38-300	12.7	- 60.88	5f-6f	8-94	8.5	- 55.47
7f-8f	18-175	10.3	- 48.28	7f-8f	22-203	10.8	- 73.49
9f-13f	1-3	33.3	+ 1.50	9f-13f	11-143	7.7	- 78.20
14f+	0-0	-	0.00	14f+	0-14	-	- 14.00

4-y-o+	W-R	Per cent	£1 Level Stake	Totals	W-R	Per cent	£1 Level Stake
5f-6f	3-35	8.6	+ 4.50	5f-6f	49-429	11.4	-111.85
7f-8f	3-57	5.3	- 19.00	7f-8f	43-435	9.9	-140.77
9f-13f	3-64	4.7	- 46.09	9f-13f	15-210	7.1	-122.79
14f+	4-24	16.7	+ 3.35	14f+	4-38	10.5	- 10.65

TYPE OF RACE

Non-Handicaps	W-R	Per cent	£1 Level Stake	Handicaps	W-R	Per cent	£1 Level Stake
2-y-o	49-386	12.7	- 85.29	2-y-o	7-73	9.6	- 9.87
3-y-o	24-207	11.6	- 82.39	3-y-o	15-219	6.8	- 120.52
4-y-o+	5-60	8.3	- 28.99	4-y-o+	7-109	6.4	- 24.75
Selling	2-20	10.0	- 10.25	Selling	0-5	-	- 5.00
Apprentice	0-4	-	- 4.00	Apprentice	2-20	10.0	- 6.00
Amat/Ladies	0-0	-	0.00	Amat/Ladies	0-9	-	- 9.00
Totals	80-677	11.8	-210.92	Totals	31-435	7.1	-175.14

COURSE GRADE

	W-R	Per cent	£1 Level Stake
Group 1	53-680	7.8	-315.98
Group 2	21-178	11.8	- 26.72
Group 3	28-195	14.4	- 39.18
Group 4	9-59	15.3	- 4.18

FIRST TIME OUT

	W-R	Per cent	£1 Level Stake
2-y-o	8-122	6.6	- 16.62
3-y-o	8-76	10.5	- 19.00
4-y-o+	2-29	6.9	- 7.50
Totals	18-227	7.9	- 43.12

JOCKEYS RIDING

	W-R	Per cent	£1 Level Stake		W-R	Per cent	£1 Level Stake
Pat Eddery	31-178	17.4	- 36.90	T Quinn	3-28	10.7	+ 1.50
J Reid	14-171	8.2	- 84.09	W R Swinburn	3-29	10.3	+ 9.38
L Dettori	12-97	12.4	- 29.74	B Raymond	2-16	12.5	- 4.67
R Perham	10-108	9.3	- 0.27	S Raymont	2-22	9.1	- 6.75
M Roberts	7-78	9.0	- 31.90	R Hughes	2-24	8.3	- 6.00
L Piggott	5-29	17.2	- 9.22	D McKeown	1-1	100.0	+ 1.75
B Thomson	4-27	14.8	+ 9.50	A Clark	1-3	33.3	+ 5.00
D O'Neill	4-40	10.0	- 4.50	W Ryan	1-6	16.7	- 3.90
K Darley	4-47	8.5	- 35.00	M Tebbutt	1-8	12.5	- 3.00
W Newnes	3-22	13.6	+ 12.25	G Carter	1-20	5.0	- 11.50

Mark Denaro	0-28	W Woods	0-4	T Williams	0-2
M Hills	0-16	Wendy Jones	0-4	A Whelan	0-1
B Rouse	0-15	A Munro	0-3	C Asmussen	0-1
G Bardwell	0-8	D Gibbs	0-3	D Holland	0-1
R Hills	0-8	G Hind	0-3	J Carroll	0-1
G Duffield	0-7	J Weaver	0-3	M Fenton	0-1
M J Kinane	0-7	N Carlisle	0-3	Mrs D McHale	0-1
W Carson	0-7	Paul Eddery	0-3	N Adams	0-1
Miss K Hannon	0-5	D Wright	0-2	S Whitworth	0-1
A McGlone	0-4	J Williams	0-2	Y Take	0-1
E Greehy	0-4	Mr C Mosse	0-2		
R Cochrane	0-4	S Dawson	0-2		

COURSE RECORD

	Total W-R	Non-Handicaps 2-y-o	3-y-o+	Handicaps 2-y-o	3-y-o+	Per cent	£1 Level Stake
Leicester	10-40	5-17	2-9	2-3	1-11	25.0	+ 37.75
Salisbury	9-66	2-30	4-15	0-0	3-21	13.6	- 2.40
Sandown	9-72	3-27	2-17	0-0	4-28	12.5	+ 4.58
Windsor	8-50	7-23	0-10	0-2	1-15	16.0	- 24.09
Newmarket	8-131	4-43	2-29	0-15	2-44	6.1	- 94.67
Newbury	7-102	2-37	3-24	0-6	2-35	6.9	- 43.02
Brighton	6-44	3-16	2-10	0-4	1-14	13.6	- 3.89
Goodwood	6-89	4-29	0-24	0-8	2-28	6.7	- 32.80
Kempton	5-71	1-18	3-24	0-3	1-26	7.0	- 46.17
Folkestone	4-23	0-10	4-8	0-1	0-4	17.4	+ 3.50
Epsom	4-27	2-9	1-6	0-1	1-11	14.8	- 6.40
York	4-39	2-14	0-4	0-4	2-17	10.3	- 5.50
Lingfield (AW)	3-14	0-0	1-7	0-1	2-6	21.4	+ 8.41
Chester	3-17	2-7	0-2	0-3	1-5	17.6	- 2.43
Chepstow	3-28	3-10	0-5	0-2	0-11	10.7	- 14.75
Doncaster	3-48	2-10	1-15	0-8	0-15	6.3	- 35.25
Beverley	2-5	0-2	1-1	1-2	0-0	40.0	+ 5.00
Pontefract	2-8	1-3	1-3	0-1	0-1	25.0	+ 1.30
Newcastle	2-10	0-2	2-5	0-0	0-3	20.0	- 3.25
Warwick	2-15	1-7	1-4	0-1	0-3	13.3	- 9.09
Haydock	2-29	2-10	0-8	0-0	0-11	6.9	- 20.75
Lingfield	2-36	1-20	0-8	1-2	0-6	5.6	- 12.00
Ascot	2-55	1-18	0-13	0-1	1-23	3.6	- 28.50
Ripon	1-2	1-1	0-0	0-0	0-1	50.0	+ 7.00
Ayr	1-7	0-1	0-2	1-1	0-3	14.3	- 4.25
Yarmouth	1-11	0-5	0-2	1-2	0-2	9.1	- 8.12
Nottingham	1-25	0-15	0-3	1-2	0-5	4.0	- 10.00
Bath	1-27	1-10	0-10	0-1	0-6	3.7	- 25.27

Thirsk	0-7	Wolverhampton (AW)	0-4	Carlisle	0-1
Redcar	0-6	Southwell (AW)	0-2	Hamilton	0-1

WINNING HORSES

	Age	Races Run	1st	2nd	3rd	Unpl	Win £
Bluegrass Prince	3	6	3	0	2	1	54,220
Venture Capitalist	5	7	1	0	0	6	52,475
Lemon Souffle	3	2	1	0	0	1	34,159
Right Win	4	3	2	0	0	1	33,324
Alriffa	3	5	2	1	0	2	17,418
Stash The Cash	3	6	2	0	0	4	17,105
Options Open	2	6	2	0	1	3	16,645
Indian Fly	3	12	3	3	0	6	14,031
Wijara	2	2	2	0	0	0	13,977
Bello Gallico	3	5	3	0	0	2	13,312
Twilight Patrol	2	5	2	1	0	2	11,513
Signs	2	4	1	1	0	2	10,406
Shamanic	2	5	2	2	0	1	10,338
Unanimous Vote	2	9	2	3	2	2	10,124
Bagshot	3	6	2	0	1	3	9,345

Gallows Corner	2	9	2	1	3	3	9,057
Soca King	2	5	2	1	1	1	8,850
Jafeica	3	8	2	1	1	4	8,669
Prussian Flag	2	5	2	0	2	1	8,577
Desert Green	5	5	1	1	0	3	8,480
Winners Choice	2	7	2	2	2	1	8,008
Ham N'Eggs	3	8	1	0	0	7	7,960
Make A Note	3	7	2	1	1	3	7,619
Femme Savante	2	6	2	2	0	2	7,585
Summit	3	7	2	1	2	2	7,476
Embankment	4	12	1	1	2	8	7,227
Queenfisher	2	5	1	0	2	2	6,840
Elfin Laughter	2	6	2	0	0	4	6,650
Flight Lieutenant	5	8	1	1	0	6	6,512
Astral Weeks	3	10	2	3	2	3	6,030
Make The Break	3	9	2	0	4	3	5,524
Mistinguett	2	3	1	0	0	2	5,390
Down D Islands	3	8	1	2	3	2	5,270
Princely Favour	4	10	1	1	0	8	5,150
Exhibit Air	4	6	2	0	1	3	5,001
Dollar Gamble	3	5	1	0	1	3	4,921
Solartica	4	7	1	1	2	3	4,811
Strutting	2	2	1	0	0	1	4,794
Reprehend	3	5	1	2	0	2	4,740
Alcove	3	10	1	1	2	6	4,709
Blurred Image	3	6	1	1	0	4	4,667
Brave Edge	3	4	1	0	0	3	4,667
Stiffelio	2	4	1	1	0	2	4,596
Singing Rock	2	8	1	0	2	5	4,478
Night Melody	4	8	1	0	2	5	4,348
Wishing	3	8	1	1	1	5	4,323
Two O'Clock Jump	2	5	1	2	1	1	4,033
Golden Lady	2	2	1	0	0	1	4,007
On The Tide	3	5	1	1	1	2	3,979
Mediate	2	9	1	1	1	6	3,915
That Old Feeling	2	2	1	0	0	1	3,864
With The Fairies	2	3	1	1	0	1	3,835
Knight Commander	2	5	1	0	2	2	3,807
Tukano	3	10	1	0	3	6	3,793
Commoner	2	2	1	0	0	1	3,725
Ffynone	2	6	1	0	2	3	3,721
Green City	2	3	1	0	0	2	3,721
Axeman	2	4	1	0	1	2	3,664
At Liberty	2	7	1	1	2	3	3,652
Moon King	2	5	1	1	1	2	3,635
Doctor's Glory	2	4	1	0	1	2	3,592
Efra	5	6	1	0	2	3	3,548
Sergeyev	2	5	1	1	2	1	3,515
Phar Lite	2	5	1	0	1	3	3,469
Fairybird	2	5	1	0	0	4	3,404
Kelly's Gold	2	6	1	1	2	2	3,393
Veuve Hoornaert	2	5	1	2	1	1	3,254
Pride Of May	3	9	1	1	0	7	3,216
Petoskin	2	9	1	1	2	5	3,202
High Typha	3	10	1	1	1	7	3,122

Dimes	2	7	1	2	0	4	3,093
Rich Victim	2	1	1	0	0	0	3,055
Unforgetableknight	2	4	1	0	0	3	3,038
Poinciana	5	5	1	0	1	3	3,002
Eighth Heaven	2	6	1	0	2	3	2,966
Last Laugh	2	5	1	0	1	3	2,936
Busy Banana	2	5	1	1	0	3	2,831
Noble Sprinter	2	3	1	0	1	1	2,827
Lucayan Cay	3	8	1	2	0	5	2,787
Coffee 'N Cream	2	5	1	1	0	3	2,722
Star Witness	2	10	1	3	1	5	2,566
Brentwood	3	8	1	2	1	4	2,554
Gallant Spirit	3	8	1	1	1	5	2,301
Our Darling Boy	2	8	1	3	0	4	2,174

WINNING OWNERS

	Races Won	Value £		Races Won	Value £
J P Hardiman	3	54,220	The Winning Team	2	6,230
Stanley E Lever	1	52,475	Lucayan Stud	2	6,191
Lord Carnarvon	3	40,809	G Howard-Spink	2	6,030
Conal Kavanagh	2	33,324	Mrs J Reglar	2	5,524
The Boardroom Syndicate	6	26,559	Exors of the late R J Shannon	1	5,270
B E Nielsen	5	22,315	C M Hamer	1	5,150
Sheikh Essa Bin Mubarak	3	19,972	Archie Hornall	2	5,001
Mohammed Suhail	3	17,612	J A Leek	1	4,921
J G Davis	2	17,105	Mrs C J Powell	1	4,740
Mrs L M Davies	2	16,645	Terry Barwick	1	4,667
Highclere Th'bred Racing Ltd	4	15,992	G S Shropshire	1	4,478
Cheveley Park Stud	3	15,104	H R H Prince Fahd Salman	1	4,007
P D Savill	4	14,797	P T Tellwright	1	3,979
Bob Lalemant	4	14,153	Mrs S H Spencer-Phillips	1	3,915
Mrs Chris Harrington	3	14,031	Mrs John Magnier	1	3,835
Roldvale Limited	2	13,499	Mrs W H Gibson Fleming	1	3,721
M M Matalon	3	13,312	Peter M Crane	1	3,721
Bruce Adams	3	12,709	Mrs P Jubert	1	3,548
Noodles Racing	3	11,401	B T Stewart-Brown	1	3,515
Robert Russell	2	10,338	R A Bernard	1	3,469
G E K Teo	2	9,345	W F Hawkings	1	3,216
M W Grant	2	9,117	Kennett Valley Farms Ltd	1	3,202
N T C (Racing) Limited	2	8,669	T S M Cunningham	1	3,122
Michael Pescod	2	8,577	T J Dale	1	3,055
Mana Al Maktoum	1	8,480	R P B Michaelson	1	2,966
Peter Hammond	1	7,960	St J O'Connell	1	2,936
N Ahamad	2	7,705	Khanmaher	1	2,827
Lady Tennant	1	7,227	A Reeves	1	2,722
K Higson	1	6,840	P B Adams	1	2,301
P & S Lever Partners	1	6,512	Jim Horgan	1	2,174

Favourites	40-134	29.9%	- 33.17	Total winning prize-money		£637,233

Longest winning sequence			2	Average SP of winner		5.5/1
Longest losing sequence			32	Return on stakes invested		-34.7%

1993 Form	182-121	15.0%	-159.43	1991 Form	126-958	13.2%	-149.42
1992 Form	154-113	13.5%	-261.59	1990 Form	73-796	9.2%	-192.68

J HANSON (Wetherby, West Yorks)

	No. of Horses	Races Run	1st	2nd	3rd	Unpl	Per cent	£1 Level Stake
2-y-o	2	4	1	1	0	2	25.0	+ 4.00
3-y-o	5	33	2	5	1	25	6.1	- 22.75
4-y-o+	0	0	0	0	0	0	-	0.00
Totals	7	37	3	6	1	27	8.1	- 18.75

Jan	Feb	Mar	Apr	May	Jun	Jul	Aug	Sep	Oct/Nov
0-0	0-0	0-0	0-2	1-7	0-6	0-4	0-3	1-6	1-9

Winning Jockeys	W-R	£1 Level Stake			W-R	£1 Level Stake
J Reid	1-4	- 0.75	A Culhane		1-10	- 3.00
M Birch	1-10	- 2.00				

Winning Courses						
Pontefract	1-1	+ 6.00	Ayr		1-3	+ 5.00
Warwick	1-2	+ 1.25				

Winning Horses	Age	Races Run	1st	2nd	3rd	Unpl	Win £
Crackhill Farm	3	6	1	0	1	4	4,093
Seckar Vale	2	3	1	1	0	1	3,854
Current Speech	3	6	1	3	0	2	3,564

Favourites	1-1	100.0%	+ 2.25	Total winning prize-money		£11,511

1993 Form	2-29	6.9%	- 5.75	1992 Form	1-13	7.7%	- 10.50

J A HARRIS (Southwell, Notts)

	No. of Horses	Races Run	1st	2nd	3rd	Unpl	Per cent	£1 Level Stake
2-y-o	4	10	0	0	2	8	-	- 10.00
3-y-o	7	24	1	0	4	19	4.2	- 7.00
4-y-o+	9	45	6	1	2	36	13.3	+ 76.90
Totals	20	79	7	1	8	63	8.9	+ 59.90

Jan	Feb	Mar	Apr	May	Jun	Jul	Aug	Sep	Oct/Nov
0-0	1-3	0-14	0-3	2-8	1-16	2-13	0-9	1-6	0-7

Winning Jockeys	W-R	£1 Level Stake				W-R	£1 Level Stake
Dale Gibson	3-26	+ 55.50	D Holland			1-2	+ 10.40
B Doyle	1-1	+ 16.00	Mr C Bonner			1-3	+ 8.00
Paul Eddery	1-1	+ 16.00					

Winning Courses							
Southwell (AW)	3-22	+ 18.40	Redcar			1-2	+ 49.00
Windsor	2-4	+ 17.50	Wolverhampton (AW)			1-12	+ 14.00

Winning Horses	Age	Races Run	1st	2nd	3rd	Unpl	Win £
Swynford Flyer	5	16	3	1	1	11	8,044
Augustan	3	7	1	0	2	4	3,418
Azureus	6	7	1	0	0	6	3,377
Certain Way	4	7	1	0	0	6	3,210
Blue Radiance	4	5	1	0	1	3	2,742

Favourites	1-6	16.7%	- 1.50	Total winning prize-money	£20,790

J L HARRIS (Melton Mowbray, Leics)

	No. of Horses	Races Run	1st	2nd	3rd	Unpl	Per cent	£1 Level Stake
2-y-o	1	2	0	0	0	2	-	- 2.00
3-y-o	8	41	3	0	3	35	7.3	- 8.75
4-y-o+	25	148	16	9	13	110	10.8	- 4.97
Totals	34	191	19	9	16	147	9.9	- 15.72

BY MONTH

2-y-o	W-R	Per cent	£1 Level Stake	3-y-o	W-R	Per cent	£1 Level Stake
January	0-0	-	0.00	January	0-2	-	- 2.00
February	0-0	-	0.00	February	0-0	-	0.00
March	0-0	-	0.00	March	0-0	-	0.00
April	0-0	-	0.00	April	0-1	-	- 1.00
May	0-0	-	0.00	May	1-11	9.1	- 8.25
June	0-0	-	0.00	June	1-5	20.0	+ 3.50
July	0-0	-	0.00	July	0-7	-	- 7.00
August	0-0	-	0.00	August	1-5	20.0	+ 16.00
September	0-0	-	0.00	September	0-5	-	- 5.00
Oct/Nov	0-2	-	- 2.00	Oct/Nov	0-5	-	- 5.00

Harris J L

4-y-o+	W-R	Per cent	£1 Level Stake	Totals	W-R	Per cent	£1 Level Stake
January	1-15	6.7	- 10.00	January	1-17	5.9	- 12.00
February	1-17	5.9	- 12.67	February	1-17	5.9	- 12.67
March	0-14	-	- 14.00	March	0-14	-	- 14.00
April	3-12	25.0	+ 29.00	April	3-13	23.1	+ 28.00
May	0-16	-	- 16.00	May	1-27	3.7	- 24.25
June	3-15	20.0	+ 5.50	June	4-20	20.0	+ 9.00
July	2-19	10.5	- 5.80	July	2-26	7.7	- 12.80
August	4-17	23.5	+ 22.00	August	5-22	22.7	+ 38.00
September	1-13	7.7	- 2.00	September	1-18	5.6	- 7.00
Oct/Nov	1-10	10.0	- 1.00	Oct/Nov	1-17	5.9	- 8.00

DISTANCE

2-y-o	W-R	Per cent	£1 Level Stake	3-y-o	W-R	Per cent	£1 Level Stake
5f-6f	0-0	-	0.00	5f-6f	0-2	-	- 2.00
7f-8f	0-2	-	- 2.00	7f-8f	2-25	8.0	- 13.75
9f-13f	0-0	-	0.00	9f-13f	0-8	-	- 8.00
14f+	0-0	-	0.00	14f+	1-6	16.7	+ 15.00

4-y-o+	W-R	Per cent	£1 Level Stake	Totals	W-R	Per cent	£1 Level Stake
5f-6f	2-30	6.7	- 4.00	5f-6f	2-32	6.3	- 6.00
7f-8f	5-50	10.0	- 4.00	7f-8f	7-77	9.1	- 19.75
9f-13f	1-29	3.4	- 20.00	9f-13f	1-37	2.7	- 28.00
14f+	8-39	20.5	+ 23.03	14f+	9-45	20.0	+ 38.03

TYPE OF RACE

Non-Handicaps	W-R	Per cent	£1 Level Stake	Handicaps	W-R	Per cent	£1 Level Stake
2-y-o	0-2	-	- 2.00	2-y-o	0-0	-	0.00
3-y-o	1-12	8.3	- 9.25	3-y-o	1-15	6.7	- 6.50
4-y-o+	5-33	15.2	- 1.67	4-y-o+	9-86	10.5	+ 1.70
Selling	0-11	-	- 11.00	Selling	0-5	-	- 5.00
Apprentice	1-4	25.0	+ 11.00	Apprentice	0-8	-	- 8.00
Amat/Ladies	0-2	-	- 2.00	Amat/Ladies	2-13	15.4	+ 17.00
Totals	7-64	10.9	- 14.92	Totals	12-127	9.4	- 0.80

COURSE GRADE	W-R	Per cent	£1 Level Stake	FIRST TIME OUT	W-R	Per cent	£1 Level Stake
Group 1	1-29	3.4	- 17.00	2-y-o	0-1	-	- 1.00
Group 2	5-18	27.8	+ 23.75	3-y-o	0-8	-	- 8.00
Group 3	6-49	12.2	+ 16.50	4-y-o+	2-21	9.5	- 1.00
Group 4	7-95	7.4	- 38.97				
				Totals	2-30	6.7	- 10.00

JOCKEYS RIDING

	W-R	Per cent	£1 Level Stake		W-R	Per cent	£1 Level Stake
Paul Eddery	5-36	13.9	- 1.97	J Carroll	1-4	25.0	+ 8.00
N Varley	2-11	18.2	+ 6.00	D Moffatt	1-6	16.7	+ 5.00
Dale Gibson	2-22	9.1	- 2.50	D Holland	1-8	12.5	- 5.25
G Parkin	1-2	50.0	+ 13.00	Mr M Mannish	1-9	11.1	0.00
K Fallon	1-2	50.0	+ 7.00	T Williams	1-9	11.1	- 4.00
S D Williams	1-2	50.0	+ 7.00	A Mackay	1-23	4.3	- 12.00
Mr I McLelland	1-3	33.3	+ 18.00				

K Darley	0-6	J Weaver	0-2	G Strange	0-1
L Dettori	0-6	P Robinson	0-2	J Dennis	0-1
J Quinn	0-4	W Ryan	0-2	J Fortune	0-1
D McKeown	0-3	A Lakeman	0-1	Miss I D W Jones	0-1
G Bardwell	0-3	A Tucker	0-1	N Carlisle	0-1
G Duffield	0-3	Bobby Elliott	0-1	R Cochrane	0-1
M Baird	0-3	D Biggs	0-1	R Hills	0-1
Mrs L Henderson	0-3	D Griffiths	0-1	R Mullen	0-1
B Doyle	0-2	G Milligan	0-1	S Lanigan	0-1

COURSE RECORD

	Total W-R	Non-Handicaps 2-y-o	Non-Handicaps 3-y-o+	Handicaps 2-y-o	Handicaps 3-y-o+	Per cent	£1 Level Stake
Wolverhampton (AW)	5-34	0-0	3-16	0-0	2-18	14.7	- 7.97
Redcar	3-8	0-0	2-2	0-0	1-6	37.5	+ 11.75
Beverley	2-8	0-0	0-0	0-0	2-8	25.0	+ 12.00
Nottingham	2-12	0-0	1-3	0-0	1-9	16.7	+ 10.00
Southwell (AW)	2-45	0-0	0-22	0-0	2-23	4.4	- 15.00
Bath	1-1	0-0	0-0	0-0	1-1	100.0	+ 7.50
Chester	1-2	0-0	0-0	0-0	1-2	50.0	+ 9.00
Newcastle	1-4	0-0	0-0	0-0	1-4	25.0	+ 8.00
Pontefract	1-6	0-0	1-2	0-0	0-4	16.7	+ 9.00
Thirsk	1-6	0-0	0-1	0-0	1-5	16.7	+ 5.00

Leicester	0-15	Yarmouth	0-4	Sandown	0-2
Doncaster	0-11	Carlisle	0-3	York	0-2
Newmarket	0-8	Lingfield (AW)	0-3	Ascot	0-1
Catterick	0-6	Hamilton	0-2	Kempton	0-1
Warwick	0-4	Ripon	0-2	Windsor	0-1

WINNING HORSES

	Age	Races Run	1st	2nd	3rd	Unpl	Win £
Iota	5	15	3	1	2	9	10,197
Tu Opes	3	9	2	0	1	6	9,605
Swordking	5	16	3	1	4	8	9,136
Top-Anna	6	10	2	1	0	7	6,248
Sir Tasker	6	18	1	3	2	12	5,572
Legend Dulac	5	12	1	0	0	11	3,964
Mohican Brave	4	6	1	0	1	4	3,158

Mary Macblain	5	8	1	0	1	6	3,152
Montone	4	9	1	1	0	7	2,843
Nordoora	5	4	1	0	0	3	2,694
Donia	5	3	1	0	1	1	2,387
Dugort Strand	3	8	1	0	0	7	2,261
Scottish Park	5	1	1	0	0	0	2,243

WINNING OWNERS

	Races Won	Value £		Races Won	Value £
Lavender Hill Leisure Ltd	5	17,090	Bob Welch	1	2,843
Mrs M L Watson	2	9,605	C R Hodson	1	2,694
P Caplan	2	6,248	J S Gowling	1	2,387
J F Coupland	1	5,572	Achill Nottingham Syndicate	1	2,261
B McAllister	1	3,964	Dick Emery	1	2,243
G W Pykett	1	3,158	J L Harris	1	2,243
D Jackson	1	3,152			

Favourites	2-6	33.3%	- 1.05	Total winning prize-money		£63,460
Longest winning sequence			2	Average SP of winner		8.2/1
Longest losing sequence			30	Return on stakes invested		-8.2%

1993 Form	12-169	7.1%	- 49.37	1991 Form	8-128	6.3%	- 35.75
1992 Form	9-132	6.8%	- 54.75	1990 Form	6-51	11.8%	+ 26.50

P W HARRIS (Berkhamsted, Herts)

	No. of Horses	Races Run	1st	2nd	3rd	Unpl	Per cent	£1 Level Stake
2-y-o	17	42	6	6	5	25	14.3	+ 26.51
3-y-o	13	68	1	3	5	59	1.5	- 62.50
4-y-o+	16	110	16	13	4	77	14.5	+ 4.94
Totals	46	220	23	22	14	161	10.5	- 31.05

BY MONTH

2-y-o	W-R	Per cent	£1 Level Stake	3-y-o	W-R	Per cent	£1 Level Stake
January	0-0	-	0.00	January	0-0	-	0.00
February	0-0	-	0.00	February	0-0	-	0.00
March	0-0	-	0.00	March	0-0	-	0.00
April	0-1	-	- 1.00	April	0-7	-	- 7.00
May	0-2	-	- 2.00	May	0-11	-	- 11.00
June	2-3	66.7	+ 52.00	June	0-10	-	- 10.00
July	2-7	28.6	+ 0.38	July	1-15	6.7	- 9.50
August	1-10	10.0	- 5.50	August	0-8	-	- 8.00
September	0-5	-	- 5.00	September	0-12	-	- 12.00
Oct/Nov	1-14	7.1	- 12.37	Oct/Nov	0-5	-	- 5.00

4-y-o+	W-R	Per cent	£1 Level Stake	Totals	W-R	Per cent	£1 Level Stake
January	0-1	-	- 1.00	January	0-1	-	- 1.00
February	2-2	100.0	+ 3.38	February	2-2	100.0	+ 3.38
March	1-2	50.0	+ 1.50	March	1-2	50.0	+ 1.50
April	2-11	18.2	- 2.90	April	2-19	10.5	- 10.90
May	4-17	23.5	+ 31.50	May	4-30	13.3	+ 18.50
June	4-18	22.2	+ 17.25	June	6-31	19.4	+ 59.25
July	1-15	6.7	- 12.12	July	4-37	10.8	- 21.24
August	1-11	9.1	- 6.67	August	2-29	6.9	- 20.17
September	1-19	5.3	- 12.00	September	1-36	2.8	- 29.00
Oct/Nov	0-14	-	- 14.00	Oct/Nov	1-33	3.0	- 31.37

DISTANCE

2-y-o	W-R	Per cent	£1 Level Stake	3-y-o	W-R	Per cent	£1 Level Stake
5f-6f	3-21	14.3	+ 4.51	5f-6f	0-10	-	- 10.00
7f-8f	3-21	14.3	+ 22.00	7f-8f	0-28	-	- 28.00
9f-13f	0-0	-	0.00	9f-13f	1-30	3.3	- 24.50
14f+	0-0	-	0.00	14f+	0-0	-	0.00

4-y-o+	W-R	Per cent	£1 Level Stake	Totals	W-R	Per cent	£1 Level Stake
5f-6f	6-21	28.6	+ 16.98	5f-6f	9-52	17.3	+ 11.49
7f-8f	4-41	9.8	- 10.00	7f-8f	7-90	7.8	- 16.00
9f-13f	5-36	13.9	+ 7.08	9f-13f	6-66	9.1	- 17.42
14f+	1-12	8.3	- 9.12	14f+	1-12	8.3	- 9.12

TYPE OF RACE

Non-Handicaps	W-R	Per cent	£1 Level Stake	Handicaps	W-R	Per cent	£1 Level Stake
2-y-o	6-42	14.3	+ 26.51	2-y-o	0-0	-	0.00
3-y-o	1-37	2.7	- 31.50	3-y-o	0-30	-	- 30.00
4-y-o+	1-7	14.3	- 4.62	4-y-o+	12-97	12.4	- 21.69
Selling	0-0	-	0.00	Selling	0-0	-	0.00
Apprentice	0-0	-	0.00	Apprentice	2-4	50.0	+ 12.25
Amat/Ladies	0-0	-	0.00	Amat/Ladies	1-3	33.3	+ 18.00
Totals	8-86	9.3	- 9.61	Totals	15-134	11.2	- 21.44

COURSE GRADE

	W-R	Per cent	£1 Level Stake
Group 1	12-114	10.5	+ 18.59
Group 2	4-38	10.5	- 15.40
Group 3	4-49	8.2	- 24.12
Group 4	3-19	15.8	- 10.12

FIRST TIME OUT

	W-R	Per cent	£1 Level Stake
2-y-o	2-17	11.8	+ 38.00
3-y-o	0-13	-	- 13.00
4-y-o+	4-16	25.0	+ 49.00
Totals	6-46	13.0	+ 74.00

187

Harris P W

JOCKEYS RIDING

	W-R	Per cent	£1 Level Stake		W-R	Per cent	£1 Level Stake
R Cochrane	7-58	12.1	+ 14.76	Pat Eddery	1-3	33.3	+ 2.50
L Dettori	4-8	50.0	+ 2.98	J Quinn	1-4	25.0	+ 17.00
W R Swinburn	3-21	14.3	+ 0.33	Miss A Elsey	1-4	25.0	+ 17.00
T Fuggle	2-12	16.7	+ 4.25	F Norton	1-5	20.0	+ 3.00
M J Kinane	1-1	100.0	+ 3.50	G Duffield	1-11	9.1	- 5.00
J Weaver	1-1	100.0	+ 0.63				

G Hind	0-14	J Reid	0-4	G Carter	0-1
P Robinson	0-14	J Williams	0-4	J Fanning	0-1
N Adams	0-10	J Fortune	0-2	J Stack	0-1
M Birch	0-9	L Piggott	0-2	R Hills	0-1
A McGlone	0-6	Stephen Davies	0-2	W Carson	0-1
S Whitworth	0-6	A Clark	0-1	W Newnes	0-1
Paul Eddery	0-5	D Biggs	0-1		
W Ryan	0-5	Dale Gibson	0-1		

COURSE RECORD

	Total W-R	Non-Handicaps 2-y-o	3-y-o+	Handicaps 2-y-o	3-y-o+	Per cent	£1 Level Stake
Lingfield (AW)	3-3	0-0	1-1	0-0	2-2	100.0	+ 5.88
Newbury	2-12	2-4	0-0	0-0	0-8	16.7	+ 13.50
Kempton	2-14	1-3	0-2	0-0	1-9	14.3	+ 41.00
Yarmouth	2-14	0-1	0-5	0-0	2-8	14.3	- 3.75
Doncaster	2-16	1-6	0-1	0-0	1-9	12.5	- 10.12
York	2-17	0-3	0-0	0-0	2-14	11.8	- 8.17
Brighton	1-2	0-0	0-1	0-0	1-1	50.0	+ 0.10
Chester	1-3	0-0	0-0	0-0	1-3	33.3	+ 7.00
Epsom	1-3	0-0	0-0	0-0	1-3	33.3	+ 5.00
Pontefract	1-4	1-1	0-3	0-0	0-0	25.0	- 2.37
Goodwood	1-6	0-2	0-1	0-0	1-3	16.7	+ 15.00
Beverley	1-7	0-0	0-1	0-0	1-6	14.3	+ 6.00
Redcar	1-9	1-2	0-0	0-0	0-7	11.1	- 4.50
Ascot	1-10	0-0	1-1	0-0	0-9	10.0	- 4.50
Thirsk	1-11	0-1	0-4	0-0	1-6	9.1	- 5.00
Haydock	1-14	0-2	0-2	0-0	1-10	7.1	- 11.12

Newmarket	0-16	Bath	0-4	Warwick	0-3
Leicester	0-7	Salisbury	0-4	Newcastle	0-2
Lingfield	0-6	Sandown	0-4	Catterick	0-1
Nottingham	0-6	Folkestone	0-3	Chepstow	0-1
Windsor	0-6	Ripon	0-3		
Wolverhampton (AW)	0-6	Southwell (AW)	0-3		

WINNING HORSES

	Age	Races Run	1st	2nd	3rd	Unpl	Win £
American Swinger	4	8	3	1	1	3	25,162
Spender	5	11	5	1	1	4	15,335
Above The Cut	2	2	2	0	0	0	11,746
Laxford Bridge	3	5	1	0	0	4	11,160
Sotoboy	2	3	2	0	0	1	8,622
So Intrepid	4	7	1	0	0	6	5,174
My Best Valentine	4	11	1	1	1	8	5,005
Blanchland	5	7	1	1	0	5	4,273
Sharp Prospect	4	8	1	2	0	5	4,078
Ever So Lyrical	4	7	1	2	0	4	3,915
Poppy Carew	2	6	1	2	2	1	3,585
George Dillingham	4	9	1	3	0	5	3,552
Smart Teacher	4	5	1	0	1	3	2,915
Supertop	6	7	1	1	0	5	2,343
Kings Assembly	2	2	1	0	0	1	844

WINNING OWNERS

	Races Won	Value £		Races Won	Value £
Mrs P W Harris	7	39,489	The Pendley Associates	1	4,078
Triple (Cr)owners I	3	25,162	The Pendley Punters	1	3,915
The Entrepreneurs	5	15,335	Triple (Cr)owners III	1	2,915
Mrs Marlene Hollis	2	8,622	Mrs G A Godfrey	1	2,343
The Valentines	1	5,005	The Everhopefuls I	1	844

Favourites	11-33	33.3%	+ 6.57	Total winning prize-money	£107,706
Longest winning sequence			3	Average SP of winner	7.2/1
Longest losing sequence			42	Return on stakes invested	-13.9%
1993 Form	23-185	12.4%	+ 61.25	1991 Form	3-74	4.1%	- 50.50
1992 Form	13-154	8.4%	- 2.00	1990 Form	8-69	11.6%	+ 3.25

R HARRIS (Exning, Suffolk)

	No. of Horses	Races Run	1st	2nd	3rd	Unpl	Per cent	£1 Level Stake
2-y-o	0	0	0	0	0	0	-	0.00
3-y-o	3	15	1	1	2	11	6.7	- 4.50
4-y-o+	4	7	0	0	0	7	-	- 7.00
Totals	7	22	1	1	2	18	4.5	- 11.50

Jan	Feb	Mar	Apr	May	Jun	Jul	Aug	Sep	Oct/Nov
0-2	0-1	1-5	0-2	0-2	0-5	0-3	0-2	0-0	0-0

Harris R

Winning Jockey	W-R	£1 Level Stake	Winning Course	W-R	£1 Level Stake
Stephen Davies	1-2	+ 8.50	Folkestone	1-3	+ 7.50

Winning Horse	Age	Races Run	1st	2nd	3rd	Unpl	Win £
Golden Hadeer	3	3	1	0	0	2	1,934

Favourites	0-0			Total winning prize-money			£1,934
1993 Form	1-35	2.9%	- 20.00				

A HARRISON (Middleham, North Yorks)

	No. of Horses	Races Run	1st	2nd	3rd	Unpl	Per cent	£1 Level Stake
2-y-o	0	0	0	0	0	0	-	0.00
3-y-o	1	4	0	0	0	4	-	- 4.00
4-y-o+	8	36	3	1	4	28	8.3	- 10.50
Totals	9	40	3	1	4	32	7.5	- 14.50

Jan	Feb	Mar	Apr	May	Jun	Jul	Aug	Sep	Oct/Nov
0-0	0-0	0-0	0-4	0-8	0-8	1-5	1-6	0-6	1-3

Winning Jockey	W-R	£1 Level Stake		W-R	£1 Level Stake
J Stack	3-24	+ 1.50			

Winning Courses					
Leicester	1-1	+ 6.50	Edinburgh	1-8	+ 1.00
Ayr	1-5	+ 4.00			

Winning Horses	Age	Races Run	1st	2nd	3rd	Unpl	Win £
Ashdren	7	11	2	0	1	8	6,331
Thisonesforalice	6	9	1	1	2	5	2,905

Favourites	0-2			Total winning prize-money			£9,236
1993 Form	1-47	2.1%	- 38.00	1991 Form	4-103	3.9%	- 78.50
1992 Form	3-68	4.4%	- 55.75	1990 Form	7-50	14.0%	- 12.12

G HARWOOD (Pulborough, West Sussex)

	No. of Horses	Races Run	1st	2nd	3rd	Unpl	Per cent	£1 Level Stake
2-y-o	14	36	3	3	4	26	8.3	- 20.80
3-y-o	15	76	16	10	11	39	21.1	+ 27.08
4-y-o+	7	45	8	10	4	23	17.8	+ 32.93
Totals	36	157	27	23	19	88	17.2	+ 39.21

BY MONTH

2-y-o	W-R	Per cent	£1 Level Stake	3-y-o	W-R	Per cent	£1 Level Stake
January	0-0	-	0.00	January	0-0	-	0.00
February	0-0	-	0.00	February	0-0	-	0.00
March	0-0	-	0.00	March	1-2	50.0	- 0.27
April	0-0	-	0.00	April	0-5	-	- 5.00
May	0-2	-	- 2.00	May	2-10	20.0	- 4.62
June	0-4	-	- 4.00	June	5-19	26.3	- 8.03
July	1-3	33.3	- 0.80	July	1-13	7.7	- 10.75
August	0-3	-	- 3.00	August	1-10	10.0	+ 16.00
September	0-11	-	- 11.00	September	4-8	50.0	+ 30.75
Oct/Nov	2-13	15.4	0.00	Oct/Nov	2-9	22.2	+ 9.00

4-y-o+	W-R	Per cent	£1 Level Stake	Totals	W-R	Per cent	£1 Level Stake
January	0-2	-	- 2.00	January	0-2	-	- 2.00
February	0-0	-	0.00	February	0-0	-	0.00
March	0-2	-	- 2.00	March	1-4	25.0	- 2.27
April	0-3	-	- 3.00	April	0-8	-	- 8.00
May	1-3	33.3	+ 18.00	May	3-15	20.0	+ 11.38
June	1-12	8.3	- 8.00	June	6-35	17.1	- 20.03
July	2-7	28.6	+ 13.50	July	4-23	17.4	+ 1.95
August	0-5	-	- 5.00	August	1-18	5.6	+ 8.00
September	0-3	-	- 3.00	September	4-22	18.2	+ 16.75
Oct/Nov	4-8	50.0	+ 24.43	Oct/Nov	8-30	26.7	+ 33.43

DISTANCE

2-y-o	W-R	Per cent	£1 Level Stake	3-y-o	W-R	Per cent	£1 Level Stake
5f-6f	3-10	30.0	+ 5.20	5f-6f	0-2	-	- 2.00
7f-8f	0-25	-	- 25.00	7f-8f	7-31	22.6	+ 6.25
9f-13f	0-1	-	- 1.00	9f-13f	8-36	22.2	+ 26.83
14f+	0-0	-	0.00	14f+	1-7	14.3	- 4.00

4-y-o+	W-R	Per cent	£1 Level Stake	Totals	W-R	Per cent	£1 Level Stake
5f-6f	0-0	-	0.00	5f-6f	3-12	25.0	+ 3.20
7f-8f	4-16	25.0	+ 14.93	7f-8f	11-72	15.3	- 3.82
9f-13f	0-13	-	- 13.00	9f-13f	8-50	16.0	+ 12.83
14f+	4-16	25.0	+ 31.00	14f+	5-23	21.7	+ 27.00

TYPE OF RACE

Non-Handicaps	W-R	Per cent	£1 Level Stake	Handicaps	W-R	Per cent	£1 Level Stake
2-y-o	3-31	9.7	- 15.80	2-y-o	0-4	-	- 4.00
3-y-o	10-36	27.8	+ 11.33	3-y-o	6-38	15.8	+ 17.75
4-y-o+	2-10	20.0	- 6.20	4-y-o+	5-32	15.6	+ 39.50
Selling	0-0	-	0.00	Selling	0-0	-	0.00
Apprentice	1-1	100.0	+ 1.63	Apprentice	0-2	-	- 2.00
Amat/Ladies	0-1	-	- 1.00	Amat/Ladies	0-2	-	- 2.00
Totals	16-79	20.3	- 10.04	Totals	11-78	14.1	+ 49.25

Harwood G

	W-R	Per cent	£1 Level Stake		W-R	Per cent	£1 Level Stake
Group 1	14-86	16.3	+ 52.21	2-y-o	0-14	-	- 14.00
Group 2	8-31	25.8	+ 7.07	3-y-o	3-15	20.0	+ 15.61
Group 3	4-29	13.8	- 18.07	4-y-o+	0-7	-	- 7.00
Group 4	1-11	9.1	- 2.00				
				Totals	3-36	8.3	- 5.39

JOCKEYS RIDING

	W-R	Per cent	£1 Level Stake		W-R	Per cent	£1 Level Stake
A Clark	8-46	17.4	+ 46.33	P Houghton	1-2	50.0	+ 0.63
Pat Eddery	5-19	26.3	- 0.64	L Dettori	1-4	25.0	- 1.75
R Cochrane	4-18	22.2	- 8.32	W R Swinburn	1-4	25.0	+ 17.00
M Perrett	4-19	21.1	+ 22.10	W Carson	1-5	20.0	- 3.00
M J Kinane	1-1	100.0	+ 4.50	T Quinn	1-6	16.7	- 4.64

M Hills	0-4	Miss A Harwood	0-2	K Darley		0-1
W Woods	0-4	R Hills	0-2	L Piggott		0-1
G Duffield	0-3	C Asmussen	0-1	Mr P P-Gordon		0-1
A McGlone	0-2	C Rutter	0-1	Paul Eddery		0-1
G Branton	0-2	D Biggs	0-1	S Mulvey		0-1
Gaye Harwood	0-2	D Wright	0-1			
J Weaver	0-2	J Reid	0-1			

COURSE RECORD

	Total W-R	Non-Handicaps 2-y-o	3-y-o+	Handicaps 2-y-o	3-y-o+	Per cent	£1 Level Stake
Newmarket	5-26	1-7	0-4	0-1	4-14	19.2	+ 53.20
Brighton	3-6	0-1	3-5	0-0	0-0	50.0	+ 0.34
Ascot	3-13	0-1	1-1	0-0	2-11	23.1	- 1.87
Goodwood	3-17	0-0	2-4	0-0	1-13	17.6	+ 22.00
Chepstow	2-5	0-1	1-2	0-0	1-2	40.0	+ 0.80
Lingfield	2-7	0-4	2-3	0-0	0-0	28.6	- 2.02
Salisbury	2-13	0-7	0-1	0-0	2-5	15.4	+ 11.50
Haydock	1-1	1-1	0-0	0-0	0-0	100.0	+ 3.00
Ripon	1-1	0-0	0-0	0-0	1-1	100.0	+ 1.25
Nottingham	1-4	0-0	1-3	0-0	0-1	25.0	- 1.37
Folkestone	1-6	1-2	0-0	0-0	0-4	16.7	+ 3.00
Kempton	1-6	0-2	1-4	0-0	0-0	16.7	- 3.75
Windsor	1-7	0-1	1-4	0-0	0-2	14.3	- 4.50
Sandown	1-8	0-1	1-3	0-0	0-4	12.5	- 5.37

Bath	0-8	Pontefract	0-3	Newcastle	0-2
Newbury	0-5	Thirsk	0-3	Warwick	0-2
Doncaster	0-3	York	0-3	Yarmouth	0-2
Lingfield (AW)	0-3	Epsom	0-2	Chester	0-1

WINNING HORSES

	Age	Races Run	1st	2nd	3rd	Unpl	Win £
Captain's Guest	4	6	3	1	0	2	61,980
Transom	3	8	3	1	3	1	17,936
Realities	4	7	2	2	0	3	17,476
Acting Brave	3	7	3	0	0	4	15,084
Kayvee	5	12	2	3	2	5	8,927
Treaty Of Peace	3	3	2	0	0	1	8,351
Lion's Mane	2	3	1	0	0	2	3,864
Mapengo	3	6	1	0	1	4	3,730
Actual Fact	2	2	1	0	0	1	3,725
Jasdan	3	7	1	2	1	3	3,678
Apache Plume	3	5	1	1	1	2	3,672
Amancio	3	6	1	2	1	2	3,469
Aeroking	3	3	1	1	0	1	3,429
Porphyrios	3	8	1	0	1	6	3,368
Chocolat De Meguro	3	5	1	2	0	2	3,260
Asian Jane	3	4	1	0	2	1	3,241
Zerali	2	4	1	0	0	3	2,954
Alqairawaan	5	8	1	3	1	3	2,635

WINNING OWNERS

	Races Won	Value £		Races Won	Value £
K J Buchanan	3	61,980	Anthony Speelman	2	7,594
K Abdulla	7	28,870	Paul H Locke	2	6,710
Seymour Cohn	3	17,936	Athos Christodoulou	1	3,368
Simon Karmel	2	17,476	T Watanabe	1	3,260
Sheikh Mohammed	3	12,023	G Harwood	1	2,635
J H Richmond-Watson	2	8,927			

Favourites	17-40	42.5%	+ 7.46	Total winning prize-money	£170,779
Longest winning sequence			2	Average SP of winner	6.3/1
Longest losing sequence			21	Return on stakes invested	25.0%
1993 Form	21-217	9.7%	- 77.01	1991 Form 55-326 16.9%	- 47.76
1992 Form	29-236	12.3%	- 81.96	1990 Form 69-396 17.4%	- 46.87

P C HASLAM (Middleham, North Yorks)

	No. of Horses	Races Run	1st	2nd	3rd	Unpl	Per cent	£1 Level Stake
2-y-o	22	79	9	8	7	55	11.4	- 12.74
3-y-o	5	42	12	6	7	17	28.6	+ 3.89
4-y-o+	11	97	15	8	13	61	15.5	- 16.74
Totals	38	218	36	22	27	133	16.5	- 25.59

BY MONTH

2-y-o	W-R	Per cent	£1 Level Stake	3-y-o	W-R	Per cent	£1 Level Stake
January	0-0	-	0.00	January	1-6	16.7	- 2.00
February	0-0	-	0.00	February	1-2	50.0	0.00
March	0-1	-	- 1.00	March	0-0	-	0.00
April	1-6	16.7	- 1.50	April	3-6	50.0	+ 7.01
May	2-11	18.2	+ 26.25	May	0-4	-	- 4.00
June	0-8	-	- 8.00	June	0-4	-	- 4.00
July	1-13	7.7	- 10.37	July	2-9	22.2	+ 4.50
August	2-17	11.8	- 5.75	August	4-8	50.0	+ 2.50
September	2-12	16.7	- 5.12	September	1-3	33.3	- 0.12
Oct/Nov	1-11	9.1	- 7.25	Oct/Nov	0-0	-	0.00

4-y-o+	W-R	Per cent	£1 Level Stake	Totals	W-R	Per cent	£1 Level Stake
January	3-16	18.8	- 3.09	January	4-22	18.2	- 5.09
February	0-10	-	- 10.00	February	1-12	8.3	- 10.00
March	2-4	50.0	+ 2.75	March	2-5	40.0	+ 1.75
April	0-7	-	- 7.00	April	4-19	21.1	- 1.49
May	4-11	36.4	+ 19.00	May	6-26	23.1	+ 41.25
June	1-16	6.3	- 11.50	June	1-28	3.6	- 23.50
July	2-16	12.5	- 6.90	July	5-38	13.2	- 12.77
August	1-8	12.5	- 4.50	August	7-33	21.2	- 7.75
September	2-7	28.6	+ 6.50	September	5-22	22.7	+ 1.26
Oct/Nov	0-2	-	- 2.00	Oct/Nov	1-13	7.7	- 9.25

DISTANCE

2-y-o	W-R	Per cent	£1 Level Stake	3-y-o	W-R	Per cent	£1 Level Stake
5f-6f	7-52	13.5	+ 1.51	5f-6f	6-17	35.3	+ 5.98
7f-8f	2-26	7.7	- 13.25	7f-8f	1-15	6.7	- 10.50
9f-13f	0-1	-	- 1.00	9f-13f	5-10	50.0	+ 8.41
14f+	0-0	-	0.00	14f+	0-0	-	0.00

4-y-o+	W-R	Per cent	£1 Level Stake	Totals	W-R	Per cent	£1 Level Stake
5f-6f	6-27	22.2	+ 4.41	5f-6f	19-96	19.8	+ 11.90
7f-8f	3-36	8.3	- 19.00	7f-8f	6-77	7.8	- 42.75
9f-13f	4-26	15.4	- 5.15	9f-13f	9-37	24.3	+ 2.26
14f+	2-8	25.0	+ 3.00	14f+	2-8	25.0	+ 3.00

TYPE OF RACE

Non-Handicaps	W-R	Per cent	£1 Level Stake	Handicaps	W-R	Per cent	£1 Level Stake
2-y-o	6-51	11.8	+ 4.13	2-y-o	1-8	12.5	- 4.00
3-y-o	3-10	30.0	- 3.99	3-y-o	5-16	31.3	+ 5.38
4-y-o+	5-19	26.3	+ 5.51	4-y-o+	9-57	15.8	- 4.00
Selling	2-23	8.7	- 15.87	Selling	1-8	12.5	- 5.75
Apprentice	1-1	100.0	+ 1.75	Apprentice	1-19	5.3	- 10.00
Amat/Ladies	0-0	-	0.00	Amat/Ladies	2-6	33.3	+ 1.25
Totals	17-104	16.3	- 8.47	Totals	19-114	16.7	- 17.12

COURSE GRADE

	W-R	Per cent	£1 Level Stake
Group 1	3-39	7.7	+ 1.00
Group 2	5-31	16.1	- 1.40
Group 3	9-56	16.1	- 4.84
Group 4	19-92	20.7	- 20.35

FIRST TIME OUT

	W-R	Per cent	£1 Level Stake
2-y-o	2-21	9.5	+ 17.50
3-y-o	1-5	20.0	- 1.00
4-y-o+	0-11	-	- 11.00
Totals	3-37	8.1	+ 5.50

JOCKEYS RIDING

	W-R	Per cent	£1 Level Stake		W-R	Per cent	£1 Level Stake
J Weaver	26-80	32.5	+ 58.31	C N Adamson	1-8	12.5	- 5.25
Mrs D Kettlewell	2-4	50.0	+ 3.25	Nicola Howarth	1-13	7.7	- 6.00
T Williams	2-19	10.5	- 7.25	D McKeown	1-18	5.6	- 6.00
L Dettori	1-3	33.3	- 0.75	J Stack	1-19	5.3	- 16.90
Carol Davison	1-7	14.3	+ 2.00				

J Quinn	0-13	M Tebbutt	0-2	K Darley	0-1
J Marshall	0-7	C Rutter	0-1	M Fenton	0-1
L Piggott	0-4	D Harrison	0-1	M Roberts	0-1
C Hodgson	0-3	D McCabe	0-1	Miss J Winter	0-1
Dale Gibson	0-2	J Gracey	0-1	Mrs A Haslam	0-1
G Duffield	0-2	J Tate	0-1	P Fessey	0-1
L Charnock	0-2	John Francome	0-1		

COURSE RECORD

	Total W-R	Non-Handicaps 2-y-o	3-y-o+	Handicaps 2-y-o	3-y-o+	Per cent	£1 Level Stake
Wolverhampton (AW)	14-58	2-16	5-13	0-0	7-29	24.1	- 3.48
Hamilton	7-25	0-3	1-5	0-1	6-16	28.0	+ 17.25
Thirsk	3-12	1-6	1-1	0-0	1-5	25.0	+ 6.35
Edinburgh	2-4	1-2	0-0	1-1	0-1	50.0	+ 2.63
Ripon	2-7	0-1	0-2	0-0	2-4	28.6	+ 4.25
Southwell (AW)	2-11	0-3	1-7	0-0	1-1	18.2	- 5.00
York	1-3	1-2	0-0	0-0	0-1	33.3	+ 31.00
Leicester	1-4	0-1	0-0	0-1	1-2	25.0	+ 3.00
Catterick	1-7	1-4	0-0	0-0	0-3	14.3	- 2.50
Newcastle	1-9	1-4	0-0	0-1	0-4	11.1	- 6.75
Beverley	1-13	0-6	1-1	0-0	0-6	7.7	- 11.09
Newmarket	1-17	1-9	0-0	0-1	0-7	5.9	- 13.25

Lingfield (AW)	0-8	Pontefract	0-4	Chester	0-1
Redcar	0-8	Brighton	0-3	Haydock	0-1
Doncaster	0-6	Carlisle	0-3	Sandown	0-1
Yarmouth	0-5	Ascot	0-1	Warwick	0-1
Nottingham	0-4	Ayr	0-1	Windsor	0-1

Haslam P C

WINNING HORSES

	Age	Races Run	1st	2nd	3rd	Unpl	Win £
Warwick Warrior	3	11	5	1	1	4	15,619
Talented Ting	5	15	2	1	1	11	13,258
Hannah's Usher	2	11	5	1	1	4	12,835
Pageboy	5	14	3	3	1	7	11,745
Pipe Major	2	4	2	1	0	1	10,774
Carrolls Marc	6	13	4	1	2	6	9,494
Red Admiral	4	11	3	1	2	5	9,251
River Junction	3	9	3	3	0	3	8,844
Dragon Man	3	6	3	0	2	1	7,731
Anorak	4	15	2	1	4	8	4,699
Rock Foundation	2	3	1	0	0	2	3,580
Rapier Point	3	5	1	0	2	2	3,056
Tee Tee Too	2	7	1	2	0	4	2,964
Suivez	4	7	1	1	0	5	2,395

WINNING OWNERS

	Races Won	Value £		Races Won	Value £
Lord Scarsdale	6	25,575	E C York	2	6,794
Martin Wickens	5	20,988	Sackville House Racing	2	6,108
Bill Fitzgerald	5	12,835	P C Haslam	2	5,978
Patrick Haslam Racing Club	3	9,570	Dunnington, Shaw & Smart	2	4,699
P I P Electrics Ltd	4	9,494	Darren Croft	1	2,964
C H Bothway	3	8,844	Mrs Jean Turpin	1	2,395

Favourites	21-47	44.7%	+ 15.91	Total winning prize-money	£116,242
Longest winning sequence			2	Average SP of winner	4.3/1
Longest losing sequence			30	Return on stakes invested	-11.7%
1993 Form	17-225	7.6%	- 61.68	1991 Form	14-145	9.7%	- 56.76
1992 Form	29-227	12.8%	- 90.30				

M J HAYNES (Epsom, Surrey)

	No. of Horses	Races Run	1st	2nd	3rd	Unpl	Per cent	£1 Level Stake
2-y-o	2	8	0	1	1	6	-	- 8.00
3-y-o	3	24	1	0	0	23	4.2	- 9.00
4-y-o+	3	11	1	0	1	9	9.1	- 7.00
Totals	8	43	2	1	2	38	4.7	- 24.00

Jan	Feb	Mar	Apr	May	Jun	Jul	Aug	Sep	Oct/Nov
0-1	0-0	0-2	2-7	0-6	0-8	0-4	0-7	0-5	0-3

196

Winning Jockeys	W-R	£1 Level Stake		W-R	£1 Level Stake
D Toole	1-5	- 1.00	J Reid	1-6	+ 9.00

Winning Courses					
Kempton	1-4	+ 11.00	Folkestone	1-7	- 3.00

Winning Horses	Age	Races Run	1st	2nd	3rd	Unpl	Win £
Kerrie-Jo	3	9	1	0	0	8	3,980
Kingsfold Pet	5	3	1	0	1	1	3,080

Favourites	1-2	50.0%	+ 2.00	Total winning prize-money		£7,060

1993 Form	4-67	6.0%	- 21.50	1991 Form	9-122	7.4%	+ 6.83
1992 Form	4-101	4.0%	- 51.00	1990 Form	9-134	6.7%	- 52.00

P HAYWARD (Netheravon, Wilts)

	No. of Horses	Races Run	1st	2nd	3rd	Unpl	Per cent	£1 Level Stake
2-y-o	0	0	0	0	0	0	-	0.00
3-y-o	2	8	2	1	0	5	25.0	+ 20.00
4-y-o+	5	13	0	2	0	11	-	- 13.00
Totals	7	21	2	3	0	16	9.5	+ 7.00

Jan	Feb	Mar	Apr	May	Jun	Jul	Aug	Sep	Oct/Nov
0-1	0-0	0-2	0-0	0-1	0-3	0-4	0-5	1-3	1-2

Winning Jockey	W-R	£1 Level Stake		W-R	£1 Level Stake
R Street	2-3	+ 25.00			

Winning Courses					
Brighton	1-1	+ 16.00	Chepstow	1-4	+ 7.00

Winning Horse	Age	Races Run	1st	2nd	3rd	Unpl	Win £
Granby Bell	3	6	2	0	0	4	7,387

Favourites	0-1			Total winning prize-money		£7,387

1993 Form	0-10			1991 Form	0-16		
1992 Form	0-2			1990 Form	1-11	9.1%	- 4.00

M J B HEATON-ELLIS (Wroughton, Wilts)

	No. of Horses	Races Run	1st	2nd	3rd	Unpl	Per cent	£1 Level Stake
2-y-o	11	37	3	5	3	26	8.1	- 14.50
3-y-o	15	72	2	2	3	65	2.8	- 60.25
4-y-o+	8	63	10	5	4	44	15.9	+ 52.50
Totals	34	172	15	12	10	135	8.7	- 22.25

BY MONTH

2-y-o	W-R	Per cent	£1 Level Stake	3-y-o	W-R	Per cent	£1 Level Stake
January	0-0	-	0.00	January	0-0	-	0.00
February	0-0	-	0.00	February	0-0	-	0.00
March	1-1	100.0	+ 8.00	March	0-1	-	- 1.00
April	0-2	-	- 2.00	April	0-3	-	- 3.00
May	0-6	-	- 6.00	May	0-8	-	- 8.00
June	0-4	-	- 4.00	June	1-15	6.7	- 11.25
July	0-2	-	- 2.00	July	0-18	-	- 18.00
August	1-4	25.0	+ 0.50	August	1-10	10.0	- 2.00
September	1-8	12.5	+ 1.00	September	0-10	-	- 10.00
Oct/Nov	0-10	-	- 10.00	Oct/Nov	0-7	-	- 7.00

4-y-o+	W-R	Per cent	£1 Level Stake	Totals	W-R	Per cent	£1 Level Stake
January	2-3	66.7	+ 18.00	January	2-3	66.7	+ 18.00
February	0-4	-	- 4.00	February	0-4	-	- 4.00
March	0-4	-	- 4.00	March	1-6	16.7	+ 3.00
April	1-8	12.5	+ 26.00	April	1-13	7.7	+ 21.00
May	1-8	12.5	+ 3.00	May	1-22	4.5	- 11.00
June	2-6	33.3	+ 13.50	June	3-25	12.0	- 1.75
July	2-6	33.3	+ 14.00	July	2-26	7.7	- 6.00
August	2-11	18.2	- 1.00	August	4-25	16.0	- 2.50
September	0-6	-	- 6.00	September	1-24	4.2	- 15.00
Oct/Nov	0-7	-	- 7.00	Oct/Nov	0-24	-	- 24.00

DISTANCE

2-y-o	W-R	Per cent	£1 Level Stake	3-y-o	W-R	Per cent	£1 Level Stake
5f-6f	3-27	11.1	- 4.50	5f-6f	1-20	5.0	- 16.25
7f-8f	0-9	-	- 9.00	7f-8f	1-27	3.7	- 19.00
9f-13f	0-1	-	- 1.00	9f-13f	0-23	-	- 23.00
14f+	0-0	-	0.00	14f+	0-2	-	- 2.00

4-y-o+	W-R	Per cent	£1 Level Stake	Totals	W-R	Per cent	£1 Level Stake
5f-6f	7-33	21.2	+ 59.50	5f-6f	11-80	13.8	+ 38.75
7f-8f	0-17	-	- 17.00	7f-8f	1-53	1.9	- 45.00
9f-13f	3-10	30.0	+ 13.00	9f-13f	3-34	8.8	- 11.00
14f+	0-3	-	- 3.00	14f+	0-5	-	- 5.00

TYPE OF RACE

Non-Handicaps	W-R	Per cent	£1 Level Stake	Handicaps	W-R	Per cent	£1 Level Stake
2-y-o	1-27	3.7	- 18.00	2-y-o	1-8	12.5	+ 1.00
3-y-o	1-23	4.3	- 15.00	3-y-o	1-42	2.4	- 38.25
4-y-o+	0-1	-	- 1.00	4-y-o+	9-55	16.4	+ 54.00
Selling	1-5	20.0	- 0.50	Selling	0-2	-	- 2.00
Apprentice	0-1	-	- 1.00	Apprentice	1-7	14.3	- 0.50
Amat/Ladies	0-0	-	0.00	Amat/Ladies	0-1	-	- 1.00
Totals	3-57	5.3	- 35.50	Totals	12-115	10.4	+ 13.25

COURSE GRADE

	W-R	Per cent	£1 Level Stake
Group 1	4-74	5.4	- 41.00
Group 2	2-26	7.7	+ 11.75
Group 3	6-51	11.8	- 2.00
Group 4	3-21	14.3	+ 9.00

FIRST TIME OUT

	W-R	Per cent	£1 Level Stake
2-y-o	1-11	9.1	- 2.00
3-y-o	0-15	-	- 15.00
4-y-o+	3-8	37.5	+ 47.00
Totals	4-34	11.8	+ 30.00

JOCKEYS RIDING

	W-R	Per cent	£1 Level Stake		W-R	Per cent	£1 Level Stake
Stephen Davies	8-84	9.5	+ 4.75	W Woods	2-10	20.0	+ 3.50
M Roberts	4-15	26.7	+ 26.00	D McCabe	1-4	25.0	+ 2.50

D Holland	0-6	Pat Eddery	0-2	G Hind	0-1
J Carroll	0-5	T Quinn	0-2	G Mitchell	0-1
R Perham	0-5	W Newnes	0-2	J Quinn	0-1
B Thomson	0-3	W Ryan	0-2	K Rutter	0-1
D Harrison	0-3	A Procter	0-1	M Hills	0-1
D Wright	0-3	A Whelan	0-1	N Adams	0-1
S Keightley	0-3	C Webb	0-1	R Hills	0-1
S Whitworth	0-3	Claire Balding	0-1	S Raymont	0-1
Dale Gibson	0-2	G Carter	0-1	T Ives	0-1
J Reid	0-2	G Duffield	0-1	T Williams	0-1

COURSE RECORD

	Total W-R	Non-Handicaps 2-y-o	Non-Handicaps 3-y-o+	Handicaps 2-y-o	Handicaps 3-y-o+	Per cent	£1 Level Stake
Windsor	3-14	1-3	0-5	0-0	2-6	21.4	+ 7.00
Newmarket	2-11	0-3	0-0	1-1	1-7	18.2	+ 4.50
Folkestone	1-3	1-2	0-0	0-1	0-0	33.3	+ 6.00
Southwell (AW)	1-5	0-0	0-0	0-0	1-5	20.0	+ 3.00
Lingfield (AW)	1-5	0-0	0-0	0-0	1-5	20.0	+ 8.00
Leicester	1-6	0-1	0-1	0-0	1-4	16.7	+ 5.00
Salisbury	1-7	0-0	0-3	0-0	1-4	14.3	+ 27.00

Heaton-Ellis M J B

Brighton	1-8	0-1	0-2	0-0	1-5	12.5	-	4.25
Chepstow	1-8	0-2	0-2	0-1	1-3	12.5	+	1.00
Haydock	1-8	0-1	0-1	0-1	1-5	12.5	+	3.00
Nottingham	1-11	0-0	1-2	0-2	0-7	9.1	-	3.00
Kempton	1-13	0-3	0-3	0-0	1-7	7.7	-	6.50

Doncaster	0-10	Epsom	0-3	Beverley	0-1
Newbury	0-10	Warwick	0-3	Chester	0-1
Lingfield	0-8	Wolverhampton (AW)	0-3	Newcastle	0-1
Bath	0-7	York	0-3	Redcar	0-1
Goodwood	0-7	Catterick	0-2	Ripon	0-1
Sandown	0-6	Ascot	0-1		
Yarmouth	0-4	Ayr	0-1		

WINNING HORSES

	Age	Races Run	1st	2nd	3rd	Unpl	Win £
Try To Please	2	7	2	0	1	4	11,005
Slivovitz	4	10	3	1	1	5	10,997
Speedy Classic	5	16	3	3	2	8	10,248
Santana Lady	5	5	2	0	0	3	7,700
Lord High Admiral	6	9	1	1	1	6	5,186
Broughton's Tango	5	5	1	0	0	4	3,158
Marjorie's Memory	3	5	1	0	0	4	3,056
Cindy's Star	3	6	1	0	0	5	2,936
Rupert's Princess	2	11	1	4	0	6	2,489

WINNING OWNERS

	Races Won	Value £		Races Won	Value £
F J Sainsbury	4	13,245	E J G Young	1	5,186
Sir Anthony Page-Wood	2	11,005	S P Lansdown	1	3,158
B H Simpson	3	10,997	M Heaton-Ellis	1	3,054
Stainless Design Services	2	7,194	Miss C Hawkings	1	2,936

Favourites	1-10	10.0%	- 3.50	Total winning prize-money		£56,774

Longest winning sequence		2	Average SP of winner	9.0/1
Longest losing sequence		26	Return on stakes invested	-12.9%

1993 Form	19-222	8.6%	- 24.10	1991 Form	0-6
1992 Form	8-138	5.8%	- 71.00		

P R HEDGER (Chichester, West Sussex)

	No. of Horses	Races Run	1st	2nd	3rd	Unpl	Per cent	£1 Level Stake
2-y-o	0	0	0	0	0	0	-	0.00
3-y-o	5	15	0	0	1	14	-	- 15.00
4-y-o+	5	28	1	5	0	22	3.6	- 20.50
Totals	10	43	1	5	1	36	2.3	- 35.50

Jan	Feb	Mar	Apr	May	Jun	Jul	Aug	Sep	Oct/Nov
0-3	1-5	0-3	0-1	0-1	0-3	0-5	0-5	0-10	0-7

Winning Jockey	W-R	£1 Level Stake	Winning Course	W-R	£1 Level Stake
S Dawson	1-10	- 2.50	Lingfield (AW)	1-14	- 6.50

Winning Horse	Age	Races Run	1st	2nd	3rd	Unpl	Win £
Lyph	8	11	1	2	0	8	2,553

Favourites	0-1		Total winning prize-money	£2,553

1993 Form	3-43	7.0%	- 31.84	1992 Form	0-17

W R HERN (Lambourn, Berks)

	No. of Horses	Races Run	1st	2nd	3rd	Unpl	Per cent	£1 Level Stake
2-y-o	14	40	9	5	5	21	22.5	+ 7.21
3-y-o	26	110	9	18	12	71	8.2	- 71.35
4-y-o+	5	30	4	7	0	19	13.3	- 2.67
Totals	45	180	22	30	17	111	12.2	- 66.81

BY MONTH

2-y-o	W-R	Per cent	£1 Level Stake	3-y-o	W-R	Per cent	£1 Level Stake
Mar/Apr	0-0	-	0.00	Mar/Apr	0-9	-	- 9.00
May	1-2	50.0	+ 2.00	May	2-16	12.5	- 11.77
June	2-3	66.7	+ 0.33	June	1-15	6.7	- 7.00
July	2-6	33.3	+ 13.63	July	2-23	8.7	- 14.00
August	3-9	33.3	+ 2.25	August	3-22	13.6	- 10.58
September	1-9	11.1	0.00	September	0-16	-	- 16.00
Oct/Nov	0-11	-	- 11.00	Oct/Nov	1-9	11.1	- 3.00

Hern W R

4-y-o+	W-R	Per cent	£1 Level Stake	Totals	W-R	Per cent	£1 Level Stake
Mar/Apr	1-2	50.0	+ 2.33	Mar/Apr	1-11	9.1	- 6.67
May	0-4	-	- 4.00	May	3-22	13.6	- 13.77
June	2-5	40.0	+ 13.00	June	5-23	21.7	+ 6.33
July	0-5	-	- 5.00	July	4-34	11.8	- 5.37
August	0-2	-	- 2.00	August	6-33	18.2	- 10.33
September	1-6	16.7	- 1.00	September	2-31	6.5	- 17.00
Oct/Nov	0-6	-	- 6.00	Oct/Nov	1-26	3.8	- 20.00

DISTANCE

2-y-o	W-R	Per cent	£1 Level Stake	3-y-o	W-R	Per cent	£1 Level Stake
5f-6f	7-19	36.8	+ 2.21	5f-6f	0-6	-	- 6.00
7f-8f	2-21	9.5	+ 5.00	7f-8f	2-20	10.0	- 7.50
9f-13f	0-0	-	0.00	9f-13f	7-76	9.2	- 49.85
14f+	0-0	-	0.00	14f+	0-8	-	- 8.00

4-y-o+	W-R	Per cent	£1 Level Stake	Totals	W-R	Per cent	£1 Level Stake
5f-6f	0-0	-	0.00	5f-6f	7-25	28.0	- 3.79
7f-8f	0-1	-	- 1.00	7f-8f	4-42	9.5	- 3.50
9f-13f	2-16	12.5	0.00	9f-13f	9-92	9.8	- 49.85
14f+	2-13	15.4	- 1.67	14f+	2-21	9.5	- 9.67

TYPE OF RACE

Non-Handicaps	W-R	Per cent	£1 Level Stake	Handicaps	W-R	Per cent	£1 Level Stake
2-y-o	8-36	22.2	+ 2.21	2-y-o	1-4	25.0	+ 5.00
3-y-o	8-81	9.9	- 45.35	3-y-o	1-29	3.4	- 26.00
4-y-o+	2-12	16.7	+ 6.00	4-y-o+	2-18	11.1	- 8.67
Selling	0-0	-	0.00	Selling	0-0	-	0.00
Apprentice	0-0	-	0.00	Apprentice	0-0	-	0.00
Amat/Ladies	0-0	-	0.00	Amat/Ladies	0-0	-	0.00
Totals	18-129	14.0	- 37.14	Totals	4-51	7.8	- 29.67

COURSE GRADE

	W-R	Per cent	£1 Level Stake
Group 1	11-95	11.6	- 39.31
Group 2	5-27	18.5	- 7.75
Group 3	6-53	11.3	- 14.75
Group 4	0-5	-	- 5.00

FIRST TIME OUT

	W-R	Per cent	£1 Level Stake
2-y-o	3-14	21.4	+ 9.00
3-y-o	2-26	7.7	- 11.50
4-y-o+	0-5	-	- 5.00
Totals	5-45	11.1	- 7.50

JOCKEYS RIDING

	W-R	Per cent	£1 Level Stake		W-R	Per cent	£1 Level Stake
W Carson	9-62	14.5	− 34.14	K Darley	1-2	50.0	+ 4.00
Paul Eddery	3-16	18.8	− 5.42	Pat Eddery	1-3	33.3	+ 4.00
L Dettori	2-4	50.0	+ 7.50	W Ryan	1-3	33.3	+ 3.50
R Hills	2-18	11.1	+ 1.75	L Piggott	1-10	10.0	+ 1.00
P Scudamore	1-1	100.0	+ 4.00	T Sprake	1-32	3.1	− 24.00

M Birch	0-5	J Reid	0-2	M J Kinane		0-1
B Raymond	0-4	B Procter	0-1	M Perrett		0-1
A McGlone	0-3	D Holland	0-1	N Carlisle		0-1
A Clark	0-2	J Weaver	0-1	W Newnes		0-1
G Duffield	0-2	John Gorton	0-1			
J Lowe	0-2	M Hills	0-1			

COURSE RECORD

	Total W-R	Non-Handicaps 2-y-o	3-y-o+	Handicaps 2-y-o	3-y-o+	Per cent	£1 Level Stake
Ripon	3-7	1-1	2-5	0-0	0-1	42.9	+ 5.42
Newbury	3-11	3-3	0-5	0-0	0-3	27.3	− 5.04
Windsor	3-14	1-1	2-11	0-0	0-2	21.4	+ 1.25
Leicester	2-6	0-1	1-3	0-0	1-2	33.3	+ 8.00
Ascot	2-9	0-1	1-3	0-1	1-4	22.2	+ 3.00
York	2-10	1-3	1-5	0-0	0-2	20.0	− 5.27
Goodwood	2-13	1-4	1-5	0-1	0-3	15.4	+ 10.00
Doncaster	2-16	1-8	1-4	0-1	0-3	12.5	− 6.00
Lingfield	1-4	0-2	1-2	0-0	0-0	25.0	− 1.50
Salisbury	1-9	0-4	0-4	0-0	1-1	11.1	− 4.67
Bath	1-11	0-0	0-9	1-1	0-1	9.1	− 2.00

Newmarket	0-13	Pontefract	0-4	Warwick	0-2
Haydock	0-11	Beverley	0-2	Newcastle	0-1
Nottingham	0-10	Brighton	0-2	Southwell (AW)	0-1
Sandown	0-7	Epsom	0-2	Yarmouth	0-1
Chepstow	0-5	Folkestone	0-2		
Chester	0-5	Kempton	0-2		

WINNING HORSES

	Age	Races Run	1st	2nd	3rd	Unpl	Win £
Harayir	2	4	2	1	1	0	46,871
Cuff Link	4	7	2	2	0	3	28,449
Wijdan	3	4	2	1	1	0	18,337
Grecian Slipper	3	6	3	0	0	3	14,301
Mack The Knife	5	8	1	3	0	4	10,029
Ikaab	2	5	2	1	0	2	9,470
Al Nufooth	2	5	2	0	0	3	8,119
Dahik	2	4	1	1	2	0	7,165
In Waiting	2	6	1	0	1	4	5,410
Farringdon Hill	3	6	1	0	1	4	3,835

Hern W R

Mihriz	2	4	1	0	0	3	3,791
Lattam	3	10	1	2	1	6	3,596
Ghaali	3	5	1	2	1	1	3,570
Campaign	3	2	1	0	0	1	3,368
Wajih	4	5	1	1	0	3	000

WINNING OWNERS

	Races Won	Value £		Races Won	Value £
Hamdan Al-Maktoum	13	100,917	Sir John Astor	1	10,029
Lord Weinstock	3	33,859	Bernard Hathaway	1	3,835
Sheikh Mohammed	4	17,669			

Favourites	8-31	25.8%	- 12.89	Total winning prize-money	£166,309

Longest winning sequence		2	Average SP of winner	4.1/1
Longest losing sequence		35	Return on stakes invested	-37.1%

1993 Form	13-157	8.3%	- 92.16	1991 Form	23-138	16.7%	- 27.87
1992 Form	17-126	13.5%	- 26.91	1990 Form	30-152	19.7%	- 45.58

LADY HERRIES (Littlehampton, West Sussex)

	No. of Horses	Races Run	1st	2nd	3rd	Unpl	Per cent	£1 Level Stake
2-y-o	7	17	4	0	1	12	23.5	+ 2.88
3-y-o	11	58	12	6	5	35	20.7	+ 37.00
4-y-o+	19	108	16	9	18	65	14.8	- 17.84
Totals	37	183	32	15	24	112	17.5	+ 22.04

BY MONTH

2-y-o	W-R	Per cent	£1 Level Stake	3-y-o	W-R	Per cent	£1 Level Stake
Mar/Apr	0-0	-	0.00	Mar/Apr	0-1	-	- 1.00
May	0-1	-	- 1.00	May	0-7	-	- 7.00
June	0-0	-	0.00	June	4-10	40.0	+ 37.50
July	2-2	100.0	+ 13.50	July	6-14	42.9	+ 18.00
August	0-3	-	- 3.00	August	1-11	9.1	0.00
September	0-3	-	- 3.00	September	1-11	9.1	- 6.50
Oct/Nov	2-8	25.0	- 3.62	Oct/Nov	0-4	-	- 4.00

4-y-o+	W-R	Per cent	£1 Level Stake	Totals	W-R	Per cent	£1 Level Stake
Mar/Apr	2-15	13.3	- 2.17	Mar/Apr	2-16	12.5	- 3.17
May	1-15	6.7	- 4.00	May	1-23	4.3	- 12.00
June	4-20	20.0	+ 2.75	June	8-30	26.7	+ 40.25
July	4-26	15.4	- 7.92	July	12-42	28.6	+ 23.58
August	3-15	20.0	+ 4.50	August	4-29	13.8	+ 1.50
September	2-10	20.0	0.00	September	3-24	12.5	- 9.50
Oct/Nov	0-7	-	- 7.00	Oct/Nov	2-19	10.5	- 14.62

DISTANCE

2-y-o	W-R	Per cent	£1 Level Stake	3-y-o	W-R	Per cent	£1 Level Stake
5f-6f	0-3	-	- 3.00	5f-6f	0-3	-	- 3.00
7f-8f	4-14	28.6	+ 5.88	7f-8f	2-18	11.1	- 5.50
9f-13f	0-0	-	0.00	9f-13f	9-32	28.1	+ 46.50
14f+	0-0	-	0.00	14f+	1-5	20.0	- 1.00

4-y-o+	W-R	Per cent	£1 Level Stake	Totals	W-R	Per cent	£1 Level Stake
5f-6f	0-1	-	- 1.00	5f-6f	0-7	-	- 7.00
7f-8f	5-36	13.9	0.00	7f-8f	11-68	16.2	+ 0.38
9f-13f	7-47	14.9	- 17.00	9f-13f	16-79	20.3	+ 29.50
14f+	4-24	16.7	+ 0.16	14f+	5-29	17.2	- 0.84

TYPE OF RACE

Non-Handicaps	W-R	Per cent	£1 Level Stake	Handicaps	W-R	Per cent	£1 Level Stake
2-y-o	4-17	23.5	+ 2.88	2-y-o	0-0	-	0.00
3-y-o	4-21	19.0	+ 24.00	3-y-o	8-32	25.0	+ 18.00
4-y-o+	3-17	17.6	- 7.50	4-y-o+	10-70	14.3	- 1.84
Selling	0-0	-	0.00	Selling	0-0	-	0.00
Apprentice	0-1	-	- 1.00	Apprentice	2-7	28.6	+ 2.75
Amat/Ladies	0-0	-	0.00	Amat/Ladies	1-18	5.6	- 15.25
Totals	11-56	19.6	+ 18.38	Totals	21-127	16.5	+ 3.66

COURSE GRADE

	W-R	Per cent	£1 Level Stake
Group 1	25-112	22.3	+ 60.29
Group 2	4-34	11.8	- 14.75
Group 3	1-30	3.3	- 22.50
Group 4	2-7	28.6	- 1.00

FIRST TIME OUT

	W-R	Per cent	£1 Level Stake
2-y-o	1-7	14.3	- 2.50
3-y-o	1-11	9.1	+ 10.00
4-y-o+	2-18	11.1	- 9.17
Totals	4-36	11.1	- 1.67

205

JOCKEYS RIDING

	W–R	Per cent	£1 Level Stake		W–R	Per cent	£1 Level Stake
K Darley	7–21	33.3	+ 4.38	N Varley	1–2	50.0	+ 0.25
J Reid	5–17	29.4	+ 12.33	K Fallon	1–4	25.0	0.00
D Harrison	4–13	30.8	+ 15.00	R Hughes	1–4	25.0	– 1.50
T Ives	3–38	7.9	+ 2.00	W Ryan	1–7	14.3	+ 4.00
M Hills	2–5	40.0	+ 9.50	J Williams	1–8	12.5	0.00
W R Swinburn	2–6	33.3	+ 6.33	Mrs M Cowdrey	1–11	9.1	– 8.25
A Clark	1–1	100.0	+ 3.50	J Quinn	1–12	8.3	+ 1.00
G Parkin	1–1	100.0	+ 6.50				

Mr P P-Gordon	0–5	T Quinn	0–2	N Kennedy	0–1
T Williams	0–4	A McGlone	0–1	P Doe	0–1
Paul Eddery	0–3	D Denby	0–1	P Robinson	0–1
G Carter	0–2	D McCabe	0–1	R Cochrane	0–1
J Tate	0–2	G Bardwell	0–1	Shona Crombie	0–1
Mr T Cuff	0–2	G Duffield	0–1		
P Quinn	0–2	J Weaver	0–1		

COURSE RECORD

	Total W–R	Non-Handicaps 2-y-o	3-y-o+	Handicaps 2-y-o	3-y-o+	Per cent	£1 Level Stake
Goodwood	5–15	0–2	1–4	0–0	4–9	33.3	+ 42.00
Sandown	4–11	1–1	1–4	0–0	2–6	36.4	+ 28.50
Ascot	3–6	1–1	1–2	0–0	1–3	50.0	+ 3.13
York	3–12	0–0	0–2	0–0	3–10	25.0	+ 6.83
Newbury	3–14	0–1	0–1	0–0	3–12	21.4	– 0.67
Newmarket	3–20	0–3	1–4	0–0	2–13	15.0	– 0.50
Ayr	2–4	1–1	1–2	0–0	0–1	50.0	+ 5.50
Folkestone	2–6	0–0	1–2	0–0	1–4	33.3	0.00
Redcar	2–11	0–0	0–3	0–0	2–8	18.2	– 4.25
Salisbury	2–13	0–1	1–3	0–0	1–9	15.4	– 0.50
Leicester	1–3	0–0	0–2	0–0	1–1	33.3	+ 4.50
Doncaster	1–10	1–2	0–1	0–0	0–7	10.0	– 8.00
Kempton	1–12	0–3	0–1	0–0	1–8	8.3	– 8.50

Windsor	0–10	Bath	0–3	Epsom	0–1
Haydock	0–7	Brighton	0–3	Pontefract	0–1
Nottingham	0–7	Chester	0–2	Warwick	0–1
Lingfield	0–5	Beverley	0–1		
Yarmouth	0–4	Chepstow	0–1		

WINNING HORSES

	Age	Races Run	1st	2nd	3rd	Unpl	Win £
Celtic Swing	2	3	3	0	0	0	103,762
Frustration	3	6	4	0	1	1	47,820
Safety In Numbers	4	6	2	0	1	3	29,383
Isle Of Pearls	4	5	3	1	1	0	18,918
Castle Courageous	7	5	2	0	1	2	16,234

Arctic Thunder	3	6	2	1	0	3	16,033
River North	4	3	1	2	0	0	10,512
Jawaal	4	7	2	1	1	3	9,815
Zajko	4	6	2	0	1	3	9,301
Minnesota Viking	3	8	2	2	0	4	8,282
Meant To Be	4	11	2	1	0	8	6,160
Polar Storm	4	8	1	0	1	6	4,436
Opaline	2	2	1	0	0	1	4,157
Taufan's Melody	3	3	1	1	0	1	3,864
Curtelace	4	8	1	0	1	6	3,730
Maidment	3	3	1	0	0	2	3,663
A Million Watts	3	8	1	0	1	6	3,262
Willow	3	7	1	0	1	5	2,959

WINNING OWNERS

	Races Won	Value £		Races Won	Value £
P D Savill	8	138,194	Charles Green	2	8,282
Lavinia Duchess of Norfolk	4	47,820	Dexam International Ltd	1	4,436
Edwin N Cohen	2	29,383	All At Sea	1	3,864
Lady Mary Mumford	4	22,394	Mrs B V Chennells	1	3,663
Mrs Berta Lazarus	3	18,918	John A Constable	1	3,262
T G Fox	2	9,815	J R M Lewis	1	2,959
Sir Roger G Gibbs	2	9,301			

Favourites	15-38	39.5%	+ 13.71	Total winning prize-money		£302,289
Longest winning sequence			3	Average SP of winner		5.4/1
Longest losing sequence			18	Return on stakes invested		12.0%
1993 Form	17-90	18.9%	+ 2.68	1991 Form	14-99	14.1%	- 6.18
1992 Form	6-77	7.8%	- 19.00	1990 Form	4-60	6.7%	- 30.70

J HETHERTON (Malton, North Yorks)

	No. of Horses	Races Run	1st	2nd	3rd	Unpl	Per cent	£1 Level Stake
2-y-o	3	16	2	2	2	10	12.5	+ 14.50
3-y-o	8	54	5	2	2	45	9.3	+ 2.50
4-y-o+	4	35	2	4	9	20	5.7	- 30.25
Totals	15	105	9	8	13	75	8.6	- 13.25

Jan	Feb	Mar	Apr	May	Jun	Jul	Aug	Sep	Oct/Nov
0-5	0-13	0-6	2-9	2-11	1-13	3-14	1-14	0-8	0-12

Winning Jockeys	W-R	£1 Level Stake				W-R	£1 Level Stake
N Kennedy	4-34	+ 17.25	B Thomson			1-2	+ 13.00
S Webster	3-11	+ 13.50	N Carlisle			1-22	- 21.00

Winning Courses							
Southwell (AW)	3-28	- 10.50	Nottingham			1-3	+ 5.00
Newcastle	2-6	+ 24.50	Pontefract			1-3	+ 0.75
Newmarket	1-3	+ 14.00	Catterick			1-6	+ 9.00

Winning Horses	Age	Races Run	1st	2nd	3rd	Unpl	Win £
Lady Silk	3	22	4	2	0	16	13,706
Manful	2	12	2	2	2	6	8,184
Absalom's Pillar	4	10	1	3	3	3	3,184
General Gubbins	3	8	1	0	0	7	3,054
Panther	4	15	1	1	5	8	2,322

Favourites	1-2	50.0%	+ 1.75	Total winning prize-money			£30,450

1993 Form	4-84	4.8%	- 14.00	1991 Form	10-91	11.0%	- 20.42
1992 Form	1-8	12.5%	- 5.25	1990 Form	4-49	8.2%	- 27.37

A HIDE (Newmarket)

	No. of Horses	Races Run	1st	2nd	3rd	Unpl	Per cent	£1 Level Stake
2-y-o	2	7	0	0	0	7	-	- 7.00
3-y-o	10	60	9	7	5	39	15.0	+ 3.13
4-y-o+	2	11	2	0	1	8	18.2	+ 7.75
Totals	14	78	11	7	6	54	14.1	+ 3.88

BY MONTH

2-y-o	W-R	Per cent	£1 Level Stake	3-y-o	W-R	Per cent	£1 Level Stake
Mar/Apr	0-0	-	0.00	Mar/Apr	1-3	33.3	+ 18.00
May	0-0	-	0.00	May	2-10	20.0	- 4.12
June	0-0	-	0.00	June	2-10	20.0	- 2.75
July	0-0	-	0.00	July	2-10	20.0	+ 5.50
August	0-2	-	- 2.00	August	1-8	12.5	- 3.50
September	0-1	-	- 1.00	September	1-12	8.3	- 3.00
Oct/Nov	0-4	-	- 4.00	Oct/Nov	0-7	-	- 7.00

4-y-o+	W-R	Per cent	£1 Level Stake	Totals	W-R	Per cent	£1 Level Stake
Mar/Apr	0-0	-	0.00	Mar/Apr	1-3	33.3	+ 18.00
May	1-2	50.0	+ 13.00	May	3-12	25.0	+ 8.88
June	1-4	25.0	- 0.25	June	3-14	21.4	- 3.00
July	0-2	-	- 2.00	July	2-12	16.7	+ 3.50
August	0-0	-	0.00	August	1-10	10.0	- 5.50
September	0-1	-	- 1.00	September	1-14	7.1	- 5.00
Oct/Nov	0-2	-	- 2.00	Oct/Nov	0-13	-	- 13.00

DISTANCE

2-y-o	W-R	Per cent	£1 Level Stake	3-y-o	W-R	Per cent	£1 Level Stake
5f-6f	0-5	-	- 5.00	5f-6f	1-7	14.3	- 2.50
7f-8f	0-2	-	- 2.00	7f-8f	2-13	15.4	+ 17.00
9f-13f	0-0	-	0.00	9f-13f	6-38	15.8	- 9.37
14f+	0-0	-	0.00	14f+	0-2	-	- 2.00

4-y-o+	W-R	Per cent	£1 Level Stake	Totals	W-R	Per cent	£1 Level Stake
5f-6f	0-0	-	0.00	5f-6f	1-12	8.3	- 7.50
7f-8f	0-0	-	0.00	7f-8f	2-15	13.3	+ 15.00
9f-13f	2-10	20.0	+ 8.75	9f-13f	8-48	16.7	- 0.62
14f+	0-1	-	- 1.00	14f+	0-3	-	- 3.00

TYPE OF RACE

Non-Handicaps	W-R	Per cent	£1 Level Stake	Handicaps	W-R	Per cent	£1 Level Stake
2-y-o	0-4	-	- 4.00	2-y-o	0-1	-	- 1.00
3-y-o	2-17	11.8	- 10.62	3-y-o	6-36	16.7	+ 16.25
4-y-o+	0-0	-	0.00	4-y-o+	1-3	33.3	+ 12.00
Selling	0-2	-	- 2.00	Selling	0-1	-	- 1.00
Apprentice	0-2	-	- 2.00	Apprentice	0-3	-	- 3.00
Amat/Ladies	0-1	-	- 1.00	Amat/Ladies	2-8	25.0	+ 0.25
Totals	2-26	7.7	- 19.62	Totals	9-52	17.3	+ 23.50

COURSE GRADE

	W-R	Per cent	£1 Level Stake
Group 1	2-33	6.1	- 20.50
Group 2	3-10	30.0	- 0.37
Group 3	5-27	18.5	+ 21.75
Group 4	1-8	12.5	+ 3.00

FIRST TIME OUT

	W-R	Per cent	£1 Level Stake
2-y-o	0-2	-	- 2.00
3-y-o	1-10	10.0	+ 11.00
4-y-o+	0-2	-	- 2.00
Totals	1-14	7.1	+ 7.00

JOCKEYS RIDING

	W-R	Per cent	£1 Level Stake		W-R	Per cent	£1 Level Stake
W Woods	6-19	31.6	+ 36.50	P Bowe	1-7	14.3	- 2.50
Miss L Hide	2-9	22.2	- 0.75	J Williams	1-8	12.5	+ 3.00
A McGlone	1-2	50.0	+ 0.63				

M Tebbutt	0-7	M Henry	0-2	M Baird	0-1
J Quinn	0-4	C Nutter	0-1	M Fenton	0-1
R Price	0-4	D Biggs	0-1	R Cochrane	0-1
B Rouse	0-2	E Johnson	0-1	S Mulvey	0-1
Dale Gibson	0-2	G Bardwell	0-1	W Ryan	0-1
K Rutter	0-2	J Stack	0-1		

COURSE RECORD

	Total W-R	Non-Handicaps 2-y-o	Non-Handicaps 3-y-o+	Handicaps 2-y-o	Handicaps 3-y-o+	Per cent	£1 Level Stake
Pontefract	2-5	0-0	0-0	0-1	2-4	40.0	+ 4.00
Ayr	1-2	0-0	0-0	0-0	1-2	50.0	+ 7.00
Brighton	1-2	0-0	1-1	0-0	0-1	50.0	+ 0.63
Redcar	1-2	0-0	0-0	0-0	1-2	50.0	+ 1.25
Southwell (AW)	1-2	0-0	0-0	0-0	1-2	50.0	+ 9.00
Lingfield	1-3	0-0	1-1	0-0	0-2	33.3	+ 0.75
Nottingham	1-4	0-1	0-0	0-0	1-3	25.0	+ 17.00
Yarmouth	1-6	0-0	0-1	0-0	1-5	16.7	- 2.25
Windsor	1-7	0-2	0-1	0-0	1-4	14.3	+ 8.00
Newmarket	1-13	0-3	0-2	0-0	1-8	7.7	- 9.50

Kempton	0-6	Goodwood	0-2	Ripon	0-1
Leicester	0-4	Newbury	0-2	Sandown	0-1
Haydock	0-3	Salisbury	0-2	Warwick	0-1
Catterick	0-2	Ascot	0-1	Wolverhampton (AW)	0-1
Doncaster	0-2	Bath	0-1		
Folkestone	0-2	Epsom	0-1		

WINNING HORSES

	Age	Races Run	1st	2nd	3rd	Unpl	Win £
Samba Sharply	3	6	3	1	1	1	23,123
Virtual Reality	3	9	2	2	1	4	9,429
Scenic Dancer	6	10	2	0	1	7	5,910
Lady-Bo-K	3	9	1	0	2	6	3,184
Orange Extreme	3	8	1	0	0	7	3,080
Legal Train	3	8	1	3	0	4	3,028
My Learned Friend	3	5	1	1	0	3	2,558

WINNING OWNERS

	Races Won	Value £		Races Won	Value £
Miss V R Jarvis	3	23,123	J P Carrington	1	3,080
Mrs Sherry Collier	2	9,429	Gerald Tams	1	3,028
Anthony Hide	2	5,910	S J Roberts	1	2,558
Ms Theresa McEvoy	1	3,184			

Favourites	5-6	83.3%	+ 12.38	Total winning prize-money		£50,311
Longest winning sequence			3	Average SP of winner		6.4/1
Longest losing sequence			18	Return on stakes invested		5.0%
1993 Form	6-89	6.7%	- 24.50	1991 Form	15-163	9.2%	- 7.92
1992 Form	5-77	6.5%	- 36.00	1990 Form	10-94	10.6%	+ 1.00

C J HILL (Barnstaple, Devon)

	No. of Horses	Races Run	1st	2nd	3rd	Unpl	Per cent	£1 Level Stake
2-y-o	12	47	5	2	1	39	10.6	- 13.20
3-y-o	1	3	0	0	0	3	-	- 3.00
4-y-o+	7	43	2	4	6	31	4.7	- 31.75
Totals	20	93	7	6	7	73	7.5	- 47.95

Jan	Feb	Mar	Apr	May	Jun	Jul	Aug	Sep	Oct/Nov
0-16	0-1	0-1	0-4	0-11	3-18	1-18	2-15	1-8	0-1

Winning Jockeys	W-R	£1 Level Stake		W-R	£1 Level Stake
J Quinn	2-24	- 16.75	D Biggs	1-1	+ 14.00
J Stack	1-1	+ 0.80	J Reid	1-2	+ 5.50
G Hind	1-1	+ 4.50	N Carlisle	1-8	0.00

Winning Courses					
Southwell (AW)	4-33	- 8.95	Nottingham	1-2	+ 3.50
Folkestone	1-2	+ 6.00	Salisbury	1-10	- 2.50

Winning Horses	Age	Races Run	1st	2nd	3rd	Unpl	Win £
Double Glow	2	7	3	0	0	4	7,492
Red River Rose	2	5	1	0	0	4	3,143
Spectator	2	8	1	1	0	6	3,104
Atlantic Way	6	9	1	4	0	4	3,047
Grand Time	5	13	1	0	2	10	2,847

Favourites	3-13	23.1%	- 3.95	Total winning prize-money		£19,632
1993 Form	27-170	15.9%	- 2.56	1991 Form	16-221	7.2%	-106.00
1992 Form	19-204	9.3%	- 66.04	1990 Form	11-125	8.8%	- 56.33

B W HILLS (Lambourn, Berks)

	No. of Horses	Races Run	1st	2nd	3rd	Unpl	Per cent	£1 Level Stake
2-y-o	52	162	15	17	22	108	9.3	- 79.39
3-y-o	37	177	23	18	19	117	13.0	- 42.20
4-y-o+	8	44	6	2	5	31	13.6	- 21.92
Totals	97	383	44	37	46	256	11.5	-143.51

BY MONTH

2-y-o	W-R	Per cent	£1 Level Stake	3-y-o	W-R	Per cent	£1 Level Stake
January	0-0	-	0.00	January	0-0	-	0.00
February	0-0	-	0.00	February	0-0	-	0.00
March	0-2	-	- 2.00	March	2-4	50.0	+ 4.00
April	0-9	-	- 9.00	April	4-24	16.7	- 6.99
May	1-5	20.0	+ 4.00	May	4-35	11.4	- 14.90
June	1-17	5.9	- 13.75	June	3-30	10.0	- 16.50
July	6-33	18.2	- 2.87	July	4-27	14.8	- 8.17
August	3-29	10.3	- 17.50	August	4-24	16.7	- 11.39
September	0-22	-	- 22.00	September	1-19	5.3	+ 22.00
Oct/Nov	4-45	8.9	- 16.27	Oct/Nov	1-14	7.1	- 10.25

4-y-o+	W-R	Per cent	£1 Level Stake	Totals	W-R	Per cent	£1 Level Stake
January	0-0	-	0.00	January	0-0	-	0.00
February	1-2	50.0	+ 3.50	February	1-2	50.0	+ 3.50
March	1-2	50.0	+ 0.10	March	3-8	37.5	+ 2.10
April	1-3	33.3	+ 1.50	April	5-36	13.9	- 14.49
May	0-12	-	- 12.00	May	5-52	9.6	- 22.90
June	0-5	-	- 5.00	June	4-52	7.7	- 35.25
July	1-8	12.5	- 2.50	July	11-68	16.2	- 13.54
August	0-4	-	- 4.00	August	7-57	12.3	- 32.89
September	0-3	-	- 3.00	September	1-44	2.3	- 3.00
Oct/Nov	2-5	40.0	- 0.52	Oct/Nov	7-64	10.9	- 27.04

DISTANCE

2-y-o	W-R	Per cent	£1 Level Stake	3-y-o	W-R	Per cent	£1 Level Stake
5f-6f	8-89	9.0	- 39.77	5f-6f	1-8	12.5	- 3.67
7f-8f	7-72	9.7	- 38.62	7f-8f	6-62	9.7	- 43.39
9f-13f	0-1	-	- 1.00	9f-13f	14-92	15.2	- 24.89
14f+	0-0	-	0.00	14f+	2-15	13.3	+ 29.75

4-y-o+	W-R	Per cent	£1 Level Stake	Totals	W-R	Per cent	£1 Level Stake
5f-6f	0-0	-	0.00	5f-6f	9-97	9.3	- 43.44
7f-8f	0-18	-	- 18.00	7f-8f	13-152	8.6	-100.01
9f-13f	3-10	30.0	+ 3.10	9f-13f	17-103	16.5	- 22.79
14f+	3-16	18.8	- 7.02	14f+	5-31	16.1	+ 22.73

TYPE OF RACE

Non-Handicaps	W-R	Per cent	£1 Level Stake	Handicaps	W-R	Per cent	£1 Level Stake
2-y-o	15-141	10.6	- 58.39	2-y-o	0-17	-	- 17.00
3-y-o	21-117	17.9	+ 8.97	3-y-o	2-53	3.8	- 44.17
4-y-o+	1-9	11.1	- 6.62	4-y-o+	5-32	15.6	- 12.30
Selling	0-3	-	- 3.00	Selling	0-3	-	- 3.00
Apprentice	0-4	-	- 4.00	Apprentice	0-2	-	- 2.00
Amat/Ladies	0-1	-	- 1.00	Amat/Ladies	0-1	-	- 1.00
Totals	37-275	13.5	- 64.04	Totals	7-108	6.5	- 79.47

COURSE GRADE

	W-R	Per cent	£1 Level Stake
Group 1	22-226	9.7	- 95.06
Group 2	8-41	19.5	- 1.54
Group 3	5-63	7.9	- 34.25
Group 4	9-53	17.0	- 12.66

FIRST TIME OUT

	W-R	Per cent	£1 Level Stake
2-y-o	2-52	3.8	- 39.50
3-y-o	5-37	13.5	- 11.00
4-y-o+	1-8	12.5	- 3.50
Totals	8-97	8.2	- 54.00

JOCKEYS RIDING

	W-R	Per cent	£1 Level Stake		W-R	Per cent	£1 Level Stake
M Hills	12-113	10.6	- 51.41	A Munro	1-2	50.0	+ 1.50
D Holland	7-44	15.9	- 12.62	S Whitworth	1-2	50.0	+ 2.33
D Harrison	6-28	21.4	+ 0.35	M Roberts	1-2	50.0	+ 0.63
Pat Eddery	5-33	15.2	+ 26.50	D McKeown	1-4	25.0	+ 2.00
B Thomson	3-30	10.0	- 18.27	K Darley	1-4	25.0	+ 1.50
R Hills	2-21	9.5	- 8.75	Stephen Davies	1-4	25.0	- 0.25
W Carson	2-26	7.7	- 21.52	Paul Eddery	1-8	12.5	- 3.50

M J Kinane	0-7	S Raymont	0-2	John Francome	0-1
R Street	0-7	T Quinn	0-2	L Dettori	0-1
S McCarthy	0-6	A Culhane	0-1	M Baird	0-1
G Duffield	0-4	D Wright	0-1	Miss J Winter	0-1
J Fortune	0-3	Dale Gibson	0-1	Mr C B Hills	0-1
J Reid	0-3	E Johnson	0-1	S Mulvey	0-1
B Russell	0-2	G Bardwell	0-1	T Williams	0-1
G Carter	0-2	J Carroll	0-1	W R Swinburn	0-1
J Quinn	0-2	J Fanning	0-1	W Woods	0-1
J Williams	0-2	J Lowe	0-1		
K Fallon	0-2	J Weaver	0-1		

COURSE RECORD

	Total W-R	Non-Handicaps 2-y-o	Non-Handicaps 3-y-o+	Handicaps 2-y-o	Handicaps 3-y-o+	Per cent	£1 Level Stake
Ayr	5-13	1-5	3-4	0-2	1-2	38.5	+ 5.73
Catterick	5-14	1-2	4-7	0-0	0-5	35.7	+ 0.99
Doncaster	5-33	1-13	4-12	0-2	0-6	15.2	+ 26.50
Newmarket	5-60	2-27	2-14	0-5	1-14	8.3	- 36.52

Hills B W

Ripon	3-9	0-2	1-5	0-0	2-2	33.3	+	5.83
Haydock	3-11	2-6	1-2	0-1	0-2	27.3	+	3.35
Lingfield	2-9	1-4	0-3	0-0	1-2	22.2		0.00
Lingfield (AW)	2-9	0-1	0-3	0-0	2-5	22.2	-	1.40
Nottingham	2-10	1-4	1-3	0-0	0-3	20.0	+	6.00
Ascot	2-12	1-5	1-5	0-0	0-2	16.7	-	5.62
Epsom	1-2	0-1	1-1	0-0	0-0	50.0	+	1.50
Brighton	1-4	0-0	1-3	0-0	0-1	25.0	-	1.37
Salisbury	1-5	1-3	0-1	0-0	0-1	20.0	+	2.00
Yarmouth	1-5	1-3	0-0	0-2	0-0	20.0	+	0.50
Wolverhampton (AW)	1-5	1-1	0-2	0-0	0-2	20.0	-	2.25
Folkestone	1-7	1-4	0-1	0-0	0-2	14.3	+	8.00
Chester	1-11	0-2	1-6	0-0	0-3	9.1	-	5.00
Bath	1-14	0-5	1-6	0-0	0-3	7.1	-	10.00
Kempton	1-16	0-4	1-7	0-0	0-5	6.3	-	11.00
Windsor	1-16	1-7	0-8	0-1	0-0	6.3	-	12.75

Newbury	0-23	Sandown	0-10	Southwell (AW)	0-2
York	0-21	Newcastle	0-7	Beverley	0-1
Goodwood	0-18	Chepstow	0-3	Edinburgh	0-1
Warwick	0-15	Pontefract	0-3		
Leicester	0-11	Redcar	0-3		

WINNING HORSES

		Races					Win
	Age	Run	1st	2nd	3rd	Unpl	£
Moonax	3	6	3	1	1	1	160,901
Bolas	3	3	2	0	0	1	86,708
Further Flight	8	8	2	0	3	3	27,914
Painted Madam	2	10	3	4	2	1	16,214
Juyush	2	5	1	1	2	1	11,063
Run Softly	3	7	2	2	0	3	10,559
Ringlet	4	6	3	1	0	2	9,319
Warning Star	2	6	2	0	1	3	7,703
La Contessa	2	5	2	1	0	2	7,257
Ritto	4	4	1	0	0	3	7,245
Tryst	3	2	2	0	0	0	6,955
Sue's Artiste	3	7	2	2	1	2	6,910
Princess Muzna	3	9	2	1	0	6	5,467
Torch Rouge	3	5	1	0	0	4	4,664
Alessia	2	3	1	0	1	1	4,513
Zingibar	2	3	1	0	1	1	4,482
New Reputation	3	8	1	1	2	4	4,464
Lipizzaner	2	5	1	1	1	2	4,373
Salam	3	9	1	1	1	6	3,545
Yacht	2	4	1	0	1	2	3,526
Lombardic	3	8	1	3	1	3	3,473
Sozzled	3	6	1	0	1	4	3,407
Tres Cher	3	9	1	1	2	5	3,322
Deliver	3	4	1	0	1	2	3,210
Charlie Sillett	2	3	1	0	0	2	3,185

Wicken Wonder	2	6	1	0	0	5	3,163
Eight Sharp	2	7	1	1	1	4	2,814
Glidingonby	3	6	1	0	0	5	2,813
As Sharp As	3	6	1	2	0	3	2,786
Recluse	3	6	1	0	1	4	2,387

WINNING OWNERS

	Races Won	Value £		Races Won	Value £
Sheikh Mohammed	5	172,518	A L R Morton	2	6,910
K Abdulla	8	110,081	J Hanson	1	4,664
S Wingfield Digby	2	27,914	D J Deer	1	4,513
Nigel S Murray	3	16,214	R D Hollingsworth	1	3,526
Hamdan Al-Maktoum	2	14,608	Mrs Robert Heathcote	1	3,407
R E Sangster	3	10,599	Kenneth B Rawlings	1	3,210
K Al-Said	3	9,948	John Sillett	1	3,185
Sir Eric Parker	3	9,319	William Heard	1	3,163
Stephen Crown	2	7,703	John Leat	1	2,814
Per A Flaate	2	7,257	D O Pickering	1	2,786

Favourites	17-47	36.2%	- 0.69	Total winning prize-money	£424,338
Longest winning sequence			2	Average SP of winner	4.4/1
Longest losing sequence			31	Return on stakes invested	-37.5%
1993 Form	39-355	11.0%	-150.21	1991 Form 99-491 20.2%	+ 7.81
1992 Form	63-424	14.9%	-101.91	1990 Form 113-579 19.5%	- 52.11

J W HILLS (Lambourn, Berks)

	No. of Horses	Races Run	1st	2nd	3rd	Unpl	Per cent	£1 Level Stake
2-y-o	15	48	6	5	7	30	12.5	- 12.95
3-y-o	18	92	10	11	13	58	10.9	- 33.50
4-y-o+	13	86	10	10	10	56	11.6	- 29.25
Totals	46	226	26	26	30	144	11.5	- 75.70

215

BY MONTH

2-y-o	W-R	Per cent	£1 Level Stake		3-y-o	W-R	Per cent	£1 Level Stake
January	0-0	-		0.00	January	0-0	-	0.00
February	0-0	-		0.00	February	0-0	-	0.00
March	0-0	-		0.00	March	0-0	-	0.00
April	0-0	-		0.00	April	2-8	25.0	+ 3.75
May	0-0	-		0.00	May	3-14	21.4	- 6.25
June	0-5	-	-	5.00	June	0-16	-	- 16.00
July	2-10	20.0	-	2.20	July	2-16	12.5	- 3.50
August	2-6	33.3	+	14.00	August	1-17	5.9	- 4.00
September	2-16	12.5	-	8.75	September	1-10	10.0	- 7.50
Oct/Nov	0-11	-	-	11.00	Oct/Nov	1-11	9.1	0.00

4-y-o+	W-R	Per cent	£1 Level Stake		Totals	W-R	Per cent	£1 Level Stake
January	2-6	33.3	+	0.75	January	2-6	33.3	+ 0.75
February	0-4	-	-	4.00	February	0-4	-	- 4.00
March	0-2	-	-	2.00	March	0-2	-	- 2.00
April	1-9	11.1	-	4.50	April	3-17	17.6	- 0.75
May	2-10	20.0	+	0.50	May	5-24	20.8	- 5.75
June	0-12	-	-	12.00	June	0-33	-	- 33.00
July	4-16	25.0	+	10.00	July	8-42	19.0	+ 4.30
August	0-10	-	-	10.00	August	3-33	9.1	0.00
September	1-9	11.1		0.00	September	4-35	11.4	- 16.25
Oct/Nov	0-8	-	-	8.00	Oct/Nov	1-30	3.3	- 19.00

DISTANCE

2-y-o	W-R	Per cent	£1 Level Stake		3-y-o	W-R	Per cent	£1 Level Stake
5f-6f	5-27	18.5	+	3.55	5f-6f	0-0	-	0.00
7f-8f	1-19	5.3	-	14.50	7f-8f	2-42	4.8	- 24.67
9f-13f	0-2	-	-	2.00	9f-13f	8-42	19.0	- 0.83
14f+	0-0	-		0.00	14f+	0-8	-	- 8.00

4-y-o+	W-R	Per cent	£1 Level Stake		Totals	W-R	Per cent	£1 Level Stake
5f-6f	1-8	12.5	-	3.50	5f-6f	6-35	17.1	+ 0.05
7f-8f	1-19	5.3	-	14.50	7f-8f	4-80	5.0	- 53.67
9f-13f	8-52	15.4	-	4.25	9f-13f	16-96	16.7	- 7.08
14f+	0-7	-	-	7.00	14f+	0-15	-	- 15.00

TYPE OF RACE

Non-Handicaps	W-R	Per cent	£1 Level Stake		Handicaps	W-R	Per cent	£1 Level Stake
2-y-o	6-41	14.6	-	5.95	2-y-o	0-6	-	- 6.00
3-y-o	7-55	12.7	-	16.00	3-y-o	2-28	7.1	- 11.00
4-y-o+	6-32	18.8	-	5.75	4-y-o+	3-44	6.8	- 20.50
Selling	1-4	25.0	-	1.50	Selling	0-1	-	- 1.00
Apprentice	0-3	-	-	3.00	Apprentice	0-5	-	- 5.00
Amat/Ladies	0-2	-	-	2.00	Amat/Ladies	1-5	20.0	+ 2.00
Totals	20-137	14.6	-	34.20	Totals	6-89	6.7	- 41.50

COURSE GRADE

	W-R	Per cent	£1 Level Stake
Group 1	10-98	10.2	- 23.33
Group 2	6-41	14.6	- 15.37
Group 3	7-64	10.9	- 23.75
Group 4	3-23	13.0	- 13.25

FIRST TIME OUT

	W-R	Per cent	£1 Level Stake
2-y-o	2-15	13.3	+ 4.00
3-y-o	3-18	16.7	- 1.92
4-y-o+	1-13	7.7	- 9.50
Totals	6-46	13.0	- 7.42

JOCKEYS RIDING

	W-R	Per cent	£1 Level Stake
M Hills	10-60	16.7	+ 8.55
A Clark	3-9	33.3	+ 0.75
D Holland	3-13	23.1	+ 0.83
R Hills	3-31	9.7	- 24.33
M Henry	2-25	8.0	- 9.50
Miss E Houghton	1-2	50.0	+ 5.00
R Cochrane	1-3	33.3	+ 1.50
K Darley	1-3	33.3	+ 4.00
Paul Eddery	1-4	25.0	+ 0.50
L Dettori	1-9	11.1	+ 4.00

D Harrison	0-14	G Bardwell	0-2	J Weaver	0-1
J Williams	0-10	G Duffield	0-2	Mr C Vigors	0-1
B Thomson	0-8	N Carlisle	0-2	Mr G J Houghton	0-1
A Munro	0-4	P Robinson	0-2	T Ives	0-1
Mr S Astaire	0-3	S Whitworth	0-2	W Carson	0-1
S Dawson	0-3	T Quinn	0-2	W Ryan	0-1
W Newnes	0-3	F Norton	0-1		
B Raymond	0-2	J Carroll	0-1		

COURSE RECORD

	Total W-R	Non-Handicaps 2-y-o	3-y-o+	Handicaps 2-y-o	3-y-o+	Per cent	£1 Level Stake
Nottingham	3-11	2-2	1-5	0-2	0-2	27.3	+ 2.25
Lingfield (AW)	3-12	0-0	3-8	0-0	0-4	25.0	- 2.25
Chester	2-4	1-1	1-1	0-0	0-2	50.0	+ 4.80
Haydock	2-4	0-0	0-1	0-0	2-3	50.0	+ 16.00
Yarmouth	2-7	0-0	1-5	0-0	1-2	28.6	+ 1.50
Newbury	2-9	0-1	2-2	0-0	0-6	22.2	+ 1.12
Newmarket	2-19	0-2	1-4	0-2	1-11	10.5	- 8.75
Kempton	1-4	1-3	0-0	0-0	0-1	25.0	+ 9.00
Redcar	1-4	0-1	1-2	0-0	0-1	25.0	+ 0.33
Ripon	1-5	0-3	0-1	0-0	1-1	20.0	- 1.50
York	1-7	0-0	1-4	0-0	0-3	14.3	+ 6.00
Windsor	1-8	0-0	1-5	0-0	0-3	12.5	- 0.50
Brighton	1-9	1-1	0-5	0-0	0-3	11.1	- 4.50
Salisbury	1-10	0-3	1-4	0-0	0-3	10.0	- 5.50
Leicester	1-11	0-6	0-3	0-0	1-2	9.1	0.00
Epsom	1-12	1-1	0-6	0-0	0-5	8.3	- 10.20
Goodwood	1-19	0-2	1-6	0-1	0-10	5.3	- 12.50

Bath	0-14	Lingfield	0-7	Warwick	0-2
Ascot	0-8	Sandown	0-7	Beverley	0-1
Chepstow	0-8	Pontefract	0-4	Folkestone	0-1
Wolverhampton (AW)	0-8	Ayr	0-2		
Doncaster	0-7	Thirsk	0-2		

WINNING HORSES

	Age	Races Run	1st	2nd	3rd	Unpl	Win £
Broadway Flyer	3	6	3	1	1	1	54,642
Glide Path	5	10	3	1	0	6	34,848
Wind In Her Hair	3	5	2	1	0	2	23,222
Cragganmore	3	5	2	0	1	2	15,684
La Riveraine	3	10	2	1	1	6	9,010
Awesome Power	8	13	3	2	4	4	8,066
Regal Fanfare	2	5	2	1	1	1	7,678
Gilderdale	12	9	1	1	2	5	4,078
Emirates Express	2	4	1	0	2	1	3,873
Castoret	8	8	1	0	1	6	3,753
Made In Heaven	2	6	1	2	2	1	3,340
Divina Mia	2	2	1	0	0	1	3,340
Perdition	4	9	1	0	0	8	2,643
Equilibrium	2	3	1	0	0	2	2,642
Karon Beach	3	4	1	1	1	1	2,544
Plain Fact	9	8	1	0	1	6	2,243

WINNING OWNERS

	Races Won	Value £		Races Won	Value £
Mrs S Bosher	3	54,642	Abbott Racing Partners	1	4,078
The Jampot Partnership	3	34,848	Sheikh Ahmed Bin Saeed		
Mrs W Tulloch	2	23,222	Al Maktoum	1	3,873
A Stoddard	2	15,684	Lady D'Avigdor-Goldsmid	1	3,753
J H Richmond-Watson	2	9,010	D J Deer	1	3,340
Garrett J Freyne	3	8,066	G R Collister	1	2,643
Michael Wauchope	2	7,678	Christopher P J Brown	1	2,642
Christopher Wright	2	5,583	Tim Newsome	1	2,544

Favourites	9-28	32.1%	- 2.03	Total winning prize-money	£181,603
Longest winning sequence			2	Average SP of winner	4.8/1
Longest losing sequence			35	Return on stakes invested	-33.5%
1993 Form	26-254	10.2%	- 64.80	1991 Form 20-191 10.5%	- 24.75
1992 Form	25-225	11.1%	- 70.33	1990 Form 28-202 13.9%	+ 20.72

P J HOBBS (Minehead, Somerset)

	No. of Horses	Races Run	1st	2nd	3rd	Unpl	Per cent	£1 Level Stake
2-y-o	0	0	0	0	0	0	-	0.00
3-y-o	1	2	0	0	0	2	-	- 2.00
4-y-o+	5	8	2	0	0	6	25.0	+ 1.00
Totals	6	10	2	0	0	8	20.0	- 1.00

Jan	Feb	Mar	Apr	May	Jun	Jul	Aug	Sep	Oct/Nov
0-0	0-0	0-1	2-2	0-1	0-0	0-2	0-0	0-1	0-3

			£1 Level					£1 Level
Winning Jockeys		W-R	Stake				W-R	Stake
K Rutter		1-1	+ 5.00	J Reid			1-3	0.00

Winning Courses								
Kempton		1-1	+ 5.00	Nottingham			1-1	+ 2.00

			Races					Win
Winning Horses		Age	Run	1st	2nd	3rd	Unpl	£
Dreams End		6	1	1	0	0	0	3,655
Elaine Tully		6	4	1	0	0	3	3,524

Favourites	1-1	100.0%	+ 2.00	Total winning prize-money				£7,179

1993 Form	0-11			1991 Form	0-11
1992 Form	2-23	8.7%	- 7.00	1990 Form	0-8

R J HODGES (Somerton, Somerset)

	No. of Horses	Races Run	1st	2nd	3rd	Unpl	Per cent	£1 Level Stake
2-y-o	6	32	1	1	6	24	3.1	- 28.50
3-y-o	6	14	0	0	0	14	-	- 14.00
4-y-o+	32	201	17	18	22	144	8.5	- 77.70
Totals	44	247	18	19	28	182	7.3	-120.20

BY MONTH

2-y-o	W-R	Per cent	£1 Level Stake	3-y-o	W-R	Per cent	£1 Level Stake
January	0-0	-	0.00	January	0-0	-	0.00
February	0-0	-	0.00	February	0-0	-	0.00
March	0-0	-	0.00	March	0-0	-	0.00
April	0-0	-	0.00	April	0-0	-	0.00
May	0-5	-	- 5.00	May	0-4	-	- 4.00
June	1-7	14.3	- 3.50	June	0-6	-	- 6.00
July	0-6	-	- 6.00	July	0-3	-	- 3.00
August	0-8	-	- 8.00	August	0-1	-	- 1.00
September	0-3	-	- 3.00	September	0-0	-	0.00
Oct/Nov	0-3	-	- 3.00	Oct/Nov	0-0	-	0.00

Hodges R J

4-y-o+	W-R	Per cent	£1 Level Stake		Totals	W-R	Per cent	£1 Level Stake
January	0-2	-	- 2.00		January	0-2	-	- 2.00
February	0-3	-	- 3.00		February	0-3	-	- 3.00
March	0-2	-	- 2.00		March	0-2	-	- 2.00
April	3-22	13.6	+ 6.25		April	3-22	13.6	+ 6.25
May	3-26	11.5	0.00		May	3-35	8.6	- 9.00
June	3-44	6.8	- 28.70		June	4-57	7.0	- 38.20
July	3-38	7.9	- 19.25		July	3-47	6.4	- 28.25
August	2-28	7.1	- 15.50		August	2-37	5.4	- 24.50
September	1-20	5.0	- 16.00		September	1-23	4.3	- 19.00
Oct/Nov	2-16	12.5	+ 2.50		Oct/Nov	2-19	10.5	- 0.50

DISTANCE

2-y-o	W-R	Per cent	£1 Level Stake	3-y-o	W-R	Per cent	£1 Level Stake
5f-6f	1-26	3.8	- 22.50	5f-6f	0-4	-	- 4.00
7f-8f	0-6	-	- 6.00	7f-8f	0-7	-	- 7.00
9f-13f	0-0	-	0.00	9f-13f	0-3	-	- 3.00
14f+	0-0	-	0.00	14f+	0-0	-	0.00

4-y-o+	W-R	Per cent	£1 Level Stake	Totals	W-R	Per cent	£1 Level Stake
5f-6f	12-116	10.3	- 34.00	5f-6f	13-146	8.9	- 60.50
7f-8f	2-43	4.7	- 30.20	7f-8f	2-56	3.6	- 43.20
9f-13f	1-36	2.8	- 28.50	9f-13f	1-39	2.6	- 31.50
14f+	2-6	33.3	+ 15.00	14f+	2-6	33.3	+ 15.00

TYPE OF RACE

Non-Handicaps	W-R	Per cent	£1 Level Stake	Handicaps	W-R	Per cent	£1 Level Stake
2-y-o	0-9	-	- 9.00	2-y-o	0-4	-	- 4.00
3-y-o	0-10	-	- 10.00	3-y-o	0-2	-	- 2.00
4-y-o+	3-22	13.6	- 9.95	4-y-o+	11-142	7.7	- 60.25
Selling	3-24	12.5	- 2.00	Selling	1-13	7.7	- 2.00
Apprentice	0-2	-	- 2.00	Apprentice	0-10	-	- 10.00
Amat/Ladies	0-1	-	- 1.00	Amat/Ladies	0-8	-	- 8.00
Totals	6-68	8.8	- 33.95	Totals	12-179	6.7	- 86.25

COURSE GRADE	W-R	Per cent	£1 Level Stake	FIRST TIME OUT	W-R	Per cent	£1 Level Stake
Group 1	5-72	6.9	- 42.50				
Group 2	4-47	8.5	- 28.20	2-y-o	0-6	-	- 6.00
Group 3	7-87	8.0	- 15.75	3-y-o	0-6	-	- 6.00
Group 4	2-41	4.9	- 33.75	4-y-o+	2-31	6.5	- 6.00
				Totals	2-43	4.7	- 18.00

JOCKEYS RIDING

	W-R	Per cent	£1 Level Stake		W-R	Per cent	£1 Level Stake
S Drowne	10-97	10.3	- 19.75	Paul Eddery	1-12	8.3	- 10.20
R Cochrane	3-22	13.6	+ 1.00	J Quinn	1-13	7.7	- 9.25
L Dettori	2-8	25.0	+ 6.00	A Munro	1-15	6.7	- 8.00

Amanda Sanders	0-13	W Carson	0-3	C Teague	0-1
F Norton	0-7	J Williams	0-2	D Biggs	0-1
Pat Eddery	0-7	M Baird	0-2	D Holland	0-1
P McCabe	0-5	T Quinn	0-2	D Toole	0-1
R Perham	0-5	W R Swinburn	0-2	K Darley	0-1
J Reid	0-4	A Daly	0-1	Mr P Macewan	0-1
M Hills	0-4	A Dicks	0-1	Mr R Johnson	0-1
Miss S Mitchell	0-4	A McGlone	0-1	N Carlisle	0-1
A Clark	0-3	A Whelan	0-1	S Whitworth	0-1
D Wright	0-3	B Doyle	0-1		

COURSE RECORD

	Total W-R	Non-Handicaps 2-y-o	3-y-o+	Handicaps 2-y-o	3-y-o+	Per cent	£1 Level Stake
Bath	3-26	0-4	1-5	0-0	2-17	11.5	+ 7.50
Newbury	2-8	0-0	0-1	0-0	2-7	25.0	+ 8.00
Chepstow	2-15	0-3	0-3	0-1	2-8	13.3	+ 1.75
Lingfield	2-19	0-3	1-4	0-0	1-12	10.5	- 8.00
Newmarket	1-3	0-0	0-1	0-0	1-2	33.3	+ 2.50
Epsom	1-5	0-0	0-1	0-0	1-4	20.0	- 0.50
Haydock	1-5	1-1	0-0	0-0	0-4	20.0	- 1.50
Brighton	1-7	0-0	1-4	0-0	0-3	14.3	- 5.20
Warwick	1-12	0-1	0-2	0-1	1-8	8.3	- 8.00
Nottingham	1-15	0-2	0-1	0-0	1-12	6.7	- 5.00
Folkestone	1-16	0-2	1-3	0-0	0-11	6.3	- 12.75
Salisbury	1-21	0-1	0-2	0-0	1-18	4.8	- 15.00
Windsor	1-21	0-3	1-4	0-0	0-14	4.8	- 10.00

Goodwood	0-17	York	0-6	Newcastle	0-2
Ascot	0-10	Sandown	0-5	Yarmouth	0-2
Wolverhampton (AW)	0-8	Southwell (AW)	0-5	Pontefract	0-1
Leicester	0-7	Ayr	0-3		
Doncaster	0-6	Kempton	0-2		

WINNING HORSES

	Age	Races Run	1st	2nd	3rd	Unpl	Win £
Ashtina	9	14	3	1	2	8	19,837
Mister Jolson	5	14	4	0	3	7	19,224
Hard To Figure	8	9	1	2	1	5	15,270
Noeprob	4	8	2	0	0	6	5,060
How's Yer Father	8	15	1	2	0	12	4,080
Pineapple Prince	4	9	1	4	1	3	3,106
Sinclair Lad	6	9	1	1	1	6	3,080

Hodges R J

Castle Maid	7	7	1	0	2	4	2,668
Commanchero	7	3	1	0	0	2	2,583
Cedar Girl	2	9	1	1	1	6	2,563
Palacegate Gold	5	12	1	0	3	8	2,534
Unveiled	6	6	1	2	0	3	2,249

WINNING OWNERS

	Races Won	Value £		Races Won	Value £
J W Mursell	6	37,077	Pineapple Clothing Company Ltd	1	3,106
Ms S A Joyner	3	19,837	Miss R Dobson	1	3,080
R J Hodges	2	5,097	R T Sercombe	1	2,668
Mrs P A Bradshaw	2	5,060	Mrs K M Burge	1	2,249
Unity Farm Holiday Centre Ltd	1	4,080			

Favourites	3-22	13.6%	- 12.95	Total winning prize-money	£82,252
Longest winning sequence			1	Average SP of winner	6.0/1
Longest losing sequence			53	Return on stakes invested	-48.7%
1993 Form	20-321	6.2%	-121.75	1991 Form	27-287	9.4%	- 93.74
1992 Form	21-371	5.7%	-167.96	1990 Form	25-245	10.2%	- 76.57

K W HOGG (Isle of Man)

	No. of Horses	Races Run	1st	2nd	3rd	Unpl	Per cent	£1 Level Stake
2-y-o	6	23	1	0	0	22	4.3	- 8.00
3-y-o	4	14	0	0	0	14	–	- 14.00
4-y-o+	4	23	2	0	2	19	8.7	- 11.50
Totals	14	60	3	0	2	55	5.0	- 33.50

Jan	Feb	Mar	Apr	May	Jun	Jul	Aug	Sep	Oct/Nov
0-0	0-0	1-2	1-16	0-5	0-12	1-11	0-10	0-4	0-0

Winning Jockeys	W-R	£1 Level Stake		W-R	£1 Level Stake
D McKeown	2-17	+ 2.50	G Hind	1-2	+ 5.00

Winning Courses					
Catterick	2-6	+ 5.50	Redcar	1-4	+ 11.00

Winning Horses	Age	Races Run	1st	2nd	3rd	Unpl	Win £
Kinoko	6	10	2	0	1	7	7,166
Castletown Count	2	5	1	0	0	4	2,679

Favourites	0-1			Total winning prize-money		£9,845
1993 Form	4-69	5.8%	- 41.62	1992 Form	4-45	8.9%	+ 6.00

222

R HOLLINSHEAD (Upper Longdon, Staffs)

	No. of Horses	Races Run	1st	2nd	3rd	Unpl	Per cent	£1 Level Stake
2-y-o	17	86	1	4	10	71	1.2	- 75.00
3-y-o	30	226	13	17	18	178	5.8	-119.50
4-y-o+	23	249	16	27	29	177	6.4	-149.75
Totals	70	561	30	48	57	426	5.3	-344.25

BY MONTH

2-y-o	W-R	Per cent	£1 Level Stake	3-y-o	W-R	Per cent	£1 Level Stake
January	0-0	-	0.00	January	0-10	-	- 10.00
February	0-0	-	0.00	February	4-13	30.8	+ 3.25
March	0-3	-	- 3.00	March	0-18	-	- 18.00
April	0-6	-	- 6.00	April	1-32	3.1	- 17.00
May	1-12	8.3	- 1.00	May	1-18	5.6	- 10.00
June	0-7	-	- 7.00	June	0-24	-	- 24.00
July	0-8	-	- 8.00	July	2-27	7.4	- 11.50
August	0-11	-	- 11.00	August	2-27	7.4	- 21.25
September	0-17	-	- 17.00	September	1-29	3.4	- 8.00
Oct/Nov	0-22	-	- 22.00	Oct/Nov	2-28	7.1	- 3.00

4-y-o+	W-R	Per cent	£1 Level Stake	Totals	W-R	Per cent	£1 Level Stake
January	5-29	17.2	- 3.50	January	5-39	12.8	- 13.50
February	3-27	11.1	- 13.50	February	7-40	17.5	- 10.25
March	1-29	3.4	- 19.00	March	1-50	2.0	- 40.00
April	2-29	6.9	- 15.00	April	3-67	4.5	- 38.00
May	4-33	12.1	- 9.75	May	6-63	9.5	- 20.75
June	0-30	-	- 30.00	June	0-61	-	- 61.00
July	0-21	-	- 21.00	July	2-56	3.6	- 40.50
August	0-22	-	- 22.00	August	2-60	3.3	- 54.25
September	1-14	7.1	- 1.00	September	2-60	3.3	- 26.00
Oct/Nov	0-15	-	- 15.00	Oct/Nov	2-65	3.1	- 40.00

DISTANCE

2-y-o	W-R	Per cent	£1 Level Stake	3-y-o	W-R	Per cent	£1 Level Stake
5f-6f	1-64	1.6	- 53.00	5f-6f	3-81	3.7	- 47.50
7f-8f	0-21	-	- 21.00	7f-8f	6-72	8.3	- 35.25
9f-13f	0-1	-	- 1.00	9f-13f	4-64	6.3	- 27.75
14f+	0-0	-	0.00	14f+	0-9	-	- 9.00

4-y-o+	W-R	Per cent	£1 Level Stake	Totals	W-R	Per cent	£1 Level Stake
5f-6f	5-57	8.8	- 24.75	5f-6f	9-202	4.5	-125.25
7f-8f	1-53	1.9	- 47.00	7f-8f	7-146	4.8	-103.25
9f-13f	6-84	7.1	- 42.25	9f-13f	10-149	6.7	- 71.00
14f+	4-55	7.3	- 35.75	14f+	4-64	6.3	- 44.75

TYPE OF RACE

Non-Handicaps	W-R	Per cent	£1 Level Stake	Handicaps	W-R	Per cent	£1 Level Stake
2-y-o	1-61	1.6	- 50.00	2-y-o	0-15	-	- 15.00
3-y-o	9-101	8.9	- 28.25	3-y-o	2-106	1.9	- 78.00
4-y-o+	6-56	10.7	- 17.50	4-y-o+	10-162	6.2	-101.25
Selling	2-27	7.4	- 21.25	Selling	0-14	-	- 14.00
Apprentice	0-3	-	- 3.00	Apprentice	0-14	-	- 14.00
Amat/Ladies	0-0	-	0.00	Amat/Ladies	0-2	-	- 2.00
Totals	18-248	7.3	-120.00	Totals	12-313	3.8	-224.25

COURSE GRADE

	W-R	Per cent	£1 Level Stake
Group 1	3-102	2.9	- 88.75
Group 2	2-74	2.7	- 59.00
Group 3	8-122	6.6	- 29.75
Group 4	17-263	6.5	-166.75

FIRST TIME OUT

	W-R	Per cent	£1 Level Stake
2-y-o	1-16	6.3	- 5.00
3-y-o	0-28	-	- 28.00
4-y-o+	0-22	-	- 22.00
Totals	1-66	1.5	- 55.00

JOCKEYS RIDING

	W-R	Per cent	£1 Level Stake		W-R	Per cent	£1 Level Stake
L Dettori	9-61	14.8	- 11.00	W R Swinburn	1-3	33.3	- 0.75
S Perks	7-143	4.9	- 99.25	R Cochrane	1-7	14.3	- 2.00
W Ryan	3-45	6.7	- 17.25	J Weaver	1-7	14.3	0.00
Paul Eddery	2-15	13.3	+ 2.00	M Humphries	1-8	12.5	- 1.00
K Darley	2-35	5.7	- 23.00	T Ives	1-23	4.3	- 2.00
A Garth	2-109	1.8	- 85.00				

D Denby	0-21	M Wigham	0-3	T Quinn	0-2
A Eddery	0-14	Miss J Southall	0-3	A McGlone	0-1
A Munro	0-8	W Carson	0-3	C Rutter	0-1
N Carlisle	0-8	D Holland	0-2	G Carter	0-1
L Aspell	0-7	J Carroll	0-2	J Williams	0-1
A Culhane	0-6	J Fanning	0-2	L Piggott	0-1
S Wynne	0-5	J Lowe	0-2	M Hills	0-1
J Fortune	0-3	Pat Eddery	0-2	M Tebbutt	0-1
J Quinn	0-3	R Price	0-2		

COURSE RECORD

	Total W-R	Non-Handicaps 2-y-o	Non-Handicaps 3-y-o+	Handicaps 2-y-o	Handicaps 3-y-o+	Per cent	£1 Level Stake
Wolverhampton (AW)	10-125	0-6	3-49	0-2	7-68	8.0	- 75.00
Lingfield (AW)	4-31	0-0	3-15	0-0	1-16	12.9	- 6.50
Beverley	2-21	0-4	1-7	0-1	1-9	9.5	+ 7.00
Leicester	2-29	0-3	2-13	0-1	0-12	6.9	- 12.00
Southwell (AW)	2-57	1-2	1-19	0-2	0-34	3.5	- 43.25

Windsor	1-1	0-0	1-1	0-0	0-0	100.0	+ 1.75
Chepstow	1-5	0-1	0-0	0-1	1-3	20.0	+ 16.00
Hamilton	1-5	0-1	1-2	0-0	0-2	20.0	+ 10.00
York	1-9	0-2	0-1	0-0	1-6	11.1	- 1.00
Carlisle	1-16	0-3	1-7	0-0	0-6	6.3	- 8.00
Thirsk	1-21	0-1	1-10	0-0	0-10	4.8	- 14.00
Chester	1-23	0-6	0-4	0-0	1-13	4.3	- 15.00
Doncaster	1-27	0-5	1-9	0-1	0-12	3.7	- 24.75
Haydock	1-32	0-9	1-4	0-1	0-18	3.1	- 29.00
Pontefract	1-34	0-4	1-9	0-2	0-19	2.9	- 25.50

Nottingham	0-23	Newmarket	0-9	Edinburgh	0-2
Ripon	0-21	Redcar	0-9	Goodwood	0-2
Newcastle	0-17	Ayr	0-5	Ascot	0-1
Catterick	0-15	Bath	0-3	Yarmouth	0-1
Warwick	0-14	Folkestone	0-3		

WINNING HORSES

	Age	Races Run	1st	2nd	3rd	Unpl	Win £
Mad Militant	5	15	2	3	0	10	13,516
Cuango	3	14	3	3	1	7	10,399
Arc Bright	4	22	3	5	4	10	9,380
Alpine Johnny	3	18	3	4	3	8	8,354
Rousitto	6	17	2	2	4	9	6,483
Respectable Jones	8	17	2	0	2	13	6,005
In The Money	5	12	1	1	2	8	5,481
Simmie's Special	6	16	2	5	4	5	5,220
King Rambo	3	4	1	0	0	3	3,702
Heathyards Lady	3	12	1	0	1	10	3,621
Dinot	3	11	1	1	2	7	3,580
The Sharp Bidder	4	15	1	0	1	13	3,420
Wheeler's Wonder	5	13	1	1	0	11	3,210
Blue Domain	3	8	1	1	0	6	3,085
Winn's Pride	3	12	1	1	1	9	3,003
Eager Deva	7	3	1	0	0	2	2,986
McGillycuddy Reeks	3	10	1	1	2	6	2,783
Chastize	3	15	1	2	1	11	2,668
C-Yer-Simmie	2	5	1	0	0	4	2,249
Abeloni	5	11	1	0	2	8	2,243

WINNING OWNERS

	Races Won	Value £		Races Won	Value £
Mrs B Facchino	6	27,494	Mrs Robert Heathcote	1	3,420
J E Bigg	7	23,214	Palacegate Corporation Ltd	1	3,210
J Pattison	3	9,151	T N Bailey	1	3,085
D Coppenhall	3	7,469	Mrs W L Bailey	1	3,003
Mrs B Ramsden	2	6,005	Mrs E G Faulkner	1	2,986
J D Graham	1	3,702	Noel Sweeney	1	2,783
L A Morgan	1	3,621	J Hardman	1	2,243

Hollinshead R

Favourites	7-37	18.9%	- 15.75	Total winning prize-money		£101,385

Longest winning sequence		2	Average SP of winner	6.4/1
Longest losing sequence		86	Return on stakes invested	-60.5%

1993 Form	44-623	7.1%	-346.60	1991 Form	31-549	5.6%	-264.91
1992 Form	60-611	9.8%	-118.14	1990 Form	41-549	7.5%	-221.15

G HOLMES (Pickering, North Yorks)

	No. of Horses	Races Run	1st	2nd	3rd	Unpl	Per cent	£1 Level Stake
2-y-o	1	1	0	0	0	1	-	- 1.00
3-y-o	1	9	2	1	2	4	22.2	- 0.50
4-y-o+	3	27	2	3	1	21	7.4	- 9.00
Totals	5	37	4	4	3	26	10.8	- 10.50

Jan	Feb	Mar	Apr	May	Jun	Jul	Aug	Sep	Oct/Nov
0-1	0-0	0-1	0-3	1-7	1-7	2-9	0-2	0-6	0-1

Winning Jockeys	W-R	£1 Level Stake			W-R	£1 Level Stake
K Fallon	2-15	- 5.50	W Newnes		1-3	+ 9.00
J Stack	1-1	+ 4.00				

Winning Courses						
Leicester	1-1	+ 2.50	Pontefract		1-2	+ 3.00
Lingfield	1-1	+ 11.00	Carlisle		1-3	+ 3.00

Winning Horses	Age	Races Run	1st	2nd	3rd	Unpl	Win £
Gymcrak Premiere	6	10	1	1	0	8	9,773
Gymcrak Flyer	3	9	2	1	2	4	6,407
Gymcrak Tycoon	5	12	1	0	1	10	2,893

Favourites	0-2	Total winning prize-money	£19,073

1993 Form	0-13

L J HOLT (Basingstoke, Hants)

	No. of Horses	Races Run	1st	2nd	3rd	Unpl	Per cent	£1 Level Stake
2-y-o	5	15	0	0	1	14	-	- 15.00
3-y-o	8	45	2	1	0	42	4.4	- 19.00
4-y-o+	13	93	12	12	11	58	12.9	- 33.42
Totals	26	153	14	13	12	114	9.2	- 67.42

BY MONTH

2-y-o	W-R	Per cent	£1 Level Stake	3-y-o	W-R	Per cent	£1 Level Stake
January	0-0	-	0.00	January	0-0	-	0.00
February	0-0	-	0.00	February	0-0	-	0.00
March	0-0	-	0.00	March	0-1	-	- 1.00
April	0-0	-	0.00	April	0-2	-	- 2.00
May	0-0	-	0.00	May	0-9	-	- 9.00
June	0-0	-	0.00	June	0-9	-	- 9.00
July	0-2	-	- 2.00	July	2-10	20.0	+ 16.00
August	0-4	-	- 4.00	August	0-7	-	- 7.00
September	0-6	-	- 6.00	September	0-6	-	- 6.00
Oct/Nov	0-3	-	- 3.00	Oct/Nov	0-1	-	- 1.00

4-y-o+	W-R	Per cent	£1 Level Stake	Totals	W-R	Per cent	£1 Level Stake
January	0-2	-	- 2.00	January	0-2	-	- 2.00
February	0-0	-	0.00	February	0-0	-	0.00
March	0-1	-	- 1.00	March	0-2	-	- 2.00
April	0-11	-	- 11.00	April	0-13	-	- 13.00
May	1-16	6.3	- 11.00	May	1-25	4.0	- 20.00
June	6-24	25.0	+ 11.08	June	6-33	18.2	+ 2.08
July	4-15	26.7	+ 1.50	July	6-27	22.2	+ 15.50
August	0-13	-	- 13.00	August	0-24	-	- 24.00
September	1-7	14.3	- 4.00	September	1-19	5.3	- 16.00
Oct/Nov	0-4	-	- 4.00	Oct/Nov	0-8	-	- 8.00

DISTANCE

2-y-o	W-R	Per cent	£1 Level Stake	3-y-o	W-R	Per cent	£1 Level Stake
5f-6f	0-15	-	- 15.00	5f-6f	2-26	7.7	0.00
7f-8f	0-0	-	0.00	7f-8f	0-9	-	- 9.00
9f-13f	0-0	-	0.00	9f-13f	0-10	-	- 10.00
14f+	0-0	-	0.00	14f+	0-0	-	0.00

4-y-o+	W-R	Per cent	£1 Level Stake	Totals	W-R	Per cent	£1 Level Stake
5f-6f	11-60	18.3	- 4.75	5f-6f	13-101	12.9	- 19.75
7f-8f	1-23	4.3	- 18.67	7f-8f	1-32	3.1	- 27.67
9f-13f	0-6	-	- 6.00	9f-13f	0-16	-	- 16.00
14f+	0-4	-	- 4.00	14f+	0-4	-	- 4.00

TYPE OF RACE

Non-Handicaps	W-R	Per cent	£1 Level Stake	Handicaps	W-R	Per cent	£1 Level Stake
2-y-o	0-13	-	- 13.00	2-y-o	0-2	-	- 2.00
3-y-o	0-19	-	- 19.00	3-y-o	1-19	5.3	- 6.00
4-y-o+	1-10	10.0	- 5.00	4-y-o+	10-71	14.1	- 20.75
Selling	0-3	-	- 3.00	Selling	0-7	-	- 7.00
Apprentice	0-0	-	0.00	Apprentice	2-9	22.2	+ 8.33
Amat/Ladies	0-0	-	0.00	Amat/Ladies	0-0	-	0.00
Totals	1-45	2.2	- 40.00	Totals	13-108	12.0	- 27.42

COURSE GRADE

	W-R	Per cent	£1 Level Stake
Group 1	7-74	9.5	- 27.50
Group 2	3-34	8.8	- 22.67
Group 3	4-24	16.7	+ 3.75
Group 4	0-21	-	- 21.00

FIRST TIME OUT

	W-R	Per cent	£1 Level Stake
2-y-o	0-4	-	- 4.00
3-y-o	0-7	-	- 7.00
4-y-o+	0-12	-	- 12.00
Totals	0-23	-	- 23.00

JOCKEYS RIDING

	W-R	Per cent	£1 Level Stake		W-R	Per cent	£1 Level Stake
A McGlone	8-61	13.1	- 9.25	Iona Wands	2-19	10.5	- 1.67
A Munro	2-4	50.0	+ 4.50	J Reid	2-35	5.7	- 27.00

N Adams	0-14	W Newnes	0-2	W Hood	0-1		
M Perrett	0-9	Aimee Cook	0-1				
C Avery	0-6	B Doyle	0-1				

COURSE RECORD

	Total W-R	Non-Handicaps 2-y-o	3-y-o+	Handicaps 2-y-o	3-y-o+	Per cent	£1 Level Stake
Brighton	2-12	0-0	0-0	0-0	2-12	16.7	- 3.67
Windsor	2-12	0-2	1-3	0-0	1-7	16.7	+ 6.00
Newcastle	1-2	0-0	0-0	0-0	1-2	50.0	+ 10.00
Chepstow	1-3	0-0	0-0	0-0	1-3	33.3	+ 0.75
Nottingham	1-3	0-0	0-0	0-0	1-3	33.3	+ 3.00
Ascot	1-5	0-0	0-0	0-1	1-4	20.0	- 1.25
Newmarket	1-5	0-1	0-0	0-1	1-3	20.0	- 0.50
Salisbury	1-6	0-0	0-3	0-0	1-3	16.7	- 3.00
Newbury	1-7	0-2	0-0	0-0	1-5	14.3	- 2.50
Sandown	1-10	0-4	0-0	0-0	1-6	10.0	+ 3.00
Epsom	1-11	0-0	0-1	0-0	1-10	9.1	- 6.00
Goodwood	1-16	0-2	0-4	0-0	1-10	6.3	- 12.25

Lingfield	0-16	Bath	0-4	Wolverhampton (AW)	0-2		
Kempton	0-11	Haydock	0-3	Ayr	0-1		
Folkestone	0-9	Lingfield (AW)	0-3	Leicester	0-1		
Warwick	0-7	York	0-3	Yarmouth	0-1		

WINNING HORSES

	Age	Races Run	1st	2nd	3rd	Unpl	Win £
Sea-Deer	5	8	4	1	1	2	19,604
Duplicity	6	9	1	2	0	6	16,310
Loch Patrick	4	4	2	0	0	2	13,844
Walnut Burl	4	11	2	3	1	5	6,086
Alltruthenight	5	9	1	2	3	3	5,940

Paddy Chalk	8	9	1	1	1	6	5,053
Sweet Magic	3	5	1	1	0	3	4,299
Patsy Grimes	4	4	1	1	0	2	3,774
Paddy's Rice	3	9	1	0	0	8	2,673

WINNING OWNERS

	Races Won	Value £		Races Won	Value £
P Cook	4	19,604	Mrs R G Wellman	2	7,726
B J Keay	1	16,310	Mrs John Crawford	1	4,299
Miss E M L Coller	2	13,844	J K Grimes	1	3,774
G Steinberg	3	12,026			

Favourites	9-21	42.9%	+ 15.58	Total winning prize-money		£77,582
Longest winning sequence			2	Average SP of winner		5.1/1
Longest losing sequence			35	Return on stakes invested		-44.1%
1993 Form	9-159	5.7%	- 74.17	1991 Form	4-160	2.5%	-131.12
1992 Form	11-146	7.5%	- 59.75	1990 Form	6-178	3.4%	-102.75

C A HORGAN (Billingbear, Berks)

	No. of Horses	Races Run	1st	2nd	3rd	Unpl	Per cent	£1 Level Stake
2-y-o	5	12	0	0	1	11	-	- 12.00
3-y-o	5	18	0	0	2	16	-	- 18.00
4-y-o+	10	50	7	5	8	30	14.0	+ 15.25
Totals	20	80	7	5	11	57	8.8	- 14.75

Jan	Feb	Mar	Apr	May	Jun	Jul	Aug	Sep	Oct/Nov
0-0	0-0	0-0	0-5	0-9	2-14	2-17	3-12	0-15	0-8

Winning Jockeys	W-R	£1 Level Stake		W-R	£1 Level Stake
D Holland	2-19	- 3.00	Paul Eddery	1-4	- 0.25
M Perrett	1-1	+ 14.00	A Clark	1-6	+ 7.00
A Munro	1-2	+ 9.00	W Woods	1-8	- 1.50

Winning Courses					
Doncaster	2-3	+ 22.00	Windsor	1-7	+ 4.00
Newmarket	2-6	+ 4.50	Salisbury	1-8	+ 7.00
Folkestone	1-3	+ 0.75			

Winning Horses	Age	Races Run	1st	2nd	3rd	Unpl	Win £
Belfry Green	4	10	3	2	1	4	34,428
Desert Time	4	5	2	0	1	2	7,216
Tiffany's Case	5	2	1	0	1	0	3,106
Pistol	4	13	1	0	4	8	3,054

Favourites	2-6	33.3%	+ 4.50	Total winning prize-money			£47,804

1993 Form	5-87	5.7%	- 45.87	1991 Form	4-105	3.8%	- 57.62
1992 Form	5-85	5.9%	- 17.00	1990 Form	3-69	4.3%	- 26.50

R F JOHNSON HOUGHTON (Didcot, Oxon)

	No. of Horses	Races Run	1st	2nd	3rd	Unpl	Per cent	£1 Level Stake
2-y-o	9	40	4	5	6	25	10.0	- 6.50
3-y-o	8	53	5	3	8	37	9.4	- 13.50
4-y-o+	1	15	2	1	0	12	13.3	+ 6.00
Totals	18	108	11	9	14	74	10.2	- 14.00

BY MONTH

2-y-o	W-R	Per cent	£1 Level Stake	3-y-o	W-R	Per cent	£1 Level Stake
January	0-0	-	0.00	January	0-0	-	0.00
February	0-0	-	0.00	February	0-1	-	- 1.00
March	0-0	-	0.00	March	0-1	-	- 1.00
April	0-0	-	0.00	April	1-1	100.0	+ 3.00
May	1-7	14.3	- 2.00	May	0-5	-	- 5.00
June	1-7	14.3	+ 4.00	June	2-10	20.0	+ 13.00
July	0-6	-	- 6.00	July	1-8	12.5	- 3.50
August	0-9	-	- 9.00	August	1-10	10.0	- 2.00
September	1-6	16.7	+ 0.50	September	0-7	-	- 7.00
Oct/Nov	1-5	20.0	+ 6.00	Oct/Nov	0-10	-	- 10.00

4-y-o+	W-R	Per cent	£1 Level Stake	Totals	W-R	Per cent	£1 Level Stake
January	0-0	-	0.00	January	0-0	-	0.00
February	0-2	-	- 2.00	February	0-3	-	- 3.00
March	0-1	-	- 1.00	March	0-2	-	- 2.00
April	0-0	-	0.00	April	1-1	100.0	+ 3.00
May	0-2	-	- 2.00	May	1-14	7.1	- 9.00
June	1-3	33.3	+ 14.00	June	4-20	20.0	+ 31.00
July	0-2	-	- 2.00	July	1-16	6.3	- 11.50
August	1-4	25.0	0.00	August	2-23	8.7	- 11.00
September	0-0	-	0.00	September	1-13	7.7	- 6.50
Oct/Nov	0-1	-	- 1.00	Oct/Nov	1-16	6.3	- 5.00

DISTANCE

2-y-o	W-R	Per cent	£1 Level Stake	3-y-o	W-R	Per cent	£1 Level Stake
5f-6f	2-26	7.7	- 10.00	5f-6f	1-11	9.1	0.00
7f-8f	2-13	15.4	+ 4.50	7f-8f	1-13	7.7	- 9.00
9f-13f	0-1	-	- 1.00	9f-13f	2-19	10.5	+ 1.00
14f+	0-0	-	0.00	14f+	1-10	10.0	- 5.50

4-y-o+	W-R	Per cent	£1 Level Stake	Totals	W-R	Per cent	£1 Level Stake
5f-6f	0-0	-	0.00	5f-6f	3-37	8.1	- 10.00
7f-8f	0-2	-	- 2.00	7f-8f	3-28	10.7	- 6.50
9f-13f	2-13	15.4	+ 8.00	9f-13f	4-33	12.1	+ 8.00
14f+	0-0	-	0.00	14f+	1-10	10.0	- 5.50

TYPE OF RACE

Non-Handicaps	W-R	Per cent	£1 Level Stake	Handicaps	W-R	Per cent	£1 Level Stake
2-y-o	3-29	10.3	- 2.00	2-y-o	0-4	-	- 4.00
3-y-o	1-16	6.3	- 12.00	3-y-o	4-37	10.8	- 1.50
4-y-o+	0-1	-	- 1.00	4-y-o+	0-5	-	- 5.00
Selling	0-5	-	- 5.00	Selling	1-2	50.0	+ 4.50
Apprentice	0-0	-	0.00	Apprentice	0-0	-	0.00
Amat/Ladies	0-1	-	- 1.00	Amat/Ladies	2-8	25.0	+ 13.00
Totals	4-52	7.7	- 21.00	Totals	7-56	12.5	+ 7.00

COURSE GRADE

	W-R	Per cent	£1 Level Stake
Group 1	4-46	8.7	- 5.00
Group 2	3-24	12.5	- 4.00
Group 3	2-23	8.7	- 5.50
Group 4	2-15	13.3	+ 0.50

FIRST TIME OUT

	W-R	Per cent	£1 Level Stake
2-y-o	1-8	12.5	+ 3.00
3-y-o	1-8	12.5	- 4.00
4-y-o+	0-1	-	- 1.00
Totals	2-17	11.8	- 2.00

JOCKEYS RIDING

	W-R	Per cent	£1 Level Stake		W-R	Per cent	£1 Level Stake
K Darley	2-4	50.0	+ 13.50	R Hills	1-3	33.3	+ 8.00
T Sprake	2-6	33.3	+ 9.00	Miss E Houghton	1-5	20.0	+ 12.00
R Cochrane	2-14	14.3	- 4.50	J Reid	1-9	11.1	- 1.00
Mr G J Houghton	1-3	33.3	+ 1.00	D Holland	1-18	5.6	- 6.00

A Tucker	0-6	M Hills	0-2	Mr F Grasso-Caprioli	0-1
J Carroll	0-4	N Varley	0-2	P Robinson	0-1
A Clark	0-3	W Carson	0-2	Pat Eddery	0-1
A McGlone	0-3	Alex Greaves	0-1	Paul Eddery	0-1
J Lowe	0-3	D Harrison	0-1	T Williams	0-1
J Quinn	0-3	G Duffield	0-1	W R Swinburn	0-1
L Piggott	0-3	J Weaver	0-1	W Ryan	0-1
J Williams	0-2	L Newton	0-1	W Woods	0-1

COURSE RECORD

	Total W-R	Non-Handicaps 2-y-o	3-y-o+	Handicaps 2-y-o	3-y-o+	Per cent	£1 Level Stake
Haydock	2-4	1-2	0-1	0-0	1-1	50.0	+ 24.00
Salisbury	2-7	0-3	1-2	0-0	1-2	28.6	+ 9.00
Beverley	1-1	0-0	0-0	1-1	0-0	100.0	+ 5.50
Hamilton	1-1	0-0	0-0	0-0	1-1	100.0	+ 10.00
Redcar	1-3	0-1	0-0	0-0	1-2	33.3	+ 1.00
Catterick	1-4	1-1	0-1	0-1	0-1	25.0	+ 7.00
Folkestone	1-4	0-0	0-0	0-0	1-4	25.0	+ 0.50
Goodwood	1-5	1-3	0-1	0-0	0-1	20.0	0.00
Newbury	1-7	0-3	0-1	0-0	1-3	14.3	+ 1.00

Chester	0-8	Ascot	0-3	Epsom	0-1
Sandown	0-8	Chepstow	0-3	Lingfield	0-1
Newmarket	0-7	Nottingham	0-3	Lingfield (AW)	0-1
Doncaster	0-5	Wolverhampton (AW)	0-3	Newcastle	0-1
Pontefract	0-5	York	0-3	Ripon	0-1
Brighton	0-4	Bath	0-2	Southwell (AW)	0-1
Leicester	0-4	Kempton	0-2		
Windsor	0-4	Warwick	0-2		

WINNING HORSES

	Age	Races Run	1st	2nd	3rd	Unpl	Win £
William Tell	3	6	2	0	0	4	12,955
Gone To Pot	3	7	1	0	1	5	7,393
Credit Squeeze	4	15	2	1	0	12	5,235
Sonic Boy	2	8	1	4	0	3	4,227
Salanka	3	12	1	1	2	8	3,518
Great Bear	2	5	1	0	0	4	3,141
Paradise Waters	2	3	1	0	0	2	3,119
Limosa	3	9	1	1	2	5	3,106
Kings Vision	2	6	1	1	1	3	2,896

WINNING OWNERS

	Races Won	Value £		Races Won	Value £
Lady Rothschild	3	16,095	Mrs Leonard Simpson	1	3,518
Lord Leverhulme	2	10,289	R Crutchley	1	3,119
R C Naylor	2	5,235	Mrs P Robeson	1	3,106
Anthony Pye-Jeary	1	4,227			

Favourites	1-15	6.7%	- 11.00	Total winning prize-money			£45,587

Longest winning sequence		2	Average SP of winner	7.5/1
Longest losing sequence		17	Return on stakes invested	-13.0%

1993 Form	7-127	5.5%	- 68.18	1991 Form	13-171	7.6%	- 57.07
1992 Form	10-132	7.6%	- 67.57	1990 Form	25-191	13.1%	- 31.02

P HOWLING (Guildford, Surrey)

	No. of Horses	Races Run	1st	2nd	3rd	Unpl	Per cent	£1 Level Stake
2-y-o	8	23	0	0	0	23	-	- 23.00
3-y-o	7	39	2	2	4	31	5.1	- 9.00
4-y-o+	18	117	2	6	6	103	1.7	- 91.00
Totals	33	179	4	8	10	157	2.2	-123.00

Jan	Feb	Mar	Apr	May	Jun	Jul	Aug	Sep	Oct/Nov
1-22	0-11	1-13	0-12	0-22	0-35	0-19	1-17	1-18	0-10

Winning Jockeys	W-R	£1 Level Stake		W-R	£1 Level Stake
Paul Eddery	3-27	+ 24.00	N Carlisle	1-18	- 13.00

Winning Courses					
Haydock	1-1	+ 12.00	Yarmouth	1-9	- 4.00
Doncaster	1-4	+ 13.00	Lingfield (AW)	1-33	- 12.00

Winning Horses	Age	Races Run	1st	2nd	3rd	Unpl	Win £
Name The Tune	3	18	2	2	4	10	9,465
Judgement Call	7	10	1	3	0	6	2,898
Tee-Emm	4	17	1	1	4	11	2,512

Favourites	0-2			Total winning prize-money			£14,875

1993 Form	10-208	4.8%	-119.92	1991 Form	6-185	3.2%	-110.50
1992 Form	3-180	1.7%	-119.37	1990 Form	6-185	3.2%	-102.50

LORD HUNTINGDON (West Ilsley, Berks)

	No. of Horses	Races Run	1st	2nd	3rd	Unpl	Per cent	£1 Level Stake
2-y-o	19	50	10	5	12	23	20.0	+ 3.62
3-y-o	36	189	35	21	30	103	18.5	- 22.56
4-y-o+	17	83	10	16	10	47	12.0	- 27.75
Totals	72	322	55	42	52	173	17.1	- 46.69

BY MONTH

2-y-o	W–R	Per cent	£1 Level Stake	3-y-o	W–R	Per cent	£1 Level Stake
January	0-0	-	0.00	January	6-15	40.0	+ 10.21
February	0-0	-	0.00	February	5-14	35.7	+ 0.40
March	0-0	-	0.00	March	4-12	33.3	+ 1.94
April	0-0	-	0.00	April	5-11	45.5	+ 11.88
May	0-0	-	0.00	May	2-18	11.1	- 13.46
June	0-3	-	- 3.00	June	2-21	9.5	- 4.00
July	3-11	27.3	+ 0.50	July	4-29	13.8	- 0.50
August	4-13	30.8	+ 4.62	August	2-25	8.0	- 18.83
September	1-11	9.1	- 7.50	September	4-22	18.2	+ 5.80
Oct/Nov	2-12	16.7	+ 9.00	Oct/Nov	1-22	4.5	- 16.00

4-y-o+	W–R	Per cent	£1 Level Stake	Totals	W–R	Per cent	£1 Level Stake
January	0-4	-	- 4.00	January	6-19	31.6	+ 6.21
February	0-5	-	- 5.00	February	5-19	26.3	- 4.60
March	0-5	-	- 5.00	March	4-17	23.5	- 3.06
April	1-7	14.3	+ 2.00	April	6-18	33.3	+ 13.88
May	1-9	11.1	- 3.00	May	3-27	11.1	- 16.46
June	0-6	-	- 6.00	June	2-30	6.7	- 13.00
July	1-9	11.1	- 3.00	July	8-49	16.3	- 3.00
August	2-11	18.2	- 3.00	August	8-49	16.3	- 17.21
September	2-15	13.3	- 5.00	September	7-48	14.6	- 6.70
Oct/Nov	3-12	25.0	+ 4.25	Oct/Nov	6-46	13.0	- 2.75

DISTANCE

2-y-o	W–R	Per cent	£1 Level Stake	3-y-o	W–R	Per cent	£1 Level Stake
5f-6f	5-26	19.2	- 3.50	5f-6f	6-29	20.7	+ 7.50
7f-8f	5-24	20.8	+ 7.12	7f-8f	22-99	22.2	+ 10.04
9f-13f	0-0	-	0.00	9f-13f	7-57	12.3	- 36.10
14f+	0-0	-	0.00	14f+	0-4	-	- 4.00

4-y-o+	W–R	Per cent	£1 Level Stake	Totals	W–R	Per cent	£1 Level Stake
5f-6f	2-14	14.3	- 6.00	5f-6f	13-69	18.8	- 2.00
7f-8f	3-37	8.1	- 13.50	7f-8f	30-160	18.8	+ 3.66
9f-13f	5-25	20.0	- 1.25	9f-13f	12-82	14.6	- 37.35
14f+	0-7	-	- 7.00	14f+	0-11	-	- 11.00

TYPE OF RACE

Non-Handicaps	W–R	Per cent	£1 Level Stake	Handicaps	W–R	Per cent	£1 Level Stake
2-y-o	9-43	20.9	+ 8.37	2-y-o	0-4	-	- 4.00
3-y-o	16-77	20.8	- 1.39	3-y-o	14-98	14.3	- 31.42
4-y-o+	5-17	29.4	+ 7.00	4-y-o+	3-59	5.1	- 39.75
Selling	6-11	54.5	+ 15.50	Selling	1-1	100.0	+ 5.00
Apprentice	0-3	-	- 3.00	Apprentice	0-3	-	- 3.00
Amat/Ladies	0-1	-	- 1.00	Amat/Ladies	1-5	20.0	+ 1.00
Totals	36-152	23.7	+ 25.48	Totals	19-170	11.2	- 72.17

COURSE GRADE

	W-R	Per cent	£1 Level Stake
Group 1	10-112	8.9	- 58.71
Group 2	10-50	20.0	+ 24.00
Group 3	9-52	17.3	- 4.00
Group 4	26-108	24.1	- 7.98

FIRST TIME OUT

	W-R	Per cent	£1 Level Stake
2-y-o	2-19	10.5	- 9.75
3-y-o	11-36	30.6	+ 23.26
4-y-o+	0-17	-	- 17.00
Totals	13-72	18.1	- 3.49

JOCKEYS RIDING

	W-R	Per cent	£1 Level Stake		W-R	Per cent	£1 Level Stake
D Harrison	21-141	14.9	- 22.46	Mr L A Urbano	1-2	50.0	+ 4.00
L Dettori	16-54	29.6	- 4.58	B Thomson	1-3	33.3	+ 8.00
M Roberts	4-10	40.0	+ 15.00	D Holland	1-3	33.3	+ 1.00
M Hills	2-6	33.3	+ 2.80	B Rouse	1-3	33.3	+ 3.00
A Munro	2-13	15.4	- 4.37	J Williams	1-4	25.0	+ 7.00
W R Swinburn	2-15	13.3	- 6.75	J Reid	1-5	20.0	- 2.83
K Darley	1-2	50.0	+ 11.00	J Weaver	1-7	14.3	- 3.50

L Piggott	0-8	Pat Eddery	0-2	Mr P P-Gordon	0-1
D McKeown	0-7	A Clark	0-1	Mrs J Crossley	0-1
D Wright	0-7	B Doyle	0-1	N Varley	0-1
J Wilkinson	0-7	B Raymond	0-1	R Hills	0-1
W Woods	0-4	C Asmussen	0-1	T Quinn	0-1
Aimee Cook	0-2	C Rutter	0-1	W Ryan	0-1
Dale Gibson	0-2	G Hind	0-1		
Mrs M Cowdrey	0-2	J Carroll	0-1		

COURSE RECORD

	Total W-R	Non-Handicaps 2-y-o	3-y-o+	Handicaps 2-y-o	3-y-o+	Per cent	£1 Level Stake
Wolverhampton (AW)	12-42	1-4	7-20	0-0	4-18	28.6	+ 2.99
Southwell (AW)	7-23	0-1	5-9	0-0	2-13	30.4	+ 2.73
Lingfield (AW)	7-28	0-0	5-13	0-0	2-15	25.0	+ 1.30
Salisbury	4-16	2-7	0-4	0-0	2-5	25.0	+ 18.00
Lingfield	4-18	2-6	0-9	0-0	2-3	22.2	+ 13.00
Epsom	3-5	1-1	0-0	0-0	2-4	60.0	+ 4.79
Windsor	3-14	1-3	1-7	0-0	1-4	21.4	+ 4.00
Bath	2-6	0-0	1-1	0-0	1-5	33.3	+ 2.00
Sandown	2-11	1-2	1-5	0-0	0-4	18.2	+ 1.50
Beverley	1-1	0-0	0-0	0-0	1-1	100.0	+ 4.50
Newcastle	1-2	0-0	0-0	0-0	1-2	50.0	+ 1.75
York	1-4	0-0	1-1	0-0	0-3	25.0	0.00
Ripon	1-5	1-1	0-1	0-0	0-3	20.0	+ 1.00
Haydock	1-6	0-0	1-3	0-0	0-3	16.7	+ 7.00
Pontefract	1-6	0-0	1-3	0-0	0-3	16.7	- 3.00
Brighton	1-7	0-1	1-2	0-0	0-4	14.3	- 4.00
Nottingham	1-7	0-1	1-2	0-1	0-3	14.3	- 0.50
Ascot	1-13	0-1	0-0	0-0	1-12	7.7	- 6.00
Leicester	1-13	0-1	1-10	0-0	0-2	7.7	- 6.00
Goodwood	1-15	1-3	0-2	0-0	0-10	6.7	- 11.75

Newbury	0-20	Chepstow	0-5	Carlisle	0-1
Newmarket	0-14	Folkestone	0-5	Redcar	0-1
Doncaster	0-11	Catterick	0-2	Thirsk	0-1
Kempton	0-10	Chester	0-2		
Warwick	0-7	Ayr	0-1		

WINNING HORSES

	Age	Races Run	1st	2nd	3rd	Unpl	Win £
Whitechapel	6	5	1	0	1	3	48,299
Penny Drops	5	4	1	0	0	3	35,406
Magic Junction	3	7	4	1	1	1	15,160
Diskette	4	8	3	2	0	3	13,089
Country Lover	3	5	2	2	0	1	9,807
Discord	8	4	1	0	1	2	8,433
Saw Mill	3	9	2	2	3	2	8,233
Off The Air	3	6	3	0	0	3	7,442
Prince Of India	2	2	1	0	0	1	6,873
Waldo	3	8	2	0	2	4	6,766
Arkady	3	7	2	2	0	3	6,415
Present Situation	3	10	2	1	4	3	6,309
Lady Williams	3	9	2	3	1	3	6,286
Success Story	3	6	2	0	0	4	5,875
Doris Doors	3	8	2	0	1	5	5,269
Far Fetched	2	1	1	0	0	0	4,264
Phantom Gold	2	2	1	0	1	0	4,188
Magongo	2	2	1	0	1	0	3,892
Twilight Sleep	2	3	1	0	1	1	3,819
Red Light	2	4	1	0	0	3	3,739
Quintus Decimus	2	2	1	0	0	1	3,739
Piquant	7	8	1	2	1	4	3,713
Akabusi	3	4	1	0	0	3	3,688
Smart Generation	3	5	1	0	1	3	3,647
Royal Hill	3	6	1	1	2	2	3,407
Colour Sergeant	6	4	1	0	0	3	3,288
L'Etat C'Est Moi	3	8	1	1	2	4	3,260
Guards Brigade	3	8	1	1	1	5	3,231
Zacaroon	3	6	1	0	1	4	3,202
Sharpening	3	6	1	1	1	3	3,024
Shamrock Fair	2	3	1	1	0	1	2,964
Varsavia	3	2	1	0	0	1	2,924
Party Line	3	3	1	0	0	2	2,920
Linger	2	4	1	0	0	3	2,875
Bangles	4	5	1	0	2	2	2,804
Lady Roxanne	5	10	1	3	1	5	2,781
Leviathan Mystery	3	2	1	0	1	0	2,385
Flora Belle	3	6	1	0	1	4	2,364
Positivo	3	7	1	1	1	4	2,243
Mariposa Lily	2	9	1	1	4	3	2,174

WINNING OWNERS

	Races Won	Value £		Races Won	Value £
The Queen	13	90,595	Lady Halifax	1	3,892
Stanley J Sharp	2	37,770	Penllyne Properties Ltd	1	3,739
Sir Gordon Brunton	4	19,643	R Van Gelder	1	3,739
M L Oberstein	3	13,089	S Hastings-Bass	1	3,688
Yoshio Asakawa	1	8,433	George Ward	1	3,647
G Cosmelli	2	8,233	George A Moore	1	3,407
Stanley Squires	3	7,442	Henryk De Kwiatkowski	1	3,260
Geoffrey C Greenwood	2	6,766	James Wigan	1	3,024
P A Leonard	2	6,490	Sultan Mohammed	1	2,924
J R Bailey	2	6,415	J Rose	1	2,804
G W Mooratoff	2	6,286	Lord Huntingdon	1	2,781
Lord Carnarvon	2	5,795	Marques De Deleitosa	1	2,385
Lord Crawshaw	2	5,269	Countess Of Lonsdale	1	2,243
Lord Weinstock	1	4,264	Lady Carolyn Warren	1	2,174

Favourites	21-68	30.9%	- 13.24	Total winning prize-money	£270,196

Longest winning sequence	4	Average SP of winner	4.0/1
Longest losing sequence	23	Return on stakes invested	-14.3%

1993 Form	40-288	13.9%	- 83.23	1991 Form	36-254	14.2%	+ 91.26
1992 Form	60-331	18.1%	+ 12.32	1990 Form	20-197	10.2%	- 53.59

D E INCISA (Middleham, North Yorks)

	No. of Horses	Races Run	1st	2nd	3rd	Unpl	Per cent	£1 Level Stake
2-y-o	1	5	0	0	0	5	-	- 5.00
3-y-o	4	40	2	1	1	36	5.0	- 24.00
4-y-o+	6	51	1	2	4	44	2.0	- 44.00
Totals	11	96	3	3	5	85	3.1	- 73.00

Jan	Feb	Mar	Apr	May	Jun	Jul	Aug	Sep	Oct/Nov
0-0	0-0	0-2	0-9	0-10	1-17	2-20	0-22	0-9	0-7

		£1 Level			£1 Level
Winning Jockey	W-R	Stake		W-R	Stake
Kim Tinkler	3-96	- 73.00			

Winning Courses					
Carlisle	2-4	+ 12.00	Nottingham	1-10	- 3.00

		Races					Win
Winning Horses	Age	Run	1st	2nd	3rd	Unpl	£
Tutu Sixtysix	3	14	2	1	1	10	5,822
Bardia	4	11	1	0	1	9	3,366

Favourites	0-0	Total winning prize-money	£9,188

1993 Form	0-59			1991 Form	4-73	5.5%	- 26.50
1992 Form	1-72	1.4%	- 59.00	1990 Form	2-67	3.0%	- 24.00

R INGRAM (Epsom, Surrey)

	No. of Horses	Races Run	1st	2nd	3rd	Unpl	Per cent	£1 Level Stake
2-y-o	5	16	1	0	0	15	6.3	- 11.50
3-y-o	2	10	0	0	0	10	-	- 10.00
4-y-o+	7	44	3	0	2	39	6.8	- 20.00
Totals	14	70	4	0	2	64	5.7	- 41.50

Jan	Feb	Mar	Apr	May	Jun	Jul	Aug	Sep	Oct/Nov
1-3	1-6	0-4	0-4	0-7	0-9	1-11	1-10	0-6	0-10

Winning Jockeys	W-R	£1 Level Stake				W-R	£1 Level Stake
Dale Gibson	2-12	- 2.50		A McGlone		1-24	- 11.00
J Weaver	1-6	0.00					

Winning Courses							
Wolverhampton (AW)	2-9	+ 2.00		Folkestone		1-10	+ 3.00
Redcar	1-2	+ 2.50					

Winning Horses	Age	Races Run	1st	2nd	3rd	Unpl	Win £
Lochore	4	6	1	0	1	4	3,524
Dam Certain	5	16	1	0	1	14	3,465
Kinnegad Kid	5	6	1	0	0	5	3,095
Tomal	2	7	1	0	0	6	2,643

Favourites	1-2	50.0%	+ 3.00	Total winning prize-money			£12,727

1993 Form	6-55	10.9%	- 0.50	1991 Form	2-27	7.4%	- 4.00
1992 Form	1-37	2.7%	- 3.00				

K T IVORY (Radlett, Herts)

	No. of Horses	Races Run	1st	2nd	3rd	Unpl	Per cent	£1 Level Stake
2-y-o	4	31	7	4	1	19	22.6	+ 6.25
3-y-o	5	29	0	1	2	26	-	- 29.00
4-y-o+	6	44	4	4	4	32	9.1	- 13.25
Totals	15	104	11	9	7	77	10.6	- 36.00

BY MONTH

2-y-o	W-R	Per cent	£1 Level Stake	3-y-o	W-R	Per cent	£1 Level Stake
January	0-0	-	0.00	January	0-1	-	- 1.00
February	0-0	-	0.00	February	0-3	-	- 3.00
March	0-1	-	- 1.00	March	0-1	-	- 1.00
April	1-4	25.0	+ 1.00	April	0-2	-	- 2.00
May	0-2	-	- 2.00	May	0-5	-	- 5.00
June	1-7	14.3	+ 2.00	June	0-3	-	- 3.00
July	3-5	60.0	+ 9.25	July	0-6	-	- 6.00
August	2-8	25.0	+ 1.00	August	0-0	-	0.00
September	0-3	-	- 3.00	September	0-4	-	- 4.00
Oct/Nov	0-1	-	- 1.00	Oct/Nov	0-4	-	- 4.00

4-y-o+	W-R	Per cent	£1 Level Stake	Totals	W-R	Per cent	£1 Level Stake
January	0-0	-	0.00	January	0-1	-	- 1.00
February	0-2	-	- 2.00	February	0-5	-	- 5.00
March	0-4	-	- 4.00	March	0-6	-	- 6.00
April	2-6	33.3	+ 7.75	April	3-12	25.0	+ 6.75
May	0-3	-	- 3.00	May	0-10	-	- 10.00
June	1-10	10.0	- 1.00	June	2-20	10.0	- 2.00
July	1-8	12.5	0.00	July	4-19	21.1	+ 3.25
August	0-6	-	- 6.00	August	2-14	14.3	- 5.00
September	0-3	-	- 3.00	September	0-10	-	- 10.00
Oct/Nov	0-2	-	- 2.00	Oct/Nov	0-7	-	- 7.00

DISTANCE

2-y-o	W-R	Per cent	£1 Level Stake	3-y-o	W-R	Per cent	£1 Level Stake
5f-6f	6-26	23.1	+ 4.75	5f-6f	0-23	-	- 23.00
7f-8f	1-5	20.0	+ 1.50	7f-8f	0-5	-	- 5.00
9f-13f	0-0	-	0.00	9f-13f	0-1	-	- 1.00
14f+	0-0	-	0.00	14f+	0-0	-	0.00

4-y-o+	W-R	Per cent	£1 Level Stake	Totals	W-R	Per cent	£1 Level Stake
5f-6f	1-13	7.7	- 5.00	5f-6f	7-62	11.3	- 23.25
7f-8f	2-20	10.0	- 1.00	7f-8f	3-30	10.0	- 4.50
9f-13f	1-11	9.1	- 7.25	9f-13f	1-12	8.3	- 8.25
14f+	0-0	-	0.00	14f+	0-0	-	0.00

TYPE OF RACE

Non-Handicaps	W-R	Per cent	£1 Level Stake	Handicaps	W-R	Per cent	£1 Level Stake
2-y-o	1-7	14.3	- 4.25	2-y-o	1-10	10.0	- 6.00
3-y-o	0-13	-	- 13.00	3-y-o	0-6	-	- 6.00
4-y-o+	1-5	20.0	+ 3.00	4-y-o+	2-28	7.1	- 14.25
Selling	6-24	25.0	+ 15.50	Selling	0-2	-	- 2.00
Apprentice	0-4	-	- 4.00	Apprentice	0-5	-	- 5.00
Amat/Ladies	0-0	-	0.00	Amat/Ladies	0-0	-	0.00
Totals	8-53	15.1	- 2.75	Totals	3-51	5.9	- 33.25

COURSE GRADE

	W-R	Per cent	£1 Level Stake
Group 1	0-16	-	- 16.00
Group 2	1-12	8.3	- 3.00
Group 3	7-48	14.6	- 2.75
Group 4	3-28	10.7	- 14.25

FIRST TIME OUT

	W-R	Per cent	£1 Level Stake
2-y-o	0-4	-	- 4.00
3-y-o	0-4	-	- 4.00
4-y-o+	1-6	16.7	- 2.25
Totals	1-14	7.1	- 10.25

JOCKEYS RIDING

	W-R	Per cent	£1 Level Stake		W-R	Per cent	£1 Level Stake
G Duffield	3-8	37.5	+ 6.25	J Stack	1-5	20.0	- 1.00
C Scally	2-18	11.1	- 4.00	D Biggs	1-6	16.7	- 1.00
G Bardwell	2-20	10.0	- 6.25	M Wigham	1-14	7.1	- 5.00
W Newnes	1-2	50.0	+ 6.00				

J Weaver	0-6	C Hodgson	0-1	L Dettori	0-1
R Cochrane	0-4	C Rutter	0-1	M Hills	0-1
N Adams	0-3	D Holland	0-1	N Carlisle	0-1
M Fenton	0-2	D Wright	0-1	Pat Eddery	0-1
N Varley	0-2	J Quinn	0-1	Paul Eddery	0-1
A McGlone	0-1	K Darley	0-1		
A Munro	0-1	K Rutter	0-1		

COURSE RECORD

	Total W-R	Non-Handicaps 2-y-o	Non-Handicaps 3-y-o+	Handicaps 2-y-o	Handicaps 3-y-o+	Per cent	£1 Level Stake
Pontefract	3-7	1-1	0-2	1-2	1-2	42.9	+ 9.75
Southwell (AW)	2-4	2-3	0-1	0-0	0-0	50.0	+ 6.00
Yarmouth	2-21	2-5	0-6	0-1	0-9	9.5	- 5.50
Beverley	1-2	1-1	0-1	0-0	0-0	50.0	+ 3.00
Bath	1-3	0-0	1-3	0-0	0-0	33.3	+ 5.00
Lingfield	1-7	0-4	1-2	0-0	0-1	14.3	+ 2.00
Warwick	1-8	0-2	0-2	0-1	1-3	12.5	- 4.25

Windsor	0-12	Nottingham	0-3	Ascot	0-1
Lingfield (AW)	0-9	Catterick	0-2	Brighton	0-1
Wolverhampton (AW)	0-4	Goodwood	0-2	Epsom	0-1
Doncaster	0-3	Redcar	0-2	Folkestone	0-1
Kempton	0-3	Salisbury	0-2	Haydock	0-1
Newmarket	0-3	Sandown	0-2		

WINNING HORSES

	Age	Races Run	1st	2nd	3rd	Unpl	Win £
Myfontaine	7	11	2	2	1	6	11,160
Delight Of Dawn	2	9	3	3	0	3	9,073
Go Likecrazy	2	11	2	1	1	7	4,858

Bold Frontier	2	7	2	0	0	5	4,673
Double Bounce	4	5	1	0	1	3	2,882
Our Shadee	4	17	1	2	2	12	2,784

WINNING OWNERS

	Races Won	Value £		Races Won	Value £
K T Ivory	10	32,547	Mrs P Scott-Dunn	1	2,882

Favourites	1-10	10.0% - 6.00	Total winning prize-money		£35,429

Longest winning sequence	2	Average SP of winner	5.2/1
Longest losing sequence	25	Return on stakes invested	-34.6%

1993 Form	2-91	2.2% - 68.50	1991 Form	5-148	3.4% - 97.00
1992 Form	9-91	9.9% + 13.23	1990 Form	7-128	5.5% - 46.00

C JAMES (Newbury, Berks)

	No. of Horses	Races Run	1st	2nd	3rd	Unpl	Per cent	£1 Level Stake
2-y-o	3	9	0	0	1	8	–	- 9.00
3-y-o	5	35	4	2	2	27	11.4	+ 47.25
4-y-o+	5	25	1	1	2	21	4.0	- 21.25
Totals	13	69	5	3	5	56	7.2	+ 17.00

Jan	Feb	Mar	Apr	May	Jun	Jul	Aug	Sep	Oct/Nov
0-1	1-3	0-0	2-8	0-6	1-18	1-7	0-8	0-10	0-8

Winning Jockeys	W-R	£1 Level Stake		W-R	£1 Level Stake
Pat Eddery	2-4	+ 6.75	J Quinn	1-4	+ 47.00
L Dettori	1-3	+ 0.25	G Bardwell	1-6	+ 15.00

Winning Courses					
Leicester	1-4	- 0.25	Windsor	1-7	+ 14.00
Goodwood	1-5	+ 46.00	Bath	1-9	- 2.00
Lingfield (AW)	1-5	- 1.75			

Winning Horses	Age	Races Run	1st	2nd	3rd	Unpl	Win £
Random	3	11	2	2	2	5	5,183
Screwball Anaconda	3	9	1	0	0	8	3,749
Knightrider	3	8	1	0	0	7	3,371
Le Baron Perche	5	1	1	0	0	0	2,976

Favourites	1-5	20.0% - 1.25	Total winning prize-money		£15,279

1993 Form	5-68	7.4% + 20.50	1991 Form	3-56	5.4% - 37.25
1992 Form	4-55	7.3% + 1.75	1990 Form	1-45	2.2% - 40.00

A P JARVIS (Aston Upthorpe, Oxon)

	No. of Horses	Races Run	1st	2nd	3rd	Unpl	Per cent	£1 Level Stake
2-y-o	8	26	4	2	2	18	15.4	- 2.00
3-y-o	7	34	1	4	4	25	2.9	- 26.50
4-y-o+	6	40	1	1	1	37	2.5	- 31.00
Totals	21	100	6	7	7	80	6.0	- 59.50

Jan	Feb	Mar	Apr	May	Jun	Jul	Aug	Sep	Oct/Nov
1-2	0-4	0-6	0-7	0-7	0-7	2-20	1-19	2-19	0-9

Winning Jockeys	W-R	£1 Level Stake		W-R	£1 Level Stake
L Dettori	3-7	+ 13.00	B Thomson	1-4	+ 7.00
D Harrison	1-1	+ 6.50	J Tate	1-5	- 3.00

Winning Courses					
Goodwood	2-9	+ 6.50	Southwell (AW)	1-3	+ 6.00
Ripon	1-2	0.00	Kempton	1-6	- 3.00
Doncaster	1-3	+ 8.00			

Winning Horses	Age	Races Run	1st	2nd	3rd	Unpl	Win £
Lennox Lewis	2	7	3	1	1	2	15,398
Sue's Return	2	6	1	1	1	3	5,361
Douce Maison	3	10	1	3	3	3	4,630
Chairmans Choice	4	7	1	1	0	5	3,348

Favourites	2-6	33.3%	- 1.00	Total winning prize-money		£28,737

1993 Form	7-133	5.3%	- 85.25	1991 Form	1-11	9.1%	- 2.00
1992 Form	2-73	2.7%	- 41.00				

M A JARVIS (Newmarket)

	No. of Horses	Races Run	1st	2nd	3rd	Unpl	Per cent	£1 Level Stake
2-y-o	11	37	0	1	4	32	-	- 37.00
3-y-o	11	64	8	10	7	39	12.5	- 8.90
4-y-o+	7	56	7	5	8	36	12.5	- 14.54
Totals	29	157	15	16	19	107	9.6	- 60.44

BY MONTH

2-y-o	W-R	Per cent	£1 Level Stake	3-y-o	W-R	Per cent	£1 Level Stake
Mar/Apr	0-0	-	0.00	Mar/Apr	4-11	36.4	+ 18.35
May	0-1	-	- 1.00	May	0-9	-	- 9.00
June	0-3	-	- 3.00	June	3-10	30.0	+ 13.50
July	0-6	-	- 6.00	July	1-10	10.0	- 7.75
August	0-9	-	- 9.00	August	0-7	-	- 7.00
September	0-7	-	- 7.00	September	0-7	-	- 7.00
Oct/Nov	0-11	-	- 11.00	Oct/Nov	0-10	-	- 10.00

4-y-o+	W-R	Per cent	£1 Level Stake	Totals	W-R	Per cent	£1 Level Stake
Mar/Apr	1-3	33.3	+ 2.50	Mar/Apr	5-14	35.7	+ 20.85
May	0-12	-	- 12.00	May	0-22	-	- 22.00
June	1-10	10.0	- 5.00	June	4-23	17.4	+ 5.50
July	2-8	25.0	+ 3.91	July	3-24	12.5	- 9.84
August	2-10	20.0	+ 4.00	August	2-26	7.7	- 12.00
September	1-9	11.1	- 3.95	September	1-23	4.3	- 17.95
Oct/Nov	0-4	-	- 4.00	Oct/Nov	0-25	-	- 25.00

DISTANCE

2-y-o	W-R	Per cent	£1 Level Stake	3-y-o	W-R	Per cent	£1 Level Stake
5f-6f	0-14	-	- 14.00	5f-6f	1-6	16.7	+ 5.00
7f-8f	0-22	-	- 22.00	7f-8f	3-38	7.9	- 6.00
9f-13f	0-1	-	- 1.00	9f-13f	3-18	16.7	- 8.15
14f+	0-0	-	0.00	14f+	1-2	50.0	+ 0.25

4-y-o+	W-R	Per cent	£1 Level Stake	Totals	W-R	Per cent	£1 Level Stake
5f-6f	1-10	10.0	- 5.00	5f-6f	2-30	6.7	- 14.00
7f-8f	5-26	19.2	+ 4.46	7f-8f	8-86	9.3	- 23.54
9f-13f	1-20	5.0	- 14.00	9f-13f	4-39	10.3	- 23.15
14f+	0-0	-	0.00	14f+	1-2	50.0	+ 0.25

TYPE OF RACE

Non-Handicaps	W-R	Per cent	£1 Level Stake	Handicaps	W-R	Per cent	£1 Level Stake
2-y-o	0-27	-	- 27.00	2-y-o	0-8	-	- 8.00
3-y-o	3-22	13.6	+ 3.25	3-y-o	5-42	11.9	- 12.15
4-y-o+	1-9	11.1	- 3.00	4-y-o+	3-36	8.3	- 17.50
Selling	2-7	28.6	- 0.04	Selling	1-3	33.3	+ 7.00
Apprentice	0-0	-	0.00	Apprentice	0-3	-	- 3.00
Amat/Ladies	0-0	-	0.00	Amat/Ladies	0-0	-	0.00
Totals	6-65	9.2	- 26.79	Totals	9-92	9.8	- 33.65

Jarvis M A

COURSE GRADE

	W-R	Per cent	£1 Level Stake
Group 1	4-68	5.9	- 47.25
Group 2	5-28	17.9	- 4.44
Group 3	3-39	7.7	- 9.75
Group 4	3-22	13.6	+ 1.00

FIRST TIME OUT

	W-R	Per cent	£1 Level Stake
2-y-o	0-11	-	- 11.00
3-y-o	2-11	18.2	+ 13.00
4-y-o+	0-6	-	- 6.00
Totals	2-28	7.1	- 4.00

JOCKEYS RIDING

	W-R	Per cent	£1 Level Stake		W-R	Per cent	£1 Level Stake
P Robinson	6-56	10.7	- 14.65	L Dettori	1-4	25.0	+ 2.00
M J Kinane	2-3	66.7	+ 3.75	Pat Eddery	1-11	9.1	- 5.50
K Darley	2-4	50.0	+ 2.96	A Munro	1-11	9.1	- 1.00
J Reid	1-3	33.3	+ 8.00	K Rutter	1-31	3.2	- 22.00

T Ives	0-8	R Painter	0-2	G Hind	0-1
W Woods	0-4	A Clark	0-1	M Roberts	0-1
J Weaver	0-3	B Thomson	0-1	Paul Eddery	0-1
B Raymond	0-2	D McKeown	0-1	R Cochrane	0-1
G Bardwell	0-2	G Carter	0-1	T Williams	0-1
J Carroll	0-2	G Duffield	0-1	W Hood	0-1

COURSE RECORD

	Total W-R	Non-Handicaps 2-y-o	3-y-o+	Handicaps 2-y-o	3-y-o+	Per cent	£1 Level Stake
Ripon	2-3	0-0	1-1	0-0	1-2	66.7	+ 1.01
York	2-5	0-0	2-2	0-0	0-3	40.0	+ 9.00
Windsor	2-6	0-1	0-1	0-0	2-4	33.3	+ 8.25
Carlisle	1-2	0-1	0-0	0-0	1-1	50.0	+ 3.00
Epsom	1-2	0-0	0-0	0-0	1-2	50.0	+ 2.50
Sandown	1-2	0-0	1-1	0-0	0-1	50.0	+ 0.25
Thirsk	1-2	0-0	1-2	0-0	0-0	50.0	+ 3.05
Leicester	1-3	0-0	1-3	0-0	0-0	33.3	+ 12.00
Warwick	1-5	0-0	0-2	0-0	1-3	20.0	+ 5.00
Brighton	1-6	0-0	0-3	0-0	1-3	16.7	- 0.50
Folkestone	1-7	0-3	0-1	0-0	1-3	14.3	+ 1.00
Lingfield	1-10	0-2	0-1	0-0	1-7	10.0	- 1.00

Newmarket	0-18	Newbury	0-5	Beverley	0-2
Haydock	0-13	Goodwood	0-4	Chester	0-2
Pontefract	0-9	Nottingham	0-4	Newcastle	0-2
Yarmouth	0-9	Salisbury	0-4	Bath	0-1
Kempton	0-8	Wolverhampton (AW)	0-4	Lingfield (AW)	0-1
Doncaster	0-7	Southwell (AW)	0-3	Redcar	0-1
Chepstow	0-5	Ayr	0-2		

244

WINNING HORSES

	Age	Races Run	1st	2nd	3rd	Unpl	Win £
Ragsat Al Omor	3	8	2	1	2	3	14,313
Diaco	9	12	3	1	1	7	7,600
Northern Union	3	2	2	0	0	0	7,530
Sakharov	5	11	2	0	0	9	6,275
Rival Bid	6	8	1	2	3	2	5,318
Northern Celadon	3	9	1	0	1	7	4,921
New Capricorn	4	8	1	1	3	3	4,836
Diabaig	3	9	1	1	1	6	4,079
Ela Man Howa	3	5	1	0	1	3	3,351
Green Golightly	3	6	1	0	0	5	3,080

WINNING OWNERS

	Races Won	Value £		Races Won	Value £
Sheikh Ahmed Al Maktoum	3	17,664	R P Marchant	1	4,921
J R Good	5	13,875	Kamal Bhatia	1	4,836
Raymond Anderson Green	3	10,610	M Sinclair	1	4,079
David Altham	1	5,318			

Favourites	5-19	26.3%	- 3.19	
Longest winning sequence			2	
Longest losing sequence			44	
1993 Form	21-150	14.0%	- 52.82	
1992 Form	28-192	14.6%	- 28.31	

Total winning prize-money			£61,301	
Average SP of winner			5.4/1	
Return on stakes invested			-38.5%	
1991 Form	24-249	9.6%	- 55.22	
1990 Form	28-258	10.9%	- 70.12	

W JARVIS (Newmarket)

	No. of Horses	Races Run	1st	2nd	3rd	Unpl	Per cent	£1 Level Stake
2-y-o	21	57	8	6	2	41	14.0	- 2.37
3-y-o	19	93	9	13	14	57	9.7	- 35.25
4-y-o+	10	51	6	4	5	36	11.8	- 1.75
Totals	50	201	23	23	21	134	11.4	- 39.37

BY MONTH

2-y-o	W-R	Per cent	£1 Level Stake	3-y-o	W-R	Per cent	£1 Level Stake
January	0-0	-	0.00	January	1-3	33.3	+ 8.00
February	0-0	-	0.00	February	0-1	-	- 1.00
March	0-0	-	0.00	March	0-0	-	0.00
April	2-3	66.7	+ 2.38	April	0-14	-	- 14.00
May	0-3	-	- 3.00	May	1-17	5.9	0.00
June	2-8	25.0	- 0.25	June	3-19	15.8	- 2.50
July	0-8	-	- 8.00	July	1-9	11.1	- 5.75
August	1-9	11.1	0.00	August	2-10	20.0	- 3.25
September	1-13	7.7	- 3.50	September	1-10	10.0	- 6.75
Oct/Nov	2-13	15.4	+ 10.00	Oct/Nov	0-10	-	- 10.00

4-y-o+	W-R	Per cent	£1 Level Stake	Totals	W-R	Per cent	£1 Level Stake
January	0-2	-	- 2.00	January	1-5	20.0	+ 6.00
February	0-1	-	- 1.00	February	0-2	-	2.00
March	0-0	-	0.00	March	0-0	-	0.00
April	1-3	33.3	+ 5.00	April	3-20	15.0	- 6.62
May	0-7	-	- 7.00	May	1-27	3.7	- 10.00
June	0-9	-	- 9.00	June	5-36	13.9	- 11.75
July	2-10	20.0	- 2.75	July	3-27	11.1	- 16.50
August	1-6	16.7	+ 5.00	August	4-25	16.0	+ 1.75
September	2-6	33.3	+ 17.00	September	4-29	13.8	+ 6.75
Oct/Nov	0-7	-	- 7.00	Oct/Nov	2-30	6.7	- 7.00

DISTANCE

2-y-o	W-R	Per cent	£1 Level Stake	3-y-o	W-R	Per cent	£1 Level Stake
5f-6f	7-32	21.9	+ 9.63	5f-6f	2-13	15.4	+ 7.75
7f-8f	1-24	4.2	- 11.00	7f-8f	4-41	9.8	- 14.75
9f-13f	0-1	-	- 1.00	9f-13f	0-27	-	- 27.00
14f+	0-0	-	0.00	14f+	3-12	25.0	- 1.25

4-y-o+	W-R	Per cent	£1 Level Stake	Totals	W-R	Per cent	£1 Level Stake
5f-6f	2-14	14.3	+ 4.00	5f-6f	11-59	18.6	+ 21.38
7f-8f	2-22	9.1	+ 2.00	7f-8f	7-87	8.0	- 23.75
9f-13f	2-14	14.3	- 6.75	9f-13f	2-42	4.8	- 34.75
14f+	0-1	-	- 1.00	14f+	3-13	23.1	- 2.25

TYPE OF RACE

Non-Handicaps	W-R	Per cent	£1 Level Stake	Handicaps	W-R	Per cent	£1 Level Stake
2-y-o	5-44	11.4	- 21.87	2-y-o	2-9	22.2	+ 10.50
3-y-o	5-59	8.5	- 17.00	3-y-o	2-27	7.4	- 19.25
4-y-o+	1-8	12.5	0.00	4-y-o+	4-41	9.8	- 4.25
Selling	1-4	25.0	+ 9.00	Selling	0-0	-	0.00
Apprentice	1-1	100.0	+ 4.00	Apprentice	2-8	25.0	- 0.50
Amat/Ladies	0-0	-	0.00	Amat/Ladies	0-0	-	0.00
Totals	13-116	11.2	- 25.87	Totals	10-85	11.8	- 13.50

COURSE GRADE

	W-R	Per cent	£1 Level Stake
Group 1	9-95	9.5	- 8.00
Group 2	5-27	18.5	+ 7.25
Group 3	4-50	8.0	- 36.00
Group 4	5-29	17.2	- 2.62

FIRST TIME OUT

	W-R	Per cent	£1 Level Stake
2-y-o	2-18	11.1	- 12.25
3-y-o	2-18	11.1	+ 10.00
4-y-o+	1-9	11.1	- 1.00
Totals	5-45	11.1	- 3.25

JOCKEYS RIDING

	W-R	Per cent	£1 Level Stake		W-R	Per cent	£1 Level Stake
M Tebbutt	5-67	7.5	- 51.87	D Harrison	1-2	50.0	+ 15.00
M J Kinane	2-3	66.7	+ 14.00	L Piggott	1-2	50.0	+ 7.50
J Weaver	2-4	50.0	+ 17.00	J Williams	1-3	33.3	+ 8.00
T Quinn	2-7	28.6	+ 13.00	A Munro	1-4	25.0	+ 1.00
M Baird	2-10	20.0	- 0.50	J Reid	1-5	20.0	- 2.25
L Dettori	2-21	9.5	- 13.25	B Thomson	1-7	14.3	+ 6.00
M Henry	1-1	100.0	+ 2.00	Pat Eddery	1-9	11.1	+ 1.00

A McGlone	0-5	A Lakeman	0-2	J Tate	0-1
G Mitchell	0-5	K Darley	0-2	K Rutter	0-1
J Stack	0-4	R Cochrane	0-2	Paul Eddery	0-1
M Hills	0-4	W Hood	0-2	S Drowne	0-1
R Hills	0-4	W Ryan	0-2	Stephen Davies	0-1
W R Swinburn	0-4	D McKeown	0-1	T Ives	0-1
M Roberts	0-3	G Bardwell	0-1	T Lucas	0-1
P Robinson	0-3	J Carroll	0-1		
W Carson	0-3	J Quinn	0-1		

COURSE RECORD

	Total W-R	Non-Handicaps 2-y-o	3-y-o+	Handicaps 2-y-o	3-y-o+	Per cent	£1 Level Stake
Chepstow	2-4	0-0	1-2	0-0	1-2	50.0	+ 2.50
Folkestone	2-6	1-3	0-2	0-0	1-1	33.3	+ 2.00
Lingfield	2-6	1-3	1-2	0-1	0-0	33.3	+ 13.75
Haydock	2-7	0-1	0-0	1-1	1-5	28.6	+ 7.50
Doncaster	2-8	0-3	0-0	1-1	1-4	25.0	+ 14.50
Newmarket	2-38	1-14	0-14	0-0	1-10	5.3	- 15.00
Carlisle	1-3	1-2	0-1	0-0	0-0	33.3	- 0.62
Chester	1-3	0-0	0-1	0-0	1-2	33.3	- 0.25
Catterick	1-4	0-0	1-2	0-0	0-2	25.0	+ 1.00
Ripon	1-4	0-0	1-2	0-0	0-2	25.0	- 0.25
Thirsk	1-4	0-0	1-4	0-0	0-0	25.0	+ 4.00
Wolverhampton (AW)	1-4	0-0	1-2	0-0	0-2	25.0	+ 7.00
York	1-5	0-0	0-1	0-0	1-4	20.0	+ 6.00
Ascot	1-7	0-0	1-2	0-0	0-5	14.3	0.00
Nottingham	1-7	1-3	0-2	0-0	0-2	14.3	- 4.00
Newbury	1-8	1-4	0-1	0-1	0-2	12.5	+ 1.00
Yarmouth	1-12	0-2	0-2	0-1	1-7	8.3	- 7.50

Jarvis W

Leicester	0-9	Kempton	0-4	Sandown	0-3
Goodwood	0-8	Newcastle	0-4	Beverley	0-2
Pontefract	0-7	Redcar	0-4	Salisbury	0-2
Lingfield (AW)	0-5	Warwick	0-4	Southwell (AW)	0-2
Brighton	0-4	Windsor	0-4	Bath	0-1
Hamilton	0-4	Epsom	0-3	Edinburgh	0-1

WINNING HORSES

	Age	Races Run	1st	2nd	3rd	Unpl	Win £
Grand Lodge	3	6	1	2	1	2	130,329
Lap Of Luxury	5	10	2	1	1	6	34,567
The Jotter	2	9	2	4	0	3	23,261
Easy Option	2	3	2	0	0	1	14,010
Keen Bid	3	12	4	2	1	5	12,266
Alasib	4	8	1	1	0	6	8,023
She's Dynamite	2	3	2	0	0	1	7,040
Meavy	4	3	1	0	0	2	5,048
Lord Olivier	4	7	1	1	0	5	4,885
Domappel	2	1	1	0	0	0	4,403
Western General	3	7	1	2	0	4	3,904
Camicia	2	8	1	1	0	6	3,692
Taffeta Silk	3	9	1	1	4	3	3,549
By Candlelight	3	4	1	0	1	2	3,545
Diplomatist	4	11	1	1	2	7	3,474
St Louis Lady	3	3	1	1	0	1	2,558

WINNING OWNERS

	Races Won	Value £		Races Won	Value £
Lord Howard De Walden	2	134,021	Miss V R Jarvis	1	4,885
I C Hill-Wood	2	34,567	Jocelyn Waller	1	4,403
Mrs Doris N Allen	2	23,261	Mrs James McAllister	1	3,904
Mrs Susan Davis	2	14,010	Highclere Th'bred Racing Ltd	1	3,549
H R H Prince Fahd Salman	4	12,266	J W Rowles	1	3,545
A Foustok	1	8,023	Michael L Page	1	3,474
Mitaab Abdullah	2	7,040	Mrs S C Thomas	1	2,558
Lord & Lady Roborough	1	5,048			

Favourites	7-26	26.9%	- 2.12	Total winning prize-money		£264,554
Longest winning sequence			2	Average SP of winner		6.0/1
Longest losing sequence			20	Return on stakes invested		-19.6%
1993 Form	21-194	10.8%	- 60.36	1991 Form	29-208	13.9%	- 43.94
1992 Form	22-183	12.0%	- 64.45	1990 Form	31-239	13.0%	- 69.91

J M JEFFERSON (Malton, North Yorks)

	No. of Horses	Races Run	1st	2nd	3rd	Unpl	Per cent	£1 Level Stake
2-y-o	2	5	0	0	0	5	–	- 5.00
3-y-o	1	3	0	0	0	3	–	- 3.00
4-y-o+	2	6	1	2	0	3	16.7	- 3.50
Totals	5	14	1	2	0	11	7.1	- 11.50

Jan	Feb	Mar	Apr	May	Jun	Jul	Aug	Sep	Oct/Nov
0-0	0-0	0-0	0-0	0-2	0-0	1-1	0-4	0-4	0-3

Winning Jockey	W-R	£1 Level Stake	Winning Course	W-R	£1 Level Stake
B Raymond	1-1	+ 1.50	Newmarket	1-1	+ 1.50

Winning Horse	Age	Races Run	1st	2nd	3rd	Unpl	Win £
Legal Flair	4	1	1	0	0	0	3,785

Favourites	1-1	100.0%	+ 1.50	Total winning prize-money	£3,785

1993 Form	0-17		1991 Form	0-19
1992 Form	0-17		1990 Form	0-26

J R JENKINS (Royston, Herts)

	No. of Horses	Races Run	1st	2nd	3rd	Unpl	Per cent	£1 Level Stake
2-y-o	7	30	0	3	0	27	–	- 30.00
3-y-o	7	28	1	1	2	24	3.6	- 22.00
4-y-o+	23	77	3	5	4	65	3.9	- 56.00
Totals	37	135	4	9	6	116	3.0	-108.00

Jan	Feb	Mar	Apr	May	Jun	Jul	Aug	Sep	Oct/Nov
0-2	0-2	0-11	1-16	0-17	3-20	0-19	0-23	0-16	0-9

Winning Jockeys	W-R	£1 Level Stake		W-R	£1 Level Stake
L Dettori	3-23	- 5.00	Pat Eddery	1-4	+ 5.00

Winning Courses					
Bath	1-4	+ 5.00	Yarmouth	1-11	- 5.00
Kempton	1-7	0.00	Windsor	1-17	- 12.00

Winning Horses	Age	Races Run	1st	2nd	3rd	Unpl	Win £
Bayrak	4	2	1	1	0	0	3,504
Lucky Tucky	3	7	1	1	1	4	3,377
Durshan	5	11	1	0	0	10	3,054
Vanroy	10	7	1	2	1	3	2,679

Favourites	2-12	16.7%	- 1.00	Total winning prize-money			£12,615

1993 Form	4-142	2.8%	-107.50	1991 Form	12-152	7.9%	- 27.87
1992 Form	12-156	7.7%	- 42.00	1990 Form	13-239	5.4%	-137.84

M JOHNSTON (Middleham, North Yorks)

	No. of Horses	Races Run	1st	2nd	3rd	Unpl	Per cent	£1 Level Stake
2-y-o	41	198	37	26	21	114	18.7	- 8.40
3-y-o	27	204	28	29	27	120	13.7	- 56.08
4-y-o+	26	247	49	37	34	127	19.8	+ 13.25
Totals	94	649	114	92	82	361	17.6	- 51.23

BY MONTH

2-y-o	W-R	Per cent	£1 Level Stake	3-y-o	W-R	Per cent	£1 Level Stake
January	0-0	-	0.00	January	1-6	16.7	- 4.00
February	0-0	-	0.00	February	3-3	100.0	+ 11.63
March	0-0	-	0.00	March	5-10	50.0	+ 8.50
April	1-11	9.1	- 7.25	April	4-19	21.1	+ 9.46
May	5-17	29.4	+ 0.56	May	0-20	-	- 20.00
June	6-24	25.0	+ 9.43	June	3-32	9.4	- 8.00
July	9-32	28.1	+ 19.96	July	5-41	12.2	- 29.67
August	8-35	22.9	+ 9.45	August	3-33	9.1	- 10.00
September	3-36	8.3	- 17.75	September	1-23	4.3	- 14.00
Oct/Nov	5-43	11.6	- 22.80	Oct/Nov	3-17	17.6	0.00

4-y-o+	W-R	Per cent	£1 Level Stake	Totals	W-R	Per cent	£1 Level Stake
January	6-22	27.3	+ 11.71	January	7-28	25.0	+ 7.71
February	4-19	21.1	- 1.25	February	7-22	31.8	+ 10.38
March	5-20	25.0	+ 3.38	March	10-30	33.3	+ 11.88
April	5-24	20.8	+ 8.50	April	10-54	18.5	+ 10.71
May	11-38	28.9	+ 9.50	May	16-75	21.3	- 9.94
June	4-33	12.1	+ 3.88	June	13-89	14.6	+ 5.31
July	4-29	13.8	- 19.47	July	18-102	17.6	- 29.18
August	5-24	20.8	+ 11.25	August	16-92	17.4	+ 10.70
September	1-19	5.3	- 17.09	September	5-78	6.4	- 48.84
Oct/Nov	4-19	21.1	+ 2.84	Oct/Nov	12-79	15.2	- 19.96

DISTANCE

2-y-o	W-R	Per cent	£1 Level Stake	3-y-o	W-R	Per cent	£1 Level Stake
5f-6f	22-123	17.9	- 20.98	5f-6f	7-55	12.7	- 22.99
7f-8f	12-69	17.4	+ 8.13	7f-8f	12-89	13.5	- 20.42
9f-13f	3-6	50.0	+ 4.45	9f-13f	9-52	17.3	- 4.67
14f+	0-0	-	0.00	14f+	0-8	-	- 8.00

4-y-o+	W-R	Per cent	£1 Level Stake	Totals	W-R	Per cent	£1 Level Stake
5f-6f	16-79	20.3	- 1.37	5f-6f	45-257	17.5	- 45.34
7f-8f	9-59	15.3	- 10.24	7f-8f	33-217	15.2	- 22.53
9f-13f	9-42	21.4	- 4.50	9f-13f	21-100	21.0	- 4.72
14f+	15-67	22.4	+ 29.36	14f+	15-75	20.0	+ 21.36

TYPE OF RACE

Non-Handicaps	W-R	Per cent	£1 Level Stake	Handicaps	W-R	Per cent	£1 Level Stake
2-y-o	27-140	19.3	- 14.85	2-y-o	8-44	18.2	+ 9.95
3-y-o	12-65	18.5	- 12.29	3-y-o	15-128	11.7	- 39.79
4-y-o+	9-33	27.3	- 1.12	4-y-o+	39-202	19.3	+ 21.87
Selling	3-20	15.0	- 5.00	Selling	1-10	10.0	- 3.00
Apprentice	0-1	-	- 1.00	Apprentice	0-5	-	- 5.00
Amat/Ladies	0-0	-	0.00	Amat/Ladies	0-1	-	- 1.00
Totals	51-259	19.7	- 34.26	Totals	63-390	16.2	- 16.97

COURSE GRADE

	W-R	Per cent	£1 Level Stake
Group 1	25-240	10.4	- 75.56
Group 2	14-95	14.7	- 12.67
Group 3	31-132	23.5	+ 21.06
Group 4	44-182	24.2	+ 15.94

FIRST TIME OUT

	W-R	Per cent	£1 Level Stake
2-y-o	6-41	14.6	- 17.75
3-y-o	2-26	7.7	- 6.62
4-y-o+	6-25	24.0	+ 12.83
Totals	14-92	15.2	- 11.54

JOCKEYS RIDING

	W-R	Per cent	£1 Level Stake		W-R	Per cent	£1 Level Stake
J Weaver	92-406	22.7	+ 58.89	M Hills	2-12	16.7	- 0.75
M Roberts	5-25	20.0	+ 3.45	T Williams	2-41	4.9	- 24.75
L Dettori	3-13	23.1	+ 9.50	W Ryan	1-2	50.0	+ 0.63
J Reid	2-4	50.0	+ 7.63	A Munro	1-3	33.3	+ 5.00
P Robinson	2-9	22.2	- 0.27	G Carter	1-5	20.0	- 1.75
Oliver Casey	2-9	22.2	- 3.81	F Norton	1-6	16.7	+ 9.00

Johnston M

D McKeown	0-24	N Kennedy	0-3	K Fallon	0-1
G Duffield	0-13	D Harrison	0-2	L Charnock	0-1
J Fanning	0-11	G Bardwell	0-2	Madeleine Smith	0-1
S Bethley	0-7	J Lowe	0-2	N Adams	0-1
N Carlisle	0-6	K Darley	0-2	P Fessey	0-1
M J Kinane	0-5	R P Elliott	0-2	Pat Eddery	0-1
R Hills	0-4	C Teague	0-1	T Ives	0-1
A Garth	0-3	D Biggs	0-1	T Quinn	0-1
A Proud	0-3	D Holland	0-1	W Carson	0-1
C Hodgson	0-3	D Moffatt	0-1	W Woods	0-1
J Carroll	0-3	Dale Gibson	0-1		
J Quinn	0-3	J Fortune	0-1		

COURSE RECORD

	Total W-R	Non-Handicaps 2-y-o	3-y-o+	Handicaps 2-y-o	3-y-o+	Per cent	£1 Level Stake
Wolverhampton (AW)	17-45	0-2	4-9	0-2	13-32	37.8	+ 43.33
Lingfield (AW)	11-39	0-0	2-6	0-1	9-32	28.2	+ 14.76
Hamilton	10-44	5-16	2-7	1-2	2-19	22.7	- 12.18
Edinburgh	7-30	2-6	1-6	1-1	3-17	23.3	- 9.87
Ayr	7-45	4-16	0-6	1-4	2-19	15.6	- 15.92
Beverley	6-18	0-3	1-2	1-1	4-12	33.3	+ 10.85
Newmarket	6-24	2-3	1-4	2-5	1-12	25.0	+ 27.50
Ripon	6-24	0-5	2-5	1-1	3-13	25.0	+ 14.00
Leicester	5-18	2-7	2-3	0-1	1-7	27.8	+ 20.00
Southwell (AW)	5-26	1-3	2-8	0-2	2-13	19.2	- 6.37
Thirsk	4-27	3-8	0-3	0-2	1-14	14.8	- 1.25
Newcastle	4-31	1-13	0-1	0-2	3-15	12.9	+ 9.96
Doncaster	4-34	0-5	1-8	0-4	3-17	11.8	- 10.10
Pontefract	3-26	1-6	1-7	0-5	1-8	11.5	- 9.25
Redcar	3-31	1-13	0-3	1-1	1-14	9.7	- 17.42
Chepstow	2-3	1-1	1-2	0-0	0-0	66.7	+ 13.75
Yarmouth	2-7	0-1	0-0	0-3	2-3	28.6	+ 6.25
Nottingham	2-11	1-4	1-2	0-1	0-4	18.2	- 7.36
Catterick	2-21	2-6	0-1	0-3	0-11	9.5	- 11.87
York	2-34	2-9	0-7	0-2	0-16	5.9	- 27.75
Lingfield	1-4	0-0	1-2	0-0	0-2	25.0	+ 1.00
Warwick	1-4	0-1	0-0	0-0	1-3	25.0	- 1.37
Windsor	1-4	0-1	0-0	0-0	1-3	25.0	0.00
Newbury	1-9	0-2	0-0	0-0	1-7	11.1	0.00
Carlisle	1-14	0-6	0-3	0-0	1-5	7.1	- 9.67
Ascot	1-17	1-3	0-3	0-0	0-11	5.9	- 13.25

Haydock	0-16	Chester	0-7	Salisbury	0-2
Goodwood	0-13	Epsom	0-7	Bath	0-1
Sandown	0-9	Folkestone	0-3	Kempton	0-1

WINNING HORSES

	Age	Races Run	1st	2nd	3rd	Unpl	Win £
Mister Baileys	3	4	1	0	1	2	131,948
Quick Ransom	6	6	1	2	0	3	62,869
Double Blue	5	17	6	4	2	5	39,418
Millstream	2	6	3	0	1	2	31,889
Star Rage	4	27	9	7	5	6	29,138
Caerphilly	2	7	2	1	1	3	27,953
Surprise Guest	3	20	6	2	3	9	22,528
Branston Abby	5	13	2	1	1	9	18,818
Ashgore	4	11	4	3	1	3	16,551
Jural	2	3	2	1	0	0	16,337
King Rat	3	18	4	4	2	8	14,918
Double Eclipse	2	2	2	0	0	0	13,333
Argyle Cavalier	4	18	4	2	5	7	12,165
Milngavie	4	26	4	5	6	11	12,060
Noosa	2	7	3	3	0	1	11,830
Russian Heroine	2	10	3	1	0	6	10,600
Jubran	8	14	2	1	2	9	9,902
Happy Hostage	3	14	3	2	5	4	9,818
Tiler	2	6	2	0	0	4	9,245
Can Can Charlie	4	19	3	4	1	11	9,131
Arak	6	7	2	0	0	5	7,881
Percy Braithwaite	2	6	2	0	1	3	7,639
Muzz	3	15	2	2	2	9	7,213
Ewald	6	7	2	1	1	3	6,941
Cavers Yangous	3	9	2	1	1	5	6,920
Rose Chime	2	10	3	0	1	6	6,855
Here Comes Risky	2	7	2	1	1	3	6,400
Miss Ritz	4	7	2	2	0	3	6,394
Croft Imperial	7	7	2	1	4	0	6,182
Indian Wedding	2	4	2	2	0	0	6,018
Wild Rose Of York	3	8	2	0	1	5	5,874
It's So Easy	3	9	2	1	0	6	5,829
Hinari Video	9	12	2	0	2	8	5,772
Double Quick	2	2	1	1	0	0	4,659
Encore Une Fois	5	8	1	0	0	7	3,834
Just Buy Baileys	2	3	1	0	1	1	3,379
Magic Times	3	5	1	0	0	4	3,366
Indian Crystal	3	14	1	1	2	10	3,348
Baileys Sunset	2	10	1	1	2	6	3,266
Loveyoumillions	2	5	1	2	0	2	3,266
Pretonic	6	7	1	1	1	4	3,080
Truben	5	3	1	0	1	1	3,028
Potsclose	3	9	1	2	1	5	2,979
Another Baileys	2	9	1	1	0	7	2,888
Deano's Beeno	2	3	1	1	1	0	2,838
Level Edge	3	7	1	1	0	5	2,759
Three Arch Bridge	2	6	1	1	1	3	2,746
Ruby Estate	3	9	1	6	0	2	2,669
Robbies Rainbow	3	9	1	2	2	4	2,659
Can She Can Can	2	4	1	1	1	1	2,642
North Ardar	4	10	1	2	1	6	2,553
Water Bebe	2	8	1	1	0	6	2,434
Euchan Falls	2	3	1	0	1	1	2,249
Benjarong	2	9	1	0	1	7	2,232

WINNING OWNERS

	Races Won	Value £		Races Won	Value £
G R Bailey Ltd (Horse Feed)	3	138,102	Julian Clopet	2	7,213
Sheikh Mohammed	7	76,179	F Leithead	2	6,920
J S Morrison	4	72,686	Mrs Margaret Pett	2	6,400
J David Abell	15	57,480	Mrs D R Schreiber	2	6,394
R W Huggins	7	44,077	M G Michaels	2	5,829
M Doyle	7	25,794	Mark Johnston Racing Ltd	2	5,772
The Middleham Partnership	4	19,351	Alex Penman	2	5,260
Mrs Elke Scullion	4	16,843	S & G Gutters	1	3,834
Brian Yeardley Continental Ltd	5	16,593	Phil Riley	1	3,379
Harvey Ashworth	4	16,551	C H Greensit	1	3,366
The 2nd Kingsley House P'ship	4	14,918	Duke Of Roxburghe	1	2,979
E H Jones (Paints) Ltd	4	12,165	Paul Dean	1	2,838
A S Robertson	4	12,060	B Coulthard	1	2,759
Mrs R J Daniels	3	11,830	R N Pennell	1	2,746
A W Robinson	4	11,773	Greenland Park Ltd	1	2,659
The Knavesmire Partnership	3	10,600	L Webster	1	2,553
Mrs B A Matthews	3	9,530	The 3rd Kingsley House		
Mrs C Robinson	2	9,245	1994 P'ship	1	2,434
D Crossland	2	7,881	R B Johnstone & R Bell	1	2,249

Favourites	49-140	35.0%	- 0.87	
Longest winning sequence			6	
Longest losing sequence			47	
1993 Form	77-519	14.8%	- 85.92	
1992 Form	53-400	13.3%	+ 2.87	

Total winning prize-money		£659,242
Average SP of winner		4.2/1
Return on stakes invested		-7.9%
1991 Form	31-287	10.8% -116.01
1990 Form	28-261	10.7% - 4.63

A P JONES (Eastbury, Berks)

	No. of Horses	Races Run	1st	2nd	3rd	Unpl	Per cent	£1 Level Stake
2-y-o	0	0	0	0	0	0	-	0.00
3-y-o	0	0	0	0	0	0	-	0.00
4-y-o+	4	38	3	6	4	25	7.9	- 12.00
Totals	4	38	3	6	4	25	7.9	- 12.00

Jan	Feb	Mar	Apr	May	Jun	Jul	Aug	Sep	Oct/Nov
0-1	0-1	0-2	0-4	1-5	0-3	0-8	0-8	1-3	1-3

Winning Jockey	W-R	£1 Level Stake			W-R	£1 Level Stake
J Williams	3-16	+ 10.00				

Winning Courses						
Chepstow	1-4	+ 3.00	Bath		1-11	- 5.00
Goodwood	1-4	+ 9.00				

Winning Horse	Age	Races Run	1st	2nd	3rd	Unpl	Win £
Kildee Lad	4	18	3	3	3	9	10,434

Favourites	1-6	16.7%	+ 1.00	Total winning prize-money			£10,434

1993 Form	3-49	6.1%	- 10.00	1991 Form	0-4
1992 Form	0-29				

BOB JONES (Newmarket)

	No. of Horses	Races Run	1st	2nd	3rd	Unpl	Per cent	£1 Level Stake
2-y-o	7	21	1	2	2	16	4.8	- 8.00
3-y-o	2	10	1	1	0	8	10.0	+ 1.00
4-y-o+	7	47	6	4	4	33	12.8	+ 11.00
Totals	16	78	8	7	6	57	10.3	+ 4.00

Jan	Feb	Mar	Apr	May	Jun	Jul	Aug	Sep	Oct/Nov
2-6	0-5	0-3	0-4	0-7	2-9	1-8	2-8	0-12	1-16

Winning Jockeys	W-R	£1 Level Stake		W-R	£1 Level Stake
M Wigham	5-38	+ 1.00	Miss D J Jones	1-6	+ 11.00
C Hodgson	1-5	+ 8.00	G Duffield	1-6	+ 7.00

Winning Courses					
Brighton	2-7	+ 12.50	York	1-3	+ 2.50
Newmarket	2-14	+ 2.00	Lingfield (AW)	1-5	+ 6.00
Warwick	1-2	+ 11.00	Southwell (AW)	1-6	+ 11.00

Winning Horses	Age	Races Run	1st	2nd	3rd	Unpl	Win £
Lookingforarainbow	6	15	3	1	1	10	15,252
Jack Button	5	15	1	3	2	9	5,483
Canovas Heart	5	5	1	0	1	3	4,013
Komplicity	3	8	1	1	0	6	3,085
Anniversaire	4	7	1	0	0	6	2,243
The Scythian	2	3	1	0	0	2	2,174

Favourites	0-2		Total winning prize-money		£32,249

1993 Form	13-128	10.2%	- 50.72	1991 Form	4-52	7.7%	- 4.00
1992 Form	11-100	11.0%	- 18.75				

D HAYDN JONES (Pontypridd, Mid-Glamorgan)

	No. of Horses	Races Run	1st	2nd	3rd	Unpl	Per cent	£1 Level Stake
2-y-o	6	36	2	4	6	24	5.6	- 9.00
3-y-o	4	20	5	2	3	10	25.0	+ 23.00
4-y-o+	9	67	4	6	8	49	6.0	- 37.00
Totals	19	123	11	12	17	83	8.9	- 23.00

BY MONTH

2-y-o	W-R	Per cent	£1 Level Stake	3-y-o	W-R	Per cent	£1 Level Stake
January	0-0	-	0.00	January	0-0	-	0.00
February	0-0	-	0.00	February	0-0	-	0.00
March	0-1	-	- 1.00	March	0-0	-	0.00
April	0-1	-	- 1.00	April	0-1	-	- 1.00
May	0-2	-	- 2.00	May	2-5	40.0	+ 10.00
June	0-4	-	- 4.00	June	1-3	33.3	+ 5.00
July	0-5	-	- 5.00	July	0-2	-	- 2.00
August	1-8	12.5	+ 13.00	August	1-4	25.0	+ 9.00
September	0-7	-	- 7.00	September	1-4	25.0	+ 3.00
Oct/Nov	1-8	12.5	- 2.00	Oct/Nov	0-1	-	- 1.00

4-y-o+	W-R	Per cent	£1 Level Stake	Totals	W-R	Per cent	£1 Level Stake
January	1-6	16.7	- 1.50	January	1-6	16.7	- 1.50
February	1-6	16.7	- 1.50	February	1-6	16.7	- 1.50
March	0-2	-	- 2.00	March	0-3	-	- 3.00
April	0-6	-	- 6.00	April	0-8	-	- 8.00
May	0-11	-	- 11.00	May	2-18	11.1	- 3.00
June	0-10	-	- 10.00	June	1-17	5.9	- 9.00
July	2-7	28.6	+ 14.00	July	2-14	14.3	+ 7.00
August	0-9	-	- 9.00	August	2-21	9.5	+ 13.00
September	0-5	-	- 5.00	September	1-16	6.3	- 9.00
Oct/Nov	0-5	-	- 5.00	Oct/Nov	1-14	7.1	- 8.00

DISTANCE

2-y-o	W-R	Per cent	£1 Level Stake	3-y-o	W-R	Per cent	£1 Level Stake
5f-6f	1-25	4.0	- 19.00	5f-6f	3-11	27.3	+ 16.50
7f-8f	1-10	10.0	+ 11.00	7f-8f	2-9	22.2	+ 6.50
9f-13f	0-1	-	- 1.00	9f-13f	0-0	-	0.00
14f+	0-0	-	0.00	14f+	0-0	-	0.00

4-y-o+	W-R	Per cent	£1 Level Stake	Totals	W-R	Per cent	£1 Level Stake
5f-6f	0-5	-	- 5.00	5f-6f	4-41	9.8	- 7.50
7f-8f	2-24	8.3	- 11.50	7f-8f	5-43	11.6	+ 6.00
9f-13f	2-28	7.1	- 10.50	9f-13f	2-29	6.9	- 11.50
14f+	0-10	-	- 10.00	14f+	0-10	-	- 10.00

TYPE OF RACE

Non-Handicaps	W-R	Per cent	£1 Level Stake	Handicaps	W-R	Per cent	£1 Level Stake
2-y-o	2-23	8.7	+ 4.00	2-y-o	0-7	-	- 7.00
3-y-o	2-6	33.3	+ 8.50	3-y-o	3-12	25.0	+ 16.50
4-y-o+	1-8	12.5	0.00	4-y-o+	3-55	5.5	- 33.00
Selling	0-8	-	- 8.00	Selling	0-1	-	- 1.00
Apprentice	0-0	-	0.00	Apprentice	0-3	-	- 3.00
Amat/Ladies	0-0	-	0.00	Amat/Ladies	0-0	-	0.00
Totals	5-45	11.1	+ 4.50	Totals	6-78	7.7	- 27.50

COURSE GRADE

	W-R	Per cent	£1 Level Stake
Group 1	1-17	5.9	- 11.00
Group 2	0-10	-	- 10.00
Group 3	1-29	3.4	- 21.00
Group 4	9-67	13.4	+ 19.00

FIRST TIME OUT

	W-R	Per cent	£1 Level Stake
2-y-o	0-6	-	- 6.00
3-y-o	1-4	25.0	+ 3.50
4-y-o+	0-9	-	- 9.00
Totals	1-19	5.3	- 11.50

JOCKEYS RIDING

	W-R	Per cent	£1 Level Stake		W-R	Per cent	£1 Level Stake
A Mackay	7-67	10.4	+ 8.50	D Harrison	1-5	20.0	+ 3.00
J Williams	2-12	16.7	- 3.00	D Holland	1-10	10.0	- 2.50

R Cochrane	0-7	D Gibbs	0-1	R Painter	0-1
D Wright	0-6	D Griffiths	0-1	S Drowne	0-1
J Reid	0-2	L Dettori	0-1	S Lanigan	0-1
S Whitworth	0-2	N Carlisle	0-1	S Mulvey	0-1
W Newnes	0-2	Paul Eddery	0-1	T Williams	0-1

COURSE RECORD

	Total W-R	Non-Handicaps 2-y-o	3-y-o+	Handicaps 2-y-o	3-y-o+	Per cent	£1 Level Stake
Wolverhampton (AW)	5-35	1-7	0-2	0-0	4-26	14.3	+ 21.00
Southwell (AW)	4-29	0-7	3-6	0-0	1-16	13.8	+ 1.00
Doncaster	1-4	1-1	0-0	0-2	0-1	25.0	+ 2.00
Nottingham	1-7	0-1	0-0	0-1	1-5	14.3	+ 1.00

Bath	0-6	Haydock	0-4	Lingfield	0-2
Leicester	0-6	Salisbury	0-4	Thirsk	0-2
Windsor	0-6	Ascot	0-2	Goodwood	0-1
Newbury	0-5	Chester	0-2	Kempton	0-1
Chepstow	0-4	Folkestone	0-2	Warwick	0-1

WINNING HORSES

	Age	Races Run	1st	2nd	3rd	Unpl	Win £
Belleminette	3	8	2	1	0	5	6,808
Premier Dance	7	13	2	2	2	7	5,797
Delrob	3	9	2	1	3	3	5,441
Q Factor	2	10	1	2	4	3	3,317
Dawalib	4	15	1	0	3	11	2,905
Quinzii Martin	6	12	1	1	2	8	2,781
Bex Hill	2	7	1	0	1	5	2,740
Keramic	3	2	1	0	0	1	2,249

WINNING OWNERS

	Races Won	Value £		Races Won	Value £
J S Fox & Sons	3	8,537	Monolithic Refractories Ltd	2	5,030
Mrs Judy Mihalop	2	6,808	H G Collis	1	3,317
Mrs E M Haydn Jones	2	5,441	R Howard Thomas	1	2,905

Favourites	2-6	33.3%	+ 4.50	Total winning prize-money	£32,037
Longest winning sequence			1	Average SP of winner	8.1/1
Longest losing sequence			25	Return on stakes invested	-18.7%
1993 Form	9-141	6.4%	- 66.25	1991 Form	2-131	1.5%	-109.50
1992 Form	5-153	3.3%	- 83.50	1990 Form	7-159	4.4%	-114.62

H THOMSON JONES (Newmarket)

	No. of Horses	Races Run	1st	2nd	3rd	Unpl	Per cent	£1 Level Stake
2-y-o	22	53	16	11	4	22	30.2	+ 34.53
3-y-o	25	141	20	27	23	71	14.2	+ 43.30
4-y-o+	0	0	0	0	0	0	–	0.00
Totals	47	194	36	38	27	93	18.6	+ 77.83

BY MONTH

2-y-o	W-R	Per cent	£1 Level Stake	3-y-o	W-R	Per cent	£1 Level Stake
Mar/Apr	0-0	–	0.00	Mar/Apr	1-7	14.3	+ 14.00
May	0-1	–	- 1.00	May	6-27	22.2	+ 19.00
June	0-4	–	- 4.00	June	3-27	11.1	- 9.37
July	0-0	–	0.00	July	2-17	11.8	+ 6.00
August	5-8	62.5	+ 7.92	August	3-23	13.0	- 9.33
September	9-22	40.9	+ 43.55	September	3-29	10.3	+ 16.00
Oct/Nov	2-18	11.1	- 11.94	Oct/Nov	2-11	18.2	+ 7.00

4-y-o+	W-R	Per cent	£1 Level Stake	Totals	W-R	Per cent	£1 Level Stake
Mar/Apr	0-0	-	0.00	Mar/Apr	1-7	14.3	+ 14.00
May	0-0	-	0.00	May	6-28	21.4	+ 18.00
June	0-0	-	0.00	June	3-31	9.7	- 13.37
July	0-0	-	0.00	July	2-17	11.8	+ 6.00
August	0-0	-	0.00	August	8-31	25.8	- 1.41
September	0-0	-	0.00	September	12-51	23.5	+ 59.55
Oct/Nov	0-0	-	0.00	Oct/Nov	4-29	13.8	- 4.94

DISTANCE

2-y-o	W-R	Per cent	£1 Level Stake	3-y-o	W-R	Per cent	£1 Level Stake
5f-6f	9-34	26.5	+ 27.40	5f-6f	4-26	15.4	- 5.37
7f-8f	7-19	36.8	+ 7.13	7f-8f	10-67	14.9	+ 14.67
9f-13f	0-0	-	0.00	9f-13f	6-43	14.0	+ 39.00
14f+	0-0	-	0.00	14f+	0-5	-	- 5.00

4-y-o+	W-R	Per cent	£1 Level Stake	Totals	W-R	Per cent	£1 Level Stake
5f-6f	0-0	-	0.00	5f-6f	13-60	21.7	+ 22.03
7f-8f	0-0	-	0.00	7f-8f	17-86	19.8	+ 21.80
9f-13f	0-0	-	0.00	9f-13f	6-43	14.0	+ 39.00
14f+	0-0	-	0.00	14f+	0-5	-	- 5.00

TYPE OF RACE

Non-Handicaps	W-R	Per cent	£1 Level Stake	Handicaps	W-R	Per cent	£1 Level Stake
2-y-o	15-50	30.0	+ 11.53	2-y-o	1-3	33.3	+ 23.00
3-y-o	11-71	15.5	+ 39.30	3-y-o	8-65	12.3	+ 5.00
4-y-o+	0-0	-	0.00	4-y-o+	0-0	-	0.00
Selling	0-0	-	0.00	Selling	0-0	-	0.00
Apprentice	1-1	100.0	+ 3.00	Apprentice	0-4	-	- 4.00
Amat/Ladies	0-0	-	0.00	Amat/Ladies	0-0	-	0.00
Totals	27-122	22.1	+ 53.83	Totals	9-72	12.5	+ 24.00

COURSE GRADE

	W-R	Per cent	£1 Level Stake
Group 1	18-91	19.8	+ 63.73
Group 2	6-37	16.2	+ 2.88
Group 3	9-55	16.4	+ 12.92
Group 4	3-11	27.3	- 1.70

FIRST TIME OUT

	W-R	Per cent	£1 Level Stake
2-y-o	7-22	31.8	+ 8.84
3-y-o	5-25	20.0	+ 29.63
4-y-o+	0-0	-	0.00
Totals	12-47	25.5	+ 38.47

Jones H Thomson

JOCKEYS RIDING

	W-R	Per cent	£1 Level Stake		W-R	Per cent	£1 Level Stake
R Hills	26-132	19.7	+ 66.32	W Ryan	1-2	50.0	+ 10.00
N Carlisle	4-20	20.0	+ 22.00	Catherine Cooper	1-10	10.0	- 6.00
K Darley	2-3	66.7	+ 4.38	W Carson	1-11	9.1	- 5.50
G Bardwell	1-1	100.0	+ 1.63				

M Roberts	0-3	Graham Thorner	0-1	Paul Eddery	0-1
B Raymond	0-2	M Birch	0-1	R Cochrane	0-1
G Duffield	0-2	M Hills	0-1	R Price	0-1
D Biggs	0-1	P Robinson	0-1		

COURSE RECORD

	Total W-R	Non-Handicaps 2-y-o	3-y-o+	Handicaps 2-y-o	3-y-o+	Per cent	£1 Level Stake
Kempton	4-11	2-3	0-4	1-1	1-3	36.4	+ 27.17
Newmarket	4-20	1-4	1-9	0-1	2-6	20.0	+ 13.33
Newcastle	3-4	1-1	1-1	0-0	1-2	75.0	+ 15.00
Bath	2-5	0-1	1-1	0-0	1-3	40.0	+ 22.50
Lingfield	2-6	1-1	0-3	0-0	1-2	33.3	+ 12.00
Haydock	2-7	0-2	2-2	0-0	0-3	28.6	+ 8.00
Redcar	2-7	2-3	0-2	0-0	0-2	28.6	- 3.12
Pontefract	2-10	2-4	0-2	0-0	0-4	20.0	- 6.83
Ascot	2-14	2-3	0-3	0-1	0-7	14.3	- 6.77
Doncaster	2-14	1-3	1-5	0-0	0-6	14.3	+ 20.00
Edinburgh	1-1	0-0	1-1	0-0	0-0	100.0	+ 1.63
Ayr	1-2	1-1	0-0	0-0	0-1	50.0	+ 6.00
Folkestone	1-3	1-1	0-0	0-0	0-2	33.3	+ 2.00
Warwick	1-4	0-0	1-3	0-0	0-1	25.0	- 2.33
Beverley	1-5	0-1	1-4	0-0	0-0	20.0	+ 1.00
Windsor	1-5	0-1	1-3	0-0	0-1	20.0	+ 8.00
Leicester	1-6	1-4	0-2	0-0	0-0	16.7	- 2.75
Nottingham	1-6	0-1	0-1	0-0	1-4	16.7	+ 5.00
Thirsk	1-6	0-1	0-3	0-0	1-2	16.7	+ 1.00
Salisbury	1-7	0-2	1-5	0-0	0-0	14.3	+ 4.00
Yarmouth	1-15	0-6	1-5	0-0	0-4	6.7	- 11.00

Newbury	0-7	Catterick	0-3	York	0-2
Chester	0-6	Ripon	0-3	Chepstow	0-1
Sandown	0-6	Brighton	0-2		
Goodwood	0-4	Hamilton	0-2		

WINNING HORSES

	Age	Races Run	1st	2nd	3rd	Unpl	Win £
Mamlakah	2	4	3	0	0	1	35,345
Bintalshaati	3	6	2	2	0	2	24,570
Hiwaya	2	5	4	1	0	0	23,240
Estimraar	3	8	3	0	2	3	17,735
Elrafa Ah	3	8	1	4	1	2	11,254

				Jones	H	Thomson	
Kayrawan	2	1	1	0	0	0	10,411
Marha	2	3	1	1	0	1	10,312
Alami	2	4	2	0	1	1	9,670
Ethbaat	3	5	2	1	0	2	8,975
Sherman	3	6	1	1	1	3	8,415
Nizaal	3	5	1	0	0	4	6,837
Kabil	2	6	1	1	0	4	4,858
Iradah	3	6	2	0	1	3	4,615
Bumaan	3	4	1	1	0	2	4,568
Tanseeq	3	6	1	0	1	4	4,276
Haddeyah	2	1	1	0	0	0	4,272
Alsakb	3	5	1	0	1	3	3,926
Shemaq	2	1	1	0	0	0	3,824
Bahith	2	2	1	1	0	0	3,813
Shafi	3	8	1	1	2	4	3,725
Sabayik	3	4	1	0	1	2	3,721
Balaabel	3	8	1	4	2	1	3,686
Sayeh	2	2	1	1	0	0	3,273
Ijlal	3	7	1	2	2	2	3,141
Watheeqah	3	6	1	0	1	4	3,132

WINNING OWNERS

	Races Won	Value £		Races Won	Value £
Hamdan Al-Maktoum	34	208,907	Khalil Al Sayegh	1	4,272
Mrs H T Jones	1	8,415			

Favourites	10-33	30.3%	- 9.50	Total winning prize-money	£221,595
Longest winning sequence			3	Average SP of winner	6.6/1
Longest losing sequence			22	Return on stakes invested	40.1%
1993 Form	28-181	15.5%	- 30.39	1991 Form	37-190	19.5%	+ 25.39
1992 Form	27-188	14.4%	- 33.53	1990 Form	34-209	16.3%	- 13.92

T M JONES (Guildford, Surrey)

	No. of Horses	Races Run	1st	2nd	3rd	Unpl	Per cent	£1 Level Stake
2-y-o	4	15	0	0	0	15	-	- 15.00
3-y-o	3	26	1	3	4	18	3.8	- 18.00
4-y-o+	1	1	0	0	0	1	-	- 1.00
Totals	8	42	1	3	4	34	2.4	- 34.00

Jan	Feb	Mar	Apr	May	Jun	Jul	Aug	Sep	Oct/Nov
0-1	0-1	0-3	0-3	0-5	1-8	0-9	0-4	0-3	0-5

Winning Jockey	W-R	£1 Level Stake	Winning Course	W-R	£1 Level Stake
R Perham	1-32	- 24.00	Lingfield	1-4	+ 4.00

Winning Horse	Age	Races Run	1st	2nd	3rd	Unpl	Win £
Rambold	3	10	1	1	0	8	3,465

Favourites	0-0			Total winning prize-money			£3,465
1993 Form	3-26	11.5%	+ 26.00	1991 Form	0-14		
1992 Form	0-12			1990 Form	2-30	6.7%	- 4.00

T THOMSON JONES (Upper Lambourn, Berks)

	No. of Horses	Races Run	1st	2nd	3rd	Unpl	Per cent	£1 Level Stake
2-y-o	4	10	1	1	1	7	10.0	- 5.67
3-y-o	5	25	0	2	2	21	-	- 25.00
4-y-o+	4	20	1	3	2	14	5.0	- 7.00
Totals	13	55	2	6	5	42	3.6	- 37.67

Jan	Feb	Mar	Apr	May	Jun	Jul	Aug	Sep	Oct/Nov
0-2	0-2	0-1	0-2	1-8	1-13	0-7	0-8	0-6	0-6

Winning Jockeys	W-R	£1 Level Stake		W-R	£1 Level Stake
D McKeown	1-4	+ 9.00	W Carson	1-6	- 1.67

Winning Courses					
Thirsk	1-3	+ 10.00	Windsor	1-3	+ 1.33

Winning Horses	Age	Races Run	1st	2nd	3rd	Unpl	Win £
High Summer	4	4	1	0	0	3	4,794
Masruf	2	4	1	1	1	1	4,150

Favourites	1-3	33.3%	+ 1.33	Total winning prize-money			£8,944
1993 Form	11-91	12.1%	- 21.41	1991 Form	7-106	6.6%	- 38.50
1992 Form	5-86	5.8%	- 42.00	1990 Form	8-131	6.1%	- 84.11

MISS GAY KELLEWAY (Newmarket)

	No. of Horses	Races Run	1st	2nd	3rd	Unpl	Per cent	£1 Level Stake
2-y-o	12	43	6	8	6	23	14.0	+ 9.75
3-y-o	6	16	1	0	2	13	6.3	- 11.00
4-y-o+	12	70	8	4	5	53	11.4	- 5.25
Totals	30	129	15	12	13	89	11.6	- 6.50

BY MONTH

2-y-o	W-R	Per cent	£1 Level Stake	3-y-o	W-R	Per cent	£1 Level Stake
January	0-0	-	0.00	January	0-1	-	- 1.00
February	0-0	-	0.00	February	0-0	-	0.00
March	0-3	-	- 3.00	March	0-0	-	0.00
April	0-3	-	- 3.00	April	0-4	-	- 4.00
May	2-6	33.3	+ 6.50	May	0-1	-	- 1.00
June	1-10	10.0	+ 3.00	June	0-2	-	- 2.00
July	0-4	-	- 4.00	July	0-4	-	- 4.00
August	0-3	-	- 3.00	August	1-4	25.0	+ 1.00
September	1-6	16.7	- 2.75	September	0-0	-	0.00
Oct/Nov	2-8	25.0	+ 16.00	Oct/Nov	0-0	-	0.00

4-y-o+	W-R	Per cent	£1 Level Stake	Totals	W-R	Per cent	£1 Level Stake
January	0-1	-	- 1.00	January	0-2	-	- 2.00
February	0-1	-	- 1.00	February	0-1	-	- 1.00
March	0-1	-	- 1.00	March	0-4	-	- 4.00
April	1-8	12.5	+ 9.00	April	1-15	6.7	+ 2.00
May	3-17	17.6	+ 10.00	May	5-24	20.8	+ 15.50
June	3-14	21.4	+ 2.25	June	4-26	15.4	+ 3.25
July	0-7	-	- 7.00	July	0-15	-	- 15.00
August	1-9	11.1	- 4.50	August	2-16	12.5	- 6.50
September	0-4	-	- 4.00	September	1-10	10.0	- 6.75
Oct/Nov	0-8	-	- 8.00	Oct/Nov	2-16	12.5	+ 8.00

DISTANCE

2-y-o	W-R	Per cent	£1 Level Stake	3-y-o	W-R	Per cent	£1 Level Stake
5f-6f	6-36	16.7	+ 16.75	5f-6f	0-2	-	- 2.00
7f-8f	0-7	-	- 7.00	7f-8f	0-10	-	- 10.00
9f-13f	0-0	-	0.00	9f-13f	0-3	-	- 3.00
14f+	0-0	-	0.00	14f+	1-1	100.0	+ 4.00

4-y-o+	W-R	Per cent	£1 Level Stake	Totals	W-R	Per cent	£1 Level Stake
5f-6f	1-5	20.0	+ 12.00	5f-6f	7-43	16.3	+ 26.75
7f-8f	2-26	7.7	- 16.25	7f-8f	2-43	4.7	- 33.25
9f-13f	5-31	16.1	+ 7.00	9f-13f	5-34	14.7	+ 4.00
14f+	0-8	-	- 8.00	14f+	1-9	11.1	- 4.00

TYPE OF RACE

Non-Handicaps	W-R	Per cent	£1 Level Stake	Handicaps	W-R	Per cent	£1 Level Stake
2-y-o	4-30	13.3	- 1.25	2-y-o	2-9	22.2	+ 15.00
3-y-o	0-5	-	- 5.00	3-y-o	0-8	-	- 8.00
4-y-o+	1-13	7.7	- 8.50	4-y-o+	7-49	14.3	+ 11.25
Selling	1-8	12.5	- 3.00	Selling	0-0	-	0.00
Apprentice	0-0	-	0.00	Apprentice	0-2	-	- 2.00
Amat/Ladies	0-0	-	0.00	Amat/Ladies	0-5	-	- 5.00
Totals	6-56	10.7	- 17.75	Totals	9-73	12.3	+ 11.25

COURSE GRADE

	W-R	Per cent	£1 Level Stake
Group 1	3-49	6.1	- 18.00
Group 2	4-17	23.5	+ 1.50
Group 3	4-31	12.9	+ 13.00
Group 4	4-32	12.5	- 3.00

FIRST TIME OUT

	W-R	Per cent	£1 Level Stake
2-y-o	0-10	-	- 10.00
3-y-o	0-6	-	- 6.00
4-y-o+	2-11	18.2	+ 17.00
Totals	2-27	7.4	+ 1.00

JOCKEYS RIDING

	W-R	Per cent	£1 Level Stake		W-R	Per cent	£1 Level Stake
R Cochrane	4-19	21.1	+ 12.25	T Williams	1-3	33.3	+ 8.00
A Munro	3-13	23.1	+ 5.25	D Holland	1-4	25.0	- 1.50
A Mackay	3-26	11.5	- 5.50	G Duffield	1-7	14.3	+ 2.00
L Charnock	1-1	100.0	+ 12.00	Stephen Davies	1-19	5.3	- 2.00

Miss L Vollaro	0-3	D Wright	0-1	Miss L Hide	0-1
W Carson	0-3	G Bardwell	0-1	Ms C Germann	0-1
J Lowe	0-2	J Reid	0-1	Paul Eddery	0-1
Justine Reader	0-2	J Tate	0-1	S Drowne	0-1
K Darley	0-2	J Weaver	0-1	T Quinn	0-1
K Fallon	0-2	L Dettori	0-1	W Newnes	0-1
Pat Eddery	0-2	M Birch	0-1	W R Swinburn	0-1
B Raymond	0-1	M J Kinane	0-1	W Woods	0-1
D McCabe	0-1	M Tebbutt	0-1		
D McKeown	0-1	M Wigham	0-1		

COURSE RECORD

	Total W-R	Non-Handicaps 2-y-o	3-y-o+	Handicaps 2-y-o	3-y-o+	Per cent	£1 Level Stake
Lingfield	3-6	3-3	0-0	0-0	0-3	50.0	+ 9.75
Warwick	2-2	0-0	0-0	0-0	2-2	100.0	+ 13.50
Newbury	2-3	0-1	0-0	1-1	1-1	66.7	+ 15.00
Beverley	2-7	1-2	1-1	0-0	0-4	28.6	+ 11.00
Pontefract	1-3	0-1	0-0	0-1	1-1	33.3	+ 6.00
Brighton	1-6	0-1	0-0	0-1	1-4	16.7	- 3.25
Lingfield (AW)	1-7	0-0	0-3	0-0	1-4	14.3	+ 2.00
Wolverhampton (AW)	1-7	0-1	1-2	0-0	0-4	14.3	- 2.50
Nottingham	1-10	0-3	0-0	0-0	1-7	10.0	+ 7.00
Newmarket	1-26	0-6	0-4	1-3	0-13	3.8	- 13.00

Southwell (AW)	0-7	Leicester	0-4	Carlisle	0-1
Yarmouth	0-6	Catterick	0-2	Chester	0-1
Doncaster	0-5	Epsom	0-2	Edinburgh	0-1
Folkestone	0-5	Haydock	0-2	Hamilton	0-1
Kempton	0-5	Salisbury	0-2	Redcar	0-1
Ascot	0-4	Sandown	0-2	Ripon	0-1

WINNING HORSES

	Age	Races Run	1st	2nd	3rd	Unpl	Win £
Wardara	2	3	2	0	0	1	14,208
Fajjoura	2	7	2	0	1	4	12,798
Father Dan	5	9	2	2	0	5	6,602
Castel Rosselo	4	8	1	1	0	6	6,073
Charlie Bigtime	4	15	2	0	1	12	5,487
Jobran	2	7	1	4	1	1	3,570
Sylvania	4	5	1	0	0	4	3,287
Mehtar	2	5	1	1	2	1	2,986
Lavender Cottage	4	9	1	1	2	5	2,925
Bobby Blue	3	3	1	0	1	1	2,785
Inderaputeri	4	10	1	0	1	8	2,050

WINNING OWNERS

	Races Won	Value £		Races Won	Value £
Miss Jo Crowley	3	16,993	Sheikh Khalifa	1	3,570
Sheikh Ahmad Yousuf Al Sabah	3	15,784	Graham Mitchell	1	3,287
Ron Dawson	4	14,484	H R H Sultan Ahmad Shah	1	2,050
Stanley Squires	2	6,602			

Favourites	3-12	25.0%	+ 2.00	Total winning prize-money	£62,770
Longest winning sequence			2	Average SP of winner	7.2/1
Longest losing sequence			26	Return on stakes invested	-4.7%
1993 Form	12-98	12.2%	- 13.70	1992 Form	0-75

P A KELLEWAY (Newmarket)

	No. of Horses	Races Run	1st	2nd	3rd	Unpl	Per cent	£1 Level Stake
2-y-o	9	26	2	3	1	20	7.7	- 11.00
3-y-o	8	46	4	8	6	28	8.7	- 9.00
4-y-o+	4	21	4	3	1	13	19.0	+ 5.00
Totals	21	93	10	14	8	61	10.8	- 15.00

BY MONTH

2-y-o	W-R	Per cent	£1 Level Stake	3-y-o	W-R	Per cent	£1 Level Stake
January	0-0	-	0.00	January	0-1	-	- 1.00
February	0-0	-	0.00	February	1-3	33.3	+ 1.00
March	0-0	-	0.00	March	0-3	-	- 3.00
April	0-1	-	- 1.00	April	1-9	11.1	+ 6.00
May	0-5	-	- 5.00	May	0-7	-	- 7.00
June	1-5	20.0	+ 8.00	June	1-5	20.0	+ 3.00
July	0-4	-	- 4.00	July	0-7	-	- 7.00
August	1-3	33.3	- 1.00	August	1-6	16.7	+ 4.00
September	0-4	-	- 4.00	September	0-2	-	- 2.00
Oct/Nov	0-4	-	- 4.00	Oct/Nov	0-3	-	- 3.00

4-y-o+	W-R	Per cent	£1 Level Stake	Totals	W-R	Per cent	£1 Level Stake
January	2-4	50.0	+ 4.00	January	2-5	40.0	+ 3.00
February	1-5	20.0	- 2.00	February	2-8	25.0	- 1.00
March	0-4	-	- 4.00	March	0-7	-	- 7.00
April	0-1	-	- 1.00	April	1-11	9.1	+ 4.00
May	0-3	-	- 3.00	May	0-15	-	- 15.00
June	1-3	33.3	+ 12.00	June	3-13	23.1	+ 23.00
July	0-0	-	0.00	July	0-11	-	- 11.00
August	0-1	-	- 1.00	August	2-10	20.0	+ 2.00
September	0-0	-	0.00	September	0-6	-	- 6.00
Oct/Nov	0-0	-	0.00	Oct/Nov	0-7	-	- 7.00

DISTANCE

2-y-o	W-R	Per cent	£1 Level Stake	3-y-o	W-R	Per cent	£1 Level Stake
5f-6f	1-11	9.1	+ 2.00	5f-6f	0-3	-	- 3.00
7f-8f	1-14	7.1	- 12.00	7f-8f	1-14	7.1	- 6.00
9f-13f	0-1	-	- 1.00	9f-13f	3-29	10.3	0.00
14f+	0-0	-	0.00	14f+	0-0	-	0.00

4-y-o+	W-R	Per cent	£1 Level Stake	Totals	W-R	Per cent	£1 Level Stake
5f-6f	0-0	-	0.00	5f-6f	1-14	7.1	- 1.00
7f-8f	0-2	-	- 2.00	7f-8f	2-30	6.7	- 20.00
9f-13f	3-14	21.4	- 3.00	9f-13f	6-44	13.6	- 4.00
14f+	1-5	20.0	+ 10.00	14f+	1-5	20.0	+ 10.00

TYPE OF RACE

Non-Handicaps	W-R	Per cent	£1 Level Stake	Handicaps	W-R	Per cent	£1 Level Stake
2-y-o	2-21	9.5	- 6.00	2-y-o	0-4	-	- 4.00
3-y-o	3-34	8.8	- 7.00	3-y-o	1-10	10.0	0.00
4-y-o+	1-6	16.7	+ 9.00	4-y-o+	3-13	23.1	- 2.00
Selling	0-1	-	- 1.00	Selling	0-0	-	0.00
Apprentice	0-0	-	0.00	Apprentice	0-2	-	- 2.00
Amat/Ladies	0-0	-	0.00	Amat/Ladies	0-2	-	- 2.00
Totals	6-62	9.7	- 5.00	Totals	4-31	12.9	- 10.00

COURSE GRADE

	W-R	Per cent	£1 Level Stake
Group 1	1-34	2.9	- 19.00
Group 2	1-8	12.5	- 6.00
Group 3	0-9	-	- 9.00
Group 4	8-42	19.0	+ 19.00

FIRST TIME OUT

	W-R	Per cent	£1 Level Stake
2-y-o	0-9	-	- 9.00
3-y-o	0-8	-	- 8.00
4-y-o+	1-4	25.0	+ 0.50
Totals	1-21	4.8	- 16.50

JOCKEYS RIDING

	W-R	Per cent	£1 Level Stake		W-R	Per cent	£1 Level Stake
Paul Eddery	4-15	26.7	- 2.00	Adelle Gibbons	1-5	20.0	+ 5.00
M Wigham	4-26	15.4	+ 14.00	D Harrison	1-7	14.3	+ 8.00

R Cochrane	0-6	C Asmussen	0-1	J Tate	0-1
T Quinn	0-6	C Avery	0-1	J Weaver	0-1
Stephen Davies	0-4	C Hodgson	0-1	L Dettori	0-1
J Quinn	0-3	D Holland	0-1	Miss S Kelleway	0-1
Pat Eddery	0-3	D McCabe	0-1	Mr T McCarthy	0-1
J Carroll	0-2	F Norton	0-1	W Carson	0-1
M Roberts	0-2	G Duffield	0-1	W Woods	0-1

COURSE RECORD

	Total W-R	Non-Handicaps 2-y-o	3-y-o+	Handicaps 2-y-o	3-y-o+	Per cent	£1 Level Stake
Southwell (AW)	4-16	1-5	2-5	0-0	1-6	25.0	+ 19.00
Lingfield (AW)	3-14	0-0	1-6	0-1	2-7	21.4	+ 8.50
Thirsk	1-1	1-1	0-0	0-0	0-0	100.0	+ 1.00
Haydock	1-3	0-0	1-3	0-0	0-0	33.3	+ 12.00
Wolverhampton (AW)	1-7	0-0	0-2	0-0	1-5	14.3	- 3.50

Newmarket	0-12	Brighton	0-2	Kempton	0-1
Ascot	0-4	Catterick	0-2	Leicester	0-1
Sandown	0-4	Chester	0-2	Nottingham	0-1
Yarmouth	0-4	Doncaster	0-2	Ripon	0-1
Hamilton	0-3	Epsom	0-2	Warwick	0-1
Newbury	0-3	Folkestone	0-2		
York	0-3	Lingfield	0-2		

WINNING HORSES

	Age	Races Run	1st	2nd	3rd	Unpl	Win £
Slight Risk	5	7	3	0	0	4	9,488
Risky Tu	3	10	2	1	2	5	5,277
Sunday News'N'Echo	3	11	1	2	1	7	3,493
Belle Genius	2	3	1	0	0	2	3,317
Dawn Rock	3	5	1	2	0	2	2,925
Abjar	4	4	1	0	0	3	2,768
My Lady Brady	2	6	1	2	0	3	2,613

WINNING OWNERS

	Races Won	Value £		Races Won	Value £
Mrs G E Kelleway	3	9,488	G Lang	1	2,925
Lewis H Norris	2	5,277	P A Kelleway	1	2,768
F M Kalla	1	3,493	T Brady	1	2,613
L J Rice	1	3,317			

Favourites	3-9	33.3%	0.00	Total winning prize-money		£29,881
Longest winning sequence			2	Average SP of winner		6.8/1
Longest losing sequence			20	Return on stakes invested		-16.1%
1993 Form	7-89	7.9%	- 15.00	1991 Form	13-156	8.3%	- 56.92
1992 Form	16-179	8.9%	- 58.72	1990 Form	8-170	4.7%	-123.20

W T KEMP (Duns, Borders)

	No. of Horses	Races Run	1st	2nd	3rd	Unpl	Per cent	£1 Level Stake
2-y-o	4	40	1	3	6	30	2.5	- 23.00
3-y-o	0	0	0	0	0	0	-	0.00
4-y-o+	2	16	2	0	1	13	12.5	+ 12.25
Totals	6	56	3	3	7	43	5.4	- 10.75

Jan	Feb	Mar	Apr	May	Jun	Jul	Aug	Sep	Oct/Nov
0-0	0-0	0-0	0-8	1-8	0-3	2-18	0-6	0-10	0-3

Winning Jockeys	W-R	£1 Level Stake			W-R	£1 Level Stake
J Weaver	2-7	+ 36.00	K Darley		1-2	+ 0.25

Winning Courses						
Edinburgh	2-17	+ 11.25	Hamilton		1-6	+ 11.00

Winning Horses	Age	Races Run	1st	2nd	3rd	Unpl	Win £
Sharp N' Smooth	7	14	2	0	1	11	6,030
Gospel Song	2	13	1	1	3	8	4,242

Favourites	1-1	100.0%	+ 1.25	Total winning prize-money	£10,272
1993 Form	0-2			1991 Form	0-3
1992 Form	0-5			1990 Form	0-13

S E KETTLEWELL (Middleham, North Yorks)

	No. of Horses	Races Run	1st	2nd	3rd	Unpl	Per cent	£1 Level Stake
2-y-o	3	8	0	0	0	8	-	- 8.00
3-y-o	2	3	0	0	0	3	-	- 3.00
4-y-o+	4	61	10	10	7	34	16.4	- 6.01
Totals	9	72	10	10	7	45	13.9	- 17.01

BY MONTH

2-y-o	W-R	Per cent	£1 Level Stake	3-y-o	W-R	Per cent	£1 Level Stake
January	0-0	-	0.00	January	0-0	-	0.00
February	0-0	-	0.00	February	0-0	-	0.00
March	0-0	-	0.00	March	0-0	-	0.00
April	0-0	-	0.00	April	0-0	-	0.00
May	0-1	-	- 1.00	May	0-0	-	0.00
June	0-0	-	0.00	June	0-1	-	- 1.00
July	0-0	-	0.00	July	0-0	-	0.00
August	0-3	-	- 3.00	August	0-0	-	0.00
September	0-4	-	- 4.00	September	0-0	-	0.00
Oct/Nov	0-0	-	0.00	Oct/Nov	0-2	-	- 2.00

4-y-o+	W-R	Per cent	£1 Level Stake	Totals	W-R	Per cent	£1 Level Stake
January	0-3	-	- 3.00	January	0-3	-	- 3.00
February	0-2	-	- 2.00	February	0-2	-	- 2.00
March	0-1	-	- 1.00	March	0-1	-	- 1.00
April	0-5	-	- 5.00	April	0-5	-	- 5.00
May	3-8	37.5	+ 15.50	May	3-9	33.3	+ 14.50
June	2-8	25.0	- 2.09	June	2-9	22.2	- 3.09
July	2-6	33.3	+ 3.00	July	2-6	33.3	+ 3.00
August	1-10	10.0	- 5.67	August	1-13	7.7	- 8.67
September	2-7	28.6	+ 5.25	September	2-11	18.2	+ 1.25
Oct/Nov	0-11	-	- 11.00	Oct/Nov	0-13	-	- 13.00

DISTANCE

2-y-o	W-R	Per cent	£1 Level Stake	3-y-o	W-R	Per cent	£1 Level Stake
5f-6f	0-3	-	- 3.00	5f-6f	0-0	-	0.00
7f-8f	0-5	-	- 5.00	7f-8f	0-0	-	0.00
9f-13f	0-0	-	0.00	9f-13f	0-3	-	- 3.00
14f+	0-0	-	0.00	14f+	0-0	-	0.00

4-y-o+	W-R	Per cent	£1 Level Stake	Totals	W-R	Per cent	£1 Level Stake
5f-6f	4-19	21.1	- 3.26	5f-6f	4-22	18.2	- 6.26
7f-8f	3-14	21.4	+ 13.00	7f-8f	3-19	15.8	+ 8.00
9f-13f	3-25	12.0	- 12.75	9f-13f	3-28	10.7	- 15.75
14f+	0-3	-	- 3.00	14f+	0-3	-	- 3.00

Kettlewell S E

TYPE OF RACE

Non-Handicaps	W-R	Per cent	£1 Level Stake	Handicaps	W-R	Per cent	£1 Level Stake
2-y-o	0-3	-	- 3.00	2-y-o	0-0	-	0.00
3-y-o	0-2	-	- 2.00	3-y-o	0-1	-	- 1.00
4-y-o+	0-8	-	- 8.00	4-y-o+	6-30	20.0	+ 5.74
Selling	1-9	11.1	- 6.00	Selling	2-4	50.0	+ 5.25
Apprentice	0-1	-	- 1.00	Apprentice	0-2	-	- 2.00
Amat/Ladies	0-2	-	- 2.00	Amat/Ladies	1-10	10.0	- 3.00
Totals	1-25	4.0	- 22.00	Totals	9-47	19.1	+ 4.99

COURSE GRADE

	W-R	Per cent	£1 Level Stake
Group 1	2-18	11.1	- 6.50
Group 2	2-14	14.3	+ 2.00
Group 3	2-16	12.5	- 10.09
Group 4	4-24	16.7	- 2.42

FIRST TIME OUT

	W-R	Per cent	£1 Level Stake
2-y-o	0-3	-	- 3.00
3-y-o	0-1	-	- 1.00
4-y-o+	0-4	-	- 4.00
Totals	0-8	-	- 8.00

JOCKEYS RIDING

	W-R	Per cent	£1 Level Stake		W-R	Per cent	£1 Level Stake
J Stack	5-13	38.5	+ 5.74	Mrs D Kettlewell	1-13	7.7	- 6.00
J Fortune	4-24	16.7	+ 5.25				

D McCabe	0-5	C N Adamson	0-1	N Adams	0-1
J Fanning	0-4	G Carter	0-1	T Ives	0-1
J Carroll	0-3	J Gracey	0-1	T Williams	0-1
R Price	0-3	J Marshall	0-1		

COURSE RECORD

	Total W-R	Non-Handicaps 2-y-o	Non-Handicaps 3-y-o+	Handicaps 2-y-o	Handicaps 3-y-o+	Per cent	£1 Level Stake
Ayr	2-3	0-0	0-1	0-0	2-2	66.7	+ 8.50
Edinburgh	2-6	0-1	0-1	0-0	2-4	33.3	+ 8.00
Hamilton	2-9	0-0	1-5	0-0	1-4	22.2	- 3.09
Lingfield	1-1	0-0	0-0	0-0	1-1	100.0	+ 6.00
Carlisle	1-3	0-0	0-0	0-0	1-3	33.3	+ 1.33
Thirsk	1-5	0-2	0-1	0-0	1-2	20.0	+ 4.00
Wolverhampton (AW)	1-6	0-1	0-1	0-0	1-4	16.7	- 2.75

Newcastle	0-5	Ripon	0-3	Lingfield (AW)	0-2
Redcar	0-5	Catterick	0-2	Newmarket	0-2
Southwell (AW)	0-4	Doncaster	0-2	York	0-2
Beverley	0-3	Goodwood	0-2	Leicester	0-1
Pontefract	0-3	Haydock	0-2	Warwick	0-1

WINNING HORSES

	Age	Races Run	1st	2nd	3rd	Unpl	Win £
Just Bob	5	19	4	2	0	13	15,310
Mbulwa	8	14	2	2	3	7	7,785
Gold Surprise	5	20	3	4	3	10	7,382
Scaraben	6	8	1	2	1	4	3,699

WINNING OWNERS

	Races Won	Value £		Races Won	Value £
J Fotherby	4	15,310	J S Calvert	3	7,382
Mrs E Stoker	2	7,785	J Tennant	1	3,699

Favourites	3-9	33.3%	- 0.09	Total winning prize-money			£34,176
Longest winning sequence			2	Average SP of winner			4.5/1
Longest losing sequence			21	Return on stakes invested			-23.6%
1993 Form	5-70	7.1%	- 29.25	1991 Form	2-17	11.8%	+ 3.00
1992 Form	5-36	13.9%	+ 9.00	1990 Form	1-17	5.9%	+ 4.00

J S KING (Swindon, Wilts)

	No. of Horses	Races Run	1st	2nd	3rd	Unpl	Per cent	£1 Level Stake
2-y-o	0	0	0	0	0	0	-	0.00
3-y-o	1	3	0	0	0	3	-	- 3.00
4-y-o+	8	21	1	2	2	16	4.8	- 13.50
Totals	9	24	1	2	2	19	4.2	- 16.50

Jan	Feb	Mar	Apr	May	Jun	Jul	Aug	Sep	Oct/Nov
0-1	0-0	0-0	0-5	0-3	0-3	0-2	1-2	0-2	0-6

Winning Jockey	W-R	£1 Level Stake	Winning Course	W-R	£1 Level Stake
R Hughes	1-7	+ 0.50	Bath	1-5	+ 2.50

Winning Horse	Age	Races Run	1st	2nd	3rd	Unpl	Win £
Chucklestone	11	8	1	2	1	4	3,397

Favourites	0-0			Total winning prize-money			£3,397
1993 Form	2-35	5.7%	- 25.00	1991 Form	0-19		
1992 Form	5-21	23.8%	+ 6.75	1990 Form	2-25	8.0%	- 11.50

MRS A L M KING (Stratford-upon-Avon, Warwicks)

	No. of Horses	Races Run	1st	2nd	3rd	Unpl	Per cent	£1 Level Stake
2-y-o	1	4	0	0	0	4	-	- 4.00
3-y-o	0	0	0	0	0	0	-	0.00
4-y-o+	4	39	4	3	4	28	10.3	+ 1.50
Totals	5	43	4	3	4	32	9.3	- 2.50

Jan	Feb	Mar	Apr	May	Jun	Jul	Aug	Sep	Oct/Nov
0-0	0-1	0-1	0-4	1-4	2-7	1-7	0-11	0-7	0-1

Winning Jockeys	W-R	£1 Level Stake			W-R	£1 Level Stake
A Garth	2-10	+ 10.00	A Munro		1-7	- 1.50
N Varley	1-1	+ 14.00				

Winning Courses						
Doncaster	1-1	+ 12.00	Pontefract		1-5	+ 0.50
Newbury	1-2	+ 5.00	Bath		1-7	+ 8.00

Winning Horses	Age	Races Run	1st	2nd	3rd	Unpl	Win £
John O'Dreams	9	14	3	0	2	9	11,944
Followmegirls	5	13	1	3	2	7	3,623

Favourites	0-1		Total winning prize-money	£15,567

1993 Form	1-35	2.9%	- 9.00	1991 Form	3-22	13.6%	+ 32.00
1992 Form	2-32	6.3%	+ 73.50	1990 Form	1-12	8.3%	+ 1.00

MRS A KNIGHT (Cullompton, Devon)

	No. of Horses	Races Run	1st	2nd	3rd	Unpl	Per cent	£1 Level Stake
2-y-o	0	0	0	0	0	0	-	0.00
3-y-o	3	12	1	0	1	10	8.3	- 5.50
4-y-o+	5	25	2	3	1	19	8.0	- 1.00
Totals	8	37	3	3	2	29	8.1	- 6.50

Jan	Feb	Mar	Apr	May	Jun	Jul	Aug	Sep	Oct/Nov
0-7	0-4	0-2	0-3	1-5	0-4	1-3	1-2	0-1	0-6

Winning Jockeys	W-R	£1 Level Stake			W-R	£1 Level Stake
R Price	2-9	+ 6.50	Sarah Thompson		1-3	+ 12.00

Winning Courses						
Salisbury	1-1	+ 14.00	Leicester		1-6	+ 0.50
Brighton	1-2	+ 7.00				

Winning Horses	Age	Races Run	1st	2nd	3rd	Unpl	Win £
Caspian Beluga	6	6	1	2	0	3	3,508
Courting Newmarket	6	14	1	1	1	11	2,988
Nuin-Tara	3	9	1	0	1	7	2,668

Favourites	0-0			Total winning prize-money			£9,164

1993 Form	7-90	7.8%	+ 4.33	1991 Form	4-50	8.0%	- 12.00
1992 Form	12-131	9.2%	+ 14.75	1990 Form	0-9		

D R LAING (Lambourn, Berks)

	No. of Horses	Races Run	1st	2nd	3rd	Unpl	Per cent	£1 Level Stake
2-y-o	5	16	1	0	3	12	6.3	- 5.00
3-y-o	2	13	0	0	1	12	-	- 13.00
4-y-o+	8	67	4	4	4	55	6.0	- 34.75
Totals	15	96	5	4	8	79	5.2	- 52.75

Jan	Feb	Mar	Apr	May	Jun	Jul	Aug	Sep	Oct/Nov
1-3	0-2	0-4	0-9	1-10	1-14	1-18	0-10	0-12	1-14

Winning Jockeys	W-R	£1 Level Stake		W-R	£1 Level Stake
S Whitworth	2-20	- 9.75	M Roberts	1-8	+ 3.00
D Holland	1-1	+ 8.00	T Williams	1-31	- 18.00

Winning Courses					
Lingfield	1-5	+ 8.00	Wolverhampton (AW)	1-9	- 2.00
Leicester	1-7	+ 2.00	Salisbury	1-10	+ 1.00
Lingfield (AW)	1-9	- 5.75			

Winning Horses	Age	Races Run	1st	2nd	3rd	Unpl	Win £
Downclose	2	6	1	0	3	2	7,987
Kintwyn	4	18	2	2	0	14	5,811
Bells Of Longwick	5	20	1	0	2	17	3,106
Proud Brigadier	6	6	1	0	0	5	2,905

Favourites	0-3			Total winning prize-money			£19,810

1993 Form	10-124	8.1%	- 42.75	1991 Form	4-100	4.0%	- 73.50
1992 Form	8-126	6.3%	- 31.50				

P LEACH (Taunton, Somerset)

	No. of Horses	Races Run	1st	2nd	3rd	Unpl	Per cent	£1 Level Stake
2-y-o	0	0	0	0	0	0	-	0.00
3-y-o	0	0	0	0	0	0	-	0.00
4-y-o+	6	13	1	0	1	11	7.7	+ 21.00
Totals	6	13	1	0	1	11	7.7	+ 21.00

Jan	Feb	Mar	Apr	May	Jun	Jul	Aug	Sep	Oct/Nov
0-1	0-4	0-0	1-3	0-3	0-2	0-0	0-0	0-0	0-0

Winning Jockey	W-R	£1 Level Stake	Winning Course	W-R	£1 Level Stake
Mr A Michael	1-2	+ 32.00	Warwick	1-1	+ 33.00

Winning Horse	Age	Races Run	1st	2nd	3rd	Unpl	Win £
Charmed Life	5	4	1	0	1	2	3,524

Favourites	0-1	Total winning prize-money	£3,524

1993 Form	3-17	17.6%	- 4.25	1991 Form	0-4		
1992 Form	0-6			1990 Form	1-14	7.1%	- 5.00

F H LEE (Wilmslow, Cheshire)

	No. of Horses	Races Run	1st	2nd	3rd	Unpl	Per cent	£1 Level Stake
2-y-o	6	23	2	4	1	16	8.7	- 17.25
3-y-o	9	60	6	8	3	43	10.0	0.00
4-y-o+	12	71	3	5	3	60	4.2	- 37.00
Totals	27	154	11	17	7	119	7.1	- 54.25

BY MONTH

2-y-o	W-R	Per cent	£1 Level Stake	3-y-o	W-R	Per cent	£1 Level Stake
January	0-0	-	0.00	January	0-0	-	0.00
February	0-0	-	0.00	February	0-0	-	0.00
March	0-0	-	0.00	March	0-0	-	0.00
April	0-0	-	0.00	April	0-3	-	- 3.00
May	0-2	-	- 2.00	May	1-9	11.1	0.00
June	1-6	16.7	- 3.00	June	2-16	12.5	+ 8.75
July	0-1	-	- 1.00	July	1-10	10.0	- 6.75
August	1-5	20.0	- 2.25	August	2-10	20.0	+ 13.00
September	0-5	-	- 5.00	September	0-7	-	- 7.00
Oct/Nov	0-4	-	- 4.00	Oct/Nov	0-5	-	- 5.00

4-y-o+	W-R	Per cent	£1 Level Stake	Totals	W-R	Per cent	£1 Level Stake
January	0-1	-	- 1.00	January	0-1	-	- 1.00
February	0-0	-	0.00	February	0-0	-	0.00
March	0-0	-	0.00	March	0-0	-	0.00
April	0-3	-	- 3.00	April	0-6	-	- 6.00
May	0-9	-	- 9.00	May	1-20	5.0	- 11.00
June	1-14	7.1	- 1.00	June	4-36	11.1	+ 4.75
July	0-17	-	- 17.00	July	1-28	3.6	- 24.75
August	2-16	12.5	+ 5.00	August	5-31	16.1	+ 15.75
September	0-6	-	- 6.00	September	0-18	-	- 18.00
Oct/Nov	0-5	-	- 5.00	Oct/Nov	0-14	-	- 14.00

DISTANCE

2-y-o	W-R	Per cent	£1 Level Stake	3-y-o	W-R	Per cent	£1 Level Stake
5f-6f	2-18	11.1	- 12.25	5f-6f	2-16	12.5	+ 14.00
7f-8f	0-5	-	- 5.00	7f-8f	3-29	10.3	- 2.25
9f-13f	0-0	-	0.00	9f-13f	1-14	7.1	- 10.75
14f+	0-0	-	0.00	14f+	0-1	-	- 1.00

4-y-o+	W-R	Per cent	£1 Level Stake	Totals	W-R	Per cent	£1 Level Stake
5f-6f	1-23	4.3	- 10.00	5f-6f	5-57	8.8	- 8.25
7f-8f	2-27	7.4	- 6.00	7f-8f	5-61	8.2	- 13.25
9f-13f	0-18	-	- 18.00	9f-13f	1-32	3.1	- 28.75
14f+	0-3	-	- 3.00	14f+	0-4	-	- 4.00

TYPE OF RACE

Non-Handicaps	W-R	Per cent	£1 Level Stake	Handicaps	W-R	Per cent	£1 Level Stake
2-y-o	2-22	9.1	- 16.25	2-y-o	0-0	-	0.00
3-y-o	1-16	6.3	- 7.00	3-y-o	5-40	12.5	+ 11.00
4-y-o+	0-5	-	- 5.00	4-y-o+	3-49	6.1	- 15.00
Selling	0-3	-	- 3.00	Selling	0-4	-	- 4.00
Apprentice	0-0	-	0.00	Apprentice	0-9	-	- 9.00
Amat/Ladies	0-0	-	0.00	Amat/Ladies	0-6	-	- 6.00
Totals	3-46	6.5	- 31.25	Totals	8-108	7.4	- 23.00

COURSE GRADE

	W-R	Per cent	£1 Level Stake
Group 1	2-62	3.2	- 28.00
Group 2	3-38	7.9	- 19.25
Group 3	2-26	7.7	- 4.00
Group 4	4-28	14.3	- 3.00

FIRST TIME OUT

	W-R	Per cent	£1 Level Stake
2-y-o	0-6	-	- 6.00
3-y-o	1-9	11.1	0.00
4-y-o+	1-12	8.3	+ 1.00
Totals	2-27	7.4	- 5.00

JOCKEYS RIDING

	W–R	Per cent	£1 Level Stake		W–R	Per cent	£1 Level Stake
S Perks	4-32	12.5	- 14.50	B Raymond	1-3	33.3	+ 10.00
K Darley	1-1	100.0	+ 2.25	N Carlisle	1-7	14.3	+ 14.00
D Holland	1-1	100.0	+ 9.00	T Ives	1-7	14.3	+ 6.00
J Reid	1-2	50.0	+ 7.00	R Lappin	1-46	2.2	- 33.00

Mr G J Houghton	0-4	C Scudder	0-1	M J Dwyer	0-1
Paul Eddery	0-4	D Griffiths	0-1	M Roberts	0-1
A Munro	0-3	D McCabe	0-1	Mark Denaro	0-1
D Wright	0-3	G Parkin	0-1	Miss E Houghton	0-1
G Carter	0-3	J Fortune	0-1	Mr G Shenkin	0-1
C Teague	0-2	J Lowe	0-1	N Connorton	0-1
J Weaver	0-2	J Stack	0-1	N Kennedy	0-1
P Robinson	0-2	J Tate	0-1	R Hills	0-1
R Cochrane	0-2	K Fallon	0-1	S Knott	0-1
A Clark	0-1	L Charnock	0-1	S Lanigan	0-1
A Culhane	0-1	L Dettori	0-1	S Webster	0-1
A Mackay	0-1	M Baird	0-1	T G McLaughlin	0-1
C N Adamson	0-1	M Hills	0-1	W R Swinburn	0-1

COURSE RECORD

	Total W–R	Non-Handicaps 2-y-o	Non-Handicaps 3-y-o+	Handicaps 2-y-o	Handicaps 3-y-o+	Per cent	£1 Level Stake
Catterick	2-7	0-0	0-1	0-0	2-6	28.6	+ 6.75
Beverley	1-2	0-0	1-1	0-0	0-1	50.0	+ 7.00
Nottingham	1-2	0-1	0-0	0-0	1-1	50.0	+ 11.00
Wolverhampton (AW)	1-3	0-0	0-2	0-0	1-1	33.3	+ 5.00
Ripon	1-6	1-1	0-2	0-0	0-3	16.7	- 3.25
York	1-9	0-1	0-0	0-0	1-8	11.1	+ 12.00
Redcar	1-10	1-1	0-0	0-0	0-9	10.0	- 7.00
Edinburgh	1-12	0-0	0-2	0-0	1-10	8.3	- 8.75
Thirsk	1-12	0-2	0-2	0-0	1-8	8.3	+ 1.00
Haydock	1-23	0-7	0-4	0-0	1-12	4.3	- 10.00

Hamilton	0-14	Leicester	0-5	Carlisle	0-1
Doncaster	0-11	Lingfield	0-4	Lingfield (AW)	0-1
Ayr	0-10	Pontefract	0-3	Newmarket	0-1
Chester	0-6	Warwick	0-3	Southwell (AW)	0-1
Goodwood	0-6	Newcastle	0-2		

WINNING HORSES

	Age	Races Run	1st	2nd	3rd	Unpl	Win £
Encore M'Lady	3	8	2	2	0	4	34,761
Beau Venture	6	9	1	2	0	6	10,625
Don't Worry Me	2	8	2	4	1	1	9,651
Pleasure Trick	3	9	2	1	0	6	7,003
To Crown It All	3	8	1	0	0	7	4,199
Move Smartly	4	10	1	1	1	7	3,391
Quarrelling	4	3	1	0	0	2	3,288
Millie's Dream	3	7	1	1	0	5	2,710

WINNING OWNERS

	Races Won	Value £		Races Won	Value £
F H Lee	3	38,049	Mrs B Facchino	2	7,003
Mrs A L Stacey	1	10,625	P Asquith	2	6,909
Michael Caveney	2	9,651	P Clinton	1	3,391

Favourites	3-15	20.0%	- 5.50	Total winning prize-money	£75,629

Longest winning sequence	1	Average SP of winner	8.1/1
Longest losing sequence	36	Return on stakes invested	-35.2%

1993 Form	11-235	4.7%	-152.50	1991 Form	30-285	10.5%	- 11.12
1992 Form	27-302	8.9%	- 77.25	1990 Form	25-256	9.8%	- 49.25

R LEE (Presteigne, Powys)

	No. of Horses	Races Run	1st	2nd	3rd	Unpl	Per cent	£1 Level Stake
2-y-o	0	0	0	0	0	0	-	0.00
3-y-o	2	7	0	1	1	5	-	- 7.00
4-y-o+	7	18	1	0	0	17	5.6	- 5.00
Totals	9	25	1	1	1	22	4.0	- 12.00

Jan	Feb	Mar	Apr	May	Jun	Jul	Aug	Sep	Oct/Nov
1-6	0-3	0-0	0-4	0-4	0-0	0-4	0-2	0-2	0-0

Winning Jockey	W-R	£1 Level Stake	Winning Course	W-R	£1 Level Stake
T Quinn	1-3	+ 10.00	Wolverhampton (AW)	1-10	+ 3.00

Winning Horse	Age	Races Run	1st	2nd	3rd	Unpl	Win £
Peak District	8	5	1	0	0	4	2,243

Favourites	0-1		Total winning prize-money	£2,243
1993 Form	2-49	4.1% - 20.00	1991 Form	2-13	15.4% + 6.00
1992 Form	3-63	4.8% - 40.50	1990 Form	0-5	

J P LEIGH (Gainsborough, Lincs)

	No. of Horses	Races Run	1st	2nd	3rd	Unpl	Per cent	£1 Level Stake
2-y-o	2	3	0	0	0	3	-	- 3.00
3-y-o	3	21	3	4	0	14	14.3	+ 0.75
4-y-o+	1	1	0	0	0	1	-	- 1.00
Totals	6	25	3	4	0	18	12.0	- 3.25

Jan	Feb	Mar	Apr	May	Jun	Jul	Aug	Sep	Oct/Nov
0-0	0-0	0-0	0-1	0-2	1-2	1-7	1-6	0-2	0-5

Winning Jockeys	W-R	£1 Level Stake			W-R	£1 Level Stake
A Culhane	1-2	+ 4.00	D McKeown		1-14	- 2.00
J Weaver	1-2	+ 1.75				

Winning Course		£1 Level Stake
Southwell (AW)	3-8	+ 13.75

Winning Horse	Age	Races Run	1st	2nd	3rd	Unpl	Win £
Johnnie The Joker	3	13	3	4	0	6	9,577

Favourites	1-3	33.3%	+ 0.75	Total winning prize-money		£9,577

1993 Form	1-41	2.4%	- 28.00	1991 Form	5-54	9.3%	- 12.00
1992 Form	1-83	1.2%	- 74.00	1990 Form	4-57	7.0%	- 17.50

G LEWIS (Epsom, Surrey)

	No. of Horses	Races Run	1st	2nd	3rd	Unpl	Per cent	£1 Level Stake
2-y-o	25	178	21	27	18	112	11.8	- 31.25
3-y-o	25	154	22	11	13	108	14.3	+ 6.01
4-y-o+	6	23	1	1	3	18	4.3	- 20.75
Totals	56	355	44	39	34	238	12.4	- 45.99

BY MONTH

2-y-o	W-R	Per cent	£1 Level Stake	3-y-o	W-R	Per cent	£1 Level Stake
January	0-0	-	0.00	January	0-0	-	0.00
February	0-0	-	0.00	February	1-2	50.0	+ 1.50
March	0-2	-	- 2.00	March	0-4	-	- 4.00
April	1-12	8.3	- 7.00	April	1-17	5.9	- 12.50
May	0-15	-	- 15.00	May	4-21	19.0	+ 8.50
June	2-24	8.3	- 10.50	June	5-33	15.2	+ 20.50
July	4-34	11.8	- 9.50	July	2-23	8.7	- 10.00
August	6-28	21.4	+ 0.75	August	3-18	16.7	- 4.87
September	5-36	13.9	- 10.50	September	4-22	18.2	- 6.12
Oct/Nov	3-27	11.1	+ 22.50	Oct/Nov	2-14	14.3	+ 13.00

4-y-o+	W-R	Per cent	£1 Level Stake	Totals	W-R	Per cent	£1 Level Stake
January	0-0	-	0.00	January	0-0	-	0.00
February	0-3	-	- 3.00	February	1-5	20.0	- 1.50
March	0-2	-	- 2.00	March	0-8	-	- 8.00
April	0-6	-	- 6.00	April	2-35	5.7	- 25.50
May	0-4	-	- 4.00	May	4-40	10.0	- 10.50
June	1-5	20.0	- 2.75	June	8-62	12.9	+ 7.25
July	0-2	-	- 2.00	July	6-59	10.2	- 21.50
August	0-1	-	- 1.00	August	9-47	19.1	- 5.12
September	0-0	-	0.00	September	9-58	15.5	- 16.62
Oct/Nov	0-0	-	0.00	Oct/Nov	5-41	12.2	+ 35.50

DISTANCE

2-y-o	W-R	Per cent	£1 Level Stake	3-y-o	W-R	Per cent	£1 Level Stake
5f-6f	14-129	10.9	- 52.25	5f-6f	5-34	14.7	- 3.37
7f-8f	7-48	14.6	+ 22.00	7f-8f	7-69	10.1	- 21.50
9f-13f	0-1	-	- 1.00	9f-13f	9-47	19.1	+ 13.88
14f+	0-0	-	0.00	14f+	1-4	25.0	+ 17.00

4-y-o+	W-R	Per cent	£1 Level Stake	Totals	W-R	Per cent	£1 Level Stake
5f-6f	0-7	-	- 7.00	5f-6f	19-170	11.2	- 62.62
7f-8f	0-7	-	- 7.00	7f-8f	14-124	11.3	- 6.50
9f-13f	1-9	11.1	- 6.75	9f-13f	10-57	17.5	+ 6.13
14f+	0-0	-	0.00	14f+	1-4	25.0	+ 17.00

TYPE OF RACE

Non-Handicaps	W-R	Per cent	£1 Level Stake	Handicaps	W-R	Per cent	£1 Level Stake
2-y-o	9-89	10.1	- 10.00	2-y-o	5-52	9.6	- 16.00
3-y-o	7-50	14.0	+ 0.01	3-y-o	14-84	16.7	+ 20.00
4-y-o+	0-9	-	- 9.00	4-y-o+	0-9	-	- 9.00
Selling	6-35	17.1	- 7.75	Selling	1-7	14.3	- 2.50
Apprentice	0-2	-	- 2.00	Apprentice	2-14	14.3	- 5.75
Amat/Ladies	0-1	-	- 1.00	Amat/Ladies	0-3	-	- 3.00
Totals	22-186	11.8	- 29.74	Totals	22-169	13.0	- 16.25

COURSE GRADE

	W-R	Per cent	£1 Level Stake
Group 1	17-140	12.1	+ 13.76
Group 2	9-76	11.8	- 27.50
Group 3	8-73	11.0	- 30.00
Group 4	10-66	15.2	- 2.25

FIRST TIME OUT

	W-R	Per cent	£1 Level Stake
2-y-o	1-24	4.2	- 19.00
3-y-o	0-22	-	- 22.00
4-y-o+	0-5	-	- 5.00
Totals	1-51	2.0	- 46.00

JOCKEYS RIDING

	W-R	Per cent	£1 Level Stake		W-R	Per cent	£1 Level Stake
Paul Eddery	17-101	16.8	- 16.62	J Williams	1-2	50.0	+ 9.00
A Whelan	8-62	12.9	+ 4.75	J Weaver	1-2	50.0	+ 32.00
Pat Eddery	6-20	30.0	+ 8.88	L Piggott	1-3	33.3	+ 7.00
M Hills	2-3	66.7	+ 27.00	R Cochrane	1-4	25.0	+ 3.00
D Wright	2-17	11.8	- 6.50	D Harrison	1-9	11.1	- 4.50
B Raymond	2-20	10.0	- 6.00	S Whitworth	1-22	4.5	- 19.00
L Dettori	1-2	50.0	+ 3.00				

J Swift	0-12	D Biggs	0-2	K Darley	0-1
N Adams	0-10	J Reid	0-2	Miss B Craven	0-1
A Lakeman	0-7	Rachel Moody	0-2	Miss C Spearing	0-1
A Munro	0-7	W Woods	0-2	Mr S Findlay	0-1
W R Swinburn	0-4	A Mackay	0-1	Mrs S Cumani	0-1
A McGlone	0-3	A Tucker	0-1	N Carlisle	0-1
B Russell	0-3	C Rutter	0-1	N Varley	0-1
G Hind	0-3	D Holland	0-1	P Houghton	0-1
J Lowe	0-3	D Toole	0-1	R Hills	0-1
J Quinn	0-3	E Johnson	0-1	R Perham	0-1
Stephen Davies	0-3	G Bardwell	0-1	S Maloney	0-1
A Clark	0-2	J Carroll	0-1	S Perks	0-1

COURSE RECORD

	Total W-R	Non-Handicaps 2-y-o	3-y-o+	Handicaps 2-y-o	3-y-o+	Per cent	£1 Level Stake
Newbury	5-15	1-5	1-2	0-2	3-6	33.3	+ 57.00
Brighton	5-20	1-5	0-6	1-2	3-7	25.0	+ 1.50
Wolverhampton (AW)	4-16	3-10	0-3	1-1	0-2	25.0	+ 5.75
Yarmouth	3-12	0-5	2-3	0-1	1-3	25.0	+ 4.00
Sandown	3-22	3-12	0-3	0-3	0-4	13.6	- 7.00
Epsom	3-24	1-8	1-5	0-0	1-11	12.5	- 9.87
Windsor	3-24	1-12	0-5	0-1	2-6	12.5	- 4.50
Ascot	2-9	0-0	2-4	0-1	0-4	22.2	+ 15.13
Southwell (AW)	2-10	1-4	0-3	1-2	0-1	20.0	+ 6.00
Lingfield (AW)	2-10	0-1	1-5	1-2	0-2	20.0	+ 1.50
Lingfield	2-28	0-13	0-5	0-1	2-9	7.1	- 14.00
Catterick	1-2	0-0	0-0	1-2	0-0	50.0	+ 9.00
Newcastle	1-2	0-0	0-1	0-0	1-1	50.0	+ 4.00
York	1-3	0-0	0-0	1-3	0-0	33.3	+ 4.00
Salisbury	1-7	1-2	0-3	0-0	0-2	14.3	- 4.00
Leicester	1-8	1-3	0-1	0-2	0-2	12.5	- 5.00
Chester	1-9	1-4	0-0	0-3	0-2	11.1	+ 1.00
Bath	1-14	0-5	0-1	0-1	1-7	7.1	- 9.50
Kempton	1-15	0-4	0-1	0-3	1-7	6.7	- 9.50
Newmarket	1-20	0-2	0-2	0-6	1-10	5.0	- 10.00
Folkestone	1-23	1-8	0-3	0-3	0-9	4.3	- 19.50

Goodwood	0-19	Nottingham	0-5	Thirsk	0-2
Redcar	0-9	Haydock	0-4	Carlisle	0-1
Doncaster	0-7	Pontefract	0-4	Hamilton	0-1
Chepstow	0-5	Warwick	0-4	Ripon	0-1

WINNING HORSES

	Age	Races Run	1st	2nd	3rd	Unpl	Win £
Lake Coniston	3	9	3	2	0	4	56,941
Silver Wedge	3	4	2	0	1	1	43,088
Circa	2	9	3	1	0	5	17,570
Kissair	3	12	4	1	0	7	17,298
Go With Bo	3	5	3	1	0	1	16,922
Robsera	3	12	4	1	0	7	16,325
Anniversarypresent	2	8	1	4	0	3	11,648
Hawaiian Dream	3	11	2	1	1	7	7,418
That Man Again	2	11	2	2	1	6	6,912
Jibereen	2	5	2	1	0	2	6,584
Don Alvaro	2	11	2	4	1	4	5,952
Bo Knows Nigel	3	3	2	1	0	0	5,770
Tachycardia	2	12	2	1	3	6	4,893
Vocal Command	2	8	2	0	2	4	4,739
Night Dance	2	2	1	0	0	1	4,172
Futuristic Brent	2	10	1	0	0	9	3,525
Solo Prize	2	12	1	2	3	6	3,493
Zuno Noelyn	3	13	1	0	1	11	3,225
Lochbroom Commando	2	11	1	3	1	6	3,054
Lively	3	9	1	0	0	8	2,795
Bitch	2	10	1	2	2	5	2,456
Mohawk Trail	5	4	1	0	0	3	2,448
Casper's Risk	2	6	1	0	0	5	2,174
Exosal	2	9	1	2	1	5	2,070

WINNING OWNERS

	Races Won	Value £		Races Won	Value £
Highclere Th'bred Racing Ltd	3	56,941	G H P Pritchard	2	5,952
Mrs Shirley Robins	2	43,088	Mrs Thelma Wade	2	4,893
David Barker	8	36,236	A R Perry	2	4,865
C F Sparrowhawk	5	22,692	G V Wright	1	4,172
Roldvale Limited	4	20,026	White Bear Limited	1	3,493
Terry Benson	4	17,298	Mrs Lyn Fatah	1	3,225
Mrs Dorothy Price	2	7,418	D Waters	1	3,054
M Jameson	2	6,912	Michael H Watt	1	2,448
H H Princess Dala			Jimmy Tarbuck	1	2,174
Abdulaziz Al-Saud	2	6,584			

Favourites	14-54	25.9%	- 0.99	Total winning prize-money £251,469
Longest winning sequence			2	Average SP of winner 6.0/1
Longest losing sequence			36	Return on stakes invested -13.0%
1993 Form	30-255	11.8%	- 60.69	1991 Form 41-355 11.5% - 42.89
1992 Form	54-355	15.2%	+ 53.64	1990 Form 26-285 9.1% -118.86

B J LLEWELLYN (Bargoed, Mid Glamorgan)

	No. of Horses	Races Run	1st	2nd	3rd	Unpl	Per cent	£1 Level Stake
2-y-o	0	0	0	0	0	0	-	0.00
3-y-o	2	2	0	0	0	2	-	- 2.00
4-y-o+	11	27	1	2	1	23	3.7	- 21.00
Totals	13	29	1	2	1	25	3.4	- 23.00

Jan	Feb	Mar	Apr	May	Jun	Jul	Aug	Sep	Oct/Nov
0-1	1-5	0-7	0-2	0-1	0-2	0-5	0-3	0-0	0-3

Winning Jockey	W-R	£1 Level Stake		Winning Course	W-R	£1 Level Stake
Mr J L Llewellyn	1-6	0.00		Wolverhampton (AW)	1-8	- 2.00

Winning Horse	Age	Races Run	1st	2nd	3rd	Unpl	Win £
Wheeler's Wonder	5	1	1	0	0	0	2,243

Favourites	0-0		Total winning prize-money	£2,243

D R LODER (Newmarket)

	No. of Horses	Races Run	1st	2nd	3rd	Unpl	Per cent	£1 Level Stake
2-y-o	19	75	23	15	11	26	30.7	- 4.01
3-y-o	14	44	11	9	4	20	25.0	+ 3.64
4-y-o+	7	29	5	6	5	13	17.2	- 11.00
Totals	40	148	39	30	20	59	26.4	- 11.37

BY MONTH

2-y-o	W-R	Per cent	£1 Level Stake	3-y-o	W-R	Per cent	£1 Level Stake
January	0-0	-	0.00	January	1-4	25.0	- 1.90
February	0-0	-	0.00	February	0-0	-	0.00
March	0-0	-	0.00	March	0-0	-	0.00
April	0-1	-	- 1.00	April	3-7	42.9	+ 1.68
May	5-7	71.4	+ 4.74	May	1-8	12.5	- 4.87
June	5-16	31.3	- 5.62	June	2-9	22.2	+ 1.00
July	6-16	37.5	+ 1.12	July	0-2	-	- 2.00
August	2-9	22.2	- 3.75	August	0-0	-	0.00
September	3-17	17.6	- 5.50	September	1-7	14.3	+ 6.00
Oct/Nov	2-9	22.2	+ 6.00	Oct/Nov	3-7	42.9	+ 3.73

4-y-o+	W-R	Per cent	£1 Level Stake	Totals	W-R	Per cent	£1 Level Stake
January	1-2	50.0	+ 4.50	January	2-6	33.3	+ 2.60
February	1-3	33.3	- 1.00	February	1-3	33.3	- 1.00
March	0-1	-	- 1.00	March	0-1	-	- 1.00
April	0-3	-	- 3.00	April	3-11	27.3	- 2.32
May	0-4	-	- 4.00	May	6-19	31.6	- 4.13
June	1-5	20.0	- 1.75	June	8-30	26.7	- 6.37
July	1-4	25.0	- 1.00	July	7-22	31.8	- 1.88
August	0-2	-	- 2.00	August	2-11	18.2	- 5.75
September	0-3	-	- 3.00	September	4-27	14.8	- 2.50
Oct/Nov	1-2	50.0	+ 1.25	Oct/Nov	6-18	33.3	+ 10.98

DISTANCE

2-y-o	W-R	Per cent	£1 Level Stake	3-y-o	W-R	Per cent	£1 Level Stake
5f-6f	18-44	40.9	+ 7.61	5f-6f	0-2	-	- 2.00
7f-8f	5-31	16.1	- 11.62	7f-8f	5-14	35.7	- 0.29
9f-13f	0-0	-	0.00	9f-13f	6-24	25.0	+ 9.93
14f+	0-0	-	0.00	14f+	0-4	-	- 4.00

4-y-o+	W-R	Per cent	£1 Level Stake	Totals	W-R	Per cent	£1 Level Stake
5f-6f	0-0	-	0.00	5f-6f	18-46	39.1	+ 5.61
7f-8f	3-11	27.3	+ 0.50	7f-8f	13-56	23.2	- 11.41
9f-13f	2-14	14.3	- 7.50	9f-13f	8-38	21.1	+ 2.43
14f+	0-4	-	- 4.00	14f+	0-8	-	- 8.00

TYPE OF RACE

Non-Handicaps	W-R	Per cent	£1 Level Stake	Handicaps	W-R	Per cent	£1 Level Stake
2-y-o	22-70	31.4	- 6.01	2-y-o	0-3	-	- 3.00
3-y-o	8-28	28.6	+ 10.13	3-y-o	3-15	20.0	- 5.49
4-y-o+	2-16	12.5	- 9.50	4-y-o+	3-13	23.1	- 1.50
Selling	1-3	33.3	+ 4.00	Selling	0-0	-	0.00
Apprentice	0-0	-	0.00	Apprentice	0-0	-	0.00
Amat/Ladies	0-0	-	0.00	Amat/Ladies	0-0	-	0.00
Totals	33-117	28.2	- 1.38	Totals	6-31	19.4	- 9.99

COURSE GRADE

	W-R	Per cent	£1 Level Stake
Group 1	13-79	16.5	- 32.42
Group 2	6-19	31.6	+ 3.15
Group 3	14-32	43.8	+ 15.92
Group 4	6-18	33.3	+ 1.98

FIRST TIME OUT

	W-R	Per cent	£1 Level Stake
2-y-o	5-19	26.3	- 1.83
3-y-o	5-12	41.7	+ 12.81
4-y-o+	1-6	16.7	+ 0.50
Totals	11-37	29.7	+ 11.48

JOCKEYS RIDING

	W-R	Per cent	£1 Level Stake		W-R	Per cent	£1 Level Stake
L Dettori	16-56	28.6	- 4.05	D Harrison	1-1	100.0	+ 7.00
G Carter	9-25	36.0	+ 1.04	T Quinn	1-2	50.0	- 0.27
K Darley	4-12	33.3	+ 12.25	M Tebbutt	1-6	16.7	- 2.75
J Weaver	4-13	30.8	- 1.47	D McCabe	1-11	9.1	- 8.00
Pat Eddery	2-6	33.3	+ 0.88				

R Cochrane	0-5	W Ryan	0-2	W R Swinburn	0-1
M J Kinane	0-4	B Thomson	0-1		
L Piggott	0-2	G Duffield	0-1		

COURSE RECORD

	Total W-R	Non-Handicaps 2-y-o	Non-Handicaps 3-y-o+	Handicaps 2-y-o	Handicaps 3-y-o+	Per cent	£1 Level Stake
Beverley	6-10	3-5	1-3	0-0	2-2	60.0	+ 8.37
Newmarket	6-26	4-16	2-7	0-0	0-3	23.1	- 0.33
Nottingham	3-4	3-3	0-1	0-0	0-0	75.0	+ 3.57
York	3-11	1-4	1-3	0-0	1-4	27.3	- 3.57
Redcar	2-3	2-2	0-0	0-0	0-1	66.7	+ 8.00
Salisbury	2-3	1-1	0-1	0-0	1-1	66.7	+ 3.10
Lingfield (AW)	2-5	0-0	0-2	0-0	2-3	40.0	+ 3.50
Sandown	2-6	2-4	0-2	0-0	0-0	33.3	- 1.52
Yarmouth	2-7	1-6	1-1	0-0	0-0	28.6	+ 9.50
Ayr	1-1	1-1	0-0	0-0	0-0	100.0	+ 2.00
Carlisle	1-1	1-1	0-0	0-0	0-0	100.0	+ 2.50
Thirsk	1-1	0-0	1-1	0-0	0-0	100.0	+ 0.80
Leicester	1-2	1-1	0-1	0-0	0-0	50.0	- 0.43
Windsor	1-2	1-2	0-0	0-0	0-0	50.0	0.00
Catterick	1-3	0-2	1-1	0-0	0-0	33.3	+ 0.25
Ripon	1-3	0-1	1-2	0-0	0-0	33.3	+ 0.25
Southwell (AW)	1-4	1-1	0-3	0-0	0-0	25.0	- 1.37
Wolverhampton (AW)	1-4	0-0	1-3	0-0	0-1	25.0	- 1.90
Pontefract	1-5	1-3	0-1	0-0	0-1	20.0	- 3.09
Haydock	1-6	0-1	1-1	0-0	0-4	16.7	0.00

Ascot	0-10	Newbury	0-4	Brighton	0-1
Doncaster	0-7	Chester	0-3	Edinburgh	0-1
Goodwood	0-6	Chepstow	0-2		
Lingfield	0-5	Kempton	0-2		

WINNING HORSES

	Age	Races Run	1st	2nd	3rd	Unpl	Win £
Maid For Walking	2	9	3	3	0	3	98,804
La Confederation	3	3	2	0	0	1	44,060
Lovely Millie	2	5	4	0	0	1	38,580
Fallow	2	8	3	3	2	0	26,035
Loyalize	2	6	3	2	0	1	25,088
Nijo	3	2	2	0	0	0	15,016

Dune River	5	8	3	1	2	2	12,694
Shortfall	3	6	2	1	0	3	10,056
Kings Cay	3	4	2	0	1	1	9,104
Tanami	2	7	2	2	0	3	8,855
Watch The Clock	2	5	2	0	1	2	7,982
Petindia	2	1	1	0	0	0	7,848
Governor George	3	5	1	2	0	2	6,315
El Supremo	2	4	1	1	1	1	4,246
Tenorio	2	3	1	0	0	2	3,939
Wigberto	2	7	1	1	2	3	3,739
Fitzrovian	3	5	1	1	1	2	3,348
Sapiston Girl	2	5	1	2	0	2	3,216
Dormy Three	4	8	1	2	1	4	3,052
Young Freeman	5	5	1	1	0	3	3,002
Bruton Stream	2	4	1	0	2	1	2,898
King Of The Horse	3	5	1	1	1	2	2,243

WINNING OWNERS

	Races Won	Value £		Races Won	Value £
Sheikh Mohammed	11	107,386	Cheveley Park Stud	2	7,982
Chris Brasher	3	98,804	P D Savill	1	7,848
Godolphin	3	34,908	Wafic Said	1	4,246
Lucayan Stud	4	16,272	Cuadra Africa	1	3,939
Sheikh Ahmed Bin Saeed			Mrs John E Guest	1	3,672
Al Maktoum	2	15,016	A M Budgett	1	3,052
Mrs P T Fenwick	3	12,694	Mrs A M Green	1	2,898
P D Player	2	10,056	Philip Tseng	1	2,243
M J Leeson	2	9,104			

Favourites	27-59	45.8%	+ 5.13	Total winning prize-money	£340,117
Longest winning sequence			3	Average SP of winner	2.5/1
Longest losing sequence			14	Return on stakes invested	-7.7%
1993 Form	45-193	23.3%	- 21.37	1992 Form	2-13	15.4%	+ 18.00

J E LONG (Plumpton, East Sussex)

	No. of Horses	Races Run	1st	2nd	3rd	Unpl	Per cent	£1 Level Stake
2-y-o	1	2	0	0	0	2	-	- 2.00
3-y-o	2	11	1	2	1	7	9.1	- 2.00
4-y-o+	14	62	0	3	4	55	-	- 62.00
Totals	17	75	1	5	5	64	1.3	- 66.00

Jan	Feb	Mar	Apr	May	Jun	Jul	Aug	Sep	Oct/Nov
0-11	0-13	0-4	1-12	0-9	0-5	0-5	0-6	0-7	0-3

Long J E

Winning Jockey	W-R	£1 Level Stake	Winning Course	W-R	£1 Level Stake
Stephen Davies	1-7	+ 2.00	Warwick	1-3	+ 6.00

Winning Horse	Age	Races Run	1st	2nd	3rd	Unpl	Win £
Mutinique	3	7	1	2	1	3	2,669

Favourites	0-0		Total winning prize-money		£2,669
1993 Form	0-66		1991 Form	0-18	
1992 Form	0-11		1990 Form	0-29	

L LUNGO (Carrutherstown, Dumfries)

	No. of Horses	Races Run	1st	2nd	3rd	Unpl	Per cent	£1 Level Stake
2-y-o	2	8	0	0	0	8	-	- 8.00
3-y-o	2	6	0	0	0	6	-	- 6.00
4-y-o+	7	21	2	2	0	17	9.5	- 13.33
Totals	11	35	2	2	0	31	5.7	- 27.33

Jan	Feb	Mar	Apr	May	Jun	Jul	Aug	Sep	Oct/Nov
0-0	0-0	1-1	0-3	0-5	0-12	0-2	0-0	0-3	1-9

Winning Jockeys	W-R	£1 Level Stake		W-R	£1 Level Stake
M Birch	1-12	- 10.33	S Copp	1-15	- 9.00

Winning Courses					
Newcastle	1-5	- 3.33	Pontefract	1-7	- 1.00

Winning Horse	Age	Races Run	1st	2nd	3rd	Unpl	Win £
Attadale	6	5	2	1	0	2	6,239

Favourites	1-2	50.0%	- 0.33	Total winning prize-money		£6,239
1993 Form	0-10			1991 Form	1-23	4.3%	- 17.00
1992 Form	0-21			1990 Form	0-2	

MRS N MACAULEY (Melton Mowbray, Leics)

	No. of Horses	Races Run	1st	2nd	3rd	Unpl	Per cent	£1 Level Stake
2-y-o	8	28	1	1	2	24	3.6	- 24.00
3-y-o	9	53	4	4	5	40	7.5	- 31.25
4-y-o+	16	110	12	8	9	81	10.9	+ 4.33
Totals	33	191	17	13	16	145	8.9	- 50.92

BY MONTH

2-y-o	W-R	Per cent	£1 Level Stake	3-y-o	W-R	Per cent	£1 Level Stake
January	0-0	-	0.00	January	0-3	-	- 3.00
February	0-0	-	0.00	February	0-1	-	- 1.00
March	0-1	-	- 1.00	March	0-1	-	- 1.00
April	0-2	-	- 2.00	April	1-6	16.7	- 1.50
May	0-2	-	- 2.00	May	2-9	22.2	+ 3.75
June	0-2	-	- 2.00	June	0-10	-	- 10.00
July	0-7	-	- 7.00	July	1-9	11.1	- 4.50
August	1-8	12.5	- 4.00	August	0-6	-	- 6.00
September	0-5	-	- 5.00	September	0-7	-	- 7.00
Oct/Nov	0-1	-	- 1.00	Oct/Nov	0-1	-	- 1.00

4-y-o+	W-R	Per cent	£1 Level Stake	Totals	W-R	Per cent	£1 Level Stake
January	1-12	8.3	+ 1.00	January	1-15	6.7	- 2.00
February	0-16	-	- 16.00	February	0-17	-	- 17.00
March	3-14	21.4	+ 21.00	March	3-16	18.8	+ 19.00
April	0-7	-	- 7.00	April	1-15	6.7	- 10.50
May	1-11	9.1	+ 4.00	May	3-22	13.6	+ 5.75
June	1-18	5.6	- 9.00	June	1-30	3.3	- 21.00
July	1-10	10.0	- 5.00	July	2-26	7.7	- 16.50
August	3-5	60.0	+ 6.33	August	4-19	21.1	- 3.67
September	1-8	12.5	+ 1.00	September	1-20	5.0	- 11.00
Oct/Nov	1-9	11.1	+ 8.00	Oct/Nov	1-11	9.1	+ 6.00

DISTANCE

2-y-o	W-R	Per cent	£1 Level Stake	3-y-o	W-R	Per cent	£1 Level Stake
5f-6f	1-24	4.2	- 20.00	5f-6f	2-18	11.1	- 9.75
7f-8f	0-4	-	- 4.00	7f-8f	0-15	-	- 15.00
9f-13f	0-0	-	0.00	9f-13f	2-20	10.0	- 6.50
14f+	0-0	-	0.00	14f+	0-0	-	0.00

4-y-o+	W-R	Per cent	£1 Level Stake	Totals	W-R	Per cent	£1 Level Stake
5f-6f	8-48	16.7	+ 18.33	5f-6f	11-90	12.2	- 11.42
7f-8f	3-38	7.9	- 3.00	7f-8f	3-57	5.3	- 22.00
9f-13f	1-20	5.0	- 7.00	9f-13f	3-40	7.5	- 13.50
14f+	0-4	-	- 4.00	14f+	0-4	-	- 4.00

TYPE OF RACE

Non-Handicaps	W-R	Per cent	£1 Level Stake	Handicaps	W-R	Per cent	£1 Level Stake
2-y-o	0-14	-	- 14.00	2-y-o	0-5	-	- 5.00
3-y-o	1-28	3.6	- 24.25	3-y-o	1-14	7.1	- 9.50
4-y-o+	4-40	10.0	+ 14.00	4-y-o+	7-58	12.1	- 8.67
Selling	2-15	13.3	- 6.50	Selling	1-4	25.0	+ 5.00
Apprentice	0-3	-	- 3.00	Apprentice	0-4	-	- 4.00
Amat/Ladies	0-1	-	- 1.00	Amat/Ladies	1-5	20.0	+ 6.00
Totals	7-101	6.9	- 34.75	Totals	10-90	11.1	- 16.17

287

Macauley Mrs N

COURSE GRADE				FIRST TIME OUT			
	W-R	Per cent	£1 Level Stake		W-R	Per cent	£1 Level Stake
Group 1	2-17	11.8	- 7.50	2-y-o	0-7	-	- 7.00
Group 2	0-9	-	- 9.00	3-y-o	0-6	-	- 6.00
Group 3	6-63	9.5	- 10.50	4-y-o+	0-12	-	- 12.00
Group 4	9-102	8.8	- 23.92				
				Totals	0-25	-	- 25.00

JOCKEYS RIDING

	W-R	Per cent	£1 Level Stake		W-R	Per cent	£1 Level Stake
L Dettori	4-23	17.4	+ 2.50	D McKeown	1-7	14.3	+ 2.00
A Clark	3-34	8.8	+ 2.50	J Weaver	1-9	11.1	+ 8.00
J Fortune	2-13	15.4	- 0.25	M Fenton	1-10	10.0	- 6.00
D Wright	1-1	100.0	+ 1.50	Amanda Sanders	1-12	8.3	- 1.00
C Rutter	1-2	50.0	+ 11.00	J Tate	1-13	7.7	- 8.67
G Carter	1-3	33.3	+ 1.50				

Dale Gibson	0-15	B Thomson	0-1	P Bowe	0-1
W Wharton	0-7	D Harrison	0-1	P Roberts	0-1
J Quinn	0-6	J Carroll	0-1	Paul Eddery	0-1
E Husband	0-4	J Edmunds	0-1	R Cochrane	0-1
A Munro	0-3	J Marshall	0-1	R Mullen	0-1
Claire Balding	0-3	J Williams	0-1	S Maloney	0-1
J Lowe	0-3	L Aspell	0-1	S Mulvey	0-1
J Fanning	0-2	M Humphries	0-1	S Perks	0-1
N Adams	0-2	Madeleine Smith	0-1		
A Scobie	0-1	N Carlisle	0-1		

COURSE RECORD

	Total W-R	Non-Handicaps 2-y-o	Non-Handicaps 3-y-o+	Handicaps 2-y-o	Handicaps 3-y-o+	Per cent	£1 Level Stake
Nottingham	3-20	1-8	0-6	0-0	2-6	15.0	+ 2.00
Wolverhampton (AW)	3-33	0-0	1-14	0-0	2-19	9.1	+ 1.50
Southwell (AW)	3-43	0-2	1-20	0-1	2-20	7.0	- 21.17
Lingfield (AW)	2-17	0-0	1-8	0-0	1-9	11.8	+ 1.00
Leicester	2-24	0-5	1-8	0-2	1-9	8.3	+ 2.00
Carlisle	1-1	0-0	1-1	0-0	0-0	100.0	+ 2.75
Sandown	1-1	0-0	0-0	0-0	1-1	100.0	+ 3.50
Newmarket	1-8	0-0	0-2	0-0	1-6	12.5	- 3.00
Yarmouth	1-8	0-2	1-3	0-2	0-1	12.5	- 3.50

Pontefract	0-5	Windsor	0-3	Redcar	0-2
Warwick	0-5	Beverley	0-2	Bath	0-1
Folkestone	0-3	Brighton	0-2	Lingfield	0-1
Haydock	0-3	Doncaster	0-2	Ripon	0-1
Thirsk	0-3	Kempton	0-2	York	0-1

WINNING HORSES

	Age	Races Run	1st	2nd	3rd	Unpl	Win £
Join The Clan	5	11	4	1	2	4	15,802
Farmer Jock	12	16	2	0	3	11	5,768
Three Of Hearts	3	8	2	1	0	5	5,269
Bentico	5	3	1	0	0	2	3,678
Everset	6	1	1	0	0	0	3,652
Elton Ledger	5	6	1	2	0	3	3,080
Maid Welcome	7	16	1	1	2	12	2,691
Letsbeonestaboutit	8	18	1	2	1	14	2,557
Blues Bay	3	6	1	1	0	4	2,342
Lady Confess	4	6	1	1	0	4	2,243
Irchester Lass	2	7	1	0	0	6	2,174
Greek Night Out	3	11	1	2	2	6	2,070

WINNING OWNERS

	Races Won	Value £		Races Won	Value £
J Redden	4	15,802	Mrs N Macauley	1	2,691
G Wiltshire	2	6,020	Stephen Roots	1	2,557
S Thompson	2	5,768	Mrs R E Tate	1	2,243
Mrs Valerie Dixon	2	5,269	D M Hacker	1	2,174
Gordon Mytton	1	3,652	Miss S E Broadley	1	2,070
The Posse	1	3,080			

Favourites	4-13	30.8%	+ 8.00	Total winning prize-money		£51,326
Longest winning sequence			2	Average SP of winner		7.2/1
Longest losing sequence			40	Return on stakes invested		-26.7%
1993 Form	12-150	8.0%	- 71.00	1991 Form	21-307	6.8%	-105.60
1992 Form	12-227	5.3%	-125.64	1990 Form	24-271	8.9%	- 66.10

J MACKIE (Church Broughton, Derbys)

	No. of Horses	Races Run	1st	2nd	3rd	Unpl	Per cent	£1 Level Stake
2-y-o	1	3	0	0	0	3	-	- 3.00
3-y-o	3	18	1	0	2	15	5.6	- 12.50
4-y-o+	5	14	2	1	0	11	14.3	- 5.00
Totals	9	35	3	1	2	29	8.6	- 20.50

Jan	Feb	Mar	Apr	May	Jun	Jul	Aug	Sep	Oct/Nov
1-3	0-2	0-1	1-1	1-11	0-3	0-2	0-1	0-5	0-6

Mackie J

Winning Jockeys	W-R	£1 Level Stake		W-R	£1 Level Stake
J Weaver	1-3	+ 2.50	L Dettori	1-4	0.00
D Moffatt	1-3	+ 2.00			

Winning Courses	W-R	£1 Level Stake		W-R	£1 Level Stake
Pontefract	1-2	+ 3.00	Wolverhampton (AW)	1-4	0.00
Carlisle	1-4	+ 1.50			

Winning Horses	Age	Races Run	1st	2nd	3rd	Unpl	Win £
Patroclus	9	4	1	1	0	2	3,262
Cheerful Groom	3	10	1	0	2	7	3,002
Must Be Magical	6	6	1	0	0	5	2,243

Favourites	1-1	100.0%	+ 3.00	Total winning prize-money		£8,507

1993 Form	4-60	6.7%	- 18.00	1991 Form	3-61	4.9%	- 30.00
1992 Form	4-58	6.9%	- 32.62	1990 Form	8-73	11.0%	+ 16.00

M J MADGWICK (Denmead, Hants)

	No. of Horses	Races Run	1st	2nd	3rd	Unpl	Per cent	£1 Level Stake
2-y-o	3	11	0	0	0	11	-	- 11.00
3-y-o	4	11	0	0	0	11	-	- 11.00
4-y-o+	2	12	1	1	0	10	8.3	- 6.00
Totals	9	34	1	1	0	32	2.9	- 28.00

Jan	Feb	Mar	Apr	May	Jun	Jul	Aug	Sep	Oct/Nov
0-2	1-2	0-1	0-3	0-5	0-6	0-5	0-4	0-5	0-1

Winning Jockey	W-R	£1 Level Stake	Winning Course	W-R	£1 Level Stake
L Dettori	1-2	+ 4.00	Lingfield (AW)	1-5	+ 1.00

Winning Horse	Age	Races Run	1st	2nd	3rd	Unpl	Win £
Ecu De France	4	10	1	1	0	8	3,377

Favourites	0-1		Total winning prize-money	£3,377

1993 Form	0-27			1991 Form	0-60		
1992 Form	0-39			1990 Form	5-65	7.7%	- 16.50

P J MAKIN (Marlborough, Wilts)

	No. of Horses	Races Run	1st	2nd	3rd	Unpl	Per cent	£1 Level Stake
2-y-o	10	26	2	2	2	20	7.7	+ 17.00
3-y-o	13	60	4	4	2	50	6.7	- 37.50
4-y-o+	13	66	3	11	4	48	4.5	- 51.50
Totals	36	152	9	17	8	118	5.9	- 72.00

Jan	Feb	Mar	Apr	May	Jun	Jul	Aug	Sep	Oct/Nov
0-1	0-3	0-0	0-3	0-18	0-22	3-21	1-16	4-33	1-35

Winning Jockeys	W-R	£1 Level Stake			W-R	£1 Level Stake
L Dettori	2-7	+ 4.50	W Newnes		1-9	- 6.00
Mr T Cuff	1-1	+ 2.00	Pat Eddery		1-11	- 5.00
A Munro	1-2	+ 6.00	M Hills		1-13	- 7.50
R Cochrane	1-7	+ 19.00	R Perham		1-39	- 22.00

Winning Courses						
Ayr	2-2	+ 9.00	Leicester		1-6	- 0.50
Windsor	2-10	+ 1.50	Sandown		1-13	- 10.00
Folkestone	1-2	+ 15.00	Kempton		1-14	- 8.00
Lingfield	1-5	+ 21.00				

Winning Horses	Age	Races Run	1st	2nd	3rd	Unpl	Win £
Wilcuma	3	8	3	0	1	4	12,812
Addicted To Love	5	8	1	2	0	5	4,464
Gentle Irony	2	5	1	0	0	4	3,580
Sharp Rebuff	3	3	1	0	0	2	3,355
Little Saboteur	5	8	1	1	1	5	3,290
Flight Master	2	2	1	0	0	1	2,986
Gone For A Burton	4	7	1	1	0	5	2,713

Favourites	3-10	30.0%	+ 4.50	Total winning prize-money		£33,199

1993 Form	13-146	8.9%	- 36.72	1991 Form	23-200	11.5%	- 44.46
1992 Form	12-162	7.4%	- 50.09	1990 Form	27-146	18.5%	- 28.65

D MARKS (Upper Lambourn, Berks)

	No. of Horses	Races Run	1st	2nd	3rd	Unpl	Per cent	£1 Level Stake
2-y-o	1	4	0	0	0	4	-	- 4.00
3-y-o	2	5	0	0	0	5	-	- 5.00
4-y-o+	5	41	1	7	6	27	2.4	- 33.50
Totals	8	50	1	7	6	36	2.0	- 42.50

Jan	Feb	Mar	Apr	May	Jun	Jul	Aug	Sep	Oct/Nov
0-5	0-2	0-4	0-2	0-4	0-8	1-7	0-6	0-6	0-6

Marks D

Winning Jockey	W-R	£1 Level Stake	Winning Course	W-R	£1 Level Stake
M Baird	1-17	- 9.50	Wolverhampton (AW)	1-14	- 6.50

Winning Horse	Age	Races Run	1st	2nd	3rd	Unpl	Win £
Arawa	4	17	1	4	2	10	2,976

Favourites	0-1			Total winning prize-money		£2,976

1993 Form	2-61	3.3%	- 39.50	1991 Form	0-41		
1992 Form	8-77	10.4%	- 14.25	1990 Form	1-32	3.1%	+ 19.00

K MCAULIFFE (Lambourn, Berks)

	No. of Horses	Races Run	1st	2nd	3rd	Unpl	Per cent	£1 Level Stake
2-y-o	8	29	2	5	2	20	6.9	+ 37.00
3-y-o	7	30	3	1	1	25	10.0	+ 14.67
4-y-o+	4	11	3	1	0	7	27.3	+ 24.25
Totals	19	70	8	7	3	52	11.4	+ 75.92

Jan	Feb	Mar	Apr	May	Jun	Jul	Aug	Sep	Oct/Nov
0-0	0-1	0-0	1-14	1-8	0-1	3-10	1-14	0-11	2-11

Winning Jockeys	W-R	£1 Level Stake		W-R	£1 Level Stake
J Tate	4-27	+ 23.25	M Perrett	1-2	+ 7.00
D Holland	2-19	+ 33.67	J Lowe	1-3	+ 31.00

Winning Courses					
Catterick	1-2	+ 32.00	Windsor	1-4	- 0.75
Doncaster	1-2	+ 13.00	Leicester	1-5	+ 16.00
Warwick	1-3	+ 6.00	Pontefract	1-7	+ 4.00
Kempton	1-4	+ 47.00	Folkestone	1-8	- 6.33

Winning Horses	Age	Races Run	1st	2nd	3rd	Unpl	Win £
Big Pat	5	3	2	1	0	0	6,753
Red Valerian	3	6	1	0	1	4	4,698
Royal Philosopher	2	4	1	0	1	2	4,590
Fairlead	4	4	1	0	0	3	3,574
Skip To Somerfield	2	2	1	1	0	0	3,141
Roses Galore	3	3	1	0	0	2	3,002
Real Popcorn	3	3	1	0	0	2	2,624

Favourites	2-5	40.0%	- 0.08	Total winning prize-money	£28,382

1993 Form	1-1	100.0%	+ 20.00

P J MCBRIDE (Newmarket)

	No. of Horses	Races Run	1st	2nd	3rd	Unpl	Per cent	£1 Level Stake
2-y-o	6	13	0	1	0	12	-	- 13.00
3-y-o	4	23	2	2	1	18	8.7	+ 1.00
4-y-o+	1	5	0	0	0	5	-	- 5.00
Totals	11	41	2	3	1	35	4.9	- 17.00

Jan	Feb	Mar	Apr	May	Jun	Jul	Aug	Sep	Oct/Nov
0-4	0-1	0-0	0-0	1-2	0-6	0-6	0-6	1-8	0-8

Winning Jockeys	W-R	£1 Level Stake				W-R	£1 Level Stake
Mrs A Farrell	1-1	+ 20.00		D McCabe		1-2	+ 1.00

Winning Courses	W-R	£1 Level Stake				W-R	£1 Level Stake
Folkestone	1-1	+ 2.00		Newbury		1-1	+ 20.00

Winning Horse	Age	Races Run	1st	2nd	3rd	Unpl	Win £
Children's Choice	3	12	2	2	0	8	8,407

Favourites	1-2	50.0%	+ 1.00	Total winning prize-money	£8,407

1993 Form	1-27	3.7%	- 21.00

M MCCORMACK (Wantage, Oxon)

	No. of Horses	Races Run	1st	2nd	3rd	Unpl	Per cent	£1 Level Stake
2-y-o	10	31	0	1	3	27	-	- 31.00
3-y-o	12	36	2	2	2	30	5.6	- 18.00
4-y-o+	7	46	2	8	2	34	4.3	- 26.00
Totals	29	113	4	11	7	91	3.5	- 75.00

Jan	Feb	Mar	Apr	May	Jun	Jul	Aug	Sep	Oct/Nov
0-0	0-0	0-5	2-10	0-16	0-21	1-17	0-14	0-17	1-13

Winning Jockeys	W-R	£1 Level Stake				W-R	£1 Level Stake
J Reid	2-22	- 2.00		B Thomson		1-6	- 1.00
G Duffield	1-5	+ 8.00					

Winning Courses	W-R	£1 Level Stake				W-R	£1 Level Stake
Warwick	1-3	+ 10.00		Lingfield (AW)		1-7	- 2.00
Doncaster	1-5	0.00		Newmarket		1-8	+ 7.00

McCormack M

Winning Horses	Age	Races Run	1st	2nd	3rd	Unpl	Win £
Windrush Lady	4	3	1	0	0	2	7,700
Inherent Magic	5	9	1	3	0	5	7,087
Pab's Choice	3	5	2	0	1	2	6,409

Favourites	1-5	20.0%	0.00	Total winning prize-money			£21,196

1993 Form	16-141	11.3%	- 8.38	1991 Form	16-145	11.0%	- 22.50
1992 Form	16-175	9.1%	- 69.97	1990 Form	5-152	3.3%	-116.25

MRS M MCCOURT (Wantage, Oxon)

	No. of Horses	Races Run	1st	2nd	3rd	Unpl	Per cent	£1 Level Stake
2-y-o	0	0	0	0	0	0	-	0.00
3-y-o	1	7	0	0	2	5	-	- 7.00
4-y-o+	5	30	2	1	2	25	6.7	- 10.37
Totals	6	37	2	1	4	30	5.4	- 17.37

Jan	Feb	Mar	Apr	May	Jun	Jul	Aug	Sep	Oct/Nov
0-0	0-0	0-0	0-5	1-9	0-5	0-7	1-5	0-2	0-4

Winning Jockey	W-R	£1 Level Stake			W-R	£1 Level Stake
B Thomson	2-7	+ 12.63				

Winning Courses						
Haydock	1-1	+ 1.63	Chepstow		1-2	+ 15.00

Winning Horse	Age	Races Run	1st	2nd	3rd	Unpl	Win £
Aughfad	8	12	2	1	2	7	6,401

Favourites	1-3	33.3%	- 0.37	Total winning prize-money		£6,401

1993 Form	0-17

P M MCENTEE (Maidenhead, Berks)

	No. of Horses	Races Run	1st	2nd	3rd	Unpl	Per cent	£1 Level Stake
2-y-o	6	25	1	0	0	24	4.0	- 18.00
3-y-o	5	14	0	0	0	14	-	- 14.00
4-y-o+	5	10	0	0	1	9	-	- 10.00
Totals	16	49	1	0	1	47	2.0	- 42.00

Jan	Feb	Mar	Apr	May	Jun	Jul	Aug	Sep	Oct/Nov
0-0	0-1	0-2	1-3	0-8	0-4	0-9	0-6	0-0	0-16

			£1 Level						£1 Level
Winning Jockey		W-R	Stake	Winning Course			W-R		Stake
B Doyle		1-4	+ 3.00	Folkestone			1-9		- 2.00

			Races						Win
Winning Horse		Age	Run	1st	2nd	3rd	Unpl		£
Lady Governor		2	11	1	0	0	10		2,217

Favourites	0-0			Total winning prize-money			£2,217
1993 Form	1-58	1.7%	- 55.00	1992 Form	1-18	5.6%	- 13.00

B A MCMAHON (Tamworth, Staffs)

	No. of Horses	Races Run	1st	2nd	3rd	Unpl	Per cent	£1 Level Stake
2-y-o	16	75	3	8	4	60	4.0	- 52.50
3-y-o	19	140	14	19	14	93	10.0	- 45.00
4-y-o+	16	147	11	19	21	96	7.5	- 70.20
Totals	51	362	28	46	39	249	7.7	-167.70

BY MONTH

2-y-o	W-R	Per cent	£1 Level Stake	3-y-o	W-R	Per cent	£1 Level Stake
January	0-0	-	0.00	January	0-2	-	- 2.00
February	0-0	-	0.00	February	0-2	-	- 2.00
March	0-1	-	- 1.00	March	0-4	-	- 4.00
April	0-4	-	- 4.00	April	2-10	20.0	- 2.50
May	0-8	-	- 8.00	May	1-16	6.3	- 9.50
June	0-10	-	- 10.00	June	2-24	8.3	- 7.50
July	3-10	30.0	+ 12.50	July	4-29	13.8	- 6.00
August	0-14	-	- 14.00	August	1-21	4.8	- 16.50
September	0-13	-	- 13.00	September	4-21	19.0	+ 16.00
Oct/Nov	0-15	-	- 15.00	Oct/Nov	0-11	-	- 11.00

4-y-o+	W-R	Per cent	£1 Level Stake	Totals	W-R	Per cent	£1 Level Stake
January	0-11	-	- 11.00	January	0-13	-	- 13.00
February	1-5	20.0	- 1.20	February	1-7	14.3	- 3.20
March	1-12	8.3	- 7.50	March	1-17	5.9	- 12.50
April	2-21	9.5	- 7.00	April	4-35	11.4	- 13.50
May	1-20	5.0	- 16.50	May	2-44	4.5	- 34.00
June	2-18	11.1	- 3.50	June	4-52	7.7	- 21.00
July	2-15	13.3	- 3.50	July	9-54	16.7	+ 3.00
August	0-16	-	- 16.00	August	1-51	2.0	- 46.50
September	1-15	6.7	- 5.00	September	5-49	10.2	- 2.00
Oct/Nov	1-14	7.1	+ 1.00	Oct/Nov	1-40	2.5	- 25.00

DISTANCE

2-y-o	W-R	Per cent	£1 Level Stake	3-y-o	W-R	Per cent	£1 Level Stake
5f-6f	3-62	4.8	- 39.50	5f-6f	7-70	10.0	- 19.00
7f-8f	0-13	-	- 13.00	7f-8f	1-31	3.2	- 24.00
9f-13f	0-0	-	0.00	9f-13f	2-28	7.1	- 13.00
14f+	0-0	-	0.00	14f+	4-11	36.4	+ 11.00

4-y-o+	W-R	Per cent	£1 Level Stake	Totals	W-R	Per cent	£1 Level Stake
5f-6f	3-55	5.5	- 28.45	5f-6f	13-187	7.0	- 86.95
7f-8f	4-55	7.3	- 30.00	7f-8f	5-99	5.1	- 67.00
9f-13f	3-29	10.3	- 10.75	9f-13f	5-57	8.8	- 23.75
14f+	1-8	12.5	- 1.00	14f+	5-19	26.3	+ 10.00

TYPE OF RACE

Non-Handicaps	W-R	Per cent	£1 Level Stake	Handicaps	W-R	Per cent	£1 Level Stake
2-y-o	1-57	1.8	- 54.00	2-y-o	2-10	20.0	+ 9.50
3-y-o	8-57	14.0	+ 5.00	3-y-o	6-73	8.2	- 40.00
4-y-o+	5-44	11.4	- 4.95	4-y-o+	6-88	6.8	- 50.25
Selling	0-11	-	- 11.00	Selling	0-10	-	- 10.00
Apprentice	0-5	-	- 5.00	Apprentice	0-4	-	- 4.00
Amat/Ladies	0-0	-	0.00	Amat/Ladies	0-3	-	- 3.00
Totals	14-174	8.0	- 69.95	Totals	14-188	7.4	- 97.75

COURSE GRADE

	W-R	Per cent	£1 Level Stake
Group 1	11-108	10.2	- 25.00
Group 2	3-38	7.9	- 15.00
Group 3	4-92	4.3	- 61.50
Group 4	10-124	8.1	- 66.20

FIRST TIME OUT

	W-R	Per cent	£1 Level Stake
2-y-o	0-16	-	- 16.00
3-y-o	1-18	5.6	- 12.50
4-y-o+	0-16	-	- 16.00
Totals	1-50	2.0	- 44.50

JOCKEYS RIDING

	W-R	Per cent	£1 Level Stake		W-R	Per cent	£1 Level Stake
J Weaver	5-25	20.0	+ 29.75	A Mackay	2-36	5.6	- 25.00
J Fortune	4-48	8.3	- 20.50	R Cochrane	1-4	25.0	- 1.00
G Carter	3-16	18.8	+ 5.25	M Tebbutt	1-5	20.0	- 1.50
T Quinn	3-30	10.0	- 16.00	B Raymond	1-6	16.7	- 1.50
K Fallon	2-9	22.2	0.00	T Williams	1-15	6.7	- 10.50
J Reid	2-12	16.7	+ 7.50	S Sanders	1-38	2.6	- 27.00
L Dettori	2-25	8.0	- 14.20				

J Bramhill	0-16	J Williams	0-2	M Hills	0-1
D Holland	0-7	M Fenton	0-2	M Perrett	0-1
T Wall	0-7	M Roberts	0-2	Miss C Froggitt	0-1
A Munro	0-5	P Robinson	0-2	Miss S Jutterstrom	0-1
G Duffield	0-4	S Whitworth	0-2	Mr E McMahon	0-1
J Lowe	0-4	T Ives	0-2	N Adams	0-1
W Carson	0-4	W Newnes	0-2	N Connorton	0-1
A Culhane	0-3	C Asmussen	0-1	N Kennedy	0-1
A Clark	0-2	D Denby	0-1	Paul Eddery	0-1
C Hodgson	0-2	Dale Gibson	0-1	Rosalyn Whittle	0-1
D Wright	0-2	F Norton	0-1	S Perks	0-1
G Bardwell	0-2	L Charnock	0-1	W Ryan	0-1
J Quinn	0-2	Le Tollboll	0-1	W Woods	0-1

COURSE RECORD

	Total W-R	Non-Handicaps 2-y-o	3-y-o+	Handicaps 2-y-o	3-y-o+	Per cent	£1 Level Stake
Wolverhampton (AW)	5-52	0-10	1-13	0-0	4-29	9.6	- 23.50
Southwell (AW)	4-40	1-4	2-17	0-1	1-18	10.0	- 15.20
Nottingham	3-29	0-6	2-10	0-0	1-13	10.3	- 4.00
Goodwood	2-7	0-2	0-0	1-1	1-4	28.6	+ 8.50
Newmarket	2-14	0-1	0-4	0-0	2-9	14.3	- 2.50
York	2-16	0-4	1-1	1-2	0-9	12.5	+ 8.00
Doncaster	2-22	0-3	2-8	0-1	0-10	9.1	- 15.00
Haydock	2-29	0-5	1-5	0-1	1-18	6.9	- 6.00
Newcastle	1-2	0-0	0-0	0-0	1-2	50.0	0.00
Thirsk	1-6	0-2	1-2	0-0	0-2	16.7	+ 5.00
Chester	1-11	0-3	1-5	0-0	0-3	9.1	- 3.00
Warwick	1-16	0-2	1-6	0-1	0-7	6.3	- 11.50
Ripon	1-17	0-4	0-4	0-1	1-8	5.9	- 13.00
Leicester	1-23	0-3	1-9	0-2	0-9	4.3	- 17.50

Pontefract	0-15	Catterick	0-7	Folkestone	0-2
Bath	0-9	Newbury	0-6	Hamilton	0-2
Beverley	0-9	Ascot	0-4	Salisbury	0-1
Ayr	0-7	Chepstow	0-4	Sandown	0-1
Carlisle	0-7	Redcar	0-3	Yarmouth	0-1

WINNING HORSES

	Age	Races Run	1st	2nd	3rd	Unpl	Win £
Silence In Court	3	9	5	1	0	3	30,476
Band On The Run	7	14	2	0	0	12	16,705
Crofters Ceildh	2	9	2	3	1	3	12,642
Wentbridge Lad	4	13	3	1	3	6	9,136
Croeso-I-Cymru	3	8	2	3	1	2	9,110
Roving Minstrel	3	14	2	4	1	7	6,256
Katy's Lad	7	9	1	3	1	4	4,256
I'm Your Lady	3	8	1	0	3	4	3,778
Swinging Tich	5	10	1	1	1	7	3,623

McMahon B A

Churchworth	3	8	1	0	0	7	3,492
Causley	9	11	1	4	1	5	3,314
Admirals Realm	5	12	1	0	3	8	3,262
Racing Brenda	3	9	1	2	1	5	3,080
Grandee	3	2	1	0	0	1	2,951
Had A Girl	3	12	1	1	1	9	2,853
Disco Boy	4	10	1	1	1	7	2,738
The Happy Fox	2	11	1	2	0	8	2,612
Well And Truly	7	10	1	2	3	4	2,243

WINNING OWNERS

	Races Won	Value £		Races Won	Value £
Peter G Freeman	9	41,855	Mrs B Facchino	1	3,492
D J Allen	2	16,705	Henry Pearce	1	3,314
Mrs Mary Meddings	2	12,642	P W Leslie	1	3,262
Mrs Richard Evans	2	9,110	G Whitaker	1	3,080
Mrs J McMahon	2	6,256	J R Smith	1	2,951
J W Butler	1	4,256	J A Forsyth	1	2,853
Michael G T Stokes	1	3,778	S P Bradford	1	2,738
D E Gregory	1	3,623	G Whitaker	1	2,612

Favourites	7-26	26.9%	– 4.25	Total winning prize-money	£122,525
Longest winning sequence			2	Average SP of winner	5.9/1
Longest losing sequence			52	Return on stakes invested	-46.3%
1993 Form	22-290	7.6%	– 44.20	1991 Form	14-277	5.1%	-150.37
1992 Form	31-316	9.8%	– 95.02	1990 Form	22-275	8.0%	– 55.74

B J MCMATH (Newmarket)

	No. of Horses	Races Run	1st	2nd	3rd	Unpl	Per cent	£1 Level Stake
2-y-o	4	6	0	1	0	5	-	– 6.00
3-y-o	5	13	1	0	0	12	7.7	0.00
4-y-o+	5	31	0	5	1	25	-	– 31.00
Totals	14	50	1	6	1	42	2.0	– 37.00

Jan	Feb	Mar	Apr	May	Jun	Jul	Aug	Sep	Oct/Nov
0-2	0-2	0-1	0-4	0-3	0-2	0-2	1-12	0-13	0-9

		£1 Level Stake			£1 Level Stake
Winning Jockey	W-R		Winning Course	W-R	
E Johnson	1-24	– 11.00	Yarmouth	1-9	+ 4.00

Winning Horse	Age	Races Run	1st	2nd	3rd	Unpl	Win £
Narbonne	3	5	1	0	0	4	3,158

Favourites	0-3			Total winning prize-money			£3,158

1993 Form	1-50	2.0%	- 45.00	1991 Form	0-32
1992 Form	1-35	2.9%	- 29.50	1990 Form	0-14

MARTYN MEADE (Malmesbury, Wilts)

	No. of Horses	Races Run	1st	2nd	3rd	Unpl	Per cent	£1 Level Stake
2-y-o	4	13	1	0	0	12	7.7	+ 21.00
3-y-o	1	4	0	0	0	4	-	- 4.00
4-y-o+	3	11	1	0	0	10	9.1	- 5.00
Totals	8	28	2	0	0	26	7.1	+ 12.00

Jan	Feb	Mar	Apr	May	Jun	Jul	Aug	Sep	Oct/Nov
0-1	1-1	0-0	0-5	0-2	0-0	0-0	0-3	1-6	0-10

Winning Jockeys	W-R	£1 Level Stake		W-R	£1 Level Stake
A Clark	1-3	+ 31.00	D Holland	1-7	- 1.00

Winning Courses					
Sandown	1-2	+ 32.00	Lingfield (AW)	1-2	+ 4.00

Winning Horses	Age	Races Run	1st	2nd	3rd	Unpl	Win £
Warning Shot	2	1	1	0	0	0	3,600
Nornax Lad	6	2	1	0	0	1	2,977

Favourites	0-0			Total winning prize-money			£6,577

1993 Form	0-2

B J MEEHAN (Upper Lambourn, Berks)

	No. of Horses	Races Run	1st	2nd	3rd	Unpl	Per cent	£1 Level Stake
2-y-o	23	103	6	8	8	81	5.8	- 53.00
3-y-o	26	170	16	20	13	121	9.4	+ 18.58
4-y-o+	9	41	2	3	6	30	4.9	- 29.17
Totals	58	314	24	31	27	232	7.6	- 63.59

BY MONTH

2-y-o	W-R	Per cent	£1 Level Stake	3-y-o	W-R	Per cent	£1 Level Stake
January	0-0	-	0.00	January	0-4	-	- 4.00
February	0-0	-	0.00	February	0-2	-	- 2.00
March	0-1	-	- 1.00	March	0-5	-	- 5.00
April	0-6	-	- 6.00	April	1-17	5.9	- 11.00
May	1-9	11.1	- 1.50	May	2-23	8.7	- 2.00
June	0-10	-	- 10.00	June	4-21	19.0	+ 54.33
July	0-18	-	- 18.00	July	2-25	8.0	- 1.00
August	2-21	9.5	- 12.00	August	4-26	15.4	+ 6.25
September	1-24	4.2	- 18.50	September	1-27	3.7	- 14.00
Oct/Nov	2-14	14.3	+ 14.00	Oct/Nov	2-20	10.0	- 3.00

4-y-o+	W-R	Per cent	£1 Level Stake	Totals	W-R	Per cent	£1 Level Stake
January	0-1	-	- 1.00	January	0-5	-	- 5.00
February	1-2	50.0	+ 2.33	February	1-4	25.0	+ 0.33
March	0-1	-	- 1.00	March	0-7	-	- 7.00
April	0-3	-	- 3.00	April	1-26	3.8	- 20.00
May	0-6	-	- 6.00	May	3-38	7.9	- 9.50
June	0-8	-	- 8.00	June	4-39	10.3	+ 36.33
July	1-5	20.0	+ 2.50	July	3-48	6.3	- 16.50
August	0-6	-	- 6.00	August	6-53	11.3	- 11.75
September	0-6	-	- 6.00	September	2-57	3.5	- 38.50
Oct/Nov	0-3	-	- 3.00	Oct/Nov	4-37	10.8	+ 8.00

DISTANCE

2-y-o	W-R	Per cent	£1 Level Stake	3-y-o	W-R	Per cent	£1 Level Stake
5f-6f	4-62	6.5	- 32.00	5f-6f	2-38	5.3	- 21.00
7f-8f	2-40	5.0	- 20.00	7f-8f	6-75	8.0	- 12.75
9f-13f	0-1	-	- 1.00	9f-13f	3-41	7.3	- 23.67
14f+	0-0	-	0.00	14f+	5-16	31.3	+ 76.00

4-y-o+	W-R	Per cent	£1 Level Stake	Totals	W-R	Per cent	£1 Level Stake
5f-6f	0-6	-	- 6.00	5f-6f	6-106	5.7	- 59.00
7f-8f	1-13	7.7	- 8.67	7f-8f	9-128	7.0	- 41.42
9f-13f	1-11	9.1	- 3.50	9f-13f	4-53	7.5	- 28.17
14f+	0-11	-	- 11.00	14f+	5-27	18.5	+ 65.00

TYPE OF RACE

Non-Handicaps	W-R	Per cent	£1 Level Stake	Handicaps	W-R	Per cent	£1 Level Stake
2-y-o	3-73	4.1	- 58.00	2-y-o	3-15	20.0	+ 20.00
3-y-o	6-44	13.6	+ 9.50	3-y-o	9-112	8.0	+ 10.08
4-y-o+	1-11	9.1	- 3.50	4-y-o+	1-24	4.2	- 19.67
Selling	0-16	-	- 16.00	Selling	0-5	-	- 5.00
Apprentice	1-2	50.0	+ 11.00	Apprentice	0-5	-	- 5.00
Amat/Ladies	0-1	-	- 1.00	Amat/Ladies	0-6	-	- 6.00
Totals	11-147	7.5	- 58.00	Totals	13-167	7.8	- 5.59

COURSE GRADE

	W-R	Per cent	£1 Level Stake
Group 1	5-113	4.4	- 71.00
Group 2	9-62	14.5	+ 10.25
Group 3	4-69	5.8	+ 10.33
Group 4	6-70	8.6	- 13.17

FIRST TIME OUT

	W-R	Per cent	£1 Level Stake
2-y-o	0-23	-	- 23.00
3-y-o	1-23	4.3	- 17.00
4-y-o+	0-8	-	- 8.00
Totals	1-54	1.9	- 48.00

JOCKEYS RIDING

	W-R	Per cent	£1 Level Stake		W-R	Per cent	£1 Level Stake
B Doyle	12-124	9.7	+ 23.50	D O'Neill	1-7	14.3	+ 6.00
J Weaver	3-15	20.0	+ 9.50	T Quinn	1-8	12.5	- 6.00
A Clark	2-8	25.0	+ 20.00	R Cochrane	1-10	10.0	- 7.25
S Whitworth	2-28	7.1	- 19.34	B Raymond	1-12	8.3	- 3.00
D Harrison	1-2	50.0	+ 13.00				

W Newnes	0-13	G Bardwell	0-2	A Munro	0-1
J Quinn	0-8	G Forster	0-2	D Biggs	0-1
T Williams	0-7	J Carroll	0-2	D Wright	0-1
C Rutter	0-5	J Williams	0-2	G Carter	0-1
Mrs J Boggis	0-5	L Piggott	0-2	G Hind	0-1
R Perham	0-5	M Roberts	0-2	J Reid	0-1
A Whelan	0-4	M Tebbutt	0-2	J Tate	0-1
Paul Eddery	0-4	Mark Denaro	0-2	L Suthern	0-1
B Thomson	0-3	Miss J Allison	0-2	M Fenton	0-1
N Adams	0-3	Pat Eddery	0-2	N Carlisle	0-1
W Ryan	0-3	W R Swinburn	0-2	S O'Gorman	0-1
A Tucker	0-2	W Woods	0-2		
B Rouse	0-2	A Culhane	0-1		

COURSE RECORD

	Total W-R	Non-Handicaps 2-y-o	Non-Handicaps 3-y-o+	Handicaps 2-y-o	Handicaps 3-y-o+	Per cent	£1 Level Stake
Brighton	6-23	2-10	2-3	0-2	2-8	26.1	+ 18.75
Wolverhampton (AW)	3-21	0-3	2-6	0-0	1-12	14.3	+ 3.50
Warwick	2-13	0-4	1-1	0-1	1-7	15.4	+ 15.00
Newbury	2-15	0-6	1-3	1-1	0-5	13.3	+ 2.00
Lingfield	2-23	0-7	1-5	0-1	1-10	8.7	+ 2.00
Ayr	1-2	0-1	0-0	0-0	1-1	50.0	+ 11.00
Hamilton	1-2	0-0	0-0	0-0	1-2	50.0	+ 2.33
Haydock	1-3	0-0	0-0	0-0	1-3	33.3	+ 2.00
Chepstow	1-5	0-1	0-1	1-1	0-2	20.0	+ 10.00
Yarmouth	1-7	0-1	0-1	0-0	1-5	14.3	+ 44.00
Salisbury	1-12	1-5	0-2	0-0	0-5	8.3	- 6.50
Lingfield (AW)	1-15	0-0	0-6	0-1	1-8	6.7	- 10.67
Leicester	1-19	0-7	1-6	0-2	0-4	5.3	- 10.00
Newmarket	1-24	0-6	0-3	1-2	0-13	4.2	- 17.00

Meehan B J

Sandown	0-20	Bath	0-10	York	0-3
Windsor	0-15	Epsom	0-10	Redcar	0-2
Folkestone	0-13	Doncaster	0-6	Chester	0-1
Goodwood	0-13	Catterick	0-5	Newcastle	0-1
Kempton	0-12	Ascot	0-4	Ripon	0-1
Nottingham	0-11	Southwell (AW)	0-3		

WINNING HORSES

	Age	Races Run	1st	2nd	3rd	Unpl	Win £
Captain Scarlet	3	9	3	1	1	4	12,049
Chris's Lad	3	12	3	2	2	5	10,357
Rowlandsons Rocks	2	8	2	1	0	5	9,531
Secundus	3	13	3	0	0	10	9,123
I Should Cocoa	2	10	2	0	1	7	7,596
Nonios	3	14	2	1	1	10	7,546
Silky Siren	5	10	1	3	2	4	4,752
Nakita	3	13	1	0	1	11	3,518
Dancing Lawyer	3	12	1	2	1	8	3,495
Tart And A Half	2	7	1	1	1	4	3,492
Tumbleweed Chapel	2	10	1	1	2	6	3,396
Bold Gem	3	12	1	3	0	8	2,786
Come On Risk Me	3	6	1	0	0	5	2,705
Kismetim	4	10	1	0	3	6	2,603
Epica	3	2	1	0	0	1	2,387

WINNING OWNERS

	Races Won	Value £		Races Won	Value £
Patrick G O'Sullivan	3	12,049	Vintage Services Limited	1	3,495
K C Gomm	3	10,357	P F Boggis	1	3,492
Rowlandsons Ltd (Jewellers)	2	9,531	The Tumbleweed Partnership	1	3,396
C J Meehan	3	9,123	F C T Wilson	1	2,786
David Abrey	2	7,596	Roldvale Limited	1	2,705
Exors of the late J P Fleming	2	7,546	R J Markwick	1	2,603
Stanley Nixon	1	4,752	Miss L Regis	1	2,387
Theobalds Stud	1	3,518			

Favourites	4-15	26.7%	- 1.92	Total winning prize-money		£85,334
Longest winning sequence			2	Average SP of winner		9.4/1
Longest losing sequence			43	Return on stakes invested		-20.3%
1993 Form	14-192	7.3%	- 92.78	1992 Form	0-2	

S MELLOR (Swindon, Wilts)

	No. of Horses	Races Run	1st	2nd	3rd	Unpl	Per cent	£1 Level Stake
2-y-o	7	25	0	1	1	23	-	- 25.00
3-y-o	1	6	0	0	0	6	-	- 6.00
4-y-o+	8	53	5	4	3	41	9.4	- 21.87
Totals	16	84	5	5	4	70	6.0	- 52.87

Jan	Feb	Mar	Apr	May	Jun	Jul	Aug	Sep	Oct/Nov
0-0	0-0	0-1	0-6	0-14	1-16	3-19	1-10	0-10	0-8

Winning Jockeys	W-R	£1 Level Stake		W-R	£1 Level Stake
M Roberts	2-4	+ 2.63	A Daly	1-6	0.00
Mr T Cuff	1-1	+ 4.50	M Wigham	1-12	+ 1.00

Winning Courses					
Carlisle	1-1	+ 5.00	Chepstow	1-3	+ 2.50
Epsom	1-2	+ 2.00	Southwell (AW)	1-3	+ 10.00
Brighton	1-3	- 0.37			

Winning Horses	Age	Races Run	1st	2nd	3rd	Unpl	Win £
Batchworth Bound	5	12	2	3	1	6	7,393
Queens Contractor	4	5	1	0	0	4	3,080
Bronze Runner	10	15	1	1	1	12	2,391
Anlace	5	8	1	0	1	6	2,262

Favourites	1-5	20.0%	- 2.37	Total winning prize-money	£15,126

1993 Form	4-56	7.1%	- 8.37	1991 Form	0-47
1992 Form	0-55			1990 Form	0-15

B R MILLMAN (Cullompton, Devon)

	No. of Horses	Races Run	1st	2nd	3rd	Unpl	Per cent	£1 Level Stake
2-y-o	4	17	1	0	3	13	5.9	+ 17.00
3-y-o	4	29	2	4	2	21	6.9	- 10.50
4-y-o+	9	40	3	2	3	32	7.5	+ 10.00
Totals	17	86	6	6	8	66	7.0	+ 16.50

Jan	Feb	Mar	Apr	May	Jun	Jul	Aug	Sep	Oct/Nov
0-0	0-1	0-0	0-6	1-7	3-17	0-15	0-11	1-16	1-13

Winning Jockeys	W-R	£1 Level Stake		W-R	£1 Level Stake
D Holland	4-12	+ 68.50	J Williams	1-12	+ 3.00
M Fenton	1-5	+ 2.00			

Winning Courses					
Chepstow	3-14	+ 13.50	Newbury	1-5	+ 21.00
Warwick	1-3	+ 12.00	Salisbury	1-9	+ 25.00

Winning Horses	Age	Races Run	1st	2nd	3rd	Unpl	Win £
World Express	4	10	2	0	0	8	7,863
Royal Seaton	5	9	1	1	1	6	5,512
Folly Finnesse	3	7	1	1	1	4	4,273
Suile Mor	2	6	1	0	1	4	2,920
Guto Nyth Bran	3	8	1	1	0	6	2,556

Favourites	1-2	50.0%	+ 1.50	Total winning prize-money		£23,123

1993 Form	6-120	5.0%	- 69.00	1991 Form	9-178	5.1%	- 84.92
1992 Form	7-107	6.5%	+ 15.00	1990 Form	12-153	7.8%	- 37.25

T G MILLS (Epsom, Surrey)

	No. of Horses	Races Run	1st	2nd	3rd	Unpl	Per cent	£1 Level Stake
2-y-o	8	40	8	3	5	24	20.0	+ 13.76
3-y-o	5	34	1	7	4	22	2.9	- 30.50
4-y-o+	8	54	7	6	5	36	13.0	+ 20.50
Totals	21	128	16	16	14	82	12.5	+ 3.76

BY MONTH

2-y-o	W-R	Per cent	£1 Level Stake	3-y-o	W-R	Per cent	£1 Level Stake
January	0-0	-	0.00	January	0-0	-	0.00
February	0-0	-	0.00	February	0-0	-	0.00
March	0-1	-	- 1.00	March	0-2	-	- 2.00
April	0-1	-	- 1.00	April	0-7	-	- 7.00
May	1-5	20.0	+ 12.00	May	0-6	-	- 6.00
June	2-5	40.0	+ 0.38	June	0-7	-	- 7.00
July	1-7	14.3	+ 2.00	July	0-2	-	- 2.00
August	2-7	28.6	+ 3.88	August	0-3	-	- 3.00
September	2-10	20.0	+ 1.50	September	1-3	33.3	+ 0.50
Oct/Nov	0-4	-	- 4.00	Oct/Nov	0-4	-	- 4.00

4-y-o+	W-R	Per cent	£1 Level Stake		Totals	W-R	Per cent	£1 Level Stake
January	0-1	-	- 1.00		January	0-1	-	- 1.00
February	0-0	-	0.00		February	0-0	-	0.00
March	1-1	100.0	+ 9.00		March	1-4	25.0	+ 6.00
April	1-10	10.0	+ 7.00		April	1-18	5.6	- 1.00
May	0-7	-	- 7.00		May	1-18	5.6	- 1.00
June	1-11	9.1	+ 1.00		June	3-23	13.0	- 5.62
July	0-8	-	- 8.00		July	1-17	5.9	- 8.00
August	2-8	25.0	+ 2.00		August	4-18	22.2	+ 2.88
September	2-7	28.6	+ 18.50		September	5-20	25.0	+ 20.50
Oct/Nov	0-1	-	- 1.00		Oct/Nov	0-9	-	- 9.00

DISTANCE

2-y-o	W-R	Per cent	£1 Level Stake		3-y-o	W-R	Per cent	£1 Level Stake
5f-6f	4-26	15.4	+ 6.63		5f-6f	0-1	-	- 1.00
7f-8f	4-14	28.6	+ 7.13		7f-8f	0-10	-	- 10.00
9f-13f	0-0	-	0.00		9f-13f	1-18	5.6	- 14.50
14f+	0-0	-	0.00		14f+	0-5	-	- 5.00

4-y-o+	W-R	Per cent	£1 Level Stake		Totals	W-R	Per cent	£1 Level Stake
5f-6f	2-15	13.3	- 5.00		5f-6f	6-42	14.3	+ 0.63
7f-8f	1-13	7.7	- 3.00		7f-8f	5-37	13.5	- 5.87
9f-13f	3-21	14.3	+ 16.50		9f-13f	4-39	10.3	+ 2.00
14f+	1-5	20.0	+ 12.00		14f+	1-10	10.0	+ 7.00

TYPE OF RACE

Non-Handicaps	W-R	Per cent	£1 Level Stake		Handicaps	W-R	Per cent	£1 Level Stake
2-y-o	5-29	17.2	+ 16.50		2-y-o	0-6	-	- 6.00
3-y-o	1-14	7.1	- 10.50		3-y-o	0-16	-	- 16.00
4-y-o+	3-10	30.0	+ 12.00		4-y-o+	3-36	8.3	+ 12.00
Selling	3-7	42.9	+ 1.26		Selling	1-4	25.0	+ 0.50
Apprentice	0-1	-	- 1.00		Apprentice	0-3	-	- 3.00
Amat/Ladies	0-0	-	0.00		Amat/Ladies	0-2	-	- 2.00
Totals	12-61	19.7	+ 18.26		Totals	4-67	6.0	- 14.50

COURSE GRADE

	W-R	Per cent	£1 Level Stake
Group 1	4-50	8.0	- 14.37
Group 2	7-26	26.9	+ 37.25
Group 3	2-32	6.3	- 15.50
Group 4	3-20	15.0	- 3.62

FIRST TIME OUT

	W-R	Per cent	£1 Level Stake
2-y-o	2-8	25.0	+ 18.00
3-y-o	0-5	-	- 5.00
4-y-o+	2-8	25.0	+ 19.00
Totals	4-21	19.0	+ 32.00

JOCKEYS RIDING

	W-R	Per cent	£1 Level Stake		W-R	Per cent	£1 Level Stake
J Reid	9-28	32.1	+ 35.25	Stephen Davies	1-9	11.1	- 6.37
D Holland	2-4	50.0	+ 15.88	T Williams	1-11	9.1	+ 10.00
L Piggott	1-3	33.3	+ 0.50	W Newnes	1-19	5.3	- 2.00
J Carroll	1-6	16.7	- 1.50				

N Gwilliams	0-9	J Quinn	0-2	N Carlisle	0-1
A Whelan	0-4	K Darley	0-2	Pat Eddery	0-1
D Toole	0-4	A Munro	0-1	R Hills	0-1
Paul Eddery	0-4	F Norton	0-1	R Price	0-1
D McKeown	0-3	J Fortune	0-1	S Whitworth	0-1
M J Kinane	0-3	L Dettori	0-1	T Quinn	0-1
A Mackay	0-2	M Hills	0-1	W Carson	0-1
G Duffield	0-2	Miss K Manzi	0-1		

COURSE RECORD

	Total W-R	Non-Handicaps 2-y-o	Non-Handicaps 3-y-o+	Handicaps 2-y-o	Handicaps 3-y-o+	Per cent	£1 Level Stake
Lingfield	3-10	1-5	1-2	0-0	1-3	30.0	+ 32.00
Folkestone	3-11	1-3	1-1	0-0	1-7	27.3	+ 5.38
Salisbury	2-4	1-1	1-1	0-0	0-2	50.0	+ 10.00
Ascot	2-9	1-4	1-1	0-0	0-4	22.2	+ 7.00
Yarmouth	1-2	1-2	0-0	0-0	0-0	50.0	+ 7.00
Brighton	1-4	1-1	0-1	0-0	0-2	25.0	- 1.25
Goodwood	1-6	1-2	0-0	0-0	0-4	16.7	- 3.37
Redcar	1-6	0-2	0-1	0-1	1-2	16.7	- 1.50
Leicester	1-8	1-2	0-4	0-1	0-1	12.5	- 0.50
Kempton	1-9	0-2	0-3	0-0	1-4	11.1	+ 8.00

Newbury	0-9	Newmarket	0-4	Pontefract	0-2
Sandown	0-7	Chepstow	0-3	Chester	0-1
Warwick	0-6	Beverley	0-2	Epsom	0-1
Windsor	0-6	Catterick	0-2	Lingfield (AW)	0-1
Nottingham	0-5	Doncaster	0-2	Ripon	0-1
Bath	0-4	Haydock	0-2	York	0-1

WINNING HORSES

	Age	Races Run	1st	2nd	3rd	Unpl	Win £
Bobzao	5	4	1	1	2	0	63,630
Fire Dome	2	4	2	0	1	1	13,669
Jonsalan	4	4	1	0	0	3	10,625
Sheila's Secret	4	13	2	2	1	8	8,812
Stevie's Wonder	4	7	2	0	0	5	7,583
Captain's Day	2	8	2	1	0	5	7,566
Greenwich Again	2	8	2	2	0	4	4,244
Media Express	2	10	1	0	2	7	3,785
Wot-If-We	2	5	1	0	2	2	3,596
Friendly Brave	4	8	1	1	0	6	3,106
Bahrain Star	3	11	1	3	1	6	2,905

WINNING OWNERS

	Races Won	Value £		Races Won	Value £
T G Mills	5	77,224	W R Norton	2	7,566
Mahmood Al-Shuaibi	3	17,454	J Humphreys Turf Accountants	2	4,244
Alan E Ward	1	10,625	Bob Merrick	1	3,596
Sherwoods Transport Ltd	2	8,812			

Favourites	6-12	50.0%	+ 8.26	Total winning prize-money	£129,520
Longest winning sequence			3	Average SP of winner	7.2/1
Longest losing sequence			31	Return on stakes invested	2.9%
1993 Form	9-125	7.2%	- 60.67		

P MITCHELL (Epsom, Surrey)

	No. of Horses	Races Run	1st	2nd	3rd	Unpl	Per cent	£1 Level Stake
2-y-o	3	6	0	0	1	5	-	- 6.00
3-y-o	6	41	3	8	5	25	7.3	- 24.25
4-y-o+	10	53	7	8	4	34	13.2	+ 27.50
Totals	19	100	10	16	10	64	10.0	- 2.75

BY MONTH

2-y-o	W-R	Per cent	£1 Level Stake	3-y-o	W-R	Per cent	£1 Level Stake
January	0-0	-	0.00	January	0-3	-	- 3.00
February	0-0	-	0.00	February	0-2	-	- 2.00
March	0-0	-	0.00	March	0-0	-	0.00
April	0-0	-	0.00	April	0-2	-	- 2.00
May	0-0	-	0.00	May	1-5	20.0	- 1.25
June	0-1	-	- 1.00	June	0-6	-	- 6.00
July	0-2	-	- 2.00	July	0-7	-	- 7.00
August	0-2	-	- 2.00	August	0-8	-	- 8.00
September	0-1	-	- 1.00	September	1-5	20.0	+ 4.00
Oct/Nov	0-0	-	0.00	Oct/Nov	1-3	33.3	+ 1.00

4-y-o+	W-R	Per cent	£1 Level Stake	Totals	W-R	Per cent	£1 Level Stake
January	1-7	14.3	+ 4.00	January	1-10	10.0	+ 1.00
February	0-2	-	- 2.00	February	0-4	-	- 4.00
March	0-2	-	- 2.00	March	0-2	-	- 2.00
April	0-2	-	- 2.00	April	0-4	-	- 4.00
May	2-8	25.0	+ 14.00	May	3-13	23.1	+ 12.75
June	0-7	-	- 7.00	June	0-14	-	- 14.00
July	0-7	-	- 7.00	July	0-16	-	- 16.00
August	1-9	11.1	- 3.00	August	1-19	5.3	- 13.00
September	1-6	16.7	+ 5.00	September	2-12	16.7	+ 8.00
Oct/Nov	2-3	66.7	+ 27.50	Oct/Nov	3-6	50.0	+ 28.50

Mitchell P

DISTANCE

	W-R	Per cent	£1 Level Stake		W-R	Per cent	£1 Level Stake
2-y-o				3-y-o			
5f-6f	0-1	-	- 1.00	5f-6f	0-1	-	- 1.00
7f-8f	0-5	-	- 5.00	7f-8f	1-11	9.1	- 7.00
9f-13f	0-0	-	0.00	9f-13f	2-22	9.1	- 9.25
14f+	0-0	-	0.00	14f+	0-7	-	- 7.00
4-y-o+				Totals			
5f-6f	0-0	-	0.00	5f-6f	0-2	-	- 2.00
7f-8f	1-20	5.0	- 9.00	7f-8f	2-36	5.6	- 21.00
9f-13f	6-31	19.4	+ 38.50	9f-13f	8-53	15.1	+ 29.25
14f+	0-2	-	- 2.00	14f+	0-9	-	- 9.00

TYPE OF RACE

Non-Handicaps	W-R	Per cent	£1 Level Stake	Handicaps	W-R	Per cent	£1 Level Stake
2-y-o	0-5	-	- 5.00	2-y-o	0-0	-	0.00
3-y-o	1-13	7.7	- 9.25	3-y-o	1-22	4.5	- 18.00
4-y-o+	0-11	-	- 11.00	4-y-o+	3-30	10.0	+ 14.00
Selling	1-3	33.3	+ 8.00	Selling	1-3	33.3	+ 6.00
Apprentice	0-0	-	0.00	Apprentice	0-4	-	- 4.00
Amat/Ladies	0-2	-	- 2.00	Amat/Ladies	3-7	42.9	+ 18.50
Totals	2-34	5.9	- 19.25	Totals	8-66	12.1	+ 16.50

COURSE GRADE

	W-R	Per cent	£1 Level Stake
Group 1	3-36	8.3	+ 7.00
Group 2	1-18	5.6	- 3.00
Group 3	2-9	22.2	+ 1.75
Group 4	4-37	10.8	- 8.50

FIRST TIME OUT

	W-R	Per cent	£1 Level Stake
2-y-o	0-3	-	- 3.00
3-y-o	0-5	-	- 5.00
4-y-o+	1-10	10.0	+ 1.00
Totals	1-18	5.6	- 7.00

JOCKEYS RIDING

	W-R	Per cent	£1 Level Stake		W-R	Per cent	£1 Level Stake
Mr T Cuff	2-2	100.0	+ 17.50	S Sanders	1-5	20.0	+ 21.00
G Duffield	2-7	28.6	+ 4.00	Mr R Teal	1-6	16.7	0.00
G Bardwell	2-12	16.7	+ 8.00	T Ives	1-12	8.3	- 1.00
J Weaver	1-2	50.0	+ 1.75				

W Newnes	0-9	T Quinn	0-2	Miss Y Haynes	0-1
D Wright	0-8	A Lakeman	0-1	Paul Eddery	0-1
S O'Gorman	0-8	A Mackay	0-1	R Hills	0-1
J Quinn	0-4	A Munro	0-1	R Hughes	0-1
A Clark	0-3	D Harrison	0-1	Stephen Davies	0-1
D Holland	0-3	G Carter	0-1	T Williams	0-1
J Reid	0-2	L Carter	0-1		
L Dettori	0-2	L Piggott	0-1		

COURSE RECORD

	Total W-R	Non-Handicaps 2-y-o	3-y-o+	Handicaps 2-y-o	3-y-o+	Per cent	£1 Level Stake
Hamilton	2-3	0-0	1-1	0-0	1-2	66.7	+ 7.75
Wolverhampton (AW)	2-5	0-0	0-0	0-0	2-5	40.0	+ 3.50
Lingfield (AW)	2-18	0-1	0-8	0-0	2-9	11.1	+ 2.00
Newbury	1-2	0-0	0-0	0-0	1-2	50.0	+ 24.00
Kempton	1-3	0-0	1-2	0-0	0-1	33.3	+ 8.00
Goodwood	1-8	0-1	0-0	0-0	1-7	12.5	- 2.00
Lingfield	1-12	0-0	0-3	0-0	1-9	8.3	+ 3.00

Epsom	0-12	Windsor	0-3	Bath	0-1
Folkestone	0-12	Leicester	0-2	Chester	0-1
Sandown	0-8	Southwell (AW)	0-2	Haydock	0-1
Brighton	0-5	Ascot	0-1	Newmarket	0-1

WINNING HORSES

	Age	Races Run	1st	2nd	3rd	Unpl	Win £
Second Chance	4	10	2	2	1	5	11,125
Ikhtiraa	4	15	3	3	0	9	10,259
Twice The Groom	4	7	2	1	0	4	7,108
Rockstine	3	16	2	4	2	8	5,820
Lear Dancer	3	10	1	3	3	3	2,540

WINNING OWNERS

	Races Won	Value £		Races Won	Value £
Down And Outs Racing	4	18,233	Mrs R A Johnson	1	2,540
J Morton	5	16,079			

Favourites	2-7	28.6%	+ 0.75	Total winning prize-money		£36,852

Longest winning sequence	3	Average SP of winner	8.7/1
Longest losing sequence	46	Return on stakes invested	-2.8%

1993 Form	9-100	9.0%	- 35.25	1991 Form	8-149	5.4%	- 63.00
1992 Form	5-107	4.7%	- 62.75	1990 Form	13-210	6.2%	-118.42

PAT MITCHELL (Newmarket)

	No. of Horses	Races Run	1st	2nd	3rd	Unpl	Per cent	£1 Level Stake
2-y-o	1	7	0	0	1	6	-	- 7.00
3-y-o	2	6	0	0	0	6	-	- 6.00
4-y-o+	7	44	2	4	2	36	4.5	- 25.50
Totals	10	57	2	4	3	48	3.5	- 38.50

Jan	Feb	Mar	Apr	May	Jun	Jul	Aug	Sep	Oct/Nov
1-3	0-5	0-6	0-3	0-4	0-3	0-7	1-10	0-10	0-6

Winning Jockeys	W-R	£1 Level Stake				W-R	£1 Level Stake
Miss A Harwood	1-1	+ 12.00	L Dettori			1-6	- 0.50

Winning Courses	W-R	£1 Level Stake				W-R	£1 Level Stake
Newmarket	1-8	+ 5.00	Lingfield (AW)			1-10	- 4.50

Winning Horse	Age	Races Run	1st	2nd	3rd	Unpl	Win £
Moujeeb	4	10	2	3	0	5	7,619

Favourites	0-5		Total winning prize-money	£7,619

1993 Form	7-147	4.8%	- 90.50	1991 Form	5-130	3.8%	- 86.00
1992 Form	10-146	6.8%	- 41.50	1990 Form	11-215	5.1%	- 62.17

D MOFFATT (Cartmel, Cumbria)

	No. of Horses	Races Run	1st	2nd	3rd	Unpl	Per cent	£1 Level Stake
2-y-o	4	16	2	0	0	14	12.5	- 1.50
3-y-o	4	13	0	1	2	10	-	- 13.00
4-y-o+	7	43	2	3	2	36	4.7	- 5.00
Totals	15	72	4	4	4	60	5.6	- 19.50

Jan	Feb	Mar	Apr	May	Jun	Jul	Aug	Sep	Oct/Nov
0-0	0-0	0-5	1-11	2-11	0-10	1-10	0-9	0-10	0-6

Winning Jockeys	W-R	£1 Level Stake				W-R	£1 Level Stake
D Moffatt	2-34	- 9.50	J Reid			1-4	+ 13.00
Dale Gibson	1-3	+ 8.00					

Winning Courses	W-R	£1 Level Stake				W-R	£1 Level Stake
Ayr	2-13	+ 19.00	Edinburgh			1-3	+ 0.50
York	1-2	+ 15.00					

Winning Horses	Age	Races Run	1st	2nd	3rd	Unpl	Win £
Key To My Heart	4	8	1	1	0	6	54,629
Seenthelight	2	7	2	0	0	5	5,270
Home Counties	5	6	1	0	0	5	3,469

Favourites	0-2			Total winning prize-money			£63,368

1993 Form	3-81	3.7%	- 57.50	1991 Form	7-94	7.4%	- 26.50
1992 Form	5-69	7.2%	- 15.50	1990 Form	1-34	2.9%	- 27.50

P MONTEITH (Rosewell, Midlothian)

	No. of Horses	Races Run	1st	2nd	3rd	Unpl	Per cent	£1 Level Stake
2-y-o	0	0	0	0	0	0	-	0.00
3-y-o	3	6	0	0	0	6	-	- 6.00
4-y-o+	13	39	2	5	7	25	5.1	- 28.25
Totals	16	45	2	5	7	31	4.4	- 34.25

Jan	Feb	Mar	Apr	May	Jun	Jul	Aug	Sep	Oct/Nov
0-0	0-0	0-3	0-0	0-4	1-11	1-13	0-8	0-5	0-1

Winning Jockeys	W-R	£1 Level Stake			W-R	£1 Level Stake
J Stack	1-10	- 7.25	J Marshall		1-15	- 7.00

Winning Courses						
Edinburgh	1-12	- 9.25	Hamilton		1-16	- 8.00

Winning Horse	Age	Races Run	1st	2nd	3rd	Unpl	Win £
Latvian	7	12	2	2	4	4	6,447

Favourites	1-1	100.0%	+ 1.75	Total winning prize-money			£6,447

1993 Form	4-61	6.6%	- 33.09	1991 Form	2-43	4.7%	- 19.50
1992 Form	0-59			1990 Form	2-61	3.3%	- 44.00

A MOORE (Brighton, East Sussex)

	No. of Horses	Races Run	1st	2nd	3rd	Unpl	Per cent	£1 Level Stake
2-y-o	6	21	0	0	0	21	-	- 21.00
3-y-o	4	18	1	0	1	16	5.6	- 12.00
4-y-o+	19	123	10	16	15	82	8.1	- 15.50
Totals	29	162	11	16	16	119	6.8	- 48.50

BY MONTH

2-y-o	W-R	Per cent	£1 Level Stake	3-y-o	W-R	Per cent	£1 Level Stake
January	0-0	-	0.00	January	0-1	-	- 1.00
February	0-0	-	0.00	February	0-0	-	0.00
March	0-0	-	0.00	March	0-0	-	0.00
April	0-0	-	0.00	April	0-0	-	0.00
May	0-0	-	0.00	May	0-0	-	0.00
June	0-2	-	- 2.00	June	0-6	-	- 6.00
July	0-4	-	- 4.00	July	1-5	20.0	+ 1.00
August	0-4	-	- 4.00	August	0-1	-	- 1.00
September	0-5	-	- 5.00	September	0-4	-	- 4.00
Oct/Nov	0-6	-	- 6.00	Oct/Nov	0-1	-	- 1.00

4-y-o+	W-R	Per cent	£1 Level Stake	Totals	W-R	Per cent	£1 Level Stake
January	5-20	25.0	+ 58.75	January	5-21	23.8	+ 57.75
February	0-18	-	- 18.00	February	0-18	-	- 18.00
March	3-17	17.6	- 2.25	March	3-17	17.6	- 2.25
April	1-8	12.5	- 3.00	April	1-8	12.5	- 3.00
May	0-12	-	- 12.00	May	0-12	-	- 12.00
June	1-17	5.9	- 8.00	June	1-25	4.0	- 16.00
July	0-10	-	- 10.00	July	1-19	5.3	- 13.00
August	0-8	-	- 8.00	August	0-13	-	- 13.00
September	0-5	-	- 5.00	September	0-14	-	- 14.00
Oct/Nov	0-8	-	- 8.00	Oct/Nov	0-15	-	- 15.00

DISTANCE

2-y-o	W-R	Per cent	£1 Level Stake	3-y-o	W-R	Per cent	£1 Level Stake
5f-6f	0-8	-	- 8.00	5f-6f	0-1	-	- 1.00
7f-8f	0-12	-	- 12.00	7f-8f	0-10	-	- 10.00
9f-13f	0-1	-	- 1.00	9f-13f	1-7	14.3	- 1.00
14f+	0-0	-	0.00	14f+	0-0	-	0.00

4-y-o+	W-R	Per cent	£1 Level Stake	Totals	W-R	Per cent	£1 Level Stake
5f-6f	2-19	10.5	- 5.00	5f-6f	2-28	7.1	- 14.00
7f-8f	1-23	4.3	- 2.00	7f-8f	1-45	2.2	- 24.00
9f-13f	5-63	7.9	- 38.50	9f-13f	6-71	8.5	- 40.50
14f+	2-18	11.1	+ 30.00	14f+	2-18	11.1	+ 30.00

TYPE OF RACE

Non-Handicaps	W-R	Per cent	£1 Level Stake	Handicaps	W-R	Per cent	£1 Level Stake
2-y-o	0-13	-	- 13.00	2-y-o	0-1	-	- 1.00
3-y-o	0-11	-	- 11.00	3-y-o	0-2	-	- 2.00
4-y-o+	4-33	12.1	+ 20.75	4-y-o+	5-62	8.1	- 11.50
Selling	0-12	-	- 12.00	Selling	2-11	18.2	- 1.75
Apprentice	0-2	-	- 2.00	Apprentice	0-5	-	- 5.00
Amat/Ladies	0-2	-	- 2.00	Amat/Ladies	0-8	-	- 8.00
Totals	4-73	5.5	- 19.25	Totals	7-89	7.9	- 29.25

COURSE GRADE					FIRST TIME OUT			
	W-R	Per cent	£1 Level Stake			W-R	Per cent	£1 Level Stake
Group 1	1-14	7.1	- 5.00	2-y-o		0-5	-	- 5.00
Group 2	2-38	5.3	- 27.00	3-y-o		0-3	-	- 3.00
Group 3	0-9	-	- 9.00	4-y-o+		3-19	15.8	+ 49.50
Group 4	8-101	7.9	- 7.50					
				Totals		3-27	11.1	+ 41.50

JOCKEYS RIDING

	W-R	Per cent	£1 Level Stake		W-R	Per cent	£1 Level Stake
N Adams	3-28	10.7	+ 7.00	Mark Denaro	1-5	20.0	+ 2.00
L Carter	2-5	40.0	+ 43.00	A Clark	1-11	9.1	- 8.25
L Dettori	2-22	9.1	- 13.75	Candy Morris	1-33	3.0	- 27.00
Paul Eddery	1-4	25.0	+ 2.50				

A Whelan	0-10	Miss J Winter	0-3	D O'Neill	0-1
T Williams	0-7	A Procter	0-2	Miss A Harwood	0-1
L Suthern	0-6	B Rouse	0-2	Mr T McCarthy	0-1
Mrs J Moore	0-5	R Cochrane	0-2	N Carlisle	0-1
J Quinn	0-4	W Woods	0-2	P McCabe	0-1
M Baird	0-4	A McGlone	0-1	W Newnes	0-1

COURSE RECORD

	Total W-R	Non-Handicaps 2-y-o	Non-Handicaps 3-y-o+	Handicaps 2-y-o	Handicaps 3-y-o+	Per cent	£1 Level Stake
Lingfield (AW)	8-78	0-1	3-24	0-1	5-52	10.3	+ 15.50
Goodwood	1-5	0-0	0-2	0-0	1-3	20.0	+ 4.00
Lingfield	1-16	0-5	0-7	0-0	1-4	6.3	- 10.00
Brighton	1-22	0-4	1-9	0-0	0-9	4.5	- 17.00

Folkestone	0-20	Kempton	0-3	Newbury	0-1
Epsom	0-4	Wolverhampton (AW)	0-2	Southwell (AW)	0-1
Windsor	0-4	Ascot	0-1		
Yarmouth	0-4	Bath	0-1		

WINNING HORSES

	Age	Races Run	1st	2nd	3rd	Unpl	Win £
One Off The Rail	4	11	2	2	0	7	6,162
Mediator	5	9	2	2	0	5	5,158
Apollo Red	5	13	2	0	3	8	5,001
Invocation	7	14	1	3	2	8	3,818
Hatta Sunshine	4	12	1	2	1	8	3,173
Carlowitz	6	9	1	1	0	7	2,899
Kentavrus Way	3	8	1	0	1	6	2,738
Kenyatta	5	13	1	4	0	8	2,385

313

WINNING OWNERS

	Races Won	Value £		Races Won	Value £
K Higson	4	11,446	C F Sparrowhawk	2	4,981
A Moore	2	5,931	R Kiernan	1	3,818
Norman Jones	2	5,158			

Favourites	1-3	33.3%	+ 0.25	Total winning prize-money	£31,334

Longest winning sequence		2	Average SP of winner	9.3/1
Longest losing sequence		54	Return on stakes invested	-29.9%

1993 Form	11-132	8.3%	- 59.00	1991 Form	1-92	1.1%	- 79.00
1992 Form	6-128	4.7%	- 40.00	1990 Form	3-80	3.8%	- 52.25

G L MOORE (Epsom, Surrey)

	No. of Horses	Races Run	1st	2nd	3rd	Unpl	Per cent	£1 Level Stake
2-y-o	18	86	4	8	8	66	4.7	- 52.12
3-y-o	24	131	11	9	9	102	8.4	- 43.87
4-y-o+	18	126	8	13	17	88	6.3	- 66.50
Totals	60	343	23	30	34	256	6.7	-162.49

BY MONTH

2-y-o	W-R	Per cent	£1 Level Stake	3-y-o	W-R	Per cent	£1 Level Stake
January	0-0	-	0.00	January	0-2	-	- 2.00
February	0-0	-	0.00	February	0-1	-	- 1.00
March	0-0	-	0.00	March	0-3	-	- 3.00
April	0-1	-	- 1.00	April	0-14	-	- 14.00
May	0-5	-	- 5.00	May	1-17	5.9	- 14.00
June	0-15	-	- 15.00	June	1-28	3.6	- 11.00
July	0-17	-	- 17.00	July	6-21	28.6	+ 5.63
August	1-23	4.3	- 10.00	August	3-24	12.5	+ 16.50
September	0-13	-	- 13.00	September	0-10	-	- 10.00
Oct/Nov	3-12	25.0	+ 8.88	Oct/Nov	0-11	-	- 11.00

4-y-o+	W-R	Per cent	£1 Level Stake	Totals	W-R	Per cent	£1 Level Stake
January	0-7	-	- 7.00	January	0-9	-	- 9.00
February	1-4	25.0	+ 2.50	February	1-5	20.0	+ 1.50
March	0-8	-	- 8.00	March	0-11	-	- 11.00
April	0-10	-	- 10.00	April	0-25	-	- 25.00
May	0-17	-	- 17.00	May	1-39	2.6	- 36.00
June	1-23	4.3	- 18.50	June	2-66	3.0	- 44.50
July	1-10	10.0	- 4.50	July	7-48	14.6	- 15.87
August	4-24	16.7	+ 4.00	August	8-71	11.3	+ 10.50
September	1-12	8.3	+ 3.00	September	1-35	2.9	- 20.00
Oct/Nov	0-11	-	- 11.00	Oct/Nov	3-34	8.8	- 13.12

DISTANCE

2-y-o	W-R	Per cent	£1 Level Stake	3-y-o	W-R	Per cent	£1 Level Stake
5f-6f	3-48	6.3	- 27.12	5f-6f	1-24	4.2	- 19.50
7f-8f	1-38	2.6	- 25.00	7f-8f	3-59	5.1	- 19.12
9f-13f	0-0	-	0.00	9f-13f	5-41	12.2	- 6.00
14f+	0-0	-	0.00	14f+	2-7	28.6	+ 0.75

4-y-o+	W-R	Per cent	£1 Level Stake	Totals	W-R	Per cent	£1 Level Stake
5f-6f	0-18	-	- 18.00	5f-6f	4-90	4.4	- 64.62
7f-8f	6-77	7.8	- 37.00	7f-8f	10-174	5.7	- 81.12
9f-13f	1-26	3.8	- 21.50	9f-13f	6-67	9.0	- 27.50
14f+	1-5	20.0	+ 10.00	14f+	3-12	25.0	+ 10.75

TYPE OF RACE

Non-Handicaps	W-R	Per cent	£1 Level Stake	Handicaps	W-R	Per cent	£1 Level Stake
2-y-o	3-46	6.5	- 24.12	2-y-o	1-16	6.3	- 4.00
3-y-o	3-43	7.0	- 33.12	3-y-o	5-62	8.1	+ 1.25
4-y-o+	2-22	9.1	- 12.50	4-y-o+	4-85	4.7	- 45.00
Selling	2-32	6.3	- 20.50	Selling	1-18	5.6	- 12.50
Apprentice	0-1	-	- 1.00	Apprentice	2-13	15.4	- 6.00
Amat/Ladies	0-0	-	0.00	Amat/Ladies	0-5	-	- 5.00
Totals	10-144	6.9	- 91.24	Totals	13-199	6.5	- 71.25

COURSE GRADE

	W-R	Per cent	£1 Level Stake
Group 1	2-112	1.8	- 91.50
Group 2	7-96	7.3	- 58.00
Group 3	2-54	3.7	- 45.62
Group 4	12-81	14.8	+ 32.63

FIRST TIME OUT

	W-R	Per cent	£1 Level Stake
2-y-o	0-18	-	- 18.00
3-y-o	0-23	-	- 23.00
4-y-o+	0-17	-	- 17.00
Totals	0-58	-	- 58.00

JOCKEYS RIDING

	W-R	Per cent	£1 Level Stake		W-R	Per cent	£1 Level Stake
B Rouse	15-176	8.5	- 72.24	A Whelan	2-11	18.2	+ 27.50
M Baird	2-8	25.0	+ 12.25	M Roberts	1-4	25.0	+ 0.50
L Suthern	2-10	20.0	- 3.00	Paul Eddery	1-9	11.1	- 2.50

Moore G L

A Clark	0-34	A McGlone	0-2	G Duffield	0-1		
A Morris	0-26	D Biggs	0-2	J Reid	0-1		
J Quinn	0-9	G Bardwell	0-2	K Darley	0-1		
B Thomson	0-4	Mr J Keller	0-2	Mr M Keller	0-1		
Candy Morris	0-4	Mrs J Moore	0-2	N Carlisle	0-1		
D Harrison	0-4	R Hughes	0-2	S Whitworth	0-1		
L Dettori	0-4	A Tucker	0-1	W Carson	0-1		
R Perham	0-4	B Doyle	0-1	W Newnes	0-1		
A Mackay	0-3	C Scudder	0-1	W R Swinburn	0-1		
Caroline Hovington	0-3	D O'Neill	0-1	W Woods	0-1		
N Adams	0-3	D Wright	0-1				

COURSE RECORD

	Total W-R	Non-Handicaps 2-y-o	3-y-o+	Handicaps 2-y-o	3-y-o+	Per cent	£1 Level Stake
Lingfield (AW)	5-33	1-1	1-10	1-2	2-20	15.2	+ 15.00
Brighton	5-43	0-9	3-11	0-2	2-21	11.6	- 14.00
Folkestone	4-28	1-9	1-8	0-1	2-10	14.3	- 2.00
Wolverhampton (AW)	2-11	0-2	0-1	0-1	2-7	18.2	+ 26.25
Lingfield	2-36	0-10	0-10	0-0	2-16	5.6	- 27.00
Catterick	1-4	1-1	0-0	0-1	0-2	25.0	- 1.62
Chepstow	1-4	0-1	1-2	0-0	0-1	25.0	- 1.12
Doncaster	1-7	0-2	1-2	0-1	0-2	14.3	- 1.50
Yarmouth	1-9	0-3	0-0	0-1	1-5	11.1	- 3.50
Newbury	1-12	0-4	0-1	0-2	1-5	8.3	+ 3.00

Epsom	0-24	Goodwood	0-11	Leicester	0-4
Sandown	0-23	Newmarket	0-10	Warwick	0-4
Windsor	0-22	Ascot	0-9	Beverley	0-2
Salisbury	0-17	Bath	0-7	York	0-2
Kempton	0-14	Nottingham	0-6	Southwell (AW)	0-1

WINNING HORSES

	Age	Races Run	1st	2nd	3rd	Unpl	Win £
Warm Spell	4	12	1	2	1	8	15,313
In Behind	3	9	3	0	0	6	8,521
The Little Ferret	4	11	2	1	2	6	7,617
Doodies Pool	4	11	2	0	2	7	5,658
Call Me Albi	3	10	2	1	1	6	4,761
Hardy Dancer	2	4	1	0	1	2	3,553
Owdbetts	2	6	1	1	0	4	3,526
Waikiki Beach	3	7	1	2	0	4	3,415
Panchellita	5	8	1	1	0	6	3,106
Go With Bo	3	4	1	0	1	2	2,898
Soaking	4	9	1	2	1	5	2,898
Shaynes Domain	3	7	1	0	0	6	2,857

Tickerty's Gift	4	8	1	0	0	7	2,489
Mister O'Grady	3	7	1	1	1	4	2,434
Roman Reel	3	10	1	0	1	8	2,387
Stoppes Brow	2	6	1	0	1	4	2,301
Deeply Vale	3	8	1	1	2	4	2,249
No Pattern	2	5	1	0	0	4	2,003

WINNING OWNERS

	Races Won	Value £		Races Won	Value £
K Higson	15	55,868	Nigel Goldman	1	2,898
Jim Horgan	3	8,521	Mrs P A Garner	1	2,857
C J Pennick	2	5,407	Peter L Higson	1	2,434

Favourites	4-22	18.2%	- 10.87	Total winning prize-money	£77,985
Longest winning sequence			3	Average SP of winner	6.8/1
Longest losing sequence			66	Return on stakes invested	-47.4%
1993 Form	13-198	6.6%	- 95.77		

G M MOORE (Middleham, North Yorks)

	No. of Horses	Races Run	1st	2nd	3rd	Unpl	Per cent	£1 Level Stake
2-y-o	2	11	0	0	1	10	-	- 11.00
3-y-o	3	9	1	0	0	8	11.1	+ 8.00
4-y-o+	13	52	5	5	4	38	9.6	- 19.20
Totals	18	72	6	5	5	56	8.3	- 22.20

Jan	Feb	Mar	Apr	May	Jun	Jul	Aug	Sep	Oct/Nov
0-3	0-3	0-2	0-8	0-6	1-12	2-12	2-12	1-8	0-6

Winning Jockeys	W-R	£1 Level Stake		W-R	£1 Level Stake
J Stack	3-15	+ 8.80	Mrs L Pearce	1-2	+ 6.00
M Tebbutt	2-10	+ 8.00			

Winning Courses	W-R	£1 Level Stake		W-R	£1 Level Stake
Redcar	2-15	- 8.20	Ayr	1-4	+ 9.00
Carlisle	1-3	+ 5.00	Beverley	1-4	+ 13.00
Pontefract	1-3	+ 2.00			

Moore G M

Winning Horses	Age	Races Run	1st	2nd	3rd	Unpl	Win £
Cool Luke	5	8	2	0	2	4	7,352
Nouvelle Cuisine	6	7	2	3	0	2	5,089
Glenugie	3	7	1	0	0	6	4,510
Flashy's Son	6	4	1	1	1	1	3,899

Favourites	2-9	22.2%	- 2.20	Total winning prize-money			£20,850

1993 Form	6-82	7.3%	- 33.93	1991 Form	7-126	5.6%	- 36.50
1992 Form	10-108	9.3%	- 42.77	1990 Form	10-154	6.5%	- 95.17

J S MOORE (Andover, Hants)

	No. of Horses	Races Run	1st	2nd	3rd	Unpl	Per cent	£1 Level Stake
2-y-o	11	41	1	0	0	40	2.4	- 7.00
3-y-o	3	15	2	1	0	12	13.3	- 3.17
4-y-o+	3	9	1	0	0	8	11.1	+ 4.00
Totals	17	65	4	1	0	60	6.2	- 6.17

Jan	Feb	Mar	Apr	May	Jun	Jul	Aug	Sep	Oct/Nov
2-4	0-2	0-1	0-4	0-8	2-12	0-10	0-10	0-7	0-7

Winning Jockeys	W-R	£1 Level Stake		W-R	£1 Level Stake
N Adams	2-14	- 2.17	A McGlone	1-9	+ 25.00
M J Dwyer	1-4	+ 9.00			

Winning Courses					
Lingfield (AW)	2-6	+ 5.83	Bath	1-9	+ 25.00
Windsor	1-6	+ 7.00			

Winning Horses	Age	Races Run	1st	2nd	3rd	Unpl	Win £
Riskie Things	3	6	2	1	0	3	5,668
Witney-De-Bergerac	2	7	1	0	0	6	3,122
Hightown-Princess	6	7	1	0	0	6	2,931

Favourites	0-1			Total winning prize-money			£11,721

1993 Form	3-87	3.4%	- 45.75	1991 Form	1-33	3.0%	- 20.00
1992 Form	2-67	3.0%	- 47.00	1990 Form	0-8		

B C MORGAN (Burton-on-Trent, Staffs)

	No. of Horses	Races Run	1st	2nd	3rd	Unpl	Per cent	£1 Level Stake
2-y-o	0	0	0	0	0	0	-	0.00
3-y-o	1	1	0	0	0	1	-	- 1.00
4-y-o+	1	5	1	1	1	2	20.0	+ 2.00
Totals	2	6	1	1	1	3	16.7	+ 1.00

Jan	Feb	Mar	Apr	May	Jun	Jul	Aug	Sep	Oct/Nov
1-5	0-0	0-0	0-0	0-0	0-1	0-0	0-0	0-0	0-0

Winning Jockey	W-R	£1 Level Stake	Winning Course	W-R	£1 Level Stake
G Bardwell	1-4	+ 3.00	Wolverhampton (AW)	1-4	+ 3.00

Winning Horse	Age	Races Run	1st	2nd	3rd	Unpl	Win £
Farndale	7	5	1	1	1	2	3,114

Favourites	0-0		Total winning prize-money	£3,114

1993 Form	0-44		1991 Form	0-39	
1992 Form	3-68	4.4% - 32.00	1990 Form	2-67	3.0% - 51.50

D MORLEY (Newmarket)

	No. of Horses	Races Run	1st	2nd	3rd	Unpl	Per cent	£1 Level Stake
2-y-o	17	67	12	9	8	38	17.9	+ 21.08
3-y-o	9	47	4	5	5	33	8.5	- 16.00
4-y-o+	5	34	7	3	2	22	20.6	+ 56.50
Totals	31	148	23	17	15	93	15.5	+ 61.58

BY MONTH

2-y-o	W-R	Per cent	£1 Level Stake	3-y-o	W-R	Per cent	£1 Level Stake
Mar/Apr	0-0	-	0.00	Mar/Apr	0-4	-	- 4.00
May	0-2	-	- 2.00	May	0-13	-	- 13.00
June	5-10	50.0	+ 6.83	June	2-12	16.7	- 4.00
July	2-11	18.2	- 0.25	July	0-6	-	- 6.00
August	3-14	21.4	+ 8.50	August	1-6	16.7	+ 7.00
September	2-15	13.3	+ 23.00	September	0-4	-	- 4.00
Oct/Nov	0-15	-	- 15.00	Oct/Nov	1-2	50.0	+ 8.00

Morley D

4-y-o+	W-R	Per cent	£1 Level Stake	Totals	W-R	Per cent	£1 Level Stake
Mar/Apr	0-2	-	- 2.00	Mar/Apr	0-6	-	- 6.00
May	0-8	-	- 8.00	May	0-23	-	- 23.00
June	2-5	40.0	+ 8.50	June	9-27	33.3	+ 11.33
July	1-4	25.0	+ 2.00	July	3-21	14.3	- 4.25
August	1-3	33.3	+ 31.00	August	5-23	21.7	+ 46.50
September	3-8	37.5	+ 29.00	September	5-27	18.5	+ 48.00
Oct/Nov	0-4	-	- 4.00	Oct/Nov	1-21	4.8	- 11.00

DISTANCE

2-y-o	W-R	Per cent	£1 Level Stake	3-y-o	W-R	Per cent	£1 Level Stake
5f-6f	9-32	28.1	+ 39.46	5f-6f	0-0	-	0.00
7f-8f	3-32	9.4	- 15.38	7f-8f	0-7	-	- 7.00
9f-13f	0-3	-	- 3.00	9f-13f	2-29	6.9	- 15.50
14f+	0-0	-	0.00	14f+	2-11	18.2	+ 6.50

4-y-o+	W-R	Per cent	£1 Level Stake	Totals	W-R	Per cent	£1 Level Stake
5f-6f	0-0	-	0.00	5f-6f	9-32	28.1	+ 39.46
7f-8f	3-10	30.0	+ 9.50	7f-8f	6-49	12.2	- 12.88
9f-13f	4-20	20.0	+ 51.00	9f-13f	6-52	11.5	+ 32.50
14f+	0-4	-	- 4.00	14f+	2-15	13.3	+ 2.50

TYPE OF RACE

Non-Handicaps	W-R	Per cent	£1 Level Stake	Handicaps	W-R	Per cent	£1 Level Stake
2-y-o	9-55	16.4	+ 13.58	2-y-o	3-10	30.0	+ 9.50
3-y-o	2-11	18.2	- 3.00	3-y-o	1-30	3.3	- 17.00
4-y-o+	0-3	-	- 3.00	4-y-o+	6-25	24.0	+ 52.50
Selling	0-3	-	- 3.00	Selling	1-3	33.3	+ 7.00
Apprentice	0-0	-	0.00	Apprentice	1-8	12.5	+ 5.00
Amat/Ladies	0-0	-	0.00	Amat/Ladies	0-0	-	0.00
Totals	11-72	15.3	+ 4.58	Totals	12-76	15.8	+ 57.00

COURSE GRADE

	W-R	Per cent	£1 Level Stake
Group 1	15-61	24.6	+100.53
Group 2	2-23	8.7	- 3.00
Group 3	5-57	8.8	- 32.45
Group 4	1-7	14.3	- 3.50

FIRST TIME OUT

	W-R	Per cent	£1 Level Stake
2-y-o	2-17	11.8	- 5.50
3-y-o	0-9	-	- 9.00
4-y-o+	1-5	20.0	+ 29.00
Totals	3-31	9.7	+ 14.50

JOCKEYS RIDING

	W–R	Per cent	£1 Level Stake		W–R	Per cent	£1 Level Stake
W Carson	7–26	26.9	+ 41.78	R Cochrane	1–2	50.0	+ 2.00
R Hills	4–22	18.2	+ 5.80	M Hills	1–5	20.0	+ 1.50
D Holland	2–3	66.7	+ 7.50	J Lowe	1–6	16.7	+ 0.50
B Raymond	2–6	33.3	+ 4.50	G Duffield	1–10	10.0	+ 1.00
M Tebbutt	2–27	7.4	– 9.00	J Dennis	1–10	10.0	+ 3.00
B Thomson	1–1	100.0	+ 33.00				

S Whitworth	0–6	D Harrison	0–2	M Birch	0–1
Paul Eddery	0–4	L Dettori	0–2	S Maloney	0–1
D McKeown	0–3	M J Kinane	0–2	T Ives	0–1
W R Swinburn	0–3	A McGlone	0–1		
W Ryan	0–3	B Rouse	0–1		

COURSE RECORD

	Total W–R	Non-Handicaps 2-y-o	3-y-o+	Handicaps 2-y-o	3-y-o+	Per cent	£1 Level Stake
Newcastle	6–13	3–6	0–1	1–2	2–4	46.2	+ 25.12
Yarmouth	4–20	2–7	0–0	1–3	1–10	20.0	+ 1.80
Newmarket	3–12	1–4	0–1	1–1	1–6	25.0	+ 64.00
Ayr	2–3	0–0	1–1	0–0	1–2	66.7	+ 14.50
Redcar	2–7	0–2	0–0	0–0	2–5	28.6	+ 13.00
Goodwood	1–2	1–1	0–0	0–0	0–1	50.0	+ 2.00
Southwell (AW)	1–2	0–0	1–1	0–0	0–1	50.0	+ 1.50
Kempton	1–4	0–2	0–1	0–0	1–1	25.0	+ 9.00
York	1–4	1–3	0–1	0–0	0–0	25.0	– 2.09
Doncaster	1–8	0–3	0–0	0–1	1–4	12.5	+ 3.00
Beverley	1–11	1–4	0–1	0–1	0–5	9.1	– 8.25

Nottingham	0–11	Ripon	0–4	Carlisle	0–1
Pontefract	0–9	Haydock	0–3	Newbury	0–1
Lingfield	0–7	Thirsk	0–3	Warwick	0–1
Ascot	0–6	Brighton	0–2	Wolverhampton (AW)	0–1
Sandown	0–5	Catterick	0–2		
Leicester	0–4	Windsor	0–2		

WINNING HORSES

	Age	Races Run	1st	2nd	3rd	Unpl	Win £
Fard	2	8	4	1	1	2	106,037
Tajdif	4	8	3	0	0	5	23,269
Fahal	2	7	3	0	1	3	20,963
Burooj	4	4	2	1	0	1	14,544
Sayl	2	5	2	0	0	3	8,055
Shashi	2	6	1	1	1	3	5,784
Karayb	2	2	1	0	0	1	5,344
Much Sought After	5	9	1	2	0	6	5,198

Morley D

Jadwal	2	5	1	1	0	3	3,589
Hawkish	5	9	1	0	2	6	3,236
Elflaa	3	7	1	2	0	4	3,202
Much Too Clever	3	7	1	2	0	4	2,970
Changing Partners	3	2	1	0	0	1	2,854
Khatir	3	8	1	0	3	4	2,736

WINNING OWNERS

	Races Won	Value £		Races Won	Value £
Hamdan Al-Maktoum	15	164,470	Mrs M F D Morley	1	3,236
Hyde Sporting Promotions Ltd	3	23,269	The MTC Partnership	1	2,970
Saif Ali	1	5,784	Lord Hartington	1	2,854
The MSA Partnership	1	5,198			

Favourites	4-16	25.0%	- 7.17	Total winning prize-money	£207,781

Longest winning sequence		3	Average SP of winner	8.1/1
Longest losing sequence		29	Return on stakes invested	41.6%

1993 Form	16-127	12.6%	- 21.00	1991 Form	20-181	11.0%	- 45.07
1992 Form	19-150	12.7%	- 17.07	1990 Form	24-238	10.1%	-102.01

D MORRIS (Newmarket)

	No. of Horses	Races Run	1st	2nd	3rd	Unpl	Per cent	£1 Level Stake
2-y-o	6	24	2	0	5	17	8.3	- 15.75
3-y-o	6	45	2	4	5	34	4.4	- 13.00
4-y-o+	10	48	7	7	2	32	14.6	+ 5.50
Totals	22	117	11	11	12	83	9.4	- 23.25

BY MONTH

2-y-o	W-R	Per cent	£1 Level Stake	3-y-o	W-R	Per cent	£1 Level Stake
January	0-0	-	0.00	January	0-1	-	- 1.00
February	0-0	-	0.00	February	0-1	-	- 1.00
March	0-0	-	0.00	March	0-1	-	- 1.00
April	0-0	-	0.00	April	0-4	-	- 4.00
May	0-1	-	- 1.00	May	0-4	-	- 4.00
June	0-3	-	- 3.00	June	0-5	-	- 5.00
July	1-5	20.0	- 1.25	July	0-6	-	- 6.00
August	0-4	-	- 4.00	August	0-10	-	- 10.00
September	1-8	12.5	- 3.50	September	2-8	25.0	+ 24.00
Oct/Nov	0-3	-	- 3.00	Oct/Nov	0-5	-	- 5.00

4-y-o+	W-R	Per cent	£1 Level Stake		Totals	W-R	Per cent	£1 Level Stake
January	0-4	-	- 4.00		January	0-5	-	- 5.00
February	1-2	50.0	+ 0.50		February	1-3	33.3	- 0.50
March	1-3	33.3	0.00		March	1-4	25.0	- 1.00
April	2-5	40.0	+ 9.00		April	2-9	22.2	+ 5.00
May	1-9	11.1	+ 4.00		May	1-14	7.1	- 1.00
June	1-7	14.3	- 1.00		June	1-15	6.7	- 9.00
July	0-5	-	- 5.00		July	1-16	6.3	- 12.25
August	1-2	50.0	+ 13.00		August	1-16	6.3	- 1.00
September	0-5	-	- 5.00		September	3-21	14.3	+ 15.50
Oct/Nov	0-6	-	- 6.00		Oct/Nov	0-14	-	- 14.00

DISTANCE

2-y-o	W-R	Per cent	£1 Level Stake		3-y-o	W-R	Per cent	£1 Level Stake
5f-6f	0-12	-	- 12.00		5f-6f	0-2	-	- 2.00
7f-8f	2-12	16.7	- 3.75		7f-8f	2-30	6.7	+ 2.00
9f-13f	0-0	-	0.00		9f-13f	0-13	-	- 13.00
14f+	0-0	-	0.00		14f+	0-0	-	0.00

4-y-o+	W-R	Per cent	£1 Level Stake		Totals	W-R	Per cent	£1 Level Stake
5f-6f	0-2	-	- 2.00		5f-6f	0-16	-	- 16.00
7f-8f	4-22	18.2	+ 7.50		7f-8f	8-64	12.5	+ 5.75
9f-13f	3-24	12.5	0.00		9f-13f	3-37	8.1	- 13.00
14f+	0-0	-	0.00		14f+	0-0	-	0.00

TYPE OF RACE

Non-Handicaps	W-R	Per cent	£1 Level Stake		Handicaps	W-R	Per cent	£1 Level Stake
2-y-o	0-13	-	- 13.00		2-y-o	1-8	12.5	- 3.50
3-y-o	0-9	-	- 9.00		3-y-o	2-26	7.7	+ 6.00
4-y-o+	3-12	25.0	+ 9.50		4-y-o+	3-31	9.7	- 5.00
Selling	2-9	22.2	+ 0.75		Selling	0-6	-	- 6.00
Apprentice	0-0	-	0.00		Apprentice	0-2	-	- 2.00
Amat/Ladies	0-0	-	0.00		Amat/Ladies	0-1	-	- 1.00
Totals	5-43	11.6	- 11.75		Totals	6-74	8.1	- 11.50

COURSE GRADE

	W-R	Per cent	£1 Level Stake
Group 1	3-39	7.7	+ 8.00
Group 2	0-11	-	- 11.00
Group 3	6-41	14.6	+ 0.25
Group 4	2-26	7.7	- 20.50

FIRST TIME OUT

	W-R	Per cent	£1 Level Stake
2-y-o	0-5	-	- 5.00
3-y-o	0-5	-	- 5.00
4-y-o+	2-10	20.0	+ 9.00
Totals	2-20	10.0	- 1.00

JOCKEYS RIDING

	W-R	Per cent	£1 Level Stake			W-R	Per cent	£1 Level Stake
Stephen Davies	6-40	15.0	+ 12.75	R Price		1-2	50.0	+ 9.00
C Hodgson	3-23	13.0	- 1.00	D McCabe		1-18	5.6	- 10.00

J Fanning	0-6	A Clark	0-1	L Piggott	0-1
D McKeown	0-3	J Lowe	0-1	M Fenton	0-1
G Hind	0-3	J Reid	0-1	Mrs L Morris	0-1
T Ives	0-3	J Stack	0-1	P Robinson	0-1
J Quinn	0-2	J Tate	0-1	S Sanders	0-1
L Dettori	0-2	J Weaver	0-1	W Woods	0-1
W Newnes	0-2	K Darley	0-1		

COURSE RECORD

	Total W-R	Non-Handicaps 2-y-o	Non-Handicaps 3-y-o+	Handicaps 2-y-o	Handicaps 3-y-o+	Per cent	£1 Level Stake
Yarmouth	2-8	1-1	0-1	1-1	0-5	25.0	+ 0.25
Epsom	1-1	0-0	0-0	0-0	1-1	100.0	+ 14.00
Hamilton	1-1	0-0	0-0	0-0	1-1	100.0	+ 7.00
Newbury	1-2	0-0	0-0	0-0	1-2	50.0	+ 9.00
Goodwood	1-5	0-0	0-0	0-2	1-3	20.0	+ 16.00
Windsor	1-6	0-0	1-3	0-0	0-3	16.7	0.00
Folkestone	1-8	0-3	0-1	0-1	1-3	12.5	- 5.00
Lingfield (AW)	1-8	0-0	1-4	0-0	0-4	12.5	- 5.50
Pontefract	1-9	0-2	1-4	0-0	0-3	11.1	- 3.00
Leicester	1-13	0-2	1-8	0-0	0-3	7.7	0.00

Newmarket	0-15	Nottingham	0-3	Beverley	0-1
Sandown	0-6	Chester	0-2	Haydock	0-1
Wolverhampton (AW)	0-6	Kempton	0-2	Lingfield	0-1
Redcar	0-5	Thirsk	0-2	Salisbury	0-1
Doncaster	0-4	York	0-2	Southwell (AW)	0-1
Edinburgh	0-3	Ascot	0-1		

WINNING HORSES

	Age	Races Run	1st	2nd	3rd	Unpl	Win £
Gadge	3	6	1	0	1	4	18,910
Lowawatha	6	15	3	5	1	6	9,955
Bobanlyn	2	7	2	0	1	4	6,492
Norman Warrior	5	9	2	0	1	6	6,449
Mr Rough	3	11	1	0	3	7	5,053
B B Glen	4	4	1	0	0	3	3,086
Pytchley Night	7	2	1	1	0	0	2,781

WINNING OWNERS

	Races Won	Value £		Races Won	Value £
J B R Leisure Ltd	1	18,910	Robin Akehurst	1	5,053
N Lunn	3	9,955	D & L Racing	1	3,086
Mrs Sheila Walker	2	6,492	J J Higgins	1	2,781
Mrs Patricia Lunn	2	6,449			

Favourites	3-11	27.3%	- 1.00	Total winning prize-money			£52,725
Longest winning sequence			2	Average SP of winner			7.5/1
Longest losing sequence			19	Return on stakes invested			-19.9%
1993 Form	18-128	14.1%	+ 36.05	1991 Form	6-88	6.8%	- 37.50
1992 Form	8-98	8.2%	- 21.75	1990 Form	2-54	3.7%	- 23.00

M P MUGGERIDGE (Newbury, Berks)

	No. of Horses	Races Run	1st	2nd	3rd	Unpl	Per cent	£1 Level Stake
2-y-o	2	9	0	0	0	9	-	- 9.00
3-y-o	3	11	0	0	1	10	-	- 11.00
4-y-o+	5	14	1	0	2	11	7.1	+ 20.00
Totals	10	34	1	0	3	30	2.9	0.00

Jan	Feb	Mar	Apr	May	Jun	Jul	Aug	Sep	Oct/Nov
0-3	0-1	1-3	0-2	0-7	0-10	0-4	0-1	0-2	0-1

Winning Jockey	W-R	£1 Level Stake	Winning Course	W-R	£1 Level Stake
D Gibbs	1-1	+ 33.00	Lingfield (AW)	1-7	+ 27.00

Winning Horse	Age	Races Run	1st	2nd	3rd	Unpl	Win £
Blue Ensign	9	1	1	0	0	0	1,749

Favourites	0-0			Total winning prize-money			£1,749
1993 Form	3-77	3.9%	- 45.25	1991 Form	3-55	5.5%	+ 48.88
1992 Form	2-46	4.3%	- 16.00	1990 Form	1-42	2.4%	- 25.00

W R MUIR (Lambourn, Berks)

	No. of Horses	Races Run	1st	2nd	3rd	Unpl	Per cent	£1 Level Stake
2-y-o	9	48	3	3	4	38	6.3	- 18.00
3-y-o	14	61	7	6	4	44	11.5	- 22.50
4-y-o+	12	71	8	8	9	46	11.3	- 20.25
Totals	35	180	18	17	17	128	10.0	- 60.75

BY MONTH

2-y-o	W-R	Per cent	£1 Level Stake	3-y-o	W-R	Per cent	£1 Level Stake
January	0-0	-	0.00	January	3-7	42.9	+ 18.50
February	0-0	-	0.00	February	1-7	14.3	- 3.75
March	0-0	-	0.00	March	1-3	33.3	- 0.25
April	0-1	-	- 1.00	April	0-3	-	- 3.00
May	0-4	-	- 4.00	May	0-7	-	- 7.00
June	0-7	-	- 7.00	June	0-6	-	- 6.00
July	0-8	-	- 8.00	July	0-9	-	- 9.00
August	1-10	10.0	+ 1.00	August	1-6	16.7	- 2.25
September	1-11	9.1	- 2.00	September	1-6	16.7	- 2.75
Oct/Nov	1-7	14.3	+ 3.00	Oct/Nov	0-7	-	- 7.00

4-y-o+	W-R	Per cent	£1 Level Stake	Totals	W-R	Per cent	£1 Level Stake
January	0-9	-	- 9.00	January	3-16	18.8	+ 9.50
February	0-8	-	- 8.00	February	1-15	6.7	- 11.75
March	0-1	-	- 1.00	March	1-4	25.0	- 1.25
April	0-2	-	- 2.00	April	0-6	-	- 6.00
May	0-5	-	- 5.00	May	0-16	-	- 16.00
June	0-10	-	- 10.00	June	0-23	-	- 23.00
July	6-13	46.2	+ 32.50	July	6-30	20.0	+ 15.50
August	2-12	16.7	- 6.75	August	4-28	14.3	- 8.00
September	0-4	-	- 4.00	September	2-21	9.5	- 8.75
Oct/Nov	0-7	-	- 7.00	Oct/Nov	1-21	4.8	- 11.00

DISTANCE

2-y-o	W-R	Per cent	£1 Level Stake	3-y-o	W-R	Per cent	£1 Level Stake
5f-6f	2-36	5.6	- 15.00	5f-6f	2-8	25.0	+ 13.00
7f-8f	1-11	9.1	- 2.00	7f-8f	3-33	9.1	- 22.50
9f-13f	0-1	-	- 1.00	9f-13f	2-20	10.0	- 13.00
14f+	0-0	-	0.00	14f+	0-0	-	0.00

4-y-o+	W-R	Per cent	£1 Level Stake	Totals	W-R	Per cent	£1 Level Stake
5f-6f	2-10	20.0	- 4.25	5f-6f	6-54	11.1	- 6.25
7f-8f	1-16	6.3	+ 1.00	7f-8f	5-60	8.3	- 23.50
9f-13f	3-28	10.7	- 10.00	9f-13f	5-49	10.2	- 24.00
14f+	2-17	11.8	- 7.00	14f+	2-17	11.8	- 7.00

TYPE OF RACE

Non-Handicaps	W-R	Per cent	£1 Level Stake	Handicaps	W-R	Per cent	£1 Level Stake
2-y-o	0-28	-	- 28.00	2-y-o	2-14	14.3	+ 7.00
3-y-o	1-26	3.8	- 23.25	3-y-o	5-28	17.9	+ 4.50
4-y-o+	3-27	11.1	- 10.50	4-y-o+	3-33	9.1	- 4.00
Selling	4-13	30.8	+ 4.50	Selling	0-5	-	- 5.00
Apprentice	0-1	-	- 1.00	Apprentice	0-5	-	- 5.00
Amat/Ladies	0-0	-	0.00	Amat/Ladies	0-0	-	0.00
Totals	8-95	8.4	- 58.25	Totals	10-85	11.8	- 2.50

COURSE GRADE

	W-R	Per cent	£1 Level Stake
Group 1	5-33	15.2	+ 4.25
Group 2	1-17	5.9	- 6.00
Group 3	1-41	2.4	- 37.75
Group 4	11-89	12.4	- 21.25

FIRST TIME OUT

	W-R	Per cent	£1 Level Stake
2-y-o	0-8	-	- 8.00
3-y-o	1-12	8.3	+ 5.00
4-y-o+	1-12	8.3	+ 5.00
Totals	2-32	6.3	+ 2.00

JOCKEYS RIDING

	W-R	Per cent	£1 Level Stake		W-R	Per cent	£1 Level Stake
J Weaver	5-21	23.8	+ 2.00	A Munro	1-5	20.0	+ 2.00
Kim McDonnell	4-35	11.4	- 8.00	W Ryan	1-5	20.0	+ 12.00
Stephen Davies	2-14	14.3	+ 2.00	D Harrison	1-8	12.5	+ 1.00
L Dettori	1-1	100.0	+ 2.25	T Quinn	1-11	9.1	- 6.50
W Carson	1-1	100.0	+ 9.00	D Holland	1-13	7.7	- 10.50

M Roberts	0-7	Antoinette Armes	0-2	J Lowe	0-1
R Cochrane	0-7	D McKeown	0-2	J Quinn	0-1
S McCarthy	0-7	Emma O'Gorman	0-2	J Stack	0-1
T Williams	0-7	M Hills	0-2	J Tate	0-1
G Bardwell	0-4	B Thomson	0-1	M Fenton	0-1
J Carroll	0-3	C Llewellyn	0-1	M J Kinane	0-1
K Darley	0-3	C N Adamson	0-1	Paul Eddery	0-1
Pat Eddery	0-3	D Wright	0-1	R Waterfield	0-1
S Mulvey	0-3	G Carter	0-1	W Woods	0-1

COURSE RECORD

	Total W-R	Non-Handicaps 2-y-o	Non-Handicaps 3-y-o+	Handicaps 2-y-o	Handicaps 3-y-o+	Per cent	£1 Level Stake
Lingfield (AW)	6-33	1-2	2-19	0-0	3-12	18.2	+ 5.50
Edinburgh	2-5	0-1	2-3	0-0	0-1	40.0	+ 9.00
Epsom	1-1	0-0	1-1	0-0	0-0	100.0	+ 2.25
Ayr	1-2	0-0	1-2	0-0	0-0	50.0	0.00
Kempton	1-4	0-0	0-0	0-1	1-3	25.0	+ 13.00
York	1-4	0-0	0-1	1-1	0-2	25.0	+ 6.00
Brighton	1-6	0-1	0-3	1-2	0-0	16.7	+ 5.00
Warwick	1-6	0-1	0-1	0-0	1-4	16.7	+ 1.00
Leicester	1-7	0-3	1-1	0-1	0-2	14.3	- 3.75
Newmarket	1-7	0-2	0-1	0-1	1-3	14.3	- 2.00
Southwell (AW)	1-12	0-4	0-3	0-2	1-3	8.3	- 7.50
Wolverhampton (AW)	1-26	0-4	0-10	0-0	1-12	3.8	- 22.25

Windsor	0-16	Nottingham	0-4	Beverley	0-1
Folkestone	0-7	Salisbury	0-4	Chester	0-1
Goodwood	0-6	Ascot	0-3	Hamilton	0-1
Yarmouth	0-5	Chepstow	0-3	Haydock	0-1
Bath	0-4	Lingfield	0-3	Redcar	0-1
Newbury	0-4	Ripon	0-2	Sandown	0-1

327

WINNING HORSES

	Age	Races Run	1st	2nd	3rd	Unpl	Win £
Rocketeer	3	10	3	1	1	5	8,968
Sue Me	2	8	1	1	2	4	6,004
Upper Grosvenor	3	10	2	0	1	7	5,999
Shabanaz	9	9	1	1	2	5	5,744
Farfelu	7	9	2	1	1	5	5,631
Cliburnel News	4	13	2	2	2	7	5,232
Dolly Face	2	11	1	1	1	8	3,468
Little Rousillon	6	6	1	0	1	4	3,418
Pish Kesh	4	7	1	2	2	2	3,288
Sagasan	3	8	1	1	1	5	2,950
Breakdancer	5	6	1	0	1	4	2,853
Gigfy	2	7	1	0	0	6	2,565
Dome Patrol	3	9	1	1	1	6	2,467

WINNING OWNERS

	Races Won	Value £		Races Won	Value £
Fayzad Thoroughbred Limited	2	9,162	Perspicacious Punters Racing Club	1	3,288
Mrs J M Muir	3	8,968	D J Deer	1	2,950
Mrs H Levy	3	8,563	J Jannaway	1	2,853
Michael Payton	1	6,004	P A Leonard	1	2,668
John O'Mulloy	2	5,631	Mrs Danita Winstanly	1	2,565
Stanley Meadows	1	3,468	Duncan J Wiltshire	1	2,467

Favourites	8-26	30.8%	- 2.25	Total winning prize-money	£58,586
Longest winning sequence			3	Average SP of winner	5.6/1
Longest losing sequence			50	Return on stakes invested	-33.8%
1993 Form	13-201	6.5%	-121.72	1991 Form	13-97	13.4%	- 9.08
1992 Form	9-174	5.2%	- 90.25				

P G MURPHY (Bristol, Avon)

	No. of Horses	Races Run	1st	2nd	3rd	Unpl	Per cent	£1 Level Stake
2-y-o	3	22	4	5	0	13	18.2	+ 10.33
3-y-o	6	60	1	0	4	55	1.7	- 39.00
4-y-o+	8	47	1	2	5	39	2.1	- 41.00
Totals	17	129	6	7	9	107	4.7	- 69.67

Jan	Feb	Mar	Apr	May	Jun	Jul	Aug	Sep	Oct/Nov
0-0	0-0	0-0	0-11	0-23	0-26	2-24	0-11	2-19	2-15

Winning Jockeys	W-R	£1 Level Stake			W-R	£1 Level Stake
S Drowne	2-23	+ 4.00	F Norton		1-5	0.00
J Williams	2-23	0.00	D Harrison		1-9	- 4.67

Winning Courses						
Warwick	2-13	- 3.67	York		1-3	+ 3.00
Bath	2-18	+ 18.00	Chepstow		1-18	- 10.00

Winning Horses	Age	Races Run	1st	2nd	3rd	Unpl	Win £
Sylvandra	2	9	2	2	0	5	8,104
Sir Joey	5	14	1	1	3	9	6,056
Winsome Wooster	3	13	1	0	2	10	4,080
Runs In The Family	2	8	1	2	0	5	3,721
Lees Please	2	5	1	1	0	3	2,726

Favourites	1-7	14.3%	- 1.00	Total winning prize-money			£24,686
1993 Form	12-169	7.1%	- 66.92	1992 Form	3-10	30.0%	+ 20.00

B W MURRAY (Malton, North Yorks)

	No. of Horses	Races Run	1st	2nd	3rd	Unpl	Per cent	£1 Level Stake
2-y-o	5	20	0	2	1	17	-	- 20.00
3-y-o	4	18	3	0	1	14	16.7	+ 13.00
4-y-o+	5	23	2	1	0	20	8.7	+ 3.00
Totals	14	61	5	3	2	51	8.2	- 4.00

Jan	Feb	Mar	Apr	May	Jun	Jul	Aug	Sep	Oct/Nov
0-0	1-2	0-2	0-5	0-8	1-7	2-10	1-13	0-6	0-8

Winning Jockeys	W-R	£1 Level Stake			W-R	£1 Level Stake
M Deering	3-21	+ 16.00	M J Dwyer		1-5	+ 4.00
J Quinn	1-4	+ 7.00				

Winning Courses						
Chester	1-1	+ 16.00	Beverley		1-9	- 2.00
Ayr	1-3	+ 10.00	Redcar		1-10	- 1.00
Southwell (AW)	1-5	+ 6.00				

Winning Horses	Age	Races Run	1st	2nd	3rd	Unpl	Win £
Maurangi	3	7	2	0	1	4	5,995
Fort Vally	4	9	1	0	0	8	3,134
Dauntless Fort	3	4	1	0	0	3	2,821
Royal Comedian	5	7	1	0	0	6	2,814

Favourites	0-2			Total winning prize-money			£14,764
1993 Form	1-44	2.3%	- 34.00	1991 Form	1-54	1.9%	- 50.00
1992 Form	0-44			1990 Form	0-29		

329

W J MUSSON (Newmarket)

	No. of Horses	Races Run	1st	2nd	3rd	Unpl	Per cent	£1 Level Stake
2-y-o	1	5	0	1	0	4	-	- 5.00
3-y-o	10	48	1	2	2	43	2.1	- 37.00
4-y-o+	12	86	7	2	2	75	8.1	- 26.50
Totals	23	139	8	5	4	122	5.8	- 68.50

Jan	Feb	Mar	Apr	May	Jun	Jul	Aug	Sep	Oct/Nov
0-8	1-4	2-11	3-17	1-20	0-16	0-19	0-14	0-13	1-17

Winning Jockeys	W-R	£1 Level Stake		W-R	£1 Level Stake
D Biggs	2-5	+ 6.00	D McCabe	1-3	+ 8.00
Pat Eddery	2-9	+ 6.00	Mrs J Musson	1-8	- 2.50
S Lanigan	2-13	+ 15.00			

Winning Courses	W-R	£1 Level Stake		W-R	£1 Level Stake
Newmarket	3-23	+ 2.00	Kempton	1-10	+ 7.00
Catterick	1-1	+ 2.00	Wolverhampton (AW)	1-11	- 3.00
Doncaster	1-10	+ 1.00	Sandown	1-13	- 6.50

Winning Horses	Age	Races Run	1st	2nd	3rd	Unpl	Win £
Swift Silver	7	7	1	0	1	5	12,660
Broughtons Formula	4	15	3	1	1	10	11,412
Bit On The Side	5	9	2	1	0	6	9,800
Rise Up Singing	6	10	1	0	0	9	5,127
Broughton Singer	3	7	1	0	0	6	4,565

Favourites	2-12	16.7%	- 3.50	Total winning prize-money		£43,564

1993 Form	12-180	6.7%	- 55.75	1991 Form	9-114	7.9%	- 51.25
1992 Form	6-130	4.6%	- 86.75	1990 Form	4-154	2.6%	-134.00

C T NASH (Wantage, Oxon)

	No. of Horses	Races Run	1st	2nd	3rd	Unpl	Per cent	£1 Level Stake
2-y-o	0	0	0	0	0	0	-	0.00
3-y-o	1	10	1	0	0	9	10.0	+ 57.00
4-y-o+	3	11	1	0	0	10	9.1	+ 40.00
Totals	4	21	2	0	0	19	9.5	+ 97.00

Jan	Feb	Mar	Apr	May	Jun	Jul	Aug	Sep	Oct/Nov
0-0	0-0	0-0	0-3	2-3	0-4	0-1	0-5	0-3	0-2

Winning Jockeys	W-R	£1 Level Stake		W-R	£1 Level Stake
Mr P Phillips	1-8	+ 43.00	R Perham	1-11	+ 56.00

Winning Courses					
Bath	1-3	+ 64.00	Warwick	1-3	+ 48.00

Winning Horses	Age	Races Run	1st	2nd	3rd	Unpl	Win £
Porte Belloch	3	10	1	0	0	9	2,628
Air Command	4	8	1	0	0	7	2,070

Favourites	0-0		Total winning prize-money	£4,698

1993 Form	0-12		1992 Form	0-8

M P NAUGHTON (Richmond, North Yorks)

	No. of Horses	Races Run	1st	2nd	3rd	Unpl	Per cent	£1 Level Stake
2-y-o	1	1	0	0	0	1	-	- 1.00
3-y-o	4	19	2	0	1	16	10.5	+ 2.33
4-y-o+	4	30	1	3	5	21	3.3	- 15.00
Totals	9	50	3	3	6	38	6.0	- 13.67

Jan	Feb	Mar	Apr	May	Jun	Jul	Aug	Sep	Oct/Nov
2-6	0-5	0-4	1-12	0-10	0-7	0-6	0-0	0-0	0-0

Winning Jockeys	W-R	£1 Level Stake		W-R	£1 Level Stake
Paul Eddery	2-15	+ 17.00	A Munro	1-4	+ 0.33

Winning Courses					
Southwell (AW)	2-8	+ 11.33	Wolverhampton (AW)	1-6	+ 11.00

Winning Horses	Age	Races Run	1st	2nd	3rd	Unpl	Win £
Shareoftheaction	3	9	2	0	1	6	5,364
Gentle Hero	8	8	1	0	0	7	3,287

Favourites	0-4		Total winning prize-money	£8,651

1993 Form	4-124	3.2%	- 78.00	1991 Form	21-201	10.4%	- 42.52
1992 Form	32-356	9.0%	-121.41	1990 Form	12-219	5.5%	-102.17

T J NAUGHTON (Epsom, Surrey)

	No. of Horses	Races Run	1st	2nd	3rd	Unpl	Per cent	£1 Level Stake
2-y-o	10	42	1	6	5	30	2.4	- 35.00
3-y-o	9	56	6	7	1	42	10.7	- 25.50
4-y-o+	13	76	5	9	4	58	6.6	- 30.00
Totals	32	174	12	22	10	130	6.9	- 90.50

BY MONTH

2-y-o	W-R	Per cent	£1 Level Stake	3-y-o	W-R	Per cent	£1 Level Stake
January	0-0	-	0.00	January	0-4	-	- 4.00
February	0-0	-	0.00	February	1-2	50.0	+ 0.25
March	0-2	-	- 2.00	March	1-4	25.0	- 0.25
April	0-1	-	- 1.00	April	0-7	-	- 7.00
May	0-1	-	- 1.00	May	0-4	-	- 4.00
June	0-9	-	- 9.00	June	0-10	-	- 10.00
July	0-4	-	- 4.00	July	3-5	60.0	+ 14.50
August	0-6	-	- 6.00	August	1-7	14.3	- 2.00
September	1-10	10.0	- 3.00	September	0-4	-	- 4.00
Oct/Nov	0-9	-	- 9.00	Oct/Nov	0-9	-	- 9.00

4-y-o+	W-R	Per cent	£1 Level Stake	Totals	W-R	Per cent	£1 Level Stake
January	0-9	-	- 9.00	January	0-13	-	- 13.00
February	0-5	-	- 5.00	February	1-7	14.3	- 4.75
March	0-2	-	- 2.00	March	1-8	12.5	- 4.25
April	0-6	-	- 6.00	April	0-14	-	- 14.00
May	0-10	-	- 10.00	May	0-15	-	- 15.00
June	2-13	15.4	- 4.00	June	2-32	6.3	- 23.00
July	0-4	-	- 4.00	July	3-13	23.1	+ 6.50
August	2-10	20.0	+ 18.00	August	3-23	13.0	+ 10.00
September	1-8	12.5	+ 1.00	September	2-22	9.1	- 6.00
Oct/Nov	0-9	-	- 9.00	Oct/Nov	0-27	-	- 27.00

DISTANCE

2-y-o	W-R	Per cent	£1 Level Stake	3-y-o	W-R	Per cent	£1 Level Stake
5f-6f	1-32	3.1	- 25.00	5f-6f	2-17	11.8	- 9.75
7f-8f	0-10	-	- 10.00	7f-8f	4-29	13.8	- 5.75
9f-13f	0-0	-	0.00	9f-13f	0-10	-	- 10.00
14f+	0-0	-	0.00	14f+	0-0	-	0.00

4-y-o+	W-R	Per cent	£1 Level Stake	Totals	W-R	Per cent	£1 Level Stake
5f-6f	2-15	13.3	+ 0.50	5f-6f	5-64	7.8	- 34.25
7f-8f	1-28	3.6	- 11.00	7f-8f	5-67	7.5	- 26.75
9f-13f	1-21	4.8	- 10.00	9f-13f	1-31	3.2	- 20.00
14f+	1-12	8.3	- 9.50	14f+	1-12	8.3	- 9.50

TYPE OF RACE

Non-Handicaps	W-R	Per cent	£1 Level Stake	Handicaps	W-R	Per cent	£1 Level Stake
2-y-o	0-31	-	- 31.00	2-y-o	1-9	11.1	- 2.00
3-y-o	1-18	5.6	- 14.25	3-y-o	5-33	15.2	- 6.25
4-y-o+	1-17	5.9	- 8.00	4-y-o+	2-46	4.3	- 26.50
Selling	1-8	12.5	+ 3.00	Selling	1-4	25.0	+ 2.50
Apprentice	0-0	-	0.00	Apprentice	0-5	-	- 5.00
Amat/Ladies	0-0	-	0.00	Amat/Ladies	0-3	-	- 3.00
Totals	3-74	4.1	- 50.25	Totals	9-100	9.0	- 40.25

COURSE GRADE

	W-R	Per cent	£1 Level Stake
Group 1	3-46	6.5	- 27.50
Group 2	0-27	-	- 27.00
Group 3	4-33	12.1	0.00
Group 4	5-68	7.4	- 36.00

FIRST TIME OUT

	W-R	Per cent	£1 Level Stake
2-y-o	0-9	-	- 9.00
3-y-o	0-9	-	- 9.00
4-y-o+	0-13	-	- 13.00
Totals	0-31	-	- 31.00

JOCKEYS RIDING

	W-R	Per cent	£1 Level Stake		W-R	Per cent	£1 Level Stake
D Holland	3-21	14.3	- 4.75	R Hills	1-2	50.0	+ 9.00
Pat Eddery	2-8	25.0	+ 4.00	A Munro	1-4	25.0	+ 13.00
Stephen Davies	2-13	15.4	- 6.75	J Weaver	1-7	14.3	- 1.50
V Halliday	2-37	5.4	- 21.50				

Paul Eddery	0-19	Mrs J Naughton	0-2	J Fortune	0-1
G Carter	0-8	P Robinson	0-2	L Dettori	0-1
A Garth	0-5	A Clark	0-1	M Fenton	0-1
D Harrison	0-5	A Eddery	0-1	M Roberts	0-1
E Johnson	0-3	A Mackay	0-1	Mr Raymond White	0-1
J Reid	0-3	A Tucker	0-1	N Adams	0-1
R Perham	0-3	D McCabe	0-1	P McCabe	0-1
A McGlone	0-2	D McKeown	0-1	S Lanigan	0-1
B Thomson	0-2	D Wright	0-1	T Quinn	0-1
G Bardwell	0-2	Dale Gibson	0-1	W Carson	0-1
J Fanning	0-2	G Duffield	0-1	W R Swinburn	0-1
J Quinn	0-2	J D Smith	0-1	W Woods	0-1

COURSE RECORD

	Total W-R	Non-Handicaps 2-y-o	Non-Handicaps 3-y-o+	Handicaps 2-y-o	Handicaps 3-y-o+	Per cent	£1 Level Stake
Southwell (AW)	2-12	0-0	1-6	0-0	1-6	16.7	- 0.75
Lingfield (AW)	2-17	0-0	1-6	0-0	1-11	11.8	- 7.25
Pontefract	1-2	0-0	0-0	0-0	1-2	50.0	+ 15.00
Hamilton	1-3	0-1	0-1	0-0	1-1	33.3	+ 3.50

Naughton T J

York	1-3	0-1	0-0	0-0	1-2	33.3	+	2.00
Doncaster	1-5	0-1	0-2	0-0	1-2	20.0	+	3.00
Nottingham	1-5	0-0	0-2	1-2	0-1	20.0	+	2.00
Chepstow	1-6	0-2	0-2	0-0	1-2	16.7	-	3.50
Warwick	1-7	0-2	1-3	0-0	0-2	14.3	+	4.00
Newmarket	1-11	0-2	0-1	0-2	1-6	9.1	-	5.50

Folkestone	0-18	Ascot	0-4	Sandown	0-2
Wolverhampton (AW)	0-12	Goodwood	0-4	Beverley	0-1
Brighton	0-9	Leicester	0-4	Carlisle	0-1
Epsom	0-9	Yarmouth	0-4	Edinburgh	0-1
Chester	0-6	Salisbury	0-3	Haydock	0-1
Lingfield	0-6	Windsor	0-3	Ripon	0-1
Bath	0-5	Newbury	0-2		
Kempton	0-5	Redcar	0-2		

WINNING HORSES

		Races					Win
	Age	Run	1st	2nd	3rd	Unpl	£
Hever Golf Rose	3	13	2	3	0	8	20,630
Milos	3	17	4	4	1	8	11,583
Comanche Companion	4	14	1	2	1	10	7,310
Cabcharge Blue	2	4	1	1	1	1	3,496
Allmosa	5	13	1	2	1	9	2,910
Call Me Blue	4	4	1	0	0	3	2,658
Splash Of Salt	4	10	1	1	1	7	2,511
Tyrian Purple	6	8	1	2	1	4	2,387

WINNING OWNERS

	Races Won	Value £		Races Won	Value £
R A Popely	6	32,213	J A Redmond	1	2,658
Drofmor Racing	1	7,310	S J Brown	1	2,511
Mrs A Wise	1	3,496	T O'Flaherty	1	2,387
The Durdans Four (II) Two	1	2,910			

Favourites	5-23	21.7%	- 0.75	Total winning prize-money			£53,485

Longest winning sequence		2	Average SP of winner	6.0/1
Longest losing sequence		46	Return on stakes invested	-52.0%

1993 Form	22-145	15.2%	- 1.18	1991 Form	6-88	6.8%	- 39.25
1992 Form	9-121	7.4%	+ 6.75				

A G NEWCOMBE (Barnstaple, Devon)

	No. of Horses	Races Run	1st	2nd	3rd	Unpl	Per cent	£1 Level Stake
2-y-o	1	1	0	1	0	0	-	- 1.00
3-y-o	3	10	0	1	3	6	-	- 10.00
4-y-o+	5	18	3	0	1	14	16.7	+ 28.00
Totals	9	29	3	2	4	20	10.3	+ 17.00

Jan	Feb	Mar	Apr	May	Jun	Jul	Aug	Sep	Oct/Nov
0-0	0-0	0-0	0-0	0-0	0-6	1-6	2-7	0-4	0-6

			£1 Level						£1 Level
Winning Jockey		W-R	Stake					W-R	Stake
S Raymont		3-8	+ 38.00						

Winning Courses								
Lingfield (AW)		2-2	+ 10.00		Warwick		1-1	+ 33.00

			Races					Win
Winning Horse		Age	Run	1st	2nd	3rd	Unpl	£
Young Fact		9	5	3	0	0	2	8,131

Favourites	0-0	Total winning prize-money	£8,131

D NICHOLLS (Thirsk, North Yorks)

	No. of Horses	Races Run	1st	2nd	3rd	Unpl	Per cent	£1 Level Stake
2-y-o	9	26	0	0	1	25	-	- 26.00
3-y-o	10	65	3	5	3	54	4.6	- 54.49
4-y-o+	15	92	13	6	11	62	14.1	- 25.63
Totals	34	183	16	11	15	141	8.7	-106.12

BY MONTH

2-y-o	W-R	Per cent	£1 Level Stake	3-y-o	W-R	Per cent	£1 Level Stake
January	0-0	-	0.00	January	0-7	-	- 7.00
February	0-0	-	0.00	February	0-1	-	- 1.00
March	0-1	-	- 1.00	March	0-3	-	- 3.00
April	0-3	-	- 3.00	April	2-7	28.6	+ 1.13
May	0-3	-	- 3.00	May	0-7	-	- 7.00
June	0-1	-	- 1.00	June	1-15	6.7	- 12.62
July	0-1	-	- 1.00	July	0-5	-	- 5.00
August	0-6	-	- 6.00	August	0-1	-	- 1.00
September	0-5	-	- 5.00	September	0-10	-	- 10.00
Oct/Nov	0-6	-	- 6.00	Oct/Nov	0-9	-	- 9.00

Nicholls D

4-y-o+	W-R	Per cent	£1 Level Stake	Totals	W-R	Per cent	£1 Level Stake
January	1-9	11.1	- 6.00	January	1-16	6.3	- 13.00
February	0-3	-	- 3.00	February	0-4	-	- 4.00
March	0-3	-	- 3.00	March	0-7	-	- 7.00
April	2-9	22.2	+ 1.50	April	4-19	21.1	- 0.37
May	1-8	12.5	+ 1.00	May	1-18	5.6	- 9.00
June	4-16	25.0	- 3.13	June	5-32	15.6	- 16.75
July	2-18	11.1	- 9.00	July	2-24	8.3	- 15.00
August	2-12	16.7	+ 3.50	August	2-19	10.5	- 3.50
September	1-6	16.7	+ 0.50	September	1-21	4.8	- 14.50
Oct/Nov	0-8	-	- 8.00	Oct/Nov	0-23	-	- 23.00

DISTANCE

2-y-o	W-R	Per cent	£1 Level Stake	3-y-o	W-R	Per cent	£1 Level Stake
5f-6f	0-17	-	- 17.00	5f-6f	2-28	7.1	- 20.12
7f-8f	0-8	-	- 8.00	7f-8f	1-28	3.6	- 25.37
9f-13f	0-1	-	- 1.00	9f-13f	0-9	-	- 9.00
14f+	0-0	-	0.00	14f+	0-0	-	0.00

4-y-o+	W-R	Per cent	£1 Level Stake	Totals	W-R	Per cent	£1 Level Stake
5f-6f	2-17	11.8	- 6.00	5f-6f	4-62	6.5	- 43.12
7f-8f	5-46	10.9	- 17.00	7f-8f	6-82	7.3	- 50.37
9f-13f	6-28	21.4	- 1.63	9f-13f	6-38	15.8	- 11.63
14f+	0-1	-	- 1.00	14f+	0-1	-	- 1.00

TYPE OF RACE

Non-Handicaps	W-R	Per cent	£1 Level Stake	Handicaps	W-R	Per cent	£1 Level Stake
2-y-o	0-20	-	- 20.00	2-y-o	0-4	-	- 4.00
3-y-o	0-15	-	- 15.00	3-y-o	2-42	4.8	- 36.99
4-y-o+	3-24	12.5	- 13.00	4-y-o+	7-54	13.0	- 18.63
Selling	2-11	18.2	0.00	Selling	1-8	12.5	+ 1.00
Apprentice	1-1	100.0	+ 4.50	Apprentice	0-1	-	- 1.00
Amat/Ladies	0-0	-	0.00	Amat/Ladies	0-3	-	- 3.00
Totals	6-71	8.5	- 43.50	Totals	10-112	8.9	- 62.62

COURSE GRADE

	W-R	Per cent	£1 Level Stake
Group 1	3-47	6.4	- 32.38
Group 2	1-37	2.7	- 27.50
Group 3	5-35	14.3	- 9.25
Group 4	7-64	10.9	- 36.99

FIRST TIME OUT

	W-R	Per cent	£1 Level Stake
2-y-o	0-8	-	- 8.00
3-y-o	0-5	-	- 5.00
4-y-o+	1-8	12.5	- 5.00
Totals	1-21	4.8	- 18.00

JOCKEYS RIDING

	W-R	Per cent	£1 Level Stake		W-R	Per cent	£1 Level Stake
Alex Greaves	11-100	11.0	- 47.13	J Lowe	1-3	33.3	- 0.62
L Dettori	1-1	100.0	+ 6.00	A Garth	1-8	12.5	- 2.50
A Eddery	1-1	100.0	+ 5.50	L Charnock	1-18	5.6	- 15.37

A Mackay	0-8	Claire Balding	0-1	Miss I D W Jones	0-1
M Birch	0-5	F Norton	0-1	Miss L Perratt	0-1
N Connorton	0-5	G Carter	0-1	Miss R Clark	0-1
J Stack	0-4	G Hind	0-1	N Carlisle	0-1
Paul Eddery	0-4	J Quinn	0-1	R Cochrane	0-1
G Duffield	0-3	J Tate	0-1	V Halliday	0-1
P McCabe	0-3	L Piggott	0-1	W Ryan	0-1
J Fanning	0-2	Lorna Vincent	0-1		
J Weaver	0-2	M J Kinane	0-1		

COURSE RECORD

	Total W-R	Non-Handicaps 2-y-o	3-y-o+	Handicaps 2-y-o	3-y-o+	Per cent	£1 Level Stake
Catterick	3-17	0-1	2-6	0-1	1-9	17.6	- 4.50
Beverley	2-8	0-0	1-2	0-0	1-6	25.0	+ 1.25
Pontefract	2-11	0-1	1-4	0-0	1-6	18.2	- 3.50
Southwell (AW)	2-12	0-1	2-8	0-0	0-3	16.7	- 2.50
Edinburgh	2-13	0-2	0-0	0-1	2-10	15.4	- 7.99
Nottingham	1-2	0-0	0-1	0-0	1-1	50.0	+ 7.00
York	1-6	0-0	0-0	0-0	1-6	16.7	+ 1.00
Ayr	1-9	0-2	0-0	0-0	1-7	11.1	- 7.38
Redcar	1-9	0-2	0-2	0-1	1-4	11.1	+ 0.50
Newcastle	1-11	0-3	0-0	0-0	1-8	9.1	- 5.00

Ripon	0-15	Lingfield (AW)	0-7	Leicester	0-3
Doncaster	0-12	Carlisle	0-6	Goodwood	0-1
Hamilton	0-10	Chester	0-5	Windsor	0-1
Wolverhampton (AW)	0-9	Haydock	0-4		
Thirsk	0-8	Newmarket	0-4		

WINNING HORSES

	Age	Races Run	1st	2nd	3rd	Unpl	Win £
Pride Of Pendle	5	17	2	1	3	11	14,758
Joseph's Wine	5	11	4	0	0	7	11,757
Sharp Sensation	4	9	1	0	0	8	3,623
Le Chic	8	6	1	0	0	5	3,460
Never In The Red	6	3	1	0	2	0	2,900
North Esk	5	6	1	2	2	1	2,872
Nineacres	3	9	1	2	1	5	2,762
Ovalworld	3	15	1	2	1	11	2,646
Elle Shaped	4	8	1	1	1	5	2,644
Waterlord	4	11	1	2	0	8	2,469
Greek Gold	5	4	1	0	1	2	2,174
Passion Sunday	3	12	1	0	0	11	1,690

WINNING OWNERS

	Races Won	Value £		Races Won	Value £
Mrs Linda Miller	2	14,758	John Wilman	1	3,460
Mrs Jennifer Houghton	4	11,757	W G Swiers	1	2,872
Consultco Ltd	2	5,369	W J Kelly	1	2,646
John Gilbertson	2	4,452	J E Marsden	1	2,644
G Chung	1	3,623	Terry Connors	1	2,174

Favourites	7-19	36.8% - 1.12	
Longest winning sequence		2	
Longest losing sequence		33	

Total winning prize-money	£53,755
Average SP of winner	3.8/1
Return on stakes invested	-58.0%

1993 Form	1-9	11.1% + 4.00

D NICHOLSON (Temple Guiting, Glos)

	No. of Horses	Races Run	1st	2nd	3rd	Unpl	Per cent	£1 Level Stake
2-y-o	0	0	0	0	0	0	-	0.00
3-y-o	3	8	0	3	1	4	-	- 8.00
4-y-o+	1	4	1	1	0	2	25.0	+ 17.00
Totals	4	12	1	4	1	6	8.3	+ 9.00

Jan	Feb	Mar	Apr	May	Jun	Jul	Aug	Sep	Oct/Nov
0-0	0-0	0-1	1-2	0-5	0-2	0-0	0-1	0-1	0-0

Winning Jockey	W-R	£1 Level Stake	Winning Course	W-R	£1 Level Stake
M Hills	1-3	+ 18.00	Newmarket	1-1	+ 20.00

Winning Horse	Age	Races Run	1st	2nd	3rd	Unpl	Win £
Silver Wisp	5	4	1	1	0	2	33,285

Favourites	0-1			Total winning prize-money		£33,285
1993 Form	0-4			1991 Form	0-8	
1992 Form	1-7	14.3%	+ 60.00	1990 Form	0-5	

J NORTON (Barnsley, South Yorks)

	No. of Horses	Races Run	1st	2nd	3rd	Unpl	Per cent	£1 Level Stake
2-y-o	0	0	0	0	0	0	-	0.00
3-y-o	1	3	0	0	0	3	-	- 3.00
4-y-o+	5	34	1	0	0	33	2.9	- 19.00
Totals	6	37	1	0	0	36	2.7	- 22.00

Jan	Feb	Mar	Apr	May	Jun	Jul	Aug	Sep	Oct/Nov
1-5	0-3	0-3	0-4	0-2	0-6	0-3	0-5	0-2	0-4

			£1 Level					£1 Level
Winning Jockey		W-R	Stake	Winning Course			W-R	Stake
J Weaver		1-5	+ 10.00	Southwell (AW)			1-14	+ 1.00

			Races					Win
Winning Horse		Age	Run	1st	2nd	3rd	Unpl	£
Diamond Inthe Dark		6	16	1	0	0	15	3,080

Favourites	0-0			Total winning prize-money		£3,080

1993 Form	0-20			1991 Form	0-17
1992 Form	0-27			1990 Form	0-39

S G NORTON (Barnsley, South Yorks)

	No. of Horses	Races Run	1st	2nd	3rd	Unpl	Per cent	£1 Level Stake
2-y-o	17	68	5	0	8	55	7.4	- 35.25
3-y-o	13	84	4	5	13	62	4.8	- 60.00
4-y-o+	7	53	3	4	5	41	5.7	- 37.77
Totals	37	205	12	9	26	158	5.9	-133.02

BY MONTH

2-y-o	W-R	Per cent	£1 Level Stake	3-y-o	W-R	Per cent	£1 Level Stake
January	0-0	-	0.00	January	0-0	-	0.00
February	0-0	-	0.00	February	0-1	-	- 1.00
March	0-1	-	- 1.00	March	0-3	-	- 3.00
April	1-8	12.5	- 3.50	April	1-15	6.7	- 6.00
May	0-4	-	- 4.00	May	0-13	-	- 13.00
June	0-6	-	- 6.00	June	1-14	7.1	- 9.50
July	3-16	18.8	+ 5.75	July	2-10	20.0	+ 0.50
August	0-13	-	- 13.00	August	0-13	-	- 13.00
September	1-7	14.3	- 0.50	September	0-7	-	- 7.00
Oct/Nov	0-13	-	- 13.00	Oct/Nov	0-8	-	- 8.00

4-y-o+	W-R	Per cent	£1 Level Stake	Totals	W-R	Per cent	£1 Level Stake
January	0-1	-	- 1.00	January	0-1	-	- 1.00
February	0-3	-	- 3.00	February	0-4	-	- 4.00
March	0-3	-	- 3.00	March	0-7	-	- 7.00
April	0-8	-	- 8.00	April	2-31	6.5	- 17.50
May	1-6	16.7	- 0.50	May	1-23	4.3	- 17.50
June	1-8	12.5	- 6.27	June	2-28	7.1	- 21.77
July	0-12	-	- 12.00	July	5-38	13.2	- 5.75
August	1-7	14.3	+ 1.00	August	1-33	3.0	- 25.00
September	0-4	-	- 4.00	September	1-18	5.6	- 11.50
Oct/Nov	0-1	-	- 1.00	Oct/Nov	0-22	-	- 22.00

Norton S G

DISTANCE

2-y-o	W-R	Per cent	£1 Level Stake	3-y-o	W-R	Per cent	£1 Level Stake
5f-6f	3-46	6.5	- 30.75	5f-6f	0-13	-	- 13.00
7f-8f	2-22	9.1	- 4.50	7f-8f	1-29	3.4	- 23.50
9f-13f	0-0	-	0.00	9f-13f	3-36	8.3	- 17.50
14f+	0-0	-	0.00	14f+	0-6	-	- 6.00

4-y-o+	W-R	Per cent	£1 Level Stake	Totals	W-R	Per cent	£1 Level Stake
5f-6f	0-9	-	- 9.00	5f-6f	3-68	4.4	- 52.75
7f-8f	0-19	-	- 19.00	7f-8f	3-70	4.3	- 47.00
9f-13f	3-18	16.7	- 2.77	9f-13f	6-54	11.1	- 20.27
14f+	0-7	-	- 7.00	14f+	0-13	-	- 13.00

TYPE OF RACE

Non-Handicaps	W-R	Per cent	£1 Level Stake	Handicaps	W-R	Per cent	£1 Level Stake
2-y-o	4-49	8.2	- 24.25	2-y-o	1-8	12.5	0.00
3-y-o	0-29	-	- 29.00	3-y-o	3-29	10.3	- 10.50
4-y-o+	2-17	11.8	- 9.77	4-y-o+	0-29	-	- 29.00
Selling	1-21	4.8	- 13.00	Selling	0-11	-	- 11.00
Apprentice	0-0	-	0.00	Apprentice	1-7	14.3	- 1.50
Amat/Ladies	0-0	-	0.00	Amat/Ladies	0-5	-	- 5.00
Totals	7-116	6.0	- 76.02	Totals	5-89	5.6	- 57.00

COURSE GRADE

	W-R	Per cent	£1 Level Stake
Group 1	1-42	2.4	- 37.00
Group 2	2-48	4.2	- 34.50
Group 3	2-48	4.2	- 39.00
Group 4	7-67	10.4	- 22.52

FIRST TIME OUT

	W-R	Per cent	£1 Level Stake
2-y-o	0-17	-	- 17.00
3-y-o	1-13	7.7	- 4.00
4-y-o+	0-6	-	- 6.00
Totals	1-36	2.8	- 27.00

JOCKEYS RIDING

	W-R	Per cent	£1 Level Stake		W-R	Per cent	£1 Level Stake
J Tate	4-33	12.1	- 11.75	D Denby	1-6	16.7	- 0.50
M Tebbutt	3-8	37.5	+ 19.00	J Fortune	1-10	10.0	- 3.50
S Maloney	2-15	13.3	- 7.77	K Darley	1-18	5.6	- 13.50

N Connorton	0-13	A Mackay	0-3	D Gibbs	0-1
T Marsden	0-12	J Weaver	0-3	D Harrison	0-1
G Hind	0-8	Paul Eddery	0-3	D Wright	0-1
K Fallon	0-8	A Munro	0-2	F Norton	0-1
J Quinn	0-6	G Duffield	0-2	G Bardwell	0-1
L Charnock	0-6	Mr G Hogan	0-2	J Carroll	0-1
T Williams	0-6	N Kennedy	0-2	L Dettori	0-1
A Garth	0-5	Sarah Senior	0-2	Mr C Bonner	0-1
D Moffatt	0-4	A Eddery	0-1	Mr R Hale	0-1
G Carter	0-4	Alex Greaves	0-1	Mrs A Farrell	0-1
O Pears	0-4	B Raymond	0-1	N Varley	0-1
T Ives	0-4	B Rouse	0-1	R Price	0-1

COURSE RECORD

	Total	Non-Handicaps		Handicaps		Per	£1 Level
	W-R	2-y-o	3-y-o+	2-y-o	3-y-o+	cent	Stake
Southwell (AW)	5-30	3-13	0-7	1-2	1-8	16.7	+ 3.75
Edinburgh	2-12	0-2	1-4	0-0	1-6	16.7	- 1.27
Pontefract	2-18	1-7	0-3	0-1	1-7	11.1	- 9.00
York	1-3	0-0	0-0	0-0	1-3	33.3	+ 2.00
Thirsk	1-7	0-2	1-3	0-0	0-2	14.3	- 1.50
Redcar	1-16	0-5	1-5	0-0	0-6	6.3	- 8.00

Beverley	0-15	Hamilton	0-10	Warwick	0-3
Doncaster	0-14	Wolverhampton (AW)	0-7	Ayr	0-2
Ripon	0-13	Newcastle	0-6	Kempton	0-2
Haydock	0-12	Nottingham	0-5	Lingfield	0-2
Catterick	0-11	Carlisle	0-4		
Chester	0-10	Newmarket	0-3		

WINNING HORSES

		Races					Win
	Age	Run	1st	2nd	3rd	Unpl	£
Slasher Jack	3	9	3	0	0	6	12,297
Rambo Waltzer	2	7	2	0	1	4	6,431
Goodbye Millie	4	9	2	2	0	5	5,132
Tidal Reach	2	4	1	0	1	2	3,393
Break The Rules	2	4	1	0	0	3	3,144
Hamadryad	6	10	1	1	0	8	2,840
Shared Risk	2	4	1	0	0	3	2,701
Gwernymynydd	3	13	1	0	2	10	2,606

WINNING OWNERS

	Races Won	Value £		Races Won	Value £
T C Chiang	3	12,297	G G Ashton	1	3,393
Keystone Racing Club P'Ship	2	6,431	P D Savill	1	3,144
S G Norton	2	5,541	D O Pickering	1	2,606
Lintscan Ltd (Corbett Bookmakers)	2	5,132			

| Favourites | 3-17 | 17.6% | - 7.02 | | Total winning prize-money | | £38,543 |

| Longest winning sequence | 2 | | Average SP of winner | 5.0/1 |
| Longest losing sequence | 38 | | Return on stakes invested | -64.9% |

| 1993 Form | 45-315 | 14.3% | - 62.44 | | 1991 Form | 19-153 | 12.4% | - 7.27 |
| 1992 Form | 27-193 | 14.0% | - 21.43 | | 1990 Form | 20-199 | 10.1% | - 39.25 |

J O'DONOGHUE (Reigate, Surrey)

	No. of Horses	Races Run	1st	2nd	3rd	Unpl	Per cent	£1 Level Stake
2-y-o	0	0	0	0	0	0	-	0.00
3-y-o	1	20	4	2	1	13	20.0	+ 19.00
4-y-o+	3	26	0	2	1	23	-	- 26.00
Totals	4	46	4	4	2	36	8.7	- 7.00

Jan	Feb	Mar	Apr	May	Jun	Jul	Aug	Sep	Oct/Nov
0-0	0-1	0-1	0-3	1-5	1-10	0-7	1-7	1-6	0-6

Winning Jockey	W-R	£1 Level Stake		W-R	£1 Level Stake
P McCabe	4-21	+ 18.00			

Winning Courses					
Doncaster	1-1	+ 12.00	Newmarket	1-5	+ 0.50
Goodwood	1-3	+ 14.00	Brighton	1-8	- 4.50

Winning Horse	Age	Races Run	1st	2nd	3rd	Unpl	Win £
Hello Mister	3	20	4	2	1	13	42,291

| Favourites | 1-3 | 33.3% | + 0.50 | | Total winning prize-money | | £42,291 |

| 1993 Form | 2-33 | 6.1% | - 11.00 | | 1991 Form | 1-15 | 6.7% | - 6.00 |
| 1992 Form | 0-11 | | | | 1990 Form | 0-16 | | |

W A O'GORMAN (Newmarket)

	No. of Horses	Races Run	1st	2nd	3rd	Unpl	Per cent	£1 Level Stake
2-y-o	11	40	2	3	6	29	5.0	- 21.00
3-y-o	6	38	2	5	3	28	5.3	- 30.00
4-y-o+	9	51	6	6	7	32	11.8	- 4.50
Totals	26	129	10	14	16	89	7.8	- 55.50

BY MONTH

2-y-o	W-R	Per cent	£1 Level Stake	3-y-o	W-R	Per cent	£1 Level Stake
January	0-0	-	0.00	January	1-2	50.0	+ 2.50
February	0-0	-	0.00	February	0-3	-	- 3.00
March	0-1	-	- 1.00	March	0-3	-	- 3.00
April	0-1	-	- 1.00	April	0-3	-	- 3.00
May	0-0	-	0.00	May	0-6	-	- 6.00
June	0-7	-	- 7.00	June	0-2	-	- 2.00
July	0-5	-	- 5.00	July	0-8	-	- 8.00
August	0-7	-	- 7.00	August	0-1	-	- 1.00
September	2-13	15.4	+ 6.00	September	1-6	16.7	- 2.50
Oct/Nov	0-6	-	- 6.00	Oct/Nov	0-4	-	- 4.00

4-y-o+	W-R	Per cent	£1 Level Stake	Totals	W-R	Per cent	£1 Level Stake
January	1-9	11.1	- 3.00	January	2-11	18.2	- 0.50
February	0-4	-	- 4.00	February	0-7	-	- 7.00
March	0-3	-	- 3.00	March	0-7	-	- 7.00
April	0-6	-	- 6.00	April	0-10	-	- 10.00
May	1-11	9.1	+ 4.00	May	1-17	5.9	- 2.00
June	2-8	25.0	+ 5.00	June	2-17	11.8	- 4.00
July	0-3	-	- 3.00	July	0-16	-	- 16.00
August	0-0	-	0.00	August	0-8	-	- 8.00
September	0-1	-	- 1.00	September	3-20	15.0	+ 2.50
Oct/Nov	2-6	33.3	+ 6.50	Oct/Nov	2-16	12.5	- 3.50

DISTANCE

2-y-o	W-R	Per cent	£1 Level Stake	3-y-o	W-R	Per cent	£1 Level Stake
5f-6f	0-25	-	- 25.00	5f-6f	1-22	4.5	- 18.50
7f-8f	2-15	13.3	+ 4.00	7f-8f	1-14	7.1	- 9.50
9f-13f	0-0	-	0.00	9f-13f	0-2	-	- 2.00
14f+	0-0	-	0.00	14f+	0-0	-	0.00

4-y-o+	W-R	Per cent	£1 Level Stake	Totals	W-R	Per cent	£1 Level Stake
5f-6f	3-17	17.6	+ 3.00	5f-6f	4-64	6.3	- 40.50
7f-8f	2-26	7.7	- 5.50	7f-8f	5-55	9.1	- 11.00
9f-13f	1-8	12.5	- 2.00	9f-13f	1-10	10.0	- 4.00
14f+	0-0	-	0.00	14f+	0-0	-	0.00

TYPE OF RACE

Non-Handicaps	W-R	Per cent	£1 Level Stake	Handicaps	W-R	Per cent	£1 Level Stake
2-y-o	2-27	7.4	- 8.00	2-y-o	0-12	-	- 12.00
3-y-o	1-10	10.0	- 6.50	3-y-o	1-28	3.6	- 23.50
4-y-o+	1-12	8.3	- 6.50	4-y-o+	5-38	13.2	+ 3.00
Selling	0-2	-	- 2.00	Selling	0-0	-	0.00
Apprentice	0-0	-	0.00	Apprentice	0-0	-	0.00
Amat/Ladies	0-0	-	0.00	Amat/Ladies	0-0	-	0.00
Totals	4-51	7.8	- 23.00	Totals	6-78	7.7	- 32.50

343

COURSE GRADE

	W-R	Per cent	£1 Level Stake
Group 1	1-44	2.3	- 29.00
Group 2	0-6	-	- 6.00
Group 3	1-25	4.0	- 15.00
Group 4	8-54	14.8	- 5.50

FIRST TIME OUT

	W-R	Per cent	£1 Level Stake
2-y-o	1-11	9.1	- 7.00
3-y-o	1-6	16.7	- 1.50
4-y-o+	1-7	14.3	- 1.00
Totals	3-24	12.5	- 9.50

JOCKEYS RIDING

	W-R	Per cent	£1 Level Stake		W-R	Per cent	£1 Level Stake
Emma O'Gorman	8-59	13.6	+ 7.00	T Ives	2-36	5.6	- 28.50
Paul Eddery	0-5			J Weaver	0-2		
L Piggott	0-4			N Adams	0-2		
A Munro	0-3			C Asmussen	0-1		
D Holland	0-3			D Harrison	0-1		
J Williams	0-3			G Carter	0-1		
L Dettori	0-3			J Lowe	0-1		

J Tate	0-1
K Darley	0-1
N Varley	0-1
T Quinn	0-1
W Ryan	0-1

COURSE RECORD

	Total W-R	Non-Handicaps 2-y-o	Non-Handicaps 3-y-o+	Handicaps 2-y-o	Handicaps 3-y-o+	Per cent	£1 Level Stake
Lingfield (AW)	4-17	0-0	1-4	0-2	3-11	23.5	+ 6.00
Southwell (AW)	4-21	2-4	1-10	0-1	1-6	19.0	+ 4.50
Beverley	1-1	0-0	0-0	0-0	1-1	100.0	+ 9.00
Doncaster	1-5	0-1	0-1	0-0	1-3	20.0	+ 10.00

Newmarket	0-28	Kempton	0-3	Thirsk	0-2
Wolverhampton (AW)	0-9	Yarmouth	0-3	Ascot	0-1
Leicester	0-8	York	0-3	Nottingham	0-1
Windsor	0-6	Bath	0-2	Redcar	0-1
Pontefract	0-4	Lingfield	0-2	Salisbury	0-1
Warwick	0-4	Newbury	0-2		
Folkestone	0-3	Sandown	0-2		

WINNING HORSES

	Age	Races Run	1st	2nd	3rd	Unpl	Win £
African Chimes	7	12	4	1	2	5	11,382
Midnight Jazz	4	9	2	3	0	4	7,130
Pleasure Beach	2	7	1	1	0	5	3,766
In Character	2	2	1	0	0	1	3,420
Berge	3	6	1	0	0	5	2,925
Cappuchino	3	6	1	2	1	2	2,467

WINNING OWNERS

	Races Won	Value £		Races Won	Value £
S Fustok	4	12,521	P B A Skegness Ltd	1	3,766
D G Wheatley	4	11,382	W A O'Gorman	1	3,420

Favourites	2-13	15.4%	- 6.50	Total winning prize-money	£31,089
Longest winning sequence			2	Average SP of winner	6.4/1
Longest losing sequence			44	Return on stakes invested	-43.0%
1993 Form	25-145	17.2%	+ 0.90	1991 Form	29-232	12.5%	- 95.24
1992 Form	27-197	13.7%	- 93.76	1990 Form	51-209	24.4%	+ 25.24

J J O'NEILL (Penrith, Cumbria)

	No. of Horses	Races Run	1st	2nd	3rd	Unpl	Per cent	£1 Level Stake
2-y-o	2	7	0	0	0	7	-	- 7.00
3-y-o	5	26	0	4	0	22	-	- 26.00
4-y-o+	7	21	1	0	1	19	4.8	- 15.00
Totals	14	54	1	4	1	48	1.9	- 48.00

Jan	Feb	Mar	Apr	May	Jun	Jul	Aug	Sep	Oct/Nov
0-0	0-0	0-0	0-9	0-10	0-18	1-8	0-3	0-6	0-0

Winning Jockey	W-R	£1 Level Stake	Winning Course	W-R	£1 Level Stake
G Parkin	1-2	+ 4.00	Carlisle	1-10	- 4.00

Winning Horse	Age	Races Run	1st	2nd	3rd	Unpl	Win £
Princess Maxine	5	2	1	0	0	1	3,002

Favourites	0-1			Total winning prize-money	£3,002
1993 Form	2-34	5.9%	- 18.50	1991 Form	2-68	2.9%	- 56.00
1992 Form	1-62	1.6%	- 52.50	1990 Form	8-37	21.6%	+ 2.00

O O'NEILL (Cheltenham, Glos)

	No. of Horses	Races Run	1st	2nd	3rd	Unpl	Per cent	£1 Level Stake
2-y-o	0	0	0	0	0	0	-	0.00
3-y-o	1	1	0	0	0	1	-	- 1.00
4-y-o+	7	27	2	1	4	20	7.4	- 11.00
Totals	8	28	2	1	4	21	7.1	- 12.00

Jan	Feb	Mar	Apr	May	Jun	Jul	Aug	Sep	Oct/Nov
0-3	0-1	0-3	0-2	0-5	2-5	0-5	0-0	0-2	0-2

Winning Jockey	W-R	£1 Level Stake					W-R	£1 Level Stake
D Griffiths	2-6	+ 10.00						

Winning Courses	W-R	£1 Level Stake					W-R	£1 Level Stake
Haydock	1-2	+ 6.00	Warwick				1-6	+ 2.00

Winning Horse	Age	Races Run	1st	2nd	3rd	Unpl	Win £
Leguard Express	6	12	2	1	4	5	5,837

Favourites	0-0		Total winning prize-money	£5,837

1993 Form	2-31	6.5%	+ 87.00	1991 Form	1-35	2.9%	- 26.00
1992 Form	0-20			1990 Form	2-50	4.0%	- 38.75

J G M O'SHEA (Welford-on-Avon, Warwicks)

	No. of Horses	Races Run	1st	2nd	3rd	Unpl	Per cent	£1 Level Stake
2-y-o	0	0	0	0	0	0	-	0.00
3-y-o	3	16	0	1	1	14	-	- 16.00
4-y-o+	11	41	4	2	2	33	9.8	- 25.50
Totals	14	57	4	3	3	47	7.0	- 41.50

Jan	Feb	Mar	Apr	May	Jun	Jul	Aug	Sep	Oct/Nov
0-1	1-5	0-2	0-2	1-9	1-15	0-10	1-8	0-2	0-3

Winning Jockeys	W-R	£1 Level Stake					W-R	£1 Level Stake
S Lanigan	1-1	+ 2.25	D McKeown				1-8	- 5.00
D Griffiths	1-2	+ 1.75	J Quinn				1-10	- 4.50

Winning Courses	W-R	£1 Level Stake					W-R	£1 Level Stake
Hamilton	2-2	+ 5.00	Wolverhampton (AW)				1-18	- 12.50
Catterick	1-3	0.00						

Winning Horses	Age	Races Run	1st	2nd	3rd	Unpl	Win £
Royal Circus	5	9	3	1	0	5	8,361
Noel	5	6	1	1	0	4	3,348

Favourites	1-5	20.0%	- 1.75	Total winning prize-money	£11,709

1993 Form	0-2		1991 Form	0-7
1992 Form	0-1		1990 Form	0-15

R J O'SULLIVAN (Bognor Regis, West Sussex)

	No. of Horses	Races Run	1st	2nd	3rd	Unpl	Per cent	£1 Level Stake
2-y-o	0	0	0	0	0	0	-	0.00
3-y-o	1	14	2	0	2	10	14.3	+ 10.50
4-y-o+	20	113	11	16	10	76	9.7	- 54.52
Totals	21	127	13	16	12	86	10.2	- 44.02

BY MONTH

2-y-o	W-R	Per cent	£1 Level Stake	3-y-o	W-R	Per cent	£1 Level Stake
January	0-0	-	0.00	January	0-0	-	0.00
February	0-0	-	0.00	February	0-1	-	- 1.00
March	0-0	-	0.00	March	0-1	-	- 1.00
April	0-0	-	0.00	April	0-1	-	- 1.00
May	0-0	-	0.00	May	0-2	-	- 2.00
June	0-0	-	0.00	June	0-2	-	- 2.00
July	0-0	-	0.00	July	1-2	50.0	+ 15.00
August	0-0	-	0.00	August	0-2	-	- 2.00
September	0-0	-	0.00	September	1-2	50.0	+ 5.50
Oct/Nov	0-0	-	0.00	Oct/Nov	0-1	-	- 1.00

4-y-o+	W-R	Per cent	£1 Level Stake	Totals	W-R	Per cent	£1 Level Stake
January	3-18	16.7	- 8.52	January	3-18	16.7	- 8.52
February	2-13	15.4	- 6.50	February	2-14	14.3	- 7.50
March	2-15	13.3	+ 11.00	March	2-16	12.5	+ 10.00
April	2-9	22.2	+ 0.25	April	2-10	20.0	- 0.75
May	0-12	-	- 12.00	May	0-14	-	- 14.00
June	1-15	6.7	- 11.75	June	1-17	5.9	- 13.75
July	1-15	6.7	- 11.00	July	2-17	11.8	+ 4.00
August	0-8	-	- 8.00	August	0-10	-	- 10.00
September	0-6	-	- 6.00	September	1-8	12.5	- 0.50
Oct/Nov	0-2	-	- 2.00	Oct/Nov	0-3	-	- 3.00

DISTANCE

2-y-o	W-R	Per cent	£1 Level Stake	3-y-o	W-R	Per cent	£1 Level Stake
5f-6f	0-0	-	0.00	5f-6f	2-6	33.3	+ 18.50
7f-8f	0-0	-	0.00	7f-8f	0-6	-	- 6.00
9f-13f	0-0	-	0.00	9f-13f	0-2	-	- 2.00
14f+	0-0	-	0.00	14f+	0-0	-	0.00

4-y-o+	W-R	Per cent	£1 Level Stake	Totals	W-R	Per cent	£1 Level Stake
5f-6f	5-33	15.2	- 4.77	5f-6f	7-39	17.9	+ 13.73
7f-8f	5-40	12.5	- 16.25	7f-8f	5-46	10.9	- 22.25
9f-13f	1-33	3.0	- 26.50	9f-13f	1-35	2.9	- 28.50
14f+	0-7	-	- 7.00	14f+	0-7	-	- 7.00

TYPE OF RACE

Non-Handicaps	W–R	Per cent	£1 Level Stake	Handicaps	W–R	Per cent	£1 Level Stake
2-y-o	0-0	–	0.00	2-y-o	0-0	–	0.00
3-y-o	0-5	–	- 5.00	3-y-o	2-9	22.2	+ 15.50
4-y-o+	4-16	25.0	- 4.37	4-y-o+	7-85	8.2	- 38.15
Selling	0-2	–	- 2.00	Selling	0-1	–	- 1.00
Apprentice	0-2	–	- 2.00	Apprentice	0-7	–	- 7.00
Amat/Ladies	0-0	–	0.00	Amat/Ladies	0-0	–	0.00
Totals	4-25	16.0	- 13.37	Totals	9-102	8.8	- 30.65

COURSE GRADE

	W–R	Per cent	£1 Level Stake
Group 1	0-28	–	- 28.00
Group 2	4-27	14.8	0.00
Group 3	0-10	–	- 10.00
Group 4	9-62	14.5	- 6.02

FIRST TIME OUT

	W–R	Per cent	£1 Level Stake
2-y-o	0-0	–	0.00
3-y-o	0-1	–	- 1.00
4-y-o+	1-19	5.3	- 14.00
Totals	1-20	5.0	- 15.00

JOCKEYS RIDING

	W–R	Per cent	£1 Level Stake		W–R	Per cent	£1 Level Stake
D Biggs	7-40	17.5	- 8.52	T Quinn	1-1	100.0	+ 3.00
A Clark	2-13	15.4	+ 21.00	Stephen Davies	1-13	7.7	- 5.50
J Quinn	2-19	10.5	- 13.00				

J D Smith	0-5	M Baird	0-2	J Reid	0-1
W Woods	0-4	M Hills	0-2	L Carter	0-1
A Tucker	0-3	R Cochrane	0-2	N Adams	0-1
L Dettori	0-3	A Martinez	0-1	N Carlisle	0-1
W Ryan	0-3	A Whelan	0-1	N Varley	0-1
B Russell	0-2	B Thomson	0-1	P McCabe	0-1
D Harrison	0-2	F Norton	0-1		
D Wright	0-2	G Hind	0-1		

COURSE RECORD

	Total W–R	Non-Handicaps 2-y-o	3-y-o+	Handicaps 2-y-o	3-y-o+	Per cent	£1 Level Stake
Lingfield (AW)	8-49	0-0	3-13	0-0	5-36	16.3	- 0.52
Brighton	2-12	0-0	0-2	0-0	2-10	16.7	- 4.75
Salisbury	1-3	0-0	1-1	0-0	0-2	33.3	- 0.25
Folkestone	1-7	0-0	0-2	0-0	1-5	14.3	+ 0.50
Lingfield	1-12	0-0	0-2	0-0	1-10	8.3	+ 5.00

Goodwood	0-12	Sandown	0-3	Epsom	0-1
Kempton	0-6	Bath	0-2	Leicester	0-1
Windsor	0-6	Newbury	0-2	Wolverhampton (AW)	0-1
Ascot	0-3	Warwick	0-2	York	0-1
Catterick	0-3	Chepstow	0-1		

WINNING HORSES

	Age	Races Run	1st	2nd	3rd	Unpl	Win £
Sir Norman Holt	5	10	3	1	3	3	11,589
Agwa	5	11	4	2	0	5	11,429
La Petite Fusee	3	14	2	0	2	10	6,491
Mighty Wrath	4	8	1	2	2	3	3,319
Masnun	9	9	1	2	1	5	3,054
Al Shaati	4	10	1	2	1	6	3,028
Little Miss Ribot	4	15	1	3	2	9	2,050

WINNING OWNERS

	Races Won	Value £		Races Won	Value £
I A Baker	8	26,047	I W Page	1	3,054
Bert Powis	2	6,491	R J O'Sullivan	1	2,050
Furlong Racing Club	1	3,319			

Favourites	5-21	23.8%	- 5.65	Total winning prize-money		£40,960
Longest winning sequence			2	Average SP of winner		5.4/1
Longest losing sequence			26	Return on stakes invested		-34.3%
1993 Form	19-153	12.4%	- 47.00	1991 Form	11-103	10.7%	+ 22.00
1992 Form	9-75	12.0%	+ 18.63	1990 Form	6-68	8.8%	- 6.50

G R OLDROYD (York, North Yorks)

	No. of Horses	Races Run	1st	2nd	3rd	Unpl	Per cent	£1 Level Stake
2-y-o	3	5	0	0	0	5	-	- 5.00
3-y-o	3	6	0	0	0	6	-	- 6.00
4-y-o+	11	47	2	4	3	38	4.3	- 30.50
Totals	17	58	2	4	3	49	3.4	- 41.50

Jan	Feb	Mar	Apr	May	Jun	Jul	Aug	Sep	Oct/Nov
0-1	0-1	0-1	0-7	0-8	0-7	1-9	0-7	1-11	0-6

Winning Jockeys	W-R	£1 Level Stake		W-R	£1 Level Stake
D Griffiths	1-3	+ 10.00	S Webster	1-36	- 32.50

Winning Courses					
Edinburgh	1-2	+ 1.50	Haydock	1-2	+ 11.00

Winning Horses	Age	Races Run	1st	2nd	3rd	Unpl	Win £
Mu-Arrik	6	11	1	2	2	6	2,864
Supreme Desire	6	6	1	0	0	5	2,775

Favourites	0-0			Total winning prize-money		£5,639
1993 Form	2-34	5.9%	- 21.50	1991 Form	5-59	8.5%	- 19.75
1992 Form	0-0			1990 Form	1-21	4.8%	- 15.50

B PALLING (Cowbridge, South Glamorgan)

	No. of Horses	Races Run	1st	2nd	3rd	Unpl	Per cent	£1 Level Stake
2-y-o	7	46	1	3	6	36	2.2	- 38.00
3-y-o	9	56	4	4	3	45	7.1	- 41.30
4-y-o+	5	20	3	1	1	15	15.0	+ 1.50
Totals	21	122	8	8	10	96	6.6	- 77.80

Jan	Feb	Mar	Apr	May	Jun	Jul	Aug	Sep	Oct/Nov
0-3	0-0	0-0	0-6	2-15	1-14	1-24	1-25	1-18	2-17

Winning Jockeys	W-R	£1 Level Stake		W-R	£1 Level Stake
Stephen Davies	3-35	- 19.00	C Rutter	1-3	+ 2.50
T Sprake	2-29	- 16.50	J Williams	1-10	- 2.00
R Hills	1-1	+ 1.20			

Winning Courses	W-R	£1 Level Stake		W-R	£1 Level Stake
Catterick	3-4	+ 6.70	York	1-3	+ 4.00
Chepstow	2-15	- 1.50	Lingfield (AW)	1-4	0.00
Goodwood	1-3	+ 6.00			

Winning Horses	Age	Races Run	1st	2nd	3rd	Unpl	Win £
Carranita	4	10	3	0	1	6	16,581
Rose Of Glenn	3	9	4	2	1	2	9,679
Havana Miss	2	5	1	0	0	4	2,248

Favourites	2-6	33.3%	- 0.80	Total winning prize-money		£28,508

1993 Form	9-118	7.6%	- 18.17	1991 Form	1-79	1.3%	- 72.00
1992 Form	8-96	8.3%	- 14.75	1990 Form	4-101	4.0%	- 47.62

C PARKER (Lockerbie, Dumfries)

	No. of Horses	Races Run	1st	2nd	3rd	Unpl	Per cent	£1 Level Stake
2-y-o	1	5	0	0	1	4	-	- 5.00
3-y-o	0	0	0	0	0	0	-	0.00
4-y-o+	3	5	1	0	0	4	20.0	+ 7.00
Totals	4	10	1	0	1	8	10.0	+ 2.00

Jan	Feb	Mar	Apr	May	Jun	Jul	Aug	Sep	Oct/Nov
0-0	0-1	0-0	0-0	1-2	0-1	0-2	0-2	0-0	0-2

Winning Jockey	W-R	£1 Level Stake	Winning Course	W-R	£1 Level Stake
J Carroll	1-4	+ 8.00	Carlisle	1-3	+ 9.00

Winning Horse	Age	Races Run	1st	2nd	3rd	Unpl	Win £
Master Of Troy	6	2	1	0	0	1	3,313

Favourites	0-1			Total winning prize-money			£3,313

1993 Form	1-8	12.5%	-	2.50	1991 Form	0-6
1992 Form	1-5	20.0%	-	1.25	1990 Form	0-15

J PARKES (Malton, North Yorks)

	No. of Horses	Races Run	1st	2nd	3rd	Unpl	Per cent	£1 Level Stake
2-y-o	1	2	0	0	0	2	-	- 2.00
3-y-o	2	6	0	0	0	6	-	- 6.00
4-y-o+	10	43	2	1	1	39	4.7	- 9.00
Totals	13	51	2	1	1	47	3.9	- 17.00

Jan	Feb	Mar	Apr	May	Jun	Jul	Aug	Sep	Oct/Nov
0-2	0-2	0-0	0-3	0-4	0-3	2-12	0-11	0-9	0-5

Winning Jockeys	W-R	£1 Level Stake		W-R	£1 Level Stake
C Rutter	1-3	+ 18.00	M Deering	1-10	+ 3.00

Winning Courses					
Newcastle	1-4	+ 9.00	Southwell (AW)	1-7	+ 14.00

Winning Horses	Age	Races Run	1st	2nd	3rd	Unpl	Win £
Ravenspur	4	7	1	0	0	6	2,642
Kilnamartyra Girl	4	12	1	1	1	9	2,551

Favourites	0-0			Total winning prize-money			£5,192

1993 Form	5-63	7.9%	- 23.67	1991 Form	3-95	3.2%	- 45.00
1992 Form	4-92	4.3%	- 70.00	1990 Form	2-90	2.2%	- 35.00

J W PAYNE (Newmarket)

	No. of Horses	Races Run	1st	2nd	3rd	Unpl	Per cent	£1 Level Stake
2-y-o	5	13	2	5	0	6	15.4	- 7.47
3-y-o	4	26	3	2	0	21	11.5	- 17.00
4-y-o+	7	55	1	4	4	46	1.8	- 49.50
Totals	16	94	6	11	4	73	6.4	- 73.97

Jan	Feb	Mar	Apr	May	Jun	Jul	Aug	Sep	Oct/Nov
0-0	0-4	0-2	0-7	1-10	2-14	2-15	0-16	1-13	0-13

Winning Jockeys	W-R	£1 Level Stake					W-R	£1 Level Stake
A Munro	3-6	+ 5.00		N Varley			1-8	- 2.50
G Bardwell	1-6	- 4.47		W Hood			1-15	- 13.00

Winning Courses						W-R	£1 Level Stake
Beverley	1-1	+ 1.00		Southwell (AW)		1-4	+ 1.50
Chester	1-1	+ 2.00		Lingfield		1-5	- 1.00
Thirsk	1-3	- 1.47		Nottingham		1-9	- 5.00

Winning Horses	Age	Races Run	1st	2nd	3rd	Unpl	Win £
Ya Malak	3	9	3	2	0	4	20,585
Valerle	2	5	1	2	0	2	3,093
Juweilla	2	4	1	3	0	0	2,920
Dancing Tralthee	4	12	1	1	2	8	2,742

Favourites	3-10	30.0%	- 3.47	Total winning prize-money		£29,340

1993 Form	11-91	12.1%	- 43.74	1991 Form	12-82	14.6%	+ 26.83
1992 Form	9-103	8.7%	- 45.40	1990 Form	4-88	4.5%	- 67.50

BRIAN ARTHUR PEARCE (Limpsfield, Surrey)

	No. of Horses	Races Run	1st	2nd	3rd	Unpl	Per cent	£1 Level Stake
2-y-o	1	2	0	0	0	2	-	- 2.00
3-y-o	4	8	1	1	0	6	12.5	- 5.90
4-y-o+	4	16	2	0	1	13	12.5	+ 3.50
Totals	9	26	3	1	1	21	11.5	- 4.40

Jan	Feb	Mar	Apr	May	Jun	Jul	Aug	Sep	Oct/Nov
0-0	0-0	0-0	0-0	2-4	0-8	1-3	0-1	0-4	0-6

Winning Jockey	W-R	£1 Level Stake			W-R	£1 Level Stake
Stephen Davies	3-11	+ 10.60				

Winning Courses					W-R	£1 Level Stake
Salisbury	1-2	+ 0.10		Wolverhampton (AW)	1-5	+ 3.50
Lingfield	1-4	+ 7.00				

Winning Horses	Age	Races Run	1st	2nd	3rd	Unpl	Win £
Distant Dynasty	4	11	2	0	1	8	6,445
Mutinique	3	2	1	1	0	0	2,888

Favourites	1-1	100.0%	+ 1.10	Total winning prize-money	£9,333

J PEARCE (Newmarket)

	No. of Horses	Races Run	1st	2nd	3rd	Unpl	Per cent	£1 Level Stake
2-y-o	8	24	2	0	1	21	8.3	- 12.50
3-y-o	9	46	6	9	0	31	13.0	+ 3.25
4-y-o+	18	113	21	9	15	68	18.6	+ 41.53
Totals	35	183	29	18	16	120	15.8	+ 32.28

BY MONTH

2-y-o	W-R	Per cent	£1 Level Stake	3-y-o	W-R	Per cent	£1 Level Stake
January	0-0	-	0.00	January	0-0	-	0.00
February	0-0	-	0.00	February	0-0	-	0.00
March	0-0	-	0.00	March	0-1	-	- 1.00
April	0-0	-	0.00	April	0-3	-	- 3.00
May	0-1	-	- 1.00	May	0-1	-	- 1.00
June	0-1	-	- 1.00	June	0-4	-	- 4.00
July	0-2	-	- 2.00	July	2-10	20.0	- 0.25
August	0-1	-	- 1.00	August	2-9	22.2	+ 13.00
September	1-6	16.7	0.00	September	1-9	11.1	- 4.50
Oct/Nov	1-13	7.7	- 7.50	Oct/Nov	1-9	11.1	+ 4.00

4-y-o+	W-R	Per cent	£1 Level Stake	Totals	W-R	Per cent	£1 Level Stake
January	3-9	33.3	+ 13.50	January	3-9	33.3	+ 13.50
February	2-9	22.2	+ 4.00	February	2-9	22.2	+ 4.00
March	0-4	-	- 4.00	March	0-5	-	- 5.00
April	2-5	40.0	+ 11.25	April	2-8	25.0	+ 8.25
May	0-11	-	- 11.00	May	0-13	-	- 13.00
June	6-19	31.6	+ 17.45	June	6-24	25.0	+ 12.45
July	2-15	13.3	- 5.67	July	4-27	14.8	- 7.92
August	2-8	25.0	+ 2.00	August	4-18	22.2	+ 14.00
September	2-12	16.7	+ 9.00	September	4-27	14.8	+ 4.50
Oct/Nov	2-21	9.5	+ 5.00	Oct/Nov	4-43	9.3	+ 1.50

DISTANCE

2-y-o	W-R	Per cent	£1 Level Stake	3-y-o	W-R	Per cent	£1 Level Stake
5f-6f	2-14	14.3	- 2.50	5f-6f	0-0	-	0.00
7f-8f	0-10	-	- 10.00	7f-8f	0-3	-	- 3.00
9f-13f	0-0	-	0.00	9f-13f	5-37	13.5	- 2.75
14f+	0-0	-	0.00	14f+	1-6	16.7	+ 9.00

4-y-o+	W-R	Per cent	£1 Level Stake	Totals	W-R	Per cent	£1 Level Stake
5f-6f	0-6	-	- 6.00	5f-6f	2-20	10.0	- 8.50
7f-8f	8-54	14.8	+ 23.00	7f-8f	8-67	11.9	+ 10.00
9f-13f	12-51	23.5	+ 23.53	9f-13f	17-88	19.3	+ 20.78
14f+	1-2	50.0	+ 1.00	14f+	2-8	25.0	+ 10.00

TYPE OF RACE

Non-Handicaps	W-R	Per cent	£1 Level Stake	Handicaps	W-R	Per cent	£1 Level Stake
2-y-o	0-15	-	- 15.00	2-y-o	1-3	33.3	+ 2.50
3-y-o	0-11	-	- 11.00	3-y-o	5-25	20.0	+ 9.25
4-y-o+	1-7	14.3	- 1.00	4-y-o+	9-55	16.4	+ 23.25
Selling	2-10	20.0	+ 11.00	Selling	2-8	25.0	+ 11.33
Apprentice	0-1	-	- 1.00	Apprentice	2-9	22.2	+ 6.50
Amat/Ladies	1-5	20.0	- 0.50	Amat/Ladies	6-34	17.6	- 3.05
Totals	4-49	8.2	- 17.50	Totals	25-134	18.7	+ 49.78

COURSE GRADE

	W-R	Per cent	£1 Level Stake
Group 1	4-49	8.2	- 6.00
Group 2	3-28	10.7	- 7.00
Group 3	11-46	23.9	+ 32.53
Group 4	11-60	18.3	+ 12.75

FIRST TIME OUT

	W-R	Per cent	£1 Level Stake
2-y-o	0-7	-	- 7.00
3-y-o	0-7	-	- 7.00
4-y-o+	2-15	13.3	+ 7.00
Totals	2-29	6.9	- 7.00

JOCKEYS RIDING

	W-R	Per cent	£1 Level Stake		W-R	Per cent	£1 Level Stake
G Bardwell	11-76	14.5	+ 9.58	Elizabeth Turner	2-7	28.6	+ 8.50
Mrs L Pearce	8-42	19.0	- 1.55	A McGlone	1-2	50.0	+ 8.00
S Lanigan	3-17	17.6	+ 14.50	L Dettori	1-3	33.3	+ 4.00
J Quinn	2-4	50.0	+ 12.25	M Wigham	1-9	11.1	0.00

J McLaughlin	0-5	K Darley	0-2	Paul Eddery	0-1
M Hills	0-3	E Johnson	0-1	R Cochrane	0-1
D Holland	0-2	G Dettori	0-1	R Price	0-1
Dale Gibson	0-2	L Charnock	0-1		
G Duffield	0-2	P McCabe	0-1		

COURSE RECORD

	Total W-R	Non-Handicaps 2-y-o	3-y-o+	Handicaps 2-y-o	3-y-o+	Per cent	£1 Level Stake
Pontefract	4-7	0-0	0-1	1-1	3-5	57.1	+ 18.50
Folkestone	4-15	0-2	2-4	0-0	2-9	26.7	+ 3.25
Wolverhampton (AW)	3-14	0-0	0-3	0-0	3-11	21.4	+ 14.50
Beverley	2-6	0-0	0-0	0-0	2-6	33.3	+ 6.00
Lingfield (AW)	2-11	0-0	0-2	0-0	2-9	18.2	+ 3.50
Yarmouth	2-14	0-0	1-6	0-0	1-8	14.3	+ 4.00
Ascot	1-1	0-0	0-0	0-0	1-1	100.0	+ 14.00
Bath	1-1	0-0	0-0	0-0	1-1	100.0	+ 3.33
Epsom	1-1	0-0	0-0	0-0	1-1	100.0	+ 9.00
Hamilton	1-1	0-0	0-0	0-0	1-1	100.0	+ 2.70
Sandown	1-3	0-1	0-0	0-0	1-2	33.3	+ 4.00

Ripon	1-4	0-1	0-0	0-0	1-3	25.0	+	6.00
Nottingham	1-5	0-0	0-0	0-0	1-5	20.0	+	10.00
Brighton	1-7	0-1	0-0	0-0	1-6	14.3	-	2.00
Warwick	1-7	0-1	0-0	0-0	1-6	14.3	-	1.00
Southwell (AW)	1-7	0-0	0-1	0-0	1-6	14.3	-	1.50
Redcar	1-8	1-4	0-0	0-0	0-4	12.5	-	2.00
Newmarket	1-22	0-4	0-4	0-0	1-14	4.5	-	11.00

Doncaster	0-7	York	0-4	Catterick	0-2
Leicester	0-7	Edinburgh	0-3	Carlisle	0-1
Lingfield	0-5	Goodwood	0-3	Haydock	0-1
Windsor	0-5	Kempton	0-3	Thirsk	0-1
Newbury	0-4	Salisbury	0-3		

WINNING HORSES

	Age	Races Run	1st	2nd	3rd	Unpl	Win £
Toujours Riviera	4	12	4	0	2	6	26,442
Mysterious Maid	7	8	3	1	3	1	12,554
Beaumont	4	9	3	0	1	5	10,832
Un Parfum De Femme	3	12	3	5	0	4	9,844
Pop To Stans	5	12	3	0	3	6	7,094
Make Time	2	4	2	0	0	2	6,645
Guesstimation	5	13	2	3	1	7	6,060
Chief Of Staff	5	8	2	0	2	4	5,590
Zonk	4	5	2	1	1	1	5,067
Brilliant	6	8	2	0	0	6	4,972
Conic Hill	3	6	1	1	0	4	4,926
Dakota Brave	3	4	1	2	0	1	2,952
Admiral Rous	3	5	1	0	0	4	2,174

WINNING OWNERS

	Races Won	Value £		Races Won	Value £
James Furlong	9	38,602	Quintet Partnership	2	6,060
D J Maden	3	12,554	The Exclusive Partnership	2	5,590
Furlong Associates Racing Club	3	11,571	Mrs Lydia Pearce	2	4,972
Garth Th'Breds Ltd	3	10,832	Mrs Anne V Holman-Chappell	1	2,952
The City Partnership	3	9,844	Cliff Woof	1	2,174

Favourites	10-31	32.3%	+ 16.08	Total winning prize-money			£105,152

Longest winning sequence			2	Average SP of winner	6.4/1
Longest losing sequence			27	Return on stakes invested	17.6%

1993 Form	14-180	7.8%	- 90.49	1991 Form	11-152	7.2%	- 92.25
1992 Form	21-166	12.7%	- 37.81	1990 Form	13-119	10.9%	- 32.00

MISS L A PERRATT (Ayr, Strathclyde)

	No. of Horses	Races Run	1st	2nd	3rd	Unpl	Per cent	£1 Level Stake
2-y-o	6	22	2	1	3	16	9.1	+ 14.00
3-y-o	3	34	1	3	1	29	2.9	- 25.00
4-y-o+	4	30	0	1	5	24	-	- 30.00
Totals	13	86	3	5	9	69	3.5	- 41.00

Jan	Feb	Mar	Apr	May	Jun	Jul	Aug	Sep	Oct/Nov
0-0	0-0	0-1	0-7	0-8	0-15	3-24	0-11	0-18	0-2

Winning Jockeys	W-R	£1 Level Stake				W-R	£1 Level Stake
B Raymond	1-3	- 1.00		J Lowe		1-10	- 1.00
N Connorton	1-5	+ 29.00					

Winning Courses							
Ayr	1-16	- 7.00		Hamilton		1-24	- 22.00
Edinburgh	1-20	+ 14.00					

Winning Horses	Age	Races Run	1st	2nd	3rd	Unpl	Win £
Leading Princess	3	11	1	2	0	8	3,453
Another Nightmare	2	4	1	1	1	1	2,583
Mister Westsound	2	5	1	0	1	3	2,564

Favourites	1-3	33.3%	- 1.00	Total winning prize-money			£8,599

1993 Form	7-157	4.5%	-115.00	1991 Form	6-73	8.2%	+ 8.50
1992 Form	10-160	6.3%	- 68.95				

R T PHILLIPS (Wantage, Oxon)

	No. of Horses	Races Run	1st	2nd	3rd	Unpl	Per cent	£1 Level Stake
2-y-o	1	2	0	0	0	2	-	- 2.00
3-y-o	9	36	2	2	3	29	5.6	- 20.20
4-y-o+	3	5	0	0	0	5	-	- 5.00
Totals	13	43	2	2	3	36	4.7	- 27.20

Jan	Feb	Mar	Apr	May	Jun	Jul	Aug	Sep	Oct/Nov
0-4	0-3	0-1	0-0	0-7	1-6	0-9	1-5	0-3	0-5

Winning Jockeys	W-R	£1 Level Stake				W-R	£1 Level Stake
R Perham	1-5	+ 3.80		M Fenton		1-5	+ 2.00

Winning Courses							
Sandown	1-2	+ 6.80		Wolverhampton (AW)		1-8	- 1.00

Winning Horses	Age	Races Run	1st	2nd	3rd	Unpl	Win £
Cashew	3	2	1	0	0	1	3,551
Shuttlecock	3	12	1	2	3	6	3,132

Favourites	0-0			Total winning prize-money			£6,683

1993 Form	1-37	2.7%	- 30.60

J A PICKERING (Hinckley, Leics)

	No. of Horses	Races Run	1st	2nd	3rd	Unpl	Per cent	£1 Level Stake
2-y-o	2	4	0	0	0	4	-	- 4.00
3-y-o	5	27	2	3	3	19	7.4	- 20.37
4-y-o+	2	2	0	0	0	2	-	- 2.00
Totals	9	33	2	3	3	25	6.1	- 26.37

Jan	Feb	Mar	Apr	May	Jun	Jul	Aug	Sep	Oct/Nov
0-0	0-3	1-1	1-5	0-3	0-6	0-2	0-1	0-4	0-8

Winning Jockeys	W-R	£1 Level Stake			W-R	£1 Level Stake
A Munro	1-3	+ 0.75	L Dettori		1-4	- 1.12

Winning Courses	W-R	£1 Level Stake			W-R	£1 Level Stake
Folkestone	1-2	+ 1.75	Lingfield (AW)		1-2	+ 0.88

Winning Horse	Age	Races Run	1st	2nd	3rd	Unpl	Win £
Nordico Princess	3	11	2	3	3	3	4,688

Favourites	0-0			Total winning prize-money			£4,688

1993 Form	0-19		1992 Form	1-4	25.0%	0.00

MRS L PIGGOTT (Newmarket)

	No. of Horses	Races Run	1st	2nd	3rd	Unpl	Per cent	£1 Level Stake
2-y-o	5	14	0	2	1	11	-	- 14.00
3-y-o	4	29	4	0	6	19	13.8	- 2.00
4-y-o+	4	12	0	0	3	9	-	- 12.00
Totals	13	55	4	2	10	39	7.3	- 28.00

Jan	Feb	Mar	Apr	May	Jun	Jul	Aug	Sep	Oct/Nov
0-3	0-5	0-3	0-4	1-5	0-8	1-6	0-8	1-7	1-6

Winning Jockeys	W-R	£1 Level Stake			W-R	£1 Level Stake
G Milligan	2-7	+ 8.00	L Piggott		1-24	- 19.50
A Munro	1-4	+ 3.50				

Winning Courses						
Brighton	2-5	+ 7.00	Leicester		1-4	+ 2.00
Redcar	1-1	+ 8.00				

Winning Horses	Age	Races Run	1st	2nd	3rd	Unpl	Win £
Possibility	3	11	2	0	1	8	4,423
Pyramus	3	11	1	0	2	8	3,541
Bassmaat	3	2	1	0	1	0	2,758

Favourites	0-3			Total winning prize-money		£10,722

1993 Form	10-75	13.3%	+ 0.61	1991 Form	15-179	8.4%	- 86.87
1992 Form	10-118	8.5%	- 68.50	1990 Form	13-193	6.7%	-122.70

M C PIPE (Wellington, Somerset)

	No. of Horses	Races Run	1st	2nd	3rd	Unpl	Per cent	£1 Level Stake
2-y-o	3	4	1	0	0	3	25.0	- 1.00
3-y-o	9	49	5	4	4	36	10.2	- 27.48
4-y-o+	17	45	6	9	4	26	13.3	+ 0.10
Totals	29	98	12	13	8	65	12.2	- 28.38

BY MONTH

2-y-o	W-R	Per cent	£1 Level Stake	3-y-o	W-R	Per cent	£1 Level Stake
January	0-0	-	0.00	January	0-0	-	0.00
February	0-0	-	0.00	February	0-0	-	0.00
March	0-0	-	0.00	March	0-1	-	- 1.00
April	0-0	-	0.00	April	1-2	50.0	- 0.50
May	0-0	-	0.00	May	1-5	20.0	- 1.75
June	0-0	-	0.00	June	0-8	-	- 8.00
July	1-2	50.0	+ 1.00	July	0-7	-	- 7.00
August	0-0	-	0.00	August	0-6	-	- 6.00
September	0-1	-	- 1.00	September	0-11	-	- 11.00
Oct/Nov	0-1	-	- 1.00	Oct/Nov	3-9	33.3	+ 7.77

4-y-o+	W-R	Per cent	£1 Level Stake	Totals	W-R	Per cent	£1 Level Stake
January	0-2	-	- 2.00	January	0-2	-	- 2.00
February	0-0	-	0.00	February	0-0	-	0.00
March	1-3	33.3	+ 3.00	March	1-4	25.0	+ 2.00
April	0-6	-	- 6.00	April	1-8	12.5	- 6.50
May	0-7	-	- 7.00	May	1-12	8.3	- 8.75
June	3-12	25.0	+ 17.60	June	3-20	15.0	+ 9.60
July	1-6	16.7	0.00	July	2-15	13.3	- 6.00
August	0-0	-	0.00	August	0-6	-	- 6.00
September	0-5	-	- 5.00	September	0-17	-	- 17.00
Oct/Nov	1-4	25.0	- 0.50	Oct/Nov	4-14	28.6	+ 6.27

DISTANCE

2-y-o	W-R	Per cent	£1 Level Stake	3-y-o	W-R	Per cent	£1 Level Stake
5f-6f	0-2	-	- 2.00	5f-6f	1-10	10.0	- 6.75
7f-8f	1-2	50.0	+ 1.00	7f-8f	1-20	5.0	- 18.50
9f-13f	0-0	-	0.00	9f-13f	3-19	15.8	- 2.23
14f+	0-0	-	0.00	14f+	0-0	-	0.00

4-y-o+	W-R	Per cent	£1 Level Stake	Totals	W-R	Per cent	£1 Level Stake
5f-6f	0-0	-	0.00	5f-6f	1-12	8.3	- 8.75
7f-8f	0-8	-	- 8.00	7f-8f	2-30	6.7	- 25.50
9f-13f	4-19	21.1	+ 5.10	9f-13f	7-38	18.4	+ 2.87
14f+	2-18	11.1	+ 3.00	14f+	2-18	11.1	+ 3.00

TYPE OF RACE

Non-Handicaps	W-R	Per cent	£1 Level Stake	Handicaps	W-R	Per cent	£1 Level Stake
2-y-o	1-3	33.3	0.00	2-y-o	0-0	-	0.00
3-y-o	4-22	18.2	- 11.48	3-y-o	0-20	-	- 20.00
4-y-o+	0-15	-	- 15.00	4-y-o+	4-22	18.2	+ 11.00
Selling	1-7	14.3	+ 1.60	Selling	1-2	50.0	+ 9.00
Apprentice	0-1	-	- 1.00	Apprentice	0-3	-	- 3.00
Amat/Ladies	0-0	-	0.00	Amat/Ladies	1-3	33.3	+ 0.50
Totals	6-48	12.5	- 25.88	Totals	6-50	12.0	- 2.50

COURSE GRADE

	W-R	Per cent	£1 Level Stake
Group 1	4-48	8.3	- 20.25
Group 2	1-9	11.1	- 7.50
Group 3	2-27	7.4	- 16.67
Group 4	5-14	35.7	+ 16.04

FIRST TIME OUT

	W-R	Per cent	£1 Level Stake
2-y-o	0-1	-	- 1.00
3-y-o	2-4	50.0	+ 0.75
4-y-o+	1-14	7.1	- 8.00
Totals	3-19	15.8	- 8.25

359

JOCKEYS RIDING

	W-R	Per cent	£1 Level Stake		W-R	Per cent	£1 Level Stake
Pat Eddery	2-7	28.6	- 1.23	C Asmussen	1-2	50.0	+ 13.00
G Carter	2-8	25.0	+ 6.60	M Hills	1-4	25.0	+ 2.00
M Roberts	2-15	13.3	- 10.25	A Munro	1-5	20.0	- 2.00
Mr J Durkan	1-1	100.0	+ 2.50	Paul Eddery	1-5	20.0	+ 1.00
D Harrison	1-1	100.0	+ 10.00				

A McGlone	0-18	F Norton	0-1	M J Kinane	0-1
L Dettori	0-4	G Bardwell	0-1	M Perrett	0-1
B Thomson	0-3	J Carroll	0-1	Mr M Burrows	0-1
S Mulvey	0-2	J Marshall	0-1	Mr Richard White	0-1
W Carson	0-2	J Reid	0-1	R Havlin	0-1
A Clark	0-1	J Stack	0-1	R Hughes	0-1
D Holland	0-1	J Tate	0-1	T Quinn	0-1
D Wright	0-1	J Weaver	0-1	W Newnes	0-1
E Husband	0-1	J Williams	0-1		

COURSE RECORD

	Total W-R	Non-Handicaps 2-y-o	3-y-o+	Handicaps 2-y-o	3-y-o+	Per cent	£1 Level Stake
Warwick	4-8	1-1	2-5	0-0	1-2	50.0	+ 11.04
Ascot	2-6	0-0	0-1	0-0	2-5	33.3	+ 12.50
Leicester	2-6	0-0	1-4	0-0	1-2	33.3	+ 4.33
Folkestone	1-1	0-0	0-0	0-0	1-1	100.0	+ 10.00
Brighton	1-4	0-0	1-4	0-0	0-0	25.0	- 2.50
Doncaster	1-5	0-0	0-2	0-0	1-3	20.0	+ 1.00
Goodwood	1-7	0-0	1-4	0-0	0-3	14.3	- 3.75

Chepstow	0-11	Newmarket	0-4	Salisbury	0-2
Sandown	0-7	Bath	0-3	Wolverhampton (AW)	0-2
Haydock	0-6	Kempton	0-3	Lingfield	0-1
Nottingham	0-6	Chester	0-2	Southwell (AW)	0-1
Epsom	0-4	Lingfield (AW)	0-2	Windsor	0-1
Newbury	0-4	Newcastle	0-2		

WINNING HORSES

	Age	Races Run	1st	2nd	3rd	Unpl	Win £
Sweet Glow	7	6	1	0	0	5	25,635
Cotteir Chief	3	9	3	2	1	3	15,207
Seasonal Splendour	4	4	2	2	0	0	11,915
Paradise Navy	5	3	1	1	0	1	6,400
Billy Cruncheon	3	9	1	1	0	7	3,692
The Laughing Lord	8	6	1	1	1	3	3,027
Anna Bannanna	2	1	1	0	0	0	2,644
Silver Pearl	3	2	1	0	0	1	2,174
Baltic Exchange	5	3	1	0	0	2	2,070

WINNING OWNERS

	Races Won	Value £		Races Won	Value £
Mrs Marilyn Fairbrother	1	25,635	Trevor Painting	1	3,692
D A Johnson	2	11,915	David R Thornton	1	3,027
James Neville	2	10,678	M C Pipe	1	2,644
W J Gredley	1	6,400	Eric Scarth	1	2,174
M & N Plant Ltd	1	4,529	Malcolm B Jones	1	2,070

Favourites	4-17	23.5%	- 7.31	Total winning prize-money	£72,765
Longest winning sequence			2	Average SP of winner	4.8/1
Longest losing sequence			26	Return on stakes invested	-29.0%
1993 Form	19-99	19.2%	+ 37.88	1991 Form	17-97	17.5%	- 2.15
1992 Form	15-95	15.8%	- 18.42	1990 Form	10-50	20.0%	+ 2.28

C L POPHAM (Taunton, Somerset)

	No. of Horses	Races Run	1st	2nd	3rd	Unpl	Per cent	£1 Level Stake
2-y-o	0	0	0	0	0	0	-	0.00
3-y-o	3	7	0	0	0	7	-	- 7.00
4-y-o+	5	8	1	0	0	7	12.5	- 1.50
Totals	8	15	1	0	0	14	6.7	- 8.50

Jan	Feb	Mar	Apr	May	Jun	Jul	Aug	Sep	Oct/Nov
0-2	0-0	0-0	0-2	0-2	1-3	0-1	0-4	0-1	0-0

Winning Jockey	W-R	£1 Level Stake	Winning Course	W-R	£1 Level Stake
D McCabe	1-2	+ 4.50	Doncaster	1-1	+ 5.50

Winning Horse	Age	Races Run	1st	2nd	3rd	Unpl	Win £
Masai Mara	6	3	1	0	0	2	2,920

Favourites	0-1	Total winning prize-money	£2,920
1993 Form	0-4	1991 Form	0-14
1992 Form	0-5	1990 Form	0-12

B PREECE (Telford, Salop)

	No. of Horses	Races Run	1st	2nd	3rd	Unpl	Per cent	£1 Level Stake
2-y-o	1	6	0	1	0	5	-	- 6.00
3-y-o	2	6	0	0	0	6	-	- 6.00
4-y-o+	8	60	3	7	6	44	5.0	- 13.00
Totals	11	72	3	8	6	55	4.2	- 25.00

Jan	Feb	Mar	Apr	May	Jun	Jul	Aug	Sep	Oct/Nov
1-6	1-7	0-7	1-8	0-6	0-7	0-10	0-6	0-6	0-9

Winning Jockey	W-R	£1 Level Stake	Winning Course	W-R	£1 Level Stake
T Wall	3-33	+ 14.00	Wolverhampton (AW)	3-52	- 5.00

Winning Horse	Age	Races Run	1st	2nd	3rd	Unpl	Win £
Jon's Choice	6	15	3	3	2	7	8,946

Favourites	0-2		Total winning prize-money	£8,946

1993 Form	0-6	1991 Form	0-6
1992 Form	0-10	1990 Form	0-74

SIR MARK PRESCOTT (Newmarket)

	No. of Horses	Races Run	1st	2nd	3rd	Unpl	Per cent	£1 Level Stake
2-y-o	27	81	16	8	5	52	19.8	- 14.52
3-y-o	24	130	30	18	18	64	23.1	+ 16.60
4-y-o+	4	26	8	4	2	12	30.8	+ 3.34
Totals	55	237	54	30	25	128	22.8	+ 5.42

BY MONTH

2-y-o	W-R	Per cent	£1 Level Stake	3-y-o	W-R	Per cent	£1 Level Stake
January	0-0	-	0.00	January	1-5	20.0	+ 7.00
February	0-0	-	0.00	February	1-5	20.0	- 3.00
March	0-0	-	0.00	March	0-2	-	- 2.00
April	0-0	-	0.00	April	2-7	28.6	+ 3.75
May	0-0	-	0.00	May	0-0	-	0.00
June	2-7	28.6	+ 8.20	June	7-21	33.3	+ 11.29
July	4-13	30.8	- 5.27	July	9-29	31.0	- 4.94
August	2-16	12.5	- 2.00	August	6-32	18.8	- 10.50
September	6-24	25.0	+ 1.38	September	2-17	11.8	- 3.00
Oct/Nov	2-21	9.5	- 16.83	Oct/Nov	2-12	16.7	+ 18.00

4-y-o+	W-R	Per cent	£1 Level Stake		Totals	W-R	Per cent	£1 Level Stake
January	0-0	-		0.00	January	1-5	20.0	+ 7.00
February	0-0	-		0.00	February	1-5	20.0	- 3.00
March	0-0	-		0.00	March	0-2	-	- 2.00
April	0-0	-		0.00	April	2-7	28.6	+ 3.75
May	0-0	-		0.00	May	0-0	-	0.00
June	1-5	20.0	-	2.75	June	10-33	30.3	+ 16.74
July	3-5	60.0	+	3.76	July	16-47	34.0	- 6.45
August	3-8	37.5	+	4.83	August	11-56	19.6	- 7.67
September	1-6	16.7	-	0.50	September	9-47	19.1	- 2.12
Oct/Nov	0-2	-	-	2.00	Oct/Nov	4-35	11.4	- 0.83

DISTANCE

2-y-o	W-R	Per cent	£1 Level Stake	3-y-o	W-R	Per cent	£1 Level Stake
5f-6f	7-44	15.9	- 15.68	5f-6f	3-18	16.7	- 0.56
7f-8f	9-36	25.0	+ 2.16	7f-8f	15-68	22.1	+ 0.39
9f-13f	0-1	-	- 1.00	9f-13f	11-40	27.5	+ 14.27
14f+	0-0	-	0.00	14f+	1-4	25.0	+ 2.50

4-y-o+	W-R	Per cent	£1 Level Stake	Totals	W-R	Per cent	£1 Level Stake
5f-6f	0-0	-	0.00	5f-6f	10-62	16.1	- 16.24
7f-8f	2-10	20.0	- 0.50	7f-8f	26-114	22.8	+ 2.05
9f-13f	4-11	36.4	- 1.54	9f-13f	15-52	28.8	+ 11.73
14f+	2-5	40.0	+ 5.38	14f+	3-9	33.3	+ 7.88

TYPE OF RACE

Non-Handicaps	W-R	Per cent	£1 Level Stake	Handicaps	W-R	Per cent	£1 Level Stake
2-y-o	14-70	20.0	- 16.02	2-y-o	2-8	25.0	+ 4.50
3-y-o	14-59	23.7	- 13.70	3-y-o	14-62	22.6	+ 31.55
4-y-o+	0-6	-	- 6.00	4-y-o+	7-19	36.8	+ 4.84
Selling	0-2	-	- 2.00	Selling	0-1	-	- 1.00
Apprentice	1-2	50.0	+ 1.25	Apprentice	0-5	-	- 5.00
Amat/Ladies	1-1	100.0	+ 3.50	Amat/Ladies	1-2	50.0	+ 3.50
Totals	30-140	21.4	- 32.97	Totals	24-97	24.7	+ 38.39

COURSE GRADE

	W-R	Per cent	£1 Level Stake
Group 1	7-60	11.7	- 11.20
Group 2	14-46	30.4	+ 15.37
Group 3	9-50	18.0	- 3.84
Group 4	24-81	29.6	+ 5.09

FIRST TIME OUT

	W-R	Per cent	£1 Level Stake
2-y-o	4-27	14.8	+ 0.70
3-y-o	2-24	8.3	- 9.90
4-y-o+	0-4	-	- 4.00
Totals	6-55	10.9	- 13.20

JOCKEYS RIDING

	W-R	Per cent	£1 Level Stake		W-R	Per cent	£1 Level Stake
G Duffield	32-137	23.4	− 7.85	P Robinson	1-1	100.0	+ 0.29
W Woods	10-19	52.6	+ 32.60	W R Swinburn	1-1	100.0	+ 2.00
C Nutter	3-27	11.1	− 10.62	Mr P P-Gordon	1-1	100.0	+ 4.50
R Perham	2-4	50.0	+ 5.75	Miss I D W Jones	1-2	50.0	+ 2.50
J Lowe	2-9	22.2	+ 9.00	D Griffiths	1-3	33.3	+ 0.25

G Carter	0-5	B Thomson	0-1	M Birch		0-1
K Darley	0-4	G Hind	0-1	M Hills		0-1
K Rutter	0-3	J Carroll	0-1	R Cochrane		0-1
M Roberts	0-3	J Quinn	0-1	S Maloney		0-1
C Hawksley	0-2	J Weaver	0-1	W Carson		0-1
D McKeown	0-2	L Carter	0-1			
T Quinn	0-2	L Dettori	0-1			

COURSE RECORD

	Total W-R	Non-Handicaps 2-y-o	Non-Handicaps 3-y-o+	Handicaps 2-y-o	Handicaps 3-y-o+	Per cent	£1 Level Stake
Wolverhampton (AW)	9-26	4-10	4-8	0-0	1-8	34.6	+ 8.59
Carlisle	5-8	0-1	3-4	0-0	2-3	62.5	+ 11.75
Redcar	5-8	1-2	1-2	1-1	2-3	62.5	+ 14.50
Hamilton	3-6	1-2	1-2	0-0	1-2	50.0	+ 0.42
Lingfield	3-7	1-2	0-2	0-0	2-3	42.9	+ 10.50
Lingfield (AW)	3-10	0-0	1-8	0-0	2-2	30.0	− 1.32
Thirsk	3-12	1-3	1-5	0-0	1-4	25.0	− 4.46
Pontefract	2-4	1-2	1-2	0-0	0-0	50.0	+ 8.25
Ascot	2-6	0-0	0-0	0-0	2-6	33.3	+ 11.50
Edinburgh	2-6	1-2	1-1	0-0	0-3	33.3	− 1.81
Folkestone	2-11	1-7	0-1	0-1	1-2	18.2	− 5.25
Southwell (AW)	2-11	0-2	1-4	0-0	1-5	18.2	− 0.75
Brighton	2-13	0-3	0-3	1-2	1-5	15.4	− 3.67
Chester	1-2	0-0	0-1	0-0	1-1	50.0	+ 2.50
Ayr	1-4	0-0	1-2	0-0	0-2	25.0	− 1.90
Catterick	1-4	0-3	0-0	0-0	1-1	25.0	− 1.12
Doncaster	1-5	1-4	0-0	0-0	0-1	20.0	+ 3.20
Bath	1-6	0-3	1-1	0-0	0-2	16.7	− 4.43
Newmarket	1-6	0-1	0-1	0-0	1-4	16.7	+ 2.00
Nottingham	1-6	1-1	0-1	0-0	0-4	16.7	− 2.75
Newcastle	1-7	0-2	0-2	0-1	1-2	14.3	− 1.50
York	1-7	0-1	0-1	0-0	1-5	14.3	+ 0.50
Yarmouth	1-9	0-3	0-3	0-0	1-3	11.1	+ 12.00
Leicester	1-10	1-5	0-3	0-0	0-2	10.0	− 8.33

Sandown	0-8	Goodwood	0-4	Ripon	0-2
Haydock	0-7	Newbury	0-3	Salisbury	0-2
Chepstow	0-5	Windsor	0-3	Beverley	0-1
Warwick	0-5	Kempton	0-2	Epsom	0-1

WINNING HORSES

	Age	Races Run	1st	2nd	3rd	Unpl	Win £
Hasten To Add	4	4	1	2	0	1	97,361
Wizard King	3	8	5	1	2	0	94,032
One Voice	4	8	5	0	2	1	18,326
Shifting Mist	3	10	5	0	1	4	15,523
Pennine Pink	3	10	4	2	2	2	11,143
Petomi	2	3	3	0	0	0	10,719
Segala	3	5	2	1	0	2	9,993
Lady Lodger	3	7	2	0	1	4	7,655
Canzonet	3	7	3	0	1	3	7,624
Red Dart	2	4	2	0	1	1	6,760
Espla	3	6	2	1	1	2	6,696
First Crush	2	4	2	1	1	0	6,562
Quiz Time	2	7	2	2	0	3	6,444
High Low	6	10	2	2	0	6	6,342
Miss Springtime	3	8	2	1	2	3	5,928
Salome's Dance	3	7	2	1	0	4	5,359
Look Daggers	2	2	1	0	0	1	3,941
Dangerous Guest	2	2	1	1	0	0	3,864
Prussia	3	5	1	1	0	3	3,800
Red Azalea	2	2	1	0	0	1	3,721
Purple Fling	3	9	1	0	1	7	3,655
Espartero	2	2	1	1	0	0	3,614
Music Maker	2	3	1	1	0	1	3,366
Level Sands	3	3	1	2	0	0	3,233
Chance Bid	2	5	1	0	1	3	3,028
Grey Again	2	2	1	0	0	1	2,421

WINNING OWNERS

	Races Won	Value £		Races Won	Value £
Pin Oak Stable	5	108,926	Lady Fairhaven	2	6,444
Sheikh Ahmed Bin Saeed			B Haggas	2	6,342
Al Maktoum	5	94,032	L A Larratt	2	5,928
Cheveley Park Stud	11	35,207	Petra Bloodstock	2	5,359
Pinnacle Racing Stable	6	21,559	W E Sturt	1	3,864
Mrs C R Philipson	5	15,523	Graham Rock	1	3,800
A E T Mines	3	10,719	Mario Lanfranchi	1	3,614
Mrs Michael Ennever	2	9,993	Lord Derby	1	3,028
Hesmonds Stud	2	7,655	Mrs F R Watts	1	2,421
Sir Mark Prescott	2	6,696			

Favourites	34-80	42.5%	+ 13.47	Total winning prize-money	£351,110
Longest winning sequence			4	Average SP of winner	3.5/1
Longest losing sequence			20	Return on stakes invested	2.3%
1993 Form	53-265	20.0%	- 42.85	1991 Form	48-238	20.2%	+ 14.32
1992 Form	50-281	17.8%	- 42.77	1990 Form	48-265	18.1%	- 35.55

R J PRICE (Leominster, H'ford & Worcs)

	No. of Horses	Races Run	1st	2nd	3rd	Unpl	Per cent	£1 Level Stake
2-y-o	1	3	0	0	0	3	-	- 3.00
3-y-o	5	11	0	0	0	11	-	- 11.00
4-y-o+	6	16	3	1	0	12	18.8	+ 18.63
Totals	12	30	3	1	0	26	10.0	+ 4.63

Jan	Feb	Mar	Apr	May	Jun	Jul	Aug	Sep	Oct/Nov
0-1	0-0	1-3	1-5	1-5	0-3	0-5	0-1	0-6	0-1

Winning Jockeys	W-R	£1 Level Stake			W-R	£1 Level Stake
T Sprake	2-13	+ 10.63	A Whelan		1-3	+ 8.00

Winning Courses	W-R	£1 Level Stake			W-R	£1 Level Stake
Haydock	1-1	+ 1.63	Bath		1-6	+ 5.00
Warwick	1-5	+ 16.00				

Winning Horses	Age	Races Run	1st	2nd	3rd	Unpl	Win £
Flakey Dove	8	2	1	0	0	1	6,367
Spot The Dove	5	5	1	1	0	3	3,652
Singing Reply	6	2	1	0	0	1	3,413

Favourites	1-2	50.0%	+ 0.63	Total winning prize-money			£13,432
1993 Form	2-29	6.9%	- 14.80	1992 Form	2-16	12.5%	+ 6.00

G A PRITCHARD-GORDON (Newmarket)

	No. of Horses	Races Run	1st	2nd	3rd	Unpl	Per cent	£1 Level Stake
2-y-o	9	31	2	6	1	22	6.5	- 22.50
3-y-o	12	44	4	4	4	32	9.1	- 9.75
4-y-o+	2	5	1	1	0	3	20.0	+ 3.00
Totals	23	80	7	11	5	57	8.8	- 29.25

Jan	Feb	Mar	Apr	May	Jun	Jul	Aug	Sep	Oct/Nov
0-0	0-2	1-3	1-8	0-12	1-24	1-19	3-12	0-0	0-0

Winning Jockeys	W-R	£1 Level Stake			W-R	£1 Level Stake
G Carter	2-4	+ 4.50	Mr P P-Gordon		1-4	+ 4.00
D Harrison	2-25	- 14.00	R Cochrane		1-6	+ 15.00
J Reid	1-1	+ 1.25				

Winning Courses	W-R	£1 Level Stake			W-R	£1 Level Stake
Yarmouth	2-10	+ 16.00	Epsom		1-3	+ 1.00
Chester	1-1	+ 3.50	Folkestone		1-4	+ 4.00
Salisbury	1-2	+ 0.25	Southwell (AW)		1-6	0.00

Winning Horses	Age	Races Run	1st	2nd	3rd	Unpl	Win £
Amin	2	6	2	3	0	1	9,001
Alzianah	3	5	1	1	0	3	5,390
Nijo	3	6	1	0	1	4	5,381
Sovinista	3	5	1	1	0	3	3,578
Daring King	4	2	1	0	0	1	2,925
Vivs Future	3	4	1	0	1	2	2,243

Favourites	2-7	28.6%	- 0.75	Total winning prize-money			£28,518

1993 Form	13-132	9.8%	- 15.75	1991 Form	14-223	6.3%	- 94.26
1992 Form	17-183	9.3%	- 63.92	1990 Form	18-201	9.0%	- 74.95

J J QUINN (Malton, North Yorks)

	No. of Horses	Races Run	1st	2nd	3rd	Unpl	Per cent	£1 Level Stake
2-y-o	1	6	2	0	1	3	33.3	+ 14.50
3-y-o	0	0	0	0	0	0	-	0.00
4-y-o+	0	0	0	0	0	0	-	0.00
Totals	1	6	2	0	1	3	33.3	+ 14.50

Jan	Feb	Mar	Apr	May	Jun	Jul	Aug	Sep	Oct/Nov
0-0	0-0	0-0	0-0	0-0	0-0	0-0	0-3	1-1	1-2

Winning Jockeys	W-R	£1 Level Stake			W-R	£1 Level Stake
D McCabe	1-1	+ 4.50	J Stack		1-2	+ 13.00

Winning Courses						
Ayr	1-1	+ 14.00	York		1-1	+ 4.50

Winning Horse	Age	Races Run	1st	2nd	3rd	Unpl	Win £
In Good Faith	2	6	2	0	1	3	11,585

Favourites	1-1	100.0%	+ 4.50	Total winning prize-money			£11,585

MRS J RAMSDEN (Thirsk, North Yorks)

	No. of Horses	Races Run	1st	2nd	3rd	Unpl	Per cent	£1 Level Stake
2-y-o	20	102	12	11	11	68	11.8	- 12.39
3-y-o	15	114	11	10	15	78	9.6	- 43.37
4-y-o+	17	114	17	8	11	78	14.9	- 5.25
Totals	52	330	40	29	37	224	12.1	- 61.01

Ramsden Mrs J

BY MONTH

2-y-o	W-R	Per cent	£1 Level Stake	3-y-o	W-R	Per cent	£1 Level Stake
January	0-0	-	0.00	January	0-4	-	- 4.00
February	0-0	-	0.00	February	0-3	-	- 3.00
March	0-0	-	0.00	March	1-7	14.3	+ 1.20
April	0-2	-	- 2.00	April	3-22	13.6	- 3.50
May	1-4	25.0	+ 1.00	May	2-21	9.5	- 10.87
June	1-11	9.1	- 6.00	June	1-11	9.1	- 5.20
July	1-20	5.0	- 16.25	July	2-15	13.3	- 0.50
August	3-24	12.5	- 3.67	August	1-9	11.1	- 1.50
September	4-21	19.0	- 4.47	September	1-12	8.3	- 6.00
Oct/Nov	2-20	10.0	+ 19.00	Oct/Nov	0-10	-	- 10.00

4-y-o+	W-R	Per cent	£1 Level Stake	Totals	W-R	Per cent	£1 Level Stake
January	0-0	-	0.00	January	0-4	-	- 4.00
February	0-0	-	0.00	February	0-3	-	- 3.00
March	1-6	16.7	+ 11.00	March	2-13	15.4	+ 12.20
April	6-22	27.3	+ 5.00	April	9-46	19.6	- 0.50
May	0-18	-	- 18.00	May	3-43	7.0	- 27.87
June	4-17	23.5	+ 5.50	June	6-39	15.4	- 5.70
July	3-12	25.0	- 0.25	July	6-47	12.8	- 17.00
August	1-15	6.7	- 9.00	August	5-48	10.4	- 14.17
September	1-13	7.7	- 3.50	September	6-46	13.0	- 13.97
Oct/Nov	1-11	9.1	+ 4.00	Oct/Nov	3-41	7.3	+ 13.00

DISTANCE

2-y-o	W-R	Per cent	£1 Level Stake	3-y-o	W-R	Per cent	£1 Level Stake
5f-6f	8-73	11.0	- 10.72	5f-6f	6-35	17.1	+ 7.00
7f-8f	4-29	13.8	- 1.67	7f-8f	2-42	4.8	- 29.87
9f-13f	0-0	-	0.00	9f-13f	3-34	8.8	- 17.50
14f+	0-0	-	0.00	14f+	0-3	-	- 3.00

4-y-o+	W-R	Per cent	£1 Level Stake	Totals	W-R	Per cent	£1 Level Stake
5f-6f	1-17	5.9	- 14.00	5f-6f	15-125	12.0	- 17.72
7f-8f	7-48	14.6	+ 2.00	7f-8f	13-119	10.9	- 29.54
9f-13f	6-37	16.2	+ 6.00	9f-13f	9-71	12.7	- 11.50
14f+	3-12	25.0	+ 0.75	14f+	3-15	20.0	- 2.25

TYPE OF RACE

Non-Handicaps	W-R	Per cent	£1 Level Stake	Handicaps	W-R	Per cent	£1 Level Stake
2-y-o	6-61	9.8	- 32.64	2-y-o	3-36	8.3	- 15.75
3-y-o	5-22	22.7	+ 6.83	3-y-o	5-81	6.2	- 44.70
4-y-o+	2-5	40.0	+ 3.50	4-y-o+	11-91	12.1	- 21.00
Selling	1-3	33.3	+ 3.00	Selling	4-5	80.0	+ 37.25
Apprentice	0-0	-	0.00	Apprentice	1-12	8.3	- 6.00
Amat/Ladies	0-0	-	0.00	Amat/Ladies	2-14	14.3	+ 8.50
Totals	14-91	15.4	- 19.31	Totals	26-239	10.9	- 41.70

COURSE GRADE					FIRST TIME OUT			
	W-R	Per cent	£1 Level Stake			W-R	Per cent	£1 Level Stake
Group 1	21-172	12.2	- 5.47	2-y-o		0-19	-	- 19.00
Group 2	3-45	6.7	- 28.62	3-y-o		3-13	23.1	+ 8.20
Group 3	9-75	12.0	- 19.75	4-y-o+		3-13	23.1	+ 15.00
Group 4	7-38	18.4	- 7.17	Totals		6-45	13.3	+ 4.20

JOCKEYS RIDING

	W-R	Per cent	£1 Level Stake		W-R	Per cent	£1 Level Stake
K Fallon	24-141	17.0	- 10.47	J Carroll	1-3	33.3	+ 10.00
J Fanning	3-35	8.6	- 6.00	D Thomas	1-5	20.0	+ 1.00
B Russell	2-21	9.5	- 10.50	J Weaver	1-6	16.7	+ 2.20
Miss B Craven	1-2	50.0	+ 15.00	M Hills	1-6	16.7	+ 1.00
W Ryan	1-2	50.0	+ 1.13	Miss F Haynes	1-7	14.3	- 1.50
D Biggs	1-2	50.0	+ 4.00	D McKeown	1-10	10.0	- 8.67
G Hind	1-2	50.0	+ 3.80	M Wigham	1-13	7.7	+ 13.00

J Quinn	0-6	S Buckley	0-2	M Henry	0-1
N Connorton	0-6	T Ives	0-2	Mr C Bonner	0-1
J Fortune	0-5	B Doyle	0-1	Mr S Swiers	0-1
K Darley	0-5	B Raymond	0-1	Pat Eddery	0-1
M Roberts	0-5	C Asmussen	0-1	R Cochrane	0-1
A Munro	0-4	C Rutter	0-1	R Hughes	0-1
B Thomson	0-3	D Holland	0-1	R Lappin	0-1
G Parkin	0-3	D McCabe	0-1	S Mulvey	0-1
J Lowe	0-3	D Moffatt	0-1	Stephen Davies	0-1
Miss E Ramsden	0-3	D Wright	0-1	T Sprake	0-1
D Harrison	0-2	Dale Gibson	0-1	W Carson	0-1
J Stack	0-2	M Baird	0-1		
Mr P Morrison	0-2	M Birch	0-1		

COURSE RECORD

	Total W-R	Non-Handicaps 2-y-o	3-y-o+	Handicaps 2-y-o	3-y-o+	Per cent	£1 Level Stake
Carlisle	6-12	2-3	1-1	0-0	3-8	50.0	+ 13.83
Newcastle	6-34	0-4	2-4	0-5	4-21	17.6	- 1.30
Nottingham	5-15	0-2	0-3	0-0	5-10	33.3	+ 15.75
Doncaster	4-46	1-5	0-2	1-9	2-30	8.7	- 5.20
Ayr	3-18	2-5	1-2	0-1	0-10	16.7	- 8.97
York	3-21	2-3	0-0	0-4	1-14	14.3	+ 13.00
Leicester	2-9	0-2	1-2	1-4	0-1	22.2	+ 6.00
Haydock	2-21	0-4	0-0	1-2	1-15	9.5	+ 11.00
Newmarket	2-22	0-1	1-5	0-4	1-12	9.1	- 10.00
Pontefract	2-28	0-7	0-0	1-4	1-17	7.1	- 18.50
Sandown	1-2	0-0	0-0	0-0	1-2	50.0	+ 4.00
Edinburgh	1-6	0-2	0-1	0-0	1-3	16.7	- 1.00
Thirsk	1-12	0-5	0-1	1-1	0-5	8.3	- 8.25
Redcar	1-13	0-5	0-0	0-1	1-7	7.7	- 3.50
Ripon	1-17	0-4	1-2	0-1	0-10	5.9	- 13.87

Beverley	0-15	Southwell (AW)	0-6	Chester	0-3
Catterick	0-12	Newbury	0-4	Wolverhampton (AW)	0-2
Hamilton	0-8	Ascot	0-3	Epsom	0-1

WINNING HORSES

		Races					Win
	Age	Run	1st	2nd	3rd	Unpl	£
Chilly Billy	2	4	1	0	1	2	61,538
Halmanerror	4	7	2	0	1	4	14,485
Rafferty's Rules	3	6	1	0	2	3	11,069
Retender	5	12	2	2	3	5	10,909
Captain Carat	3	17	2	3	5	7	10,343
Fame Again	2	8	2	1	1	4	9,650
Hazard A Guess	4	6	2	0	1	3	9,591
Vocalize	2	7	1	3	0	3	7,960
Balzino	5	6	2	0	0	4	7,695
Montone	4	6	2	2	1	1	6,668
Let's Get Lost	5	11	2	0	2	7	6,602
Tulu	3	7	2	2	0	3	6,400
Barato	3	14	2	0	0	12	5,303
Self Expression	6	18	2	1	1	14	4,968
Jungle Patrol	2	6	1	1	2	2	4,450
Travelling Light	8	1	1	0	0	0	3,915
Northern Influence	2	5	1	2	0	2	3,623
Playing For Time	2	3	1	2	0	0	3,552
Kemo Sabo	2	8	1	1	3	3	3,540
Deliver	3	4	1	1	0	2	3,395
Winterbound	2	8	1	0	1	6	3,368
Dynamic Deluxe	3	9	1	0	0	8	3,054
Arctic Diamond	3	4	1	0	0	3	2,942
On A Pedestal	2	6	1	0	0	5	2,902
Lucky Magpie	2	8	1	0	0	7	2,864
Battle Colours	5	13	1	0	2	10	2,795
Royal Explorer	2	7	1	1	1	4	2,766
Clifton Beat	3	6	1	1	1	3	2,749
Petal's Jarred	4	5	1	0	0	4	1,574

WINNING OWNERS

	Races Won	Value £		Races Won	Value £
G E Shouler	2	69,498	L C and A E Sigsworth	1	3,623
P A Leonard	4	17,800	Jonathan Ramsden	1	3,552
Mrs Joan Smith (Lincoln)	2	14,485	Paul H Locke	1	3,540
Colin Webster	3	13,109	Kenneth B Rawlings	1	3,395
Godolphin	1	11,069	Miss P Zygmant	1	3,079
Prestige Racing Club Ltd	3	10,408	D Morrison	1	3,054
Mrs J R Ramsden	2	9,650	Mrs B D Southam	1	2,942
Mrs D Ridley	2	9,591	Harry Rishworth	1	2,902
C Mauritzon	2	6,668	M R Charlton	1	2,864
Mark Houlston	2	6,400	Tony Fawcett	1	2,795
David R Young	2	5,303	Lord Downshire	1	2,749
Mrs H M Carr	1	4,450	R C Moody	1	2,255
Mrs J Ramsden	1	3,915	Lt D J Lewis	1	1,574

Favourites	11-59	18.6%	- 25.26	Total winning prize-money			£220,668
Longest winning sequence			3	Average SP of winner			5.7/1
Longest losing sequence			23	Return on stakes invested			-18.5%
1993 Form	30-278	10.8%	- 55.63	1991 Form	38-294	12.9%	- 123.50
1992 Form	23-249	9.2%	- 87.12	1990 Form	26-239	10.9%	- 104.32

MRS M REVELEY (Lingdale, Co Cleveland)

	No. of Horses	Races Run	1st	2nd	3rd	Unpl	Per cent	£1 Level Stake
2-y-o	16	73	1	8	4	60	1.4	- 71.38
3-y-o	25	134	22	14	11	87	16.4	+ 36.94
4-y-o+	63	387	59	56	51	221	15.2	- 18.99
Totals	104	594	82	78	66	368	13.8	- 53.43

BY MONTH

2-y-o	W-R	Per cent	£1 Level Stake	3-y-o	W-R	Per cent	£1 Level Stake
January	0-0	-	0.00	January	0-0	-	0.00
February	0-0	-	0.00	February	0-0	-	0.00
March	0-1	-	- 1.00	March	1-7	14.3	- 4.25
April	0-3	-	- 3.00	April	5-19	26.3	- 2.63
May	0-4	-	- 4.00	May	4-19	21.1	+ 33.86
June	0-4	-	- 4.00	June	0-18	-	- 18.00
July	0-14	-	- 14.00	July	5-23	21.7	+ 2.71
August	1-11	9.1	- 9.38	August	1-20	5.0	- 17.25
September	0-18	-	- 18.00	September	3-14	21.4	+ 6.00
Oct/Nov	0-18	-	- 18.00	Oct/Nov	3-14	21.4	+ 36.50

Reveley Mrs M

4-y-o+	W-R	Per cent	£1 Level Stake	Totals	W-R	Per cent	£1 Level Stake
January	3-10	30.0	+ 6.25	January	3-10	30.0	+ 6.25
February	4-12	33.3	- 0.40	February	4-12	33.3	- 0.40
March	6-22	27.3	+ 6.28	March	7-30	23.3	+ 1.03
April	3-33	9.1	- 11.25	April	8-55	14.5	- 16.88
May	2-34	5.9	- 16.25	May	6-57	10.5	+ 13.61
June	6-50	12.0	- 13.37	June	6-72	8.3	- 35.37
July	13-74	17.6	- 10.12	July	18-111	16.2	- 21.41
August	12-55	21.8	+ 20.74	August	14-86	16.3	- 5.89
September	6-48	12.5	+ 14.30	September	9-80	11.3	+ 2.30
Oct/Nov	4-49	8.2	- 15.17	Oct/Nov	7-81	8.6	+ 3.33

DISTANCE

2-y-o	W-R	Per cent	£1 Level Stake	3-y-o	W-R	Per cent	£1 Level Stake
5f-6f	0-33	-	- 33.00	5f-6f	1-17	5.9	+ 17.00
7f-8f	1-37	2.7	- 35.38	7f-8f	7-54	13.0	- 7.13
9f-13f	0-3	-	- 3.00	9f-13f	13-55	23.6	+ 29.57
14f+	0-0	-	0.00	14f+	1-8	12.5	- 2.50

4-y-o+	W-R	Per cent	£1 Level Stake	Totals	W-R	Per cent	£1 Level Stake
5f-6f	4-17	23.5	+ 10.00	5f-6f	5-67	7.5	- 6.00
7f-8f	18-114	15.8	+ 11.66	7f-8f	26-205	12.7	- 30.85
9f-13f	22-163	13.5	- 28.17	9f-13f	35-221	15.8	- 1.60
14f+	15-93	16.1	- 12.48	14f+	16-101	15.8	- 14.98

TYPE OF RACE

Non-Handicaps	W-R	Per cent	£1 Level Stake	Handicaps	W-R	Per cent	£1 Level Stake
2-y-o	0-43	-	- 43.00	2-y-o	0-19	-	- 19.00
3-y-o	12-50	24.0	+ 32.94	3-y-o	6-63	9.5	- 16.50
4-y-o+	16-48	33.3	+ 30.99	4-y-o+	38-286	13.3	- 53.23
Selling	5-27	18.5	- 14.13	Selling	0-10	-	- 10.00
Apprentice	1-3	33.3	+ 9.00	Apprentice	1-25	4.0	- 19.50
Amat/Ladies	0-1	-	- 1.00	Amat/Ladies	3-19	15.8	+ 50.00
Totals	34-172	19.8	+ 14.80	Totals	48-422	11.4	- 68.23

COURSE GRADE

	W-R	Per cent	£1 Level Stake
Group 1	20-188	10.6	- 51.51
Group 2	18-132	13.6	+ 41.96
Group 3	12-153	7.8	-109.46
Group 4	32-121	26.4	+ 65.58

FIRST TIME OUT

	W-R	Per cent	£1 Level Stake
2-y-o	0-16	-	- 16.00
3-y-o	6-22	27.3	+ 73.50
4-y-o+	8-58	13.8	- 4.37
Totals	14-96	14.6	+ 53.13

JOCKEYS RIDING

	W-R	Per cent	£1 Level Stake		W-R	Per cent	£1 Level Stake
K. Darley	52-267	19.5	+ 2.59	Miss S Bainbridge	1-3	33.3	+ 31.00
J Fortune	6-32	18.8	+ 9.25	Mr M A Naughton	1-3	33.3	+ 23.00
G Parkin	5-46	10.9	- 16.25	T Quinn	1-5	20.0	+ 4.00
R Cochrane	4-15	26.7	+ 8.50	N Connorton	1-5	20.0	+ 3.00
S Copp	4-35	11.4	+ 22.50	Claire Balding	1-5	20.0	+ 8.00
D Moffatt	4-45	8.9	- 34.02	J Fanning	1-10	10.0	- 1.00
Renee Kierans	1-1	100.0	+ 8.00				

J Lowe	0-15	L Dettori	0-2	M J Kinane	0-1
D McKeown	0-12	M Herrington	0-2	Madeleine Smith	0-1
Dale Gibson	0-4	Mr M Buckley	0-2	Miss A Yardley	0-1
K Fallon	0-4	Pat Eddery	0-2	Miss J Russell	0-1
M Hills	0-4	S Maloney	0-2	Mr L Donnelly	0-1
M Roberts	0-4	S Perks	0-2	Mrs L Pearce	0-1
Mr E Babington	0-4	T Ives	0-2	Mrs M Cowdrey	0-1
W Woods	0-4	W Ryan	0-2	N Adams	0-1
C Rutter	0-3	A Munro	0-1	N Kennedy	0-1
G Duffield	0-3	Alex Greaves	0-1	P Fessey	0-1
M Birch	0-3	B Raymond	0-1	Paul Eddery	0-1
Mr S Swiers	0-3	D Harrison	0-1	R Price	0-1
N Varley	0-3	D Wright	0-1	S D Williams	0-1
A Mackay	0-2	G Carter	0-1	S Whitworth	0-1
B Thomson	0-2	J Quinn	0-1	V Halliday	0-1
J Carroll	0-2	J Weaver	0-1	W Newnes	0-1
J Marshall	0-2	J Williams	0-1	Wendy Jones	0-1
J Stack	0-2	M Baird	0-1		
L Charnock	0-2	M J Dwyer	0-1		

COURSE RECORD

	Total W-R	Non-Handicaps 2-y-o	Non-Handicaps 3-y-o+	Handicaps 2-y-o	Handicaps 3-y-o+	Per cent	£1 Level Stake
Redcar	13-81	0-12	1-15	0-1	12-53	16.0	+ 66.08
Southwell (AW)	11-25	0-0	4-7	0-0	7-18	44.0	+ 36.08
Wolverhampton (AW)	7-26	0-0	5-10	0-0	2-16	26.9	+ 1.17
Haydock	6-22	0-1	0-1	0-1	6-19	27.3	+ 21.83
Catterick	6-27	1-2	2-7	0-0	3-18	22.2	+ 30.87
Hamilton	6-40	0-4	2-10	0-0	4-26	15.0	- 15.59
Ayr	5-23	0-2	4-7	0-0	1-14	21.7	- 4.84
Carlisle	4-19	0-3	3-5	0-0	1-11	21.1	+ 8.13
Doncaster	4-40	0-1	2-6	0-0	2-33	10.0	- 5.00
Edinburgh	3-20	0-3	2-4	0-0	1-13	15.0	- 10.17
Ripon	3-27	0-3	2-3	0-0	1-21	11.1	- 17.12
Newcastle	3-49	0-5	1-7	0-7	2-30	6.1	- 25.50
Yarmouth	2-9	0-1	2-3	0-0	0-5	22.2	- 1.25
Pontefract	2-29	0-2	2-7	0-4	0-16	6.9	- 22.75
Sandown	1-2	0-0	0-0	0-0	1-2	50.0	+ 5.00
Lingfield (AW)	1-2	0-0	0-1	0-0	1-1	50.0	+ 1.50
Chester	1-7	0-0	0-1	0-0	1-6	14.3	+ 1.00
Leicester	1-15	0-2	0-4	0-0	1-9	6.7	- 12.25
Thirsk	1-17	0-4	0-5	0-0	1-8	5.9	- 8.00
Newmarket	1-21	0-0	0-3	0-1	1-17	4.8	- 12.00
Nottingham	1-23	0-2	1-4	0-2	0-15	4.3	- 20.62

Beverley	0-36	Goodwood	0-3	Kempton	0-1
York	0-22	Warwick	0-2	Newbury	0-1
Epsom	0-3	Ascot	0-1	Windsor	0-1

WINNING HORSES

	Age	Races Run	1st	2nd	3rd	Unpl	Win £
Penny A Day	4	9	4	4	0	1	23,819
Shadows Of Silver	6	6	4	1	0	1	20,192
Batabanoo	5	6	3	0	0	3	17,822
Cutthroat Kid	4	10	4	1	0	5	15,924
Themaam	5	12	4	3	2	3	13,487
Parliament Piece	8	10	4	1	1	4	12,166
Wolf Power	4	16	3	5	1	7	9,936
Foundry Lane	3	9	2	2	3	2	8,788
Sweet Mignonette	6	10	2	0	0	8	8,117
Spring Loaded	3	7	3	1	1	2	7,961
Nashville Star	3	11	3	2	1	5	7,905
Second Colours	4	7	3	1	0	3	7,805
Billy Bushwacker	3	6	2	1	1	2	7,185
Slmaat	3	8	2	0	0	6	7,091
Roar On Tour	5	4	2	0	0	2	6,991
Old Red	4	12	2	4	2	4	6,828
Keep Your Distance	4	16	2	4	2	8	6,774
Father Hayes	6	4	2	1	0	1	6,606
Hickleton Lady	3	8	2	1	1	4	6,357
Fearless Wonder	3	7	2	0	1	4	6,316
Princess Maxine	5	5	2	0	1	2	5,768
Out Of Favour	3	2	2	0	0	0	5,668
Lady Donoghue	5	9	1	2	2	4	5,618
Kayartis	5	2	2	0	0	0	5,248
Winter Scout	6	7	2	0	1	4	5,130
Taroudant	7	6	1	0	1	4	4,997
Bold Amusement	4	6	1	1	0	4	4,581
Brodessa	8	9	2	1	3	3	4,429
Sunderland Echo	5	7	1	2	1	3	3,630
Essayeffsee	5	10	1	0	2	7	3,600
Avishayes	7	11	1	0	2	8	3,422
White Willow	5	11	1	1	3	6	3,348
Mondragon	4	7	1	1	1	4	3,292
Surrey Dancer	6	8	1	2	0	5	3,231
Steel Sovereign	3	9	1	0	0	8	2,915
Durgams First	2	12	1	5	2	4	2,848
Uncle Doug	3	7	1	1	1	4	2,840
Mystic Memory	5	8	1	3	2	2	2,827
Hit The Canvas	3	3	1	1	0	1	2,743
Elle Shaped	4	4	1	0	0	3	2,726
Mr Abbot	4	1	1	0	0	0	2,646
Peep O Day	3	1	1	0	0	0	2,565

WINNING OWNERS

	Races Won	Value £		Races Won	Value £
P D Savill	24	82,538	Carnoustie Racing Club Ltd	2	5,473
G A Farndon	7	24,254	Mrs J M Allen	2	5,248
J Good	4	23,819	John Hughes	2	5,130
Mrs R H Corbett	4	20,192	David Bell	1	4,581
Wetherby Racing Bureau Plc	4	13,487	R W S Jevon	2	4,429
Mrs S D Murray	3	10,591	Northeast Press Limited	1	3,630
A Sharratt	2	8,788	P Davidson-Brown	1	3,422
Ron Whitehead	2	8,117	Mrs H North	1	3,348
T S Child	2	7,185	D Young	1	3,292
A Flannigan	2	6,828	Laurel (Leisure) Ltd	1	3,231
A F Gleeson	2	6,606	Roland Hope	1	2,915
Mrs Linda Leech	2	6,357	Mrs S Todd	1	2,848
William A Davies	2	6,316	D D Saul	1	2,840
J Fox	2	5,768	Simple Technology UK Ltd	1	2,726
C C Buckley	1	5,618	John L Holdroyd	1	2,565

Favourites	29-96	30.2%	- 15.59	Total winning prize-money		£292,138
Longest winning sequence			2	Average SP of winner		5.6/1
Longest losing sequence			26	Return on stakes invested		-9.0%
1993 Form	83-519	16.0%	- 97.21	1991 Form	34-226	15.0%	- 56.47
1992 Form	68-326	20.9%	- 2.87	1990 Form	15-146	10.3%	+ 1.42

G RICHARDS (Greystoke, Cumbria)

	No. of Horses	Races Run	1st	2nd	3rd	Unpl	Per cent	£1 Level Stake
2-y-o	0	0	0	0	0	0	-	0.00
3-y-o	0	0	0	0	0	0	-	0.00
4-y-o+	3	9	2	2	2	3	22.2	+ 7.00
Totals	3	9	2	2	2	3	22.2	+ 7.00

Jan	Feb	Mar	Apr	May	Jun	Jul	Aug	Sep	Oct/Nov
0-0	0-0	1-2	1-2	0-3	0-0	0-0	0-0	0-2	0-0

Winning Jockeys	W-R	£1 Level Stake			W-R	£1 Level Stake
Mr R Hale	1-2	+ 2.00	J Lowe		1-3	+ 9.00

Winning Course		
Hamilton	2-5	+ 11.00

Winning Horse	Age	Races Run	1st	2nd	3rd	Unpl	Win £
Sweet City	9	3	2	0	1	0	5,453

Favourites	0-0		Total winning prize-money			£5,453
1993 Form	0-3		1991 Form	0-28		
1992 Form	0-6		1990 Form	2-17	11.8%	+ 5.50

B RICHMOND (Wellingore, Lincs)

	No. of Horses	Races Run	1st	2nd	3rd	Unpl	Per cent	£1 Level Stake
2-y-o	1	6	0	0	1	5	-	- 6.00
3-y-o	0	0	0	0	0	0	-	0.00
4-y-o+	1	18	2	2	4	10	11.1	- 8.17
Totals	2	24	2	2	5	15	8.3	- 14.17

Jan	Feb	Mar	Apr	May	Jun	Jul	Aug	Sep	Oct/Nov
0-3	0-1	0-3	0-0	0-3	0-1	0-1	0-6	2-4	0-2

Winning Jockey	W-R	£1 Level Stake				W-R	£1 Level Stake
Miss I D W Jones	2-3	+ 6.83					

Winning Courses							
Yarmouth	1-1	+ 3.33		Pontefract		1-2	+ 3.50

Winning Horse	Age	Races Run	1st	2nd	3rd	Unpl	Win £
Modest Hope	7	18	2	2	4	10	6,203

Favourites	1-4	25.0%	+ 1.50	Total winning prize-money		£6,203
1993 Form	3-50	6.0%	+ 10.00	1991 Form	0-7	
1992 Form	0-20			1990 Form	0-17	

G RIMMER (Newmarket)

	No. of Horses	Races Run	1st	2nd	3rd	Unpl	Per cent	£1 Level Stake
2-y-o	5	9	0	0	0	9	-	- 9.00
3-y-o	9	25	2	2	0	21	8.0	0.00
4-y-o+	3	8	0	0	0	8	-	- 8.00
Totals	17	42	2	2	0	38	4.8	- 17.00

Jan	Feb	Mar	Apr	May	Jun	Jul	Aug	Sep	Oct/Nov
0-0	0-0	0-0	0-0	0-0	0-0	1-12	0-12	1-8	0-10

Winning Jockeys	W-R	£1 Level Stake				W-R	£1 Level Stake
G Hind	1-3	+ 10.00		R Price		1-25	- 13.00

Winning Courses							
Lingfield	1-3	+ 10.00		Yarmouth		1-3	+ 9.00

Winning Horses	Age	Races Run	1st	2nd	3rd	Unpl	Win £
Superluminal	3	5	1	1	0	3	3,574
Exotic Forest	3	2	1	0	0	1	3,132

Favourites	0-0	Total winning prize-money	£6,706

B S ROTHWELL (Upper Hemsley, York)

	No. of Horses	Races Run	1st	2nd	3rd	Unpl	Per cent	£1 Level Stake
2-y-o	6	30	1	3	1	25	3.3	- 19.00
3-y-o	7	43	1	1	3	38	2.3	- 17.00
4-y-o+	6	40	4	2	2	32	10.0	- 6.50
Totals	19	113	6	6	6	95	5.3	- 42.50

Jan	Feb	Mar	Apr	May	Jun	Jul	Aug	Sep	Oct/Nov
1-7	0-2	0-6	0-15	0-15	0-20	2-13	2-12	1-11	0-12

Winning Jockeys	W-R	£1 Level Stake			W-R	£1 Level Stake
M Fenton	4-19	+ 21.50	L Charnock		1-12	+ 14.00
Alex Greaves	1-8	- 4.00				

Winning Courses						
Nottingham	2-6	+ 6.50	Haydock		1-1	+ 25.00
Southwell (AW)	2-15	0.00	Beverley		1-12	+ 5.00

Winning Horses	Age	Races Run	1st	2nd	3rd	Unpl	Win £
Queens Consul	4	18	4	2	2	10	14,148
Ochos Rios	3	15	1	0	1	13	4,822
Runforaction	2	12	1	2	0	9	2,651

Favourites	1-1	100.0%	+ 3.00	Total winning prize-money	£21,621

1993 Form	4-124	3.2%	- 60.00	1991 Form	0-5
1992 Form	3-60	5.0%	- 31.00		

M J RYAN (Newmarket)

	No. of Horses	Races Run	1st	2nd	3rd	Unpl	Per cent	£1 Level Stake
2-y-o	11	35	3	0	0	32	8.6	- 5.00
3-y-o	8	89	7	7	7	68	7.9	- 38.87
4-y-o+	11	90	12	12	9	57	13.3	- 10.92
Totals	30	214	22	19	16	157	10.3	- 54.79

BY MONTH

2-y-o	W-R	Per cent	£1 Level Stake		3-y-o	W-R	Per cent	£1 Level Stake
January	0-0	-		0.00	January	2-7	28.6	- 1.87
February	0-0	-		0.00	February	0-4	-	- 4.00
March	0-0	-		0.00	March	0-2	-	- 2.00
April	0-0	-		0.00	April	0-7	-	- 7.00
May	1-5	20.0	+	2.00	May	0-10	-	- 10.00
June	0-1	-	-	1.00	June	1-12	8.3	- 8.50
July	0-1	-	-	1.00	July	2-14	14.3	- 4.50
August	0-5	-	-	5.00	August	0-12	-	- 12.00
September	1-6	16.7		0.00	September	0-8	-	- 8.00
Oct/Nov	1-17	5.9		0.00	Oct/Nov	2-13	15.4	+ 19.00

4-y-o+	W-R	Per cent	£1 Level Stake		Totals	W-R	Per cent	£1 Level Stake
January	2-6	33.3	+	4.75	January	4-13	30.8	+ 2.88
February	0-2	-	-	2.00	February	0-6	-	- 6.00
March	0-5	-	-	5.00	March	0-7	-	- 7.00
April	3-10	30.0	+	12.00	April	3-17	17.6	+ 5.00
May	1-14	7.1	-	11.00	May	2-29	6.9	- 19.00
June	1-12	8.3	-	5.00	June	2-25	8.0	- 14.50
July	1-13	7.7	-	5.00	July	3-28	10.7	- 10.50
August	2-9	22.2	+	6.00	August	2-26	7.7	- 11.00
September	1-11	9.1	-	2.00	September	2-25	8.0	- 10.00
Oct/Nov	1-8	12.5	-	3.67	Oct/Nov	4-38	10.5	+ 15.33

DISTANCE

2-y-o	W-R	Per cent	£1 Level Stake		3-y-o	W-R	Per cent	£1 Level Stake
5f-6f	1-13	7.7	-	6.00	5f-6f	1-13	7.7	- 9.50
7f-8f	2-22	9.1	+	1.00	7f-8f	4-52	7.7	- 14.87
9f-13f	0-0	-		0.00	9f-13f	1-22	4.5	- 18.00
14f+	0-0	-		0.00	14f+	1-2	50.0	+ 3.50

4-y-o+	W-R	Per cent	£1 Level Stake		Totals	W-R	Per cent	£1 Level Stake
5f-6f	2-7	28.6	+	10.00	5f-6f	4-33	12.1	- 5.50
7f-8f	6-42	14.3	-	4.92	7f-8f	12-116	10.3	- 18.79
9f-13f	3-26	11.5	-	5.50	9f-13f	4-48	8.3	- 23.50
14f+	1-15	6.7	-	10.50	14f+	2-17	11.8	- 7.00

TYPE OF RACE

Non-Handicaps	W-R	Per cent	£1 Level Stake		Handicaps	W-R	Per cent	£1 Level Stake
2-y-o	1-24	4.2	-	17.00	2-y-o	2-9	22.2	+ 14.00
3-y-o	0-13	-	-	13.00	3-y-o	5-67	7.5	- 48.37
4-y-o+	0-4	-	-	4.00	4-y-o+	12-70	17.1	+ 9.08
Selling	1-6	16.7	+	20.00	Selling	1-12	8.3	- 6.50
Apprentice	0-1	-	-	1.00	Apprentice	0-7	-	- 7.00
Amat/Ladies	0-0	-		0.00	Amat/Ladies	0-1	-	- 1.00
Totals	2-48	4.2	-	15.00	Totals	20-166	12.0	- 39.79

COURSE GRADE

	W-R	Per cent	£1 Level Stake
Group 1	4-55	7.3	- 20.50
Group 2	4-20	20.0	+ 11.00
Group 3	8-80	10.0	- 36.17
Group 4	6-59	10.2	- 9.12

FIRST TIME OUT

	W-R	Per cent	£1 Level Stake
2-y-o	1-11	9.1	- 4.00
3-y-o	1-8	12.5	- 5.62
4-y-o+	2-11	18.2	+ 4.50
Totals	4-30	13.3	- 5.12

JOCKEYS RIDING

	W-R	Per cent	£1 Level Stake		W-R	Per cent	£1 Level Stake
D Biggs	6-53	11.3	+ 1.38	G Carter	3-11	27.3	+ 17.50
A Clark	5-37	13.5	- 0.67	P McCabe	3-29	10.3	- 15.50
G Bardwell	4-20	20.0	- 0.50	G Duffield	1-6	16.7	+ 1.00

M Baird	0-12	G Eblet	0-3	K Darley	0-1
P Robinson	0-12	A McGlone	0-2	Miss L Hide	0-1
T Ives	0-10	M Tebbutt	0-2	W Carson	0-1
A Tucker	0-8	D Holland	0-1		
N Adams	0-4	J Lowe	0-1		

COURSE RECORD

	Total W-R	Non-Handicaps 2-y-o	Non-Handicaps 3-y-o+	Handicaps 2-y-o	Handicaps 3-y-o+	Per cent	£1 Level Stake
Leicester	4-25	0-8	0-4	0-1	4-12	16.0	- 0.17
Lingfield (AW)	3-17	0-0	0-1	0-0	3-16	17.6	- 3.50
Brighton	2-4	0-0	0-0	1-1	1-3	50.0	+ 11.00
Salisbury	2-4	1-1	0-0	0-0	1-3	50.0	+ 12.00
Nottingham	2-12	0-0	0-0	0-0	2-12	16.7	- 0.50
Yarmouth	2-26	0-5	0-3	0-3	2-15	7.7	- 18.50
Epsom	1-3	0-0	0-1	0-0	1-2	33.3	+ 3.00
Doncaster	1-6	0-2	0-1	1-1	0-2	16.7	+ 11.00
Haydock	1-6	0-0	0-2	0-0	1-4	16.7	- 1.50
Warwick	1-7	0-1	0-0	0-1	1-5	14.3	+ 1.00
Kempton	1-11	0-1	0-1	0-1	1-8	9.1	- 4.00
Folkestone	1-13	0-2	1-2	0-1	0-8	7.7	+ 13.00
Southwell (AW)	1-16	0-1	0-4	0-0	1-11	6.3	- 13.62

Newmarket	0-9	Ascot	0-3	Wolverhampton (AW)	0-3
Lingfield	0-7	Beverley	0-3	Chester	0-2
Sandown	0-7	Chepstow	0-3	Redcar	0-2
Goodwood	0-5	Edinburgh	0-3	Newcastle	0-1
Bath	0-4	Newbury	0-3	Thirsk	0-1
Pontefract	0-4	Windsor	0-3	York	0-1

WINNING HORSES

	Age	Races Run	1st	2nd	3rd	Unpl	Win £
Island Knight	5	13	4	3	1	5	16,976
Just Harry	3	16	4	1	1	10	12,024
Duffertoes	2	7	3	0	0	4	11,374
Jolis Absent	4	8	3	0	0	5	11,198
Kingchip Boy	5	18	2	4	2	10	8,317
Misty Silks	4	17	2	1	3	11	7,705
Prima Silk	3	15	1	1	1	12	3,785
Joli's Great	6	4	1	0	0	3	3,314
Chilly Lad	3	13	1	3	0	9	3,028
Chantelys	3	10	1	1	1	7	2,174

WINNING OWNERS

	Races Won	Value £		Races Won	Value £
P E Axon	6	24,681	Four Jays Racing Partnership	2	8,317
Miss Laura Shally	4	12,024	D Bell	2	5,202
Mrs Patricia J Williams	3	11,374	Three Ply Racing	1	3,785
Peter Hart	3	11,198	Enterprise Markets Ltd	1	3,314

Favourites	9-30	30.0%	+ 6.21	Total winning prize-money	£79,895
Longest winning sequence			2	Average SP of winner	6.2/1
Longest losing sequence			28	Return on stakes invested	-25.6%
1993 Form	26-189	13.8%	- 12.54	1991 Form 23-234 9.8% - 63.50	
1992 Form	22-182	12.1%	- 38.74	1990 Form 32-233 13.7% - 0.16	

MISS B SANDERS (Epsom, Surrey)

	No. of Horses	Races Run	1st	2nd	3rd	Unpl	Per cent	£1 Level Stake
2-y-o	2	4	0	0	0	4	–	- 4.00
3-y-o	2	7	1	0	1	5	14.3	+ 1.00
4-y-o+	11	52	5	4	5	38	9.6	- 13.17
Totals	15	63	6	4	6	47	9.5	- 16.17

Jan	Feb	Mar	Apr	May	Jun	Jul	Aug	Sep	Oct/Nov
0-5	1-2	1-3	0-6	1-9	1-14	0-8	1-10	1-4	0-2

Winning Jockeys	W-R	£1 Level Stake				W-R	£1 Level Stake
W Newnes	2-21	- 8.50	D Wright			1-7	- 2.00
Mr T Cuff	1-3	+ 14.00	M Roberts			1-7	+ 1.00
W Carson	1-3	+ 1.33					

Winning Courses							
Brighton	2-6	+ 18.50	Salisbury			1-2	+ 2.33
Lingfield (AW)	2-11	- 1.00	Sandown			1-10	- 2.00

Winning Horses	Age	Races Run	1st	2nd	3rd	Unpl	Win £
Lunar Risk	4	8	1	0	0	7	5,174
Moscow Road	3	3	1	0	0	2	3,453
Ice Rebel	4	5	1	0	1	3	3,260
Running Glimpse	6	13	1	3	2	7	3,173
Mr Copyforce	4	9	1	0	2	6	3,085
Wild Strawberry	5	2	1	0	0	1	2,717

Favourites	1-9	11.1%	- 4.67	Total winning prize-money			£20,861

1993 Form	7-65	10.8%	+ 57.00	1991 Form	7-84	8.3%	- 21.00
1992 Form	4-77	5.2%	- 39.00	1990 Form	4-71	5.6%	- 35.50

M S SAUNDERS (Wells, Somerset)

	No. of Horses	Races Run	1st	2nd	3rd	Unpl	Per cent	£1 Level Stake
2-y-o	5	16	2	2	0	12	12.5	- 3.00
3-y-o	5	36	3	2	2	29	8.3	- 20.93
4-y-o+	7	15	0	0	2	13	-	- 15.00
Totals	17	67	5	4	4	54	7.5	- 38.93

Jan	Feb	Mar	Apr	May	Jun	Jul	Aug	Sep	Oct/Nov
0-3	0-3	0-1	0-10	0-10	2-8	2-11	1-10	0-7	0-4

Winning Jockeys	W-R	£1 Level Stake		W-R	£1 Level Stake
N Adams	4-30	- 8.93	R Price	1-8	- 1.00

Winning Courses					
Lingfield	2-4	+ 9.00	Brighton	1-3	+ 0.75
Bath	2-19	- 7.68			

Winning Horses	Age	Races Run	1st	2nd	3rd	Unpl	Win £
Napoleon Star	3	19	3	1	2	13	7,941
Astral Invader	2	9	2	2	0	5	5,176

Favourites	0-1	Total winning prize-money	£13,118

1993 Form	1-30	3.3%	- 22.50

DR J D SCARGILL (Newmarket)

	No. of Horses	Races Run	1st	2nd	3rd	Unpl	Per cent	£1 Level Stake
2-y-o	8	20	0	4	4	12	-	- 20.00
3-y-o	8	37	3	2	2	30	8.1	- 23.17
4-y-o+	6	28	2	2	5	19	7.1	- 9.33
Totals	22	85	5	8	11	61	5.9	- 52.50

Jan	Feb	Mar	Apr	May	Jun	Jul	Aug	Sep	Oct/Nov
1-5	1-4	1-4	0-4	1-10	0-11	1-12	0-16	0-7	0-12

Winning Jockeys	W-R	£1 Level Stake			W-R	£1 Level Stake
D Holland	2-8	+ 10.67	G Hind		1-6	- 1.00
K Rutter	2-9	- 0.17				

Winning Courses					
Lingfield (AW)	2-10	- 1.17	Southwell (AW)	1-4	+ 1.00
Doncaster	1-1	+ 16.00	Lingfield	1-8	- 6.33

Winning Horses	Age	Races Run	1st	2nd	3rd	Unpl	Win £
Our Rita	5	6	2	1	1	2	51,359
Herr Trigger	3	5	2	1	1	1	5,091
Lady Tjonger	3	7	1	0	1	5	2,681

Favourites	1-8	12.5%	- 6.33	Total winning prize-money	£59,131

1993 Form	11-119	9.2%	- 21.37	1991 Form	7-172	4.1%	-141.87
1992 Form	9-116	7.8%	- 32.34	1990 Form	18-185	9.7%	- 37.56

A A SCOTT (Newmarket)

	No. of Horses	Races Run	1st	2nd	3rd	Unpl	Per cent	£1 Level Stake
2-y-o	28	77	8	11	8	50	10.4	- 49.82
3-y-o	18	80	14	5	11	50	17.5	- 1.98
4-y-o+	7	40	8	4	2	26	20.0	+ 30.50
Totals	53	197	30	20	21	126	15.2	- 21.30

BY MONTH

2-y-o	W-R	Per cent	£1 Level Stake	3-y-o	W-R	Per cent	£1 Level Stake
January	0-0	-	0.00	January	0-0	-	0.00
February	0-0	-	0.00	February	0-0	-	0.00
March	0-0	-	0.00	March	0-1	-	- 1.00
April	0-0	-	0.00	April	2-11	18.2	+ 4.50
May	0-4	-	- 4.00	May	3-15	20.0	- 3.87
June	1-5	20.0	- 2.90	June	4-16	25.0	+ 8.35
July	3-23	13.0	- 12.50	July	4-24	16.7	- 8.96
August	2-18	11.1	- 9.67	August	1-10	10.0	+ 2.00
September	2-27	7.4	- 20.75	September	0-3	-	- 3.00
Oct/Nov	0-0	-	0.00	Oct/Nov	0-0	-	0.00

4-y-o+	W-R	Per cent	£1 Level Stake	Totals	W-R	Per cent	£1 Level Stake
January	0-0	-	0.00	January	0-0	-	0.00
February	0-1	-	- 1.00	February	0-1	-	- 1.00
March	1-2	50.0	+ 9.00	March	1-3	33.3	+ 8.00
April	1-8	12.5	- 4.50	April	3-19	15.8	0.00
May	2-6	33.3	+ 8.00	May	5-25	20.0	+ 0.13
June	0-4	-	- 4.00	June	5-25	20.0	+ 1.45
July	3-9	33.3	+ 26.50	July	10-56	17.9	+ 5.04
August	0-7	-	- 7.00	August	3-35	8.6	- 14.67
September	1-3	33.3	+ 3.50	September	3-33	9.1	- 20.25
Oct/Nov	0-0	-	0.00	Oct/Nov	0-0	-	0.00

DISTANCE

2-y-o	W-R	Per cent	£1 Level Stake	3-y-o	W-R	Per cent	£1 Level Stake
5f-6f	4-39	10.3	- 27.65	5f-6f	4-19	21.1	- 0.75
7f-8f	4-37	10.8	- 21.17	7f-8f	8-40	20.0	+ 0.27
9f-13f	0-1	-	- 1.00	9f-13f	2-21	9.5	- 1.50
14f+	0-0	-	0.00	14f+	0-0	-	0.00

4-y-o+	W-R	Per cent	£1 Level Stake	Totals	W-R	Per cent	£1 Level Stake
5f-6f	1-3	33.3	+ 4.00	5f-6f	9-61	14.8	- 24.40
7f-8f	7-27	25.9	+ 36.50	7f-8f	19-104	18.3	+ 15.60
9f-13f	0-9	-	- 9.00	9f-13f	2-31	6.5	- 11.50
14f+	0-1	-	- 1.00	14f+	0-1	-	- 1.00

TYPE OF RACE

Non-Handicaps	W-R	Per cent	£1 Level Stake	Handicaps	W-R	Per cent	£1 Level Stake
2-y-o	8-66	12.1	- 38.82	2-y-o	0-7	-	- 7.00
3-y-o	10-53	18.9	- 2.08	3-y-o	4-27	14.8	+ 0.10
4-y-o+	1-12	8.3	- 5.50	4-y-o+	6-23	26.1	+ 34.00
Selling	1-4	25.0	+ 3.00	Selling	0-2	-	- 2.00
Apprentice	0-0	-	0.00	Apprentice	0-1	-	- 1.00
Amat/Ladies	0-0	-	0.00	Amat/Ladies	0-2	-	- 2.00
Totals	20-135	14.8	- 43.40	Totals	10-62	16.1	+ 22.10

Scott A A

<table>
<tr><th colspan="4">COURSE GRADE</th><th></th><th colspan="4">FIRST TIME OUT</th></tr>
<tr><th></th><th>W-R</th><th>Per cent</th><th>£1 Level Stake</th><th></th><th></th><th>W-R</th><th>Per cent</th><th>£1 Level Stake</th></tr>
<tr><td>Group 1</td><td>19-116</td><td>16.4</td><td>- 7.65</td><td>2-y-o</td><td></td><td>1-28</td><td>3.6</td><td>- 24.00</td></tr>
<tr><td>Group 2</td><td>4-32</td><td>12.5</td><td>- 11.50</td><td>3-y-o</td><td></td><td>4-18</td><td>22.2</td><td>+ 3.13</td></tr>
<tr><td>Group 3</td><td>2-35</td><td>5.7</td><td>- 15.50</td><td>4-y-o+</td><td></td><td>1-7</td><td>14.3</td><td>+ 4.00</td></tr>
<tr><td>Group 4</td><td>5-14</td><td>35.7</td><td>+ 13.35</td><td></td><td></td><td></td><td></td><td></td></tr>
<tr><td></td><td></td><td></td><td></td><td>Totals</td><td></td><td>6-53</td><td>11.3</td><td>- 16.87</td></tr>
</table>

JOCKEYS RIDING

<table>
<tr><th></th><th>W-R</th><th>Per cent</th><th>£1 Level Stake</th><th></th><th>W-R</th><th>Per cent</th><th>£1 Level Stake</th></tr>
<tr><td>J Tate</td><td>9-44</td><td>20.5</td><td>+ 26.85</td><td>W Carson</td><td>2-9</td><td>22.2</td><td>- 4.09</td></tr>
<tr><td>W R Swinburn</td><td>8-51</td><td>15.7</td><td>- 0.57</td><td>D Biggs</td><td>1-1</td><td>100.0</td><td>+ 5.50</td></tr>
<tr><td>B Raymond</td><td>7-41</td><td>17.1</td><td>- 13.24</td><td>W Ryan</td><td>1-4</td><td>25.0</td><td>- 1.50</td></tr>
<tr><td>J Fortune</td><td>2-7</td><td>28.6</td><td>+ 5.75</td><td></td><td></td><td></td><td></td></tr>
</table>

<table>
<tr><td>R Hills</td><td>0-8</td><td>B Rouse</td><td>0-1</td><td>K Fallon</td><td>0-1</td></tr>
<tr><td>Pat Eddery</td><td>0-4</td><td>Dale Gibson</td><td>0-1</td><td>M Roberts</td><td>0-1</td></tr>
<tr><td>W Newnes</td><td>0-4</td><td>G Carter</td><td>0-1</td><td>Miss T Bracegirdle</td><td>0-1</td></tr>
<tr><td>B Thomson</td><td>0-3</td><td>G Hind</td><td>0-1</td><td>Mr P P-Gordon</td><td>0-1</td></tr>
<tr><td>J Quinn</td><td>0-3</td><td>J Carroll</td><td>0-1</td><td>N Adams</td><td>0-1</td></tr>
<tr><td>M Tebbutt</td><td>0-3</td><td>J Stack</td><td>0-1</td><td>Paul Eddery</td><td>0-1</td></tr>
<tr><td>K Darley</td><td>0-2</td><td>J Williams</td><td>0-1</td><td></td><td></td></tr>
</table>

COURSE RECORD

<table>
<tr><th></th><th>Total W-R</th><th colspan="2">Non-Handicaps</th><th colspan="2">Handicaps</th><th>Per cent</th><th>£1 Level Stake</th></tr>
<tr><th></th><th></th><th>2-y-o</th><th>3-y-o+</th><th>2-y-o</th><th>3-y-o+</th><th></th><th></th></tr>
<tr><td>Newmarket</td><td>8-37</td><td>3-18</td><td>3-9</td><td>0-2</td><td>2-8</td><td>21.6</td><td>+ 6.06</td></tr>
<tr><td>Sandown</td><td>4-12</td><td>2-5</td><td>1-4</td><td>0-0</td><td>1-3</td><td>33.3</td><td>+ 0.41</td></tr>
<tr><td>Wolverhampton (AW)</td><td>2-4</td><td>0-0</td><td>0-0</td><td>0-0</td><td>2-4</td><td>50.0</td><td>+ 10.50</td></tr>
<tr><td>Kempton</td><td>2-8</td><td>0-3</td><td>1-1</td><td>0-1</td><td>1-3</td><td>25.0</td><td>+ 15.38</td></tr>
<tr><td>Haydock</td><td>2-9</td><td>1-2</td><td>1-4</td><td>0-0</td><td>0-3</td><td>22.2</td><td>- 3.50</td></tr>
<tr><td>Catterick</td><td>1-1</td><td>1-1</td><td>0-0</td><td>0-0</td><td>0-0</td><td>100.0</td><td>+ 2.75</td></tr>
<tr><td>Bath</td><td>1-2</td><td>0-1</td><td>1-1</td><td>0-0</td><td>0-0</td><td>50.0</td><td>+ 4.50</td></tr>
<tr><td>Chester</td><td>1-2</td><td>0-0</td><td>0-0</td><td>0-0</td><td>1-2</td><td>50.0</td><td>+ 5.00</td></tr>
<tr><td>Folkestone</td><td>1-2</td><td>0-1</td><td>0-0</td><td>0-0</td><td>1-1</td><td>50.0</td><td>+ 0.10</td></tr>
<tr><td>Southwell (AW)</td><td>1-2</td><td>0-0</td><td>1-2</td><td>0-0</td><td>0-0</td><td>50.0</td><td>+ 5.00</td></tr>
<tr><td>Chepstow</td><td>1-3</td><td>0-2</td><td>1-1</td><td>0-0</td><td>0-0</td><td>33.3</td><td>+ 10.00</td></tr>
<tr><td>Ripon</td><td>1-4</td><td>0-0</td><td>0-3</td><td>0-0</td><td>1-1</td><td>25.0</td><td>+ 3.50</td></tr>
<tr><td>Newcastle</td><td>1-6</td><td>0-2</td><td>1-2</td><td>0-1</td><td>0-1</td><td>16.7</td><td>+ 3.00</td></tr>
<tr><td>Salisbury</td><td>1-7</td><td>0-1</td><td>1-5</td><td>0-0</td><td>0-1</td><td>14.3</td><td>- 3.75</td></tr>
<tr><td>Goodwood</td><td>1-9</td><td>0-2</td><td>0-0</td><td>0-0</td><td>1-7</td><td>11.1</td><td>+ 2.00</td></tr>
<tr><td>Thirsk</td><td>1-10</td><td>0-3</td><td>1-3</td><td>0-1</td><td>0-3</td><td>10.0</td><td>- 7.25</td></tr>
<tr><td>Newbury</td><td>1-11</td><td>1-4</td><td>0-5</td><td>0-0</td><td>0-2</td><td>9.1</td><td>- 7.00</td></tr>
</table>

<table>
<tr><td>Doncaster</td><td>0-9</td><td>Lingfield</td><td>0-5</td><td>Ayr</td><td>0-1</td></tr>
<tr><td>Yarmouth</td><td>0-8</td><td>Warwick</td><td>0-5</td><td>Brighton</td><td>0-1</td></tr>
<tr><td>York</td><td>0-8</td><td>Nottingham</td><td>0-4</td><td>Epsom</td><td>0-1</td></tr>
<tr><td>Ascot</td><td>0-5</td><td>Pontefract</td><td>0-4</td><td>Hamilton</td><td>0-1</td></tr>
<tr><td>Beverley</td><td>0-5</td><td>Redcar</td><td>0-3</td><td></td><td></td></tr>
<tr><td>Leicester</td><td>0-5</td><td>Windsor</td><td>0-3</td><td></td><td></td></tr>
</table>

WINNING HORSES

	Age	Races Run	1st	2nd	3rd	Unpl	Win £
Fraam	5	7	2	1	2	2	58,762
Tabook	3	6	2	0	1	3	28,562
Mahool	5	14	5	1	0	8	23,222
Desert Symphony	3	8	3	1	0	4	10,343
Desert Conqueror	3	13	2	2	1	8	9,537
Lammtarra	2	1	1	0	0	0	8,773
Monaassib	3	5	2	0	1	2	8,730
Done Well	2	5	1	1	1	2	4,558
Mowlaie	3	6	1	0	1	4	4,500
Cadeaux Tryst	2	4	1	0	0	3	4,007
Wakeel	2	4	1	1	1	1	3,835
Istinsaar	3	6	1	1	1	3	3,788
Hindaawee	2	4	1	1	1	1	3,778
Lynton Lad	2	3	1	1	1	0	3,663
Tamayaz	2	2	1	0	0	1	3,647
Top Guide	3	1	1	0	0	0	3,621
Rotherfield Park	2	5	1	0	0	4	3,466
Kanat Lee	3	2	1	0	0	1	3,254
Swedish Invader	3	3	1	0	1	1	2,905
Elton Ledger	5	3	1	1	0	1	2,076

WINNING OWNERS

	Races Won	Value £		Races Won	Value £
Maktoum Al Maktoum	20	150,038	Hamdan Al-Maktoum	1	3,788
A A Scott	6	25,298	Uplands Bloodstock	1	3,663
Saeed Maktoum Al Maktoum	1	8,773	The Pure Gold Partnership	1	3,466

Favourites	12-41	29.3%	- 2.13	Total winning prize-money		£195,025
Longest winning sequence			2	Average SP of winner		4.9/1
Longest losing sequence			23	Return on stakes invested		-10.8%
1993 Form	20-197	10.2%	- 52.88	1991 Form	23-225	10.2%	-104.93
1992 Form	38-322	11.8%	-124.45	1990 Form	29-194	14.9%	- 78.07

J R SHAW (Newmarket)

	No. of Horses	Races Run	1st	2nd	3rd	Unpl	Per cent	£1 Level Stake
2-y-o	1	1	0	0	0	1	-	- 1.00
3-y-o	6	16	1	1	0	14	6.3	- 5.00
4-y-o+	3	5	0	1	1	3	-	- 5.00
Totals	10	22	1	2	1	18	4.5	- 11.00

Shaw J R

Jan	Feb	Mar	Apr	May	Jun	Jul	Aug	Sep	Oct/Nov
0-0	0-0	0-0	1-8	0-5	0-9	0-0	0-0	0-0	0-0

Winning Jockey	W-R	£1 Level Stake	Winning Course	W-R	£1 Level Stake
N Connorton	1-3	+ 8.00	Thirsk	1-3	+ 8.00

Winning Horse	Age	Races Run	1st	2nd	3rd	Unpl	Win £
Unprejudice	3	3	1	0	0	2	3,377

Favourites	0-0		Total winning prize-money	£3,377

1993 Form	0-0		1991 Form	0-13		
1992 Form	0-0		1990 Form	2-30	6.7%	- 20.88

J J SHEEHAN (Findon, West Sussex)

	No. of Horses	Races Run	1st	2nd	3rd	Unpl	Per cent	£1 Level Stake
2-y-o	1	3	0	0	0	3	-	- 3.00
3-y-o	1	3	0	0	0	3	-	- 3.00
4-y-o+	4	36	3	4	2	27	8.3	- 11.80
Totals	6	42	3	4	2	33	7.1	- 17.80

Jan	Feb	Mar	Apr	May	Jun	Jul	Aug	Sep	Oct/Nov
0-1	0-3	0-5	0-1	0-1	1-8	0-7	2-10	0-0	0-6

Winning Jockeys	W-R	£1 Level Stake		W-R	£1 Level Stake
N Varley	2-3	+ 19.00	Mr C Bonner	1-1	+ 1.20

Winning Courses					
Kempton	2-6	+ 16.00	Windsor	1-3	- 0.80

Winning Horse	Age	Races Run	1st	2nd	3rd	Unpl	Win £
Rock Legend	6	13	3	1	0	9	9,294

Favourites	1-1	100.0%	+ 1.20	Total winning prize-money	£9,294

MISS L C SIDDALL (Tadcaster, North Yorks)

	No. of Horses	Races Run	1st	2nd	3rd	Unpl	Per cent	£1 Level Stake
2-y-o	3	14	0	0	1	13	-	- 14.00
3-y-o	4	33	2	0	3	28	6.1	- 16.50
4-y-o+	12	75	3	8	4	60	4.0	- 21.00
Totals	19	122	5	8	8	101	4.1	- 51.50

Jan	Feb	Mar	Apr	May	Jun	Jul	Aug	Sep	Oct/Nov
0-0	0-0	0-1	0-5	1-19	1-20	0-25	0-15	1-20	2-17

Winning Jockeys		W-R	£1 Level Stake					W-R	£1 Level Stake
D Harrison		3-24	+ 26.00		D McCabe			1-27	- 16.00
W Newnes		1-5	+ 4.50						

Winning Courses									
Newmarket		4-18	+ 45.50		Newcastle			1-6	+ 1.00

Winning Horses	Age	Races Run	1st	2nd	3rd	Unpl	Win £
Takadou	3	15	2	0	3	10	8,458
Different Times	4	15	2	1	1	11	8,099
Primo Figlio	4	9	1	2	0	6	5,166

Favourites	0-6			Total winning prize-money			£21,723

1993 Form	10-114	8.8%	+ 8.00	1991 Form	2-64	3.1%	- 54.67
1992 Form	4-107	3.7%	- 62.00	1990 Form	4-98	4.1%	- 61.25

R SIMPSON (Newport, Gwent)

	No. of Horses	Races Run	1st	2nd	3rd	Unpl	Per cent	£1 Level Stake
2-y-o	7	24	0	2	3	19	-	- 24.00
3-y-o	10	41	2	3	3	33	4.9	- 21.00
4-y-o+	12	55	2	3	3	47	3.6	- 37.00
Totals	29	120	4	8	9	99	3.3	- 82.00

Jan	Feb	Mar	Apr	May	Jun	Jul	Aug	Sep	Oct/Nov
0-0	0-2	0-0	0-6	3-24	1-22	0-17	0-19	0-20	0-10

Winning Jockeys		W-R	£1 Level Stake					W-R	£1 Level Stake
A Clark		2-6	+ 14.00		S Whitworth			2-31	- 13.00

Winning Courses									
Brighton		2-7	+ 6.00		Leicester			1-8	+ 5.00
Newmarket		1-3	+ 9.00						

Winning Horses	Age	Races Run	1st	2nd	3rd	Unpl	Win £
Mount Leinster	3	8	1	1	1	5	4,007
Araboybill	3	7	1	0	1	5	3,443
Cross Mags	7	4	1	0	0	3	2,931
Terrhars	6	7	1	0	0	6	2,686

Favourites	0-2			Total winning prize-money			£13,066

1993 Form	5-82	6.1%	- 35.00	1991 Form	5-104	4.8%	- 44.67
1992 Form	11-121	9.1%	- 48.32	1990 Form	6-96	6.3%	- 23.50

MRS P SLY (Peterborough, Cambs)

	No. of Horses	Races Run	1st	2nd	3rd	Unpl	Per cent	£1 Level Stake
2-y-o	3	10	0	1	0	9	-	- 10.00
3-y-o	0	0	0	0	0	0	-	0.00
4-y-o+	2	10	1	2	2	5	10.0	+ 5.00
Totals	5	20	1	3	2	14	5.0	- 5.00

Jan	Feb	Mar	Apr	May	Jun	Jul	Aug	Sep	Oct/Nov
0-0	0-0	0-0	0-0	1-3	0-6	0-3	0-2	0-3	0-3

Winning Jockey	W-R	£1 Level Stake	Winning Course	W-R	£1 Level Stake
M Birch	1-3	+ 12.00	Catterick	1-3	+ 12.00

Winning Horse	Age	Races Run	1st	2nd	3rd	Unpl	Win £
Superoo	8	7	1	2	2	2	4,308

Favourites	0-1		Total winning prize-money	£4,308

B SMART (Lambourn, Berks)

	No. of Horses	Races Run	1st	2nd	3rd	Unpl	Per cent	£1 Level Stake
2-y-o	6	20	0	2	1	17	-	- 20.00
3-y-o	6	17	0	1	0	16	-	- 17.00
4-y-o+	4	18	1	0	1	16	5.6	- 9.00
Totals	16	55	1	3	2	49	1.8	- 46.00

Jan	Feb	Mar	Apr	May	Jun	Jul	Aug	Sep	Oct/Nov
0-0	0-1	0-0	0-2	0-7	0-12	1-10	0-4	0-8	0-11

Winning Jockey	W-R	£1 Level Stake	Winning Course	W-R	£1 Level Stake
W Newnes	1-7	+ 2.00	Chepstow	1-2	+ 7.00

Winning Horse	Age	Races Run	1st	2nd	3rd	Unpl	Win £
Alaskan Princess	4	9	1	0	0	8	3,175

Favourites	0-1		Total winning prize-money	£3,175

1993 Form	3-52	5.8%	- 4.00	1991 Form	0-5
1992 Form	2-23	8.7%	- 9.67	1990 Form	0-5

A SMITH (Beverley, North Humberside)

	No. of Horses	Races Run	1st	2nd	3rd	Unpl	Per cent	£1 Level Stake
2-y-o	5	14	0	0	1	13	-	- 14.00
3-y-o	1	2	0	0	0	2	-	- 2.00
4-y-o+	3	9	1	0	2	6	11.1	- 3.00
Totals	9	25	1	0	3	21	4.0	- 19.00

Jan	Feb	Mar	Apr	May	Jun	Jul	Aug	Sep	Oct/Nov
0-0	0-0	0-0	0-5	1-6	0-1	0-5	0-1	0-2	0-5

Winning Jockey	W-R	£1 Level Stake	Winning Course	W-R	£1 Level Stake
M Birch	1-9	- 3.00	Thirsk	1-4	+ 2.00

Winning Horse	Age	Races Run	1st	2nd	3rd	Unpl	Win £
Calamanco	4	6	1	0	2	3	3,948

Favourites	0-0		Total winning prize-money	£3,948

1993 Form	3-37	8.1%	+ 37.50	1991 Form	1-113	0.9%	-101.00
1992 Form	3-63	4.8%	- 35.50	1990 Form	1-28	3.6%	- 20.00

C SMITH (Wellingore, Lincs)

	No. of Horses	Races Run	1st	2nd	3rd	Unpl	Per cent	£1 Level Stake
2-y-o	3	18	1	4	2	11	5.6	- 11.00
3-y-o	4	22	1	0	2	19	4.5	- 1.00
4-y-o+	7	49	5	4	7	33	10.2	- 5.25
Totals	14	89	7	8	11	63	7.9	- 17.25

Jan	Feb	Mar	Apr	May	Jun	Jul	Aug	Sep	Oct/Nov
0-7	0-4	0-5	0-7	3-10	2-11	2-19	0-10	0-7	0-9

Winning Jockeys	W-R	£1 Level Stake		W-R	£1 Level Stake
K Rutter	4-49	- 17.75	J Tate	1-4	+ 0.50
W Ryan	1-2	+ 13.00	N Varley	1-8	+ 13.00

Winning Courses					
Doncaster	2-6	+ 30.00	Yarmouth	1-5	- 1.75
Hamilton	1-1	+ 6.00	Wolverhampton (AW)	1-6	0.00
Lingfield	1-1	+ 3.50	Catterick	1-11	+ 4.00

Smith C

Winning Horses	Age	Races Run	1st	2nd	3rd	Unpl	Win £
Moshaajir	4	8	2	1	0	5	7,314
Arctic Guest	4	16	2	1	2	11	6,302
Vayello	3	14	1	0	2	11	3,525
Raindeer Quest	2	5	1	0	1	3	2,811
Mrs Jawleyford	6	8	1	0	2	5	2,762

Favourites	1-4	25.0%	- 0.75	Total winning prize-money			£22,713

1993 Form	4-42	9.5%	- 18.00	1992 Form	0-2

C A SMITH (Hanley Swan, H'ford & Worcs)

	No. of Horses	Races Run	1st	2nd	3rd	Unpl	Per cent	£1 Level Stake
2-y-o	3	13	1	0	0	12	7.7	+ 4.00
3-y-o	6	22	0	1	1	20	-	- 22.00
4-y-o+	1	6	0	1	0	5	-	- 6.00
Totals	10	41	1	2	1	37	2.4	- 24.00

Jan	Feb	Mar	Apr	May	Jun	Jul	Aug	Sep	Oct/Nov
0-0	0-0	0-2	0-5	0-5	1-5	0-9	0-8	0-2	0-5

Winning Jockey	W-R	£1 Level Stake	Winning Course	W-R	£1 Level Stake
T G McLaughlin	1-1	+ 16.00	Wolverhampton (AW)	1-4	+ 13.00

Winning Horse	Age	Races Run	1st	2nd	3rd	Unpl	Win £
Magical Belle	2	5	1	0	0	4	2,512

Favourites	0-0	Total winning prize-money		£2,512

1993 Form	1-60	1.7%	- 51.00	1991 Form	2-33	6.1%	+ 14.00
1992 Form	0-63						

D J G MURRAY SMITH (Upper Lambourn, Berks)

	No. of Horses	Races Run	1st	2nd	3rd	Unpl	Per cent	£1 Level Stake
2-y-o	8	25	1	1	4	19	4.0	- 18.00
3-y-o	4	38	4	2	5	27	10.5	- 17.00
4-y-o+	1	10	2	3	2	3	20.0	0.00
Totals	13	73	7	6	11	49	9.6	- 35.00

Jan	Feb	Mar	Apr	May	Jun	Jul	Aug	Sep	Oct/Nov
1-3	1-3	1-5	1-7	0-12	1-10	0-9	1-11	1-9	0-4

Winning Jockeys	W-R	£1 Level Stake		W-R	£1 Level Stake
T Quinn	2-8	+ 3.50	A Mackay	1-6	+ 1.00
J Tate	2-10	- 0.50	C Rutter	1-7	0.00
D Biggs	1-2	+ 1.00			

Winning Courses	W-R	£1 Level Stake		W-R	£1 Level Stake
Lingfield (AW)	4-12	+ 7.50	Brighton	1-4	+ 3.50
Chester	1-1	+ 6.00	Folkestone	1-4	0.00

Winning Horses	Age	Races Run	1st	2nd	3rd	Unpl	Win £
Beverly Knight	4	10	2	3	2	3	6,374
Prince Danzig	3	12	2	0	1	9	6,037
Tonka	2	6	1	0	1	4	5,118
Norfolk Lavender	3	7	1	1	0	5	2,977
Bold Mick	3	13	1	1	2	9	2,385

Favourites	1-6	16.7%	- 2.00	Total winning prize-money		£22,890

1993 Form	6-48	12.5%	+ 47.00	1991 Form	7-76	9.2%	- 12.00
1992 Form	2-36	5.6%	- 27.50	1990 Form	9-100	9.0%	- 40.69

DENYS SMITH (Bishop Auckland, Co Durham)

	No. of Horses	Races Run	1st	2nd	3rd	Unpl	Per cent	£1 Level Stake
2-y-o	4	17	1	0	1	15	5.9	- 7.50
3-y-o	7	48	3	4	7	34	6.3	- 29.12
4-y-o+	10	95	4	7	8	76	4.2	- 67.25
Totals	21	160	8	11	16	125	5.0	-103.87

Jan	Feb	Mar	Apr	May	Jun	Jul	Aug	Sep	Oct/Nov
0-0	0-3	0-5	2-18	0-19	1-35	3-32	1-21	1-18	0-9

Winning Jockeys	W-R	£1 Level Stake		W-R	£1 Level Stake
C Teague	3-69	- 43.00	Miss M Carson	1-8	+ 1.00
J Weaver	2-11	- 5.37	D McKeown	1-10	- 4.00
K Darley	1-1	+ 8.50			

Winning Courses	W-R	£1 Level Stake		W-R	£1 Level Stake
Edinburgh	4-21	+ 2.13	Catterick	1-7	+ 3.00
Hamilton	2-23	- 8.00	Thirsk	1-14	- 6.00

Winning Horses	Age	Races Run	1st	2nd	3rd	Unpl	Win £
Spanish Verdict	7	16	2	0	1	13	14,949
Grey Toppa	3	12	2	2	0	8	5,529
The Happy Loon	3	9	1	2	0	6	4,988
The Dandy Don	5	11	1	1	1	8	4,395
Imperial Bid	6	11	1	2	0	8	2,801
Ramborette	2	5	1	0	0	4	2,167

Favourites	2-3	66.7%	+ 2.63	Total winning prize-money			£34,828

1993 Form	12-159	7.5%	- 63.50	1991 Form	9-207	4.3%	-144.25
1992 Form	15-149	10.1%	- 39.59	1990 Form	8-215	3.7%	-172.13

J L SPEARING (Alcester, Warwicks)

	No. of Horses	Races Run	1st	2nd	3rd	Unpl	Per cent	£1 Level Stake
2-y-o	5	22	0	0	2	20	-	- 22.00
3-y-o	7	30	0	1	2	27	-	- 30.00
4-y-o+	13	74	8	2	6	58	10.8	- 18.65
Totals	25	126	8	3	10	105	6.3	- 70.65

Jan	Feb	Mar	Apr	May	Jun	Jul	Aug	Sep	Oct/Nov
0-5	0-7	0-3	0-14	3-23	1-13	4-21	0-5	0-14	0-21

Winning Jockeys	W-R	£1 Level Stake		W-R	£1 Level Stake
G Hind	2-13	- 7.40	Miss C Spearing	1-4	+ 0.50
A Mackay	2-34	- 1.00	Paul Eddery	1-5	+ 1.00
J Weaver	1-4	- 2.75	D Wright	1-12	- 7.00

Winning Courses	W-R			W-R	
Hamilton	2-5	+ 4.50	Sandown	1-4	+ 2.00
Beverley	2-10	+ 13.10	Ayr	1-7	- 5.75
Kempton	1-1	+ 2.50	Bath	1-7	+ 5.00

Winning Horses	Age	Races Run	1st	2nd	3rd	Unpl	Win £
Jucea	5	12	2	2	0	8	7,746
Magic Orb	4	4	1	0	0	3	6,018
Dominuet	9	12	2	0	1	9	5,480
Roxy River	5	3	1	0	0	2	3,818
Miss Vaxette	5	6	1	0	0	5	2,644
Hataal	5	8	1	0	1	6	2,449

Favourites	3-6	50.0%	+ 1.85	Total winning prize-money			£28,154

1993 Form	18-176	10.2%	- 15.85	1991 Form	12-177	6.8%	- 64.75
1992 Form	15-204	7.4%	- 84.29	1990 Form	13-176	7.4%	-103.37

A C STEWART (Newmarket)

	No. of Horses	Races Run	1st	2nd	3rd	Unpl	Per cent	£1 Level Stake
2-y-o	11	27	1	6	2	18	3.7	- 23.00
3-y-o	22	89	13	14	6	56	14.6	- 28.94
4-y-o+	5	34	8	6	6	14	23.5	- 4.69
Totals	38	150	22	26	14	88	14.7	- 56.63

BY MONTH

2-y-o	W-R	Per cent	£1 Level Stake	3-y-o	W-R	Per cent	£1 Level Stake
Mar/Apr	0-0	-	0.00	Mar/Apr	0-3	-	- 3.00
May	0-0	-	0.00	May	1-21	4.8	- 18.00
June	0-0	-	0.00	June	7-18	38.9	+ 12.93
July	0-2	-	- 2.00	July	1-14	7.1	- 11.50
August	0-7	-	- 7.00	August	4-11	36.4	+ 12.63
September	1-9	11.1	- 5.00	September	0-10	-	- 10.00
Oct/Nov	0-9	-	- 9.00	Oct/Nov	0-12	-	- 12.00

4-y-o+	W-R	Per cent	£1 Level Stake	Totals	W-R	Per cent	£1 Level Stake
Mar/Apr	1-3	33.3	+ 1.33	Mar/Apr	1-6	16.7	- 1.67
May	1-7	14.3	- 4.25	May	2-28	7.1	- 22.25
June	0-4	-	- 4.00	June	7-22	31.8	+ 8.93
July	2-8	25.0	+ 2.10	July	3-24	12.5	- 11.40
August	2-5	40.0	+ 1.75	August	6-23	26.1	+ 7.38
September	2-4	50.0	+ 1.38	September	3-23	13.0	- 13.62
Oct/Nov	0-3	-	- 3.00	Oct/Nov	0-24	-	- 24.00

DISTANCE

2-y-o	W-R	Per cent	£1 Level Stake	3-y-o	W-R	Per cent	£1 Level Stake
5f-6f	0-4	-	- 4.00	5f-6f	0-0	-	0.00
7f-8f	1-23	4.3	- 19.00	7f-8f	5-31	16.1	- 14.80
9f-13f	0-0	-	0.00	9f-13f	5-46	10.9	- 23.14
14f+	0-0	-	0.00	14f+	3-12	25.0	+ 9.00

4-y-o+	W-R	Per cent	£1 Level Stake	Totals	W-R	Per cent	£1 Level Stake
5f-6f	0-2	-	- 2.00	5f-6f	0-6	-	- 6.00
7f-8f	3-16	18.8	- 5.92	7f-8f	9-70	12.9	- 39.72
9f-13f	5-16	31.3	+ 3.23	9f-13f	10-62	16.1	- 19.91
14f+	0-0	-	0.00	14f+	3-12	25.0	+ 9.00

Stewart A C

TYPE OF RACE

Non-Handicaps	W-R	Per cent	£1 Level Stake	Handicaps	W-R	Per cent	£1 Level Stake
2-y-o	1-22	4.5	- 18.00	2-y-o	0-5	-	- 5.00
3-y-o	8-57	14.0	- 27.44	3-y-o	4-25	16.0	- 6.50
4-y-o+	4-7	57.1	+ 9.13	4-y-o+	2-23	8.7	- 17.90
Selling	0-0	-	0.00	Selling	0-0	-	0.00
Apprentice	1-5	20.0	- 0.67	Apprentice	0-3	-	- 3.00
Amat/Ladies	0-0	-	0.00	Amat/Ladies	2-3	66.7	+ 12.75
Totals	14-91	15.4	- 36.98	Totals	8-59	13.6	- 19.65

COURSE GRADE

	W-R	Per cent	£1 Level Stake
Group 1	6-69	8.7	- 45.37
Group 2	3-22	13.6	+ 4.00
Group 3	11-51	21.6	- 12.72
Group 4	2-8	25.0	- 2.54

FIRST TIME OUT

	W-R	Per cent	£1 Level Stake
2-y-o	0-11	-	- 11.00
3-y-o	0-22	-	- 22.00
4-y-o+	2-5	40.0	+ 2.08
Totals	2-38	5.3	- 30.92

JOCKEYS RIDING

	W-R	Per cent	£1 Level Stake		W-R	Per cent	£1 Level Stake
M Roberts	6-38	15.8	- 15.25	Mr V Lukanuik	2-3	66.7	+ 12.75
W Carson	4-21	19.0	- 6.99	C Dykes	1-4	25.0	+ 0.33
S Whitworth	4-41	9.8	- 25.57	Pat Eddery	1-4	25.0	+ 1.00
R Hills	3-14	21.4	0.00	J Carroll	1-6	16.7	- 3.90

A Mackay	0-3	Bill Smith	0-1	L Dettori	0-1
M Birch	0-2	F Norton	0-1	M Hills	0-1
A Clark	0-1	G Duffield	0-1	M J Kinane	0-1
A Eddery	0-1	J Dennis	0-1	W Ryan	0-1
Adele Shelford	0-1	J Quinn	0-1		
B Thomson	0-1	L Aspell	0-1		

COURSE RECORD

	Total W-R	Non-Handicaps 2-y-o	3-y-o+	Handicaps 2-y-o	3-y-o+	Per cent	£1 Level Stake
Pontefract	4-7	0-0	1-3	0-1	3-3	57.1	+ 4.48
Hamilton	3-3	1-1	2-2	0-0	0-0	100.0	+ 4.30
Yarmouth	3-16	0-4	2-9	0-0	1-3	18.8	- 1.50
Newmarket	2-15	0-2	2-5	0-0	0-8	13.3	- 4.25
Folkestone	1-1	0-0	1-1	0-0	0-0	100.0	+ 3.33
Edinburgh	1-2	0-1	1-1	0-0	0-0	50.0	- 0.87
Kempton	1-5	0-1	1-2	0-0	0-2	20.0	- 2.00
Lingfield	1-5	0-1	1-4	0-0	0-0	20.0	+ 6.00
Salisbury	1-5	0-1	0-2	0-0	1-2	20.0	+ 7.00

Nottingham	1-6	0-2	0-2	0-0	1-2	16.7	-	1.00
Brighton	1-7	0-1	1-4	0-0	0-2	14.3	-	4.00
Doncaster	1-7	0-2	0-1	0-1	1-3	14.3	-	4.50
Newbury	1-11	0-0	0-6	0-0	1-5	9.1	-	6.00
Ascot	1-13	0-1	1-5	0-0	0-7	7.7	-	10.62

Leicester	0-7	Warwick	0-4	Carlisle	0-1
Windsor	0-5	Beverley	0-3	Chester	0-1
Bath	0-4	Epsom	0-2	Ripon	0-1
Goodwood	0-4	Newcastle	0-2	Thirsk	0-1
Haydock	0-4	Redcar	0-2		
Sandown	0-4	York	0-2		

WINNING HORSES

		Races					Win
	Age	Run	1st	2nd	3rd	Unpl	£
Wagon Master	4	6	3	1	2	0	87,412
Mareha	3	8	3	3	0	2	11,967
Honey Mount	3	8	2	1	1	4	8,333
Mo-Addab	4	10	2	2	1	5	7,635
Cast The Line	4	7	2	1	2	2	7,149
Rumi	3	7	2	1	0	4	6,051
Dalu	3	2	1	1	0	0	3,577
Vlaminck	3	4	1	0	1	2	3,521
Alfawz Alwasheek	3	4	1	1	0	2	3,342
Red Bustaan	2	3	1	1	0	1	2,898
Brumon	3	6	1	0	0	5	2,831
Alqaswar	3	5	1	0	0	4	2,758
Mister Kite	3	7	1	2	0	4	2,504
Fawaran	4	6	1	1	1	3	2,070

WINNING OWNERS

	Races Won	Value £		Races Won	Value £
Hamdan Al-Maktoum	8	105,026	Sir Stephen Hastings	2	6,051
Sheikh Ahmed Al Maktoum	3	8,998	R Collins	1	3,521
Cliveden Stud	2	8,333	S Corman Ltd	1	2,831
S J Hammond	2	7,635	Mrs H R Slack	1	2,504
D P Barrie	2	7,149			

Favourites	11-27	40.7%	- 1.21	Total winning prize-money				£152,047
Longest winning sequence			2	Average SP of winner				3.2/1
Longest losing sequence			26	Return on stakes invested				-37.8%
1993 Form	11-120	9.2%	- 43.27	1991 Form	29-194	14.9%	-	2.19
1992 Form	22-129	17.1%	- 28.70	1990 Form	40-234	17.1%	-	81.52

W STOREY (Consett, Co Durham)

	No. of Horses	Races Run	1st	2nd	3rd	Unpl	Per cent	£1 Level Stake
2-y-o	1	1	0	0	0	1	-	- 1.00
3-y-o	5	10	0	1	0	9	-	- 10.00
4-y-o+	3	14	1	1	1	11	7.1	+ 7.00
Totals	9	25	1	2	1	21	4.0	- 4.00

Jan	Feb	Mar	Apr	May	Jun	Jul	Aug	Sep	Oct/Nov
0-0	0-0	0-0	0-0	0-1	0-3	0-4	1-4	0-8	0-5

Winning Jockey	W-R	£1 Level Stake	Winning Course	W-R	£1 Level Stake
R Havlin	1-6	+ 15.00	Edinburgh	1-3	+ 18.00

Winning Horse	Age	Races Run	1st	2nd	3rd	Unpl	Win £
Master Hyde	5	8	1	1	1	5	2,840

Favourites	0-1		Total winning prize-money	£2,840

1993 Form	0-21			1991 Form	2-35	5.7%	- 16.50
1992 Form	2-51	3.9%	- 20.50	1990 Form	0-49		

M R STOUTE (Newmarket)

	No. of Horses	Races Run	1st	2nd	3rd	Unpl	Per cent	£1 Level Stake
2-y-o	74	176	31	26	22	97	17.6	- 36.38
3-y-o	61	315	60	38	50	167	19.0	- 29.19
4-y-o+	21	99	17	12	15	55	17.2	- 3.79
Totals	156	590	108	76	87	319	18.3	- 69.36

BY MONTH

2-y-o	W-R	Per cent	£1 Level Stake	3-y-o	W-R	Per cent	£1 Level Stake
Mar/Apr	0-1	-	- 1.00	Mar/Apr	8-44	18.2	+ 2.89
May	0-5	-	- 5.00	May	16-61	26.2	+ 24.01
June	3-11	27.3	+ 11.12	June	12-68	17.6	- 28.22
July	4-13	30.8	+ 7.08	July	9-46	19.6	- 9.03
August	5-35	14.3	- 18.81	August	9-41	22.0	+ 9.83
September	12-61	19.7	- 6.64	September	4-30	13.3	- 11.17
Oct/Nov	7-50	14.0	- 23.13	Oct/Nov	2-25	8.0	- 16.50

4-y-o+	W-R	Per cent	£1 Level Stake	Totals	W-R	Per cent	£1 Level Stake
Mar/Apr	1-16	6.3	- 9.00	Mar/Apr	9-61	14.8	- 7.11
May	2-15	13.3	- 6.00	May	18-81	22.2	+ 13.01
June	1-13	7.7	- 5.00	June	16-92	17.4	- 22.10
July	5-17	29.4	+ 24.00	July	18-76	23.7	+ 22.05
August	2-14	14.3	- 5.25	August	16-90	17.8	- 14.23
September	4-17	23.5	- 1.50	September	20-108	18.5	- 19.31
Oct/Nov	2-7	28.6	- 0.04	Oct/Nov	11-82	13.4	- 39.67

DISTANCE

2-y-o	W-R	Per cent	£1 Level Stake	3-y-o	W-R	Per cent	£1 Level Stake
5f-6f	14-63	22.2	+ 22.06	5f-6f	3-12	25.0	- 2.36
7f-8f	17-111	15.3	- 56.44	7f-8f	18-134	13.4	- 47.25
9f-13f	0-2	-	- 2.00	9f-13f	36-156	23.1	+ 12.92
14f+	0-0	-	0.00	14f+	3-13	23.1	+ 7.50

4-y-o+	W-R	Per cent	£1 Level Stake	Totals	W-R	Per cent	£1 Level Stake
5f-6f	0-6	-	- 6.00	5f-6f	17-81	21.0	+ 13.70
7f-8f	7-28	25.0	+ 5.75	7f-8f	42-273	15.4	- 97.94
9f-13f	10-55	18.2	+ 6.46	9f-13f	46-213	21.6	+ 17.38
14f+	0-10	-	- 10.00	14f+	3-23	13.0	- 2.50

TYPE OF RACE

Non-Handicaps	W-R	Per cent	£1 Level Stake	Handicaps	W-R	Per cent	£1 Level Stake
2-y-o	30-166	18.1	- 32.38	2-y-o	1-9	11.1	- 3.00
3-y-o	36-187	19.3	- 25.20	3-y-o	23-125	18.4	- 2.61
4-y-o+	10-60	16.7	- 17.04	4-y-o+	6-38	15.8	+ 8.25
Selling	0-0	-	0.00	Selling	0-0	-	0.00
Apprentice	0-0	-	0.00	Apprentice	0-1	-	- 1.00
Amat/Ladies	2-2	100.0	+ 5.62	Amat/Ladies	0-2	-	- 2.00
Totals	78-415	18.8	- 69.00	Totals	30-175	17.1	- 0.36

COURSE GRADE

	W-R	Per cent	£1 Level Stake
Group 1	64-392	16.3	- 53.81
Group 2	21-78	26.9	+ 11.35
Group 3	18-96	18.8	- 18.54
Group 4	5-24	20.8	- 8.36

FIRST TIME OUT

	W-R	Per cent	£1 Level Stake
2-y-o	5-74	6.8	- 51.75
3-y-o	9-61	14.8	- 1.36
4-y-o+	3-20	15.0	+ 5.00
Totals	17-155	11.0	- 48.11

JOCKEYS RIDING

	W-R	Per cent	£1 Level Stake		W-R	Per cent	£1 Level Stake
W R Swinburn	38-216	17.6	- 1.64	L Dettori	2-11	18.2	- 6.70
B Raymond	10-43	23.3	- 13.55	G Hind	2-12	16.7	0.00
K Darley	7-34	20.6	- 6.52	D McKeown	2-13	15.4	- 1.43
Paul Eddery	7-40	17.5	- 14.43	P Robinson	2-15	13.3	- 8.25
D Holland	6-23	26.1	+ 8.83	W Carson	2-16	12.5	- 8.50
M J Kinane	4-15	26.7	+ 8.50	T Quinn	1-2	50.0	+ 5.00
J Reid	4-16	25.0	- 6.00	J Weaver	1-3	33.3	+ 1.50
Pat Eddery	4-25	16.0	- 2.90	J Quinn	1-3	33.3	+ 2.00
Mrs M Cowdrey	2-3	66.7	+ 4.62	G Carter	1-5	20.0	0.00
M Roberts	2-5	40.0	+ 4.73	W Woods	1-6	16.7	- 3.62
R Cochrane	2-8	25.0	- 0.50	M Fenton	1-7	14.3	- 1.50
J Tate	2-8	25.0	+ 14.00	W Ryan	1-8	12.5	- 5.50
A Munro	2-9	22.2	+ 0.50	P D'Arcy	1-13	7.7	- 7.00

K Bradshaw	0-6	B Rouse	0-1	M J Dwyer	0-1
M Hills	0-5	C Asmussen	0-1	M Tebbutt	0-1
L Piggott	0-3	C Dwyer	0-1	Mr P P-Gordon	0-1
T Ives	0-3	K Fallon	0-1	Wally Swinburn	0-1
A Clark	0-2	K Rutter	0-1		
F Norton	0-2	M Birch	0-1		

COURSE RECORD

	Total W-R	Non-Handicaps 2-y-o	Non-Handicaps 3-y-o+	Handicaps 2-y-o	Handicaps 3-y-o+	Per cent	£1 Level Stake
Newmarket	11-106	6-37	5-43	0-3	0-23	10.4	- 40.54
York	8-33	1-5	5-16	0-0	2-12	24.2	+ 20.62
Ascot	8-57	2-13	4-23	0-0	2-21	14.0	- 7.42
Goodwood	7-26	1-2	3-13	1-1	2-10	26.9	+ 19.10
Newcastle	6-20	2-5	1-3	0-0	3-12	30.0	+ 1.35
Haydock	6-25	2-4	2-10	0-0	2-11	24.0	- 4.38
Chester	5-17	1-3	1-7	0-1	3-6	29.4	+ 8.67
Ayr	4-8	0-1	3-5	0-0	1-2	50.0	+ 1.13
Thirsk	4-10	1-2	3-7	0-0	0-1	40.0	+ 8.20
Redcar	4-11	0-3	3-6	0-0	1-2	36.4	+ 2.42
Lingfield	4-12	1-3	3-7	0-0	0-2	33.3	+ 0.99
Ripon	4-14	0-2	1-4	0-0	3-8	28.6	+ 5.07
Leicester	4-17	3-10	1-4	0-0	0-3	23.5	- 0.71
Doncaster	4-26	2-10	2-11	0-1	0-4	15.4	- 4.50
Sandown	4-29	1-7	2-15	0-0	1-7	13.8	- 8.50
Bath	3-8	1-1	1-6	0-0	1-1	37.5	+ 2.23
Nottingham	3-12	1-8	1-2	0-0	1-2	25.0	+ 7.00
Windsor	3-14	0-1	1-8	0-0	2-5	21.4	+ 0.75
Epsom	3-19	0-0	2-12	0-0	1-7	15.8	- 3.00
Chepstow	2-5	2-3	0-1	0-0	0-1	40.0	+ 2.25
Warwick	2-6	0-0	0-3	0-0	2-3	33.3	+ 3.50
Newbury	2-23	1-7	0-8	0-0	1-8	8.7	- 13.17
Yarmouth	2-25	1-11	0-4	0-2	1-8	8.0	- 16.50
Folkestone	1-3	0-1	1-2	0-0	0-0	33.3	- 1.09
Southwell (AW)	1-4	0-1	1-3	0-0	0-0	25.0	- 2.27
Catterick	1-5	0-1	1-3	0-1	0-0	20.0	- 2.50
Pontefract	1-8	1-5	0-2	0-0	0-1	12.5	- 6.56
Kempton	1-20	0-4	1-12	0-0	0-4	5.0	- 14.50

Salisbury	0-10	Wolverhampton (AW)	0-4	Hamilton	0-1
Beverley	0-6	Carlisle	0-1		
Brighton	0-4	Edinburgh	0-1		

WINNING HORSES

	Age	Races Run	1st	2nd	3rd	Unpl	Win £
Ezzoud	5	4	2	1	0	1	328,958
Gay Gallanta	2	5	2	1	1	1	103,289
Foyer	3	5	2	0	1	2	75,894
Sacrament	3	7	4	0	0	3	70,603
Soviet Line	4	9	4	2	0	3	68,996
Hawajiss	3	6	2	0	2	2	66,719
Desert Shot	4	10	3	1	2	4	51,976
Dancing Bloom	4	6	2	1	1	2	40,246
Raah Algharb	2	9	3	2	2	2	39,983
Sadler's Image	3	7	4	0	1	2	38,758
Hawker's News	3	3	2	0	0	1	35,315
Monaassabaat	3	9	2	1	3	3	23,071
Red Carnival	2	2	2	0	0	0	22,219
Pure Grain	2	5	2	1	1	1	21,585
Green Crusader	3	9	2	2	1	4	21,532
Dahyah	4	6	2	1	0	3	20,031
Knave's Ash	3	4	1	0	1	2	19,088
Zilzal Zamaan	3	7	3	2	0	2	18,518
Annus Mirabilis	2	4	2	1	0	1	15,225
Just Happy	3	4	2	0	0	2	14,846
Munnaya	3	3	1	0	1	1	14,020
Zafaaf	3	5	2	0	0	3	13,353
Three In One	3	8	2	2	2	2	13,320
Darrery	4	5	1	1	2	1	12,393
Blushing Flame	3	8	2	0	0	6	12,328
Desert Fighter	3	10	3	1	1	5	11,299
Kamaa Taraani	2	2	1	0	0	1	10,673
Always Aloof	3	6	2	1	1	2	9,192
Highland Dress	5	7	2	1	1	3	8,974
Jabaroot	3	3	1	0	0	2	8,500
Daawe	3	7	2	1	0	4	8,303
Convoy Point	3	8	2	1	1	4	8,284
Alfaaselah	2	5	2	1	0	2	8,214
Lazienki	3	8	2	1	0	5	8,121
Mellaby	6	2	1	0	1	0	7,635
Jaawis	3	8	2	0	4	2	7,347
Mr Diamond	3	7	2	1	1	3	7,273
Amidst	3	8	1	1	0	6	5,995
Subzero	2	7	1	2	2	2	5,479
Night Hero	2	2	1	1	0	0	5,443
Nuriva	2	3	1	0	0	2	4,813
Golden Ball	3	8	1	2	2	3	4,653
Flight Soundly	2	4	1	0	0	3	4,634
Blue Ocean	2	2	1	1	0	0	4,618
Tajannab	3	9	1	3	3	2	4,503

Stoute M R

Brave Revival	2	5	1	1	1	2	4,304
King Balant	2	4	1	1	0	2	4,175
Desert Courier	2	1	1	0	0	0	4,150
Zilayah	2	3	1	0	1	1	4,093
Dance A Dream	2	3	1	1	0	1	4,093
High Standard	2	3	1	0	0	2	3,941
Ela-Aristokrati	2	5	1	2	0	2	3,918
Star Of Zilzal	2	2	1	0	1	0	3,892
Hedera	2	1	1	0	0	0	3,749
Takkatamm	2	4	1	1	0	2	3,710
Singspiel	2	3	1	1	0	1	3,673
Ketabi	3	5	1	1	1	2	3,664
Opera Lover	2	4	1	0	0	3	3,617
Mistress Gwyn	3	5	1	0	1	3	3,553
Little Sister	3	6	1	1	1	3	3,522
Footlight Fantasy	3	4	1	0	0	3	3,521
Zifta	3	5	1	1	0	3	3,418
Neptunalia	3	4	1	0	1	2	3,140
Brave Vanessa	3	7	1	2	2	2	2,765
Desert Maiden	3	6	1	2	1	2	2,743
Sariyaa	3	5	1	1	1	2	2,673
Jundi	3	3	1	0	0	2	2,395

WINNING OWNERS

	Races Won	Value £		Races Won	Value £
Maktoum Al Maktoum	37	679,388	S Hanson	2	9,192
Cheveley Park Stud	19	256,027	Sultan Mohammed	2	8,284
Sheikh Mohammed	20	228,784	P D Savill	1	5,479
Sheikh Ahmed Al Maktoum	6	50,962	Mrs Doreen M Swinburn	1	4,150
Lord Weinstock	4	48,422	Andreas Michael	1	3,918
Mana Al Maktoum	6	34,574	Peter R Pritchard	1	3,553
R Barnett	2	21,585	Helena Springfield Ltd	1	3,521
W H Scott	2	13,320	Mrs Denis Haynes	1	3,140
Sir Evelyn De Rothschild	2	10,629			

Favourites	47-124	37.9%	+ 3.65		Total winning prize-money			£1,384,928

Longest winning sequence		3
Longest losing sequence		27

Average SP of winner		3.8/1
Return on stakes invested		-11.2%

1993 Form	65-420	15.5%	- 70.50		1991 Form	83-413	20.1%	- 57.70
1992 Form	74-449	16.5%	-129.10		1990 Form	78-428	18.2%	-116.07

A P STRINGER (Thirsk, North Yorks)

	No. of Horses	Races Run	1st	2nd	3rd	Unpl	Per cent	£1 Level Stake
2-y-o	0	0	0	0	0	0	-	0.00
3-y-o	0	0	0	0	0	0	-	0.00
4-y-o+	4	17	1	1	1	14	5.9	- 12.00
Totals	4	17	1	1	1	14	5.9	- 12.00

Jan	Feb	Mar	Apr	May	Jun	Jul	Aug	Sep	Oct/Nov
0-6	0-0	0-0	1-3	0-7	0-1	0-0	0-0	0-0	0-0

Winning Jockey	W-R	£1 Level Stake	Winning Course	W-R	£1 Level Stake
A Munro	1-2	+ 3.00	Southwell (AW)	1-9	- 4.00

Winning Horse	Age	Races Run	1st	2nd	3rd	Unpl	Win £
Nellie's Gamble	4	7	1	0	0	6	3,028

Favourites	1-2	50.0%	+ 3.00	Total winning prize-money	£3,028

1993 Form	6-56	10.7%	- 21.12	1991 Form	4-84	4.8%	- 39.00
1992 Form	6-72	8.3%	+ 35.50	1990 Form	5-77	6.5%	- 10.50

MRS A SWINBANK (Richmond, North Yorks)

	No. of Horses	Races Run	1st	2nd	3rd	Unpl	Per cent	£1 Level Stake
2-y-o	3	11	0	0	0	11	-	- 11.00
3-y-o	4	10	0	0	1	9	-	- 10.00
4-y-o+	8	40	1	2	3	34	2.5	- 33.00
Totals	15	61	1	2	4	54	1.6	- 54.00

Jan	Feb	Mar	Apr	May	Jun	Jul	Aug	Sep	Oct/Nov
0-3	0-1	0-2	0-5	0-10	0-11	1-12	0-9	0-5	0-3

Winning Jockey	W-R	£1 Level Stake	Winning Course	W-R	£1 Level Stake
J Weaver	1-3	+ 4.00	Redcar	1-8	- 1.00

Winning Horse	Age	Races Run	1st	2nd	3rd	Unpl	Win £
Colorful Ambition	4	7	1	2	3	1	3,136

Favourites	0-1	Total winning prize-money	£3,136

1993 Form	0-45	1992 Form	0-4

D T THOM (Newmarket)

	No. of Horses	Races Run	1st	2nd	3rd	Unpl	Per cent	£1 Level Stake
2-y-o	3	14	0	2	1	11	-	- 14.00
3-y-o	2	9	0	0	0	9	-	- 9.00
4-y-o+	9	68	9	3	9	47	13.2	+ 3.25
Totals	14	91	9	5	10	67	9.9	- 19.75

Jan	Feb	Mar	Apr	May	Jun	Jul	Aug	Sep	Oct/Nov
0-3	0-4	1-3	1-10	1-14	0-13	1-11	2-13	3-11	0-9

Winning Jockeys	W-R	£1 Level Stake		W-R	£1 Level Stake
L Newton	2-5	+ 13.25	Stephen Davies	1-4	+ 2.00
D McCabe	2-7	+ 4.50	M Roberts	1-4	+ 2.00
E Guest	1-2	+ 4.50	Miss I D W Jones	1-6	+ 2.00
Pat Eddery	1-3	+ 12.00			

Winning Courses	W-R	£1 Level Stake		W-R	£1 Level Stake
Salisbury	2-2	+ 9.25	Thirsk	1-4	+ 2.00
Folkestone	1-2	+ 4.00	Leicester	1-5	+ 1.50
York	1-2	+ 13.00	Nottingham	1-6	+ 9.00
Chepstow	1-3	+ 4.50	Newmarket	1-13	- 9.00

Winning Horses	Age	Races Run	1st	2nd	3rd	Unpl	Win £
Ball Gown	4	10	4	1	1	4	17,341
Ballerina Bay	6	12	2	0	2	8	10,335
Wayne County	4	7	2	1	0	4	6,571
Tyrone Flyer	5	7	1	1	1	4	3,002

Favourites	2-10	20.0%	- 2.75	Total winning prize-money		£37,249

1993 Form	5-73	6.8%	- 33.17	1991 Form	3-104	2.9%	- 55.00
1992 Form	7-146	4.8%	- 83.75	1990 Form	11-130	8.5%	- 21.63

C W THORNTON (Middleham, North Yorks)

	No. of Horses	Races Run	1st	2nd	3rd	Unpl	Per cent	£1 Level Stake
2-y-o	14	61	3	6	5	47	4.9	- 45.50
3-y-o	13	62	5	3	8	46	8.1	- 35.00
4-y-o+	6	26	3	2	3	18	11.5	+ 22.75
Totals	33	149	11	11	16	111	7.4	- 57.75

BY MONTH

2-y-o	W-R	Per cent	£1 Level Stake	3-y-o	W-R	Per cent	£1 Level Stake
Mar/Apr	0-3	-	- 3.00	Mar/Apr	1-10	10.0	- 4.50
May	0-9	-	- 9.00	May	0-8	-	- 8.00
June	0-1	-	- 1.00	June	0-8	-	- 8.00
July	1-9	11.1	- 2.50	July	3-9	33.3	+ 11.75
August	0-12	-	- 12.00	August	0-9	-	- 9.00
September	1-14	7.1	- 10.00	September	1-13	7.7	- 9.25
Oct/Nov	1-13	7.7	- 8.00	Oct/Nov	0-5	-	- 5.00

4-y-o+	W-R	Per cent	£1 Level Stake	Totals	W-R	Per cent	£1 Level Stake
Mar/Apr	1-5	20.0	- 4.00	Mar/Apr	2-18	11.1	- 11.50
May	0-5	-	- 5.00	May	0-22	-	- 22.00
June	1-4	25.0	- 0.25	June	1-13	7.7	- 9.25
July	0-3	-	- 3.00	July	4-21	19.0	+ 6.25
August	1-3	33.3	+ 31.00	August	1-24	4.2	+ 10.00
September	0-4	-	- 4.00	September	2-31	6.5	- 23.25
Oct/Nov	0-2	-	- 2.00	Oct/Nov	1-20	5.0	- 15.00

DISTANCE

2-y-o	W-R	Per cent	£1 Level Stake	3-y-o	W-R	Per cent	£1 Level Stake
5f-6f	1-40	2.5	- 33.50	5f-6f	0-5	-	- 5.00
7f-8f	2-20	10.0	- 11.00	7f-8f	0-22	-	- 22.00
9f-13f	0-1	-	- 1.00	9f-13f	5-31	16.1	- 4.00
14f+	0-0	-	0.00	14f+	0-4	-	- 4.00

4-y-o+	W-R	Per cent	£1 Level Stake	Totals	W-R	Per cent	£1 Level Stake
5f-6f	0-0	-	0.00	5f-6f	1-45	2.2	- 38.50
7f-8f	1-5	20.0	+ 29.00	7f-8f	3-47	6.4	- 4.00
9f-13f	2-13	15.4	+ 1.75	9f-13f	7-45	15.6	- 3.25
14f+	0-8	-	- 8.00	14f+	0-12	-	- 12.00

TYPE OF RACE

Non-Handicaps	W-R	Per cent	£1 Level Stake	Handicaps	W-R	Per cent	£1 Level Stake
2-y-o	2-37	5.4	- 28.00	2-y-o	0-14	-	- 14.00
3-y-o	1-23	4.3	- 20.50	3-y-o	2-26	7.7	- 16.25
4-y-o+	0-2	-	- 2.00	4-y-o+	2-20	10.0	- 5.25
Selling	3-14	21.4	+ 37.50	Selling	0-4	-	- 4.00
Apprentice	0-1	-	- 1.00	Apprentice	0-3	-	- 3.00
Amat/Ladies	0-0	-	0.00	Amat/Ladies	1-5	20.0	- 1.25
Totals	6-77	7.8	- 14.00	Totals	5-72	6.9	- 43.75

403

Thornton C W

<table>
<tr><td colspan="4" style="text-align:center">COURSE GRADE</td><td colspan="4" style="text-align:center">FIRST TIME OUT</td></tr>
<tr><td></td><td>W-R</td><td>Per cent</td><td>£1 Level Stake</td><td></td><td>W-R</td><td>Per cent</td><td>£1 Level Stake</td></tr>
<tr><td>Group 1</td><td>2-54</td><td>3.7</td><td>- 47.75</td><td>2-y-o</td><td>0-14</td><td>-</td><td>- 14.00</td></tr>
<tr><td>Group 2</td><td>2-24</td><td>8.3</td><td>+ 14.00</td><td>3-y-o</td><td>1-13</td><td>7.7</td><td>- 10.50</td></tr>
<tr><td>Group 3</td><td>5-46</td><td>10.9</td><td>- 11.00</td><td>4-y-o+</td><td>1-6</td><td>16.7</td><td>+ 5.00</td></tr>
<tr><td>Group 4</td><td>2-25</td><td>8.0</td><td>- 13.00</td><td></td><td></td><td></td><td></td></tr>
<tr><td></td><td></td><td></td><td></td><td>Totals</td><td>2-33</td><td>6.1</td><td>- 19.50</td></tr>
</table>

JOCKEYS RIDING

	W-R	Per cent	£1 Level Stake		W-R	Per cent	£1 Level Stake
D McKeown	7-57	12.3	- 21.50	A Mackay	1-12	8.3	+ 22.00
W Ryan	1-2	50.0	+ 9.00	J Fanning	1-27	3.7	- 20.00
Mr C Bonner	1-2	50.0	+ 1.75				

G Mills	0-7	J Lowe	0-2	Mrs D Kettlewell	0-1
Dale Gibson	0-4	L Charnock	0-2	N Carlisle	0-1
T Williams	0-4	Pat Eddery	0-2	N Varley	0-1
M Birch	0-3	A McGlone	0-1	Paul Eddery	0-1
M Tebbutt	0-3	D Griffiths	0-1	R Hills	0-1
D Wright	0-2	J Weaver	0-1	R Price	0-1
G Bardwell	0-2	K Fallon	0-1	S Maloney	0-1
G Duffield	0-2	Mr D Parker	0-1	W R Swinburn	0-1
J Carroll	0-2	Mr J Weymes	0-1		

COURSE RECORD

	Total W-R	Non-Handicaps 2-y-o	3-y-o+	Handicaps 2-y-o	3-y-o+	Per cent	£1 Level Stake
Hamilton	4-18	1-7	0-1	0-1	3-9	22.2	+ 6.00
Edinburgh	1-7	1-2	0-1	0-0	0-4	14.3	- 2.00
Thirsk	1-7	0-3	1-1	0-0	0-3	14.3	+ 27.00
Carlisle	1-8	0-1	0-1	0-0	1-6	12.5	- 1.00
Redcar	1-8	1-3	0-3	0-1	0-1	12.5	- 4.00
Haydock	1-9	0-3	0-0	0-0	1-6	11.1	- 5.25
Beverley	1-10	0-4	1-1	0-1	0-4	10.0	+ 1.00
Newcastle	1-11	0-3	1-4	0-1	0-3	9.1	- 8.50

Ayr	0-12	Doncaster	0-6	Kempton	0-1
York	0-11	Leicester	0-4	Newmarket	0-1
Pontefract	0-10	Nottingham	0-4	Southwell (AW)	0-1
Ripon	0-9	Newbury	0-2	Warwick	0-1
Catterick	0-8	Ascot	0-1		

WINNING HORSES

	Age	Races Run	1st	2nd	3rd	Unpl	Win £
Chantry Beath	3	11	2	3	2	4	5,983
Contract Elite	4	9	1	1	3	4	5,508
Lucidity	2	7	1	1	0	5	3,704
Rosmarino	4	5	1	0	0	4	3,525
Last Roundup	2	3	1	1	0	1	3,382
Albeit	4	6	1	0	0	5	3,028
Seminole Wind	3	9	1	0	2	6	2,976
Zirconium	2	9	1	1	2	5	2,738
All In The Mind	3	5	1	0	1	3	2,580
Typographer	3	4	1	0	0	3	2,420

WINNING OWNERS

	Races Won	Value £		Races Won	Value £
Guy Reed	6	18,956	Brian Whitelaw	1	5,508
Racegoers Club Chantry			W G Pallister	1	2,976
Beath Owners	2	5,983	Simon Brown	1	2,420

Favourites	3-8	37.5%	+ 2.25	Total winning prize-money		£35,843
Longest winning sequence			1	Average SP of winner		7.3/1
Longest losing sequence			37	Return on stakes invested		-38.8%
1993 Form	2-98	2.0%	- 70.00	1991 Form	9-102	8.8% - 54.17
1992 Form	2-94	2.1%	- 84.00	1990 Form	12-146	8.2% - 47.06

C TINKLER (Malton, North Yorks)

	No. of Horses	Races Run	1st	2nd	3rd	Unpl	Per cent	£1 Level Stake
2-y-o	4	17	0	0	2	15	–	- 17.00
3-y-o	2	6	0	0	0	6	–	- 6.00
4-y-o+	4	19	1	0	1	17	5.3	- 12.00
Totals	10	42	1	0	3	38	2.4	- 35.00

Jan	Feb	Mar	Apr	May	Jun	Jul	Aug	Sep	Oct/Nov
0-1	0-3	0-0	0-2	0-11	1-10	0-9	0-3	0-1	0-2

Winning Jockey	W-R	£1 Level Stake	Winning Course	W-R	£1 Level Stake
S Maloney	1-5	+ 2.00	Ayr	1-2	+ 5.00

Tinkler C

Winning Horse	Age	Races Run	1st	2nd	3rd	Unpl	Win £
Wild Prospect	6	9	1	0	0	8	2,788

Favourites	0-1			Total winning prize-money			£2,788
1993 Form	3-123	2.4%	-109.04	1991 Form	15-188	8.0%	- 69.09
1992 Form	5-139	3.6%	- 51.50	1990 Form	28-284	9.9%	-135.39

N TINKLER (Malton, North Yorks)

	No. of Horses	Races Run	1st	2nd	3rd	Unpl	Per cent	£1 Level Stake
2-y-o	5	34	2	2	1	29	5.9	- 5.00
3-y-o	1	2	0	0	0	2	-	- 2.00
4-y-o+	19	82	1	5	8	68	1.2	- 77.00
Totals	25	118	3	7	9	99	2.5	- 84.00

Jan	Feb	Mar	Apr	May	Jun	Jul	Aug	Sep	Oct/Nov
0-3	0-1	0-3	0-16	1-26	0-19	1-15	1-9	0-15	0-11

Winning Jockeys	W-R	£1 Level Stake			W-R	£1 Level Stake
Kim Tinkler	2-55	- 26.00	L Charnock		1-10	- 5.00

Winning Courses					
Catterick	1-3	+ 9.00	Edinburgh	1-7	- 2.00
Leicester	1-4	+ 13.00			

Winning Horses	Age	Races Run	1st	2nd	3rd	Unpl	Win £
Vain Prince	7	11	1	1	0	9	2,879
Samaka Hara	2	8	1	0	0	7	2,477
My First Paige	2	12	1	1	0	10	2,280

Favourites	0-2			Total winning prize-money			£7,636
1993 Form	15-141	10.6%	- 46.40	1991 Form	13-197	6.6%	-110.64
1992 Form	9-150	6.0%	- 90.92	1990 Form	17-300	5.7%	-231.34

J A R TOLLER (Newmarket)

	No. of Horses	Races Run	1st	2nd	3rd	Unpl	Per cent	£1 Level Stake
2-y-o	6	20	3	1	1	15	15.0	+ 0.75
3-y-o	5	17	1	1	1	14	5.9	- 6.00
4-y-o+	6	36	5	5	3	23	13.9	- 3.50
Totals	17	73	9	7	5	52	12.3	- 8.75

Jan	Feb	Mar	Apr	May	Jun	Jul	Aug	Sep	Oct/Nov
0-0	0-0	0-0	0-3	1-8	3-15	2-18	3-15	0-11	0-3

Winning Jockeys	W-R	£1 Level Stake				W-R	£1 Level Stake
W Newnes	5-21	+ 20.50		T Williams		1-1	+ 3.00
K Darley	2-7	+ 8.50		Paul Eddery		1-7	- 3.75

Winning Courses							
Yarmouth	3-13	+ 4.50		Leicester		1-1	+ 2.25
Wolverhampton (AW)	2-7	+ 8.00		Kempton		1-5	+ 8.00
Haydock	1-1	+ 3.50		Newmarket		1-11	0.00

Winning Horses	Age	Races Run	1st	2nd	3rd	Unpl	Win £
Dry Point	8	12	4	1	0	7	16,096
Bide Our Time	2	4	1	0	1	2	4,440
Landlord	2	2	1	0	0	1	4,093
Miasma	2	6	1	1	0	4	3,773
Tartan Gem	3	5	1	1	0	3	3,266
Rolling Waters	4	9	1	3	2	3	2,381

Favourites	3-6	50.0%	+ 3.75	Total winning prize-money			£34,049

1993 Form	3-44	6.8%	- 20.56	1991 Form	4-66	6.1%	- 42.12
1992 Form	9-60	15.0%	- 15.44	1990 Form	7-84	8.3%	- 46.75

M H TOMPKINS (Newmarket)

	No. of Horses	Races Run	1st	2nd	3rd	Unpl	Per cent	£1 Level Stake
2-y-o	24	89	9	6	9	65	10.1	- 59.28
3-y-o	21	147	16	20	11	100	10.9	- 79.40
4-y-o+	16	90	10	5	10	65	11.1	- 9.37
Totals	61	326	35	31	30	230	10.7	-148.05

BY MONTH

2-y-o	W-R	Per cent	£1 Level Stake	3-y-o	W-R	Per cent	£1 Level Stake
January	0-0	-	0.00	January	0-3	-	- 3.00
February	0-0	-	0.00	February	0-0	-	0.00
March	0-0	-	0.00	March	0-5	-	- 5.00
April	0-2	-	- 2.00	April	2-20	10.0	- 15.65
May	0-3	-	- 3.00	May	5-25	20.0	- 5.92
June	3-11	27.3	- 4.26	June	3-35	8.6	- 25.08
July	1-17	5.9	- 14.00	July	1-16	6.3	- 12.75
August	1-13	7.7	- 6.50	August	2-14	14.3	- 2.00
September	3-20	15.0	- 12.52	September	2-19	10.5	- 5.00
Oct/Nov	1-23	4.3	- 17.00	Oct/Nov	1-10	10.0	- 5.00

4-y-o+	W-R	Per cent	£1 Level Stake		Totals	W-R	Per cent	£1 Level Stake
January	0-1	-	- 1.00		January	0-4	-	- 4.00
February	0-1	-	- 1.00		February	0-1	-	- 1.00
March	0-3	-	- 3.00		March	0-8	-	- 8.00
April	2-12	16.7	+ 0.50		April	4-34	11.8	- 17.15
May	5-14	35.7	+ 19.13		May	10-42	23.8	+ 10.21
June	1-14	7.1	- 5.00		June	7-60	11.7	- 34.34
July	1-10	10.0	- 1.00		July	3-43	7.0	- 27.75
August	0-5	-	- 5.00		August	3-32	9.4	- 13.50
September	0-10	-	- 10.00		September	5-49	10.2	- 27.52
Oct/Nov	1-20	5.0	- 3.00		Oct/Nov	3-53	5.7	- 25.00

DISTANCE

2-y-o	W-R	Per cent	£1 Level Stake		3-y-o	W-R	Per cent	£1 Level Stake
5f-6f	7-48	14.6	- 27.78		5f-6f	3-24	12.5	- 14.15
7f-8f	2-40	5.0	- 30.50		7f-8f	5-51	9.8	- 23.25
9f-13f	0-1	-	- 1.00		9f-13f	6-59	10.2	- 35.67
14f+	0-0	-	0.00		14f+	2-13	15.4	- 6.33

4-y-o+	W-R	Per cent	£1 Level Stake		Totals	W-R	Per cent	£1 Level Stake
5f-6f	2-12	16.7	+ 1.50		5f-6f	12-84	14.3	- 40.43
7f-8f	3-27	11.1	+ 2.00		7f-8f	10-118	8.5	- 51.75
9f-13f	4-39	10.3	- 9.87		9f-13f	10-99	10.1	- 46.54
14f+	1-12	8.3	- 3.00		14f+	3-25	12.0	- 9.33

TYPE OF RACE

Non-Handicaps	W-R	Per cent	£1 Level Stake		Handicaps	W-R	Per cent	£1 Level Stake
2-y-o	6-61	9.8	- 42.14		2-y-o	0-18	-	- 18.00
3-y-o	8-56	14.3	- 26.75		3-y-o	8-75	10.7	- 36.65
4-y-o+	2-20	10.0	+ 1.50		4-y-o+	6-50	12.0	- 6.37
Selling	2-17	11.8	- 12.64		Selling	1-7	14.3	- 0.50
Apprentice	0-2	-	- 2.00		Apprentice	2-19	10.5	- 3.50
Amat/Ladies	0-1	-	- 1.00		Amat/Ladies	0-0	-	0.00
Totals	18-157	11.5	- 83.03		Totals	17-169	10.1	- 65.02

COURSE GRADE

	W-R	Per cent	£1 Level Stake
Group 1	10-127	7.9	- 62.12
Group 2	3-34	8.8	- 17.77
Group 3	11-109	10.1	- 70.53
Group 4	11-56	19.6	+ 2.37

FIRST TIME OUT

	W-R	Per cent	£1 Level Stake
2-y-o	0-24	-	- 24.00
3-y-o	0-20	-	- 20.00
4-y-o+	1-15	6.7	- 4.00
Totals	1-59	1.7	- 48.00

JOCKEYS RIDING

	W-R	Per cent	£1 Level Stake		W-R	Per cent	£1 Level Stake
P Robinson	22-202	10.9	- 85.81	Ronnie Beggan	1-1	100.0	+ 5.00
S Mulvey	7-71	9.9	- 31.54	M Birch	1-2	50.0	+ 3.50
K Darley	3-10	30.0	- 1.58	Dale Gibson	1-4	25.0	- 1.62

J Gotobed	0-11	D Holland	0-1	S Maloney	0-1
R Hills	0-6	F Norton	0-1	S Whitworth	0-1
D Wright	0-4	G Bardwell	0-1	T Ives	0-1
M Tebbutt	0-2	Mr G Hogan	0-1	T Quinn	0-1
N Kennedy	0-2	R Cochrane	0-1		
D Denby	0-1	R Price	0-1		

COURSE RECORD

	Total W-R	Non-Handicaps 2-y-o	3-y-o+	Handicaps 2-y-o	3-y-o+	Per cent	£1 Level Stake
Hamilton	6-13	2-3	1-3	0-0	3-7	46.2	+ 2.09
Carlisle	4-13	0-1	2-7	0-0	2-5	30.8	+ 3.35
Warwick	3-15	0-3	2-4	0-2	1-6	20.0	+ 8.75
Newmarket	3-57	0-18	2-10	0-3	1-26	5.3	- 40.00
Edinburgh	2-3	1-1	0-0	0-0	1-2	66.7	+ 11.50
Ascot	2-4	0-0	0-2	0-0	2-2	50.0	+ 10.00
Nottingham	2-9	1-4	0-2	0-0	1-3	22.2	- 3.75
York	2-17	0-1	1-2	0-0	1-14	11.8	- 3.00
Chester	1-4	0-0	0-1	0-1	1-2	25.0	+ 5.00
Redcar	1-5	0-1	1-1	0-1	0-2	20.0	+ 0.50
Folkestone	1-8	1-4	0-0	0-0	0-4	12.5	- 5.90
Catterick	1-10	0-1	1-5	0-0	0-4	10.0	- 8.33
Haydock	1-10	1-2	0-0	0-0	0-8	10.0	- 7.62
Lingfield	1-11	1-3	0-4	0-1	0-3	9.1	- 9.27
Sandown	1-12	0-2	0-4	1-1	0-5	8.3	- 5.50
Doncaster	1-13	0-3	0-2	0-0	1-8	7.7	- 2.00
Pontefract	1-15	0-4	0-8	0-1	1-2	6.7	- 8.50
Leicester	1-24	0-5	0-6	0-1	1-12	4.2	- 15.00
Yarmouth	1-30	1-7	0-9	0-2	0-12	3.3	- 27.37

Beverley	0-8	Lingfield (AW)	0-4	Southwell (AW)	0-2
Windsor	0-8	Goodwood	0-3	Epsom	0-1
Brighton	0-7	Newbury	0-3	Kempton	0-1
Ayr	0-5	Chepstow	0-2	Newcastle	0-1
Thirsk	0-5	Ripon	0-2	Wolverhampton (AW)	0-1

WINNING HORSES

	Age	Races Run	1st	2nd	3rd	Unpl	Win £
Ringmaster	3	11	3	1	2	5	21,141
Halkopous	8	8	2	0	1	5	12,328
Cabcharge Blue	2	10	4	1	2	3	9,760
Virkon Venture	6	9	2	0	1	6	7,980
Blue Grotto	4	4	1	0	0	3	7,765

Tompkins M H

Lunar Mission	3	7	2	0	0	5	6,540
Gilt Throne	7	13	2	1	1	9	6,423
Galora	2	8	2	1	0	5	5,517
Memorable	3	6	2	1	1	2	5,277
The Flying Phantom	3	13	1	5	1	6	5,115
Time For Action	2	4	1	0	1	2	4,678
Don't Jump	4	4	1	1	0	2	4,013
Walsham Whisper	3	13	1	4	1	7	3,948
The Multiyorker	3	12	1	2	0	9	3,921
Bajan	3	10	1	0	1	8	3,850
Cool Edge	3	5	1	0	1	3	3,582
St Martha	4	12	1	0	2	9	3,469
Elsdon	3	5	1	0	0	4	3,443
Candane	3	6	1	2	0	3	3,202
Super Sonata	2	5	1	1	0	3	3,054
Ziffany	2	8	1	2	2	3	2,900
Bures	3	8	1	2	1	4	2,746
Bradwell	3	10	1	1	1	7	2,735
Overpower	10	11	1	1	3	6	2,406

WINNING OWNERS

	Races Won	Value £		Races Won	Value £
D Fisher	3	21,141	Multiyork Ltd	1	3,921
Athos Christodoulou	2	12,328	J A Fuller	1	3,850
B Schmidt-Bodner	4	11,940	Henry B H Chan	1	3,582
P D Savill	4	11,817	Michael H Keogh	1	3,469
Computer Cab Racing Club	4	9,760	Bryan Platts	1	3,443
Mrs J Auchincloss	2	7,980	Mark Tompkins Racing	1	3,202
Mrs Carol Davis	1	7,765	Jack Maxwell	1	3,054
P H Betts (Holdings) Ltd	1	5,115	Lady Nelson Of Stafford	1	2,900
Mrs G A E Smith	1	4,678	John Wimbs	1	2,746
Mrs O M Weston	1	4,013	P F Riseborough	1	2,735
J H Ellis	1	3,948	M P Bowring	1	2,406

Favourites	16-40	40.0%	+ 6.70	Total winning prize-money		£135,791

Longest winning sequence		2	Average SP of winner	4.1/1
Longest losing sequence		31	Return on stakes invested	-45.4%

1993 Form	28-298	9.4%	-119.74	1991 Form	42-411	10.2%	-115.54
1992 Form	42-372	11.3%	- 88.35	1990 Form	46-435	10.6%	-161.69

D R TUCKER (Cullompton, Devon)

	No. of Horses	Races Run	1st	2nd	3rd	Unpl	Per cent	£1 Level Stake
2-y-o	0	0	0	0	0	0	–	0.00
3-y-o	3	13	0	1	0	12	–	– 13.00
4-y-o+	1	4	1	0	0	3	25.0	+ 30.00
Totals	4	17	1	1	0	15	5.9	+ 17.00

Jan	Feb	Mar	Apr	May	Jun	Jul	Aug	Sep	Oct/Nov
0-0	0-1	0-0	0-0	0-1	1-7	0-3	0-1	0-3	0-1

Winning Jockey	W-R	£1 Level Stake	Winning Course	W-R	£1 Level Stake
Miss S Rowe	1-2	+ 32.00	Chepstow	1-6	+ 28.00

Winning Horse	Age	Races Run	1st	2nd	3rd	Unpl	Win £
Dontdressfordinner	4	4	1	0	0	3	2,584

Favourites	0-0		Total winning prize-money	£2,584

1993 Form	1-18	5.6%	– 8.50	1991 Form	0-26
1992 Form	1-66	1.5%	– 49.00	1990 Form	0-15

W G M TURNER (Sherborne, Dorset)

	No. of Horses	Races Run	1st	2nd	3rd	Unpl	Per cent	£1 Level Stake
2-y-o	8	28	2	4	4	18	7.1	– 18.50
3-y-o	12	46	3	6	3	34	6.5	– 6.00
4-y-o+	14	52	3	6	3	40	5.8	– 13.00
Totals	34	126	8	16	10	92	6.3	– 37.50

Jan	Feb	Mar	Apr	May	Jun	Jul	Aug	Sep	Oct/Nov
1-12	0-7	0-12	1-12	1-23	1-16	2-14	1-8	1-15	0-7

Winning Jockeys	W-R	£1 Level Stake		W-R	£1 Level Stake
T Sprake	3-51	– 16.00	P McCabe	1-9	– 4.00
N Connorton	1-1	+ 3.50	D McCabe	1-16	+ 10.00
J D Smith	1-6	+ 7.00	A Daly	1-26	– 21.00

Winning Courses					
Beverley	3-10	+ 25.50	Leicester	1-5	+ 4.00
Wolverhampton (AW)	3-20	+ 19.00	Warwick	1-11	– 6.00

Winning Horses	Age	Races Run	1st	2nd	3rd	Unpl	Win £
Royal Interval	4	12	1	2	0	9	5,920
Dee-Lady	2	7	1	2	1	3	3,636
Olympic Way	5	6	1	1	0	4	3,465
Lying Eyes	3	7	1	1	0	5	2,794
Sleeptite	4	1	1	0	0	0	2,786
Flair Lady	3	8	1	2	1	4	2,760
Move With Edes	2	2	1	0	0	1	2,742
St Kitts	3	6	1	2	0	3	2,504

Favourites	0-5			Total winning prize-money			£26,606
1993 Form	13-142	9.2%	- 15.00	1991 Form	2-61	3.3%	- 38.50
1992 Form	11-111	9.9%	- 4.12	1990 Form	2-88	2.3%	- 62.50

M D I USHER (Swindon, Wilts)

	No. of Horses	Races Run	1st	2nd	3rd	Unpl	Per cent	£1 Level Stake
2-y-o	9	51	1	0	1	49	2.0	- 45.00
3-y-o	6	41	1	4	6	30	2.4	- 34.00
4-y-o+	11	104	10	8	12	74	9.6	- 6.00
Totals	26	196	12	12	19	153	6.1	- 85.00

BY MONTH

2-y-o	W-R	Per cent	£1 Level Stake	3-y-o	W-R	Per cent	£1 Level Stake
January	0-0	-	0.00	January	0-0	-	0.00
February	0-0	-	0.00	February	0-0	-	0.00
March	0-0	-	0.00	March	0-0	-	0.00
April	1-6	16.7	0.00	April	0-5	-	- 5.00
May	0-2	-	- 2.00	May	0-7	-	- 7.00
June	0-7	-	- 7.00	June	0-7	-	- 7.00
July	0-5	-	- 5.00	July	0-6	-	- 6.00
August	0-11	-	- 11.00	August	0-3	-	- 3.00
September	0-9	-	- 9.00	September	1-8	12.5	- 1.00
Oct/Nov	0-11	-	- 11.00	Oct/Nov	0-5	-	- 5.00

4-y-o+	W-R	Per cent	£1 Level Stake	Totals	W-R	Per cent	£1 Level Stake
January	0-0	-	0.00	January	0-0	-	0.00
February	1-3	33.3	+ 3.50	February	1-3	33.3	+ 3.50
March	0-1	-	- 1.00	March	0-1	-	- 1.00
April	1-15	6.7	- 7.00	April	2-26	7.7	- 12.00
May	1-16	6.3	- 3.00	May	1-25	4.0	- 12.00
June	1-10	10.0	- 1.00	June	1-24	4.2	- 15.00
July	3-17	17.6	+ 19.00	July	3-28	10.7	+ 8.00
August	1-17	5.9	- 2.00	August	1-31	3.2	- 16.00
September	2-15	13.3	- 4.50	September	3-32	9.4	- 14.50
Oct/Nov	0-10	-	- 10.00	Oct/Nov	0-26	-	- 26.00

DISTANCE

2-y-o	W-R	Per cent	£1 Level Stake	3-y-o	W-R	Per cent	£1 Level Stake
5f-6f	1-40	2.5	- 34.00	5f-6f	0-8	-	- 8.00
7f-8f	0-11	-	- 11.00	7f-8f	1-10	10.0	- 3.00
9f-13f	0-0	-	0.00	9f-13f	0-21	-	- 21.00
14f+	0-0	-	0.00	14f+	0-2	-	- 2.00

4-y-o+	W-R	Per cent	£1 Level Stake	Totals	W-R	Per cent	£1 Level Stake
5f-6f	2-38	5.3	- 23.00	5f-6f	3-86	3.5	- 65.00
7f-8f	5-33	15.2	+ 10.00	7f-8f	6-54	11.1	- 4.00
9f-13f	3-26	11.5	+ 14.00	9f-13f	3-47	6.4	- 7.00
14f+	0-7	-	- 7.00	14f+	0-9	-	- 9.00

TYPE OF RACE

Non-Handicaps	W-R	Per cent	£1 Level Stake	Handicaps	W-R	Per cent	£1 Level Stake
2-y-o	0-32	-	- 32.00	2-y-o	0-9	-	- 9.00
3-y-o	0-24	-	- 24.00	3-y-o	0-11	-	- 11.00
4-y-o+	2-15	13.3	+ 4.50	4-y-o+	4-72	5.6	- 40.50
Selling	1-7	14.3	- 1.00	Selling	0-4	-	- 4.00
Apprentice	0-0	-	0.00	Apprentice	5-19	26.3	+ 35.00
Amat/Ladies	0-0	-	0.00	Amat/Ladies	0-3	-	- 3.00
Totals	3-78	3.8	- 52.50	Totals	9-118	7.6	- 32.50

COURSE GRADE

	W-R	Per cent	£1 Level Stake
Group 1	4-78	5.1	- 30.00
Group 2	2-24	8.3	- 10.00
Group 3	5-58	8.6	- 15.50
Group 4	1-36	2.8	- 29.50

FIRST TIME OUT

	W-R	Per cent	£1 Level Stake
2-y-o	1-9	11.1	- 3.00
3-y-o	0-5	-	- 5.00
4-y-o+	2-11	18.2	+ 3.50
Totals	3-25	12.0	- 4.50

JOCKEYS RIDING

	W-R	Per cent	£1 Level Stake		W-R	Per cent	£1 Level Stake
C N Adamson	5-51	9.8	+ 3.00	T Quinn	1-1	100.0	+ 7.00
B Thomson	2-5	40.0	+ 14.50	L Dettori	1-3	33.3	+ 3.50
R Street	2-49	4.1	- 35.00	J Weaver	1-4	25.0	+ 5.00

R Price	0-29	B Rouse	0-1	N Adams	0-1
D Harrison	0-11	C Avery	0-1	N Carlisle	0-1
J Williams	0-7	C Hodgson	0-1	R Cochrane	0-1
M Wigham	0-6	Colin Williams	0-1	Rhona Gent	0-1
R Perham	0-5	J Carroll	0-1	S McCarthy	0-1
A Clark	0-3	J Osborne	0-1	Stephen Davies	0-1
Mrs A Usher	0-3	J Quinn	0-1	T Ives	0-1
A Munro	0-1	K Darley	0-1	W R Swinburn	0-1
A Tucker	0-1	M Baird	0-1		

COURSE RECORD

	Total W-R	Non-Handicaps 2-y-o	3-y-o+	Handicaps 2-y-o	3-y-o+	Per cent	£1 Level Stake
Sandown	2-12	0-0	0-3	0-3	2-6	16.7	+ 13.00
Bath	2-13	0-3	0-1	0-0	2-9	15.4	+ 1.00
Kempton	2-13	0-0	0-7	0-1	2-5	15.4	+ 10.00
Lingfield (AW)	1-4	0-1	1-2	0-0	0-1	25.0	+ 2.50
Nottingham	1-5	0-1	0-0	0-0	1-4	20.0	+ 4.00
Brighton	1-6	1-1	0-2	0-0	0-3	16.7	0.00
Chepstow	1-9	0-1	1-2	0-1	0-5	11.1	+ 4.00
Leicester	1-9	0-3	0-0	0-0	1-6	11.1	- 2.50
Lingfield	1-9	0-4	0-0	0-1	1-4	11.1	- 1.00

Wolverhampton (AW)	0-15	York	0-5	Ayr	0-1
Windsor	0-13	Salisbury	0-4	Beverley	0-1
Newbury	0-12	Southwell (AW)	0-4	Carlisle	0-1
Newmarket	0-10	Thirsk	0-4	Hamilton	0-1
Ascot	0-8	Warwick	0-4	Haydock	0-1
Folkestone	0-8	Yarmouth	0-4	Newcastle	0-1
Goodwood	0-7	Pontefract	0-3	Redcar	0-1
Doncaster	0-6	Epsom	0-2		

WINNING HORSES

		Races					Win
	Age	Run	1st	2nd	3rd	Unpl	£
Whatever's Right	5	11	4	0	1	6	14,118
Allesca	4	16	3	2	3	8	9,012
Bayin	5	13	1	1	2	9	3,818
Zermatt	4	13	1	2	1	9	3,368
Sparkling Roberta	3	11	1	1	2	7	3,136
Paley Prince	8	14	1	0	1	12	2,479
Saxon Heir	2	12	1	0	0	11	2,422

WINNING OWNERS

	Races Won	Value £		Races Won	Value £
M S Thurgood	4	14,118	M Hopkins	1	3,136
Trevor Barker	2	6,240	G A Summers	1	2,819
Miss D G Kerr	2	6,193	Shirval Partners	1	2,479
Clairtex Gwent	1	3,368			

Favourites	2-10	20.0%	+ 0.50	Total winning prize-money	£38,351
Longest winning sequence			1	Average SP of winner	8.3/1
Longest losing sequence			34	Return on stakes invested	-43.4%

1993 Form	11-177	6.2%	- 97.99	1991 Form	4-166	2.4%	-141.68
1992 Form	3-136	2.2%	- 93.00	1990 Form	12-289	4.2%	-101.62

R VOORSPUY (Polegate, East Sussex)

	No. of Horses	Races Run	1st	2nd	3rd	Unpl	Per cent	£1 Level Stake
2-y-o	1	5	0	0	0	5	-	- 5.00
3-y-o	2	5	0	0	0	5	-	- 5.00
4-y-o+	8	31	1	1	4	25	3.2	- 24.50
Totals	11	41	1	1	4	35	2.4	- 34.50

Jan	Feb	Mar	Apr	May	Jun	Jul	Aug	Sep	Oct/Nov
0-1	0-0	0-5	0-6	0-6	1-9	0-9	0-2	0-1	0-2

Winning Jockey	W-R	£1 Level Stake	Winning Course	W-R	£1 Level Stake
N Adams	1-14	- 7.50	Folkestone	1-7	- 0.50

Winning Horse	Age	Races Run	1st	2nd	3rd	Unpl	Win £
Peach Brandy	5	5	1	1	1	2	2,870

Favourites	0-0			Total winning prize-money		£2,870
1993 Form	0-90			1991 Form	5-58	8.6%	+ 36.50
1992 Form	2-66	3.0%	- 48.50	1990 Form	1-50	2.0%	- 29.00

J S WAINWRIGHT (Malton, North Yorks)

	No. of Horses	Races Run	1st	2nd	3rd	Unpl	Per cent	£1 Level Stake
2-y-o	6	27	0	1	3	23	-	- 27.00
3-y-o	4	29	2	2	1	24	6.9	- 14.00
4-y-o+	3	10	0	0	0	10	-	- 10.00
Totals	13	66	2	3	4	57	3.0	- 51.00

Jan	Feb	Mar	Apr	May	Jun	Jul	Aug	Sep	Oct/Nov
0-3	0-0	0-3	0-5	0-8	0-9	1-13	1-16	0-7	0-2

Winning Jockeys	W-R	£1 Level Stake			W-R	£1 Level Stake
D McKeown	1-5	+ 7.00	J Fanning		1-15	- 12.00

Winning Course			
Carlisle	2-7	+ 8.00	

Winning Horses	Age	Races Run	1st	2nd	3rd	Unpl	Win £
Lightning Quest	3	10	1	1	1	7	3,000
Karseam	3	7	1	0	0	6	2,521

Favourites	0-0		Total winning prize-money	£5,521

1993 Form	3-90	3.3%	- 62.50	1991 Form	5-137	3.6%	- 61.50
1992 Form	1-77	1.3%	- 56.00	1990 Form	3-141	2.1%	-105.00

N J H WALKER (Wantage, Oxon)

	No. of Horses	Races Run	1st	2nd	3rd	Unpl	Per cent	£1 Level Stake
2-y-o	0	0	0	0	0	0	-	0.00
3-y-o	1	3	0	0	0	3	-	- 3.00
4-y-o+	9	52	11	5	9	27	21.2	+ 30.63
Totals	10	55	11	5	9	30	20.0	+ 27.63

BY MONTH

2-y-o	W-R	Per cent	£1 Level Stake	3-y-o	W-R	Per cent	£1 Level Stake
January	0-0	-	0.00	January	0-0	-	0.00
February	0-0	-	0.00	February	0-0	-	0.00
March	0-0	-	0.00	March	0-0	-	0.00
April	0-0	-	0.00	April	0-0	-	0.00
May	0-0	-	0.00	May	0-1	-	- 1.00
June	0-0	-	0.00	June	0-0	-	0.00
July	0-0	-	0.00	July	0-0	-	0.00
August	0-0	-	0.00	August	0-2	-	- 2.00
September	0-0	-	0.00	September	0-0	-	0.00
Oct/Nov	0-0	-	0.00	Oct/Nov	0-0	-	0.00

4-y-o+	W-R	Per cent	£1 Level Stake	Totals	W-R	Per cent	£1 Level Stake
January	1-7	14.3	+ 6.00	January	1-7	14.3	+ 6.00
February	2-6	33.3	− 0.87	February	2-6	33.3	− 0.87
March	1-5	20.0	0.00	March	1-5	20.0	0.00
April	1-1	100.0	+ 1.50	April	1-1	100.0	+ 1.50
May	1-6	16.7	+ 11.00	May	1-7	14.3	+ 10.00
June	0-8	−	− 8.00	June	0-8	−	− 8.00
July	0-4	−	− 4.00	July	0-4	−	− 4.00
August	3-6	50.0	+ 15.00	August	3-8	37.5	+ 13.00
September	1-3	33.3	+ 10.00	September	1-3	33.3	+ 10.00
Oct/Nov	1-6	16.7	0.00	Oct/Nov	1-6	16.7	0.00

DISTANCE

2-y-o	W-R	Per cent	£1 Level Stake	3-y-o	W-R	Per cent	£1 Level Stake
5f-6f	0-0	−	0.00	5f-6f	0-0	−	0.00
7f-8f	0-0	−	0.00	7f-8f	0-3	−	− 3.00
9f-13f	0-0	−	0.00	9f-13f	0-0	−	0.00
14f+	0-0	−	0.00	14f+	0-0	−	0.00

4-y-o+	W-R	Per cent	£1 Level Stake	Totals	W-R	Per cent	£1 Level Stake
5f-6f	0-1	−	− 1.00	5f-6f	0-1	−	− 1.00
7f-8f	4-23	17.4	+ 24.00	7f-8f	4-26	15.4	+ 21.00
9f-13f	7-26	26.9	+ 9.63	9f-13f	7-26	26.9	+ 9.63
14f+	0-2	−	− 2.00	14f+	0-2	−	− 2.00

TYPE OF RACE

Non-Handicaps	W-R	Per cent	£1 Level Stake	Handicaps	W-R	Per cent	£1 Level Stake
2-y-o	0-0	−	0.00	2-y-o	0-0	−	0.00
3-y-o	0-0	−	0.00	3-y-o	0-3	−	− 3.00
4-y-o+	8-16	50.0	+ 40.13	4-y-o+	2-31	6.5	− 7.00
Selling	0-0	−	0.00	Selling	0-0	−	0.00
Apprentice	0-0	−	0.00	Apprentice	1-3	33.3	− 0.50
Amat/Ladies	0-0	−	0.00	Amat/Ladies	0-2	−	− 2.00
Totals	8-16	50.0	+ 40.13	Totals	3-39	7.7	− 12.50

COURSE GRADE

	W-R	Per cent	£1 Level Stake
Group 1	1-16	6.3	+ 1.00
Group 2	4-9	44.4	+ 23.50
Group 3	2-10	20.0	0.00
Group 4	4-20	20.0	+ 3.13

FIRST TIME OUT

	W-R	Per cent	£1 Level Stake
2-y-o	0-0	−	0.00
3-y-o	0-1	−	− 1.00
4-y-o+	2-8	25.0	+ 7.63
Totals	2-9	22.2	+ 6.63

417

JOCKEYS RIDING

	W-R	Per cent	£1 Level Stake		W-R	Per cent	£1 Level Stake
D Gibbs	3-14	21.4	+ 10.50	G Carter	1-2	50.0	+ 4.00
D McCabe	2-4	50.0	+ 6.00	L Dettori	1-4	25.0	- 1.37
R Cochrane	2-7	28.6	+ 17.00	S Dawson	1-11	9.1	+ 2.00
Pat Eddery	1-2	50.0	+ 0.50				

J Reid	0-2	A Clark	0-1	T Quinn		0-1
Paul Eddery	0-2	Miss H Kington	0-1	W Carson		0-1
R Perham	0-2	Mr J Durkan	0-1			

COURSE RECORD

	Total W-R	Non-Handicaps 2-y-o	3-y-o+	Handicaps 2-y-o	3-y-o+	Per cent	£1 Level Stake
Lingfield (AW)	4-12	0-0	3-6	0-0	1-6	33.3	+ 11.13
Lingfield	3-3	0-0	1-1	0-0	2-2	100.0	+ 27.00
Leicester	1-3	0-0	1-1	0-0	0-2	33.3	+ 3.00
Brighton	1-4	0-0	1-1	0-0	0-3	25.0	- 1.50
Chepstow	1-4	0-0	1-1	0-0	0-3	25.0	0.00
Sandown	1-4	0-0	1-1	0-0	0-3	25.0	+ 13.00

Southwell (AW)	0-4	Kempton	0-2	Thirsk		0-1
Doncaster	0-3	Nottingham	0-2	Warwick		0-1
Newmarket	0-3	Ascot	0-1	Windsor		0-1
Wolverhampton (AW)	0-3	Chester	0-1			
Goodwood	0-2	Newbury	0-1			

WINNING HORSES

		Races					Win
	Age	Run	1st	2nd	3rd	Unpl	£
Elementary	11	10	3	1	3	3	8,594
View From Above	8	8	3	0	2	3	8,563
Helios	6	9	2	2	1	4	7,853
Nashaat	6	13	2	1	2	8	7,165
Noblely	7	5	1	1	1	2	3,231

WINNING OWNERS

	Races Won	Value £		Races Won	Value £
Paul Green	6	17,157	D H Cowgill	1	3,231
Mrs Christine Painting	4	15,018			

Favourites	2-8	25.0%	- 3.00	Total winning prize-money	£35,406

Longest winning sequence		2	Average SP of winner	6.5/1
Longest losing sequence		13	Return on stakes invested	50.2%

1993 Form	0-5

C F WALL (Newmarket)

	No. of Horses	Races Run	1st	2nd	3rd	Unpl	Per cent	£1 Level Stake
2-y-o	9	32	3	2	3	24	9.4	- 17.87
3-y-o	11	47	7	3	1	36	14.9	- 5.65
4-y-o+	6	32	2	2	4	24	6.3	- 20.50
Totals	26	111	12	7	8	84	10.8	- 44.02

BY MONTH

2-y-o	W-R	Per cent	£1 Level Stake	3-y-o	W-R	Per cent	£1 Level Stake
January	0-0	-	0.00	January	0-0	-	0.00
February	0-0	-	0.00	February	0-1	-	- 1.00
March	0-0	-	0.00	March	1-2	50.0	+ 1.50
April	0-0	-	0.00	April	0-4	-	- 4.00
May	0-2	-	- 2.00	May	0-5	-	- 5.00
June	0-3	-	- 3.00	June	0-4	-	- 4.00
July	0-6	-	- 6.00	July	1-11	9.1	- 8.90
August	2-5	40.0	+ 5.13	August	1-10	10.0	+ 2.00
September	1-7	14.3	- 3.00	September	2-8	25.0	- 0.75
Oct/Nov	0-9	-	- 9.00	Oct/Nov	2-2	100.0	+ 14.50

4-y-o+	W-R	Per cent	£1 Level Stake	Totals	W-R	Per cent	£1 Level Stake
January	0-1	-	- 1.00	January	0-1	-	- 1.00
February	0-5	-	- 5.00	February	0-6	-	- 6.00
March	0-3	-	- 3.00	March	1-5	20.0	- 1.50
April	1-7	14.3	0.00	April	1-11	9.1	- 4.00
May	0-5	-	- 5.00	May	0-12	-	- 12.00
June	0-3	-	- 3.00	June	0-10	-	- 10.00
July	0-1	-	- 1.00	July	1-18	5.6	- 15.90
August	0-1	-	- 1.00	August	3-16	18.8	+ 6.13
September	0-2	-	- 2.00	September	3-17	17.6	- 5.75
Oct/Nov	1-4	25.0	+ 0.50	Oct/Nov	3-15	20.0	+ 6.00

DISTANCE

2-y-o	W-R	Per cent	£1 Level Stake	3-y-o	W-R	Per cent	£1 Level Stake
5f-6f	1-20	5.0	- 12.50	5f-6f	1-11	9.1	- 7.50
7f-8f	2-12	16.7	- 5.37	7f-8f	6-28	21.4	+ 9.85
9f-13f	0-0	-	0.00	9f-13f	0-8	-	- 8.00
14f+	0-0	-	0.00	14f+	0-0	-	0.00

4-y-o+	W-R	Per cent	£1 Level Stake	Totals	W-R	Per cent	£1 Level Stake
5f-6f	0-8	-	- 8.00	5f-6f	2-39	5.1	- 28.00
7f-8f	1-11	9.1	- 4.00	7f-8f	9-51	17.6	+ 0.48
9f-13f	1-9	11.1	- 4.50	9f-13f	1-17	5.9	- 12.50
14f+	0-4	-	- 4.00	14f+	0-4	-	- 4.00

Wall C F

TYPE OF RACE

Non-Handicaps	W-R	Per cent	£1 Level Stake	Handicaps	W-R	Per cent	£1 Level Stake
2-y-o	2-24	8.3	- 13.87	2-y-o	1-8	12.5	- 4.00
3-y-o	0-11	-	- 11.00	3-y-o	5-30	16.7	+ 5.75
4-y-o+	0-5	-	- 5.00	4-y-o+	2-21	9.5	- 9.50
Selling	1-4	25.0	- 0.50	Selling	0-1	-	- 1.00
Apprentice	0-0	-	0.00	Apprentice	1-6	16.7	- 3.90
Amat/Ladies	0-0	-	0.00	Amat/Ladies	0-1	-	- 1.00
Totals	3-44	6.8	- 30.37	Totals	9-67	13.4	- 13.65

COURSE GRADE

	W-R	Per cent	£1 Level Stake
Group 1	6-35	17.1	+ 7.75
Group 2	1-15	6.7	- 12.90
Group 3	3-34	8.8	- 19.00
Group 4	2-27	7.4	- 19.87

FIRST TIME OUT

	W-R	Per cent	£1 Level Stake
2-y-o	0-9	-	- 9.00
3-y-o	2-10	20.0	+ 2.50
4-y-o+	0-6	-	- 6.00
Totals	2-25	8.0	- 12.50

JOCKEYS RIDING

	W-R	Per cent	£1 Level Stake		W-R	Per cent	£1 Level Stake
W Woods	4-40	10.0	- 20.50	L Dettori	1-5	20.0	+ 2.50
G Duffield	3-12	25.0	+ 2.25	N Carlisle	1-8	12.5	- 5.37
Pat Eddery	1-1	100.0	+ 8.00	C Webb	1-8	12.5	- 5.90
K Fallon	1-2	50.0	+ 10.00				

	W-R			W-R			W-R
A McGlone	0-6	R Hills	0-2	K Darley	0-1
M Tebbutt	0-6	D Biggs	0-1	M Hills	0-1
K Rutter	0-3	D Holland	0-1	Mrs C Wall	0-1
S Webster	0-3	Dale Gibson	0-1	R Cochrane	0-1
G Carter	0-2	J Carroll	0-1	S Mulvey	0-1
P Robinson	0-2	J Lowe	0-1	Stephen Davies	0-1

COURSE RECORD

	Total W-R	Non-Handicaps 2-y-o	3-y-o+	Handicaps 2-y-o	3-y-o+	Per cent	£1 Level Stake
Newmarket	2-5	0-0	0-0	0-1	2-4	40.0	+ 6.00
Thirsk	1-1	0-0	0-0	0-0	1-1	100.0	+ 1.10
Newbury	1-2	0-0	0-1	0-0	1-1	50.0	+ 5.00
Newcastle	1-2	0-0	0-0	0-0	1-2	50.0	+ 10.00
Haydock	1-4	0-1	0-0	0-0	1-3	25.0	+ 5.00
Windsor	1-4	1-1	0-1	0-0	0-2	25.0	+ 3.50
Doncaster	1-6	0-2	0-0	0-2	1-2	16.7	- 2.25
Warwick	1-6	1-3	0-1	0-0	0-2	16.7	- 3.37
Yarmouth	1-7	0-4	0-1	1-1	0-1	14.3	- 3.00
Lingfield (AW)	1-8	0-0	0-2	0-0	1-6	12.5	- 3.50
Leicester	1-9	0-3	1-3	0-0	0-3	11.1	- 5.50

Nottingham	0-8	Ascot	0-2	Edinburgh	0-1
Kempton	0-6	Brighton	0-2	Epsom	0-1
Sandown	0-6	Catterick	0-2	Goodwood	0-1
Folkestone	0-5	Chester	0-2	Hamilton	0-1
Salisbury	0-4	Lingfield	0-2	Redcar	0-1
Pontefract	0-3	Bath	0-1	Wolverhampton (AW)	0-1
Ripon	0-3	Beverley	0-1		
Southwell (AW)	0-3	Carlisle	0-1		

WINNING HORSES

	Age	Races Run	1st	2nd	3rd	Unpl	Win £
Polish Admiral	3	9	4	0	1	4	31,051
Missed Flight	4	4	1	0	1	2	18,156
Donna Viola	2	7	2	2	0	3	8,304
Amoret	3	1	1	0	0	0	3,844
Admirals Secret	5	10	1	1	2	6	3,184
Almasi	2	9	1	0	3	5	3,153
Sarmatian	3	12	1	2	0	9	2,873
Admirals Flame	3	8	1	1	0	6	2,406

WINNING OWNERS

	Races Won	Value £		Races Won	Value £
Walter Grubmuller	6	51,613	Mrs C A Wall	1	3,184
Kieran D Scott	2	8,304	The Equema Partnership	1	3,153
Dr B Lischka	1	3,844	David Allan	1	2,873

Favourites	7-14	50.0%	+ 9.98	Total winning prize-money			£72,971
Longest winning sequence			1	Average SP of winner			4.6/1
Longest losing sequence			44	Return on stakes invested			-39.7%
1993 Form	13-108	12.0%	- 18.62	1991 Form	7-135	5.2%	- 83.77
1992 Form	7-152	4.6%	- 88.80	1990 Form	15-159	9.4%	- 70.56

P T WALWYN (Lambourn, Berks)

	No. of Horses	Races Run	1st	2nd	3rd	Unpl	Per cent	£1 Level Stake
2-y-o	17	56	9	14	8	25	16.1	- 21.57
3-y-o	15	99	16	12	12	59	16.2	+ 7.87
4-y-o+	2	25	4	5	4	12	16.0	+ 7.50
Totals	34	180	29	31	24	96	16.1	- 6.20

421

Walwyn P T

BY MONTH

2-y-o	W-R	Per cent	£1 Level Stake	3-y-o	W-R	Per cent	£1 Level Stake
Mar/Apr	0-0	-	0.00	Mar/Apr	5-18	27.8	- 2.79
May	0-2	-	- 2.00	May	2-16	12.5	0.00
June	0-4	-	- 4.00	June	4-19	21.1	- 2.17
July	1-7	14.3	- 1.00	July	2-14	14.3	+ 7.00
August	3-12	25.0	- 0.77	August	2-13	15.4	+ 20.50
September	2-19	10.5	- 11.75	September	1-11	9.1	- 6.67
Oct/Nov	3-12	25.0	- 2.05	Oct/Nov	0-8	-	- 8.00

4-y-o+	W-R	Per cent	£1 Level Stake	Totals	W-R	Per cent	£1 Level Stake
Mar/Apr	0-1	-	- 1.00	Mar/Apr	5-19	26.3	- 3.79
May	0-2	-	- 2.00	May	2-20	10.0	- 4.00
June	0-5	-	- 5.00	June	4-28	14.3	- 11.17
July	0-3	-	- 3.00	July	3-24	12.5	+ 3.00
August	2-6	33.3	+ 5.00	August	7-31	22.6	+ 24.73
September	2-5	40.0	+ 16.50	September	5-35	14.3	- 1.92
Oct/Nov	0-3	-	- 3.00	Oct/Nov	3-23	13.0	- 13.05

DISTANCE

2-y-o	W-R	Per cent	£1 Level Stake	3-y-o	W-R	Per cent	£1 Level Stake
5f-6f	5-34	14.7	- 13.02	5f-6f	1-17	5.9	- 12.67
7f-8f	4-22	18.2	- 8.55	7f-8f	11-63	17.5	+ 12.71
9f-13f	0-0	-	0.00	9f-13f	3-17	17.6	+ 5.83
14f+	0-0	-	0.00	14f+	1-2	50.0	+ 2.00

4-y-o+	W-R	Per cent	£1 Level Stake	Totals	W-R	Per cent	£1 Level Stake
5f-6f	3-11	27.3	+ 6.50	5f-6f	9-62	14.5	- 19.19
7f-8f	0-3	-	- 3.00	7f-8f	15-88	17.0	+ 1.16
9f-13f	1-11	9.1	+ 4.00	9f-13f	4-28	14.3	+ 9.83
14f+	0-0	-	0.00	14f+	1-2	50.0	+ 2.00

TYPE OF RACE

Non-Handicaps	W-R	Per cent	£1 Level Stake	Handicaps	W-R	Per cent	£1 Level Stake
2-y-o	8-48	16.7	- 17.07	2-y-o	1-8	12.5	- 4.50
3-y-o	10-39	25.6	+ 4.04	3-y-o	6-58	10.3	+ 5.83
4-y-o+	1-3	33.3	0.00	4-y-o+	2-13	15.4	+ 1.50
Selling	0-0	-	0.00	Selling	0-0	-	0.00
Apprentice	0-0	-	0.00	Apprentice	1-2	50.0	+ 13.00
Amat/Ladies	0-2	-	- 2.00	Amat/Ladies	0-7	-	- 7.00
Totals	19-92	20.7	- 15.03	Totals	10-88	11.4	+ 8.83

COURSE GRADE

	W-R	Per cent	£1 Level Stake
Group 1	12-85	14.1	- 7.39
Group 2	9-38	23.7	+ 13.56
Group 3	6-43	14.0	- 3.25
Group 4	2-14	14.3	- 9.12

FIRST TIME OUT

	W-R	Per cent	£1 Level Stake
2-y-o	2-17	11.8	- 7.00
3-y-o	4-15	26.7	- 1.29
4-y-o+	0-2	-	- 2.00
Totals	6-34	17.6	- 10.29

JOCKEYS RIDING

	W-R	Per cent	£1 Level Stake		W-R	Per cent	£1 Level Stake
R Hills	6-24	25.0	+ 10.25	M Henry	1-1	100.0	+ 14.00
Pat Eddery	5-12	41.7	+ 0.68	K Darley	1-2	50.0	+ 0.50
D Holland	4-13	30.8	+ 33.33	P Robinson	1-3	33.3	+ 3.00
W Carson	4-30	13.3	- 13.79	D Harrison	1-5	20.0	+ 1.50
Paul Eddery	3-25	12.0	- 5.00	J Weaver	1-7	14.3	0.00
J Carroll	2-9	22.2	- 1.67				

M Hills	0-5	B Thomson	0-2	L Charnock	0-1
A Mackay	0-4	D McKeown	0-2	L Dettori	0-1
Marchione Blandford	0-4	D Wright	0-2	M Birch	0-1
Miss S Nugent	0-4	G Duffield	0-2	M Roberts	0-1
A Munro	0-3	B Doyle	0-1	Mr C Vigors	0-1
J Reid	0-3	D Biggs	0-1	N Carlisle	0-1
R Cochrane	0-3	G Carter	0-1	Richard Linley	0-1
W R Swinburn	0-3	J D Smith	0-1	S Perks	0-1

COURSE RECORD

	Total W-R	Non-Handicaps 2-y-o	Non-Handicaps 3-y-o+	Handicaps 2-y-o	Handicaps 3-y-o+	Per cent	£1 Level Stake
Thirsk	4-7	0-0	2-3	0-0	2-4	57.1	+ 19.00
Newmarket	4-19	1-4	1-4	1-3	1-8	21.1	+ 14.20
Redcar	3-3	0-0	2-2	0-0	1-1	100.0	+ 10.83
Nottingham	2-6	1-1	0-2	0-0	1-3	33.3	+ 5.50
Haydock	2-7	1-3	1-2	0-0	0-2	28.6	+ 3.00
Kempton	2-7	0-2	2-3	0-0	0-2	28.6	+ 0.33
Catterick	1-2	0-0	1-1	0-0	0-1	50.0	+ 0.50
Yarmouth	1-2	0-0	0-0	0-0	1-2	50.0	+ 6.00
Ayr	1-3	0-0	0-1	0-0	1-2	33.3	+ 1.33
Brighton	1-4	1-1	0-1	0-0	0-2	25.0	- 2.27
York	1-5	1-3	0-0	0-0	0-2	20.0	- 0.50
Leicester	1-6	1-2	0-1	0-0	0-3	16.7	- 2.75
Folkestone	1-7	0-1	1-3	0-0	0-3	14.3	- 4.62
Hamilton	1-7	1-4	0-0	0-0	0-3	14.3	- 1.00
Ascot	1-8	0-2	0-2	0-1	1-3	12.5	+ 7.00
Lingfield	1-8	0-2	1-4	0-0	0-2	12.5	+ 2.00
Windsor	1-9	0-1	0-4	0-0	1-4	11.1	+ 2.00
Newbury	1-12	1-6	0-1	0-1	0-4	8.3	- 8.75

423

Salisbury	0-12	Doncaster	0-5	Lingfield (AW)	0-1
Goodwood	0-9	Ripon	0-4	Newcastle	0-1
Bath	0-6	Epsom	0-3	Southwell (AW)	0-1
Chepstow	0-6	Carlisle	0-2	Wolverhampton (AW)	0-1
Sandown	0-6	Beverley	0-1		

WINNING HORSES

	Age	Races Run	1st	2nd	3rd	Unpl	Win £
Tom Morgan	3	11	4	0	0	7	14,317
Sheppard's Cross	3	7	2	1	0	4	11,283
Oare Sparrow	4	12	3	3	1	5	10,639
Devotee	3	12	3	1	3	5	10,474
Murajja	2	2	2	0	0	0	8,933
Muhab	2	5	2	2	0	1	8,642
Mnaafa	3	9	2	1	3	3	6,919
Munwar	2	2	1	0	1	0	6,323
Stalled	4	13	1	2	3	7	5,322
Ben Gunn	2	5	2	0	0	3	4,072
Makhraj	3	3	1	0	0	2	3,904
Iltimas	2	3	1	2	0	0	3,647
Ehtefaal	3	4	1	0	2	1	3,538
Thabit	3	4	1	1	0	2	3,377
Midwich Cuckoo	2	6	1	2	1	2	3,233
Razinah	3	5	1	0	0	4	2,986
Asdaf	3	7	1	1	2	3	2,685

WINNING OWNERS

	Races Won	Value £		Races Won	Value £
Hamdan Al-Maktoum	13	50,955	Mrs R B Kennard	1	7,730
Michael White	4	17,509	Lady Eliza Mays-Smith	1	5,322
Mrs Henry Keswick	4	13,872	Maj & Mrs Kennard & Partners	1	3,553
Bloomsbury Stud	3	10,474	P T Walwyn	2	880

Favourites	12-38	31.6%	- 1.19	Total winning prize-money	£110,295

Longest winning sequence	2	Average SP of winner	5.0/1
Longest losing sequence	18	Return on stakes invested	-3.4%

1993 Form	17-190	8.9%	- 53.87	1991 Form	24-262	9.2%	-101.99
1992 Form	22-229	9.6%	- 65.60	1990 Form	48-312	15.4%	+ 36.45

MARTYN WANE (Richmond, North Yorks)

	No. of Horses	Races Run	1st	2nd	3rd	Unpl	Per cent	£1 Level Stake
2-y-o	0	0	0	0	0	0	-	0.00
3-y-o	3	18	1	2	2	13	5.6	- 5.00
4-y-o+	8	44	2	4	7	31	4.5	- 26.80
Totals	11	62	3	6	9	44	4.8	- 31.80

Jan	Feb	Mar	Apr	May	Jun	Jul	Aug	Sep	Oct/Nov
0-1	0-1	0-3	0-4	0-10	0-11	0-13	3-9	0-6	0-4

Winning Jockeys	W-R	£1 Level Stake					W-R	£1 Level Stake
B Thomson	2-5	+ 12.20		K Fallon			1-4	+ 9.00

Winning Courses	W-R	£1 Level Stake					W-R	£1 Level Stake
Epsom	1-1	+ 7.20		Nottingham			1-2	+ 11.00
Folkestone	1-1	+ 8.00						

Winning Horses	Age	Races Run	1st	2nd	3rd	Unpl	Win £
Invigilate	5	11	2	1	2	6	6,264
Diamond Crown	3	8	1	1	1	5	2,174

Favourites	0-0	Total winning prize-money	£8,438

1993 Form	5-66	7.6%	+ 6.33

MRS B WARING (Chippenham, Wilts)

	No. of Horses	Races Run	1st	2nd	3rd	Unpl	Per cent	£1 Level Stake
2-y-o	0	0	0	0	0	0	-	0.00
3-y-o	1	5	0	1	0	4	-	- 5.00
4-y-o+	8	27	2	1	4	20	7.4	+ 5.00
Totals	9	32	2	2	4	24	6.3	0.00

Jan	Feb	Mar	Apr	May	Jun	Jul	Aug	Sep	Oct/Nov
0-4	0-4	0-2	1-2	1-1	0-7	0-5	0-3	0-2	0-2

Winning Jockey	W-R	£1 Level Stake					W-R	£1 Level Stake
C Rutter	2-10	+ 22.00						

Winning Courses	W-R	£1 Level Stake					W-R	£1 Level Stake
Brighton	1-1	+ 16.00		Doncaster			1-3	+ 12.00

Waring Mrs B

Winning Horses	Age	Races Run	1st	2nd	3rd	Unpl	Win £
Lucknam Style	6	13	1	0	3	9	3,339
Altermeera	6	2	1	0	0	1	3,132

Favourites	0-1			Total winning prize-money			£6,471

1993 Form	2-45	4.4%	- 26.00	1991 Form	6-111	5.4%	- 35.00
1992 Form	3-106	2.8%	- 75.75	1990 Form	5-83	6.0%	+ 20.25

F WATSON (Sedgefield, Co Cleveland)

	No. of Horses	Races Run	1st	2nd	3rd	Unpl	Per cent	£1 Level Stake
2-y-o	1	4	0	0	0	4	-	- 4.00
3-y-o	1	5	0	0	0	5	-	- 5.00
4-y-o+	2	17	2	2	1	12	11.8	+ 20.25
Totals	4	26	2	2	1	21	7.7	+ 11.25

Jan	Feb	Mar	Apr	May	Jun	Jul	Aug	Sep	Oct/Nov
0-0	0-0	0-0	0-2	0-2	2-3	0-8	0-5	0-5	0-1

Winning Jockey	W-R	£1 Level Stake		W-R	£1 Level Stake
N Connorton	2-15	+ 22.25			

Winning Courses					
Catterick	1-3	+ 0.25	Edinburgh	1-8	+ 26.00

Winning Horse	Age	Races Run	1st	2nd	3rd	Unpl	Win £
Great Oration	5	9	2	2	1	4	5,552

Favourites	1-3	33.3%	+ 0.25	Total winning prize-money			£5,552

1993 Form	0-15	1991 Form	0-1
1992 Form	0-6	1990 Form	0-8

J W WATTS (Richmond, North Yorks)

	No. of Horses	Races Run	1st	2nd	3rd	Unpl	Per cent	£1 Level Stake
2-y-o	12	36	3	0	8	25	8.3	- 22.00
3-y-o	10	56	7	8	4	37	12.5	- 3.25
4-y-o+	7	55	4	7	7	37	7.3	- 18.00
Totals	29	147	14	15	19	99	9.5	- 43.25

BY MONTH

2-y-o	W-R	Per cent	£1 Level Stake	3-y-o	W-R	Per cent	£1 Level Stake
Mar/Apr	0-0	-	0.00	Mar/Apr	2-15	13.3	- 4.75
May	0-2	-	- 2.00	May	1-9	11.1	- 5.50
June	0-1	-	- 1.00	June	2-8	25.0	+ 10.00
July	1-4	25.0	+ 0.33	July	2-5	40.0	+ 16.00
August	2-12	16.7	- 2.33	August	0-7	-	- 7.00
September	0-11	-	- 11.00	September	0-7	-	- 7.00
Oct/Nov	0-6	-	- 6.00	Oct/Nov	0-5	-	- 5.00

4-y-o+	W-R	Per cent	£1 Level Stake	Totals	W-R	Per cent	£1 Level Stake
Mar/Apr	1-7	14.3	- 6.00	Mar/Apr	3-22	13.6	- 10.75
May	2-12	16.7	+ 1.50	May	3-23	13.0	- 6.00
June	0-7	-	- 7.00	June	2-16	12.5	+ 2.00
July	0-9	-	- 9.00	July	3-18	16.7	+ 7.33
August	0-6	-	- 6.00	August	2-25	8.0	- 15.33
September	1-7	14.3	- 4.50	September	1-25	4.0	- 22.50
Oct/Nov	0-7	-	- 7.00	Oct/Nov	0-18	-	- 18.00

DISTANCE

2-y-o	W-R	Per cent	£1 Level Stake	3-y-o	W-R	Per cent	£1 Level Stake
5f-6f	3-23	13.0	- 9.00	5f-6f	6-20	30.0	+ 29.25
7f-8f	0-13	-	- 13.00	7f-8f	0-16	-	- 16.00
9f-13f	0-0	-	0.00	9f-13f	1-17	5.9	- 13.50
14f+	0-0	-	0.00	14f+	0-3	-	- 3.00

4-y-o+	W-R	Per cent	£1 Level Stake	Totals	W-R	Per cent	£1 Level Stake
5f-6f	1-5	20.0	+ 16.00	5f-6f	10-48	20.8	+ 36.25
7f-8f	1-31	3.2	- 28.50	7f-8f	1-60	1.7	- 57.50
9f-13f	1-8	12.5	0.00	9f-13f	2-25	8.0	- 13.50
14f+	1-11	9.1	- 5.50	14f+	1-14	7.1	- 8.50

TYPE OF RACE

Non-Handicaps	W-R	Per cent	£1 Level Stake	Handicaps	W-R	Per cent	£1 Level Stake
2-y-o	2-22	9.1	- 16.00	2-y-o	1-9	11.1	- 1.00
3-y-o	3-28	10.7	- 14.25	3-y-o	4-28	14.3	+ 11.00
4-y-o+	2-13	15.4	- 2.50	4-y-o+	2-40	5.0	- 13.50
Selling	0-4	-	- 4.00	Selling	0-1	-	- 1.00
Apprentice	0-0	-	0.00	Apprentice	0-1	-	- 1.00
Amat/Ladies	0-0	-	0.00	Amat/Ladies	0-1	-	- 1.00
Totals	7-67	10.4	- 36.75	Totals	7-80	8.8	- 6.50

COURSE GRADE

	W-R	Per cent	£1 Level Stake
Group 1	5-76	6.6	- 24.00
Group 2	2-27	7.4	- 9.00
Group 3	6-29	20.7	- 1.25
Group 4	1-15	6.7	- 9.00

FIRST TIME OUT

	W-R	Per cent	£1 Level Stake
2-y-o	1-12	8.3	- 7.67
3-y-o	1-10	10.0	- 2.00
4-y-o+	1-7	14.3	+ 14.00
Totals	3-29	10.3	+ 4.33

JOCKEYS RIDING

	W-R	Per cent	£1 Level Stake		W-R	Per cent	£1 Level Stake
N Connorton	4-36	11.1	- 17.67	J Carroll	1-4	25.0	+ 8.00
G Duffield	2-20	10.0	+ 9.00	J Fanning	1-5	20.0	+ 10.00
J Reid	1-2	50.0	+ 1.50	M J Kinane	1-6	16.7	+ 2.00
Pat Eddery	1-3	33.3	- 0.75	L Dettori	1-8	12.5	0.00
K Darley	1-3	33.3	+ 3.00	B Thomson	1-28	3.6	- 26.33

J Lowe	0-9	J Tate	0-1	P Robinson	0-1
W R Swinburn	0-6	K Fallon	0-1	Paul Eddery	0-1
D Harrison	0-2	L Piggott	0-1	T Ives	0-1
J Weaver	0-2	M Birch	0-1	W Carson	0-1
A Mackay	0-1	M Hills	0-1	W Ryan	0-1
B Raymond	0-1	Mr S Swiers	0-1		

COURSE RECORD

	Total W-R	Non-Handicaps 2-y-o	Non-Handicaps 3-y-o+	Handicaps 2-y-o	Handicaps 3-y-o+	Per cent	£1 Level Stake
Beverley	4-11	1-1	3-7	0-0	0-3	36.4	+ 7.08
Newcastle	2-11	0-2	1-5	0-0	1-4	18.2	- 3.00
Sandown	1-2	0-0	1-1	0-0	0-1	50.0	+ 6.00
Southwell (AW)	1-3	0-0	0-1	0-0	1-2	33.3	+ 3.00
Hamilton	1-4	1-2	0-2	0-0	0-0	25.0	- 2.33
Thirsk	1-4	0-1	0-1	0-0	1-2	25.0	+ 8.00
Pontefract	1-6	0-0	0-3	1-1	0-2	16.7	+ 2.00
Haydock	1-10	0-2	0-2	0-0	1-6	10.0	+ 5.00
Doncaster	1-13	0-3	0-2	0-2	1-6	7.7	+ 8.00
Ripon	1-13	0-1	0-4	0-0	1-8	7.7	- 7.00

Ayr	0-18	Edinburgh	0-4	Carlisle	0-1
Newmarket	0-11	Leicester	0-4	Kempton	0-1
Redcar	0-8	Nottingham	0-4	Wolverhampton (AW)	0-1
York	0-7	Ascot	0-3		
Catterick	0-6	Chester	0-2		

WINNING HORSES

	Age	Races Run	1st	2nd	3rd	Unpl	Win £
Chatoyant	4	5	1	1	1	2	21,480
Lepine	3	10	3	0	1	6	12,010
Sagebrush Roller	6	12	2	3	1	6	7,526
Colway Rake	3	9	2	0	1	6	6,383
Time Of Trouble	2	9	1	0	4	4	5,618
Madly Sharp	3	6	1	3	0	2	5,134
Bridge Of Fire	2	3	1	0	0	2	3,864
Northward Hoe	3	5	1	1	0	3	3,342
Good Hand	8	11	1	1	0	9	3,128
Rosey Nosey	2	5	1	0	1	3	2,887

WINNING OWNERS

	Races Won	Value £		Races Won	Value £
Lord Derby	1	21,480	R Coleman	2	6,383
Lord Swaythling	4	17,144	Mrs M M Haggas	1	3,128
Sheikh Mohammed	3	12,824	Gerald Cooper	1	2,887
A K Collins	2	7,526			

Favourites	4-14	28.6%	- 3.25	Total winning prize-money	£71,370
Longest winning sequence			2	Average SP of winner	6.4/1
Longest losing sequence			35	Return on stakes invested	-29.4%

1993 Form	17-161	10.6%	- 29.51	1991 Form	14-192	7.3%	- 136.44
1992 Form	17-162	10.5%	- 7.75	1990 Form	27-228	11.8%	- 74.77

E WEYMES (Middleham, North Yorks)

	No. of Horses	Races Run	1st	2nd	3rd	Unpl	Per cent	£1 Level Stake
2-y-o	8	55	7	5	6	37	12.7	- 5.75
3-y-o	6	51	6	6	5	34	11.8	+ 8.50
4-y-o+	5	22	0	0	4	18	-	- 22.00
Totals	19	128	13	11	15	89	10.2	- 19.25

BY MONTH

2-y-o	W-R	Per cent	£1 Level Stake	3-y-o	W-R	Per cent	£1 Level Stake
Mar/Apr	1-6	16.7	- 3.25	Mar/Apr	1-5	20.0	+ 8.00
May	2-8	25.0	+ 2.50	May	1-7	14.3	+ 14.00
June	2-11	18.2	+ 1.25	June	0-9	-	- 9.00
July	1-9	11.1	- 6.25	July	1-11	9.1	- 8.00
August	0-6	-	- 6.00	August	2-12	16.7	+ 2.50
September	0-8	-	- 8.00	September	0-4	-	- 4.00
Oct/Nov	1-7	14.3	+ 14.00	Oct/Nov	1-3	33.3	+ 5.00

Weymes E

4-y-o+	W-R	Per cent	£1 Level Stake	Totals	W-R	Per cent	£1 Level Stake
Mar/Apr	0-0	-	0.00	Mar/Apr	2-11	18.2	+ 4.75
May	0-2	-	- 2.00	May	3-17	17.6	+ 14.50
June	0-3	-	- 3.00	June	2-23	8.7	- 10.75
July	0-4	-	- 4.00	July	2-24	8.3	- 18.25
August	0-5	-	- 5.00	August	2-23	8.7	- 8.50
September	0-3	-	- 3.00	September	0-15	-	- 15.00
Oct/Nov	0-5	-	- 5.00	Oct/Nov	2-15	13.3	+ 14.00

DISTANCE

2-y-o	W-R	Per cent	£1 Level Stake	3-y-o	W-R	Per cent	£1 Level Stake
5f-6f	6-47	12.8	- 18.75	5f-6f	2-23	8.7	+ 1.00
7f-8f	1-8	12.5	+ 13.00	7f-8f	1-20	5.0	- 7.00
9f-13f	0-0	-	0.00	9f-13f	2-5	40.0	+ 9.50
14f+	0-0	-	0.00	14f+	1-3	33.3	+ 5.00

4-y-o+	W-R	Per cent	£1 Level Stake	Totals	W-R	Per cent	£1 Level Stake
5f-6f	0-3	-	- 3.00	5f-6f	8-73	11.0	- 20.75
7f-8f	0-5	-	- 5.00	7f-8f	2-33	6.1	+ 1.00
9f-13f	0-14	-	- 14.00	9f-13f	2-19	10.5	- 4.50
14f+	0-0	-	0.00	14f+	1-3	33.3	+ 5.00

TYPE OF RACE

Non-Handicaps	W-R	Per cent	£1 Level Stake	Handicaps	W-R	Per cent	£1 Level Stake
2-y-o	4-34	11.8	- 18.00	2-y-o	1-14	7.1	+ 7.00
3-y-o	2-13	15.4	+ 14.50	3-y-o	4-34	11.8	- 2.00
4-y-o+	0-1	-	- 1.00	4-y-o+	0-19	-	- 19.00
Selling	2-8	25.0	+ 4.25	Selling	0-0	-	0.00
Apprentice	0-1	-	- 1.00	Apprentice	0-1	-	- 1.00
Amat/Ladies	0-0	-	0.00	Amat/Ladies	0-3	-	- 3.00
Totals	8-57	14.0	- 1.25	Totals	5-71	7.0	- 18.00

COURSE GRADE

	W-R	Per cent	£1 Level Stake
Group 1	5-58	8.6	- 29.00
Group 2	0-29	-	- 29.00
Group 3	2-22	9.1	+ 3.50
Group 4	6-19	31.6	+ 35.25

FIRST TIME OUT

	W-R	Per cent	£1 Level Stake
2-y-o	0-8	-	- 8.00
3-y-o	2-6	33.3	+ 28.00
4-y-o+	0-5	-	- 5.00
Totals	2-19	10.5	+ 15.00

430

JOCKEYS RIDING

	W-R	Per cent	£1 Level Stake		W-R	Per cent	£1 Level Stake
D Harrison	4-11	36.4	+ 12.25	Dale Gibson	1-1	100.0	+ 7.00
K Darley	2-7	28.6	+ 0.50	A Garth	1-4	25.0	+ 9.00
G Hind	2-27	7.4	- 3.75	N Kennedy	1-6	16.7	- 3.25
D McKeown	2-35	5.7	- 4.00				

A Culhane	0-4	R Cochrane	0-3	M Birch	0-1
E Guest	0-3	W R Swinburn	0-3	M Hills	0-1
J Fortune	0-3	J Quinn	0-2	S D Williams	0-1
J Marshall	0-3	L Dettori	0-2	S Knott	0-1
J Stack	0-3	B Russell	0-1	S Maloney	0-1
Mr J Weymes	0-3	K Fallon	0-1	W Ryan	0-1

COURSE RECORD

	Total W-R	Non-Handicaps 2-y-o	3-y-o+	Handicaps 2-y-o	3-y-o+	Per cent	£1 Level Stake
Carlisle	3-3	2-2	1-1	0-0	0-0	100.0	+ 30.75
Newcastle	2-20	0-4	0-2	0-2	2-12	10.0	+ 1.00
Wolverhampton (AW)	1-1	0-0	0-0	0-0	1-1	100.0	+ 7.00
Southwell (AW)	1-2	0-0	1-1	0-0	0-1	50.0	+ 4.50
Pontefract	1-5	0-2	0-0	1-2	0-1	20.0	+ 16.00
Edinburgh	1-6	1-2	0-0	0-0	0-4	16.7	0.00
Hamilton	1-7	1-2	0-0	0-1	0-4	14.3	- 2.50
Doncaster	1-8	1-2	0-0	0-3	0-3	12.5	- 5.75
Haydock	1-9	1-4	0-1	0-1	0-3	11.1	- 6.25
Ayr	1-11	0-3	0-0	0-2	1-6	9.1	- 8.00

Redcar	0-12	York	0-4	Kempton	0-1
Ripon	0-9	Newmarket	0-3	Newbury	0-1
Catterick	0-7	Chester	0-2	Nottingham	0-1
Beverley	0-6	Yarmouth	0-2	Windsor	0-1
Thirsk	0-6	Ascot	0-1		

WINNING HORSES

	Age	Races Run	1st	2nd	3rd	Unpl	Win £
New Inn	3	8	3	1	1	3	9,037
Distinctive Air	3	9	1	0	0	8	6,840
Grate British	2	7	1	0	0	6	3,626
Impulsive Air	2	5	1	2	1	1	3,532
Oriental Air	3	11	1	1	3	6	3,089
Special-K	2	7	1	0	1	5	3,002
Simand	2	8	1	0	1	6	2,877
Loganberry	2	4	1	0	0	3	2,876
Rich Harmony	3	7	1	1	0	5	2,577
Sly Dancer	2	8	1	2	2	3	2,406
Arasong	2	11	1	1	1	8	2,388

WINNING OWNERS

	Races Won	Value £		Races Won	Value £
T A Scothern	5	18,426	W G Martin	1	2,877
Mrs Christine Sharratt	3	9,037	Mrs R L Heaton	1	2,876
Mrs M Ashby	1	3,626	Mrs P M Weymes	1	2,406
G Falshaw	1	3,002			

Favourites	4-7	57.1%	+ 3.75	Total winning prize-money	£42,250
Longest winning sequence			1	Average SP of winner	7.4/1
Longest losing sequence			25	Return on stakes invested	-15.0%
1993 Form	10-95	10.5%	+ 16.25	1991 Form	2-68	2.9%	- 56.00
1992 Form	12-78	15.4%	- 22.71	1990 Form	5-122	4.1%	- 85.00

J WHARTON (Melton Mowbray, Leics)

	No. of Horses	Races Run	1st	2nd	3rd	Unpl	Per cent	£1 Level Stake
2-y-o	10	36	2	5	2	27	5.6	- 23.00
3-y-o	9	53	2	5	5	41	3.8	- 35.00
4-y-o+	7	66	10	15	6	35	15.2	+ 9.50
Totals	26	155	14	25	13	103	9.0	- 48.50

BY MONTH

2-y-o	W-R	Per cent	£1 Level Stake	3-y-o	W-R	Per cent	£1 Level Stake
January	0-0	-	0.00	January	0-3	-	- 3.00
February	0-0	-	0.00	February	0-3	-	- 3.00
March	0-2	-	- 2.00	March	0-2	-	- 2.00
April	0-2	-	- 2.00	April	0-6	-	- 6.00
May	2-7	28.6	+ 6.00	May	1-9	11.1	+ 0.50
June	0-5	-	- 5.00	June	0-3	-	- 3.00
July	0-3	-	- 3.00	July	0-6	-	- 6.00
August	0-2	-	- 2.00	August	0-7	-	- 7.00
September	0-6	-	- 6.00	September	1-5	20.0	+ 3.50
Oct/Nov	0-9	-	- 9.00	Oct/Nov	0-9	-	- 9.00

4-y-o+	W-R	Per cent	£1 Level Stake	Totals	W-R	Per cent	£1 Level Stake
January	1-6	16.7	- 2.00	January	1-9	11.1	- 5.00
February	0-4	-	- 4.00	February	0-7	-	- 7.00
March	1-1	100.0	+ 8.50	March	1-5	20.0	+ 4.50
April	0-7	-	- 7.00	April	0-15	-	- 15.00
May	1-11	9.1	- 7.00	May	4-27	14.8	- 0.50
June	1-11	9.1	- 7.50	June	1-19	5.3	- 15.50
July	1-6	16.7	- 2.00	July	1-15	6.7	- 11.00
August	0-2	-	- 2.00	August	0-11	-	- 11.00
September	1-3	33.3	+ 4.00	September	2-14	14.3	+ 1.50
Oct/Nov	4-15	26.7	+ 28.50	Oct/Nov	4-33	12.1	+ 10.50

DISTANCE

2-y-o	W-R	Per cent	£1 Level Stake	3-y-o	W-R	Per cent	£1 Level Stake
5f-6f	2-28	7.1	- 15.00	5f-6f	0-14	-	- 14.00
7f-8f	0-8	-	- 8.00	7f-8f	0-18	-	- 18.00
9f-13f	0-0	-	0.00	9f-13f	2-21	9.5	- 3.00
14f+	0-0	-	0.00	14f+	0-0	-	0.00

4-y-o+	W-R	Per cent	£1 Level Stake	Totals	W-R	Per cent	£1 Level Stake
5f-6f	2-10	20.0	+ 18.00	5f-6f	4-52	7.7	- 11.00
7f-8f	3-28	10.7	- 8.00	7f-8f	3-54	5.6	- 34.00
9f-13f	4-18	22.2	+ 1.50	9f-13f	6-39	15.4	- 1.50
14f+	1-10	10.0	- 2.00	14f+	1-10	10.0	- 2.00

TYPE OF RACE

Non-Handicaps	W-R	Per cent	£1 Level Stake	Handicaps	W-R	Per cent	£1 Level Stake
2-y-o	2-26	7.7	- 13.00	2-y-o	0-4	-	- 4.00
3-y-o	0-22	-	- 22.00	3-y-o	2-23	8.7	- 5.00
4-y-o+	6-19	31.6	+ 15.00	4-y-o+	4-42	9.5	- 0.50
Selling	0-12	-	- 12.00	Selling	0-3	-	- 3.00
Apprentice	0-0	-	0.00	Apprentice	0-4	-	- 4.00
Amat/Ladies	0-0	-	0.00	Amat/Ladies	0-0	-	0.00
Totals	8-79	10.1	- 32.00	Totals	6-76	7.9	- 16.50

COURSE GRADE

	W-R	Per cent	£1 Level Stake
Group 1	3-32	9.4	+ 5.00
Group 2	1-14	7.1	- 4.50
Group 3	8-54	14.8	- 1.50
Group 4	2-55	3.6	- 47.50

FIRST TIME OUT

	W-R	Per cent	£1 Level Stake
2-y-o	0-9	-	- 9.00
3-y-o	0-9	-	- 9.00
4-y-o+	0-7	-	- 7.00
Totals	0-25	-	- 25.00

JOCKEYS RIDING

	W-R	Per cent	£1 Level Stake		W-R	Per cent	£1 Level Stake
K Darley	3-10	30.0	+ 9.50	W Newnes	1-3	33.3	+ 4.00
J Williams	3-46	6.5	- 34.50	P Robinson	1-8	12.5	+ 1.50
J Weaver	2-3	66.7	+ 15.00	A Mackay	1-8	12.5	0.00
J Quinn	2-17	11.8	+ 12.00	A Clark	1-9	11.1	- 5.00

Wharton J

M Birch	0-10	Paul Eddery	0-2	J D Smith	0-1
J Reid	0-4	S D Williams	0-2	L Dettori	0-1
R Cochrane	0-4	B Doyle	0-1	M Baird	0-1
J Fanning	0-3	B Rouse	0-1	M J Kinane	0-1
N Adams	0-3	B Russell	0-1	M Wigham	0-1
D McKeown	0-2	C Dwyer	0-1	P McCabe	0-1
G Parkin	0-2	D Holland	0-1	T G McLaughlin	0-1
K Fallon	0-2	G Carter	0-1	W Ryan	0-1
N Carlisle	0-2	J Carroll	0-1		

COURSE RECORD

	Total W-R	Non-Handicaps 2-y-o	3-y-o+	Handicaps 2-y-o	3-y-o+	Per cent	£1 Level Stake
Leicester	3-10	1-2	1-6	0-0	1-2	30.0	+ 11.50
Nottingham	2-27	0-7	1-6	0-1	1-13	7.4	- 16.00
Sandown	1-1	0-0	0-0	0-0	1-1	100.0	+ 7.50
Chepstow	1-2	0-0	0-0	0-0	1-2	50.0	+ 5.00
Haydock	1-3	0-1	0-0	0-0	1-2	33.3	+ 18.00
Yarmouth	1-4	0-0	1-2	0-0	0-2	25.0	+ 4.00
Redcar	1-5	0-0	0-0	0-1	1-4	20.0	+ 4.50
Beverley	1-8	1-3	0-0	0-0	0-5	12.5	- 3.00
Doncaster	1-11	0-2	1-3	0-1	0-5	9.1	- 3.50
Wolverhampton (AW)	1-15	0-4	1-4	0-0	0-7	6.7	- 11.50
Southwell (AW)	1-28	0-8	1-14	0-0	0-6	3.6	- 24.00

Newmarket	0-10	Newcastle	0-3	Kempton	0-2
Thirsk	0-5	Pontefract	0-3	Newbury	0-2
Warwick	0-5	Ripon	0-3	Chester	0-1
Catterick	0-4	Folkestone	0-2	Edinburgh	0-1

WINNING HORSES

	Age	Races Run	1st	2nd	3rd	Unpl	Win £
Bescaby Boy	8	12	3	3	1	5	10,755
Sharp Falcon	3	12	2	2	4	4	6,578
Blowedifiknow	4	10	2	2	0	6	6,101
First Gold	5	19	2	5	2	10	5,807
Clairification	4	12	2	3	3	4	5,533
Panikin	6	7	1	0	0	6	4,039
Just Fizzy	2	8	1	1	0	6	2,705
Poly Lane	2	2	1	1	0	0	2,649

WINNING OWNERS

	Races Won	Value £		Races Won	Value £
Mrs S M Moore	3	10,755	Dr T J Molony	2	5,533
K D Standen	3	8,456	P W Lambert	1	4,039
G W Mills	2	6,578	J Rose	1	2,705
Hickling & Squires Ltd	2	6,101			

Favourites	5-11	45.5%	+ 11.50	Total winning prize-money			£44,167
Longest winning sequence			2	Average SP of winner			6.6/1
Longest losing sequence			28	Return on stakes invested			-31.3%
1993 Form	15-166	9.0%	- 51.11	1991 Form	11-119	9.2%	- 30.17
1992 Form	18-156	11.5%	+ 31.95	1990 Form	15-198	7.6%	- 38.00

R M WHITAKER (Wetherby, West Yorks)

	No. of Horses	Races Run	1st	2nd	3rd	Unpl	Per cent	£1 Level Stake
2-y-o	10	53	2	9	4	38	3.8	- 45.25
3-y-o	10	64	4	4	2	54	6.3	- 18.00
4-y-o+	12	100	10	5	12	73	10.0	- 19.62
Totals	32	217	16	18	18	165	7.4	- 82.87

BY MONTH

2-y-o	W-R	Per cent	£1 Level Stake	3-y-o	W-R	Per cent	£1 Level Stake
Mar/Apr	2-8	25.0	- 1.00	Mar/Apr	0-10	-	- 9.00
May	0-6	-	- 6.00	May	0-16	-	- 16.00
June	0-4	-	- 4.00	June	2-9	22.2	+ 19.00
July	0-7	-	- 7.00	July	2-11	18.2	+ 7.00
August	0-10	-	- 10.00	August	0-9	-	- 9.00
September	0-13	-	- 13.00	September	0-6	-	- 6.00
Oct/Nov	0-5	-	- 5.00	Oct/Nov	0-3	-	- 3.00

4-y-o+	W-R	Per cent	£1 Level Stake	Totals	W-R	Per cent	£1 Level Stake
Mar/Apr	0-10	-	- 9.00	Mar/Apr	2-28	7.1	- 19.00
May	2-18	11.1	- 6.00	May	2-40	5.0	- 28.00
June	1-10	10.0	- 5.00	June	3-23	13.0	+ 10.00
July	0-19	-	- 19.00	July	2-37	5.4	- 19.00
August	2-19	10.5	- 6.62	August	2-38	5.3	- 25.62
September	3-15	20.0	+ 16.00	September	3-34	8.8	- 3.00
Oct/Nov	2-9	22.2	+ 11.00	Oct/Nov	2-17	11.8	+ 3.00

DISTANCE

2-y-o	W-R	Per cent	£1 Level Stake	3-y-o	W-R	Per cent	£1 Level Stake
5f-6f	2-48	4.2	- 40.25	5f-6f	3-16	18.8	+ 15.00
7f-8f	0-4	-	- 4.00	7f-8f	0-27	-	- 27.00
9f-13f	0-1	-	- 1.00	9f-13f	1-14	7.1	+ 1.00
14f+	0-0	-	0.00	14f+	0-7	-	- 7.00

4-y-o+	W-R	Per cent	£1 Level Stake	Totals	W-R	Per cent	£1 Level Stake
5f-6f	5-41	12.2	+ 0.38	5f-6f	10-105	9.5	- 24.87
7f-8f	1-33	3.0	- 30.00	7f-8f	1-64	1.6	- 61.00
9f-13f	1-15	6.7	- 8.00	9f-13f	2-30	6.7	- 8.00
14f+	3-11	27.3	+ 18.00	14f+	3-18	16.7	+ 11.00

TYPE OF RACE

Non-Handicaps	W-R	Per cent	£1 Level Stake	Handicaps	W-R	Per cent	£1 Level Stake
2-y-o	2-39	5.1	- 31.25	2-y-o	0-10	-	- 10.00
3-y-o	2-21	9.5	+ 7.00	3-y-o	1-31	3.2	- 24.00
4-y-o+	0-5	-	- 5.00	4-y-o+	6-76	7.9	- 15.00
Selling	2-11	18.2	+ 1.00	Selling	1-12	8.3	- 1.00
Apprentice	0-1	-	- 1.00	Apprentice	2-8	25.0	- 0.62
Amat/Ladies	0-0	-	0.00	Amat/Ladies	0-3	-	- 3.00
Totals	6-77	7.8	- 29.25	Totals	10-140	7.1	- 53.62

COURSE GRADE

	W-R	Per cent	£1 Level Stake
Group 1	2-63	3.2	- 41.00
Group 2	6-67	9.0	- 17.00
Group 3	5-53	9.4	- 5.00
Group 4	3-34	8.8	- 19.87

FIRST TIME OUT

	W-R	Per cent	£1 Level Stake
2-y-o	0-10	-	- 10.00
3-y-o	0-10	-	- 10.00
4-y-o+	0-12	-	- 12.00
Totals	0-32	-	- 32.00

JOCKEYS RIDING

	W-R	Per cent	£1 Level Stake		W-R	Per cent	£1 Level Stake
A Culhane	10-128	7.8	- 43.25	A Mackay	1-5	20.0	+ 8.00
M Hills	1-1	100.0	+ 12.00	A Clark	1-7	14.3	- 2.00
L Aspell	1-2	50.0	+ 3.00	Dale Gibson	1-28	3.6	- 17.00
J Stack	1-4	25.0	- 1.62				

N Varley	0-5	A Eddery	0-1	P Fessey	0-1
D Wright	0-4	A Munro	0-1	R Painter	0-1
J Lowe	0-3	Alex Greaves	0-1	S Maloney	0-1
J Quinn	0-3	D Biggs	0-1	S Perks	0-1
G Parkin	0-2	D Denby	0-1	Stephen Davies	0-1
J Fanning	0-2	G Bardwell	0-1	T Ives	0-1
J Tate	0-2	K Darley	0-1	W Carson	0-1
Miss S Brotherton	0-2	L Charnock	0-1	W Ryan	0-1
N Carlisle	0-2	Mr S Whitaker	0-1		

COURSE RECORD

	Total W-R	Non-Handicaps 2-y-o	3-y-o+	Handicaps 2-y-o	3-y-o+	Per cent	£1 Level Stake
Redcar	3-19	0-2	1-4	0-0	2-13	15.8	+ 12.00
Nottingham	2-7	0-0	0-1	0-1	2-5	28.6	+ 16.00
Catterick	2-19	1-2	1-5	0-2	0-10	10.5	- 7.25
Beverley	2-20	0-7	0-3	0-0	2-10	10.0	- 8.00
Thirsk	2-25	1-5	1-8	0-1	0-11	8.0	- 17.00
Chepstow	1-3	0-0	1-1	0-0	0-2	33.3	+ 10.00
Chester	1-3	0-0	0-0	0-0	1-3	33.3	+ 8.00
Edinburgh	1-7	0-1	0-0	0-1	1-5	14.3	- 4.62
Doncaster	1-8	0-1	0-1	0-0	1-6	12.5	- 1.00
York	1-14	0-2	0-0	0-0	1-12	7.1	+ 1.00

Ripon	0-18	Newmarket	0-4	Ascot	0-1
Ayr	0-11	Hamilton	0-3	Brighton	0-1
Bath	0-7	Carlisle	0-2	Goodwood	0-1
Haydock	0-7	Epsom	0-2	Newbury	0-1
Newcastle	0-7	Folkestone	0-2	Salisbury	0-1
Sandown	0-7	Southwell (AW)	0-2	Yarmouth	0-1
Leicester	0-5	Warwick	0-2		
Pontefract	0-5	Windsor	0-2		

WINNING HORSES

	Age	Races Run	1st	2nd	3rd	Unpl	Win £
First Bid	7	17	3	1	3	10	15,333
The Fed	4	17	3	2	4	8	9,819
Seigneurial	2	8	2	0	1	5	8,041
Petrina Bay	3	7	2	0	0	5	5,471
Scored Again	4	11	1	0	0	10	5,053
Alacrity	3	7	1	1	1	4	2,854
Hot Off The Press	4	7	1	0	0	6	2,532
Eluned May	3	6	1	0	0	5	2,389
Resolute Bay	8	12	1	0	3	8	2,294
Hope Hall	6	5	1	0	0	4	2,268

WINNING OWNERS

	Races Won	Value £		Races Won	Value £
Thomlinson's	3	15,333	Derek D Clee	2	4,800
The PBT Group	3	13,094	G F Pemberton	1	2,854
The Country Lane Partnership	3	9,819	Mrs Jean P Clee	1	2,389
G S Goodyear	2	5,471	R M Whitaker	1	2,294

Favourites	3-14	21.4%	- 3.62	Total winning prize-money	£56,054

Longest winning sequence	1	Average SP of winner	7.4/1
Longest losing sequence	35	Return on stakes invested	-38.2%

1993 Form	22-327	6.7%	- 101.42	1991 Form	24-286	8.4%	- 87.80
1992 Form	23-295	7.8%	- 107.49	1990 Form	36-380	9.5%	- 82.40

J WHITE (Wendover, Bucks)

	No. of Horses	Races Run	1st	2nd	3rd	Unpl	Per cent	£1 Level Stake
2-y-o	5	11	0	0	0	11	-	- 11.00
3-y-o	9	28	1	1	0	26	3.6	- 24.75
4-y-o+	18	61	3	8	4	46	4.9	- 44.50
Totals	32	100	4	9	4	83	4.0	- 80.25

Jan	Feb	Mar	Apr	May	Jun	Jul	Aug	Sep	Oct/Nov
0-2	0-4	0-4	0-7	0-13	3-25	0-16	1-9	0-10	0-10

Winning Jockeys	W-R	£1 Level Stake		W-R	£1 Level Stake
T Quinn	3-7	+ 9.50	J Williams	1-20	- 16.75

Winning Courses	W-R	£1 Level Stake		W-R	£1 Level Stake
Brighton	2-7	+ 4.00	Epsom	1-4	+ 1.50
Chepstow	1-2	+ 1.25			

Winning Horses	Age	Races Run	1st	2nd	3rd	Unpl	Win £
Shikari's Son	7	13	3	3	0	7	13,186
Bird Island	3	2	1	0	0	1	2,206

Favourites	3-5	60.0%	+ 6.75	Total winning prize-money	£15,392

1993 Form	11-101	10.9%	- 21.38	1991 Form	5-106	4.7%	- 36.00
1992 Form	9-98	9.2%	- 62.75	1990 Form	2-88	2.3%	- 72.00

K WHITE (Aston Munslow, Salop)

	No. of Horses	Races Run	1st	2nd	3rd	Unpl	Per cent	£1 Level Stake
2-y-o	0	0	0	0	0	0	-	0.00
3-y-o	2	10	0	0	2	8	-	- 10.00
4-y-o+	5	28	2	2	2	22	7.1	+ 7.00
Totals	7	38	2	2	4	30	5.3	- 3.00

Jan	Feb	Mar	Apr	May	Jun	Jul	Aug	Sep	Oct/Nov
2-9	0-2	0-2	0-4	0-8	0-3	0-5	0-3	0-2	0-0

Winning Jockey	W-R	£1 Level Stake	Winning Course	W-R	£1 Level Stake
J Williams	2-12	+ 23.00	Wolverhampton (AW)	2-28	+ 7.00

Winning Horse	Age	Races Run	1st	2nd	3rd	Unpl	Win £
Maple Bay	5	12	2	1	1	8	6,264

Favourites	0-0			Total winning prize-money			£6,264

1993 Form	0-33			1991 Form	3-32	9.4%	+ 27.00
1992 Form	0-41			1990 Form	1-46	2.2%	- 37.00

MISS A J WHITFIELD (Lambourn, Berks)

	No. of Horses	Races Run	1st	2nd	3rd	Unpl	Per cent	£1 Level Stake
2-y-o	1	1	0	0	0	1	-	- 1.00
3-y-o	3	23	1	2	4	16	4.3	- 21.09
4-y-o+	3	15	0	0	1	14	-	- 15.00
Totals	7	39	1	2	5	31	2.6	- 37.09

Jan	Feb	Mar	Apr	May	Jun	Jul	Aug	Sep	Oct/Nov
0-3	0-1	0-2	0-2	0-1	0-7	0-6	0-3	1-7	0-7

Winning Jockey	W-R	£1 Level Stake	Winning Course	W-R	£1 Level Stake
R Painter	1-4	- 2.09	Folkestone	1-3	- 1.09

Winning Horse	Age	Races Run	1st	2nd	3rd	Unpl	Win £
Shadow Leader	3	11	1	2	3	5	2,701

Favourites	1-3	33.3%	- 1.09	Total winning prize-money			£2,701

1993 Form	0-32			1991 Form	3-74	4.1%	- 29.00
1992 Form	7-50	14.0%	+ 19.50	1990 Form	4-58	6.9%	- 12.00

P WIGHAM (Malton, North Yorks)

	No. of Horses	Races Run	1st	2nd	3rd	Unpl	Per cent	£1 Level Stake
2-y-o	0	0	0	0	0	0	-	0.00
3-y-o	0	0	0	0	0	0	-	0.00
4-y-o+	3	17	2	6	2	7	11.8	- 2.50
Totals	3	17	2	6	2	7	11.8	- 2.50

Jan	Feb	Mar	Apr	May	Jun	Jul	Aug	Sep	Oct/Nov
0-0	0-0	0-0	0-0	0-3	0-2	0-5	1-5	1-2	0-0

439

Wigham P

C P WILDMAN (Salisbury, Wilts)

	No. of Horses	Races Run	1st	2nd	3rd	Unpl	Per cent	£1 Level Stake
2-y-o	0	0	0	0	0	0	-	0.00
3-y-o	4	17	1	1	0	15	5.9	- 6.00
4-y-o+	6	53	3	6	6	38	5.7	- 42.87
Totals	10	70	4	7	6	53	5.7	- 48.87

Jan	Feb	Mar	Apr	May	Jun	Jul	Aug	Sep	Oct/Nov
2-11	2-13	0-9	0-1	0-9	0-7	0-3	0-7	0-5	0-5

Winning Jockeys	W-R	£1 Level Stake		W-R	£1 Level Stake
C Rutter	2-23	- 8.00	Paul Eddery	1-2	+ 0.38
D McCabe	1-2	+ 1.75			

Winning Course		
Lingfield (AW)	4-31	- 9.87

Winning Horses	Age	Races Run	1st	2nd	3rd	Unpl	Win £
Sarum	8	11	2	0	3	6	5,927
Leviathan Mystery	3	1	1	0	0	0	3,085
Head Turner	6	14	1	5	2	6	2,713

Favourites	3-4	75.0%	+ 6.13	Total winning prize-money		£11,725

1993 Form	2-43	4.7%	- 24.00	1991 Form	3-31	9.7%	- 8.00
1992 Form	3-34	8.8%	- 22.25	1990 Form	3-45	6.7%	+ 6.00

C N WILLIAMS (Newmarket)

	No. of Horses	Races Run	1st	2nd	3rd	Unpl	Per cent	£1 Level Stake
2-y-o	3	15	5	1	0	9	33.3	+ 12.25
3-y-o	3	18	0	2	1	15	-	- 18.00
4-y-o+	7	18	0	2	2	14	-	- 18.00
Totals	13	51	5	5	3	38	9.8	- 23.75

Jan	Feb	Mar	Apr	May	Jun	Jul	Aug	Sep	Oct/Nov
0-1	0-2	0-1	0-2	0-5	0-8	0-4	2-9	3-7	0-12

Winning Jockeys	W-R	£1 Level Stake		W-R	£1 Level Stake
J Quinn	3-23	- 4.25	P Robinson	2-8	+ 0.50

Winning Courses	W-R	£1 Level Stake		W-R	£1 Level Stake
Brighton	1-1	+ 2.50	Newbury	1-3	+ 0.75
Lingfield	1-2	+ 3.00	Newmarket	1-6	+ 4.00
Goodwood	1-3	+ 2.00			

Winning Horses	Age	Races Run	1st	2nd	3rd	Unpl	Win £
Lab Test	2	6	3	0	0	3	37,615
Sapphire Son	2	8	2	1	0	5	5,560

Favourites	4-8	50.0%	+ 9.25	Total winning prize-money			£43,175
1993 Form	3-41	7.3%	- 27.75	1991 Form	2-36	5.6%	- 26.09
1992 Form	3-34	8.8%	- 25.00	1990 Form	4-60	6.7%	- 15.50

D L WILLIAMS (Newbury, Berks)

	No. of Horses	Races Run	1st	2nd	3rd	Unpl	Per cent	£1 Level Stake
2-y-o	1	1	0	0	0	1	-	- 1.00
3-y-o	1	2	0	0	0	2	-	- 2.00
4-y-o+	6	36	6	1	1	28	16.7	+ 37.00
Totals	8	39	6	1	1	31	15.4	+ 34.00

Jan	Feb	Mar	Apr	May	Jun	Jul	Aug	Sep	Oct/Nov
0-2	2-4	0-0	0-2	0-5	0-4	0-3	3-6	1-8	0-5

Winning Jockeys	W-R	£1 Level Stake		W-R	£1 Level Stake
D Griffiths	3-6	+ 24.50	N Varley	1-4	+ 0.50
Miss S Higgins	2-9	+ 29.00			

Winning Courses	W-R	£1 Level Stake		W-R	£1 Level Stake
Pontefract	2-2	+ 22.00	Salisbury	1-2	+ 2.50
Wolverhampton (AW)	2-5	+ 33.00	Goodwood	1-5	+ 1.50

Winning Horses	Age	Races Run	1st	2nd	3rd	Unpl	Win £
Seaside Minstrel	6	23	4	1	1	17	14,474
Super Heights	6	5	2	0	0	3	4,313

Favourites	1-2	50.0%	+	2.00	Total winning prize-money		£18,787

1993 Form	0-17				1991 Form	0-4
1992 Form	0-20					

R J R WILLIAMS (Newmarket)

	No. of Horses	Races Run	1st	2nd	3rd	Unpl	Per cent	£1 Level Stake
2-y-o	10	32	2	3	2	25	6.3	- 15.33
3-y-o	10	66	6	5	9	46	9.1	+ 1.90
4-y-o+	7	77	6	11	6	54	7.8	- 15.50
Totals	27	175	14	19	17	125	8.0	- 28.93

BY MONTH

2-y-o	W-R	Per cent	£1 Level Stake	3-y-o	W-R	Per cent	£1 Level Stake
January	0-0	-	0.00	January	0-0	-	0.00
February	0-0	-	0.00	February	0-0	-	0.00
March	0-0	-	0.00	March	0-1	-	- 1.00
April	0-0	-	0.00	April	0-7	-	- 7.00
May	1-3	33.3	+ 12.00	May	1-7	14.3	+ 19.00
June	0-3	-	- 3.00	June	1-10	10.0	+ 1.00
July	0-3	-	- 3.00	July	2-19	10.5	- 7.50
August	0-5	-	- 5.00	August	1-9	11.1	- 1.60
September	1-7	14.3	- 5.33	September	0-5	-	- 5.00
Oct/Nov	0-11	-	- 11.00	Oct/Nov	1-8	12.5	+ 4.00

4-y-o+	W-R	Per cent	£1 Level Stake	Totals	W-R	Per cent	£1 Level Stake
January	1-2	50.0	+ 5.00	January	1-2	50.0	+ 5.00
February	0-1	-	- 1.00	February	0-1	-	- 1.00
March	0-0	-	0.00	March	0-1	-	- 1.00
April	1-10	10.0	+ 3.00	April	1-17	5.9	- 4.00
May	2-11	18.2	+ 13.00	May	4-21	19.0	+ 44.00
June	0-18	-	- 18.00	June	1-31	3.2	- 20.00
July	1-14	7.1	- 9.50	July	3-36	8.3	- 20.00
August	0-12	-	- 12.00	August	1-26	3.8	- 18.60
September	1-6	16.7	+ 7.00	September	2-18	11.1	- 3.33
Oct/Nov	0-3	-	- 3.00	Oct/Nov	1-22	4.5	- 10.00

DISTANCE

2-y-o	W-R	Per cent	£1 Level Stake	3-y-o	W-R	Per cent	£1 Level Stake
5f-6f	1-14	7.1	+ 1.00	5f-6f	4-21	19.0	+ 15.40
7f-8f	1-18	5.6	- 16.33	7f-8f	1-21	4.8	+ 5.00
9f-13f	0-0	-	0.00	9f-13f	1-23	4.3	- 17.50
14f+	0-0	-	0.00	14f+	0-1	-	- 1.00

4-y-o+	W-R	Per cent	£1 Level Stake	Totals	W-R	Per cent	£1 Level Stake
5f-6f	0-17	-	- 17.00	5f-6f	5-52	9.6	- 0.60
7f-8f	5-28	17.9	+ 18.50	7f-8f	7-67	10.4	+ 7.17
9f-13f	0-23	-	- 23.00	9f-13f	1-46	2.2	- 40.50
14f+	1-9	11.1	+ 6.00	14f+	1-10	10.0	+ 5.00

TYPE OF RACE

Non-Handicaps	W-R	Per cent	£1 Level Stake	Handicaps	W-R	Per cent	£1 Level Stake
2-y-o	2-26	7.7	- 9.33	2-y-o	0-6	-	- 6.00
3-y-o	0-24	-	- 24.00	3-y-o	4-30	13.3	+ 6.40
4-y-o+	0-11	-	- 11.00	4-y-o+	5-50	10.0	+ 2.50
Selling	0-3	-	- 3.00	Selling	0-1	-	- 1.00
Apprentice	0-2	-	- 2.00	Apprentice	3-20	15.0	+ 20.50
Amat/Ladies	0-0	-	0.00	Amat/Ladies	0-2	-	- 2.00
Totals	2-66	3.0	- 49.33	Totals	12-109	11.0	+ 20.40

COURSE GRADE

	W-R	Per cent	£1 Level Stake
Group 1	3-72	4.2	- 47.93
Group 2	2-38	5.3	- 17.00
Group 3	2-33	6.1	+ 2.00
Group 4	7-32	21.9	+ 34.00

FIRST TIME OUT

	W-R	Per cent	£1 Level Stake
2-y-o	0-10	-	- 10.00
3-y-o	0-10	-	- 10.00
4-y-o+	1-7	14.3	0.00
Totals	1-27	3.7	- 20.00

JOCKEYS RIDING

	W-R	Per cent	£1 Level Stake		W-R	Per cent	£1 Level Stake
Sarah Thompson	6-40	15.0	+ 25.00	D Biggs	2-20	10.0	+ 4.00
G Duffield	2-4	50.0	+ 15.40	Paul Eddery	1-7	14.3	- 5.33
G Bardwell	2-19	10.5	+ 2.00	R Cochrane	1-38	2.6	- 23.00

D Harrison	0-4	T Williams	0-2	J Tate	0-1
M Fenton	0-4	W Carson	0-2	M J Kinane	0-1
M Hills	0-4	W Woods	0-2	M Roberts	0-1
C Hodgson	0-3	A Munro	0-1	Miss B Craven	0-1
T Quinn	0-3	B Rouse	0-1	Mrs M Cowdrey	0-1
A Clark	0-2	D Holland	0-1	N Varley	0-1
J Reid	0-2	D Wright	0-1	Pat Eddery	0-1
N Adams	0-2	G Carter	0-1	R Hills	0-1
T Ives	0-2	J Lowe	0-1	Tracy Johnson	0-1

COURSE RECORD

	Total W-R	Non-Handicaps 2-y-o	3-y-o+	Handicaps 2-y-o	3-y-o+	Per cent	£1 Level Stake
Catterick	3-4	0-0	0-1	0-0	3-3	75.0	+ 32.00
Haydock	2-5	2-2	0-0	0-0	0-3	40.0	+ 11.67
Chester	2-7	0-0	0-2	0-0	2-5	28.6	+ 14.00
Nottingham	2-12	0-2	0-2	0-0	2-8	16.7	+ 23.00
Warwick	1-2	0-0	0-0	0-0	1-2	50.0	+ 11.00
York	1-4	0-1	0-0	0-0	1-3	25.0	+ 3.40
Wolverhampton (AW)	1-4	0-0	0-2	0-0	1-2	25.0	+ 3.00
Lingfield (AW)	1-6	0-0	0-3	0-0	1-3	16.7	- 0.50
Southwell (AW)	1-8	0-0	0-4	0-0	1-4	12.5	- 3.50

Newmarket	0-18	Brighton	0-4	Newcastle	0-3
Lingfield	0-14	Ripon	0-4	Salisbury	0-3
Ascot	0-12	Thirsk	0-4	Epsom	0-2
Kempton	0-11	Windsor	0-4	Folkestone	0-2
Yarmouth	0-9	Beverley	0-3	Redcar	0-2
Doncaster	0-6	Goodwood	0-3	Bath	0-1
Edinburgh	0-6	Leicester	0-3	Pontefract	0-1
Sandown	0-5	Newbury	0-3		

WINNING HORSES

	Age	Races Run	1st	2nd	3rd	Unpl	Win £
Doyce	5	7	1	1	2	3	29,163
Insider Trader	3	13	4	2	2	5	24,234
On Y Va	7	13	3	1	1	8	9,341
Ludgate	2	5	1	1	0	3	7,162
Buddy's Friend	6	12	2	1	1	8	5,189
Dansu	2	8	1	0	1	6	3,616
Al Jinn	3	8	1	1	0	6	2,807
Galway Blazer	3	10	1	0	0	9	2,070

WINNING OWNERS

	Races Won	Value £		Races Won	Value £
Lord Matthews	7	62,628	Lady Matthews	1	3,616
Marriott Stables Ltd	3	9,341	Greg Gregory	1	2,807
Colin G R Booth	2	5,189			

Favourites	2-14	14.3%	- 7.83	Total winning prize-money	£83,580
Longest winning sequence			2	Average SP of winner	9.4/1
Longest losing sequence			37	Return on stakes invested	-16.5%

1993 Form	16-217	7.4%	-104.34	1991 Form	20-186	10.8%	- 7.96
1992 Form	14-137	10.2%	- 34.97	1990 Form	15-171	8.8%	- 47.67

S C WILLIAMS (Newmarket)

	No. of Horses	Races Run	1st	2nd	3rd	Unpl	Per cent	£1 Level Stake
2-y-o	3	10	0	0	0	10	-	- 10.00
3-y-o	11	72	9	11	5	47	12.5	- 22.98
4-y-o+	6	38	6	2	5	25	15.8	- 3.25
Totals	20	120	15	13	10	82	12.5	- 36.23

BY MONTH

2-y-o	W-R	Per cent	£1 Level Stake	3-y-o	W-R	Per cent	£1 Level Stake
January	0-0	-	0.00	January	0-0	-	0.00
February	0-0	-	0.00	February	0-2	-	- 2.00
March	0-0	-	0.00	March	1-3	33.3	+ 6.00
April	0-0	-	0.00	April	1-9	11.1	- 7.56
May	0-0	-	0.00	May	3-18	16.7	- 2.75
June	0-0	-	0.00	June	1-13	7.7	- 3.50
July	0-1	-	- 1.00	July	2-9	22.2	+ 0.50
August	0-2	-	- 2.00	August	0-6	-	- 6.00
September	0-2	-	- 2.00	September	0-8	-	- 8.00
Oct/Nov	0-5	-	- 5.00	Oct/Nov	1-4	25.0	+ 0.33

4-y-o+	W-R	Per cent	£1 Level Stake	Totals	W-R	Per cent	£1 Level Stake
January	0-0	-	0.00	January	0-0	-	0.00
February	0-2	-	- 2.00	February	0-4	-	- 4.00
March	0-2	-	- 2.00	March	1-5	20.0	+ 4.00
April	1-3	33.3	+ 2.50	April	2-12	16.7	- 5.06
May	2-5	40.0	+ 4.25	May	5-23	21.7	+ 1.50
June	0-4	-	- 4.00	June	1-17	5.9	- 7.50
July	1-6	16.7	+ 1.00	July	3-16	18.8	+ 0.50
August	0-3	-	- 3.00	August	0-11	-	- 11.00
September	0-6	-	- 6.00	September	0-16	-	- 16.00
Oct/Nov	2-7	28.6	+ 6.00	Oct/Nov	3-16	18.8	+ 1.33

DISTANCE

2-y-o	W-R	Per cent	£1 Level Stake	3-y-o	W-R	Per cent	£1 Level Stake
5f-6f	0-0	-	0.00	5f-6f	0-4	-	- 4.00
7f-8f	0-10	-	- 10.00	7f-8f	3-34	8.8	- 14.06
9f-13f	0-0	-	0.00	9f-13f	6-31	19.4	- 1.92
14f+	0-0	-	0.00	14f+	0-3	-	- 3.00

4-y-o+	W-R	Per cent	£1 Level Stake	Totals	W-R	Per cent	£1 Level Stake
5f-6f	3-16	18.8	+ 0.25	5f-6f	3-20	15.0	- 3.75
7f-8f	1-11	9.1	- 5.50	7f-8f	4-55	7.3	- 29.56
9f-13f	2-11	18.2	+ 2.00	9f-13f	8-42	19.0	+ 0.08
14f+	0-0	-	0.00	14f+	0-3	-	- 3.00

TYPE OF RACE

Non-Handicaps	W-R	Per cent	£1 Level Stake	Handicaps	W-R	Per cent	£1 Level Stake
2-y-o	0-4	-	- 4.00	2-y-o	0-0	-	0.00
3-y-o	6-36	16.7	- 5.81	3-y-o	3-33	9.1	- 14.17
4-y-o+	2-6	33.3	+ 3.25	4-y-o+	4-30	13.3	- 4.50
Selling	0-5	-	- 5.00	Selling	0-1	-	- 1.00
Apprentice	0-1	-	- 1.00	Apprentice	0-4	-	- 4.00
Amat/Ladies	0-0	-	0.00	Amat/Ladies	0-0	-	0.00
Totals	8-52	15.4	- 12.56	Totals	7-68	10.3	- 23.67

COURSE GRADE

	W-R	Per cent	£1 Level Stake
Group 1	0-26	-	- 26.00
Group 2	1-22	4.5	- 16.50
Group 3	3-30	10.0	- 14.00
Group 4	11-42	26.2	+ 20.27

FIRST TIME OUT

	W-R	Per cent	£1 Level Stake
2-y-o	0-3	-	- 3.00
3-y-o	1-10	10.0	- 7.25
4-y-o+	0-4	-	- 4.00
Totals	1-17	5.9	- 14.25

JOCKEYS RIDING

	W-R	Per cent	£1 Level Stake		W-R	Per cent	£1 Level Stake
K Darley	5-19	26.3	+ 17.00	L Aspell	1-1	100.0	+ 2.25
A Munro	2-8	25.0	- 1.06	J Carroll	1-2	50.0	+ 0.75
G Hind	2-9	22.2	+ 2.50	B Thomson	1-5	20.0	+ 1.00
J Tate	2-15	13.3	- 2.00	P McCabe	1-16	6.3	- 11.67

A Mackay	0-6	S Sanders	0-2	J Quinn	0-1
K Fallon	0-4	W R Swinburn	0-2	S Maloney	0-1
J Weaver	0-3	A Culhane	0-1	S Mulvey	0-1
L Dettori	0-3	A Whelan	0-1	Stephen Davies	0-1
M Fenton	0-3	C Hodgson	0-1	T Quinn	0-1
D Harrison	0-2	G Bardwell	0-1	W Ryan	0-1
K Rutter	0-2	G Carter	0-1	W Woods	0-1
M Wigham	0-2	G Duffield	0-1		
R Cochrane	0-2	J Fortune	0-1		

COURSE RECORD

	Total W-R	Non-Handicaps 2-y-o	3-y-o+	Handicaps 2-y-o	3-y-o+	Per cent	£1 Level Stake
Edinburgh	3-6	0-0	1-2	0-0	2-4	50.0	+ 11.25
Catterick	2-4	0-1	1-2	0-0	1-1	50.0	+ 7.25
Pontefract	2-5	0-0	1-3	0-0	1-2	40.0	+ 6.50
Lingfield (AW)	2-5	0-0	2-5	0-0	0-0	40.0	+ 5.44
Folkestone	2-6	0-1	1-2	0-0	1-3	33.3	+ 6.33
Warwick	1-1	0-0	1-1	0-0	0-0	100.0	+ 5.00
Hamilton	1-3	0-0	1-2	0-0	0-1	33.3	+ 1.50
Thirsk	1-5	0-1	0-2	0-0	1-2	20.0	+ 0.50
Wolverhampton (AW)	1-13	0-1	0-3	0-0	1-9	7.7	- 8.00

Newmarket	0-12	Bath	0-2	Doncaster	0-1
Ripon	0-6	Brighton	0-2	Epsom	0-1
Nottingham	0-5	Carlisle	0-2	Lingfield	0-1
Redcar	0-5	Goodwood	0-2	Newbury	0-1
Southwell (AW)	0-5	Haydock	0-2	Newcastle	0-1
Yarmouth	0-5	Kempton	0-2	Sandown	0-1
Beverley	0-4	York	0-2	Windsor	0-1
Leicester	0-4	Ayr	0-1		
Salisbury	0-3	Chepstow	0-1		

WINNING HORSES

	Age	Races Run	1st	2nd	3rd	Unpl	Win £
Jato	5	15	3	2	2	8	10,570
Greenback	3	11	3	0	1	7	7,684
Francia	4	7	2	0	1	4	7,556
Phylian	3	7	2	0	0	5	5,100
Wonderful Day	3	6	1	0	0	5	3,366
Barti-Ddu	3	11	1	3	1	6	2,857
Eager Deva	7	6	1	0	1	4	2,807
Flamingo Times	3	5	1	0	0	4	2,504
Environmentalist	3	6	1	1	0	4	2,243

WINNING OWNERS

	Races Won	Value £		Races Won	Value £
Mrs Marion E Southcott	5	15,670	Patrick Veitch	1	2,807
D A Shekells	2	7,556	Patrick McGlone	1	2,504
Mrs V Vilain	2	5,217	Mrs L J Ward	1	2,467
Maurice Kirby	1	3,366	Ron Dawson	1	2,243
Miss L J Ward	1	2,857			

Favourites	5-8	62.5%	+ 8.77	Total winning prize-money		£44,687
Longest winning sequence			2	Average SP of winner		4.6/1
Longest losing sequence			36	Return on stakes invested		-30.2%

MRS S D WILLIAMS (South Molton, Devon)

	No. of Horses	Races Run	1st	2nd	3rd	Unpl	Per cent	£1 Level Stake
2-y-o	0	0	0	0	0	0	-	0.00
3-y-o	0	0	0	0	0	0	-	0.00
4-y-o+	3	19	1	2	4	12	5.3	- 11.00
Totals	3	19	1	2	4	12	5.3	- 11.00

Jan	Feb	Mar	Apr	May	Jun	Jul	Aug	Sep	Oct/Nov
0-2	0-1	0-2	0-2	0-3	0-1	1-4	0-3	0-1	0-0

Winning Jockey	W-R	£1 Level Stake	Winning Course	W-R	£1 Level Stake
T G McLaughlin	1-4	+ 4.00	Chepstow	1-2	+ 6.00

Winning Horse	Age	Races Run	1st	2nd	3rd	Unpl	Win £
Young Duke	6	9	1	1	1	6	3,058

Favourites	0-1		Total winning prize-money	£3,058
1993 Form	1-25	4.0%	- 21.00	

D A WILSON (Epsom, Surrey)

	No. of Horses	Races Run	1st	2nd	3rd	Unpl	Per cent	£1 Level Stake
2-y-o	3	8	0	0	0	8	-	- 8.00
3-y-o	4	30	2	2	2	24	6.7	- 11.75
4-y-o+	10	75	5	12	1	57	6.7	- 42.35
Totals	17	113	7	14	3	89	6.2	- 62.10

Jan	Feb	Mar	Apr	May	Jun	Jul	Aug	Sep	Oct/Nov
0-13	0-5	2-7	0-7	1-11	3-24	0-14	0-17	1-11	0-4

Winning Jockeys	W-R	£1 Level Stake			W-R	£1 Level Stake
R Cochrane	1-1	+ 7.50	B Thomson		1-7	- 0.50
D Harrison	1-2	+ 5.65	G Carter		1-15	- 9.50
T Williams	1-2	+ 2.50	N Gwilliams		1-18	- 3.00
Mr T Cuff	1-2	+ 1.25				

Winning Courses					
Epsom	2-11	+ 12.50	Lingfield (AW)	2-23	- 10.85
Salisbury	2-11	- 2.25	Lingfield	1-4	+ 2.50

Winning Horses	Age	Races Run	1st	2nd	3rd	Unpl	Win £
Neither Nor	5	10	2	0	0	8	18,018
Nordance Prince	3	7	2	2	2	1	13,785
Medland	4	14	2	4	0	8	4,581
Nobby Barnes	5	14	1	2	0	11	3,072

Favourites	2-12	16.7%	- 4.25	Total winning prize-money		£39,455
1993 Form	25-206	12.1%	- 30.75	1991 Form	11-177	6.2%	- 90.00
1992 Form	10-156	6.4%	- 79.25	1990 Form	19-197	9.6%	- 83.54

MISS S J WILTON (Stoke-on-Trent, Staffs)

	No. of Horses	Races Run	1st	2nd	3rd	Unpl	Per cent	£1 Level Stake
2-y-o	1	2	0	0	0	2	-	- 2.00
3-y-o	0	0	0	0	0	0	-	0.00
4-y-o+	6	25	3	2	3	17	12.0	+ 10.50
Totals	7	27	3	2	3	19	11.1	+ 8.50

Jan	Feb	Mar	Apr	May	Jun	Jul	Aug	Sep	Oct/Nov
0-2	0-1	0-4	1-4	0-6	1-5	1-1	0-1	0-3	0-0

Winning Jockeys	W-R	£1 Level Stake		W-R	£1 Level Stake
A Mackay	2-4	+ 5.50	J Lowe	1-10	+ 16.00

Winning Course		
Wolverhampton (AW)	3-14	+ 21.50

Winning Horse	Age	Races Run	1st	2nd	3rd	Unpl	Win £
Ivan The Terrible	6	10	3	1	1	5	10,622

Favourites	0-1	Total winning prize-money		£10,622
1993 Form	0-11	1991 Form	1-18	5.6%	- 16.20
1992 Form	0-18	1990 Form	0-7	

S WOODMAN (East Lavant, W Sussex)

	No. of Horses	Races Run	1st	2nd	3rd	Unpl	Per cent	£1 Level Stake
2-y-o	0	0	0	0	0	0	-	0.00
3-y-o	0	0	0	0	0	0	-	0.00
4-y-o+	4	15	1	3	1	10	6.7	- 7.00
Totals	4	15	1	3	1	10	6.7	- 7.00

Jan	Feb	Mar	Apr	May	Jun	Jul	Aug	Sep	Oct/Nov
0-0	0-0	0-0	0-2	0-0	0-2	0-4	0-3	0-2	1-2

Winning Jockey	W-R	£1 Level Stake	Winning Course	W-R	£1 Level Stake
M Fenton	1-1	+ 7.00	Folkestone	1-3	+ 5.00

Winning Horse	Age	Races Run	1st	2nd	3rd	Unpl	Win £
By Arrangement	5	9	1	3	1	4	2,381

Favourites	0-0	Total winning prize-money	£2,381

1993 Form	0-11	1991 Form	0-2
1992 Form	0-7	1990 Form	0-15

S P C WOODS (Newmarket)

	No. of Horses	Races Run	1st	2nd	3rd	Unpl	Per cent	£1 Level Stake
2-y-o	6	25	2	7	6	10	8.0	- 6.33
3-y-o	7	44	4	6	6	28	9.1	- 31.99
4-y-o+	5	43	6	12	3	22	14.0	- 2.87
Totals	18	112	12	25	15	60	10.7	- 41.19

BY MONTH

2-y-o	W-R	Per cent	£1 Level Stake	3-y-o	W-R	Per cent	£1 Level Stake
January	0-0	-	0.00	January	0-0	-	0.00
February	0-0	-	0.00	February	0-0	-	0.00
March	0-0	-	0.00	March	0-0	-	0.00
April	0-2	-	- 2.00	April	1-7	14.3	- 4.12
May	0-1	-	- 1.00	May	1-5	20.0	- 2.00
June	1-5	20.0	+ 12.00	June	0-8	-	- 8.00
July	0-4	-	- 4.00	July	0-7	-	- 7.00
August	0-6	-	- 6.00	August	0-5	-	- 5.00
September	1-4	25.0	- 2.33	September	0-6	-	- 6.00
Oct/Nov	0-3	-	- 3.00	Oct/Nov	2-6	33.3	+ 0.13

4-y-o+	W–R	Per cent	£1 Level Stake	Totals	W–R	Per cent	£1 Level Stake
January	1-6	16.7	0.00	January	1-6	16.7	0.00
February	0-4	–	– 4.00	February	0-4	–	– 4.00
March	0-3	–	– 3.00	March	0-3	–	– 3.00
April	1-4	25.0	+ 13.00	April	2-13	15.4	+ 6.88
May	0-2	–	– 2.00	May	1-8	12.5	– 5.00
June	1-5	20.0	– 2.25	June	2-18	11.1	+ 1.75
July	2-6	33.3	+ 5.50	July	2-17	11.8	– 5.50
August	0-5	–	– 5.00	August	0-16	–	– 16.00
September	1-3	33.3	– 0.12	September	2-13	15.4	– 8.45
Oct/Nov	0-5	–	– 5.00	Oct/Nov	2-14	14.3	– 7.87

DISTANCE

2-y-o	W–R	Per cent	£1 Level Stake	3-y-o	W–R	Per cent	£1 Level Stake
5f-6f	1-15	6.7	+ 2.00	5f-6f	0-0	–	0.00
7f-8f	1-10	10.0	– 8.33	7f-8f	1-18	5.6	– 15.12
9f-13f	0-0	–	0.00	9f-13f	1-19	5.3	– 16.00
14f+	0-0	–	0.00	14f+	2-7	28.6	– 0.87

4-y-o+	W–R	Per cent	£1 Level Stake	Totals	W–R	Per cent	£1 Level Stake
5f-6f	0-1	–	– 1.00	5f-6f	1-16	6.3	+ 1.00
7f-8f	2-18	11.1	– 9.25	7f-8f	4-46	8.7	– 32.70
9f-13f	1-11	9.1	– 8.12	9f-13f	2-30	6.7	– 24.12
14f+	3-13	23.1	+ 15.50	14f+	5-20	25.0	+ 14.63

TYPE OF RACE

Non-Handicaps	W–R	Per cent	£1 Level Stake	Handicaps	W–R	Per cent	£1 Level Stake
2-y-o	2-20	10.0	– 1.33	2-y-o	0-5	–	– 5.00
3-y-o	3-28	10.7	– 19.74	3-y-o	1-12	8.3	– 8.25
4-y-o+	3-21	14.3	– 9.37	4-y-o+	2-17	11.8	+ 4.50
Selling	0-4	–	– 4.00	Selling	0-2	–	– 2.00
Apprentice	0-0	–	0.00	Apprentice	0-1	–	– 1.00
Amat/Ladies	0-0	–	0.00	Amat/Ladies	1-2	50.0	+ 5.00
Totals	8-73	11.0	– 34.44	Totals	4-39	10.3	– 6.75

COURSE GRADE

	W–R	Per cent	£1 Level Stake
Group 1	5-43	11.6	– 24.11
Group 2	2-12	16.7	+ 8.00
Group 3	0-23	–	– 23.00
Group 4	5-34	14.7	– 2.08

FIRST TIME OUT

	W–R	Per cent	£1 Level Stake
2-y-o	1-6	16.7	+ 11.00
3-y-o	0-7	–	– 7.00
4-y-o+	1-5	20.0	+ 1.00
Totals	2-18	11.1	+ 5.00

451

Woods S P C

	W-R	Per cent	£1 Level Stake			W-R	Per cent	£1 Level Stake
W Woods	10-84	11.9	- 37.19	D Biggs		1-8	12.5	+ 9.00
Miss L Hide	1-1	100.0	+ 6.00					

G Duffield	0-3	D Wright	0-1	Mr D McCain	0-1
A Clark	0-2	J Quinn	0-1	N Carlisle	0-1
N Varley	0-2	K Rutter	0-1	W Newnes	0-1
V Smith	0-2	M Fenton	0-1	W Ryan	0-1
C Webb	0-1	M Tebbutt	0-1		

COURSE RECORD

	Total W-R	Non-Handicaps 2-y-o	3-y-o+	Handicaps 2-y-o	3-y-o+	Per cent	£1 Level Stake
Doncaster	2-5	0-2	1-1	0-0	1-2	40.0	+ 4.38
Southwell (AW)	2-17	1-3	1-10	0-0	0-4	11.8	- 9.33
Haydock	1-1	0-0	1-1	0-0	0-0	100.0	+ 1.88
Salisbury	1-1	1-1	0-0	0-0	0-0	100.0	+ 16.00
Newbury	1-3	0-0	1-3	0-0	0-0	33.3	- 0.12
Warwick	1-3	0-0	0-1	0-0	1-2	33.3	+ 1.50
Folkestone	1-5	0-1	0-1	0-0	1-3	20.0	+ 12.00
Lingfield (AW)	1-6	0-0	1-6	0-0	0-0	16.7	- 3.25
Brighton	1-7	0-0	1-7	0-0	0-0	14.3	- 4.00
Newmarket	1-19	0-3	0-5	0-4	1-7	5.3	- 15.25

Yarmouth	0-11	Wolverhampton (AW)	0-3	Lingfield	0-1
Leicester	0-5	York	0-3	Newcastle	0-1
Sandown	0-4	Epsom	0-2	Redcar	0-1
Goodwood	0-3	Ascot	0-1	Ripon	0-1
Nottingham	0-3	Ayr	0-1	Thirsk	0-1
Pontefract	0-3	Beverley	0-1		

WINNING HORSES

	Age	Races Run	1st	2nd	3rd	Unpl	Win £
Trans Siberia	3	6	2	3	1	0	9,877
Marathia	4	20	3	6	2	9	9,104
Mistle Cat	4	4	1	1	0	2	5,274
Pearl Venture	2	5	1	0	2	2	3,778
Rad	4	10	1	2	0	7	3,688
Phoenix Venture	3	6	1	1	1	3	3,649
Shanghai Venture	3	8	1	1	1	5	3,342
Pierre Bosco	2	9	1	4	0	4	2,838
Spanish Storm	5	7	1	3	0	3	2,577

WINNING OWNERS

	Races Won	Value £		Races Won	Value £
S P C Woods	4	12,791	The Storm Syndicate	2	5,415
Dr Frank S B Chao	3	10,769	P K Chu	1	5,274
H Laska	2	9,877			

Favourites	7-19	36.8%	+ 1.81	Total winning prize-money	£44,126
Longest winning sequence			2	Average SP of winner	4.9/1
Longest losing sequence			23	Return on stakes invested	-36.8%
1993 Form	9-143	6.3%	- 82.92	1992 Form 10-83 12.0%	+ 15.50

G WRAGG (Newmarket)

	No. of Horses	Races Run	1st	2nd	3rd	Unpl	Per cent	£1 Level Stake
2-y-o	16	46	8	7	9	22	17.4	- 6.46
3-y-o	23	102	16	13	10	63	15.7	+ 6.38
4-y-o+	7	34	8	5	11	10	23.5	+ 22.00
Totals	46	182	32	25	30	95	17.6	+ 21.92

BY MONTH

2-y-o	W-R	Per cent	£1 Level Stake	3-y-o	W-R	Per cent	£1 Level Stake
January	0-0	-	0.00	January	0-0	-	0.00
February	0-0	-	0.00	February	0-0	-	0.00
March	0-0	-	0.00	March	0-1	-	- 1.00
April	0-0	-	0.00	April	0-18	-	- 18.00
May	0-0	-	0.00	May	3-11	27.3	+ 8.00
June	1-4	25.0	- 1.00	June	4-23	17.4	- 7.50
July	3-13	23.1	+ 2.63	July	3-11	27.3	- 1.37
August	2-13	15.4	- 4.09	August	2-10	20.0	+ 16.00
September	2-8	25.0	+ 4.00	September	4-19	21.1	+ 19.25
Oct/Nov	0-8	-	- 8.00	Oct/Nov	0-9	-	- 9.00

4-y-o+	W-R	Per cent	£1 Level Stake	Totals	W-R	Per cent	£1 Level Stake
January	0-0	-	0.00	January	0-0	-	0.00
February	0-0	-	0.00	February	0-0	-	0.00
March	1-2	50.0	+ 2.50	March	1-3	33.3	+ 1.50
April	0-4	-	- 4.00	April	0-22	-	- 22.00
May	0-4	-	- 4.00	May	3-15	20.0	+ 4.00
June	3-8	37.5	+ 20.50	June	8-35	22.9	+ 12.00
July	1-6	16.7	+ 7.00	July	7-30	23.3	+ 8.26
August	2-2	100.0	+ 3.50	August	6-25	24.0	+ 15.41
September	1-6	16.7	- 1.50	September	7-33	21.2	+ 21.75
Oct/Nov	0-2	-	- 2.00	Oct/Nov	0-19	-	- 19.00

DISTANCE

2-y-o	W–R	Per cent	£1 Level Stake	3-y-o	W–R	Per cent	£1 Level Stake
5f-6f	6-25	24.0	+ 4.54	5f-6f	3-6	50.0	+ 8.00
7f-8f	2-21	9.5	- 11.00	7f-8f	6-44	13.6	+ 0.63
9f-13f	0-0	-	0.00	9f-13f	5-46	10.9	- 4.25
14f+	0-0	-	0.00	14f+	2-6	33.3	+ 2.00

4-y-o+	W–R	Per cent	£1 Level Stake	Totals	W–R	Per cent	£1 Level Stake
5f-6f	0-0	-	0.00	5f-6f	9-31	29.0	+ 12.54
7f-8f	0-9	-	- 9.00	7f-8f	8-74	10.8	- 19.37
9f-13f	6-20	30.0	+ 10.50	9f-13f	11-66	16.7	+ 6.25
14f+	2-5	40.0	+ 20.50	14f+	4-11	36.4	+ 22.50

TYPE OF RACE

Non-Handicaps	W–R	Per cent	£1 Level Stake	Handicaps	W–R	Per cent	£1 Level Stake
2-y-o	8-45	17.8	- 5.46	2-y-o	0-1	-	- 1.00
3-y-o	11-63	17.5	+ 13.13	3-y-o	5-38	13.2	- 5.75
4-y-o+	7-28	25.0	+ 26.83	4-y-o+	0-4	-	- 4.00
Selling	0-0	-	0.00	Selling	0-0	-	0.00
Apprentice	0-0	-	0.00	Apprentice	0-1	-	- 1.00
Amat/Ladies	1-2	50.0	- 0.83	Amat/Ladies	0-0	-	0.00
Totals	27-138	19.6	+ 33.67	Totals	5-44	11.4	- 11.75

COURSE GRADE

	W–R	Per cent	£1 Level Stake
Group 1	17-97	17.5	+ 26.21
Group 2	1-19	5.3	- 15.25
Group 3	9-56	16.1	- 8.29
Group 4	5-10	50.0	+ 19.25

FIRST TIME OUT

	W–R	Per cent	£1 Level Stake
2-y-o	0-16	-	- 16.00
3-y-o	2-23	8.7	- 13.75
4-y-o+	2-7	28.6	+ 3.50
Totals	4-46	8.7	- 26.25

JOCKEYS RIDING

	W–R	Per cent	£1 Level Stake		W–R	Per cent	£1 Level Stake
M Hills	16-93	17.2	+ 26.04	W Ryan	1-2	50.0	+ 5.50
P Robinson	3-7	42.9	+ 9.25	D Holland	1-2	50.0	+ 19.00
Paul Eddery	3-24	12.5	- 12.42	R Cochrane	1-2	50.0	- 0.50
F Norton	2-24	8.3	- 16.00	M J Kinane	1-2	50.0	+ 0.38
J Carroll	1-1	100.0	+ 3.00	Miss A Harwood	1-2	50.0	- 0.83
L Dettori	1-2	50.0	+ 2.50	R Hills	1-4	25.0	+ 3.00

G Duffield	0-3	D Gibbs	0-1	M Birch	0-1
Pat Eddery	0-3	G Carter	0-1	W Newnes	0-1
B Raymond	0-1	J Fortune	0-1	W Woods	0-1
B Thomson	0-1	J Weaver	0-1		
C Asmussen	0-1	K Darley	0-1		

COURSE RECORD

	Total W-R	Non-Handicaps 2-y-o	3-y-o+	Handicaps 2-y-o	3-y-o+	Per cent	£1 Level Stake
Kempton	3-8	1-1	2-7	0-0	0-0	37.5	+ 12.50
Doncaster	3-13	0-2	3-7	0-0	0-4	23.1	+ 5.00
Yarmouth	3-20	1-7	2-8	0-0	0-5	15.0	- 11.62
Newmarket	3-23	2-13	1-9	0-0	0-1	13.0	- 13.37
Wolverhampton (AW)	2-3	0-0	1-1	0-0	1-2	66.7	+ 15.50
Windsor	2-6	1-1	1-4	0-0	0-1	33.3	+ 8.33
York	2-6	1-3	1-2	0-0	0-1	33.3	+ 6.00
Nottingham	2-7	1-3	0-3	0-0	1-1	28.6	+ 3.00
Sandown	2-7	0-0	2-6	0-0	0-1	28.6	+ 15.17
Ascot	2-14	0-3	2-9	0-0	0-2	14.3	+ 12.00
Hamilton	1-1	0-0	0-0	0-0	1-1	100.0	+ 3.00
Lingfield (AW)	1-1	0-0	1-1	0-0	0-0	100.0	+ 3.50
Edinburgh	1-2	0-0	0-1	0-0	1-1	50.0	+ 1.00
Salisbury	1-2	0-0	1-1	0-0	0-1	50.0	+ 1.75
Southwell (AW)	1-2	0-0	0-0	0-0	1-2	50.0	+ 1.25
Ayr	1-3	0-0	1-1	0-0	0-2	33.3	+ 10.00
Newbury	1-7	1-4	0-3	0-0	0-0	14.3	- 5.09
Leicester	1-9	0-2	1-5	0-0	0-2	11.1	+ 2.00

Goodwood	0-8	Beverley	0-3	Ripon	0-2
Haydock	0-7	Chepstow	0-3	Carlisle	0-1
Pontefract	0-7	Redcar	0-3	Newcastle	0-1
Chester	0-4	Brighton	0-2	Warwick	0-1
Thirsk	0-4	Lingfield	0-2		

WINNING HORSES

	Age	Races Run	1st	2nd	3rd	Unpl	Win £
Owington	3	5	3	0	1	1	143,342
Arcadian Heights	6	5	2	0	2	1	133,334
Young Buster	6	6	2	1	2	1	28,723
Beneficial	4	6	1	0	1	4	22,494
Ingozi	3	7	2	1	0	4	15,114
Baltic Raider	2	4	2	1	0	1	9,078
So Sedulous	3	4	2	1	1	0	8,474
Lalindi	3	10	2	1	1	6	6,701
Rainbow Walk	4	4	2	0	1	1	6,283
Chez Catalan	3	8	2	1	2	3	5,777
Pentire	2	5	1	0	3	1	5,152
Jumilla	2	5	1	2	1	1	5,068
Iblis	2	5	1	1	1	2	5,068
Dr Edgar	2	3	1	0	0	2	4,407
Sadler's Walk	3	3	1	0	0	2	4,150
Alusha	2	2	1	1	0	0	4,012
Stylish Ways	2	3	1	0	1	1	3,793
Red October	3	3	1	2	0	0	3,723
Dreams	3	5	1	0	0	4	3,596
Blue Lion	4	8	1	3	3	1	3,551
Norma's Lady	3	7	1	1	3	2	3,496
Conic Hill	3	6	1	1	1	3	2,777

WINNING OWNERS

	Races Won	Value £		Races Won	Value £
Baron G Von Ullmann	3	143,342	A E Oppenheimer	2	15,114
J L C Pearce	4	139,111	Mrs Nicola Bscher	3	13,542
Mollers Racing	5	41,163	Sheikh Mohammed	1	5,068
Sir Philip Oppenheimer	11	41,129	Mrs Nigel Elwes	1	3,596
Exors Of The Late			Sheikh Ahmed Bin Saeed		
Sir Robin McAlpine	1	22,494	Al Maktoum	1	3,551

Favourites	13-35	37.1%	+ 5.92	Total winning prize-money	£428,111
Longest winning sequence			3	Average SP of winner	5.4/1
Longest losing sequence			24	Return on stakes invested	12.0%
1993 Form	35-202	17.3%	- 25.64	1991 Form	51-220	23.2%	+ 27.73
1992 Form	45-214	21.0%	- 33.35	1990 Form	32-224	14.3%	+ 0.57

TRAINERS WITH NO WINNERS 1994

	No. of Horses	Races Run	2nd	3rd	Unpl
R Allan	6	20	0	0	20
P Asquith	1	1	0	0	1
N M Babbage	1	1	0	0	1
K C Bailey	1	1	0	1	0
J Balding	11	57	2	5	50
G Barnett	7	20	0	2	18
M F Barraclough	4	11	0	0	11
L J Barratt	7	34	3	2	29
A Barrow	4	12	0	0	12
C R Barwell	1	7	0	0	7
B P J Baugh	6	23	0	0	23
P Beaumont	1	2	0	0	2
J A Bennett	6	36	3	4	29
M Bielby	5	19	0	2	17
T T Bill	2	3	0	0	3
J J Birkett	1	2	0	0	2
K Bishop	9	28	1	4	23
P A Blockley	3	11	0	0	11
J R Bostock	5	12	0	2	10
Mrs S C Bradburne	10	25	0	1	24
Mrs S Bramall	2	2	0	0	2
K S Bridgwater	10	16	0	0	16
R Brotherton	10	26	1	2	23
R H Buckler	4	11	0	1	10
E T Buckley	1	1	0	0	1
I Campbell	11	27	3	0	24
Mark Campion	12	55	4	5	46
S W Campion	2	3	0	0	3
T Casey	3	8	0	0	8
R Champion	5	13	0	0	13
M J Charles	4	16	1	0	15
G F H Charles-Jones	1	4	0	0	4

	No. of Horses	Races Run	2nd	3rd	Unpl
P C Clarke	1	2	0	0	2
W Clay	4	7	0	0	7
T T Clement	9	25	0	0	25
S Coathup	8	30	0	0	30
W S Cunningham	2	4	0	0	4
R Curtis	12	53	3	1	49
T A K Cuthbert	2	5	0	0	5
P T Dalton	4	24	2	3	19
B De Haan	1	1	0	0	1
J Dooler	6	23	0	0	23
C J Drewe	4	17	0	1	16
M W Eckley	6	21	0	1	20
D Eddy	2	5	0	0	5
J A C Edwards	1	2	0	0	2
M W Ellerby	5	24	1	4	19
G P Enright	5	23	0	0	23
T J Etherington	5	6	1	2	3
T Fairhurst	2	2	0	0	2
J Ffitch-Heyes	13	44	1	3	40
G Fierro	10	21	0	1	20
A G Foster	18	50	3	4	43
R G Frost	2	2	0	0	2
D T Garraton	1	7	0	1	6
T R George	4	6	0	0	6
J S Haldane	2	2	0	0	2
G A Ham	3	8	0	0	8
A A Hambly	2	4	2	0	2
C J Hemsley	7	27	0	0	27
N J Henderson	1	1	0	0	1
R P C Hoad	9	28	0	1	27
H S Howe	1	4	0	0	4
A P James	6	18	0	1	17
Mrs A E Jermy	3	11	0	0	11
Mrs L C Jewell	4	14	0	1	13
J H Johnson	1	1	0	0	1
A W Jones	4	13	1	1	11
G H Jones	1	3	0	0	3
P J Jones	2	4	0	0	4
F Jordan	10	40	1	4	35
Mrs J Jordan	4	11	0	0	11
R T Juckes	7	19	1	1	17
G P Kelly	5	17	1	2	14
D W Kent	5	10	2	3	5
T Kersey	4	20	0	1	19
Miss H C Knight	3	9	2	2	5
S G Knight	4	15	0	4	11
R Lamb	2	4	0	0	4
M R Leach	4	9	0	0	9
N P Littmoden	7	19	1	1	17
L R Lloyd-James	7	27	3	1	23
Mrs M E Long	4	8	0	0	8
C J Mann	3	5	0	0	5
R Manning	1	4	0	0	4
R F Marvin	2	10	1	0	9
D McCain	4	19	1	0	18
J C McConnochie	1	1	0	0	1

	No. of Horses	Races Run	2nd	3rd	Unpl
T P McGovern	5	13	0	0	13
R M McKellar	4	7	0	0	7
M G Meagher	10	39	1	2	36
Miss M K Milligan	1	1	0	0	1
N R Mitchell	3	9	0	0	9
J Mooney	4	22	0	0	22
K A Morgan	4	12	0	1	11
J W Mullins	2	9	0	0	9
F Murphy	6	18	0	2	16
Mrs A M Naughton	5	14	1	0	13
D A Nolan	7	31	0	2	29
R O'Leary	1	2	0	0	2
F O'Mahony	4	11	1	2	8
J A B Old	5	5	0	0	5
E H Owen	1	1	0	0	1
Mrs H Parrott	1	1	0	0	1
J Peacock	5	11	0	1	10
R E Peacock	8	33	0	0	33
A W Potts	8	24	1	0	23
P A Pritchard	3	5	0	0	5
R Rowe	7	11	0	1	10
O Sherwood	1	2	0	0	2
S Sherwood	3	4	0	0	4
J P Smith	4	11	1	0	10
N A Smith	3	14	2	0	12
Mrs S J Smith	4	9	2	1	6
R C Spicer	21	86	1	2	83
B Stevens	1	1	0	0	1
M Tate	3	6	0	0	6
T P Tate	1	2	0	1	1
R Thompson	9	24	1	0	23
Ronald Thompson	9	27	2	1	24
V Thompson	3	8	0	0	8
N B Thomson	1	1	0	0	1
G Thorner	2	4	0	0	4
A Turnell	1	13	1	2	10
W G Turner	1	1	0	0	1
N A Twiston-Davies	4	10	0	1	9
R J Weaver	11	24	0	2	22
J Webber	1	3	0	0	3
C Weedon	5	11	0	0	11
Capt J Wilson	15	62	4	4	54
K G Wingrove	8	32	0	2	30
D J Wintle	2	12	1	0	11
R D E Woodhouse	2	5	0	0	5
F J Yardley	2	17	2	1	14
G H Yardley	1	1	0	0	1

WINNING OVERSEAS TRAINERS 1994

A FABRE (France)

	No. of Horses	Races Run	1st	2nd	3rd	Unpl	Per cent	£1 Level Stake
2-y-o	1	1	1	0	0	0	100.0	+ 2.50
3-y-o	4	4	0	0	0	4	-	- 4.00
4-y-o+	6	8	2	1	0	5	25.0	+ 14.00
Totals	11	13	3	1	0	9	23.1	+ 12.50

Jan	Feb	Mar	Apr	May	Jun	Jul	Aug	Sep	Oct/Nov
0-0	0-0	0-0	0-3	0-0	1-6	0-1	0-0	0-1	2-2

Winning Jockeys	W-R	£1 Level Stake			W-R	£1 Level Stake
T Jarnet	2-5	+ 11.50	S Guillot		1-1	+ 8.00

Winning Courses						
Newmarket	2-5	+ 7.50	Epsom		1-4	+ 9.00

Winning Horses	Age	Races Run	1st	2nd	3rd	Unpl	Win £
Dernier Empereur	4	1	1	0	0	0	165,948
Pennekamp	2	1	1	0	0	0	96,585
Apple Tree	5	3	1	1	0	1	91,950

Favourites	1-3	33.3%	+ 0.50	Total winning prize-money		£354,483

1993 Form	3-15	20.0%	- 3.17	1991 Form	5-12	41.7%	+ 15.94
1992 Form	4-20	20.0%	- 3.54	1990 Form	2-7	28.6%	- 1.49

H IBRAHIM (Dubai)

	No. of Horses	Races Run	1st	2nd	3rd	Unpl	Per cent	£1 Level Stake
2-y-o	0	0	0	0	0	0	-	0.00
3-y-o	4	6	2	1	1	2	33.3	+ 10.00
4-y-o+	7	12	1	2	0	9	8.3	- 6.50
Totals	11	18	3	3	1	11	16.7	+ 3.50

Jan	Feb	Mar	Apr	May	Jun	Jul	Aug	Sep	Oct/Nov
0-0	0-0	0-0	1-8	0-1	1-6	1-3	0-0	0-0	0-0

Winning Jockeys	W-R	£1 Level Stake			W-R	£1 Level Stake
Pat Eddery	1-1	+ 8.00	L Dettori		1-5	+ 2.00
G Hind	1-2	+ 3.50				

Winning Courses						
Epsom	1-2	+ 5.00	Newmarket		1-8	+ 1.00
York	1-3	+ 2.50				

Winning Horses	Age	Races Run	1st	2nd	3rd	Unpl	Win £
Balanchine	3	2	1	1	0	0	147,500
Cezanne	5	2	1	0	0	1	36,390
Seismograph	3	2	1	0	0	1	5,390

Favourites	0-3			Total winning prize-money			£189,280

M KAUNTZE (Ireland)

	No. of Horses	Races Run	1st	2nd	3rd	Unpl	Per cent	£1 Level Stake
2-y-o	1	1	0	0	1	0	-	- 1.00
3-y-o	2	3	0	0	0	3	-	- 3.00
4-y-o+	3	8	2	1	0	5	25.0	- 4.81
Totals	6	12	2	1	1	8	16.7	- 8.81

Jan	Feb	Mar	Apr	May	Jun	Jul	Aug	Sep	Oct/Nov
0-0	0-0	0-0	0-0	1-3	0-5	1-1	0-2	0-0	0-1

Winning Jockeys	W-R	£1 Level Stake			W-R	£1 Level Stake
J Williams	1-1	+ 0.36	L Dettori		1-1	+ 0.83

Winning Courses						
Chepstow	1-1	+ 0.83	Lingfield		1-2	- 0.64

Winning Horses	Age	Races Run	1st	2nd	3rd	Unpl	Win £
Shrewd Idea	4	2	1	1	0	0	8,149
Royal Ballerina	4	4	1	0	0	3	6,207

Favourites	2-2	100.0%	+ 1.19	Total winning prize-money		£14,356

1993 Form	0-5			1991 Form	1-3	33.3%	+ 1.00
1992 Form	1-7	14.3%	- 2.50	1990 Form	2-3	66.7%	+ 7.25

A SMITH (Belgium)

	No. of Horses	Races Run	1st	2nd	3rd	Unpl	Per cent	£1 Level Stake
2-y-o	1	1	0	0	0	1	-	- 1.00
3-y-o	2	8	1	0	0	7	12.5	+ 7.00
4-y-o+	4	23	0	4	1	18	-	- 23.00
Totals	7	32	1	4	1	26	3.1	- 17.00

Jan	Feb	Mar	Apr	May	Jun	Jul	Aug	Sep	Oct/Nov
0-12	1-10	0-6	0-0	0-2	0-2	0-0	0-0	0-0	0-0

Winning Jockey	W-R	£1 Level Stake	Winning Course	W-R	£1 Level Stake
L Dettori	1-5	+ 10.00	Lingfield (AW)	1-26	- 11.00

Winning Horse	Age	Races Run	1st	2nd	3rd	Unpl	Win £
Old Hook	3	5	1	0	0	4	2,400

Favourites	0-2			Total winning prize-money		£2,400

1993 Form	1-17	5.9%	+ 4.00	1991 Form	0-0	
1992 Form	0-0			1990 Form	0-5	

T STACK (Ireland)

	No. of Horses	Races Run	1st	2nd	3rd	Unpl	Per cent	£1 Level Stake
2-y-o	1	1	0	0	0	1	-	- 1.00
3-y-o	3	4	1	0	0	3	25.0	+ 9.00
4-y-o+	1	1	0	0	0	1	-	- 1.00
Totals	5	6	1	0	0	5	16.7	+ 7.00

Jan	Feb	Mar	Apr	May	Jun	Jul	Aug	Sep	Oct/Nov
0-0	0-0	0-0	1-3	0-0	0-2	0-0	0-0	0-1	0-0

Winning Jockey	W-R	£1 Level Stake	Winning Course	W-R	£1 Level Stake
J Reid	1-2	+ 11.00	Newmarket	1-3	+ 10.00

Winning Horse	Age	Races Run	1st	2nd	3rd	Unpl	Win £
Las Meninas	3	2	1	0	0	1	112,705

Favourites	0-1			Total winning prize-money		£112,705

1993 Form	1-1	100.0%	+ 11.00	1991 Form	1-5	20.0%	+ 4.00
1992 Form	0-6			1990 Form	0-4		

A VANDERHAEGHEN (Belgium)

	No. of Horses	Races Run	1st	2nd	3rd	Unpl	Per cent	£1 Level Stake
2-y-o	0	0	0	0	0	0	-	0.00
3-y-o	0	0	0	0	0	0	-	0.00
4-y-o+	3	5	1	0	0	4	20.0	- 1.25
Totals	3	5	1	0	0	4	20.0	- 1.25

Jan	Feb	Mar	Apr	May	Jun	Jul	Aug	Sep	Oct/Nov
0-0	0-0	0-0	0-0	0-0	1-4	0-0	0-1	0-0	0-0

Winning Jockey	W-R	£1 Level Stake	Winning Course	W-R	£1 Level Stake
M Servranckx	1-5	- 1.25	Lingfield	1-2	+ 1.75

Winning Horse	Age	Races Run	1st	2nd	3rd	Unpl	Win £
Myasha	5	3	1	0	0	2	3,290

Favourites	0-0			Total winning prize-money			£3,290

OVERSEAS TRAINERS WITH NO WINNERS 1994

	No. of Horses	Races Run	2nd	3rd	Unpl
J S O Arthur (Jer)	1	1	1	0	0
J S Bolger (Ire)	4	5	1	0	4
Mrs Bollack (Fra)	1	1	0	0	1
W Boniface (USA)	1	1	0	0	1
F Boutin (Fra)	4	4	1	1	2
W P Browne (Ire)	1	1	0	0	1
J Burns (Ire)	1	1	0	0	1
D Carroll (Ire)	1	1	0	0	1
R Collet (Fra)	2	2	0	1	1
C Collins (Ire)	1	1	0	0	1
N Draper (Ire)	1	1	0	0	1
P J Flynn (Ire)	1	1	0	0	1
J E Hammond (Fra)	2	2	1	0	1
Mrs C Head (Fra)	4	4	0	0	4
H Jentzsch (Ger)	1	1	0	0	1
B V Kelly (Ire)	1	1	1	0	0
E Lellouche (Fra)	1	2	0	1	1
J Lesbordes (Fra)	1	1	0	0	1
P Matthews (Ire)	1	1	0	0	1
J J McLoughlin (Ire)	1	1	0	0	1
N Meade (Ire)	1	1	0	0	1
A P O'Brien (Ire)	2	2	0	0	2
M V O'Brien (Ire)	1	1	0	0	1
P O'Leary (Ire)	1	1	0	0	1
John Oxx (Ire)	5	6	1	0	5
Paul Smith (Bel)	2	2	0	0	2
D K Weld (Ire)	7	7	1	2	4
A Woehler (Ger)	1	1	0	0	1

COURSE SECTION

ASCOT (Group 1)

Leading Trainers 1990-94

	Total W-R	Non-handicaps 2-y-o	3-y-o+	Handicaps 2-y-o	3-y-o+	Per cent	£1 Level Stake
M R Stoute	27-177	5-35	14-80	0-2	8-60	15.3	+ 0.05
J H M Gosden	23-133	4-17	12-55	0-1	7-60	17.3	- 25.66
H R A Cecil	22-99	3-19	14-61	0-0	5-19	22.2	+ 73.85
P F I Cole	20-105	11-37	5-28	0-3	4-37	19.0	+ 8.88
R Hannon	19-241	9-69	3-49	2-15	5-108	7.9	+ 44.50
L M Cumani	17-109	6-20	8-47	0-0	3-42	15.6	- 7.23
J L Dunlop	17-123	5-27	6-49	0-2	6-45	13.8	+ 13.07
G Wragg	15-74	4-15	9-41	0-0	2-18	20.3	+ 22.80
D R C Elsworth	15-120	6-21	1-34	0-3	8-62	12.5	+ 62.58
C E Brittain	15-228	3-52	5-83	2-4	5-89	6.6	- 47.50
Lord Huntingdon	13-77	0-3	6-17	0-1	7-56	16.9	+ 53.92
G Harwood	10-102	0-13	6-30	0-2	4-57	9.8	- 4.44
I A Balding	10-111	0-19	2-29	0-2	8-61	9.0	+ 14.80
H Thomson Jones	8-65	5-26	1-15	0-1	2-23	12.3	- 9.94
R Charlton	7-46	2-9	2-7	0-1	3-29	15.2	- 0.09
R Akehurst	7-62	0-0	0-5	0-1	7-56	11.3	+ 18.83
B W Hills	7-83	4-19	3-35	0-1	0-28	8.4	- 35.42
G Lewis	6-41	0-6	2-9	1-6	3-20	14.6	+ 32.63
M H Tompkins	6-41	0-4	0-3	0-0	6-34	14.6	+ 4.50
M Johnston	6-45	3-7	1-9	0-0	2-29	13.3	+ 0.92
P Chapple-Hyam	5-62	3-22	2-31	0-1	0-8	8.1	- 48.13
J Berry	5-74	3-36	0-14	0-0	2-24	6.8	- 44.75

Leading Jockeys

	Total W-R	Per cent	£1 Level Stake	Best Trainer	W-R	Per cent	£1 Level Stake
Pat Eddery	42-251	16.7	+ 35.95	M R Stoute	7-25	28.0	+ 23.86
L Dettori	32-249	12.9	- 1.25	L M Cumani	14-71	19.7	+ 14.04
W Carson	32-251	12.7	- 71.01	J L Dunlop	10-56	17.9	- 11.42
M Roberts	28-252	11.1	- 42.46	C E Brittain	9-118	7.6	- 43.50
W R Swinburn	23-199	11.6	- 30.15	M R Stoute	9-70	12.9	- 12.29
T Quinn	17-163	10.4	- 31.42	P F I Cole	10-49	20.4	+ 19.25
A Munro	16-123	13.0	+ 12.86	P F I Cole	7-33	21.2	- 11.97
J Reid	14-187	7.5	- 51.13	P Chapple-Hyam	5-31	16.1	- 17.13
R Cochrane	13-172	7.6	+ 2.50	G Harwood	4-37	10.8	+ 31.00
M J Kinane	11-83	13.3	+ 39.00	H R A Cecil	3-8	37.5	+ 21.00
M Hills	9-129	7.0	- 54.34	G Wragg	6-23	26.1	+ 18.66
R Hills	8-98	8.2	+ 19.73	H Thomson Jones	7-51	13.7	- 0.27

How the Favourites Fared

Non-handicaps	W-R	Per cent	£1 Level Stake	Handicaps	W-R	Per cent	£1 Level Stake
2-y-o	38-101	37.6	- 3.47	2-y-o	0-10	-	- 10.00
3-y-o	22-56	39.3	+ 0.26	3-y-o	3-29	10.3	- 13.50
Weight-for-age	33-83	39.8	+ 4.90	All-aged	28-126	22.2	- 9.15
Totals	93-240	38.8	+ 1.69	Totals	31-165	18.8	- 32.65
All favs	124-405	30.6	- 30.96				

Leading Trainers by Month at Ascot

March/Apr

	Total W-R	Non-handicaps 2-y-o	3-y-o+	Handicaps 2-y-o	3-y-o+	Per cent	£1 Level Stake
Lord Huntingdon	3-4	0-0	2-2	0-0	1-2	75.0	+ 6.83
M R Stoute	2-6	0-0	1-4	0-0	1-2	33.3	+ 2.25
R Hannon	2-7	2-2	0-1	0-0	0-4	28.6	- 1.63
J A B Old	1-1	0-0	1-1	0-0	0-0	100.0	+ 33.00
M H Tompkins	1-1	0-0	0-0	0-0	1-1	100.0	+ 5.50

May

	Total W-R	Non-handicaps 2-y-o	3-y-o+	Handicaps 2-y-o	3-y-o+	Per cent	£1 Level Stake
P F I Cole	3-6	1-1	1-3	0-0	1-2	50.0	+ 7.60
M R Stoute	2-5	0-0	2-5	0-0	0-0	40.0	+ 5.50
J Berry	1-1	1-1	0-0	0-0	0-0	100.0	+ 2.00
B Hanbury	1-1	0-0	1-1	0-0	0-0	100.0	+ 1.00
M Johnston	1-1	0-0	1-1	0-0	0-0	100.0	+ 10.00

June

	Total W-R	Non-handicaps 2-y-o	3-y-o+	Handicaps 2-y-o	3-y-o+	Per cent	£1 Level Stake
P F I Cole	12-46	8-15	2-13	0-0	2-18	26.1	+ 34.45
H R A Cecil	12-48	0-2	9-33	0-0	3-13	25.0	+ 63.75
G Wragg	11-34	3-5	7-23	0-0	1-6	32.4	+ 47.64
R Hannon	10-115	3-30	2-33	0-0	5-52	8.7	+ 87.88
M R Stoute	8-70	1-7	6-46	0-0	1-17	11.4	- 14.63

July

	Total W-R	Non-handicaps 2-y-o	3-y-o+	Handicaps 2-y-o	3-y-o+	Per cent	£1 Level Stake
H R A Cecil	6-17	2-5	3-10	0-0	1-2	35.3	+ 29.63
D R C Elsworth	5-16	2-5	0-2	0-0	3-9	31.3	+ 22.75
M R Stoute	5-29	2-5	2-13	0-0	1-11	17.2	+ 4.13
B W Hills	3-13	3-8	0-2	0-0	0-3	23.1	+ 4.71
I A Balding	3-16	0-4	0-2	0-0	3-10	18.8	+ 24.50

September

	Total W-R	Non-handicaps 2-y-o	3-y-o+	Handicaps 2-y-o	3-y-o+	Per cent	£1 Level Stake
L M Cumani	9-44	5-15	2-10	0-0	2-19	20.5	+ 21.03
J H M Gosden	7-33	1-7	6-9	0-1	0-16	21.2	- 9.02
M R Stoute	7-47	2-17	2-8	0-1	3-21	14.9	+ 6.48
J L Dunlop	6-32	3-8	1-9	0-1	2-14	18.8	+ 6.87
M H Tompkins	4-13	0-0	0-0	0-0	4-13	30.8	+ 14.00

Oct/Nov

	Total W-R	Non-handicaps 2-y-o	3-y-o+	Handicaps 2-y-o	3-y-o+	Per cent	£1 Level Stake
J H M Gosden	6-19	2-5	1-5	0-0	3-9	31.6	+ 3.16
L M Cumani	4-14	1-3	3-9	0-0	0-2	28.6	- 3.01
D R C Elsworth	4-18	2-5	0-3	0-3	2-7	22.2	+ 25.33
C E Brittain	3-19	0-6	0-2	1-2	2-9	15.8	+ 32.00
G Harwood	3-19	0-6	2-3	0-2	1-8	15.8	- 9.04

AYR (Group 1)

Leading Trainers 1990-94

	Total W-R	Non-handicaps 2-y-o	3-y-o+	Handicaps 2-y-o	3-y-o+	Per cent	£1 Level Stake
J Berry	29-231	15-77	8-35	0-22	6-97	12.6	- 54.35
B W Hills	19-49	4-13	10-20	0-2	5-14	38.8	+ 13.38
M H Easterby	18-103	3-16	2-11	1-13	12-63	17.5	- 23.10
P Chapple-Hyam	16-40	9-18	3-8	1-1	3-13	40.0	+ 23.38
Mrs M Reveley	16-82	2-11	9-26	0-2	5-43	19.5	- 13.27
Mrs J Ramsden	14-66	4-10	4-7	1-5	5-44	21.2	- 7.38
M Johnston	14-101	6-26	1-16	1-7	6-52	13.9	- 23.44
A Bailey	13-96	1-19	2-19	2-9	8-49	13.5	- 26.72
F H Lee	12-110	1-20	1-17	1-4	9-69	10.9	- 28.38
T D Barron	9-51	1-5	0-6	3-5	5-35	17.6	- 6.54
M H Tompkins	9-64	0-11	3-11	0-6	6-36	14.1	- 1.50
M P Naughton	7-70	0-2	0-15	0-1	7-52	10.0	- 24.75
M Brittain	7-93	0-14	0-7	0-7	7-65	7.5	- 8.75
J L Dunlop	6-20	3-7	2-4	0-3	1-6	30.0	- 5.76
M R Stoute	6-20	0-4	3-8	0-0	3-8	30.0	- 0.88
Sir M Prescott	6-24	2-5	3-6	0-1	1-12	25.0	- 9.10
J H M Gosden	6-31	1-2	2-17	0-0	3-12	19.4	- 5.29
I A Balding	5-13	0-0	1-6	0-0	4-7	38.5	+ 13.50
D Morley	5-14	0-1	2-7	0-0	3-6	35.7	+ 20.25
P C Haslam	5-16	0-1	0-4	0-0	5-11	31.3	- 1.90
H Thomson Jones	5-22	2-8	2-4	0-0	1-10	22.7	+ 11.38
D Moffatt	5-43	1-5	0-19	1-1	3-18	11.6	+ 18.00

Leading Jockeys

	Total W-R	Per cent	£1 Level Stake	Best Trainer	W-R	Per cent	£1 Level Stake
K Darley	47-213	22.1	- 17.04	Mrs M Reveley	12-41	29.3	+ 3.97
J Carroll	20-159	12.6	- 50.81	J Berry	14-103	13.6	- 33.55
K Fallon	16-133	12.0	- 44.70	Mrs J Ramsden	6-20	30.0	+ 7.53
D Holland	14-50	28.0	+ 5.16	B W Hills	7-15	46.7	+ 11.42
D McKeown	14-109	12.8	- 54.66	J W Watts	3-15	20.0	- 6.27
J Weaver	12-81	14.8	- 35.17	M Johnston	7-34	20.6	- 4.92
M Birch	12-92	13.0	- 11.56	M H Easterby	5-39	12.8	- 15.31
W Carson	11-51	21.6	- 10.22	J L Dunlop	3-9	33.3	- 1.30
J Fortune	10-74	13.5	+ 2.75	S E Kettlewell	2-6	33.3	+ 4.00
S Maloney	10-81	12.3	- 11.04	M H Easterby	5-13	38.5	+ 6.46
M Hills	9-47	19.1	+ 13.41	B W Hills	4-11	36.4	- 0.00
A Mackay	9-108	8.3	- 45.59	A Bailey	6-47	12.8	- 13.09

How the Favourites Fared

Non-handicaps	W-R	Per cent	£1 Level Stake	Handicaps	W-R	Per cent	£1 Level Stake
2-y-o	41-89	46.1	- 4.96	2-y-o	7-23	30.4	- 4.71
3-y-o	14-36	38.9	- 8.13	3-y-o	12-45	26.7	- 11.94
Weight-for-age	31-74	41.9	- 11.28	All-aged	47-154	30.5	- 4.73
Totals	86-199	43.2	- 24.37	Totals	66-222	29.7	- 21.38
All favs	152-421	36.1	- 45.75				

Leading Trainers by Month at Ayr

March/Apr

	Total W-R	Non-handicaps 2-y-o	3-y-o+	Handicaps 2-y-o	3-y-o+	Per cent	£1 Level Stake
B W Hills	2-2	0-0	2-2	0-0	0-0	100.0	+ 4.12
M Johnston	2-4	0-0	1-1	0-0	1-3	50.0	+ 14.00
Mrs J Ramsden	2-5	0-0	1-1	0-0	1-4	40.0	+ 4.75
J Berry	2-10	1-1	0-4	0-0	1-5	20.0	- 2.20
M Brittain	2-15	0-2	0-3	0-0	2-10	13.3	+ 24.00

May

	Total W-R	Non-handicaps 2-y-o	3-y-o+	Handicaps 2-y-o	3-y-o+	Per cent	£1 Level Stake
J Berry	5-15	3-5	2-3	0-0	0-7	33.3	+ 9.75
J H M Gosden	2-2	0-0	1-1	0-0	1-1	100.0	+ 3.91
M H Tompkins	2-3	0-0	1-1	0-0	1-2	66.7	+ 12.00
P Chapple-Hyam	2-3	0-0	1-2	0-0	1-1	66.7	+ 2.79
M H Easterby	2-4	0-1	0-0	0-0	2-3	50.0	+ 7.00

June

	Total W-R	Non-handicaps 2-y-o	3-y-o+	Handicaps 2-y-o	3-y-o+	Per cent	£1 Level Stake
P Chapple-Hyam	4-10	1-2	1-3	0-0	2-5	40.0	+ 10.32
F H Lee	4-19	1-5	0-1	0-0	3-13	21.1	+ 9.00
J Berry	4-32	1-17	0-3	0-0	3-12	12.5	- 11.38
M H Easterby	3-10	2-6	1-1	0-0	0-3	30.0	- 4.51
M R Channon	2-3	1-2	1-1	0-0	0-0	66.7	+ 2.38

July

	Total W-R	Non-handicaps 2-y-o	3-y-o+	Handicaps 2-y-o	3-y-o+	Per cent	£1 Level Stake
Mrs M Reveley	10-39	1-5	6-14	0-0	3-20	25.6	+ 8.70
A Bailey	9-35	0-4	1-7	1-3	7-21	25.7	+ 7.78
J Berry	9-56	3-16	4-15	0-4	2-21	16.1	- 22.42
M H Easterby	7-40	1-7	1-4	0-3	5-26	17.5	- 16.58
F H Lee	7-40	0-5	1-6	1-3	5-26	17.5	+ 0.63

August

	Total W-R	Non-handicaps 2-y-o	3-y-o+	Handicaps 2-y-o	3-y-o+	Per cent	£1 Level Stake
B W Hills	4-6	1-2	2-2	0-1	1-1	66.7	+ 7.23
N Bycroft	3-8	0-0	0-0	0-0	3-8	37.5	+ 14.33
M Johnston	3-14	1-2	0-2	0-3	2-7	21.4	+ 3.75
J Berry	3-18	1-4	2-5	0-2	0-7	16.7	+ 20.58
R M Whitaker	2-3	0-0	2-2	0-1	0-0	66.7	+ 29.00

September

	Total W-R	Non-handicaps 2-y-o	3-y-o+	Handicaps 2-y-o	3-y-o+	Per cent	£1 Level Stake
B W Hills	9-24	3-8	4-8	0-1	2-7	37.5	+ 5.75
M H Tompkins	7-42	0-9	2-6	0-5	5-22	16.7	+ 5.50
P Chapple-Hyam	6-11	4-5	1-2	1-1	0-3	54.5	+ 18.70
Mrs J Ramsden	6-29	3-6	1-2	1-4	1-17	20.7	- 6.72
R Charlton	4-6	2-2	0-0	0-0	2-4	66.7	+ 16.00

Oct/Nov

	Total W-R	Non-handicaps 2-y-o	3-y-o+	Handicaps 2-y-o	3-y-o+	Per cent	£1 Level Stake
T D Barron	2-2	0-0	0-0	1-1	1-1	100.0	+ 9.50
J Berry	2-10	2-6	0-2	0-1	0-1	20.0	- 6.18
W W Haigh	1-2	0-0	1-1	0-0	0-1	50.0	+ 6.00
S G Norton	1-2	0-1	1-1	0-0	0-0	50.0	+ 15.00
Mrs N Macauley	1-2	1-1	0-1	0-0	0-0	50.0	+ 1.25

BATH (Group 3)

Leading Trainers 1990-94

	Total W-R	Non-handicaps 2-y-o	3-y-o+	Handicaps 2-y-o	3-y-o+	Per cent	£1 Level Stake
B W Hills	18-93	2-20	11-39	1-2	4-32	19.4	- 25.00
I A Balding	18-117	2-26	4-41	0-3	12-47	15.4	- 22.07
R Hannon	17-138	6-50	4-36	1-6	6-46	12.3	- 48.76
P F I Cole	16-123	5-30	5-42	0-2	6-49	13.0	- 30.62
R J Hodges	15-161	1-15	2-38	0-1	12-107	9.3	- 26.29
J Berry	13-58	9-25	3-9	0-4	1-20	22.4	- 2.84
R Charlton	12-30	5-8	6-20	0-0	1-2	40.0	+ 8.58
D R C Elsworth	11-52	3-14	4-18	0-1	4-19	21.2	+ 27.33
R Akehurst	10-48	0-5	2-8	0-0	8-35	20.8	+ 36.50
G Harwood	10-48	1-8	9-20	0-1	0-19	20.8	- 1.85
G Lewis	10-55	1-18	4-10	0-5	5-22	18.2	- 3.13
M R Channon	10-84	5-30	2-20	0-4	3-30	11.9	- 7.27
C J Hill	9-88	0-18	1-17	1-1	7-52	10.2	- 38.42
W R Hern	8-45	0-3	3-26	2-2	3-14	17.8	+ 6.00
J L Dunlop	8-51	1-11	2-13	0-0	5-27	15.7	- 19.93
H R A Cecil	7-12	2-2	4-9	0-0	1-1	58.3	+ 7.54
H Thomson Jones	7-18	4-6	2-4	0-0	1-8	38.9	+ 38.00
J S King	7-24	0-1	0-1	0-0	7-22	29.2	+ 20.50
M R Stoute	7-27	1-3	5-19	0-0	1-5	25.9	- 2.77
Lord Huntingdon	6-29	1-6	1-7	1-1	3-15	20.7	- 6.09
D W P Arbuthnot	6-35	3-9	1-7	0-1	2-18	17.1	+ 22.60
J W Hills	6-55	2-10	1-19	0-2	3-24	10.9	- 23.50

Leading Jockeys

	Total W-R	Per cent	£1 Level Stake	Best Trainer	W-R	Per cent	£1 Level Stake
Pat Eddery	33-110	30.0	+ 0.78	B W Hills	8-19	42.1	+ 1.73
J Williams	26-228	11.4	+ 3.13	D R C Elsworth	7-24	29.2	+ 38.00
J Reid	23-131	17.6	+ 14.69	I A Balding	4-19	21.1	+ 8.10
T Quinn	23-142	16.2	+ 47.99	P F I Cole	9-65	13.8	+ 1.72
R Cochrane	13-82	15.9	- 33.81	I A Balding	3-18	16.7	- 1.67
Paul Eddery	13-83	15.7	- 30.22	G Lewis	3-19	15.8	- 6.25
A Munro	13-91	14.3	- 24.15	P F I Cole	3-17	17.6	- 8.33
A Clark	11-100	11.0	+ 29.20	G Harwood	3-18	16.7	- 6.05
W Carson	10-67	14.9	- 13.72	W R Hern	3-10	30.0	+ 12.25
G Duffield	9-68	13.2	- 31.52	Sir M Prescott	4-18	22.2	- 10.52
L Dettori	9-72	12.5	- 31.17	I A Balding	4-16	25.0	- 2.50
D Holland	9-117	7.7	- 60.98	B W Hills	4-34	11.8	- 12.58

How the Favourites Fared

Non-handicaps	W-R	Per cent	£1 Level Stake	Handicaps	W-R	Per cent	£1 Level Stake
2-y-o	31-83	37.3	- 14.95	2-y-o	4-10	40.0	+ 4.75
3-y-o	40-78	51.3	+ 6.97	3-y-o	16-46	34.8	+ 11.17
Weight-for-age	15-36	41.7	- 0.33	All-aged	36-136	26.5	- 15.43
Totals	86-197	43.7	- 8.31	Totals	56-192	29.2	+ 0.49
All favs	142-389	36.5	- 7.82				

Leading Trainers by Month at Bath

March/Apr	Total W-R	Non-handicaps 2-y-o	3-y-o+	Handicaps 2-y-o	3-y-o+	Per cent	£1 Level Stake
J Berry	2-6	0-3	2-3	0-0	0-0	33.3	- 2.13
J L Dunlop	2-6	0-1	1-2	0-0	1-3	33.3	- 0.55
G Lewis	2-6	1-3	0-1	0-0	1-2	33.3	+ 5.00
P F I Cole	2-14	0-1	1-8	0-0	1-5	14.3	+ 5.50
R J Hodges	2-14	1-1	0-5	0-0	1-8	14.3	+ 35.00

May	Total W-R	Non-handicaps 2-y-o	3-y-o+	Handicaps 2-y-o	3-y-o+	Per cent	£1 Level Stake
G Harwood	6-12	1-1	5-10	0-0	0-1	50.0	+ 10.12
R Charlton	5-10	0-0	5-10	0-0	0-0	50.0	+ 2.43
B W Hills	5-20	0-1	2-11	0-0	3-8	25.0	- 5.65
I A Balding	4-32	0-2	2-19	0-0	2-11	12.5	- 12.83
R Hannon	4-33	1-10	2-12	0-0	1-11	12.1	- 4.25

June	Total W-R	Non-handicaps 2-y-o	3-y-o+	Handicaps 2-y-o	3-y-o+	Per cent	£1 Level Stake
R J Hodges	7-26	0-1	2-8	0-0	5-17	26.9	+ 14.88
I A Balding	4-17	0-2	1-9	0-0	3-6	23.5	+ 6.08
J W Hills	3-7	1-1	1-3	0-0	1-3	42.9	+ 12.00
R Akehurst	3-8	0-1	2-2	0-0	1-5	37.5	+ 35.75
J L Dunlop	3-9	0-1	1-4	0-0	2-4	33.3	+ 2.25

July	Total W-R	Non-handicaps 2-y-o	3-y-o+	Handicaps 2-y-o	3-y-o+	Per cent	£1 Level Stake
B W Hills	7-15	1-3	6-10	0-0	0-2	46.7	+ 4.02
J Berry	5-16	4-8	1-1	0-0	0-7	31.3	+ 12.54
P F I Cole	5-25	2-6	1-8	0-0	2-11	20.0	- 6.90
R Hannon	5-26	1-11	1-2	0-0	3-13	19.2	- 5.27
I A Balding	4-25	0-5	0-6	0-0	4-14	16.0	- 6.67

August	Total W-R	Non-handicaps 2-y-o	3-y-o+	Handicaps 2-y-o	3-y-o+	Per cent	£1 Level Stake
H Thomson Jones	3-4	1-1	1-1	0-0	1-2	75.0	+ 15.50
Lord Huntingdon	3-9	0-1	1-2	0-0	2-6	33.3	+ 0.91
M R Channon	3-12	2-5	1-3	0-1	0-3	25.0	- 0.75
R Hannon	3-13	1-4	1-3	0-1	1-5	23.1	- 2.68
G Lewis	2-2	0-0	2-2	0-0	0-0	100.0	+ 11.00

September	Total W-R	Non-handicaps 2-y-o	3-y-o+	Handicaps 2-y-o	3-y-o+	Per cent	£1 Level Stake
I A Balding	5-25	2-14	0-4	0-3	3-4	20.0	+ 6.85
D R C Elsworth	4-10	2-4	1-3	0-0	1-3	40.0	+ 18.33
H Candy	4-14	0-2	4-4	0-1	0-7	28.6	+ 7.87
P F I Cole	4-24	2-8	1-4	0-2	1-10	16.7	+ 1.50
H R A Cecil	3-3	1-1	2-2	0-0	0-0	100.0	+ 4.04

Oct/Nov	Total W-R	Non-handicaps 2-y-o	3-y-o+	Handicaps 2-y-o	3-y-o+	Per cent	£1 Level Stake
H Thomson Jones	2-2	2-2	0-0	0-0	0-0	100.0	+ 8.00
Bob Jones	2-3	1-2	0-0	0-0	1-1	66.7	+ 19.50
C J Hill	2-6	0-0	0-3	1-1	1-2	33.3	+ 4.25
N A Callaghan	1-1	0-0	1-1	0-0	0-0	100.0	+ 4.50
R Akehurst	1-2	0-1	0-0	0-0	1-1	50.0	+ 3.50

BEVERLEY (Group 3)

Leading Trainers 1990-94

	Total W-R	Non-handicaps 2-y-o	3-y-o+	Handicaps 2-y-o	3-y-o+	Per cent	£1 Level Stake
M H Easterby	25-194	8-67	3-31	1-15	13-81	12.9	- 56.22
J Berry	23-163	17-99	2-33	1-10	3-21	14.1	- 57.38
H R A Cecil	15-42	2-7	10-28	0-0	3-7	35.7	- 4.08
I A Balding	15-47	2-6	2-13	0-0	11-28	31.9	+ 7.07
Mrs M Reveley	15-102	4-16	1-10	0-4	10-72	14.7	- 30.51
R M Whitaker	15-131	2-28	4-30	0-6	9-67	11.5	- 4.38
M Brittain	15-143	3-43	2-19	0-4	10-77	10.5	- 0.75
R Hollinshead	13-131	4-31	2-36	0-1	7-63	9.9	- 34.95
M Johnston	12-71	1-17	4-12	1-4	6-38	16.9	- 17.87
T D Barron	12-104	1-16	1-14	0-6	10-68	11.5	- 30.78
D R Loder	11-19	7-9	1-4	0-0	3-6	57.9	+ 13.74
L M Cumani	11-27	1-1	9-19	0-0	1-7	40.7	+ 2.63
M R Channon	11-40	4-11	1-5	0-4	6-20	27.5	+ 25.55
S G Norton	10-74	1-14	2-15	0-2	7-43	13.5	+ 2.73
M R Stoute	9-40	0-6	9-22	0-0	0-12	22.5	- 17.32
J W Watts	9-40	2-8	6-13	0-2	1-17	22.5	+ 9.40
J L Spearing	9-60	1-6	2-11	0-1	6-42	15.0	+ 13.73
P F I Cole	8-18	2-8	5-7	0-0	1-3	44.4	+ 9.57
J L Dunlop	8-33	2-8	1-8	0-2	5-15	24.2	- 1.51
D Morley	8-50	2-8	1-9	0-1	5-32	16.0	- 7.92
J R Fanshawe	7-30	0-2	3-13	0-0	4-15	23.3	+ 14.00
M Bell	7-31	3-12	0-3	0-2	4-14	22.6	+ 3.33

Leading Jockeys

	Total W-R	Per cent	£1 Level Stake	Best Trainer	W-R	Per cent	£1 Level Stake
K Darley	50-265	18.9	- 28.07	M H Easterby	7-19	36.8	+ 8.89
M Birch	20-201	10.0	- 85.52	M H Easterby	10-85	11.8	- 33.27
J Lowe	20-221	9.0	- 73.20	Mrs M Reveley	6-19	31.6	+ 31.00
W Ryan	16-87	18.4	- 10.50	H R A Cecil	10-25	40.0	- 0.60
G Duffield	16-100	16.0	- 0.82	J W Watts	4-11	36.4	+ 21.25
J Carroll	16-119	13.4	- 55.53	J Berry	14-82	17.1	- 34.53
W Carson	15-69	21.7	- 16.36	J L Dunlop	4-10	40.0	+ 3.39
L Dettori	13-46	28.3	+ 6.39	L M Cumani	4-6	66.7	+ 4.98
M Roberts	13-54	24.1	+ 6.49	C E Brittain	4-14	28.6	+ 7.83
W R Swinburn	12-51	23.5	- 7.23	M R Stoute	5-15	33.3	- 2.73
D Holland	12-64	18.8	+ 1.50	B W Hills	4-17	23.5	+ 0.25
B Raymond	12-82	14.6	- 17.38	B A McMahon	2-7	28.6	+ 12.00

How the Favourites Fared

Non-handicaps	W-R	Per cent	£1 Level Stake	Handicaps	W-R	Per cent	£1 Level Stake
2-y-o	57-128	44.5	- 7.64	2-y-o	4-15	26.7	+ 0.25
3-y-o	28-63	44.4	+ 2.16	3-y-o	17-58	29.3	- 17.28
Weight-for-age	36-86	41.9	- 16.86	All-aged	63-206	30.6	- 1.56
Totals	121-277	43.7	- 22.34	Totals	84-279	30.1	- 18.59
All favs	205-556	36.9	- 40.93				

Leading Trainers by Month at Beverley

March/Apr

	Total W-R	Non-handicaps 2-y-o	3-y-o+	Handicaps 2-y-o	3-y-o+	Per cent	£1 Level Stake
J W Watts	5-12	0-0	4-7	0-0	1-5	41.7	+ 22.50
R Hollinshead	5-28	1-5	0-11	0-0	4-12	17.9	- 0.80
J Berry	4-23	3-13	1-4	0-0	0-6	17.4	- 8.60
H R A Cecil	3-6	0-0	3-6	0-0	0-0	50.0	- 0.10
M R Channon	3-6	0-0	1-2	0-0	2-4	50.0	+ 17.50

May

	Total W-R	Non-handicaps 2-y-o	3-y-o+	Handicaps 2-y-o	3-y-o+	Per cent	£1 Level Stake
S G Norton	6-14	1-2	1-4	0-0	4-8	42.9	+ 26.73
M H Easterby	6-41	2-15	0-9	0-0	4-17	14.6	- 4.00
M R Stoute	4-8	0-0	4-7	0-0	0-1	50.0	+ 2.98
J Berry	4-31	3-22	1-8	0-0	0-1	12.9	- 17.50
M Brittain	4-36	1-16	1-3	0-0	2-17	11.1	- 0.50

June

	Total W-R	Non-handicaps 2-y-o	3-y-o+	Handicaps 2-y-o	3-y-o+	Per cent	£1 Level Stake
M Brittain	6-29	1-7	0-0	0-0	5-22	20.7	+ 46.50
H R A Cecil	5-8	0-0	3-6	0-0	2-2	62.5	+ 5.93
J Berry	5-25	4-18	0-4	0-0	1-3	20.0	- 3.50
M H Easterby	5-28	4-11	0-1	0-0	1-16	17.9	- 9.36
P F I Cole	4-6	0-0	3-4	0-0	1-2	66.7	+ 5.16

July

	Total W-R	Non-handicaps 2-y-o	3-y-o+	Handicaps 2-y-o	3-y-o+	Per cent	£1 Level Stake
D R Loder	7-8	6-7	0-0	0-0	1-1	87.5	+ 9.74
J Berry	7-36	6-25	0-5	0-0	1-6	19.4	- 6.28
M H Easterby	7-54	1-20	0-8	0-3	6-23	13.0	- 7.88
I A Balding	6-15	0-1	0-1	0-0	6-13	40.0	+ 8.25
Mrs M Reveley	6-30	1-2	1-4	0-0	4-24	20.0	- 0.92

August

	Total W-R	Non-handicaps 2-y-o	3-y-o+	Handicaps 2-y-o	3-y-o+	Per cent	£1 Level Stake
M H Easterby	4-24	1-4	2-6	0-6	1-8	16.7	- 7.65
I A Balding	3-5	1-2	0-0	0-0	2-3	60.0	+ 4.13
R Hannon	2-3	0-0	0-0	2-3	0-0	66.7	+ 8.00
H R A Cecil	2-5	1-1	1-3	0-0	0-1	40.0	- 1.29
J L Harris	2-5	0-1	1-1	0-0	1-3	40.0	+ 6.63

September

	Total W-R	Non-handicaps 2-y-o	3-y-o+	Handicaps 2-y-o	3-y-o+	Per cent	£1 Level Stake
R M Whitaker	5-16	0-4	1-2	0-4	4-6	31.3	+ 22.00
L M Cumani	3-6	1-1	1-2	0-0	1-3	50.0	+ 3.75
J L Dunlop	3-7	1-5	1-1	0-0	1-1	42.9	+ 6.10
B W Hills	3-7	1-1	2-5	0-0	0-1	42.9	+ 4.75
H Thomson Jones	2-4	2-3	0-1	0-0	0-0	50.0	+ 3.88

BRIGHTON (Group 2)

Leading Trainers 1990-94

	Total W-R	Non-handicaps 2-y-o	3-y-o+	Handicaps 2-y-o	3-y-o+	Per cent	£1 Level Stake
R Hannon	39-219	19-63	12-59	1-12	7-85	17.8	- 16.18
L M Cumani	27-64	6-11	14-38	1-2	6-13	42.2	+ 15.12
R Akehurst	23-106	0-4	8-26	0-1	15-75	21.7	+ 31.88
Sir M Prescott	19-77	1-15	6-17	2-6	10-39	24.7	+ 9.91
P F I Cole	19-132	3-29	11-51	1-5	4-47	14.4	- 65.41
R J Hodges	17-133	0-1	2-24	0-0	15-108	12.8	- 34.60
J L Dunlop	15-74	3-17	5-24	0-6	7-27	20.3	- 8.60
M J Ryan	14-49	3-5	0-7	1-1	10-36	28.6	+ 31.38
G Harwood	12-54	1-6	10-35	0-1	1-12	22.2	- 11.69
G Lewis	12-83	2-20	1-23	3-5	6-35	14.5	+ 0.67
J H M Gosden	11-38	2-2	8-31	0-0	1-5	28.9	- 8.19
M A Jarvis	11-45	0-4	5-20	0-1	6-20	24.4	+ 19.75
C A Cyzer	10-78	2-8	3-32	0-0	5-38	12.8	+ 3.45
J White	9-35	0-4	1-10	0-0	8-21	25.7	+ 4.75
R Boss	9-37	2-5	1-7	0-2	6-23	24.3	+ 22.53
B J Meehan	9-38	4-15	2-5	1-4	2-14	23.7	+ 15.97
B W Hills	8-33	0-3	5-21	1-1	2-8	24.2	- 3.65
W Carter	8-57	1-6	0-12	0-1	7-38	14.0	- 15.75
S Dow	8-99	1-16	3-24	0-5	4-54	8.1	- 39.13
J Berry	7-32	3-13	0-1	2-7	2-11	21.9	- 5.25
R J O'Sullivan	7-53	0-0	0-12	0-0	7-41	13.2	+ 38.75
M R Channon	7-85	3-25	1-12	0-6	3-42	8.2	- 49.27

Leading Jockeys

	Total W-R	Per cent	£1 Level Stake	Best Trainer	W-R	Per cent	£1 Level Stake
T Quinn	46-252	18.3	+ 5.50	R Akehurst	10-32	31.3	+ 30.13
W Carson	44-165	26.7	+ 23.45	R J Hodges	9-34	26.5	+ 14.10
M Roberts	31-141	22.0	- 10.85	R Boss	4-9	44.4	+ 16.13
J Reid	28-222	12.6	- 62.24	R Hannon	6-33	18.2	+ 13.93
Pat Eddery	27-109	24.8	- 13.51	R Hannon	4-19	21.1	- 10.74
L Dettori	26-110	23.6	- 12.24	L M Cumani	16-31	51.6	+ 28.90
R Cochrane	26-151	17.2	- 40.96	G Harwood	6-22	27.3	- 8.53
G Duffield	24-126	19.0	- 3.47	Sir M Prescott	15-63	23.8	+ 1.03
A Munro	24-135	17.8	- 15.85	R Akehurst	4-7	57.1	+ 19.75
B Rouse	13-156	8.3	- 62.00	G L Moore	4-39	10.3	- 12.50
D Holland	10-78	12.8	- 39.17	B W Hills	4-15	26.7	+ 1.13
Paul Eddery	9-91	9.9	- 33.82	G Lewis	4-34	11.8	+ 1.00

How the Favourites Fared

Non-handicaps	W-R	Per cent	£1 Level Stake	Handicaps	W-R	Per cent	£1 Level Stake
2-y-o	49-99	49.5	+ 7.68	2-y-o	6-17	35.3	+ 2.80
3-y-o	38-86	44.2	- 5.71	3-y-o	18-55	32.7	- 10.84
Weight-for-age	41-96	42.7	- 11.86	All-aged	59-200	29.5	- 18.63
Totals	128-281	45.6	- 9.89	Totals	83-272	30.5	- 26.67
All favs	211-553	38.2	- 36.56				

472

Leading Trainers by Month at Brighton

March/Apr

	Total W-R	Non-handicaps 2-y-o	3-y-o+	Handicaps 2-y-o	3-y-o+	Per cent	£1 Level Stake
R Hannon	8-47	1-5	5-24	0-0	2-18	17.0	- 5.24
R J Hodges	7-27	0-0	1-6	0-0	6-21	25.9	+ 13.50
P F I Cole	6-25	1-1	5-18	0-0	0-6	24.0	- 12.27
Sir M Prescott	5-10	0-0	3-5	0-0	2-5	50.0	+ 10.88
C E Brittain	4-14	0-0	4-10	0-0	0-4	28.6	+ 14.01

May

	Total W-R	Non-handicaps 2-y-o	3-y-o+	Handicaps 2-y-o	3-y-o+	Per cent	£1 Level Stake
R Hannon	8-34	5-13	2-5	0-0	1-16	23.5	+ 15.85
M A Jarvis	6-15	0-0	4-12	0-0	2-3	40.0	+ 21.25
R Akehurst	5-19	0-1	1-6	0-0	4-12	26.3	+ 16.50
J L Dunlop	4-11	0-1	1-5	0-0	3-5	36.4	+ 16.00
J Berry	3-9	2-5	0-0	0-0	1-4	33.3	+ 3.08

June

	Total W-R	Non-handicaps 2-y-o	3-y-o+	Handicaps 2-y-o	3-y-o+	Per cent	£1 Level Stake
P F I Cole	5-21	1-4	3-7	0-0	1-10	23.8	- 4.76
R Hannon	5-37	2-11	2-11	0-0	1-15	13.5	- 12.48
R J Hodges	4-19	0-0	1-4	0-0	3-15	21.1	- 5.85
L M Cumani	3-9	0-0	3-8	0-0	0-1	33.3	- 0.30
L J Holt	3-9	0-0	0-1	0-0	3-8	33.3	+ 4.33

July

	Total W-R	Non-handicaps 2-y-o	3-y-o+	Handicaps 2-y-o	3-y-o+	Per cent	£1 Level Stake
R Boss	3-5	1-1	0-0	0-0	2-4	60.0	+ 20.91
J White	3-6	0-1	0-1	0-0	3-4	50.0	+ 7.00
A C Stewart	2-2	0-0	2-2	0-0	0-0	100.0	+ 2.61
L G Cottrell	2-3	0-0	1-2	0-0	1-1	66.7	+ 2.95
Mrs N Macauley	2-5	0-0	0-2	0-0	2-3	40.0	+ 3.75

August

	Total W-R	Non-handicaps 2-y-o	3-y-o+	Handicaps 2-y-o	3-y-o+	Per cent	£1 Level Stake
L M Cumani	10-13	3-3	1-2	0-0	6-8	76.9	+ 19.14
Sir M Prescott	9-28	1-5	1-6	1-2	6-15	32.1	+ 8.50
R Akehurst	7-22	0-0	3-6	0-0	4-16	31.8	+ 14.63
R Hannon	7-48	3-11	3-12	1-6	0-19	14.6	- 19.84
G L Moore	5-20	0-3	3-7	0-2	2-8	25.0	+ 9.00

September

	Total W-R	Non-handicaps 2-y-o	3-y-o+	Handicaps 2-y-o	3-y-o+	Per cent	£1 Level Stake
R Hannon	8-33	7-18	0-5	0-4	1-6	24.2	- 2.68
M J Ryan	5-6	1-1	0-0	1-1	3-4	83.3	+ 27.50
L M Cumani	5-20	2-7	3-10	0-1	0-2	25.0	- 4.63
G Lewis	4-13	2-6	0-1	1-2	1-4	30.8	+ 17.00
J H M Gosden	3-8	2-2	1-5	0-0	0-1	37.5	+ 3.50

Oct/Nov

	Total W-R	Non-handicaps 2-y-o	3-y-o+	Handicaps 2-y-o	3-y-o+	Per cent	£1 Level Stake
L M Cumani	4-5	1-1	2-3	1-1	0-0	80.0	+ 5.44
G Wragg	2-4	1-1	1-3	0-0	0-0	50.0	+ 2.50
R Akehurst	1-1	0-0	0-0	0-0	1-1	100.0	+ 2.75
G Harwood	1-2	0-0	0-1	0-0	1-1	50.0	+ 2.33
W Carter	1-2	0-0	0-0	0-0	1-2	50.0	+ 5.00

CARLISLE (Group 4)

Leading Trainers 1990-94

	Total W-R	Non-handicaps 2-y-o	3-y-o+	Handicaps 2-y-o	3-y-o+	Per cent	£1 Level Stake
J Berry	27-125	11-54	11-45	0-0	5-26	21.6	+ 21.48
Sir M Prescott	16-42	3-8	7-16	0-0	6-18	38.1	+ 28.34
M H Tompkins	13-42	2-4	6-18	0-0	5-20	31.0	+ 15.95
Mrs M Reveley	13-65	0-7	5-21	0-0	8-37	20.0	+ 7.45
Mrs J Ramsden	11-46	4-12	1-6	0-0	6-28	23.9	+ 18.83
M Johnston	10-55	1-10	3-17	0-0	6-28	18.2	+ 46.53
M H Easterby	10-82	4-28	3-23	0-0	3-31	12.2	- 49.68
S G Norton	8-33	1-5	4-15	0-0	3-13	24.2	+ 21.63
N Tinkler	7-25	2-6	2-9	0-0	3-10	28.0	+ 18.28
R M Whitaker	6-35	2-4	3-12	0-0	1-19	17.1	+ 19.50
Denys Smith	6-43	1-6	1-9	0-0	4-28	14.0	0.00
J L Dunlop	5-8	1-3	2-2	0-0	2-3	62.5	+ 13.12
Miss S E Hall	5-20	0-6	2-7	0-0	3-7	25.0	+ 1.91
T D Barron	5-34	0-7	3-10	0-0	2-17	14.7	+ 1.00
E J Alston	5-38	0-7	0-10	0-0	5-21	13.2	+ 11.50
R Hollinshead	5-86	1-16	3-31	0-0	1-39	5.8	- 18.50
W Jarvis	4-12	2-3	2-5	0-0	0-4	33.3	+ 0.88
W W Haigh	4-24	0-3	4-8	0-0	0-13	16.7	+ 13.60
J W Watts	4-28	0-3	1-11	0-0	3-14	14.3	+ 4.33
G M Moore	4-34	0-6	1-14	0-0	3-14	11.8	- 11.00
J Etherington	4-37	2-14	1-9	0-0	1-14	10.8	- 2.65
M W Easterby	4-38	0-13	0-8	0-0	4-17	10.5	- 17.38

Leading Jockeys

	Total W-R	Per cent	£1 Level Stake	Best Trainer	W-R	Per cent	£1 Level Stake
G Duffield	24-108	22.2	+ 3.72	Sir M Prescott	14-35	40.0	+ 28.84
D McKeown	23-126	18.3	+ 27.86	M Johnston	4-18	22.2	+ 1.19
K Darley	21-130	16.2	- 20.51	Mrs M Reveley	6-19	31.6	+ 8.16
J Carroll	18-116	15.5	- 29.43	J Berry	16-80	20.0	- 10.43
P Robinson	13-34	38.2	+ 31.43	M H Tompkins	8-23	34.8	+ 13.35
K Fallon	11-84	13.1	- 12.75	Mrs J Ramsden	4-9	44.4	+ 8.75
A Culhane	8-43	18.6	+ 29.50	R M Whitaker	6-27	22.2	+ 27.50
M Birch	8-98	8.2	- 57.00	M H Easterby	5-42	11.9	- 22.00
O Pears	7-34	20.6	+ 8.29	S G Norton	3-10	30.0	+ 8.88
Kim Tinkler	7-50	14.0	+ 6.00	N Tinkler	4-19	21.1	+ 14.50
L Charnock	6-89	6.7	- 34.75	Denys Smith	2-9	22.2	+ 13.00
B Raymond	5-26	19.2	- 1.71	J L Dunlop	1-1	100.0	+ 0.62

How the Favourites Fared

Non-handicaps	W-R	Per cent	£1 Level Stake	Handicaps	W-R	Per cent	£1 Level Stake
2-y-o	16-49	32.7	- 8.00	2-y-o	0-0	-	0.00
3-y-o	27-51	52.9	+ 4.35	3-y-o	14-40	35.0	+ 0.03
Weight-for-age	17-56	30.4	- 8.83	All-aged	20-93	21.5	- 26.62
Totals	60-156	38.5	- 12.48	Totals	34-133	25.6	- 26.59
All favs	94-289	32.5	- 39.07				

Leading Trainers by Month at Carlisle

March/Apr

	Total W-R	Non-handicaps 2-y-o	3-y-o+	Handicaps 2-y-o	3-y-o+	Per cent	£1 Level Stake
J Berry	6-20	3-6	3-10	0-0	0-4	30.0	+ 0.25
M H Tompkins	4-10	0-0	2-4	0-0	2-6	40.0	+ 8.73
W Jarvis	2-2	1-1	1-1	0-0	0-0	100.0	+ 4.88
M R Stoute	2-3	0-0	2-2	0-0	0-1	66.7	+ 0.20
J Etherington	2-7	1-2	0-2	0-0	1-3	28.6	+ 4.25

May

	Total W-R	Non-handicaps 2-y-o	3-y-o+	Handicaps 2-y-o	3-y-o+	Per cent	£1 Level Stake
J Berry	7-36	3-15	3-15	0-0	1-6	19.4	+ 18.60
Sir M Prescott	5-13	1-2	1-5	0-0	3-6	38.5	+ 11.91
M H Tompkins	5-18	1-1	2-9	0-0	2-8	27.8	+ 8.25
Mrs J Ramsden	4-12	0-1	0-0	0-0	4-11	33.3	+ 17.25
M Johnston	4-18	1-2	1-8	0-0	2-8	22.2	+ 13.50

June

	Total W-R	Non-handicaps 2-y-o	3-y-o+	Handicaps 2-y-o	3-y-o+	Per cent	£1 Level Stake
J Berry	9-37	2-15	3-13	0-0	4-9	24.3	+ 9.22
Mrs M Reveley	6-20	0-2	3-7	0-0	3-11	30.0	+ 2.33
Mrs J Ramsden	4-12	2-3	1-1	0-0	1-8	33.3	+ 6.25
Denys Smith	4-14	1-2	0-3	0-0	3-9	28.6	+ 15.00
M H Tompkins	4-14	1-3	2-5	0-0	1-6	28.6	- 1.02

July

	Total W-R	Non-handicaps 2-y-o	3-y-o+	Handicaps 2-y-o	3-y-o+	Per cent	£1 Level Stake
Sir M Prescott	4-6	0-0	3-4	0-0	1-2	66.7	+ 4.75
Mrs M Reveley	3-10	0-1	1-3	0-0	2-6	30.0	- 0.38
M H Easterby	3-12	1-3	2-5	0-0	0-4	25.0	- 3.88
J L Dunlop	2-2	1-1	0-0	0-0	1-1	100.0	+ 3.00
J J O'Neill	2-4	0-0	0-1	0-0	2-3	50.0	+ 7.00

August

	Total W-R	Non-handicaps 2-y-o	3-y-o+	Handicaps 2-y-o	3-y-o+	Per cent	£1 Level Stake
Sir M Prescott	2-3	0-0	1-1	0-0	1-2	66.7	+ 7.00
B Hanbury	1-1	0-0	0-0	0-0	1-1	100.0	+ 7.00
S Mellor	1-1	0-0	1-1	0-0	0-0	100.0	+ 5.00
M P Naughton	1-2	0-0	0-0	0-0	1-2	50.0	+ 11.00
S G Norton	1-2	0-0	0-1	0-0	1-1	50.0	+ 4.00

September

	Total W-R	Non-handicaps 2-y-o	3-y-o+	Handicaps 2-y-o	3-y-o+	Per cent	£1 Level Stake
J G FitzGerald	2-2	2-2	0-0	0-0	0-0	100.0	+ 8.50
J Berry	2-13	2-10	0-1	0-0	0-2	15.4	+ 3.00
B R Cambidge	1-1	0-0	0-0	0-0	1-1	100.0	+ 3.50
D Morley	1-1	0-0	1-1	0-0	0-0	100.0	+ 1.10
A Smith	1-1	0-0	0-0	0-0	1-1	100.0	+ 11.00

CATTERICK (Group 4)

Leading Trainers 1990-94

	Total W-R	Non-handicaps 2-y-o	3-y-o+	Handicaps 2-y-o	3-y-o+	Per cent	£1 Level Stake
J Berry	32-208	17-99	7-41	3-22	5-46	15.4	- 59.10
Mrs M Reveley	20-89	1-11	8-26	0-6	11-46	22.5	+ 44.76
T D Barron	20-108	6-25	3-15	2-10	9-58	18.5	+ 27.05
B W Hills	18-50	2-6	15-33	0-1	1-10	36.0	+ 21.88
M H Easterby	12-156	3-54	3-32	2-11	4-59	7.7	-100.56
Sir M Prescott	11-46	5-21	4-11	0-1	2-13	23.9	- 7.31
H R A Cecil	10-20	1-2	9-16	0-0	0-2	50.0	+ 9.58
S G Norton	10-55	2-11	2-24	0-3	6-17	18.2	- 6.65
M W Easterby	10-78	3-28	1-12	0-7	6-31	12.8	- 13.15
R M Whitaker	10-98	2-24	1-22	0-6	7-46	10.2	- 17.40
G Wragg	9-25	1-2	7-21	0-0	1-2	36.0	+ 27.41
J H M Gosden	8-25	1-4	7-18	0-0	0-3	32.0	- 0.08
M Johnston	8-70	3-21	1-9	1-8	3-32	11.4	- 23.46
L M Cumani	7-14	0-0	6-13	0-0	1-1	50.0	- 1.25
M R Stoute	7-31	1-4	6-25	0-1	0-1	22.6	- 12.67
M Bell	6-25	1-8	3-7	1-2	1-8	24.0	+ 3.53
Miss S E Hall	6-34	2-8	3-10	0-2	1-14	17.6	+ 17.62
M H Tompkins	6-34	2-10	3-12	0-2	1-10	17.6	- 9.86
M P Naughton	6-57	0-1	0-15	0-0	6-41	10.5	- 25.96
R Hollinshead	6-88	2-15	2-32	1-5	1-36	6.8	- 18.20
W A O'Gorman	5-10	5-9	0-0	0-0	0-1	50.0	+ 11.30
M O'Neill	5-24	0-3	0-4	1-1	4-16	20.8	+ 26.50

Leading Jockeys

	Total W-R	Per cent	£1 Level Stake	Best Trainer	W-R	Per cent	£1 Level Stake
K Darley	35-185	18.9	- 6.54	Mrs M Reveley	9-25	36.0	+ 31.20
J Carroll	28-160	17.5	- 27.43	J Berry	22-113	19.5	- 13.30
J Fortune	16-99	16.2	+ 3.87	L M Cumani	3-6	50.0	- 0.95
M Birch	15-157	9.6	- 51.29	M H Easterby	6-76	7.9	- 61.04
G Duffield	14-103	13.6	- 20.85	Sir M Prescott	8-36	22.2	- 6.30
J Lowe	13-144	9.0	- 3.87	Mrs M Reveley	3-15	20.0	+ 7.00
W Ryan	12-59	20.3	- 13.48	H R A Cecil	8-14	57.1	+ 12.92
N Connorton	12-75	16.0	- 4.93	Miss S E Hall	4-19	21.1	+ 19.71
Alex Greaves	12-77	15.6	+ 3.88	T D Barron	10-55	18.2	+ 18.88
J Fanning	12-149	8.1	- 33.26	T D Barron	3-9	33.3	+ 8.00
O Pears	11-61	18.0	+ 25.76	S G Norton	6-23	26.1	+ 7.01
L Charnock	11-133	8.3	+ 31.00	M J Camacho	2-8	25.0	+ 7.00

How the Favourites Fared

Non-handicaps	W-R	Per cent	£1 Level Stake	Handicaps	W-R	Per cent	£1 Level Stake
2-y-o	45-105	42.9	- 7.11	2-y-o	7-18	38.9	+ 1.43
3-y-o	47-82	57.3	+ 10.57	3-y-o	12-46	26.1	- 13.25
Weight-for-age	37-69	53.6	+ 12.32	All-aged	33-133	24.8	- 31.49
Totals	129-256	50.4	+ 15.78	Totals	52-197	26.4	- 43.31
All favs	181-453	40.0	- 27.53				

Leading Trainers by Month at Catterick

March/Apr

	Total W-R	Non-handicaps 2-y-o	3-y-o+	Handicaps 2-y-o	3-y-o+	Per cent	£1 Level Stake
J Berry	9-34	4-13	3-9	0-0	2-12	26.5	+ 6.02
T D Barron	4-20	0-3	0-4	0-0	4-13	20.0	+ 1.25
B W Hills	3-4	0-0	3-4	0-0	0-0	75.0	+ 3.25
G Wragg	3-4	0-0	3-4	0-0	0-0	75.0	+ 5.41
M Bell	3-7	1-2	2-4	0-0	0-1	42.9	- 0.04

May

	Total W-R	Non-handicaps 2-y-o	3-y-o+	Handicaps 2-y-o	3-y-o+	Per cent	£1 Level Stake
G Wragg	2-2	0-0	2-2	0-0	0-0	100.0	+ 10.50
B W Hills	2-3	0-0	2-3	0-0	0-0	66.7	+ 4.63
R M Whitaker	2-8	0-1	1-5	0-0	1-2	25.0	+ 7.50
T D Barron	2-9	1-3	0-1	0-0	1-5	22.2	- 0.80
R Hollinshead	2-11	1-2	0-5	0-0	1-4	18.2	- 3.00

June

	Total W-R	Non-handicaps 2-y-o	3-y-o+	Handicaps 2-y-o	3-y-o+	Per cent	£1 Level Stake
J Berry	7-29	4-14	1-6	0-0	2-9	24.1	- 2.24
S G Norton	4-9	0-2	2-5	0-0	2-2	44.4	+ 7.50
P F I Cole	4-12	2-4	2-6	0-0	0-2	33.3	- 0.79
L M Cumani	3-3	0-0	3-3	0-0	0-0	100.0	+ 1.69
W Jarvis	2-2	0-0	2-2	0-0	0-0	100.0	+ 7.50

July

	Total W-R	Non-handicaps 2-y-o	3-y-o+	Handicaps 2-y-o	3-y-o+	Per cent	£1 Level Stake
Mrs M Reveley	8-26	0-4	3-8	0-0	5-14	30.8	+ 12.07
J Berry	8-49	3-27	3-12	1-1	1-9	16.3	- 15.92
M H Easterby	8-50	3-19	2-8	0-1	3-22	16.0	- 24.56
B W Hills	5-11	0-0	5-10	0-0	0-1	45.5	+ 13.19
Sir M Prescott	5-12	2-5	1-3	0-0	2-4	41.7	+ 0.19

August

	Total W-R	Non-handicaps 2-y-o	3-y-o+	Handicaps 2-y-o	3-y-o+	Per cent	£1 Level Stake
Mrs M Reveley	3-10	1-2	1-1	0-1	1-6	30.0	- 2.18
R M Whitaker	3-12	0-3	0-1	0-1	3-7	25.0	+ 19.10
N A Callaghan	2-2	1-1	0-0	1-1	0-0	100.0	+ 4.00
T D Barron	2-7	1-2	0-1	0-1	1-3	28.6	+ 12.00
R Hollinshead	2-7	0-1	1-2	1-2	0-2	28.6	+ 3.80

September

	Total W-R	Non-handicaps 2-y-o	3-y-o+	Handicaps 2-y-o	3-y-o+	Per cent	£1 Level Stake
Mrs M Reveley	3-8	0-0	0-1	0-1	3-6	37.5	+ 5.38
T D Barron	3-10	1-2	0-1	2-4	0-3	30.0	+ 13.38
J H M Gosden	2-3	0-0	2-3	0-0	0-0	66.7	+ 5.25
J L Dunlop	1-1	1-1	0-0	0-0	0-0	100.0	+ 0.80
P J Feilden	1-1	0-0	0-0	0-0	1-1	100.0	+ 6.50

Oct/Nov

	Total W-R	Non-handicaps 2-y-o	3-y-o+	Handicaps 2-y-o	3-y-o+	Per cent	£1 Level Stake
B W Hills	6-18	2-6	3-8	0-1	1-3	33.3	+ 7.09
T D Barron	4-21	2-5	1-2	0-4	1-10	19.0	+ 16.63
J Berry	4-45	4-27	0-1	0-10	0-7	8.9	- 19.25
H R A Cecil	3-6	1-1	2-5	0-0	0-0	50.0	+ 3.75
G Wragg	3-10	1-2	1-6	0-0	1-2	30.0	+ 13.00

CHEPSTOW (Group 3)

Leading Trainers 1990-94

	Total W-R	Non-handicaps 2-y-o	Non-handicaps 3-y-o+	Handicaps 2-y-o	Handicaps 3-y-o+	Per cent	£1 Level Stake
R Hannon	19-144	10-54	3-25	2-11	4-54	13.2	- 45.74
R J Hodges	13-117	0-6	0-17	0-2	13-92	11.1	- 21.79
H R A Cecil	11-33	2-8	6-19	0-0	3-6	33.3	+ 14.57
L M Cumani	9-20	0-0	7-15	1-1	1-4	45.0	+ 1.77
H Candy	9-45	1-6	4-14	0-1	4-24	20.0	+ 53.35
B W Hills	8-40	1-7	6-17	0-1	1-15	20.0	+ 20.05
B R Millman	8-66	2-9	1-13	0-2	5-42	12.1	+ 68.00
P F I Cole	8-78	5-34	0-27	0-2	3-15	10.3	- 10.17
J Berry	7-27	3-12	3-8	0-2	1-5	25.9	+ 1.33
R Hollinshead	6-49	1-8	0-11	0-3	5-27	12.2	+ 29.00
H Thomson Jones	5-12	1-3	2-6	0-0	2-3	41.7	+ 16.40
M R Stoute	5-18	4-9	1-7	0-0	0-2	27.8	+ 6.20
J H M Gosden	5-22	1-5	3-12	0-0	1-5	22.7	- 3.11
R Charlton	5-22	1-9	2-10	1-1	1-2	22.7	+ 4.00
P T Walwyn	5-29	0-7	3-12	0-2	2-8	17.2	- 2.47
P Chapple-Hyam	5-30	1-14	4-9	0-0	0-7	16.7	- 0.50
M C Pipe	5-36	0-1	0-12	0-0	5-23	13.9	- 2.88
J L Dunlop	5-50	1-20	3-12	0-0	1-18	10.0	- 28.58
J M Bradley	5-59	0-2	2-14	0-0	3-43	8.5	- 8.50
M Johnston	4-8	1-1	2-4	0-1	1-2	50.0	+ 22.50
Sir M Prescott	4-26	1-9	3-11	0-1	0-5	15.4	- 12.03
Lord Huntingdon	4-26	0-5	3-9	0-0	1-12	15.4	+ 6.00

Leading Jockeys

	Total W-R	Per cent	£1 Level Stake	Best Trainer	W-R	Per cent	£1 Level Stake
J Williams	19-160	11.9	+ 56.96	B R Millman	3-15	20.0	+ 76.00
M Roberts	15-41	36.6	+ 41.02	M C Pipe	3-4	75.0	+ 7.13
L Dettori	14-58	24.1	- 12.97	L M Cumani	7-11	63.6	+ 6.10
J Reid	12-95	12.6	- 25.56	P Chapple-Hyam	3-11	27.3	+ 6.50
T Sprake	10-69	14.5	- 6.12	R J Hodges	7-28	25.0	+ 21.13
T Quinn	9-92	9.8	- 25.51	P F I Cole	3-38	7.9	- 16.67
W Ryan	8-39	20.5	+ 25.83	H R A Cecil	4-15	26.7	+ 4.08
Pat Eddery	8-49	16.3	- 16.92	R Lee	1-1	100.0	+ 7.00
A Munro	8-56	14.3	+ 3.31	L M Cumani	1-1	100.0	+ 0.91
D Harrison	7-48	14.6	+ 17.00	B J Meehan	1-1	100.0	+ 14.00
C Rutter	7-73	9.6	- 16.00	H Candy	3-15	20.0	+ 12.00
R Perham	7-77	9.1	- 30.25	R Hannon	5-38	13.2	- 7.75

How the Favourites Fared

Non-handicaps	W-R	Per cent	£1 Level Stake	Handicaps	W-R	Per cent	£1 Level Stake
2-y-o	12-56	21.4	- 28.26	2-y-o	5-11	45.5	+ 3.85
3-y-o	27-51	52.9	+ 6.03	3-y-o	9-21	42.9	+ 6.34
Weight-for-age	26-54	48.1	- 2.98	All-aged	34-122	27.9	- 3.01
Totals	65-161	40.4	- 25.21	Totals	48-154	31.2	+ 7.18
All favs	113-315	35.9	- 18.03				

Leading Trainers by Month at Chepstow

May

	Total W-R	Non-handicaps 2-y-o	3-y-o+	Handicaps 2-y-o	3-y-o+	Per cent	£1 Level Stake
R J Hodges	4-20	0-2	0-1	0-0	4-17	20.0	- 5.88
H Candy	3-7	0-0	3-5	0-0	0-2	42.9	+ 30.85
H Thomson Jones	2-2	0-0	2-2	0-0	0-0	100.0	+ 1.90
M D I Usher	2-5	0-0	2-4	0-0	0-1	40.0	+ 10.38
J L Dunlop	2-6	0-0	2-4	0-0	0-2	33.3	- 1.83

June

	Total W-R	Non-handicaps 2-y-o	3-y-o+	Handicaps 2-y-o	3-y-o+	Per cent	£1 Level Stake
J Berry	4-10	1-5	3-4	0-0	0-1	40.0	- 1.08
P F I Cole	4-17	2-6	0-6	0-0	2-5	23.5	- 0.17
R Hannon	4-23	3-7	0-2	0-0	1-14	17.4	- 6.25
P T Walwyn	3-5	0-0	1-2	0-0	2-3	60.0	+ 18.30
H R A Cecil	3-6	0-0	3-6	0-0	0-0	50.0	+ 7.33

July

	Total W-R	Non-handicaps 2-y-o	3-y-o+	Handicaps 2-y-o	3-y-o+	Per cent	£1 Level Stake
R Hannon	7-27	2-5	2-8	1-2	2-12	25.9	+ 3.91
L M Cumani	5-7	0-0	4-6	0-0	1-1	71.4	+ 5.78
R J Hodges	5-26	0-1	0-6	0-0	5-19	19.2	+ 11.08
H R A Cecil	3-8	0-0	3-7	0-0	0-1	37.5	- 4.02
M C Pipe	3-8	0-0	0-1	0-0	3-7	37.5	+ 7.13

August

	Total W-R	Non-handicaps 2-y-o	3-y-o+	Handicaps 2-y-o	3-y-o+	Per cent	£1 Level Stake
L M Cumani	4-5	0-0	3-3	1-1	0-1	80.0	+ 3.99
M R Stoute	4-6	4-5	0-0	0-0	0-1	66.7	+ 13.87
B Palling	3-11	0-3	1-2	0-1	2-5	27.3	+ 37.50
R Hannon	3-20	2-10	0-0	1-4	0-6	15.0	- 9.40
B R Millman	2-11	1-2	0-1	0-1	1-7	18.2	+ 68.00

September

	Total W-R	Non-handicaps 2-y-o	3-y-o+	Handicaps 2-y-o	3-y-o+	Per cent	£1 Level Stake
J Berry	2-3	1-2	0-0	0-0	1-1	66.7	+ 14.50
P Chapple-Hyam	2-3	0-1	2-2	0-0	0-0	66.7	+ 9.00
R Hannon	2-11	1-5	1-3	0-0	0-3	18.2	+ 1.00
P Butler	1-1	0-0	1-1	0-0	0-0	100.0	+ 8.00
B W Hills	1-1	0-0	1-1	0-0	0-0	100.0	+ 0.57

Oct/Nov

	Total W-R	Non-handicaps 2-y-o	3-y-o+	Handicaps 2-y-o	3-y-o+	Per cent	£1 Level Stake
B W Hills	3-10	1-3	1-2	0-0	1-5	30.0	+ 31.75
H R A Cecil	3-11	2-4	0-4	0-0	1-3	27.3	+ 8.50
J H M Gosden	3-11	1-5	1-1	0-0	1-5	27.3	+ 4.25
R Hannon	3-52	2-24	0-9	0-5	1-14	5.8	- 24.00
M Johnston	2-3	0-0	1-1	0-1	1-1	66.7	+ 11.75

CHESTER (Group 2)

Leading Trainers 1990-94

	Total W-R	Non-handicaps 2-y-o	3-y-o+	Handicaps 2-y-o	3-y-o+	Per cent	£1 Level Stake
B W Hills	21-79	4-14	12-39	1-1	4-25	26.6	+ 20.04
J H M Gosden	17-60	3-6	9-26	0-0	5-28	28.3	+ 15.10
M R Stoute	16-64	4-9	6-25	0-2	6-28	25.0	- 2.54
R Hannon	15-69	8-27	2-8	3-11	2-23	21.7	- 9.95
J Berry	15-130	8-49	1-9	2-12	4-60	11.5	- 35.63
H R A Cecil	12-41	3-8	8-22	0-0	1-11	29.3	- 9.52
A Bailey	12-100	0-19	4-16	0-2	8-63	12.0	- 15.58
P F I Cole	11-57	8-17	2-24	1-3	0-13	19.3	- 29.17
C E Brittain	11-72	5-15	4-25	0-3	2-29	15.3	+ 14.95
R Hollinshead	9-140	3-40	2-25	0-7	4-68	6.4	- 60.25
B A McMahon	8-65	0-11	1-13	0-4	7-37	12.3	+ 23.46
E J Alston	7-61	1-12	2-8	1-1	3-40	11.5	+ 11.00
G Lewis	6-24	5-12	0-0	0-4	1-8	25.0	+ 10.41
F H Lee	6-46	2-11	0-6	0-1	4-28	13.0	- 7.50
R M Whitaker	5-24	0-3	0-0	0-0	5-21	20.8	+ 26.00
J W Watts	5-32	2-3	0-1	1-2	2-26	15.6	+ 2.50
M H Easterby	5-47	2-13	1-4	0-6	2-24	10.6	- 14.25
S G Norton	5-53	1-16	0-9	0-2	4-26	9.4	- 11.75
M H Tompkins	4-18	0-1	0-1	0-3	4-13	22.2	+ 22.00
J D Bethell	4-20	1-2	0-1	0-2	3-15	20.0	+ 8.83
P Chapple-Hyam	4-20	2-4	2-11	0-0	0-5	20.0	- 4.15
G Wragg	4-26	0-4	4-12	0-1	0-9	15.4	- 11.63

Leading Jockeys

	Total W-R	Per cent	£1 Level Stake	Best Trainer	W-R	Per cent	£1 Level Stake
Pat Eddery	26-97	26.8	- 15.68	B W Hills	7-13	53.8	+ 10.58
M Roberts	17-89	19.1	+ 17.51	C E Brittain	7-36	19.4	+ 29.75
A Munro	16-100	16.0	- 28.95	C E Brittain	2-5	40.0	- 0.80
W R Swinburn	13-67	19.4	+ 0.61	M R Stoute	5-26	19.2	- 7.39
D Holland	12-69	17.4	+ 14.50	B W Hills	6-22	27.3	+ 19.00
J Carroll	12-94	12.8	- 46.99	J Berry	9-72	12.5	- 36.62
T Quinn	11-59	18.6	- 16.37	P F I Cole	6-32	18.8	- 14.45
Paul Eddery	11-61	18.0	- 4.98	G Lewis	4-10	40.0	+ 11.66
L Dettori	10-62	16.1	- 12.43	J H M Gosden	3-6	50.0	+ 14.00
W Ryan	10-63	15.9	- 11.85	H R A Cecil	5-19	26.3	- 2.85
K Darley	10-69	14.5	- 12.10	P S Felgate	1-1	100.0	+ 10.00
W Carson	8-71	11.3	- 39.40	B W Hills	2-6	33.3	+ 5.00

How the Favourites Fared

Non-handicaps	W-R	Per cent	£1 Level Stake	Handicaps	W-R	Per cent	£1 Level Stake
2-y-o	37-78	47.4	- 0.06	2-y-o	3-14	21.4	- 5.87
3-y-o	26-44	59.1	+ 13.62	3-y-o	9-35	25.7	- 2.00
Weight-for-age	13-32	40.6	- 1.41	All-aged	28-102	27.5	- 6.66
Totals	76-154	49.4	+ 12.15	Totals	40-151	26.5	- 14.53
All favs	116-305	38.0	- 2.38				

Leading Trainers by Month at Chester

May

	Total W-R	Non-handicaps 2-y-o	3-y-o+	Handicaps 2-y-o	3-y-o+	Per cent	£1 Level Stake
B W Hills	9-39	0-3	7-24	0-0	2-12	23.1	- 0.15
J H M Gosden	8-21	0-0	4-10	0-0	4-11	38.1	+ 24.75
R Hannon	7-26	6-10	1-6	0-0	0-10	26.9	+ 4.01
H R A Cecil	6-14	0-0	6-13	0-0	0-1	42.9	+ 2.01
M R Stoute	6-24	0-0	2-15	0-0	4-9	25.0	+ 0.94

June

	Total W-R	Non-handicaps 2-y-o	3-y-o+	Handicaps 2-y-o	3-y-o+	Per cent	£1 Level Stake
P F I Cole	4-7	3-3	1-2	0-0	0-2	57.1	+ 3.91
B A McMahon	3-8	0-4	1-1	0-0	2-3	37.5	+ 8.13
A Bailey	3-10	0-2	2-4	0-0	1-4	30.0	+ 2.17
R Hannon	2-5	0-1	1-1	0-0	1-3	40.0	+ 1.67
B W Hills	2-5	0-0	2-3	0-0	0-2	40.0	+ 0.94

July

	Total W-R	Non-handicaps 2-y-o	3-y-o+	Handicaps 2-y-o	3-y-o+	Per cent	£1 Level Stake
G Lewis	5-9	4-6	0-0	0-1	1-2	55.6	+ 15.41
J H M Gosden	5-9	2-2	3-5	0-0	0-2	55.6	+ 6.13
P F I Cole	4-14	3-5	1-6	0-0	0-3	28.6	- 5.33
A Bailey	4-21	0-5	1-3	0-0	3-13	19.0	+ 16.50
H R A Cecil	3-6	2-2	1-2	0-0	0-2	50.0	+ 0.15

August

	Total W-R	Non-handicaps 2-y-o	3-y-o+	Handicaps 2-y-o	3-y-o+	Per cent	£1 Level Stake
R Hannon	4-11	1-4	0-1	3-5	0-1	36.4	+ 5.71
B W Hills	3-11	1-4	1-5	0-0	1-2	27.3	- 1.26
J Berry	3-30	2-12	0-1	0-7	1-10	10.0	- 4.00
R Hollinshead	3-30	1-8	1-6	0-2	1-14	10.0	+ 10.00
G Wragg	2-7	0-1	2-2	0-1	0-3	28.6	+ 1.50

September

	Total W-R	Non-handicaps 2-y-o	3-y-o+	Handicaps 2-y-o	3-y-o+	Per cent	£1 Level Stake
J D Bethell	2-2	1-1	0-0	0-0	1-1	100.0	+ 11.33
M R Stoute	2-6	1-2	1-3	0-0	0-1	33.3	+ 2.17
J L Dunlop	1-1	0-0	1-1	0-0	0-0	100.0	+ 2.75
J L Harris	1-1	0-0	0-0	0-0	1-1	100.0	+ 10.00
D Murray Smith	1-1	0-0	0-0	1-1	0-0	100.0	+ 6.00

Oct/Nov

	Total W-R	Non-handicaps 2-y-o	3-y-o+	Handicaps 2-y-o	3-y-o+	Per cent	£1 Level Stake
B W Hills	6-15	3-5	1-2	1-1	1-7	40.0	+ 27.00
M R Stoute	3-7	2-3	1-1	0-1	0-2	42.9	+ 2.17
J W Watts	3-7	0-1	0-0	1-1	2-5	42.9	+ 13.00
M J Camacho	3-9	1-1	0-1	0-1	2-6	33.3	+ 3.50
C E Brittain	3-16	3-6	0-1	0-3	0-6	18.8	- 5.80

DONCASTER (Group 1)

Leading Trainers 1990-94

	Total W-R	Non-handicaps 2-y-o	Non-handicaps 3-y-o+	Handicaps 2-y-o	Handicaps 3-y-o+	Per cent	£1 Level Stake
J H M Gosden	36-142	12-37	14-61	1-2	9-42	25.4	+ 35.60
H R A Cecil	31-105	12-27	18-64	0-0	1-14	29.5	+ 19.59
B W Hills	30-130	6-41	20-55	0-4	4-30	23.1	+ 36.82
R Hannon	27-249	11-69	7-57	4-36	5-87	10.8	- 84.05
J Berry	22-137	10-58	4-23	0-11	8-45	16.1	+ 60.77
Mrs J Ramsden	20-182	2-19	3-19	4-20	11-124	11.0	- 0.88
M R Stoute	19-111	8-39	7-40	2-7	2-25	17.1	- 5.28
R W Armstrong	15-48	7-13	4-14	0-4	4-17	31.3	+ 59.34
Mrs M Reveley	15-120	0-12	3-11	0-8	12-89	12.5	- 22.75
J L Dunlop	14-97	3-29	3-28	2-7	6-33	14.4	+ 10.43
L M Cumani	13-80	0-11	7-36	0-2	6-31	16.3	- 18.68
M Johnston	13-133	2-27	3-22	0-13	8-71	9.8	- 44.60
M H Easterby	12-138	3-31	1-13	4-17	4-77	8.7	- 28.75
G Wragg	11-56	3-9	5-27	0-0	3-20	19.6	- 3.92
I A Balding	11-72	2-17	3-16	0-4	6-35	15.3	+ 14.28
A C Stewart	9-45	1-11	4-13	0-2	4-19	20.0	+ 11.00
M R Channon	8-61	4-18	1-10	0-5	3-28	13.1	+ 11.85
C E Brittain	8-146	0-28	4-50	1-10	3-58	5.5	- 82.67
R Hollinshead	8-204	0-47	3-53	0-15	5-89	3.9	-112.29
H Thomson Jones	7-43	4-14	3-15	0-1	0-13	16.3	+ 13.38
M A Jarvis	7-49	2-12	2-11	0-4	3-22	14.3	- 23.20
F H Lee	7-98	1-13	0-17	0-14	6-54	7.1	- 24.00

Leading Jockeys

	Total W-R	Per cent	£1 Level Stake	Best Trainer	W-R	Per cent	£1 Level Stake
Pat Eddery	46-216	21.3	+ 34.46	B W Hills	7-19	36.8	+ 47.45
W Carson	31-238	13.0	- 71.87	J H M Gosden	5-14	35.7	+ 6.00
K Darley	29-222	13.1	- 8.98	Mrs M Reveley	7-41	17.1	+ 2.25
L Dettori	25-194	12.9	- 55.62	J H M Gosden	5-22	22.7	+ 6.50
M Hills	23-154	14.9	+ 14.29	B W Hills	9-49	18.4	- 11.59
W R Swinburn	22-170	12.9	- 33.84	M R Stoute	7-47	14.9	- 5.00
M Roberts	21-194	10.8	- 71.44	A C Stewart	5-25	20.0	+ 8.50
W Ryan	19-147	12.9	- 34.48	H R A Cecil	10-39	25.6	+ 12.38
B Raymond	17-132	12.9	- 8.73	R Hannon	3-20	15.0	- 4.92
R Cochrane	17-186	9.1	- 66.25	J H M Gosden	3-12	25.0	+ 14.57
J Carroll	16-151	10.6	- 10.03	J Berry	13-90	14.4	+ 27.77
J Reid	16-162	9.9	- 69.39	R Hannon	5-44	11.4	- 9.00

How the Favourites Fared

Non-handicaps	W-R	Per cent	£1 Level Stake	Handicaps	W-R	Per cent	£1 Level Stake
2-y-o	53-153	34.6	- 29.77	2-y-o	7-33	21.2	- 4.50
3-y-o	27-68	39.7	- 3.30	3-y-o	13-55	23.6	- 9.69
Weight-for-age	47-110	42.7	+ 2.85	All-aged	61-211	28.9	+ 16.94
Totals	127-331	38.4	- 30.22	Totals	81-299	27.1	+ 2.75
All favs	208-630	33.0	- 27.47				

Leading Trainers by Month at Doncaster

March/Apr

	Total W-R	Non-handicaps 2-y-o	3-y-o+	Handicaps 2-y-o	3-y-o+	Per cent	£1 Level Stake
J Berry	13-37	4-15	4-7	0-0	5-15	35.1	+ 92.10
B W Hills	10-25	1-5	8-16	0-0	1-4	40.0	+ 13.88
Mrs J Ramsden	5-44	0-1	1-9	0-0	4-34	11.4	+ 13.50
M R Channon	4-22	2-4	0-7	0-0	2-11	18.2	+ 9.85
C E Brittain	4-36	0-0	3-20	0-0	1-16	11.1	- 11.42

May

	Total W-R	Non-handicaps 2-y-o	3-y-o+	Handicaps 2-y-o	3-y-o+	Per cent	£1 Level Stake
H R A Cecil	6-13	0-0	6-12	0-0	0-1	46.2	+ 8.61
B W Hills	5-18	1-3	4-7	0-0	0-8	27.8	+ 4.54
M R Stoute	4-12	1-2	1-4	0-0	2-6	33.3	+ 10.00
F H Lee	4-18	1-2	0-2	0-0	3-14	22.2	+ 18.00
J W Watts	4-23	0-1	0-3	0-0	4-19	17.4	- 0.25

June

	Total W-R	Non-handicaps 2-y-o	3-y-o+	Handicaps 2-y-o	3-y-o+	Per cent	£1 Level Stake
J H M Gosden	5-7	0-1	3-4	0-0	2-2	71.4	+ 5.80
M H Easterby	4-21	2-9	1-3	0-0	1-9	19.0	+ 4.50
R W Armstrong	3-5	1-1	0-0	0-0	2-4	60.0	+ 8.25
A C Stewart	3-5	0-0	1-2	0-0	2-3	60.0	+ 7.50
G Wragg	3-7	0-0	0-1	0-0	3-6	42.9	+ 9.50

July

	Total W-R	Non-handicaps 2-y-o	3-y-o+	Handicaps 2-y-o	3-y-o+	Per cent	£1 Level Stake
I A Balding	4-8	0-2	1-1	0-0	3-5	50.0	+ 7.13
R Hannon	4-15	3-7	0-2	0-0	1-6	26.7	- 4.75
L M Cumani	3-6	0-0	1-2	0-0	2-4	50.0	+ 1.61
Mrs M Reveley	3-12	0-3	0-2	0-0	3-7	25.0	+ 10.50
M Johnston	3-13	1-2	0-2	0-0	2-9	23.1	+ 13.00

September

	Total W-R	Non-handicaps 2-y-o	3-y-o+	Handicaps 2-y-o	3-y-o+	Per cent	£1 Level Stake
R Hannon	14-89	1-19	6-18	3-20	4-32	15.7	+ 25.20
J H M Gosden	13-51	4-8	6-30	0-0	3-13	25.5	+ 21.58
M R Stoute	10-49	5-12	3-19	2-6	0-12	20.4	+ 5.13
H R A Cecil	9-39	3-8	6-25	0-0	0-6	23.1	- 1.00
B W Hills	6-51	1-13	3-22	0-3	2-13	11.8	+ 11.53

Oct/Nov

	Total W-R	Non-handicaps 2-y-o	3-y-o+	Handicaps 2-y-o	3-y-o+	Per cent	£1 Level Stake
J H M Gosden	14-60	7-25	3-15	1-2	3-18	23.3	+ 24.52
H R A Cecil	12-33	9-17	3-11	0-0	0-5	36.4	+ 23.64
R W Armstrong	7-19	4-8	2-4	0-3	1-4	36.8	+ 50.50
J L Dunlop	7-43	3-18	1-6	1-5	2-14	16.3	+ 19.88
B W Hills	6-29	3-18	2-6	0-1	1-4	20.7	+ 8.00

Leading Trainers 1990-94

	Total W-R	Non-handicaps 2-y-o	3-y-o+	Handicaps 2-y-o	3-y-o+	Per cent	£1 Level Stake
J Berry	39-185	21-93	11-34	0-5	7-53	21.1	- 21.35
M Johnston	15-83	5-22	3-13	3-3	4-45	18.1	- 32.99
M P Naughton	15-96	0-2	1-27	0-0	14-67	15.6	+ 46.98
M H Tompkins	11-26	4-8	2-7	0-1	5-10	42.3	+ 26.15
Sir M Prescott	11-47	4-14	4-14	0-0	3-19	23.4	- 0.96
M H Easterby	9-47	4-16	1-8	0-1	4-22	19.1	- 18.68
S G Norton	9-56	1-15	5-19	0-1	3-21	16.1	- 0.22
P C Haslam	8-30	2-7	1-3	1-1	4-19	26.7	+ 3.94
Mrs M Reveley	8-67	2-11	2-13	0-0	4-43	11.9	- 33.41
T D Barron	8-72	1-15	2-15	0-1	5-41	11.1	- 31.52
J H M Gosden	7-21	2-6	4-11	0-0	1-4	33.3	- 1.73
J L Spearing	7-43	0-9	0-3	0-1	7-30	16.3	- 11.13
D W Chapman	7-81	2-6	0-7	0-0	5-68	8.6	- 4.25
Denys Smith	7-86	3-19	0-12	0-1	4-54	8.1	- 26.25
M D Hammond	6-31	1-4	0-1	0-0	5-26	19.4	+ 7.88
A Harrison	6-38	1-7	2-7	0-1	3-23	15.8	+ 1.50
R M Whitaker	6-45	1-7	0-8	0-2	5-28	13.3	- 7.03
B W Hills	5-14	0-2	4-9	0-0	1-3	35.7	+ 0.10
M J Camacho	5-16	0-3	2-4	0-0	3-9	31.3	+ 3.48
J Etherington	5-19	2-6	2-5	0-1	1-7	26.3	+ 18.25
N Tinkler	5-24	1-3	1-7	0-0	3-14	20.8	- 0.90
R Allan	5-35	1-6	1-6	0-0	3-23	14.3	- 1.63

Leading Jockeys

	Total W-R	Per cent	£1 Level Stake	Best Trainer	W-R	Per cent	£1 Level Stake
K Darley	35-169	20.7	- 39.36	J L Spearing	5-12	41.7	+ 10.50
J Carroll	30-161	18.6	- 50.99	J Berry	24-98	24.5	- 22.24
J Weaver	28-92	30.4	+ 49.11	M Johnston	8-25	32.0	- 3.07
G Duffield	24-123	19.5	- 18.11	Sir M Prescott	8-36	22.2	+ 2.29
K Fallon	15-136	11.0	- 20.77	M P Naughton	4-30	13.3	+ 16.25
D McKeown	13-123	10.6	- 71.91	J Berry	3-7	42.9	+ 11.50
J Fanning	13-167	7.8	- 17.01	Miss L A Perratt	3-33	9.1	- 1.95
N Connorton	12-85	14.1	+ 74.48	M J Camacho	5-10	50.0	+ 9.48
J Fortune	11-87	12.6	- 8.19	L M Cumani	2-4	50.0	- 0.76
G Hind	8-54	14.8	- 30.59	J H M Gosden	4-9	44.4	+ 0.78
S Webster	8-79	10.1	- 14.50	J Etherington	1-1	100.0	+ 3.50
J Lowe	7-160	4.4	-131.07	Sir M Prescott	2-9	22.2	- 4.25

How the Favourites Fared

Non-handicaps	W-R	Per cent	£1 Level Stake	Handicaps	W-R	Per cent	£1 Level Stake
2-y-o	43-92	46.7	- 2.57	2-y-o	2-4	50.0	+ 1.80
3-y-o	25-39	64.1	+ 13.76	3-y-o	12-25	48.0	+ 2.78
Weight-for-age	34-60	56.7	+ 12.81	All-aged	49-163	30.1	- 11.22
Totals	102-191	53.4	+ 24.00	Totals	63-192	32.8	- 6.64
All favs	165-383	43.1	+ 17.36				

Leading Trainers by Month at Edinburgh

March/Apr

	Total W-R	Non-handicaps 2-y-o	3-y-o+	Handicaps 2-y-o	3-y-o+	Per cent	£1 Level Stake
J Berry	5-16	3-5	2-6	0-0	0-5	31.3	+ 12.49
Sir M Prescott	4-5	0-0	2-3	0-0	2-2	80.0	+ 7.85
J H M Gosden	2-2	0-0	2-2	0-0	0-0	100.0	+ 1.87
Mrs J Ramsden	2-13	0-0	1-5	0-0	1-8	15.4	- 3.50
M J Camacho	1-1	0-0	0-0	0-0	1-1	100.0	+ 1.38

May

	Total W-R	Non-handicaps 2-y-o	3-y-o+	Handicaps 2-y-o	3-y-o+	Per cent	£1 Level Stake
J Berry	8-24	3-8	1-5	0-0	4-11	33.3	+ 26.88
M Johnston	4-17	2-4	1-5	0-0	1-8	23.5	- 4.02
J G FitzGerald	3-8	0-0	2-4	0-0	1-4	37.5	+ 4.75
T D Barron	3-11	0-1	2-3	0-0	1-7	27.3	+ 0.25
M H Tompkins	2-2	0-0	1-1	0-0	1-1	100.0	+ 8.50

June

	Total W-R	Non-handicaps 2-y-o	3-y-o+	Handicaps 2-y-o	3-y-o+	Per cent	£1 Level Stake
J Berry	12-45	6-19	6-13	0-0	0-13	26.7	- 12.81
B W Hills	4-9	0-0	3-7	0-0	1-2	44.4	+ 2.60
R M Whitaker	4-15	1-1	0-3	0-0	3-11	26.7	+ 14.60
M P Naughton	4-27	0-0	1-9	0-0	3-18	14.8	+ 24.50
M Bell	3-5	0-0	0-1	0-0	3-4	60.0	+ 5.20

July

	Total W-R	Non-handicaps 2-y-o	3-y-o+	Handicaps 2-y-o	3-y-o+	Per cent	£1 Level Stake
J Berry	9-42	6-26	1-6	0-0	2-10	21.4	- 13.71
M P Naughton	6-19	0-0	0-6	0-0	6-13	31.6	+ 5.88
M D Hammond	4-13	1-3	0-1	0-0	3-9	30.8	+ 5.88
M Johnston	4-14	0-2	2-4	0-0	2-8	28.6	- 5.27
Denys Smith	4-22	1-5	0-2	0-0	3-15	18.2	+ 17.50

August

	Total W-R	Non-handicaps 2-y-o	3-y-o+	Handicaps 2-y-o	3-y-o+	Per cent	£1 Level Stake
M H Easterby	3-6	1-2	0-0	0-1	2-3	50.0	+ 5.83
Mrs M Reveley	3-8	0-1	1-2	0-0	2-5	37.5	+ 3.33
M Johnston	2-13	0-3	0-0	2-2	0-8	15.4	- 3.50
J Berry	2-17	2-9	0-0	0-2	0-6	11.8	- 12.94
R Boss	1-1	0-0	0-0	0-0	1-1	100.0	+ 6.00

September

	Total W-R	Non-handicaps 2-y-o	3-y-o+	Handicaps 2-y-o	3-y-o+	Per cent	£1 Level Stake
Mrs M Reveley	3-9	1-3	1-1	0-0	1-5	33.3	+ 5.47
P C Haslam	2-3	1-1	0-0	1-1	0-1	66.7	+ 7.00
J Pearce	2-3	0-0	0-0	0-1	2-2	66.7	+ 7.25
A Harrison	2-4	1-1	0-0	0-1	1-2	50.0	+ 12.00
M P Naughton	2-7	0-0	0-1	0-0	2-6	28.6	+ 12.50

Oct/Nov

	Total W-R	Non-handicaps 2-y-o	3-y-o+	Handicaps 2-y-o	3-y-o+	Per cent	£1 Level Stake
R Hannon	3-3	3-3	0-0	0-0	0-0	100.0	+ 6.35
M H Tompkins	3-7	2-3	0-1	0-0	1-3	42.9	+ 4.95
A Bailey	2-3	0-0	0-0	0-0	2-3	66.7	+ 15.50
P J Makin	2-4	1-1	0-2	0-0	1-1	50.0	+ 7.00
C Tinkler	2-7	0-3	1-1	0-0	1-3	28.6	+ 8.50

EPSOM (Group 1)

Leading Trainers 1990-94

	Total W-R	Non-handicaps 2-y-o	3-y-o+	Handicaps 2-y-o	3-y-o+	Per cent	£1 Level Stake
R Hannon	15-126	5-31	4-35	0-4	6-56	11.9	- 39.40
J Berry	12-47	5-18	2-2	0-0	5-27	25.5	+ 10.94
D R C Elsworth	10-55	1-4	6-31	0-0	3-20	18.2	+ 11.85
R Akehurst	10-65	1-4	1-7	0-0	8-54	15.4	+ 10.03
Lord Huntingdon	8-20	2-3	2-4	0-1	4-12	40.0	+ 37.66
C E Brittain	8-56	2-4	4-28	0-1	2-23	14.3	+ 25.50
G Lewis	8-94	2-29	3-24	0-2	3-39	8.5	- 51.79
M R Stoute	7-49	0-0	4-32	0-0	3-17	14.3	- 17.25
J L Dunlop	6-27	1-6	4-12	1-1	0-8	22.2	- 4.38
P F I Cole	5-53	1-14	2-22	0-0	2-17	9.4	- 21.25
H R A Cecil	4-19	0-1	2-15	0-0	2-3	21.1	+ 3.83
A C Stewart	4-20	0-0	3-12	0-1	1-7	20.0	- 4.29
J W Hills	4-26	1-1	1-10	0-0	2-15	15.4	- 5.20
M McCormack	3-9	0-0	1-2	0-0	2-7	33.3	+ 24.50
M A Jarvis	3-10	0-1	1-2	0-0	2-7	30.0	+ 12.50
A Fabre (Fra)	3-12	0-0	3-12	0-0	0-0	25.0	+ 9.88
H Thomson Jones	3-16	0-1	1-4	0-0	2-11	18.8	+ 5.33
P Chapple-Hyam	3-19	0-1	3-14	0-0	0-4	15.8	- 4.75
R J Hodges	3-21	0-0	0-2	0-0	3-19	14.3	- 3.50
M Bell	3-23	2-6	0-4	0-1	1-12	13.0	+ 7.25
P T Walwyn	3-26	0-0	1-7	0-1	2-18	11.5	+ 12.00
L J Holt	3-27	0-3	0-2	0-0	3-22	11.1	0.00

Leading Jockeys

	Total W-R	Per cent	£1 Level Stake	Best Trainer	W-R	Per cent	£1 Level Stake
M Roberts	24-133	18.0	+ 20.07	C E Brittain	5-30	16.7	+ 19.00
Pat Eddery	21-132	15.9	- 28.88	J Berry	5-17	29.4	- 1.96
J Reid	16-101	15.8	+ 2.37	L J Holt	3-16	18.8	+ 11.00
W Carson	14-86	16.3	- 2.14	J L Dunlop	4-15	26.7	- 0.62
L Dettori	11-81	13.6	- 14.88	Lord Huntingdon	2-3	66.7	+ 11.62
R Cochrane	10-66	15.2	- 5.62	D A Wilson	1-1	100.0	+ 7.50
T Quinn	9-98	9.2	- 51.75	R Akehurst	3-21	14.3	- 5.75
A Munro	8-57	14.0	+ 42.00	Lord Huntingdon	2-6	33.3	+ 22.00
R Hills	5-32	15.6	- 3.87	J W Hills	2-6	33.3	- 0.20
C Asmussen	4-16	25.0	+ 22.88	J Berry	1-1	100.0	+ 7.00
J Williams	4-35	11.4	+ 2.00	D R C Elsworth	2-9	22.2	+ 12.00
D Holland	4-37	10.8	- 3.50	M J Heaton-Ellis	1-2	50.0	+ 5.00

How the Favourites Fared

Non-handicaps	W-R	Per cent	£1 Level Stake	Handicaps	W-R	Per cent	£1 Level Stake
2-y-o	11-32	34.4	- 5.43	2-y-o	3-3	100.0	+ 9.25
3-y-o	20-50	40.0	+ 3.63	3-y-o	8-35	22.9	- 8.04
Weight-for-age	11-22	50.0	+ 2.42	All-aged	11-72	15.3	- 29.52
Totals	42-104	40.4	+ 0.62	Totals	22-110	20.0	- 28.31
All favs	64-214	29.9	- 27.69				

Leading Trainers by Month at Epsom

March/Apr

	Total W-R	Non-handicaps 2-y-o	Non-handicaps 3-y-o+	Handicaps 2-y-o	Handicaps 3-y-o+	Per cent	£1 Level Stake
J Berry	2-3	1-1	0-0	0-0	1-2	66.7	+ 2.13
G Harwood	1-1	0-0	1-1	0-0	0-0	100.0	+ 2.13
R J Hodges	1-1	0-0	0-0	0-0	1-1	100.0	+ 6.00
A C Stewart	1-1	0-0	1-1	0-0	0-0	100.0	+ 0.91
Lord Huntingdon	1-1	0-0	0-0	0-0	1-1	100.0	+ 2.75

June

	Total W-R	Non-handicaps 2-y-o	Non-handicaps 3-y-o+	Handicaps 2-y-o	Handicaps 3-y-o+	Per cent	£1 Level Stake
R Hannon	10-87	4-20	3-26	0-0	3-41	11.5	- 39.90
J Berry	7-31	4-14	0-0	0-0	3-17	22.6	+ 5.41
C E Brittain	7-46	2-3	3-24	0-0	2-19	15.2	+ 30.00
R Akehurst	6-39	0-2	1-4	0-0	5-33	15.4	+ 5.90
M R Stoute	6-44	0-0	3-29	0-0	3-15	13.6	- 17.25

July

	Total W-R	Non-handicaps 2-y-o	Non-handicaps 3-y-o+	Handicaps 2-y-o	Handicaps 3-y-o+	Per cent	£1 Level Stake
R Akehurst	3-11	0-0	0-2	0-0	3-9	27.3	+ 15.63
D R C Elsworth	2-2	0-0	2-2	0-0	0-0	100.0	+ 2.60
G Lewis	2-8	0-2	0-3	0-0	2-3	25.0	+ 11.50
M J Bolton	1-1	0-0	0-0	0-0	1-1	100.0	+ 12.00
J L Dunlop	1-1	0-0	1-1	0-0	0-0	100.0	+ 1.75

August

	Total W-R	Non-handicaps 2-y-o	Non-handicaps 3-y-o+	Handicaps 2-y-o	Handicaps 3-y-o+	Per cent	£1 Level Stake
Lord Huntingdon	3-8	1-2	0-1	0-0	2-5	37.5	+ 2.28
G Lewis	3-18	1-6	2-4	0-1	0-7	16.7	- 10.54
R J Hodges	2-5	0-0	0-0	0-0	2-5	40.0	+ 5.50
J Berry	2-8	0-2	1-1	0-0	1-5	25.0	+ 6.91
P F I Cole	2-10	0-5	1-2	0-0	1-3	20.0	- 0.50

September

	Total W-R	Non-handicaps 2-y-o	Non-handicaps 3-y-o+	Handicaps 2-y-o	Handicaps 3-y-o+	Per cent	£1 Level Stake
H Candy	1-1	0-0	0-0	0-0	1-1	100.0	+ 5.00
J L Dunlop	1-1	0-0	0-0	1-1	0-0	100.0	+ 4.50
D R C Elsworth	1-1	0-0	0-0	0-0	1-1	100.0	+ 6.50
J Berry	1-2	0-0	1-1	0-0	0-1	50.0	- 0.50
Lord Huntingdon	1-2	0-0	1-1	0-1	0-0	50.0	+ 15.00

FOLKESTONE (Group 4)

Leading Trainers 1990-94

	Total W-R	Non-handicaps 2-y-o	3-y-o+	Handicaps 2-y-o	3-y-o+	Per cent	£1 Level Stake
R Hannon	23-143	7-54	10-36	1-10	5-43	16.1	- 24.04
G Harwood	21-61	5-12	13-28	0-0	3-21	34.4	+ 36.90
R Akehurst	17-99	2-13	4-29	0-2	11-55	17.2	+ 13.75
P F I Cole	14-72	7-20	4-25	1-5	2-22	19.4	+ 13.03
J Berry	10-39	5-21	5-11	0-5	0-2	25.6	- 12.22
J Pearce	10-41	0-5	5-15	0-0	5-21	24.4	+ 7.75
J L Dunlop	10-45	1-13	4-11	1-1	4-20	22.2	- 3.01
M R Channon	10-66	4-28	1-16	2-4	3-18	15.2	- 10.25
N A Callaghan	8-42	2-8	2-13	3-7	1-14	19.0	- 7.38
S Dow	8-85	2-16	0-22	0-3	6-44	9.4	+ 47.88
D W P Arbuthnot	7-28	2-8	0-7	1-2	4-11	25.0	+ 28.00
Sir M Prescott	7-42	3-18	1-9	0-4	3-11	16.7	- 3.50
G L Moore	7-45	1-13	2-12	0-3	4-17	15.6	+ 2.25
G Lewis	7-116	1-31	2-29	1-8	3-48	6.0	- 73.13
L M Cumani	6-22	1-5	5-14	0-0	0-3	27.3	+ 0.85
Mrs L Piggott	6-35	0-7	4-13	0-1	2-14	17.1	- 1.67
P T Walwyn	6-37	1-11	4-13	0-1	1-12	16.2	- 4.33
W Carter	6-53	2-14	2-14	0-3	2-22	11.3	- 5.38
C E Brittain	6-55	0-11	2-16	1-1	3-27	10.9	+ 11.83
Mrs J Cecil	5-9	2-4	1-2	0-0	2-3	55.6	+ 14.83
B Hanbury	5-15	1-2	3-7	0-0	1-6	33.3	+ 9.83
H R A Cecil	5-18	1-4	4-14	0-0	0-0	27.8	- 6.05

Leading Jockeys

	Total W-R	Per cent	£1 Level Stake	Best Trainer	W-R	Per cent	£1 Level Stake
R Cochrane	28-131	21.4	- 24.04	G Harwood	9-18	50.0	+ 17.63
Pat Eddery	27-91	29.7	- 16.18	G Harwood	5-6	83.3	+ 2.03
T Quinn	25-163	15.3	+ 56.41	P F I Cole	9-41	22.0	- 1.64
B Rouse	16-173	9.2	- 81.73	G L Moore	6-29	20.7	+ 13.75
G Duffield	15-101	14.9	- 19.17	Sir M Prescott	6-35	17.1	- 13.50
Paul Eddery	15-113	13.3	+ 1.41	P Chapple-Hyam	3-4	75.0	+ 21.50
M Roberts	13-73	17.8	+ 14.96	A C Stewart	3-6	50.0	+ 11.38
W Carson	12-45	26.7	+ 1.84	J L Dunlop	3-8	37.5	+ 6.50
W Newnes	12-143	8.4	- 66.12	Miss B Sanders	2-15	13.3	+ 1.00
L Piggott	11-41	26.8	+ 5.75	J Berry	3-3	100.0	+ 3.62
A Munro	11-68	16.2	- 6.59	P F I Cole	2-4	50.0	+ 8.00
L Dettori	11-73	15.1	- 11.50	L M Cumani	2-8	25.0	- 2.25

How the Favourites Fared

Non-handicaps	W-R	Per cent	£1 Level Stake	Handicaps	W-R	Per cent	£1 Level Stake
2-y-o	39-111	35.1	- 12.07	2-y-o	8-18	44.4	+ 6.30
3-y-o	31-66	47.0	- 4.39	3-y-o	14-37	37.8	+ 6.54
Weight-for-age	44-78	56.4	+ 32.54	All-aged	44-152	28.9	- 12.89
Totals	114-255	44.7	+ 16.08	Totals	66-207	31.9	- 0.05
All favs	180-462	39.0	+ 16.03				

Leading Trainers by Month at Folkestone

March/Apr

	Total W-R	Non-handicaps 2-y-o	Non-handicaps 3-y-o+	Handicaps 2-y-o	Handicaps 3-y-o+	Per cent	£1 Level Stake
R Hannon	7-28	1-3	6-16	0-0	0-9	25.0	- 2.56
P F I Cole	4-14	0-0	3-10	0-0	1-4	28.6	- 2.47
R J Hodges	4-15	0-0	3-8	0-0	1-7	26.7	+ 5.25
P T Walwyn	3-5	0-0	3-5	0-0	0-0	60.0	+ 0.58
Mrs L Piggott	3-7	0-0	1-3	0-0	2-4	42.9	+ 14.50

May

	Total W-R	Non-handicaps 2-y-o	Non-handicaps 3-y-o+	Handicaps 2-y-o	Handicaps 3-y-o+	Per cent	£1 Level Stake
J Berry	2-2	1-1	1-1	0-0	0-0	100.0	+ 2.12
G Harwood	2-2	0-0	2-2	0-0	0-0	100.0	+ 2.08
N A Callaghan	2-8	1-2	1-4	0-0	0-2	25.0	- 1.40
H Candy	1-1	0-0	0-0	0-0	1-1	100.0	+ 2.75
J T Gifford	1-1	0-0	0-0	0-0	1-1	100.0	+ 5.50

June

	Total W-R	Non-handicaps 2-y-o	Non-handicaps 3-y-o+	Handicaps 2-y-o	Handicaps 3-y-o+	Per cent	£1 Level Stake
J Pearce	4-5	0-0	1-1	0-0	3-4	80.0	+ 12.38
G Harwood	3-5	1-1	2-3	0-0	0-1	60.0	+ 1.24
S Dow	3-12	1-3	0-2	0-0	2-7	25.0	+ 7.38
D W P Arbuthnot	2-2	0-0	0-0	0-0	2-2	100.0	+ 20.00
G Lewis	2-11	1-4	1-3	0-0	0-4	18.2	0.00

July

	Total W-R	Non-handicaps 2-y-o	Non-handicaps 3-y-o+	Handicaps 2-y-o	Handicaps 3-y-o+	Per cent	£1 Level Stake
N A Callaghan	4-12	1-2	0-1	2-4	1-5	33.3	+ 0.93
R Hannon	4-13	1-3	1-4	1-3	1-3	30.8	+ 8.89
B W Hills	3-4	0-0	2-3	0-0	1-1	75.0	+ 3.76
J L Dunlop	3-6	0-0	1-2	1-1	1-3	50.0	+ 4.44
W Carter	3-8	2-4	0-0	0-0	1-4	37.5	+ 22.00

August

	Total W-R	Non-handicaps 2-y-o	Non-handicaps 3-y-o+	Handicaps 2-y-o	Handicaps 3-y-o+	Per cent	£1 Level Stake
J Pearce	3-4	0-0	2-2	0-0	1-2	75.0	+ 8.88
R Akehurst	3-10	0-1	0-1	0-0	3-8	30.0	+ 9.50
W Carter	3-11	0-2	2-4	0-0	1-5	27.3	+ 6.63
G Harwood	3-12	0-0	2-5	0-0	1-7	25.0	+ 13.86
W Jarvis	2-3	0-0	0-0	0-0	2-3	66.7	+ 4.00

September

	Total W-R	Non-handicaps 2-y-o	Non-handicaps 3-y-o+	Handicaps 2-y-o	Handicaps 3-y-o+	Per cent	£1 Level Stake
G Harwood	4-12	0-3	3-7	0-0	1-2	33.3	+ 15.50
L M Cumani	3-6	1-2	2-4	0-0	0-0	50.0	+ 5.00
J Berry	3-8	3-7	0-0	0-1	0-0	37.5	+ 2.50
J L Dunlop	3-8	0-1	2-2	0-0	1-5	37.5	+ 2.30
J Pearce	3-10	0-1	2-6	0-0	1-3	30.0	+ 8.50

Oct/Nov

	Total W-R	Non-handicaps 2-y-o	Non-handicaps 3-y-o+	Handicaps 2-y-o	Handicaps 3-y-o+	Per cent	£1 Level Stake
R Hannon	7-45	5-22	1-8	0-6	1-9	15.6	- 9.00
G Harwood	6-19	4-8	1-4	0-0	1-7	31.6	+ 10.37
B Hanbury	4-7	1-2	3-3	0-0	0-2	57.1	+ 12.33
P F I Cole	4-19	3-8	0-6	1-5	0-0	21.1	+ 24.75
R Akehurst	4-31	0-6	1-8	0-2	3-15	12.9	- 16.00

489

GOODWOOD (Group 1)

Leading Trainers 1990-94

	Total W-R	Non-handicaps 2-y-o	3-y-o+	Handicaps 2-y-o	3-y-o+	Per cent	£1 Level Stake
R Hannon	39-370	12-124	11-86	2-29	14-131	10.5	- 61.54
I A Balding	27-135	5-37	10-45	2-3	10-50	20.0	+ 62.33
J H M Gosden	26-122	6-18	8-57	2-3	10-44	21.3	+ 41.95
J L Dunlop	26-176	7-68	11-43	2-11	6-54	14.8	- 53.43
H R A Cecil	22-85	8-15	13-48	0-1	1-21	25.9	+ 10.97
M R Stoute	19-94	4-17	10-39	1-4	4-34	20.2	+ 2.03
P F I Cole	18-110	6-38	7-37	0-1	5-34	16.4	- 7.81
D R C Elsworth	17-155	6-36	3-52	0-2	8-65	11.0	- 45.68
L M Cumani	15-78	1-6	8-40	0-0	6-32	19.2	+ 5.78
R Akehurst	14-104	0-7	4-19	1-5	9-73	13.5	- 12.54
G Lewis	13-93	3-35	4-16	2-16	4-26	14.0	+ 12.07
R Charlton	12-52	1-13	4-13	0-1	7-25	23.1	+ 9.58
B W Hills	10-96	2-24	8-41	0-4	0-27	10.4	- 40.58
Lord Huntingdon	9-53	1-7	5-17	0-2	3-27	17.0	+ 28.38
D A Wilson	9-55	0-2	0-0	0-0	9-53	16.4	- 2.67
M R Channon	9-91	4-28	1-15	0-14	4-34	9.9	+ 7.67
J Berry	9-98	4-29	1-16	3-18	1-35	9.2	- 48.09
Lady Herries	8-40	1-7	2-9	0-2	5-22	20.0	+ 31.50
S Dow	8-62	2-19	3-13	1-2	2-28	12.9	+ 17.58
G Harwood	8-139	2-23	3-47	0-4	3-65	5.8	- 67.75
W R Hern	7-44	4-10	2-18	0-2	1-14	15.9	- 0.46
B Hanbury	7-45	0-6	2-17	0-1	5-21	15.6	- 8.08

Leading Jockeys

	Total W-R	Per cent	£1 Level Stake	Best Trainer	W-R	Per cent	£1 Level Stake
W Carson	50-293	17.1	- 75.29	J L Dunlop	16-79	20.3	- 30.16
Pat Eddery	46-238	19.3	- 37.58	H R A Cecil	9-19	47.4	+ 8.53
J Reid	42-235	17.9	+ 45.87	R Hannon	8-38	21.1	+ 13.93
L Dettori	30-196	15.3	- 46.27	L M Cumani	11-44	25.0	+ 6.27
R Cochrane	28-213	13.1	- 5.85	I A Balding	10-32	31.3	+ 52.30
M Roberts	26-203	12.8	- 17.92	R Hannon	4-27	14.8	+ 14.79
A Munro	24-137	17.5	+ 23.56	Lord Huntingdon	4-10	40.0	+ 42.25
T Quinn	22-233	9.4	- 70.67	P F I Cole	11-67	16.4	+ 13.50
M Hills	21-126	16.7	+ 43.16	J W Hills	5-24	20.8	+ 13.00
D Holland	16-81	19.8	+109.38	D A Wilson	2-2	100.0	+ 7.25
Paul Eddery	16-152	10.5	- 65.16	G Lewis	5-40	12.5	+ 0.25
W R Swinburn	12-127	9.4	- 58.63	M R Stoute	7-33	21.2	+ 4.18

How the Favourites Fared

Non-handicaps	W-R	Per cent	£1 Level Stake	Handicaps	W-R	Per cent	£1 Level Stake
2-y-o	66-124	53.2	+ 33.52	2-y-o	7-30	23.3	- 3.25
3-y-o	32-93	34.4	- 10.51	3-y-o	12-68	17.6	- 25.08
Weight-for-age	30-87	34.5	- 12.51	All-aged	39-177	22.0	- 31.41
Totals	128-304	42.1	+ 10.50	Totals	58-275	21.1	- 59.74
All favs	186-579	32.1	- 49.24				

Leading Trainers by Month at Goodwood

May

	Total W-R	Non-handicaps 2-y-o	3-y-o+	Handicaps 2-y-o	3-y-o+	Per cent	£1 Level Stake
R Hannon	10-69	1-23	4-23	0-0	5-23	14.5	- 12.96
J H M Gosden	8-23	0-1	3-15	0-0	5-7	34.8	+ 18.60
I A Balding	5-24	1-2	3-19	0-0	1-3	20.8	+ 33.50
J L Dunlop	5-31	2-9	3-10	0-0	0-12	16.1	- 15.94
H R A Cecil	4-14	0-0	4-11	0-0	0-3	28.6	+ 1.00

June

	Total W-R	Non-handicaps 2-y-o	3-y-o+	Handicaps 2-y-o	3-y-o+	Per cent	£1 Level Stake
J L Dunlop	7-32	3-14	2-5	0-0	2-13	21.9	- 10.06
D A Wilson	6-17	0-0	0-0	0-0	6-17	35.3	+ 17.08
P F I Cole	5-16	1-5	1-6	0-0	3-5	31.3	+ 17.12
M R Channon	5-24	2-8	1-9	0-0	2-7	20.8	+ 35.50
B Hanbury	4-10	0-0	2-6	0-0	2-4	40.0	+ 5.42

July

	Total W-R	Non-handicaps 2-y-o	3-y-o+	Handicaps 2-y-o	3-y-o+	Per cent	£1 Level Stake
R Hannon	12-100	3-31	2-16	2-10	5-43	12.0	+ 20.94
H R A Cecil	8-31	5-7	3-13	0-0	0-11	25.8	+ 2.64
I A Balding	7-40	0-11	4-9	0-0	3-20	17.5	+ 9.03
L M Cumani	5-32	0-1	2-14	0-0	3-17	15.6	+ 0.83
J H M Gosden	5-38	1-4	1-16	0-0	3-18	13.2	+ 16.25

August

	Total W-R	Non-handicaps 2-y-o	3-y-o+	Handicaps 2-y-o	3-y-o+	Per cent	£1 Level Stake
I A Balding	8-31	0-7	2-9	2-2	4-13	25.8	+ 5.50
J L Dunlop	7-34	2-15	3-7	1-1	1-11	20.6	- 4.43
R Hannon	7-58	2-20	3-11	0-8	2-19	12.1	- 13.57
P F I Cole	5-19	0-6	4-9	0-0	1-4	26.3	+ 14.25
H R A Cecil	5-23	2-5	3-14	0-0	0-4	21.7	- 9.05

September

	Total W-R	Non-handicaps 2-y-o	3-y-o+	Handicaps 2-y-o	3-y-o+	Per cent	£1 Level Stake
M R Stoute	5-18	1-3	4-9	0-0	0-6	27.8	- 2.49
J H M Gosden	5-20	1-6	2-9	1-1	1-4	25.0	+ 21.50
R Akehurst	4-11	0-0	0-2	1-1	3-8	36.4	+ 16.33
I A Balding	4-22	3-11	0-2	0-1	1-8	18.2	+ 14.80
B W Hills	3-4	1-1	2-2	0-0	0-1	75.0	+ 7.83

Oct/Nov

	Total W-R	Non-handicaps 2-y-o	3-y-o+	Handicaps 2-y-o	3-y-o+	Per cent	£1 Level Stake
R Hannon	5-35	2-15	1-6	0-5	2-9	14.3	+ 18.25
J H M Gosden	4-13	3-5	1-4	0-1	0-3	30.8	- 4.90
H R A Cecil	3-6	0-0	2-4	0-1	1-1	50.0	+ 21.50
C A Cyzer	2-3	0-0	1-1	0-0	1-2	66.7	+ 19.00
Mrs J Cecil	2-3	0-0	0-0	0-1	2-2	66.7	+ 15.50

HAMILTON (Group 3)

Leading Trainers 1990-94

	Total W-R	Non-handicaps 2-y-o	3-y-o+	Handicaps 2-y-o	3-y-o+	Per cent	£1 Level Stake
J Berry	57-286	25-108	18-70	4-19	10-89	19.9	- 20.65
Mrs M Reveley	31-141	4-22	10-41	0-2	17-76	22.0	- 24.44
M Johnston	28-173	10-42	5-39	1-6	12-86	16.2	- 26.34
P C Haslam	19-103	1-15	6-21	0-5	12-62	18.4	+ 20.25
M H Tompkins	17-66	6-17	6-15	0-5	5-29	25.8	+ 4.83
B Hanbury	13-36	2-5	6-17	1-1	4-13	36.1	+ 25.18
M Bell	13-37	6-11	5-11	0-4	2-11	35.1	+ 2.21
Miss L A Perratt	13-124	1-28	3-18	1-8	8-70	10.5	+ 1.50
S G Norton	11-69	2-14	4-19	0-2	5-34	15.9	- 2.13
Sir M Prescott	9-38	3-8	2-10	0-2	4-18	23.7	- 14.47
Mrs J Ramsden	9-58	0-11	1-10	0-2	8-35	15.5	- 4.13
Denys Smith	9-95	0-13	6-27	0-2	3-53	9.5	- 40.75
M H Easterby	8-60	2-13	2-10	1-9	3-28	13.3	+ 9.91
C W Thornton	8-64	1-10	2-12	0-2	5-40	12.5	- 22.50
E J Alston	8-84	1-11	2-20	0-0	5-53	9.5	- 5.25
A Bailey	7-49	0-8	0-6	1-1	6-34	14.3	+ 14.50
A C Stewart	6-8	1-1	4-4	0-0	1-3	75.0	+ 7.30
J Etherington	6-28	1-4	4-10	0-3	1-11	21.4	- 1.35
T D Barron	6-56	2-10	0-9	2-5	2-32	10.7	- 28.03
D Moffatt	6-65	2-15	1-12	0-2	3-36	9.2	+ 1.50
M P Naughton	6-74	0-1	1-26	0-0	5-47	8.1	- 18.75
R Hannon	5-14	1-2	2-6	1-3	1-3	35.7	+ 7.18

Leading Jockeys

	Total W-R	Per cent	£1 Level Stake	Best Trainer	W-R	Per cent	£1 Level Stake
J Carroll	51-241	21.2	- 20.43	J Berry	41-165	24.8	+ 2.59
K Darley	49-254	19.3	- 57.57	Mrs M Reveley	17-54	31.5	+ 6.35
D McKeown	30-190	15.8	- 20.71	M Johnston	7-40	17.5	- 5.12
J Weaver	26-108	24.1	+ 26.47	M Johnston	9-37	24.3	- 6.91
G Duffield	20-133	15.0	- 57.92	Sir M Prescott	7-27	25.9	- 6.75
J Lowe	20-219	9.1	- 38.75	M J Bolton	4-12	33.3	+ 12.50
K Fallon	18-201	9.0	- 67.00	E J Alston	4-30	13.3	+ 0.75
J Fanning	17-166	10.2	- 42.07	Miss L A Perratt	3-35	8.6	+ 6.00
P Robinson	14-36	38.9	+ 20.11	M H Tompkins	7-23	30.4	+ 4.86
J Fortune	14-105	13.3	+ 4.23	Mrs M Reveley	2-4	50.0	+ 6.00
B Raymond	13-51	25.5	+ 11.38	B Hanbury	9-20	45.0	+ 15.31
A Mackay	10-100	10.0	- 1.50	A Bailey	3-19	15.8	+ 2.00

How the Favourites Fared

Non-handicaps	W-R	Per cent	£1 Level Stake	Handicaps	W-R	Per cent	£1 Level Stake
2-y-o	43-104	41.3	- 12.87	2-y-o	6-18	33.3	+ 5.04
3-y-o	44-80	55.0	+ 10.32	3-y-o	18-51	35.3	- 2.74
Weight-for-age	34-72	47.2	+ 5.61	All-aged	63-199	31.7	+ 1.46
Totals	121-256	47.3	+ 3.06	Totals	87-268	32.5	+ 3.76
All favs	208-524	39.7	+ 6.82				

492

Leading Trainers by Month at Hamilton

March/Apr	Total W-R	Non-handicaps 2-y-o	3-y-o+	Handicaps 2-y-o	3-y-o+	Per cent	£1 Level Stake
J Berry	12-47	4-14	6-12	0-0	2-21	25.5	+ 25.17
E J Alston	6-16	1-2	1-5	0-0	4-9	37.5	+ 34.75
Mrs J Ramsden	4-18	0-0	0-4	0-0	4-14	22.2	- 2.38
S G Norton	4-24	0-3	1-9	0-0	3-12	16.7	+ 12.00
Mrs M Reveley	3-13	0-1	2-7	0-0	1-5	23.1	- 0.63

May	Total W-R	Non-handicaps 2-y-o	3-y-o+	Handicaps 2-y-o	3-y-o+	Per cent	£1 Level Stake
J Berry	12-58	8-26	2-13	0-0	2-19	20.7	- 6.52
M H Tompkins	8-24	1-6	5-8	0-0	2-10	33.3	+ 15.58
Miss L A Perratt	5-18	0-2	1-1	0-0	4-15	27.8	+ 24.00
M Johnston	5-39	2-9	2-13	0-0	1-17	12.8	- 16.52
Mrs M Reveley	4-21	1-5	1-6	0-0	2-10	19.0	- 6.13

June	Total W-R	Non-handicaps 2-y-o	3-y-o+	Handicaps 2-y-o	3-y-o+	Per cent	£1 Level Stake
M Johnston	9-31	5-8	1-6	0-0	3-17	29.0	+ 3.93
J Berry	8-47	3-17	4-15	0-0	1-15	17.0	- 18.68
A C Stewart	4-4	0-0	3-3	0-0	1-1	100.0	+ 5.30
S G Norton	4-11	1-3	2-2	0-0	1-6	36.4	+ 9.25
M H Tompkins	3-8	2-3	1-3	0-0	0-2	37.5	+ 3.38

July	Total W-R	Non-handicaps 2-y-o	3-y-o+	Handicaps 2-y-o	3-y-o+	Per cent	£1 Level Stake
Mrs M Reveley	17-51	2-9	7-17	0-1	8-24	33.3	+ 5.31
J Berry	16-69	8-31	2-14	2-7	4-17	23.2	- 8.97
P C Haslam	8-20	1-2	2-5	0-1	5-12	40.0	+ 22.75
M Johnston	6-43	2-12	1-6	1-4	3-21	14.0	- 18.27
C Tinkler	4-13	1-7	1-2	0-1	2-3	30.8	+ 0.45

August	Total W-R	Non-handicaps 2-y-o	3-y-o+	Handicaps 2-y-o	3-y-o+	Per cent	£1 Level Stake
J Berry	5-18	1-5	3-5	0-0	1-8	27.8	+ 6.09
P C Haslam	3-10	0-0	1-1	0-0	2-9	30.0	+ 1.00
Mrs M Reveley	3-12	1-4	0-2	0-0	2-6	25.0	+ 3.00
Sir M Prescott	2-3	0-0	0-0	0-0	2-3	66.7	+ 3.05
J W Watts	2-3	2-3	0-0	0-0	0-0	66.7	+ 1.67

September	Total W-R	Non-handicaps 2-y-o	3-y-o+	Handicaps 2-y-o	3-y-o+	Per cent	£1 Level Stake
B Hanbury	8-18	2-5	4-8	1-1	1-4	44.4	+ 17.21
Sir M Prescott	4-12	3-4	1-4	0-1	0-3	33.3	- 0.13
R Hannon	3-5	1-2	1-2	1-1	0-0	60.0	+ 9.38
M Bell	3-6	1-1	2-2	0-2	0-1	50.0	+ 4.25
Mrs M Reveley	3-22	0-1	0-6	0-1	3-14	13.6	- 6.75

Oct/Nov	Total W-R	Non-handicaps 2-y-o	3-y-o+	Handicaps 2-y-o	3-y-o+	Per cent	£1 Level Stake
J Berry	2-6	1-3	1-1	0-2	0-0	33.3	+ 3.25
M H Tompkins	2-11	0-1	0-0	0-4	2-6	18.2	- 0.50
M W Easterby	1-1	0-0	1-1	0-0	0-0	100.0	+ 10.00
D T Thom	1-1	1-1	0-0	0-0	0-0	100.0	+ 11.00
B Ellison	1-1	0-0	1-1	0-0	0-0	100.0	+ 7.00

HAYDOCK (Group 1)

Leading Trainers 1990–94

	Total W–R	Non-handicaps 2-y-o	3-y-o+	Handicaps 2-y-o	3-y-o+	Per cent	£1 Level Stake
J H M Gosden	27-94	4-11	16-57	0-0	7-26	28.7	+ 47.49
H R A Cecil	21-57	4-8	15-31	0-0	2-18	36.8	+ 30.82
J L Dunlop	20-96	6-26	6-23	1-1	7-46	20.8	+ 2.91
J Berry	19-209	5-71	6-47	3-29	5-62	9.1	– 89.00
R Hannon	15-101	10-29	1-28	1-4	3-40	14.9	– 16.08
B W Hills	14-76	5-20	8-27	0-2	1-27	18.4	– 19.27
R Hollinshead	14-191	2-51	5-40	1-10	6-90	7.3	– 37.53
H Thomson Jones	13-53	5-15	4-19	0-1	4-18	24.5	+ 31.74
M R Stoute	13-82	4-13	7-39	0-1	2-29	15.9	– 38.40
M H Easterby	13-131	5-33	1-11	1-11	6-76	9.9	– 59.50
L M Cumani	12-70	2-8	5-30	0-0	5-32	17.1	– 2.99
F H Lee	12-133	2-29	1-23	1-4	8-77	9.0	– 44.00
R Boss	11-29	2-11	3-8	1-1	5-9	37.9	+ 46.25
M H Tompkins	11-79	3-9	2-21	1-8	5-41	13.9	– 27.78
B A McMahon	11-141	2-25	1-38	1-2	7-76	7.8	– 24.17
R Charlton	10-44	2-5	4-17	0-0	4-22	22.7	– 6.19
Mrs M Reveley	10-58	0-6	0-8	0-2	10-42	17.2	+ 16.00
P T Walwyn	9-39	2-11	2-10	0-0	5-18	23.1	+ 11.00
P F I Cole	9-59	2-20	4-21	1-2	2-16	15.3	+ 6.91
Mrs J Ramsden	9-107	1-20	2-7	1-6	5-74	8.4	– 47.25
W Jarvis	8-38	1-5	2-13	1-2	4-18	21.1	+ 16.13
R J R Williams	7-26	3-4	1-4	0-1	3-17	26.9	+ 13.04

Leading Jockeys

	Total W–R	Per cent	£1 Level Stake	Best Trainer	W–R	Per cent	£1 Level Stake
Pat Eddery	32-106	30.2	+ 37.53	H R A Cecil	5-8	62.5	+ 4.48
W Ryan	26-139	18.7	+ 23.61	H R A Cecil	13-31	41.9	+ 24.35
L Dettori	23-125	18.4	– 15.69	L M Cumani	5-21	23.8	+ 0.32
M Roberts	21-113	18.6	+ 1.39	J H M Gosden	3-4	75.0	+ 4.51
R Hills	19-113	16.8	– 9.06	H Thomson Jones	10-42	23.8	+ 7.74
J Carroll	19-186	10.2	– 54.09	J Berry	11-114	9.6	– 55.25
M Hills	17-98	17.3	+ 8.20	B W Hills	5-26	19.2	– 11.49
B Raymond	17-128	13.3	– 38.13	B Hanbury	3-21	14.3	– 10.00
K Darley	16-126	12.7	– 0.07	Mrs M Reveley	4-18	22.2	+ 12.33
J Reid	15-85	17.6	– 1.73	J L Dunlop	4-7	57.1	+ 12.60
Paul Eddery	15-92	16.3	– 17.84	M R Stoute	3-19	15.8	– 7.26
W Carson	15-96	15.6	– 40.17	J L Dunlop	4-25	16.0	– 12.40

How the Favourites Fared

Non-handicaps	W–R	Per cent	£1 Level Stake	Handicaps	W–R	Per cent	£1 Level Stake
2-y-o	50-114	43.9	+ 0.24	2-y-o	3-22	13.6	– 11.75
3-y-o	37-90	41.1	– 8.93	3-y-o	10-57	17.5	– 28.39
Weight-for-age	31-79	39.2	– 6.66	All-aged	44-202	21.8	– 52.38
Totals	118-283	41.7	– 15.35	Totals	57-281	20.3	– 92.52
All favs	175-564	31.0	–107.87				

Leading Trainers by Month at Haydock

March/Apr	Total W-R	Non-handicaps 2-y-o	3-y-o+	Handicaps 2-y-o	3-y-o+	Per cent	£1 Level Stake
R Charlton	3-4	0-0	3-3	0-0	0-1	75.0	+ 1.96
T D Barron	2-3	0-0	2-3	0-0	0-0	66.7	+ 11.50
M R Channon	2-3	1-1	1-1	0-0	0-1	66.7	+ 4.25
M H Easterby	2-9	2-3	0-3	0-0	0-3	22.2	- 3.75
R Hannon	2-13	1-3	0-6	0-0	1-4	15.4	- 2.00

May	Total W-R	Non-handicaps 2-y-o	3-y-o+	Handicaps 2-y-o	3-y-o+	Per cent	£1 Level Stake
H Thomson Jones	6-15	3-4	3-8	0-0	0-3	40.0	+ 12.74
B W Hills	5-9	1-1	4-6	0-0	0-2	55.6	+ 15.01
P F I Cole	5-13	2-2	2-8	0-0	1-3	38.5	+ 14.91
M R Stoute	5-20	0-0	5-14	0-0	0-6	25.0	- 7.12
G Wragg	3-5	0-0	2-4	0-0	1-1	60.0	+ 3.75

June	Total W-R	Non-handicaps 2-y-o	3-y-o+	Handicaps 2-y-o	3-y-o+	Per cent	£1 Level Stake
R F J Houghton	4-6	1-2	0-0	0-0	3-4	66.7	+ 36.25
B W Hills	4-9	0-2	3-4	0-0	1-3	44.4	+ 5.25
J L Dunlop	4-15	0-3	1-3	0-0	3-9	26.7	+ 20.43
R Hollinshead	4-22	0-4	1-4	0-0	3-14	18.2	+ 27.00
M Brittain	2-4	2-2	0-0	0-0	0-2	50.0	+ 19.00

July	Total W-R	Non-handicaps 2-y-o	3-y-o+	Handicaps 2-y-o	3-y-o+	Per cent	£1 Level Stake
H R A Cecil	8-13	2-2	4-8	0-0	2-3	61.5	+ 26.54
J H M Gosden	6-16	0-1	6-12	0-0	0-3	37.5	+ 7.41
M P Naughton	3-8	0-0	0-1	0-0	3-7	37.5	+ 8.50
J L Dunlop	3-9	0-0	1-4	0-0	2-5	33.3	0.00
M H Easterby	3-10	2-6	0-0	0-0	1-4	30.0	+ 2.25

August	Total W-R	Non-handicaps 2-y-o	3-y-o+	Handicaps 2-y-o	3-y-o+	Per cent	£1 Level Stake
F H Lee	7-28	1-6	0-2	1-1	5-19	25.0	+ 27.00
R Hollinshead	5-26	1-7	2-6	1-2	1-11	19.2	+ 11.10
J Berry	5-32	2-11	2-6	0-5	1-10	15.6	- 15.58
J H M Gosden	4-15	1-1	2-9	0-0	1-5	26.7	+ 0.51
M H Easterby	4-20	0-3	0-0	1-2	3-15	20.0	+ 14.50

September	Total W-R	Non-handicaps 2-y-o	3-y-o+	Handicaps 2-y-o	3-y-o+	Per cent	£1 Level Stake
J H M Gosden	11-34	2-5	6-21	0-0	3-8	32.4	+ 44.00
R Hannon	6-31	3-10	1-9	1-3	1-9	19.4	+ 11.88
J L Dunlop	6-36	4-13	1-7	1-1	0-15	16.7	- 11.40
B A McMahon	6-47	1-9	1-8	1-1	3-29	12.8	+ 9.50
H R A Cecil	5-15	1-3	4-5	0-0	0-7	33.3	+ 6.23

Oct/Nov	Total W-R	Non-handicaps 2-y-o	3-y-o+	Handicaps 2-y-o	3-y-o+	Per cent	£1 Level Stake
H R A Cecil	3-8	1-3	2-2	0-0	0-3	37.5	+ 8.83
L M Cumani	3-8	1-2	0-1	0-0	2-5	37.5	+ 10.90
Mrs J Ramsden	3-18	0-2	1-2	1-3	1-11	16.7	+ 14.00
P J Bevan	2-3	0-0	0-0	0-1	2-2	66.7	+ 27.00
R Hannon	2-6	2-2	0-0	0-1	0-3	33.3	+ 6.50

KEMPTON (Group 1)

Leading Trainers 1990-94

	Total W-R	Non-handicaps 2-y-o	3-y-o+	Handicaps 2-y-o	3-y-o+	Per cent	£1 Level Stake
R Hannon	33-307	14-87	7-81	1-15	11-124	10.7	- 61.70
R Charlton	16-70	6-15	9-34	0-1	1-20	22.9	+ 28.48
J L Dunlop	16-130	2-35	9-54	0-1	5-40	12.3	- 13.27
J H M Gosden	15-103	1-7	11-74	0-1	3-21	14.6	- 35.93
D R C Elsworth	14-131	3-21	7-64	0-0	4-46	10.7	- 11.76
M R Stoute	12-86	4-21	5-47	2-2	1-16	14.0	- 39.33
I A Balding	12-110	3-23	5-39	0-3	4-45	10.9	- 8.50
P T Walwyn	11-69	1-13	4-25	0-0	6-31	15.9	+ 19.71
C E Brittain	11-125	0-17	5-59	1-4	5-45	8.8	- 36.29
G Wragg	9-41	2-5	5-26	0-0	2-10	22.0	+ 11.67
J R Fanshawe	9-56	2-9	5-26	0-2	2-19	16.1	+ 27.33
M J Ryan	9-69	0-3	4-11	0-1	5-54	13.0	+ 21.00
Lord Huntingdon	9-72	1-9	4-26	0-2	4-35	12.5	- 6.38
B W Hills	9-81	2-26	5-37	0-0	2-18	11.1	- 8.17
P F I Cole	9-104	3-25	2-39	1-3	3-37	8.7	- 62.15
H Thomson Jones	8-43	4-7	1-21	1-1	2-14	18.6	+ 14.29
H R A Cecil	8-45	0-4	8-33	0-0	0-8	17.8	- 9.08
B Hanbury	8-51	1-6	5-21	0-2	2-22	15.7	+ 18.98
H Candy	8-65	0-4	2-30	0-1	6-30	12.3	+100.00
G Lewis	8-94	3-28	0-15	0-8	5-43	8.5	- 32.38
M J Haynes	7-39	2-8	2-13	0-0	3-18	17.9	+ 57.00
R F J Houghton	7-42	1-13	5-14	0-3	1-12	16.7	+ 33.50

Leading Jockeys

	Total W-R	Per cent	£1 Level Stake	Best Trainer	W-R	Per cent	£1 Level Stake
Pat Eddery	50-236	21.2	+ 44.26	R Charlton	11-42	26.2	+ 18.98
W Carson	31-223	13.9	- 45.93	J L Dunlop	5-43	11.6	- 9.50
A Munro	21-136	15.4	+ 41.51	C E Brittain	2-2	100.0	+ 15.00
M Roberts	20-197	10.2	- 52.79	C E Brittain	5-63	7.9	- 12.00
T Quinn	19-193	9.8	-106.09	P F I Cole	6-65	9.2	- 48.65
L Dettori	19-208	9.1	- 64.05	R Hannon	2-17	11.8	+ 11.00
R Cochrane	19-213	8.9	- 48.87	I A Balding	5-25	20.0	+ 12.00
W R Swinburn	18-157	11.5	- 48.11	M R Stoute	6-43	14.0	- 19.95
J Reid	16-183	8.7	- 45.45	R Hannon	5-23	21.7	+ 1.30
J Williams	13-184	7.1	- 45.90	D R C Elsworth	7-48	14.6	+ 16.50
Paul Eddery	12-120	10.0	+ 15.80	G Lewis	3-33	9.1	+ 4.50
W Ryan	11-75	14.7	+ 6.51	H R A Cecil	4-19	21.1	- 3.87

How the Favourites Fared

Non-handicaps	W-R	Per cent	£1 Level Stake	Handicaps	W-R	Per cent	£1 Level Stake
2-y-o	29-75	38.7	- 3.50	2-y-o	5-14	35.7	+ 8.75
3-y-o	34-94	36.2	- 10.18	3-y-o	15-48	31.3	+ 11.51
Weight-for-age	18-58	31.0	- 7.92	All-aged	28-162	17.3	- 45.13
Totals	81-227	35.7	- 21.60	Totals	48-224	21.4	- 24.87
All favs	129-451	28.6	- 46.47				

Leading Trainers by Month at Kempton

March/Apr

	Total W-R	Non-handicaps 2-y-o	3-y-o+	Handicaps 2-y-o	3-y-o+	Per cent	£1 Level Stake
R Hannon	12-87	6-20	4-27	0-0	2-40	13.8	- 19.25
J L Dunlop	7-39	0-0	6-26	0-0	1-13	17.9	+ 26.50
P T Walwyn	5-21	0-0	2-5	0-0	3-16	23.8	+ 33.33
M J Ryan	4-14	0-1	2-2	0-0	2-11	28.6	+ 29.50
M J Haynes	4-16	2-5	1-5	0-0	1-6	25.0	+ 31.00

May

	Total W-R	Non-handicaps 2-y-o	3-y-o+	Handicaps 2-y-o	3-y-o+	Per cent	£1 Level Stake
P F I Cole	5-32	3-4	0-16	0-0	2-12	15.6	- 14.43
Mrs J Cecil	4-9	0-0	3-8	0-0	1-1	44.4	+ 7.55
H R A Cecil	4-16	0-0	4-11	0-0	0-5	25.0	- 2.83
I A Balding	4-25	0-0	3-12	0-0	1-13	16.0	+ 9.00
D R C Elsworth	4-25	0-1	2-19	0-0	2-5	16.0	+ 11.41

June

	Total W-R	Non-handicaps 2-y-o	3-y-o+	Handicaps 2-y-o	3-y-o+	Per cent	£1 Level Stake
D R C Elsworth	4-22	0-1	3-13	0-0	1-8	18.2	+ 11.83
R Hannon	4-24	2-6	0-7	0-0	2-11	16.7	+ 5.50
Lord Huntingdon	3-10	0-0	1-5	0-0	2-5	30.0	+ 5.25
R Charlton	3-10	0-0	3-9	0-0	0-1	30.0	+ 21.00
N A Callaghan	2-5	0-0	0-1	0-0	2-4	40.0	+ 8.00

July

	Total W-R	Non-handicaps 2-y-o	3-y-o+	Handicaps 2-y-o	3-y-o+	Per cent	£1 Level Stake
P T Walwyn	3-7	1-2	0-3	0-0	2-2	42.9	+ 11.00
R Charlton	3-10	1-1	2-6	0-0	0-3	30.0	+ 0.15
J H M Gosden	3-13	0-1	1-8	0-0	2-4	23.1	+ 4.12
R Hannon	3-26	1-9	0-5	0-0	2-12	11.5	- 7.70
H Candy	2-3	0-0	0-1	0-0	2-2	66.7	+ 43.00

August

	Total W-R	Non-handicaps 2-y-o	3-y-o+	Handicaps 2-y-o	3-y-o+	Per cent	£1 Level Stake
R Hannon	4-33	2-16	0-1	1-7	1-9	12.1	- 10.00
H Thomson Jones	3-5	2-3	0-0	0-0	1-2	60.0	+ 11.25
C E Brittain	3-7	0-0	1-1	1-2	1-4	42.9	+ 16.00
G Wragg	2-3	2-3	0-0	0-0	0-0	66.7	+ 5.67
W R Hern	2-6	0-4	0-0	0-0	2-2	33.3	+ 14.00

September

	Total W-R	Non-handicaps 2-y-o	3-y-o+	Handicaps 2-y-o	3-y-o+	Per cent	£1 Level Stake
M R Stoute	8-30	4-18	2-8	2-2	0-2	26.7	+ 0.55
R Charlton	7-29	4-11	2-9	0-0	1-9	24.1	+ 1.83
I A Balding	6-36	2-15	2-6	0-3	2-12	16.7	+ 15.00
R Hannon	6-72	2-30	1-12	0-8	3-22	8.3	+ 10.50
G Wragg	5-13	0-2	3-7	0-0	2-4	38.5	+ 17.50

LEICESTER (Group 3)

Leading Trainers 1990-94

	Total W-R	Non-handicaps 2-y-o	3-y-o+	Handicaps 2-y-o	3-y-o+	Per cent	£1 Level Stake
R Hannon	28-177	13-89	8-32	4-12	3-44	15.8	+ 5.50
H R A Cecil	24-96	9-38	14-50	0-0	1-8	25.0	- 20.41
J H M Gosden	21-87	8-31	10-41	0-1	3-14	24.1	- 20.68
M R Stoute	18-79	11-41	7-30	0-0	0-8	22.8	+ 4.46
J L Dunlop	18-99	6-44	5-29	1-4	6-22	18.2	+ 0.42
P F I Cole	13-92	6-35	5-35	1-8	1-14	14.1	- 25.05
M J Ryan	12-88	0-23	1-14	0-2	11-49	13.6	- 7.42
J Berry	10-81	3-39	5-17	2-14	0-11	12.3	- 28.89
G Wragg	9-50	2-16	6-22	0-1	1-11	18.0	+ 9.77
M Bell	9-79	5-30	2-16	0-5	2-28	11.4	- 6.25
M A Jarvis	8-48	0-8	5-23	1-3	2-14	16.7	+ 15.63
M C Pipe	7-30	1-2	2-14	0-0	4-14	23.3	+ 29.96
P T Walwyn	7-34	2-12	3-11	0-1	2-10	20.6	+ 40.50
G Lewis	7-46	4-17	2-9	0-6	1-14	15.2	- 2.52
Mrs J Cecil	6-18	3-10	3-7	0-0	0-1	33.3	+ 7.63
R Charlton	6-31	2-8	3-16	0-0	1-7	19.4	- 8.15
W R Hern	6-37	1-9	4-18	0-0	1-10	16.2	- 9.45
G Harwood	6-39	0-12	4-19	0-1	2-7	15.4	- 2.03
M Johnston	6-41	2-14	2-8	0-3	2-16	14.6	+ 3.00
Sir M Prescott	6-42	4-19	1-11	1-1	0-11	14.3	- 5.16
Lord Huntingdon	6-45	1-9	4-25	0-0	1-11	13.3	+ 6.50
B Hanbury	6-62	3-25	1-24	0-0	2-13	9.7	- 20.63

Leading Jockeys

	Total W-R	Per cent	£1 Level Stake	Best Trainer	W-R	Per cent	£1 Level Stake
Pat Eddery	31-138	22.5	+ 4.35	R Hannon	6-18	33.3	+ 12.00
L Dettori	28-179	15.6	- 9.58	J L Dunlop	3-6	50.0	+ 10.83
W Carson	26-144	18.1	- 51.21	J H M Gosden	5-9	55.6	+ 0.03
T Quinn	24-148	16.2	+ 33.79	P F I Cole	10-50	20.0	+ 10.88
M Roberts	24-173	13.9	- 59.86	C E Brittain	4-40	10.0	- 22.71
W Ryan	22-190	11.6	- 74.87	H R A Cecil	13-51	25.5	- 5.58
W R Swinburn	19-111	17.1	- 42.67	M R Stoute	9-27	33.3	- 4.22
Paul Eddery	16-121	13.2	- 23.60	Mrs J Cecil	4-13	30.8	+ 4.13
R Cochrane	15-152	9.9	- 67.96	G Harwood	3-17	17.6	- 5.52
J Reid	14-96	14.6	- 19.53	R Hannon	4-19	21.1	+ 9.75
J Williams	14-132	10.6	+ 60.90	M Williams	3-4	75.0	+ 35.40
J Weaver	12-61	19.7	+ 81.75	M Johnston	2-10	20.0	+ 14.75

How the Favourites Fared

Non-handicaps	W-R	Per cent	£1 Level Stake	Handicaps	W-R	Per cent	£1 Level Stake
2-y-o	64-144	44.4	+ 12.05	2-y-o	8-26	30.8	- 1.58
3-y-o	52-133	39.1	- 11.97	3-y-o	12-49	24.5	- 0.77
Weight-for-age	15-50	30.0	- 9.60	All-aged	24-120	20.0	- 26.46
Totals	131-327	40.1	- 9.52	Totals	44-195	22.6	- 28.81
All favs	175-522	33.5	- 38.33				

Leading Trainers by Month at Leicester

March/Apr

	Total W-R	Non-handicaps 2-y-o	3-y-o+	Handicaps 2-y-o	3-y-o+	Per cent	£1 Level Stake
M R Stoute	5-16	0-0	5-15	0-0	0-1	31.3	+ 24.03
H R A Cecil	4-14	0-0	3-12	0-0	1-2	28.6	+ 1.81
M Bell	4-19	3-6	0-7	0-0	1-6	21.1	+ 4.50
Lord Huntingdon	3-8	0-0	3-7	0-0	0-1	37.5	+ 13.50
P F I Cole	3-13	0-0	2-10	0-0	1-3	23.1	- 0.93

May

	Total W-R	Non-handicaps 2-y-o	3-y-o+	Handicaps 2-y-o	3-y-o+	Per cent	£1 Level Stake
J Berry	4-13	2-9	2-4	0-0	0-0	30.8	+ 20.80
R Hannon	4-23	2-13	2-3	0-0	0-7	17.4	+ 16.00
H Thomson Jones	3-7	2-2	1-4	0-0	0-1	42.9	- 1.09
J H M Gosden	3-11	0-0	3-9	0-0	0-2	27.3	- 1.82
Mrs J Cecil	2-2	0-0	2-2	0-0	0-0	100.0	+ 3.50

June

	Total W-R	Non-handicaps 2-y-o	3-y-o+	Handicaps 2-y-o	3-y-o+	Per cent	£1 Level Stake
J H M Gosden	6-12	2-3	4-7	0-0	0-2	50.0	+ 2.17
M W Easterby	2-3	1-2	0-0	0-0	1-1	66.7	+ 12.50
R Charlton	2-5	0-2	1-1	0-0	1-2	40.0	+ 1.00
H R A Cecil	2-6	0-1	2-5	0-0	0-0	33.3	- 1.20
P S Felgate	2-7	0-0	0-1	0-0	2-6	28.6	+ 5.50

July

	Total W-R	Non-handicaps 2-y-o	3-y-o+	Handicaps 2-y-o	3-y-o+	Per cent	£1 Level Stake
H R A Cecil	7-14	1-2	6-11	0-0	0-1	50.0	+ 2.52
B A McMahon	4-19	2-2	2-8	0-3	0-6	21.1	+ 8.00
M J Ryan	4-20	0-5	1-3	0-1	3-11	20.0	+ 7.25
G Lewis	3-5	2-2	1-1	0-1	0-1	60.0	+ 6.08
P F I Cole	3-15	2-5	1-7	0-1	0-2	20.0	- 1.50

August

	Total W-R	Non-handicaps 2-y-o	3-y-o+	Handicaps 2-y-o	3-y-o+	Per cent	£1 Level Stake
R Hannon	5-10	1-4	1-1	1-1	2-4	50.0	+ 13.25
M Johnston	2-3	0-0	1-1	0-0	1-2	66.7	+ 10.00
J L Dunlop	2-7	0-3	0-0	0-0	2-4	28.6	+ 5.33
I A Balding	1-1	0-0	1-1	0-0	0-0	100.0	+ 3.50
W R Hern	1-1	0-0	1-1	0-0	0-0	100.0	+ 2.25

September

	Total W-R	Non-handicaps 2-y-o	3-y-o+	Handicaps 2-y-o	3-y-o+	Per cent	£1 Level Stake
J H M Gosden	5-14	3-6	0-4	0-0	2-4	35.7	+ 7.70
M R Stoute	3-12	2-9	1-2	0-0	0-1	25.0	+ 0.17
Mrs J Ramsden	3-13	0-2	2-6	1-4	0-1	23.1	+ 5.50
J L Dunlop	3-18	3-15	0-1	0-1	0-1	16.7	- 8.55
Lady Herries	2-4	0-1	0-0	0-0	2-3	50.0	+ 14.50

Oct/Nov

	Total W-R	Non-handicaps 2-y-o	3-y-o+	Handicaps 2-y-o	3-y-o+	Per cent	£1 Level Stake
R Hannon	10-51	7-36	2-4	1-5	0-6	19.6	+ 11.75
J L Dunlop	8-39	3-23	2-9	1-3	2-4	20.5	+ 8.16
H R A Cecil	8-40	7-26	1-12	0-0	0-2	20.0	- 17.05
M R Stoute	7-31	7-28	0-2	0-0	0-1	22.6	- 16.27
Sir M Prescott	4-18	3-14	0-1	1-1	0-2	22.2	+ 14.67

LINGFIELD TURF (Group 2)

Leading Trainers 1990-94

	Total W-R	Non-handicaps 2-y-o	3-y-o+	Handicaps 2-y-o	3-y-o+	Per cent	£1 Level Stake
R Hannon	22-198	10-78	7-48	1-13	4-59	11.1	- 94.55
R Akehurst	18-154	0-23	2-36	0-4	16-91	11.7	- 25.42
B W Hills	14-43	6-16	2-12	1-1	5-14	32.6	+ 29.35
G Harwood	14-62	3-14	6-25	0-2	5-21	22.6	- 2.03
M R Stoute	13-56	4-15	9-28	0-1	0-12	23.2	- 18.74
J Berry	13-62	9-37	2-10	0-3	2-12	21.0	+ 2.52
P F I Cole	13-100	3-31	6-42	0-2	4-25	13.0	- 21.72
L M Cumani	11-24	1-1	10-21	0-0	0-2	45.8	+ 16.63
J H M Gosden	11-58	4-18	7-30	0-0	0-10	19.0	- 30.14
J L Dunlop	11-95	3-38	5-27	0-3	3-27	11.6	- 51.13
H R A Cecil	10-35	3-8	6-23	0-0	1-4	28.6	- 9.52
Sir M Prescott	10-45	2-15	3-13	0-2	5-15	22.2	- 2.38
C E Brittain	10-75	1-17	4-22	0-1	5-35	13.3	- 31.40
M R Channon	9-67	2-21	2-10	1-7	4-29	13.4	- 4.00
G Lewis	9-108	4-44	1-19	0-5	4-40	8.3	- 51.13
I A Balding	8-46	0-7	7-19	0-0	1-20	17.4	- 15.22
Lord Huntingdon	8-49	3-16	2-21	1-1	2-11	16.3	+ 4.04
Pat Mitchell	7-69	1-16	0-11	0-4	6-38	10.1	- 26.92
R J Hodges	7-92	1-12	1-13	0-2	5-65	7.6	- 27.75
R Charlton	6-20	1-4	4-11	0-0	1-5	30.0	+ 11.43
H Thomson Jones	6-25	1-5	4-14	0-0	1-6	24.0	+ 19.67
B Hanbury	6-34	2-8	1-9	0-1	3-16	17.6	+ 27.00

Leading Jockeys

	Total W-R	Per cent	£1 Level Stake	Best Trainer	W-R	Per cent	£1 Level Stake
T Quinn	29-197	14.7	- 8.88	P F I Cole	10-57	17.5	- 4.72
R Cochrane	28-156	17.9	+ 58.61	G Harwood	5-13	38.5	+ 12.42
W Carson	25-95	26.3	+ 3.53	J L Dunlop	6-18	33.3	- 1.11
J Reid	20-121	16.5	- 6.08	I A Balding	2-3	66.7	+ 1.03
M Hills	19-89	21.3	+ 3.90	M Bell	4-13	30.8	+ 2.50
L Dettori	19-101	18.8	- 19.68	L M Cumani	4-8	50.0	+ 3.25
M Roberts	19-134	14.2	+ 18.48	A C Stewart	4-9	44.4	+ 13.10
W Newnes	16-138	11.6	- 20.75	C C Elsey	4-14	28.6	+ 15.50
D Holland	15-74	20.3	+ 41.44	B W Hills	4-11	36.4	+ 16.00
R Hills	14-71	19.7	+ 31.75	M R Channon	4-5	80.0	+ 24.25
B Raymond	11-77	14.3	- 7.75	R Hannon	2-7	28.6	- 1.00
S O'Gorman	11-88	12.5	- 14.92	Pat Mitchell	6-29	20.7	+ 6.08

How the Favourites Fared

Non-handicaps	W-R	Per cent	£1 Level Stake	Handicaps	W-R	Per cent	£1 Level Stake
2-y-o	41-124	33.1	- 31.80	2-y-o	6-14	42.9	+ 7.83
3-y-o	32-80	40.0	- 8.19	3-y-o	14-47	29.8	- 4.42
Weight-for-age	40-79	50.6	+ 8.00	All-aged	44-180	24.4	- 30.01
Totals	113-283	39.9	- 31.99	Totals	64-241	26.6	- 26.60
All favs	177-524	33.8	- 58.59				

Leading Trainers by Month at Lingfield Turf

March/Apr	Total W-R	Non-handicaps 2-y-o	3-y-o+	Handicaps 2-y-o	3-y-o+	Per cent	£1 Level Stake
H Thomson Jones	1-1	0-0	1-1	0-0	0-0	100.0	+ 12.00
M McCormack	1-1	0-0	0-0	0-0	1-1	100.0	+ 12.00
Lord Huntingdon	1-1	0-0	1-1	0-0	0-0	100.0	+ 3.33
M Bell	1-1	1-1	0-0	0-0	0-0	100.0	+ 1.50
K R Burke	1-1	0-0	0-0	0-0	1-1	100.0	+ 5.50

May	Total W-R	Non-handicaps 2-y-o	3-y-o+	Handicaps 2-y-o	3-y-o+	Per cent	£1 Level Stake
M R Stoute	7-22	0-0	7-18	0-0	0-4	31.8	+ 3.80
R Hannon	7-54	1-15	5-18	0-0	1-21	13.0	- 29.88
J H M Gosden	4-11	0-0	4-9	0-0	0-2	36.4	+ 2.03
N A Callaghan	4-20	1-5	1-3	0-0	2-12	20.0	+ 3.50
G Lewis	4-33	0-11	1-10	0-0	3-12	12.1	+ 2.75

June	Total W-R	Non-handicaps 2-y-o	3-y-o+	Handicaps 2-y-o	3-y-o+	Per cent	£1 Level Stake
R Hannon	7-31	3-8	2-10	0-0	2-13	22.6	- 5.17
J L Dunlop	5-15	1-2	2-6	0-0	2-7	33.3	- 2.25
R Charlton	4-5	0-0	3-4	0-0	1-1	80.0	+ 14.43
G Harwood	4-10	0-0	3-8	0-0	1-2	40.0	+ 12.48
R Akehurst	4-33	0-2	0-11	0-0	4-20	12.1	+ 4.75

July	Total W-R	Non-handicaps 2-y-o	3-y-o+	Handicaps 2-y-o	3-y-o+	Per cent	£1 Level Stake
G Harwood	4-10	1-1	1-2	0-0	2-7	40.0	+ 6.25
R Akehurst	4-24	0-3	0-2	0-1	4-18	16.7	- 4.50
L M Cumani	3-5	0-0	3-5	0-0	0-0	60.0	+ 2.42
J Berry	3-8	2-5	0-0	0-2	1-1	37.5	+ 3.95
G Lewis	3-14	3-6	0-1	0-3	0-4	21.4	- 0.38

August	Total W-R	Non-handicaps 2-y-o	3-y-o+	Handicaps 2-y-o	3-y-o+	Per cent	£1 Level Stake
G Harwood	4-6	2-2	0-0	0-0	2-4	66.7	+ 11.08
P F I Cole	3-7	0-2	2-3	0-0	1-2	42.9	+ 14.33
R Hannon	3-23	3-12	0-6	0-2	0-3	13.0	- 9.00
N J H Walker	2-2	0-0	1-1	0-0	1-1	100.0	+ 15.00
A Hide	2-4	0-0	0-1	0-0	2-3	50.0	+ 10.00

September	Total W-R	Non-handicaps 2-y-o	3-y-o+	Handicaps 2-y-o	3-y-o+	Per cent	£1 Level Stake
B W Hills	6-9	4-6	1-2	0-0	1-1	66.7	+ 27.73
J H M Gosden	3-13	2-8	1-4	0-0	0-1	23.1	- 7.41
R Bastiman	2-2	0-0	0-0	0-0	2-2	100.0	+ 11.00
G Wragg	2-3	1-1	1-2	0-0	0-0	66.7	+ 18.00
D Morley	2-4	1-3	0-0	0-0	1-1	50.0	+ 14.50

Oct/Nov	Total W-R	Non-handicaps 2-y-o	3-y-o+	Handicaps 2-y-o	3-y-o+	Per cent	£1 Level Stake
M R Stoute	3-13	3-10	0-1	0-1	0-1	23.1	- 7.55
R Akehurst	3-18	0-5	1-3	0-1	2-9	16.7	+ 16.00
R Hannon	3-18	2-6	0-3	0-2	1-7	16.7	+ 2.00
Mrs J Cecil	2-4	2-2	0-0	0-0	0-2	50.0	+ 7.00
D W P Arbuthnot	2-5	1-1	0-1	1-1	0-2	40.0	+ 20.00

LINGFIELD ALL-WEATHER (Group 4)

Leading Trainers 1990-94

	Total W-R	Non-handicaps 2-y-o	3-y-o+	Handicaps 2-y-o	3-y-o+	Per cent	£1 Level Stake
W A O'Gorman	36-166	3-13	17-55	2-9	14-89	21.7	+ 10.02
R J O'Sullivan	34-203	0-0	7-35	0-0	27-168	16.7	+ 2.60
M Johnston	29-130	2-5	5-23	0-2	22-100	22.3	+ 24.28
Lord Huntingdon	24-106	0-8	11-42	0-3	13-53	22.6	+ 4.76
B W Hills	23-70	1-9	11-26	0-2	11-33	32.9	- 10.00
C C Elsey	23-147	2-12	4-27	0-1	17-107	15.6	- 0.69
A Moore	23-235	0-14	6-84	0-1	17-136	9.8	- 1.50
P F I Cole	22-101	4-31	11-34	2-5	5-31	21.8	- 27.29
Sir M Prescott	20-89	4-24	7-29	0-2	9-34	22.5	- 18.69
P Mitchell	20-139	0-8	3-29	0-3	17-99	14.4	+ 10.83
S Dow	19-187	3-16	3-56	1-6	12-109	10.2	- 29.17
C A Cyzer	18-129	0-8	6-43	0-0	12-78	14.0	- 30.68
D Murray Smith	17-80	2-8	7-24	0-4	8-44	21.3	+ 20.81
R Hollinshead	16-84	0-5	12-37	0-1	4-41	19.0	- 14.57
R Hannon	16-129	5-33	5-35	0-13	6-48	12.4	+ 9.66
J Berry	15-71	5-18	4-22	0-1	6-30	21.1	- 15.58
M J Ryan	14-93	1-5	2-13	0-0	11-75	15.1	- 13.82
W R Muir	13-91	1-7	7-39	0-2	5-43	14.3	- 21.98
D R C Elsworth	12-57	6-15	2-19	2-2	2-21	21.1	- 12.70
N A Callaghan	12-71	7-14	2-19	1-9	2-29	16.9	+ 10.17
Dr J D Scargill	12-90	3-14	2-25	0-0	7-51	13.3	- 4.44
M R Channon	12-106	2-15	6-43	0-3	4-45	11.3	- 21.50

Leading Jockeys

	Total W-R	Per cent	£1 Level Stake	Best Trainer	W-R	Per cent	£1 Level Stake
T Quinn	61-327	18.7	- 22.37	P F I Cole	10-57	17.5	- 31.01
J Williams	51-388	13.1	- 51.02	D R C Elsworth	10-34	29.4	+ 3.05
L Dettori	48-157	30.6	+ 87.53	Lord Huntingdon	6-15	40.0	+ 13.80
D Biggs	39-346	11.3	- 96.17	R J O'Sullivan	21-116	18.1	+ 15.48
Emma O'Gorman	38-165	23.0	+ 34.72	W A O'Gorman	31-135	23.0	+ 23.09
M Hills	31-196	15.8	- 45.17	B W Hills	9-24	37.5	- 0.59
D McKeown	29-154	18.8	+ 17.80	Lord Huntingdon	6-27	22.2	- 7.50
J Quinn	29-403	7.2	-152.59	R Akehurst	2-5	40.0	+ 10.33
N Adams	28-339	8.3	- 19.92	A Moore	7-54	13.0	+ 48.50
G Duffield	24-124	19.4	- 31.10	Sir M Prescott	15-50	30.0	- 7.23
W Ryan	24-157	15.3	- 54.50	R Hollinshead	6-19	31.6	- 1.07
W Newnes	21-194	10.8	- 74.32	C C Elsey	8-36	22.2	+ 9.68

How the Favourites Fared

Non-handicaps	W-R	Per cent	£1 Level Stake	Handicaps	W-R	Per cent	£1 Level Stake
2-y-o	35-88	39.8	- 5.68	2-y-o	6-20	30.0	+ 1.75
3-y-o	59-134	44.0	- 11.05	3-y-o	28-78	35.9	- 15.96
Weight-for-age	70-203	34.5	- 36.34	All-aged	138-480	28.8	- 61.86
Totals	164-425	38.6	- 53.07	Totals	172-578	29.8	- 76.07
All favs	336-1003	33.5	-129.14				

Leading Trainers by Month at Lingfield (AW)

January

	Total W-R	Non-handicaps		Handicaps		Per cent	£1 Level Stake
		2-y-o	3-y-o+	2-y-o	3-y-o+		
W A O'Gorman	11-33	0-0	4-14	0-0	7-19	33.3	+ 18.25
R Hollinshead	10-22	0-0	7-11	0-0	3-11	45.5	+ 22.93

February

	Total W-R	Non-handicaps		Handicaps		Per cent	£1 Level Stake
		2-y-o	3-y-o+	2-y-o	3-y-o+		
M Johnston	11-39	0-0	2-5	0-0	9-34	28.2	+ 12.25
Lord Huntingdon	7-18	0-0	2-6	0-0	5-12	38.9	+ 6.55

March

	Total W-R	Non-handicaps		Handicaps		Per cent	£1 Level Stake
		2-y-o	3-y-o+	2-y-o	3-y-o+		
R J O'Sullivan	8-43	0-0	1-10	0-0	7-33	18.6	+ 13.50
W A O'Gorman	6-25	0-0	3-10	0-0	3-15	24.0	+ 4.33

April

	Total W-R	Non-handicaps		Handicaps		Per cent	£1 Level Stake
		2-y-o	3-y-o+	2-y-o	3-y-o+		
Sir M Prescott	5-8	0-0	3-3	0-0	2-5	62.5	+ 3.40
N A Callaghan	2-2	1-1	1-1	0-0	0-0	100.0	+ 10.25

May

	Total W-R	Non-handicaps		Handicaps		Per cent	£1 Level Stake
		2-y-o	3-y-o+	2-y-o	3-y-o+		
G Lewis	2-4	0-0	0-1	0-0	2-3	50.0	+ 8.50
M Dixon	2-4	0-0	1-1	0-0	1-3	50.0	+ 4.50

June

	Total W-R	Non-handicaps		Handicaps		Per cent	£1 Level Stake
		2-y-o	3-y-o+	2-y-o	3-y-o+		
P A Kelleway	3-4	0-0	2-3	0-0	1-1	75.0	+ 25.50
J Berry	2-2	1-1	0-0	0-0	1-1	100.0	+ 5.50

July

	Total W-R	Non-handicaps		Handicaps		Per cent	£1 Level Stake
		2-y-o	3-y-o+	2-y-o	3-y-o+		
P F I Cole	3-4	0-0	2-3	0-0	1-1	75.0	+ 0.83
Sir M Prescott	3-9	0-0	0-3	0-0	3-6	33.3	- 0.33

August

	Total W-R	Non-handicaps		Handicaps		Per cent	£1 Level Stake
		2-y-o	3-y-o+	2-y-o	3-y-o+		
C A Cyzer	6-20	0-3	0-0	0-0	6-17	30.0	+ 14.13
Mrs L Piggott	3-4	0-0	1-1	0-0	2-3	75.0	+ 16.20

September

	Total W-R	Non-handicaps		Handicaps		Per cent	£1 Level Stake
		2-y-o	3-y-o+	2-y-o	3-y-o+		
G Lewis	2-3	0-1	1-1	1-1	0-0	66.7	+ 20.00
B W Hills	2-4	0-0	1-2	0-0	1-2	50.0	+ 6.50

October

	Total W-R	Non-handicaps		Handicaps		Per cent	£1 Level Stake
		2-y-o	3-y-o+	2-y-o	3-y-o+		
W A O'Gorman	2-6	0-1	2-4	0-0	0-1	33.3	+ 2.13
C R Nelson	1-1	0-0	0-0	0-0	1-1	100.0	+ 6.50

November

	Total W-R	Non-handicaps		Handicaps		Per cent	£1 Level Stake
		2-y-o	3-y-o+	2-y-o	3-y-o+		
B W Hills	7-24	1-5	2-3	0-2	4-14	29.2	- 5.27
W A O'Gorman	6-31	1-7	1-5	2-6	2-13	19.4	+ 15.38

December

	Total W-R	Non-handicaps		Handicaps		Per cent	£1 Level Stake
		2-y-o	3-y-o+	2-y-o	3-y-o+		
R J O'Sullivan	9-30	0-0	0-2	0-0	9-28	30.0	+ 24.13
D R C Elsworth	6-14	5-7	0-3	1-1	0-3	42.9	+ 6.75

NEWBURY (Group 1)

Leading Trainers 1990-94

	Total W-R	Non-handicaps 2-y-o	3-y-o+	Handicaps 2-y-o	3-y-o+	Per cent	£1 Level Stake
R Hannon	42-452	15-187	11-84	4-35	12-146	9.3	- 161.08
P Chapple-Hyam	30-92	20-49	8-26	1-3	1-14	32.6	+ 26.54
J H M Gosden	29-129	4-19	16-74	0-0	9-36	22.5	+ 34.67
H R A Cecil	23-97	3-15	16-66	0-0	4-16	23.7	+ 1.69
R Charlton	19-116	4-38	8-41	0-4	7-33	16.4	+ 21.88
J L Dunlop	17-178	3-51	7-65	1-7	6-55	9.6	- 79.61
I A Balding	17-192	3-58	4-48	0-2	10-84	8.9	- 45.55
M R Stoute	16-113	4-27	8-53	0-2	4-31	14.2	- 13.75
L M Cumani	15-72	4-9	6-30	0-1	5-32	20.8	- 16.89
B W Hills	14-142	5-50	4-47	0-1	5-44	9.9	- 29.90
P F I Cole	14-162	7-59	4-50	0-9	3-44	8.6	- 55.54
C E Brittain	11-147	2-33	4-57	1-6	4-51	7.5	- 66.17
D R C Elsworth	11-161	3-46	0-52	1-6	7-57	6.8	- 60.50
G Lewis	10-67	2-29	1-7	1-8	6-23	14.9	+ 69.67
Lord Huntingdon	10-131	0-25	3-28	1-3	6-75	7.6	- 56.50
P T Walwyn	9-100	4-27	0-31	1-4	4-38	9.0	- 37.25
J Berry	8-50	6-17	1-12	0-7	1-14	16.0	+ 2.67
W R Hern	8-51	5-12	2-28	0-0	1-11	15.7	- 14.54
B Hanbury	8-64	3-20	4-22	0-0	1-22	12.5	- 27.34
Lady Herries	5-31	0-1	0-2	0-0	5-28	16.1	+ 12.83
J W Hills	5-57	0-16	2-12	0-0	3-29	8.8	- 19.88
R Akehurst	5-71	0-10	0-2	1-4	4-55	7.0	- 43.50

Leading Jockeys

	Total W-R	Per cent	£1 Level Stake	Best Trainer	W-R	Per cent	£1 Level Stake
Pat Eddery	51-289	17.6	- 10.12	R Charlton	10-48	20.8	+ 2.38
W Carson	41-264	15.5	- 44.36	J L Dunlop	10-66	15.2	- 22.61
L Dettori	35-217	16.1	+ 33.70	L M Cumani	9-35	25.7	- 1.25
J Reid	35-229	15.3	- 63.99	P Chapple-Hyam	18-50	36.0	+ 8.17
M Roberts	34-266	12.8	- 56.10	R Hannon	7-47	14.9	- 18.68
W R Swinburn	25-189	13.2	- 47.20	M R Stoute	5-45	11.1	- 12.00
R Cochrane	22-200	11.0	- 35.97	I A Balding	8-36	22.2	+ 14.95
T Quinn	21-226	9.3	- 85.45	P F I Cole	10-95	10.5	- 46.95
M Hills	13-146	8.9	- 48.96	G Wragg	3-14	21.4	+ 1.54
A Munro	11-121	9.1	- 40.87	W A O'Gorman	2-2	100.0	+ 4.03
D Harrison	10-78	12.8	+ 4.00	J W Hills	3-11	27.3	+ 16.00
D Holland	9-89	10.1	+ 7.17	B W Hills	5-32	15.6	+ 16.00

How the Favourites Fared

Non-handicaps	W-R	Per cent	£1 Level Stake	Handicaps	W-R	Per cent	£1 Level Stake
2-y-o	59-127	46.5	+ 7.47	2-y-o	8-21	38.1	+ 8.16
3-y-o	32-82	39.0	+ 0.77	3-y-o	15-60	25.0	- 11.35
Weight-for-age	20-61	32.8	- 1.79	All-aged	37-137	27.0	+ 17.20
Totals	111-270	41.1	+ 6.45	Totals	60-218	27.5	+ 14.01
All favs	171-488	35.0	+ 20.46				

Leading Trainers by Month at Newbury

March/Apr	Total W-R	Non-handicaps 2-y-o	3-y-o+	Handicaps 2-y-o	3-y-o+	Per cent	£1 Level Stake
P Chapple-Hyam	11-22	3-3	7-13	0-0	1-6	50.0	+ 31.89
H R A Cecil	7-23	0-0	6-21	0-0	1-2	30.4	+ 13.03
R Hannon	7-56	2-11	3-26	0-0	2-19	12.5	+ 22.50
I A Balding	4-31	0-2	1-19	0-0	3-10	12.9	+ 18.50
J L Dunlop	4-40	0-0	3-24	0-0	1-16	10.0	- 27.02

May	Total W-R	Non-handicaps 2-y-o	3-y-o+	Handicaps 2-y-o	3-y-o+	Per cent	£1 Level Stake
R Hannon	11-73	4-30	6-21	0-0	1-22	15.1	- 13.11
I A Balding	5-27	0-6	2-10	0-0	3-11	18.5	+ 24.00
J H M Gosden	5-27	0-0	5-22	0-0	0-5	18.5	- 3.55
P F I Cole	5-37	3-12	2-14	0-0	0-11	13.5	- 21.20
P Chapple-Hyam	4-13	4-6	0-6	0-0	0-1	30.8	+ 10.29

June	Total W-R	Non-handicaps 2-y-o	3-y-o+	Handicaps 2-y-o	3-y-o+	Per cent	£1 Level Stake
R Hannon	6-61	4-34	0-8	0-0	2-19	9.8	- 27.35
A C Stewart	4-6	0-0	2-2	0-0	2-4	66.7	+ 10.75
R Charlton	4-14	1-4	1-4	0-0	2-6	28.6	+ 0.25
W R Hern	3-10	3-4	0-3	0-0	0-3	30.0	+ 1.33
L M Cumani	3-12	0-0	2-8	0-0	1-4	25.0	- 3.00

July	Total W-R	Non-handicaps 2-y-o	3-y-o+	Handicaps 2-y-o	3-y-o+	Per cent	£1 Level Stake
L M Cumani	6-11	0-0	3-6	0-0	3-5	54.5	+ 15.13
J H M Gosden	5-9	0-0	2-5	0-0	3-4	55.6	+ 19.58
H R A Cecil	4-9	0-1	3-6	0-0	1-2	44.4	+ 4.79
P Chapple-Hyam	4-12	4-9	0-2	0-0	0-1	33.3	- 0.77
R Hannon	4-63	3-38	0-11	0-0	1-14	6.3	- 29.87

August	Total W-R	Non-handicaps 2-y-o	3-y-o+	Handicaps 2-y-o	3-y-o+	Per cent	£1 Level Stake
P Chapple-Hyam	5-15	5-10	0-2	0-0	0-3	33.3	- 3.78
J L Dunlop	4-16	1-8	1-3	1-1	1-4	25.0	+ 10.33
R Hannon	4-76	0-33	1-10	1-7	2-26	5.3	- 54.50
J Berry	3-9	2-5	0-0	0-0	1-4	33.3	+ 7.83
J H M Gosden	3-14	1-6	1-5	0-0	1-3	21.4	- 3.30

September	Total W-R	Non-handicaps 2-y-o	3-y-o+	Handicaps 2-y-o	3-y-o+	Per cent	£1 Level Stake
R Hannon	7-63	1-24	1-7	2-14	3-18	11.1	- 24.75
J H M Gosden	5-19	1-6	2-5	0-0	2-8	26.3	- 0.25
J L Dunlop	4-23	2-13	1-3	0-2	1-5	17.4	+ 7.50
M R Stoute	3-18	2-9	0-3	0-0	1-6	16.7	- 0.17
B W Hills	3-20	1-12	0-0	0-0	2-8	15.0	+ 1.10

Oct/Nov	Total W-R	Non-handicaps 2-y-o	3-y-o+	Handicaps 2-y-o	3-y-o+	Per cent	£1 Level Stake
R Charlton	6-27	2-12	3-6	0-4	1-5	22.2	+ 1.13
J H M Gosden	6-28	2-6	2-16	0-0	2-6	21.4	+ 19.08
G B Balding	4-13	0-1	1-1	1-2	2-9	30.8	+ 44.50
L M Cumani	4-18	3-4	1-6	0-1	0-7	22.2	- 2.88
M R Stoute	4-21	2-7	1-7	0-2	1-5	19.0	+ 13.00

NEWCASTLE (Group 1)

Leading Trainers 1990-94

	Total W-R	Non-handicaps 2-y-o	3-y-o+	Handicaps 2-y-o	3-y-o+	Per cent	£1 Level Stake
J Berry	25-154	12-63	7-27	0-11	6-53	16.2	- 53.25
Mrs M Reveley	19-144	2-19	2-20	1-11	14-94	13.2	- 50.64
M R Stoute	18-62	7-16	7-21	0-1	4-24	29.0	- 20.82
H R A Cecil	13-38	4-9	6-17	0-0	3-12	34.2	- 6.44
Mrs J Ramsden	13-99	1-20	3-11	0-9	9-59	13.1	- 27.01
J W Watts	12-74	2-14	4-18	0-1	6-41	16.2	- 19.33
M H Easterby	12-130	2-31	1-14	0-7	9-78	9.2	- 65.08
D Morley	11-40	5-12	0-9	1-2	5-17	27.5	+ 19.22
M Johnston	11-90	2-30	1-7	1-4	7-49	12.2	- 0.24
Sir M Prescott	10-34	2-9	1-7	1-3	6-15	29.4	+ 7.24
J H M Gosden	9-25	0-4	6-15	0-0	3-6	36.0	+ 10.42
M J Camacho	9-38	1-8	3-6	0-0	5-24	23.7	+ 32.70
L M Cumani	8-20	2-3	4-12	0-0	2-5	40.0	+ 4.74
R Hannon	8-30	2-10	4-9	0-1	2-10	26.7	+ 15.42
B W Hills	8-36	2-7	4-18	0-0	2-11	22.2	- 3.67
T D Barron	7-58	1-11	1-8	0-4	5-35	12.1	- 17.50
B Beasley	6-17	2-4	0-3	0-1	4-9	35.3	+ 43.50
J L Dunlop	6-25	2-8	1-4	0-1	3-12	24.0	- 1.87
M Bell	6-31	4-10	0-3	0-2	2-16	19.4	- 15.72
B Hanbury	6-32	3-9	1-16	0-0	2-7	18.8	+ 4.63
W Jarvis	5-21	2-7	1-4	0-0	2-10	23.8	+ 13.75
H Thomson Jones	5-23	1-6	1-5	0-1	3-11	21.7	+ 13.00

Leading Jockeys

	Total W-R	Per cent	£1 Level Stake	Best Trainer	W-R	Per cent	£1 Level Stake
K Darley	27-189	14.3	- 74.58	Mrs M Reveley	6-43	14.0	- 21.14
J Carroll	22-149	14.8	- 31.08	J Berry	16-97	16.5	- 26.58
W Carson	20-55	36.4	+ 20.37	D Morley	5-14	35.7	+ 5.22
D McKeown	18-125	14.4	- 37.51	J W Watts	7-21	33.3	+ 4.19
M Birch	16-144	11.1	- 54.96	M H Easterby	6-72	8.3	- 43.29
G Duffield	15-82	18.3	+ 1.65	Sir M Prescott	8-25	32.0	+ 6.98
Pat Eddery	12-42	28.6	- 16.13	M R Stoute	4-6	66.7	- 0.40
W Ryan	12-70	17.1	- 16.33	H R A Cecil	4-17	23.5	- 6.46
N Connorton	12-79	15.2	- 5.30	Miss S E Hall	5-22	22.7	+ 11.50
J Lowe	12-139	8.6	- 45.87	Mrs M Reveley	4-23	17.4	- 8.25
K Fallon	11-118	9.3	- 44.34	Mrs J Ramsden	4-24	16.7	- 10.59
L Dettori	10-43	23.3	+ 3.76	L M Cumani	6-9	66.7	+ 13.51

How the Favourites Fared

Non-handicaps	W-R	Per cent	£1 Level Stake	Handicaps	W-R	Per cent	£1 Level Stake
2-y-o	45-89	50.6	- 3.05	2-y-o	4-14	28.6	+ 0.63
3-y-o	12-38	31.6	- 11.08	3-y-o	15-44	34.1	- 3.95
Weight-for-age	28-57	49.1	- 5.96	All-aged	42-148	28.4	- 22.82
Totals	85-184	46.2	- 20.09	Totals	61-206	29.6	- 26.14
All favs	146-390	37.4	- 46.23				

Leading Trainers by Month at Newcastle

March/Apr

	Total W-R	Non-handicaps 2-y-o	3-y-o+	Handicaps 2-y-o	3-y-o+	Per cent	£1 Level Stake
Mrs J Ramsden	7-23	0-0	3-8	0-0	4-15	30.4	+ 20.33
J Berry	6-31	5-10	0-9	0-0	1-12	19.4	- 10.98
M J Camacho	5-9	0-0	2-4	0-0	3-5	55.6	+ 42.00
J W Watts	5-16	0-0	3-10	0-0	2-6	31.3	+ 4.30
M R Stoute	3-4	0-0	3-4	0-0	0-0	75.0	+ 0.96

May

	Total W-R	Non-handicaps 2-y-o	3-y-o+	Handicaps 2-y-o	3-y-o+	Per cent	£1 Level Stake
J Berry	7-13	2-6	3-4	0-0	2-3	53.8	+ 19.78
Sir M Prescott	2-2	0-0	0-0	0-0	2-2	100.0	+ 3.33
H Thomson Jones	2-5	0-0	1-2	0-0	1-3	40.0	+ 9.00
M Johnston	2-8	1-4	0-1	0-0	1-3	25.0	- 0.17
Mrs M Reveley	2-17	1-2	0-7	0-0	1-8	11.8	- 11.05

June

	Total W-R	Non-handicaps 2-y-o	3-y-o+	Handicaps 2-y-o	3-y-o+	Per cent	£1 Level Stake
H R A Cecil	5-8	2-2	3-3	0-0	0-3	62.5	+ 0.40
M R Stoute	5-18	2-3	1-4	0-0	2-11	27.8	- 10.23
J H M Gosden	4-7	0-0	1-4	0-0	3-3	57.1	+ 19.90
P T Walwyn	3-5	0-0	2-2	0-0	1-3	60.0	+ 4.50
D Morley	3-6	2-3	0-1	0-0	1-2	50.0	+ 8.62

July

	Total W-R	Non-handicaps 2-y-o	3-y-o+	Handicaps 2-y-o	3-y-o+	Per cent	£1 Level Stake
Mrs M Reveley	6-21	1-4	0-1	0-0	5-16	28.6	+ 15.41
M R Stoute	5-13	2-2	2-6	0-0	1-5	38.5	- 1.38
J Berry	5-21	3-9	2-2	0-2	0-8	23.8	- 6.25
Mrs J Ramsden	4-11	1-2	0-1	0-1	3-7	36.4	+ 7.41
W Jarvis	3-4	1-1	1-1	0-0	1-2	75.0	+ 16.75

August

	Total W-R	Non-handicaps 2-y-o	3-y-o+	Handicaps 2-y-o	3-y-o+	Per cent	£1 Level Stake
L M Cumani	3-4	0-0	2-2	0-0	1-2	75.0	+ 8.61
B W Hills	3-12	1-3	1-4	0-0	1-5	25.0	+ 1.25
M R Stoute	3-14	2-5	0-2	0-1	1-6	21.4	- 2.83
Mrs M Reveley	3-25	0-4	1-3	0-4	2-14	12.0	- 4.25
M H Easterby	3-29	0-8	0-1	0-6	3-14	10.3	- 7.57

September

	Total W-R	Non-handicaps 2-y-o	3-y-o+	Handicaps 2-y-o	3-y-o+	Per cent	£1 Level Stake
J L Dunlop	3-5	1-3	0-0	0-0	2-2	60.0	+ 3.13
J Berry	2-7	0-3	1-3	0-0	1-1	28.6	+ 1.50
R Hannon	2-7	0-3	2-4	0-0	0-0	28.6	+ 2.50
B A McMahon	1-1	0-0	0-0	0-0	1-1	100.0	+ 1.00
N A Graham	1-1	1-1	0-0	0-0	0-0	100.0	+ 8.50

Oct/Nov

	Total W-R	Non-handicaps 2-y-o	3-y-o+	Handicaps 2-y-o	3-y-o+	Per cent	£1 Level Stake
J H M Gosden	5-11	0-3	5-7	0-0	0-1	45.5	- 2.48
D Morley	4-13	2-5	0-3	0-0	2-5	30.8	+ 3.10
M H Easterby	4-15	1-3	0-1	0-1	3-10	26.7	+ 6.62
Mrs M Reveley	4-29	0-3	0-1	1-7	3-18	13.8	- 14.75
L M Cumani	3-7	2-3	1-3	0-0	0-1	42.9	+ 1.02

NEWMARKET ROWLEY MILE (Group 1)

Leading Trainers 1990-94

	Total W-R	Non-handicaps 2-y-o	3-y-o+	Handicaps 2-y-o	3-y-o+	Per cent	£1 Level Stake
H R A Cecil	39-214	11-59	25-125	0-0	3-30	18.2	- 51.37
J H M Gosden	35-211	3-36	24-112	0-3	8-60	16.6	- 5.13
M R Stoute	32-232	12-87	18-107	0-7	2-31	13.8	- 9.21
L M Cumani	30-224	9-73	13-94	0-3	8-54	13.4	- 68.01
B W Hills	29-248	8-68	10-98	0-7	11-75	11.7	- 82.28
R Hannon	25-339	10-100	8-85	2-38	5-116	7.4	-170.28
C E Brittain	21-282	3-73	11-120	1-9	6-80	7.4	- 79.75
J L Dunlop	18-172	3-42	11-64	0-9	4-57	10.5	- 67.65
J Berry	12-91	4-22	4-27	1-12	3-30	13.2	+ 6.07
P Chapple-Hyam	11-78	4-34	6-33	1-3	0-8	14.1	+ 0.20
J R Fanshawe	11-109	2-24	4-48	1-4	4-33	10.1	- 17.90
P F I Cole	10-120	4-46	4-39	1-9	1-26	8.3	- 13.88
A Fabre (Fra)	9-23	5-6	4-16	0-0	0-1	39.1	+ 26.92
M Johnston	9-62	2-7	1-11	3-13	3-31	14.5	+ 25.50
P T Walwyn	9-66	3-14	4-30	0-2	2-20	13.6	- 12.59
G Harwood	9-129	0-32	3-42	0-2	6-53	7.0	- 6.63
G Wragg	8-82	5-24	3-43	0-1	0-14	9.8	- 35.38
G Lewis	7-53	1-15	0-5	2-13	4-20	13.2	+ 34.00
H Thomson Jones	7-63	1-11	5-25	0-3	1-24	11.1	- 24.92
I A Balding	7-73	1-15	4-22	0-3	2-33	9.6	- 27.29
M Bell	7-112	2-38	2-27	0-5	3-42	6.3	- 42.50
M H Tompkins	7-115	2-37	2-18	0-10	3-50	6.1	- 61.00

Leading Jockeys

	Total W-R	Per cent	£1 Level Stake	Best Trainer	W-R	Per cent	£1 Level Stake
Pat Eddery	69-352	19.6	- 12.62	H R A Cecil	14-44	31.8	- 2.56
W R Swinburn	43-267	16.1	+ 12.70	M R Stoute	14-91	15.4	- 14.26
W Carson	41-360	11.4	- 69.59	J L Dunlop	13-67	19.4	+ 2.85
L Dettori	39-344	11.3	- 89.24	L M Cumani	18-114	15.8	- 17.28
M Roberts	37-361	10.2	- 97.78	C E Brittain	16-133	12.0	+ 7.75
M Hills	21-217	9.7	- 48.60	B W Hills	10-60	16.7	+ 2.40
R Cochrane	19-233	8.2	- 17.66	G Harwood	3-41	7.3	+ 0.50
J Reid	17-207	8.2	- 31.55	P Chapple-Hyam	3-37	8.1	- 10.80
T Quinn	17-221	7.7	- 57.94	P F I Cole	6-67	9.0	+ 7.75
D Holland	15-138	10.9	- 56.87	B W Hills	9-66	13.6	- 21.50
R Hills	15-156	9.6	- 12.37	H Thomson Jones	4-49	8.2	- 28.42
G Duffield	13-121	10.7	+ 11.38	Sir M Prescott	4-15	26.7	+ 11.50

How the Favourites Fared

Non-handicaps	W-R	Per cent	£1 Level Stake	Handicaps	W-R	Per cent	£1 Level Stake
2-y-o	56-140	40.0	+ 5.71	2-y-o	4-32	12.5	- 10.50
3-y-o	51-131	38.9	- 15.86	3-y-o	6-51	11.8	- 24.00
Weight-for-age	35-100	35.0	- 8.61	All-aged	33-136	24.3	- 9.19
Totals	142-371	38.3	- 18.76	Totals	43-219	19.6	- 43.69
All favs	185-590	31.4	- 62.45				

Leading Trainers by Month at Newmarket (Rowley Mile)

March/Apr

	Total W-R	Non-handicaps 2-y-o	3-y-o+	Handicaps 2-y-o	3-y-o+	Per cent	£1 Level Stake
H R A Cecil	15-67	0-0	14-59	0-0	1-8	22.4	+ 5.69
J H M Gosden	12-62	0-0	8-46	0-0	4-16	19.4	+ 10.13
R Hannon	10-80	4-11	3-42	0-0	3-27	12.5	- 16.38
C E Brittain	8-69	0-3	6-46	0-0	2-20	11.6	+ 12.75
M R Stoute	6-55	0-1	6-44	0-0	0-10	10.9	- 16.67

May

	Total W-R	Non-handicaps 2-y-o	3-y-o+	Handicaps 2-y-o	3-y-o+	Per cent	£1 Level Stake
R Hannon	9-59	3-14	5-25	0-0	1-20	15.3	- 19.91
H R A Cecil	8-42	0-2	7-37	0-0	1-3	19.0	- 22.04
J Berry	7-29	3-8	3-10	0-0	1-11	24.1	+ 15.57
J L Dunlop	7-29	0-1	6-20	0-0	1-8	24.1	+ 5.27
J H M Gosden	7-32	0-0	6-26	0-0	1-6	21.9	+ 4.87

September

	Total W-R	Non-handicaps 2-y-o	3-y-o+	Handicaps 2-y-o	3-y-o+	Per cent	£1 Level Stake
P Chapple-Hyam	3-12	2-10	0-0	1-1	0-1	25.0	+ 31.20
M R Stoute	3-22	2-14	1-3	0-3	0-2	13.6	+ 4.00
L M Cumani	2-11	1-7	0-1	0-1	1-2	18.2	- 2.25
J H M Gosden	2-11	2-8	0-0	0-0	0-3	18.2	+ 10.00
C E Brittain	2-24	1-14	0-2	0-2	1-6	8.3	- 12.50

Oct/Nov

	Total W-R	Non-handicaps 2-y-o	3-y-o+	Handicaps 2-y-o	3-y-o+	Per cent	£1 Level Stake
B W Hills	19-124	6-47	6-26	0-5	7-46	15.3	- 18.78
M R Stoute	19-129	10-70	7-38	0-4	2-17	14.7	+ 19.25
L M Cumani	16-116	8-66	5-19	0-2	3-29	13.8	- 39.60
H R A Cecil	15-95	10-53	4-26	0-0	1-16	15.8	- 29.53
J H M Gosden	14-106	1-28	10-40	0-3	3-35	13.2	- 30.13

NEWMARKET JULY COURSE (Group 1)

Leading Trainers 1990-94

	Total W-R	Non-handicaps 2-y-o	3-y-o+	Handicaps 2-y-o	3-y-o+	Per cent	£1 Level Stake
R Hannon	32-219	14-94	8-35	5-21	5-69	14.6	- 15.34
H R A Cecil	24-106	9-29	12-55	0-0	3-22	22.6	- 28.01
J H M Gosden	21-119	4-25	12-60	0-1	5-33	17.6	- 4.36
L M Cumani	20-115	4-20	11-58	0-1	5-36	17.4	- 29.76
M R Stoute	20-116	12-52	5-31	1-3	2-30	17.2	- 29.76
P F I Cole	15-56	8-21	4-18	1-5	2-12	26.8	+ 8.25
J L Dunlop	14-82	3-38	6-16	0-2	5-26	17.1	- 7.55
C E Brittain	14-170	5-64	6-49	0-7	3-50	8.2	- 68.13
R Charlton	13-39	7-14	5-11	0-1	1-13	33.3	+ 32.23
M Bell	13-93	2-26	3-16	4-13	4-38	14.0	- 7.78
G Wragg	10-64	4-19	3-23	0-1	3-21	15.6	- 19.26
A C Stewart	9-44	0-6	5-16	0-0	4-22	20.5	+ 42.10
M A Jarvis	7-55	0-13	2-8	0-3	5-31	12.7	- 7.50
B W Hills	7-72	3-28	1-15	0-1	3-28	9.7	- 22.25
G Harwood	6-41	1-7	2-16	0-1	3-17	14.6	+ 26.45
R Akehurst	6-42	1-4	2-6	0-0	3-32	14.3	- 3.88
J R Fanshawe	6-59	0-9	2-19	0-1	4-30	10.2	- 7.13
N A Callaghan	6-89	3-39	2-18	0-7	1-25	6.7	- 54.54
B Hanbury	6-92	1-43	0-25	0-2	5-22	6.5	- 28.50
P Chapple-Hyam	5-20	3-11	0-4	0-0	2-5	25.0	+ 8.80
W R Hern	5-31	2-10	3-14	0-0	0-7	16.1	- 6.38
R W Armstrong	5-45	5-19	0-10	0-1	0-15	11.1	- 17.29

Leading Jockeys

	Total W-R	Per cent	£1 Level Stake	Best Trainer	W-R	Per cent	£1 Level Stake
L Dettori	37-219	16.9	- 36.28	L M Cumani	10-46	21.7	- 16.12
Pat Eddery	35-201	17.4	- 56.76	H R A Cecil	9-24	37.5	+ 8.85
W Carson	34-193	17.6	+ 22.67	J L Dunlop	10-34	29.4	+ 14.70
M Roberts	32-198	16.2	+ 1.67	C E Brittain	10-73	13.7	- 7.12
W R Swinburn	30-174	17.2	- 5.89	M R Stoute	8-35	22.9	+ 4.21
B Raymond	16-132	12.1	- 59.05	R Hannon	5-20	25.0	+ 0.36
T Quinn	14-80	17.5	+ 25.13	P F I Cole	6-22	27.3	+ 4.38
J Reid	13-99	13.1	- 21.21	T G Mills	3-6	50.0	+ 7.33
A Munro	13-127	10.2	- 59.91	P F I Cole	4-12	33.3	+ 4.13
M Hills	12-94	12.8	+ 3.63	M Bell	6-26	23.1	+ 19.13
R Cochrane	12-148	8.1	- 50.09	G Wragg	2-3	66.7	+ 11.00
L Piggott	11-74	14.9	- 0.99	R Hannon	5-11	45.5	+ 17.41

How the Favourites Fared

Non-handicaps	W-R	Per cent	£1 Level Stake	Handicaps	W-R	Per cent	£1 Level Stake
2-y-o	56-116	48.3	+ 18.20	2-y-o	8-20	40.0	+ 7.71
3-y-o	29-70	41.4	+ 0.74	3-y-o	12-56	21.4	- 10.62
Weight-for-age	31-70	44.3	+ 0.91	All-aged	25-115	21.7	- 36.35
Totals	116-256	45.3	+ 19.85	Totals	45-191	23.6	- 39.26
All favs	161-447	36.0	- 19.41				

Leading Trainers by Month at Newmarket (July)

June

	Total W-R	Non-handicaps 2-y-o	3-y-o+	Handicaps 2-y-o	3-y-o+	Per cent	£1 Level Stake
J H M Gosden	6-27	0-4	5-16	0-0	1-7	22.2	+ 6.11
H R A Cecil	5-21	1-3	3-14	0-0	1-4	23.8	- 2.77
J R Fanshawe	4-17	0-0	1-7	0-0	3-10	23.5	+ 21.00
R Hannon	4-32	2-13	1-8	0-0	1-11	12.5	- 13.17
J L Dunlop	3-9	1-4	2-3	0-0	0-2	33.3	- 0.93

July

	Total W-R	Non-handicaps 2-y-o	3-y-o+	Handicaps 2-y-o	3-y-o+	Per cent	£1 Level Stake
R Hannon	17-113	8-49	5-16	1-4	3-44	15.0	- 22.75
H R A Cecil	15-58	7-18	7-28	0-0	1-12	25.9	- 5.29
J H M Gosden	9-58	3-13	4-26	0-1	2-18	15.5	- 23.84
M R Stoute	8-48	5-21	2-14	0-1	1-12	16.7	- 11.93
L M Cumani	8-52	0-5	5-27	0-0	3-20	15.4	- 4.06

August

	Total W-R	Non-handicaps 2-y-o	3-y-o+	Handicaps 2-y-o	3-y-o+	Per cent	£1 Level Stake
R Hannon	11-74	4-32	2-11	4-17	1-14	14.9	+ 20.58
M R Stoute	10-51	6-25	2-9	1-2	1-15	19.6	- 6.67
L M Cumani	9-39	3-11	4-16	0-1	2-11	23.1	- 9.13
P F I Cole	7-21	4-7	2-6	1-5	0-3	33.3	+ 7.25
R Charlton	6-19	4-8	2-4	0-1	0-6	31.6	+ 14.44

NOTTINGHAM (Group 3)

Leading Trainers 1990-94

	Total W-R	Non-handicaps 2-y-o	3-y-o+	Handicaps 2-y-o	3-y-o+	Per cent	£1 Level Stake
H R A Cecil	30-78	11-30	18-44	0-0	1-4	38.5	+ 14.64
J L Dunlop	21-111	6-41	7-31	2-4	6-35	18.9	- 25.67
P F I Cole	16-80	7-31	6-21	0-4	3-24	20.0	+ 4.21
J H M Gosden	13-42	1-4	11-29	0-1	1-8	31.0	+ 12.75
D Morley	13-83	2-25	2-14	0-1	9-43	15.7	+ 13.63
R Hannon	13-121	5-63	4-16	2-14	2-28	10.7	- 54.15
R Charlton	11-36	4-16	5-14	0-0	2-6	30.6	+ 12.69
Mrs J Ramsden	11-92	1-12	0-7	0-3	10-70	12.0	- 10.92
L M Cumani	10-32	4-9	5-18	0-0	1-5	31.3	+ 7.57
J Berry	10-101	6-62	2-22	2-12	0-5	9.9	- 52.53
P T Walwyn	9-34	4-10	4-10	0-1	1-13	26.5	+ 5.67
R M Whitaker	9-52	1-10	1-11	0-3	7-28	17.3	+ 21.00
R J Hodges	9-79	0-4	1-15	0-1	8-59	11.4	+ 32.00
J Wharton	9-84	3-25	3-16	0-3	3-40	10.7	+ 6.00
B A McMahon	9-111	2-25	4-30	0-1	3-55	8.1	- 42.00
Sir M Prescott	8-41	3-13	0-4	0-0	5-24	19.5	+ 27.38
M J Ryan	8-54	0-3	1-7	0-2	7-42	14.8	+ 8.50
B Hanbury	8-58	2-22	4-21	0-3	2-12	13.8	- 4.25
M Johnston	7-41	1-12	4-12	1-2	1-15	17.1	- 15.26
G Wragg	7-42	4-16	2-18	0-1	1-7	16.7	- 13.50
F H Lee	7-47	0-5	2-9	0-0	5-33	14.9	+ 61.00
B W Hills	7-58	3-24	2-21	1-3	1-10	12.1	- 8.50

Leading Jockeys

	Total W-R	Per cent	£1 Level Stake	Best Trainer	W-R	Per cent	£1 Level Stake
W Carson	37-193	19.2	+ 1.76	J L Dunlop	7-35	20.0	- 12.98
Pat Eddery	33-128	25.8	- 23.23	R Charlton	8-14	57.1	+ 12.20
L Dettori	29-157	18.5	- 21.57	L M Cumani	5-15	33.3	+ 3.17
W Ryan	21-167	12.6	- 68.29	H R A Cecil	13-38	34.2	- 1.04
M Roberts	18-160	11.3	- 37.24	C E Brittain	3-27	11.1	- 18.12
Paul Eddery	17-120	14.2	- 9.56	Mrs J Cecil	4-10	40.0	+ 3.03
T Quinn	15-99	15.2	- 5.26	P F I Cole	8-36	22.2	+ 3.01
W R Swinburn	14-102	13.7	+ 18.84	J R Fanshawe	2-10	20.0	+ 5.88
R Cochrane	13-112	11.6	- 42.37	R Charlton	2-3	66.7	+ 14.50
A Munro	11-128	8.6	- 32.54	P F I Cole	5-15	33.3	+ 7.46
D Harrison	10-45	22.2	+ 38.63	Lord Huntingdon	4-9	44.4	+ 16.63
M Hills	10-108	9.3	- 62.42	M Bell	3-16	18.8	- 5.17

How the Favourites Fared

Non-handicaps	W-R	Per cent	£1 Level Stake	Handicaps	W-R	Per cent	£1 Level Stake
2-y-o	62-142	43.7	+ 1.93	2-y-o	5-20	25.0	- 8.26
3-y-o	55-106	51.9	+ 19.34	3-y-o	15-56	26.8	- 5.61
Weight-for-age	27-60	45.0	+ 7.98	All-aged	41-168	24.4	- 12.94
Totals	144-308	46.8	+ 29.25	Totals	61-244	25.0	- 26.81
All favs	205-552	37.1	+ 2.44				

Leading Trainers by Month at Nottingham

March/Apr

	Total W-R	Non-handicaps 2-y-o	3-y-o+	Handicaps 2-y-o	3-y-o+	Per cent	£1 Level Stake
H R A Cecil	9-16	0-1	9-15	0-0	0-0	56.3	- 0.14
J L Dunlop	6-21	0-1	5-12	0-0	1-8	28.6	- 5.29
Mrs J Ramsden	4-20	0-1	0-4	0-0	4-15	20.0	+ 1.50
Lord Huntingdon	3-7	0-0	2-4	0-0	1-3	42.9	+ 16.00
C Tinkler	3-13	0-1	1-5	0-0	2-7	23.1	+ 10.33

May

	Total W-R	Non-handicaps 2-y-o	3-y-o+	Handicaps 2-y-o	3-y-o+	Per cent	£1 Level Stake
H R A Cecil	3-4	1-1	2-3	0-0	0-0	75.0	+ 5.18
M Bell	3-6	2-2	0-1	0-0	1-3	50.0	+ 7.33
J H M Gosden	2-6	0-0	1-5	0-0	1-1	33.3	+ 1.50
R J R Williams	2-7	0-1	0-0	0-0	2-6	28.6	+ 28.00
B A McMahon	2-10	0-2	0-2	0-0	2-6	20.0	+ 2.50

June

	Total W-R	Non-handicaps 2-y-o	3-y-o+	Handicaps 2-y-o	3-y-o+	Per cent	£1 Level Stake
H R A Cecil	5-14	2-4	2-9	0-0	1-1	35.7	+ 3.12
F H Lee	3-7	0-1	1-1	0-0	2-5	42.9	+ 48.00
B Hanbury	3-8	1-1	1-5	0-0	1-2	37.5	+ 11.50
P F I Cole	3-9	1-2	2-5	0-0	0-2	33.3	+ 3.54
I A Balding	3-10	0-0	3-6	0-0	0-4	30.0	+ 9.00

July

	Total W-R	Non-handicaps 2-y-o	3-y-o+	Handicaps 2-y-o	3-y-o+	Per cent	£1 Level Stake
Sir M Prescott	3-6	1-1	0-1	0-0	2-4	50.0	+ 12.13
B W Hills	3-7	1-3	2-2	0-0	0-2	42.9	+ 12.00
P F I Cole	3-12	1-2	1-2	0-0	1-8	25.0	+ 6.94
J L Dunlop	3-12	2-4	0-4	0-0	1-4	25.0	- 5.67
Mrs J Ramsden	3-12	0-2	0-0	0-0	3-10	25.0	+ 8.75

August

	Total W-R	Non-handicaps 2-y-o	3-y-o+	Handicaps 2-y-o	3-y-o+	Per cent	£1 Level Stake
M J Ryan	3-7	0-0	0-1	0-0	3-6	42.9	+ 20.50
D Morley	3-8	0-2	0-1	0-0	3-5	37.5	+ 14.00
P F I Cole	3-13	1-5	1-4	0-0	1-4	23.1	+ 5.00
L M Cumani	2-2	1-1	1-1	0-0	0-0	100.0	+ 5.38
P T Walwyn	2-2	1-1	0-0	0-0	1-1	100.0	+ 13.50

September

	Total W-R	Non-handicaps 2-y-o	3-y-o+	Handicaps 2-y-o	3-y-o+	Per cent	£1 Level Stake
J H M Gosden	6-11	1-3	5-7	0-0	0-1	54.5	+ 24.88
R Hannon	6-40	2-25	3-5	1-6	0-4	15.0	- 11.32
D Morley	5-21	1-7	1-2	0-1	3-11	23.8	+ 19.75
R M Whitaker	4-21	1-8	1-3	0-3	2-7	19.0	+ 8.50
Mrs J Cecil	3-3	3-3	0-0	0-0	0-0	100.0	+ 4.78

Oct/Nov

	Total W-R	Non-handicaps 2-y-o	3-y-o+	Handicaps 2-y-o	3-y-o+	Per cent	£1 Level Stake
H R A Cecil	8-18	5-12	3-6	0-0	0-0	44.4	+ 13.90
M Johnston	3-10	1-2	2-3	0-1	0-4	30.0	- 4.56
P F I Cole	3-14	3-12	0-0	0-1	0-1	21.4	+ 3.85
J L Dunlop	3-14	2-11	0-0	0-1	1-2	21.4	- 7.83
D Morley	3-15	1-10	1-2	0-0	1-3	20.0	- 1.88

PONTEFRACT (Group 3)

Leading Trainers 1990-94

	Total W-R	Non-handicaps 2-y-o	3-y-o+	Handicaps 2-y-o	3-y-o+	Per cent	£1 Level Stake
R Hollinshead	25-197	8-44	7-51	0-10	10-92	12.7	- 83.08
H R A Cecil	18-37	3-4	15-33	0-0	0-0	48.6	+ 19.70
Mrs M Reveley	17-99	0-17	5-21	2-11	10-50	17.2	- 8.03
J Berry	17-145	10-71	4-24	0-12	3-38	11.7	- 46.40
Mrs J Ramsden	17-151	1-21	0-15	1-11	15-104	11.3	- 76.21
M H Tompkins	13-96	5-26	4-32	1-8	3-30	13.5	- 14.31
B A McMahon	12-108	0-9	4-43	0-0	8-56	11.1	- 11.00
M Johnston	11-86	4-23	3-19	1-10	3-34	12.8	+ 5.75
J L Dunlop	8-22	2-5	3-6	1-1	2-10	36.4	+ 23.22
I A Balding	8-45	4-10	3-19	0-3	1-13	17.8	- 11.80
J A Glover	8-69	2-9	1-10	0-4	5-46	11.6	- 11.90
S G Norton	8-93	3-25	0-22	1-7	4-39	8.6	- 53.38
A C Stewart	7-26	0-1	3-17	0-2	4-6	26.9	- 8.00
B Hanbury	7-28	0-2	4-14	0-2	3-10	25.0	- 7.81
H Thomson Jones	7-32	5-8	1-9	1-5	0-10	21.9	- 6.29
G Wragg	7-36	0-1	6-26	0-3	1-6	19.4	+ 6.81
M H Easterby	7-124	1-40	2-16	0-15	4-53	5.6	- 87.88
W Jarvis	6-26	0-3	4-12	1-3	1-8	23.1	+ 11.25
M R Stoute	6-33	3-10	3-18	0-1	0-4	18.2	- 18.38
J H M Gosden	6-34	1-3	4-25	0-0	1-6	17.6	- 6.72
M J Ryan	5-16	0-0	1-2	1-2	3-12	31.3	+ 28.00
G Harwood	5-23	1-5	2-11	0-0	2-7	21.7	- 6.76

Leading Jockeys

	Total W-R	Per cent	£1 Level Stake	Best Trainer	W-R	Per cent	£1 Level Stake
K Darley	24-189	12.7	- 87.95	Mrs M Reveley	7-34	20.6	+ 0.13
M Roberts	22-97	22.7	+ 22.61	A C Stewart	4-11	36.4	- 1.48
L Dettori	19-104	18.3	+ 5.71	L M Cumani	4-9	44.4	+ 3.12
W Ryan	18-89	20.2	- 36.29	H R A Cecil	10-23	43.5	+ 5.68
K Fallon	18-137	13.1	+ 75.35	J J O'Neill	3-8	37.5	+ 2.75
A Munro	16-102	15.7	+ 9.73	W A O'Gorman	3-7	42.9	+ 2.48
D McKeown	15-182	8.2	- 106.44	Mrs J Ramsden	4-22	18.2	- 8.29
W R Swinburn	13-55	23.6	- 5.89	B Hanbury	3-3	100.0	+ 5.01
R Hills	13-76	17.1	- 5.79	H Thomson Jones	7-24	29.2	+ 1.71
B Raymond	13-87	14.9	- 30.84	B Hanbury	4-11	36.4	+ 0.69
J Quinn	13-119	10.9	- 21.42	J Pearce	2-2	100.0	+ 14.25
J Carroll	13-132	9.8	- 63.30	J Berry	9-87	10.3	- 32.03

How the Favourites Fared

Non-handicaps	W-R	Per cent	£1 Level Stake	Handicaps	W-R	Per cent	£1 Level Stake
2-y-o	54-105	51.4	+ 18.91	2-y-o	7-22	31.8	+ 7.30
3-y-o	31-78	39.7	- 4.86	3-y-o	14-39	35.9	+ 0.33
Weight-for-age	31-69	44.9	+ 8.33	All-aged	60-189	31.7	- 3.26
Totals	116-252	46.0	+ 22.38	Totals	81-250	32.4	+ 4.37
All favs	197-502	39.2	+ 26.75				

Leading Trainers by Month at Pontefract

March/Apr	Total W-R	Non-handicaps 2-y-o	3-y-o+	Handicaps 2-y-o	3-y-o+	Per cent	£1 Level Stake
H R A Cecil	7-8	0-0	7-8	0-0	0-0	87.5	+ 11.35
J Berry	7-31	4-11	2-8	0-0	1-12	22.6	+ 4.10
Mrs J Ramsden	5-29	0-4	0-4	0-0	5-21	17.2	- 10.63
R Hollinshead	5-37	1-9	0-9	0-0	4-19	13.5	+ 0.54
G Wragg	4-20	0-0	4-18	0-0	0-2	20.0	+ 1.81

May	Total W-R	Non-handicaps 2-y-o	3-y-o+	Handicaps 2-y-o	3-y-o+	Per cent	£1 Level Stake
B Hanbury	4-4	0-0	3-3	0-0	1-1	100.0	+ 9.63
Miss S E Hall	3-5	0-0	2-3	0-0	1-2	60.0	+ 25.00
M H Tompkins	3-9	1-2	2-5	0-0	0-2	33.3	+ 17.44
C J Hill	2-2	0-0	0-0	0-0	2-2	100.0	+ 13.50
W A O'Gorman	2-3	2-2	0-0	0-0	0-1	66.7	+ 4.50

June	Total W-R	Non-handicaps 2-y-o	3-y-o+	Handicaps 2-y-o	3-y-o+	Per cent	£1 Level Stake
J A Glover	4-14	2-3	1-1	0-0	1-10	28.6	+ 6.50
R Hollinshead	4-30	2-11	0-4	0-0	2-15	13.3	- 20.34
Mrs V Aconley	3-3	0-0	1-1	0-0	2-2	100.0	+ 16.50
H R A Cecil	3-9	1-1	2-8	0-0	0-0	33.3	- 1.00
Denys Smith	3-10	0-3	0-2	0-0	3-5	30.0	+ 7.00

July	Total W-R	Non-handicaps 2-y-o	3-y-o+	Handicaps 2-y-o	3-y-o+	Per cent	£1 Level Stake
R Hollinshead	7-29	3-5	1-9	0-0	3-15	24.1	+ 4.49
H R A Cecil	4-7	0-0	4-7	0-0	0-0	57.1	+ 10.52
F H Lee	3-10	0-0	0-2	0-0	3-8	30.0	+ 16.50
S C Williams	2-2	0-0	1-1	0-0	1-1	100.0	+ 9.50
J A Glover	2-3	0-0	0-0	0-0	2-3	66.7	+ 3.60

August	Total W-R	Non-handicaps 2-y-o	3-y-o+	Handicaps 2-y-o	3-y-o+	Per cent	£1 Level Stake
Mrs M Reveley	8-19	0-0	4-10	1-3	3-6	42.1	+ 30.63
A C Stewart	4-5	0-0	2-2	0-1	2-2	80.0	+ 7.38
R Hollinshead	4-27	1-6	3-10	0-2	0-9	14.8	- 16.52
I A Balding	3-10	3-5	0-1	0-1	0-3	30.0	- 2.33
S G Norton	3-15	2-6	0-1	1-2	0-6	20.0	- 8.06

September	Total W-R	Non-handicaps 2-y-o	3-y-o+	Handicaps 2-y-o	3-y-o+	Per cent	£1 Level Stake
B A McMahon	4-10	0-1	1-2	0-0	3-7	40.0	+ 24.00
H Thomson Jones	3-6	2-3	0-1	1-1	0-1	50.0	+ 7.25
J D Bethell	3-9	0-1	0-0	0-0	3-8	33.3	+ 8.50
Mrs J Ramsden	3-16	0-1	0-1	1-3	2-11	18.8	- 6.75
M R Stoute	2-8	0-2	2-5	0-0	0-1	25.0	- 0.75

Oct/Nov	Total W-R	Non-handicaps 2-y-o	3-y-o+	Handicaps 2-y-o	3-y-o+	Per cent	£1 Level Stake
M Johnston	6-18	2-4	2-3	1-6	1-5	33.3	+ 44.50
J L Dunlop	4-8	1-3	0-0	1-1	2-4	50.0	+ 21.30
R Bastiman	3-8	0-0	1-2	0-0	2-6	37.5	+ 75.00
Mrs M Reveley	3-25	0-3	0-2	0-7	3-13	12.0	- 5.00
R Hollinshead	3-39	1-6	2-13	0-7	0-13	7.7	- 28.75

REDCAR (Group 2)

Leading Trainers 1990-94

	Total W-R	Non-handicaps 2-y-o	3-y-o+	Handicaps 2-y-o	3-y-o+	Per cent	£1 Level Stake
Mrs M Reveley	50-320	4-57	9-55	1-15	36-193	15.6	+ 49.23
M H Easterby	22-216	9-92	3-22	5-22	5-80	10.2	- 77.72
J Berry	21-173	12-86	3-22	1-21	5-44	12.1	- 33.09
Sir M Prescott	13-43	1-10	6-11	1-3	5-19	30.2	+ 16.58
J H M Gosden	13-69	4-19	6-30	0-2	3-18	18.8	- 26.32
H Thomson Jones	12-48	5-13	3-11	0-2	4-22	25.0	+ 6.65
R M Whitaker	12-161	3-49	2-31	1-7	6-74	7.5	- 38.45
M Johnston	11-131	5-47	1-16	1-11	4-57	8.4	- 53.81
R Hollinshead	10-94	2-19	2-19	0-4	6-52	10.6	- 28.20
W Carter	9-36	0-8	1-2	1-5	7-21	25.0	+ 18.00
J W Hills	9-45	1-8	2-10	0-0	6-27	20.0	+ 7.50
L M Cumani	9-47	1-14	7-19	0-1	1-13	19.1	- 11.38
M Bell	8-36	5-16	1-4	0-2	2-14	22.2	- 0.08
H R A Cecil	8-38	1-10	6-21	0-0	1-7	21.1	- 16.09
J L Dunlop	8-40	3-8	1-9	1-2	3-21	20.0	- 12.70
P Calver	8-58	1-12	3-11	1-2	3-33	13.8	+ 50.33
P W Harris	7-26	1-3	1-4	0-0	5-19	26.9	+ 24.25
R Hannon	7-32	5-20	1-4	1-3	0-5	21.9	- 6.31
M R Stoute	7-35	1-12	5-11	0-1	1-11	20.0	- 12.22
Denys Smith	7-93	3-18	0-6	0-4	4-65	7.5	- 49.58
T D Barron	7-97	2-25	1-10	1-6	3-56	7.2	- 44.75
Lady Herries	6-16	0-1	0-3	0-0	6-12	37.5	+ 2.49

Leading Jockeys

	Total W-R	Per cent	£1 Level Stake	Best Trainer	W-R	Per cent	£1 Level Stake
K Darley	50-263	19.0	+ 35.69	Mrs M Reveley	25-99	25.3	+ 56.50
M Birch	24-205	11.7	- 74.40	M H Easterby	10-102	9.8	- 48.04
Paul Eddery	20-91	22.0	+ 29.93	P W Harris	2-3	66.7	+ 12.75
G Duffield	20-134	14.9	- 21.66	Sir M Prescott	9-32	28.1	+ 3.09
K Fallon	18-167	10.8	- 45.93	Denys Smith	4-15	26.7	- 1.08
R Hills	17-100	17.0	- 15.15	H Thomson Jones	9-36	25.0	+ 3.28
J Carroll	17-155	11.0	- 40.13	J Berry	9-86	10.5	- 32.37
W Ryan	16-99	16.2	- 13.44	H R A Cecil	5-26	19.2	- 10.09
D McKeown	16-159	10.1	- 71.70	W W Haigh	3-19	15.8	- 2.25
J Lowe	14-218	6.4	- 86.28	Mrs M Reveley	8-64	12.5	- 8.28
L Dettori	13-71	18.3	- 1.49	L M Cumani	4-17	23.5	+ 0.13
J Fortune	13-138	9.4	- 47.63	L M Cumani	4-16	25.0	- 0.25

How the Favourites Fared

Non-handicaps	W-R	Per cent	£1 Level Stake	Handicaps	W-R	Per cent	£1 Level Stake
2-y-o	52-137	38.0	- 18.19	2-y-o	9-26	34.6	+ 4.61
3-y-o	22-55	40.0	- 8.63	3-y-o	19-57	33.3	- 2.97
Weight-for-age	44-84	52.4	+ 6.51	All-aged	65-215	30.2	+ 3.77
Totals	118-276	42.8	- 20.31	Totals	93-298	31.2	+ 5.41
All favs	211-574	36.8	- 14.90				

Leading Trainers by Month at Redcar

March/Apr	Total W-R	Non-handicaps 2-y-o	3-y-o+	Handicaps 2-y-o	3-y-o+	Per cent	£1 Level Stake
Mrs M Reveley	2-5	1-1	0-1	0-0	1-3	40.0	+ 1.38
L M Cumani	1-1	0-0	1-1	0-0	0-0	100.0	+ 4.50
M W Eckley	1-1	0-0	0-0	0-0	1-1	100.0	+ 10.00
J L Harris	1-1	0-0	0-0	0-0	1-1	100.0	+ 11.00
M Dods	1-2	0-0	0-0	0-0	1-2	50.0	+ 11.00

May	Total W-R	Non-handicaps 2-y-o	3-y-o+	Handicaps 2-y-o	3-y-o+	Per cent	£1 Level Stake
Mrs M Reveley	8-41	0-3	0-9	0-0	8-29	19.5	+ 26.50
J Berry	7-27	4-10	2-8	0-0	1-9	25.9	+ 19.00
M R Stoute	4-7	0-0	4-5	0-0	0-2	57.1	+ 9.37
P Calver	3-8	0-0	2-5	0-0	1-3	37.5	+ 24.50
Denys Smith	3-9	2-3	0-3	0-0	1-3	33.3	+ 5.50

June	Total W-R	Non-handicaps 2-y-o	3-y-o+	Handicaps 2-y-o	3-y-o+	Per cent	£1 Level Stake
J H M Gosden	4-8	0-0	3-5	0-0	1-3	50.0	- 0.13
J Berry	4-28	2-16	1-5	0-0	1-7	14.3	+ 6.40
C W C Elsey	3-5	0-0	1-3	0-0	2-2	60.0	+ 23.21
H R A Cecil	3-6	0-0	3-5	0-0	0-1	50.0	+ 0.50
J W Hills	3-7	0-0	0-1	0-0	3-6	42.9	+ 12.33

July	Total W-R	Non-handicaps 2-y-o	3-y-o+	Handicaps 2-y-o	3-y-o+	Per cent	£1 Level Stake
Mrs M Reveley	15-60	3-15	2-4	0-0	10-41	25.0	+ 50.70
J Berry	6-26	4-16	0-3	0-0	2-7	23.1	+ 2.28
R M Whitaker	6-26	2-8	0-1	0-0	4-17	23.1	+ 22.55
L M Cumani	3-6	0-1	2-3	0-0	1-2	50.0	+ 2.88
Sir M Prescott	3-7	1-3	0-1	0-0	2-3	42.9	+ 6.00

August	Total W-R	Non-handicaps 2-y-o	3-y-o+	Handicaps 2-y-o	3-y-o+	Per cent	£1 Level Stake
M H Easterby	10-41	3-14	2-6	3-9	2-12	24.4	+ 9.98
Mrs M Reveley	10-75	0-12	4-22	0-2	6-39	13.3	- 8.50
H Thomson Jones	6-11	2-2	2-3	0-0	2-6	54.5	+ 7.77
R Hollinshead	5-25	1-4	1-6	0-1	3-14	20.0	- 4.70
W Jarvis	4-5	0-0	0-1	0-0	4-4	80.0	+ 10.88

September	Total W-R	Non-handicaps 2-y-o	3-y-o+	Handicaps 2-y-o	3-y-o+	Per cent	£1 Level Stake
Mrs M Reveley	6-41	0-12	0-4	1-7	5-18	14.6	+ 25.50
M Bell	3-9	1-3	1-1	0-1	1-4	33.3	+ 11.50
W Carter	3-10	0-2	0-0	0-2	3-6	30.0	+ 19.50
P T Walwyn	2-2	0-0	0-0	0-0	2-2	100.0	+ 15.50
R Charlton	2-2	1-1	1-1	0-0	0-0	100.0	+ 9.00

Oct/Nov	Total W-R	Non-handicaps 2-y-o	3-y-o+	Handicaps 2-y-o	3-y-o+	Per cent	£1 Level Stake
R Hannon	6-29	4-19	1-4	1-2	0-4	20.7	- 8.31
Mrs M Reveley	6-52	0-8	1-3	0-6	5-35	11.5	- 9.90
J L Dunlop	5-22	3-7	0-4	0-1	2-10	22.7	- 4.20
M H Easterby	5-40	2-19	0-1	2-4	1-16	12.5	- 0.25
M J Camacho	4-20	0-8	2-3	0-1	2-8	20.0	- 0.97

RIPON (Group 2)

Leading Trainers 1990-94

	Total W-R	Non-handicaps 2-y-o	3-y-o+	Handicaps 2-y-o	3-y-o+	Per cent	£1 Level Stake
J Berry	23-148	13-78	3-16	1-11	6-43	15.5	- 34.74
H R A Cecil	22-45	2-3	18-33	0-0	2-9	48.9	+ 4.62
M H Easterby	18-210	6-61	3-22	0-8	9-119	8.6	-111.37
M R Stoute	14-53	1-5	7-22	0-0	6-26	26.4	+ 12.60
M Johnston	12-81	1-20	2-10	2-4	7-47	14.8	- 5.88
J H M Gosden	11-41	0-1	7-33	0-0	4-7	26.8	- 8.99
Mrs M Reveley	11-92	0-6	4-19	0-2	7-65	12.0	- 37.79
P C Haslam	10-63	2-11	1-11	0-2	7-39	15.9	+ 29.75
J W Watts	10-71	3-14	0-17	0-0	7-40	14.1	+ 13.00
B W Hills	8-38	1-7	4-17	0-0	3-14	21.1	- 6.94
Miss S E Hall	8-83	1-25	3-25	0-1	4-32	9.6	- 43.18
L M Cumani	7-28	1-1	5-21	0-0	1-6	25.0	- 9.45
J L Dunlop	7-29	1-7	2-5	0-1	4-16	24.1	+ 7.30
J Etherington	6-49	2-15	3-13	0-1	1-20	12.2	- 15.79
M Brittain	6-94	0-13	0-7	1-5	5-69	6.4	- 39.00
R M Whitaker	6-106	2-23	2-29	0-2	2-52	5.7	- 55.95
R Hollinshead	6-112	0-20	1-30	0-2	5-60	5.4	- 55.79
Sir M Prescott	5-17	1-1	1-4	0-0	3-12	29.4	+ 7.96
R W Armstrong	5-23	0-1	1-6	0-0	4-16	21.7	+ 27.50
J Wharton	5-27	0-3	1-7	0-1	4-16	18.5	+ 4.50
D Morley	5-28	0-2	1-9	0-0	4-17	17.9	- 2.45
B A McMahon	5-53	1-9	2-15	0-2	2-27	9.4	- 25.42

Leading Jockeys

	Total W-R	Per cent	£1 Level Stake	Best Trainer	W-R	Per cent	£1 Level Stake
K Darley	28-176	15.9	- 45.41	Mrs M Reveley	6-33	18.2	- 13.12
M Birch	19-179	10.6	- 53.58	M H Easterby	11-100	11.0	- 34.24
W Ryan	17-91	18.7	- 37.69	H R A Cecil	11-22	50.0	+ 4.22
D McKeown	17-138	12.3	- 22.38	J W Watts	5-18	27.8	+ 16.00
J Carroll	15-117	12.8	- 20.33	J Berry	13-70	18.6	+ 0.67
N Connorton	13-113	11.5	- 28.04	Miss S E Hall	6-40	15.0	- 9.67
J Lowe	13-172	7.6	- 66.42	Mrs M Reveley	5-29	17.2	+ 5.33
J Weaver	11-59	18.6	+ 7.57	M Johnston	6-17	35.3	+ 21.00
G Duffield	11-87	12.6	- 32.17	J H M Gosden	2-3	66.7	+ 2.38
M Roberts	10-51	19.6	- 15.60	A C Stewart	4-7	57.1	+ 5.25
R Cochrane	10-53	18.9	+ 11.26	G Harwood	2-3	66.7	+ 5.75
A Culhane	10-109	9.2	- 25.20	R M Whitaker	6-69	8.7	- 18.95

How the Favourites Fared

Non-handicaps	W-R	Per cent	£1 Level Stake	Handicaps	W-R	Per cent	£1 Level Stake
2-y-o	34-86	39.5	- 18.45	2-y-o	1-8	12.5	- 4.87
3-y-o	34-60	56.7	+ 5.54	3-y-o	17-61	27.9	- 12.09
Weight-for-age	27-53	50.9	+ 13.12	All-aged	41-146	28.1	- 6.50
Totals	95-199	47.7	+ 0.21	Totals	59-215	27.4	- 23.46
All favs	154-414	37.2	- 23.25				

518

Leading Trainers by Month at Ripon

March/Apr

	Total W-R	Non-handicaps 2-y-o	3-y-o+	Handicaps 2-y-o	3-y-o+	Per cent	£1 Level Stake
J Berry	10-38	5-19	0-7	0-0	5-12	26.3	+ 13.06
J H M Gosden	6-10	0-0	4-7	0-0	2-3	60.0	+ 7.77
M R Stoute	4-7	0-0	3-4	0-0	1-3	57.1	+ 11.78
H R A Cecil	4-9	0-0	4-9	0-0	0-0	44.4	- 0.31
J L Dunlop	4-11	0-0	2-5	0-0	2-6	36.4	+ 14.13

May

	Total W-R	Non-handicaps 2-y-o	3-y-o+	Handicaps 2-y-o	3-y-o+	Per cent	£1 Level Stake
H R A Cecil	3-3	0-0	2-2	0-0	1-1	100.0	+ 5.41
A C Stewart	2-2	0-0	1-1	0-0	1-1	100.0	+ 2.24
M R Stoute	2-5	0-0	1-4	0-0	1-1	40.0	+ 0.13
J W Watts	2-6	0-0	0-2	0-0	2-4	33.3	+ 8.00
M Johnston	2-6	0-1	0-0	0-0	2-5	33.3	+ 8.00

June

	Total W-R	Non-handicaps 2-y-o	3-y-o+	Handicaps 2-y-o	3-y-o+	Per cent	£1 Level Stake
H R A Cecil	5-9	1-1	4-7	0-0	0-1	55.6	+ 3.25
M R Stoute	5-14	0-0	2-8	0-0	3-6	35.7	+ 17.33
J Pearce	4-10	0-1	1-1	0-0	3-8	40.0	+ 13.88
M Brittain	3-16	0-5	0-1	0-0	3-10	18.8	+ 4.50
J Berry	3-23	2-13	1-1	0-0	0-9	13.0	- 5.20

July

	Total W-R	Non-handicaps 2-y-o	3-y-o+	Handicaps 2-y-o	3-y-o+	Per cent	£1 Level Stake
J H M Gosden	3-9	0-1	2-6	0-0	1-2	33.3	- 2.01
Mrs M Reveley	3-11	0-0	1-2	0-0	2-9	27.3	+ 8.50
J W Watts	3-12	2-5	0-1	0-0	1-6	25.0	+ 6.50
J Berry	3-15	2-10	0-2	0-0	1-3	20.0	- 4.67
M H Easterby	3-24	0-5	1-2	0-0	2-17	12.5	+ 0.63

August

	Total W-R	Non-handicaps 2-y-o	3-y-o+	Handicaps 2-y-o	3-y-o+	Per cent	£1 Level Stake
M H Easterby	8-74	2-17	1-4	0-8	5-45	10.8	- 31.12
H R A Cecil	6-17	1-2	4-9	0-0	1-6	35.3	- 3.02
M Johnston	6-33	0-8	0-1	2-4	4-20	18.2	+ 7.63
J Berry	6-59	4-30	1-2	1-11	0-16	10.2	- 27.93
J Etherington	5-21	1-6	3-5	0-1	1-9	23.8	+ 3.21

September

	Total W-R	Non-handicaps 2-y-o	3-y-o+	Handicaps 2-y-o	3-y-o+	Per cent	£1 Level Stake
H R A Cecil	2-3	0-0	2-2	0-0	0-1	66.7	+ 0.20
M R Channon	1-1	0-0	1-1	0-0	0-0	100.0	+ 8.00
P A Kelleway	1-2	0-1	1-1	0-0	0-0	50.0	+ 7.00
G Wragg	1-2	0-0	0-1	0-0	1-1	50.0	+ 4.00
D W Chapman	1-3	0-0	0-0	0-0	1-3	33.3	+ 14.00

SALISBURY (Group 2)

Leading Trainers 1990-94

	Total W-R	Non-handicaps 2-y-o	3-y-o+	Handicaps 2-y-o	3-y-o+	Per cent	£1 Level Stake
R Hannon	44-331	18-140	14-65	0-4	12-122	13.3	- 38.42
G Harwood	20-88	6-29	4-21	2-2	8-36	22.7	- 1.02
D R C Elsworth	18-165	5-44	4-45	0-0	9-76	10.9	- 49.25
I A Balding	15-135	3-46	5-40	0-0	7-49	11.1	- 43.76
P F I Cole	14-93	7-37	3-25	0-1	4-30	15.1	- 10.85
J L Dunlop	14-116	4-41	4-33	0-1	6-41	12.1	- 28.52
J H M Gosden	13-37	4-10	8-21	0-0	1-6	35.1	+ 45.00
L M Cumani	11-31	2-5	8-18	0-0	1-8	35.5	+ 21.91
R Charlton	10-66	4-25	3-30	0-0	3-11	15.2	- 33.75
D A Wilson	9-57	0-4	0-1	0-0	9-52	15.8	+ 2.75
Lord Huntingdon	9-64	2-19	4-25	0-0	3-20	14.1	- 11.18
R Akehurst	8-69	3-14	0-19	0-0	5-36	11.6	- 18.50
H R A Cecil	6-24	0-1	6-21	0-0	0-2	25.0	- 9.20
P Chapple-Hyam	6-24	5-14	1-7	0-0	0-3	25.0	- 0.50
J R Fanshawe	6-25	1-2	3-13	0-1	2-9	24.0	+ 17.50
M R Stoute	6-30	1-18	2-9	0-0	3-3	20.0	- 8.27
M Bell	6-34	2-7	1-5	0-1	3-21	17.6	+ 18.25
J W Hills	6-47	3-14	2-9	0-0	1-24	12.8	- 2.05
H Candy	6-66	3-17	1-18	0-0	2-31	9.1	+ 19.00
G Lewis	6-68	5-27	1-14	0-1	0-26	8.8	- 37.02
G B Balding	6-110	1-22	2-17	0-1	3-70	5.5	- 59.25
A C Stewart	5-23	0-2	1-11	0-0	4-10	21.7	+ 14.00

Leading Jockeys

	Total W-R	Per cent	£1 Level Stake	Best Trainer	W-R	Per cent	£1 Level Stake
J Reid	27-172	15.7	- 35.23	R Hannon	6-32	18.8	+ 2.28
Pat Eddery	25-127	19.7	- 17.86	R Charlton	5-17	29.4	- 4.57
R Cochrane	24-171	14.0	- 56.10	G Harwood	10-32	31.3	- 6.06
J Williams	23-232	9.9	- 39.74	D R C Elsworth	8-56	14.3	- 6.74
W Carson	20-149	13.4	- 57.89	J L Dunlop	7-32	21.9	- 2.52
L Dettori	19-112	17.0	+ 27.36	L M Cumani	5-12	41.7	+ 13.58
W R Swinburn	14-55	25.5	+ 35.48	J R Fanshawe	3-5	60.0	+ 17.50
T Quinn	14-135	10.4	- 57.94	P F I Cole	7-53	13.2	- 14.77
M Roberts	13-80	16.3	- 10.35	G Harwood	2-3	66.7	+ 2.50
A Munro	11-83	13.3	- 17.67	P F I Cole	2-5	40.0	+ 7.73
B Rouse	11-157	7.0	- 76.25	R Hannon	6-37	16.2	- 1.75
M Hills	10-63	15.9	- 6.15	J W Hills	4-13	30.8	+ 22.95

How the Favourites Fared

Non-handicaps	W-R	Per cent	£1 Level Stake	Handicaps	W-R	Per cent	£1 Level Stake
2-y-o	43-118	36.4	- 18.99	2-y-o	2-3	66.7	+ 0.92
3-y-o	33-82	40.2	- 6.62	3-y-o	13-37	35.1	+ 14.26
Weight-for-age	14-26	53.8	+ 3.06	All-aged	32-160	20.0	- 45.85
Totals	90-226	39.8	- 22.55	Totals	47-200	23.5	- 30.67
All favs	137-426	32.2	- 53.22				

Leading Trainers by Month at Salisbury

March/Apr

	Total W-R	Non-handicaps 2-y-o	3-y-o+	Handicaps 2-y-o	3-y-o+	Per cent	£1 Level Stake
L M Cumani	2-4	0-0	2-4	0-0	0-0	50.0	+ 13.38
I A Balding	2-9	0-0	1-7	0-0	1-2	22.2	- 2.50
R Hannon	2-17	0-0	1-8	0-0	1-9	11.8	- 5.50
R F J Houghton	1-1	0-0	1-1	0-0	0-0	100.0	+ 3.00
A C Stewart	1-1	0-0	0-0	0-0	1-1	100.0	+ 10.00

May

	Total W-R	Non-handicaps 2-y-o	3-y-o+	Handicaps 2-y-o	3-y-o+	Per cent	£1 Level Stake
R Hannon	11-63	3-15	5-20	0-0	3-28	17.5	+ 14.10
G Harwood	4-14	0-0	3-11	0-0	1-3	28.6	- 6.18
J R Fanshawe	3-8	0-0	2-6	0-0	1-2	37.5	+ 13.50
M McCormack	3-14	3-5	0-5	0-0	0-4	21.4	- 6.01
D R C Elsworth	3-29	0-2	1-14	0-0	2-13	10.3	- 12.88

June

	Total W-R	Non-handicaps 2-y-o	3-y-o+	Handicaps 2-y-o	3-y-o+	Per cent	£1 Level Stake
R Hannon	7-73	2-33	3-15	0-0	2-25	9.6	- 18.88
J L Dunlop	6-30	1-4	2-11	0-0	3-15	20.0	+ 2.48
I A Balding	6-41	1-11	1-9	0-0	4-21	14.6	- 3.50
P F I Cole	5-23	2-8	0-6	0-0	3-9	21.7	+ 8.95
D R C Elsworth	4-32	2-9	1-6	0-0	1-17	12.5	- 14.63

July

	Total W-R	Non-handicaps 2-y-o	3-y-o+	Handicaps 2-y-o	3-y-o+	Per cent	£1 Level Stake
R Hannon	6-39	3-17	2-6	0-0	1-16	15.4	- 1.45
G Harwood	5-16	3-7	0-2	0-0	2-7	31.3	+ 9.10
D R C Elsworth	3-18	0-3	1-4	0-0	2-11	16.7	+ 5.00
Lord Huntingdon	2-3	0-0	1-2	0-0	1-1	66.7	+ 12.50
Lady Herries	2-8	1-2	0-0	0-0	1-6	25.0	- 0.50

August

	Total W-R	Non-handicaps 2-y-o	3-y-o+	Handicaps 2-y-o	3-y-o+	Per cent	£1 Level Stake
R Hannon	11-74	6-36	2-11	0-4	3-23	14.9	- 19.70
G Harwood	5-23	1-6	1-3	2-2	1-12	21.7	- 5.54
J H M Gosden	4-8	0-0	3-6	0-0	1-2	50.0	+ 20.20
R Charlton	4-15	3-8	1-6	0-0	0-1	26.7	- 5.13
R Akehurst	3-10	1-1	0-3	0-0	2-6	30.0	+ 9.25

September

	Total W-R	Non-handicaps 2-y-o	3-y-o+	Handicaps 2-y-o	3-y-o+	Per cent	£1 Level Stake
P Chapple-Hyam	3-8	3-6	0-0	0-0	0-2	37.5	+ 5.25
P F I Cole	3-12	2-8	1-2	0-0	0-2	25.0	+ 9.25
G Harwood	3-13	1-8	0-1	0-0	2-4	23.1	+ 16.00
J L Dunlop	3-26	2-18	0-2	0-0	1-6	11.5	- 9.00
R Hannon	3-40	3-27	0-2	0-0	0-11	7.5	- 19.50

Oct/Nov

	Total W-R	Non-handicaps 2-y-o	3-y-o+	Handicaps 2-y-o	3-y-o+	Per cent	£1 Level Stake
D R C Elsworth	4-13	2-7	0-2	0-0	2-4	30.8	+ 17.00
R Hannon	4-25	1-12	1-3	0-0	2-10	16.0	+ 12.50
J H M Gosden	3-6	2-5	1-1	0-0	0-0	50.0	+ 15.75
B Hanbury	1-1	0-0	1-1	0-0	0-0	100.0	+ 2.50
A Hide	1-1	0-0	0-0	0-0	1-1	100.0	+ 16.00

SANDOWN (Group 1)

Leading Trainers 1990-94

	Total W-R	Non-handicaps 2-y-o	3-y-o+	Handicaps 2-y-o	3-y-o+	Per cent	£1 Level Stake
R Hannon	40-308	13-111	8-59	1-11	18-127	13.0	- 57.97
M R Stoute	24-157	7-27	12-80	0-3	5-47	15.3	- 42.03
J H M Gosden	20-92	0-5	14-55	0-0	6-32	21.7	+ 8.54
J L Dunlop	18-113	6-34	6-30	0-0	6-49	15.9	+ 3.38
R Akehurst	17-127	0-3	0-19	0-4	17-101	13.4	- 14.88
P F I Cole	16-112	6-28	4-40	1-7	5-37	14.3	- 12.30
I A Balding	14-99	4-23	3-23	0-0	7-53	14.1	- 5.68
H R A Cecil	13-79	5-14	7-51	0-0	1-14	16.5	- 38.83
G Harwood	12-74	1-9	5-29	1-2	5-34	16.2	- 13.00
C E Brittain	12-144	1-32	6-47	0-2	5-63	8.3	- 10.43
J Berry	11-60	1-10	8-25	0-8	2-17	18.3	- 0.62
J R Fanshawe	11-60	1-7	5-22	0-1	5-30	18.3	+ 36.98
M R Channon	11-76	3-23	0-11	2-9	6-33	14.5	+ 11.05
Lord Huntingdon	10-79	3-15	3-22	0-2	4-40	12.7	- 24.13
B W Hills	10-86	4-23	5-46	1-2	0-15	11.6	- 2.25
D R C Elsworth	8-131	1-18	4-55	0-3	3-55	6.1	- 87.50
Lady Herries	7-42	1-5	1-8	0-0	5-29	16.7	+ 30.50
G B Balding	7-49	0-7	4-12	0-1	3-29	14.3	- 0.33
L M Cumani	7-61	0-3	5-42	0-0	2-16	11.5	- 19.63
G Lewis	7-90	5-34	1-15	0-10	1-31	7.8	- 49.33
W R Hern	6-39	2-6	4-25	0-0	0-8	15.4	- 11.42
P J Makin	6-41	0-6	3-16	0-0	3-19	14.6	+ 1.13

Leading Jockeys

	Total W-R	Per cent	£1 Level Stake	Best Trainer	W-R	Per cent	£1 Level Stake
Pat Eddery	55-284	19.4	- 32.43	R Hannon	9-38	23.7	- 3.70
M Roberts	42-262	16.0	- 7.46	C E Brittain	8-81	9.9	- 10.00
T Quinn	34-209	16.3	+ 24.96	P F I Cole	12-63	19.0	+ 9.20
L Dettori	32-184	17.4	+ 14.44	J H M Gosden	6-20	30.0	+ 8.25
W Carson	30-242	12.4	- 78.65	J L Dunlop	7-40	17.5	- 9.24
W R Swinburn	29-179	16.2	- 22.95	M R Stoute	11-51	21.6	+ 0.69
J Reid	19-201	9.5	- 73.00	R Hannon	5-33	15.2	- 2.50
R Cochrane	18-173	10.4	- 39.09	I A Balding	4-20	20.0	- 1.25
M Hills	13-107	12.1	- 21.32	M Bell	3-14	21.4	- 1.20
A Munro	12-110	10.9	- 53.81	H Candy	2-2	100.0	+ 5.25
W Ryan	10-59	16.9	+ 0.57	H R A Cecil	3-17	17.6	- 4.31
D Harrison	10-83	12.0	+ 14.00	Lord Huntingdon	4-23	17.4	+ 4.50

How the Favourites Fared

Non-handicaps	W-R	Per cent	£1 Level Stake	Handicaps	W-R	Per cent	£1 Level Stake
2-y-o	42-104	40.4	- 2.48	2-y-o	2-20	10.0	- 10.50
3-y-o	31-85	36.5	- 9.08	3-y-o	26-87	29.9	+ 3.80
Weight-for-age	28-81	34.6	- 11.70	All-aged	45-152	29.6	+ 5.62
Totals	101-270	37.4	- 23.26	Totals	73-259	28.2	- 1.08
All favs	174-529	32.9	- 24.34				

Leading Trainers by Month at Sandown

March/Apr

	Total W-R	Non-handicaps 2-y-o	3-y-o+	Handicaps 2-y-o	3-y-o+	Per cent	£1 Level Stake
R Hannon	7-49	1-17	2-13	0-0	4-19	14.3	+ 7.08
J L Dunlop	5-20	0-0	4-13	0-0	1-7	25.0	+ 7.38
P F I Cole	4-24	1-5	2-13	0-0	1-6	16.7	+ 9.50
C E Brittain	4-26	1-3	2-15	0-0	1-8	15.4	+ 16.00
J H M Gosden	3-7	0-0	3-6	0-0	0-1	42.9	+ 10.25

May

	Total W-R	Non-handicaps 2-y-o	3-y-o+	Handicaps 2-y-o	3-y-o+	Per cent	£1 Level Stake
M R Stoute	7-36	0-5	7-26	0-0	0-5	19.4	+ 2.29
R Hannon	7-47	3-13	1-13	0-0	3-21	14.9	- 14.03
I A Balding	5-16	1-2	1-6	0-0	3-8	31.3	+ 18.44
Lord Huntingdon	4-6	1-1	2-4	0-0	1-1	66.7	+ 18.00
J L Dunlop	3-12	0-0	1-6	0-0	2-6	25.0	+ 3.88

June

	Total W-R	Non-handicaps 2-y-o	3-y-o+	Handicaps 2-y-o	3-y-o+	Per cent	£1 Level Stake
R Hannon	6-37	2-11	1-10	0-0	3-16	16.2	- 7.70
M R Stoute	5-14	3-3	1-7	0-0	1-4	35.7	+ 2.78
J H M Gosden	5-15	0-1	3-11	0-0	2-3	33.3	+ 0.58
B W Hills	3-9	1-2	2-6	0-0	0-1	33.3	+ 7.38
J R Fanshawe	3-10	0-0	0-3	0-0	3-7	30.0	+ 9.00

July

	Total W-R	Non-handicaps 2-y-o	3-y-o+	Handicaps 2-y-o	3-y-o+	Per cent	£1 Level Stake
R Hannon	11-93	3-39	2-12	0-0	6-42	11.8	- 38.63
R Akehurst	10-47	0-3	0-5	0-0	10-39	21.3	+ 25.50
M R Stoute	7-43	3-7	2-12	0-0	2-24	16.3	- 4.83
P F I Cole	5-21	2-4	0-7	0-0	3-10	23.8	+ 5.70
I A Balding	5-28	2-7	1-5	0-0	2-16	17.9	- 6.13

August

	Total W-R	Non-handicaps 2-y-o	3-y-o+	Handicaps 2-y-o	3-y-o+	Per cent	£1 Level Stake
J L Dunlop	4-16	2-7	1-3	0-0	1-6	25.0	+ 11.88
R Hannon	4-40	2-11	0-7	1-8	1-14	10.0	- 27.27
J W Hills	3-9	1-1	1-5	1-1	0-2	33.3	+ 46.00
J Berry	3-11	0-0	2-3	0-4	1-4	27.3	+ 3.13
J R Fanshawe	3-13	1-1	1-4	0-1	1-7	23.1	+ 10.38

September

	Total W-R	Non-handicaps 2-y-o	3-y-o+	Handicaps 2-y-o	3-y-o+	Per cent	£1 Level Stake
R Hannon	5-42	2-20	2-4	0-3	1-15	11.9	+ 22.58
P F I Cole	4-27	2-11	0-3	1-2	1-11	14.8	- 10.50
J H M Gosden	3-16	0-3	3-6	0-0	0-7	18.8	- 8.75
J W Payne	2-4	1-1	0-1	0-1	1-1	50.0	+ 5.00
H Thomson Jones	2-6	2-2	0-0	0-0	0-4	33.3	+ 2.00

SOUTHWELL ALL-WEATHER (Group 4)

Leading Trainers 1990-94

	Total W-R	Non-handicaps 2-y-o	3-y-o+	Handicaps 2-y-o	3-y-o+	Per cent	£1 Level Stake
T D Barron	63-316	4-26	27-100	1-14	31-176	19.9	- 12.54
D W Chapman	50-499	2-29	27-162	0-10	21-298	10.0	-158.51
W A O'Gorman	44-225	19-46	13-73	3-12	9-94	19.6	+ 3.13
J Berry	40-252	21-106	5-56	1-11	13-79	15.9	- 45.83
S G Norton	34-169	12-49	9-35	2-13	11-72	20.1	+ 41.13
R Hollinshead	30-388	4-53	12-145	2-15	12-175	7.7	-192.94
C J Hill	29-190	4-20	7-71	3-7	15-92	15.3	- 50.38
Sir M Prescott	26-134	4-48	15-38	0-2	7-46	19.4	- 26.66
M Johnston	26-159	2-17	11-42	0-9	13-91	16.4	- 20.45
Lord Huntingdon	24-99	2-12	16-43	0-2	6-42	24.2	+ 7.32
Mrs N Macauley	20-276	1-24	6-103	1-10	12-139	7.2	-104.42
J G FitzGerald	19-142	5-27	9-43	0-1	5-71	13.4	- 18.09
S R Bowring	19-195	0-9	4-43	0-5	15-138	9.7	- 2.50
C N Allen	18-148	2-24	8-39	1-8	7-77	12.2	- 16.23
M J Ryan	15-84	2-6	4-18	0-3	9-57	17.9	+ 8.03
M Bell	15-90	6-22	4-29	0-2	5-37	16.7	+ 4.29
W W Haigh	14-104	1-7	6-42	0-2	7-53	13.5	- 6.14
M Brittain	14-179	2-27	9-42	0-6	3-104	7.8	- 66.50
C R Nelson	13-36	2-7	8-19	0-0	3-10	36.1	+ 24.66
P F I Cole	13-70	5-31	3-17	1-6	4-16	18.6	- 9.97
M W Easterby	13-139	6-72	1-10	3-13	3-44	9.4	- 61.68
B A McMahon	13-195	1-21	7-69	0-2	5-103	6.7	- 98.15

Leading Jockeys

	Total W-R	Per cent	£1 Level Stake	Best Trainer	W-R	Per cent	£1 Level Stake
Alex Greaves	57-270	21.1	- 2.81	T D Barron	47-188	25.0	- 17.79
G Duffield	43-266	16.2	- 57.28	Sir M Prescott	20-89	22.5	- 16.41
J Quinn	38-502	7.6	-203.67	C J Hill	10-48	20.8	- 20.92
D McKeown	37-335	11.0	-105.40	M Johnston	10-36	27.8	- 0.82
S Wood	36-408	8.8	-162.39	D W Chapman	29-269	10.8	-104.52
Emma O'Gorman	35-224	15.6	- 45.40	W A O'Gorman	33-180	18.3	- 18.40
D Biggs	33-196	16.8	+ 36.84	M J Ryan	9-29	31.0	+ 18.38
G Bardwell	30-320	9.4	- 54.17	C J Hill	8-44	18.2	- 7.92
L Dettori	25-125	20.0	- 23.58	D R Loder	6-13	46.2	+ 3.03
J Fanning	25-316	7.9	- 90.71	P C Haslam	3-17	17.6	- 5.17
D Holland	24-95	25.3	+ 26.54	B W Hills	4-12	33.3	- 3.14
A Munro	22-171	12.9	- 35.99	P F I Cole	3-7	42.9	+ 8.50

How the Favourites Fared

Non-handicaps	W-R	Per cent	£1 Level Stake	Handicaps	W-R	Per cent	£1 Level Stake
2-y-o	68-181	37.6	- 23.86	2-y-o	11-35	31.4	+ 5.51
3-y-o	74-164	45.1	- 4.67	3-y-o	35-111	31.5	- 19.73
Weight-for-age	110-266	41.4	- 6.29	All-aged	137-483	28.4	- 57.86
Totals	252-611	41.2	- 34.82	Totals	183-629	29.1	- 72.08
All favs	435-1240	35.1	-106.90				

Leading Trainers by Month at Southwell (AW)

January	Total W-R	Non-handicaps 2-y-o	3-y-o+	Handicaps 2-y-o	3-y-o+	Per cent	£1 Level Stake
T D Barron	24-99	0-0	15-47	0-0	9-52	24.2	- 9.94
D W Chapman	21-119	0-0	13-49	0-0	8-70	17.6	+ 37.68

February	Total W-R	Non-handicaps 2-y-o	3-y-o+	Handicaps 2-y-o	3-y-o+	Per cent	£1 Level Stake
T D Barron	15-56	0-0	4-20	0-0	11-36	26.8	+ 9.65
T Thomson Jones	6-9	0-0	1-1	0-0	5-8	66.7	+ 10.58

March	Total W-R	Non-handicaps 2-y-o	3-y-o+	Handicaps 2-y-o	3-y-o+	Per cent	£1 Level Stake
W A O'Gorman	6-21	0-0	5-10	0-0	1-11	28.6	+ 3.14
S G Norton	5-18	0-0	0-4	0-0	5-14	27.8	+ 13.00

April	Total W-R	Non-handicaps 2-y-o	3-y-o+	Handicaps 2-y-o	3-y-o+	Per cent	£1 Level Stake
S G Norton	3-10	0-4	3-4	0-0	0-2	30.0	+ 13.00
A P Stringer	2-3	0-0	0-1	0-0	2-2	66.7	+ 13.00

May	Total W-R	Non-handicaps 2-y-o	3-y-o+	Handicaps 2-y-o	3-y-o+	Per cent	£1 Level Stake
J Berry	7-35	4-13	0-12	0-0	3-10	20.0	- 0.02
Sir M Prescott	5-10	1-1	3-5	0-0	1-4	50.0	+ 5.85

June	Total W-R	Non-handicaps 2-y-o	3-y-o+	Handicaps 2-y-o	3-y-o+	Per cent	£1 Level Stake
J Berry	10-40	6-24	0-5	0-0	4-11	25.0	+ 13.24
Sir M Prescott	5-24	0-7	4-9	0-0	1-8	20.8	- 4.27

July	Total W-R	Non-handicaps 2-y-o	3-y-o+	Handicaps 2-y-o	3-y-o+	Per cent	£1 Level Stake
S G Norton	10-32	4-15	2-3	1-1	3-13	31.3	+ 28.88
W A O'Gorman	6-18	6-11	0-1	0-0	0-6	33.3	+ 17.80

August	Total W-R	Non-handicaps 2-y-o	3-y-o+	Handicaps 2-y-o	3-y-o+	Per cent	£1 Level Stake
M W Easterby	6-39	3-21	1-1	2-3	0-14	15.4	- 3.80
Mrs N Macauley	5-11	0-1	1-2	0-0	4-8	45.5	+ 35.83

September	Total W-R	Non-handicaps 2-y-o	3-y-o+	Handicaps 2-y-o	3-y-o+	Per cent	£1 Level Stake
W A O'Gorman	5-10	4-5	1-3	0-1	0-1	50.0	+ 32.00
Lord Huntingdon	3-5	0-2	1-1	0-0	2-2	60.0	+ 13.50

November	Total W-R	Non-handicaps 2-y-o	3-y-o+	Handicaps 2-y-o	3-y-o+	Per cent	£1 Level Stake
S G Norton	9-35	5-11	1-3	1-9	2-12	25.7	+ 21.75
W A O'Gorman	8-29	5-8	1-8	1-4	1-9	27.6	+ 20.25

December	Total W-R	Non-handicaps 2-y-o	3-y-o+	Handicaps 2-y-o	3-y-o+	Per cent	£1 Level Stake
T D Barron	10-44	2-9	2-7	1-7	5-21	22.7	+ 6.50
W A O'Gorman	7-30	3-13	2-5	2-6	0-6	23.3	- 6.73

THIRSK (Group 2)

Leading Trainers 1990-94

	Total W-R	Non-handicaps 2-y-o	3-y-o+	Handicaps 2-y-o	3-y-o+	Per cent	£1 Level Stake
M H Easterby	18-168	7-70	2-24	0-11	9-63	10.7	- 32.00
R M Whitaker	15-121	4-22	5-37	1-6	5-56	12.4	- 20.67
J L Dunlop	13-32	2-7	5-14	0-0	6-11	40.6	+ 25.41
T D Barron	13-130	3-25	0-13	2-3	8-89	10.0	- 35.92
J Berry	13-135	4-65	5-25	0-9	4-36	9.6	- 87.62
H R A Cecil	12-28	3-4	7-18	0-1	2-5	42.9	+ 2.27
M Johnston	12-82	4-18	3-14	0-4	5-46	14.6	+ 13.75
Sir M Prescott	9-39	3-13	2-9	2-4	2-13	23.1	+ 5.29
F H Lee	9-65	1-11	0-10	1-5	7-39	13.8	+ 8.50
Mrs J Ramsden	8-60	3-17	1-5	2-4	2-34	13.3	- 6.00
D W Chapman	8-71	0-3	0-3	0-1	8-64	11.3	+ 48.50
R Hollinshead	8-93	2-15	6-35	0-2	0-41	8.6	- 43.88
M J Camacho	6-25	1-4	1-7	2-2	2-12	24.0	+ 21.50
M R Stoute	6-34	2-7	4-20	0-0	0-7	17.6	- 11.76
P C Haslam	6-40	2-14	1-3	0-2	3-21	15.0	- 9.58
Mrs J Cecil	5-11	1-1	2-4	1-1	1-5	45.5	+ 12.58
W Jarvis	5-12	2-2	3-9	0-0	0-1	41.7	+ 14.30
G Wragg	5-18	1-4	3-8	0-0	1-6	27.8	+ 2.01
J R Fanshawe	5-19	1-5	2-8	0-1	2-5	26.3	- 0.11
P Calver	5-49	0-4	2-10	0-1	3-34	10.2	- 4.50
Mrs M Reveley	5-52	0-11	0-14	0-2	5-25	9.6	- 15.25
M W Easterby	5-121	3-64	0-12	0-2	2-43	4.1	-103.50

Leading Jockeys

	Total W-R	Per cent	£1 Level Stake	Best Trainer	W-R	Per cent	£1 Level Stake
G Duffield	29-113	25.7	+ 16.99	Sir M Prescott	9-32	28.1	+ 12.29
M Birch	21-172	12.2	- 44.62	M H Easterby	12-74	16.2	+ 1.85
D McKeown	14-129	10.9	- 26.18	M Johnston	4-20	20.0	+ 12.00
J Weaver	13-63	20.6	+ 31.23	P C Haslam	3-8	37.5	+ 10.35
J Carroll	13-115	11.3	- 42.83	J Berry	8-71	11.3	- 38.08
J Fortune	13-118	11.0	- 8.10	S E Kettlewell	3-7	42.9	+ 36.00
K Darley	13-177	7.3	-105.10	R Hannon	2-4	50.0	+ 3.75
R Hills	12-60	20.0	- 21.48	H Thomson Jones	3-13	23.1	- 1.08
K Fallon	12-108	11.1	+ 11.75	Mrs J Ramsden	3-13	23.1	+ 6.25
W Ryan	11-53	20.8	- 5.35	H R A Cecil	5-13	38.5	- 3.00
S Wood	10-63	15.9	+ 66.50	D W Chapman	7-32	21.9	+ 61.50
A Culhane	10-99	10.1	- 29.17	R M Whitaker	10-73	13.7	- 3.17

How the Favourites Fared

Non-handicaps	W-R	Per cent	£1 Level Stake	Handicaps	W-R	Per cent	£1 Level Stake
2-y-o	33-89	37.1	- 11.25	2-y-o	5-16	31.3	- 2.15
3-y-o	37-82	45.1	- 12.90	3-y-o	10-26	38.5	+ 7.28
Weight-for-age	25-47	53.2	+ 9.37	All-aged	28-140	20.0	- 45.37
Totals	95-218	43.6	- 14.78	Totals	43-182	23.6	- 40.24
All favs	138-400	34.5	- 55.02				

Leading Trainers by Month at Thirsk

March/Apr	Total W-R	Non-handicaps 2-y-o	3-y-o+	Handicaps 2-y-o	3-y-o+	Per cent	£1 Level Stake
M Johnston	4-12	0-1	2-4	0-0	2-7	33.3	+ 23.00
J Berry	4-28	2-10	2-12	0-0	0-6	14.3	- 16.00
M H Easterby	4-35	1-6	1-11	0-0	2-18	11.4	- 10.85
M McCormack	3-6	0-0	2-4	0-0	1-2	50.0	+ 10.75
G Wragg	3-6	0-0	2-4	0-0	1-2	50.0	+ 7.88

May	Total W-R	Non-handicaps 2-y-o	3-y-o+	Handicaps 2-y-o	3-y-o+	Per cent	£1 Level Stake
M H Easterby	7-54	1-20	1-8	0-0	5-26	13.0	+ 9.25
R M Whitaker	6-40	1-9	3-10	0-0	2-21	15.0	+ 13.50
J L Dunlop	4-8	1-1	3-4	0-0	0-3	50.0	+ 10.47
W Jarvis	4-8	2-2	2-6	0-0	0-0	50.0	+ 10.30
P C Haslam	4-12	2-5	0-0	0-0	2-7	33.3	+ 10.32

June	Total W-R	Non-handicaps 2-y-o	3-y-o+	Handicaps 2-y-o	3-y-o+	Per cent	£1 Level Stake
J L Dunlop	4-5	1-1	0-1	0-0	3-3	80.0	+ 22.03
J W Watts	2-3	1-1	0-0	0-0	1-2	66.7	+ 10.91
J R Fanshawe	2-3	0-0	1-2	0-0	1-1	66.7	+ 2.14
F H Lee	2-4	1-1	0-0	0-0	1-3	50.0	+ 2.50
M H Easterby	2-13	1-9	0-0	0-0	1-4	15.4	+ 3.00

July	Total W-R	Non-handicaps 2-y-o	3-y-o+	Handicaps 2-y-o	3-y-o+	Per cent	£1 Level Stake
Mrs J Ramsden	5-13	1-4	1-1	2-4	1-4	38.5	+ 16.50
J M Bradley	4-8	0-0	0-0	0-0	4-8	50.0	+ 20.83
Sir M Prescott	3-10	1-3	1-3	0-0	1-4	30.0	- 2.46
C F Wall	2-2	0-0	0-0	0-0	2-2	100.0	+ 4.60
S P C Woods	2-2	1-1	1-1	0-0	0-0	100.0	+ 7.25

August	Total W-R	Non-handicaps 2-y-o	3-y-o+	Handicaps 2-y-o	3-y-o+	Per cent	£1 Level Stake
T D Barron	6-30	1-5	0-2	2-2	3-21	20.0	+ 5.50
J Berry	6-34	1-18	3-5	0-5	2-6	17.6	- 13.28
H R A Cecil	5-11	0-1	3-7	0-0	2-3	45.5	+ 3.46
D W Chapman	5-27	0-2	0-1	0-0	5-24	18.5	+ 61.50
Sir M Prescott	4-15	2-7	0-1	2-3	0-4	26.7	+ 15.00

September	Total W-R	Non-handicaps 2-y-o	3-y-o+	Handicaps 2-y-o	3-y-o+	Per cent	£1 Level Stake
H R A Cecil	3-5	2-2	1-2	0-1	0-0	60.0	+ 0.45
Mrs M Reveley	3-14	0-3	0-2	0-1	3-8	21.4	+ 13.50
M A Jarvis	2-2	1-1	1-1	0-0	0-0	100.0	+ 4.45
B A McMahon	2-5	0-1	1-2	0-0	1-2	40.0	+ 21.00
M R Stoute	2-5	1-4	1-1	0-0	0-0	40.0	- 0.96

WARWICK (Group 4)

Leading Trainers 1990-94

	Total W-R	Non-handicaps 2-y-o	3-y-o+	Handicaps 2-y-o	3-y-o+	Per cent	£1 Level Stake
J Berry	21-120	7-53	6-27	3-16	5-24	17.5	+ 7.38
H R A Cecil	13-39	4-6	8-30	0-1	1-2	33.3	- 2.86
P Chapple-Hyam	11-42	3-12	5-17	1-2	2-11	26.2	+ 15.36
J L Dunlop	10-52	1-7	5-20	1-6	3-19	19.2	- 6.58
R Charlton	9-28	0-1	5-17	1-1	3-9	32.1	+ 12.83
M Bell	9-40	6-16	3-9	0-3	0-12	22.5	+ 2.91
G Lewis	9-51	6-13	1-15	0-6	2-17	17.6	+ 35.98
P F I Cole	9-83	2-17	4-30	1-9	2-27	10.8	- 32.88
G B Balding	8-40	1-3	0-6	0-2	7-29	20.0	+ 26.25
I A Balding	8-52	2-8	5-22	0-5	1-17	15.4	- 26.11
R Hannon	8-112	1-34	2-28	1-12	4-38	7.1	- 68.47
M C Pipe	7-33	1-1	3-12	0-0	3-20	21.2	- 4.21
M R Stoute	7-34	3-9	2-16	0-0	2-9	20.6	- 11.87
B A McMahon	7-69	0-7	1-21	0-2	6-39	10.1	- 27.13
R Hollinshead	7-72	1-13	3-24	1-2	2-33	9.7	- 21.50
J H M Gosden	6-31	0-2	6-25	0-0	0-4	19.4	- 4.52
L G Cottrell	6-32	1-5	1-14	0-0	4-13	18.8	+ 70.00
R Akehurst	6-37	0-2	0-5	0-0	6-30	16.2	+ 5.50
B W Hills	6-61	1-13	3-28	0-2	2-18	9.8	- 38.64
J W Hills	5-34	0-7	3-12	0-0	2-15	14.7	- 6.39
P G Murphy	5-37	3-6	0-9	0-2	2-20	13.5	- 2.42
H Candy	5-47	0-3	3-22	0-3	2-19	10.6	- 16.00

Leading Jockeys

	Total W-R	Per cent	£1 Level Stake	Best Trainer	W-R	Per cent	£1 Level Stake
W Carson	23-95	24.2	- 19.93	P T Walwyn	3-4	75.0	+ 2.48
Pat Eddery	19-65	29.2	+ 2.60	R Charlton	4-10	40.0	+ 5.01
A Munro	16-93	17.2	- 10.33	R Akehurst	3-6	50.0	+ 9.00
J Reid	15-79	19.0	- 1.29	R Hannon	3-11	27.3	+ 0.91
Paul Eddery	15-99	15.2	+ 5.93	G Lewis	7-24	29.2	+ 44.48
J Williams	15-152	9.9	+ 19.00	G B Balding	6-18	33.3	+ 30.00
T Quinn	14-122	11.5	- 1.00	P F I Cole	5-42	11.9	- 3.00
M Hills	12-61	19.7	+ 10.08	M Bell	4-11	36.4	+ 6.53
W R Swinburn	12-63	19.0	+ 2.61	M R Stoute	4-13	30.8	- 1.77
M Roberts	11-43	25.6	+ 12.68	C E Brittain	3-18	16.7	+ 9.50
W Ryan	11-71	15.5	- 27.31	H R A Cecil	9-18	50.0	+ 3.69
R Cochrane	9-50	18.0	- 22.90	I A Balding	3-10	30.0	- 1.50

How the Favourites Fared

Non-handicaps	W-R	Per cent	£1 Level Stake	Handicaps	W-R	Per cent	£1 Level Stake
2-y-o	28-86	32.6	- 25.84	2-y-o	6-21	28.6	- 6.22
3-y-o	35-71	49.3	+ 0.30	3-y-o	14-39	35.9	+ 5.40
Weight-for-age	28-66	42.4	+ 11.81	All-aged	31-145	21.4	- 50.21
Totals	91-223	40.8	- 13.73	Totals	51-205	24.9	- 51.03
All favs	142-428	33.2	- 64.76				

Leading Trainers by Month at Warwick

March/Apr

	Total W-R	Non-handicaps 2-y-o	3-y-o+	Handicaps 2-y-o	3-y-o+	Per cent	£1 Level Stake
J Berry	9-35	4-14	4-11	0-0	1-10	25.7	+ 13.91
B A McMahon	4-15	0-2	1-5	0-0	3-8	26.7	+ 8.50
K T Ivory	4-19	0-3	0-4	0-0	4-12	21.1	+ 39.25
R Charlton	3-10	0-0	1-8	0-0	2-2	30.0	- 0.27
P Chapple-Hyam	3-11	0-0	3-9	0-0	0-2	27.3	+ 16.00

May

	Total W-R	Non-handicaps 2-y-o	3-y-o+	Handicaps 2-y-o	3-y-o+	Per cent	£1 Level Stake
J W Hills	3-7	0-0	2-4	0-0	1-3	42.9	+ 4.25
M Bell	3-13	2-6	1-2	0-0	0-5	23.1	- 0.97
G B Balding	3-16	1-2	0-2	0-0	2-12	18.8	+ 14.00
W J Haggas	2-3	0-0	2-3	0-0	0-0	66.7	+ 9.00
R Akehurst	2-5	0-1	0-0	0-0	2-4	40.0	+ 5.00

June

	Total W-R	Non-handicaps 2-y-o	3-y-o+	Handicaps 2-y-o	3-y-o+	Per cent	£1 Level Stake
J L Dunlop	4-9	1-1	1-3	0-0	2-5	44.4	+ 0.84
R Charlton	3-4	0-0	2-2	0-0	1-2	75.0	+ 12.80
H R A Cecil	3-11	1-2	2-9	0-0	0-0	27.3	- 6.99
J Berry	3-17	1-9	1-5	0-0	1-3	17.6	+ 4.00
P Chapple-Hyam	2-2	0-0	2-2	0-0	0-0	100.0	+ 3.75

July

	Total W-R	Non-handicaps 2-y-o	3-y-o+	Handicaps 2-y-o	3-y-o+	Per cent	£1 Level Stake
J Berry	4-24	0-11	0-2	2-6	2-5	16.7	- 7.28
W R Hern	3-3	0-0	3-3	0-0	0-0	100.0	+ 2.98
M A Jarvis	3-3	0-0	1-1	0-0	2-2	100.0	+ 13.80
G Lewis	3-6	3-4	0-0	0-1	0-1	50.0	+ 4.48
B W Hills	3-13	1-2	2-6	0-0	0-5	23.1	- 3.30

August

	Total W-R	Non-handicaps 2-y-o	3-y-o+	Handicaps 2-y-o	3-y-o+	Per cent	£1 Level Stake
P Chapple-Hyam	3-6	1-2	0-2	1-1	1-1	50.0	+ 5.54
H Candy	3-9	0-0	3-6	0-1	0-2	33.3	+ 8.00
R Hollinshead	2-4	0-0	2-4	0-0	0-0	50.0	+ 4.00
K O C-Brown	1-1	0-0	0-0	0-0	1-1	100.0	+ 6.50
D R C Elsworth	1-1	1-1	0-0	0-0	0-0	100.0	+ 2.25

Oct/Nov

	Total W-R	Non-handicaps 2-y-o	3-y-o+	Handicaps 2-y-o	3-y-o+	Per cent	£1 Level Stake
H R A Cecil	4-8	3-4	1-3	0-1	0-0	50.0	+ 8.87
I A Balding	3-16	2-7	1-2	0-5	0-2	18.8	- 8.52
P F I Cole	3-24	2-10	0-5	1-5	0-4	12.5	+ 4.50
J Wharton	2-7	1-3	0-1	0-1	1-2	28.6	+ 29.00
J H M Gosden	2-7	0-1	2-5	0-0	0-1	28.6	- 0.77

WINDSOR (Group 3)

Leading Trainers 1990-94

	Total W-R	Non-handicaps 2-y-o	3-y-o+	Handicaps 2-y-o	3-y-o+	Per cent	£1 Level Stake
R Hannon	43-239	23-99	5-42	4-20	11-78	18.0	- 10.05
H R A Cecil	13-38	0-3	10-31	0-0	3-4	34.2	+ 6.25
L M Cumani	10-33	0-0	9-24	0-1	1-8	30.3	- 7.26
I A Balding	10-53	2-8	3-23	0-0	5-22	18.9	- 12.73
P J Makin	9-43	1-7	6-19	0-0	2-17	20.9	- 6.35
M A Jarvis	8-34	0-4	2-14	0-1	6-15	23.5	+ 3.90
G Harwood	8-36	1-2	3-18	0-0	4-16	22.2	- 1.81
W R Hern	8-47	2-4	5-31	0-0	1-12	17.0	- 14.75
J Berry	8-50	4-29	1-3	3-9	0-9	16.0	- 20.40
Lord Huntingdon	8-50	3-12	3-23	0-0	2-15	16.0	- 6.48
M J Heaton-Ellis	8-50	2-10	0-15	0-0	6-25	16.0	+ 21.00
D R C Elsworth	8-63	2-15	5-26	0-1	1-21	12.7	- 22.75
P F I Cole	8-74	3-27	1-17	0-4	4-26	10.8	- 19.30
M R Stoute	7-42	1-7	1-17	0-0	5-18	16.7	- 16.33
N A Callaghan	7-43	1-8	1-4	0-4	5-27	16.3	+ 9.00
G Lewis	7-92	4-38	0-16	1-5	2-33	7.6	- 53.67
J L Dunlop	6-34	0-8	2-12	1-3	3-11	17.6	+ 2.63
J W Hills	6-34	1-5	3-15	0-2	2-12	17.6	+ 21.75
R Charlton	6-35	2-10	2-15	0-2	2-8	17.1	- 4.18
H Candy	6-44	0-8	1-19	1-1	4-16	13.6	+ 31.88
J H M Gosden	6-48	0-0	4-40	0-1	2-7	12.5	- 3.50
C J Benstead	6-50	0-5	0-7	0-1	6-37	12.0	- 12.67

Leading Jockeys

	Total W-R	Per cent	£1 Level Stake	Best Trainer	W-R	Per cent	£1 Level Stake
Pat Eddery	53-221	24.0	- 41.56	R Hannon	14-48	29.2	- 4.55
L Dettori	26-141	18.4	- 29.32	L M Cumani	8-23	34.8	- 3.62
J Reid	18-161	11.2	- 28.50	R Hannon	4-19	21.1	+ 13.50
M Roberts	17-127	13.4	- 51.66	Lord Huntingdon	3-4	75.0	+ 13.90
R Cochrane	16-116	13.8	+ 12.50	I A Balding	4-14	28.6	+ 8.20
T Quinn	15-146	10.3	- 5.26	C J Benstead	4-10	40.0	+ 13.33
A Munro	13-115	11.3	- 15.91	J D Bethell	2-5	40.0	+ 23.00
W Carson	13-138	9.4	- 80.84	W R Hern	5-25	20.0	- 6.50
W R Swinburn	12-70	17.1	- 26.30	R Hannon	2-3	66.7	+ 2.67
M Hills	11-86	12.8	- 19.54	J W Hills	3-11	27.3	+ 3.75
Paul Eddery	10-129	7.8	- 70.46	G Lewis	5-36	13.9	- 8.67
B Raymond	8-56	14.3	- 14.37	R Hannon	3-7	42.9	+ 4.13

How the Favourites Fared

Non-handicaps	W-R	Per cent	£1 Level Stake	Handicaps	W-R	Per cent	£1 Level Stake
2-y-o	43-98	43.9	+ 1.06	2-y-o	6-22	27.3	- 2.12
3-y-o	22-49	44.9	- 0.97	3-y-o	13-56	23.2	- 22.41
Weight-for-age	23-70	32.9	- 3.67	All-aged	30-107	28.0	- 17.42
Totals	88-217	40.6	- 3.58	Totals	49-185	26.5	- 41.95
All favs	137-402	34.1	- 45.53				

Leading Trainers by Month at Windsor

March/Apr

	Total W-R	Non-handicaps 2-y-o	3-y-o+	Handicaps 2-y-o	3-y-o+	Per cent	£1 Level Stake
R Hannon	9-24	6-11	1-7	0-0	2-6	37.5	+ 26.75
H Candy	2-3	0-0	0-1	0-0	2-2	66.7	+ 27.00
H R A Cecil	2-3	0-0	2-3	0-0	0-0	66.7	+ 3.13
M J Ryan	1-1	0-0	0-0	0-0	1-1	100.0	+ 4.50
K R Burke	1-1	0-0	1-1	0-0	0-0	100.0	+ 7.00

May

	Total W-R	Non-handicaps 2-y-o	3-y-o+	Handicaps 2-y-o	3-y-o+	Per cent	£1 Level Stake
R Hannon	6-25	2-7	0-6	0-0	4-12	24.0	+ 18.58
G Harwood	2-3	0-0	2-2	0-0	0-1	66.7	+ 4.50
J W Hills	2-6	0-0	1-3	0-0	1-3	33.3	+ 22.50
J White	2-19	0-0	2-15	0-0	0-4	10.5	- 10.50
R W Armstrong	1-1	0-0	0-0	0-0	1-1	100.0	+ 16.00

June

	Total W-R	Non-handicaps 2-y-o	3-y-o+	Handicaps 2-y-o	3-y-o+	Per cent	£1 Level Stake
R Hannon	7-45	5-21	1-5	0-0	1-19	15.6	- 18.56
N A Callaghan	4-16	1-4	0-0	0-0	3-12	25.0	+ 8.00
L M Cumani	3-6	0-0	2-4	0-0	1-2	50.0	+ 4.00
M A Jarvis	3-9	0-1	1-4	0-0	2-4	33.3	+ 8.40
I A Balding	3-11	1-2	1-4	0-0	1-5	27.3	+ 4.60

July

	Total W-R	Non-handicaps 2-y-o	3-y-o+	Handicaps 2-y-o	3-y-o+	Per cent	£1 Level Stake
R Hannon	13-85	6-38	2-14	2-6	3-27	15.3	- 28.53
H R A Cecil	6-13	0-0	5-12	0-0	1-1	46.2	+ 7.42
Lord Huntingdon	6-21	2-7	2-6	0-0	2-8	28.6	+ 12.90
D R C Elsworth	6-25	2-6	4-10	0-0	0-9	24.0	+ 6.50
P J Makin	5-18	0-3	3-6	0-0	2-9	27.8	+ 1.74

August

	Total W-R	Non-handicaps 2-y-o	3-y-o+	Handicaps 2-y-o	3-y-o+	Per cent	£1 Level Stake
R Hannon	8-60	4-22	1-10	2-14	1-14	13.3	- 8.30
W R Hern	6-23	1-2	4-15	0-0	1-6	26.1	+ 2.00
J Berry	5-13	1-3	1-2	3-8	0-0	38.5	+ 5.00
M J Heaton-Ellis	4-11	1-2	0-4	0-0	3-5	36.4	+ 9.50
L M Cumani	4-13	0-0	4-10	0-1	0-2	30.8	- 4.09

WOLVERHAMPTON ALL-WEATHER (Group 4)

Leading Trainers 1990-94

	Total W-R	Non-handicaps 2-y-o	Non-handicaps 3-y-o+	Handicaps 2-y-o	Handicaps 3-y-o+	Per cent	£1 Level Stake
M Johnston	17-45	0-2	4-9	0-2	13-32	37.8	+ 43.33
J Berry	15-79	4-17	7-28	0-3	4-31	19.0	- 14.40
P C Haslam	14-58	2-16	5-13	0-0	7-29	24.1	- 3.49
Lord Huntingdon	12-44	1-5	7-20	0-0	4-19	27.3	+ 0.98
R Hollinshead	11-134	0-8	3-50	0-4	8-72	8.2	- 80.25
Sir M Prescott	9-26	4-10	4-8	0-0	1-8	34.6	+ 8.59
A Bailey	9-55	1-4	3-18	0-2	5-31	16.4	- 4.45
Mrs M Reveley	7-26	0-0	5-10	0-0	2-16	26.9	+ 1.16
T D Barron	7-31	0-0	1-9	0-0	6-22	22.6	+ 25.75
B A McMahon	7-56	1-12	2-15	0-0	4-29	12.5	- 6.00
J L Harris	6-36	0-0	3-16	0-0	3-20	16.7	+ 3.03
D Haydn Jones	5-35	1-7	0-2	0-0	4-26	14.3	+ 21.00
P D Evans	5-62	0-3	3-22	2-3	0-34	8.1	- 37.38
G Lewis	4-16	3-10	0-3	1-1	0-2	25.0	+ 5.75
J A Glover	4-16	2-4	0-1	0-0	2-11	25.0	+ 14.13
M R Channon	4-25	1-9	0-5	1-1	2-10	16.0	+ 3.25
R Bastiman	3-9	0-0	2-4	0-0	1-5	33.3	+ 2.13
W J Haggas	3-10	0-0	2-8	0-0	1-2	30.0	+ 1.38
R Ingram	3-10	0-0	0-0	0-0	3-10	30.0	+ 7.00
P S Felgate	3-13	0-0	0-2	0-0	3-11	23.1	+ 7.00
J Pearce	3-14	0-0	0-3	0-0	3-11	21.4	+ 14.50
Miss S J Wilton	3-14	0-0	2-8	0-0	1-6	21.4	+ 21.50

Leading Jockeys

	Total W-R	Per cent	£1 Level Stake	Best Trainer	W-R	Per cent	£1 Level Stake
J Weaver	31-108	28.7	+ 37.25	M Johnston	15-33	45.5	+ 37.08
L Dettori	14-83	16.9	- 32.40	R Hollinshead	5-29	17.2	- 2.50
K Darley	12-59	20.3	- 4.68	Mrs M Reveley	5-10	50.0	+ 1.29
J Williams	10-88	11.4	+ 1.13	D Haydn Jones	2-10	20.0	- 1.00
A Mackay	9-85	10.6	- 9.75	D Haydn Jones	3-18	16.7	+ 29.00
G Duffield	8-31	25.8	- 4.41	Sir M Prescott	6-14	42.9	+ 4.09
Paul Eddery	8-77	10.4	- 25.22	J L Harris	4-14	28.6	+ 11.03
D Harrison	7-37	18.9	+ 4.75	Lord Huntingdon	4-19	21.1	- 1.75
G Bardwell	6-45	13.3	+ 1.75	C N Allen	3-8	37.5	+ 5.75
T Williams	6-46	13.0	- 17.50	P C Haslam	2-11	18.2	+ 0.75
A Clark	6-53	11.3	+ 17.25	Mrs N Macauley	2-11	18.2	+ 21.00
D Wright	6-60	10.0	- 30.20	A Bailey	5-22	22.7	+ 5.30

How the Favourites Fared

Non-handicaps	W-R	Per cent	£1 Level Stake	Handicaps	W-R	Per cent	£1 Level Stake
2-y-o	13-25	52.0	+ 6.59	2-y-o	1-4	25.0	- 2.17
3-y-o	10-27	37.0	- 7.92	3-y-o	8-16	50.0	+ 2.27
Weight-for-age	25-64	39.1	- 7.59	All-aged	35-105	33.3	+ 7.56
Totals	48-116	41.4	- 8.92	Totals	44-125	35.2	+ 7.66
All favs	92-241	38.2	- 1.26				

Leading Trainers by Month at Wolverhampton (AW)

January

	Total W-R	Non-handicaps 2-y-o	3-y-o+	Handicaps 2-y-o	3-y-o+	Per cent	£1 Level Stake
M Johnston	4-11	0-0	0-1	0-0	4-10	36.4	+ 6.83
Lord Huntingdon	3-8	0-0	1-5	0-0	2-3	37.5	+ 6.71
P C Haslam	3-16	0-0	2-5	0-0	1-11	18.8	- 3.09

February

	Total W-R	Non-handicaps 2-y-o	3-y-o+	Handicaps 2-y-o	3-y-o+	Per cent	£1 Level Stake
R Hollinshead	5-21	0-0	3-13	0-0	2-8	23.8	0.00
J Berry	3-13	0-0	3-8	0-0	0-5	23.1	+ 4.00
D L Williams	2-4	0-0	2-2	0-0	0-2	50.0	+ 34.00

March

	Total W-R	Non-handicaps 2-y-o	3-y-o+	Handicaps 2-y-o	3-y-o+	Per cent	£1 Level Stake
M Johnston	3-4	0-0	0-1	0-0	3-3	75.0	+ 13.00
Mrs M Reveley	3-11	0-0	2-5	0-0	1-6	27.3	- 3.71
P C Haslam	2-2	0-0	1-1	0-0	1-1	100.0	+ 4.75

April

	Total W-R	Non-handicaps 2-y-o	3-y-o+	Handicaps 2-y-o	3-y-o+	Per cent	£1 Level Stake
Mrs M Reveley	3-3	0-0	3-3	0-0	0-0	100.0	+ 3.87
M J Camacho	1-1	0-0	1-1	0-0	0-0	100.0	+ 3.50
W J Haggas	1-1	0-0	1-1	0-0	0-0	100.0	+ 1.00

May

	Total W-R	Non-handicaps 2-y-o	3-y-o+	Handicaps 2-y-o	3-y-o+	Per cent	£1 Level Stake
J Berry	2-5	1-1	1-2	0-0	0-2	40.0	+ 2.33
P S Felgate	1-2	0-0	0-0	0-0	1-2	50.0	+ 2.50
J A R Toller	1-2	0-0	1-1	0-0	0-1	50.0	+ 9.00

June

	Total W-R	Non-handicaps 2-y-o	3-y-o+	Handicaps 2-y-o	3-y-o+	Per cent	£1 Level Stake
J Berry	4-12	1-3	2-4	0-0	1-5	33.3	+ 1.83
P S Felgate	2-3	0-0	0-0	0-0	2-3	66.7	+ 12.50
M Johnston	2-4	0-1	1-1	0-0	1-2	50.0	+ 16.00

July

	Total W-R	Non-handicaps 2-y-o	3-y-o+	Handicaps 2-y-o	3-y-o+	Per cent	£1 Level Stake
Sir M Prescott	3-4	1-2	1-1	0-0	1-1	75.0	+ 3.19
M R Channon	3-7	1-3	0-1	0-0	2-3	42.9	+ 15.75
A Bailey	3-8	0-1	2-4	0-0	1-3	37.5	+ 3.30

August

	Total W-R	Non-handicaps 2-y-o	3-y-o+	Handicaps 2-y-o	3-y-o+	Per cent	£1 Level Stake
P C Haslam	4-13	1-6	1-3	0-0	2-4	30.8	+ 5.00
D Haydn Jones	2-7	1-2	0-0	0-0	1-5	28.6	+ 27.00
J A R Toller	1-1	0-0	1-1	0-0	0-0	100.0	+ 3.00

September

	Total W-R	Non-handicaps 2-y-o	3-y-o+	Handicaps 2-y-o	3-y-o+	Per cent	£1 Level Stake
P C Haslam	3-11	1-6	0-0	0-0	2-5	27.3	- 0.75
G Lewis	1-1	1-1	0-0	0-0	0-0	100.0	+ 1.50
G Wragg	1-1	0-0	0-0	0-0	1-1	100.0	+ 16.00

October

	Total W-R	Non-handicaps 2-y-o	3-y-o+	Handicaps 2-y-o	3-y-o+	Per cent	£1 Level Stake
J A Glover	2-2	1-1	0-0	0-0	1-1	100.0	+ 17.50
A Bailey	2-3	1-1	0-1	0-0	1-1	66.7	+ 13.00
P Mitchell	2-4	0-0	0-0	0-0	2-4	50.0	+ 4.50

YARMOUTH (Group 3)

Leading Trainers 1990-94

	Total W-R	Non-handicaps 2-y-o	3-y-o+	Handicaps 2-y-o	3-y-o+	Per cent	£1 Level Stake
H R A Cecil	30-100	11-36	16-51	0-1	3-12	30.0	- 13.26
J H M Gosden	20-97	5-21	12-57	0-0	3-19	20.6	- 6.07
M H Tompkins	20-152	8-57	4-32	1-12	7-51	13.2	- 28.35
G Wragg	19-93	6-36	9-32	1-2	3-23	20.4	+ 28.14
M R Stoute	19-106	8-47	8-33	0-4	3-22	17.9	- 21.74
C E Brittain	19-161	4-39	7-48	2-4	6-70	11.8	+ 0.37
A C Stewart	15-69	4-19	5-30	0-0	6-20	21.7	+ 0.02
D Morley	14-96	8-30	2-12	1-3	3-51	14.6	- 0.78
H Thomson Jones	12-74	5-29	4-22	0-1	3-22	16.2	- 3.43
Mrs N Macauley	12-76	1-19	3-10	0-4	8-43	15.8	+ 32.78
L M Cumani	12-90	5-26	5-45	0-1	2-18	13.3	- 32.95
M J Ryan	10-138	0-24	2-29	0-7	8-78	7.2	- 85.00
J Berry	9-31	7-20	2-4	0-2	0-5	29.0	+ 22.70
B W Hills	9-31	4-13	3-8	0-2	2-8	29.0	+ 10.41
J W Hills	9-38	1-9	4-13	0-0	4-16	23.7	+ 21.38
M Bell	9-80	4-23	0-2	2-11	3-44	11.3	- 5.26
J Pearce	9-81	1-7	4-32	0-0	4-42	11.1	+ 4.50
B Hanbury	9-82	4-35	3-23	0-5	2-19	11.0	- 34.59
N A Callaghan	8-51	1-19	2-7	2-5	3-20	15.7	- 13.00
W J Haggas	8-54	2-15	1-11	2-9	3-19	14.8	+ 12.38
D Morris	8-57	2-6	3-14	1-6	2-31	14.0	- 0.25
Sir M Prescott	8-60	2-28	0-7	0-1	6-24	13.3	+ 19.87

Leading Jockeys

	Total W-R	Per cent	£1 Level Stake	Best Trainer	W-R	Per cent	£1 Level Stake
M Roberts	39-222	17.6	+ 50.21	C E Brittain	13-70	18.6	+ 37.70
L Dettori	26-162	16.0	- 37.79	L M Cumani	8-38	21.1	- 12.82
R Hills	24-136	17.6	- 6.77	H Thomson Jones	11-51	21.6	+ 15.57
W Ryan	23-132	17.4	- 42.91	H R A Cecil	13-45	28.9	- 9.36
G Duffield	23-139	16.5	+ 37.98	Sir M Prescott	7-33	21.2	+ 45.25
P Robinson	19-108	17.6	- 19.24	M H Tompkins	10-53	18.9	- 7.74
M Hills	19-122	15.6	- 19.25	J W Hills	5-12	41.7	+ 21.50
Pat Eddery	18-64	28.1	- 3.23	H R A Cecil	3-8	37.5	- 2.98
W R Swinburn	18-128	14.1	- 17.95	D Morley	3-12	25.0	+ 1.30
R Cochrane	16-116	13.8	+ 6.48	M H Tompkins	3-21	14.3	+ 8.50
M Tebbutt	12-104	11.5	- 37.75	W Jarvis	5-35	14.3	- 3.75
G Bardwell	12-120	10.0	- 10.71	K T Ivory	4-26	15.4	+ 7.13

How the Favourites Fared

Non-handicaps	W-R	Per cent	£1 Level Stake	Handicaps	W-R	Per cent	£1 Level Stake
2-y-o	61-140	43.6	- 9.52	2-y-o	11-26	42.3	+ 4.80
3-y-o	36-71	50.7	+ 2.58	3-y-o	11-43	25.6	- 16.49
Weight-for-age	35-83	42.2	+ 2.49	All-aged	48-186	25.8	- 43.23
Totals	132-294	44.9	- 4.45	Totals	70-255	27.5	- 54.92
All favs	202-549	36.8	- 59.37				

Leading Trainers by Month at Yarmouth

June

	Total W-R	Non-handicaps 2-y-o	Non-handicaps 3-y-o+	Handicaps 2-y-o	Handicaps 3-y-o+	Per cent	£1 Level Stake
G Wragg	8-28	2-3	4-18	0-0	2-7	28.6	+ 11.24
A C Stewart	6-15	0-0	2-9	0-0	4-6	40.0	+ 6.48
M H Tompkins	6-45	5-16	0-11	0-0	1-18	13.3	- 6.75
J H M Gosden	5-21	0-1	5-19	0-0	0-1	23.8	- 5.72
C E Brittain	5-39	1-3	3-16	0-0	1-20	12.8	- 12.25

July

	Total W-R	Non-handicaps 2-y-o	Non-handicaps 3-y-o+	Handicaps 2-y-o	Handicaps 3-y-o+	Per cent	£1 Level Stake
M H Tompkins	10-53	3-23	1-11	1-1	5-18	18.9	- 3.60
H R A Cecil	9-17	2-2	7-15	0-0	0-0	52.9	+ 7.79
D Morley	7-27	3-8	2-5	0-0	2-14	25.9	+ 31.93
M R Stoute	6-15	2-4	3-5	0-0	1-6	40.0	+ 11.00
M Bell	6-19	4-8	0-2	0-0	2-9	31.6	+ 13.74

August

	Total W-R	Non-handicaps 2-y-o	Non-handicaps 3-y-o+	Handicaps 2-y-o	Handicaps 3-y-o+	Per cent	£1 Level Stake
H R A Cecil	9-20	5-9	4-9	0-0	0-2	45.0	+ 4.39
W J Haggas	6-18	2-7	0-1	2-3	2-7	33.3	+ 41.04
J Pearce	5-18	0-0	2-6	0-0	3-12	27.8	+ 35.00
M R Stoute	5-29	3-17	2-6	0-0	0-6	17.2	- 5.39
Sir M Prescott	4-14	2-3	0-3	0-0	2-8	28.6	+ 16.37

September

	Total W-R	Non-handicaps 2-y-o	Non-handicaps 3-y-o+	Handicaps 2-y-o	Handicaps 3-y-o+	Per cent	£1 Level Stake
H R A Cecil	8-23	3-9	2-7	0-1	3-6	34.8	+ 2.62
P W Harris	5-10	0-1	0-0	0-0	5-9	50.0	+ 27.00
J H M Gosden	5-21	2-4	1-11	0-0	2-6	23.8	+ 12.88
J Berry	4-9	3-5	1-2	0-0	0-2	44.4	+ 28.75
R W Armstrong	3-9	1-2	0-2	2-2	0-3	33.3	+ 25.50

Oct/Nov

	Total W-R	Non-handicaps 2-y-o	Non-handicaps 3-y-o+	Handicaps 2-y-o	Handicaps 3-y-o+	Per cent	£1 Level Stake
J H M Gosden	6-14	3-9	3-5	0-0	0-0	42.9	+ 11.35
C E Brittain	3-17	0-6	1-4	1-1	1-6	17.6	+ 20.62
N A Callaghan	2-3	0-1	0-0	1-1	1-1	66.7	+ 6.00
J W Hills	2-7	0-2	1-4	0-0	1-1	28.6	+ 10.00
R Hannon	2-8	1-5	0-0	1-2	0-1	25.0	+ 1.00

YORK (Group 1)

Leading Trainers 1990-94

	Total W-R	Non-handicaps 2-y-o	3-y-o+	Handicaps 2-y-o	3-y-o+	Per cent	£1 Level Stake
J H M Gosden	34-125	6-17	18-58	0-2	10-48	27.2	+ 22.61
H R A Cecil	26-114	6-14	13-66	1-2	6-32	22.8	- 21.37
M R Stoute	26-143	1-17	19-64	0-1	6-61	18.2	+ 7.76
R Hannon	22-192	13-72	3-23	2-18	4-79	11.5	- 53.01
J L Dunlop	19-89	8-22	6-31	0-4	5-32	21.3	- 9.25
M H Easterby	17-178	2-21	2-11	2-20	11-126	9.6	- 56.42
L M Cumani	16-91	0-5	13-44	0-2	3-40	17.6	- 7.47
P F I Cole	15-67	13-32	2-23	0-1	0-11	22.4	+ 13.34
C E Brittain	13-149	2-25	6-57	0-3	5-64	8.7	- 40.40
J Berry	12-117	6-33	0-16	2-12	4-56	10.3	- 63.86
R Charlton	10-46	5-10	1-11	0-2	4-23	21.7	+ 8.75
M Johnston	10-87	5-19	0-12	0-4	5-52	11.5	- 22.38
B W Hills	10-126	1-27	5-53	0-1	4-45	7.9	- 55.92
P Chapple-Hyam	9-44	6-17	1-13	0-2	2-12	20.5	+ 0.02
M Bell	7-41	1-7	1-6	2-9	3-19	17.1	+ 25.00
M Feth-Godley	6-22	0-1	0-0	0-1	6-20	27.3	+ 35.50
W Jarvis	6-42	1-12	2-14	2-3	1-13	14.3	- 3.67
T D Barron	6-43	0-4	0-1	2-10	4-28	14.0	+ 19.00
D R C Elsworth	6-53	1-6	3-26	0-1	2-20	11.3	- 5.50
B Hanbury	6-63	4-13	0-19	0-1	2-30	9.5	- 24.13
Mrs M Reveley	6-74	0-11	0-3	1-4	5-56	8.1	- 36.25
I A Balding	6-80	0-10	1-17	0-2	5-51	7.5	- 36.50

Leading Jockeys

	Total W-R	Per cent	£1 Level Stake	Best Trainer	W-R	Per cent	£1 Level Stake
Pat Eddery	49-239	20.5	+ 7.59	H R A Cecil	8-25	32.0	- 4.48
W Carson	39-265	14.7	- 76.64	J L Dunlop	11-40	27.5	+ 0.66
M Roberts	35-243	14.4	+ 3.96	C E Brittain	9-78	11.5	- 0.62
L Dettori	34-198	17.2	+ 11.31	L M Cumani	12-46	26.1	+ 12.40
W R Swinburn	23-205	11.2	- 49.43	M R Stoute	13-71	18.3	+ 20.61
A Munro	17-144	11.8	- 31.15	P F I Cole	8-26	30.8	+ 13.35
J Reid	15-134	11.2	- 19.14	P Chapple-Hyam	5-24	20.8	- 4.10
R Cochrane	14-147	9.5	- 74.92	R Charlton	3-4	75.0	+ 15.00
M Birch	13-155	8.4	- 58.17	M H Easterby	11-101	10.9	- 15.67
D Holland	12-69	17.4	+ 24.13	P Chapple-Hyam	3-3	100.0	+ 12.13
W Ryan	12-86	14.0	+ 16.95	H R A Cecil	6-32	18.8	- 13.15
M Hills	11-114	9.6	- 24.92	B W Hills	5-33	15.2	+ 4.83

How the Favourites Fared

Non-handicaps	W-R	Per cent	£1 Level Stake	Handicaps	W-R	Per cent	£1 Level Stake
2-y-o	53-119	44.5	+ 4.45	2-y-o	5-27	18.5	- 10.66
3-y-o	26-74	35.1	- 22.62	3-y-o	16-56	28.6	+ 10.85
Weight-for-age	20-70	28.6	- 21.12	All-aged	48-154	31.2	+ 41.79
Totals	99-263	37.6	- 39.29	Totals	69-237	29.1	+ 41.98
All favs	168-500	33.6	+ 2.69				

Leading Trainers by Month at York

May

	Total W-R	Non-handicaps 2-y-o	3-y-o+	Handicaps 2-y-o	3-y-o+	Per cent	£1 Level Stake
M R Stoute	12-44	0-2	9-24	0-0	3-18	27.3	+ 18.31
H R A Cecil	7-30	2-2	4-20	0-0	1-8	23.3	- 13.54
J L Dunlop	4-17	0-0	3-9	0-0	1-8	23.5	+ 8.50
P Chapple-Hyam	4-20	3-6	0-6	0-0	1-8	20.0	- 6.60
R Hannon	4-38	0-9	2-7	0-0	2-22	10.5	+ 3.50

June

	Total W-R	Non-handicaps 2-y-o	3-y-o+	Handicaps 2-y-o	3-y-o+	Per cent	£1 Level Stake
H R A Cecil	6-8	1-1	4-4	0-0	1-3	75.0	+ 9.08
J L Dunlop	3-12	0-2	2-7	0-0	1-3	25.0	- 2.35
M R Stoute	3-16	0-0	3-10	0-0	0-6	18.8	- 7.76
M R Channon	2-3	0-1	0-0	0-0	2-2	66.7	+ 30.50
P F I Cole	2-5	2-2	0-3	0-0	0-0	40.0	+ 3.73

July

	Total W-R	Non-handicaps 2-y-o	3-y-o+	Handicaps 2-y-o	3-y-o+	Per cent	£1 Level Stake
J H M Gosden	4-7	0-0	3-4	0-0	1-3	57.1	+ 2.50
H R A Cecil	4-10	1-1	2-5	0-0	1-4	40.0	+ 8.78
P F I Cole	4-11	3-6	1-3	0-0	0-2	36.4	- 2.01
R Hannon	4-21	4-12	0-2	0-0	0-7	19.0	- 6.70
J L Dunlop	3-12	3-6	0-0	0-0	0-6	25.0	- 6.32

August

	Total W-R	Non-handicaps 2-y-o	3-y-o+	Handicaps 2-y-o	3-y-o+	Per cent	£1 Level Stake
L M Cumani	8-37	0-1	8-18	0-0	0-18	21.6	+ 9.80
R Hannon	8-70	7-31	1-9	0-6	0-24	11.4	- 27.19
P F I Cole	6-22	6-11	0-8	0-0	0-3	27.3	+ 17.63
H R A Cecil	6-42	2-5	1-22	0-1	3-14	14.3	- 15.28
M R Stoute	6-54	1-10	4-21	0-1	1-22	11.1	+ 8.83

September

	Total W-R	Non-handicaps 2-y-o	3-y-o+	Handicaps 2-y-o	3-y-o+	Per cent	£1 Level Stake
J H M Gosden	7-18	0-1	5-12	0-0	2-5	38.9	+ 4.99
L M Cumani	5-14	0-1	3-8	0-0	2-5	35.7	+ 7.69
C E Brittain	5-18	1-3	2-6	0-2	2-7	27.8	+ 24.50
M Feth-Godley	3-6	0-0	0-0	0-1	3-5	50.0	+ 18.50
R Boss	2-2	2-2	0-0	0-0	0-0	100.0	+ 10.00

Oct/Nov

	Total W-R	Non-handicaps 2-y-o	3-y-o+	Handicaps 2-y-o	3-y-o+	Per cent	£1 Level Stake
J H M Gosden	15-33	6-11	6-12	0-0	3-10	45.5	+ 23.12
J L Dunlop	5-21	3-9	0-4	0-2	2-6	23.8	- 2.26
R Hannon	5-32	2-12	0-2	2-9	1-9	15.6	- 0.13
M H Easterby	5-40	1-5	1-3	1-9	2-23	12.5	- 9.25
E Weymes	3-7	1-2	0-0	0-3	2-2	42.9	+ 11.25

TRAINERS' FAVOURITES AT ASCOT 1990-94

	Total W-R	Non-handicaps 2-y-o	3-y-o+	Handicaps 2-y-o	3-y-o+	Per cent	£1 Level Stake
J H M Gosden	15-40	4-7	6-14	0-0	5-19	37.5	+ 6.26
P F I Cole	9-13	5-8	3-3	0-1	1-1	69.2	+ 10.38
G Wragg	9-17	4-7	4-6	0-0	1-4	52.9	+ 17.05
M R Stoute	9-35	1-8	6-15	0-0	2-12	25.7	- 9.28
J L Dunlop	7-20	3-9	3-7	0-0	1-4	35.0	+ 0.08
L M Cumani	7-22	4-5	3-10	0-0	0-7	31.8	- 4.46
H R A Cecil	7-31	2-10	4-15	0-0	1-6	22.6	- 6.89
G Harwood	5-11	0-0	4-6	0-1	1-4	45.5	+ 5.73
R Hannon	4-20	2-7	1-7	0-0	1-6	20.0	- 4.24
Lady Herries	3-3	1-1	0-0	0-0	2-2	100.0	+ 6.13
C A Cyzer	3-4	0-0	0-0	0-0	3-4	75.0	+ 11.75
R W Armstrong	3-5	2-2	0-1	0-0	1-2	60.0	+ 7.25
P Chapple-Hyam	3-11	2-6	1-4	0-0	0-1	27.3	- 6.13
B Hanbury	2-3	0-0	2-3	0-0	0-0	66.7	+ 2.00
P T Walwyn	2-3	0-1	0-0	0-0	2-2	66.7	+ 5.88
A C Stewart	2-3	0-0	1-1	0-0	1-2	66.7	+ 2.88
Sir M Prescott	2-4	0-0	1-1	0-0	1-3	50.0	+ 5.70
M H Tompkins	2-5	0-0	0-1	0-0	2-4	40.0	+ 6.00
C E Brittain	2-7	0-1	2-2	0-0	0-4	28.6	- 1.00
H Thomson Jones	2-9	2-7	0-0	0-1	0-1	22.2	- 4.27
R Charlton	2-9	0-3	2-2	0-1	0-3	22.2	- 3.84
Lord Huntingdon	2-10	0-1	1-1	0-0	1-8	20.0	- 5.42
B W Hills	2-12	1-1	1-9	0-0	0-2	16.7	- 5.62

TRAINERS' FAVOURITES AT AYR 1990-94

	Total W-R	Non-handicaps 2-y-o	3-y-o+	Handicaps 2-y-o	3-y-o+	Per cent	£1 Level Stake
J Berry	12-30	6-13	5-7	0-3	1-7	40.0	- 7.10
B W Hills	10-21	2-4	6-12	0-1	2-4	47.6	+ 3.05
M H Easterby	8-19	3-8	1-2	1-2	3-7	42.1	- 1.31
P Chapple-Hyam	7-14	5-9	2-4	0-0	0-1	50.0	- 3.99
Mrs M Reveley	7-21	1-1	4-6	0-2	2-12	33.3	- 4.61
Mrs J Ramsden	7-26	4-5	0-2	1-2	2-17	26.9	- 4.14
M R Stoute	6-9	0-1	3-4	0-0	3-4	66.7	+ 10.13
Sir M Prescott	5-10	2-3	2-3	0-0	1-4	50.0	+ 0.91
J L Dunlop	5-13	3-6	1-3	0-1	1-3	38.5	- 2.00
P C Haslam	4-7	0-0	0-2	0-0	4-5	57.1	+ 3.86
T D Barron	4-8	1-1	0-1	1-2	2-4	50.0	+ 5.96
M Johnston	4-12	2-4	0-1	1-1	1-6	33.3	- 2.94
I A Balding	3-3	0-0	0-0	0-0	3-3	100.0	+ 7.50
M J Camacho	3-4	0-0	0-1	0-0	3-3	75.0	+ 8.38
F H Lee	3-9	0-2	0-0	0-0	3-7	33.3	- 0.12
A Bailey	3-11	0-1	1-3	0-1	2-6	27.3	- 4.21
J W Watts	3-11	1-2	0-1	0-3	2-5	27.3	- 2.27
J H M Gosden	3-12	0-1	2-5	0-0	1-6	25.0	- 4.79
J F Bottomley	2-3	1-1	0-0	0-0	1-2	66.7	+ 7.00
D W Chapman	2-4	0-0	1-1	1-1	0-2	50.0	+ 1.48
Miss S E Hall	2-4	0-0	1-3	0-0	1-1	50.0	+ 6.00
S E Kettlewell	2-4	0-0	1-2	0-0	1-2	50.0	+ 4.50
M P Naughton	2-6	0-0	0-0	0-0	2-6	33.3	+ 0.25
R M Whitaker	2-6	0-1	0-0	0-0	2-5	33.3	+ 4.50

TRAINERS' FAVOURITES AT BATH 1990-94

	Total W-R	Non-handicaps 2-y-o	3-y-o+	Handicaps 2-y-o	3-y-o+	Per cent	£1 Level Stake
R Hannon	10-26	4-9	3-7	0-3	3-7	38.5	+ 3.24
I A Balding	10-27	1-4	4-11	0-0	5-12	37.0	+ 9.68
B W Hills	9-20	1-2	5-7	0-0	3-11	45.0	+ 3.13
R Charlton	7-11	1-1	5-9	0-0	1-1	63.6	+ 7.55
J Berry	7-20	4-8	3-7	0-0	0-5	35.0	- 2.83
G Harwood	6-11	0-2	6-7	0-1	0-1	54.5	+ 5.62
P F I Cole	6-36	1-10	2-8	0-0	3-18	16.7	- 19.61
M R Channon	5-8	2-3	2-2	0-0	1-3	62.5	+ 8.73
Sir M Prescott	5-9	2-4	3-4	0-0	0-1	55.6	+ 0.15
C J Hill	5-10	0-0	0-0	1-1	4-9	50.0	+ 13.08
R Akehurst	5-12	0-0	0-0	0-0	5-12	41.7	+ 6.00
J L Dunlop	5-13	1-4	2-2	0-0	2-7	38.5	+ 0.84
M R Stoute	4-5	1-1	2-3	0-0	1-1	80.0	+ 5.98
G Lewis	4-8	0-3	2-2	0-0	2-3	50.0	+ 5.38
R J Hodges	4-19	0-0	0-1	0-0	4-18	21.1	- 5.12
H Candy	3-4	0-0	3-3	0-1	0-0	75.0	+ 6.07
H R A Cecil	3-6	0-0	2-5	0-0	1-1	50.0	+ 1.55
Lord Huntingdon	3-6	0-0	1-2	1-1	1-3	50.0	+ 0.91
D R C Elsworth	3-8	1-2	1-4	0-0	1-2	37.5	+ 2.83
W R Hern	3-8	0-0	1-3	0-0	2-5	37.5	+ 0.50
L G Cottrell	2-3	1-1	0-1	0-0	1-1	66.7	+ 7.50
M J Ryan	2-4	1-1	0-2	1-1	0-0	50.0	+ 4.50
J W Hills	2-5	1-1	0-0	0-0	1-4	40.0	0.00
D Marks	1-1	0-0	1-1	0-0	0-0	100.0	+ 5.00

TRAINERS' FAVOURITES AT BEVERLEY 1990-94

	Total W-R	Non-handicaps 2-y-o	3-y-o+	Handicaps 2-y-o	3-y-o+	Per cent	£1 Level Stake
H R A Cecil	12-24	2-5	8-15	0-0	2-4	50.0	+ 3.69
M H Easterby	11-29	5-12	3-5	1-2	2-10	37.9	+ 3.54
J Berry	11-31	10-22	1-6	0-1	0-2	35.5	- 5.13
Mrs M Reveley	10-28	2-5	1-3	0-0	7-20	35.7	- 5.84
I A Balding	9-16	2-2	2-5	0-0	5-9	56.3	+ 7.45
D R Loder	8-10	5-6	0-1	0-0	3-3	80.0	+ 8.75
M R Stoute	7-13	0-0	7-10	0-0	0-3	53.8	+ 3.31
L M Cumani	7-14	1-1	5-11	0-0	1-2	50.0	+ 1.30
M Johnston	5-11	0-1	2-2	0-0	3-8	45.5	- 1.20
J L Dunlop	5-15	1-5	0-2	0-2	4-6	33.3	+ 0.49
R Hollinshead	5-16	2-4	1-4	0-0	2-8	31.3	+ 2.10
P F I Cole	4-5	0-1	3-3	0-0	1-1	80.0	+ 4.07
J L Spearing	4-8	0-0	1-1	0-0	3-7	50.0	+ 5.23
J W Watts	4-8	1-2	3-4	0-0	0-2	50.0	+ 2.40
D Morley	4-14	0-1	1-4	0-0	3-9	28.6	+ 0.33
T D Barron	4-16	0-1	0-1	0-1	4-13	25.0	- 3.77
P C Haslam	3-5	2-2	1-1	0-0	0-2	60.0	+ 0.73
S G Norton	3-6	1-1	0-1	0-0	2-4	50.0	+ 1.73
B Hanbury	3-8	1-1	1-2	0-0	1-5	37.5	+ 2.57
M Bell	3-11	2-5	0-1	0-1	1-4	27.3	- 5.17
R Hannon	2-2	0-0	1-1	1-1	0-0	100.0	+ 5.00
R Bastiman	2-2	0-0	1-1	0-0	1-1	100.0	+ 3.60
P Calver	2-3	0-0	0-0	0-0	2-3	66.7	+ 6.50
H J Collingridge	2-3	1-1	0-0	0-0	1-2	66.7	+ 1.88

TRAINERS' FAVOURITES AT BRIGHTON 1990-94

	Total W-R	Non-handicaps 2-y-o	3-y-o+	Handicaps 2-y-o	3-y-o+	Per cent	£1 Level Stake
R Hannon	21-53	15-25	4-8	0-1	2-19	39.6	- 1.75
L M Cumani	16-29	3-4	8-16	1-2	4-7	55.2	+ 8.55
Sir M Prescott	13-30	1-4	5-5	0-1	7-20	43.3	+ 3.41
P F I Cole	8-19	2-5	6-10	0-0	0-4	42.1	- 3.98
R J Hodges	8-29	0-0	2-4	0-0	6-25	27.6	- 1.85
J H M Gosden	7-12	1-1	6-10	0-0	0-1	58.3	+ 0.31
G Harwood	7-14	0-2	6-10	0-0	1-2	50.0	+ 0.31
G Lewis	7-17	1-7	1-1	2-2	3-7	41.2	+ 10.67
J L Dunlop	7-18	1-1	3-7	0-1	3-9	38.9	+ 1.41
B W Hills	5-12	0-1	3-8	1-1	1-2	41.7	+ 2.36
R Akehurst	5-16	0-0	1-3	0-0	4-13	31.3	+ 2.88
Lord Huntingdon	4-7	1-1	1-3	0-0	2-3	57.1	+ 4.90
M J Ryan	4-10	1-1	0-0	0-0	3-9	40.0	+ 5.88
J Berry	4-13	1-3	0-1	2-4	1-5	30.8	- 2.00
C J Benstead	3-3	0-0	1-1	0-0	2-2	100.0	+ 5.48
J White	3-3	0-0	0-0	0-0	3-3	100.0	+ 7.00
M A Jarvis	3-4	0-0	1-1	0-0	2-3	75.0	+ 8.50
L J Holt	3-6	0-0	0-0	0-0	3-6	50.0	+ 6.33
W Carter	3-6	1-1	0-0	0-0	2-5	50.0	+ 4.25
B J Meehan	3-6	2-3	0-0	0-0	1-3	50.0	- 0.03
S Dow	3-7	0-0	2-4	0-0	1-3	42.9	+ 2.38
R Charlton	3-8	1-1	2-7	0-0	0-0	37.5	- 2.27
I A Balding	3-11	0-2	3-5	0-0	0-4	27.3	- 4.11
R Boss	3-11	1-2	1-1	0-0	1-8	27.3	- 2.96

TRAINERS' FAVOURITES AT CARLISLE 1990-94

	Total W-R	Non-handicaps 2-y-o	3-y-o+	Handicaps 2-y-o	3-y-o+	Per cent	£1 Level Stake
J Berry	9-32	3-13	5-14	0-0	1-5	28.1	- 9.52
M H Easterby	7-14	4-6	1-3	0-0	2-5	50.0	+ 5.70
Mrs M Reveley	7-17	0-0	3-5	0-0	4-12	41.2	+ 5.21
Sir M Prescott	6-13	0-0	4-6	0-0	2-7	46.2	+ 3.89
M H Tompkins	5-11	0-0	2-5	0-0	3-6	45.5	+ 2.46
J L Dunlop	4-5	0-0	2-2	0-0	2-3	80.0	+ 13.87
N Tinkler	3-4	1-1	1-1	0-0	1-2	75.0	+ 3.95
W Jarvis	3-4	2-2	1-2	0-0	0-0	75.0	+ 4.38
Miss S E Hall	3-6	0-0	1-3	0-0	2-3	50.0	+ 5.91
Mrs J Ramsden	3-13	2-3	0-1	0-0	1-9	23.1	- 4.92
W J Haggas	2-2	0-0	2-2	0-0	0-0	100.0	+ 2.32
M R Stoute	2-4	0-0	2-3	0-0	0-1	50.0	- 0.80
M Johnston	2-8	0-0	1-3	0-0	1-5	25.0	- 2.81
M W Easterby	2-10	0-2	0-2	0-0	2-6	20.0	- 2.37
B R Cambidge	1-1	0-0	0-0	0-0	1-1	100.0	+ 3.50
C W C Elsey	1-1	0-0	1-1	0-0	0-0	100.0	+ 1.00
P S Felgate	1-1	0-0	0-0	0-0	1-1	100.0	+ 1.88
J A R Toller	1-1	0-0	1-1	0-0	0-0	100.0	+ 0.08
E Weymes	1-1	1-1	0-0	0-0	0-0	100.0	+ 1.75
G Wragg	1-1	0-0	1-1	0-0	0-0	100.0	+ 0.29
C Tinkler	1-1	0-0	0-0	0-0	1-1	100.0	+ 4.00
R Earnshaw	1-1	0-0	0-0	0-0	1-1	100.0	+ 4.00
M R Channon	1-1	0-0	1-1	0-0	0-0	100.0	+ 0.53
B Beasley	1-1	0-0	1-1	0-0	0-0	100.0	+ 0.73

TRAINERS' FAVOURITES AT CATTERICK 1990-94

	Total W-R	Non-handicaps 2-y-o	3-y-o+	Handicaps 2-y-o	3-y-o+	Per cent	£1 Level Stake
J Berry	16-35	7-15	6-11	3-5	0-4	45.7	+ 2.15
B W Hills	11-25	1-3	10-19	0-1	0-2	44.0	+ 0.66
Mrs M Reveley	7-12	1-1	4-4	0-0	2-7	58.3	+ 4.77
Sir M Prescott	7-15	3-7	2-4	0-0	2-4	46.7	+ 1.46
T D Barron	7-17	3-4	0-4	1-1	3-8	41.2	+ 4.06
M H Easterby	7-28	1-10	3-6	1-2	2-10	25.0	- 11.56
J H M Gosden	6-7	1-1	5-6	0-0	0-0	85.7	+ 7.43
L M Cumani	6-8	0-0	5-7	0-0	1-1	75.0	+ 2.64
M Bell	5-8	1-2	3-4	0-0	1-2	62.5	+ 3.54
M R Stoute	5-11	1-2	4-8	0-0	0-1	45.5	- 0.09
J R Fanshawe	4-6	2-3	2-2	0-0	0-1	66.7	+ 1.80
H R A Cecil	4-8	0-1	4-5	0-0	0-2	50.0	- 0.91
S G Norton	4-9	1-1	1-3	0-1	2-4	44.4	+ 0.86
W A O'Gorman	3-3	3-3	0-0	0-0	0-0	100.0	+ 2.30
M J Camacho	3-4	1-1	1-1	1-1	0-1	75.0	+ 6.41
Miss S E Hall	3-5	1-2	2-3	0-0	0-0	60.0	+ 4.12
M H Tompkins	3-5	2-3	1-1	0-0	0-1	60.0	+ 0.40
M P Naughton	3-6	0-0	0-0	0-0	3-6	50.0	+ 3.55
M Johnston	3-7	1-2	1-1	0-0	1-4	42.9	+ 1.30
M R Channon	3-7	0-3	0-0	0-0	3-4	42.9	+ 7.63
P F I Cole	3-9	2-7	1-2	0-0	0-0	33.3	- 4.09
M W Easterby	3-9	2-4	1-2	0-0	0-3	33.3	- 1.64
B Palling	2-2	0-0	2-2	0-0	0-0	100.0	+ 3.20
J Etherington	2-3	0-0	1-2	0-0	1-1	66.7	+ 3.13

TRAINERS' FAVOURITES AT CHEPSTOW 1990-94

	Total W-R	Non-handicaps 2-y-o	3-y-o+	Handicaps 2-y-o	3-y-o+	Per cent	£1 Level Stake
L M Cumani	8-11	0-0	6-7	1-1	1-3	72.7	+ 7.51
R Hannon	7-15	2-4	1-2	1-2	3-7	46.7	+ 8.26
H R A Cecil	6-13	0-2	4-8	0-0	2-3	46.2	- 0.94
J Berry	5-7	2-4	3-3	0-0	0-0	71.4	+ 3.84
B W Hills	5-9	0-1	5-7	0-1	0-0	55.6	+ 3.55
G Harwood	4-8	0-2	3-3	0-0	1-3	50.0	+ 1.90
R J Hodges	4-10	0-1	0-0	0-0	4-9	40.0	+ 4.46
J L Dunlop	4-14	0-3	3-4	0-0	1-7	28.6	- 3.57
M R Stoute	3-8	3-3	0-4	0-0	0-1	37.5	+ 0.87
W R Hern	2-3	0-0	2-3	0-0	0-0	66.7	+ 0.40
H Thomson Jones	2-3	0-0	2-3	0-0	0-0	66.7	+ 0.90
P T Walwyn	2-3	0-0	2-2	0-1	0-0	66.7	+ 0.23
M A Jarvis	2-4	1-2	1-2	0-0	0-0	50.0	+ 3.00
W Jarvis	2-4	0-0	0-2	0-0	2-2	50.0	+ 2.25
J R Fanshawe	2-4	1-1	1-2	0-0	0-1	50.0	+ 2.00
R Hollinshead	2-5	0-0	0-1	0-1	2-3	40.0	+ 6.50
J H M Gosden	2-5	0-1	2-3	0-0	0-1	40.0	- 1.36
B R Millman	2-5	1-2	0-0	0-0	1-3	40.0	+ 2.00
R Akehurst	2-7	0-0	0-1	0-0	2-6	28.6	- 1.12
M C Pipe	2-7	0-0	0-2	0-0	2-5	28.6	- 1.37
R Charlton	2-7	0-3	1-3	0-0	1-1	28.6	- 0.99
Sir M Prescott	2-8	0-1	2-5	0-0	0-2	25.0	- 5.03
I A Balding	2-9	0-1	2-3	0-0	0-5	22.2	- 3.75
G Lewis	2-9	0-2	2-4	0-1	0-2	22.2	- 5.63

TRAINERS' FAVOURITES AT CHESTER 1990-94

	Total W-R	Non-handicaps 2-y-o	3-y-o+	Handicaps 2-y-o	3-y-o+	Per cent	£1 Level Stake
R Hannon	11-24	6-12	1-3	2-5	2-4	45.8	+ 4.23
B W Hills	11-25	2-4	6-11	0-0	3-10	44.0	+ 6.03
H R A Cecil	10-19	3-6	7-12	0-0	0-1	52.6	+ 1.99
J H M Gosden	9-20	3-4	4-8	0-0	2-8	45.0	+ 7.49
P F I Cole	8-14	6-11	2-2	0-0	0-1	57.1	+ 2.08
M R Stoute	8-15	4-4	3-7	0-0	1-4	53.3	+ 1.96
J Berry	5-21	1-5	0-2	1-1	3-13	23.8	- 0.75
A Bailey	4-11	0-0	1-1	0-2	3-8	36.4	+ 1.92
G Wragg	3-6	0-1	3-4	0-1	0-0	50.0	+ 3.38
L M Cumani	2-2	0-0	2-2	0-0	0-0	100.0	+ 2.50
J W Hills	2-3	0-0	1-1	0-0	1-2	66.7	+ 1.30
P Chapple-Hyam	2-3	1-1	1-1	0-0	0-1	66.7	+ 1.85
M J Camacho	2-4	0-0	0-1	0-0	2-3	50.0	+ 5.88
M H Easterby	2-5	1-2	1-1	0-1	0-1	40.0	+ 2.25
J W Watts	2-5	1-2	0-0	0-0	1-3	40.0	+ 8.00
C E Brittain	2-7	2-4	0-0	0-0	0-3	28.6	- 2.80
F H Lee	2-8	0-0	0-1	0-0	2-7	25.0	+ 1.00
L G Cottrell	1-1	0-0	0-0	0-0	1-1	100.0	+ 3.50
R M Whitaker	1-1	0-0	0-0	0-0	1-1	100.0	+ 3.00
E J Alston	1-1	0-0	0-0	0-0	1-1	100.0	+ 6.00
J W Payne	1-1	0-0	1-1	0-0	0-0	100.0	+ 2.00
B R Millman	1-1	0-0	0-0	0-0	1-1	100.0	+ 3.33
J R Fanshawe	1-1	0-0	0-0	0-0	1-1	100.0	+ 1.50
Mrs V Aconley	1-1	0-0	0-0	0-0	1-1	100.0	+ 3.00

TRAINERS' FAVOURITES AT DONCASTER 1990-94

	Total W-R	Non-handicaps 2-y-o	3-y-o+	Handicaps 2-y-o	3-y-o+	Per cent	£1 Level Stake
H R A Cecil	18-42	7-15	10-20	0-0	1-7	42.9	+ 0.36
J H M Gosden	17-44	4-11	8-19	0-0	5-14	38.6	- 0.73
B W Hills	16-29	3-7	10-17	0-0	3-5	55.2	+ 15.45
R Hannon	12-33	6-15	3-7	0-2	3-9	36.4	+ 2.00
L M Cumani	8-23	0-2	5-16	0-0	3-5	34.8	- 0.68
R W Armstrong	7-10	3-3	3-3	0-0	1-4	70.0	+ 9.34
I A Balding	6-9	0-0	2-3	0-0	4-6	66.7	+ 8.79
M R Stoute	6-27	3-10	1-10	1-3	1-4	22.2	- 2.27
M Johnston	5-13	0-0	1-3	0-1	4-9	38.5	+ 10.25
J Berry	5-19	4-14	0-1	0-0	1-4	26.3	- 2.23
P Chapple-Hyam	4-8	4-7	0-0	0-1	0-0	50.0	+ 1.36
Mrs M Reveley	4-17	0-1	1-3	0-2	3-11	23.5	- 1.50
J L Dunlop	4-19	1-8	0-4	1-1	2-6	21.1	- 4.82
Mrs J Ramsden	4-28	0-2	1-2	1-6	2-18	14.3	- 8.75
M A Jarvis	3-6	2-2	1-1	0-1	0-2	50.0	+ 1.80
D R C Elsworth	3-8	1-1	0-3	0-0	2-4	37.5	+ 8.50
G Wragg	3-8	2-4	1-2	0-0	0-2	37.5	+ 0.08
R Hollinshead	3-9	0-1	2-5	0-1	1-2	33.3	- 2.79
A C Stewart	3-9	0-0	1-3	0-1	2-5	33.3	+ 1.00
R Akehurst	3-10	0-0	0-1	0-0	3-9	30.0	+ 2.75
J W Watts	3-11	1-2	0-1	0-3	2-5	27.3	- 1.75
M H Easterby	3-14	1-4	0-0	0-0	2-10	21.4	- 0.75
J G FitzGerald	2-4	0-0	2-3	0-0	0-1	50.0	+ 2.50
M McCormack	2-4	0-0	0-2	0-0	2-2	50.0	+ 5.00

TRAINERS' FAVOURITES AT EDINBURGH 1990-94

	Total W-R	Non-handicaps 2-y-o	3-y-o+	Handicaps 2-y-o	3-y-o+	Per cent	£1 Level Stake
J Berry	21-42	15-26	4-6	0-0	2-10	50.0	+ 6.17
M Johnston	10-18	2-5	3-3	1-1	4-9	55.6	+ 8.51
M H Easterby	7-14	3-5	0-1	0-1	4-7	50.0	+ 5.83
M H Tompkins	6-9	2-3	2-3	0-0	2-3	66.7	+ 6.15
J H M Gosden	6-11	1-3	4-5	0-0	1-3	54.5	+ 4.78
Sir M Prescott	6-17	2-5	2-6	0-0	2-6	35.3	- 0.46
Mrs M Reveley	5-20	2-2	2-4	0-0	1-14	25.0	- 11.41
M J Camacho	4-5	0-0	2-2	0-0	2-3	80.0	+ 6.48
B W Hills	4-5	0-0	3-3	0-0	1-2	80.0	+ 4.61
T D Barron	4-6	1-2	1-1	0-0	2-3	66.7	+ 7.73
P C Haslam	4-9	1-2	1-2	1-1	1-4	44.4	+ 1.45
M P Naughton	4-10	0-1	0-1	0-0	4-8	40.0	+ 1.88
J L Spearing	4-12	0-1	0-0	0-0	4-11	33.3	+ 3.88
M Bell	3-4	1-2	0-0	0-0	2-2	75.0	+ 3.23
L M Cumani	3-5	0-0	2-3	0-0	1-2	60.0	+ 0.62
Denys Smith	3-5	0-0	0-0	0-0	3-5	60.0	+ 3.26
N Tinkler	3-5	1-1	0-2	0-0	2-2	60.0	+ 8.10
R Hannon	2-2	2-2	0-0	0-0	0-0	100.0	+ 3.35
H Thomson Jones	2-2	0-0	2-2	0-0	0-0	100.0	+ 1.80
A N Lee	2-2	0-0	1-1	0-0	1-1	100.0	+ 3.13
J R Fanshawe	2-2	0-0	2-2	0-0	0-0	100.0	+ 2.63
C W C Elsey	2-3	0-0	2-2	0-0	0-1	66.7	+ 2.10
J Etherington	2-3	0-0	2-3	0-0	0-0	66.7	0.00
E Weymes	2-3	0-0	1-1	0-0	1-2	66.7	+ 0.80

TRAINERS' FAVOURITES AT EPSOM 1990-94

	Total W-R	Non-handicaps 2-y-o	3-y-o+	Handicaps 2-y-o	3-y-o+	Per cent	£1 Level Stake
J Berry	5-9	2-4	2-2	0-0	1-3	55.6	+ 1.45
J L Dunlop	5-10	0-1	4-6	1-1	0-2	50.0	+ 8.63
R Hannon	5-22	2-5	1-5	0-0	2-12	22.7	- 2.40
M R Stoute	4-8	0-0	3-5	0-0	1-3	50.0	+ 3.75
G Lewis	4-12	1-1	3-4	0-0	0-7	33.3	- 0.79
Lord Huntingdon	3-5	2-2	0-1	0-0	1-2	60.0	+ 3.00
D R C Elsworth	3-10	0-1	3-6	0-0	0-3	30.0	- 2.14
P Chapple-Hyam	2-3	0-0	2-3	0-0	0-0	66.7	+ 2.25
Miss B Sanders	2-4	0-0	0-0	0-0	2-4	50.0	+ 6.00
A C Stewart	2-5	0-0	2-3	0-0	0-2	40.0	- 1.29
J H M Gosden	2-5	0-0	2-4	0-0	0-1	40.0	- 0.50
J W Hills	2-6	1-1	1-1	0-0	0-4	33.3	- 0.20
H R A Cecil	2-8	0-1	1-6	0-0	1-1	25.0	- 1.67
R Akehurst	2-10	0-0	1-1	0-0	1-9	20.0	- 3.62
B Hanbury	1-1	0-0	0-0	0-0	1-1	100.0	+ 1.10
M A Jarvis	1-1	0-0	0-0	0-0	1-1	100.0	+ 3.50
D Morley	1-1	0-0	0-0	0-0	1-1	100.0	+ 3.00
M J Ryan	1-1	0-0	0-0	0-0	1-1	100.0	+ 5.00
F H Lee	1-1	0-0	0-0	0-0	1-1	100.0	+ 1.50
D Burchell	1-1	0-0	1-1	0-0	0-0	100.0	+ 0.80
R J O'Sullivan	1-1	0-0	0-0	0-0	1-1	100.0	+ 4.50
J White	1-1	0-0	0-0	0-0	1-1	100.0	+ 4.50
P A Kelleway	1-2	1-1	0-1	0-0	0-0	50.0	+ 0.63
M Bell	1-2	1-2	0-0	0-0	0-0	50.0	+ 1.75

TRAINERS' FAVOURITES AT FOLKESTONE 1990-94

	Total W-R	Non-handicaps 2-y-o	3-y-o+	Handicaps 2-y-o	3-y-o+	Per cent	£1 Level Stake
G Harwood	13-27	4-9	9-14	0-0	0-4	48.1	- 2.60
R Hannon	11-34	5-16	4-12	0-1	2-5	32.4	- 7.15
J Berry	8-16	4-10	4-4	0-2	0-0	50.0	+ 3.54
R Akehurst	8-20	0-0	3-6	0-0	5-14	40.0	+ 5.26
N A Callaghan	6-14	2-5	2-6	1-1	1-2	42.9	+ 2.63
J Pearce	5-11	0-0	2-3	0-0	3-8	45.5	+ 9.63
J L Dunlop	5-12	1-3	3-3	1-1	0-5	41.7	- 0.01
P F I Cole	5-13	1-2	3-3	1-1	0-7	38.5	+ 0.28
J H M Gosden	4-6	0-0	4-6	0-0	0-0	66.7	+ 1.86
D R C Elsworth	4-7	1-2	2-4	1-1	0-0	57.1	+ 4.43
P T Walwyn	4-8	0-2	4-6	0-0	0-0	50.0	- 0.32
Sir M Prescott	4-10	2-3	1-1	0-1	1-5	40.0	+ 2.50
W Jarvis	3-3	0-0	1-1	0-0	2-2	100.0	+ 6.88
Mrs L Piggott	3-5	0-1	2-2	0-0	1-2	60.0	+ 6.50
H R A Cecil	3-6	1-2	2-4	0-0	0-0	50.0	- 0.80
M H Tompkins	3-6	2-2	0-2	0-0	1-2	50.0	+ 0.98
W J Haggas	3-6	1-3	0-1	0-0	2-2	50.0	+ 2.53
L M Cumani	3-8	0-1	3-6	0-0	0-1	37.5	+ 1.35
R J Hodges	3-9	0-0	2-3	0-0	1-6	33.3	+ 2.25
M R Channon	3-11	1-5	0-1	1-1	1-4	27.3	- 0.75
A Bailey	2-2	0-0	0-0	1-1	1-1	100.0	+ 5.25
J R Fanshawe	2-2	1-1	0-0	0-0	1-1	100.0	+ 4.91
T G Mills	2-2	1-1	1-1	0-0	0-0	100.0	+ 4.38
G L Moore	2-2	0-0	1-1	0-0	1-1	100.0	+ 4.25

TRAINERS' FAVOURITES AT GOODWOOD 1990-94

	Total W-R	Non-handicaps 2-y-o	3-y-o+	Handicaps 2-y-o	3-y-o+	Per cent	£1 Level Stake
J H M Gosden	14-37	5-8	3-13	1-2	5-14	37.8	+ 2.35
I A Balding	12-23	4-7	5-10	0-1	3-5	52.2	+ 15.09
J L Dunlop	12-31	5-10	5-9	1-3	1-9	38.7	- 5.24
H R A Cecil	11-25	7-8	4-12	0-1	0-4	44.0	+ 2.35
M R Stoute	8-23	2-4	5-13	0-0	1-6	34.8	+ 0.19
R Hannon	8-41	4-12	4-12	0-3	0-14	19.5	- 22.79
L M Cumani	7-15	0-0	4-10	0-0	3-5	46.7	+ 10.52
R Charlton	6-16	1-4	4-9	0-0	1-3	37.5	+ 2.08
R Akehurst	6-19	0-0	2-2	0-0	4-17	31.6	+ 1.38
J Berry	6-20	4-7	1-3	1-8	0-2	30.0	- 0.59
G Lewis	5-7	0-0	1-2	2-2	2-3	71.4	+ 11.01
P F I Cole	5-14	4-9	1-3	0-0	0-2	35.7	- 4.55
D R C Elsworth	5-16	2-4	1-4	0-0	2-8	31.3	- 2.18
M C Pipe	3-4	0-0	2-3	0-0	1-1	75.0	+ 8.25
Lord Huntingdon	3-7	1-1	2-2	0-0	0-4	42.9	+ 2.88
L J Holt	3-9	0-0	1-1	0-0	2-8	33.3	+ 5.25
Lady Herries	3-10	1-2	0-1	0-0	2-7	30.0	+ 0.50
P Chapple-Hyam	3-10	3-7	0-1	0-0	0-2	30.0	- 3.40
D A Wilson	3-11	0-0	0-0	0-0	3-11	27.3	- 0.92
G Harwood	3-23	2-9	1-10	0-0	0-4	13.0	- 15.75
W A O'Gorman	2-2	2-2	0-0	0-0	0-0	100.0	+ 2.44
J M P Eustace	2-2	1-1	0-0	0-0	1-1	100.0	+ 9.00
T J Naughton	2-4	0-1	0-0	0-0	2-3	50.0	+ 5.25
A C Stewart	2-5	1-1	0-2	0-0	1-2	40.0	+ 4.00

TRAINERS' FAVOURITES AT HAMILTON 1990-94

	Total W-R	Non-handicaps 2-y-o	3-y-o+	Handicaps 2-y-o	3-y-o+	Per cent	£1 Level Stake
J Berry	32-69	14-31	12-19	1-4	5-15	46.4	+ 10.25
Mrs M Reveley	16-41	0-3	7-12	0-0	9-26	39.0	- 0.64
M H Tompkins	9-22	3-4	4-9	0-1	2-8	40.9	- 2.90
M Johnston	9-26	4-6	1-5	0-0	4-15	34.6	- 6.57
P C Haslam	8-12	0-0	1-3	0-0	7-9	66.7	+ 11.75
Sir M Prescott	8-13	2-3	2-3	0-0	4-7	61.5	+ 6.54
M Bell	8-15	4-6	3-6	0-1	1-2	53.3	+ 2.46
Mrs J Ramsden	6-18	0-4	1-2	0-1	5-11	33.3	- 1.12
J Etherington	4-5	1-1	3-4	0-0	0-0	80.0	+ 6.65
B Hanbury	4-6	0-0	2-3	1-1	1-2	66.7	+ 7.23
A C Stewart	4-6	0-0	4-4	0-0	0-2	66.7	+ 1.55
C W Thornton	4-9	0-0	2-2	0-0	2-7	44.4	+ 2.00
S G Norton	4-12	0-1	2-4	0-0	2-7	33.3	+ 2.63
C Tinkler	4-14	1-3	1-5	0-1	2-5	28.6	- 2.14
S E Kettlewell	3-3	0-0	1-1	0-0	2-2	100.0	+ 6.66
W Bentley	3-4	0-0	3-3	0-0	0-1	75.0	+ 6.88
P J Makin	3-4	0-1	3-3	0-0	0-0	75.0	+ 3.83
Miss L A Perratt	3-11	1-1	0-0	0-1	2-9	27.3	- 1.75
I A Balding	2-2	0-0	1-1	0-0	1-1	100.0	+ 8.25
P Calver	2-2	0-0	1-1	0-0	1-1	100.0	+ 4.10
L M Cumani	2-2	0-0	0-0	0-0	2-2	100.0	+ 2.16
P S Felgate	2-2	2-2	0-0	0-0	0-0	100.0	+ 2.08
J W Watts	2-2	2-2	0-0	0-0	0-0	100.0	+ 2.67
M D Hammond	2-2	0-0	1-1	0-0	1-1	100.0	+ 4.13

TRAINERS' FAVOURITES AT HAYDOCK 1990-94

	Total W-R	Non-handicaps 2-y-o	3-y-o+	Handicaps 2-y-o	3-y-o+	Per cent	£1 Level Stake
J H M Gosden	11-23	2-4	5-8	0-0	4-11	47.8	+ 8.49
H R A Cecil	10-26	2-5	7-14	0-0	1-7	38.5	- 2.13
B W Hills	9-22	4-5	5-11	0-0	0-6	40.9	- 2.52
J L Dunlop	9-28	2-9	3-8	1-1	3-10	32.1	- 2.42
M H Tompkins	7-16	2-2	2-5	0-0	3-9	43.8	+ 4.23
M R Stoute	7-27	3-8	4-12	0-1	0-6	25.9	- 12.23
R Charlton	6-18	1-1	3-9	0-0	2-8	33.3	- 2.69
L M Cumani	6-22	1-3	2-11	0-0	3-8	27.3	- 6.04
R Hannon	5-22	4-6	0-8	0-0	1-8	22.7	- 8.07
Mrs J Ramsden	5-26	1-2	1-2	0-2	3-20	19.2	- 11.75
R Boss	4-6	1-1	1-1	1-1	1-3	66.7	+ 10.25
G Harwood	4-8	1-1	1-5	0-0	2-2	50.0	+ 9.38
M H Easterby	4-19	4-7	0-1	0-0	0-11	21.1	- 8.50
J Berry	4-23	1-5	1-5	0-4	2-9	17.4	- 4.00
G Wragg	3-5	1-1	1-3	0-0	1-1	60.0	+ 2.55
W Jarvis	3-5	0-0	1-2	0-1	2-2	60.0	+ 5.13
P T Walwyn	3-6	1-2	1-2	0-0	1-2	50.0	+ 2.75
H Thomson Jones	3-7	3-6	0-0	0-0	0-1	42.9	- 1.26
F H Lee	3-14	0-1	0-0	1-1	2-12	21.4	- 2.50
R J R Williams	2-2	1-1	0-0	0-0	1-1	100.0	+ 2.55
W J Haggas	2-3	0-0	2-3	0-0	0-0	66.7	+ 1.25
P Chapple-Hyam	2-3	2-3	0-0	0-0	0-0	66.7	+ 2.05
Bob Jones	2-3	0-0	2-3	0-0	0-0	66.7	+ 0.53
A C Stewart	2-4	0-0	2-2	0-0	0-2	50.0	+ 1.50

TRAINERS' FAVOURITES AT KEMPTON 1990-94

	Total W-R	Non-handicaps 2-y-o	Non-handicaps 3-y-o+	Handicaps 2-y-o	Handicaps 3-y-o+	Per cent	£1 Level Stake
R Hannon	10-39	3-10	2-7	0-3	5-19	25.6	− 4.92
M R Stoute	8-18	4-5	2-7	1-1	1-5	44.4	+ 6.18
J H M Gosden	8-26	0-1	7-19	0-1	1-5	30.8	− 0.67
R Charlton	7-22	4-5	3-12	0-0	0-5	31.8	− 1.02
P F I Cole	6-18	3-9	2-7	1-1	0-1	33.3	− 1.65
H Thomson Jones	4-7	2-2	1-3	0-0	1-2	57.1	+ 5.30
B W Hills	4-10	1-3	2-5	0-0	1-2	40.0	+ 4.00
D R C Elsworth	4-15	1-3	3-10	0-0	0-2	26.7	− 2.26
H R A Cecil	4-16	0-2	4-12	0-0	0-2	25.0	− 6.95
Mrs J Cecil	3-5	0-0	2-2	0-0	1-3	60.0	+ 4.55
C E Brittain	3-7	0-0	2-4	0-0	1-3	42.9	+ 5.21
B Hanbury	3-7	1-1	2-3	0-0	0-3	42.9	+ 1.48
P T Walwyn	3-9	1-3	2-3	0-0	0-3	33.3	+ 2.38
W R Hern	3-10	0-3	2-4	0-0	1-3	30.0	− 0.52
G Lewis	3-10	1-2	0-0	0-2	2-6	30.0	+ 2.13
G Harwood	3-11	0-1	2-4	1-1	0-5	27.3	− 1.46
R Akehurst	3-14	0-0	0-1	0-1	3-12	21.4	+ 0.50
L M Cumani	3-14	1-1	2-10	0-0	0-3	21.4	− 5.87
J L Dunlop	3-14	1-2	0-5	0-0	2-7	21.4	+ 0.73
R F J Houghton	2-2	0-0	1-1	0-0	1-1	100.0	+ 2.00
M Bell	2-4	1-1	0-0	0-0	1-3	50.0	+ 1.83
L J Holt	2-5	0-0	1-1	0-0	1-4	40.0	+ 2.08
J R Fanshawe	2-5	1-2	0-0	0-1	1-2	40.0	+ 1.83
Sir M Prescott	2-6	0-0	1-2	0-1	1-3	33.3	+ 0.60

TRAINERS' FAVOURITES AT LEICESTER 1990-94

	Total W-R	Non-handicaps 2-y-o	Non-handicaps 3-y-o+	Handicaps 2-y-o	Handicaps 3-y-o+	Per cent	£1 Level Stake
H R A Cecil	16-31	6-12	10-17	0-0	0-2	51.6	+ 2.22
M R Stoute	12-31	8-16	4-13	0-0	0-2	38.7	− 8.04
J H M Gosden	11-25	6-10	3-11	0-0	2-4	44.0	− 0.90
J L Dunlop	8-19	3-6	3-8	1-2	1-3	42.1	+ 2.60
R Hannon	8-22	4-10	2-5	2-3	0-4	36.4	+ 7.00
H Thomson Jones	5-7	3-3	1-3	0-0	1-1	71.4	+ 4.26
J Berry	5-15	2-8	2-3	1-1	0-3	33.3	− 1.39
P F I Cole	5-15	1-5	3-7	1-2	0-1	33.3	− 3.55
N A Callaghan	4-5	1-1	2-2	0-0	1-2	80.0	+ 10.60
R Charlton	4-9	1-1	2-6	0-0	1-2	44.4	+ 0.35
M J Ryan	4-11	0-0	1-2	0-0	3-9	36.4	+ 3.08
Mrs J Cecil	3-4	2-2	1-1	0-0	0-1	75.0	+ 4.13
R F J Houghton	3-5	0-1	3-3	0-0	0-1	60.0	+ 2.55
D R Loder	3-5	2-4	1-1	0-0	0-0	60.0	+ 1.83
M C Pipe	3-6	0-0	1-1	0-0	2-5	50.0	+ 7.63
Sir M Prescott	3-6	2-2	1-4	0-0	0-0	50.0	− 0.15
M Johnston	3-6	1-3	1-2	0-0	1-1	50.0	+ 4.00
L M Cumani	3-10	3-6	0-3	0-0	0-1	30.0	− 1.17
G Harwood	3-12	0-1	3-10	0-0	0-1	25.0	− 4.02
P T Walwyn	2-2	1-1	1-1	0-0	0-0	100.0	+ 4.50
C F Wall	2-2	0-0	1-1	0-0	1-1	100.0	+ 8.00
P Chapple-Hyam	2-2	2-2	0-0	0-0	0-0	100.0	+ 1.17
M Williams	2-2	2-2	0-0	0-0	0-0	100.0	+ 3.40
W A O'Gorman	2-3	0-1	1-1	1-1	0-0	66.7	+ 3.83

TRAINERS' FAVOURITES AT LINGFIELD (TURF) 1990-94

	Total W-R	Non-handicaps 2-y-o	Non-handicaps 3-y-o+	Handicaps 2-y-o	Handicaps 3-y-o+	Per cent	£1 Level Stake
R Hannon	12-32	5-11	5-13	0-0	2-8	37.5	+ 0.63
M R Stoute	10-21	4-6	6-11	0-0	0-4	47.6	+ 0.02
G Harwood	10-23	2-7	4-8	0-0	4-8	43.5	+ 8.90
J H M Gosden	9-21	3-6	6-12	0-0	0-3	42.9	- 3.99
H R A Cecil	8-18	2-4	5-11	0-0	1-3	44.4	- 4.27
B W Hills	6-8	1-2	2-2	1-1	2-3	75.0	+ 9.36
L M Cumani	6-14	1-1	5-13	0-0	0-0	42.9	+ 0.30
P F I Cole	6-18	2-7	2-8	0-0	2-3	33.3	- 5.05
R Akehurst	6-25	0-2	1-3	0-0	5-20	24.0	- 4.67
I A Balding	5-10	0-0	4-6	0-0	1-4	50.0	+ 4.28
G Lewis	5-13	2-5	1-1	0-0	2-7	38.5	+ 2.88
C E Brittain	4-7	0-3	3-3	0-0	1-1	57.1	+ 4.35
Sir M Prescott	4-10	0-2	3-5	0-0	1-3	40.0	- 0.88
J Berry	4-16	1-7	2-3	0-0	1-6	25.0	- 4.06
J L Dunlop	4-17	1-3	1-6	0-0	2-8	23.5	- 7.62
Pat Mitchell	3-5	0-0	0-0	0-0	3-5	60.0	+ 7.58
Lord Huntingdon	3-12	1-5	0-3	1-1	1-3	25.0	- 1.29
W Jarvis	2-3	1-2	0-0	0-0	1-1	66.7	+ 3.75
J W Payne	2-3	1-1	0-0	0-0	1-2	66.7	+ 3.62
P Chapple-Hyam	2-3	0-1	2-2	0-0	0-0	66.7	+ 2.63
R W Armstrong	2-4	0-0	0-0	0-0	2-4	50.0	+ 2.41
N A Callaghan	2-4	1-2	0-0	0-0	1-2	50.0	+ 2.38
H Candy	2-4	0-1	1-2	0-0	1-1	50.0	+ 4.50
C N Williams	2-4	2-2	0-0	0-0	0-2	50.0	+ 3.75

TRAINERS' FAVOURITES AT LINGFIELD (AW) 1990-94

	Total W-R	Non-handicaps 2-y-o	Non-handicaps 3-y-o+	Handicaps 2-y-o	Handicaps 3-y-o+	Per cent	£1 Level Stake
B W Hills	18-40	1-7	9-18	0-0	8-15	45.0	- 4.47
P F I Cole	16-33	4-12	8-12	1-2	3-7	48.5	+ 0.71
W A O'Gorman	13-51	1-1	8-25	1-3	3-22	25.5	- 19.01
Sir M Prescott	12-31	3-5	4-14	0-0	5-12	38.7	- 7.93
R J O'Sullivan	12-35	0-0	2-3	0-0	10-32	34.3	+ 4.48
M Johnston	12-40	1-2	5-9	0-1	6-28	30.0	- 4.70
Lord Huntingdon	11-29	0-1	5-13	0-1	6-14	37.9	+ 1.43
J Berry	10-21	2-5	3-6	0-0	5-10	47.6	+ 7.91
W R Muir	6-14	0-0	5-11	0-0	1-3	42.9	+ 1.53
M J Ryan	6-15	0-0	1-3	0-0	5-12	40.0	+ 3.43
C P Wildman	6-15	0-0	1-2	0-0	5-13	40.0	+ 5.88
R Hollinshead	6-16	0-0	6-12	0-0	0-4	37.5	- 5.32
R Hannon	6-23	2-8	3-8	0-1	1-6	26.1	- 4.84
C C Elsey	6-24	1-1	1-4	0-0	4-19	25.0	- 6.44
D R C Elsworth	5-6	3-3	1-1	0-0	1-2	83.3	+ 6.05
C A Cyzer	5-10	0-0	1-2	0-0	4-8	50.0	+ 5.73
Dr J D Scargill	5-10	1-1	0-2	0-0	4-7	50.0	+ 7.73
J H M Gosden	5-10	2-2	0-2	1-2	2-4	50.0	+ 3.65
J Pearce	5-11	0-0	4-5	0-0	1-6	45.5	+ 7.88
D Murray Smith	5-15	1-1	2-7	0-0	2-7	33.3	+ 0.48
R Akehurst	5-20	0-0	1-7	0-0	4-13	25.0	- 6.77
P W Harris	4-5	0-0	1-1	0-0	3-4	80.0	+ 7.38
M Fetherston-Godley	4-8	2-3	1-2	0-0	1-3	50.0	+ 4.58
K O C-Brown	4-11	0-0	0-1	0-0	4-10	36.4	+ 8.75

TRAINERS' FAVOURITES AT NEWBURY 1990-94

	Total W-R	Non-handicaps 2-y-o	Non-handicaps 3-y-o+	Handicaps 2-y-o	Handicaps 3-y-o+	Per cent	£1 Level Stake
P Chapple-Hyam	21-31	16-22	4-7	1-1	0-1	67.7	+ 18.85
R Hannon	17-47	6-14	6-10	3-9	2-14	36.2	+ 1.93
J H M Gosden	14-38	3-7	6-22	0-0	5-9	36.8	+ 8.91
H R A Cecil	13-39	3-10	10-24	0-0	0-5	33.3	- 8.44
L M Cumani	11-28	3-7	4-7	0-0	4-14	39.3	+ 2.79
J L Dunlop	6-13	0-0	3-5	1-1	2-7	46.2	+ 6.31
M R Stoute	6-20	0-1	4-13	0-1	2-5	30.0	+ 1.42
R Charlton	6-25	1-5	3-11	0-0	2-9	24.0	- 8.25
W R Hern	4-8	4-5	0-2	0-0	0-1	50.0	- 0.54
Lord Huntingdon	4-12	0-0	0-3	1-1	3-8	33.3	+ 12.00
D R C Elsworth	4-13	1-5	0-3	0-0	3-5	30.8	+ 5.50
P F I Cole	4-15	2-9	2-4	0-1	0-1	26.7	- 6.04
J Berry	3-6	3-5	0-0	0-0	0-1	50.0	+ 1.33
B W Hills	3-15	2-5	0-4	0-0	1-6	20.0	- 4.90
P T Walwyn	3-15	2-4	0-5	0-0	1-6	20.0	- 3.75
C W C Elsey	2-2	0-0	2-2	0-0	0-0	100.0	+ 6.00
B Hanbury	2-3	0-0	1-1	0-0	1-2	66.7	+ 2.16
M H Easterby	2-4	0-0	0-0	0-0	2-4	50.0	+ 4.83
Lady Herries	2-4	0-0	0-0	0-0	2-4	50.0	+ 5.00
G Lewis	2-5	1-1	0-0	0-2	1-2	40.0	+ 2.67
M R Channon	2-5	1-2	0-0	1-1	0-2	40.0	+ 4.50
I A Balding	2-9	1-4	0-1	0-0	1-4	22.2	- 0.38
R Akehurst	2-14	0-0	0-0	0-0	2-14	14.3	- 6.50
D Marks	1-1	0-0	0-0	0-0	1-1	100.0	+ 5.50

TRAINERS' FAVOURITES AT NEWCASTLE 1990-94

	Total W-R	Non-handicaps 2-y-o	Non-handicaps 3-y-o+	Handicaps 2-y-o	Handicaps 3-y-o+	Per cent	£1 Level Stake
M R Stoute	12-23	6-9	4-8	0-0	2-6	52.2	- 4.94
Mrs M Reveley	12-25	1-3	1-1	1-1	9-20	48.0	+ 12.87
J Berry	11-27	7-13	3-6	0-1	1-7	40.7	+ 1.09
H R A Cecil	10-16	3-5	5-6	0-0	2-5	62.5	+ 1.43
J W Watts	7-13	2-3	2-4	0-0	3-6	53.8	+ 3.81
L M Cumani	5-8	1-1	3-5	0-0	1-2	62.5	+ 0.23
R Hannon	5-8	2-4	2-2	0-0	1-2	62.5	+ 5.42
M Bell	5-12	4-5	0-1	0-1	1-5	41.7	- 1.20
Mrs J Ramsden	5-19	1-2	0-1	0-3	4-13	26.3	- 4.54
M H Easterby	5-25	1-6	1-4	0-0	3-15	20.0	- 10.57
M J Camacho	4-5	0-0	1-2	0-0	3-3	80.0	+ 8.20
J H M Gosden	4-11	0-1	3-8	0-0	1-2	36.4	- 4.08
Sir M Prescott	4-12	0-1	1-4	0-2	3-5	33.3	- 1.48
M Johnston	3-6	1-2	1-1	0-0	1-3	50.0	- 0.24
B W Hills	3-8	2-2	1-4	0-0	0-2	37.5	+ 0.08
J L Dunlop	3-11	1-2	0-2	0-0	2-7	27.3	- 4.87
W R Hern	2-2	1-1	1-1	0-0	0-0	100.0	+ 1.57
P T Walwyn	2-2	0-0	2-2	0-0	0-0	100.0	+ 1.50
Miss S E Hall	2-3	1-2	0-0	1-1	0-0	66.7	+ 2.50
G Wragg	2-5	0-1	2-3	0-0	0-1	40.0	- 0.25
M R Channon	2-5	0-1	1-2	1-1	0-1	40.0	+ 2.75
D Morley	2-6	1-4	0-0	0-0	1-2	33.3	- 2.28
R Allan	1-1	0-0	0-0	0-0	1-1	100.0	+ 2.00
A Bailey	1-1	1-1	0-0	0-0	0-0	100.0	+ 1.75

TRAINERS' FAVOURITES AT NEWMARKET (ROWLEY) 1990-94

	Total W-R	Non-handicaps 2-y-o	3-y-o+	Handicaps 2-y-o	3-y-o+	Per cent	£1 Level Stake
H R A Cecil	22-65	6-19	15-40	0-0	1-6	33.8	- 17.12
L M Cumani	14-37	5-11	8-14	0-2	1-10	37.8	- 4.34
J H M Gosden	14-61	1-11	9-29	0-2	4-19	23.0	- 13.95
B W Hills	13-33	2-6	5-8	0-0	6-19	39.4	+ 11.48
M R Stoute	10-30	3-7	7-19	0-2	0-2	33.3	- 4.54
R Hannon	9-29	6-13	2-7	1-3	0-6	31.0	- 2.61
J L Dunlop	7-20	2-3	4-11	0-0	1-6	35.0	- 0.48
A Fabre (Fra)	5-9	4-4	1-4	0-0	0-1	55.6	+ 3.62
P Chapple-Hyam	5-14	3-10	2-4	0-0	0-0	35.7	- 0.54
I A Balding	4-6	1-1	3-5	0-0	0-0	66.7	+ 7.71
P F I Cole	4-10	3-6	1-2	0-0	0-2	40.0	+ 0.63
J Berry	3-7	2-3	1-2	0-0	0-2	42.9	- 1.18
W R Hern	3-8	1-2	2-4	0-0	0-2	37.5	- 0.50
M Johnston	3-8	1-1	0-1	0-1	2-5	37.5	+ 8.50
Mrs J Ramsden	3-9	0-0	0-2	1-2	2-5	33.3	+ 0.63
C E Brittain	3-10	0-0	2-3	1-1	0-6	30.0	+ 1.75
J R Fanshawe	3-10	1-1	1-4	0-1	1-4	30.0	+ 1.60
P T Walwyn	3-12	1-2	2-9	0-0	0-1	25.0	- 6.97
R Boss	2-3	2-3	0-0	0-0	0-0	66.7	+ 4.33
D R Loder	2-3	1-2	1-1	0-0	0-0	66.7	+ 5.10
M H Tompkins	2-4	1-1	0-0	0-0	1-3	50.0	+ 5.00
M A Jarvis	2-5	0-1	2-2	0-0	0-2	40.0	+ 0.80
J W Hills	2-5	0-0	1-1	0-1	1-3	40.0	+ 3.75
W Jarvis	2-6	2-3	0-2	0-0	0-1	33.3	- 0.55

TRAINERS' FAVOURITES AT NEWMARKET (JULY) 1990-94

	Total W-R	Non-handicaps 2-y-o	3-y-o+	Handicaps 2-y-o	3-y-o+	Per cent	£1 Level Stake
H R A Cecil	17-44	6-14	9-23	0-0	2-7	38.6	- 2.24
R Hannon	15-36	8-16	4-9	2-2	1-9	41.7	+ 12.79
L M Cumani	11-30	2-5	8-14	0-0	1-11	36.7	- 5.62
P F I Cole	9-14	4-6	3-5	1-2	1-1	64.3	+ 16.88
M R Stoute	9-20	7-13	2-6	0-0	0-1	45.0	- 0.89
J H M Gosden	9-30	2-4	5-14	0-1	2-11	30.0	- 9.10
R Charlton	6-11	3-5	3-6	0-0	0-0	54.5	+ 1.99
J L Dunlop	6-12	2-4	3-4	0-0	1-4	50.0	+ 3.20
G Wragg	5-13	2-5	1-3	0-0	2-5	38.5	+ 2.24
M A Jarvis	4-8	0-1	2-2	0-0	2-5	50.0	+ 8.00
D R Loder	3-3	3-3	0-0	0-0	0-0	100.0	+ 3.57
A C Stewart	3-5	0-0	2-2	0-0	1-3	60.0	+ 6.35
R Akehurst	3-8	1-1	1-1	0-0	1-6	37.5	+ 4.13
W R Hern	3-8	2-4	1-3	0-0	0-1	37.5	- 0.87
M Bell	3-10	0-1	2-3	1-2	0-4	30.0	- 2.77
C E Brittain	3-14	1-1	2-4	0-1	0-8	21.4	- 6.37
R Boss	2-2	0-0	1-1	0-0	1-1	100.0	+ 9.25
R W Armstrong	2-4	2-3	0-0	0-0	0-1	50.0	+ 1.38
D R C Elsworth	2-4	1-1	1-2	0-0	0-1	50.0	+ 2.75
P J Makin	2-4	0-0	1-2	0-0	1-2	50.0	+ 1.88
C A Cyzer	2-4	0-0	0-0	0-0	2-4	50.0	+ 4.00
T G Mills	2-4	0-0	0-1	0-0	2-3	50.0	+ 4.33
C A Horgan	2-5	0-0	0-0	0-0	2-5	40.0	+ 5.50
G Harwood	2-7	1-1	1-4	0-0	0-2	28.6	- 2.05

TRAINERS' FAVOURITES AT NOTTINGHAM 1990-94

	Total W-R	Non-handicaps 2-y-o	3-y-o+	Handicaps 2-y-o	3-y-o+	Per cent	£1 Level Stake
H R A Cecil	21-38	5-10	16-28	0-0	0-0	55.3	+ 3.17
J L Dunlop	13-30	4-11	5-8	0-0	4-11	43.3	+ 1.72
J H M Gosden	8-15	0-2	7-11	0-0	1-2	53.3	+ 8.76
P F I Cole	8-17	5-10	1-1	0-0	2-6	47.1	+ 7.99
R Hannon	8-20	2-6	4-7	1-2	1-5	40.0	+ 4.10
R Charlton	6-11	3-6	2-3	0-0	1-2	54.5	+ 2.70
J Berry	6-22	4-11	2-9	0-1	0-1	27.3	- 7.53
L M Cumani	5-11	1-3	3-7	0-0	1-1	45.5	+ 1.70
M Johnston	5-12	1-3	3-5	1-2	0-2	41.7	- 2.26
W Jarvis	4-7	2-3	2-2	0-1	0-1	57.1	+ 2.40
D Morley	4-9	2-4	0-0	0-0	2-5	44.4	+ 3.63
M J Camacho	3-3	0-0	1-1	0-0	2-2	100.0	+ 9.00
G Harwood	3-3	0-0	3-3	0-0	0-0	100.0	+ 2.41
R M Whitaker	3-4	0-0	1-1	0-0	2-3	75.0	+ 16.50
W J Haggas	3-4	1-1	1-1	0-1	1-1	75.0	+ 4.00
J Wharton	3-5	1-1	1-1	0-0	1-3	60.0	+ 6.50
J R Fanshawe	3-5	1-2	1-2	1-1	0-0	60.0	+ 2.36
C E Brittain	3-6	2-3	1-2	0-0	0-1	50.0	+ 1.61
B A McMahon	3-6	0-0	2-2	0-0	1-4	50.0	+ 6.50
Mrs J Cecil	3-7	2-5	0-1	0-0	1-1	42.9	+ 0.03
J W Hills	3-8	1-2	2-2	0-0	0-4	37.5	+ 3.25
Mrs M Reveley	3-9	0-2	1-1	0-1	2-5	33.3	+ 3.88
Mrs J Ramsden	3-17	0-0	0-3	0-2	3-12	17.6	- 7.75
A Bailey	2-2	0-0	0-0	0-0	2-2	100.0	+ 6.50

TRAINERS' FAVOURITES AT PONTEFRACT 1990-94

	Total W-R	Non-handicaps 2-y-o	3-y-o+	Handicaps 2-y-o	3-y-o+	Per cent	£1 Level Stake
R Hollinshead	13-22	5-8	2-3	0-0	6-11	59.1	+ 10.68
H R A Cecil	12-15	3-3	9-12	0-0	0-0	80.0	+ 16.45
Mrs J Ramsden	12-39	0-3	0-2	1-4	11-30	30.8	+ 2.46
Mrs M Reveley	7-18	0-1	2-5	0-1	5-11	38.9	+ 2.48
J Berry	7-22	5-8	2-9	0-0	0-5	31.8	- 1.15
A C Stewart	5-9	0-0	2-5	0-1	3-3	55.6	+ 2.25
M R Stoute	5-10	3-4	2-4	0-0	0-2	50.0	+ 0.11
M Johnston	5-12	2-4	2-4	0-1	1-3	41.7	+ 5.75
I A Balding	5-13	3-3	2-6	0-0	0-4	38.5	- 3.12
H Thomson Jones	4-6	4-4	0-2	0-0	0-0	66.7	+ 0.71
L M Cumani	4-9	1-2	3-6	0-0	0-1	44.4	- 0.68
M H Easterby	4-9	0-2	1-1	0-0	3-6	44.4	+ 3.63
M H Tompkins	4-9	2-4	2-2	0-1	0-2	44.4	+ 4.69
J H M Gosden	4-12	1-1	2-6	0-0	1-5	33.3	- 1.71
J D Bethell	3-5	0-0	0-0	0-0	3-5	60.0	+ 12.50
M J Camacho	3-5	0-0	0-0	0-0	3-5	60.0	+ 8.50
Sir M Prescott	3-5	0-0	2-2	0-1	1-2	60.0	+ 2.75
J L Dunlop	3-6	1-1	1-2	0-0	1-3	50.0	- 0.03
B Hanbury	3-6	0-0	1-1	0-0	2-4	50.0	+ 0.82
G Harwood	3-6	1-1	2-5	0-0	0-0	50.0	+ 1.50
J A Glover	3-6	1-1	1-1	0-0	1-4	50.0	+ 1.10
Lord Huntingdon	3-7	0-1	2-3	0-0	1-3	42.9	+ 2.80
G Wragg	3-8	0-0	3-7	0-0	0-1	37.5	- 1.19
Miss S E Hall	2-2	1-1	0-0	0-0	1-1	100.0	+ 8.83

TRAINERS' FAVOURITES AT REDCAR 1990-94

	Total W-R	Non-handicaps 2-y-o	3-y-o+	Handicaps 2-y-o	3-y-o+	Per cent	£1 Level Stake
Mrs M Reveley	18-45	3-4	4-7	0-1	11-33	40.0	+ 8.45
M H Easterby	10-35	4-11	2-6	1-4	3-14	28.6	- 8.66
J H M Gosden	8-19	2-6	4-10	0-0	2-3	42.1	- 0.82
J Berry	8-28	2-13	1-6	1-2	4-7	28.6	- 4.08
Sir M Prescott	7-16	1-3	3-5	1-1	2-7	43.8	+ 3.88
J L Dunlop	6-11	2-2	1-3	1-1	2-5	54.5	+ 3.80
H Thomson Jones	6-13	4-6	2-4	0-0	0-3	46.2	- 2.34
Lady Herries	5-6	0-0	0-0	0-0	5-6	83.3	+ 8.00
M Bell	5-7	3-4	1-2	0-0	1-1	71.4	+ 4.68
R Hannon	5-10	3-6	1-2	1-2	0-0	50.0	+ 3.69
M R Stoute	5-11	1-3	3-4	0-0	1-4	45.5	- 0.71
H R A Cecil	5-17	0-5	4-8	0-0	1-4	29.4	- 8.42
R Hollinshead	4-7	1-2	1-2	0-0	2-3	57.1	+ 4.80
M J Camacho	4-8	0-1	2-2	0-0	2-5	50.0	+ 2.79
M Johnston	4-15	1-4	1-3	0-1	2-7	26.7	- 4.38
W Jarvis	3-4	0-0	1-2	0-0	2-2	75.0	+ 1.95
W Carter	3-4	0-0	0-0	1-2	2-2	75.0	+ 6.25
P C Haslam	3-7	0-0	2-4	0-1	1-2	42.9	+ 0.50
M D Hammond	3-7	0-0	0-0	0-0	3-7	42.9	+ 6.00
F H Lee	3-8	1-1	0-0	1-1	1-6	37.5	+ 2.25
R M Whitaker	3-15	1-5	0-2	0-0	2-8	20.0	- 4.45
L M Cumani	3-20	0-7	3-5	0-0	0-8	15.0	- 14.62
Denys Smith	2-2	1-1	0-0	0-0	1-1	100.0	+ 1.67
N Tinkler	2-2	0-0	2-2	0-0	0-0	100.0	+ 2.36

TRAINERS' FAVOURITES AT RIPON 1990-94

	Total W-R	Non-handicaps 2-y-o	3-y-o+	Handicaps 2-y-o	3-y-o+	Per cent	£1 Level Stake
H R A Cecil	19-32	1-2	17-26	0-0	1-4	59.4	+ 4.63
J Berry	11-26	8-17	2-6	0-2	1-1	42.3	+ 3.44
J H M Gosden	9-16	0-0	6-12	0-0	3-4	56.3	+ 3.53
M H Easterby	9-26	3-8	2-4	0-0	4-14	34.6	- 2.37
L M Cumani	6-11	0-0	5-10	0-0	1-1	54.5	+ 4.80
M R Stoute	6-14	1-2	2-2	0-0	3-10	42.9	+ 2.31
Mrs M Reveley	5-16	0-0	3-5	0-0	2-11	31.3	- 1.79
J L Dunlop	4-12	0-3	1-2	0-1	3-6	33.3	- 3.20
G Harwood	3-4	0-0	1-2	0-0	2-2	75.0	+ 7.00
D Morley	3-5	0-1	1-1	0-0	2-3	60.0	+ 3.55
Miss S E Hall	3-6	0-1	1-1	0-0	2-4	50.0	+ 5.70
W J Haggas	3-6	2-2	0-0	0-0	1-4	50.0	+ 3.63
P C Haslam	3-7	0-0	0-1	0-0	3-6	42.9	+ 4.25
B W Hills	3-12	1-2	1-5	0-0	1-5	25.0	- 3.53
M A Jarvis	2-2	0-0	1-1	0-0	1-1	100.0	+ 2.01
G Lewis	2-2	1-1	0-0	0-0	1-1	100.0	+ 2.36
J L Spearing	2-2	0-0	0-0	0-0	2-2	100.0	+ 3.00
Capt J Wilson	2-2	0-0	0-0	0-0	2-2	100.0	+ 11.50
P Wigham	2-3	0-0	1-1	0-0	1-2	66.7	+ 5.75
J Wharton	2-3	0-1	0-0	0-0	2-2	66.7	+ 6.00
J Pearce	2-4	0-0	1-1	0-0	1-3	50.0	+ 1.88
M R Channon	2-4	1-1	1-1	0-0	0-2	50.0	+ 0.60
R Charlton	2-4	0-0	1-2	0-0	1-2	50.0	- 0.33
M J Camacho	2-5	0-1	1-1	0-0	1-3	40.0	+ 1.13

TRAINERS' FAVOURITES AT SALISBURY 1990-94

	Total W-R	Non-handicaps 2-y-o	3-y-o+	Handicaps 2-y-o	3-y-o+	Per cent	£1 Level Stake
G Harwood	13-29	3-10	3-7	2-2	5-10	44.8	+ 8.75
R Hannon	13-46	8-21	3-9	0-3	2-13	28.3	- 11.54
D R C Elsworth	7-27	3-8	1-6	0-0	3-13	25.9	- 2.99
R Charlton	6-12	2-6	2-3	0-0	2-3	50.0	+ 1.76
P F I Cole	6-17	4-10	1-3	0-0	1-4	35.3	- 1.59
L M Cumani	5-9	0-0	5-8	0-0	0-1	55.6	+ 2.08
H R A Cecil	5-10	0-0	5-9	0-0	0-1	50.0	+ 0.47
M R Stoute	5-11	1-4	2-5	0-0	2-2	45.5	+ 1.73
J L Dunlop	5-15	1-4	2-6	0-0	2-5	33.3	+ 0.98
J H M Gosden	4-10	0-1	4-7	0-0	0-2	40.0	0.00
G Lewis	4-11	3-5	1-3	0-0	0-3	36.4	+ 1.48
I A Balding	4-21	2-6	0-6	0-0	2-9	19.0	- 8.26
Lady Herries	3-5	1-1	0-0	0-0	2-4	60.0	+ 9.50
J W Hills	3-6	2-4	1-1	0-0	0-1	50.0	+ 2.45
P Chapple-Hyam	3-6	2-4	1-2	0-0	0-0	50.0	+ 1.75
Lord Huntingdon	3-10	0-1	2-4	0-0	1-5	30.0	- 0.68
D R Laing	2-2	0-0	1-1	0-0	1-1	100.0	+ 6.25
M McCormack	2-2	2-2	0-0	0-0	0-0	100.0	+ 2.74
D R Loder	2-2	1-1	0-0	0-0	1-1	100.0	+ 4.10
C J Hill	2-4	0-0	0-0	0-0	2-4	50.0	+ 7.00
L J Holt	2-4	1-1	0-0	0-0	1-3	50.0	+ 2.00
M C Pipe	2-4	0-0	0-1	0-0	2-3	50.0	+ 4.75
A C Stewart	2-4	0-0	1-2	0-0	1-2	50.0	+ 3.50
J Berry	2-6	1-1	0-3	0-0	1-2	33.3	+ 1.33

TRAINERS' FAVOURITES AT SANDOWN 1990-94

	Total W-R	Non-handicaps 2-y-o	3-y-o+	Handicaps 2-y-o	3-y-o+	Per cent	£1 Level Stake
R Hannon	17-45	8-16	1-5	0-1	8-23	37.8	+ 0.12
J H M Gosden	10-24	0-1	7-11	0-0	3-12	41.7	+ 8.80
H R A Cecil	9-32	4-8	4-19	0-0	1-5	28.1	- 11.08
M R Stoute	8-25	4-7	4-10	0-1	0-7	32.0	- 5.35
G Harwood	7-16	0-2	5-10	0-1	2-3	43.8	+ 4.51
J L Dunlop	7-19	2-7	2-4	0-0	3-8	36.8	+ 5.14
R Akehurst	6-22	0-1	0-2	0-2	6-17	27.3	+ 3.88
J Berry	5-18	0-2	4-9	0-3	1-4	27.8	- 2.36
M R Channon	4-7	2-3	0-1	0-0	2-3	57.1	+ 5.55
J R Fanshawe	4-7	0-0	2-3	0-0	2-4	57.1	+ 6.48
D R Loder	4-7	3-5	0-1	0-0	1-1	57.1	+ 3.17
P F I Cole	4-14	2-6	1-5	1-2	0-1	28.6	- 1.80
I A Balding	4-15	1-3	1-6	0-0	2-6	26.7	- 2.31
R Simpson	3-5	0-0	2-2	0-0	1-3	60.0	+ 6.35
P J Makin	3-7	0-0	1-3	0-0	2-4	42.9	+ 1.13
G Wragg	3-7	1-3	2-3	0-0	0-1	42.9	- 2.38
B Hanbury	3-9	0-2	0-2	0-0	3-5	33.3	- 0.66
M Bell	3-9	3-6	0-1	0-1	0-1	33.3	- 1.45
Sir M Prescott	3-10	0-0	2-3	0-4	1-3	30.0	+ 1.50
B W Hills	3-15	2-5	1-8	0-0	0-2	20.0	- 6.74
C A Cyzer	2-2	0-0	1-1	0-0	1-1	100.0	+ 5.50
W R Hern	2-3	2-2	0-1	0-0	0-0	66.7	+ 0.83
M P Naughton	2-4	0-0	0-0	0-0	2-4	50.0	+ 2.91
M C Pipe	2-4	0-0	1-1	0-0	1-3	50.0	+ 0.80

TRAINERS' FAVOURITES AT SOUTHWELL (AW) 1990-94

	Total W-R	Non-handicaps 2-y-o	Non-handicaps 3-y-o+	Handicaps 2-y-o	Handicaps 3-y-o+	Per cent	£1 Level Stake
T D Barron	32-81	3-3	18-39	1-3	10-36	39.5	+ 4.96
D W Chapman	27-57	0-0	19-35	0-1	8-21	47.4	+ 9.30
W A O'Gorman	22-67	8-13	7-27	1-3	6-24	32.8	- 8.15
J Berry	19-50	11-27	2-7	1-3	5-13	38.0	+ 11.09
Sir M Prescott	16-41	3-11	9-14	0-2	4-14	39.0	- 0.99
C J Hill	15-42	2-3	4-12	2-2	7-25	35.7	- 4.96
M Johnston	13-33	0-2	6-9	0-0	7-22	39.4	+ 7.31
Lord Huntingdon	12-33	1-3	8-18	0-0	3-12	36.4	- 0.69
R Hollinshead	11-32	2-5	4-14	0-0	5-13	34.4	- 4.26
S G Norton	8-24	3-8	4-8	0-2	1-6	33.3	+ 3.30
C R Nelson	6-9	1-2	4-5	0-0	1-2	66.7	+ 4.16
T Thomson Jones	6-10	0-0	1-1	0-0	5-9	60.0	+ 10.09
P S Felgate	6-11	0-0	1-1	0-0	5-10	54.5	+ 10.45
B W Hills	6-12	0-2	4-6	0-0	2-4	50.0	- 0.15
M J Ryan	6-13	1-2	2-3	0-0	3-8	46.2	+ 2.71
D R Loder	6-14	4-5	2-6	0-0	0-3	42.9	+ 0.19
J G FitzGerald	6-15	2-4	4-5	0-0	0-6	40.0	- 1.17
P F I Cole	6-19	2-6	2-9	0-1	2-3	31.6	- 2.71
C Tinkler	5-8	0-0	0-0	0-0	5-8	62.5	+ 4.51
M W Easterby	5-11	3-6	0-0	1-2	1-3	45.5	+ 0.83
Mrs M Reveley	5-12	0-0	2-3	0-0	3-9	41.7	+ 1.08
C N Allen	5-12	0-2	2-2	1-1	2-7	41.7	+ 1.78
M C Chapman	5-13	0-0	1-3	0-0	4-10	38.5	+ 4.75
J A Glover	5-16	0-3	0-0	0-0	5-13	31.3	+ 4.75

TRAINERS' FAVOURITES AT THIRSK 1990-94

	Total W-R	Non-handicaps 2-y-o	Non-handicaps 3-y-o+	Handicaps 2-y-o	Handicaps 3-y-o+	Per cent	£1 Level Stake
H R A Cecil	9-15	3-4	5-8	0-0	1-3	60.0	+ 2.78
J L Dunlop	8-14	0-1	3-5	0-0	5-8	57.1	+ 3.91
M H Easterby	7-27	3-12	0-2	0-2	4-11	25.9	- 4.50
J Berry	7-33	3-17	3-7	0-2	1-7	21.2	- 16.86
Sir M Prescott	5-10	1-3	1-3	1-1	2-3	50.0	+ 3.79
G Harwood	4-5	0-0	4-5	0-0	0-0	80.0	+ 1.46
P C Haslam	4-6	2-2	1-1	0-1	1-2	66.7	+ 5.42
M R Stoute	4-15	1-2	3-9	0-0	0-4	26.7	- 6.75
J R Fanshawe	3-4	1-1	1-2	0-0	1-1	75.0	+ 5.89
N Tinkler	3-6	0-1	3-4	0-0	0-1	50.0	+ 1.74
J H M Gosden	3-6	0-0	3-5	0-0	0-1	50.0	+ 0.90
M W Easterby	3-8	3-5	0-0	0-0	0-3	37.5	+ 0.38
P Chapple-Hyam	3-9	0-2	3-5	0-0	0-2	33.3	- 3.70
T D Barron	3-15	1-3	0-2	1-1	1-9	20.0	- 2.50
M J Camacho	2-2	0-0	0-0	1-1	1-1	100.0	+ 4.50
B Hanbury	2-3	1-1	0-1	0-0	1-1	66.7	+ 2.40
M A Jarvis	2-3	1-1	1-2	0-0	0-0	66.7	+ 3.45
R Hannon	2-4	0-1	2-2	0-0	0-1	50.0	+ 1.25
B W Hills	2-4	0-1	1-1	0-0	1-2	50.0	+ 0.91
R Hollinshead	2-4	0-0	2-3	0-0	0-1	50.0	+ 1.38
Mrs J Ramsden	2-4	0-0	1-2	0-0	1-2	50.0	+ 3.25
Mrs J Cecil	2-4	0-0	1-2	1-1	0-1	50.0	+ 1.50
D W Chapman	2-5	0-0	0-0	0-0	2-5	40.0	+ 4.00
P F I Cole	2-5	1-1	1-2	0-0	0-2	40.0	- 1.14

TRAINERS' FAVOURITES AT WARWICK 1990-94

	Total W-R	Non-handicaps 2-y-o	Non-handicaps 3-y-o+	Handicaps 2-y-o	Handicaps 3-y-o+	Per cent	£1 Level Stake
H R A Cecil	10-19	3-5	7-14	0-0	0-0	52.6	+ 0.13
J L Dunlop	6-12	1-2	2-2	1-2	2-6	50.0	+ 2.82
I A Balding	6-15	2-2	3-7	0-2	1-4	40.0	− 0.94
P Chapple-Hyam	5-7	3-5	2-2	0-0	0-0	71.4	+ 2.86
M R Stoute	5-9	3-3	1-3	0-0	1-3	55.6	+ 1.13
J Berry	5-17	1-9	1-4	2-2	1-2	29.4	− 4.86
R Hollinshead	4-6	1-2	2-3	1-1	0-0	66.7	+ 7.00
J W Hills	4-7	0-0	3-3	0-0	1-4	57.1	+ 5.61
R Charlton	4-7	0-0	2-5	0-0	2-2	57.1	+ 1.91
M Bell	4-8	3-5	1-1	0-1	0-1	50.0	+ 4.41
B A McMahon	4-11	0-0	1-2	0-0	3-9	36.4	+ 2.38
J H M Gosden	4-13	0-1	4-10	0-0	0-2	30.8	− 0.52
R Hannon	4-17	1-7	0-3	1-3	2-4	23.5	− 3.46
L M Cumani	3-4	0-0	3-3	0-0	0-1	75.0	+ 1.99
G Lewis	3-5	2-3	0-0	0-0	1-2	60.0	+ 5.48
R Akehurst	3-6	0-0	0-0	0-0	3-6	50.0	+ 6.50
W R Hern	3-6	0-0	3-3	0-0	0-3	50.0	+ 0.60
M C Pipe	3-9	0-0	2-4	0-0	1-5	33.3	− 1.56
P T Walwyn	2-2	0-0	2-2	0-0	0-0	100.0	+ 2.38
Mrs J Cecil	2-3	0-0	0-0	1-1	1-2	66.7	+ 1.58
J W Payne	2-4	2-3	0-0	0-1	0-0	50.0	− 0.33
Sir M Prescott	2-5	0-1	0-1	0-1	2-2	40.0	+ 1.63
Lady Herries	2-5	0-0	1-2	0-1	1-2	40.0	+ 0.50
R J Hodges	2-6	0-0	1-1	0-0	1-5	33.3	+ 0.50

TRAINERS' FAVOURITES AT WINDSOR 1990-94

	Total W-R	Non-handicaps 2-y-o	Non-handicaps 3-y-o+	Handicaps 2-y-o	Handicaps 3-y-o+	Per cent	£1 Level Stake
R Hannon	19-48	13-23	2-11	2-3	2-11	39.6	+ 1.00
L M Cumani	8-16	0-0	7-12	0-1	1-3	50.0	+ 2.76
H R A Cecil	5-9	0-0	3-7	0-0	2-2	55.6	+ 1.04
M R Stoute	5-9	1-3	0-0	0-0	4-6	55.6	+ 5.68
I A Balding	5-10	2-3	0-2	0-0	3-5	50.0	+ 1.82
P J Makin	5-12	0-0	5-8	0-0	0-4	41.7	+ 1.82
J Berry	5-19	1-9	1-1	3-5	0-4	26.3	− 1.00
C F Wall	4-4	3-3	1-1	0-0	0-0	100.0	+ 6.98
M Bell	4-8	2-5	0-0	0-0	2-3	50.0	+ 2.60
G Harwood	4-9	0-1	2-5	0-0	2-3	44.4	+ 0.44
M A Jarvis	4-10	0-0	1-2	0-0	3-8	40.0	+ 0.15
J L Dunlop	3-6	0-0	2-3	0-1	1-2	50.0	+ 2.63
N A Callaghan	3-7	1-1	0-0	0-2	2-4	42.9	+ 3.50
D R C Elsworth	3-9	0-1	2-5	0-1	1-2	33.3	+ 3.50
R Charlton	3-10	1-2	0-5	0-0	2-3	30.0	+ 0.58
W R Hern	3-11	0-1	2-7	0-0	1-3	27.3	− 1.75
P F I Cole	3-13	1-7	1-1	0-0	1-5	23.1	− 6.54
N Tinkler	2-2	0-0	1-1	0-0	1-1	100.0	+ 5.23
Lord Huntingdon	2-2	2-2	0-0	0-0	0-0	100.0	+ 1.87
D R Loder	2-2	2-2	0-0	0-0	0-0	100.0	+ 3.00
C R Nelson	2-3	1-1	0-0	0-0	1-2	66.7	+ 1.75
G Wragg	2-3	0-0	2-3	0-0	0-0	66.7	+ 3.71
J R Fanshawe	2-3	0-0	2-2	0-0	0-1	66.7	+ 2.50
C J Benstead	2-5	0-0	0-0	0-0	2-5	40.0	+ 1.83

TRAINERS' FAVOURITES AT WOLVERHAMPTON (AW) 1993-94

	Total W-R	Non-handicaps 2-y-o	3-y-o+	Handicaps 2-y-o	3-y-o+	Per cent	£1 Level Stake
P C Haslam	10-18	1-1	3-7	0-0	6-10	55.6	+ 14.52
M Johnston	8-12	0-0	3-3	0-0	5-9	66.7	+ 11.50
Sir M Prescott	7-10	3-3	3-3	0-0	1-4	70.0	+ 5.59
J Berry	7-16	2-5	3-6	0-2	2-3	43.8	- 2.40
Lord Huntingdon	6-17	1-3	1-5	0-0	4-9	35.3	- 4.64
A Bailey	4-8	0-0	2-2	0-0	2-6	50.0	+ 4.30
Mrs M Reveley	4-8	0-0	3-4	0-0	1-4	50.0	- 0.33
R Hollinshead	4-19	0-2	1-8	0-0	3-9	21.1	- 5.75
R Charlton	2-2	1-1	1-1	0-0	0-0	100.0	+ 1.33
W J Haggas	2-3	0-0	1-2	0-0	1-1	66.7	+ 1.88
M R Channon	2-4	1-2	0-1	1-1	0-0	50.0	+ 4.75
J H M Gosden	2-5	0-0	2-4	0-0	0-1	40.0	- 2.31
B A McMahon	2-6	0-0	0-1	0-0	2-5	33.3	+ 1.25
P D Evans	2-9	0-0	2-6	0-0	0-3	22.2	- 3.87
I A Balding	1-1	0-0	1-1	0-0	0-0	100.0	+ 1.00
P F I Cole	1-1	1-1	0-0	0-0	0-0	100.0	+ 3.00
B W Hills	1-1	1-1	0-0	0-0	0-0	100.0	+ 1.75
G Wragg	1-1	0-0	1-1	0-0	0-0	100.0	+ 0.50
J Mackie	1-1	0-0	1-1	0-0	0-0	100.0	+ 3.00
D Burchell	1-1	0-0	0-0	0-0	1-1	100.0	+ 1.38
G C Bravery	1-1	1-1	0-0	0-0	0-0	100.0	+ 1.88
D J S Cosgrove	1-1	0-0	1-1	0-0	0-0	100.0	+ 2.50
S C Williams	1-1	0-0	0-0	0-0	1-1	100.0	+ 4.00
P Mitchell	1-2	0-0	0-0	0-0	1-2	50.0	+ 2.00

TRAINERS' FAVOURITES AT YARMOUTH 1990-94

	Total W-R	Non-handicaps 2-y-o	3-y-o+	Handicaps 2-y-o	3-y-o+	Per cent	£1 Level Stake
H R A Cecil	23-48	10-22	10-22	0-0	3-4	47.9	+ 2.66
J H M Gosden	10-27	1-4	8-15	0-0	1-8	37.0	- 2.07
A C Stewart	9-20	2-5	3-8	0-0	4-7	45.0	+ 2.03
C E Brittain	8-13	3-5	3-3	0-0	2-5	61.5	+ 11.44
M H Tompkins	8-17	5-8	1-4	1-2	1-3	47.1	+ 0.66
G Wragg	8-22	4-11	4-7	0-0	0-4	36.4	- 3.35
M R Stoute	7-18	3-8	3-5	0-0	1-5	38.9	- 1.74
Mrs L Piggott	6-12	1-2	3-4	0-0	2-6	50.0	+ 3.33
J Berry	6-13	4-8	2-3	0-0	0-2	46.2	+ 5.71
D Morley	5-12	3-5	1-1	0-0	1-6	41.7	+ 1.73
M Bell	5-14	3-6	0-0	1-2	1-6	35.7	+ 0.75
W J Haggas	4-9	0-1	1-2	2-3	1-3	44.4	+ 0.38
B W Hills	4-10	2-4	1-3	0-1	1-2	40.0	- 0.09
N A Callaghan	4-12	1-5	1-2	1-2	1-3	33.3	- 0.50
J L Dunlop	3-5	0-0	1-2	0-0	2-3	60.0	+ 1.21
M Johnston	3-6	1-1	0-0	0-0	2-5	50.0	+ 3.75
R Hannon	3-8	0-3	0-0	2-2	1-3	37.5	+ 2.38
B Hanbury	3-9	2-4	1-2	0-1	0-2	33.3	- 0.09
H Thomson Jones	3-10	3-6	0-2	0-0	0-2	30.0	- 1.93
Mrs M Reveley	3-10	1-2	2-3	0-0	0-5	30.0	- 3.56
J Pearce	3-10	0-0	1-4	0-0	2-6	30.0	- 0.50
J R Fanshawe	3-11	0-0	2-6	0-0	1-5	27.3	- 0.77
G Lewis	3-12	2-4	0-2	0-0	1-6	25.0	- 5.45
M J Ryan	3-12	0-0	0-1	0-2	3-9	25.0	+ 4.00

TRAINERS' FAVOURITES AT YORK 1990-94

	Total W-R	Non-handicaps 2-y-o	3-y-o+	Handicaps 2-y-o	3-y-o+	Per cent	£1 Level Stake
J H M Gosden	15-33	2-3	6-15	0-1	7-14	45.5	+ 13.91
H R A Cecil	14-47	4-8	9-34	0-0	1-5	29.8	- 20.75
J L Dunlop	11-23	6-12	2-4	0-0	3-7	47.8	+ 4.93
M R Stoute	10-42	0-9	7-21	0-0	3-12	23.8	- 10.94
P F I Cole	7-10	7-9	0-0	0-0	0-1	70.0	+ 7.85
M Johnston	6-13	3-4	0-1	0-0	3-8	46.2	+ 11.13
L M Cumani	6-26	0-2	5-13	0-1	1-10	23.1	- 12.97
M H Easterby	6-31	0-1	1-2	1-4	4-24	19.4	- 2.42
J Berry	5-6	3-4	0-0	1-1	1-1	83.3	+ 5.64
R Hannon	5-16	3-9	1-1	1-2	0-4	31.3	- 0.84
P Chapple-Hyam	4-8	4-5	0-0	0-1	0-2	50.0	+ 1.03
E Weymes	3-3	2-2	0-0	0-0	1-1	100.0	+ 5.75
Lady Herries	3-4	0-0	0-0	0-0	3-4	75.0	+ 6.93
Mrs J Cecil	3-7	1-1	1-2	0-2	1-2	42.9	+ 2.50
D R Loder	3-7	1-2	1-2	0-0	1-3	42.9	+ 0.43
W R Hern	3-8	1-3	2-4	0-0	0-1	37.5	- 1.54
B Hanbury	3-9	3-4	0-1	0-1	0-3	33.3	- 2.22
G Wragg	3-10	2-5	1-3	0-0	0-2	30.0	- 1.62
R Charlton	3-13	1-3	0-2	0-1	2-7	23.1	- 0.37
I A Balding	3-17	0-4	0-3	0-0	3-10	17.6	- 2.50
B W Hills	3-19	1-7	1-7	0-0	1-5	15.8	- 5.92
M Fetherston-Godley	2-2	0-0	0-0	0-0	2-2	100.0	+ 10.00
Sir M Prescott	2-4	0-0	0-0	0-0	2-4	50.0	+ 7.25
T D Barron	2-5	0-0	0-0	0-1	2-4	40.0	+ 7.00

TOP PERCENTAGE COURSES FOR FAVOURITES 1990-94

	W-R	Per cent	£1 Level Stake		W-R	Per cent	£1 Level Stake
Edinburgh	165-383	43.1	+ 17.36	Newbury	171-488	35.0	+ 20.46
Catterick	181-453	40.0	- 27.53	Thirsk	138-400	34.5	- 55.02
Hamilton	208-524	39.7	+ 6.82	Windsor	137-402	34.1	- 45.53
Pontefract	197-502	39.2	+ 26.75	Lingfield	177-524	33.8	- 58.59
Folkestone	180-462	39.0	+ 16.03	York	168-500	33.6	+ 2.69
Brighton	211-553	38.2	- 36.56	Leicester	175-522	33.5	- 38.33
Wolverhampton*	92-241	38.2	- 1.26	Lingfield (AW)	336-1003	33.5	-129.14
Chester	116-305	38.0	- 2.38	Warwick	142-428	33.2	- 64.76
Newcastle	146-390	37.4	- 46.23	Doncaster	208-630	33.0	- 27.47
Ripon	154-414	37.2	- 23.25	Sandown	174-529	32.9	- 24.34
Nottingham	205-552	37.1	+ 2.44	Carlisle	94-289	32.5	- 39.07
Beverley	205-556	36.9	- 40.93	Salisbury	137-426	32.2	- 53.22
Redcar	211-574	36.8	- 14.90	Goodwood	186-579	32.1	- 49.24
Yarmouth	202-549	36.8	- 59.37	Newmarket (R)	185-590	31.4	- 62.45
Bath	142-389	36.5	- 7.82	Haydock	175-564	31.0	-107.87
Ayr	152-421	36.1	- 45.75	Ascot	124-405	30.6	- 30.96
Newmarket (J)	161-447	36.0	- 19.41	Epsom	64-214	29.9	- 27.69
Chepstow	113-315	35.9	- 18.03	Kempton	129-451	28.6	- 46.47
Southwell (AW)	435-1240	35.1	-106.90				

*All Weather since December 1993
(J) July Course
(R) Rowley Mile

FAVOURITES' PERFORMANCE BY TYPE OF RACE 1990-94

Non-h'caps	W-R	Per cent	£1 Level Stake	Handicaps	W-R	Per cent	£1 Level Stake
2-y-o	1641-3944	41.6	-204.72	2-y-o	192-675	28.4	- 23.67
3-y-o	1259-2856	44.1	- 92.70	3-y-o	539-1864	28.9	-208.68
Weight/age	1196-2858	41.8	- 45.60	All-aged	1697-6371	26.6	-685.23
Totals	4096-9658	42.4	-343.02	Totals	2428-8910	27.3	-917.58
All Favs	6524-18568	35.1	-1260.60				

When there is more than one favourite in a race then the £1 stake has been equally divided on each one. Only one favourite is counted for each race.

FOR SALE

A unique opportunity to obtain all, or part, of a Bloodstock Breeding and
Racing library gathered over the last 35 years.

General Stud Books 1897–1988 (Vols 19–41)
American Stud Books 1946–1990 (Vols 20; 22–30 + 5 supplements)
French Stud Books 1947–1991 (Vols 28–43)
German Stud Books 1929–1987 (Vols 19–32)
Italian Stud Books 1956–1987 (Vols 18, 19; 21–25)
Statistical Abstract 1958–1971 (13 specially bound volumes)
Statistical Record 1971–1993 (23 leather bound vols)
Statistical Record Jump Annuals 1985–1992/93 (9 vols)
Abrege des Courses Plates (France) 1966–1991 (26 vols)
Thoroughbred Times Statistical Review (USA) 1988–1992 (5 vols)
Thoroughbred Times Sires of Winners (USA) 1989–1992 (4 vols)
Registered Thoroughbred Names (Lexington) 1988
Bloodstock Breeders' Annual Review 1959–1981 (22 vols)
Non-Thoroughbred Register 1974–1993 (20 vols)
Register of Thoroughbred Stallions 1954–1983 (15 vols + 9 supps)
Weatherbys Stallion Book 1985–1994 (10 vols)
Sires for 1990–1994 (5 vols)
Etalons de Pur Sang (France) 1957; 1971/72; 1979–1990 (11 vols + 7
  supps)
Stalloni Purosangue (Italy) 1971–1980 (3 vols)
Thoroughbred Times Stallion Directory (USA) 1989–1992 (4 vols)
Keylock's Dams of Winners 1915–1989 (7 vols)
Mares de Gagnants (France) 1941–1987 (7 vols)
American Produce Records 1930–1991 (2 sets, 30 vols, both in binders)
Pedigrees of Leading Winners 1912–1984 (3 vols + supp)
Bend Or Graded & Group Winners 1973–1990 (2 vols)
Pattern Races/Thoroughbred Breeder Magazine 1978–1994 (14 vols in
  binders)
Timeform 'Racehorses of' 1960–1993 (34 vols)
Timeform 'Chasers and Hurdlers' 1988/89–1993/94 (6 vols)
Directory of the Turf/Turf Directory 1976; 1980; 1984–1994 (12 vols)
Raceform Annuals 1982–1991 (10 vols)
Chaseform Annual 1992/93 only
French Races Past (Flat) 1965; 1966; 1969–1990 (24 vols, many leather
  bound)

Inspection of all volumes welcomed

Please contact Martin Pickering by telephone, or Fax, on (01707) 655269,
or write to 69 Northlands, Potters Bar, Hertfordshire EN6 5JD.

TRAINER SUMMARIES

WINNING FLAT TRAINERS 1994

	Total W-R	2-y-o	3-y-o	4-y-o+	Per cent	£1 Level Stake
J Berry	123-911	60-409	30-216	33-286	13.5	-271.06
M Johnston	114-649	37-198	28-204	49-247	17.6	- 51.23
R Hannon	111-1112	57-478	41-454	13-180	10.0	-386.06
M R Stoute	108-590	31-176	60-315	17-99	18.3	- 69.36
J H M Gosden	93-521	9-70	72-369	12-82	17.9	- 80.00
J L Dunlop	82-503	24-176	35-228	23-99	16.3	- 78.54
Mrs M Reveley	82-594	1-73	22-134	59-387	13.8	- 53.43
H R A Cecil	76-324	26-90	47-205	3-29	23.5	- 28.91
M R Channon	73-628	41-290	13-170	19-168	11.6	-180.52
P F I Cole	68-580	28-219	35-284	5-77	11.7	-153.43
Lord Huntingdon	55-322	10-50	35-189	10-83	17.1	- 46.19
M Bell	55-382	27-142	17-178	11-62	14.4	- 97.49
Sir Mark Prescott	54-237	16-81	30-130	8-26	22.8	+ 5.42
I A Balding	51-385	5-84	31-174	15-127	13.2	- 92.71
R Charlton	48-228	22-77	22-118	4-33	21.1	- 8.85
R Akehurst	48-369	2-31	5-84	41-254	13.0	- 4.01
L M Cumani	47-269	5-40	28-166	14-63	17.5	- 41.31
G Lewis	44-355	21-178	22-154	1-23	12.4	- 45.99
B W Hills	44-383	15-162	23-177	6-44	11.5	-143.51
Mrs J Ramsden	40-330	12-102	11-114	17-114	12.1	- 61.01
D R Loder	39-148	23-75	11-44	5-29	26.4	- 11.37
P Chapple-Hyam	39-222	22-88	15-107	2-27	17.6	- 29.08
T D Barron	37-232	5-29	10-52	22-151	15.9	+ 43.00
H Thomson Jones	36-194	16-53	20-141	0-0	18.6	+ 77.83
P C Haslam	36-218	9-79	12-42	15-97	16.5	- 25.59
M H Tompkins	35-326	9-89	16-147	10-90	10.7	-148.05
G Wragg	32-182	8-46	16-102	8-34	17.6	+ 21.92
Lady Herries	32-183	4-17	12-58	16-108	17.5	+ 22.04
M H Easterby	31-392	10-162	11-143	10-87	7.9	-178.87
A A Scott	30-197	8-77	14-80	8-40	15.2	- 21.30
R Hollinshead	30-561	1-86	13-226	16-249	5.3	-344.25
P T Walwyn	29-180	9-56	16-99	4-25	16.1	- 6.20
J Pearce	29-183	2-24	6-46	21-113	15.8	+ 32.28
C E Brittain	29-442	5-84	16-191	8-167	6.6	-202.43
B A McMahon	28-362	3-75	14-140	11-147	7.7	-167.70
G Harwood	27-157	3-36	16-76	8-45	17.2	+ 39.21
A Bailey	26-215	2-22	2-67	22-126	12.1	- 43.70
J W Hills	26-226	6-48	10-92	10-86	11.5	- 75.70
B Hanbury	25-221	8-57	11-108	6-56	11.3	- 87.70
J R Fanshawe	24-249	6-55	14-118	4-76	9.6	- 76.63
B J Meehan	24-314	6-103	16-170	2-41	7.6	- 63.59
Mrs J Cecil	23-132	3-26	14-70	6-36	17.4	+ 28.08
D Morley	23-148	12-67	4-47	7-34	15.5	+ 61.58
R W Armstrong	23-187	5-40	15-119	3-28	12.3	+ 61.54
W Jarvis	23-201	8-57	9-93	6-51	11.4	- 39.37
P W Harris	23-220	6-42	1-68	16-110	10.5	- 30.55
G L Moore	23-343	4-86	11-131	8-126	6.7	-162.49
A C Stewart	22-150	1-27	13-89	8-34	14.7	- 56.63
W J Haggas	22-155	1-22	15-93	6-40	14.2	+ 18.20
W R Hern	22-180	9-40	9-110	4-30	12.2	- 66.81
M J Ryan	22-214	3-35	7-89	12-90	10.3	- 54.79
E J Alston	20-282	1-17	6-75	13-190	7.1	- 67.45
J L Harris	19-191	0-2	3-41	16-148	9.9	- 15.72
C A Cyzer	19-248	3-23	10-107	6-118	7.7	- 67.80

	Total W-R	2-y-o	3-y-o	4-y-o+	Per cent	£1 Level Stake
W R Muir	18-180	3-48	7-61	8-71	10.0	- 60.75
R J Hodges	18-247	1-32	0-14	17-201	7.3	-120.20
Mrs N Macauley	17-191	1-28	4-53	12-110	8.9	- 50.92
T G Mills	16-128	8-40	1-34	7-54	12.5	+ 3.76
D Nicholls	16-183	0-26	3-65	13-92	8.7	-106.12
J L Eyre	16-196	2-36	4-39	10-121	8.2	- 42.85
R M Whitaker	16-217	2-53	4-64	10-100	7.4	- 82.87
S Dow	16-227	4-56	4-63	8-108	7.0	- 88.37
S C Williams	15-120	0-10	9-72	6-38	12.5	- 36.23
Miss Gay Kelleway	15-129	6-43	1-16	8-70	11.6	- 6.00
M A Jarvis	15-157	0-37	8-64	7-56	9.6	- 60.44
D W P Arbuthnot	15-162	5-45	3-31	7-86	9.3	- 42.37
M J B Heaton-Ellis	15-172	3-37	2-72	10-63	8.7	- 22.25
C N Allen	14-125	1-23	10-77	3-25	11.2	- 15.62
R Boss	14-126	2-26	10-75	2-25	11.1	- 14.17
J W Watts	14-147	3-36	7-56	4-55	9.5	- 43.25
L J Holt	14-153	0-15	2-45	12-93	9.2	- 67.42
J Wharton	14-155	2-36	2-53	10-66	9.0	- 48.50
R J R Williams	14-175	2-32	6-66	6-77	8.0	- 28.93
D R C Elsworth	14-232	1-36	6-117	7-79	6.0	-135.99
R J O'Sullivan	13-127	0-0	2-14	11-113	10.2	- 43.52
E Weymes	13-128	7-55	6-51	0-22	10.2	- 19.25
H Candy	13-136	2-24	9-93	2-19	9.6	- 28.02
M C Pipe	12-98	1-4	5-49	6-45	12.2	- 28.38
M D Hammond	12-108	0-0	3-19	9-89	11.1	- 6.00
C F Wall	12-111	3-32	7-47	2-32	10.8	- 44.02
S R Bowring	12-112	0-0	7-51	5-61	10.7	+ 5.50
S P C Woods	12-112	2-25	4-44	6-43	10.7	- 41.19
T J Naughton	12-174	1-42	6-56	5-76	6.9	- 90.50
M D I Usher	12-196	1-51	1-41	10-104	6.1	- 85.00
S G Norton	12-205	5-68	4-84	3-53	5.9	-133.02
N J H Walker	11-55	0-0	0-3	11-52	20.0	+ 27.63
A Hide	11-78	0-7	9-60	2-11	14.1	+ 3.88
K T Ivory	11-104	7-31	0-29	4-44	10.6	- 36.00
R F Johnson Houghton	11-108	4-40	5-53	2-15	10.2	- 14.00
Miss S E Hall	11-114	2-37	5-31	4-46	9.6	- 33.50
D Morris	11-117	2-24	2-45	7-48	9.4	- 23.25
D Haydn Jones	11-123	2-36	5-20	4-67	8.9	- 23.00
M Dods	11-143	2-17	2-28	7-98	7.7	- 44.75
C W Thornton	11-149	3-61	5-62	3-26	7.4	- 57.75
F H Lee	11-154	2-23	6-60	3-71	7.1	- 54.25
H J Collingridge	11-156	0-16	1-60	10-80	7.1	- 53.00
A Moore	11-162	0-21	1-18	10-123	6.8	- 48.50
D W Chapman	11-177	0-11	0-23	11-143	6.2	- 84.05
M Brittain	11-188	0-17	0-72	11-99	5.9	- 75.00
S E Kettlewell	10-72	0-8	0-3	10-61	13.9	- 17.01
P S Felgate	10-92	0-0	0-7	10-85	10.9	+ 11.50
P A Kelleway	10-93	2-26	4-46	4-21	10.8	- 15.00
P Mitchell	10-100	0-6	3-41	7-53	10.0	- 2.75
W A O'Gorman	10-129	2-40	2-38	6-51	7.8	- 55.50
J D Bethell	10-171	3-31	0-64	7-76	5.8	- 42.67
J A R Toller	9-73	3-20	1-17	5-36	12.3	- 8.75
K R Burke	9-81	0-11	3-27	6-43	11.1	- 22.52
D T Thom	9-91	0-14	0-9	9-68	9.9	- 19.75
J Hetherton	9-105	2-16	5-54	2-35	8.6	- 13.25
G B Balding	9-110	0-0	5-49	4-61	8.2	- 12.75

	Total W-R	2-y-o	3-y-o	4-y-o+	Per cent	£1 Level Stake
N A Callaghan	9-111	3-37	6-73	0-1	8.1	- 31.75
B Beasley	9-112	0-10	1-14	8-88	8.0	- 33.50
J A Glover	9-124	4-30	1-47	4-47	7.3	- 60.52
P J Makin	9-152	2-26	4-60	3-66	5.9	- 72.00
P D Evans	9-168	0-20	2-61	7-87	5.4	- 91.87
R Bastiman	8-65	0-0	0-6	8-59	12.3	- 16.27
K McAuliffe	8-70	2-29	3-30	3-11	11.4	+ 75.92
Bob Jones	8-78	1-21	1-10	6-47	10.3	+ 4.00
C J Benstead	8-82	2-29	3-30	3-23	9.8	- 14.27
M J Camacho	8-105	0-23	2-41	6-41	7.6	- 59.75
N A Graham	8-112	2-19	5-67	1-26	7.1	- 60.00
B Palling	8-122	1-46	4-56	3-20	6.6	- 77.80
J L Spearing	8-126	0-22	0-30	8-74	6.3	- 70.65
W G M Turner	8-126	2-28	3-46	3-52	6.3	- 37.50
K O Cunningham-Brown	8-137	1-12	1-18	6-107	5.8	+ 59.00
W J Musson	8-139	0-5	1-48	7-86	5.8	- 68.50
J M Bradley	8-144	0-13	1-27	7-104	5.6	- 54.67
Denys Smith	8-160	1-17	3-48	4-95	5.0	-103.87
M W Easterby	8-234	2-124	2-56	4-54	3.4	-168.86
J E Banks	7-63	3-18	2-23	2-22	11.1	+ 27.25
D J G Murray Smith	7-73	1-25	4-38	2-10	9.6	- 35.00
R M Flower	7-73	0-6	2-15	5-52	9.6	- 13.17
J A Harris	7-79	0-10	1-24	6-45	8.9	+ 59.90
G A Pritchard-Gordon	7-80	2-31	4-44	1-5	8.8	- 29.25
C A Horgan	7-80	0-12	0-18	7-50	8.8	- 14.75
C Smith	7-89	1-18	1-22	5-49	7.9	- 17.25
C J Hill	7-93	5-47	0-3	2-43	7.5	- 47.95
P Calver	7-106	2-12	1-21	4-73	6.6	- 15.75
D A Wilson	7-113	0-8	2-30	5-75	6.2	- 62.10
M J Fetherston-Godley	7-113	4-36	2-49	1-28	6.2	- 51.00
J G FitzGerald	7-124	0-28	1-16	6-80	5.6	- 97.02
D N Chappell	6-18	4-7	2-10	0-1	33.3	+ 15.48
D L Williams	6-39	0-1	0-2	6-36	15.4	+ 34.00
Miss B Sanders	6-63	0-4	1-7	5-52	9.5	- 16.17
P D Cundell	6-71	0-10	0-19	6-42	8.5	- 16.00
G M Moore	6-72	0-11	1-9	5-52	8.3	- 22.20
L G Cottrell	6-74	2-16	0-9	4-49	8.1	- 38.95
R Guest	6-75	0-9	4-41	2-25	8.0	- 30.50
W W Haigh	6-86	0-5	1-28	5-53	7.0	- 46.50
B R Millman	6-86	1-17	2-29	3-40	7.0	+ 16.50
J W Payne	6-94	2-13	3-26	1-55	6.4	- 73.97
A P Jarvis	6-100	4-26	1-34	1-40	6.0	- 59.50
B S Rothwell	6-113	1-30	1-43	4-40	5.3	- 42.50
P G Murphy	6-129	4-22	1-60	1-47	4.7	- 69.67
C W Fairhurst	6-179	4-41	0-61	2-77	3.4	-117.56
B Gubby	5-49	0-14	0-9	5-26	10.2	- 8.17
C N Williams	5-51	5-15	0-18	0-18	9.8	- 23.75
W Bentley	5-53	1-25	0-3	4-25	9.4	+ 18.88
J Akehurst	5-59	1-19	2-22	2-18	8.5	+ 2.50
B W Murray	5-61	0-20	3-18	2-23	8.2	- 4.00
M S Saunders	5-67	2-16	3-36	0-15	7.5	- 38.93
C James	5-69	0-9	4-35	1-25	7.2	+ 17.00
J F Bottomley	5-69	1-25	0-4	4-40	7.2	- 35.90
C W C Elsey	5-78	0-16	1-38	4-24	6.4	- 29.70
S Mellor	5-84	0-25	0-6	5-53	6.0	- 52.87
Dr J D Scargill	5-85	0-20	3-37	2-28	5.9	- 52.50

	Total W-R	2-y-o	3-y-o	4-y-o+	Per cent	£1 Level Stake
C C Elsey	5-88	0-9	2-48	3-31	5.7	- 30.25
J J Bridger	5-90	0-22	3-31	2-37	5.6	- 49.00
D R Laing	5-96	1-16	0-13	4-67	5.2	- 52.75
Miss L C Siddall	5-122	0-14	2-33	3-75	4.1	- 51.50
M Blanshard	5-147	3-33	0-63	2-51	3.4	- 95.75
N Bycroft	5-156	1-24	1-73	3-59	3.2	- 66.50
G Holmes	4-37	0-1	2-9	2-27	10.8	- 10.50
Mrs A L M King	4-43	0-4	0-0	4-39	9.3	- 2.50
C R Egerton	4-43	2-14	0-15	2-14	9.3	+ 4.25
J O'Donoghue	4-46	0-0	4-20	0-26	8.7	- 7.00
Mrs L Piggott	4-55	0-14	4-29	0-12	7.3	- 28.00
J G M O'Shea	4-57	0-0	0-16	4-41	7.0	- 41.50
J S Moore	4-65	1-41	2-15	1-9	6.2	- 6.17
D Burchell	4-69	0-3	0-8	4-58	5.8	- 48.12
C P Wildman	4-70	0-0	1-17	3-53	5.7	- 48.87
R Ingram	4-70	1-16	0-10	3-44	5.7	- 41.50
D Moffatt	4-72	2-16	0-13	2-43	5.6	- 19.50
D J S Cosgrove	4-97	1-24	0-39	3-34	4.1	- 78.25
J White	4-100	0-11	1-28	3-61	4.0	- 80.25
M C Chapman	4-106	0-0	4-43	0-63	3.8	- 9.00
M McCormack	4-113	0-31	2-36	2-46	3.5	- 75.00
R Simpson	4-120	0-24	2-41	2-55	3.3	- 82.00
J R Jenkins	4-135	0-30	1-28	3-77	3.0	-108.00
P Howling	4-179	0-23	2-39	2-117	2.2	-123.00
C P E Brooks	3-12	0-0	0-0	3-12	25.0	+ 4.00
A Fabre (Fra)	3-13	1-1	0-4	2-8	23.1	+ 12.50
H Ibrahim (UAE)	3-18	0-0	2-6	1-12	16.7	+ 3.50
Mrs S M Austin	3-22	0-4	0-0	3-18	13.6	+ 9.50
J P Leigh	3-25	0-3	3-21	0-1	12.0	- 3.25
Brian Arthur Pearce	3-26	0-2	1-8	2-16	11.5	- 4.40
Miss S J Wilton	3-27	0-2	0-0	3-25	11.1	+ 8.50
S Gollings	3-28	0-0	2-11	1-17	10.7	- 0.75
A G Newcombe	3-29	0-1	0-10	3-18	10.3	+ 17.00
R J Price	3-30	0-3	0-11	3-16	10.0	+ 4.63
T W Donnelly	3-30	0-0	0-3	3-27	10.0	+ 8.00
J Mackie	3-35	0-3	1-18	2-14	8.6	- 20.50
J Hanson	3-37	1-4	2-33	0-0	8.1	- 18.75
Mrs A Knight	3-37	0-0	1-12	2-25	8.1	- 6.50
A P Jones	3-38	0-0	0-0	3-38	7.9	- 12.00
A Harrison	3-40	0-0	0-4	3-36	7.5	- 14.50
J J Sheehan	3-42	0-3	0-3	3-36	7.1	- 17.80
M P Naughton	3-50	0-1	2-19	1-30	6.0	- 13.67
J R Bosley	3-52	0-0	0-12	3-40	5.8	- 5.50
G C Bravery	3-54	1-20	1-22	1-12	5.6	- 44.12
W T Kemp	3-56	1-40	0-0	2-16	5.4	- 10.75
K W Hogg	3-60	1-23	0-14	2-23	5.0	- 33.50
Martyn Wane	3-62	0-0	1-18	2-44	4.8	- 31.80
G H Eden	3-63	1-4	2-24	0-35	4.8	- 28.00
J Etherington	3-70	0-11	1-33	2-26	4.3	- 41.25
B Preece	3-72	0-6	0-6	3-60	4.2	- 25.00
J M P Eustace	3-86	1-27	1-22	1-37	3.5	- 56.20
Miss L A Perratt	3-86	2-22	1-34	0-30	3.5	- 41.00
D E Incisa	3-96	0-5	2-40	1-51	3.1	- 73.00
N Tinkler	3-118	2-34	0-2	1-82	2.5	- 84.00
J J Quinn	2-6	2-6	0-0	0-0	33.3	+ 14.50
G Richards	2-9	0-0	0-0	2-9	22.2	+ 7.00

	Total W-R	2-y-o	3-y-o	4-y-o+	Per cent	£1 Level Stake
P J Hobbs	2-10	0-0	0-2	2-8	20.0	- 1.00
N A Gaselee	2-12	0-0	0-1	2-11	16.7	+ 15.00
M Kauntze (Ire)	2-12	0-1	0-3	2-8	16.7	- 8.81
P Wigham	2-17	0-0	0-0	2-17	11.8	- 2.50
M J Bolton	2-18	0-0	0-2	2-16	11.1	+ 29.00
P Hayward	2-21	0-0	2-8	0-13	9.5	+ 7.00
C T Nash	2-21	0-0	1-10	1-11	9.5	+ 97.00
N Chamberlain	2-22	0-3	0-0	2-19	9.1	+ 28.00
B Richmond	2-24	0-6	0-0	2-18	8.3	- 14.17
R E Barr	2-25	0-0	0-0	2-25	8.0	- 8.50
F Watson	2-26	0-4	0-5	2-17	7.7	+ 11.25
O O'Neill	2-28	0-0	0-1	2-27	7.1	- 12.00
Martyn Meade	2-28	1-13	0-4	1-11	7.1	+ 12.00
P J Bevan	2-31	0-11	0-2	2-18	6.5	- 3.00
Mrs Barbara Waring	2-32	0-0	0-5	2-27	6.3	0.00
J A Pickering	2-33	0-4	2-27	0-2	6.1	- 26.37
L Lungo	2-35	0-8	0-6	2-21	5.7	- 27.33
R A Fahey	2-35	0-21	2-14	0-0	5.7	- 5.00
Mrs M McCourt	2-37	0-0	0-7	2-30	5.4	- 17.37
K White	2-38	0-0	0-10	2-28	5.3	- 3.00
W M Brisbourne	2-38	0-4	2-22	0-12	5.3	- 13.25
P J McBride	2-41	0-13	2-23	0-5	4.9	- 17.00
B R Cambidge	2-42	0-0	0-0	2-42	4.8	- 20.00
J R Arnold	2-42	2-31	0-4	0-7	4.8	- 22.67
G Rimmer	2-42	0-9	2-25	0-8	4.8	- 17.00
M J Haynes	2-43	0-8	1-24	1-11	4.7	- 24.00
R Dickin	2-43	0-3	0-14	2-26	4.7	- 19.50
R T Phillips	2-43	0-2	2-36	0-5	4.7	- 27.20
P Monteith	2-45	0-0	0-6	2-39	4.4	- 34.25
J Parkes	2-51	0-2	0-6	2-43	3.9	- 17.00
C D Broad	2-52	0-6	0-11	2-35	3.8	- 26.00
T Thomson Jones	2-55	1-10	0-25	1-20	3.6	- 37.67
Pat Mitchell	2-57	0-7	0-6	2-44	3.5	- 38.50
C B B Booth	2-58	0-6	1-33	1-19	3.4	- 37.00
G R Oldroyd	2-58	0-5	0-6	2-47	3.4	- 41.50
J M Carr	2-59	0-14	0-9	2-36	3.4	- 44.00
T H Caldwell	2-60	1-22	0-4	1-34	3.3	- 48.00
J S Wainwright	2-66	0-27	2-29	0-10	3.0	- 51.00
A L Forbes	2-67	0-5	2-20	0-42	3.0	- 60.20
W L Barker	2-75	0-4	1-14	1-57	2.7	- 40.00
D R Gandolfo	1-2	0-0	1-2	0-0	50.0	+ 7.00
B J Curley	1-3	0-0	0-0	1-3	33.3	+ 4.00
D H Barons	1-5	0-0	1-5	0-0	20.0	+ 4.00
A Vanderhaeghen (Ger)	1-5	0-0	0-0	1-5	20.0	- 1.25
B C Morgan	1-6	0-0	0-1	1-5	16.7	+ 1.00
T Stack (Ire)	1-6	0-1	1-4	0-1	16.7	+ 7.00
C Parker	1-10	0-5	0-0	1-5	10.0	+ 2.00
Mrs P A Barker	1-10	0-0	0-0	1-10	10.0	+ 3.00
D Nicholson	1-12	0-0	0-8	1-4	8.3	+ 9.00
P Leach	1-13	0-0	0-0	1-13	7.7	+ 21.00
E Dunlop	1-13	1-12	0-1	0-0	7.7	- 9.00
J M Jefferson	1-14	0-5	0-3	1-6	7.1	- 11.50
S Woodman	1-15	0-0	0-0	1-15	6.7	- 7.00
C L Popham	1-15	0-0	0-7	1-8	6.7	- 8.50
D R Tucker	1-17	0-0	0-13	1-4	5.9	+ 17.00
A P Stringer	1-17	0-0	0-0	1-17	5.9	- 12.00

	Total W-R	2-y-o	3-y-o	4-y-o+	Per cent	£1 Level Stake
Mrs S D Williams	1-19	0-0	0-0	1-19	5.3	- 11.00
Mrs P Sly	1-20	0-10	0-0	1-10	5.0	- 5.00
A Chamberlain	1-21	0-0	0-0	1-21	4.8	- 4.00
P J Feilden	1-22	0-0	0-0	1-22	4.5	- 17.50
J R Shaw	1-22	0-1	1-16	0-5	4.5	- 11.00
R Harris	1-22	0-0	1-15	0-7	4.5	- 11.00
J S King	1-24	0-0	0-3	1-21	4.2	- 16.50
A Smith	1-25	0-14	0-2	1-9	4.0	- 19.00
W Storey	1-25	0-1	0-10	1-14	4.0	- 4.00
R Lee	1-25	0-0	0-7	1-18	4.0	- 12.00
Miss J S Doyle	1-25	0-6	0-8	1-11	4.0	- 12.00
B J Llewellyn	1-29	0-0	0-2	1-27	3.4	- 23.00
R F Fisher	1-30	1-5	0-15	0-10	3.3	- 9.00
A Smith (Bel)	1-32	0-1	1-8	0-23	3.1	- 17.00
M J Madgwick	1-34	0-11	0-11	1-12	2.9	- 28.00
M P Muggeridge	1-34	0-9	0-11	1-14	2.9	0.00
J Norton	1-37	0-0	0-3	1-34	2.7	- 22.00
Miss A J Whitfield	1-39	0-1	1-23	0-15	2.6	- 37.09
B Forsey	1-40	0-0	0-0	1-40	2.5	- 19.00
B Ellison	1-40	0-6	0-6	1-28	2.5	- 19.00
D J S Ffrench Davis	1-40	1-17	0-18	0-5	2.5	- 29.00
R Voorspuy	1-41	0-5	0-5	1-31	2.4	- 34.50
C A Smith	1-41	1-13	0-22	0-6	2.4	- 24.00
T M Jones	1-42	0-15	1-26	0-1	2.4	- 34.00
C Tinkler	1-42	0-17	0-6	1-19	2.4	- 35.00
T Dyer	1-42	0-8	0-3	1-31	2.4	- 34.00
P R Hedger	1-43	0-0	0-15	1-28	2.3	- 35.50
M Dixon	1-46	0-9	0-19	1-18	2.2	- 43.90
P Burgoyne	1-48	0-0	0-2	1-46	2.1	- 41.00
P M McEntee	1-49	1-25	0-14	0-10	2.0	- 42.00
R W Emery	1-49	0-0	0-12	1-37	2.0	- 39.00
D Marks	1-50	0-4	0-5	1-41	2.0	- 42.50
B J McMath	1-50	0-6	1-13	0-31	2.0	- 37.00
P Butler	1-51	0-7	1-21	0-23	2.0	- 17.00
J J O'Neill	1-54	0-7	0-26	1-21	1.9	- 48.00
B Smart	1-55	0-20	0-17	1-18	1.8	- 46.00
Mrs V Aconley	1-59	0-5	0-17	1-37	1.7	- 51.00
Mrs A Swinbank	1-61	0-11	0-10	1-40	1.6	- 54.00
J E Long	1-75	0-2	1-11	0-62	1.3	- 66.00
R J Baker	1-83	0-10	0-28	1-45	1.2	- 70.00

WINNING FLAT JOCKEYS 1994

	1st	2nd	3rd	Unpl	Total Mts	Per cent	£1 Level Stake
L Dettori	233	243	164	677	1317	17.7	- 192.91
J Weaver	198	149	134	579	1060	18.7	+ 171.15
Pat Eddery	154	110	79	458	801	19.2	- 27.40
K Darley	154	124	115	550	943	16.3	- 125.26
T Quinn	112	118	120	559	909	12.3	- 191.26
J Reid	98	86	75	437	696	14.1	- 84.69
M Hills	88	78	65	412	643	13.7	- 45.02
W Carson	88	93	86	385	652	13.5	- 214.28
Paul Eddery	83	65	79	507	734	11.3	- 233.22
J Carroll	82	50	71	440	643	12.8	- 198.06
M Roberts	81	71	75	537	764	10.6	- 169.12
W R Swinburn	75	80	71	301	527	14.2	- 74.35
W Ryan	70	69	52	323	514	13.6	- 124.87
D Harrison	65	59	68	364	556	11.7	- 0.88
R Cochrane	63	66	70	406	605	10.4	- 172.78
G Duffield	62	45	45	352	504	12.3	- 172.29
R Hills	59	80	53	260	452	13.1	+ 11.10
G Carter	57	67	44	349	517	11.0	- 194.21
D Holland	56	51	43	281	431	13.0	+ 43.60
J Fortune	55	58	52	348	513	10.7	- 126.15
A Munro	52	48	55	218	373	13.9	+ 2.98
W Woods	50	43	43	275	411	12.2	- 99.63
P Robinson	50	45	44	326	465	10.8	- 172.94
K Fallon	47	46	62	277	432	10.9	- 95.19
A Clark	47	45	37	377	506	9.3	- 94.78
J Quinn	41	68	73	601	783	5.2	- 357.75
B Raymond	40	34	32	172	278	14.4	- 80.83
B Thomson	40	32	37	247	356	11.2	- 13.46
G Hind	35	34	28	238	335	10.4	- 105.62
G Bardwell	35	34	27	369	465	7.5	- 200.66
W Newnes	33	26	37	337	433	7.6	- 140.77
J Williams	33	58	50	420	561	5.9	- 292.93
A McGlone	31	21	18	283	353	8.8	- 164.79
A Mackay	31	21	41	397	490	6.3	- 163.75
D McKeown	31	55	48	367	501	6.2	- 262.12
M Birch	28	28	34	306	396	7.1	- 219.08
J Lowe	25	31	33	398	487	5.1	- 225.87
D Biggs	24	17	25	182	248	9.7	- 61.64
M J Kinane	23	18	21	86	148	15.5	- 1.04
R Price	22	14	19	272	327	6.7	- 117.75
Dale Gibson	22	20	31	322	395	5.6	- 123.12
N Connorton	21	28	26	213	288	7.3	- 58.92
S Whitworth	21	34	19	270	344	6.1	- 224.64
C Rutter	20	18	25	236	299	6.7	- 120.37
L Charnock	20	26	36	339	421	4.8	- 178.12
R Hughes	19	15	21	110	165	11.5	- 38.12
L Piggott	19	15	24	147	205	9.3	- 101.94
N Carlisle	19	22	24	281	346	5.5	- 201.62
T Williams	19	17	31	333	400	4.8	- 224.50
B Rouse	18	19	29	185	251	7.2	- 111.24
M Tebbutt	17	20	19	190	246	6.9	- 133.87
R Perham	17	21	17	229	284	6.0	- 57.72
M Wigham	16	21	14	170	221	7.2	- 51.50
A Culhane	15	19	18	178	230	6.5	- 99.25

	1st	2nd	3rd	Unpl	Total Mts	Per cent	£1 Level Stake
S Webster	14	16	14	140	184	7.6	- 63.50
T Sprake	14	25	19	186	244	5.7	-126.97
J Fanning	14	28	38	352	432	3.2	-291.06
T Ives	13	12	28	191	244	5.3	-128.38
Alex Greaves	12	7	13	96	128	9.4	- 71.13
S D Williams	12	17	12	140	181	6.6	- 87.20
N Adams	12	21	24	445	502	2.4	-414.60
S Perks	11	17	23	147	198	5.6	-136.75
S Raymont	8	6	13	49	76	10.5	+ 0.86
M Perrett	6	2	4	63	75	8.0	- 9.90
Kim Tinkler	5	6	7	137	155	3.2	-103.00
Kim McDonnell	4	5	4	29	42	9.5	- 15.00
E Guest	4	2	2	40	48	8.3	+ 6.00
R Lappin	4	8	2	57	71	5.6	- 41.12
R Street	4	5	8	58	75	5.3	- 33.00
C Dwyer	3	1	0	22	26	11.5	- 10.00
C Nutter	3	4	2	22	31	9.7	- 14.62
T Wall	3	6	5	54	68	4.4	- 21.00
T Jarnet	2	0	0	3	5	40.0	+ 11.50
T Lucas	2	2	4	74	82	2.4	- 76.49
S Dawson	2	6	5	75	88	2.3	- 67.50
Ronnie Beggan	1	0	0	0	1	100.0	+ 5.00
P Scudamore	1	0	0	0	1	100.0	+ 4.00
S Guillot	1	0	0	0	1	100.0	+ 8.00
Le Tollboll	1	0	1	1	3	33.3	+ 0.25
Lorna Vincent	1	0	0	3	4	25.0	- 1.00
M Servranckx	1	0	0	4	5	20.0	- 1.25
P D'Arcy	1	1	3	8	13	7.7	- 7.00
V Smith	1	0	2	17	20	5.0	+ 6.00
M McAndrew	1	3	1	20	25	4.0	- 13.00
W Hood	1	2	1	21	25	4.0	- 23.00
C Asmussen	1	3	6	24	34	2.9	- 19.00
Candy Morris	1	1	4	47	53	1.9	- 47.00
S O'Gorman	1	4	5	46	56	1.8	- 48.00
E Johnson	1	5	0	56	62	1.6	- 49.00
A Tucker	1	5	6	96	108	0.9	- 95.00

WINNING APPRENTICES 1994

	1st	2nd	3rd	Unpl	Total Mts	Per cent	£1 Level Stake
Stephen Davies	41	48	39	318	446	9.2	-118.64
M Fenton	39	35	32	278	384	10.2	-172.31
J Tate	33	32	27	253	345	9.6	- 85.57
J Stack	28	27	27	196	278	10.1	- 91.05
B Doyle	26	35	43	280	384	6.8	- 6.83
D Griffiths	19	7	13	113	152	12.5	- 13.71
D McCabe	17	18	12	135	182	9.3	- 20.25
A Whelan	16	15	17	130	178	9.0	- 16.75
S Maloney	15	17	28	209	269	5.6	-174.02
N Varley	15	24	28	220	287	5.2	-139.75
D Wright	15	17	18	344	394	3.8	-304.20
S Drowne	14	14	12	135	175	8.0	- 47.00
K Rutter	13	12	13	125	163	8.0	- 54.92

	1st	2nd	3rd	Unpl	Total Mts	Per cent	£1 Level Stake
J Marshall	12	12	20	134	178	6.7	− 51.25
S Sanders	11	18	21	121	171	6.4	− 21.35
F Norton	11	10	16	183	220	5.0	−133.00
S Mulvey	10	9	6	80	105	9.5	− 46.04
R Painter	10	15	11	86	122	8.2	− 48.46
D Moffatt	10	9	16	116	151	6.6	− 64.52
P McCabe	10	13	15	129	167	6.0	− 96.17
C Hodgson	10	13	11	136	170	5.9	−101.12
M Baird	9	10	13	157	189	4.8	−100.25
Emma O'Gorman	8	6	7	45	66	12.1	0.00
G Parkin	8	8	4	56	76	10.5	− 17.75
N Kennedy	8	7	18	162	195	4.1	− 85.00
A Garth	8	12	17	169	206	3.9	−118.75
Sarah Thompson	7	6	2	30	45	15.6	+ 35.00
S Lanigan	7	3	1	63	74	9.5	− 3.75
H Bastiman	6	1	5	29	41	14.6	− 18.27
M J Dwyer	6	4	1	45	56	10.7	+ 11.75
R Havlin	6	5	6	51	68	8.8	− 12.25
C N Adamson	6	6	8	59	79	7.6	− 22.25
D O'Neill	5	6	9	39	59	8.5	− 10.50
S Copp	5	9	5	41	60	8.3	+ 3.50
P Roberts	5	7	6	58	76	6.6	− 60.95
J D Smith	5	3	9	76	93	5.4	− 28.00
C Teague	5	9	10	107	131	3.8	− 82.00
L Aspell	4	1	1	15	21	19.0	− 7.65
D Gibbs	4	4	7	15	30	13.3	+ 28.50
M Deering	4	2	1	40	47	8.5	+ 3.00
M Henry	4	5	7	32	48	8.3	− 14.50
R Waterfield	4	7	4	41	56	7.1	− 21.75
P Fessey	4	6	7	49	66	6.1	− 45.76
Ruth Coulter	3	1	2	13	19	15.8	+ 3.20
L Carter	3	2	2	13	20	15.0	+ 40.00
G Mitchell	3	1	3	13	20	15.0	+ 1.50
A Procter	3	0	1	30	34	8.8	− 15.37
Iona Wands	3	2	2	34	41	7.3	− 18.17
B Russell	3	5	4	71	83	3.6	− 63.50
L Newton	3	8	5	71	87	3.4	− 62.75
V Halliday	3	6	7	88	104	2.9	− 79.50
C Hawksley	3	6	5	106	120	2.5	−104.00
Elizabeth Turner	2	0	0	6	8	25.0	+ 7.50
N Hall	2	0	0	9	11	18.2	+ 2.50
Kimberley Hart	2	0	2	7	11	18.2	+ 12.00
T Fuggle	2	0	0	10	12	16.7	+ 4.25
Oliver Casey	2	2	1	7	12	16.7	− 6.81
G Milligan	2	1	1	9	13	15.4	+ 2.00
S Eiffert	2	2	2	11	17	11.8	− 3.50
C Scally	2	0	2	16	20	10.0	− 6.00
Amanda Sanders	2	2	2	23	29	6.9	− 1.00
M Humphries	2	1	1	26	30	6.7	− 6.00
Aimee Cook	2	0	3	25	30	6.7	− 1.12
L Suthern	2	4	3	26	35	5.7	− 28.00
G Strange	2	4	4	28	38	5.3	− 20.00
P Bowe	2	7	5	31	45	4.4	− 38.40
A Daly	2	3	4	48	57	3.5	− 46.00
D Denby	2	3	5	52	62	3.2	− 35.50
T G McLaughlin	2	8	3	64	77	2.6	− 52.00

	1st	2nd	3rd	Unpl	Total Mts	Per cent	£1 Level Stake
Richard Edwards	1	0	0	0	1	100.0	+ 2.25
C Dykes	1	0	1	2	4	25.0	+ 0.33
P Houghton	1	1	0	3	5	20.0	- 2.37
Adelle Gibbons	1	0	1	3	5	20.0	+ 5.00
G Macdonald	1	1	0	3	5	20.0	- 0.50
D Thomas	1	0	2	3	6	16.7	0.00
Carol Davison	1	1	1	4	7	14.3	+ 2.00
G Faulkner	1	0	1	5	7	14.3	+ 10.00
S Richardson	1	1	0	5	7	14.3	+ 8.00
Jo Hunnam	1	1	2	4	8	12.5	- 6.00
D Meredith	1	0	0	9	10	10.0	+ 7.00
Catherine Cooper	1	1	0	8	10	10.0	- 6.00
C Webb	1	0	1	10	12	8.3	- 9.90
J Dennis	1	1	3	8	13	7.7	0.00
D Toole	1	0	2	12	15	6.7	- 11.00
W Hawksley	1	0	0	15	16	6.3	+ 5.00
Nicola Howarth	1	1	1	15	18	5.6	- 11.00
R Moogan	1	3	4	11	19	5.3	- 16.50
M Kneafsey	1	1	1	16	19	5.3	+ 32.00
O Pears	1	3	1	16	21	4.8	- 6.00
C Munday	1	1	2	33	37	2.7	- 27.00
N Gwilliams	1	1	1	43	46	2.2	- 31.00
V Slattery	1	0	1	45	47	2.1	- 30.00
A Eddery	1	2	5	48	56	1.8	- 49.50
Mark Denaro	1	8	6	46	61	1.6	- 54.00
Claire Balding	1	3	4	59	67	1.5	- 54.00

WINNING AMATEUR RIDERS 1994

	1st	2nd	3rd	Unpl	Total Mts	Per cent	£1 Level Stake
Mrs L Pearce	9	7	10	30	56	16.1	- 7.55
T Cuff	7	3	2	20	32	21.9	+ 25.25
Miss A Elsey	4	2	0	13	19	21.1	+ 31.30
Mrs M Cowdrey	4	1	3	14	22	18.2	- 8.38
Miss I D W Jones	4	5	6	23	38	10.5	- 15.67
A Balding	3	2	1	2	8	37.5	+ 11.00
C Bonner	3	1	1	6	11	27.3	+ 5.95
Miss L Hide	3	2	0	7	12	25.0	+ 3.25
Mrs D Kettlewell	3	5	1	12	21	14.3	- 6.75
T McCarthy	2	0	0	5	7	28.6	+ 1.75
V Lukanuik	2	0	0	6	8	25.0	+ 7.75
Miss S Higgins	2	0	0	7	9	22.2	+ 29.00
Miss A Harwood	2	3	0	7	12	16.7	+ 2.17
Miss E Houghton	2	0	0	10	12	16.7	+ 12.00
P P-Gordon	2	2	3	7	14	14.3	- 0.50
Mrs D Arbuthnot	2	3	1	13	19	10.5	- 7.50
Renee Kierans	1	0	0	0	1	100.0	+ 8.00
Miss S Rowe	1	0	0	1	2	50.0	+ 32.00
L A Urbano	1	1	0	0	2	50.0	+ 4.00
A Michael	1	0	1	0	2	50.0	+ 32.00
Miss J Feilden	1	0	0	2	3	33.3	+ 1.50
Mrs L Fahey	1	0	0	2	3	33.3	+ 18.00
Miss S Bainbridge	1	0	0	2	3	33.3	+ 31.00

	1st	2nd	3rd	Unpl	Total Mts	Per cent	£1 Level Stake
Mrs A Dennis	1	0	0	2	3	33.3	+ 7.00
M A Naughton	1	0	0	2	3	33.3	+ 23.00
R Teal	1	0	1	4	6	16.7	0.00
Miss C Spearing	1	0	0	5	6	16.7	- 1.50
Mrs M Busby	1	0	0	5	6	16.7	+ 5.00
J L Llewellyn	1	0	1	4	6	16.7	0.00
Miss B Craven	1	0	0	5	6	16.7	+ 11.00
I McLelland	1	0	1	5	7	14.3	+ 14.00
R Hale	1	0	1	5	7	14.3	- 3.00
Miss D J Jones	1	0	0	6	7	14.3	+ 10.00
Miss C Metcalfe	1	0	0	6	7	14.3	+ 34.00
Mrs J Musson	1	0	1	6	8	12.5	- 2.50
J Durkan	1	0	1	6	8	12.5	- 4.50
Miss F Haynes	1	1	0	6	8	12.5	- 2.50
P Phillips	1	0	0	7	8	12.5	+ 43.00
G J Houghton	1	3	1	4	9	11.1	- 5.00
Mrs J Crossley	1	2	2	4	9	11.1	+ 2.00
Mrs A Farrell	1	1	1	7	10	10.0	+ 11.00
Miss M Carson	1	0	2	7	10	10.0	- 1.00
M Mannish	1	0	0	9	10	10.0	- 1.00
Mrs H Noonan	1	0	0	12	13	7.7	0.00
Miss A Purdy	1	1	1	11	14	7.1	+ 7.00
Miss R Clark	1	0	0	15	16	6.3	- 12.00
Mrs S Bosley	1	5	3	21	30	3.3	- 19.00

LEADING TRAINERS' AND OWNERS' PRIZE MONEY 1994

	Races Won	Value £		Races Won	Value £
M R Stoute	108	1,384,928	Hamdan Al-Maktoum	133	1,875,132
J L Dunlop	82	1,309,562	Sheikh Mohammed	125	1,727,614
H R A Cecil	76	1,046,674	Maktoum Al Maktoum	57	829,427
J H M Gosden	93	774,152	K Abdulla	56	523,430
M Johnston	114	659,242	Cheveley Park Stud	50	392,365
R Hannon	111	637,233	P D Savill	52	300,571
J Berry	123	473,209	R E Sangster	28	253,266
P F I Cole	68	472,439	J C Smith	13	209,719
L M Cumani	47	456,652	Lord Howard De Walden	12	183,393
G Wragg	32	428,111	Gary A Tanaka	1	165,948
B W Hills	44	424,338	J L C Pearce	6	151,970
I A Balding	51	407,795	H R H Prince Fahd Salman	34	149,021
M R Channon	73	375,791	Sheikh Ahmed Al Maktoum	23	147,502
R W Armstrong	23	361,693	Maktoum Al Maktoum	1	147,500
R Akehurst	48	360,730	Godolphin	11	145,374
A Fabre (Fra)	3	354,483	Baron G Von Ullmann	3	143,342
Sir M Prescott	54	351,110	H R H Sultan Ahmad Shah	9	141,340
D R Loder	39	340,117	G R Bailey Ltd (Horse Feed)	3	138,102

LEADING TRAINERS FIRST TIME OUT 1990-94

	Total W-R	2-y-o	3-y-o	4-y-o+	Per cent	£1 Level Stake
H R A Cecil	147-569	53-205	83-315	11-49	25.8	- 48.48
J H M Gosden	118-642	35-178	63-382	20-82	18.4	+ 12.72
M R Stoute	104-675	40-295	49-315	15-65	15.4	-149.57
J Berry	90-619	55-382	23-157	12-80	14.5	- 69.35
P F I Cole	84-594	50-281	27-225	7-88	14.1	-169.65
R Hannon	81-933	38-497	35-324	8-112	8.7	-296.75
B W Hills	71-573	20-246	40-271	11-56	12.4	-137.48
J L Dunlop	62-573	24-260	25-227	13-86	10.8	-188.19
L M Cumani	59-422	20-123	28-241	11-58	14.0	-113.64
R Charlton	57-265	25-109	25-128	7-28	21.5	+ 66.71
P Chapple-Hyam	53-239	33-133	17-90	3-16	22.2	+ 14.69
Lord Huntingdon	48-340	6-103	33-150	9-87	14.1	+ 2.85
H Thomson Jones	45-235	25-97	20-121	0-17	19.1	+ 5.51
G Harwood	43-335	9-105	27-169	7-61	12.8	-128.20
C E Brittain	42-561	9-209	18-220	15-132	7.5	-161.04
Sir Mark Prescott	40-282	15-138	22-113	3-31	14.2	- 80.35
M Johnston	40-291	14-120	13-97	13-74	13.7	+ 10.52
I A Balding	37-379	12-154	17-153	8-72	9.8	- 97.96
G Wragg	36-234	11-77	18-121	7-36	15.4	- 31.71
Mrs M Reveley	34-325	2-75	10-83	22-167	10.5	- 58.62
M Bell	33-308	13-153	18-118	2-37	10.7	-134.98
D R C Elsworth	30-338	12-112	7-125	11-101	8.9	- 24.37
W A O'Gorman	28-156	8-74	11-51	9-31	17.9	+ 1.07
W R Hern	28-209	13-73	12-116	3-20	13.4	- 60.49
A C Stewart	27-237	5-58	17-154	5-25	11.4	- 58.09
P T Walwyn	26-233	8-97	15-109	3-27	11.2	- 33.06
J W Watts	25-171	7-60	10-81	8-30	14.6	+ 26.85
R Akehurst	24-275	0-41	6-68	18-166	8.7	- 88.44
Mrs J Ramsden	23-215	3-71	11-74	9-70	10.7	- 41.22
M R Channon	23-254	16-123	4-77	3-54	9.1	- 65.32
W J Haggas	22-161	2-63	13-70	7-28	13.7	+ 12.74
J R Fanshawe	22-250	6-94	14-123	2-33	8.8	- 29.65
B Hanbury	21-302	7-122	10-142	4-38	7.0	-163.14
W Jarvis	20-250	10-107	8-105	2-38	8.0	-111.10
D R Loder	19-76	9-39	6-22	4-15	25.0	+ 28.61
R W Armstrong	19-180	9-66	7-84	3-30	10.6	- 49.73
R Hollinshead	19-408	2-135	9-141	8-132	4.7	-164.11
Mrs J Cecil	18-164	5-68	8-68	5-28	11.0	- 36.07
H Candy	18-204	5-64	9-94	4-46	8.8	+ 20.05
T D Barron	18-215	4-62	9-68	5-85	8.4	- 87.25
M H Tompkins	18-358	3-146	6-108	9-104	5.0	-187.00
J W Hills	17-206	5-77	8-75	4-54	8.3	- 32.67
M H Easterby	17-374	8-164	4-111	5-99	4.5	-230.60
S G Norton	16-171	5-68	6-62	5-41	9.4	- 40.75
M A Jarvis	16-208	4-80	10-96	2-32	7.7	- 58.70
D W P Arbuthnot	15-128	4-35	2-43	9-50	11.7	- 13.00
R J Hodges	14-233	2-30	1-46	11-157	6.0	- 71.87
M J Ryan	13-145	3-39	3-45	7-61	9.0	- 37.87
R M Whitaker	13-233	5-73	3-80	5-80	5.6	- 63.75
J Etherington	12-136	6-59	4-57	2-20	8.8	- 13.25
M McCormack	12-141	3-51	5-54	4-36	8.5	- 15.63
M C Pipe	11-100	1-6	4-18	6-76	11.0	- 43.65
M J Camacho	11-118	2-39	3-36	6-43	9.3	- 13.25
G B Balding	11-139	1-33	3-45	7-61	7.9	- 11.37

	Total W-R	2-y-o	3-y-o	4-y-o+	Per cent	£1 Level Stake
P W Harris	11-159	2-55	3-67	6-37	6.9	+ 47.00
B A McMahon	11-244	1-67	3-67	7-110	4.5	- 27.50
M J B Heaton-Ellis	10-108	3-44	3-41	4-23	9.3	+ 21.90
Mrs L Piggott	10-125	1-41	8-55	1-29	8.0	- 61.25
D Morley	10-166	8-66	1-72	1-28	6.0	- 81.00
F H Lee	10-179	1-48	3-62	6-69	5.6	- 54.00
G Lewis	10-241	5-120	3-88	2-33	4.1	-131.12
D Morris	9-77	2-19	1-16	6-42	11.7	- 1.75
R Guest	9-118	3-38	3-51	3-29	7.6	- 49.45
J Pearce	9-119	0-23	1-37	8-59	7.6	- 24.62
R J R Williams	9-133	2-42	3-55	4-36	6.8	- 40.25
P C Haslam	9-139	4-60	4-39	1-40	6.5	- 28.42
P A Kelleway	9-147	4-69	3-52	2-26	6.1	- 80.87
J Wharton	9-156	2-45	3-48	4-63	5.8	- 2.50
N A Callaghan	9-162	3-73	4-68	2-21	5.6	- 85.37
C A Cyzer	9-170	2-43	5-85	2-42	5.3	- 46.50
D W Chapman	9-180	0-21	1-45	8-114	5.0	- 89.10
P J Makin	9-186	1-47	5-83	3-56	4.8	-114.75
J G FitzGerald	9-198	0-51	4-68	5-79	4.5	-123.75

LEADING TRAINERS SECOND TIME OUT 1990-94

	Total W-R	2-y-o	3-y-o	4-y-o+	Per cent	£1 Level Stake
H R A Cecil	146-429	43-99	97-287	6-43	34.0	+ 21.72
J H M Gosden	132-504	27-99	89-331	16-74	26.2	- 47.47
R Hannon	119-869	74-457	38-308	7-104	13.7	-288.16
M R Stoute	105-525	39-175	54-288	12-62	20.0	-176.94
L M Cumani	97-359	24-84	66-222	7-53	27.0	- 71.86
J L Dunlop	93-507	38-218	42-214	13-75	18.3	- 61.85
J Berry	89-590	59-361	21-153	9-76	15.1	-126.73
B W Hills	78-481	30-174	44-253	4-54	16.2	-148.10
P F I Cole	76-492	41-219	28-201	7-72	15.4	-137.73
G Harwood	56-272	13-68	38-154	5-50	20.6	- 3.96
Lord Huntingdon	54-288	10-66	23-142	21-80	18.8	+ 7.19
R Charlton	53-217	22-70	27-121	4-26	24.4	- 4.81
C E Brittain	47-481	14-153	21-207	12-121	9.8	-192.71
P Chapple-Hyam	43-193	29-94	13-84	1-15	22.3	- 13.20
G Wragg	43-206	21-59	16-115	6-32	20.9	- 35.73
Sir Mark Prescott	43-251	16-113	23-108	4-30	17.1	- 80.13
M Bell	42-274	30-133	12-109	0-32	15.3	- 48.71
M Johnston	41-265	14-111	15-88	12-66	15.5	- 44.10
I A Balding	41-329	19-117	18-145	4-67	12.5	- 86.81
A C Stewart	37-189	5-29	27-135	5-25	19.6	- 43.06
Mrs M Reveley	37-295	6-71	10-76	21-148	12.5	- 78.97
M H Tompkins	37-318	15-129	12-98	10-91	11.6	- 77.11
D R C Elsworth	33-290	15-88	8-117	10-85	11.4	- 92.86
H Thomson Jones	32-199	18-74	13-110	1-15	16.1	- 51.16
P T Walwyn	32-217	13-83	12-108	7-26	14.7	+ 25.59
T D Barron	31-197	6-57	10-63	15-77	15.7	- 9.51
M R Channon	29-236	15-109	8-77	6-50	12.3	- 41.99
R Akehurst	29-252	3-38	6-61	20-153	11.5	+ 10.89
B Hanbury	28-260	16-98	8-124	4-38	10.8	-115.29
Mrs J Cecil	27-130	12-48	11-59	4-23	20.8	+ 29.35

	Total W-R	2-y-o	3-y-o	4-y-o+	Per cent	£1 Level Stake
B A McMahon	25-219	2-60	7-65	16-94	11.4	- 32.13
M H Easterby	24-342	13-149	6-105	5-88	7.0	-192.54
R Hollinshead	23-374	7-121	7-136	9-117	6.1	-170.05
J W Hills	22-192	7-67	11-75	4-50	11.5	- 71.00
R W Armstrong	21-145	13-48	6-74	2-23	14.5	+ 12.30
W Jarvis	21-201	11-69	7-96	3-36	10.4	- 97.94
J R Fanshawe	21-210	9-64	9-117	3-29	10.0	- 96.05
W J Haggas	20-129	8-44	11-61	1-24	15.5	+ 15.44
W R Hern	20-158	7-40	11-100	2-18	12.7	- 78.99
Mrs J Ramsden	20-205	5-67	5-72	10-66	9.8	-110.32
G Lewis	20-226	12-111	6-84	2-31	8.8	-122.27
D R Loder	19-63	13-30	4-20	2-13	30.2	- 5.88
W A O'Gorman	19-128	7-59	6-41	6-28	14.8	- 64.56
D Morley	17-144	7-52	5-66	5-26	11.8	- 21.34
P J Makin	17-155	4-36	9-71	4-48	11.0	- 43.88
S G Norton	17-158	6-64	5-60	6-34	10.8	- 56.12
Lady Herries	16-94	3-21	5-30	8-43	17.0	+ 23.38
J W Watts	16-155	6-50	7-75	3-30	10.3	- 73.71
M A Jarvis	16-187	4-62	10-94	2-31	8.6	-112.57
M J Camacho	14-106	1-33	5-36	8-37	13.2	- 20.36
P W Harris	14-145	4-49	4-60	6-36	9.7	- 31.99
M C Pipe	13-83	0-6	2-16	11-61	15.7	- 13.27
N A Callaghan	13-145	7-71	5-59	1-15	9.0	- 56.57
J A R Toller	12-63	5-13	4-30	3-20	19.0	+ 13.67
R Boss	12-123	6-45	4-59	2-19	9.8	- 64.99
M J Ryan	12-134	2-33	5-44	5-57	9.0	- 40.71
P A Kelleway	12-135	5-59	4-54	3-22	8.9	- 47.79
D W Chapman	12-161	3-19	1-42	8-100	7.5	- 22.71
R J R Williams	11-118	6-31	3-53	2-34	9.3	- 35.34
J Wharton	11-129	4-38	3-43	4-48	8.5	- 39.50
J G FitzGerald	11-158	3-46	4-55	4-57	7.0	- 72.17
H Candy	11-167	4-39	4-87	3-41	6.6	- 80.42
R J Hodges	11-194	1-26	2-40	8-128	5.7	- 95.75
C J Hill	10-126	1-28	3-35	6-63	7.9	- 36.76
M McCormack	10-129	3-46	4-49	3-34	7.8	- 67.98
M Brittain	10-195	3-66	4-66	3-63	5.1	- 72.92
R M Whitaker	10-211	4-68	3-75	3-68	4.7	-143.25
C R Nelson	9-72	5-20	1-35	3-17	12.5	- 7.93
P Calver	9-75	0-18	4-30	5-27	12.0	+ 11.60
N A Graham	9-86	4-24	3-41	2-21	10.5	- 22.04
C N Allen	9-99	2-32	6-37	1-30	9.1	- 51.51
D W P Arbuthnot	9-115	2-30	2-41	5-44	7.8	- 49.37
R F Johnson Houghton	9-117	5-52	2-51	2-14	7.7	- 44.72
Mrs N Macauley	9-121	2-32	3-40	4-49	7.4	- 55.25
Denys Smith	9-124	6-42	2-42	1-40	7.3	- 85.38
C A Cyzer	9-153	2-31	1-80	6-42	5.9	- 75.50
F H Lee	9-168	5-46	1-60	3-62	5.4	-120.75
M W Easterby	9-179	4-111	1-35	4-33	5.0	-128.95

LEADING TRAINERS BY MONTH 1990-94

January

	Total W-R	2-y-o	3-y-o	4-y-o+	Per cent	£1 Level Stake
T D Barron	26-117	0-0	14-48	12-69	22.2	- 19.94
D W Chapman	22-135	0-0	4-29	18-106	16.3	+ 24.69
R Hollinshead	20-120	0-0	4-37	16-83	16.7	- 24.44
W A O'Gorman	19-73	0-0	7-32	12-41	26.0	+ 16.34
M Johnston	16-67	0-0	3-20	13-47	23.9	+ 15.21
Lord Huntingdon	12-36	0-0	11-25	1-11	33.3	+ 24.59
A Bailey	9-64	0-0	2-21	7-43	14.1	+ 4.63
C C Elsey	8-33	0-0	1-6	7-27	24.2	+ 36.83
M J Ryan	8-43	0-0	2-10	6-33	18.6	- 9.49
J Berry	8-52	0-0	5-25	3-27	15.4	+ 5.00
C J Hill	8-66	0-0	4-14	4-52	12.1	- 42.16
D J G Murray Smith	7-21	0-0	5-11	2-10	33.3	+ 28.31
P A Kelleway	7-36	0-0	2-13	5-23	19.4	- 7.25
P C Haslam	7-44	0-0	2-11	5-33	15.9	- 10.76
R J O'Sullivan	7-46	0-0	0-0	7-46	15.2	- 19.77
C N Allen	7-60	0-0	7-41	0-19	11.7	- 12.33
R Bastiman	6-17	0-0	2-3	4-14	35.3	+ 9.88
R Akehurst	6-28	0-0	2-2	4-26	21.4	+ 13.06
P Mitchell	6-38	0-0	0-8	6-30	15.8	+ 3.50
A Moore	6-41	0-0	0-3	6-38	14.6	+ 43.25
J L Harris	6-44	0-0	1-8	5-36	13.6	- 3.25
M C Chapman	6-47	0-0	1-12	5-35	12.8	+ 2.50
Mrs N Macauley	6-77	0-0	5-28	1-49	7.8	- 47.37

February

	Total W-R	2-y-o	3-y-o	4-y-o+	Per cent	£1 Level Stake
T D Barron	21-80	0-0	8-29	13-51	26.3	+ 19.28
M Johnston	19-62	0-0	12-20	7-42	30.6	+ 30.94
R Hollinshead	12-91	0-0	7-31	5-60	13.2	- 24.02
Lord Huntingdon	11-46	0-0	7-25	4-21	23.9	- 4.35
T Thomson Jones	8-17	0-0	0-2	8-15	47.1	+ 19.59
C N Allen	8-56	0-0	6-40	2-16	14.3	- 17.14
Dr J D Scargill	7-32	0-0	2-8	5-24	21.9	+ 7.23
C J Hill	7-43	0-0	3-10	4-33	16.3	+ 10.35
W A O'Gorman	7-62	0-0	3-26	4-36	11.3	- 31.88
D W Chapman	7-114	0-0	2-22	5-92	6.1	- 84.67
B W Hills	6-14	0-0	4-11	2-3	42.9	+ 0.76
C P Wildman	6-32	0-0	0-3	6-29	18.8	+ 5.13
J Berry	6-34	0-0	4-16	2-18	17.6	- 4.06
C C Elsey	6-35	0-0	2-12	4-23	17.1	+ 7.60
R J O'Sullivan	6-40	0-0	1-3	5-37	15.0	- 3.50
N A Graham	5-12	0-0	2-5	3-7	41.7	+ 6.55
K R Burke	5-15	0-0	1-3	4-12	33.3	+ 9.23
D Haydn Jones	5-19	0-0	0-1	5-18	26.3	+ 13.25
J Pearce	5-34	0-0	2-5	3-29	14.7	- 7.00
Mrs A Knight	5-37	0-0	0-0	5-37	13.5	+ 46.50

March

	Total W-R	2-y-o	3-y-o	4-y-o+	Per cent	£1 Level Stake
J Berry	36-146	13-51	12-52	11-43	24.7	+ 77.31
M R Channon	18-76	4-10	3-28	11-38	23.7	+ 68.10
W A O'Gorman	16-63	1-5	9-27	6-31	25.4	+ 3.95
T D Barron	16-96	0-9	4-26	12-61	16.7	+ 5.75
B W Hills	14-42	1-5	10-28	3-9	33.3	+ 4.06
M Johnston	14-85	0-4	7-33	7-48	16.5	- 21.82
M Bell	13-74	3-12	9-42	1-20	17.6	- 10.41
C E Brittain	13-94	0-0	4-50	9-44	13.8	- 11.59
Mrs M Reveley	12-57	1-6	1-13	10-38	21.1	+ 1.53
Lord Huntingdon	12-59	0-0	7-32	5-27	20.3	+ 5.19
R Hannon	11-113	2-19	9-56	0-38	9.7	- 68.39
Mrs J Ramsden	10-73	0-1	4-36	6-36	13.7	+ 6.45
Sir Mark Prescott	9-31	0-0	9-27	0-4	29.0	+ 2.26
R J O'Sullivan	9-52	0-0	0-2	9-50	17.3	+ 55.50
S G Norton	9-54	0-3	6-33	3-18	16.7	+ 9.00
D W Chapman	8-94	0-2	0-18	8-74	8.5	- 57.87
Mrs N Macauley	7-64	0-2	2-26	5-36	10.9	+ 15.50
M Brittain	7-90	1-14	3-35	3-41	7.8	- 51.25
W W Haigh	6-19	0-0	0-2	6-17	31.6	+ 17.75
J H M Gosden	6-25	0-0	6-23	0-2	24.0	+ 3.99
R Boss	6-27	2-3	4-16	0-8	22.2	+ 17.25
B A McMahon	6-48	0-3	1-16	5-29	12.5	+ 42.30
R Hollinshead	6-171	1-18	4-64	1-89	3.5	-102.00
M C Pipe	5-18	0-0	1-3	4-15	27.8	- 0.97
G Wragg	5-27	0-0	4-19	1-8	18.5	- 14.18
P F I Cole	5-28	1-1	3-21	1-6	17.9	- 10.00
H J Collingridge	5-30	0-0	0-9	5-21	16.7	+ 70.00
P Mitchell	5-31	1-2	0-11	4-18	16.1	+ 4.50
S Dow	5-62	1-3	2-21	2-38	8.1	- 13.00
M R Stoute	4-13	0-0	4-10	0-3	30.8	+ 2.96
P C Haslam	4-21	0-1	1-7	3-13	19.0	+ 4.48
J G FitzGerald	4-22	0-1	1-1	3-20	18.2	+ 31.25
D R C Elsworth	4-25	0-0	1-9	3-16	16.0	- 9.37
D A Wilson	4-26	0-0	1-2	3-24	15.4	+ 16.15
C C Elsey	4-26	0-0	0-7	4-19	15.4	- 13.75
Mrs A Knight	4-31	0-0	0-1	4-30	12.9	- 5.50
R Akehurst	4-33	0-0	0-4	4-29	12.1	- 8.25
M W Easterby	4-33	1-13	0-8	3-12	12.1	- 4.00
M J Ryan	4-38	0-0	2-11	2-27	10.5	- 6.00
P A Kelleway	4-39	0-5	1-17	3-17	10.3	- 18.12
A Moore	4-41	0-0	0-6	4-35	9.8	- 17.25
C N Allen	4-44	1-3	2-22	1-19	9.1	+ 18.75
J Etherington	3-5	0-0	1-2	2-3	60.0	+ 24.00
G B Balding	3-11	0-0	0-0	3-11	27.3	+ 14.50
C R Nelson	3-13	0-0	1-7	2-6	23.1	- 5.24
G Harwood	3-16	0-0	3-7	0-9	18.8	- 9.04
D W P Arbuthnot	3-17	0-0	0-4	3-13	17.6	- 5.75
M J Camacho	3-20	0-0	1-5	2-15	15.0	+ 5.00
C J Hill	3-21	0-0	2-5	1-16	14.3	- 4.25
K O Cunningham-Brown	3-26	0-1	0-3	3-22	11.5	- 2.75
C A Cyzer	3-34	0-1	0-15	3-18	8.8	- 17.50
C Tinkler	3-35	1-6	1-12	1-17	8.6	- 19.25
G Lewis	3-36	1-3	2-22	0-11	8.3	- 18.62
E J Alston	3-42	1-9	0-7	2-26	7.1	- 5.00

April

	Total W-R	2-y-o	3-y-o	4-y-o+	Per cent	£1 Level Stake
J Berry	81-419	40-166	26-167	15-86	19.3	- 14.88
R Hannon	70-491	24-104	38-283	8-104	14.3	- 53.07
H R A Cecil	68-207	0-1	57-169	11-37	32.9	+ 11.86
J L Dunlop	43-262	0-5	30-178	13-79	16.4	- 29.96
J H M Gosden	39-190	0-0	28-139	11-51	20.5	+ 0.67
M R Stoute	30-194	0-2	24-154	6-38	15.5	- 48.81
C E Brittain	30-245	1-9	16-143	13-93	12.2	+ 34.22
P F I Cole	30-252	3-31	24-172	3-49	11.9	-118.84
Mrs J Ramsden	29-206	0-10	13-94	16-102	14.1	- 70.81
Sir Mark Prescott	24-94	0-0	17-70	7-24	25.5	+ 3.52
M Johnston	24-171	1-28	15-77	8-66	14.0	- 9.59
M Bell	24-175	8-39	14-101	2-35	13.7	- 44.50
R Hollinshead	24-297	4-47	7-136	13-114	8.1	- 66.67
P Chapple-Hyam	23-96	4-8	15-74	4-14	24.0	+ 31.00
R J Hodges	21-154	2-2	2-25	17-127	13.6	+ 9.13
B W Hills	21-222	0-20	16-165	5-37	9.5	- 74.12
Mrs M Reveley	20-122	1-11	7-36	12-75	16.4	- 34.45
Lord Huntingdon	19-97	0-0	12-56	7-41	19.6	+ 21.80
P T Walwyn	19-108	0-0	13-84	6-24	17.6	+ 21.49
J W Watts	18-114	0-4	12-77	6-33	15.8	+ 11.47
M R Channon	17-167	11-50	6-63	0-54	10.2	- 55.39
M H Easterby	17-215	6-56	5-83	6-76	7.9	-121.61
G Wragg	16-124	1-3	11-91	4-30	12.9	- 48.15
I A Balding	16-141	0-2	11-89	5-50	11.3	- 43.37
M J Camacho	15-74	0-3	4-35	11-36	20.3	+ 45.26
W J Haggas	14-56	1-2	12-41	1-13	25.0	+ 42.67
G Harwood	14-87	0-1	12-57	2-29	16.1	- 31.96
M A Jarvis	14-89	0-2	12-69	2-18	15.7	+ 49.15
B A McMahon	14-122	0-19	6-39	8-64	11.5	- 9.50
L M Cumani	13-121	0-0	9-95	4-26	10.7	- 49.70
T D Barron	13-127	1-19	5-39	7-69	10.2	- 29.00
Mrs J Cecil	12-50	1-1	6-34	5-15	24.0	+ 27.13
M J Ryan	12-96	0-5	5-32	7-59	12.5	+ 20.38
B Hanbury	12-129	0-6	7-94	5-29	9.3	- 58.75
G Lewis	12-175	4-46	5-94	3-35	6.9	- 68.50
M Brittain	12-252	1-38	4-106	7-108	4.8	-105.00
M McCormack	11-70	0-5	6-36	5-29	15.7	+ 48.25
E J Alston	11-77	2-11	3-17	6-49	14.3	+ 18.25
S G Norton	11-113	1-18	6-64	4-31	9.7	- 24.00
R Akehurst	11-123	0-1	1-17	10-105	8.9	- 38.50
M H Tompkins	11-124	0-17	5-62	6-45	8.9	- 60.52
A C Stewart	10-59	0-1	6-44	4-14	16.9	+ 6.47
W A O'Gorman	10-62	6-16	4-25	0-21	16.1	- 24.37
R Charlton	10-70	0-3	9-56	1-11	14.3	- 36.54
C A Cyzer	10-102	0-1	4-63	6-38	9.8	+ 42.50
J Wharton	9-70	4-19	1-17	4-34	12.9	+ 24.00
W Jarvis	9-91	4-12	3-59	2-20	9.9	- 44.32
M W Easterby	9-124	2-50	2-33	5-41	7.3	- 66.97
H Thomson Jones	8-63	0-0	8-55	0-8	12.7	- 9.40
W J Musson	8-79	0-2	1-25	7-52	10.1	- 3.25
P C Haslam	8-82	2-20	4-25	2-37	9.8	- 13.49
J R Fanshawe	8-102	0-1	5-76	3-25	7.8	- 33.00
D R C Elsworth	8-126	0-8	2-64	6-54	6.3	- 62.37

May

	Total W-R	2-y-o	3-y-o	4-y-o+	Per cent	£1 Level Stake
J Berry	108-590	62-270	27-193	19-127	18.3	+ 13.54
R Hannon	98-701	36-203	49-374	13-124	14.0	- 138.13
M R Stoute	80-338	2-14	62-272	16-52	23.7	- 13.65
H R A Cecil	74-268	4-10	67-220	3-38	27.6	- 38.87
J H M Gosden	59-259	0-5	49-204	10-50	22.8	- 2.01
J L Dunlop	51-292	4-27	38-196	9-69	17.5	- 61.04
B W Hills	47-315	4-42	36-206	7-67	14.9	- 85.92
P F I Cole	45-355	18-62	19-215	8-78	12.7	- 146.24
M Johnston	42-257	10-49	13-102	19-106	16.3	- 12.30
M H Tompkins	38-222	5-42	21-109	12-71	17.1	+ 70.28
I A Balding	38-244	2-15	21-147	15-82	15.6	+ 37.41
L M Cumani	33-181	1-3	25-146	7-32	18.2	- 51.28
G Harwood	32-165	2-7	25-115	5-43	19.4	- 6.32
Mrs M Reveley	32-203	5-30	9-62	18-111	15.8	+ 18.19
M Bell	31-200	13-54	17-113	1-33	15.5	- 25.23
M H Easterby	31-333	10-100	9-125	12-108	9.3	- 120.25
Sir Mark Prescott	25-105	2-4	19-74	4-27	23.8	- 13.62
P Chapple-Hyam	25-109	10-24	15-74	0-11	22.9	- 15.77
R Charlton	25-116	2-5	18-89	5-22	21.6	+ 16.70
B Hanbury	25-181	3-23	18-120	4-38	13.8	- 19.71
R Akehurst	25-191	0-6	7-60	18-125	13.1	- 21.17
C E Brittain	25-327	2-27	13-189	10-111	7.6	- 82.71
J R Fanshawe	24-125	0-6	22-99	2-20	19.2	+ 59.36
R Hollinshead	24-341	3-62	11-138	10-141	7.0	- 139.12
G Wragg	22-127	5-10	12-89	5-28	17.3	- 23.54
H Thomson Jones	22-132	6-11	16-108	0-13	16.7	- 24.70
G Lewis	22-206	4-57	17-109	1-40	10.7	- 15.89
R M Whitaker	22-215	6-38	6-89	10-88	10.2	+ 14.55
M R Channon	22-233	9-82	2-87	11-64	9.4	- 103.92
J W Hills	21-139	0-6	11-76	10-57	15.1	- 15.67
S G Norton	19-127	2-19	8-67	9-41	15.0	- 19.51
J W Watts	19-146	2-17	8-82	9-47	13.0	- 5.02
P T Walwyn	19-153	0-8	14-118	5-27	12.4	- 8.79
T D Barron	19-161	4-32	5-49	10-80	11.8	- 32.95
Mrs J Ramsden	19-193	3-19	9-85	7-89	9.8	- 72.04
Mrs J Cecil	18-91	0-3	12-62	6-26	19.8	+ 5.60
Lord Huntingdon	18-119	3-12	6-66	9-41	15.1	- 38.05
D R C Elsworth	18-218	0-17	7-120	11-81	8.3	- 37.02
W Jarvis	16-128	5-15	7-82	4-31	12.5	- 33.27
R J R Williams	15-94	5-15	4-36	6-43	16.0	+ 62.26
M J Ryan	15-121	2-12	3-44	10-65	12.4	- 4.12
N A Callaghan	15-137	3-38	11-81	1-18	10.9	- 12.90
W J Haggas	14-98	0-8	12-69	2-21	14.3	- 9.65
A C Stewart	14-100	0-0	10-81	4-19	14.0	- 43.89
J Wharton	14-111	5-22	3-35	6-54	12.6	+ 52.95
M A Jarvis	14-130	1-13	10-84	3-33	10.8	- 49.04
R J Hodges	13-217	0-15	1-40	12-162	6.0	- 117.12
Mrs N Macauley	12-97	1-10	5-38	6-49	12.4	+ 30.75
R Boss	12-105	4-19	5-62	3-24	11.4	- 28.37
M McCormack	12-117	5-21	5-49	2-47	10.3	- 49.86
M Brittain	12-255	3-71	2-89	7-95	4.7	- 111.17

June

	Total W-R	2-y-o	3-y-o	4-y-o+	Per cent	£1 Level Stake
J Berry	109-647	54-337	43-209	12-101	16.8	-153.02
R Hannon	88-754	40-269	40-359	8-126	11.7	-183.77
H R A Cecil	84-289	10-35	69-216	5-38	29.1	+ 43.57
P F I Cole	79-370	33-111	37-191	9-68	21.4	+ 49.29
J L Dunlop	76-337	10-66	53-210	13-61	22.6	+ 19.93
J H M Gosden	69-303	5-19	53-227	11-57	22.8	- 20.36
M R Stoute	58-335	10-32	40-251	8-52	17.3	-103.06
L M Cumani	49-226	1-8	45-175	3-43	21.7	- 56.40
I A Balding	42-282	4-35	25-162	13-85	14.9	- 21.17
M Johnston	39-268	14-60	14-107	11-101	14.6	+ 9.88
B W Hills	39-274	6-45	30-182	3-47	14.2	-116.72
C E Brittain	38-359	7-67	24-176	7-116	10.6	- 89.99
Sir Mark Prescott	37-185	7-43	26-111	4-31	20.0	- 11.70
R Charlton	36-121	5-20	27-78	4-23	29.8	+ 55.95
G Wragg	35-142	6-16	22-98	7-28	24.6	+ 49.97
M R Channon	34-259	13-98	13-97	8-64	13.1	- 28.86
M H Easterby	33-385	13-140	12-126	8-119	8.6	-211.36
R Akehurst	32-223	1-19	8-59	23-145	14.3	+ 24.79
B Hanbury	31-216	6-38	16-135	9-43	14.4	- 59.22
M H Tompkins	29-311	10-84	12-141	7-86	9.3	-173.08
D R C Elsworth	28-243	3-33	12-124	13-86	11.5	- 16.79
G Lewis	28-267	12-93	13-130	3-44	10.5	- 83.45
Lord Huntingdon	26-139	2-18	12-79	12-42	18.7	+ 77.25
S G Norton	26-167	4-36	13-77	9-54	15.6	- 43.58
G Harwood	26-193	3-20	19-129	4-44	13.5	- 35.22
M Bell	26-234	10-72	12-131	4-31	11.1	- 36.59
P T Walwyn	25-166	2-16	16-111	7-39	15.1	+ 18.28
R M Whitaker	25-225	4-41	10-93	11-91	11.1	+ 0.48
R Hollinshead	25-334	4-67	6-131	15-136	7.5	-112.96
A C Stewart	24-116	0-0	20-97	4-19	20.7	- 25.11
P Chapple-Hyam	24-123	11-41	13-74	0-8	19.5	- 25.60
H Thomson Jones	24-160	6-32	17-117	1-11	15.0	+ 13.64
M A Jarvis	23-154	4-23	14-83	5-48	14.9	- 21.50
F H Lee	23-187	5-34	7-73	11-80	12.3	+ 6.00
Mrs M Reveley	22-236	0-27	2-68	20-141	9.3	-145.49
R J Hodges	22-259	1-15	1-40	20-204	8.5	- 99.47
J R Fanshawe	21-158	2-15	14-118	5-25	13.3	- 26.50
D Morley	20-124	6-16	8-77	6-31	16.1	- 13.09
D A Wilson	19-126	0-3	2-24	17-99	15.1	- 7.54
Mrs J Ramsden	18-194	4-41	4-77	10-76	9.3	- 89.12
B A McMahon	18-213	1-40	5-71	12-102	8.5	- 73.62
P S Felgate	17-84	0-10	1-20	16-54	20.2	+ 49.70
W R Hern	17-93	4-11	7-68	6-14	18.3	- 3.97
P J Makin	17-122	1-11	11-65	5-46	13.9	- 17.36
W Jarvis	17-152	6-32	7-79	4-41	11.2	- 77.10
M Brittain	17-223	5-71	3-71	9-81	7.6	- 50.00
W A O'Gorman	16-90	10-42	1-25	5-23	17.8	- 21.57
J Pearce	16-99	0-2	2-33	14-64	16.2	- 8.29
R W Armstrong	16-115	3-12	10-75	3-28	13.9	- 4.19
M P Naughton	16-127	0-0	4-23	12-104	12.6	- 9.75
L J Holt	16-143	1-26	5-48	10-69	11.2	- 25.17
J W Hills	16-145	1-20	8-68	7-57	11.0	- 34.17
T D Barron	16-159	6-35	6-50	4-74	10.1	- 48.37

July

	Total W-R	2-y-o	3-y-o	4-y-o+	Per cent	£1 Level Stake
J Berry	120-734	74-421	27-198	19-115	16.3	-258.38
R Hannon	112-792	58-374	39-310	15-108	14.1	-128.04
H R A Cecil	104-282	29-57	71-199	4-26	36.9	+ 79.21
Mrs M Reveley	80-355	9-61	26-105	45-189	22.5	+ 48.93
J H M Gosden	68-309	10-37	45-218	13-54	22.0	- 9.30
P F I Cole	62-315	27-113	25-143	10-59	19.7	- 37.50
L M Cumani	61-247	4-24	47-178	10-45	24.7	+ 2.54
B W Hills	60-295	17-85	36-169	7-41	20.3	- 8.65
M R Stoute	57-321	17-68	30-206	10-47	17.8	- 69.78
I A Balding	53-299	7-58	27-146	19-95	17.7	- 23.42
M H Easterby	53-396	16-146	17-123	20-127	13.4	-157.71
Sir Mark Prescott	49-208	11-67	31-112	7-29	23.6	- 42.73
M Johnston	48-309	20-83	20-127	8-99	15.5	- 85.83
J L Dunlop	48-311	15-118	26-142	7-51	15.4	- 93.57
G Lewis	43-252	23-112	14-114	6-26	17.1	- 31.78
M Bell	41-249	25-102	11-112	5-35	16.5	- 55.70
G Harwood	37-186	7-25	21-111	9-50	19.9	- 15.03
R Akehurst	35-249	1-28	5-67	29-154	14.1	- 32.28
D R C Elsworth	34-220	8-44	20-103	6-73	15.5	- 5.13
R Hollinshead	33-362	10-74	14-153	9-135	9.1	-190.27
R Charlton	32-144	12-37	15-80	5-27	22.2	+ 6.91
G Wragg	32-145	13-40	16-74	3-31	22.1	+ 4.78
M H Tompkins	31-277	15-113	6-83	10-81	11.2	-145.85
B Hanbury	30-180	10-52	13-91	7-37	16.7	- 35.70
F H Lee	30-205	4-36	13-81	13-88	14.6	+ 32.38
Lord Huntingdon	29-167	7-31	11-87	11-49	17.4	- 11.48
Mrs J Ramsden	27-183	8-63	10-62	9-58	14.8	- 17.93
B A McMahon	27-223	7-39	8-80	12-104	12.1	- 56.04
A Bailey	26-126	3-25	5-34	18-67	20.6	+ 43.00
M R Channon	26-240	9-112	12-77	5-51	10.8	- 60.21
P T Walwyn	25-153	7-32	13-96	5-25	16.3	+ 40.80
C E Brittain	25-372	7-100	13-168	5-104	6.7	-187.10
W R Hern	24-121	8-21	11-80	5-20	19.8	- 10.33
M J Ryan	24-151	2-27	11-52	11-72	15.9	- 20.96
T D Barron	24-215	6-51	6-59	12-105	11.2	- 66.90
P J Makin	23-112	3-18	13-59	7-35	20.5	+ 8.37
P C Haslam	23-128	3-31	9-43	11-54	18.0	- 10.25
A C Stewart	22-129	3-15	16-91	3-23	17.1	+ 2.92
R Boss	22-131	5-41	12-62	5-28	16.8	+ 2.07
J W Hills	22-160	5-28	9-72	8-60	13.8	- 29.02
R F Johnson Houghton	21-99	8-33	11-55	2-11	21.2	+ 20.90
M P Naughton	21-143	0-4	2-16	19-123	14.7	- 37.16
M A Jarvis	20-140	2-29	3-75	15-36	14.3	- 49.04
N A Callaghan	20-152	7-56	9-69	4-27	13.2	- 58.49
R M Whitaker	20-227	4-46	6-81	10-100	8.8	-105.32
D Morley	19-109	6-26	5-56	8-27	17.4	+ 27.93
R W Armstrong	19-117	7-27	7-68	5-22	16.2	- 26.23
W Jarvis	19-136	3-27	8-75	8-34	14.0	- 25.50
M W Easterby	19-213	10-115	1-46	8-52	8.9	- 75.92
R J Hodges	19-222	2-19	0-36	17-167	8.6	- 79.71
W A O'Gorman	18-105	13-50	5-36	0-19	17.1	- 19.01
H Thomson Jones	18-116	6-23	11-88	1-5	15.5	- 26.57
C A Cyzer	18-173	1-25	9-84	8-64	10.4	- 54.09
J L Spearing	17-135	2-23	2-27	13-85	12.6	- 14.12

August

	Total W-R	2-y-o	3-y-o	4-y-o+	Per cent	£1 Level Stake
R Hannon	98-724	63-394	26-248	9-82	13.5	-186.98
J Berry	81-603	44-358	27-143	10-102	13.4	-180.86
L M Cumani	64-243	11-37	45-172	8-34	26.3	- 11.43
H R A Cecil	58-249	17-64	38-166	3-19	23.3	- 68.34
M R Stoute	57-359	27-130	27-188	3-41	15.9	- 64.30
B W Hills	56-317	16-116	31-170	9-31	17.7	- 63.99
P F I Cole	50-300	25-146	16-116	9-38	16.7	- 33.96
M H Easterby	49-353	19-160	18-113	12-80	13.9	- 58.42
J H M Gosden	48-278	5-38	36-203	7-37	17.3	- 18.46
J L Dunlop	48-293	21-143	21-105	6-45	16.4	- 37.67
Sir Mark Prescott	45-193	17-71	18-84	10-38	23.3	+ 46.53
Mrs M Reveley	44-302	3-61	13-83	28-158	14.6	- 68.99
I A Balding	40-275	15-76	19-126	6-73	14.5	- 59.18
M Johnston	35-268	13-88	10-94	12-86	13.1	- 36.17
R Charlton	33-143	17-48	14-80	2-15	23.1	+ 6.56
G Harwood	32-201	9-39	20-128	3-34	15.9	+ 0.06
G Lewis	32-230	16-119	6-78	10-33	13.9	- 42.03
H Thomson Jones	31-134	12-42	18-85	1-7	23.1	+ 17.12
R Hollinshead	30-325	9-89	11-122	10-114	9.2	-129.32
P Chapple-Hyam	29-116	18-58	11-51	0-7	25.0	+ 1.34
W R Hern	29-135	6-27	20-95	3-13	21.5	+ 0.91
R Akehurst	29-211	3-26	5-65	21-120	13.7	+ 11.13
C E Brittain	28-324	8-92	14-140	6-92	8.6	-110.63
M Bell	27-224	17-100	8-96	2-28	12.1	- 35.13
G Wragg	25-130	11-44	11-70	3-16	19.2	- 16.34
Lord Huntingdon	25-199	6-39	10-104	9-56	12.6	- 57.66
M R Channon	24-245	14-126	8-80	2-39	9.8	- 65.54
M H Tompkins	23-195	8-83	9-57	6-55	11.8	- 56.73
A C Stewart	22-127	0-21	19-85	3-21	17.3	- 37.35
W Jarvis	22-136	5-45	12-65	5-26	16.2	- 4.26
F H Lee	22-182	6-41	5-58	11-83	12.1	+ 2.00
P C Haslam	21-126	4-46	10-42	7-38	16.7	+ 1.50
B Hanbury	21-211	7-81	7-97	7-33	10.0	- 53.92
W J Haggas	20-110	7-36	9-44	4-30	18.2	+ 53.53
P T Walwyn	20-162	8-55	10-87	2-20	12.3	- 43.04
C A Cyzer	20-174	2-24	10-90	8-60	11.5	- 16.04
H Candy	19-138	5-31	9-73	5-34	13.8	+ 39.26
Mrs N Macauley	19-153	5-51	2-46	12-56	12.4	- 33.27
R M Whitaker	19-233	3-69	4-79	12-85	8.2	- 70.52
S Dow	18-140	5-42	7-53	6-45	12.9	- 2.59
T D Barron	18-173	7-51	6-49	5-73	10.4	- 43.05
J Pearce	17-94	0-5	7-41	10-48	18.1	+ 35.63
Mrs J Ramsden	17-165	7-66	5-53	5-46	10.3	- 54.74
R J Hodges	17-211	0-20	2-31	15-160	8.1	- 69.00
M J Ryan	16-105	1-19	7-44	8-42	15.2	+ 17.25
D Morley	16-113	5-38	9-52	2-23	14.2	+ 19.55
M A Jarvis	16-145	3-37	6-69	7-39	11.0	- 44.49
J W Hills	16-158	8-41	2-61	6-56	10.1	- 0.17
W R Muir	14-89	7-37	4-22	3-30	15.7	- 18.33
J R Fanshawe	14-138	5-39	9-80	0-19	10.1	- 61.88
D R C Elsworth	14-190	6-55	4-73	4-62	7.4	-111.12

September

	Total W-R	2-y-o	3-y-o	4-y-o+	Per cent	£1 Level Stake
J H M Gosden	92-361	28-91	48-215	16-55	25.5	+ 97.23
R Hannon	79-764	43-417	21-247	15-100	10.3	-159.67
M R Stoute	65-373	35-188	21-144	9-41	17.4	- 83.50
J L Dunlop	61-422	33-218	21-148	7-56	14.5	- 94.57
H R A Cecil	51-232	23-81	27-134	1-17	22.0	- 62.76
B W Hills	51-355	21-159	27-163	3-33	14.4	- 67.87
J Berry	48-535	30-302	13-148	5-85	9.0	-210.51
L M Cumani	46-275	20-84	21-158	5-33	16.7	- 53.41
R Charlton	37-179	19-85	14-75	4-19	20.7	+ 33.59
Mrs M Reveley	35-245	6-69	9-56	20-120	14.3	+ 11.26
I A Balding	35-318	11-140	14-105	10-73	11.0	- 18.73
H Thomson Jones	34-181	21-74	12-97	1-10	18.8	+ 45.79
G Wragg	32-156	7-47	21-93	4-16	20.5	+ 62.03
Lord Huntingdon	30-216	6-65	13-99	11-52	13.9	+ 11.06
B Hanbury	28-217	13-99	12-97	3-21	12.9	- 13.24
P F I Cole	28-309	19-173	6-91	3-45	9.1	-127.51
C E Brittain	28-376	12-149	12-152	4-75	7.4	-141.56
M H Tompkins	27-268	8-115	13-76	6-77	10.1	-101.22
Sir Mark Prescott	26-184	13-92	9-61	4-31	14.1	- 34.61
G Lewis	26-216	14-127	10-75	2-14	12.0	- 39.17
R Akehurst	25-208	6-39	5-55	14-114	12.0	+ 10.50
R W Armstrong	23-130	9-50	10-59	4-21	17.7	+179.75
P Chapple-Hyam	22-133	19-81	3-40	0-12	16.5	- 15.31
Mrs J Ramsden	22-177	10-65	7-57	5-55	12.4	- 60.72
R M Whitaker	22-223	5-84	6-75	11-64	9.9	- 41.67
G Harwood	21-189	4-62	16-99	1-28	11.1	- 54.67
D Morley	20-130	5-47	10-59	5-24	15.4	+ 54.33
D R C Elsworth	20-221	11-88	5-74	4-59	9.0	- 86.12
M Johnston	20-264	9-100	7-88	4-76	7.6	-127.58
M H Easterby	20-293	8-138	6-73	6-82	6.8	-149.81
M Bell	18-195	12-106	6-67	0-22	9.2	- 71.13
A C Stewart	17-119	2-29	10-75	5-15	14.3	- 37.41
J W Hills	17-153	4-52	7-57	6-44	11.1	- 21.75
W Jarvis	17-161	6-62	7-68	4-31	10.6	- 34.70
B A McMahon	17-205	3-52	5-57	9-96	8.3	- 29.62
J R Fanshawe	16-157	6-57	9-76	1-24	10.2	- 48.12
M R Channon	16-221	8-121	3-60	5-40	7.2	- 78.62
Mrs J Cecil	15-90	12-44	1-31	2-15	16.7	+ 11.04
P T Walwyn	15-199	8-78	5-93	2-28	7.5	- 92.79
W J Haggas	14-107	5-46	7-37	2-24	13.1	- 27.29
C A Cyzer	14-133	4-29	6-66	4-38	10.5	+ 8.00
H Candy	14-159	2-50	9-75	3-34	8.8	- 56.41
M A Jarvis	13-135	7-47	2-59	4-29	9.6	- 40.92
T D Barron	13-137	8-45	1-50	4-42	9.5	- 41.87
Lady Herries	12-79	0-13	5-32	7-34	15.2	- 2.73
R Boss	12-82	5-42	5-34	2-6	14.6	- 8.87
M J Camacho	11-86	4-31	3-18	4-37	12.8	+ 29.88
J Pearce	11-96	2-16	2-34	7-46	11.5	- 14.25
W R Hern	11-128	5-38	4-74	2-16	8.6	- 66.76
M C Pipe	10-58	2-9	3-27	5-22	17.2	+ 10.98
C F Wall	10-95	2-37	6-48	2-10	10.5	- 29.00
M J Ryan	10-110	3-26	2-37	5-47	9.1	- 47.25
P W Harris	10-114	0-28	4-50	6-36	8.8	- 43.75
W Carter	10-120	2-40	5-38	3-42	8.3	+ 32.73

October/November

	Total W-R	2-y-o	3-y-o	4-y-o+	Per cent	£1 Level Stake
J H M Gosden	101-485	42-175	44-248	15-62	20.8	- 41.86
R Hannon	80-795	60-476	16-226	4-93	10.1	-255.04
H R A Cecil	69-318	45-159	21-146	3-13	21.7	- 16.86
B W Hills	61-383	23-179	29-170	9-34	15.9	- 17.86
M R Stoute	57-366	35-231	19-107	3-28	15.6	- 61.59
L M Cumani	54-283	24-122	26-137	4-24	19.1	- 32.32
J L Dunlop	54-401	28-215	20-146	6-40	13.5	- 60.45
M Johnston	43-341	16-154	16-98	11-89	12.6	- 17.16
P F I Cole	38-339	30-216	5-84	3-39	11.2	- 9.33
J Berry	34-401	23-244	8-95	3-62	8.5	-136.11
G Harwood	32-276	8-117	15-116	9-43	11.6	- 76.96
C E Brittain	32-408	10-175	12-128	10-105	7.8	- 80.30
D R C Elsworth	30-242	18-119	4-66	8-57	12.4	+ 9.26
Mrs M Reveley	30-259	3-66	9-53	18-140	11.6	- 35.39
G Lewis	28-215	15-117	10-61	3-37	13.0	+ 89.15
Sir Mark Prescott	28-226	16-158	7-48	5-20	12.4	- 36.91
R Akehurst	28-276	0-58	10-85	18-133	10.1	- 81.50
M H Tompkins	28-345	9-155	6-72	13-118	8.1	-119.75
M H Easterby	27-243	14-98	3-72	10-73	11.1	- 8.63
Mrs J Cecil	26-122	14-69	11-43	1-10	21.3	+ 79.48
R Charlton	25-137	14-72	10-52	1-13	18.2	+ 12.64
T D Barron	25-201	9-64	7-62	9-75	12.4	+ 19.88
G Wragg	24-176	8-63	15-99	1-14	13.6	- 28.72
J W Hills	24-220	3-96	10-66	11-58	10.9	- 41.41
Lord Huntingdon	24-279	6-88	12-123	6-68	8.6	- 96.13
B Hanbury	23-166	9-80	14-72	0-14	13.9	- 27.38
H Thomson Jones	23-166	15-88	8-71	0-7	13.9	+ 13.40
M J Camacho	20-117	2-40	4-30	14-47	17.1	+ 2.50
W A O'Gorman	20-150	13-71	3-49	4-30	13.3	- 23.74
P Chapple-Hyam	19-123	17-89	2-31	0-3	15.4	- 46.48
M J Ryan	19-205	4-63	7-78	8-64	9.3	- 41.46
R Hollinshead	19-447	8-197	6-151	5-99	4.3	-205.75
R W Armstrong	18-123	12-58	3-48	3-17	14.6	+ 6.21
J R Fanshawe	18-185	11-89	6-68	1-28	9.7	- 14.74
W Jarvis	18-187	9-92	7-68	2-27	9.6	- 64.51
S G Norton	18-193	6-98	7-70	5-25	9.3	- 39.82
N A Callaghan	16-120	14-90	2-27	0-3	13.3	+ 8.00
M R Channon	16-230	10-133	4-48	2-49	7.0	- 73.25
A C Stewart	15-177	8-45	7-115	0-17	8.5	- 77.94
M C Pipe	14-64	1-6	6-23	7-35	21.9	+ 24.65
D Morley	14-175	6-80	7-67	1-28	8.0	- 81.27
Mrs J Ramsden	14-179	5-71	4-51	5-57	7.8	- 69.67
C J Hill	13-95	4-23	1-32	8-40	13.7	- 11.58
E J Alston	13-129	1-16	6-41	6-72	10.1	+ 13.00
M Bell	13-168	7-105	5-52	1-11	7.7	- 32.12
M A Jarvis	13-193	5-96	5-64	3-33	6.7	-105.45
P T Walwyn	13-204	7-94	5-92	1-18	6.4	-114.69
H Candy	12-159	3-47	7-85	2-27	7.5	- 48.50
I A Balding	12-201	6-102	2-60	4-39	6.0	-148.03
R Boss	11-106	9-59	1-34	1-13	10.4	- 44.79
G B Balding	11-128	1-36	2-34	8-58	8.6	- 12.12
A Bailey	11-137	4-41	0-32	7-64	8.0	- 47.75

LEADING TRAINERS BY TYPE OF RACE 1990-94

2-y-o Non-Handicaps

	W-R	Per cent	£1 Level Stake		W-R	Per cent	£1 Level Stake
R Hannon	260-1783	14.6	- 456.64	J Berry	243-1434	16.9	-363.20
P F I Cole	140-737	19.0	- 64.54	H R A Cecil	128-401	31.9	+ 3.73
M R Stoute	120-616	19.5	- 136.31	J L Dunlop	93-696	13.4	-278.09
P Chapple-Hyam	88-332	26.5	- 2.50	J H M Gosden	88-350	25.1	+ 11.10
M Bell	77-421	18.3	- 91.75	B W Hills	77-594	13.0	-189.85
R Charlton	66-247	26.7	+ 80.74	H Thomson Jones	63-247	25.5	+ 13.36
M Johnston	61-383	15.9	- 42.97	L M Cumani	59-261	22.6	+ 1.70
W A O'Gorman	56-245	22.9	- 30.71	Sir Mark Prescott	56-349	16.0	- 78.05
G Lewis	53-424	12.5	- 39.25	M R Channon	52-464	11.2	-128.21
G Wragg	51-211	24.2	+ 3.47	M H Easterby	49-517	9.5	-282.81
B Hanbury	44-322	13.7	- 73.24	D R C Elsworth	44-332	13.3	- 60.86
I A Balding	42-383	11.0	- 120.96	D R Loder	39-140	27.9	- 15.71
R W Armstrong	38-174	21.8	+ 61.06	M H Tompkins	38-383	9.9	-162.79
C E Brittain	37-548	6.8	- 344.68	W Jarvis	34-246	13.8	- 65.56
Mrs J Cecil	33-163	20.2	+ 16.99	R Hollinshead	33-536	6.2	-285.62
P T Walwyn	30-260	11.5	- 85.56	S G Norton	27-226	11.9	- 84.42
G Harwood	27-239	11.3	- 136.69	W R Hern	26-148	17.6	- 44.73
R Boss	26-196	13.3	- 63.34	D Morley	23-166	13.9	+ 3.58
J R Fanshawe	23-202	11.4	- 49.17	T D Barron	22-181	12.2	- 74.97
N A Callaghan	22-213	10.3	- 56.27	Lord Huntingdon	22-216	10.2	-108.37
R M Whitaker	20-239	8.4	- 96.47	J W Watts	18-152	11.8	- 66.75
J Etherington	18-187	9.6	- 43.77	M A Jarvis	18-198	9.1	-102.12
Mrs J Ramsden	18-203	8.9	- 107.65	J W Hills	17-212	8.0	- 82.75
E Weymes	16-114	14.0	+ 12.00	W J Haggas	16-138	11.6	- 50.33
R F J Houghton	15-197	7.6	- 90.74	P C Haslam	14-142	9.9	- 26.48
Mrs M Reveley	14-195	7.2	- 107.30	C R Nelson	13-62	21.0	+ 19.57
A C Stewart	13-98	13.3	- 17.31	J W Payne	13-108	12.0	- 63.12
M W Easterby	13-318	4.1	- 230.65	F H Lee	12-171	7.0	-111.00
C Tinkler	12-200	6.0	- 115.38	J Wharton	11-115	9.6	- 13.87
J M P Eustace	11-135	8.1	- 72.82	C F Wall	11-155	7.1	- 92.82
M McCormack	11-177	6.2	- 102.26	S Dow	11-185	5.9	- 80.12

3-y-o Non-Handicaps

	W-R	Per cent	£1 Level Stake		W-R	Per cent	£1 Level Stake
H R A Cecil	296-998	29.7	- 13.64	J H M Gosden	229-1020	22.5	- 94.82
L M Cumani	159-685	23.2	- 147.74	M R Stoute	156-823	19.0	-164.57
B W Hills	154-795	19.4	- 98.05	R Hannon	120-828	14.5	-186.78
J L Dunlop	112-597	18.8	- 66.83	J Berry	96-471	20.4	- 53.65
P F I Cole	89-617	14.4	- 216.65	G Harwood	87-418	20.8	- 72.22
G Wragg	84-410	20.5	+ 8.30	R Charlton	76-327	23.2	- 2.20
C E Brittain	73-665	11.0	- 149.00	Lord Huntingdon	63-337	18.7	+ 44.61
Sir Mark Prescott	62-227	27.3	+ 3.08	A C Stewart	56-360	15.6	-100.25
I A Balding	55-421	13.1	- 104.16	H Thomson Jones	51-300	17.0	- 12.46
W R Hern	51-357	14.3	- 146.71	P Chapple-Hyam	50-257	19.5	- 53.68
B Hanbury	49-404	12.1	- 84.92	J R Fanshawe	46-321	14.3	+ 19.47
P T Walwyn	45-310	14.5	- 58.31	M Johnston	41-231	17.7	- 48.51
D R C Elsworth	36-412	8.7	- 222.77	R Hollinshead	36-486	7.4	-184.87
W J Haggas	35-175	20.0	- 11.35	M H Tompkins	35-231	15.2	- 23.03
W Jarvis	32-302	10.6	- 137.07	Mrs J Cecil	30-170	17.6	- 14.51
Mrs M Reveley	29-148	19.6	+ 14.57	M A Jarvis	29-251	11.6	- 59.74

	W-R	Per cent	£1 Level Stake		W-R	Per cent	£1 Level Stake
H Candy	29-256	11.3	- 14.15	M Bell	28-214	13.1	- 81.69
J W Hills	27-211	12.8	- 50.04	T D Barron	26-136	19.1	- 7.51
G Lewis	25-223	11.2	- 96.04	P J Makin	24-179	13.4	- 14.97
W A O'Gorman	22-115	19.1	- 28.48	R Boss	22-154	14.3	- 28.41
S G Norton	22-156	14.1	- 3.57	N A Callaghan	21-145	14.5	- 8.24
M R Channon	21-241	8.7	- 125.18	D R Loder	20-65	30.8	+ 20.22
R W Armstrong	20-199	10.1	- 80.09	M H Easterby	19-191	9.9	- 77.10
C A Cyzer	18-264	6.8	- 99.09	P A Kelleway	17-206	8.3	- 81.00
Mrs J Ramsden	15-104	14.4	- 7.22	C N Allen	15-114	13.2	- 34.60
R F J Houghton	15-132	11.4	- 55.90	M McCormack	15-140	10.7	- 35.47
R Akehurst	14-155	9.0	- 77.42	B A McMahon	14-200	7.0	-107.93
J A R Toller	13-103	12.6	- 39.31	C F Wall	13-135	9.6	- 59.35
D Morley	13-140	9.3	- 72.07	Mrs N Macauley	13-169	7.7	- 86.02
J G FitzGerald	12-124	9.7	- 12.07	Mrs L Piggott	12-149	8.1	- 90.25
R M Whitaker	12-171	7.0	- 33.12	Miss S E Hall	11-76	14.5	- 21.68
J W Payne	11-82	13.4	+ 6.21	C R Nelson	11-93	11.8	- 37.74
J Pearce	11-97	11.3	- 7.75	J W Watts	11-150	7.3	- 85.81
P W Harris	11-175	6.3	- 11.50				

4-y-o+ Non-Handicaps

	W-R	Per cent	£1 Level Stake		W-R	Per cent	£1 Level Stake
J H M Gosden	48-189	25.4	+ 37.66	M R Stoute	43-183	23.5	+ 9.86
J Berry	37-189	19.6	- 46.74	R Hannon	33-213	15.5	+ 6.60
Mrs M Reveley	29-131	22.1	- 12.30	J L Dunlop	26-116	22.4	+ 25.61
D W Chapman	24-165	14.5	- 68.11	C E Brittain	24-247	9.7	- 31.83
H R A Cecil	23-116	19.8	- 31.09	R Hollinshead	23-214	10.7	-102.24
Lord Huntingdon	21-79	26.6	+ 65.63	I A Balding	21-107	19.6	- 39.46
L M Cumani	20-114	17.5	- 22.93	B A McMahon	20-173	11.6	+ 0.43
J Wharton	18-76	23.7	+ 29.84	B W Hills	18-92	19.6	- 5.10
G Wragg	18-108	16.7	+ 22.58	R Akehurst	18-138	13.0	- 1.97
Sir Mark Prescott	17-47	36.2	+ 0.22	W A O'Gorman	17-79	21.5	- 20.59
T D Barron	17-90	18.9	- 23.79	M Johnston	16-98	16.3	- 32.96
M H Tompkins	15-109	13.8	+ 16.72	M J Camacho	14-51	27.5	+ 22.20
J W Hills	14-76	18.4	- 5.24	A Bailey	14-83	16.9	- 23.78
M C Pipe	14-89	15.7	- 30.14	B Hanbury	13-59	22.0	- 13.83
P J Makin	12-72	16.7	- 20.47	P F I Cole	12-112	10.7	- 49.48
A C Stewart	11-46	23.9	+ 1.64	M R Channon	11-54	20.4	+ 34.50
M J Ryan	10-57	17.5	- 13.83	J Pearce	10-79	12.7	- 38.11
G Harwood	10-80	12.5	- 10.15	Mrs N Macauley	10-112	8.9	- 25.12
D R C Elsworth	10-133	7.5	- 34.37	P C Haslam	9-43	20.9	+ 23.84
W W Haigh	9-54	16.7	+ 29.00	M H Easterby	9-55	16.4	- 13.37
P T Walwyn	9-59	15.3	+ 27.91	J L Harris	9-82	11.0	- 14.17
N Tinkler	9-123	7.3	- 81.79	N J H Walker	8-18	44.4	+ 38.13
G Lewis	8-52	15.4	- 11.50	W Jarvis	8-55	14.5	- 2.62
D Burchell	8-60	13.3	+ 48.75	J G FitzGerald	8-75	10.7	- 34.77
T G Mills	7-21	33.3	+ 36.50	W R Hern	7-28	25.0	+ 13.65
D R Loder	7-36	19.4	+ 8.83	P A Kelleway	7-44	15.9	0.00
C A Cyzer	7-71	9.9	- 3.35	R J Hodges	7-92	7.6	- 65.95
A Moore	7-103	6.8	+ 6.75	Mrs J Cecil	6-24	25.0	+ 5.80
K R Burke	6-29	20.7	+ 0.48	M Bell	6-40	15.0	- 8.90
D Morris	6-41	14.6	- 2.50	S G Norton	6-42	14.3	- 13.89
N A Callaghan	6-43	14.0	- 16.77	G B Balding	6-44	13.6	- 18.37
W R Muir	6-57	10.5	- 31.97	M McCormack	6-91	6.6	- 45.87
M P Naughton	6-111	5.4	- 66.37				

Selling Non-Handicaps

	W-R	Per cent	£1 Level Stake		W-R	Per cent	£1 Level Stake
J Berry	80-474	16.9	- 89.70	M H Easterby	26-185	14.1	- 77.13
G Lewis	21-120	17.5	- 0.84	Mrs M Reveley	19-105	18.1	- 27.12
R Hannon	18-137	13.1	- 19.75	M R Channon	18-161	11.2	- 60.22
N Tinkler	16-126	12.7	- 47.85	R Hollinshead	16-135	11.9	- 30.21
M H Tompkins	16-160	10.0	- 103.11	M W Easterby	15-194	7.7	- 107.98
M Johnston	14-102	13.7	- 33.57	P F I Cole	12-63	19.0	+ 4.32
R M Whitaker	12-124	9.7	- 44.17	Mrs J Ramsden	11-56	19.6	- 11.57
Lord Huntingdon	10-31	32.3	+ 23.00	M A Jarvis	9-32	28.1	+ 12.71
J Wharton	9-80	11.3	+ 5.50	W G M Turner	9-100	9.0	+ 6.00
D R Loder	8-12	66.7	+ 20.83	Sir Mark Prescott	8-52	15.4	- 13.34
J Pearce	8-72	11.1	- 18.00	N A Callaghan	8-75	10.7	- 33.02
K T Ivory	8-84	9.5	- 13.50	R J Hodges	8-111	7.2	- 47.87
M Feth-Godley	7-41	17.1	+ 16.50	D Morris	7-42	16.7	+ 11.75
C W Thornton	7-50	14.0	+ 33.50	C N Allen	7-58	12.1	+ 11.00
T D Barron	7-70	10.0	- 13.37	J L Harris	7-76	9.2	- 9.37
P C Haslam	7-76	9.2	- 33.25	C Tinkler	7-84	8.3	- 47.75
M Brittain	7-122	5.7	- 65.67				

Apprentice Non-Handicaps

	W-R	Per cent	£1 Level Stake		W-R	Per cent	£1 Level Stake
L M Cumani	9-38	23.7	- 17.52	B W Hills	8-18	44.4	+ 1.58
G Harwood	6-12	50.0	+ 14.16	Sir Mark Prescott	5-9	55.6	+ 7.20
J H M Gosden	5-15	33.3	+ 6.49	I A Balding	5-18	27.8	+ 4.12
P F I Cole	5-21	23.8	- 9.70	M R Stoute	4-9	44.4	+ 1.59
H R A Cecil	4-16	25.0	- 7.17	W J Haggas	3-5	60.0	+ 10.00
P T Walwyn	3-6	50.0	+ 2.05	C E Brittain	3-7	42.9	+ 8.80
G Wragg	3-7	42.9	+ 1.91	Mrs M Reveley	3-10	30.0	+ 7.57
M H Tompkins	3-13	23.1	- 3.68	R Hannon	3-18	16.7	- 6.25
B A McMahon	3-27	11.1	+ 3.50	D W Chapman	2-5	40.0	+ 0.10
M A Jarvis	2-5	40.0	0.00	B Hanbury	2-7	28.6	+ 11.00
W Jarvis	2-7	28.6	+ 0.88	J White	2-7	28.6	+ 2.67
R Guest	2-9	22.2	- 3.50	M R Channon	2-9	22.2	- 3.12
H Candy	2-10	20.0	+ 8.00	J L Harris	2-10	20.0	+ 22.00
Mrs L Piggott	2-10	20.0	+ 0.50	M Bell	2-11	18.2	- 5.17
J W Hills	2-12	16.7	- 6.20	A C Stewart	2-15	13.3	- 7.42
C A Cyzer	2-17	11.8	- 7.90	R Hollinshead	2-33	6.1	- 21.00

Amateur Non-Handicaps

	W-R	Per cent	£1 Level Stake		W-R	Per cent	£1 Level Stake
B W Hills	5-11	45.5	+ 2.12	M R Stoute	4-9	44.4	+ 5.25
L M Cumani	3-4	75.0	+ 3.57	M C Pipe	3-5	60.0	+ 1.09
H R A Cecil	3-8	37.5	+ 3.14	J W Hills	3-8	37.5	+ 4.75
R F J Houghton	3-10	30.0	+ 36.25	J H M Gosden	3-10	30.0	+ 0.63
G Harwood	3-15	20.0	- 5.60	J Pearce	3-16	18.8	+ 3.50
R Charlton	2-3	66.7	+ 2.88	D L Williams	2-4	50.0	+ 34.00
Lord Huntingdon	2-5	40.0	+ 2.38	H Thomson Jones	2-7	28.6	+ 2.67
D W Chapman	2-10	20.0	+ 44.75				

2-y-o Handicaps

	W-R	Per cent	£1 Level Stake		W-R	Per cent	£1 Level Stake
R Hannon	53-396	13.4	- 9.06	J Berry	35-332	10.5	-122.76
G Lewis	19-153	12.4	+ 0.58	T D Barron	18-96	18.8	+ 26.01
M H Easterby	18-167	10.8	+ 3.45	M Johnston	17-122	13.9	- 18.42
N A Callaghan	14-81	17.3	- 4.70	J L Dunlop	14-84	16.7	+ 24.18
M Bell	14-130	10.8	+ 10.38	P F I Cole	12-96	12.5	- 16.87
M R Channon	12-145	8.3	- 31.50	Mrs J Ramsden	11-102	10.8	- 37.75
C E Brittain	10-69	14.5	+ 61.00	W A O'Gorman	10-72	13.9	- 7.00
B W Hills	8-48	16.7	+ 11.88	W R Muir	8-50	16.0	+ 16.00
D R C Elsworth	7-29	24.1	+ 29.25	F H Lee	7-59	11.9	+ 1.00
Sir Mark Prescott	7-61	11.5	- 8.50	Mrs M Reveley	7-81	8.6	- 19.62
M H Tompkins	7-127	5.5	- 76.09	M J Camacho	6-19	31.6	+ 58.50
J R Fanshawe	6-26	23.1	+ 18.38	M Feth-Godley	6-41	14.6	+ 5.00
Lord Huntingdon	6-42	14.3	- 5.17	A Bailey	6-44	13.6	+ 8.25
M R Stoute	6-45	13.3	+ 2.00	B J Meehan	6-47	12.8	+ 15.50
W Jarvis	5-35	14.3	+ 14.83	R Boss	5-36	13.9	- 6.50
W J Haggas	5-36	13.9	- 13.83	M J Ryan	5-45	11.1	- 3.00
M W Easterby	5-98	5.1	- 62.00	R Hollinshead	5-121	4.1	- 64.00

3-y-o Handicaps

	W-R	Per cent	£1 Level Stake		W-R	Per cent	£1 Level Stake
R Hannon	105-1117	9.4	- 202.16	J L Dunlop	96-531	18.1	- 36.06
J H M Gosden	78-436	17.9	+ 18.08	M Johnston	70-481	14.6	- 9.94
M R Stoute	66-483	13.7	- 97.80	J Berry	66-568	11.6	- 99.00
Sir Mark Prescott	64-339	18.9	+ 2.45	I A Balding	54-371	14.6	- 24.08
M Bell	51-458	11.1	- 34.27	B W Hills	50-425	11.8	-130.45
H R A Cecil	48-231	20.8	+ 1.84	L M Cumani	48-323	14.9	- 32.42
P F I Cole	43-362	11.9	- 28.09	G Lewis	42-372	11.3	- 7.00
M H Easterby	42-459	9.2	- 177.87	C E Brittain	38-470	8.1	- 72.00
H Thomson Jones	37-307	12.1	+ 39.31	J W Watts	34-281	12.1	- 38.74
G Harwood	34-299	11.4	- 55.48	B Hanbury	33-276	12.0	- 74.08
T D Barron	32-285	11.2	- 81.32	Mrs J Ramsden	32-346	9.2	-127.40
R Charlton	31-178	17.4	- 6.89	Mrs M Reveley	31-243	12.8	- 57.96
M J Ryan	31-265	11.7	- 43.99	J R Fanshawe	31-275	11.3	- 73.68
Lord Huntingdon	31-311	10.0	- 96.01	M H Tompkins	31-315	9.8	-145.52
A C Stewart	30-201	14.9	- 49.32	P T Walwyn	30-351	8.5	- 73.18
R Akehurst	29-245	11.8	- 41.77	G Wragg	26-215	12.1	- 32.50
F H Lee	25-277	9.0	- 24.75	N A Callaghan	24-225	10.7	- 53.00
D Morley	24-227	10.6	- 41.22	R W Armstrong	23-202	11.4	+ 50.24
Lady Herries	22-101	21.8	+ 51.60	S G Norton	22-223	9.9	- 79.65
M R Channon	21-235	8.9	- 29.34	R Hollinshead	21-469	4.5	-275.42
P J Makin	19-167	11.4	- 65.61	M A Jarvis	19-227	8.4	- 98.82
P C Haslam	18-140	12.9	- 53.88	W J Haggas	18-140	12.9	+ 22.46
W Jarvis	18-181	9.9	- 70.37	S Dow	17-197	8.6	- 13.42
J W Hills	17-197	8.6	- 47.75	R F J Houghton	17-215	7.9	- 77.25
C J Hill	16-114	14.0	+ 5.46	Mrs J Cecil	16-120	13.3	+ 25.33
D R C Elsworth	16-211	7.6	- 77.50	T J Naughton	15-88	17.0	+ 13.08
C F Wall	15-172	8.7	- 57.95	W A O'Gorman	15-190	7.9	- 96.58
B A McMahon	15-211	7.1	- 105.42	R J R Williams	14-131	10.7	- 18.57
C A Cyzer	14-186	7.5	- 49.50	R Boss	14-192	7.3	- 87.50

4-y-o+ Handicaps

	W-R	Per cent	£1 Level Stake		W-R	Per cent	£1 Level Stake
Mrs M Reveley	123-731	16.8	- 46.41	R Akehurst	111-740	15.0	+ 67.50
M Johnston	81-630	12.9	- 19.88	R J Hodges	76-813	9.3	-211.18
T D Barron	69-547	12.6	- 55.10	M H Easterby	58-577	10.1	-201.09
R Hollinshead	57-712	8.0	-252.44	J Berry	52-512	10.2	- 94.15
M J Ryan	50-379	13.2	- 9.04	Lord Huntingdon	46-297	15.5	+ 21.18
R J O'Sullivan	44-370	11.9	+ 8.48	Mrs J Ramsden	44-424	10.4	-151.32
R M Whitaker	44-446	9.9	- 48.15	B A McMahon	44-492	8.9	-111.86
R Hannon	43-526	8.2	-146.27	M P Naughton	43-534	8.1	-163.49
D W Chapman	43-724	5.9	-294.96	I A Balding	42-335	12.5	+ 28.50
J L Dunlop	41-302	13.6	- 51.61	A Bailey	41-337	12.2	- 54.59
E J Alston	41-374	11.0	+ 6.23	D R C Elsworth	40-331	12.1	+ 53.76
F H Lee	40-404	9.9	- 72.37	J L Spearing	38-400	9.5	-108.97
C E Brittain	38-489	7.8	-118.84	D W P Arbuthnot	36-299	12.0	+ 40.71
P W Harris	34-206	16.5	+ 57.56	M H Tompkins	34-370	9.2	-106.37
C A Cyzer	33-256	12.9	- 4.46	P S Felgate	33-265	12.5	- 16.92
Mrs N Macauley	33-366	9.0	- 59.27	D A Wilson	32-414	7.7	-194.22
M Brittain	32-521	6.1	-137.00	J H M Gosden	31-167	18.6	+ 37.42
S G Norton	31-197	15.7	+ 9.37	J W Hills	31-270	11.5	- 11.76
M R Channon	31-324	9.6	- 46.75	R Bastiman	30-234	12.8	+ 37.25
R J R Williams	29-265	10.9	- 19.15	C J Hill	29-293	9.9	- 80.83
J D Bethell	28-274	10.2	- 10.50	P F I Cole	27-236	11.4	- 49.12
M A Jarvis	26-164	15.9	+ 7.13	B W Hills	26-181	14.4	- 36.87
J A Glover	26-215	12.1	+ 18.75	G B Balding	26-272	9.6	- 9.39
Lady Herries	25-194	12.9	- 10.99	G Harwood	24-179	13.4	+ 55.76
P C Haslam	24-191	12.6	- 43.96	P Calver	24-201	11.9	+ 12.58
C C Elsey	24-208	11.5	- 32.32	D Morley	23-135	17.0	+ 42.00
Sir Mark Prescott	23-144	16.0	- 23.04	M C Pipe	23-146	15.8	+ 1.13
M J Camacho	23-175	13.1	- 17.11	M D Hammond	22-223	9.9	- 47.99
J L Harris	22-266	8.3	- 53.55	H J Collingridge	22-277	7.9	- 89.00
B Hanbury	21-156	13.5	+ 7.88	J Pearce	21-203	10.3	- 46.12
M W Easterby	21-211	10.0	- 36.41	S R Bowring	21-214	9.8	+ 17.00
C J Benstead	21-219	9.6	- 63.92	W Jarvis	20-149	13.4	+ 0.50
K O C-Brown	20-228	8.8	+137.13	L G Cottrell	20-243	8.2	- 69.17
Mrs A Knight	19-161	11.8	+ 8.58	D Morris	19-187	10.2	- 4.25
Capt J Wilson	19-190	10.0	+ 20.71	W Carter	19-224	8.5	- 85.00
W J Musson	19-279	6.8	-128.50	B R Millman	19-317	6.0	-119.00
R Charlton	18-97	18.6	+ 49.86	P T Walwyn	18-113	15.9	+ 35.00
L M Cumani	18-115	15.7	- 14.04	W A O'Gorman	18-179	10.1	- 43.75
J W Watts	18-209	8.6	- 44.42	J Wharton	18-242	7.4	- 24.30
L J Holt	18-269	6.7	-130.42	Denys Smith	18-275	6.5	-154.08
S Dow	18-276	6.5	- 92.62	Mrs L Piggott	17-130	13.1	- 18.54
W W Haigh	17-172	9.9	- 51.14	C Tinkler	17-176	9.7	- 58.68
M Dods	17-181	9.4	- 16.90	P Howling	17-412	4.1	-256.37
M J Heaton-Ellis	16-119	13.4	+ 70.00	R Boss	16-120	13.3	+ 6.50
Bob Jones	16-122	13.1	- 7.50	R W Armstrong	16-129	12.4	- 20.19
M McCormack	16-130	12.3	+ 11.25	P Mitchell	16-188	8.5	- 42.42
C A Horgan	16-191	8.4	- 16.37	G M Moore	16-271	5.9	-127.35
A Hide	15-123	12.2	+ 38.50	T Thomson Jones	15-131	11.5	- 10.03
H Candy	15-182	8.2	- 29.37	D Haydn Jones	15-215	7.0	- 92.37
E A Wheeler	14-123	11.4	+ 8.50	R C Spicer	14-128	10.9	+ 2.75
K T Ivory	14-155	9.0	- 10.52	D T Thom	14-156	9.0	- 50.30
W R Muir	14-164	8.5	- 44.50	Miss B Sanders	14-168	8.3	- 51.17
Dr J D Scargill	14-179	7.8	- 84.14	Pat Mitchell	14-213	6.6	- 91.42
M Blanshard	14-264	5.3	-139.00	Miss S E Hall	13-115	11.3	- 24.17

	W-R	Per cent	£1 Level Stake		W-R	Per cent	£1 Level Stake
J White	13-121	10.7	- 8.50	A P Stringer	13-124	10.5	- 3.00
G Lewis	13-155	8.4	- 44.12	M Feth-Godley	13-173	7.5	- 73.12
T Casey	12-124	9.7	- 32.67	M O'Neill	12-138	8.7	+ 7.25
Miss L A Perrat	12-140	8.6	- 34.00	P J Makin	12-167	7.2	- 26.00
G Wragg	11-70	15.7	- 3.70	S E Kettlewell	11-76	14.5	+ 8.24
J A R Toller	11-96	11.5	- 12.00	B Beasley	11-109	10.1	+ 22.00
A Harrison	11-114	9.6	- 43.12	J Mackie	11-131	8.4	- 1.50
D R Laing	11-147	7.5	- 41.50	T J Naughton	11-157	7.0	- 35.75
Mrs Barbara Waring	11-179	6.1	- 47.25	J M Bradley	11-184	6.0	- 86.42
Miss L Siddall	11-215	5.1	- 86.42	W R Hern	10-69	14.5	- 9.92
A C Stewart	10-74	13.5	- 22.40	Miss G Kelleway	10-75	13.3	+ 9.75
P D Cundell	10-76	13.2	+ 19.50	Mrs J Cecil	10-84	11.9	- 19.62
J M P Eustace	10-96	10.4	- 14.50	J Akehurst	10-99	10.1	- 15.62
J R Fanshawe	10-100	10.0	- 9.00	D Moffatt	10-118	8.5	- 14.50
J L Eyre	10-123	8.1	- 18.10	W J Haggas	10-128	7.8	- 8.67
G L Moore	10-143	7.0	- 68.00	A Moore	10-180	5.6	- 82.50
J G FitzGerald	10-190	5.3	- 100.75	N Bycroft	10-201	5.0	- 68.75
M D I Usher	10-239	4.2	- 139.50				

Selling Handicaps

	W-R	Per cent	£1 Level Stake		W-R	Per cent	£1 Level Stake
Mrs J Ramsden	11-43	25.6	+ 37.75	R Bastiman	10-48	20.8	+ 25.83
J Berry	9-81	11.1	+ 14.78	Sir Mark Prescott	7-30	23.3	+ 14.05
R M Whitaker	7-61	11.5	+ 1.00	R Akehurst	6-25	24.0	+ 10.38
C N Allen	6-42	14.3	+ 13.00	R Hollinshead	6-62	9.7	- 8.00
R J Hodges	6-76	7.9	- 32.75	M P Naughton	5-29	17.2	- 1.07
C A Cyzer	5-38	13.2	+ 7.63	M H Tompkins	5-42	11.9	- 2.50
M H Easterby	5-54	9.3	- 13.12	M Brittain	5-73	6.8	- 25.75
M A Jarvis	4-16	25.0	+ 15.50	D Morley	4-17	23.5	+ 13.13
A Moore	4-30	13.3	+ 4.25	M J Ryan	4-36	11.1	- 0.50
C J Hill	4-40	10.0	- 1.67	G Lewis	4-45	8.9	- 19.37
M R Channon	4-45	8.9	- 15.50	J Pearce	4-50	8.0	- 19.87
S E Kettlewell	3-10	30.0	+ 4.75	D W P Arbuthnot	3-11	27.3	+ 36.75
J W Hills	3-14	21.4	+ 18.00	J Balding	3-18	16.7	+ 9.25
S Dow	3-20	15.0	+ 7.50	I Campbell	3-21	14.3	+ 20.00
M Blanshard	3-22	13.6	+ 21.00	M C Pipe	3-22	13.6	+ 9.00
N Tinkler	3-28	10.7	- 1.75	Mrs N Macauley	3-28	10.7	+ 21.50
J Wharton	3-29	10.3	+ 4.00	J G FitzGerald	3-32	9.4	- 4.00
J L Spearing	3-33	9.1	- 12.50	M Johnston	3-36	8.3	- 15.67
Mrs M Reveley	3-38	7.9	- 19.12	J White	3-40	7.5	- 16.50
T D Barron	3-41	7.3	- 7.00	P C Haslam	3-56	5.4	- 43.00

Apprentice Handicaps

	W-R	Per cent	£1 Level Stake		W-R	Per cent	£1 Level Stake
Mrs M Reveley	15-73	20.5	+ 9.46	J Berry	13-69	18.8	+ 23.40
R J R Williams	11-65	16.9	+ 54.46	G Lewis	9-40	22.5	+ 17.75
Mrs J Ramsden	9-59	15.3	- 15.42	R Hannon	9-117	7.7	- 58.62
M D I Usher	8-51	15.7	+ 46.00	M H Tompkins	8-68	11.8	- 7.50
R M Flower	7-19	36.8	+ 35.50	M W Easterby	7-27	25.9	+ 14.50
H Candy	7-46	15.2	+ 30.50	M R Channon	7-49	14.3	+ 3.13
R Akehurst	7-58	12.1	- 15.09	D A Wilson	7-64	10.9	- 13.17
R Hollinshead	7-97	7.2	- 43.25	D T Thom	6-21	28.6	+ 16.25
B W Hills	6-28	21.4	+ 3.48	C J Hill	6-42	14.3	- 2.00
J M Bradley	6-45	13.3	+ 20.00	T D Barron	6-49	12.2	+ 19.00
P C Haslam	6-52	11.5	+ 12.00	F H Lee	6-61	9.8	- 4.75
W J Musson	6-62	9.7	+ 3.25	J L Eyre	5-24	20.8	+ 15.00
M J Heaton-Ellis	5-26	19.2	+ 2.00	D R C Elsworth	5-30	16.7	+ 0.50
J A Glover	5-32	15.6	+ 17.00	S G Norton	5-39	12.8	+ 10.00
B A McMahon	5-41	12.2	+ 39.00	Lord Huntingdon	5-42	11.9	- 24.18
A Bailey	5-51	9.8	- 20.75	G B Balding	5-68	7.4	- 25.75
R J Hodges	5-85	5.9	- 47.92	Lady Herries	4-21	19.0	- 0.45
W Jarvis	4-22	18.2	- 10.12	M J Ryan	4-29	13.8	+ 1.50
C A Cyzer	4-37	10.8	- 3.00	L J Holt	4-38	10.5	+ 4.83
M Bell	4-41	9.8	- 18.00	K O C-Brown	4-46	8.7	+ 1.00
I A Balding	4-48	8.3	- 16.25				

Amateur Handicaps

	W-R	Per cent	£1 Level Stake		W-R	Per cent	£1 Level Stake
D A Wilson	20-117	17.1	+ 0.75	J Pearce	17-96	17.7	+ 0.83
I A Balding	11-37	29.7	+ 22.71	Mrs M Reveley	8-51	15.7	+ 53.00
P Mitchell	6-30	20.0	+ 6.75	S Dow	6-37	16.2	+ 29.50
P J Feilden	6-54	11.1	- 4.50	M J Haynes	5-24	20.8	+ 23.50
D W P Arbuthnot	5-24	20.8	+ 14.50	A Hide	5-34	14.7	+ 4.25
D T Thom	4-27	14.8	+ 5.50	J L Spearing	4-39	10.3	- 19.25
P F I Cole	3-17	17.6	+ 7.50	J W Hills	3-17	17.6	+ 2.38
S E Kettlewell	3-20	15.0	+ 11.75	R F J Houghton	3-23	13.0	+ 9.00
J R Bosley	3-26	11.5	+ 9.00	Lady Herries	3-30	10.0	- 13.25
G Harwood	3-33	9.1	- 10.50	A C Stewart	2-4	50.0	+ 11.75
W J Haggas	2-4	50.0	+ 9.38	Sir Mark Prescott	2-5	40.0	+ 3.00
B Richmond	2-5	40.0	+ 33.33	P Calver	2-7	28.6	+ 5.50
M C Pipe	2-7	28.6	+ 5.50	C W C Elsey	2-8	25.0	+ 0.30
D R C Elsworth	2-10	20.0	+ 0.33	B Gubby	2-10	20.0	+ 9.00
L G Cottrell	2-11	18.2	+ 9.50	C W Thornton	2-11	18.2	- 2.75
P C Haslam	2-12	16.7	- 4.75	Lord Huntingdon	2-12	16.7	+ 1.00
J L Harris	2-16	12.5	+ 14.00	R M Whitaker	2-17	11.8	+ 1.50
M Bell	2-20	10.0	+ 5.00	H J Collingridge	2-21	9.5	+ 47.00
F H Lee	2-22	9.1	+ 12.00	A W Jones	2-24	8.3	- 4.00
M P Naughton	2-24	8.3	- 16.00	E J Alston	2-25	8.0	- 4.00
W J Musson	2-28	7.1	- 19.25	Mrs J Ramsden	2-31	6.5	- 8.50
G B Balding	2-35	5.7	- 16.50	R J Hodges	2-38	5.3	+ 3.00

LEADING TRAINERS' FAVOURITES 1990-1994

	W-R	Per cent	£1 Level Stake	% of Runners that Started Favourite	% of Winners that Started Favourite
H R A Cecil	287-675	42.5	- 54.57	36.5	56.4
J Berry	272-737	36.9	- 18.10	17.7	43.0
R Hannon	242-716	33.8	- 44.20	13.7	37.5
J H M Gosden	238-598	39.8	+ 28.86	26.8	48.7
M R Stoute	195-507	38.5	- 23.38	22.0	47.8
J L Dunlop	177-460	38.5	+ 30.94	19.5	45.9
L M Cumani	161-433	37.2	- 42.01	27.5	50.3
B W Hills	152-425	35.8	- 27.63	19.0	42.5
P F I Cole	139-378	36.8	- 46.68	16.3	39.9
Sir M Prescott	131-323	40.6	+ 22.82	25.1	51.8
Mrs M Reveley	117-339	34.5	- 14.86	18.7	41.5
M Johnston	113-333	33.9	- 1.40	15.7	37.3
G Harwood	102-255	40.0	+ 15.21	19.1	50.7
M H Easterby	92-316	29.1	- 43.54	13.9	39.8
R Charlton	90-237	38.0	- 4.36	25.7	44.8
I A Balding	89-260	34.2	+ 11.02	14.6	37.4
P Chapple-Hyam	76-172	44.2	- 9.65	21.0	47.8
M Bell	71-223	31.8	- 47.55	14.4	35.5
Lord Huntingdon	71-233	30.5	- 15.74	16.7	33.6
G Wragg	68-190	35.8	- 14.84	18.2	34.9
M H Tompkins	67-208	32.2	- 24.41	11.3	34.7
T D Barron	66-210	31.4	- 4.20	13.9	32.8
R Akehurst	65-251	25.9	- 15.21	15.8	32.2
R Hollinshead	62-187	33.2	- 13.34	6.5	30.1
W A O'Gorman	61-180	33.9	- 35.00	19.7	43.0
A C Stewart	60-182	33.0	- 28.51	22.0	48.4
Mrs J Ramsden	59-250	23.6	- 63.14	18.0	37.6
G Lewis	55-195	28.2	- 20.75	12.1	28.2
D R Loder	53-114	46.5	+ 18.48	32.2	61.6
M R Channon	53-183	29.0	- 2.80	10.5	29.6
H Thomson Jones	50-149	33.6	- 32.96	15.5	30.9
B Hanbury	49-160	30.6	- 24.54	12.1	28.7
C E Brittain	44-142	31.0	- 11.09	5.6	19.6
P C Haslam	43-110	39.1	+ 12.71	13.5	44.8
W R Hern	43-129	33.3	- 28.58	17.1	41.0
J R Fanshawe	43-133	32.3	+ 7.35	12.9	34.1
P T Walwyn	42-150	28.0	- 40.00	12.8	30.0
D R C Elsworth	42-153	27.5	- 15.38	10.1	25.8
M A Jarvis	41-107	38.3	+ 16.01	10.6	35.3
W Jarvis	38-114	33.3	- 9.51	11.1	30.2
P J Makin	37-119	31.1	+ 0.56	14.8	44.0
J W Hills	35-135	25.9	- 35.10	12.3	28.0
D W Chapman	34-102	33.3	- 12.31	6.8	35.8
M J Ryan	34-113	30.1	+ 9.86	10.7	27.2
R W Armstrong	33-100	33.0	- 4.38	13.1	32.4
R J Hodges	33-147	22.4	- 21.55	10.0	29.7
M J Camacho	32-68	47.1	+ 45.52	11.9	42.7
W J Haggas	32-100	32.0	- 12.97	14.5	33.3
Mrs J Cecil	32-102	31.4	- 9.68	17.1	32.0
J W Watts	31-100	31.0	- 5.99	11.2	34.8
N A Callaghan	31-114	27.2	- 16.84	12.6	29.8
S G Norton	30-100	30.0	- 11.00	9.4	24.4
Lady Herries	29-78	37.2	+ 20.11	15.3	39.7

	W-R	Per cent	£1 Level Stake	% of Runners that Started Favourite	% of Winners that Started Favourite
M C Pipe	28-92	30.4	- 8.82	21.0	38.4
J Pearce	28-98	28.6	+ 8.65	12.3	31.8
A Bailey	27-90	30.0	+ 6.55	9.6	31.0
C J Hill	26-95	27.4	- 7.96	11.7	32.5
B A McMahon	26-111	23.4	- 30.95	7.3	22.2
F H Lee	25-95	26.3	+ 0.88	7.7	24.0
D Morley	24-99	24.2	- 28.50	11.7	23.5
R Boss	23-83	27.7	- 9.62	10.8	26.4
M W Easterby	23-91	25.3	- 22.67	8.0	30.7
Mrs L Piggott	21-65	32.3	- 4.29	10.5	40.4
R M Whitaker	21-88	23.9	- 7.66	5.8	17.4
C A Cyzer	20-55	36.4	+ 14.63	5.2	21.1
N Tinkler	20-59	33.9	+ 5.34	6.5	35.1
Miss S E Hall	19-45	42.2	+ 24.36	8.8	36.5
C F Wall	19-57	33.3	+ 0.23	8.6	35.2
P W Harris	19-66	28.8	+ 7.69	9.4	27.1
R J R Williams	19-77	24.7	- 17.39	8.7	24.1
J Wharton	18-46	39.1	+ 24.14	5.8	24.7
J Etherington	18-60	30.0	- 12.98	8.1	33.3
D A Wilson	18-82	22.0	- 10.04	9.7	25.0
H Candy	17-52	32.7	+ 4.83	6.0	21.5
J L Spearing	17-53	32.1	+ 10.36	6.2	25.8
J G FitzGerald	17-61	27.9	- 12.71	7.4	26.2
C Tinkler	17-66	25.8	- 13.31	8.5	32.7
L J Holt	17-67	25.4	+ 4.16	8.4	38.6
P Calver	16-46	34.8	+ 17.85	8.9	31.4
J A Glover	16-50	32.0	+ 10.10	7.8	30.8
Mrs N Macauley	16-60	26.7	+ 4.63	5.2	18.6
M P Naughton	16-69	23.2	- 16.41	7.3	22.2
G B Balding	16-79	20.3	- 16.34	9.6	23.9
Dr J D Scargill	15-46	32.6	- 0.48	6.8	30.0
R J O'Sullivan	15-67	22.4	- 15.02	12.7	25.9
Denys Smith	14-29	48.3	+ 12.41	3.3	26.9
P A Kelleway	14-42	33.3	- 4.42	6.1	25.9
M McCormack	14-54	25.9	- 0.48	7.4	24.6
W R Muir	14-55	25.5	- 14.97	8.4	26.4
S Dow	14-58	24.1	- 12.91	5.3	18.4
R F J Houghton	14-60	23.3	- 26.37	8.2	21.2
E Weymes	13-28	46.4	+ 11.54	5.7	31.0
C J Benstead	13-35	37.1	+ 14.19	6.3	35.1
R Guest	13-39	33.3	+ 2.51	8.1	31.0
R Bastiman	13-42	31.0	+ 12.18	7.7	24.5
P S Felgate	13-44	29.5	- 0.96	8.4	29.5
T J Naughton	13-54	24.1	- 1.64	10.2	26.5
J W Payne	12-44	27.3	- 9.86	9.6	28.6
C N Allen	12-47	25.5	- 12.93	6.0	20.3
J White	11-25	44.0	+ 9.87	5.1	35.5
E J Alston	11-43	25.6	+ 6.90	5.0	15.3
J A R Toller	10-27	37.0	- 1.87	8.3	31.3
C N Williams	10-28	35.7	+ 10.66	12.6	58.8
J Akehurst	10-38	26.3	- 2.11	11.0	32.3
G M Moore	10-41	24.4	- 10.15	7.6	25.6
D W P Arbuthnot	10-54	18.5	- 12.87	7.1	12.8

TRAINER SECTION

(IRISH FLAT SEASON 1994)

P ASPELL

	No. of Horses	Races Run	1st	2nd	3rd	Unpl	Per cent	£1 Level Stake
2-y-o	0	0	0	0	0	0	–	0.00
3-y-o	8	64	2	4	13	45	3.1	- 49.75
4-y-o+	7	31	2	4	7	18	6.5	- 19.50
Totals	15	95	4	8	20	63	4.2	- 69.25

Mar/Apr	May	Jun	Jul	Aug	Sep	Oct/Nov
0-9	2-14	1-15	0-15	1-14	0-9	0-19

Winning Jockey	W-R	£1 Level Stake			W-R	£1 Level Stake
W J O'Connor	4-53	- 27.25				

Winning Courses						
Clonmel	1-5	- 1.75	Killarney		1-9	- 5.00
The Curragh	1-8	- 0.50	Roscommon		1-11	0.00

Winning Horses	Age	Races Run	1st	2nd	3rd	Unpl	Win £
Limbo Lady	4	8	1	3	2	2	4,110
Nemuro	6	4	1	0	1	2	3,450
House Music	3	11	1	2	4	4	2,228
Pleasant Outlook	3	11	1	0	1	9	2,228

Favourites	0-3		Total winning prize-money	£12,017

1993 Form	4-70	5.7%	- 26.00	1992 Form	0-10

F BERRY

	No. of Horses	Races Run	1st	2nd	3rd	Unpl	Per cent	£1 Level Stake
2-y-o	0	0	0	0	0	0	–	0.00
3-y-o	4	27	0	3	2	22	–	- 27.00
4-y-o+	4	24	2	2	3	17	8.3	+ 2.00
Totals	8	51	2	5	5	39	3.9	- 25.00

Mar/Apr	May	Jun	Jul	Aug	Sep	Oct/Nov
0-4	0-5	0-9	0-4	1-8	1-9	0-12

Winning Jockeys	W-R	£1 Level Stake		W-R	£1 Level Stake
J F Egan	1-2	+ 13.00	Joanna Morgan	1-2	+ 9.00

Winning Course		
The Curragh	2-13	+ 13.00

Winning Horse	Age	Races Run	1st	2nd	3rd	Unpl	Win £
Another Sky-Lark	6	13	2	2	3	6	16,325

Favourites	0-3			Total winning prize-money		£16,325

1993 Form	2-17	11.8%	- 5.50	1991 Form	0-12
1992 Form	0-10				

J S BOLGER

	No. of Horses	Races Run	1st	2nd	3rd	Unpl	Per cent	£1 Level Stake
2-y-o	53	188	42	25	29	92	22.3	+ 5.01
3-y-o	46	236	40	37	24	135	16.9	- 11.34
4-y-o+	28	165	26	15	13	111	15.8	+ 56.15
Totals	127	589	108	77	66	338	18.3	+ 49.82

BY MONTH

2-y-o	W-R	Per cent	£1 Level Stake	3-y-o	W-R	Per cent	£1 Level Stake
Mar/Apr	3-10	30.0	- 2.35	Mar/Apr	7-28	25.0	+ 17.00
May	4-14	28.6	- 7.47	May	6-32	18.8	- 4.40
June	8-24	33.3	+ 9.80	June	6-38	15.8	- 13.37
July	7-29	24.1	- 0.44	July	10-37	27.0	+ 34.25
August	10-35	28.6	+ 8.97	August	5-47	10.6	- 22.75
September	2-35	5.7	- 13.00	September	3-28	10.7	- 10.20
Oct/Nov	8-41	19.5	+ 9.50	Oct/Nov	3-26	11.5	- 11.87

4-y-o+	W-R	Per cent	£1 Level Stake	Totals	W-R	Per cent	£1 Level Stake
Mar/Apr	2-15	13.3	- 2.50	Mar/Apr	12-53	22.6	+ 12.15
May	5-23	21.7	+ 23.38	May	15-69	21.7	+ 11.51
June	3-34	8.8	- 20.42	June	17-96	17.7	- 23.99
July	3-25	12.0	- 2.25	July	20-91	22.0	+ 31.56
August	6-26	23.1	+ 34.44	August	21-108	19.4	+ 20.66
September	2-18	11.1	+ 7.50	September	7-81	8.6	- 15.70
Oct/Nov	5-24	20.8	+ 16.00	Oct/Nov	16-91	17.6	+ 13.63

DISTANCE

2-y-o	W-R	Per cent	£1 Level Stake	3-y-o	W-R	Per cent	£1 Level Stake
5f-6f	21-79	26.6	+ 12.11	5f-6f	2-17	11.8	- 5.62
7f-8f	19-104	18.3	- 10.10	7f-8f	9-81	11.1	- 14.50
9f-13f	2-4	50.0	+ 4.00	9f-13f	28-132	21.2	+ 7.78
14f+	0-1	-	- 1.00	14f+	1-6	16.7	+ 1.00

Bolger J S

4-y-o+	W-R	Per cent	£1 Level Stake	Totals	W-R	Per cent	£1 Level Stake
5f-6f	2-34	5.9	- 6.00	5f-6f	25-130	19.2	+ 0.49
7f-8f	6-35	17.1	+ 1.27	7f-8f	34-220	15.5	- 23.33
9f-13f	16-70	22.9	+ 72.88	9f-13f	46-206	22.3	+ 84.66
14f+	2-26	7.7	- 12.00	14f+	3-33	9.1	- 12.00

TYPE OF RACE

Non-Handicaps	W-R	Per cent	£1 Level Stake	Handicaps	W-R	Per cent	£1 Level Stake
2-y-o	36-164	22.0	- 11.91	2-y-o	6-24	25.0	+ 16.92
3-y-o	30-151	19.9	+ 6.16	3-y-o	10-76	13.2	- 8.50
4-y-o+	8-48	16.7	- 9.23	4-y-o+	15-103	14.6	+ 45.00
Apprentice	0-1	-	- 1.00	Apprentice	2-14	14.3	+ 5.38
Amat/Ladies	1-7	14.3	+ 8.00	Amat/Ladies	0-1	-	- 1.00
Totals	75-371	20.2	- 7.98	Totals	33-218	15.1	+ 57.80

FIRST TIME OUT

	W-R	Per cent	£1 Level Stake
2-y-o	11-53	20.8	+ 3.13
3-y-o	8-46	17.4	- 4.20
4-y-o+	4-27	14.8	+ 5.50
Totals	23-126	18.3	+ 4.43

JOCKEYS RIDING

	W-R	Per cent	£1 Level Stake		W-R	Per cent	£1 Level Stake
K J Manning	80-401	20.0	- 18.06	A P McCoy	2-7	28.6	+ 6.38
J A Heffernan	15-91	16.5	+ 46.00	J P Murtagh	1-1	100.0	+ 1.75
T E Durcan	5-29	17.2	+ 20.75	Mr F Cooper	1-2	50.0	+ 13.00
Joanna Morgan	3-8	37.5	+ 23.00	D Quirke	1-10	10.0	- 3.00

B A Hunter	0-15	M W Martin	0-3	Miss I Leahy	0-1
Mrs C Barker	0-6	R M Burke	0-3	S Craine	0-1
J F Egan	0-4	N G McCullagh	0-2		
W R Swinburn	0-4	D G O'Shea	0-1		

COURSE RECORD

	Total W-R	Non-Handicaps 2-y-o	3-y-o+	Handicaps 2-y-o	3-y-o+	Per cent	£1 Level Stake
The Curragh	20-135	8-43	9-38	1-3	2-51	14.8	- 8.32
Leopardstown	18-91	4-23	7-34	1-3	6-31	19.8	+ 25.18
Naas	8-43	4-16	1-9	1-5	2-13	18.6	+ 6.08
Tipperary	6-28	1-11	2-11	1-1	2-5	21.4	+ 2.13
Mallow	5-9	3-3	0-4	1-1	1-1	55.6	+ 10.23
Gowran Park	5-38	4-10	1-17	0-3	0-8	13.2	- 10.01
Down Royal	4-8	2-2	1-2	0-0	1-4	50.0	+ 13.50
Killarney	4-14	1-2	3-7	0-0	0-5	28.6	- 0.20
Ballinrobe	4-15	1-2	2-7	1-1	0-5	26.7	+ 3.05
Dundalk	4-19	2-6	1-8	0-1	1-4	21.1	- 3.75
Navan	4-21	1-8	0-5	0-0	3-8	19.0	+ 13.80
Tralee	4-21	2-4	1-9	0-2	1-6	19.0	+ 2.58
Roscommon	4-31	0-7	2-13	0-1	2-10	12.9	- 3.75
Sligo	3-6	1-2	1-2	0-0	1-2	50.0	+ 22.50
Clonmel	3-13	0-0	3-9	0-0	0-4	23.1	+ 7.25
Fairyhouse	3-21	1-6	0-9	0-0	2-6	14.3	- 3.00
Thurles	2-3	0-0	2-3	0-0	0-0	66.7	+ 6.50
Wexford	2-9	0-0	1-3	0-0	1-6	22.2	- 2.75
Galway	2-33	0-7	1-6	0-2	1-18	6.1	- 19.00
Downpatrick	1-2	0-0	1-2	0-0	0-0	50.0	- 0.20
Bellewstown	1-5	0-2	0-1	0-0	1-2	20.0	+ 8.00
Punchestown	1-6	1-3	0-3	0-0	0-0	16.7	- 2.00

Listowel	0-16	Limerick		0-2

WINNING HORSES

	Age	Races Run	1st	2nd	3rd	Unpl	Win £
Eva Luna	2	6	5	0	1	0	131,386
Ballykett Nancy	3	11	6	2	0	3	48,605
Perfect Impostor	4	4	1	0	1	2	28,850
Wild Bluebell	2	5	3	1	0	1	22,758
Zavaleta	3	5	2	0	0	3	21,125
Nordic Oak	6	8	2	1	0	5	20,250
Royal Vision	5	8	2	1	0	5	19,900
Al Mohaajir	3	6	3	1	0	2	14,387
Via Lombardia	2	4	2	1	1	0	13,831
Camisha	3	4	2	1	1	0	10,302
Lovely Ali	5	5	3	0	0	2	9,955
Garamendi	2	4	2	0	2	0	9,316
Desert Style	2	5	2	1	2	0	8,631
Taibhseach	2	2	1	0	0	1	8,625
Mohaajir	3	2	2	0	0	0	8,245
Goodies Two Step	4	5	1	0	0	4	8,220
Pennine Tune	5	5	2	0	0	3	8,135
Raghida	2	4	2	1	0	1	7,905
Antiquity	3	8	2	2	1	3	7,893
Diamond Display	3	9	3	1	1	4	7,880
Gallardini	5	8	2	0	0	6	6,852
Giulio Romano	3	8	1	2	1	4	6,850

Foravella	2	8	2	1	0	5	5,994
Nordic Queen	4	8	2	3	2	1	5,653
Rondelli	4	10	1	0	0	9	5,520
Ckr Sport	2	4	1	0	0	3	5,480
Kerry Project	2	2	1	0	0	1	5,206
Rigobertha	2	4	1	1	0	2	5,206
Bluffing	2	5	1	2	2	0	5,206
Magic Rimsh	3	7	2	3	1	1	4,970
Liffey's Secret	3	6	2	2	0	2	4,968
Arctic Park	3	6	2	0	1	3	4,455
Nordic Sensation	5	10	2	2	1	5	4,453
Ivory Frontier	4	5	1	1	1	2	4,410
Northern Frontier	3	3	1	0	0	2	4,140
Kly Green	3	5	1	1	1	2	4,140
Irrestible Lady	3	7	1	0	1	5	4,110
River Project	2	5	1	1	1	2	3,770
Persian Creek	5	13	1	2	3	7	3,768
Pozzoli	2	6	1	2	1	2	3,768
Nordic Brief	5	6	1	0	0	5	3,768
Book Project	2	4	1	2	1	0	3,768
Mini Project	2	1	1	0	0	0	3,768
Keep Bobbin Up	2	1	1	0	0	0	3,768
French Project	2	2	1	0	0	1	3,768
Mystic Shadow	2	4	1	1	1	1	3,768
Something Bright	2	1	1	0	0	0	3,768
Prosaic Star	2	3	1	0	0	2	3,768
Aliuska	2	3	2	0	0	1	3,613
Mining Project	2	6	1	0	2	3	3,308
Lord Bentley	4	10	1	1	2	6	3,105
Zanella	2	7	1	1	2	3	3,085
Corso	2	5	1	1	2	1	3,083
Blitzer	2	5	1	1	0	3	3,083
Boristova	2	5	1	3	1	0	3,083
Nordic Colours	3	7	1	0	0	6	2,913
Bubbly Prospect	3	9	1	1	2	5	2,900
Osvaldo	5	8	1	0	0	7	2,740
Kartlos	5	4	1	0	0	3	2,740
Galavotti	5	4	1	0	0	3	2,740
Ballykett Lady	4	4	1	1	0	2	2,740
Nordic Valley	3	5	1	0	1	3	2,243
Nordic Flavour	3	7	1	1	0	5	2,243
Northern Bars	3	4	1	0	0	3	2,243
Dallachio	3	5	1	0	1	3	2,228
Smaointeach	3	5	1	1	0	3	2,228
Maroondah	2	5	1	0	0	4	2,226
Nordic Crown	3	4	1	0	1	2	2,226
Greenspan	2	3	1	0	1	1	2,226
Gold Depositor	2	2	1	0	0	1	2,055
Rustavi	3	9	1	4	2	2	1,541
Double Pendant	3	5	1	0	1	3	1,380

WINNING OWNERS

	Races Won	Value £		Races Won	Value £
Mrs Catherine Shubotham	12	171,052	C K R Racing Club	1	5,480
Mrs J S Bolger	26	115,634	Jerry Moynihan	1	5,206
D H W Dobson	15	52,991	Mrs David Nagle	1	5,206
N Keating	6	48,605	Hamad Ali	2	4,970
Maktoum Al Maktoum	10	42,938	Patrick H Burns	2	4,455
Dr Michael Smurfit	5	39,812	Thomas McDonogh	2	4,453
Ballylinch Stud	5	28,580	Mrs Una Manning	1	3,768
Michael H Keogh	4	16,028	Dermot McGovern	1	3,768
T F Brennan	2	10,618	Mrs Seamus Hayes	1	3,768
T Lucas	1	8,220	D Bernie	1	3,105
Niall Quinn	2	7,905	Stephen Keating	1	2,740
Peter J P Gleeson	2	7,150	J P Hill	1	2,226
Mrs A J F O'Reilly	2	7,010	P J O'Donovan	1	1,541

Favourites	37-103	35.9%	- 10.59	Total winning prize-money		£607,225
Longest winning sequence			3	Average SP of winner		4.9/1
Longest losing sequence			23	Return on stakes invested		8.5%
1993 Form	57-520	11.0%	-232.19	1991 Form	111-622	17.8%	-124.92
1992 Form	119-671	17.7%	-160.84	1990 Form	125-562	22.2%	- 95.72

W T BOURKE

	No. of Horses	Races Run	1st	2nd	3rd	Unpl	Per cent	£1 Level Stake
2-y-o	0	0	0	0	0	0	-	0.00
3-y-o	0	0	0	0	0	0	-	0.00
4-y-o+	1	12	2	0	0	10	16.7	+ 7.00
Totals	1	12	2	0	0	10	16.7	+ 7.00

Mar/Apr	May	Jun	Jul	Aug	Sep	Oct/Nov
0-0	0-1	0-1	0-2	1-3	1-2	0-3

Winning Jockeys	W-R	£1 Level Stake		W-R	£1 Level Stake
J A Heffernan	1-1	+ 7.00	D G O'Shea	1-9	+ 2.00

Winning Courses					
Mallow	1-1	+ 10.00	Clonmel	1-1	+ 7.00

Winning Horse	Age	Races Run	1st	2nd	3rd	Unpl	Win £
Kess	5	12	2	0	0	10	4,453

Favourites	0-1		Total winning prize-money	£4,453
1993 Form	0-7		1990 Form	0-2

V BOWENS

	No. of Horses	Races Run	1st	2nd	3rd	Unpl	Per cent	£1 Level Stake
2-y-o	0	0	0	0	0	0	-	0.00
3-y-o	2	7	2	1	0	4	28.6	+ 8.00
4-y-o+	4	10	1	1	0	8	10.0	- 4.00
Totals	6	17	3	2	0	12	17.6	+ 4.00

Mar/Apr	May	Jun	Jul	Aug	Sep	Oct/Nov
0-3	1-4	0-1	1-2	1-2	0-1	0-4

Winning Jockeys	W-R	£1 Level Stake		W-R	£1 Level Stake
P Shanahan	1-1	+ 6.00	R Fitzpatrick	1-4	+ 4.00
D G O'Shea	1-3	+ 3.00			

Winning Courses	W-R	£1 Level Stake		W-R	£1 Level Stake
The Curragh	1-2	+ 6.00	Leopardstown	1-6	+ 1.00
Mallow	1-2	+ 4.00			

Winning Horses	Age	Races Run	1st	2nd	3rd	Unpl	Win £
Sweetest Thing	3	4	2	1	0	1	6,850
Mayfield Prince	5	6	1	1	0	4	2,228

Favourites	0-0			Total winning prize-money			£9,078
1993 Form	0-37			1991 Form	1-52	1.9%	- 41.00
1992 Form	7-85	8.2%	- 16.75	1990 Form	2-40	5.0%	- 26.00

M BREW

	No. of Horses	Races Run	1st	2nd	3rd	Unpl	Per cent	£1 Level Stake
2-y-o	1	1	0	0	0	1	-	- 1.00
3-y-o	1	5	0	0	0	5	-	- 5.00
4-y-o+	3	4	1	0	0	3	25.0	- 0.50
Totals	5	10	1	0	0	9	10.0	- 6.50

Mar/Apr	May	Jun	Jul	Aug	Sep	Oct/Nov
0-1	0-1	0-2	0-1	0-3	0-0	1-2

Winning Jockey	W-R	£1 Level Stake	Winning Course	W-R	£1 Level Stake
J J Behan	1-1	+ 2.50	Down Royal	1-2	+ 1.50

Winning Horse	Age	Races Run	1st	2nd	3rd	Unpl	Win £
Asta Madera	4	1	1	0	0	0	1,541

Favourites	1-1	100.0%	+ 2.50	Total winning prize-money		£1,541
1993 Form	0-5			1992 Form	0-5	

LIAM BROWNE

	No. of Horses	Races Run	1st	2nd	3rd	Unpl	Per cent	£1 Level Stake
2-y-o	8	22	1	2	1	18	4.5	- 17.00
3-y-o	9	38	1	2	1	34	2.6	- 32.00
4-y-o+	4	17	0	1	1	15	-	- 17.00
Totals	21	77	2	5	3	67	2.6	- 66.00

Mar/Apr	May	Jun	Jul	Aug	Sep	Oct/Nov
0-5	0-14	1-19	0-9	1-15	0-12	0-3

Winning Jockeys	W-R	£1 Level Stake		W-R	£1 Level Stake
C Roche	1-7	- 2.00	J F Egan	1-10	- 4.00

Winning Courses	W-R	£1 Level Stake		W-R	£1 Level Stake
Leopardstown	1-11	- 6.00	The Curragh	1-23	- 17.00

Winning Horses	Age	Races Run	1st	2nd	3rd	Unpl	Win £
Gold Anchor	2	1	1	0	0	0	5,206
Fairy Water	3	4	1	0	0	3	2,400

Favourites	0-1			Total winning prize-money		£7,606
1993 Form	11-117	9.4%	- 40.80	1991 Form	9-128	7.0%	- 43.12
1992 Form	8-130	6.2%	- 83.04	1990 Form	13-202	6.4%	-121.25

J BURNS

	No. of Horses	Races Run	1st	2nd	3rd	Unpl	Per cent	£1 Level Stake
2-y-o	3	6	0	0	0	6	-	- 6.00
3-y-o	17	97	5	15	12	65	5.2	- 49.00
4-y-o+	5	20	3	2	3	12	15.0	- 4.50
Totals	25	123	8	17	15	83	6.5	- 59.50

Mar/Apr	May	Jun	Jul	Aug	Sep	Oct/Nov
1-9	1-27	0-18	1-25	3-22	2-13	0-9

Winning Jockeys	W-R	£1 Level Stake		W-R	£1 Level Stake
J P Murtagh	3-14	+ 13.00	W J Smith	1-4	+ 1.00
N G McCullagh	2-20	- 9.50	C Roche	1-8	+ 3.00
W Carson	1-2	+ 8.00			

Winning Courses	W-R	£1 Level Stake		W-R	£1 Level Stake
Down Royal	2-7	+ 6.00	Dundalk	1-6	- 1.50
Fairyhouse	1-3	+ 7.00	The Curragh	1-18	- 8.00
Mallow	1-4	+ 7.00	Leopardstown	1-24	- 18.00
Killarney	1-5	+ 4.00			

Winning Horses	Age	Races Run	1st	2nd	3rd	Unpl	Win £
Memories	3	7	1	2	0	4	8,625
Aster Aweke	4	4	2	1	1	0	6,338
Welcome Wish	3	8	1	1	1	5	3,427
Jenbro	3	7	1	0	1	5	2,740
Beauchamp Image	3	6	1	1	0	4	2,226
Adolescence	4	5	1	0	1	3	1,541
Salience	3	4	1	1	0	2	1,383

Favourites	0-8			Total winning prize-money			£26,280

1993 Form	1-95	1.1%	- 84.00	1992 Form	7-56	12.5%	- 4.25

M J BYRNE

	No. of Horses	Races Run	1st	2nd	3rd	Unpl	Per cent	£1 Level Stake
2-y-o	0	0	0	0	0	0	-	0.00
3-y-o	1	7	1	1	0	5	14.3	- 1.50
4-y-o+	2	3	0	0	0	3	-	- 3.00
Totals	3	10	1	1	0	8	10.0	- 4.50

Mar/Apr	May	Jun	Jul	Aug	Sep	Oct/Nov
0-2	1-2	0-1	0-1	0-2	0-2	0-0

Winning Jockey	W-R	£1 Level Stake	Winning Course		W-R	£1 Level Stake
R Hughes	1-4	+ 1.50	Mallow		1-1	+ 4.50

Winning Horse	Age	Races Run	1st	2nd	3rd	Unpl	Win £
The Cushman	3	7	1	1	0	5	2,228

Favourites	0-0			Total winning prize-money			£2,228

J M CANTY

	No. of Horses	Races Run	1st	2nd	3rd	Unpl	Per cent	£1 Level Stake
2-y-o	2	5	0	0	1	4	-	- 5.00
3-y-o	2	12	2	0	0	10	16.7	+ 3.00
4-y-o+	11	58	5	3	6	44	8.6	- 16.00
Totals	15	75	7	3	7	58	9.3	- 18.00

Mar/Apr	May	Jun	Jul	Aug	Sep	Oct/Nov
0-6	0-5	2-12	0-9	1-13	0-14	4-16

Winning Jockeys	W-R	£1 Level Stake		W-R	£1 Level Stake
P M Donohue	2-16	- 5.00	D O'Callaghan	1-5	+ 4.00
J J Behan	1-3	+ 4.00	D G O'Shea	1-10	+ 5.00
P P Murphy	1-3	+ 5.00	P V Gilson	1-19	- 12.00

Winning Courses					
Gowran Park	3-8	+ 10.00	Roscommon	1-7	+ 2.00
Dundalk	1-5	+ 3.00	Galway	1-9	+ 6.00
Tipperary	1-6	+ 1.00			

Winning Horses	Age	Races Run	1st	2nd	3rd	Unpl	Win £
My Gossip	4	9	2	0	2	5	6,508
Euphoric	3	9	2	0	0	7	4,966
Bavarian Ballad	4	6	1	0	0	5	3,768
Super Flame	7	3	1	0	1	1	2,742
Veritable Gallery	4	6	1	0	0	5	2,226

Favourites	1-8	12.5%	- 3.00	Total winning prize-money		£20,210

1993 Form	6-80	7.5%	- 47.50	1991 Form	3-72	4.2%	- 40.00
1992 Form	1-58	1.7%	- 56.56	1990 Form	6-55	10.9%	- 28.62

D CARROLL

	No. of Horses	Races Run	1st	2nd	3rd	Unpl	Per cent	£1 Level Stake
2-y-o	0	0	0	0	0	0	-	0.00
3-y-o	2	10	0	0	0	10	-	- 10.00
4-y-o+	2	8	1	0	0	7	12.5	+ 7.00
Totals	4	18	1	0	0	17	5.6	- 3.00

Mar/Apr	May	Jun	Jul	Aug	Sep	Oct/Nov
0-3	1-7	0-3	0-0	0-0	0-2	0-3

Winning Jockey	W-R	£1 Level Stake	Winning Course	W-R	£1 Level Stake
D G O'Shea	1-3	+ 12.00	Navan	1-1	+ 14.00

Winning Horse	Age	Races Run	1st	2nd	3rd	Unpl	Win £
Noble Sam	5	5	1	0	0	4	2,760

Favourites	0-1	Total winning prize-money	£2,760

1993 Form   0-16

N CASSIDY

	No. of Horses	Races Run	1st	2nd	3rd	Unpl	Per cent	£1 Level Stake
2-y-o	0	0	0	0	0	0	-	0.00
3-y-o	0	0	0	0	0	0	-	0.00
4-y-o+	4	10	1	0	0	9	10.0	+ 11.00
Totals	4	10	1	0	0	9	10.0	+ 11.00

Mar/Apr	May	Jun	Jul	Aug	Sep	Oct/Nov
0-1	0-1	1-3	0-3	0-2	0-0	0-0

Winning Jockey	W-R	£1 Level Stake	Winning Course	W-R	£1 Level Stake
Mr T J Beattie	1-3	+ 18.00	Limerick	1-1	+ 20.00

Winning Horse	Age	Races Run	1st	2nd	3rd	Unpl	Win £
Indiana Gold	6	6	1	0	0	5	2,228

Favourites	0-0	Total winning prize-money	£2,228
1993 Form	0-2		

NOEL T CHANCE

	No. of Horses	Races Run	1st	2nd	3rd	Unpl	Per cent	£1 Level Stake
2-y-o	0	0	0	0	0	0	-	0.00
3-y-o	3	27	1	3	3	20	3.7	- 18.00
4-y-o+	2	11	1	1	1	8	9.1	- 4.00
Totals	5	38	2	4	4	28	5.3	- 22.00

Mar/Apr	May	Jun	Jul	Aug	Sep	Oct/Nov
0-2	1-5	0-3	1-5	0-10	0-8	0-5

Winning Jockeys	W-R	£1 Level Stake		W-R	£1 Level Stake
J F Egan	1-4	+ 3.00	J J Behan	1-9	0.00

Winning Courses					
Ballinrobe	1-2	+ 5.00	Dundalk	1-5	+ 4.00

Winning Horses	Age	Races Run	1st	2nd	3rd	Unpl	Win £
Royal Thimble	3	15	1	3	2	9	2,228
Pearl Dawn	4	10	1	1	1	7	2,226

Favourites	0-0	Total winning prize-money	£4,455

1993 Form	4-31	12.9%	+ 3.10	1991 Form	0-38		
1992 Form	0-21			1990 Form	1-32	3.1%	- 21.00

MRS P COLLIER

	No. of Horses	Races Run	1st	2nd	3rd	Unpl	Per cent	£1 Level Stake
2-y-o	0	0	0	0	0	0	-	0.00
3-y-o	0	0	0	0	0	0	-	0.00
4-y-o+	1	5	1	1	0	3	20.0	0.00
Totals	1	5	1	1	0	3	20.0	0.00

Mar/Apr	May	Jun	Jul	Aug	Sep	Oct/Nov
0-0	0-0	0-0	0-0	1-1	0-3	0-1

Winning Jockey	W-R	£1 Level Stake	Winning Course	W-R	£1 Level Stake
M J Cullen	1-3	+ 2.00	Roscommon	1-2	+ 3.00

Winning Horse	Age	Races Run	1st	2nd	3rd	Unpl	Win £
Kawa-Kawa	7	5	1	1	0	3	2,226

Favourites	1-3	33.3%	+ 2.00	Total winning prize-money	£2,226

1993 Form	0-6		1991 Form	0-0		
1992 Form	0-0		1990 Form	1-2	50.0%	+ 15.00

C COLLINS

	No. of Horses	Races Run	1st	2nd	3rd	Unpl	Per cent	£1 Level Stake
2-y-o	17	68	8	9	9	42	11.8	- 21.68
3-y-o	18	124	14	14	13	83	11.3	- 49.60
4-y-o+	8	54	7	9	7	31	13.0	+ 16.30
Totals	43	246	29	32	29	156	11.8	- 54.98

BY MONTH

2-y-o	W-R	Per cent	£1 Level Stake	3-y-o	W-R	Per cent	£1 Level Stake
Mar/Apr	0-1	-	- 1.00	Mar/Apr	2-20	10.0	- 4.75
May	2-8	25.0	- 0.93	May	1-15	6.7	- 10.50
June	2-12	16.7	+ 6.50	June	3-20	15.0	- 7.00
July	0-9	-	- 9.00	July	1-19	5.3	- 15.75
August	1-8	12.5	- 5.25	August	6-21	28.6	+ 6.40
September	2-13	15.4	- 4.00	September	1-13	7.7	- 2.00
Oct/Nov	1-17	5.9	- 8.00	Oct/Nov	0-16	-	- 16.00

Collins C

4-y-o+	W-R	Per cent	£1 Level Stake	Totals	W-R	Per cent	£1 Level Stake
Mar/Apr	2-9	22.2	+ 15.80	Mar/Apr	4-30	13.3	+ 10.05
May	0-6	-	- 6.00	May	3-29	10.3	- 17.43
June	1-6	16.7	- 2.50	June	6-38	15.8	- 3.00
July	2-7	28.6	+ 9.00	July	3-35	8.6	- 15.75
August	0-6	-	- 6.00	August	7-35	20.0	- 4.85
September	0-7	-	- 7.00	September	3-33	9.1	- 13.00
Oct/Nov	2-13	15.4	+ 13.00	Oct/Nov	3-46	6.5	- 11.00

DISTANCE

2-y-o	W-R	Per cent	£1 Level Stake	3-y-o	W-R	Per cent	£1 Level Stake
5f-6f	5-38	13.2	- 7.93	5f-6f	3-25	12.0	- 5.25
7f-8f	3-29	10.3	- 12.75	7f-8f	5-53	9.4	- 36.60
9f-13f	0-0	-	0.00	9f-13f	6-46	13.0	- 7.75
14f+	0-1	-	- 1.00	14f+	0-0	-	0.00

4-y-o+	W-R	Per cent	£1 Level Stake	Totals	W-R	Per cent	£1 Level Stake
5f-6f	3-10	30.0	+ 24.00	5f-6f	11-73	15.1	+ 10.82
7f-8f	4-22	18.2	+ 14.30	7f-8f	12-104	11.5	- 35.05
9f-13f	0-17	-	- 17.00	9f-13f	6-63	9.5	- 24.75
14f+	0-5	-	- 5.00	14f+	0-6	-	- 6.00

TYPE OF RACE

Non-Handicaps	W-R	Per cent	£1 Level Stake	Handicaps	W-R	Per cent	£1 Level Stake
2-y-o	7-58	12.1	- 16.18	2-y-o	1-10	10.0	- 5.50
3-y-o	11-72	15.3	- 20.60	3-y-o	3-48	6.3	- 25.00
4-y-o+	0-4	-	- 4.00	4-y-o+	7-48	14.6	+ 22.30
Apprentice	0-1	-	- 1.00	Apprentice	0-3	-	- 3.00
Amat/Ladies	0-2	-	- 2.00	Amat/Ladies	0-0	-	0.00
Totals	18-137	13.1	- 43.78	Totals	11-109	10.1	- 11.20

FIRST TIME OUT

	W-R	Per cent	£1 Level Stake
2-y-o	0-16	-	- 16.00
3-y-o	1-18	5.6	- 5.00
4-y-o+	2-7	28.6	+ 17.80
Totals	3-41	7.3	- 3.20

JOCKEYS RIDING

	W-R	Per cent	£1 Level Stake		W-R	Per cent	£1 Level Stake
P V Gilson	23-168	13.7	- 27.53	P Carberry	1-1	100.0	+ 12.00
S Craine	3-13	23.1	+ 1.75	R M Burke	1-10	10.0	+ 1.00
J F Egan	1-1	100.0	+ 10.80				

J J Mullins	0-13	D G O'Shea	0-3	N G McCullagh	0-1
Anne Corish	0-10	D Hogan	0-1	P J Smullen	0-1
A C O'Brien	0-9	G Bardwell	0-1	P Shanahan	0-1
Joanna Morgan	0-6	Miss M Olivefalk	0-1		
P M Donohue	0-5	Miss S Collins	0-1		

COURSE RECORD

	Total W-R	Non-Handicaps 2-y-o	Non-Handicaps 3-y-o+	Handicaps 2-y-o	Handicaps 3-y-o+	Per cent	£1 Level Stake
The Curragh	6-49	2-13	1-11	0-2	3-23	12.2	- 10.50
Tipperary	5-21	2-10	3-8	0-1	0-2	23.8	- 6.43
Leopardstown	5-35	1-6	0-14	1-1	3-14	14.3	+ 16.30
Tramore	3-8	0-0	2-3	0-0	1-5	37.5	+ 11.75
Tralee	3-10	1-1	1-5	0-0	1-4	30.0	+ 12.40
Downpatrick	1-2	0-0	1-2	0-0	0-0	50.0	+ 1.50
Bellewstown	1-4	0-1	0-1	0-0	1-2	25.0	+ 4.00
Sligo	1-5	1-3	0-0	0-0	0-2	20.0	- 3.50
Down Royal	1-5	0-2	0-1	0-0	1-2	20.0	+ 8.00
Ballinrobe	1-6	0-0	1-2	0-1	0-3	16.7	- 3.75
Navan	1-11	0-3	1-4	0-0	0-4	9.1	+ 2.00
Galway	1-16	0-3	1-2	0-1	0-10	6.3	- 12.75

Naas	0-25	Listowel	0-6	Clonmel	0-2
Gowran Park	0-12	Mallow	0-6	Laytown	0-1
Dundalk	0-7	Roscommon	0-6		
Fairyhouse	0-6	Punchestown	0-3		

WINNING HORSES

	Age	Races Run	1st	2nd	3rd	Unpl	Win £
Kill The Crab	2	7	3	2	2	0	22,253
Kiltimony	4	8	3	0	0	5	19,480
One False Move	3	8	2	1	1	4	15,325
Soreze	2	4	2	1	1	0	11,487
General Chaos	4	10	2	0	2	6	11,162
Miss Sacha	3	4	1	0	1	2	8,627
Incharder	3	7	2	2	1	2	5,825
Tirols Result	2	6	1	0	1	4	5,206
Jingling Silver	3	9	2	0	0	7	5,138
Make That Call	3	7	1	1	1	4	4,110
Faydora	2	7	1	1	2	3	3,768
Musical Sunset	3	6	1	0	1	4	3,450
Ladies Gallery	4	12	1	3	1	7	3,425
Vittoria Colonna	3	6	1	1	2	2	3,425

Welcome Guest	3	8	1	2	1	4	2,911
Opulent	3	6	1	0	2	3	2,760
Leonbruno	2	3	1	1	0	1	2,228
Bank Statement	3	9	1	3	2	3	2,226
Day Light	3	5	1	2	0	2	1,541
Madame Minister	4	3	1	0	0	2	1,370

WINNING OWNERS

	Races Won	Value £		Races Won	Value £
Mrs C Collins	6	28,728	James McNeil	1	3,450
James Fennelly	3	22,253	C Humphries	1	3,425
Cyril Humphris	2	14,128	Donal O'Buachalla	1	3,425
Mrs H R Norton	2	11,487	David F Howard	1	3,425
J N Anthony	2	11,162	James McNeil	1	2,911
Lucayan Stud	1	8,627	A C Behan	1	2,760
Mrs G W Jennings	2	5,825	P D Savill	1	2,226
Statenprojekt BV	1	5,206	Lord Harrington	1	1,541
J H McLoughlin	1	3,768	J P Foley	1	1,370

Favourites	11-30	36.7%	+ 0.97	Total winning prize-money	£135,716

Longest winning sequence		2	Average SP of winner	5.6/1
Longest losing sequence		32	Return on stakes invested	-22.3%

1993 Form	22-216	10.2%	- 82.51	1991 Form	22-208	10.6%	- 73.25
1992 Form	16-167	9.6%	- 78.45	1990 Form	19-255	7.5%	-119.27

J G COOGAN

	No. of Horses	Races Run	1st	2nd	3rd	Unpl	Per cent	£1 Level Stake
2-y-o	5	19	3	4	2	10	15.8	+ 0.50
3-y-o	10	71	3	6	6	56	4.2	- 56.90
4-y-o+	4	8	0	0	0	8	–	- 8.00
Totals	19	98	6	10	8	74	6.1	- 64.40

Mar/Apr	May	Jun	Jul	Aug	Sep	Oct/Nov
0-12	1-11	0-21	4-24	0-17	1-7	0-6

Winning Jockeys	W-R	£1 Level Stake		W-R	£1 Level Stake
B Coogan	3-35	- 22.40	P V Gilson	1-3	+ 3.00
P P Murphy	1-1	+ 8.00	P Shanahan	1-13	- 7.00

Winning Courses					
Bellewstown	2-7	+ 1.50	Downpatrick	1-1	+ 1.10
Dundalk	2-10	+ 4.00	Listowel	1-2	+ 7.00

Winning Horses	Age	Races Run	1st	2nd	3rd	Unpl	Win £
Suga Hawk	2	8	1	2	2	3	4,110
Double Risk	2	3	1	2	0	0	3,085
Nun's Island	3	9	1	0	0	8	2,742
The Mardyke	3	10	1	0	3	6	2,742
Ballynakelly	2	2	1	0	0	1	2,228
Hania	3	4	1	0	0	3	1,553

Favourites	3-7	42.9%	+ 3.60	Total winning prize-money			£16,460
1993 Form	3-101	3.0%	- 84.50	1991 Form	5-67	7.5%	- 16.50
1992 Form	7-75	9.3%	- 41.50	1990 Form	1-26	3.8%	- 18.00

R J COTTER

	No. of Horses	Races Run	1st	2nd	3rd	Unpl	Per cent	£1 Level Stake
2-y-o	1	5	0	0	1	4	-	- 5.00
3-y-o	0	0	0	0	0	0	-	0.00
4-y-o+	2	8	1	0	1	6	12.5	0.00
Totals	3	13	1	0	2	10	7.7	- 5.00

Mar/Apr	May	Jun	Jul	Aug	Sep	Oct/Nov
0-1	0-0	1-5	0-2	0-4	0-1	0-0

Winning Jockey	W-R	£1 Level Stake	Winning Course	W-R	£1 Level Stake
D G O'Shea	1-7	+ 1.00	Tipperary	1-2	+ 6.00

Winning Horse	Age	Races Run	1st	2nd	3rd	Unpl	Win £
Simply Phrased	5	5	1	0	1	3	2,742

Favourites	0-2		Total winning prize-money		£2,742
1993 Form	0-8		1991 Form	0-2	
1992 Form	0-2		1990 Form	0-1	

M CUNNINGHAM

	No. of Horses	Races Run	1st	2nd	3rd	Unpl	Per cent	£1 Level Stake
2-y-o	1	3	0	0	1	2	-	- 3.00
3-y-o	1	2	0	0	0	2	-	- 2.00
4-y-o+	4	12	5	0	2	5	41.7	+ 4.75
Totals	6	17	5	0	3	9	29.4	- 0.25

Cunningham M

Mar/Apr	May	Jun	Jul	Aug	Sep	Oct/Nov
1-2	1-3	1-1	2-3	0-2	0-3	0-3

Winning Jockeys	W-R	£1 Level Stake			W-R	£1 Level Stake
Joanna Morgan	3-5	+ 5.75	J F Egan		1-2	+ 2.00
B J Walsh	1-1	+ 1.00				

Winning Courses						
Down Royal	1-1	+ 1.25	The Curragh		1-2	+ 2.00
Tipperary	1-1	+ 2.50	Tralee		1-2	0.00
Leopardstown	1-2	+ 3.00				

Winning Horse	Age	Races Run	1st	2nd	3rd	Unpl	Win £
Dairine's Delight	4	8	5	0	1	2	22,847

Favourites	4-6	66.7%	+ 5.75	Total winning prize-money			£22,847

1993 Form	2-20	10.0%	- 4.50	1991 Form	2-86	2.3%	- 67.00
1992 Form	0-54			1990 Form	7-84	8.3%	- 36.75

G A CUSACK

	No. of Horses	Races Run	1st	2nd	3rd	Unpl	Per cent	£1 Level Stake
2-y-o	5	10	1	0	1	8	10.0	- 8.00
3-y-o	0	0	0	0	0	0	-	0.00
4-y-o+	1	3	0	0	0	3	-	- 3.00
Totals	6	13	1	0	1	11	7.7	- 11.00

Mar/Apr	May	Jun	Jul	Aug	Sep	Oct/Nov
0-0	0-0	0-1	0-1	0-1	1-3	0-7

Winning Jockey	W-R	£1 Level Stake	Winning Course	W-R	£1 Level Stake
P J Smullen	1-8	- 6.00	Down Royal	1-2	0.00

Winning Horse	Age	Races Run	1st	2nd	3rd	Unpl	Win £
Danalia	2	2	1	0	1	0	2,055

Favourites	1-1	100.0%	+ 1.00	Total winning prize-money			£2,055

P J DEEGAN

	No. of Horses	Races Run	1st	2nd	3rd	Unpl	Per cent	£1 Level Stake
2-y-o	1	4	0	0	0	4	-	- 4.00
3-y-o	0	0	0	0	0	0	-	0.00
4-y-o+	2	12	2	0	0	10	16.7	+ 12.00
Totals	3	16	2	0	0	14	12.5	+ 8.00

Mar/Apr	May	Jun	Jul	Aug	Sep	Oct/Nov
0-1	0-2	1-3	1-4	0-1	0-3	0-2

Winning Jockey	W-R	£1 Level Stake	Winning Course	W-R	£1 Level Stake
R M Burke	2-8	+ 16.00	Naas	2-4	+ 20.00

Winning Horse	Age	Races Run	1st	2nd	3rd	Unpl	Win £
Another Flyer	4	10	2	0	0	8	5,482

Favourites	0-0	Total winning prize-money		£5,482
1993 Form	0-16	1991 Form	0-23	
1992 Form	0-34	1990 Form	0-2	

F DOYLE

	No. of Horses	Races Run	1st	2nd	3rd	Unpl	Per cent	£1 Level Stake
2-y-o	0	0	0	0	0	0	-	0.00
3-y-o	0	0	0	0	0	0	-	0.00
4-y-o+	4	22	2	1	5	14	9.1	+ 6.00
Totals	4	22	2	1	5	14	9.1	+ 6.00

Mar/Apr	May	Jun	Jul	Aug	Sep	Oct/Nov
0-1	1-4	1-4	0-6	0-6	0-1	0-0

Winning Jockeys	W-R	£1 Level Stake		W-R	£1 Level Stake
Mrs C Doyle	1-5	+ 10.00	N G McCullagh	1-7	+ 6.00

Winning Courses	W-R	£1 Level Stake		W-R	£1 Level Stake
The Curragh	1-2	+ 13.00	Killarney	1-5	+ 8.00

Winning Horses	Age	Races Run	1st	2nd	3rd	Unpl	Win £
Myro Balanne	4	6	1	0	2	3	3,450
Up She Flew	4	7	1	1	0	5	3,425

Favourites	0-0			Total winning prize-money		£6,875
1993 Form	1-12	8.3%	+ 14.00	1991 Form	0-4	
1992 Form	0-1					

611

F DUNNE

	No. of Horses	Races Run	1st	2nd	3rd	Unpl	Per cent	£1 Level Stake
2-y-o	5	14	0	0	0	14	-	- 14.00
3-y-o	3	10	1	0	3	6	10.0	- 4.50
4-y-o+	6	11	0	0	0	11	-	- 11.00
Totals	14	35	1	0	3	31	2.9	- 29.50

Mar/Apr	May	Jun	Jul	Aug	Sep	Oct/Nov
0-1	0-8	1-4	0-6	0-8	0-7	0-1

Winning Jockey	W-R	£1 Level Stake	Winning Course	W-R	£1 Level Stake
J P Murtagh	1-14	- 8.50	The Curragh	1-7	- 1.50

Winning Horse	Age	Races Run	1st	2nd	3rd	Unpl	Win £
Better Choice	3	3	1	0	0	2	2,400

Favourites	0-1		Total winning prize-money	£2,400

1993 Form	9-87	10.3%	- 8.00	1991 Form	10-139	7.2%	- 47.50
1992 Form	10-138	7.2%	- 53.92	1990 Form	3-55	5.5%	- 39.25

FRANCIS ENNIS

	No. of Horses	Races Run	1st	2nd	3rd	Unpl	Per cent	£1 Level Stake
2-y-o	1	6	0	1	0	5	-	- 6.00
3-y-o	1	2	0	0	0	2	-	- 2.00
4-y-o+	2	14	1	3	1	9	7.1	- 8.00
Totals	4	22	1	4	1	16	4.5	- 16.00

Mar/Apr	May	Jun	Jul	Aug	Sep	Oct/Nov
0-5	0-1	1-4	0-3	0-1	0-4	0-4

Winning Jockey	W-R	£1 Level Stake	Winning Course	W-R	£1 Level Stake
W J Smith	1-8	- 2.00	Wexford	1-3	+ 3.00

Winning Horse	Age	Races Run	1st	2nd	3rd	Unpl	Win £
Nora Ann	5	8	1	2	1	4	2,228

Favourites	0-2		Total winning prize-money	£2,228

1993 Form	2-11	18.2%	- 2.25	1991 Form	0-15		
1992 Form	0-4			1990 Form	0-16		

A D EVANS

	No. of Horses	Races Run	1st	2nd	3rd	Unpl	Per cent	£1 Level Stake
2-y-o	0	0	0	0	0	0	-	0.00
3-y-o	0	0	0	0	0	0	-	0.00
4-y-o+	4	15	1	2	0	12	6.7	0.00
Totals	4	15	1	2	0	12	6.7	0.00

Mar/Apr	May	Jun	Jul	Aug	Sep	Oct/Nov
0-0	0-3	0-3	0-1	1-5	0-2	0-1

Winning Jockey	W-R	£1 Level Stake	Winning Course	W-R	£1 Level Stake
W J Smith	1-8	+ 7.00	Tralee	1-2	+ 13.00

Winning Horse	Age	Races Run	1st	2nd	3rd	Unpl	Win £
Southern Rule	7	8	1	0	0	7	3,425

Favourites	0-0		Total winning prize-money	£3,425

1993 Form	0-13	1991 Form	0-2
1992 Form	0-9	1990 Form	0-6

S FAHEY

	No. of Horses	Races Run	1st	2nd	3rd	Unpl	Per cent	£1 Level Stake
2-y-o	0	0	0	0	0	0	-	0.00
3-y-o	0	0	0	0	0	0	-	0.00
4-y-o+	1	9	1	2	1	5	11.1	+ 2.00
Totals	1	9	1	2	1	5	11.1	+ 2.00

Mar/Apr	May	Jun	Jul	Aug	Sep	Oct/Nov
0-0	0-0	0-0	0-0	0-2	0-3	1-4

Winning Jockey	W-R	£1 Level Stake	Winning Course	W-R	£1 Level Stake
P J Smullen	1-4	+ 7.00	Punchestown	1-1	+ 10.00

Winning Horse	Age	Races Run	1st	2nd	3rd	Unpl	Win £
Chuck's Treasure	5	9	1	2	1	5	2,740

Favourites	0-0		Total winning prize-money	£2,740

1993 Form	0-2	1991 Form	0-2

I FERGUSON

	No. of Horses	Races Run	1st	2nd	3rd	Unpl	Per cent	£1 Level Stake
2-y-o	0	0	0	0	0	0	–	0.00
3-y-o	0	0	0	0	0	0	–	0.00
4-y-o+	1	6	2	0	1	3	33.3	+ 7.00
Totals	1	6	2	0	1	3	33.3	+ 7.00

Mar/Apr	May	Jun	Jul	Aug	Sep	Oct/Nov
0-0	0-1	1-1	1-2	0-0	0-2	0-0

Winning Jockey	W-R	£1 Level Stake			W-R	£1 Level Stake
A P McCoy	2-2	+ 11.00				

Winning Courses						
Sligo	1-1	+ 7.00	Bellewstown		1-2	+ 3.00

Winning Horse	Age	Races Run	1st	2nd	3rd	Unpl	Win £
Huncheon Chance	4	6	2	0	1	3	4,968

Favourites	1-1	100.0%	+ 4.00	Total winning prize-money		£4,968
1993 Form	0-1			1991 Form	0-2	
1992 Form	0-3			1990 Form	0-1	

OLIVER FINNEGAN

	No. of Horses	Races Run	1st	2nd	3rd	Unpl	Per cent	£1 Level Stake
2-y-o	0	0	0	0	0	0	–	0.00
3-y-o	0	0	0	0	0	0	–	0.00
4-y-o+	4	20	3	1	3	13	15.0	+ 7.00
Totals	4	20	3	1	3	13	15.0	+ 7.00

Mar/Apr	May	Jun	Jul	Aug	Sep	Oct/Nov
0-0	0-2	0-3	0-5	1-3	1-3	1-4

Winning Jockeys	W-R	£1 Level Stake			W-R	£1 Level Stake
P P Murphy	2-8	+ 10.00	E Ahern		1-1	+ 8.00

Winning Courses						
Dundalk	2-7	+ 9.00	Galway		1-3	+ 8.00

Winning Horse	Age	Races Run	1st	2nd	3rd	Unpl	Win £
Ardlea House	5	12	3	1	3	5	7,878

Favourites	0-1			Total winning prize-money		£7,878
1993 Form	1-17	5.9%	- 10.00	1991 Form	0-11	
1992 Form	1-29	3.4%	- 8.00	1990 Form	0-8	

F FLOOD

	No. of Horses	Races Run	1st	2nd	3rd	Unpl	Per cent	£1 Level Stake
2-y-o	1	3	0	0	0	3	-	- 3.00
3-y-o	1	3	0	0	1	2	-	- 3.00
4-y-o+	3	23	2	1	1	19	8.7	- 12.00
Totals	5	29	2	1	2	24	6.9	- 18.00

Mar/Apr	May	Jun	Jul	Aug	Sep	Oct/Nov
0-3	1-5	0-2	0-5	1-4	0-6	0-4

Winning Jockeys	W-R	£1 Level Stake		W-R	£1 Level Stake
L Dettori	1-1	+ 6.50	L J Fleming	1-6	- 2.50

Winning Courses	W-R	£1 Level Stake		W-R	£1 Level Stake
Downpatrick	1-2	+ 1.50	The Curragh	1-6	+ 1.50

Winning Horses	Age	Races Run	1st	2nd	3rd	Unpl	Win £
Loughmogue	4	11	1	0	0	10	4,110
Annadot	4	11	1	1	1	8	1,713

Favourites	0-1	Total winning prize-money	£5,823

1993 Form	1-8	12.5%	+ 3.00	1991 Form	3-14	21.4%	+ 11.25
1992 Form	1-12	8.3%	- 5.00	1990 Form	2-7	28.6%	+ 2.40

P J FLYNN

	No. of Horses	Races Run	1st	2nd	3rd	Unpl	Per cent	£1 Level Stake
2-y-o	10	44	4	2	4	34	9.1	- 17.83
3-y-o	12	86	10	4	13	59	11.6	- 13.25
4-y-o+	20	88	13	9	6	60	14.8	- 0.96
Totals	42	218	27	15	23	153	12.4	- 32.04

BY MONTH

2-y-o	W-R	Per cent	£1 Level Stake	3-y-o	W-R	Per cent	£1 Level Stake
Mar/Apr	0-0	-	0.00	Mar/Apr	3-14	21.4	+ 2.75
May	0-0	-	0.00	May	0-13	-	- 13.00
June	0-1	-	- 1.00	June	1-11	9.1	- 3.50
July	2-5	40.0	+ 2.17	July	1-11	9.1	- 8.00
August	0-4	-	- 4.00	August	0-6	-	- 6.00
September	0-15	-	- 15.00	September	0-11	-	- 11.00
Oct/Nov	2-19	10.5	0.00	Oct/Nov	5-20	25.0	+ 25.50

Flynn P J

4-y-o+	W-R	Per cent	£1 Level Stake	Totals	W-R	Per cent	£1 Level Stake
Mar/Apr	2-10	20.0	+ 6.00	Mar/Apr	5-24	20.8	+ 8.75
May	3-22	13.6	- 13.71	May	3-35	8.6	- 26.71
June	1-15	6.7	- 7.00	June	2-27	7.4	- 11.50
July	2-16	12.5	+ 3.50	July	5-32	15.6	- 2.33
August	2-6	33.3	+ 4.75	August	2-16	12.5	- 5.25
September	1-7	14.3	+ 2.00	September	1-33	3.0	- 24.00
Oct/Nov	2-12	16.7	+ 3.50	Oct/Nov	9-51	17.6	+ 29.00

DISTANCE

2-y-o	W-R	Per cent	£1 Level Stake	3-y-o	W-R	Per cent	£1 Level Stake
5f-6f	0-8	-	- 8.00	5f-6f	2-10	20.0	+ 9.00
7f-8f	4-33	12.1	- 6.83	7f-8f	3-31	9.7	- 13.75
9f-13f	0-3	-	- 3.00	9f-13f	5-42	11.9	- 5.50
14f+	0-0	-	0.00	14f+	0-3	-	- 3.00

4-y-o+	W-R	Per cent	£1 Level Stake	Totals	W-R	Per cent	£1 Level Stake
5f-6f	3-10	30.0	+ 8.50	5f-6f	5-28	17.9	+ 9.50
7f-8f	0-11	-	- 11.00	7f-8f	7-75	9.3	- 31.58
9f-13f	7-36	19.4	+ 8.79	9f-13f	12-81	14.8	+ 0.29
14f+	3-31	9.7	- 7.25	14f+	3-34	8.8	- 10.25

TYPE OF RACE

Non-Handicaps	W-R	Per cent	£1 Level Stake	Handicaps	W-R	Per cent	£1 Level Stake
2-y-o	2-34	5.9	- 24.33	2-y-o	2-10	20.0	+ 6.50
3-y-o	4-39	10.3	- 13.25	3-y-o	5-43	11.6	- 5.00
4-y-o+	3-12	25.0	+ 4.29	4-y-o+	8-69	11.6	- 10.00
Apprentice	0-1	-	- 1.00	Apprentice	2-5	40.0	+ 13.00
Amat/Ladies	1-3	33.3	- 0.25	Amat/Ladies	0-2	-	- 2.00
Totals	10-89	11.2	- 34.54	Totals	17-129	13.2	+ 2.50

FIRST TIME OUT

	W-R	Per cent	£1 Level Stake
2-y-o	0-9	-	- 9.00
3-y-o	1-12	8.3	- 9.25
4-y-o+	3-20	15.0	- 9.71
Totals	4-41	9.8	- 27.96

JOCKEYS RIDING

	W-R	Per cent	£1 Level Stake		W-R	Per cent	£1 Level Stake
J F Egan	13-115	11.3	- 28.08	J P Murtagh	1-2	50.0	+ 1.00
M Duffy	2-7	28.6	- 3.21	D G O'Shea	1-4	25.0	- 1.00
J J Behan	2-14	14.3	+ 7.00	Mr E Norris	1-6	16.7	- 3.25
B J Halligan	1-1	100.0	+ 6.00	R Fitzpatrick	1-6	16.7	+ 3.00
Mr D Marnane	1-1	100.0	+ 16.00	Joanna Morgan	1-7	14.3	- 0.50
J F Clarke	1-1	100.0	+ 8.00	J R Barry	1-27	3.7	- 19.00
T E Durcan	1-1	100.0	+ 8.00				

G M Moylan	0-4	G Dickie	0-1	Miss C E Hyde	0-1
P V Gilson	0-4	I Browne	0-1	R V Skelly	0-1
P Carberry	0-3	J Cornally	0-1	W J O'Connor	0-1
S P Cooke	0-2	K J Manning	0-1	W J Smith	0-1
A J Beale	0-1	K P Gaule	0-1	W J Supple	0-1
D Mason	0-1	M J Kinane	0-1		

COURSE RECORD

	Total W-R	Non-Handicaps 2-y-o	3-y-o+	Handicaps 2-y-o	3-y-o+	Per cent	£1 Level Stake
The Curragh	5-38	0-7	1-9	0-0	4-22	13.2	+ 7.00
Killarney	3-14	0-0	1-5	0-0	2-9	21.4	- 4.00
Naas	3-15	0-2	2-2	0-2	1-9	20.0	+ 2.25
Gowran Park	3-20	1-3	1-6	1-3	0-8	15.0	+ 6.50
Galway	2-22	0-5	0-1	1-2	1-14	9.1	+ 0.50
Ballinrobe	1-1	0-0	0-0	0-0	1-1	100.0	+ 4.00
Sligo	1-2	0-0	0-0	0-0	1-2	50.0	+ 6.00
Down Royal	1-2	1-1	0-0	0-0	0-1	50.0	- 0.33
Downpatrick	1-3	0-0	1-1	0-0	0-2	33.3	- 1.71
Fairyhouse	1-4	0-0	0-1	0-0	1-3	25.0	+ 7.00
Dundalk	1-4	0-1	0-0	0-1	1-2	25.0	+ 2.50
Roscommon	1-5	0-1	0-1	0-0	1-3	20.0	+ 4.00
Bellewstown	1-5	0-1	0-0	0-0	1-4	20.0	- 2.50
Tralee	1-7	0-3	1-1	0-0	0-3	14.3	- 4.25
Clonmel	1-8	0-0	0-3	0-0	1-5	12.5	+ 1.00
Leopardstown	1-18	0-1	1-10	0-1	0-6	5.6	- 10.00

Listowel	0-8	Navan	0-7	Wexford	0-4
Mallow	0-8	Tramore	0-6	Punchestown	0-3
Tipperary	0-8	Thurles	0-4	Laytown	0-2

WINNING HORSES

	Age	Races Run	1st	2nd	3rd	Unpl	Win £
Double On	3	10	4	1	3	2	26,842
Onomatopoeia	4	8	1	2	1	4	9,975
Cheviot Amble	6	7	1	1	1	4	8,625
Matchless Prince	4	11	3	1	0	7	8,567
For Reg	5	3	1	0	0	2	6,850
Uncle Baby	6	4	2	0	0	2	5,695

Flynn P J

Oh'Cecilia	2	8	2	2	0	4	5,651
Hind Vision	4	10	2	0	1	7	4,453
How's It Goin	3	9	1	0	2	6	4,140
Main Refrain	3	10	1	1	2	6	4,140
Kinnincha	2	5	1	0	1	3	3,768
Guided Tour	3	8	1	1	2	4	3,450
Kerryhead Girl	4	3	1	0	0	2	3,450
Lady's Vision	3	11	1	1	1	8	3,425
The Barracuda	3	9	1	0	1	7	3,083
Ger's Royale	3	6	1	0	1	4	3,083
White's Island	2	2	1	0	0	1	2,740
Thatch And Gold	6	5	1	0	0	4	2,569
Aries Girl	5	4	1	1	0	2	1,553

WINNING OWNERS

	Races Won	Value £		Races Won	Value £
Joseph Christie	4	26,842	E Hannan	1	4,140
Dr Michael Smurfit	2	12,050	Mrs J Dermot Cantillon	1	4,140
Mrs Patrick Flynn	4	10,104	John Bernard O'Connor	1	3,768
David O'Reilly	1	9,975	J A O'Gorman	1	3,450
Mrs Patte O'Reilly	3	8,567	James R Browne	1	3,450
D H O'Reilly	1	6,850	Ms L Sutton	1	3,083
N P Doyle	2	5,695	Simply Great Syndicate	1	2,740
Lockforbes Racing Syndicate	2	5,651	W E Sturt	1	1,553

Favourites	9-28	32.1%	+ 2.96	Total winning prize-money		£112,057
Longest winning sequence			2	Average SP of winner		5.9/1
Longest losing sequence			36	Return on stakes invested		-14.7%
1993 Form	17-195	8.7%	- 73.00	1991 Form	16-166	9.6% - 49.37
1992 Form	22-181	12.2%	- 71.72	1990 Form	15-154	9.7% - 61.27

D GILLESPIE

	No. of Horses	Races Run	1st	2nd	3rd	Unpl	Per cent	£1 Level Stake
2-y-o	12	41	2	3	3	33	4.9	- 33.25
3-y-o	11	48	2	4	3	39	4.2	- 27.00
4-y-o+	4	24	2	4	3	15	8.3	- 11.75
Totals	27	113	6	11	9	87	5.3	- 72.00

Mar/Apr	May	Jun	Jul	Aug	Sep	Oct/Nov
0-13	0-18	2-15	1-19	1-15	2-14	0-19

Winning Jockeys	W-R	£1 Level Stake				W-R	£1 Level Stake
P Shanahan	2-19	- 11.25	B Fenton			1-3	+ 0.25
C Roche	1-1	+ 8.00	P J Smullen			1-14	- 6.00
P Carberry	1-2	+ 11.00					

Winning Courses							
Limerick	1-1	+ 3.00	Killarney			1-3	+ 6.00
Tralee	1-2	+ 1.75	Downpatrick			1-3	+ 0.25
Fairyhouse	1-3	+ 5.00	Leopardstown			1-7	+ 6.00

Winning Horses	Age	Races Run	1st	2nd	3rd	Unpl	Win £
Champagne Hurley	3	9	2	1	1	5	7,537
Legal Adviser	7	4	1	1	0	2	3,427
Onenineten	2	7	1	1	1	4	3,425
Bounty Guard	2	4	1	0	0	3	2,228
Fleeting Vision	5	10	1	3	2	4	1,541

Favourites	0-2			Total winning prize-money			£18,159

1993 Form	10-159	6.3%	- 77.42	1991 Form	17-162	10.5%	- 62.49
1992 Form	14-199	7.0%	-129.50				

J T GORMAN

	No. of Horses	Races Run	1st	2nd	3rd	Unpl	Per cent	£1 Level Stake
2-y-o	5	17	0	0	1	16	-	- 17.00
3-y-o	7	45	1	5	6	33	2.2	- 40.50
4-y-o+	4	23	0	3	0	20	-	- 23.00
Totals	16	85	1	8	7	69	1.2	- 80.50

Mar/Apr	May	Jun	Jul	Aug	Sep	Oct/Nov
0-13	0-14	0-9	0-3	0-14	0-14	1-18

Winning Jockey	W-R	£1 Level Stake	Winning Course	W-R	£1 Level Stake
M J Kinane	1-1	+ 3.50	Navan	1-8	- 3.50

Winning Horse	Age	Races Run	1st	2nd	3rd	Unpl	Win £
Lesley's Angel	3	9	1	2	1	5	2,740

Favourites	1-4	25.0%	+ 0.50	Total winning prize-money		£2,740

1993 Form	4-74	5.4%	- 13.00	1991 Form	2-81	2.5%	- 65.00
1992 Form	1-72	1.4%	- 51.00	1990 Form	5-44	11.4%	+ 9.00

M J GRASSICK

	No. of Horses	Races Run	1st	2nd	3rd	Unpl	Per cent	£1 Level Stake
2-y-o	8	21	2	4	2	13	9.5	- 12.27
3-y-o	10	50	1	5	3	41	2.0	- 29.00
4-y-o+	1	1	1	0	0	0	100.0	+ 3.50
Totals	19	72	4	9	5	54	5.6	- 37.77

Mar/Apr	May	Jun	Jul	Aug	Sep	Oct/Nov
1-8	0-6	1-4	0-12	2-13	0-16	0-13

Winning Jockeys	W-R	£1 Level Stake		W-R	£1 Level Stake
M J Grassick	1-1	+ 3.50	W J Supple	1-10	- 3.00
R Hughes	1-9	+ 12.00	J F Egan	1-16	- 14.27

Winning Courses					
Mallow	1-1	+ 20.00	Tipperary	1-3	- 1.27
Sligo	1-3	+ 4.00	Naas	1-5	- 0.50

Winning Horses	Age	Races Run	1st	2nd	3rd	Unpl	Win £
High Charger	2	4	1	1	1	1	3,768
Hi Handsome	3	8	1	0	0	7	2,243
Ground Shot	2	4	1	1	0	2	2,226
Drums Of Freedom	4	1	1	0	0	0	100

Favourites	1-3	33.3%	- 1.27	Total winning prize-money		£8,337
1993 Form	16-119	13.4%	- 34.12	1991 Form	8-119	6.7%	- 61.50
1992 Form	14-134	10.4%	- 31.20	1990 Form	16-185	8.6%	- 81.70

M HALFORD

	No. of Horses	Races Run	1st	2nd	3rd	Unpl	Per cent	£1 Level Stake
2-y-o	3	6	0	1	0	5	-	- 6.00
3-y-o	9	43	3	0	5	35	7.0	- 23.00
4-y-o+	6	12	0	0	0	12	-	- 12.00
Totals	18	61	3	1	5	52	4.9	- 41.00

Mar/Apr	May	Jun	Jul	Aug	Sep	Oct/Nov
1-6	0-17	0-3	0-7	0-6	2-9	0-13

Winning Jockeys	W-R	£1 Level Stake		W-R	£1 Level Stake
W J O'Connor	2-14	- 2.00	P V Gilson	1-13	- 5.00

Winning Courses					
Galway	1-1	+ 6.50	Dundalk	1-4	+ 4.00
The Curragh	1-4	+ 0.50			

Winning Horses	Age	Races Run	1st	2nd	3rd	Unpl	Win £
Queen Of All Birds	3	10	2	0	1	7	6,875
Port Queen	3	5	1	0	0	4	2,226

Favourites	0-1			Total winning prize-money			£9,101

1993 Form	5-68	7.4%	- 40.50	1991 Form	6-79	7.6%	- 40.75
1992 Form	5-103	4.9%	- 79.17	1990 Form	3-87	3.4%	- 64.00

A A HAMBLY

	No. of Horses	Races Run	1st	2nd	3rd	Unpl	Per cent	£1 Level Stake
2-y-o	1	2	1	0	0	1	50.0	+ 6.00
3-y-o	3	8	0	0	2	6	-	- 8.00
4-y-o+	1	4	0	0	0	4	-	- 4.00
Totals	5	14	1	0	2	11	7.1	- 6.00

Mar/Apr	May	Jun	Jul	Aug	Sep	Oct/Nov
0-0	0-0	0-5	0-2	1-3	0-4	0-0

Winning Jockey	W-R	£1 Level Stake	Winning Course	W-R	£1 Level Stake
W J O'Connor	1-1	+ 7.00	Leopardstown	1-3	+ 5.00

Winning Horse	Age	Races Run	1st	2nd	3rd	Unpl	Win £
Johns Conqueror	2	2	1	0	0	1	5,206

Favourites	0-0	Total winning prize-money	£5,206

D HANLEY

	No. of Horses	Races Run	1st	2nd	3rd	Unpl	Per cent	£1 Level Stake
2-y-o	9	20	1	1	5	13	5.0	- 14.50
3-y-o	11	37	4	3	6	24	10.8	- 10.50
4-y-o+	5	15	1	1	2	11	6.7	- 4.00
Totals	25	72	6	5	13	48	8.3	- 29.00

Mar/Apr	May	Jun	Jul	Aug	Sep	Oct/Nov
1-1	1-6	1-7	0-8	1-15	1-16	1-19

Winning Jockeys	W-R	£1 Level Stake		W-R	£1 Level Stake
N G McCullagh	5-53	- 18.00	P Carberry	1-4	+ 4.00

Winning Courses					
Naas	2-3	+ 19.00	Roscommon	1-7	- 1.50
Ballinrobe	1-2	+ 1.50	Gowran Park	1-11	- 7.00
Leopardstown	1-5	+ 3.00			

Winning Horses	Age	Races Run	1st	2nd	3rd	Unpl	Win £
Corporate Sport	4	4	1	0	0	3	6,900
Gallic Victory	3	7	2	0	1	4	4,966
Sandy Desert	3	5	1	1	1	2	3,450
Salmon River	3	7	1	1	0	5	3,425
Clearwater Lady	2	6	1	1	0	4	3,083

Favourites	0-4			Total winning prize-money			£21,824

1993 Form	8-33	24.2%	+ 44.25	1991 Form	3-22	13.6%	+ 1.50
1992 Form	5-35	14.3%	- 7.90	1990 Form	0-6		

J C HARLEY

	No. of Horses	Races Run	1st	2nd	3rd	Unpl	Per cent	£1 Level Stake
2-y-o	2	4	0	0	1	3	-	- 4.00
3-y-o	7	17	0	3	1	13	-	- 17.00
4-y-o+	7	25	4	1	1	19	16.0	+ 15.10
Totals	16	46	4	4	3	35	8.7	- 5.90

Mar/Apr	May	Jun	Jul	Aug	Sep	Oct/Nov
0-6	3-5	1-11	0-12	0-3	0-7	0-2

Winning Jockey	W-R	£1 Level Stake		W-R	£1 Level Stake
R M Burke	4-31	+ 9.10			

Winning Courses					
Gowran Park	2-4	+ 24.00	Downpatrick	1-3	+ 0.50
Dundalk	1-1	+ 7.60			

Winning Horses	Age	Races Run	1st	2nd	3rd	Unpl	Win £
Masai Warrior	7	3	1	0	0	2	2,760
My Trelawny	4	4	1	1	0	2	2,740
Tinco Paleno	10	5	1	0	1	3	2,228
Sensitive King	6	5	1	0	0	4	1,553

Favourites	1-3	33.3%	+ 0.50	Total winning prize-money			£9,281
1993 Form	6-73	8.2%	- 27.00	1992 Form	4-79	5.1%	- 48.75

MRS JOHN HARRINGTON

	No. of Horses	Races Run	1st	2nd	3rd	Unpl	Per cent	£1 Level Stake
2-y-o	0	0	0	0	0	0	-	0.00
3-y-o	0	0	0	0	0	0	-	0.00
4-y-o+	2	5	1	2	0	2	20.0	+ 3.00
Totals	2	5	1	2	0	2	20.0	+ 3.00

Mar/Apr	May	Jun	Jul	Aug	Sep	Oct/Nov
0-0	0-0	0-1	1-2	0-0	0-2	0-0

Winning Jockey	W-R	£1 Level Stake	Winning Course	W-R	£1 Level Stake
P Carberry	1-2	+ 6.00	Dundalk	1-1	+ 7.00

Winning Horse	Age	Races Run	1st	2nd	3rd	Unpl	Win £
Oh So Grumpy	6	4	1	1	0	2	2,228

Favourites	0-0		Total winning prize-money	£2,228

1993 Form	0-1		1992 Form	1-8	12.5%	+ 1.00

J L HASSETT

	No. of Horses	Races Run	1st	2nd	3rd	Unpl	Per cent	£1 Level Stake
2-y-o	0	0	0	0	0	0	-	0.00
3-y-o	2	3	1	0	0	2	33.3	+ 1.00
4-y-o+	1	4	0	0	0	4	-	- 4.00
Totals	3	7	1	0	0	6	14.3	- 3.00

Mar/Apr	May	Jun	Jul	Aug	Sep	Oct/Nov
0-0	0-1	1-2	0-0	0-4	0-0	0-0

Winning Jockey	W-R	£1 Level Stake	Winning Course	W-R	£1 Level Stake
Joanna Morgan	1-4	0.00	Sligo	1-1	+ 3.00

Winning Horse	Age	Races Run	1st	2nd	3rd	Unpl	Win £
Millionetta	3	2	1	0	0	1	2,740

Favourites	0-0		Total winning prize-money	£2,740

1993 Form	0-14		1991 Form	0-0
1992 Form	0-7		1990 Form	0-8

J C HAYDEN

	No. of Horses	Races Run	1st	2nd	3rd	Unpl	Per cent	£1 Level Stake
2-y-o	4	14	0	1	0	13	–	- 14.00
3-y-o	3	23	1	2	4	16	4.3	- 20.25
4-y-o+	4	10	1	2	1	6	10.0	- 2.00
Totals	11	47	2	5	5	35	4.3	- 36.25

Mar/Apr	May	Jun	Jul	Aug	Sep	Oct/Nov
0-3	1-5	1-10	0-6	0-9	0-6	0-8

Winning Jockeys	W-R	£1 Level Stake		W-R	£1 Level Stake
Mr P M Kelly	1-2	+ 6.00	W J Supple	1-21	- 18.25

Winning Courses	W-R	£1 Level Stake		W-R	£1 Level Stake
Gowran Park	1-1	+ 7.00	Mallow	1-3	- 0.25

Winning Horses	Age	Races Run	1st	2nd	3rd	Unpl	Win £
Herbert Lodge	5	3	1	2	0	0	2,742
Terrible Confusion	3	8	1	1	2	4	2,228

Favourites	1-4	25.0%	- 1.25	Total winning prize-money		£4,970
1993 Form	0-19			1991 Form	7-65	10.8%	- 16.95
1992 Form	5-45	11.1%	- 15.75	1990 Form	5-185	2.7%	-148.00

M HOURIGAN

	No. of Horses	Races Run	1st	2nd	3rd	Unpl	Per cent	£1 Level Stake
2-y-o	2	2	0	0	0	2	–	- 2.00
3-y-o	0	0	0	0	0	0	–	0.00
4-y-o+	10	32	6	4	4	18	18.8	+ 8.88
Totals	12	34	6	4	4	20	17.6	+ 6.88

Mar/Apr	May	Jun	Jul	Aug	Sep	Oct/Nov
1-2	0-1	0-3	0-5	3-11	1-5	1-7

Winning Jockeys	W-R	£1 Level Stake		W-R	£1 Level Stake
C Everard	1-1	+ 1.25	P Shanahan	1-3	- 0.12
R Hughes	1-2	+ 5.00	B Fenton	1-5	- 2.25
J P Murtagh	1-2	+ 11.00	Joanna Morgan	1-5	+ 8.00

Winning Courses	W-R	£1 Level Stake		W-R	£1 Level Stake
Navan	1-1	+ 1.25	Tipperary	1-2	+ 0.75
Ballinrobe	1-1	+ 1.88	Listowel	1-2	+ 11.00
Punchestown	1-1	+ 12.00	Tralee	1-5	+ 2.00

Winning Horses	Age	Races Run	1st	2nd	3rd	Unpl	Win £
Tropical Lake	4	6	3	0	0	3	20,955
Commodity Market	4	8	2	2	1	3	4,966
Back To Black	5	4	1	1	0	2	3,768

Favourites	2-3	66.7%	+ 2.00	Total winning prize-money			£29,689

1993 Form	1-6	16.7%	+ 5.00	1991 Form	0-0		
1992 Form	0-10			1990 Form	0-3		

D T HUGHES

	No. of Horses	Races Run	1st	2nd	3rd	Unpl	Per cent	£1 Level Stake
2-y-o	1	6	0	0	0	6	-	- 6.00
3-y-o	0	0	0	0	0	0	-	0.00
4-y-o+	7	22	1	2	2	17	4.5	- 18.50
Totals	8	28	1	2	2	23	3.6	- 24.50

Mar/Apr	May	Jun	Jul	Aug	Sep	Oct/Nov
0-2	0-0	0-4	0-0	1-9	0-4	0-9

Winning Jockey	W-R	£1 Level Stake	Winning Course	W-R	£1 Level Stake
P P Murphy	1-20	- 16.50	Fairyhouse	1-1	+ 2.50

Winning Horse	Age	Races Run	1st	2nd	3rd	Unpl	Win £
Touchdown	7	4	1	1	1	1	3,768

Favourites	1-1	100.0%	+ 2.50	Total winning prize-money			£3,768

1993 Form	7-71	9.9%	- 27.50	1991 Form	0-45		
1992 Form	3-40	7.5%	- 11.00	1990 Form	2-65	3.1%	- 55.67

M KAUNTZE

	No. of Horses	Races Run	1st	2nd	3rd	Unpl	Per cent	£1 Level Stake
2-y-o	12	27	3	5	3	16	11.1	- 15.82
3-y-o	14	80	6	16	7	51	7.5	- 35.00
4-y-o+	5	24	5	2	0	17	20.8	+ 2.03
Totals	31	131	14	23	10	84	10.7	- 48.79

BY MONTH

2-y-o	W-R	Per cent	£1 Level Stake	3-y-o	W-R	Per cent	£1 Level Stake
Mar/Apr	0-0	-	0.00	Mar/Apr	2-10	20.0	+ 2.00
May	0-1	-	- 1.00	May	0-19	-	- 19.00
June	0-2	-	- 2.00	June	0-13	-	- 13.00
July	1-5	20.0	- 3.82	July	0-10	-	- 10.00
August	1-7	14.3	- 1.00	August	3-14	21.4	+ 11.00
September	0-5	-	- 5.00	September	1-8	12.5	0.00
Oct/Nov	1-7	14.3	- 3.00	Oct/Nov	0-6	-	- 6.00

4-y-o+	W-R	Per cent	£1 Level Stake	Totals	W-R	Per cent	£1 Level Stake
Mar/Apr	1-5	20.0	+ 4.00	Mar/Apr	3-15	20.0	+ 6.00
May	1-2	50.0	- 0.47	May	1-22	4.5	- 20.47
June	0-3	-	- 3.00	June	0-18	-	- 18.00
July	0-2	-	- 2.00	July	1-17	5.9	- 15.82
August	1-5	20.0	+ 2.00	August	5-26	19.2	+ 12.00
September	1-3	33.3	+ 2.00	September	2-16	12.5	- 3.00
Oct/Nov	1-4	25.0	- 0.50	Oct/Nov	2-17	11.8	- 9.50

DISTANCE

2-y-o	W-R	Per cent	£1 Level Stake	3-y-o	W-R	Per cent	£1 Level Stake
5f-6f	0-6	-	- 6.00	5f-6f	3-24	12.5	+ 2.00
7f-8f	3-20	15.0	- 8.82	7f-8f	0-22	-	- 22.00
9f-13f	0-0	-	0.00	9f-13f	3-30	10.0	- 11.00
14f+	0-1	-	- 1.00	14f+	0-4	-	- 4.00

4-y-o+	W-R	Per cent	£1 Level Stake	Totals	W-R	Per cent	£1 Level Stake
5f-6f	0-1	-	- 1.00	5f-6f	3-31	9.7	- 5.00
7f-8f	1-6	16.7	- 1.00	7f-8f	4-48	8.3	- 31.82
9f-13f	4-17	23.5	+ 4.03	9f-13f	7-47	14.9	- 6.97
14f+	0-0	-	0.00	14f+	0-5	-	- 5.00

TYPE OF RACE

Non-Handicaps	W-R	Per cent	£1 Level Stake	Handicaps	W-R	Per cent	£1 Level Stake
2-y-o	3-26	11.5	- 14.82	2-y-o	0-1	-	- 1.00
3-y-o	3-34	8.8	- 13.50	3-y-o	3-41	7.3	- 16.50
4-y-o+	3-9	33.3	+ 5.03	4-y-o+	2-15	13.3	- 3.00
Apprentice	0-0	-	0.00	Apprentice	0-1	-	- 1.00
Amat/Ladies	0-4	-	- 4.00	Amat/Ladies	0-0	-	0.00
Totals	9-73	12.3	- 27.29	Totals	5-58	8.6	- 21.50

FIRST TIME OUT

	W-R	Per cent	£1 Level Stake
2-y-o	0-12	-	- 12.00
3-y-o	2-14	14.3	- 2.00
4-y-o+	1-5	20.0	- 3.47
Totals	3-31	9.7	- 17.47

JOCKEYS RIDING

	W-R	Per cent	£1 Level Stake
W J O'Connor	14-108	13.0	- 25.79

Miss S Kauntze	0-4	A J Nolan	0-1	N G McCullagh	0-1
W J Supple	0-3	C Everard	0-1	P Braiden	0-1
P Carberry	0-2	G M Moylan	0-1	P Shanahan	0-1
R Fitzpatrick	0-2	J F Egan	0-1	P V Gilson	0-1
R Hughes	0-2	M Fenton	0-1	R V Skelly	0-1

COURSE RECORD

	Total W-R	Non-Handicaps 2-y-o	3-y-o+	Handicaps 2-y-o	3-y-o+	Per cent	£1 Level Stake
The Curragh	3-37	0-5	2-14	0-0	1-18	8.1	- 21.00
Sligo	2-3	0-0	1-2	0-0	1-1	66.7	+ 15.00
Navan	2-6	1-2	1-1	0-0	0-3	33.3	+ 5.50
Gowran Park	2-8	1-2	1-4	0-0	0-2	25.0	- 0.47
Mallow	1-3	0-0	1-2	0-0	0-1	33.3	+ 6.00
Galway	1-5	0-0	0-1	0-1	1-3	20.0	0.00
Tipperary	1-7	0-0	0-3	0-0	1-4	14.3	0.00
Dundalk	1-9	0-2	0-5	0-0	1-2	11.1	- 2.00
Down Royal	1-12	1-1	0-6	0-0	0-5	8.3	- 10.82

Leopardstown	0-20	Bellewstown	0-1	Roscommon	0-1
Naas	0-8	Clonmel	0-1	Tralee	0-1
Fairyhouse	0-5	Laytown	0-1		
Punchestown	0-2	Listowel	0-1		

WINNING HORSES

	Age	Races Run	1st	2nd	3rd	Unpl	Win £
Royal Ballerina	4	3	2	1	0	0	28,520
The Puzzler	3	9	1	3	0	5	8,625
Shankar	3	5	1	2	0	2	6,900
Devil's Holiday	4	6	2	1	0	3	6,165
Venusia	2	3	1	1	0	1	4,110
Vitus	2	3	1	0	0	2	3,768
Maid Of Kashmir	3	6	1	1	2	2	3,450

Kauntze M

Bold Encounter	3	9	1	1	1	6	2,569
Flame Of Persia	4	11	1	0	0	10	2,243
Tiger Bittern	3	8	1	1	1	5	2,226
Final Contract	3	6	1	0	0	5	2,226
Tea Service	2	4	1	1	1	1	2,055

WINNING OWNERS

	Races Won	Value £		Races Won	Value £
Mitsuo Haga	5	36,740	Lady Clague	1	2,569
Sheikh Mohammed	3	14,778	E Flynn	1	2,243
Lady Richard Wellesley	1	8,625	Mrs E M Burke	1	2,226
Sheikh Ahmed Al Maktoum	1	3,450	Mrs Alan Dargan	1	2,226

Favourites	4-17	23.5%	- 5.79	Total winning prize-money	£72,857

Longest winning sequence		3	Average SP of winner	4.9/1
Longest losing sequence		44	Return on stakes invested	-37.2%

1993 Form	13-127	10.2%	- 26.83	1991 Form	19-184	10.3%	- 86.80
1992 Form	16-142	11.3%	- 55.33	1990 Form	29-226	12.8%	- 60.94

E J KEARNS

	No. of Horses	Races Run	1st	2nd	3rd	Unpl	Per cent	£1 Level Stake
2-y-o	0	0	0	0	0	0	-	0.00
3-y-o	0	0	0	0	0	0	-	0.00
4-y-o+	2	6	1	1	1	3	16.7	+ 5.00
Totals	2	6	1	1	1	3	16.7	+ 5.00

Mar/Apr	May	Jun	Jul	Aug	Sep	Oct/Nov
0-2	1-2	0-0	0-0	0-2	0-0	0-0

		£1 Level			£1 Level
Winning Jockey	W-R	Stake	Winning Course	W-R	Stake
J P Murtagh	1-1	+ 10.00	Mallow	1-1	+ 10.00

		Races					Win
Winning Horse	Age	Run	1st	2nd	3rd	Unpl	£
Tranquil Beauty	5	5	1	1	1	2	2,228

Favourites	0-0	Total winning prize-money	£2,228

1993 Form	1-9	11.1%	- 2.00	1991 Form	0-3	
1992 Form	0-12					

B V KELLY

	No. of Horses	Races Run	1st	2nd	3rd	Unpl	Per cent	£1 Level Stake
2-y-o	5	15	1	0	0	14	6.7	+ 19.00
3-y-o	4	18	0	0	1	17	-	- 18.00
4-y-o+	4	12	0	2	0	10	-	- 12.00
Totals	13	45	1	2	1	41	2.2	- 11.00

Mar/Apr	May	Jun	Jul	Aug	Sep	Oct/Nov
0-7	0-4	0-2	1-10	0-12	0-4	0-6

Winning Jockey	W-R	£1 Level Stake	Winning Course	W-R	£1 Level Stake
Joanna Morgan	1-9	+ 25.00	Galway	1-6	+ 28.00

Winning Horse	Age	Races Run	1st	2nd	3rd	Unpl	Win £
Lady Blayney	2	4	1	0	0	3	4,110

Favourites	0-0			Total winning prize-money		£4,110
1993 Form	6-64	9.4%	+ 3.50	1991 Form	9-107	8.4%	- 27.00
1992 Form	4-98	4.1%	- 73.67	1990 Form	4-76	5.3%	- 54.75

D P KELLY

	No. of Horses	Races Run	1st	2nd	3rd	Unpl	Per cent	£1 Level Stake
2-y-o	0	0	0	0	0	0	-	0.00
3-y-o	3	7	0	0	0	7	-	- 7.00
4-y-o+	8	28	2	0	1	25	7.1	- 5.00
Totals	11	35	2	0	1	32	5.7	- 12.00

Mar/Apr	May	Jun	Jul	Aug	Sep	Oct/Nov
0-4	0-6	1-10	0-3	0-5	0-1	1-6

Winning Jockeys	W-R	£1 Level Stake		W-R	£1 Level Stake
L O'Shea	1-1	+ 11.00	Joanna Morgan	1-3	+ 8.00

Winning Course			
The Curragh	2-8	+ 15.00	

Winning Horse	Age	Races Run	1st	2nd	3rd	Unpl	Win £
Three Musketeers	5	8	2	0	0	6	7,193

Favourites	0-2			Total winning prize-money		£7,193
1993 Form	4-47	8.5%	- 10.50	1991 Form	0-14	
1992 Form	3-35	8.6%	+ 10.00			

V KENNEDY

	No. of Horses	Races Run	1st	2nd	3rd	Unpl	Per cent	£1 Level Stake
2-y-o	1	1	0	0	0	1	-	- 1.00
3-y-o	2	4	0	0	0	4	-	- 4.00
4-y-o+	5	34	3	4	0	27	8.8	- 16.75
Totals	8	39	3	4	0	32	7.7	- 21.75

Mar/Apr	May	Jun	Jul	Aug	Sep	Oct/Nov
1-4	0-4	1-7	0-5	1-4	0-6	0-9

Winning Jockeys	W-R	£1 Level Stake			W-R	£1 Level Stake
T E Durcan	1-4	+ 3.00	P Shanahan		1-9	- 2.00
J J Behan	1-5	- 1.75				

Winning Courses		£1 Level Stake				£1 Level Stake
Tramore	1-2	+ 1.25	Dundalk		1-4	+ 3.00
Gowran Park	1-3	+ 4.00				

Winning Horses	Age	Races Run	1st	2nd	3rd	Unpl	Win £
Scalp	4	7	1	1	0	5	2,760
Sir Alwah	5	10	1	2	0	7	2,228
Kephren	5	6	1	1	0	4	2,226

Favourites	1-5	20.0%	- 1.75	Total winning prize-money	£7,215

1993 Form	0-26			1991 Form	1-67	1.5%	- 54.00
1992 Form	1-37	2.7%	- 28.00	1990 Form	3-46	6.5%	- 10.00

J E KIELY

	No. of Horses	Races Run	1st	2nd	3rd	Unpl	Per cent	£1 Level Stake
2-y-o	0	0	0	0	0	0	-	0.00
3-y-o	1	4	0	1	0	3	-	- 4.00
4-y-o+	4	9	2	1	1	5	22.2	- 4.25
Totals	5	13	2	2	1	8	15.4	- 8.25

Mar/Apr	May	Jun	Jul	Aug	Sep	Oct/Nov
0-0	0-1	1-2	0-1	0-0	1-6	0-3

Winning Jockey	W-R	£1 Level Stake		W-R	£1 Level Stake
M J Kinane	2-2	+ 2.75			

Winning Courses		£1 Level Stake			£1 Level Stake
Clonmel	1-2	+ 0.25	Listowel	1-4	- 1.50

Winning Horses	Age	Races Run	1st	2nd	3rd	Unpl	Win £
Kate Fisher	5	1	1	0	0	0	3,768
Jupiter Jimmy	5	4	1	1	1	1	2,228

Favourites	2-3	66.7%	+ 1.75	Total winning prize-money			£5,996

1993 Form	0-3		1991 Form	0-2
1992 Form	0-6		1990 Form	0-15

T KINANE

	No. of Horses	Races Run	1st	2nd	3rd	Unpl	Per cent	£1 Level Stake
2-y-o	0	0	0	0	0	0	-	0.00
3-y-o	6	40	1	5	7	27	2.5	- 27.00
4-y-o+	1	1	0	0	0	1	-	- 1.00
Totals	7	41	1	5	7	28	2.4	- 28.00

Mar/Apr	May	Jun	Jul	Aug	Sep	Oct/Nov
0-1	0-5	0-2	0-6	1-8	0-6	0-13

Winning Jockey	W-R	£1 Level Stake	Winning Course	W-R	£1 Level Stake
D J Smith	1-18	- 5.00	Tipperary	1-1	+ 12.00

Winning Horse	Age	Races Run	1st	2nd	3rd	Unpl	Win £
Imposing Time	3	11	1	1	2	7	2,740

Favourites	0-1	Total winning prize-money	£2,740

1993 Form	0-18		1991 Form	0-3
1992 Form	0-7			

F J LACY

	No. of Horses	Races Run	1st	2nd	3rd	Unpl	Per cent	£1 Level Stake
2-y-o	0	0	0	0	0	0	-	0.00
3-y-o	2	9	0	0	0	9	-	- 9.00
4-y-o+	2	4	1	0	0	3	25.0	+ 1.00
Totals	4	13	1	0	0	12	7.7	- 8.00

Mar/Apr	May	Jun	Jul	Aug	Sep	Oct/Nov
0-0	0-3	0-2	0-4	0-2	0-1	1-1

Lacy F J

Winning Jockey	W-R	£1 Level Stake	Winning Course	W-R	£1 Level Stake
Mr A E Lacy	1-1	+ 4.00	Galway	1-2	+ 3.00

Winning Horse	Age	Races Run	1st	2nd	3rd	Unpl	Win £
Divinity Run	5	1	1	0	0	0	4,410

Favourites	0-0		Total winning prize-money		£4,410
1993 Form	0-2		1991 Form	0-5	
1992 Form	0-11		1990 Form	0-4	

T F LACY

	No. of Horses	Races Run	1st	2nd	3rd	Unpl	Per cent	£1 Level Stake
2-y-o	3	10	0	0	2	8	-	- 10.00
3-y-o	1	6	0	0	0	6	-	- 6.00
4-y-o+	6	21	1	1	0	19	4.8	- 15.50
Totals	10	37	1	1	2	33	2.7	- 31.50

Mar/Apr	May	Jun	Jul	Aug	Sep	Oct/Nov
0-4	0-8	0-8	1-8	0-8	0-0	0-1

Winning Jockey	W-R	£1 Level Stake	Winning Course	W-R	£1 Level Stake
P J Smullen	1-27	- 21.50	Ballinrobe	1-2	+ 3.50

Winning Horse	Age	Races Run	1st	2nd	3rd	Unpl	Win £
Vicosa	5	3	1	1	0	1	2,909

Favourites	0-0			Total winning prize-money			£2,909
1993 Form	7-86	8.1%	- 18.00	1991 Form	0-89		
1992 Form	3-87	3.4%	- 75.25	1990 Form	2-62	3.2%	- 51.00

B LAWLOR

	No. of Horses	Races Run	1st	2nd	3rd	Unpl	Per cent	£1 Level Stake
2-y-o	2	2	0	0	0	2	-	- 2.00
3-y-o	0	0	0	0	0	0	-	- 0.00
4-y-o+	4	17	1	2	1	13	5.9	- 9.00
Totals	6	19	1	2	1	15	5.3	- 11.00

Mar/Apr	May	Jun	Jul	Aug	Sep	Oct/Nov
0-3	0-3	1-4	0-4	0-2	0-2	0-1

632

Winning Jockey	W-R	£1 Level Stake	Winning Course	W-R	£1 Level Stake
B Coogan	1-6	+ 2.00	The Curragh	1-4	+ 4.00

Winning Horse	Age	Races Run	1st	2nd	3rd	Unpl	Win £
Sand Or Stone	6	12	1	2	1	8	2,400

Favourites	0-1			Total winning prize-money			£2,400

1993 Form	1-27	3.7%	- 15.00	1991 Form	2-13	15.4%	+ 1.50
1992 Form	0-10			1990 Form	0-5		

AUGUSTINE LEAHY

	No. of Horses	Races Run	1st	2nd	3rd	Unpl	Per cent	£1 Level Stake
2-y-o	7	32	2	5	2	23	6.3	- 18.25
3-y-o	7	37	5	3	3	26	13.5	- 12.17
4-y-o+	12	32	0	3	2	27	-	- 32.00
Totals	26	101	7	11	7	76	6.9	- 62.42

Mar/Apr	May	Jun	Jul	Aug	Sep	Oct/Nov
0-15	3-19	0-12	0-11	2-16	1-12	1-16

Winning Jockeys	W-R	£1 Level Stake		W-R	£1 Level Stake
B Fenton	3-43	- 28.67	D G O'Shea	1-7	- 4.25
G M Moylan	1-1	+ 5.00	C Roche	1-11	- 6.50
J J Behan	1-3	+ 8.00			

Winning Courses					
Naas	1-2	+ 9.00	Tralee	1-11	- 4.50
Tramore	1-5	+ 1.00	Mallow	1-12	- 9.25
Galway	1-6	- 2.50	Tipperary	1-12	- 7.50
Killarney	1-9	- 4.67			

Winning Horses	Age	Races Run	1st	2nd	3rd	Unpl	Win £
Zoe Baird	3	13	2	2	1	8	5,651
Phardy	3	8	1	0	1	6	3,768
Sea Fisher	3	6	1	0	1	4	3,452
Barrichello	3	1	1	0	0	0	2,742
Fleet Petite	2	4	1	0	1	2	2,740
Be My Folly	2	7	1	2	0	4	2,228

Favourites	2-8	25.0%	- 1.75	Total winning prize-money			£20,581

1993 Form	2-89	2.2%	- 72.00	1991 Form	1-106	0.9%	- 91.00
1992 Form	8-91	8.8%	- 44.67	1990 Form	11-107	10.3%	- 31.50

ANDREW LEE

	No. of Horses	Races Run	1st	2nd	3rd	Unpl	Per cent	£1 Level Stake
2-y-o	2	3	1	1	0	1	33.3	+ 2.50
3-y-o	0	0	0	0	0	0	-	0.00
4-y-o+	1	1	0	0	0	1	-	- 1.00
Totals	3	4	1	1	0	2	25.0	+ 1.50

Mar/Apr	May	Jun	Jul	Aug	Sep	Oct/Nov
0-0	0-1	0-0	0-0	0-1	0-0	1-2

Winning Jockey	W-R	£1 Level Stake	Winning Course	W-R	£1 Level Stake
C O'Brien	1-2	+ 3.50	Gowran Park	1-1	+ 4.50

Winning Horse	Age	Races Run	1st	2nd	3rd	Unpl	Win £
Fair Lane Lady	2	2	1	1	0	0	3,768

Favourites	0-0	Total winning prize-money	£3,768

EDWARD LYNAM

	No. of Horses	Races Run	1st	2nd	3rd	Unpl	Per cent	£1 Level Stake
2-y-o	6	23	0	3	2	18	-	- 23.00
3-y-o	6	29	1	1	2	25	3.4	- 20.00
4-y-o+	7	21	4	0	2	15	19.0	+ 3.50
Totals	19	73	5	4	6	58	6.8	- 39.50

Mar/Apr	May	Jun	Jul	Aug	Sep	Oct/Nov
0-6	0-12	3-13	0-7	0-13	2-14	0-8

Winning Jockeys	W-R	£1 Level Stake		W-R	£1 Level Stake
M J Kinane	1-1	+ 3.00	P Shanahan	1-13	- 8.50
P Carberry	1-2	+ 7.00	D A O'Sullivan	1-13	- 2.00
J P Murtagh	1-7	- 2.00			

Winning Courses					
Tipperary	1-2	+ 3.00	Galway	1-5	+ 4.00
Ballinrobe	1-3	+ 1.50	The Curragh	1-17	- 6.00
Listowel	1-3	+ 1.00			

Winning Horses	Age	Races Run	1st	2nd	3rd	Unpl	Win £
Atmospheric Blues	5	5	2	0	0	3	5,142
Kurdistan	4	2	1	0	0	1	3,768
Jakdul	3	6	1	1	1	3	3,425
Rustic-Ort	6	3	1	0	0	2	2,228

Favourites	3-6	50.0%	+ 7.50	Total winning prize-money			£14,562
1993 Form	8-110	7.3%	- 28.50	1991 Form	1-93	1.1%	- 87.50
1992 Form	5-92	5.4%	- 35.50	1990 Form	4-144	2.8%	-127.67

G M LYONS

	No. of Horses	Races Run	1st	2nd	3rd	Unpl	Per cent	£1 Level Stake
2-y-o	4	12	1	2	0	9	8.3	- 3.00
3-y-o	0	0	0	0	0	0	-	0.00
4-y-o+	3	8	0	0	0	8	-	- 8.00
Totals	7	20	1	2	0	17	5.0	- 11.00

Mar/Apr	May	Jun	Jul	Aug	Sep	Oct/Nov
0-0	0-3	0-0	0-4	0-6	0-1	1-6

Winning Jockey	W-R	£1 Level Stake	Winning Course	W-R	£1 Level Stake
J P Murtagh	1-4	+ 5.00	Navan	1-2	+ 7.00

Winning Horse	Age	Races Run	1st	2nd	3rd	Unpl	Win £
Maelalong	2	5	1	1	0	3	3,768

Favourites	0-0		Total winning prize-money	£3,768

PEADAR MATTHEWS

	No. of Horses	Races Run	1st	2nd	3rd	Unpl	Per cent	£1 Level Stake
2-y-o	2	6	0	0	1	5	-	- 6.00
3-y-o	2	9	1	0	0	8	11.1	+ 8.00
4-y-o+	2	8	0	0	1	7	-	- 8.00
Totals	6	23	1	0	2	20	4.3	- 6.00

Mar/Apr	May	Jun	Jul	Aug	Sep	Oct/Nov
1-3	0-2	0-4	0-3	0-3	0-3	0-5

Winning Jockey	W-R	£1 Level Stake	Winning Course	W-R	£1 Level Stake
J F Egan	1-7	+ 10.00	The Curragh	1-4	+ 13.00

Matthews Peadar

Winning Horse	Age	Races Run	1st	2nd	3rd	Unpl	Win £
Quintiliani	3	5	1	0	0	4	14,375

Favourites	0-0				Total winning prize-money		£14,375

1993 Form	1-19	5.3%	- 10.00	1991 Form	1-3	33.3%	+ 18.00
1992 Form	0-21			1990 Form	0-28		

D G MCARDLE

	No. of Horses	Races Run	1st	2nd	3rd	Unpl	Per cent	£1 Level Stake
2-y-o	0	0	0	0	0	0	-	0.00
3-y-o	1	2	0	0	0	2	-	- 2.00
4-y-o+	4	27	4	5	4	14	14.8	+ 23.00
Totals	5	29	4	5	4	16	13.8	+ 21.00

Mar/Apr	May	Jun	Jul	Aug	Sep	Oct/Nov
0-2	1-7	0-4	2-7	0-2	1-2	0-5

Winning Jockey	W-R	£1 Level Stake			W-R	£1 Level Stake
W J Smith	4-15	+ 35.00				

Winning Courses						
Roscommon	2-3	+ 21.00	Galway		1-3	+ 6.00
Listowel	1-1	+ 16.00				

Winning Horses	Age	Races Run	1st	2nd	3rd	Unpl	Win £
Albona	6	11	3	1	2	5	8,567
Vistage	6	6	1	0	2	3	3,768

Favourites	0-3				Total winning prize-money		£12,334

1993 Form	1-24	4.2%	- 7.00	1992 Form	0-5

PETER MCCREERY

	No. of Horses	Races Run	1st	2nd	3rd	Unpl	Per cent	£1 Level Stake
2-y-o	1	1	0	0	0	1	-	- 1.00
3-y-o	7	23	2	0	1	20	8.7	- 10.90
4-y-o+	4	14	0	1	2	11	-	- 14.00
Totals	12	38	2	1	3	32	5.3	- 25.90

Mar/Apr	May	Jun	Jul	Aug	Sep	Oct/Nov
0-5	2-8	0-2	0-6	0-6	0-4	0-7

Winning Jockeys	W-R	£1 Level Stake			W-R	£1 Level Stake
Paul Eddery	1-1	+ 9.00	W J Supple		1-3	- 0.90

Winning Courses						
Clonmel	1-3	- 0.90	The Curragh		1-4	+ 6.00

Winning Horse	Age	Races Run	1st	2nd	3rd	Unpl	Win £
Majestic Man	3	5	2	0	1	2	6,338

Favourites	1-1	100.0%	+ 1.10	Total winning prize-money		£6,338

1993 Form	2-46	4.3%	- 16.00	1991 Form	0-3		
1992 Form	0-16			1990 Form	2-27	7.4%	- 1.00

M A MCCULLAGH

	No. of Horses	Races Run	1st	2nd	3rd	Unpl	Per cent	£1 Level Stake
2-y-o	0	0	0	0	0	0	-	0.00
3-y-o	1	6	0	0	0	6	-	- 6.00
4-y-o+	2	14	4	3	1	6	28.6	+ 9.00
Totals	3	20	4	3	1	12	20.0	+ 3.00

Mar/Apr	May	Jun	Jul	Aug	Sep	Oct/Nov
0-0	0-2	0-2	3-4	1-2	0-6	0-4

Winning Jockeys	W-R	£1 Level Stake			W-R	£1 Level Stake
N G McCullagh	2-7	+ 3.50	D M McCullagh		2-7	+ 5.50

Winning Courses						
Bellewstown	1-1	+ 6.50	Killarney		1-2	+ 3.00
Leopardstown	1-2	+ 5.00	Galway		1-5	- 1.50

Winning Horse	Age	Races Run	1st	2nd	3rd	Unpl	Win £
Wesbest	5	13	4	3	1	5	23,294

Favourites	2-2	100.0%	+ 6.50	Total winning prize-money		£23,294

1993 Form	0-17			1991 Form	0-3
1992 Form	3-11	27.3%	+ 13.50	1990 Form	0-6

NEIL S MCGRATH

	No. of Horses	Races Run	1st	2nd	3rd	Unpl	Per cent	£1 Level Stake
2-y-o	4	12	1	2	0	9	8.3	+ 1.00
3-y-o	6	29	0	0	0	29	-	- 29.00
4-y-o+	0	0	0	0	0	0	-	0.00
Totals	10	41	1	2	0	38	2.4	- 28.00

Mar/Apr	May	Jun	Jul	Aug	Sep	Oct/Nov
1-4	0-6	0-7	0-1	0-11	0-4	0-8

Winning Jockey	W-R	£1 Level Stake	Winning Course	W-R	£1 Level Stake
J F Egan	1-8	+ 5.00	The Curragh	1-11	+ 2.00

Winning Horse	Age	Races Run	1st	2nd	3rd	Unpl	Win £
Double Quick	2	3	1	0	0	2	5,244

Favourites	0-0			Total winning prize-money		£5,244

1993 Form	1-45	2.2%	- 39.00	1991 Form	0-32		
1992 Form	3-51	5.9%	- 14.00	1990 Form	3-43	7.0%	- 29.50

J J MCLOUGHLIN

	No. of Horses	Races Run	1st	2nd	3rd	Unpl	Per cent	£1 Level Stake
2-y-o	4	21	2	2	1	16	9.5	- 6.75
3-y-o	10	61	7	6	3	45	11.5	+ 22.00
4-y-o+	5	22	0	4	3	15	-	- 22.00
Totals	19	104	9	12	7	76	8.7	- 6.75

Mar/Apr	May	Jun	Jul	Aug	Sep	Oct/Nov
0-13	0-4	0-12	3-18	2-15	1-18	3-24

Winning Jockeys	W-R	£1 Level Stake		W-R	£1 Level Stake
N G McCullagh	4-36	+ 12.25	W J Smith	2-8	+ 9.00
P J Smullen	3-14	+ 18.00			

Winning Courses					
The Curragh	2-27	- 8.00	Naas	1-5	+ 6.00
Bellewstown	1-2	+ 11.00	Tipperary	1-9	- 5.75
Ballinrobe	1-3	+ 10.00	Gowran Park	1-10	- 4.00
Roscommon	1-3	+ 18.00	Leopardstown	1-13	- 2.00

Winning Horses	Age	Races Run	1st	2nd	3rd	Unpl	Win £
Model Show	3	9	2	1	0	6	6,850
Noble Choice	3	9	2	1	0	6	6,167
Life Is Precious	2	10	1	0	1	8	3,768
Robert's Toy	3	8	1	1	0	6	3,425
Moments To Care	3	7	1	0	0	6	2,740
Fill The Bill	2	4	1	2	0	1	2,740
Graceful Resign	3	6	1	0	1	4	2,226

Favourites	0-4			Total winning prize-money			£27,916

1993 Form	0-59			1991 Form	13-181	7.2%	- 93.50
1992 Form	15-162	9.3%	- 75.18	1990 Form	15-172	8.7%	- 42.50

A J MCNAMARA

	No. of Horses	Races Run	1st	2nd	3rd	Unpl	Per cent	£1 Level Stake
2-y-o	0	0	0	0	0	0	-	0.00
3-y-o	1	2	0	0	0	2	-	- 2.00
4-y-o+	1	8	3	0	0	5	37.5	+ 21.50
Totals	2	10	3	0	0	7	30.0	+ 19.50

Mar/Apr	May	Jun	Jul	Aug	Sep	Oct/Nov
0-1	1-3	1-2	1-1	0-2	0-1	0-0

Winning Jockey	W-R	£1 Level Stake				W-R	£1 Level Stake
J J Behan	3-6	+ 23.50					

Winning Courses							
Wexford	1-1	+ 4.50		Tramore		1-2	+ 15.00
Thurles	1-2	+ 5.00					

Winning Horse	Age	Races Run	1st	2nd	3rd	Unpl	Win £
Von Carty	5	8	3	0	0	5	7,849

Favourites	0-2		Total winning prize-money			£7,849

1993 Form	0-13			1991 Form	0-32		
1992 Form	0-14			1990 Form	1-36	2.8%	- 10.00

NOEL MEADE

	No. of Horses	Races Run	1st	2nd	3rd	Unpl	Per cent	£1 Level Stake
2-y-o	17	52	6	6	7	33	11.5	- 8.75
3-y-o	22	108	11	4	9	84	10.2	- 45.97
4-y-o+	17	41	4	6	4	27	9.8	- 17.25
Totals	56	201	21	16	20	144	10.4	- 71.97

BY MONTH

2-y-o	W-R	Per cent	£1 Level Stake	3-y-o	W-R	Per cent	£1 Level Stake
Mar/Apr	0-2	-	- 2.00	Mar/Apr	0-14	-	- 14.00
May	0-1	-	- 1.00	May	2-17	11.8	- 10.37
June	2-3	66.7	+ 12.00	June	2-17	11.8	- 2.43
July	2-5	40.0	+ 3.75	July	2-18	11.1	- 7.17
August	1-9	11.1	- 4.50	August	1-12	8.3	- 5.50
September	1-13	7.7	+ 2.00	September	3-13	23.1	+ 5.50
Oct/Nov	0-19	-	- 19.00	Oct/Nov	1-17	5.9	- 12.00

4-y-o+	W-R	Per cent	£1 Level Stake	Totals	W-R	Per cent	£1 Level Stake
Mar/Apr	0-2	-	- 2.00	Mar/Apr	0-18	-	- 18.00
May	1-9	11.1	- 3.50	May	3-27	11.1	- 14.87
June	1-8	12.5	+ 1.00	June	5-28	17.9	+ 10.57
July	0-7	-	- 7.00	July	4-30	13.3	- 10.42
August	0-3	-	- 3.00	August	2-24	8.3	- 13.00
September	0-6	-	- 6.00	September	4-32	12.5	+ 1.50
Oct/Nov	2-6	33.3	+ 3.25	Oct/Nov	3-42	7.1	- 27.75

DISTANCE

2-y-o	W-R	Per cent	£1 Level Stake	3-y-o	W-R	Per cent	£1 Level Stake
5f-6f	5-20	25.0	+ 17.75	5f-6f	1-16	6.3	- 3.00
7f-8f	1-30	3.3	- 24.50	7f-8f	2-24	8.3	- 16.43
9f-13f	0-2	-	- 2.00	9f-13f	7-62	11.3	- 27.04
14f+	0-0	-	0.00	14f+	1-6	16.7	+ 0.50

4-y-o+	W-R	Per cent	£1 Level Stake	Totals	W-R	Per cent	£1 Level Stake
5f-6f	0-2	-	- 2.00	5f-6f	6-38	15.8	+ 12.75
7f-8f	0-7	-	- 7.00	7f-8f	3-61	4.9	- 47.93
9f-13f	3-21	14.3	- 6.25	9f-13f	10-85	11.8	- 35.29
14f+	1-11	9.1	- 2.00	14f+	2-17	11.8	- 1.50

TYPE OF RACE

Non-Handicaps	W-R	Per cent	£1 Level Stake	Handicaps	W-R	Per cent	£1 Level Stake
2-y-o	6-49	12.2	- 5.75	2-y-o	0-3	-	- 3.00
3-y-o	10-67	14.9	- 11.47	3-y-o	1-39	2.6	- 32.50
4-y-o+	2-8	25.0	- 0.25	4-y-o+	2-28	7.1	- 12.00
Apprentice	0-2	-	- 2.00	Apprentice	0-2	-	- 2.00
Amat/Ladies	0-1	-	- 1.00	Amat/Ladies	0-2	-	- 2.00
Totals	18-127	14.2	- 20.47	Totals	3-74	4.1	- 51.50

FIRST TIME OUT

	W-R	Per cent	£1 Level Stake
2-y-o	2-17	11.8	+ 1.50
3-y-o	1-18	5.6	- 14.00
4-y-o+	1-16	6.3	- 7.00
Totals	4-51	7.8	- 19.50

JOCKEYS RIDING

	W-R	Per cent	£1 Level Stake		W-R	Per cent	£1 Level Stake
P Carberry	8-70	11.4	- 35.05	M J Kinane	1-2	50.0	+ 1.25
N G McCullagh	4-25	16.0	- 2.00	P Shanahan	1-3	33.3	+ 1.00
S Craine	4-37	10.8	- 3.50	Joanna Morgan	1-15	6.7	- 10.67
R Hughes	2-14	14.3	+ 12.00				

W J Supple	0-6	D J O'Donohoe	0-2	B J Halligan	0-1
Mr D Marnane	0-4	J A Heffernan	0-2	G M Moylan	0-1
R M Burke	0-4	J J Behan	0-2	L Dettori	0-1
J F Egan	0-3	W Carson	0-2	P P Murphy	0-1
M Hunt	0-3	W J O'Connor	0-2	P V Gilson	0-1

COURSE RECORD

	Total W-R	Non-Handicaps 2-y-o	Non-Handicaps 3-y-o+	Handicaps 2-y-o	Handicaps 3-y-o+	Per cent	£1 Level Stake
The Curragh	5-38	3-16	1-8	0-0	1-14	13.2	+ 14.00
Dundalk	4-12	1-2	3-4	0-2	0-4	33.3	+ 4.70
Fairyhouse	2-8	0-2	2-5	0-0	0-1	25.0	+ 3.50
Tipperary	2-11	0-2	2-6	0-0	0-3	18.2	- 3.25
Sligo	1-2	1-2	0-0	0-0	0-0	50.0	0.00
Wexford	1-3	0-0	1-1	0-0	0-2	33.3	+ 1.33
Punchestown	1-3	0-0	1-2	0-0	0-1	33.3	+ 2.00
Down Royal	1-4	0-0	1-1	0-0	0-3	25.0	0.00
Clonmel	1-5	0-0	0-3	0-0	1-2	20.0	+ 4.00
Roscommon	1-10	0-1	1-6	0-0	0-3	10.0	- 3.50
Galway	1-12	0-2	0-3	0-0	1-7	8.3	- 5.00
Leopardstown	1-26	1-10	0-9	0-0	0-7	3.8	- 22.75

Meade Noel

Naas	0-13	Ballinrobe	0-4	Downpatrick	0-1
Navan	0-13	Mallow	0-4	Killarney	0-1
Gowran Park	0-8	Bellewstown	0-3	Laytown	0-1
Listowel	0-8	Thurles	0-3	Limerick	0-1
Tramore	0-5	Tralee	0-2		

WINNING HORSES

		Races					Win
	Age	Run	1st	2nd	3rd	Unpl	£
Viaticum	2	5	2	0	0	3	12,393
Tante Zoe	2	5	2	0	2	1	12,052
Regal Access	3	6	1	1	0	4	6,850
Dardjini	4	5	2	0	0	3	5,502
Persian Symphony	3	8	2	0	0	6	4,966
Father Sky	3	3	2	0	0	1	4,966
Woody	3	8	1	0	0	7	4,110
Monkstown Major	3	3	2	0	1	0	3,781
Cockney Lad	5	2	1	1	0	0	3,768
Rocket Dancer	8	2	1	0	0	1	3,598
Distant Lover	2	5	1	1	1	2	3,083
Anita's Galaxy	2	5	1	1	0	3	2,911
Mobile Miss	3	7	1	1	1	4	2,742
Peruke	3	6	1	0	0	5	2,400
Stage Left Even	3	6	1	0	1	4	2,228

WINNING OWNERS

	Races Won	Value £		Races Won	Value £
S Kiernan	2	12,393	D Daly	1	3,768
Kenneth Parkhill	2	12,052	Kerr Technology Ltd	1	3,598
Mrs Rita Polly	1	6,850	Liam Doherty	1	3,083
The High Street Racing Syndicate	2	5,502	Arthur M McMurray	1	2,911
Sheikh Mohammed	2	4,966	C P Brady	1	2,742
P M Hunt	2	4,966	Mrs A S O'Brien	1	2,400
Owen Keane	1	4,110	Anthony Wai-Kwan Yip	1	2,228
James B McDonnell	2	3,781			

Favourites	5-19	26.3%	- 7.30	Total winning prize-money			£75,350
Longest winning sequence			2	Average SP of winner			5.1/1
Longest losing sequence			24	Return on stakes invested			-35.8%
1993 Form	21-194	10.8%	- 16.00	1991 Form	17-207	8.2%	-123.39
1992 Form	18-170	10.6%	- 61.54	1990 Form	14-209	6.7%	-129.13

J E MULHERN

	No. of Horses	Races Run	1st	2nd	3rd	Unpl	Per cent	£1 Level Stake
2-y-o	2	5	0	0	0	5	-	- 5.00
3-y-o	3	25	2	1	4	18	8.0	- 9.00
4-y-o+	2	14	0	0	0	14	-	- 14.00
Totals	7	44	2	1	4	37	4.5	- 28.00

Mar/Apr	May	Jun	Jul	Aug	Sep	Oct/Nov
1-3	0-7	0-9	0-6	0-7	0-4	1-8

Winning Jockeys	W-R	£1 Level Stake		W-R	£1 Level Stake
C Roche	1-2	+ 6.00	T E Durcan	1-3	+ 5.00

Winning Courses	W-R	£1 Level Stake		W-R	£1 Level Stake
Fairyhouse	1-1	+ 7.00	Leopardstown	1-16	- 8.00

Winning Horse	Age	Races Run	1st	2nd	3rd	Unpl	Win £
Little Musgrave	3	14	2	1	4	7	7,565

Favourites	0-2		Total winning prize-money	£7,565

1993 Form	3-56	5.4%	- 27.17	1991 Form	2-50	4.0%	- 34.00
1992 Form	4-76	5.3%	- 35.00	1990 Form	4-44	9.1%	- 22.25

ANTHONY MULLINS

	No. of Horses	Races Run	1st	2nd	3rd	Unpl	Per cent	£1 Level Stake
2-y-o	2	5	1	0	1	3	20.0	- 1.60
3-y-o	2	19	2	2	1	14	10.5	- 10.75
4-y-o+	4	9	1	0	1	7	11.1	- 2.00
Totals	8	33	4	2	3	24	12.1	- 14.35

Mar/Apr	May	Jun	Jul	Aug	Sep	Oct/Nov
0-2	1-2	0-8	0-2	1-5	0-7	2-7

Winning Jockeys	W-R	£1 Level Stake		W-R	£1 Level Stake
P Carberry	2-4	+ 4.25	J A Heffernan	1-2	+ 5.00
J P Murtagh	1-2	+ 1.40			

Winning Courses	W-R	£1 Level Stake		W-R	£1 Level Stake
Tipperary	2-2	+ 6.25	Dundalk	1-1	+ 2.40
Naas	1-1	+ 6.00			

Mullins Anthony

Winning Horses	Age	Races Run	1st	2nd	3rd	Unpl	Win £
Out In The Sun	3	9	2	2	1	4	5,502
Kharasar	4	5	1	0	1	3	4,110
Federico	2	1	1	0	0	0	3,083

Favourites	1-1	100.0%	+ 2.25	Total winning prize-money			£12,695

1993 Form	0-28			1991 Form	0-12		
1992 Form	0-11			1990 Form	1-31	3.2%	- 27.50

P MULLINS

	No. of Horses	Races Run	1st	2nd	3rd	Unpl	Per cent	£1 Level Stake
2-y-o	2	10	0	0	3	7	-	- 10.00
3-y-o	4	19	1	0	0	18	5.3	- 11.00
4-y-o+	11	35	3	2	4	26	8.6	- 20.00
Totals	17	64	4	2	7	51	6.3	- 41.00

Mar/Apr	May	Jun	Jul	Aug	Sep	Oct/Nov
0-2	0-7	1-14	0-8	1-9	2-12	0-12

Winning Jockeys	W-R	£1 Level Stake			W-R	£1 Level Stake
J J Behan	2-16	- 6.00	P Shanahan		1-6	+ 2.00
G Coogan	1-1	+ 4.00				

Winning Courses						
Galway	2-8	+ 8.00	Tramore		1-3	- 1.00
Thurles	1-3	+ 2.00				

Winning Horses	Age	Races Run	1st	2nd	3rd	Unpl	Win £
No Dunce	4	6	2	1	0	3	9,720
Bernard's Toy	3	8	1	0	0	7	3,425
Gambolling Doc	4	3	1	0	1	1	2,228

Favourites	1-1	100.0%	+ 1.00	Total winning prize-money			£15,373

1993 Form	10-97	10.3%	- 15.08	1991 Form	1-48	2.1%	- 42.00
1992 Form	3-56	5.4%	+ 6.00	1990 Form	10-147	6.8%	- 65.30

W P MULLINS

	No. of Horses	Races Run	1st	2nd	3rd	Unpl	Per cent	£1 Level Stake
2-y-o	0	0	0	0	0	0	-	0.00
3-y-o	3	10	1	1	2	6	10.0	- 1.00
4-y-o+	11	48	1	4	2	41	2.1	- 40.00
Totals	14	58	2	5	4	47	3.4	- 41.00

Mar/Apr	May	Jun	Jul	Aug	Sep	Oct/Nov
1-3	0-8	1-16	0-9	0-10	0-5	0-7

Winning Jockeys	W-R	£1 Level Stake		W-R	£1 Level Stake
G Dickie	1-1	+ 8.00	J J Behan	1-4	+ 4.00

Winning Courses	W-R	£1 Level Stake		W-R	£1 Level Stake
Clonmel	1-5	+ 3.00	The Curragh	1-8	+ 1.00

Winning Horses	Age	Races Run	1st	2nd	3rd	Unpl	Win £
Meglio Che Posso	3	6	1	0	2	3	4,110
Sharp Invite	7	5	1	1	0	3	2,243

Favourites	0-4	Total winning prize-money	£6,353

1993 Form	9-73	12.3%	- 24.25	1991 Form	4-59	6.8%	- 28.00
1992 Form	7-99	7.1%	- 56.75	1990 Form	4-27	14.8%	+ 2.00

DANIEL J MURPHY

	No. of Horses	Races Run	1st	2nd	3rd	Unpl	Per cent	£1 Level Stake
2-y-o	4	14	1	1	3	9	7.1	- 5.00
3-y-o	9	55	2	4	8	41	3.6	- 37.00
4-y-o+	3	13	3	0	2	8	23.1	+ 12.00
Totals	16	82	6	5	13	58	7.3	- 30.00

Mar/Apr	May	Jun	Jul	Aug	Sep	Oct/Nov
1-8	2-16	2-15	1-16	0-14	0-3	0-10

Winning Jockeys	W-R	£1 Level Stake		W-R	£1 Level Stake
P Shanahan	3-14	+ 13.00	C Roche	1-8	- 1.50
R V Skelly	1-6	+ 7.00	P J Smullen	1-12	- 6.50

Winning Courses	W-R	£1 Level Stake		W-R	£1 Level Stake
Dundalk	2-10	+ 12.00	Naas	1-4	+ 5.00
Thurles	1-2	+ 4.50	Tramore	1-4	+ 1.50
Sligo	1-2	+ 7.00			

Murphy Daniel J

Winning Horses	Age	Races Run	1st	2nd	3rd	Unpl	Win £
Final Favour	5	7	2	0	1	4	4,488
Dick Ching	2	6	1	0	0	5	3,770
Yonoka	5	4	1	0	1	2	2,228
Good Connection	3	3	1	0	0	2	2,228
Wolfies Rascal	3	7	1	0	2	4	2,226

Favourites	0-4			Total winning prize-money			£14,940

1993 Form	4-91	4.4%	- 45.50	1991 Form	2-69	2.9%	- 58.00
1992 Form	6-79	7.6%	- 14.50	1990 Form	8-55	14.5%	- 7.18

J G MURPHY

	No. of Horses	Races Run	1st	2nd	3rd	Unpl	Per cent	£1 Level Stake
2-y-o	1	2	0	1	1	0	-	- 2.00
3-y-o	1	4	0	0	0	4	-	- 4.00
4-y-o+	1	5	1	0	0	4	20.0	+ 6.00
Totals	3	11	1	1	1	8	9.1	0.00

Mar/Apr	May	Jun	Jul	Aug	Sep	Oct/Nov
0-1	0-1	0-3	0-4	1-1	0-1	0-0

Winning Jockey	W-R	£1 Level Stake	Winning Course	W-R	£1 Level Stake
P J Smullen	1-2	+ 9.00	Tramore	1-1	+ 10.00

Winning Horse	Age	Races Run	1st	2nd	3rd	Unpl	Win £
Shpeel	4	5	1	0	0	4	2,226

Favourites	0-0		Total winning prize-money		£2,226

1993 Form	1-13	7.7%	- 6.00	1991 Form	0-10
1992 Form	0-6				

JOHN W NICHOLSON

	No. of Horses	Races Run	1st	2nd	3rd	Unpl	Per cent	£1 Level Stake
2-y-o	1	1	0	0	0	1	-	- 1.00
3-y-o	1	5	1	0	0	4	20.0	+ 8.00
4-y-o+	0	0	0	0	0	0	-	0.00
Totals	2	6	1	0	0	5	16.7	+ 7.00

Mar/Apr	May	Jun	Jul	Aug	Sep	Oct/Nov
1-3	0-2	0-0	0-0	0-1	0-0	0-0

Winning Jockey	W-R	£1 Level Stake	Winning Course	W-R	£1 Level Stake
Joanna Morgan	1-3	+ 10.00	Down Royal	1-1	+ 12.00

Winning Horse	Age	Races Run	1st	2nd	3rd	Unpl	Win £
Jenny Jingle	3	5	1	0	0	4	1,380

Favourites	0-1		Total winning prize-money	£1,380

1993 Form	0-5

A P O'BRIEN

	No. of Horses	Races Run	1st	2nd	3rd	Unpl	Per cent	£1 Level Stake
2-y-o	19	59	5	7	6	41	8.5	- 28.10
3-y-o	25	152	22	14	15	101	14.5	- 42.49
4-y-o+	30	132	20	10	13	89	15.2	- 17.77
Totals	74	343	47	31	34	231	13.7	- 88.36

BY MONTH

2-y-o	W-R	Per cent	£1 Level Stake	3-y-o	W-R	Per cent	£1 Level Stake
Mar/Apr	0-0	-	0.00	Mar/Apr	2-13	15.4	+ 4.33
May	2-5	40.0	+ 1.40	May	1-23	4.3	- 15.50
June	0-4	-	- 4.00	June	7-24	29.2	+ 4.88
July	2-10	20.0	+ 2.50	July	7-39	17.9	- 4.20
August	1-6	16.7	+ 6.00	August	4-26	15.4	- 7.50
September	0-11	-	- 11.00	September	0-14	-	- 14.00
Oct/Nov	0-23	-	- 23.00	Oct/Nov	1-13	7.7	- 10.50

4-y-o+	W-R	Per cent	£1 Level Stake	Totals	W-R	Per cent	£1 Level Stake
Mar/Apr	0-12	-	- 12.00	Mar/Apr	2-25	8.0	- 7.67
May	4-24	16.7	+ 5.50	May	7-52	13.5	- 8.60
June	1-26	3.8	- 20.00	June	8-54	14.8	- 19.12
July	7-27	25.9	+ 17.00	July	16-76	21.1	+ 15.30
August	3-20	15.0	- 11.00	August	8-52	15.4	- 12.50
September	2-13	15.4	- 2.27	September	2-38	5.3	- 27.27
Oct/Nov	3-10	30.0	+ 5.00	Oct/Nov	4-46	8.7	- 28.50

DISTANCE

	W-R	Per cent	£1 Level Stake		W-R	Per cent	£1 Level Stake
2-y-o				3-y-o			
5f-6f	2-25	8.0	- 18.60	5f-6f	2-16	12.5	- 5.50
7f-8f	3-33	9.1	- 8.50	7f-8f	7-40	17.5	- 2.60
9f-13f	0-1	-	- 1.00	9f-13f	10-87	11.5	- 39.29
14f+	0-0	-	0.00	14f+	3-9	33.3	+ 4.90

	W-R	Per cent	£1 Level Stake		W-R	Per cent	£1 Level Stake
4-y-o+				Totals			
5f-6f	0-4	-	- 4.00	5f-6f	4-45	8.9	- 28.10
7f-8f	7-29	24.1	+ 8.25	7f-8f	17-102	16.7	- 2.85
9f-13f	6-61	9.8	- 17.00	9f-13f	16-149	10.7	- 57.29
14f+	7-38	18.4	- 5.02	14f+	10-47	21.3	- 0.12

TYPE OF RACE

	W-R	Per cent	£1 Level Stake		W-R	Per cent	£1 Level Stake
Non-Handicaps				Handicaps			
2-y-o	5-53	9.4	- 22.10	2-y-o	0-5	-	- 5.00
3-y-o	10-73	13.7	- 28.02	3-y-o	12-74	16.2	- 9.47
4-y-o+	7-51	13.7	- 9.77	4-y-o+	9-64	14.1	- 18.90
Apprentice	0-2	-	- 2.00	Apprentice	1-9	11.1	- 1.00
Amat/Ladies	1-6	16.7	+ 3.00	Amat/Ladies	2-6	33.3	+ 4.90
Totals	23-185	12.4	- 58.89	Totals	24-158	15.2	- 29.47

FIRST TIME OUT

	W-R	Per cent	£1 Level Stake
2-y-o	1-18	5.6	- 11.00
3-y-o	2-24	8.3	- 8.50
4-y-o+	4-30	13.3	- 5.52
Totals	7-72	9.7	- 25.02

JOCKEYS RIDING

	W-R	Per cent	£1 Level Stake		W-R	Per cent	£1 Level Stake
C Roche	30-160	18.8	- 15.89	G M Moylan	1-4	25.0	+ 5.00
Miss F M Crowley	3-7	42.9	+ 8.40	K P Gaule	1-5	20.0	+ 6.00
J F Egan	3-19	15.8	+ 3.50	J P Murtagh	1-7	14.3	- 4.62
Mr A P O'Brien	2-5	40.0	+ 6.75	J A Heffernan	1-7	14.3	0.00
S P Kelly	2-40	5.0	- 25.00	D G O'Shea	1-9	11.1	- 6.00
B J Walsh	1-1	100.0	+ 7.00	M J Cullen	1-23	4.3	- 17.50

W J Supple	0-12	P V Gilson	0-2	M Holbrook	0-1
P Shanahan	0-6	R M Burke	0-2	M J Kinane	0-1
N G McCullagh	0-4	T Horgan	0-2	Mr A J Martin	0-1
S Craine	0-4	W J O'Connor	0-2	Mr G R Ryan	0-1
Mr G F Ryan	0-3	C F Swan	0-1	Paul Eddery	0-1
N T Egan	0-3	E Ahern	0-1	R Hughes	0-1
A J Nolan	0-2	J J Behan	0-1	S M Kelly	0-1
Mr F McGirr	0-2	Joanna Morgan	0-1	W J Smith	0-1

COURSE RECORD

	Total	Non-Handicaps		Handicaps		Per	£1 Level
	W-R	2-y-o	3-y-o+	2-y-o	3-y-o+	cent	Stake
The Curragh	6-60	0-10	4-24	0-1	2-25	10.0	- 23.25
Wexford	5-12	0-0	1-2	0-0	4-10	41.7	+ 6.10
Tipperary	5-28	1-8	3-13	0-0	1-7	17.9	- 5.10
Leopardstown	5-37	2-5	1-17	0-1	2-14	13.5	- 0.50
Naas	4-16	0-3	1-6	0-0	3-7	25.0	+ 3.71
Gowran Park	4-31	0-5	2-12	0-0	2-14	12.9	- 5.50
Navan	3-11	1-7	1-2	0-0	1-2	27.3	+ 0.40
Killarney	3-17	0-1	0-5	0-0	3-11	17.6	+ 8.50
Bellewstown	2-7	1-2	1-2	0-0	0-3	28.6	+ 2.75
Tramore	2-9	0-0	1-5	0-0	1-4	22.2	- 4.10
Clonmel	2-10	0-0	1-6	0-0	1-4	20.0	+ 0.73
Galway	2-28	0-3	1-8	0-1	1-16	7.1	- 17.10
Punchestown	1-3	0-1	0-1	0-0	1-1	33.3	+ 2.50
Dundalk	1-7	0-0	1-3	0-1	0-3	14.3	- 4.50
Tralee	1-8	0-0	0-3	0-0	1-5	12.5	- 3.00
Listowel	1-13	0-4	0-1	0-0	1-8	7.7	- 4.00

Mallow	0-11	Fairyhouse	0-5	Limerick	0-3
Roscommon	0-8	Ballinrobe	0-4	Sligo	0-3
Thurles	0-7	Downpatrick	0-3	Down Royal	0-2

WINNING HORSES

		Races					Win
	Age	Run	1st	2nd	3rd	Unpl	£
Wandering Thoughts	5	13	3	1	3	6	24,102
Dancing Sunset	3	4	2	1	1	0	19,855
Moorefield Girl	5	7	4	1	0	2	16,911
Bob Barnes	3	9	3	0	1	5	12,330
Na-Ammah	4	6	2	0	0	4	10,868
Acumen	3	18	3	1	2	12	10,620
Two Shonas	3	9	3	0	1	5	9,617
Glounthaune Garden	2	3	1	0	0	2	8,625
Holiway Star	4	5	3	0	1	1	8,563
Magic Feeling	4	3	1	1	0	1	6,850
Hamseh	3	7	2	3	1	1	6,165
White Satin	2	3	1	0	2	0	5,480
Glowing Lines	4	14	2	2	2	8	4,983
Sign Of Peace	3	9	2	1	1	5	4,970

Kelly's Pearl	7	4	1	0	1	2	4,795
Metroella	3	7	1	0	0	5	4,495
Kiladante	5	7	1	1	0	5	3,795
Donleole	2	2	1	1	0	0	3,770
Petite Fantasy	2	7	1	0	1	3	3,768
Knight Of Vision	3	11	1	1	1	8	3,452
Trillick	4	7	1	0	1	5	3,425
Hero's Honour	2	1	1	0	0	0	2,913
Rockfield Native	4	3	1	0	0	2	2,913
Petit Nom	3	5	1	0	0	4	2,740
Dancing At Lunasa	3	6	1	2	1	2	2,740
An Gabh Dubh	3	9	1	0	2	6	2,228
Katies Holme	3	7	1	0	0	6	2,226
Putty Road	4	1	1	0	0	0	2,226
Diaki	3	1	1	0	0	0	2,226

WINNING OWNERS

	Races Won	Value £		Races Won	Value £
Mrs A M O'Brien	10	31,871	Seamus O'Farrell	1	4,795
W Mythen	3	24,102	M Hanrahan	1	4,495
Patrick H Burns	2	19,855	William Feighery	1	3,795
Mrs J M Ryan	5	18,155	M Moloney	1	3,770
James Patrick Killeen	4	16,911	S Bolger	1	3,452
John Malone	4	15,838	Fergus McGirr	1	3,425
Joseph Crowley	3	10,620	M F McKeon	1	2,913
Mrs P O'Connor	3	10,446	James Shanahan	1	2,740
J R Curran	3	9,617	Philip De Vere Hunt	1	2,226
T F Roe	1	8,625			

Favourites	22-47	46.8%	+ 20.14	Total winning prize-money £197,651
Longest winning sequence			3	Average SP of winner 4.4/1
Longest losing sequence			34	Return on stakes invested -25.8%
1993 Form	20-175	11.4%	- 46.62	

CHARLES O'BRIEN

	No. of Horses	Races Run	1st	2nd	3rd	Unpl	Per cent	£1 Level Stake
2-y-o	11	17	2	4	2	9	11.8	- 8.75
3-y-o	16	67	2	13	3	49	3.0	- 57.50
4-y-o+	4	9	1	1	3	4	11.1	- 6.90
Totals	31	93	5	18	8	62	5.4	- 73.15

Mar/Apr	May	Jun	Jul	Aug	Sep	Oct/Nov
0-7	0-17	2-13	0-10	1-16	1-15	1-15

Winning Jockeys	W-R	£1 Level Stake		W-R	£1 Level Stake
C Roche	4-59	- 41.25	P V Gilson	1-17	- 14.90

Winning Courses					
Leopardstown	2-22	- 17.40	Roscommon	1-4	+ 3.00
The Curragh	2-23	- 14.75			

Winning Horses	Age	Races Run	1st	2nd	3rd	Unpl	Win £
Burden Of Proof	2	2	2	0	0	0	22,456
Lake Kariba	3	5	1	1	0	3	5,147
Portrait Gallery	4	5	1	1	2	1	3,768
Valmarana	3	6	1	2	0	3	2,226

Favourites	3-15	20.0%	- 8.15	Total winning prize-money	£33,597
1993 Form	10-69	14.5%	- 21.15		

M V O'BRIEN

	No. of Horses	Races Run	1st	2nd	3rd	Unpl	Per cent	£1 Level Stake
2-y-o	0	0	0	0	0	0	-	0.00
3-y-o	0	0	0	0	0	0	-	0.00
4-y-o+	2	6	4	1	0	1	66.7	+ 8.63
Totals	2	6	4	1	0	1	66.7	+ 8.63

Mar/Apr	May	Jun	Jul	Aug	Sep	Oct/Nov
0-1	1-1	1-2	0-0	1-1	1-1	0-0

Winning Jockeys	W-R	£1 Level Stake		W-R	£1 Level Stake
C Roche	3-4	+ 8.38	L Piggott	1-2	+ 0.25

Winning Courses					
The Curragh	2-4	+ 5.25	Tipperary	1-1	+ 1.38
Naas	1-1	+ 2.00			

Winning Horses	Age	Races Run	1st	2nd	3rd	Unpl	Win £
Mysterious Ways	4	4	3	0	0	1	17,530
College Chapel	4	2	1	1	0	0	14,475

Favourites	3-5	60.0%	+ 2.63	Total winning prize-money	£32,005

1993 Form	6-19	31.6%	+ 4.40	1991 Form	36-105	34.3%	+ 9.79
1992 Form	19-53	35.8%	+ 1.32	1990 Form	37-119	31.1%	+ 0.64

E J O'GRADY

	No. of Horses	Races Run	1st	2nd	3rd	Unpl	Per cent	£1 Level Stake
2-y-o	4	13	1	1	0	11	7.7	- 7.50
3-y-o	4	16	1	1	0	14	6.3	- 5.00
4-y-o+	7	27	3	1	2	21	11.1	- 2.50
Totals	15	56	5	3	2	46	8.9	- 15.00

Mar/Apr	May	Jun	Jul	Aug	Sep	Oct/Nov
0-1	0-3	1-10	2-14	0-7	2-8	0-13

Winning Jockeys	W-R	£1 Level Stake		W-R	£1 Level Stake
M J Kinane	2-4	+ 7.50	W J Smith	1-2	+ 9.00
P J Smullen	2-6	+ 12.50			

Winning Courses	W-R	£1 Level Stake		W-R	£1 Level Stake
Galway	2-6	+ 11.00	Naas	1-7	- 1.50
Down Royal	1-3	+ 0.50	The Curragh	1-8	+ 7.00

Winning Horses	Age	Races Run	1st	2nd	3rd	Unpl	Win £
Rudi's Pride	3	5	1	0	0	4	4,110
Sea Gale	6	6	1	0	1	4	3,768
Pilgrim Bay	4	8	1	0	1	6	3,768
Lenni Lenape	2	2	1	0	0	1	2,740
Champagne 'N Roses	4	4	1	1	0	2	1,541

Favourites	1-5	20.0%	- 1.50	Total winning prize-money			£15,926
1993 Form	12-83	14.5%	- 1.18	1991 Form	6-106	5.7%	- 16.00
1992 Form	5-108	4.6%	- 86.10	1990 Form	4-136	2.9%	-128.35

PAT O'LEARY

	No. of Horses	Races Run	1st	2nd	3rd	Unpl	Per cent	£1 Level Stake
2-y-o	2	2	0	0	0	2	-	- 2.00
3-y-o	3	8	0	0	1	7	-	- 8.00
4-y-o+	7	28	2	4	2	20	7.1	- 9.00
Totals	12	38	2	4	3	29	5.3	- 19.00

Mar/Apr	May	Jun	Jul	Aug	Sep	Oct/Nov
1-5	0-5	0-7	0-2	1-5	0-10	0-4

Winning Jockeys	W-R	£1 Level Stake		W-R	£1 Level Stake
J J Behan	1-2	+ 6.00	N G McCullagh	1-5	+ 6.00

Winning Courses	W-R	£1 Level Stake		W-R	£1 Level Stake
Naas	1-2	+ 6.00	Ballinrobe	1-2	+ 9.00

Winning Horses	Age	Races Run	1st	2nd	3rd	Unpl	Win £
Man' Of Arran	4	4	1	0	0	3	3,105
Texas Friday	4	10	1	0	2	7	2,226

Favourites	0-1			Total winning prize-money			£5,331

1993 Form	2-49	4.1%	- 25.00	1991 Form	0-20		
1992 Form	3-26	11.5%	- 15.10	1990 Form	0-18		

T O'NEILL

	No. of Horses	Races Run	1st	2nd	3rd	Unpl	Per cent	£1 Level Stake
2-y-o	1	3	0	0	1	2	-	- 3.00
3-y-o	3	10	0	1	1	8	-	- 10.00
4-y-o+	2	11	2	2	2	5	18.2	+ 9.25
Totals	6	24	2	3	4	15	8.3	- 3.75

Mar/Apr	May	Jun	Jul	Aug	Sep	Oct/Nov
0-0	0-1	0-3	0-1	2-9	0-4	0-6

Winning Jockeys	W-R	£1 Level Stake			W-R	£1 Level Stake
B Fenton	1-2	+ 15.00	J F Egan		1-3	+ 0.25

Winning Course			
Laytown	2-4	+ 16.25	

Winning Horses	Age	Races Run	1st	2nd	3rd	Unpl	Win £
Bolero Dancer	6	7	1	2	1	3	2,055
Ardee Flo Jo	6	4	1	0	1	2	2,055

Favourites	1-1	100.0%	+ 2.25	Total winning prize-money			£4,110

1993 Form	1-17	5.9%	- 6.00	1991 Form	1-19	5.3%	- 6.00
1992 Form	0-3			1990 Form	0-6		

E M O'SULLIVAN

	No. of Horses	Races Run	1st	2nd	3rd	Unpl	Per cent	£1 Level Stake
2-y-o	0	0	0	0	0	0	-	0.00
3-y-o	0	0	0	0	0	0	-	0.00
4-y-o+	3	3	1	0	0	2	33.3	+ 10.00
Totals	3	3	1	0	0	2	33.3	+ 10.00

Mar/Apr	May	Jun	Jul	Aug	Sep	Oct/Nov
0-0	1-1	0-0	0-2	0-0	0-0	0-0

Winning Jockey	W-R	£1 Level Stake	Winning Course	W-R	£1 Level Stake
Mrs F A O'Sullivan	1-1	+ 12.00	Killarney	1-2	+ 11.00

Winning Horse	Age	Races Run	1st	2nd	3rd	Unpl	Win £
Sam Vaughan	5	1	1	0	0	0	3,452

Favourites	0-0		Total winning prize-money		£3,452
1993 Form	0-0		1991 Form	0-4	
1992 Form	0-6		1990 Form	0-1	

K F O'SULLIVAN

	No. of Horses	Races Run	1st	2nd	3rd	Unpl	Per cent	£1 Level Stake
2-y-o	3	11	0	0	2	9	-	- 11.00
3-y-o	4	16	1	0	0	15	6.3	- 7.50
4-y-o+	0	0	0	0	0	0	-	0.00
Totals	7	27	1	0	2	24	3.7	- 18.50

Mar/Apr	May	Jun	Jul	Aug	Sep	Oct/Nov
0-3	1-5	0-2	0-3	0-5	0-6	0-3

Winning Jockey	W-R	£1 Level Stake	Winning Course	W-R	£1 Level Stake
J F Egan	1-7	+ 1.50	Dundalk	1-1	+ 7.50

Winning Horse	Age	Races Run	1st	2nd	3rd	Unpl	Win £
Trigger Happy John	3	5	1	0	0	4	2,228

Favourites	0-0			Total winning prize-money		£2,228
1993 Form	2-20	10.0%	- 2.00	1991 Form	0-8	
1992 Form	2-31	6.5%	- 20.67			

M A O'TOOLE

	No. of Horses	Races Run	1st	2nd	3rd	Unpl	Per cent	£1 Level Stake
2-y-o	2	6	0	0	0	6	-	- 6.00
3-y-o	10	55	3	2	5	45	5.5	- 32.00
4-y-o+	6	10	0	1	1	8	-	- 10.00
Totals	18	71	3	3	6	59	4.2	- 48.00

Mar/Apr	May	Jun	Jul	Aug	Sep	Oct/Nov
0-2	0-15	0-9	3-18	0-14	0-6	0-7

Winning Jockey	W-R	£1 Level Stake			W-R	£1 Level Stake
J F Egan	3-31	- 8.00				

Winning Courses						
Killarney	1-1	+ 8.00	Galway		1-7	- 1.00
Bellewstown	1-4	+ 4.00				

Winning Horses	Age	Races Run	1st	2nd	3rd	Unpl	Win £
Blake's Hotel	3	4	2	0	0	2	6,852
Royal Crimson	3	8	1	0	1	6	4,110

Favourites	1-5	20.0%	+ 1.00	Total winning prize-money	£10,962

1993 Form	3-67	4.5%	- 25.00	1991 Form	6-120	5.0%	- 82.50
1992 Form	9-107	8.4%	- 63.93	1990 Form	12-126	9.5%	- 18.75

MISS I T OAKES

	No. of Horses	Races Run	1st	2nd	3rd	Unpl	Per cent	£1 Level Stake
2-y-o	1	1	0	0	0	1	-	- 1.00
3-y-o	1	10	2	0	1	7	20.0	+ 1.75
4-y-o+	3	15	0	2	0	13	-	- 15.00
Totals	5	26	2	2	1	21	7.7	- 14.25

Mar/Apr	May	Jun	Jul	Aug	Sep	Oct/Nov
0-1	0-7	1-5	1-4	0-3	0-3	0-3

Winning Jockeys	W-R	£1 Level Stake			W-R	£1 Level Stake
N G McCullagh	1-4	+ 5.00	W J Supple		1-7	- 4.25

Winning Courses						
Roscommon	1-1	+ 1.75	The Curragh		1-4	+ 5.00

Winning Horse	Age	Races Run	1st	2nd	3rd	Unpl	Win £
Concept House	3	10	2	0	1	7	5,823

Favourites	1-1	100.0%	+ 1.75	Total winning prize-money	£5,823

1993 Form	2-38	5.3%	- 13.00

JOHN M OXX

	No. of Horses	Races Run	1st	2nd	3rd	Unpl	Per cent	£1 Level Stake
2-y-o	18	33	13	6	6	8	39.4	+ 29.47
3-y-o	62	232	48	28	45	111	20.7	- 1.71
4-y-o+	8	17	2	7	1	7	11.8	+ 1.00
Totals	88	282	63	41	52	126	22.3	+ 28.76

BY MONTH

2-y-o	W-R	Per cent	£1 Level Stake	3-y-o	W-R	Per cent	£1 Level Stake
Mar/Apr	0-0	-	0.00	Mar/Apr	6-26	23.1	+ 1.94
May	0-0	-	0.00	May	4-14	28.6	+ 3.83
June	0-0	-	0.00	June	6-24	25.0	+ 13.32
July	0-1	-	- 1.00	July	8-43	18.6	- 6.58
August	2-3	66.7	+ 9.25	August	13-51	25.5	- 7.20
September	3-11	27.3	- 0.75	September	6-42	14.3	- 4.02
Oct/Nov	8-18	44.4	+ 21.97	Oct/Nov	5-32	15.6	- 3.00

4-y-o+	W-R	Per cent	£1 Level Stake	Totals	W-R	Per cent	£1 Level Stake
Mar/Apr	0-3	-	- 3.00	Mar/Apr	6-29	20.7	- 1.06
May	0-1	-	- 1.00	May	4-15	26.7	+ 2.83
June	1-4	25.0	+ 9.00	June	7-28	25.0	+ 22.32
July	0-2	-	- 2.00	July	8-46	17.4	- 9.58
August	1-4	25.0	+ 1.00	August	16-58	27.6	+ 3.05
September	0-3	-	- 3.00	September	9-56	16.1	- 7.77
Oct/Nov	0-0	-	0.00	Oct/Nov	13-50	26.0	+ 18.97

DISTANCE

2-y-o	W-R	Per cent	£1 Level Stake	3-y-o	W-R	Per cent	£1 Level Stake
5f-6f	3-6	50.0	+ 14.00	5f-6f	2-9	22.2	- 4.52
7f-8f	10-27	37.0	+ 15.47	7f-8f	12-67	17.9	- 20.22
9f-13f	0-0	-	0.00	9f-13f	31-136	22.8	+ 18.53
14f+	0-0	-	0.00	14f+	3-20	15.0	+ 4.50

4-y-o+	W-R	Per cent	£1 Level Stake	Totals	W-R	Per cent	£1 Level Stake
5f-6f	0-0	-	0.00	5f-6f	5-15	33.3	+ 9.48
7f-8f	0-4	-	- 4.00	7f-8f	22-98	22.4	- 8.75
9f-13f	1-8	12.5	- 3.00	9f-13f	32-144	22.2	+ 15.53
14f+	1-5	20.0	+ 8.00	14f+	4-25	16.0	+ 12.50

TYPE OF RACE

Non-Handicaps	W-R	Per cent	£1 Level Stake	Handicaps	W-R	Per cent	£1 Level Stake
2-y-o	13-33	39.4	+ 29.47	2-y-o	0-0	-	0.00
3-y-o	34-159	21.4	- 32.46	3-y-o	11-67	16.4	+ 20.75
4-y-o+	1-9	11.1	+ 4.00	4-y-o+	1-7	14.3	- 2.00
Apprentice	0-0	-	0.00	Apprentice	0-1	-	- 1.00
Amat/Ladies	3-6	50.0	+ 10.00	Amat/Ladies	0-0	-	0.00
Totals	51-207	24.6	+ 11.01	Totals	12-75	16.0	+ 17.75

FIRST TIME OUT

	W-R	Per cent	£1 Level Stake
2-y-o	8-18	44.4	+ 19.55
3-y-o	15-62	24.2	+ 9.74
4-y-o+	1-8	12.5	+ 5.00
Totals	24-88	27.3	+ 34.29

JOCKEYS RIDING

	W-R	Per cent	£1 Level Stake		W-R	Per cent	£1 Level Stake
J P Murtagh	33-124	26.6	+ 25.91	D G O'Shea	3-33	9.1	- 15.00
M J Kinane	8-21	38.1	- 1.00	J Reid	1-1	100.0	+ 12.00
C Roche	4-11	36.4	+ 10.00	P V Gilson	1-1	100.0	+ 2.50
D Hogan	4-49	8.2	- 19.33	Joanna Morgan	1-2	50.0	+ 3.50
Miss L Robinson	3-3	100.0	+ 13.00	N G McCullagh	1-2	50.0	+ 15.00
R Hughes	3-8	37.5	+ 7.38	G Mosse	1-4	25.0	- 2.20

W J Supple	0-6	W J O'Connor	0-2	M Roberts	0-1
L Dettori	0-3	C Everard	0-1	Mr J R Banahan	0-1
R M Burke	0-3	J J Behan	0-1	Sinead O'Keeffe	0-1
Miss L Dykes	0-2	J Quinn	0-1	W Carson	0-1

COURSE RECORD

	Total W-R	Non-Handicaps 2-y-o	Non-Handicaps 3-y-o+	Handicaps 2-y-o	Handicaps 3-y-o+	Per cent	£1 Level Stake
The Curragh	14-84	3-13	6-42	0-0	5-29	16.7	+ 17.25
Leopardstown	13-62	3-7	6-35	0-0	4-20	21.0	+ 20.19
Gowran Park	5-14	0-1	5-12	0-0	0-1	35.7	- 1.45
Tipperary	5-15	1-1	4-14	0-0	0-0	33.3	+ 0.05
Naas	5-17	2-2	2-11	0-0	1-4	29.4	+ 12.00
Navan	3-4	2-3	1-1	0-0	0-0	75.0	+ 6.17
Roscommon	3-15	1-1	2-13	0-0	0-1	20.0	- 7.68
Fairyhouse	3-17	1-3	2-9	0-0	0-5	17.6	- 9.40
Dundalk	2-7	0-0	2-6	0-0	0-1	28.6	+ 3.00
Tralee	2-8	0-0	2-5	0-0	0-3	25.0	+ 1.50
Listowel	2-9	0-1	2-4	0-0	0-4	22.2	- 4.52

Oxx John M

Galway	2-15	0-1	1-9	0-0	1-5	13.3	-	5.75
Sligo	1-1	0-0	1-1	0-0	0-0	100.0	+	0.90
Down Royal	1-2	0-0	0-0	0-0	1-2	50.0	+	3.00
Wexford	1-2	0-0	1-2	0-0	0-0	50.0	+	1.00
Thurles	1-3	0-0	1-3	0-0	0-0	33.3	-	0.50

Killarney   0-4   Mallow   0-2   Tramore   0-1

WINNING HORSES

	Age	Races Run	1st	2nd	3rd	Unpl	Win £
Karikata	3	12	4	3	3	2	31,800
Cajarian	3	5	2	1	1	1	23,000
Heart Lake	3	5	3	1	0	1	21,935
Ozette	3	9	4	0	1	4	19,351
Elupa	3	8	3	0	1	4	19,236
Witness Box	7	1	1	0	0	0	15,750
Flag Fen	3	3	2	1	0	0	15,126
Ridgewood Ben	3	5	1	2	1	1	14,375
Ridgewood Pearl	2	2	1	0	1	0	14,375
Kotama	3	2	2	0	0	0	12,765
Manntari	3	2	1	0	0	1	8,625
Icy Tundra	3	9	1	0	2	6	6,850
Ros Castle	3	2	2	0	0	0	6,169
Musical Insight	3	3	1	1	0	1	5,480
Manashar	2	3	1	1	0	1	5,480
Khaytada	2	2	1	1	0	0	5,480
Charillus	2	1	1	0	0	0	5,206
Adjareli	2	1	1	0	0	0	5,206
Jane Digby	2	1	1	0	0	0	5,206
Johansson	2	1	1	0	0	0	5,206
First Eleven	2	3	1	0	1	1	5,138
Niyazi	3	1	1	0	0	0	4,795
Tarziyana	3	2	1	1	0	0	4,653
Zabargar	3	5	1	0	1	3	4,110
Suekar	4	3	1	1	0	1	4,110
Tirmizi	3	3	1	0	1	1	4,110
Niyampour	3	2	1	0	0	1	4,110
Teinein	3	3	1	0	1	1	4,110
Treasurer	2	3	1	1	0	1	4,110
Daryabad	2	2	1	0	0	1	3,768
Tarajan	2	2	1	0	0	1	3,768
Sannkaya	2	1	1	0	0	0	3,768
Night City	3	2	1	0	0	1	3,450
Katiniyd	3	5	1	0	2	2	3,427
Bhavnagar	3	2	1	1	0	0	3,425
Taidja	3	6	1	1	2	2	3,425
Sharadiya	3	3	1	0	1	1	3,425
Bayariyka	3	4	1	1	1	1	3,425
Shadirwan	3	5	1	0	3	1	3,425
Caladira	3	2	1	0	0	1	3,425
Sorb Apple	3	1	1	0	0	0	3,425

Madaraka	3	5	1	1	1	2	3,083
Mediation	2	3	1	0	1	1	3,083
Simafar	3	5	1	1	0	3	2,740
Masawa	3	5	1	0	0	4	2,740
Safkana	3	3	1	0	1	1	2,740
Paliapour	3	4	1	0	1	2	2,226
Alaiyda	3	5	1	0	2	2	2,226
Balanak	3	3	1	2	0	0	2,226

WINNING OWNERS

	Races Won	Value £		Races Won	Value £
H H Aga Khan	34	167,394	Lady Clague	2	8,563
Sheikh Mohammed	16	95,790	Dundalk Racing Club	1	5,206
Mrs Anne Coughlan	2	28,750	T J Monaghan	1	4,110
T Keena	3	19,236	Takahiro Wada	1	4,110
Sheikh Ahmed Al Maktoum	3	15,926			

Favourites	30-81	37.0%	+ 4.97	Total winning prize-money	£349,085

Longest winning sequence		3	Average SP of winner	3.9/1
Longest losing sequence		17	Return on stakes invested	10.2%

1993 Form	80-327	24.5%	- 17.70	1991 Form	93-403	23.1%	+ 7.22
1992 Form	85-356	23.9%	- 36.00	1990 Form	65-376	17.3%	- 95.59

K PRENDERGAST

	No. of Horses	Races Run	1st	2nd	3rd	Unpl	Per cent	£1 Level Stake
2-y-o	24	97	8	9	11	69	8.2	- 51.85
3-y-o	25	177	11	17	13	136	6.2	- 83.00
4-y-o+	10	81	6	7	9	59	7.4	- 35.00
Totals	59	355	25	33	33	264	7.0	-169.85

BY MONTH

2-y-o	W-R	Per cent	£1 Level Stake	3-y-o	W-R	Per cent	£1 Level Stake
Mar/Apr	1-5	20.0	+ 4.00	Mar/Apr	1-16	6.3	- 11.00
May	0-7	-	- 7.00	May	1-15	6.7	- 7.00
June	1-14	7.1	- 7.50	June	1-29	3.4	- 23.00
July	2-13	15.4	- 6.50	July	2-26	7.7	+ 4.00
August	1-18	5.6	- 9.00	August	3-46	6.5	- 22.50
September	1-16	6.3	- 6.00	September	3-21	14.3	+ 0.50
Oct/Nov	2-24	8.3	- 19.85	Oct/Nov	0-24	-	- 24.00

4-y-o+	W-R	Per cent	£1 Level Stake	Totals	W-R	Per cent	£1 Level Stake
Mar/Apr	1-9	11.1	+ 2.00	Mar/Apr	3-30	10.0	- 5.00
May	0-14	-	- 14.00	May	1-36	2.8	- 28.00
June	2-15	13.3	- 4.00	June	4-58	6.9	- 34.50
July	1-12	8.3	- 3.00	July	5-51	9.8	- 5.50
August	1-9	11.1	- 5.00	August	5-73	6.8	- 36.50
September	0-9	-	- 9.00	September	4-46	8.7	- 14.50
Oct/Nov	1-13	7.7	- 2.00	Oct/Nov	3-61	4.9	- 45.85

DISTANCE

2-y-o	W-R	Per cent	£1 Level Stake	3-y-o	W-R	Per cent	£1 Level Stake
5f-6f	2-42	4.8	- 29.00	5f-6f	2-44	4.5	- 32.00
7f-8f	6-52	11.5	- 19.85	7f-8f	4-53	7.5	- 17.50
9f-13f	0-2	-	- 2.00	9f-13f	4-71	5.6	- 34.50
14f+	0-1	-	- 1.00	14f+	1-9	11.1	+ 1.00

4-y-o+	W-R	Per cent	£1 Level Stake	Totals	W-R	Per cent	£1 Level Stake
5f-6f	1-7	14.3	- 0.50	5f-6f	5-93	5.4	- 61.50
7f-8f	2-25	8.0	- 5.00	7f-8f	12-130	9.2	- 42.35
9f-13f	2-38	5.3	- 22.50	9f-13f	6-111	5.4	- 59.00
14f+	1-11	9.1	- 7.00	14f+	2-21	9.5	- 7.00

TYPE OF RACE

Non-Handicaps	W-R	Per cent	£1 Level Stake	Handicaps	W-R	Per cent	£1 Level Stake
2-y-o	8-81	9.9	- 35.85	2-y-o	0-16	-	- 16.00
3-y-o	8-87	9.2	- 24.00	3-y-o	3-86	3.5	- 55.00
4-y-o+	0-11	-	- 11.00	4-y-o+	6-63	9.5	- 17.00
Apprentice	0-1	-	- 1.00	Apprentice	0-10	-	- 10.00
Amat/Ladies	0-0	-	0.00	Amat/Ladies	0-0	-	0.00
Totals	16-180	8.9	- 71.85	Totals	9-175	5.1	- 98.00

FIRST TIME OUT

	W-R	Per cent	£1 Level Stake
2-y-o	3-23	13.0	- 5.25
3-y-o	1-24	4.2	- 15.00
4-y-o+	1-10	10.0	+ 1.00
Totals	5-57	8.8	- 19.25

JOCKEYS RIDING

	W-R	Per cent	£1 Level Stake		W-R	Per cent	£1 Level Stake
W J Supple	19-237	8.0	- 96.85	P Shanahan	1-2	50.0	+ 9.00
J F Clarke	3-47	6.4	- 21.50	B J Walsh	1-14	7.1	- 9.50
Mr G J Harford	1-1	100.0	+ 3.00				

J Cornally	0-9	D Hogan	0-2	J P Murtagh	0-1
I Browne	0-8	G Coogan	0-2	Joanna Morgan	0-1
G Dickie	0-5	K J Manning	0-2	Mr J K Connolly	0-1
A J Nolan	0-4	N G McCullagh	0-2	Mr P J Prendergast	0-1
D G O'Shea	0-4	P P Murphy	0-2	S Clancy	0-1
S Craine	0-4	B Fenton	0-1	W J Smith	0-1
C Roche	0-2	J A Heffernan	0-1		

COURSE RECORD

	Total W-R	Non-Handicaps 2-y-o	Non-Handicaps 3-y-o+	Handicaps 2-y-o	Handicaps 3-y-o+	Per cent	£1 Level Stake
Leopardstown	4-55	1-15	1-12	0-2	2-26	7.3	- 22.00
The Curragh	4-77	2-22	1-16	0-1	1-38	5.2	- 48.00
Roscommon	3-18	1-2	2-11	0-1	0-4	16.7	+ 1.00
Ballinrobe	2-7	0-0	0-1	0-1	2-5	28.6	+ 12.50
Galway	2-21	0-4	1-2	0-3	1-12	9.5	+ 3.00
Tipperary	2-24	1-8	1-13	0-0	0-3	8.3	- 14.10
Tramore	1-6	0-0	0-2	0-0	1-4	16.7	+ 4.00
Listowel	1-6	0-0	1-1	0-1	0-4	16.7	+ 3.00
Bellewstown	1-7	1-1	0-1	0-0	0-5	14.3	- 4.50
Laytown	1-7	0-0	0-2	0-0	1-5	14.3	- 3.00
Fairyhouse	1-8	1-2	0-3	0-0	0-3	12.5	- 5.75
Tralee	1-10	0-0	1-4	0-1	0-5	10.0	- 3.50
Dundalk	1-14	1-5	0-1	0-1	0-7	7.1	- 4.00
Gowran Park	1-31	0-8	0-10	0-3	1-10	3.2	- 24.50

Naas	0-27	Mallow	0-3	Killarney	0-2
Navan	0-10	Punchestown	0-3	Thurles	0-1
Clonmel	0-6	Sligo	0-3	Wexford	0-1
Down Royal	0-6	Downpatrick	0-2		

WINNING HORSES

	Age	Races Run	1st	2nd	3rd	Unpl	Win £
Blues Composer	5	15	3	1	2	9	9,080
Diligent Dodger	3	11	1	0	0	10	8,625
Regal Domain	3	11	2	0	0	9	7,535
Fakhira	2	7	1	0	1	5	5,244
Meaghers	2	5	1	0	2	2	5,206
Anemone Garden	2	9	1	1	0	7	5,206
Yankee Singer	3	14	1	3	4	6	4,110
Something Super	3	11	1	0	0	10	4,110
Oscar Schindler	2	1	1	0	0	0	4,110
Thatcher Molloy	3	3	1	0	0	2	3,450

Al Naayy	3	11	1	4	2	4	3,425
Desert Calm	5	17	1	1	1	14	3,425
Flora Wood	4	4	1	0	0	3	3,105
Blue Kestrel	2	7	1	1	1	4	3,085
Nayil	2	3	1	0	1	1	3,083
I'm Supposin	2	2	1	0	1	0	2,740
Mile A Minute	3	13	1	0	0	12	2,569
Thistle Hill	3	8	1	0	0	7	2,226
Glamour Game	3	7	1	2	2	2	2,226
Genuine Leader	2	6	1	0	0	5	2,226
Asawir	3	4	1	0	0	3	2,226
Lake Of Loughrea	4	4	1	1	0	2	2,055

WINNING OWNERS

	Races Won	Value £		Races Won	Value £
Hamdan Al-Maktoum	4	13,978	Oliver Lehane	1	4,110
Mrs D M Donohoe	2	11,194	Mrs C McNulty	1	3,425
Mrs Kevin Prendergast	3	10,665	Dominic Fagan	1	3,085
Aidan Walsh	3	9,080	A D Brennan	1	2,740
Robert Scott	2	7,535	P Conlan	1	2,226
T F Roe	1	5,206	Hadi Al-Tajir	1	2,226
Michael O'Donnell	1	5,206	M A Ryan	1	2,226
J P Hardiman	1	4,110	Bezwell Fixings Ltd	1	2,055

Favourites	6-30	20.0% - 9.35	Total winning prize-money		£89,067
Longest winning sequence		2	Average SP of winner		6.4/1
Longest losing sequence		56	Return on stakes invested		-47.8%
1993 Form	40-423	9.5% - 155.82	1991 Form	36-467	7.7% - 214.25
1992 Form	30-373	8.0% - 196.85	1990 Form	59-533	11.1% - 159.45

P PRENDERGAST

	No. of Horses	Races Run	1st	2nd	3rd	Unpl	Per cent	£1 Level Stake
2-y-o	5	18	1	4	2	11	5.6	- 16.27
3-y-o	5	31	1	3	3	24	3.2	- 28.62
4-y-o+	5	31	5	5	5	16	16.1	+ 15.00
Totals	15	80	7	12	10	51	8.8	- 29.89

Mar/Apr	May	Jun	Jul	Aug	Sep	Oct/Nov
1-9	2-9	1-15	0-14	3-8	0-8	0-17

Winning Jockeys	W-R	£1 Level Stake			W-R	£1 Level Stake
R Fitzpatrick	2-10	+ 16.00	P M Donohue		1-4	- 1.00
W J Supple	1-2	+ 2.00	T P Treacy		1-5	+ 8.00
D G O'Shea	1-2	- 0.27	J J Behan		1-16	- 13.62

Winning Courses	W-R	£1 Level Stake			W-R	£1 Level Stake
The Curragh	2-18	+ 8.00	Roscommon		1-1	+ 1.38
Clonmel	1-1	+ 3.00	Mallow		1-2	- 0.27
Tramore	1-1	+ 12.00	Tralee		1-4	- 1.00

Winning Horses	Age	Races Run	1st	2nd	3rd	Unpl	Win £
Soundproof	4	5	1	0	0	4	16,250
Macgillycuddy	5	11	2	2	4	3	10,960
Take No Chances	4	12	1	3	1	7	6,325
Life Dancing	3	13	1	2	2	8	3,968
Winter Belle	6	2	1	0	0	1	2,228
Vail Star	2	8	1	4	1	2	2,226

Favourites	2-8	25.0%	- 3.89	Total winning prize-money			£41,957

1993 Form	7-88	8.0%	- 29.40	1991 Form	5-69	7.2%	- 31.50
1992 Form	11-82	13.4%	- 26.37	1990 Form	7-69	10.1%	- 33.95

T A REGAN

	No. of Horses	Races Run	1st	2nd	3rd	Unpl	Per cent	£1 Level Stake
2-y-o	3	11	1	1	0	9	9.1	+ 6.00
3-y-o	1	11	1	3	2	5	9.1	- 6.00
4-y-o+	1	1	0	0	0	1	-	- 1.00
Totals	5	23	2	4	2	15	8.7	- 1.00

Mar/Apr	May	Jun	Jul	Aug	Sep	Oct/Nov
0-2	1-3	0-2	0-2	0-4	0-3	1-7

Winning Jockeys	W-R	£1 Level Stake		W-R	£1 Level Stake
R Hughes	1-7	- 2.00	A J Nolan	1-7	+ 10.00

Winning Courses	W-R	£1 Level Stake		W-R	£1 Level Stake
Mallow	1-2	+ 3.00	Dundalk	1-4	+ 13.00

Winning Horses	Age	Races Run	1st	2nd	3rd	Unpl	Win £
Miss Potter	3	11	1	3	2	5	2,228
Brighton Lodge	2	5	1	0	0	4	2,226

Favourites	1-2	50.0%	+ 3.00	Total winning prize-money			£4,455
1993 Form	0-11			1991 Form	0-34		
1992 Form	0-13			1990 Form	3-55	5.5%	- 36.75

M ROBINSON

	No. of Horses	Races Run	1st	2nd	3rd	Unpl	Per cent	£1 Level Stake
2-y-o	2	7	1	0	1	5	14.3	+ 8.00
3-y-o	0	0	0	0	0	0	-	0.00
4-y-o+	1	1	0	0	0	1	-	- 1.00
Totals	3	8	1	0	1	6	12.5	+ 7.00

Mar/Apr	May	Jun	Jul	Aug	Sep	Oct/Nov
0-0	0-1	0-0	0-1	1-3	0-2	0-1

Winning Jockey	W-R	£1 Level Stake	Winning Course	W-R	£1 Level Stake
D J O'Donohoe	1-1	+ 14.00	Fairyhouse	1-1	+ 14.00

Winning Horse	Age	Races Run	1st	2nd	3rd	Unpl	Win £
Loving Contract	2	5	1	0	1	3	3,425

Favourites	0-0		Total winning prize-money	£3,425

W M ROPER

	No. of Horses	Races Run	1st	2nd	3rd	Unpl	Per cent	£1 Level Stake
2-y-o	0	0	0	0	0	0	-	0.00
3-y-o	4	15	1	0	0	14	6.7	0.00
4-y-o+	4	7	1	1	1	4	14.3	+ 6.00
Totals	8	22	2	1	1	18	9.1	+ 6.00

Mar/Apr	May	Jun	Jul	Aug	Sep	Oct/Nov
1-3	0-6	1-5	0-3	0-0	0-3	0-2

Winning Jockeys	W-R	£1 Level Stake		W-R	£1 Level Stake
D J O'Donohoe	1-3	+ 10.00	N G McCullagh	1-4	+ 11.00

Winning Courses					
Gowran Park	1-2	+ 13.00	Roscommon	1-4	+ 9.00

Winning Horses	Age	Races Run	1st	2nd	3rd	Unpl	Win £
Moneybroker	3	2	1	0	0	1	2,760
Millenium Lass	6	3	1	0	0	2	2,228

Favourites	0-0		Total winning prize-money	£4,988

1993 Form	1-22	4.5%	- 11.00	1991 Form	2-33	6.1%	- 11.00
1992 Form	1-31	3.2%	- 26.00	1990 Form	0-17		

T STACK

	No. of Horses	Races Run	1st	2nd	3rd	Unpl	Per cent	£1 Level Stake
2-y-o	13	44	2	5	7	30	4.5	- 34.00
3-y-o	29	134	15	12	12	95	11.2	- 39.60
4-y-o+	9	41	2	3	1	35	4.9	- 23.00
Totals	51	219	19	20	20	160	8.7	- 96.60

BY MONTH

2-y-o	W-R	Per cent	£1 Level Stake	3-y-o	W-R	Per cent	£1 Level Stake
Mar/Apr	0-4	-	- 4.00	Mar/Apr	0-13	-	- 13.00
May	1-7	14.3	- 0.50	May	3-25	12.0	- 5.25
June	0-7	-	- 7.00	June	3-36	8.3	- 19.10
July	0-3	-	- 3.00	July	4-22	18.2	+ 3.00
August	0-7	-	- 7.00	August	4-23	17.4	+ 1.75
September	0-3	-	- 3.00	September	1-11	9.1	- 3.00
Oct/Nov	1-13	7.7	- 9.50	Oct/Nov	0-4	-	- 4.00

4-y-o+	W-R	Per cent	£1 Level Stake	Totals	W-R	Per cent	£1 Level Stake
Mar/Apr	1-7	14.3	0.00	Mar/Apr	1-24	4.2	- 17.00
May	0-8	-	- 8.00	May	4-40	10.0	- 13.75
June	0-8	-	- 8.00	June	3-51	5.9	- 34.10
July	0-6	-	- 6.00	July	4-31	12.9	- 6.00
August	1-7	14.3	+ 4.00	August	5-37	13.5	- 1.25
September	0-2	-	- 2.00	September	1-16	6.3	- 8.00
Oct/Nov	0-3	-	- 3.00	Oct/Nov	1-20	5.0	- 16.50

DISTANCE

2-y-o	W-R	Per cent	£1 Level Stake	3-y-o	W-R	Per cent	£1 Level Stake
5f-6f	1-21	4.8	- 14.50	5f-6f	6-39	15.4	- 2.00
7f-8f	1-22	4.5	- 18.50	7f-8f	3-46	6.5	- 26.10
9f-13f	0-0	-	0.00	9f-13f	6-45	13.3	- 7.50
14f+	0-1	-	- 1.00	14f+	0-4	-	- 4.00

4-y-o+	W-R	Per cent	£1 Level Stake	Totals	W-R	Per cent	£1 Level Stake
5f-6f	0-10	-	- 10.00	5f-6f	7-70	10.0	- 26.50
7f-8f	1-13	7.7	- 2.00	7f-8f	5-81	6.2	- 46.60
9f-13f	1-17	5.9	- 10.00	9f-13f	7-62	11.3	- 17.50
14f+	0-1	-	- 1.00	14f+	0-6	-	- 6.00

TYPE OF RACE

Non-Handicaps	W–R	Per cent	£1 Level Stake	Handicaps	W–R	Per cent	£1 Level Stake
2-y-o	2-38	5.3	- 28.00	2-y-o	0-6	-	- 6.00
3-y-o	9-76	11.8	- 18.75	3-y-o	4-50	8.0	- 22.10
4-y-o+	1-21	4.8	- 14.00	4-y-o+	1-18	5.6	- 7.00
Apprentice	0-2	-	- 2.00	Apprentice	1-4	25.0	+ 2.00
Amat/Ladies	1-4	25.0	- 0.75	Amat/Ladies	0-0	-	0.00
Totals	13-141	9.2	- 63.50	Totals	6-78	7.7	- 33.10

FIRST TIME OUT

	W–R	Per cent	£1 Level Stake
2-y-o	0-12	-	- 12.00
3-y-o	2-29	6.9	- 20.00
4-y-o+	1-9	11.1	- 2.00
Totals	3-50	6.0	- 34.00

JOCKEYS RIDING

	W–R	Per cent	£1 Level Stake		W–R	Per cent	£1 Level Stake
S Craine	16-157	10.2	- 52.85	Mr S P Hennessy	1-2	50.0	+ 1.25
W J Smith	2-10	20.0	+ 5.00				

	W–R		W–R		W–R
D W O'Sullivan	0-15	A J Nolan	0-1	L Piggott	0-1
P P O'Grady	0-7	H R H Princess Haya	0-1	Miss C E Hyde	0-1
P P Murphy	0-5	J F Clarke	0-1	Miss R Hickey	0-1
W J Supple	0-4	J F Egan	0-1	Miss S Bottani	0-1
C P Dunne	0-2	J G Power	0-1	R Fitzpatrick	0-1
P V Gilson	0-2	J Reid	0-1	S P Kelly	0-1
R Hughes	0-2	K J Manning	0-1		

COURSE RECORD

	Total W–R	Non-Handicaps 2-y-o	3-y-o+	Handicaps 2-y-o	3-y-o+	Per cent	£1 Level Stake
Tramore	2-4	0-0	2-4	0-0	0-0	50.0	+ 11.25
Clonmel	2-5	0-0	2-3	0-0	0-2	40.0	+ 11.00
Roscommon	2-11	0-0	1-8	0-1	1-2	18.2	- 0.10
Killarney	2-14	0-1	2-10	0-0	0-3	14.3	- 4.00
Leopardstown	2-22	1-3	0-9	0-1	1-9	9.1	- 9.50
Laytown	1-1	0-0	1-1	0-0	0-0	100.0	+ 2.50
Bellewstown	1-2	0-1	1-1	0-0	0-0	50.0	+ 4.00
Fairyhouse	1-5	0-2	1-2	0-0	0-1	20.0	- 1.75
Listowel	1-6	0-0	0-2	0-1	1-3	16.7	+ 2.00
Dundalk	1-9	1-4	0-1	0-0	0-4	11.1	- 5.50
Gowran Park	1-10	0-1	0-4	0-0	1-5	10.0	- 1.00
Tralee	1-13	0-1	0-6	0-1	1-5	7.7	- 2.00
Naas	1-14	0-4	1-6	0-0	0-4	7.1	- 9.50
The Curragh	1-35	0-8	0-9	0-1	1-17	2.9	- 26.00

Tipperary	0-18	Ballinrobe	0-9	Wexford	0-3
Galway	0-11	Mallow	0-9	Limerick	0-1
Navan	0-10	Sligo	0-5	Thurles	0-1

WINNING HORSES

	Age	Races Run	1st	2nd	3rd	Unpl	Win £
One Man Band	3	10	2	1	2	5	6,508
Snowing	3	6	2	0	1	3	6,508
Dark Poet	3	5	2	1	1	1	5,670
Sir Silver Sox	2	3	1	1	1	0	5,244
El Zorro Dorado	4	12	1	1	1	9	5,138
Tourandot	3	10	2	1	1	6	4,797
Bold Emir	3	5	1	2	0	2	4,112
Musical Banker	3	1	1	0	0	0	3,450
Glimmering Girl	3	12	1	1	0	10	2,740
Crystal Voice	4	7	1	2	0	4	2,243
Saltonic	3	8	1	0	0	7	2,228
Perilous Plight	3	9	1	1	1	6	2,228
Tordo	3	4	1	0	1	2	2,228
Siren	3	6	1	0	1	4	2,228
Faldberg	2	2	1	0	0	1	2,226

WINNING OWNERS

	Races Won	Value £		Races Won	Value £
Mrs T Stack	6	16,288	R E Sangster	1	5,138
T Corden	3	9,790	Thomas R Wolohan	1	2,228
P Piller	2	6,508	Mrs John Magnier	1	2,228
Jermome S Moss	2	5,670	Mrs Jane Rowlinson	1	2,228
M A Begley	1	5,244	G Cosmelli	1	2,226

Favourites	5-19	26.3%	- 4.60	Total winning prize-money			£57,548
Longest winning sequence			2	Average SP of winner			5.4/1
Longest losing sequence			26	Return on stakes invested			-44.1%

1993 Form	12-172	7.0%	-105.37	1991 Form	49-263	18.6%	+ 22.70
1992 Form	20-199	10.1%	- 78.70	1990 Form	22-216	10.2%	-101.10

F SUTHERLAND

	No. of Horses	Races Run	1st	2nd	3rd	Unpl	Per cent	£1 Level Stake
2-y-o	1	6	0	0	0	6	-	- 6.00
3-y-o	0	0	0	0	0	0	-	0.00
4-y-o+	1	1	1	0	0	0	100.0	+ 10.00
Totals	2	7	1	0	0	6	14.3	+ 4.00

Mar/Apr	May	Jun	Jul	Aug	Sep	Oct/Nov
0-1	0-1	1-2	0-1	0-1	0-1	0-0

Winning Jockey	W-R	£1 Level Stake	Winning Course	W-R	£1 Level Stake
C O'Brien	1-1	+ 10.00	Limerick	1-1	+ 10.00

Winning Horse	Age	Races Run	1st	2nd	3rd	Unpl	Win £
Malmsey	6	1	1	0	0	0	2,228

Favourites	0-0		Total winning prize-money		£2,228
1993 Form	0-2		1992 Form	0-4	

ADRIAN TAYLOR

	No. of Horses	Races Run	1st	2nd	3rd	Unpl	Per cent	£1 Level Stake
2-y-o	0	0	0	0	0	0	-	0.00
3-y-o	1	4	0	0	0	4	-	- 4.00
4-y-o+	3	20	2	1	0	17	10.0	- 8.50
Totals	4	24	2	1	0	21	8.3	- 12.50

Mar/Apr	May	Jun	Jul	Aug	Sep	Oct/Nov
0-2	1-4	1-8	0-5	0-5	0-0	0-0

Winning Jockey	W-R	£1 Level Stake		W-R	£1 Level Stake
G M Moylan	2-7	+ 4.50			

Winning Courses					
Down Royal	1-3	+ 3.00	Tralee	1-3	+ 2.50

Winning Horse	Age	Races Run	1st	2nd	3rd	Unpl	Win £
Mystical City	4	13	2	1	0	10	4,281

Favourites	0-0			Total winning prize-money			£4,281
1993 Form	2-24	8.3%	- 6.00	1991 Form	1-22	4.5%	- 1.00
1992 Form	2-22	9.1%	+ 14.00	1990 Form	1-28	3.6%	- 15.00

WILBERT TOLERTON

	No. of Horses	Races Run	1st	2nd	3rd	Unpl	Per cent	£1 Level Stake
2-y-o	0	0	0	0	0	0	-	0.00
3-y-o	1	3	0	0	0	3	-	- 3.00
4-y-o+	5	15	3	0	2	10	20.0	+ 24.40
Totals	6	18	3	0	2	13	16.7	+ 21.40

Mar/Apr	May	Jun	Jul	Aug	Sep	Oct/Nov
0-1	1-2	0-1	1-4	1-5	0-1	0-4

Winning Jockey	W-R	£1 Level Stake			W-R	£1 Level Stake
W J Smith	3-14	+ 25.40				

Winning Courses						
Laytown	1-1	+ 6.00	Down Royal		1-7	- 0.60
Downpatrick	1-2	+ 24.00				

Winning Horses	Age	Races Run	1st	2nd	3rd	Unpl	Win £
Nabeel	8	6	2	0	2	2	3,604
Elegant Isle	10	5	1	0	0	4	1,553

Favourites	0-0	Total winning prize-money	£5,157

1993 Form	0-15			1991 Form	0-2
1992 Form	1-13	7.7%	+ 8.00		

S TREACY

	No. of Horses	Races Run	1st	2nd	3rd	Unpl	Per cent	£1 Level Stake
2-y-o	0	0	0	0	0	0	-	0.00
3-y-o	2	8	1	1	1	5	12.5	- 1.00
4-y-o+	2	2	0	0	0	2	-	- 2.00
Totals	4	10	1	1	1	7	10.0	- 3.00

Mar/Apr	May	Jun	Jul	Aug	Sep	Oct/Nov
0-0	0-0	0-1	0-0	0-0	0-5	1-4

Winning Jockey	W-R	£1 Level Stake	Winning Course	W-R	£1 Level Stake
P P Murphy	1-6	+ 1.00	Gowran Park	1-2	+ 5.00

Winning Horse	Age	Races Run	1st	2nd	3rd	Unpl	Win £
Bolino Star	3	5	1	1	1	2	2,740

Favourites	0-0	Total winning prize-money	£2,740

1993 Form	2-11	18.2%	- 3.25	1991 Form	0-1
1992 Form	0-6				

T WALKER

	No. of Horses	Races Run	1st	2nd	3rd	Unpl	Per cent	£1 Level Stake
2-y-o	0	0	0	0	0	0	-	0.00
3-y-o	0	0	0	0	0	0	-	0.00
4-y-o+	2	10	2	0	0	8	20.0	+ 10.00
Totals	2	10	2	0	0	8	20.0	+ 10.00

Mar/Apr	May	Jun	Jul	Aug	Sep	Oct/Nov
0-1	1-1	1-3	0-0	0-3	0-1	0-1

Winning Jockey	W-R	£1 Level Stake					
G M Moylan	2-6	+ 14.00					

Winning Courses						W-R	£1 Level Stake
Killarney	1-1	+ 10.00		Wexford		1-2	+ 7.00

Winning Horse	Age	Races Run	1st	2nd	3rd	Unpl	Win £
Marian Year	8	9	2	0	0	7	6,192

Favourites	0-0		Total winning prize-money		£6,192
1993 Form	0-12		1991 Form	0-18	
1992 Form	0-14		1990 Form	0-2	

JOHN J WALSH

	No. of Horses	Races Run	1st	2nd	3rd	Unpl	Per cent	£1 Level Stake
2-y-o	1	2	0	0	0	2	-	- 2.00
3-y-o	1	11	0	1	1	9	-	- 11.00
4-y-o+	2	12	1	2	1	8	8.3	- 6.00
Totals	4	25	1	3	2	19	4.0	- 19.00

Mar/Apr	May	Jun	Jul	Aug	Sep	Oct/Nov
0-0	0-5	0-4	0-5	1-8	0-3	0-0

Winning Jockey	W-R	£1 Level Stake	Winning Course		W-R	£1 Level Stake
R Fitzpatrick	1-2	+ 4.00	Tramore		1-1	+ 5.00

Winning Horse	Age	Races Run	1st	2nd	3rd	Unpl	Win £
Alberta Rose	5	9	1	2	1	5	2,569

Favourites	0-1			Total winning prize-money		£2,569
1993 Form	0-10			1991 Form	0-7	
1992 Form	1-10	10.0%	- 1.00	1990 Form	0-9	

T M WALSH

	No. of Horses	Races Run	1st	2nd	3rd	Unpl	Per cent	£1 Level Stake
2-y-o	2	5	0	4	0	1	-	- 5.00
3-y-o	1	3	1	0	0	2	33.3	+ 2.00
4-y-o+	4	12	0	0	2	10	-	- 12.00
Totals	7	20	1	4	2	13	5.0	- 15.00

Mar/Apr	May	Jun	Jul	Aug	Sep	Oct/Nov
0-2	0-1	0-5	0-2	1-3	0-3	0-4

Winning Jockey	W-R	£1 Level Stake	Winning Course	W-R	£1 Level Stake
W J Smith	1-3	+ 2.00	Tramore	1-1	+ 4.00

Winning Horse	Age	Races Run	1st	2nd	3rd	Unpl	Win £
Quasimodo	3	3	1	0	0	2	2,226

Favourites	0-1		Total winning prize-money	£2,226

1993 Form	5-46	10.9%	+ 2.90	1991 Form	1-26	3.8%	- 18.50
1992 Form	3-45	6.7%	- 16.00				

D K WELD

	No. of Horses	Races Run	1st	2nd	3rd	Unpl	Per cent	£1 Level Stake
2-y-o	53	155	35	29	21	70	22.6	- 46.81
3-y-o	61	300	40	28	35	197	13.3	-111.81
4-y-o+	37	157	25	25	23	84	15.9	- 63.03
Totals	151	612	100	82	79	351	16.3	-221.65

BY MONTH

2-y-o	W-R	Per cent	£1 Level Stake	3-y-o	W-R	Per cent	£1 Level Stake
Mar/Apr	1-7	14.3	- 3.50	Mar/Apr	1-33	3.0	- 28.00
May	3-11	27.3	- 5.18	May	7-38	18.4	- 4.50
June	4-18	22.2	- 9.03	June	8-60	13.3	- 19.00
July	7-24	29.2	- 0.42	July	9-48	18.8	- 17.32
August	5-31	16.1	- 15.88	August	5-51	9.8	- 26.87
September	11-29	37.9	+ 5.60	September	6-29	20.7	+ 7.75
Oct/Nov	4-35	11.4	- 18.40	Oct/Nov	4-41	9.8	- 23.87

671

Weld D K

4-y-o+	W-R	Per cent	£1 Level Stake	Totals	W-R	Per cent	£1 Level Stake
Mar/Apr	0-11	-	- 11.00	Mar/Apr	2-51	3.9	- 42.50
May	3-20	15.0	- 9.45	May	13-69	18.8	- 19.13
June	3-20	15.0	- 8.00	June	15-98	15.3	- 36.03
July	3-28	10.7	- 16.75	July	19-100	19.0	- 34.49
August	10-42	23.8	- 12.25	August	20-124	16.1	- 55.00
September	4-17	23.5	+ 6.25	September	21-75	28.0	+ 19.60
Oct/Nov	2-19	10.5	- 11.83	Oct/Nov	10-95	10.5	- 54.10

DISTANCE

2-y-o	W-R	Per cent	£1 Level Stake	3-y-o	W-R	Per cent	£1 Level Stake
5f-6f	9-57	15.8	- 37.08	5f-6f	5-52	9.6	- 29.25
7f-8f	24-94	25.5	- 11.40	7f-8f	16-115	13.9	- 38.94
9f-13f	1-3	33.3	+ 1.00	9f-13f	16-125	12.8	- 45.62
14f+	1-1	100.0	+ 0.67	14f+	3-8	37.5	+ 2.00

4-y-o+	W-R	Per cent	£1 Level Stake	Totals	W-R	Per cent	£1 Level Stake
5f-6f	2-20	10.0	- 9.00	5f-6f	16-129	12.4	- 75.33
7f-8f	6-35	17.1	- 7.60	7f-8f	46-244	18.9	- 57.94
9f-13f	8-64	12.5	- 38.03	9f-13f	25-192	13.0	- 82.65
14f+	9-38	23.7	- 8.40	14f+	13-47	27.7	- 5.73

TYPE OF RACE

Non-Handicaps	W-R	Per cent	£1 Level Stake	Handicaps	W-R	Per cent	£1 Level Stake
2-y-o	30-137	21.9	- 49.96	2-y-o	5-18	27.8	+ 3.15
3-y-o	26-181	14.4	- 69.44	3-y-o	11-106	10.4	- 48.12
4-y-o+	15-53	28.3	- 9.38	4-y-o+	9-85	10.6	- 40.15
Apprentice	1-6	16.7	+ 5.00	Apprentice	1-11	9.1	- 5.50
Amat/Ladies	2-12	16.7	- 4.25	Amat/Ladies	0-3	-	- 3.00
Totals	74-389	19.0	-128.03	Totals	26-223	11.7	- 93.62

FIRST TIME OUT

	W-R	Per cent	£1 Level Stake
2-y-o	14-53	26.4	- 18.48
3-y-o	6-61	9.8	- 22.25
4-y-o+	5-37	13.5	- 15.75
Totals	25-151	16.6	- 56.48

JOCKEYS RIDING

	W-R	Per cent	£1 Level Stake		W-R	Per cent	£1 Level Stake
M J Kinane	67-302	22.2	- 63.32	L Cummins	1-2	50.0	+ 9.00
D J O'Donohoe	16-124	12.9	- 49.43	W Carson	1-2	50.0	+ 5.50
P Shanahan	12-125	9.6	- 77.40	W J Smith	1-18	5.6	- 14.75
Miss U Smyth	2-5	40.0	+ 2.75				

Mr J A Nash	0-7	B J Halligan	0-1	Miss M Burns	0-1
S M McGovern	0-7	D O'Callaghan	0-1	Mr D Marnane	0-1
B Coogan	0-4	L O'Shea	0-1	Mr K Dempsey	0-1
R Dolan	0-4	M McGovern	0-1	Mr P J Prendergast	0-1
D V Smith	0-3	Miss J McDowell	0-1		

COURSE RECORD

	Total W-R	Non-Handicaps 2-y-o	3-y-o+	Handicaps 2-y-o	3-y-o+	Per cent	£1 Level Stake
Leopardstown	19-107	3-25	12-45	0-2	4-35	17.8	- 21.12
Galway	12-39	6-8	2-10	1-2	3-19	30.8	- 2.50
The Curragh	11-117	5-29	2-36	0-2	4-50	9.4	- 62.91
Tralee	8-22	1-3	3-9	1-1	3-9	36.4	+ 10.10
Listowel	7-15	3-3	0-2	1-1	3-9	46.7	+ 12.78
Gowran Park	7-39	2-11	3-14	1-3	1-11	17.9	- 17.48
Naas	6-45	2-10	3-19	0-3	1-13	13.3	- 17.55
Roscommon	5-21	2-6	2-10	1-1	0-4	23.8	+ 0.98
Tipperary	5-45	4-11	1-25	0-1	0-8	11.1	- 29.60
Down Royal	4-13	0-4	3-7	0-0	1-2	30.8	+ 0.67
Fairyhouse	4-24	1-7	3-10	0-0	0-7	16.7	- 14.82
Killarney	3-14	0-1	2-6	0-0	1-7	21.4	- 1.87
Tramore	2-8	0-0	2-6	0-0	0-2	25.0	- 3.20
Ballinrobe	2-10	1-2	1-6	0-0	0-2	20.0	- 3.38
Laytown	1-3	0-0	1-1	0-0	0-2	33.3	+ 0.50
Downpatrick	1-6	0-0	1-6	0-0	0-0	16.7	+ 1.00
Clonmel	1-8	0-0	1-6	0-0	0-2	12.5	- 3.00
Dundalk	1-18	0-5	1-9	0-1	0-3	5.6	- 15.50
Navan	1-20	0-5	1-6	0-0	0-9	5.0	- 16.75

Sligo	0-9	Punchestown	0-6	Limerick	0-1
Bellewstown	0-7	Thurles	0-6		
Mallow	0-7	Wexford	0-2		

WINNING HORSES

	Age	Races Run	1st	2nd	3rd	Unpl	Win £
Vintage Crop	7	4	3	1	0	0	100,722
Definite Article	2	2	2	0	0	0	65,868
Saibot	5	7	2	0	2	3	29,652
Treble Bob	4	5	4	0	0	1	24,203
Artema	3	4	1	0	2	1	24,000
Jahid	2	5	2	1	2	0	19,581
Free To Speak	2	5	4	0	0	1	17,683

Kayfa	5	7	2	2	1	2	17,400
Unusual Heat	4	5	2	1	1	1	17,250
Market Slide	3	4	1	1	0	2	14,875
El Caid	3	7	3	0	0	4	14,387
Tropical	4	1	1	0	0	0	14,375
Humbel	2	2	2	0	0	0	13,831
Low Key Affair	3	3	2	1	0	0	12,393
Theatre Flight	3	10	2	3	2	3	11,645
Bryn Clovis	3	6	3	0	1	2	10,106
King Leon	2	4	2	0	1	1	9,590
Kilconnel	3	6	3	0	1	2	8,734
City Nights	3	3	1	1	1	0	8,625
Poetical Justice	3	5	2	1	1	1	6,875
Nassau	7	6	1	0	0	5	6,850
Loki	6	1	1	0	0	0	6,850
Political Domain	4	7	2	2	1	2	6,338
Boscabel	2	5	2	2	0	1	6,167
In Anticipation	3	4	2	0	0	2	6,165
Katie McLain	3	8	2	1	2	3	5,668
Feeling Of Power	2	4	1	1	0	2	5,480
Union Decree	2	3	1	1	0	1	5,480
Duke Of Aragon	2	5	1	0	1	3	5,244
Sharpness In Mind	2	3	1	1	1	0	5,206
Beating The Buzz	2	4	1	1	0	2	5,206
Journey Of Hope	2	4	1	0	1	2	5,206
Delightful Chime	2	3	1	0	0	2	5,206
Nautical Pet	2	1	1	0	0	0	5,206
Copper Mountain	3	6	2	0	0	4	4,968
Limanda	3	11	2	2	2	5	4,463
Bawader	2	3	1	1	0	1	4,453
Blazing Spectacle	4	6	2	0	2	2	4,281
Sprint For Gold	3	6	1	2	1	2	4,110
Dancing Action	3	5	1	0	0	4	4,110
Storm Ashore	2	1	1	0	0	0	4,110
Munif	2	3	1	2	0	0	4,110
Minstrelina	2	3	1	0	1	1	3,770
Desert Lily	2	1	1	0	0	0	3,770
Alterezza	7	6	1	2	1	2	3,768
Sharp Point	2	4	1	2	0	1	3,768
Key Import	2	6	1	1	1	3	3,768
Keep The Pace	2	2	1	0	0	1	3,768
Glamour Model	2	1	1	0	0	0	3,768
Off'N'Way	2	2	1	0	1	0	3,768
Moy Water	2	2	1	0	0	1	3,768
Devastating Storm	3	5	1	0	1	3	3,427
Deelish	3	8	1	1	0	6	3,427
Swift Tern	3	5	1	1	0	3	3,427
Portenza	3	6	1	1	0	4	3,425
Usman	3	7	1	2	1	3	3,425
Baydur	3	2	1	0	0	1	3,425
Brief Reunion	3	4	1	0	0	3	3,425
Pendolino	3	7	1	0	1	5	3,425
Ciseaux	5	6	1	1	1	3	3,105
Rockwood	2	2	1	0	1	0	3,083
Municipal	3	3	1	0	0	2	2,740
Moobakkr	3	2	1	0	0	1	2,228

Sir Slaves	4	4	1	1	0	2	2,226
In Common	2	6	1	1	1	3	2,226
Brief Merger	4	11	1	0	3	7	2,226
Persian View	4	2	1	0	0	1	2,055
Kuwah	3	6	1	0	1	4	1,541
Baas	3	2	1	0	0	1	1,541

WINNING OWNERS

	Races Won	Value £		Races Won	Value £
Moyglare Stud Farm	30	198,180	Landon Knight	2	5,668
Dr Michael Smurfit	13	172,177	J R Brown	1	5,244
Hamdan Al-Maktoum	7	33,454	Ovidstown Investments Ltd	2	4,968
Saleh Y Al-Homaisi	2	27,425	Thomas McDonogh	1	3,770
Mrs J Maxwell Moran	6	18,840	The Sussex Stud Limited	1	3,770
Vincent Loughnane	2	17,400	M G Hynes	1	3,768
Thomas T S Liang	2	17,250	H E The President of Ireland	1	3,768
M Benacerraf	3	14,387	Mrs Sonia Rogers	1	3,427
Godolphin	1	14,375	Michael Hilary Burke	1	3,427
Andrea Schiavi	4	11,655	Ballylinch Stud	1	3,425
Mrs Anne F Thorington	2	11,645	Metabolic Inc	1	3,425
Frank Stronach	2	9,590	G Olivero	1	3,105
Michael H Watt	2	9,076	Sportsworld Syndicate	1	2,740
E K Gaylord II	1	8,625	Mrs A J F O'Reilly	1	2,226
Mrs C L Weld	2	6,852	Miss K McGann	1	2,226
Miss Philomena O'Brien	1	6,850	Finbarr Sheehy	1	2,055
Sheikh Mohammed	2	6,167			

Favourites	57-169	33.7%	- 11.65	Total winning prize-money		£640,959
Longest winning sequence			3	Average SP of winner		2.9/1
Longest losing sequence			37	Return on stakes invested		-36.2%
1993 Form	109-552	19.7%	- 72.34	1991 Form	120-645	18.6%	-119.34
1992 Form	106-597	17.8%	-179.63	1990 Form	82-559	14.7%	-266.83

TRAINERS WITH NO WINNERS IN IRELAND 1994

	No. of Horses	Races Run	2nd	3rd	Unpl
J F Bailey Jnr	6	36	6	4	26
J R Banahan	2	4	1	0	3
D J Barry	1	2	0	0	2
P Beirne	6	17	0	2	15
N C Bell	4	10	0	0	10
Thomas Bergin	7	19	0	0	19
J A Berry	1	1	0	0	1
Ms M Dowdall Blake	1	2	0	0	2
J Brassil	2	2	1	0	1
Martin Brassil	5	10	0	0	10
M S Brosnan	2	6	0	0	6
W P Browne	6	28	3	1	24
Mrs S Burke	1	13	0	0	13
P Burke	3	10	0	0	10
Thomas Bustin	1	1	0	0	1
A Butler	2	2	1	0	1
J P Byrne	8	30	2	2	26
T Carmody	2	8	0	0	8
Peter Casey	8	15	1	0	14
P J Casserly	1	1	0	0	1
Ms E Cassidy	3	17	0	0	17
Henry Cleary	2	4	0	0	4
J Collins	1	1	0	0	1
Luke Comer	8	22	1	1	20
M J Corbett	1	3	0	0	3
J Cox	4	16	0	0	16
J S Cullen	1	4	0	0	4
James William Cullen	1	2	0	0	2
M Cullinane	2	10	0	0	10
Gerald Cully	2	4	0	0	4
Ronald Curran	1	1	0	0	1
J P Daly	2	6	0	0	6
H De Bromhead	2	2	0	0	2
P Delaney	1	1	0	0	1
C P Donoghue	1	6	1	3	2
N Draper	1	1	0	0	1
P C Duffy	5	10	0	0	10
T Duggan	2	12	0	1	11
B W Duke	1	2	0	0	2
H Eastwood	2	2	0	0	2
P A Fahy	4	21	1	1	19
W Fennin	3	9	0	0	9
Mrs E Finn	1	1	0	0	1
M Flynn	5	19	0	0	19
T Foley	2	6	0	1	5
Mrs Ian Fox	1	2	0	0	2
Noel Furlong	1	2	1	0	1
J Geoghegan	1	6	0	0	6
J G Groome	4	16	0	0	16
E P Harty	3	17	0	0	17
Mrs Seamus Hayes	1	3	0	0	3
P Henley	3	5	0	0	5
Ms E C Holdsworth	4	9	0	0	9

	No. of Horses	Races Run	2nd	3rd	Unpl
John Houghton	2	10	1	0	9
G T Hourigan	4	14	0	1	13
P Hughes	4	17	1	1	15
R Jennings	3	8	0	2	6
J P Kavanagh	3	8	1	0	7
G Kelleher	1	2	0	0	2
P G Kelly	4	14	1	0	13
T A Kent	1	4	0	2	2
C Kinane	1	1	0	0	1
Basil King	1	1	0	0	1
D Kinsella	3	12	0	0	12
P J Lally	2	14	0	0	14
Adam Lord	1	4	0	0	4
M M Lynch	2	4	0	0	4
Niall Madden	2	15	4	2	9
C P Magnier	3	10	0	0	10
M V Manning	4	9	0	0	9
A J Martin	3	11	0	1	10
P Martin	8	36	4	0	32
W J Martin	2	9	0	0	9
A J Maxwell	15	56	3	5	48
S Maye	1	1	0	0	1
H McCaffrey	3	8	0	0	8
T G McCourt	4	19	3	3	13
M McDonagh	3	6	0	1	5
J G McDonnell	1	2	0	0	2
D McDonogh	2	7	0	1	6
Michael McElhone	3	8	2	0	6
D J McGrath	1	1	0	0	1
Miss M McGuinness	1	4	0	0	4
Patrick G McHale	1	7	0	1	6
Miss A M McMahon	3	16	3	1	12
E McNamara	2	10	0	2	8
E P Mitchell	5	31	2	1	28
P J Molloy	4	9	0	0	9
A L T Moore	8	17	0	0	17
Ms J Morgan	5	9	0	0	9
J Morrison	5	19	2	0	17
T B Naughton	2	2	0	0	2
P E I Newell	1	4	0	0	4
Robert Norris	2	4	0	0	4
P O'Brady	1	1	0	0	1
M J P O'Brien	4	12	1	1	10
V T O'Brien	1	2	1	0	1
E O'Connell	1	1	0	0	1
J A O'Connell	1	8	0	0	8
M J O'Connor	2	9	0	0	9
J O'Haire	1	2	0	0	2
T J O'Mara	4	18	0	1	17
Mrs O M Pearse	2	6	0	0	6
F W Pennicott	6	31	1	0	30
M Phelan	1	7	0	0	7
G Power	2	2	0	0	2
M Purcell	1	1	0	0	1
M Quaid	1	5	0	0	5

	No. of Horses	Races Run	2nd	3rd	Unpl
D J Reddan	4	11	0	0	11
L T Reilly	2	10	0	0	10
W Rock	2	4	0	0	4
Ms Rosemary Rooney	1	1	0	0	1
P Rooney	1	1	0	0	1
J H Scott	1	3	0	0	3
R V Shaw	1	3	0	0	3
J Sheahan	1	1	0	0	1
J C Shearman	1	4	0	0	4
D T Sheridan	1	1	0	0	1
Laurence Skelly	1	1	0	0	1
G Stack	2	8	0	1	7
Capt D G Swan	7	10	0	0	10
T Taaffe	1	2	0	0	2
M J Tynan	1	1	0	0	1
J Weld	3	14	0	0	14
O Weldon	6	30	1	0	29
John A White	1	1	0	0	1
Miss A M Winters	1	1	0	0	1
L Woods	1	1	0	0	1
Patrick Woods	4	14	2	3	9
L Young	1	2	0	0	2

OVERSEAS TRAINERS WITH WINNERS IN IRELAND 1994

M BELL (England)

	No. of Horses	Races Run	1st	2nd	3rd	Unpl	Per cent	£1 Level Stake
2-y-o	2	2	1	0	0	1	50.0	+ 4.50
3-y-o	0	0	0	0	0	0	-	0.00
4-y-o+	0	0	0	0	0	0	-	0.00
Totals	2	2	1	0	0	1	50.0	+ 4.50

Mar/Apr	May	Jun	Jul	Aug	Sep	Oct/Nov
0-0	0-0	0-0	0-0	1-2	0-0	0-0

Winning Jockey	W-R	£1 Level Stake	Winning Course	W-R	£1 Level Stake
M Fenton	1-2	+ 4.50	The Curragh	1-2	+ 4.50

Winning Horse	Age	Races Run	1st	2nd	3rd	Unpl	Win £
Smart Guest	2	1	1	0	0	0	14,375

Favourites	0-0		Total winning prize-money	£14,375

1993 Form	0-0	1991 Form	0-3
1992 Form	0-4	1990 Form	0-3

J BERRY (England)

	No. of Horses	Races Run	1st	2nd	3rd	Unpl	Per cent	£1 Level Stake
2-y-o	2	2	0	0	0	2	-	- 2.00
3-y-o	1	1	0	0	1	0	-	- 1.00
4-y-o+	3	4	1	1	1	1	25.0	- 1.00
Totals	6	7	1	1	2	3	14.3	- 4.00

Mar/Apr	May	Jun	Jul	Aug	Sep	Oct/Nov
0-0	0-0	1-4	0-0	0-2	0-1	0-0

Winning Jockey	W-R	£1 Level Stake	Winning Course	W-R	£1 Level Stake
C Roche	1-2	+ 1.00	Tipperary	1-2	+ 1.00

Winning Horse	Age	Races Run	1st	2nd	3rd	Unpl	Win £
Sabre Rattler	4	2	1	1	0	0	8,627

Favourites	1-1	100.0%	+ 2.00	Total winning prize-money	£8,627

1993 Form	1-5	20.0%	+ 3.00	1991 Form	0-7		
1992 Form	1-3	33.3%	- 1.47	1990 Form	2-9	22.2%	+ 3.00

F BOUTIN (France)

	No. of Horses	Races Run	1st	2nd	3rd	Unpl	Per cent	£1 Level Stake
2-y-o	0	0	0	0	0	0	-	0.00
3-y-o	1	1	1	0	0	0	100.0	+ 0.90
4-y-o+	0	0	0	0	0	0	-	0.00
Totals	1	1	1	0	0	0	100.0	+ 0.90

Mar/Apr	May	Jun	Jul	Aug	Sep	Oct/Nov
0-0	0-0	0-0	0-0	0-0	1-1	0-0

Winning Jockey	W-R	£1 Level Stake	Winning Course	W-R	£1 Level Stake
M J Kinane	1-1	+ 0.90	The Curragh	1-1	+ 0.90

Winning Horse	Age	Races Run	1st	2nd	3rd	Unpl	Win £
Eternal Reve	3	1	1	0	0	0	14,375

Favourites	1-1	100.0%	+ 0.90	Total winning prize-money	£14,375

1993 Form	0-1		1991 Form	0-1
1992 Form	0-0		1990 Form	0-1

C E BRITTAIN (England)

	No. of Horses	Races Run	1st	2nd	3rd	Unpl	Per cent	£1 Level Stake
2-y-o	0	0	0	0	0	0	-	0.00
3-y-o	1	1	0	0	0	1	-	- 1.00
4-y-o+	2	2	1	0	0	1	50.0	+ 1.50
Totals	3	3	1	0	0	2	33.3	+ 0.50

Mar/Apr	May	Jun	Jul	Aug	Sep	Oct/Nov
0-0	0-0	1-2	0-0	0-0	0-1	0-0

Winning Jockey	W-R	£1 Level Stake	Winning Course	W-R	£1 Level Stake
M Roberts	1-2	+ 1.50	The Curragh	1-2	+ 1.50

Winning Horse	Age	Races Run	1st	2nd	3rd	Unpl	Win £
Alflora	5	1	1	0	0	0	27,250

Favourites	0-0		Total winning prize-money	£27,250

1993 Form	0-4			1991 Form	0-1		
1992 Form	4-9	44.4%	+ 4.83	1990 Form	2-7	28.6%	+ 2.50

M R CHANNON (England)

	No. of Horses	Races Run	1st	2nd	3rd	Unpl	Per cent	£1 Level Stake
2-y-o	3	3	0	0	0	3	-	- 3.00
3-y-o	2	4	1	1	0	2	25.0	0.00
4-y-o+	0	0	0	0	0	0	-	0.00
Totals	5	7	1	1	0	5	14.3	- 3.00

Mar/Apr	May	Jun	Jul	Aug	Sep	Oct/Nov
0-0	0-1	1-1	0-0	0-4	0-1	0-0

Winning Jockey	W-R	£1 Level Stake	Winning Course	W-R	£1 Level Stake
Paul Eddery	1-2	+ 2.00	Leopardstown	1-4	0.00

Winning Horse	Age	Races Run	1st	2nd	3rd	Unpl	Win £
Great Deeds	3	3	1	0	0	2	14,375

Favourites	1-2	50.0%	+ 2.00	Total winning prize-money	£14,375

1993 Form	0-0			1991 Form	1-2	50.0%	+ 11.00
1992 Form	0-1						

P CHAPPLE-HYAM (England)

	No. of Horses	Races Run	1st	2nd	3rd	Unpl	Per cent	£1 Level Stake
2-y-o	2	2	0	1	0	1	-	- 2.00
3-y-o	2	2	1	0	1	0	50.0	+ 0.25
4-y-o+	1	1	0	0	0	1	-	- 1.00
Totals	5	5	1	1	1	2	20.0	- 2.75

Mar/Apr	May	Jun	Jul	Aug	Sep	Oct/Nov
0-0	1-1	0-2	0-1	0-1	0-0	0-0

Winning Jockey	W-R	£1 Level Stake	Winning Course	W-R	£1 Level Stake
J Reid	1-4	- 1.75	The Curragh	1-3	- 0.75

Winning Horse	Age	Races Run	1st	2nd	3rd	Unpl	Win £
Turtle Island	3	1	1	0	0	0	131,550

Favourites	1-3	33.3%	- 0.75	Total winning prize-money	£131,550

1993 Form	1-3	33.3%	- 0.25	1991 Form	0-1	
1992 Form	2-6	33.3%	+ 0.23			

J L DUNLOP (England)

	No. of Horses	Races Run	1st	2nd	3rd	Unpl	Per cent	£1 Level Stake
2-y-o	2	2	0	0	0	2	-	- 2.00
3-y-o	4	4	1	0	1	2	25.0	- 0.50
4-y-o+	7	8	0	1	0	7	-	- 8.00
Totals	13	14	1	1	1	11	7.1	- 10.50

Mar/Apr	May	Jun	Jul	Aug	Sep	Oct/Nov
0-0	1-2	0-3	0-3	0-0	0-4	0-2

Winning Jockey	W-R	£1 Level Stake	Winning Course	W-R	£1 Level Stake
W Carson	1-6	- 2.50	The Curragh	1-10	- 6.50

Winning Horse	Age	Races Run	1st	2nd	3rd	Unpl	Win £
Mehthaaf	3	1	1	0	0	0	98,550

Favourites	0-1		Total winning prize-money	£98,550

1993 Form	1-7	14.3%	- 2.67	1991 Form	0-2		
1992 Form	1-2	50.0%	+ 8.00	1990 Form	2-8	25.0%	- 2.63

J H M GOSDEN (England)

	No. of Horses	Races Run	1st	2nd	3rd	Unpl	Per cent	£1 Level Stake
2-y-o	0	0	0	0	0	0	-	0.00
3-y-o	1	1	0	0	1	0	-	- 1.00
4-y-o+	4	5	1	1	1	2	20.0	- 3.00
Totals	5	6	1	1	2	2	16.7	- 4.00

Mar/Apr	May	Jun	Jul	Aug	Sep	Oct/Nov
0-0	0-1	1-2	0-0	0-1	0-2	0-0

Winning Jockey	W-R	£1 Level Stake	Winning Course	W-R	£1 Level Stake
L Dettori	1-5	- 3.00	The Curragh	1-3	- 1.00

Winning Horse	Age	Races Run	1st	2nd	3rd	Unpl	Win £
Del Deya	4	2	1	1	0	0	26,250

Favourites	1-5	20.0%	- 3.00	Total winning prize-money		£26,250

1993 Form	1-4	25.0%	+ 4.00	1991 Form	0-2
1992 Form	1-4	25.0%	- 0.25	1990 Form	0-2

B HANBURY (England)

	No. of Horses	Races Run	1st	2nd	3rd	Unpl	Per cent	£1 Level Stake
2-y-o	0	0	0	0	0	0	-	0.00
3-y-o	1	1	0	0	0	1	-	- 1.00
4-y-o+	2	2	1	0	1	0	50.0	+ 2.50
Totals	3	3	1	0	1	1	33.3	+ 1.50

Mar/Apr	May	Jun	Jul	Aug	Sep	Oct/Nov
0-0	0-1	0-0	0-0	1-1	0-1	0-0

Winning Jockey	W-R	£1 Level Stake	Winning Course	W-R	£1 Level Stake
L Piggott	1-1	+ 3.50	The Curragh	1-3	+ 1.50

Winning Horse	Age	Races Run	1st	2nd	3rd	Unpl	Win £
Bin Ajwaad	4	1	1	0	0	0	14,375

Favourites	0-1		Total winning prize-money	£14,375

1993 Form	1-2	50.0%	+ 0.50	1991 Form	1-4	25.0%	+ 0.50
1992 Form	0-1			1990 Form	1-3	33.3%	+ 0.50

R HANNON (England)

	No. of Horses	Races Run	1st	2nd	3rd	Unpl	Per cent	£1 Level Stake
2-y-o	3	3	0	1	0	2	-	- 3.00
3-y-o	2	3	0	1	0	2	-	- 3.00
4-y-o+	3	3	2	0	1	0	66.7	+ 9.38
Totals	8	9	2	2	1	4	22.2	+ 3.38

Mar/Apr	May	Jun	Jul	Aug	Sep	Oct/Nov
0-0	0-1	1-2	0-0	1-4	0-1	0-1

Winning Jockeys	W-R	£1 Level Stake			W-R	£1 Level Stake
L Piggott	1-1	+ 1.38	W R Swinburn		1-1	+ 9.00

Winning Courses	W-R	£1 Level Stake			W-R	£1 Level Stake
Leopardstown	1-2	+ 8.00	The Curragh		1-7	- 4.62

Winning Horses	Age	Races Run	1st	2nd	3rd	Unpl	Win £
Right Win	4	1	1	0	0	0	23,000
Surprise Offer	4	1	1	0	0	0	14,375

Favourites	1-2	50.0%	+ 0.38	Total winning prize-money			£37,375
1993 Form	1-4	25.0%	+ 0.33	1991 Form	2-4	50.0%	+ 6.50
1992 Form	1-4	25.0%	+ 7.00	1990 Form	2-4	50.0%	+ 2.75

B W HILLS (England)

	No. of Horses	Races Run	1st	2nd	3rd	Unpl	Per cent	£1 Level Stake
2-y-o	0	0	0	0	0	0	-	0.00
3-y-o	1	1	1	0	0	0	100.0	+ 2.50
4-y-o+	1	1	0	0	0	1	-	- 1.00
Totals	2	2	1	0	0	1	50.0	+ 1.50

Mar/Apr	May	Jun	Jul	Aug	Sep	Oct/Nov
0-0	0-0	0-0	1-1	0-1	0-0	0-0

Winning Jockey	W-R	£1 Level Stake	Winning Course	W-R	£1 Level Stake
Pat Eddery	1-1	+ 2.50	The Curragh	1-1	+ 2.50

Winning Horse	Age	Races Run	1st	2nd	3rd	Unpl	Win £
Bolas	3	1	1	0	0	0	130,850

Favourites	1-1	100.0%	+ 2.50	Total winning prize-money			£130,850
1993 Form	1-2	50.0%	+ 7.00	1991 Form	1-8	12.5%	- 1.00
1992 Form	1-7	14.3%	- 3.00	1990 Form	4-15	26.7%	- 0.87

H IBRAHIM (Dubai)

	No. of Horses	Races Run	1st	2nd	3rd	Unpl	Per cent	£1 Level Stake
2-y-o	0	0	0	0	0	0	-	0.00
3-y-o	1	1	1	0	0	0	100.0	+ 5.00
4-y-o+	0	0	0	0	0	0	-	0.00
Totals	1	1	1	0	0	0	100.0	+ 5.00

Mar/Apr	May	Jun	Jul	Aug	Sep	Oct/Nov
0-0	0-0	1-1	0-0	0-0	0-0	0-0

Winning Jockey	W-R	£1 Level Stake	Winning Course	W-R	£1 Level Stake
L Dettori	1-1	+ 5.00	The Curragh	1-1	+ 5.00

Winning Horse	Age	Races Run	1st	2nd	3rd	Unpl	Win £
Balanchine	3	1	1	0	0	0	348,000

Favourites	0-0	Total winning prize-money	£348,000

M S JOHNSTON (England)

	No. of Horses	Races Run	1st	2nd	3rd	Unpl	Per cent	£1 Level Stake
2-y-o	4	4	3	1	0	0	75.0	+ 6.90
3-y-o	0	0	0	0	0	0	-	0.00
4-y-o+	0	0	0	0	0	0	-	0.00
Totals	4	4	3	1	0	0	75.0	+ 6.90

Mar/Apr	May	Jun	Jul	Aug	Sep	Oct/Nov
0-0	0-0	0-0	1-1	2-3	0-0	0-0

Winning Jockeys	W-R	£1 Level Stake		W-R	£1 Level Stake
L Dettori	1-1	+ 0.90	J Weaver	1-2	+ 2.50
M Roberts	1-1	+ 3.50			

Winning Course		
The Curragh	3-4	+ 6.90

Winning Horses	Age	Races Run	1st	2nd	3rd	Unpl	Win £
Loveyoumillions	2	1	1	0	0	0	74,000
Millstream	2	1	1	0	0	0	15,375
Jural	2	1	1	0	0	0	14,375

Favourites	2-2	100.0%	+ 4.40	Total winning prize-money	£103,750
1993 Form	0-1			1991 Form	0-1
1992 Form	0-5			1990 Form	0-2

P A KELLEWAY (England)

	No. of Horses	Races Run	1st	2nd	3rd	Unpl	Per cent	£1 Level Stake
2-y-o	1	1	1	0	0	0	100.0	+ 20.00
3-y-o	0	0	0	0	0	0	-	0.00
4-y-o+	0	0	0	0	0	0	-	0.00
Totals	1	1	1	0	0	0	100.0	+ 20.00

Mar/Apr	May	Jun	Jul	Aug	Sep	Oct/Nov
0-0	0-0	0-0	0-0	0-0	1-1	0-0

Winning Jockey	W-R	£1 Level Stake	Winning Course	W-R	£1 Level Stake
J Weaver	1-1	+ 20.00	The Curragh	1-1	+ 20.00

Winning Horse	Age	Races Run	1st	2nd	3rd	Unpl	Win £
Belle Genius	2	1	1	0	0	0	65,100

Favourites	0-0		Total winning prize-money	£65,100

1991 Form	0-1

M R STOUTE (England)

	No. of Horses	Races Run	1st	2nd	3rd	Unpl	Per cent	£1 Level Stake
2-y-o	0	0	0	0	0	0	-	0.00
3-y-o	1	1	0	1	0	0	-	- 1.00
4-y-o+	4	4	1	1	1	1	25.0	+ 0.50
Totals	5	5	1	2	1	1	20.0	- 0.50

Mar/Apr	May	Jun	Jul	Aug	Sep	Oct/Nov
0-0	0-1	0-0	0-1	0-2	1-1	0-0

Winning Jockey	W-R	£1 Level Stake	Winning Course	W-R	£1 Level Stake
M J Kinane	1-2	+ 2.50	Leopardstown	1-1	+ 3.50

Winning Horse	Age	Races Run	1st	2nd	3rd	Unpl	Win £
Cezanne	5	1	1	0	0	0	97,800

Favourites	0-0		Total winning prize-money	£97,800

1993 Form	0-4			1991 Form	0-4		
1992 Form	1-5	20.0%	- 1.50	1990 Form	1-4	25.0%	- 1.75

OVERSEAS TRAINERS WITH NO WINNERS IN IRELAND 1994

	No. of Horses	Races Run	2nd	3rd	Unpl
C N Allen (Eng)	1	1	0	0	1
R W Armstrong (Eng)	1	2	1	0	1
J R Arnold (Eng)	1	1	0	0	1
J E Banks (Eng)	1	1	0	0	1
R Boss (Eng)	1	1	0	0	1
H R A Cecil (Eng)	1	1	1	0	0
Mrs J Cecil (Eng)	2	2	1	0	1
R Charlton (Eng)	1	1	1	0	0
P F I Cole (Eng)	2	2	0	1	1
L Cumani (Eng)	2	2	0	2	0
C W C Elsey (Eng)	1	1	0	0	1
A Fabre (Fra)	4	4	1	0	3
J R Fanshawe (Eng)	1	1	0	0	1
A G Foster (Eng)	1	1	0	0	1
R Guest (Eng)	1	1	0	1	0
W Haggas (Eng)	1	1	0	0	1
J W Hills (Eng)	1	1	0	0	1
W Jarvis (Eng)	1	2	0	1	1
D R Loder (Eng)	1	1	0	0	1
P J McBride (Eng)	1	1	0	1	0
D J G Murray Smith (Eng)	1	1	0	0	1
J E Pease (Fra)	1	1	0	0	1
Miss L Perratt (Eng)	1	1	0	0	1
A Renzoni (Ita)	1	1	0	0	1
Dr J Scargill (Eng)	1	1	0	0	1
A A Scott (Eng)	1	1	0	0	1
M H Tompkins (Eng)	1	1	0	0	1
S P C Woods (Eng)	1	1	0	1	0

COURSE SECTION

(IRISH FLAT 1990-94)

BALLINROBE

Leading Trainers 1990-94

	Total W-R	Non-handicaps 2-y-o	3-y-o+	Handicaps 2-y-o	3-y-o+	Per cent	£1 Level Stake
J S Bolger	10-37	2-7	4-19	1-1	3-10	27.0	+ 2.54
D K Weld	7-41	1-10	3-17	0-0	3-14	17.1	- 19.26
John M Oxx	6-7	0-1	5-5	0-0	1-1	85.7	+ 9.13
D Gillespie	5-26	0-3	2-10	0-0	3-13	19.2	- 5.48
B V Kelly	3-12	1-2	0-4	0-0	2-6	25.0	+ 26.00
Edward Lynam	3-17	0-2	1-5	0-0	2-10	17.6	- 5.17
K Prendergast	3-24	0-5	0-6	0-1	3-12	12.5	+ 8.50
G T Hourigan	2-3	1-2	1-1	0-0	0-0	66.7	+ 11.00
D Hanley	2-6	0-2	1-2	0-0	1-2	33.3	+ 7.50
Noel T Chance	2-8	0-1	2-4	0-0	0-3	25.0	+ 16.00
T F Lacy	2-10	1-1	0-5	0-0	1-4	20.0	- 1.50
P Prendergast	2-13	0-2	1-4	0-0	1-7	15.4	- 6.90
M J Grassick	2-14	1-2	0-3	0-0	1-9	14.3	- 3.00
J J McLoughlin	2-16	1-2	1-4	0-1	0-9	12.5	+ 10.00
C Collins	2-17	0-0	1-6	0-1	1-10	11.8	- 9.25
Daniel J Murphy	2-18	0-3	0-8	0-1	2-6	11.1	+ 4.50
T Stack	2-26	0-4	2-15	0-0	0-7	7.7	- 18.75
M Hourigan	1-1	0-0	0-0	0-0	1-1	100.0	+ 1.88
T G McCourt	1-1	0-0	0-0	0-0	1-1	100.0	+ 10.00
Pat O'Leary	1-3	0-0	0-0	0-0	1-3	33.3	+ 8.00
W M Roper	1-3	0-1	0-0	0-0	1-2	33.3	+ 2.00
W P Mullins	1-3	0-0	0-0	0-0	1-3	33.3	+ 1.00

Leading Jockeys

	Total W-R	Per cent	£1 Level Stake	Best Trainer	W-R	Per cent	£1 Level Stake
W J Supple	10-32	31.3	+ 36.40	J S Bolger	4-9	44.4	+ 5.50
M J Kinane	9-35	25.7	- 11.20	D K Weld	6-28	21.4	- 11.25
N G McCullagh	6-28	21.4	+ 11.25	Pat O'Leary	1-1	100.0	+ 10.00
J P Murtagh	5-14	35.7	+ 5.47	John M Oxx	4-5	80.0	+ 7.47
K J Manning	5-31	16.1	- 6.95	J S Bolger	4-13	30.8	+ 5.05
S Craine	5-39	12.8	- 16.50	T Stack	2-24	8.3	- 16.75
J F Egan	4-24	16.7	- 1.00	M J Grassick	2-3	66.7	+ 8.00
B J Walsh	3-6	50.0	+ 9.50	A P O'Brien	1-1	100.0	+ 5.00
J J Behan	3-20	15.0	+ 3.10	P Prendergast	2-6	33.3	+ 0.10
P Shanahan	3-30	10.0	- 21.37	M Hourigan	1-1	100.0	+ 1.88
R Hughes	3-33	9.1	- 18.67	G T Hourigan	1-1	100.0	+ 5.00
M Fenton	2-12	16.7	- 1.75	Augustine Leahy	1-2	50.0	+ 1.25

How the Favourites Fared

Non-handicaps	W-R	Per cent	£1 Level Stake	Handicaps	W-R	Per cent	£1 Level Stake
2-y-o	3-10	30.0	- 2.13	2-y-o	1-1	100.0	+ 0.67
3-y-o	2-3	66.7	+ 2.50	3-y-o	1-6	16.7	- 3.62
Weight-for-age	12-29	41.4	+ 7.13	All-aged	9-29	31.0	- 4.27
Totals	17-42	40.5	+ 7.50	Totals	11-36	30.6	- 7.22
All favs	28-78	35.9	+ 0.28				

BELLEWSTOWN

Leading Trainers 1990-94

	Total W-R	Non-handicaps 2-y-o	3-y-o+	Handicaps 2-y-o	3-y-o+	Per cent	£1 Level Stake
K Prendergast	8-42	4-10	2-11	0-0	2-21	19.0	- 8.83
D K Weld	5-40	1-10	4-12	0-0	0-18	12.5	- 18.50
J S Bolger	4-24	1-6	1-8	0-0	2-10	16.7	- 1.00
John M Oxx	3-10	0-0	2-7	0-0	1-3	30.0	+ 3.50
F Dunne	3-11	0-4	1-2	0-0	2-5	27.3	+ 10.50
J G Coogan	3-19	1-8	1-4	0-0	1-7	15.8	- 4.50
M A O'Toole	3-25	0-5	2-8	0-0	1-12	12.0	- 13.08
E J O'Grady	2-8	1-1	0-2	0-0	1-5	25.0	+ 27.00
A P O'Brien	2-9	1-3	1-2	0-0	0-4	22.2	+ 0.75
B V Kelly	2-11	0-2	0-1	0-0	2-8	18.2	- 1.00
M J Grassick	2-13	0-2	2-9	0-0	0-2	15.4	- 9.10
C Collins	2-15	0-2	0-7	0-0	2-6	13.3	+ 8.00
P J Flynn	2-15	1-2	0-1	0-0	1-12	13.3	- 1.50
M Kauntze	2-24	1-7	0-6	0-0	1-11	8.3	- 18.05
M A McCullagh	1-2	0-0	0-0	0-0	1-2	50.0	+ 5.50
I Ferguson	1-2	0-0	0-0	0-0	1-2	50.0	+ 3.00
P Beirne	1-2	1-1	0-0	0-0	0-1	50.0	+ 2.00
Noel T Chance	1-3	0-0	1-3	0-0	0-0	33.3	+ 5.00
J J McLoughlin	1-6	0-2	0-0	0-0	1-4	16.7	+ 7.00
P Prendergast	1-7	0-2	0-1	0-0	1-4	14.3	- 3.50
J T Gorman	1-7	0-1	0-0	0-0	1-6	14.3	+ 2.00
C P Magnier	1-8	0-0	0-4	0-0	1-4	12.5	+ 9.00

Leading Jockeys

	Total W-R	Per cent	£1 Level Stake	Best Trainer	W-R	Per cent	£1 Level Stake
M J Kinane	8-33	24.2	- 3.13	D K Weld	5-25	20.0	- 3.50
J P Murtagh	6-32	18.8	+ 6.00	F Dunne	2-4	50.0	+ 6.50
S Craine	5-34	14.7	- 1.00	B V Kelly	2-4	50.0	+ 6.00
P V Gilson	4-30	13.3	- 15.20	J G Coogan	1-1	100.0	+ 5.00
R M Burke	3-27	11.1	+ 4.00	C Collins	1-1	100.0	+ 14.00
Mr A P O'Brien	2-3	66.7	+ 3.00	A P O'Brien	1-1	100.0	+ 1.75
B J Walsh	2-7	28.6	+ 7.50	K Prendergast	2-7	28.6	+ 7.50
J A Heffernan	2-9	22.2	+ 11.00	A P O'Brien	1-2	50.0	+ 5.00
B Coogan	2-12	16.7	- 3.50	J G Coogan	2-11	18.2	- 2.50
M Fenton	2-17	11.8	+ 9.50	Edward Lynam	1-3	33.3	+ 2.50
C Roche	2-19	10.5	- 12.25	J S Bolger	2-11	18.2	- 4.25
W J Supple	2-21	9.5	- 17.00	K Prendergast	2-6	33.3	- 2.00

How the Favourites Fared

Non-handicaps	W-R	Per cent	£1 Level Stake	Handicaps	W-R	Per cent	£1 Level Stake
2-y-o	8-13	61.5	+ 5.04	2-y-o	0-0	-	0.00
3-y-o	0-0	-	0.00	3-y-o	0-0	-	0.00
Weight-for-age	8-21	38.1	- 3.03	All-aged	11-26	42.3	+ 8.75
Totals	16-34	47.1	+ 2.01	Totals	11-26	42.3	+ 8.75
All favs	27-60	45.0	+ 10.76				

CLONMEL

Leading Trainers 1990-94

	Total W-R	Non-handicaps 2-y-o	3-y-o+	Handicaps 2-y-o	3-y-o+	Per cent	£1 Level Stake
J S Bolger	10-48	0-0	7-30	0-0	3-18	20.8	+ 0.65
D K Weld	7-26	0-0	5-16	0-0	2-10	26.9	+ 11.80
John M Oxx	5-13	0-0	5-11	0-0	0-2	38.5	- 2.56
J J McLoughlin	4-8	0-0	0-2	0-0	4-6	50.0	+ 22.00
Noel Meade	4-16	0-0	2-10	0-0	2-6	25.0	+ 8.50
A P O'Brien	4-17	0-0	3-10	0-0	1-7	23.5	+ 10.73
K Prendergast	4-34	0-0	2-17	0-0	2-17	11.8	- 2.00
P J Flynn	3-30	0-0	1-13	0-0	2-17	10.0	- 8.50
P Aspell	2-6	0-0	2-3	0-0	0-3	33.3	+ 3.25
P Prendergast	2-8	0-0	2-7	0-0	0-1	25.0	- 2.10
Capt D G Swan	2-9	0-0	1-8	0-0	1-1	22.2	+ 10.33
Daniel J Murphy	2-12	0-0	1-5	0-0	1-7	16.7	- 4.25
T Stack	2-13	0-0	2-10	0-0	0-3	15.4	+ 3.00
W P Mullins	2-13	0-0	1-9	0-0	1-4	15.4	- 0.50
Augustine Leahy	2-29	0-0	1-23	0-0	1-6	6.9	- 8.00
W T Bourke	1-1	0-0	0-0	0-0	1-1	100.0	+ 7.00
J P Kavanagh	1-4	0-0	1-3	0-0	0-1	25.0	- 1.50
J E Kiely	1-4	0-0	1-3	0-0	0-1	25.0	- 1.75
E McNamara	1-4	0-0	1-3	0-0	0-1	25.0	+ 3.00
T A Regan	1-5	0-0	0-3	0-0	1-2	20.0	- 2.75
Peter McCreery	1-5	0-0	0-3	0-0	1-2	20.0	- 2.90
F Berry	1-5	0-0	0-2	0-0	1-3	20.0	- 1.00

Leading Jockeys

	Total W-R	Per cent	£1 Level Stake	Best Trainer	W-R	Per cent	£1 Level Stake
M J Kinane	8-23	34.8	+ 6.20	D K Weld	4-12	33.3	+ 8.80
W J Supple	8-40	20.0	- 0.90	J S Bolger	3-6	50.0	+ 5.00
C Roche	7-31	22.6	- 10.39	J S Bolger	3-18	16.7	- 7.60
J P Murtagh	6-25	24.0	- 11.81	John M Oxx	4-11	36.4	- 2.06
J A Heffernan	4-16	25.0	+ 16.00	J S Bolger	3-7	42.9	+ 17.00
J J Behan	4-18	22.2	+ 2.40	W P Mullins	2-3	66.7	+ 9.50
S Craine	3-29	10.3	- 9.00	Noel Meade	2-6	33.3	+ 7.00
N G McCullagh	3-33	9.1	- 11.00	J J McLoughlin	2-4	50.0	+ 9.00
D J O'Donohoe	2-7	28.6	+ 2.00	D K Weld	2-5	40.0	+ 4.00
W J Smith	2-17	11.8	0.00	T Stack	1-1	100.0	+ 8.00
W J O'Connor	2-26	7.7	- 16.75	P Aspell	2-6	33.3	+ 3.25
J F Egan	2-36	5.6	- 19.00	A P O'Brien	1-1	100.0	+ 8.00

How the Favourites Fared

Non-handicaps	W-R	Per cent	£1 Level Stake	Handicaps	W-R	Per cent	£1 Level Stake
2-y-o	0-0	-	0.00	2-y-o	0-0	-	0.00
3-y-o	2-12	16.7	- 7.20	3-y-o	2-5	40.0	- 0.90
Weight-for-age	19-31	61.3	+ 8.53	All-aged	6-20	30.0	- 1.75
Totals	21-43	48.8	+ 1.33	Totals	8-25	32.0	- 2.65
All favs	29-68	42.6	- 1.32				

THE CURRAGH

Leading Trainers 1990-94

	Total W-R	Non-handicaps 2-y-o	3-y-o+	Handicaps 2-y-o	3-y-o+	Per cent	£1 Level Stake
J S Bolger	115-738	49-225	37-262	4-20	25-231	15.6	-120.04
John M Oxx	88-535	21-135	45-262	0-3	22-135	16.4	- 17.42
D K Weld	63-604	15-158	28-204	2-10	18-232	10.4	-320.64
K Prendergast	35-510	10-139	10-150	1-14	14-207	6.9	-238.72
C Collins	24-281	7-61	6-90	1-7	10-123	8.5	-104.50
T Stack	20-229	4-55	8-84	1-6	7-84	8.7	- 60.12
M Kauntze	19-179	7-53	8-71	0-2	4-53	10.6	- 44.33
P J Flynn	14-137	1-19	4-31	0-3	9-84	10.2	+ 1.00
Noel Meade	13-176	4-44	4-43	1-4	4-85	7.4	- 54.00
A P O'Brien	10-82	0-18	4-27	0-1	6-36	12.2	- 20.25
D P Kelly	7-41	0-4	0-6	1-3	6-28	17.1	+ 37.50
F Dunne	7-63	1-14	3-20	0-1	3-28	11.1	+ 4.50
P Prendergast	7-97	1-23	1-22	1-5	4-47	7.2	- 22.60
W P Mullins	6-53	0-2	0-15	0-4	6-32	11.3	- 11.00
Liam Browne	6-159	3-52	2-47	0-8	1-52	3.8	- 98.00
R Hannon (Eng)	5-16	2-8	3-8	0-0	0-0	31.3	+ 4.96
P F I Cole (Eng)	5-17	0-2	5-14	0-0	0-1	29.4	+ 2.63
C E Brittain (Eng)	5-18	1-5	4-13	0-0	0-0	27.8	- 2.67
J L Dunlop (Eng)	5-26	2-6	3-20	0-0	0-0	19.2	- 2.80
B W Hills (Eng)	5-27	0-5	4-21	0-0	1-1	18.5	- 1.50
T M Walsh	5-44	0-3	1-13	0-1	4-27	11.4	+ 7.50
M A O'Toole	5-94	1-18	0-27	1-4	3-45	5.3	- 26.00

Leading Jockeys

	Total W-R	Per cent	£1 Level Stake	Best Trainer	W-R	Per cent	£1 Level Stake
C Roche	85-445	19.1	- 68.71	J S Bolger	74-326	22.7	- 16.21
M J Kinane	74-504	14.7	-197.79	D K Weld	53-395	13.4	-167.62
J P Murtagh	35-285	12.3	- 98.31	John M Oxx	28-211	13.3	- 68.81
L Piggott	31-127	24.4	- 16.54	R Hannon (Eng)	2-2	100.0	+ 4.71
W J Supple	31-341	9.1	- 42.17	K Prendergast	14-118	11.9	- 3.67
R Hughes	25-284	8.8	- 98.63	John M Oxx	10-50	20.0	+ 0.97
S Craine	23-360	6.4	-194.12	T Stack	17-177	9.6	- 53.12
W J O'Connor	22-227	9.7	- 80.83	M Kauntze	16-122	13.1	- 21.83
P V Gilson	22-292	7.5	-133.25	C Collins	11-136	8.1	- 46.50
K J Manning	17-261	6.5	-165.32	J S Bolger	16-148	10.8	- 69.32
J Reid	16-79	20.3	+ 25.55	John M Oxx	1-1	100.0	+ 12.00
P Shanahan	16-284	5.6	-209.75	C Collins	7-54	13.0	- 20.50

How the Favourites Fared

Non-handicaps	W-R	Per cent	£1 Level Stake	Handicaps	W-R	Per cent	£1 Level Stake
2-y-o	71-178	39.9	- 19.80	2-y-o	4-15	26.7	+ 1.75
3-y-o	37-88	42.0	- 0.92	3-y-o	6-24	25.0	- 4.42
Weight-for-age	56-165	33.9	- 20.64	All-aged	38-165	23.0	- 23.25
Totals	164-431	38.1	- 41.36	Totals	48-204	23.5	- 25.92
All favs	212-635	33.4	- 67.28				

DOWN ROYAL

Leading Trainers 1990-94

	Total W-R	Non-handicaps 2-y-o	3-y-o+	Handicaps 2-y-o	3-y-o+	Per cent	£1 Level Stake
J S Bolger	15-42	4-15	7-18	1-1	3-8	35.7	+ 22.06
D K Weld	13-55	1-12	9-31	0-1	3-11	23.6	- 11.77
M Kauntze	8-48	2-11	3-22	0-0	3-15	16.7	- 17.21
M J Grassick	7-30	2-7	3-12	0-0	2-11	23.3	- 4.52
J C Hayden	5-14	2-4	3-7	0-0	0-3	35.7	+ 13.80
C Collins	5-22	2-6	0-8	0-0	3-8	22.7	+ 4.75
B V Kelly	5-40	2-11	2-13	0-0	1-16	12.5	- 20.50
John M Oxx	4-16	0-0	3-12	0-0	1-4	25.0	- 6.17
E J O'Grady	4-18	1-4	0-4	0-0	3-10	22.2	+ 10.92
Liam Browne	3-11	2-3	1-7	0-0	0-1	27.3	+ 5.35
J Burns	3-12	1-2	2-7	0-0	0-3	25.0	+ 7.50
F Dunne	3-15	0-3	1-8	0-0	2-4	20.0	+ 5.25
P Prendergast	2-6	0-1	1-1	0-0	1-4	33.3	+ 6.00
Daniel J Murphy	2-10	2-4	0-2	0-1	0-3	20.0	+ 11.50
Adrian Taylor	2-10	0-1	1-5	0-0	1-4	20.0	+ 17.00
M Cunningham	2-13	0-2	0-3	0-0	2-8	15.4	- 8.25
J J McLoughlin	2-14	0-0	0-4	0-0	2-10	14.3	- 5.50
V Bowens	2-16	0-2	0-6	0-0	2-8	12.5	- 0.75
Noel Meade	2-23	1-5	1-11	0-0	0-7	8.7	- 14.50
John W Nicholson	1-1	0-0	0-0	0-0	1-1	100.0	+ 12.00
G T Hourigan	1-2	0-1	0-0	0-0	1-1	50.0	+ 13.00
G A Cusack	1-2	1-1	0-1	0-0	0-0	50.0	0.00

Leading Jockeys

	Total W-R	Per cent	£1 Level Stake	Best Trainer	W-R	Per cent	£1 Level Stake
C Roche	8-16	50.0	+ 14.78	J S Bolger	7-10	70.0	+ 17.28
P Shanahan	8-34	23.5	- 4.44	D K Weld	4-17	23.5	- 4.73
P V Gilson	7-18	38.9	+ 5.75	C Collins	4-9	44.4	+ 4.75
W J O'Connor	6-43	14.0	+ 0.62	M Kauntze	5-29	17.2	- 6.38
J P Murtagh	5-13	38.5	+ 6.83	John M Oxx	3-7	42.9	- 2.17
M J Kinane	5-19	26.3	- 2.33	D K Weld	3-11	27.3	+ 1.25
N G McCullagh	5-22	22.7	+ 3.80	F Dunne	2-3	66.7	+ 14.00
K J Manning	5-29	17.2	- 7.75	M J Grassick	3-8	37.5	+ 1.25
W J Supple	5-32	15.6	- 11.50	J S Bolger	3-12	25.0	+ 2.00
M Fenton	4-15	26.7	+ 10.25	P Prendergast	1-1	100.0	+ 5.00
J A Heffernan	4-24	16.7	+ 6.75	J S Bolger	2-9	22.2	+ 3.50
W J Smith	4-52	7.7	- 33.93	D K Weld	2-12	16.7	- 5.33

How the Favourites Fared

Non-handicaps	W-R	Per cent	£1 Level Stake	Handicaps	W-R	Per cent	£1 Level Stake
2-y-o	14-27	51.9	+ 0.30	2-y-o	1-1	100.0	+ 0.50
3-y-o	3-15	20.0	- 7.90	3-y-o	1-4	25.0	- 1.50
Weight-for-age	11-29	37.9	- 8.77	All-aged	17-36	47.2	+ 11.02
Totals	28-71	39.4	- 16.37	Totals	19-41	46.3	+ 10.02
All favs	47-112	42.0	- 6.35				

DOWNPATRICK

Leading Trainers 1990-94

	Total	Non-handicaps		Handicaps		Per	£1 Level
	W–R	2-y-o	3-y-o+	2-y-o	3-y-o+	cent	Stake
M J Grassick	3–11	0–0	3–11	0–0	0–0	27.3	+ 0.30
Peter Casey	3–13	0–0	2–10	0–0	1–3	23.1	+ 5.50
D K Weld	3–19	0–0	3–19	0–0	0–0	15.8	– 4.00
F Dunne	2–4	0–0	1–3	0–0	1–1	50.0	+ 4.00
F Flood	2–4	0–0	1–2	0–0	1–2	50.0	+ 0.90
J S Bolger	2–6	0–0	2–6	0–0	0–0	33.3	+ 3.30
K Prendergast	2–10	0–0	2–7	0–0	0–3	20.0	– 2.50
Francis Ennis	1–1	0–0	1–1	0–0	0–0	100.0	+ 4.50
Miss I T Oakes	1–2	0–0	1–2	0–0	0–0	50.0	+ 15.00
T O'Neill	1–3	0–0	1–3	0–0	0–0	33.3	+ 10.00
P Hughes	1–3	0–0	1–2	0–0	0–1	33.3	– 1.33
T Stack	1–3	0–0	1–2	0–0	0–1	33.3	– 1.00
J F Bailey Jnr	1–3	0–0	1–3	0–0	0–0	33.3	+ 18.00
Noel T Chance	1–4	0–0	1–2	0–0	0–2	25.0	– 1.90
J G Coogan	1–4	0–0	1–4	0–0	0–0	25.0	– 1.90
M A O'Toole	1–5	0–0	0–3	0–0	1–2	20.0	+ 3.00
J Burns	1–5	0–0	1–5	0–0	0–0	20.0	+ 10.00
Wilbert Tolerton	1–5	0–0	0–4	0–0	1–1	20.0	+ 21.00
D Gillespie	1–5	0–0	0–2	0–0	1–3	20.0	– 1.75
J C Harley	1–5	0–0	0–3	0–0	1–2	20.0	– 1.50
P J Flynn	1–6	0–0	1–4	0–0	0–2	16.7	– 4.71
Daniel J Murphy	1–6	0–0	1–4	0–0	0–2	16.7	– 1.00

Leading Jockeys

	Total	Per	£1 Level			Per	£1 Level
	W–R	cent	Stake	Best Trainer	W–R	cent	Stake
W J Smith	4–16	25.0	+ 27.00	J P Byrne	1–1	100.0	+ 6.00
C Everard	2–5	40.0	+ 2.60	Francis Ennis	1–1	100.0	+ 4.50
J A Heffernan	2–6	33.3	+ 22.50	J F Bailey Jnr	1–1	100.0	+ 20.00
B J Walsh	2–7	28.6	+ 0.50	K Prendergast	2–4	50.0	+ 3.50
K J Manning	2–9	22.2	– 5.40	J S Bolger	1–2	50.0	– 0.20
P Shanahan	2–10	20.0	+ 1.00	D K Weld	2–8	25.0	+ 3.00
R Hughes	2–10	20.0	+ 2.50	M J Grassick	1–2	50.0	+ 2.50
R M Burke	2–11	18.2	– 4.00	F Dunne	1–1	100.0	+ 2.50
J P Murtagh	1–1	100.0	+ 3.50	F Dunne	1–1	100.0	+ 3.50
B Fenton	1–1	100.0	+ 2.25	D Gillespie	1–1	100.0	+ 2.25
C O'Dwyer	1–2	50.0	– 0.60	F Flood	1–1	100.0	+ 0.40
M Fenton	1–2	50.0	+ 5.00	Peter Casey	1–1	100.0	+ 6.00

How the Favourites Fared

		Per	£1 Level			Per	£1 Level
Non-handicaps	W–R	cent	Stake	Handicaps	W–R	cent	Stake
2-y-o	0–0	–	0.00	2-y-o	0–0	–	0.00
3-y-o	2–5	40.0	– 0.65	3-y-o	0–0	–	0.00
Weight-for-age	11–27	40.7	– 3.77	All-aged	2–8	25.0	– 1.00
Totals	13–32	40.6	– 4.42	Totals	2–8	25.0	– 1.00
All favs	15–40	37.5	– 5.42				

693

DUNDALK

Leading Trainers 1990-94

	Total W-R	Non-handicaps 2-y-o	3-y-o+	Handicaps 2-y-o	3-y-o+	Per cent	£1 Level Stake
J S Bolger	20-88	9-31	7-37	1-2	3-18	22.7	- 21.15
John M Oxx	18-65	4-12	13-40	0-0	1-13	27.7	- 4.17
D K Weld	16-105	3-30	6-34	0-3	7-38	15.2	- 45.59
Noel Meade	8-50	2-11	3-13	0-2	3-24	16.0	- 4.68
K Prendergast	8-82	2-18	2-21	0-2	4-41	9.8	- 35.73
F Dunne	6-32	0-7	3-14	0-0	3-11	18.8	+ 13.75
M Kauntze	5-47	1-12	2-17	0-0	2-18	10.6	- 12.20
Oliver Finnegan	4-20	0-0	0-1	0-0	4-19	20.0	+ 24.00
J C Harley	3-11	0-1	0-1	0-0	3-9	27.3	+ 12.10
V Kennedy	3-18	0-1	0-4	0-0	3-13	16.7	+ 4.00
J C Hayden	3-21	0-4	0-6	0-0	3-11	14.3	+ 6.25
Daniel J Murphy	3-28	1-6	0-6	0-2	2-14	10.7	+ 7.00
Edward Lynam	3-34	1-10	1-4	0-0	1-20	8.8	- 8.50
D Gillespie	3-35	1-12	0-5	0-1	2-17	8.6	- 18.10
P J Flynn	2-11	0-2	0-2	0-1	2-6	18.2	- 1.00
T A Regan	2-15	1-7	0-3	1-1	0-4	13.3	+ 11.00
T Stack	2-15	1-8	0-1	0-0	1-6	13.3	- 2.50
Liam Browne	2-17	2-12	0-4	0-0	0-1	11.8	- 8.38
J G Coogan	2-22	1-5	0-9	0-0	1-8	9.1	- 8.00
M J Grassick	2-27	0-7	0-5	0-0	2-15	7.4	- 18.25
C Collins	2-35	0-10	1-12	0-0	1-13	5.7	- 28.00
Mrs John Harrington	1-1	0-0	1-1	0-0	0-0	100.0	+ 7.00

Leading Jockeys

	Total W-R	Per cent	£1 Level Stake	Best Trainer	W-R	Per cent	£1 Level Stake
M J Kinane	16-77	20.8	- 30.81	D K Weld	12-59	20.3	- 23.63
J P Murtagh	14-71	19.7	- 14.60	John M Oxx	11-29	37.9	- 0.00
C Roche	13-54	24.1	- 8.12	J S Bolger	12-39	30.8	- 1.12
P V Gilson	10-54	18.5	+ 2.25	F Dunne	3-5	60.0	+ 20.25
P Carberry	9-36	25.0	+ 16.20	Noel Meade	5-12	41.7	+ 14.70
W J Supple	8-68	11.8	- 29.02	J S Bolger	4-16	25.0	- 2.27
P Shanahan	7-55	12.7	- 0.58	Daniel J Murphy	2-3	66.7	+ 19.00
K J Manning	6-53	11.3	- 19.75	J S Bolger	4-21	19.0	- 5.75
W J O'Connor	6-65	9.2	- 34.20	M Kauntze	4-39	10.3	- 19.20
D Hogan	5-27	18.5	+ 13.50	John M Oxx	3-16	18.8	+ 1.50
R Hughes	5-56	8.9	- 36.87	M J Grassick	2-6	33.3	+ 2.75
J J Behan	4-22	18.2	+ 17.63	Oliver Finnegan	2-3	66.7	+ 25.00

How the Favourites Fared

Non-handicaps	W-R	Per cent	£1 Level Stake	Handicaps	W-R	Per cent	£1 Level Stake
2-y-o	16-33	48.5	+ 2.21	2-y-o	0-2	-	- 2.00
3-y-o	17-23	73.9	+ 13.09	3-y-o	4-10	40.0	- 0.69
Weight-for-age	11-26	42.3	- 3.55	All-aged	11-46	23.9	- 14.02
Totals	44-82	53.7	+ 11.75	Totals	15-58	25.9	- 16.71
All favs	59-140	42.1	- 4.96				

694

FAIRYHOUSE

Leading Trainers 1990-94

	Total W-R	Non-handicaps 2-y-o	3-y-o+	Handicaps 2-y-o	3-y-o+	Per cent	£1 Level Stake
John M Oxx	16-65	6-18	7-27	0-0	3-20	24.6	- 13.76
D K Weld	15-104	4-31	8-40	0-1	3-32	14.4	- 44.78
J S Bolger	14-97	7-34	4-35	0-1	3-27	14.4	- 44.23
Noel Meade	7-35	0-9	4-18	0-1	3-7	20.0	+ 23.00
P J Flynn	4-19	1-2	0-5	0-1	3-11	21.1	+ 9.00
D Gillespie	4-21	0-8	1-7	0-0	3-6	19.0	+ 0.75
M Kauntze	4-41	1-15	3-15	0-0	0-11	9.8	- 21.75
K Prendergast	4-63	2-18	1-24	0-1	1-20	6.3	- 40.75
D T Hughes	3-10	0-1	2-6	0-0	1-3	30.0	+ 6.50
D Hanley	3-12	3-4	0-5	0-0	0-3	25.0	+ 11.50
T Stack	3-15	0-5	3-5	0-1	0-4	20.0	- 4.50
P Prendergast	2-10	1-4	0-2	1-1	0-3	20.0	+ 6.73
J J McLoughlin	2-23	0-3	0-7	0-0	2-13	8.7	- 11.25
C Collins	2-33	0-12	1-13	0-0	1-8	6.1	- 18.00
Liam Browne	2-34	1-15	1-12	0-0	0-7	5.9	- 10.00
B W Hills (Eng)	1-1	0-0	1-1	0-0	0-0	100.0	+ 6.00
M Robinson	1-1	1-1	0-0	0-0	0-0	100.0	+ 14.00
J F Bailey Jnr	1-3	0-0	1-2	0-0	0-1	33.3	+ 2.50
J E Mulhern	1-7	0-0	1-5	0-0	0-2	14.3	+ 1.00
W P Mullins	1-7	0-1	1-3	0-1	0-2	14.3	- 1.50
V Bowens	1-8	0-2	1-4	0-0	0-2	12.5	+ 3.00
E J O'Grady	1-9	1-4	0-3	0-0	0-2	11.1	- 6.50

Leading Jockeys

	Total W-R	Per cent	£1 Level Stake	Best Trainer	W-R	Per cent	£1 Level Stake
M J Kinane	19-75	25.3	- 4.54	D K Weld	15-66	22.7	- 6.77
J P Murtagh	10-41	24.4	- 3.23	John M Oxx	9-25	36.0	+ 2.77
R Hughes	9-49	18.4	+ 6.23	D Hanley	3-4	75.0	+ 19.50
C Roche	7-45	15.6	- 22.95	J S Bolger	7-32	21.9	- 9.95
P Carberry	4-17	23.5	+ 21.00	Noel Meade	4-12	33.3	+ 26.00
K J Manning	4-38	10.5	- 6.50	J S Bolger	3-22	13.6	- 5.50
N G McCullagh	4-43	9.3	- 14.75	Noel Meade	2-2	100.0	+ 14.50
S Craine	4-48	8.3	- 23.00	P J Flynn	1-2	50.0	+ 3.00
D G O'Shea	3-32	9.4	- 17.25	John M Oxx	2-9	22.2	+ 2.50
J R Barry	2-2	100.0	+ 6.63	P J Flynn	1-1	100.0	+ 5.00
Miss S Kauntze	2-4	50.0	+ 3.00	M Kauntze	2-3	66.7	+ 4.00
T E Durcan	2-5	40.0	+ 7.50	J E Mulhern	1-1	100.0	+ 7.00

How the Favourites Fared

Non-handicaps	W-R	Per cent	£1 Level Stake	Handicaps	W-R	Per cent	£1 Level Stake
2-y-o	15-28	53.6	+ 3.79	2-y-o	0-1	-	- 1.00
3-y-o	5-9	55.6	+ 2.52	3-y-o	2-11	18.2	- 3.25
Weight-for-age	14-32	43.8	- 1.24	All-aged	4-15	26.7	- 2.37
Totals	34-69	49.3	+ 5.07	Totals	6-27	22.2	- 6.62
All favs	40-96	41.7	- 1.55				

GALWAY

Leading Trainers 1990-94

	Total W-R	Non-handicaps 2-y-o	Non-handicaps 3-y-o+	Handicaps 2-y-o	Handicaps 3-y-o+	Per cent	£1 Level Stake
D K Weld	47-167	16-32	13-47	1-7	17-81	28.1	+ 3.70
J S Bolger	14-152	4-32	6-37	0-7	4-76	9.2	-101.74
P J Flynn	12-88	0-10	6-21	1-2	5-55	13.6	- 23.25
John M Oxx	10-63	2-7	5-31	0-0	3-25	15.9	- 1.75
T Stack	7-44	1-3	4-20	0-0	2-21	15.9	- 6.95
K Prendergast	7-80	0-14	1-15	2-7	4-44	8.8	- 17.00
Noel Meade	7-83	0-15	1-15	0-3	6-50	8.4	- 49.00
C Collins	6-63	0-11	4-17	0-4	2-31	9.5	- 33.50
M Kauntze	5-24	1-6	0-4	0-3	4-11	20.8	+ 18.50
Augustine Leahy	4-33	0-6	1-9	0-2	3-16	12.1	- 10.00
P Mullins	4-36	1-4	0-11	0-0	3-21	11.1	+ 36.00
P Prendergast	3-21	1-6	1-6	1-2	0-7	14.3	+ 0.50
E J O'Grady	3-24	0-7	0-8	0-0	3-9	12.5	+ 1.00
B V Kelly	3-24	1-5	0-5	0-2	2-12	12.5	+ 34.00
M Halford	3-25	0-2	1-7	0-0	2-16	12.0	- 3.00
M J Grassick	3-27	0-4	1-8	0-1	2-14	11.1	+ 12.00
M Cunningham	3-27	0-4	0-7	0-0	3-16	11.1	+ 4.00
J J McLoughlin	3-43	0-1	0-5	1-2	2-35	7.0	- 8.00
A P O'Brien	3-45	0-5	1-14	0-2	2-24	6.7	- 30.85
D G McArdle	2-4	0-0	0-0	0-0	2-4	50.0	+ 22.00
M A McCullagh	2-8	0-0	0-1	0-0	2-7	25.0	+ 12.50
D Hanley	2-9	0-0	1-5	0-0	1-4	22.2	+ 13.50

Leading Jockeys

	Total W-R	Per cent	£1 Level Stake	Best Trainer	W-R	Per cent	£1 Level Stake
M J Kinane	43-137	31.4	+ 12.56	D K Weld	40-126	31.7	+ 10.66
S Craine	12-110	10.9	- 44.20	T Stack	5-33	15.2	- 11.95
J P Murtagh	10-71	14.1	+ 35.50	John M Oxx	3-29	10.3	- 16.50
P Shanahan	10-85	11.8	- 22.45	C Collins	4-21	19.0	+ 0.25
P V Gilson	8-74	10.8	- 19.75	M Halford	2-10	20.0	+ 4.50
C Roche	8-76	10.5	- 58.18	J S Bolger	7-52	13.5	- 36.08
K J Manning	7-79	8.9	- 32.15	J S Bolger	5-47	10.6	- 25.15
M Fenton	5-36	13.9	+ 1.00	Augustine Leahy	2-11	18.2	+ 4.00
N G McCullagh	5-83	6.0	- 16.50	M A McCullagh	2-5	40.0	+ 15.50
J F Egan	5-87	5.7	- 62.50	P J Flynn	4-37	10.8	- 18.50
J J Behan	4-46	8.7	- 7.50	Adrian Taylor	1-3	33.3	+ 18.00
R M Burke	4-52	7.7	- 23.50	K Prendergast	2-12	16.7	+ 8.50

How the Favourites Fared

Non-handicaps	W-R	Per cent	£1 Level Stake	Handicaps	W-R	Per cent	£1 Level Stake
2-y-o	20-31	64.5	+ 6.76	2-y-o	2-7	28.6	- 1.50
3-y-o	3-5	60.0	+ 3.80	3-y-o	5-8	62.5	+ 3.03
Weight-for-age	15-49	30.6	- 15.84	All-aged	19-80	23.8	- 18.52
Totals	38-85	44.7	- 5.28	Totals	26-95	27.4	- 16.99
All favs	64-180	35.6	- 22.27				

GOWRAN PARK

Leading Trainers 1990-94

	Total W-R	Non-handicaps 2-y-o	3-y-o+	Handicaps 2-y-o	3-y-o+	Per cent	£1 Level Stake
D K Weld	33-152	9-39	17-61	2-14	5-38	21.7	- 26.53
J S Bolger	25-155	12-47	6-56	3-18	4-34	16.1	- 42.80
John M Oxx	19-84	3-26	15-43	0-4	1-11	22.6	- 25.94
M Kauntze	9-48	6-15	2-14	1-6	0-13	18.8	- 6.92
A P O'Brien	7-46	0-12	2-14	1-1	4-19	15.2	+ 4.50
P J Flynn	7-70	3-15	2-25	1-7	1-23	10.0	- 23.00
K Prendergast	7-118	0-33	4-39	0-14	3-32	5.9	- 82.45
J J McLoughlin	5-37	0-8	1-11	1-3	3-15	13.5	+ 1.75
J M Canty	4-21	1-5	0-2	0-3	3-11	19.0	+ 2.00
T Stack	3-32	0-6	0-12	1-2	2-12	9.4	- 12.50
D Gillespie	3-33	0-11	1-10	0-4	2-8	9.1	- 14.25
C Collins	3-50	1-16	2-20	0-1	0-13	6.0	- 32.00
Noel Meade	3-52	0-19	2-17	1-4	0-12	5.8	- 43.52
J C Harley	2-8	0-1	0-0	0-1	2-6	25.0	+ 20.00
Charles O'Brien	2-12	1-5	1-7	0-0	0-0	16.7	- 4.50
W P Mullins	2-25	0-6	0-6	2-5	0-8	8.0	- 8.00
M A O'Toole	2-31	0-3	0-9	0-1	2-18	6.5	- 19.75
J C Hayden	2-32	1-11	0-8	0-1	1-12	6.3	- 17.00
Andrew Lee	1-1	1-1	0-0	0-0	0-0	100.0	+ 4.50
S Treacy	1-3	0-0	1-2	0-1	0-0	33.3	+ 4.00
B Lawlor	1-3	0-0	0-1	0-0	1-2	33.3	+ 6.00
J R Banahan	1-3	0-1	1-2	0-0	0-0	33.3	+ 4.00

Leading Jockeys

	Total W-R	Per cent	£1 Level Stake	Best Trainer	W-R	Per cent	£1 Level Stake
M J Kinane	28-113	24.8	- 17.25	D K Weld	23-93	24.7	- 9.55
C Roche	17-94	18.1	- 19.77	J S Bolger	13-61	21.3	- 8.27
J P Murtagh	14-83	16.9	- 16.04	John M Oxx	9-39	23.1	- 13.79
W J O'Connor	9-79	11.4	- 37.92	M Kauntze	9-33	27.3	+ 8.08
N G McCullagh	8-77	10.4	- 1.25	J J McLoughlin	3-14	21.4	+ 3.75
R Hughes	7-80	8.8	- 32.75	M Halford	1-1	100.0	+ 7.00
K J Manning	7-83	8.4	- 47.66	J S Bolger	6-39	15.4	- 10.66
P Shanahan	6-87	6.9	- 61.00	D K Weld	3-26	11.5	- 14.00
S Craine	5-92	5.4	- 67.02	T Stack	3-28	10.7	- 8.50
D J O'Donohoe	4-10	40.0	+ 5.77	D K Weld	4-9	44.4	+ 6.77
J F Egan	4-64	6.3	- 38.00	P J Flynn	4-33	12.1	- 7.00
P V Gilson	4-84	4.8	- 63.93	Charles O'Brien	2-5	40.0	+ 2.50

How the Favourites Fared

Non-handicaps	W-R	Per cent	£1 Level Stake	Handicaps	W-R	Per cent	£1 Level Stake
2-y-o	18-42	42.9	- 4.65	2-y-o	5-13	38.5	+ 2.15
3-y-o	7-22	31.8	- 6.03	3-y-o	1-9	11.1	- 5.00
Weight-for-age	20-41	48.8	+ 0.35	All-aged	12-38	31.6	- 1.10
Totals	45-105	42.9	- 10.33	Totals	18-60	30.0	- 3.95
All favs	63-165	38.2	- 14.28				

KILLARNEY

Leading Trainers 1990-94

	Total W-R	Non-handicaps 2-y-o	3-y-o+	Handicaps 2-y-o	3-y-o+	Per cent	£1 Level Stake
J S Bolger	16-66	2-6	7-28	0-0	7-32	24.2	- 18.94
D K Weld	12-50	1-3	9-24	0-0	2-23	24.0	- 16.02
T Stack	12-54	1-4	8-30	0-0	3-20	22.2	- 6.50
P J Flynn	7-39	0-1	1-9	0-0	6-29	17.9	- 16.95
John M Oxx	6-19	0-0	6-18	0-0	0-1	31.6	- 8.13
M Halford	3-19	0-0	0-4	0-0	3-15	15.8	- 4.50
A P O'Brien	3-19	0-1	0-5	0-0	3-13	15.8	+ 6.50
K Prendergast	3-24	0-2	3-12	0-0	0-10	12.5	- 13.13
Neil S McGrath	2-6	0-0	0-0	0-0	2-6	33.3	+ 2.50
M J Grassick	2-11	0-0	2-5	0-0	0-6	18.2	+ 3.80
Edward Lynam	2-12	0-0	0-7	0-0	2-5	16.7	+ 12.00
E J O'Grady	2-17	0-1	0-6	0-0	2-10	11.8	0.00
J J McLoughlin	2-20	0-1	0-2	0-0	2-17	10.0	- 12.43
Augustine Leahy	2-36	0-2	1-18	0-0	1-16	5.6	- 26.67
P Burke	1-1	0-0	1-1	0-0	0-0	100.0	+ 2.25
M A O'Toole	1-2	0-0	0-0	0-0	1-2	50.0	+ 7.00
H De Bromhead	1-2	0-0	0-0	0-0	1-2	50.0	+ 15.00
K F O'Sullivan	1-2	0-0	0-1	0-0	1-1	50.0	+ 2.33
E M O'Sullivan	1-4	0-0	1-3	0-0	0-1	25.0	+ 9.00
M A McCullagh	1-5	0-0	0-2	0-0	1-3	20.0	0.00
M J Corbett	1-5	0-0	0-1	0-0	1-4	20.0	+ 4.00
F Doyle	1-5	0-0	0-1	0-0	1-4	20.0	+ 8.00

Leading Jockeys

	Total W-R	Per cent	£1 Level Stake	Best Trainer	W-R	Per cent	£1 Level Stake
M J Kinane	16-56	28.6	- 11.21	D K Weld	11-34	32.4	- 1.51
C Roche	13-52	25.0	+ 0.99	J S Bolger	8-26	30.8	- 6.76
S Craine	12-71	16.9	- 24.65	T Stack	10-45	22.2	- 6.90
J F Egan	6-45	13.3	- 5.25	P J Flynn	2-17	11.8	- 9.75
J P Murtagh	5-23	21.7	- 1.50	John M Oxx	2-7	28.6	- 2.50
D G O'Shea	4-35	11.4	+ 26.80	P J Flynn	1-1	100.0	+ 2.00
N G McCullagh	4-37	10.8	+ 0.57	J J McLoughlin	2-11	18.2	- 3.43
L Piggott	3-5	60.0	+ 1.43				
P Shanahan	3-21	14.3	- 12.13	Liam Browne	1-1	100.0	+ 4.00
K J Manning	3-24	12.5	- 13.95	J S Bolger	3-16	18.8	- 5.95
W J O'Connor	3-31	9.7	- 18.78	M Kauntze	1-6	16.7	- 4.78
G M Moylan	2-7	28.6	+ 13.00	A P O'Brien	1-1	100.0	+ 8.00

How the Favourites Fared

Non-handicaps	W-R	Per cent	£1 Level Stake	Handicaps	W-R	Per cent	£1 Level Stake
2-y-o	4-5	80.0	+ 2.47	2-y-o	0-0	-	0.00
3-y-o	11-14	78.6	+ 7.27	3-y-o	4-10	40.0	- 1.25
Weight-for-age	15-34	44.1	- 6.77	All-aged	16-45	35.6	- 2.65
Totals	30-53	56.6	+ 2.97	Totals	20-55	36.4	- 3.90
All favs	50-108	46.3	- 0.93				

LAYTOWN

Leading Trainers 1990-94

	Total W-R	Non-handicaps 2-y-o	3-y-o+	Handicaps 2-y-o	3-y-o+	Per cent	£1 Level Stake
D K Weld	4-16	0-0	3-6	0-0	1-10	25.0	- 1.00
K Prendergast	4-24	0-0	0-8	0-0	4-16	16.7	+ 1.13
T O'Neill	3-7	0-0	0-4	0-0	3-3	42.9	+ 24.25
Noel Meade	2-6	0-0	1-1	0-0	1-5	33.3	+ 14.00
P Martin	2-7	0-0	1-2	0-0	1-5	28.6	+ 14.50
M A O'Toole	2-23	0-0	0-7	0-0	2-16	8.7	- 14.00
Wilbert Tolerton	1-3	0-0	0-1	0-0	1-2	33.3	+ 4.00
T Stack	1-3	0-0	1-2	0-0	0-1	33.3	+ 0.50
B V Kelly	1-6	0-0	1-2	0-0	0-4	16.7	- 1.67
Noel T Chance	1-6	0-0	1-4	0-0	0-2	16.7	+ 1.00
D J Reddan	1-7	0-0	0-2	0-0	1-5	14.3	+ 0.50
P Prendergast	1-8	0-0	1-2	0-0	0-6	12.5	- 2.00
J T Gorman	1-8	0-0	1-5	0-0	0-3	12.5	0.00
Daniel J Murphy	1-8	0-0	1-4	0-0	0-4	12.5	- 6.43
Peter Casey	1-11	0-0	0-4	0-0	1-7	9.1	+ 2.00

Leading Jockeys

	Total W-R	Per cent	£1 Level Stake	Best Trainer	W-R	Per cent	£1 Level Stake
W J Smith	4-16	25.0	+ 9.50	D K Weld	2-6	33.3	- 0.50
P Carberry	3-5	60.0	+ 22.00	Noel Meade	2-3	66.7	+ 17.00
S Craine	3-17	17.6	- 1.17	J T Gorman	1-2	50.0	+ 6.00
R M Burke	2-12	16.7	+ 20.00	P Martin	1-1	100.0	+ 16.00
J F Egan	2-16	12.5	- 6.25	T O'Neill	1-2	50.0	+ 1.25
Mr J K Connolly	1-1	100.0	+ 3.33	K Prendergast	1-1	100.0	+ 3.33
Mr D Marnane	1-2	50.0	+ 0.50	M A O'Toole	1-2	50.0	+ 0.50
Mr G J Harford	1-3	33.3	+ 1.00	K Prendergast	1-1	100.0	+ 3.00
B Fenton	1-3	33.3	+ 14.00	T O'Neill	1-1	100.0	+ 16.00
P Shanahan	1-6	16.7	0.00	D K Weld	1-3	33.3	+ 3.00
R V Skelly	1-6	16.7	+ 5.00	T O'Neill	1-1	100.0	+ 10.00
P V Gilson	1-8	12.5	- 3.50	P Martin	1-1	100.0	+ 3.50

How the Favourites Fared

Non-handicaps	W-R	Per cent	£1 Level Stake	Handicaps	W-R	Per cent	£1 Level Stake
2-y-o	0-0	-	0.00	2-y-o	0-0	-	0.00
3-y-o	0-0	-	0.00	3-y-o	0-0	-	0.00
Weight-for-age	3-11	27.3	- 2.93	All-aged	4-15	26.7	- 4.95
Totals	3-11	27.3	- 2.93	Totals	4-15	26.7	- 4.95
All favs	7-26	26.9	- 7.88				

Leading Trainers 1990-94

	Total W-R	Non-handicaps 2-y-o	3-y-o+	Handicaps 2-y-o	3-y-o+	Per cent	£1 Level Stake
D K Weld	96-509	16-106	55-210	2-9	23-184	18.9	- 95.66
J S Bolger	96-520	31-129	33-210	5-15	27-166	18.5	- 69.47
John M Oxx	67-333	15-58	37-176	0-3	15-96	20.1	+ 4.56
K Prendergast	28-347	5-72	9-120	2-11	12-144	8.1	-152.36
C Collins	17-145	6-36	7-67	1-3	3-39	11.7	- 20.38
T Stack	17-151	3-31	6-67	0-1	8-52	11.3	- 36.25
J E Mulhern	8-85	0-7	3-31	0-1	5-46	9.4	- 20.17
Noel Meade	8-134	2-25	3-47	0-2	3-60	6.0	- 60.72
M Kauntze	7-148	2-36	3-58	0-4	2-50	4.7	- 96.75
A P O'Brien	6-56	2-11	1-20	0-3	3-22	10.7	- 10.50
Charles O'Brien	5-36	1-6	4-29	0-0	0-1	13.9	- 14.15
M A O'Toole	5-73	0-12	2-18	1-2	2-41	6.8	- 35.00
P Prendergast	4-27	0-4	0-8	0-0	4-15	14.8	+ 15.50
M J Grassick	4-55	0-9	2-23	0-2	2-21	7.3	- 34.50
J J McLoughlin	4-83	0-15	1-28	0-3	3-37	4.8	- 42.50
R Hannon (Eng)	3-6	2-3	1-3	0-0	0-0	50.0	+ 18.00
Daniel J Murphy	3-28	1-4	1-14	0-0	1-10	10.7	+ 4.00
W P Mullins	3-30	0-1	0-13	0-1	3-15	10.0	- 8.00
E J O'Grady	3-48	1-10	0-15	0-2	2-21	6.3	- 24.50
J M Canty	3-52	0-6	1-12	0-1	2-33	5.8	- 41.70
P J Flynn	3-72	0-7	2-27	0-2	1-36	4.2	- 55.50
P Chapple-Hyam (Eng)	2-4	1-3	1-1	0-0	0-0	50.0	+ 3.25

Leading Jockeys

	Total W-R	Per cent	£1 Level Stake	Best Trainer	W-R	Per cent	£1 Level Stake
M J Kinane	85-339	25.1	- 5.14	D K Weld	80-306	26.1	- 1.89
C Roche	63-323	19.5	- 62.53	J S Bolger	52-221	23.5	- 22.83
J P Murtagh	42-250	16.8	- 15.24	John M Oxx	37-150	24.7	+ 44.86
P V Gilson	28-218	12.8	- 57.14	C Collins	14-89	15.7	+ 11.07
S Craine	25-253	9.9	- 95.67	T Stack	15-121	12.4	- 17.75
K J Manning	21-178	11.8	- 70.13	J S Bolger	20-124	16.1	- 33.13
P Shanahan	19-211	9.0	-111.99	D K Weld	10-85	11.8	- 31.74
R Hughes	17-173	9.8	- 62.10	John M Oxx	5-22	22.7	- 5.35
W J Supple	13-219	5.9	-133.75	J S Bolger	6-48	12.5	- 14.25
J Reid	10-43	23.3	+ 5.10	J E Mulhern	2-3	66.7	+ 10.33
P Carberry	9-54	16.7	+ 44.50	Noel Meade	5-30	16.7	+ 34.00
D G O'Shea	8-109	7.3	- 66.83	John M Oxx	6-37	16.2	- 10.33

How the Favourites Fared

Non-handicaps	W-R	Per cent	£1 Level Stake	Handicaps	W-R	Per cent	£1 Level Stake
2-y-o	45-103	43.7	- 12.58	2-y-o	6-11	54.5	+ 5.48
3-y-o	24-67	35.8	- 18.65	3-y-o	5-17	29.4	- 1.25
Weight-for-age	66-141	46.8	+ 9.63	All-aged	27-128	21.1	- 33.76
Totals	135-311	43.4	- 21.60	Totals	38-156	24.4	- 29.53
All favs	173-467	37.0	- 51.13				

LIMERICK

Leading Trainers 1990-94

	Total W-R	Non-handicaps 2-y-o	Non-handicaps 3-y-o+	Handicaps 2-y-o	Handicaps 3-y-o+	Per cent	£1 Level Stake
P J Flynn	8-36	0-3	2-14	0-1	6-18	22.2	+ 3.00
J S Bolger	7-38	2-4	3-24	0-0	2-10	18.4	- 4.21
D K Weld	6-52	3-8	2-29	0-1	1-14	11.5	- 33.23
Liam Browne	4-15	1-3	3-10	0-0	0-2	26.7	- 2.38
J C Hayden	3-12	1-3	0-5	0-0	2-4	25.0	+ 11.00
C Collins	3-14	0-0	2-8	0-0	1-6	21.4	+ 2.67
D Gillespie	3-16	2-5	0-5	0-1	1-5	18.8	- 5.57
J J McLoughlin	2-12	0-0	0-4	0-0	2-8	16.7	0.00
M J Grassick	2-25	0-2	2-14	0-1	0-8	8.0	- 1.75
S Treacy	1-1	0-0	0-0	0-0	1-1	100.0	+ 3.50
F Sutherland	1-1	0-0	1-1	0-0	0-0	100.0	+ 10.00
Charles O'Brien	1-1	0-0	1-1	0-0	0-0	100.0	+ 1.00
N Cassidy	1-1	0-0	0-0	0-0	1-1	100.0	+ 20.00
D P Kelly	1-3	0-0	1-2	0-0	0-1	33.3	+ 14.00
W M Roper	1-4	0-0	0-2	0-0	1-2	25.0	+ 7.00
M Kauntze	1-5	0-0	1-3	0-0	0-2	20.0	- 2.25
J T Gorman	1-5	0-0	1-2	0-0	0-3	20.0	+ 16.00
J C Harley	1-6	0-0	1-3	0-0	0-3	16.7	+ 5.00
M A O'Toole	1-8	0-0	1-3	0-0	0-5	12.5	- 6.10
John M Oxx	1-8	0-0	1-8	0-0	0-0	12.5	- 6.50
M Cunningham	1-8	1-1	0-4	0-0	0-3	12.5	+ 3.00
Daniel J Murphy	1-10	0-1	1-5	0-0	0-4	10.0	- 4.00

Leading Jockeys

	Total W-R	Per cent	£1 Level Stake	Best Trainer	W-R	Per cent	£1 Level Stake
M J Kinane	7-35	20.0	- 14.33	D K Weld	6-31	19.4	- 12.23
C Roche	6-25	24.0	+ 2.54	J S Bolger	5-19	26.3	+ 5.79
P V Gilson	5-27	18.5	- 10.83	Charles O'Brien	1-1	100.0	+ 1.00
S Craine	4-34	11.8	- 19.87	Liam Browne	2-6	33.3	+ 1.38
P Shanahan	3-17	17.6	- 0.67	D Gillespie	2-3	66.7	+ 5.33
J F Egan	3-21	14.3	- 7.75	P J Flynn	3-13	23.1	+ 0.25
R M Burke	3-22	13.6	+ 3.00	J J McLoughlin	1-1	100.0	+ 4.00
W J O'Connor	3-23	13.0	- 3.50	C Collins	1-1	100.0	+ 6.00
W J Supple	3-24	12.5	- 8.25	M J Grassick	1-2	50.0	+ 0.25
J R Barry	2-7	28.6	- 0.25	P J Flynn	2-3	66.7	+ 3.75
N G McCullagh	2-23	8.7	- 5.00	M Cunningham	1-1	100.0	+ 10.00
R Hughes	2-29	6.9	- 3.00	D T Hughes	1-7	14.3	- 2.00

How the Favourites Fared

Non-handicaps	W-R	Per cent	£1 Level Stake	Handicaps	W-R	Per cent	£1 Level Stake
2-y-o	5-10	50.0	- 1.98	2-y-o	0-1	-	- 1.00
3-y-o	2-12	16.7	- 7.60	3-y-o	0-2	-	- 2.00
Weight-for-age	9-17	52.9	+ 2.65	All-aged	5-21	23.8	- 8.65
Totals	16-39	41.0	- 6.93	Totals	5-24	20.8	- 11.65
All favs	21-63	33.3	- 18.58				

LISTOWEL

Leading Trainers 1990-94

	Total W-R	Non-handicaps 2-y-o	3-y-o+	Handicaps 2-y-o	3-y-o+	Per cent	£1 Level Stake
D K Weld	22-63	10-15	3-14	1-4	8-30	34.9	+ 23.80
John M Oxx	8-36	2-7	4-16	0-0	2-13	22.2	- 12.80
J S Bolger	8-69	5-20	1-24	1-6	1-19	11.6	- 35.63
T Stack	4-35	0-9	2-11	0-1	2-14	11.4	- 14.50
K Prendergast	3-23	1-4	1-6	0-4	1-9	13.0	+ 3.00
J Morrison	2-8	0-1	0-1	0-0	2-6	25.0	+ 13.00
J G Coogan	2-13	1-7	1-4	0-0	0-2	15.4	+ 17.00
Edward Lynam	2-14	0-3	1-2	0-2	1-7	14.3	+ 5.00
M Kauntze	2-17	0-2	0-1	2-3	0-11	11.8	- 2.00
T F Lacy	2-18	0-2	0-7	0-0	2-9	11.1	0.00
W P Mullins	2-22	0-2	0-6	1-2	1-12	9.1	- 6.00
M Halford	2-26	0-7	0-4	0-1	2-14	7.7	- 12.50
Augustine Leahy	2-36	0-12	0-8	0-4	2-12	5.6	- 24.67
M Hourigan	1-2	0-0	0-0	0-0	1-2	50.0	+ 11.00
D G McArdle	1-3	0-0	0-1	0-0	1-2	33.3	+ 14.00
H De Bromhead	1-4	0-1	0-1	0-0	1-2	25.0	+ 1.00
M Purcell	1-4	0-0	1-2	0-0	0-2	25.0	+ 1.50
J E Kiely	1-6	0-0	1-2	0-0	0-4	16.7	- 3.50
Neil S McGrath	1-7	0-2	1-1	0-2	0-2	14.3	+ 4.00
F Flood	1-7	0-2	0-3	0-0	1-2	14.3	+ 1.00
D Hanley	1-7	0-1	1-4	0-0	0-2	14.3	0.00
V Bowens	1-8	0-4	1-2	0-0	0-2	12.5	+ 2.00

Leading Jockeys

	Total W-R	Per cent	£1 Level Stake	Best Trainer	W-R	Per cent	£1 Level Stake
M J Kinane	22-64	34.4	+ 12.07	D K Weld	17-46	37.0	+ 17.73
C Roche	7-41	17.1	- 18.38	J S Bolger	6-23	26.1	- 3.13
R M Burke	4-37	10.8	- 11.25	M Halford	2-2	100.0	+ 11.50
S Craine	4-53	7.5	- 26.00	T Stack	3-29	10.3	- 13.00
J P Murtagh	3-27	11.1	- 18.00	John M Oxx	3-18	16.7	- 9.00
P V Gilson	3-36	8.3	- 12.20	Edward Lynam	1-1	100.0	+ 14.00
N G McCullagh	3-52	5.8	- 15.00	J M Canty	1-1	100.0	+ 20.00
D J O'Donohoe	2-6	33.3	+ 9.00	D K Weld	2-5	40.0	+ 10.00
R V Skelly	2-12	16.7	+ 3.38	J Morrison	1-1	100.0	+ 12.00
Joanna Morgan	2-18	11.1	0.00	M Hourigan	1-1	100.0	+ 12.00
W J Smith	2-21	9.5	- 2.67	D G McArdle	1-1	100.0	+ 16.00
D G O'Shea	2-29	6.9	- 17.00	Augustine Leahy	1-2	50.0	+ 5.00

How the Favourites Fared

Non-handicaps	W-R	Per cent	£1 Level Stake	Handicaps	W-R	Per cent	£1 Level Stake
2-y-o	13-19	68.4	+ 8.16	2-y-o	2-5	40.0	+ 1.25
3-y-o	1-6	16.7	- 4.27	3-y-o	0-0	-	0.00
Weight-for-age	10-20	50.0	+ 6.06	All-aged	8-32	25.0	- 1.67
Totals	24-45	53.3	+ 9.95	Totals	10-37	27.0	- 0.42
All favs	34-82	41.5	+ 9.53				

MALLOW

Leading Trainers 1990-94

	Total W-R	Non-handicaps 2-y-o	3-y-o+	Handicaps 2-y-o	3-y-o+	Per cent	£1 Level Stake
J S Bolger	13-52	7-15	3-23	1-2	2-12	25.0	+ 2.83
John M Oxx	11-33	3-6	7-23	0-0	1-4	33.3	- 10.39
D K Weld	8-57	2-13	6-34	0-3	0-7	14.0	- 25.84
J J McLoughlin	6-16	0-1	1-5	0-2	5-8	37.5	+ 9.00
Liam Browne	4-16	2-3	1-9	0-0	1-4	25.0	+ 0.30
C Collins	4-21	1-3	3-14	0-0	0-4	19.0	+ 20.50
T Stack	4-45	0-3	3-31	0-1	1-10	8.9	- 32.75
J G Coogan	3-12	1-5	1-4	1-2	0-1	25.0	+ 2.50
P Prendergast	3-20	2-4	1-14	0-0	0-2	15.0	- 12.97
D Gillespie	3-25	1-3	0-10	1-5	1-7	12.0	- 7.90
P J Flynn	3-49	0-13	1-16	0-2	2-18	6.1	- 21.50
J T Gorman	2-20	0-3	0-8	0-1	2-8	10.0	- 2.00
E J O'Grady	2-22	0-4	1-9	1-2	0-7	9.1	- 15.10
M J Grassick	2-27	0-5	2-14	0-1	0-7	7.4	- 3.25
W T Bourke	1-1	0-0	0-0	0-0	1-1	100.0	+ 10.00
E J Kearns	1-1	0-0	0-0	0-0	1-1	100.0	+ 10.00
M J Byrne	1-1	0-0	1-1	0-0	0-0	100.0	+ 4.50
S Treacy	1-2	0-0	0-0	0-0	1-2	50.0	+ 1.25
Henry Cleary	1-2	0-0	1-2	0-0	0-0	50.0	+ 3.00
D T Hughes	1-3	0-1	1-1	0-0	0-1	33.3	+ 2.00
J M Canty	1-3	0-0	0-1	0-0	1-2	33.3	+ 0.50
E O'Connell	1-3	0-0	0-1	0-0	1-2	33.3	0.00

Leading Jockeys

	Total W-R	Per cent	£1 Level Stake	Best Trainer	W-R	Per cent	£1 Level Stake
C Roche	12-55	21.8	+ 15.40	J S Bolger	7-32	21.9	+ 2.10
J P Murtagh	8-31	25.8	- 4.55	John M Oxx	7-15	46.7	+ 0.45
R Hughes	7-33	21.2	+ 8.70	John M Oxx	2-2	100.0	+ 1.40
M J Kinane	6-49	12.2	- 26.84	D K Weld	6-33	18.2	- 10.84
S Craine	6-58	10.3	- 33.25	T Stack	3-33	9.1	- 23.25
N G McCullagh	5-32	15.6	- 7.50	J J McLoughlin	2-5	40.0	+ 1.00
P Shanahan	5-41	12.2	- 22.25	J S Bolger	1-1	100.0	+ 0.50
D G O'Shea	4-20	20.0	+ 1.48	W T Bourke	1-1	100.0	+ 10.00
K J Manning	4-27	14.8	- 11.27	J S Bolger	4-8	50.0	+ 7.73
D V Smith	2-9	22.2	- 1.00	Henry Cleary	1-1	100.0	+ 4.00
B Coogan	2-10	20.0	+ 2.00	J G Coogan	2-7	28.6	+ 5.00
R V Skelly	2-17	11.8	+ 1.50	P Prendergast	1-2	50.0	+ 1.50

How the Favourites Fared

Non-handicaps	W-R	Per cent	£1 Level Stake	Handicaps	W-R	Per cent	£1 Level Stake
2-y-o	15-21	71.4	+ 10.22	2-y-o	2-5	40.0	- 0.40
3-y-o	8-14	57.1	+ 2.92	3-y-o	3-7	42.9	+ 0.18
Weight-for-age	10-27	37.0	- 0.60	All-aged	6-15	40.0	- 0.08
Totals	33-62	53.2	+ 12.54	Totals	11-27	40.7	- 0.30
All favs	44-89	49.4	+ 12.24				

NAAS

Leading Trainers 1990-94

	Total W-R	Non-handicaps 2-y-o	3-y-o+	Handicaps 2-y-o	3-y-o+	Per cent	£1 Level Stake
J S Bolger	30-173	15-52	5-48	5-25	5-48	17.3	- 26.08
D K Weld	30-200	9-47	11-83	1-12	9-58	15.0	- 47.23
John M Oxx	22-101	5-19	11-49	0-4	6-29	21.8	- 6.18
P J Flynn	7-49	1-11	2-8	0-3	4-27	14.3	+ 4.75
C Collins	7-77	4-19	1-28	0-5	2-25	9.1	- 52.08
K Prendergast	7-148	2-39	4-52	0-12	1-45	4.7	-115.00
M J Grassick	5-33	2-8	2-13	0-4	1-8	15.2	- 6.75
Liam Browne	5-38	2-15	2-13	1-3	0-7	13.2	+ 17.50
A P O'Brien	4-22	0-7	1-6	0-1	3-8	18.2	- 2.29
J J McLoughlin	4-39	1-6	1-10	0-4	2-19	10.3	- 6.00
M Kauntze	4-44	0-17	3-11	1-4	0-12	9.1	- 18.50
Noel Meade	4-62	0-13	2-23	0-6	2-20	6.5	- 38.25
W P Mullins	3-17	0-0	2-5	0-0	1-12	17.6	- 3.75
T F Lacy	3-31	0-3	1-15	0-1	2-12	9.7	- 1.00
M A O'Toole	3-32	1-10	1-11	1-2	0-9	9.4	- 13.50
E J O'Grady	3-34	1-7	1-13	1-3	0-11	8.8	- 6.50
F Dunne	3-39	1-10	1-15	0-1	1-13	7.7	- 3.17
T Stack	3-50	0-12	2-24	0-1	1-13	6.0	- 32.00
D Hanley	2-7	0-3	0-1	0-0	2-3	28.6	+ 15.00
P J Deegan	2-10	0-2	0-6	0-0	2-2	20.0	+ 14.00
Augustine Leahy	2-18	0-8	0-3	2-3	0-4	11.1	- 2.00
Edward Lynam	2-37	0-7	1-18	0-5	1-7	5.4	- 11.00

Leading Jockeys

	Total W-R	Per cent	£1 Level Stake	Best Trainer	W-R	Per cent	£1 Level Stake
C Roche	24-90	26.7	+ 11.18	J S Bolger	19-50	38.0	+ 23.85
M J Kinane	19-82	23.2	- 12.74	D K Weld	16-73	21.9	- 15.24
P Shanahan	13-103	12.6	- 22.20	D K Weld	6-45	13.3	- 0.87
J P Murtagh	12-77	15.6	- 7.42	John M Oxx	10-46	21.7	- 4.80
R Hughes	10-93	10.8	- 17.50	M J Grassick	3-9	33.3	+ 5.75
D G O'Shea	8-60	13.3	- 13.63	John M Oxx	4-15	26.7	- 6.63
J F Egan	8-82	9.8	- 19.75	P J Flynn	5-30	16.7	+ 8.25
K J Manning	7-79	8.9	- 38.92	J S Bolger	7-35	20.0	+ 5.08
J J Behan	6-38	15.8	+ 23.50	Liam Browne	3-7	42.9	+ 22.50
R M Burke	6-70	8.6	- 15.92	P J Deegan	2-6	33.3	+ 18.00
W J O'Connor	6-81	7.4	- 24.00	M Kauntze	3-36	8.3	- 18.50
P V Gilson	6-94	6.4	- 68.31	Charles O'Brien	1-4	25.0	+ 2.50

How the Favourites Fared

Non-handicaps	W-R	Per cent	£1 Level Stake	Handicaps	W-R	Per cent	£1 Level Stake
2-y-o	22-49	44.9	- 0.71	2-y-o	1-13	7.7	- 11.70
3-y-o	6-24	25.0	- 8.90	3-y-o	3-11	27.3	- 2.75
Weight-for-age	12-39	30.8	- 9.43	All-aged	14-45	31.1	+ 3.49
Totals	40-112	35.7	- 19.04	Totals	18-69	26.1	- 10.96
All favs	58-181	32.0	- 30.00				

NAVAN

Leading Trainers 1990-94

	Total W-R	Non-handicaps 2-y-o	3-y-o+	Handicaps 2-y-o	3-y-o+	Per cent	£1 Level Stake
J S Bolger	19-90	10-36	5-33	0-0	4-21	21.1	+ 5.62
John M Oxx	12-42	6-14	6-20	0-0	0-8	28.6	- 2.76
M Kauntze	5-32	1-10	3-10	0-0	1-12	15.6	- 8.25
K Prendergast	5-87	1-29	2-24	0-0	2-34	5.7	- 52.40
A P O'Brien	4-18	1-10	2-5	0-0	1-3	22.2	- 2.10
D K Weld	4-82	2-24	2-34	0-0	0-24	4.9	- 56.75
Noel Meade	3-57	1-16	1-22	0-0	1-19	5.3	- 39.00
C Collins	3-58	0-13	2-26	0-0	1-19	5.2	- 33.00
Liam Browne	2-11	2-7	0-3	0-0	0-1	18.2	- 0.50
M Halford	2-15	1-3	1-4	0-0	0-8	13.3	+ 1.00
T F Lacy	2-16	0-3	1-5	0-0	1-8	12.5	- 4.25
D T Hughes	2-21	0-4	0-5	0-0	2-12	9.5	- 1.00
T Stack	2-39	0-13	2-16	0-0	0-10	5.1	- 32.50
M Hourigan	1-1	0-0	0-0	0-0	1-1	100.0	+ 1.25
G M Lyons	1-2	1-2	0-0	0-0	0-0	50.0	+ 7.00
C P Magnier	1-3	0-0	0-0	0-0	1-3	33.3	+ 6.00
D Carroll	1-3	0-1	0-1	0-0	1-1	33.3	+ 12.00
Mrs Ian Fox	1-3	0-0	0-2	0-0	1-1	33.3	+ 12.00
J E Mulhern	1-5	0-1	1-2	0-0	0-2	20.0	+ 3.00
J M Canty	1-7	0-0	1-2	0-0	0-5	14.3	- 2.67
P Mullins	1-7	0-3	1-2	0-0	0-2	14.3	+ 1.00
D Hanley	1-8	0-2	1-5	0-0	0-1	12.5	- 4.75

Leading Jockeys

	Total W-R	Per cent	£1 Level Stake	Best Trainer	W-R	Per cent	£1 Level Stake
C Roche	17-54	31.5	+ 19.04	J S Bolger	12-37	32.4	+ 1.31
J P Murtagh	13-44	29.5	+ 29.90	John M Oxx	8-18	44.4	+ 9.40
K J Manning	7-56	12.5	- 2.95	J S Bolger	5-24	20.8	+ 13.30
W J O'Connor	6-48	12.5	- 17.25	M Kauntze	5-20	25.0	+ 3.75
P V Gilson	4-57	7.0	- 29.62	C Collins	2-24	8.3	- 8.00
S Craine	4-66	6.1	- 48.00	T Stack	2-26	7.7	- 19.50
M Fenton	3-15	20.0	+ 12.00	Noel Meade	1-1	100.0	+ 7.00
M J Kinane	3-51	5.9	- 37.25	D K Weld	2-41	4.9	- 31.75
R Hughes	3-60	5.0	- 45.25	John M Oxx	2-5	40.0	+ 3.25
P P Murphy	2-18	11.1	+ 2.00	D T Hughes	2-7	28.6	+ 13.00
P Carberry	2-24	8.3	- 10.50	A P O'Brien	1-1	100.0	+ 3.50
R M Burke	2-29	6.9	- 4.00	J E Mulhern	1-2	50.0	+ 6.00

How the Favourites Fared

	W-R	Per cent	£1 Level Stake		W-R	Per cent	£1 Level Stake
Non-handicaps				Handicaps			
2-y-o	16-29	55.2	+ 6.28	2-y-o	0-0	-	0.00
3-y-o	6-19	31.6	- 4.52	3-y-o	1-5	20.0	- 1.00
Weight-for-age	9-15	60.0	+ 10.28	All-aged	3-22	13.6	- 11.75
Totals	31-63	49.2	+ 12.04	Totals	4-27	14.8	- 12.75
All favs	35-90	38.9	- 0.71				

PUNCHESTOWN

Leading Trainers 1990-94

	Total W-R	Non-handicaps 2-y-o	3-y-o+	Handicaps 2-y-o	3-y-o+	Per cent	£1 Level Stake
J S Bolger	4-17	3-8	0-7	0-0	1-2	23.5	- 6.54
John M Oxx	2-11	2-5	0-2	0-0	0-4	18.2	- 3.00
M Kauntze	2-11	1-4	0-3	0-0	1-4	18.2	+ 4.00
K Prendergast	2-19	0-6	0-4	0-0	2-9	10.5	- 4.50
M Hourigan	1-1	0-0	1-1	0-0	0-0	100.0	+ 12.00
S Fahey	1-1	0-0	0-0	0-0	1-1	100.0	+ 10.00
Edward Lynam	1-2	0-0	0-0	0-0	1-2	50.0	+ 7.00
J E Mulhern	1-2	0-0	1-2	0-0	0-0	50.0	+ 2.00
Liam Browne	1-5	1-3	0-1	0-0	0-1	20.0	+ 4.00
A P O'Brien	1-6	0-3	0-2	0-0	1-1	16.7	- 0.50
P Mullins	1-9	0-2	1-3	0-0	0-4	11.1	0.00
M J Grassick	1-11	0-5	1-1	0-0	0-5	9.1	+ 2.00
Noel Meade	1-12	0-1	1-4	0-0	0-7	8.3	- 7.00
D K Weld	1-23	0-6	0-8	0-0	1-9	4.3	- 18.00

Leading Jockeys

	Total W-R	Per cent	£1 Level Stake	Best Trainer	W-R	Per cent	£1 Level Stake
J P Murtagh	2-10	20.0	+ 5.00	M Hourigan	1-1	100.0	+ 12.00
W J O'Connor	2-11	18.2	+ 4.00	M Kauntze	2-10	20.0	+ 5.00
C Roche	2-12	16.7	- 3.87	A P O'Brien	1-2	50.0	+ 3.50
K J Manning	2-14	14.3	+ 3.00	M J Grassick	1-3	33.3	+ 10.00
W J Supple	2-18	11.1	- 8.67	J S Bolger	1-2	50.0	- 0.67
A J Beale	1-1	100.0	+ 3.00	J E Mulhern	1-1	100.0	+ 3.00
C Everard	1-3	33.3	- 0.50	J S Bolger	1-2	50.0	+ 0.67
P J Smullen	1-5	20.0	+ 6.00	S Fahey	1-1	100.0	+ 10.00
J A Heffernan	1-8	12.5	+ 1.00	Edward Lynam	1-1	100.0	+ 8.00
P Carberry	1-10	10.0	- 5.00	Noel Meade	1-5	20.0	0.00
S Craine	1-12	8.3	- 3.00	Liam Browne	1-1	100.0	+ 8.00
J F Egan	1-14	7.1	- 11.00				

How the Favourites Fared

Non-handicaps	W-R	Per cent	£1 Level Stake	Handicaps	W-R	Per cent	£1 Level Stake
2-y-o	3-7	42.9	- 1.04	2-y-o	0-0	-	0.00
3-y-o	0-1	-	- 1.00	3-y-o	0-0	-	0.00
Weight-for-age	2-5	40.0	+ 2.00	All-aged	4-8	50.0	+ 11.50
Totals	5-13	38.5	- 0.04	Totals	4-8	50.0	+ 11.50
All favs	9-21	42.9	+ 11.46				

ROSCOMMON

Leading Trainers 1990-94

	Total W-R	Non-handicaps 2-y-o	3-y-o+	Handicaps 2-y-o	3-y-o+	Per cent	£1 Level Stake
J S Bolger	20-110	9-32	5-48	0-2	6-28	18.2	- 15.28
John M Oxx	16-59	4-5	10-40	0-0	2-14	27.1	- 14.83
K Prendergast	15-97	5-20	6-43	0-2	4-32	15.5	+ 12.58
D K Weld	14-101	5-30	5-37	1-2	3-32	13.9	- 27.95
T Stack	10-45	0-7	8-27	0-1	2-10	22.2	+ 17.78
J M Canty	4-22	0-6	1-5	0-0	3-11	18.2	+ 4.50
Noel Meade	4-40	1-9	3-18	0-0	0-13	10.0	- 12.25
J J McLoughlin	3-25	0-8	1-7	0-0	2-10	12.0	+ 5.25
D Gillespie	3-39	0-8	1-9	0-2	2-20	7.7	- 23.00
D G McArdle	2-3	0-0	0-0	0-0	2-3	66.7	+ 21.00
D Hanley	2-8	1-1	1-6	0-0	0-1	25.0	- 0.50
P Prendergast	2-12	0-6	1-3	0-0	1-3	16.7	- 7.73
M Kauntze	2-15	0-4	2-8	0-0	0-3	13.3	- 3.50
P Aspell	2-15	0-0	2-9	0-0	0-6	13.3	+ 5.00
M A O'Toole	2-20	0-4	0-5	0-0	2-11	10.0	+ 2.00
P J Flynn	2-23	1-6	0-7	0-0	1-10	8.7	- 8.00
F Dunne	2-33	0-12	0-11	0-1	2-9	6.1	- 23.50
T J O'Mara	1-1	0-0	0-0	0-0	1-1	100.0	+ 9.00
P Burke	1-2	0-0	0-0	0-1	1-1	50.0	+ 7.00
E P Mitchell	1-2	0-0	0-0	1-1	0-1	50.0	+ 11.00
Mrs P Collier	1-2	0-0	0-0	0-0	1-2	50.0	+ 3.00
Adrian Taylor	1-3	0-1	0-1	0-0	1-1	33.3	+ 4.00

Leading Jockeys

	Total W-R	Per cent	£1 Level Stake	Best Trainer	W-R	Per cent	£1 Level Stake
C Roche	14-61	23.0	+ 9.54	J S Bolger	9-40	22.5	- 3.21
M J Kinane	14-85	16.5	- 28.70	D K Weld	9-64	14.1	- 20.52
W J Supple	11-67	16.4	- 10.00	J S Bolger	5-17	29.4	+ 9.00
S Craine	10-74	13.5	- 18.22	T Stack	8-38	21.1	+ 10.28
J P Murtagh	8-68	11.8	- 41.66	John M Oxx	6-26	23.1	- 8.66
N G McCullagh	6-57	10.5	- 5.75	J J McLoughlin	3-11	27.3	+ 19.25
K J Manning	6-73	8.2	- 36.25	J S Bolger	3-28	10.7	- 9.75
R M Burke	4-31	12.9	- 3.50	K Prendergast	3-10	30.0	+ 13.00
W J O'Connor	4-55	7.3	- 27.00	M Kauntze	2-14	14.3	- 2.50
R Hughes	4-56	7.1	- 31.10	D Hanley	1-1	100.0	+ 1.00
D J O'Donohoe	3-16	18.8	+ 11.00	D K Weld	2-7	28.6	+ 7.00
J J Behan	3-23	13.0	+ 1.38	P Prendergast	1-1	100.0	+ 1.38

How the Favourites Fared

Non-handicaps	W-R	Per cent	£1 Level Stake	Handicaps	W-R	Per cent	£1 Level Stake
2-y-o	9-27	33.3	- 6.35	2-y-o	0-2	-	- 2.00
3-y-o	6-20	30.0	- 6.47	3-y-o	4-12	33.3	- 0.85
Weight-for-age	15-36	41.7	- 3.79	All-aged	4-31	12.9	- 17.32
Totals	30-83	36.1	- 16.61	Totals	8-45	17.8	- 20.17
All favs	38-128	29.7	- 36.78				

SLIGO

Leading Trainers 1990-94

	Total W-R	Non-handicaps 2-y-o	3-y-o+	Handicaps 2-y-o	3-y-o+	Per cent	£1 Level Stake
D K Weld	13-56	4-10	5-29	0-0	4-17	23.2	- 4.60
Noel Meade	8-22	2-7	2-7	0-0	4-8	36.4	+ 2.85
M J Grassick	8-38	2-11	3-16	0-0	3-11	21.1	+ 12.00
P J Flynn	5-19	0-1	2-4	0-0	3-14	26.3	+ 2.88
J S Bolger	4-33	1-10	2-14	0-0	1-9	12.1	+ 5.50
John M Oxx	3-11	0-1	2-8	0-0	1-2	27.3	+ 5.40
C Collins	3-20	3-6	0-9	0-0	0-5	15.0	- 1.00
O Weldon	2-5	0-0	0-2	0-0	2-3	40.0	+ 15.00
M Kauntze	2-6	0-1	1-2	0-0	1-3	33.3	+ 12.00
J Burns	2-6	1-3	1-2	0-0	0-1	33.3	+ 8.00
M Halford	2-7	1-1	1-3	0-0	0-3	28.6	+ 7.00
J T Gorman	2-7	1-1	0-1	0-0	1-5	28.6	+ 17.00
Daniel J Murphy	2-7	0-4	2-3	0-0	0-0	28.6	+ 5.50
J C Hayden	2-10	1-3	1-5	0-0	0-2	20.0	+ 2.25
D Gillespie	2-27	0-5	2-12	0-0	0-10	7.4	- 19.00
K Prendergast	2-30	0-7	1-12	0-0	1-11	6.7	- 22.25
J L Hassett	1-1	0-0	1-1	0-0	0-0	100.0	+ 3.00
I Ferguson	1-1	0-0	0-0	0-0	1-1	100.0	+ 7.00
C P Magnier	1-2	0-0	0-1	0-0	1-1	50.0	+ 3.00
Thomas Bergin	1-2	0-0	1-2	0-0	0-0	50.0	+ 7.00
Anthony Mullins	1-2	0-1	1-1	0-0	0-0	50.0	+ 1.50
L T Reilly	1-3	0-0	0-0	0-0	1-3	33.3	+ 18.00

Leading Jockeys

	Total W-R	Per cent	£1 Level Stake	Best Trainer	W-R	Per cent	£1 Level Stake
M J Kinane	12-42	28.6	+ 5.81	D K Weld	11-35	31.4	+ 10.91
R Hughes	6-33	18.2	- 1.40	Noel Meade	2-4	50.0	+ 1.60
P Shanahan	5-29	17.2	0.00	J Burns	2-3	66.7	+ 11.00
J F Egan	5-32	15.6	- 9.12	P J Flynn	3-10	30.0	+ 1.63
S Craine	5-35	14.3	- 17.50	Noel Meade	2-7	28.6	- 0.50
J A Heffernan	3-15	20.0	+ 15.00	O Weldon	2-3	66.7	+ 17.00
P V Gilson	3-17	17.6	+ 2.00	C Collins	3-12	25.0	+ 7.00
D G O'Shea	3-18	16.7	+ 0.50	E J O'Grady	1-1	100.0	+ 4.00
W J O'Connor	3-21	14.3	+ 10.00	M Kauntze	2-5	40.0	+ 13.00
K J Manning	3-26	11.5	- 3.50	J S Bolger	2-13	15.4	+ 0.50
W J Supple	3-38	7.9	- 21.00	M J Grassick	1-1	100.0	+ 6.00
N G McCullagh	3-40	7.5	- 25.00	Noel Meade	2-2	100.0	+ 6.00

How the Favourites Fared

Non-handicaps	W-R	Per cent	£1 Level Stake	Handicaps	W-R	Per cent	£1 Level Stake
2-y-o	7-19	36.8	- 4.05	2-y-o	0-0	-	0.00
3-y-o	6-14	42.9	+ 1.71	3-y-o	0-1	-	- 1.00
Weight-for-age	7-22	31.8	- 2.97	All-aged	6-28	21.4	- 11.90
Totals	20-55	36.4	- 5.31	Totals	6-29	20.7	- 12.90
All favs	26-84	31.0	- 18.21				

708

THURLES

Leading Trainers 1990-94

	Total W-R	Non-handicaps 2-y-o	3-y-o+	Handicaps 2-y-o	3-y-o+	Per cent	£1 Level Stake
J S Bolger	5-21	0-0	4-17	0-0	1-4	23.8	+ 26.50
P J Flynn	3-19	0-0	3-13	0-0	0-6	15.8	- 8.55
D K Weld	3-21	0-0	2-18	0-0	1-3	14.3	+ 11.75
E J O'Grady	2-6	0-0	1-4	0-0	1-2	33.3	+ 7.25
John M Oxx	2-7	0-0	2-7	0-0	0-0	28.6	+ 0.50
Noel Meade	2-9	0-0	2-8	0-0	0-1	22.2	+ 5.00
P Mullins	2-15	0-0	2-9	0-0	0-6	13.3	+ 3.00
F Flood	1-3	0-0	0-0	0-0	1-3	33.3	- 0.25
Daniel J Murphy	1-5	0-0	0-1	0-0	1-4	20.0	+ 1.50
K Prendergast	1-8	0-0	1-6	0-0	0-2	12.5	- 4.25
A J McNamara	1-8	0-0	0-3	0-0	1-5	12.5	- 1.00
T Stack	1-8	0-0	1-6	0-0	0-2	12.5	- 6.27
Pat O'Leary	1-9	0-0	1-5	0-0	0-4	11.1	+ 6.00

Leading Jockeys

	Total W-R	Per cent	£1 Level Stake	Best Trainer	W-R	Per cent	£1 Level Stake
M J Kinane	3-9	33.3	+ 5.00	F Flood	1-1	100.0	+ 1.75
P Shanahan	3-15	20.0	+ 15.75	D K Weld	2-7	28.6	+ 16.75
K J Manning	2-11	18.2	- 1.50	J S Bolger	2-3	66.7	+ 6.50
C Roche	2-17	11.8	- 1.50	Daniel J Murphy	1-1	100.0	+ 5.50
G Coogan	1-1	100.0	+ 4.00	P Mullins	1-1	100.0	+ 4.00
M Duffy	1-3	33.3	- 1.27	P J Flynn	1-2	50.0	- 0.27
M F Ryan	1-3	33.3	+ 2.00	Noel Meade	1-1	100.0	+ 4.00
A P McCoy	1-3	33.3	+ 18.00	J S Bolger	1-2	50.0	+ 19.00
T E Durcan	1-4	25.0	+ 4.00	J S Bolger	1-1	100.0	+ 7.00
C Everard	1-5	20.0	+ 6.00	E J O'Grady	1-1	100.0	+ 4.00
T P Treacy	1-5	20.0	+ 8.00	P Mullins	1-3	33.3	+ 10.00
J J Behan	1-6	16.7	+ 1.00	A J McNamara	1-1	100.0	+ 6.00

How the Favourites Fared

Non-handicaps	W-R	Per cent	£1 Level Stake	Handicaps	W-R	Per cent	£1 Level Stake
2-y-o	0-0	-	0.00	2-y-o	0-0	-	0.00
3-y-o	2-8	25.0	- 4.02	3-y-o	0-0	-	0.00
Weight-for-age	3-12	25.0	- 6.04	All-aged	2-8	25.0	- 2.50
Totals	5-20	25.0	- 10.06	Totals	2-8	25.0	- 2.50
All favs	7-28	25.0	- 12.56				

TIPPERARY

Leading Trainers 1990-94

	Total W-R	Non-handicaps 2-y-o	Non-handicaps 3-y-o+	Handicaps 2-y-o	Handicaps 3-y-o+	Per cent	£1 Level Stake
D K Weld	35-177	7-43	22-95	1-2	5-37	19.8	- 44.28
J S Bolger	33-175	14-54	11-88	1-3	7-30	18.9	- 60.49
John M Oxx	25-87	6-15	18-61	0-0	1-11	28.7	+ 3.67
K Prendergast	16-118	6-33	7-59	0-0	3-26	13.6	- 25.88
T Stack	12-96	3-16	7-60	1-4	1-16	12.5	- 20.94
Noel Meade	8-47	2-13	4-20	0-0	2-14	17.0	- 13.63
D Gillespie	6-36	2-13	3-9	0-1	1-13	16.7	+ 9.63
C Collins	6-53	2-16	4-27	0-1	0-9	11.3	- 33.43
M Kauntze	5-33	1-6	2-17	0-0	2-10	15.2	- 15.00
A P O'Brien	5-36	1-13	3-15	0-0	1-8	13.9	- 13.10
M J Grassick	4-25	2-4	2-16	0-0	0-5	16.0	+ 1.23
Augustine Leahy	4-56	0-18	2-24	0-0	2-14	7.1	- 34.75
B V Kelly	3-15	0-0	0-8	0-0	3-7	20.0	+ 15.00
J G Coogan	3-21	3-14	0-3	0-1	0-3	14.3	- 4.50
Anthony Mullins	2-5	0-1	1-3	0-0	1-1	40.0	+ 3.25
J Berry (Eng)	2-5	0-0	2-5	0-0	0-0	40.0	+ 5.00
D Hanley	2-7	0-1	2-4	0-0	0-2	28.6	+ 8.10
Daniel J Murphy	2-16	0-3	1-10	0-0	1-3	12.5	+ 4.00
J M Canty	2-20	0-7	1-6	0-0	1-7	10.0	- 6.50
P Prendergast	2-21	0-7	1-10	0-0	1-4	9.5	- 13.40
J Burns	2-24	1-11	1-10	0-0	0-3	8.3	- 12.75
P Mullins	2-32	0-11	2-10	0-0	0-11	6.3	- 10.00

Leading Jockeys

	Total W-R	Per cent	£1 Level Stake	Best Trainer	W-R	Per cent	£1 Level Stake
M J Kinane	34-130	26.2	+ 2.75	D K Weld	30-105	28.6	+ 13.05
C Roche	26-117	22.2	- 31.22	J S Bolger	18-73	24.7	- 24.00
J P Murtagh	22-81	27.2	+ 22.33	John M Oxx	16-37	43.2	+ 18.33
S Craine	17-132	12.9	- 31.96	T Stack	11-71	15.5	+ 0.06
K J Manning	16-85	18.8	+ 20.87	J S Bolger	12-46	26.1	+ 9.37
W J Supple	10-91	11.0	- 27.20	K Prendergast	5-34	14.7	- 1.30
P Shanahan	10-103	9.7	- 55.58	D K Weld	5-45	11.1	- 30.33
P V Gilson	9-95	9.5	- 51.68	C Collins	5-30	16.7	- 15.43
R Hughes	7-68	10.3	- 28.37	John M Oxx	5-10	50.0	+ 16.63
W J O'Connor	5-68	7.4	- 43.50	M Kauntze	4-25	16.0	- 9.50
P Carberry	4-30	13.3	- 14.00	Anthony Mullins	2-2	100.0	+ 6.25
N G McCullagh	4-79	5.1	- 48.25	J E Mulhern	1-1	100.0	+ 2.50

How the Favourites Fared

Non-handicaps	W-R	Per cent	£1 Level Stake	Handicaps	W-R	Per cent	£1 Level Stake
2-y-o	27-56	48.2	- 2.14	2-y-o	3-3	100.0	+ 3.10
3-y-o	14-31	45.2	+ 2.29	3-y-o	5-9	55.6	+ 6.25
Weight-for-age	36-78	46.2	- 0.56	All-aged	13-39	33.3	- 6.77
Totals	77-165	46.7	- 0.41	Totals	21-51	41.2	+ 2.58
All favs	98-216	45.4	+ 2.17				

TRALEE

Leading Trainers 1990-94

	Total W-R	Non-handicaps 2-y-o	3-y-o+	Handicaps 2-y-o	3-y-o+	Per cent	£1 Level Stake
D K Weld	33-102	7-14	12-38	1-5	13-45	32.4	+ 10.96
J S Bolger	17-111	9-22	3-43	1-5	4-41	15.3	- 35.18
John M Oxx	12-43	1-3	10-27	0-0	1-13	27.9	- 8.20
C Collins	7-53	1-11	4-20	0-0	2-22	13.2	- 15.35
Augustine Leahy	5-51	0-12	0-14	0-4	5-21	9.8	- 25.00
T Stack	5-57	1-8	2-23	0-2	2-24	8.8	- 36.33
D Gillespie	4-23	1-6	3-5	0-2	0-10	17.4	+ 1.75
K Prendergast	4-33	0-2	1-9	1-4	2-18	12.1	+ 4.00
M Cunningham	3-12	0-0	0-3	0-0	3-9	25.0	+ 10.00
M Kauntze	3-15	1-2	2-5	0-0	0-8	20.0	- 0.20
A P O'Brien	3-16	0-0	0-7	0-0	3-9	18.8	+ 0.50
P Prendergast	3-28	1-8	0-6	0-1	2-13	10.7	- 16.25
M McDonagh	2-5	0-2	0-0	0-0	2-3	40.0	+ 8.75
M Hourigan	2-7	0-0	0-2	0-0	2-5	28.6	+ 11.00
P Mullins	2-10	0-2	1-3	0-1	1-4	20.0	+ 6.00
Noel Meade	2-20	0-1	1-4	0-1	1-14	10.0	- 12.00
P J Flynn	2-37	0-7	1-5	0-2	1-23	5.4	- 31.00
B Lawlor	1-1	0-0	1-1	0-0	0-0	100.0	+ 4.50
W P Browne	1-3	0-0	1-2	0-0	0-1	33.3	- 0.50
A D Evans	1-4	0-0	0-0	0-0	1-4	25.0	+ 11.00
P Henley	1-4	0-0	0-2	0-0	1-2	25.0	+ 4.00
H De Bromhead	1-4	0-1	0-1	0-0	1-2	25.0	+ 5.00

Leading Jockeys

	Total W-R	Per cent	£1 Level Stake	Best Trainer	W-R	Per cent	£1 Level Stake
M J Kinane	30-88	34.1	+ 16.69	D K Weld	26-71	36.6	+ 13.94
J P Murtagh	10-54	18.5	- 7.73	John M Oxx	5-17	29.4	- 4.48
C Roche	8-62	12.9	- 40.53	J S Bolger	6-37	16.2	- 24.86
W J Supple	8-65	12.3	- 18.65	J S Bolger	3-13	23.1	- 3.90
P V Gilson	7-41	17.1	+ 3.65	C Collins	5-19	26.3	+ 9.15
K J Manning	6-53	11.3	- 24.99	J S Bolger	4-23	17.4	+ 0.58
S Craine	6-68	8.8	- 38.25	T Stack	3-38	7.9	- 21.75
R M Burke	5-34	14.7	+ 23.00	M Hourigan	1-1	100.0	+ 10.00
P Shanahan	5-54	9.3	- 37.35	D K Weld	2-10	20.0	- 2.60
W J Smith	4-32	12.5	+ 25.50	Edward Lynam	1-2	50.0	+ 19.00
D Hogan	3-12	25.0	- 3.93	John M Oxx	3-7	42.9	+ 1.07
J A Heffernan	3-20	15.0	+ 5.50	J S Bolger	3-11	27.3	+ 14.50

How the Favourites Fared

Non-handicaps	W-R	Per cent	£1 Level Stake	Handicaps	W-R	Per cent	£1 Level Stake
2-y-o	14-25	56.0	+ 1.15	2-y-o	1-5	20.0	- 2.25
3-y-o	4-8	50.0	+ 1.30	3-y-o	1-3	33.3	+ 1.33
Weight-for-age	23-40	57.5	+ 12.22	All-aged	16-57	28.1	- 16.85
Totals	41-73	56.2	+ 14.67	Totals	18-65	27.7	- 17.77
All favs	59-138	42.8	- 3.10				

TRAMORE

Leading Trainers 1990-94

	Total W-R	Non-handicaps 2-y-o	3-y-o+	Handicaps 2-y-o	3-y-o+	Per cent	£1 Level Stake
K Prendergast	7-29	0-0	3-13	0-0	4-16	24.1	+ 7.40
C Collins	6-18	0-0	3-8	0-0	3-10	33.3	+ 12.88
T Stack	5-10	0-0	4-8	0-0	1-2	50.0	+ 16.75
P Mullins	4-17	0-0	3-8	0-0	1-9	23.5	- 8.47
W P Mullins	4-19	0-0	1-8	0-0	3-11	21.1	- 1.25
D K Weld	4-31	0-0	4-22	0-0	0-9	12.9	- 16.20
A P O'Brien	3-15	0-0	1-7	0-0	2-8	20.0	- 4.10
Daniel J Murphy	3-16	0-0	2-11	0-0	1-5	18.8	+ 6.50
M A McCullagh	2-2	0-0	0-0	0-0	2-2	100.0	+ 5.50
P Prendergast	2-4	0-0	1-2	0-0	1-2	50.0	+ 11.10
E P Harty	2-4	0-0	2-4	0-0	0-0	50.0	+ 33.00
John M Oxx	2-5	0-0	2-4	0-0	0-1	40.0	- 0.70
Liam Browne	2-6	0-0	1-3	0-0	1-3	33.3	- 1.27
W P Browne	2-9	0-0	2-6	0-0	0-3	22.2	+ 0.67
Edward Lynam	2-13	0-0	1-6	0-0	1-7	15.4	- 1.00
Augustine Leahy	2-22	0-0	2-12	0-0	0-10	9.1	- 1.00
P J Flynn	2-23	0-0	1-7	0-0	1-16	8.7	- 17.25
Mrs John Harrington	1-1	0-0	1-1	0-0	0-0	100.0	+ 8.00
A L T Moore	1-2	0-0	1-2	0-0	0-0	50.0	+ 0.25
John J Walsh	1-2	0-0	0-0	0-0	1-2	50.0	+ 4.00
Mrs P Collier	1-2	0-0	1-2	0-0	0-0	50.0	+ 15.00
V Kennedy	1-3	0-0	1-2	0-0	0-1	33.3	+ 0.25

Leading Jockeys

	Total W-R	Per cent	£1 Level Stake	Best Trainer	W-R	Per cent	£1 Level Stake
J J Behan	9-32	28.1	+ 10.40	P Mullins	2-4	50.0	- 0.33
P V Gilson	6-19	31.6	+ 17.25	C Collins	4-10	40.0	+ 14.25
R Hughes	6-30	20.0	+ 3.15	W P Browne	2-2	100.0	+ 7.67
S Craine	4-16	25.0	+ 7.50	T Stack	4-7	57.1	+ 16.50
J P Murtagh	4-20	20.0	+ 7.30	John M Oxx	2-3	66.7	+ 1.30
D G O'Shea	4-24	16.7	+ 4.00	W P Mullins	1-1	100.0	+ 4.00
W J Smith	4-34	11.8	- 17.33	D K Weld	2-9	22.2	+ 1.00
N G McCullagh	4-46	8.7	- 26.75	M A McCullagh	1-1	100.0	+ 4.00
B J Walsh	3-13	23.1	+ 0.40	K Prendergast	3-7	42.9	+ 6.40
C Everard	2-9	22.2	+ 1.00	E P Harty	1-1	100.0	+ 2.00
D J O'Donohoe	2-12	16.7	- 7.20	D K Weld	2-8	25.0	- 3.20
G M Moylan	2-12	16.7	- 2.75	Augustine Leahy	1-1	100.0	+ 5.00

How the Favourites Fared

Non-handicaps	W-R	Per cent	£1 Level Stake	Handicaps	W-R	Per cent	£1 Level Stake
2-y-o	0-0	-	0.00	2-y-o	0-0	-	0.00
3-y-o	2-7	28.6	- 2.25	3-y-o	2-2	100.0	+ 3.00
Weight-for-age	21-38	55.3	+ 9.38	All-aged	13-38	34.2	- 4.69
Totals	23-45	51.1	+ 7.13	Totals	15-40	37.5	- 1.69
All favs	38-85	44.7	+ 5.44				

WEXFORD

Leading Trainers 1990-94

	Total W-R	Non-handicaps 2-y-o	Non-handicaps 3-y-o+	Handicaps 2-y-o	Handicaps 3-y-o+	Per cent	£1 Level Stake
John M Oxx	17-30	0-0	14-24	0-0	3-6	56.7	+ 18.93
A P O'Brien	7-19	0-0	2-5	0-0	5-14	36.8	+ 4.60
J S Bolger	6-42	0-0	4-25	0-0	2-17	14.3	- 14.85
P Mullins	5-23	0-0	2-11	0-0	3-12	21.7	+ 5.08
M J Grassick	3-13	0-0	2-8	0-0	1-5	23.1	+ 1.00
K Prendergast	3-17	0-0	2-10	0-0	1-7	17.6	- 5.33
P J Flynn	3-20	0-0	0-5	0-0	3-15	15.0	+ 5.50
J J McLoughlin	2-6	0-0	0-2	0-0	2-4	33.3	+ 13.50
Noel Meade	2-8	0-0	1-3	0-0	1-5	25.0	+ 0.67
C Collins	2-9	0-0	2-5	0-0	0-4	22.2	+ 8.00
A J McNamara	1-1	0-0	0-0	0-0	1-1	100.0	+ 4.50
F Flood	1-3	0-0	1-1	0-0	0-2	33.3	+ 2.50
M J P O'Brien	1-3	0-0	1-3	0-0	0-0	33.3	+ 0.50
M A O'Toole	1-4	0-0	0-0	0-0	1-4	25.0	+ 3.00
J Morrison	1-4	0-0	0-0	0-0	1-4	25.0	+ 5.00
Francis Ennis	1-5	0-0	0-0	0-0	1-5	20.0	+ 1.00
T Walker	1-6	0-0	0-1	0-0	1-5	16.7	+ 3.00
E J O'Grady	1-8	0-0	0-6	0-0	1-2	12.5	+ 3.00
J C Harley	1-8	0-0	0-2	0-0	1-6	12.5	0.00
Augustine Leahy	1-9	0-0	1-5	0-0	0-4	11.1	- 5.50
J M Canty	1-13	0-0	1-3	0-0	0-10	7.7	- 11.56

Leading Jockeys

	Total W-R	Per cent	£1 Level Stake	Best Trainer	W-R	Per cent	£1 Level Stake
J P Murtagh	14-32	43.8	+ 8.93	John M Oxx	11-17	64.7	+ 9.18
C Roche	6-26	23.1	- 7.90	A P O'Brien	4-8	50.0	+ 5.60
K J Manning	5-22	22.7	- 3.85	J S Bolger	3-12	25.0	- 4.35
D G O'Shea	3-13	23.1	- 1.25	John M Oxx	2-2	100.0	+ 6.25
M J Kinane	3-14	21.4	+ 0.50	John M Oxx	2-2	100.0	+ 5.50
S Craine	3-23	13.0	- 10.06	P Mullins	2-4	50.0	+ 7.50
J F Egan	3-27	11.1	- 5.75	P J Flynn	2-10	20.0	+ 9.00
J R Barry	2-11	18.2	+ 2.33	P Mullins	2-5	40.0	+ 8.33
P V Gilson	2-19	10.5	- 2.00	C Collins	2-6	33.3	+ 11.00
R Hughes	2-23	8.7	- 15.17	Noel Meade	1-2	50.0	+ 2.33
Mrs S McCarthy	1-2	50.0	+ 1.25	P Mullins	1-2	50.0	+ 1.25
Miss F M Crowley	1-2	50.0	+ 2.50	A P O'Brien	1-2	50.0	+ 2.50

How the Favourites Fared

Non-handicaps	W-R	Per cent	£1 Level Stake	Handicaps	W-R	Per cent	£1 Level Stake
2-y-o	0-0	-	0.00	2-y-o	0-0	-	0.00
3-y-o	4-10	40.0	- 0.71	3-y-o	3-4	75.0	+ 2.50
Weight-for-age	13-24	54.2	+ 1.65	All-aged	9-25	36.0	+ 4.68
Totals	17-34	50.0	+ 0.94	Totals	12-29	41.4	+ 7.18
All favs	29-63	46.0	+ 8.12				

TRAINERS' FAVOURITES AT THE CURRAGH 1990-94

	Total W-R	Non-handicaps 2-y-o	3-y-o+	Handicaps 2-y-o	3-y-o+	Per cent	£1 Level Stake
J S Bolger	49-119	25-51	17-39	1-5	6-24	41.2	+ 0.89
D K Weld	34-130	10-35	14-41	1-3	9-51	26.2	- 25.87
John M Oxx	30-103	9-24	14-47	0-0	7-32	29.1	- 14.78
K Prendergast	12-24	2-6	6-10	1-2	3-6	50.0	+ 20.28
C Collins	7-25	1-1	2-5	0-2	4-17	28.0	+ 5.00
P J Flynn	4-9	0-0	0-1	0-0	4-8	44.4	+ 19.50
M Kauntze	4-17	1-3	3-12	0-0	0-2	23.5	- 7.83
A P O'Brien	3-8	0-0	1-3	0-0	2-5	37.5	+ 4.75
P F I Cole (Eng)	3-9	0-1	3-8	0-0	0-0	33.3	- 1.37
R Hannon (Eng)	2-2	0-0	2-2	0-0	0-0	100.0	+ 2.63
P T Walwyn (Eng)	2-2	0-0	2-2	0-0	0-0	100.0	+ 2.67
M S Johnston (Eng)	2-3	2-2	0-0	0-0	0-1	66.7	+ 3.40
C E Brittain (Eng)	2-4	1-2	1-2	0-0	0-0	50.0	- 0.17
P Chapple-Hyam (Eng)	2-5	0-2	2-3	0-0	0-0	40.0	- 1.02
B W Hills (Eng)	2-6	0-0	1-5	0-0	1-1	33.3	+ 1.00
J H M Gosden (Eng)	2-6	0-1	2-5	0-0	0-0	33.3	- 0.25
T Stack	2-13	1-2	0-4	0-0	1-7	15.4	- 7.20
P Prendergast	2-14	0-2	1-3	1-2	0-7	14.3	- 6.10
I A Balding (Eng)	1-1	1-1	0-0	0-0	0-0	100.0	+ 1.75
W R Hern (Eng)	1-1	0-0	1-1	0-0	0-0	100.0	+ 1.50
H T Jones (Eng)	1-1	0-0	1-1	0-0	0-0	100.0	+ 1.10
F Boutin (Fra)	1-1	0-0	1-1	0-0	0-0	100.0	+ 0.90
G Wragg (Eng)	1-1	0-0	1-1	0-0	0-0	100.0	+ 0.80
J L Dunlop (Eng)	1-2	1-2	0-0	0-0	0-0	50.0	- 0.38

TRAINERS' FAVOURITES AT LEOPARDSTOWN 1990-94

	Total W-R	Non-handicaps 2-y-o	3-y-o+	Handicaps 2-y-o	3-y-o+	Per cent	£1 Level Stake
D K Weld	50-141	7-23	32-67	0-1	11-50	35.5	- 1.26
J S Bolger	46-112	18-42	16-39	4-7	8-24	41.1	+ 0.80
John M Oxx	30-72	8-12	16-40	0-0	6-20	41.7	+ 12.77
K Prendergast	5-20	0-2	2-4	1-1	2-13	25.0	- 4.77
M Kauntze	3-18	1-6	2-7	0-1	0-4	16.7	- 9.75
M A O'Toole	2-3	0-0	1-1	1-1	0-1	66.7	+ 2.50
Charles O'Brien	2-6	0-2	2-4	0-0	0-0	33.3	- 1.40
C Collins	2-7	0-1	2-5	0-0	0-1	28.6	- 1.43
T Stack	2-7	0-0	1-4	0-0	1-3	28.6	+ 2.25
Noel Meade	2-8	1-2	1-2	0-0	0-4	25.0	- 3.22
H R A Cecil (Eng)	1-1	0-0	1-1	0-0	0-0	100.0	+ 0.50
P F I Cole (Eng)	1-1	0-0	1-1	0-0	0-0	100.0	+ 3.00
J Berry (Eng)	1-1	1-1	0-0	0-0	0-0	100.0	+ 0.53
B V Kelly	1-2	0-0	1-1	0-0	0-1	50.0	+ 1.25
B W Hills (Eng)	1-2	0-0	1-2	0-0	0-0	50.0	+ 0.75
J E Hammond (Fra)	1-2	0-0	1-2	0-0	0-0	50.0	- 0.33
M R Channon (Eng)	1-2	0-0	1-2	0-0	0-0	50.0	+ 2.00
P Chapple-Hyam (Eng)	1-2	1-2	0-0	0-0	0-0	50.0	+ 0.75
P Prendergast	1-3	0-0	0-0	0-0	1-3	33.3	+ 1.50
J J McLoughlin	1-3	0-0	1-1	0-0	0-2	33.3	+ 0.50
J M Canty	1-3	0-0	1-2	0-0	0-1	33.3	- 1.20
R Hannon (Eng)	1-3	1-2	0-1	0-0	0-0	33.3	0.00
M R Stoute (Eng)	1-4	1-2	0-2	0-0	0-0	25.0	- 1.75
P J Flynn	1-6	0-1	1-2	0-0	0-3	16.7	- 3.50

TOP PERCENTAGE COURSES FOR FAVOURITES 1990-94

	W-R	Per cent	£1 Level Stake		W-R	Per cent	£1 Level Stake
Mallow	44-89	49.4	+ 12.24	Navan	35-90	38.9	- 0.71
Killarney	50-108	46.3	- 0.93	Gowran	63-165	38.2	- 14.28
Wexford	29-63	46.0	+ 8.12	Downpatrick	15-40	37.5	- 5.42
Tipperary	98-216	45.4	+ 2.17	Leopardstown	173-467	37.0	- 51.13
Bellewstown	27-60	45.0	+ 10.76	Ballinrobe	28-78	35.9	+ 0.28
Phoenix	47-105	44.8	+ 0.86	Galway	64-180	35.6	- 22.27
Tramore	38-85	44.7	+ 5.44	The Curragh	212-635	33.4	- 67.28
Punchestown	9-21	42.9	+ 11.46	Limerick	21-63	33.3	- 18.58
Tralee	59-138	42.8	- 3.10	Naas	58-181	32.0	- 30.00
Clonmel	29-68	42.6	- 1.32	Sligo	26-84	31.0	- 18.21
Dundalk	59-140	42.1	- 4.96	Roscommon	38-128	29.7	- 36.78
Down Royal	47-112	42.0	- 6.35	Laytown	7-26	26.9	- 7.88
Fairyhouse	40-96	41.7	- 1.55	Thurles	7-28	25.0	- 12.56
Listowel	34-82	41.5	+ 9.53				

FAVOURITES' PERFORMANCE BY TYPE OF RACE 1990-94

Non-h'caps	W-R	Per cent	£1 Level Stake	Handicaps	W-R	Per cent	£1 Level Stake
2-y-o	360-761	47.3	- 9.94	2-y-o	29-87	33.3	- 5.95
3-y-o	181-450	40.2	- 44.99	3-y-o	55-167	32.9	- 13.09
Weight/age	446-1039	42.9	- 18.60	All-aged	286-1044	27.4	-149.88
Totals	987-2250	43.9	- 73.53	Totals	370-1298	28.5	-168.92
All Favs	1357-3548	38.2	- 242.45				

When there is more than one favourite in a race then the £1 stake has been equally divided on each one. Only one favourite is counted for each race.

FOR SALE

A unique opportunity to obtain all, or part, of a Bloodstock Breeding and Racing library gathered over the last 35 years.

General Stud Books 1897–1988 (Vols 19–41)
American Stud Books 1946–1990 (Vols 20; 22–30 + 5 supplements)
French Stud Books 1947–1991 (Vols 28–43)
German Stud Books 1929–1987 (Vols 19–32)
Italian Stud Books 1956–1987 (Vols 18, 19; 21–25)
Statistical Abstract 1958–1971 (13 specially bound volumes)
Statistical Record 1971–1993 (23 leather bound vols)
Statistical Record Jump Annuals 1985–1992/93 (9 vols)
Abrege des Courses Plates (*France*) 1966–1991 (26 vols)
Thoroughbred Times Statistical Review (*USA*) 1988–1992 (5 vols)
Thoroughbred Times Sires of Winners (*USA*) 1989–1992 (4 vols)
Registered Thoroughbred Names (*Lexington*) 1988
Bloodstock Breeders' Annual Review 1959–1981 (22 vols)
Non-Thoroughbred Register 1974–1993 (20 vols)
Register of Thoroughbred Stallions 1954–1983 (15 vols + 9 supps)
Weatherbys Stallion Book 1985–1994 (10 vols)
Sires for 1990–1994 (5 vols)
Etalons de Pur Sang (*France*) 1957; 1971/72; 1979–1990 (11 vols + 7 supps)
Stalloni Purosangue (*Italy*) 1971–1980 (3 vols)
Thoroughbred Times Stallion Directory (*USA*) 1989–1992 (4 vols)
Keylock's Dams of Winners 1915–1989 (7 vols)
Mares de Gagnants (*France*) 1941–1987 (7 vols)
American Produce Records 1930–1991 (2 sets, 30 vols, both in binders)
Pedigrees of Leading Winners 1912–1984 (3 vols + supp)
Bend Or Graded & Group Winners 1973–1990 (2 vols)
Pattern Races/Thoroughbred Breeder Magazine 1978–1994 (14 vols in binders)
Timeform 'Racehorses of' 1960–1993 (34 vols)
Timeform 'Chasers and Hurdlers' 1988/89–1993/94 (6 vols)
Directory of the Turf/Turf Directory 1976; 1980; 1984–1994 (12 vols)
Raceform Annuals 1982–1991 (10 vols)
Chaseform Annual 1992/93 only
French Races Past (*Flat*) 1965; 1966; 1969–1990 (24 vols, many leather bound)

Inspection of all volumes welcomed

Please contact Martin Pickering by telephone, or Fax, on (01707) 655269, or write to 69 Northlands, Potters Bar, Hertfordshire EN6 5JD.

IRISH TRAINER SUMMARIES

WINNING FLAT TRAINERS IN IRELAND 1994

	Total W-R	2-y-o	3-y-o	4-y-o+	Per cent	£1 Level Stake
J S Bolger	108-589	42-188	40-236	26-165	18.3	+ 49.82
D K Weld	100-612	35-155	40-300	25-157	16.3	-221.65
John M Oxx	63-282	13-33	48-232	2-17	22.3	+ 28.76
A P O'Brien	47-343	5-59	22-152	20-132	13.7	- 88.36
C Collins	29-246	8-68	14-124	7-54	11.8	- 54.98
P J Flynn	27-218	4-44	10-86	13-88	12.4	- 32.04
K Prendergast	25-355	8-97	11-177	6-81	7.0	-169.85
Noel Meade	21-201	6-52	11-108	4-41	10.4	- 71.97
T Stack	19-219	2-44	15-134	2-41	8.7	- 96.60
M Kauntze	14-131	3-27	6-80	5-24	10.7	- 48.79
J J McLoughlin	9-104	2-21	7-61	0-22	8.7	- 6.75
J Burns	8-123	0-6	5-97	3-20	6.5	- 59.50
J M Canty	7-75	0-5	2-12	5-58	9.3	- 18.00
P Prendergast	7-80	1-18	1-31	5-31	8.8	- 29.89
Augustine Leahy	7-101	2-32	5-37	0-32	6.9	- 62.42
M Hourigan	6-34	0-2	0-0	6-32	17.6	+ 6.88
D Hanley	6-72	1-20	4-37	1-15	8.3	- 29.00
Daniel J Murphy	6-82	1-14	2-55	3-13	7.3	- 30.00
J G Coogan	6-98	3-19	3-71	0-8	6.1	- 64.40
D Gillespie	6-113	2-41	2-48	2-24	5.3	- 72.00
M Cunningham	5-17	0-3	0-2	5-12	29.4	- 0.25
E J O'Grady	5-56	1-13	1-16	3-27	8.9	- 15.00
Edward Lynam	5-73	0-23	1-29	4-21	6.8	- 39.50
Charles O'Brien	5-93	2-17	2-67	1-9	5.4	- 73.15
M V O'Brien	4-6	0-0	0-0	4-6	66.7	+ 8.63
M A McCullagh	4-20	0-0	0-6	4-14	20.0	+ 3.00
D G McArdle	4-29	0-0	0-2	4-27	13.8	+ 21.00
Anthony Mullins	4-33	1-5	2-19	1-9	12.1	- 14.35
J C Harley	4-46	0-4	0-17	4-25	8.7	- 5.90
P Mullins	4-64	0-10	1-19	3-35	6.3	- 41.00
M J Grassick	4-72	2-21	1-50	1-1	5.6	- 37.77
P Aspell	4-95	0-0	2-64	2-31	4.2	- 69.25
M S Johnston (Eng)	3-4	3-4	0-0	0-0	75.0	+ 6.90
A J McNamara	3-10	0-0	0-2	3-8	30.0	+ 19.50
V Bowens	3-17	0-0	2-7	1-10	17.6	+ 4.00
Wilbert Tolerton	3-18	0-0	0-3	3-15	16.7	+ 21.40
Oliver Finnegan	3-20	0-0	0-0	3-20	15.0	+ 7.00
V Kennedy	3-39	0-1	0-4	3-34	7.7	- 21.75
M Halford	3-61	0-6	3-43	0-12	4.9	- 41.00
M A O'Toole	3-71	0-6	3-55	0-10	4.2	- 48.00
I Ferguson	2-6	0-0	0-0	2-6	33.3	+ 7.00
R Hannon (Eng)	2-9	0-3	0-3	2-3	22.2	+ 3.38
T Walker	2-10	0-0	0-0	2-10	20.0	+ 10.00
W T Bourke	2-12	0-0	0-0	2-12	16.7	+ 7.00
J E Kiely	2-13	0-0	0-4	2-9	15.4	- 8.25
P J Deegan	2-16	0-4	0-0	2-12	12.5	+ 8.00
W M Roper	2-22	0-0	1-15	1-7	9.1	+ 8.00
F Doyle	2-22	0-0	0-0	2-22	9.1	+ 6.00
T A Regan	2-23	1-11	1-11	0-1	8.7	- 1.00
T O'Neill	2-24	0-3	0-10	2-11	8.3	- 3.75
Adrian Taylor	2-24	0-0	0-4	2-20	8.3	- 12.50
Miss I T Oakes	2-26	0-1	2-10	0-15	7.7	- 14.25
F Flood	2-29	0-3	0-3	2-23	6.9	- 18.00
D P Kelly	2-35	0-0	0-7	2-28	5.7	- 12.00

718

	Total W-R	2-y-o	3-y-o	4-y-o+	Per cent	£1 Level Stake
Noel T Chance	2-38	0-0	1-27	1-11	5.3	- 22.00
Peter McCreery	2-38	0-1	2-23	0-14	5.3	- 25.90
Pat O'Leary	2-38	0-2	0-8	2-28	5.3	- 19.00
J E Mulhern	2-44	0-5	2-25	0-14	4.5	- 28.00
J C Hayden	2-47	0-14	1-23	1-10	4.3	- 36.25
F Berry	2-51	0-0	0-27	2-24	3.9	- 25.00
W P Mullins	2-58	0-0	1-10	1-48	3.4	- 41.00
Liam Browne	2-77	1-22	1-38	0-17	2.6	- 66.00
F Boutin (Fra)	1-1	0-0	1-1	0-0	100.0	+ 0.90
P A Kelleway (Eng)	1-1	1-1	0-0	0-0	100.0	+ 20.00
H Ibrahim (UAE)	1-1	0-0	1-1	0-0	100.0	+ 5.00
B W Hills (Eng)	1-2	0-0	1-1	0-1	50.0	+ 1.50
M Bell (Eng)	1-2	1-2	0-0	0-0	50.0	+ 4.50
C E Brittain (Eng)	1-3	0-0	0-1	1-2	33.3	+ 0.50
B Hanbury (Eng)	1-3	0-0	0-1	1-2	33.3	+ 1.50
E M O'Sullivan	1-3	0-0	0-0	1-3	33.3	+ 10.00
Andrew Lee	1-4	1-3	0-0	0-1	25.0	+ 1.50
Mrs John Harrington	1-5	0-0	0-0	1-5	20.0	+ 3.00
M R Stoute (Eng)	1-5	0-0	0-1	1-4	20.0	- 0.50
Mrs P Collier	1-5	0-0	0-0	1-5	20.0	0.00
P Chapple-Hyam (Eng)	1-5	0-2	1-2	0-1	20.0	- 2.75
E J Kearns	1-6	0-0	0-0	1-6	16.7	+ 5.00
J H M Gosden (Eng)	1-6	0-0	0-1	1-5	16.7	- 4.00
John W Nicholson	1-6	0-1	1-5	0-0	16.7	+ 7.00
J L Hassett	1-7	0-0	1-3	0-4	14.3	- 3.00
J Berry (Eng)	1-7	0-2	0-1	1-4	14.3	- 4.00
M R Channon (Eng)	1-7	0-3	1-4	0-0	14.3	- 3.00
F Sutherland	1-7	0-6	0-0	1-1	14.3	+ 4.00
M Robinson	1-8	1-7	0-0	0-1	12.5	+ 7.00
S Fahey	1-9	0-0	0-0	1-9	11.1	+ 2.00
S Treacy	1-10	0-0	1-8	0-2	10.0	- 3.00
M Brew	1-10	0-1	0-5	1-4	10.0	- 6.50
N Cassidy	1-10	0-0	0-0	1-10	10.0	+ 11.00
M J Byrne	1-10	0-0	1-7	0-3	10.0	- 4.50
J G Murphy	1-11	0-2	0-4	1-5	9.1	0.00
R J Cotter	1-13	0-5	0-0	1-8	7.7	- 5.00
F J Lacy	1-13	0-0	0-9	1-4	7.7	- 8.00
G A Cusack	1-13	1-10	0-0	0-3	7.7	- 11.00
J L Dunlop (Eng)	1-14	0-2	1-4	0-8	7.1	- 10.50
A A Hambly	1-14	1-2	0-8	0-4	7.1	- 6.00
A D Evans	1-15	0-0	0-0	1-15	6.7	0.00
D Carroll	1-18	0-0	0-10	1-8	5.6	- 3.00
B Lawlor	1-19	0-2	0-0	1-17	5.3	- 11.00
T M Walsh	1-20	0-5	1-3	0-12	5.0	- 15.00
G M Lyons	1-20	1-12	0-0	0-8	5.0	- 11.00
Francis Ennis	1-22	0-6	0-2	1-14	4.5	- 16.00
Peadar Matthews	1-23	0-6	1-9	0-8	4.3	- 6.00
John J Walsh	1-25	0-2	0-11	1-12	4.0	- 19.00
K F O'Sullivan	1-27	0-11	1-16	0-0	3.7	- 18.50
D T Hughes	1-28	0-6	0-0	1-22	3.6	- 24.50
F Dunne	1-35	0-14	1-10	0-11	2.9	- 29.50
T F Lacy	1-37	0-10	0-6	1-21	2.7	- 31.50
T Kinane	1-41	0-0	1-40	0-1	2.4	- 28.00
Neil S McGrath	1-41	1-12	0-29	0-0	2.4	- 28.00
B V Kelly	1-45	1-15	0-18	0-12	2.2	- 11.00
J T Gorman	1-85	0-17	1-45	0-23	1.2	- 80.50

WINNING FLAT JOCKEYS IN IRELAND 1994

	1st	2nd	3rd	Unpl	Total Mts	Per cent	£1 Level Stake
M J Kinane	84	72	49	163	368	22.8	- 74.92
K J Manning	80	65	54	247	446	17.9	- 63.06
C Roche	48	45	38	198	329	14.6	- 86.76
J P Murtagh	45	34	31	118	228	19.7	+ 3.94
J F Egan	29	24	30	273	356	8.1	-136.30
P V Gilson	28	35	44	194	301	9.3	-133.93
P Shanahan	25	22	29	220	296	8.4	-163.27
W J Supple	24	39	41	318	422	5.7	-263.25
S Craine	23	24	25	238	310	7.4	-157.60
N G McCullagh	22	25	34	207	288	7.6	- 95.75
W J O'Connor	21	41	21	192	275	7.6	-147.04
D J O'Donohoe	18	13	20	109	160	11.3	- 57.43
J A Heffernan	18	7	12	125	162	11.1	- 3.00
W J Smith	17	14	14	144	189	9.0	- 22.35
P Carberry	15	11	11	116	153	9.8	- 58.80
Joanna Morgan	15	13	13	154	195	7.7	- 50.92
J J Behan	15	15	22	182	234	6.4	-121.37
D G O'Shea	12	10	12	153	187	6.4	-103.52
P J Smullen	11	10	7	116	144	7.6	- 50.50
R Hughes	9	12	15	88	124	7.3	- 44.12
T E Durcan	8	7	4	63	82	9.8	- 8.25
R M Burke	7	9	8	93	117	6.0	- 41.90
B Fenton	6	7	6	65	84	7.1	- 46.67
P P Murphy	6	7	7	104	124	4.8	- 78.50
G M Moylan	6	9	7	113	135	4.4	- 88.50
R Fitzpatrick	5	16	11	111	143	3.5	- 94.00
A P McCoy	4	1	1	10	16	25.0	+ 10.38
L Dettori	4	3	4	15	26	15.4	- 8.60
B Coogan	4	5	4	37	50	8.0	- 29.40
D Hogan	4	5	12	34	55	7.3	- 25.33
J F Clarke	4	3	3	47	57	7.0	- 22.50
L Piggott	3	1	2	1	7	42.9	+ 2.13
Miss L Robinson	3	0	1	0	4	75.0	+ 12.00
Miss F M Crowley	3	1	0	4	8	37.5	+ 7.40
B J Walsh	3	1	3	12	19	15.8	- 4.50
W Carson	3	3	3	16	25	12.0	- 4.00
P M Donohue	3	1	1	26	31	9.7	- 17.00
M Roberts	2	1	0	2	5	40.0	+ 3.00
Paul Eddery	2	1	1	5	9	22.2	+ 5.00
M Duffy	2	1	0	6	9	22.2	- 5.21
C O'Brien	2	2	0	1	5	40.0	+ 11.50
J Weaver	2	1	0	3	6	33.3	+ 19.50
A P O'Brien	2	0	0	3	5	40.0	+ 6.75
Miss U Smyth	2	0	1	3	6	33.3	+ 1.75
J Reid	2	4	4	3	13	15.4	+ 2.25
D M McCullagh	2	1	1	8	12	16.7	+ 0.50
M J Cullen	2	0	1	29	32	6.3	- 21.50
S P Kelly	2	2	3	50	57	3.5	- 42.00
Pat Eddery	1	0	0	2	3	33.3	+ 0.50
G Mosse	1	1	0	2	4	25.0	- 2.20
M Fenton	1	0	0	2	3	33.3	+ 3.50
L Cummins	1	0	0	5	6	16.7	+ 5.00
L J Fleming	1	0	0	7	8	12.5	- 4.50

	1st	2nd	3rd	Unpl	Total Mts	Per cent	£1 Level Stake
K P Gaule	1	0	0	7	8	12.5	+ 3.00
M J Grassick	1	0	0	0	1	100.0	+ 3.50
A E Lacy	1	0	0	0	1	100.0	+ 4.00
Mrs F A O'Sullivan	1	0	0	0	1	100.0	+ 12.00
G J Harford	1	0	0	1	2	50.0	+ 2.00
S P Hennessy	1	0	0	1	2	50.0	+ 1.25
F Cooper	1	0	1	0	2	50.0	+ 13.00
P M Kelly	1	1	0	1	3	33.3	+ 5.00
T J Beattie	1	0	0	2	3	33.3	+ 18.00
Mrs C Doyle	1	0	1	3	5	20.0	+ 10.00
E Norris	1	0	0	5	6	16.7	- 3.25
D Marnane	1	3	3	2	9	11.1	+ 8.00
W R Swinburn	1	2	3	4	10	10.0	0.00
G Dickie	1	1	0	10	12	8.3	- 3.00
L O'Shea	1	0	0	12	13	7.7	- 1.00
D Quirke	1	0	0	12	13	7.7	- 6.00
D O'Callaghan	1	1	1	14	17	5.9	- 8.00
D A O'Sullivan	1	0	1	16	18	5.6	- 7.00
D J Smith	1	4	4	10	19	5.3	- 6.00
R V Skelly	1	0	2	18	21	4.8	- 8.00
T P Treacy	1	0	3	21	25	4.0	- 12.00
J R Barry	1	7	5	20	33	3.0	- 25.00
B J Halligan	1	0	0	34	35	2.9	- 28.00
E Ahern	1	3	4	28	36	2.8	- 27.00
G Coogan	1	5	3	37	46	2.2	- 41.00
C Everard	1	2	2	46	51	2.0	- 48.75
A J Nolan	1	0	1	61	63	1.6	- 46.00

LEADING TRAINERS' AND OWNERS' PRIZE MONEY 1994

	Races Won	Value £		Races Won	Value £
D K Weld	100	640,959	Maktoum Al Maktoum	11	390,938
J S Bolger	108	607,225	Dr Michael Smurfit	20	224,039
John M Oxx	63	349,085	Moyglare Stud Farm	30	198,180
H Ibrahim (UAE)	1	348,000	Mrs Catherine Shubotham	12	171,052
A P O'Brien	47	197,651	H H Aga Khan	34	167,394
C Collins	29	135,716	Sheikh Mohammed	26	165,826
P Chapple-Hyam (Eng)	1	131,550	Hamdan Al-Maktoum	12	145,982
B W Hills (Eng)	1	130,850	R E Sangster	2	136,688
P J Flynn	27	112,057	K Abdullah	1	130,850
M S Johnston (Eng)	3	103,750	Mrs J S Bolger	26	115,634
J L Dunlop (Eng)	1	98,550	Godolphin	2	112,175
M R Stoute (Eng)	1	97,800	M Doyle	1	74,000
K Prendergast	25	89,067	L J Rice	1	65,100
Noel Meade	21	75,350	D H W Dobson	15	52,991
M Kauntze	14	72,857	N Keating	6	48,605
P A Kelleway (Eng)	1	65,100	Sheikh Ahmed Al Maktoum	5	45,626
T Stack	19	57,548	Mitsuo Haga	5	36,740
P Prendergast	7	41,957	Ballylinch Stud	6	32,005
R Hannon (Eng)	2	37,375	Mrs A M O'Brien	10	31,871
Charles O'Brien	5	33,597	Mrs Anne Coughlan	3	31,490

LEADING IRISH TRAINERS FIRST TIME OUT 1990-94

	Total W-R	2-y-o	3-y-o	4-y-o+	Per cent	£1 Level Stake
J S Bolger	127-693	65-273	36-269	26-151	18.3	-196.24
John M Oxx	112-494	39-152	69-309	4-33	22.7	+ 36.63
D K Weld	103-720	42-263	41-294	20-163	14.3	-290.14
T Stack	25-251	6-77	9-125	10-49	10.0	- 75.52
M Kauntze	22-185	11-81	9-82	2-22	11.9	- 56.04
K Prendergast	17-340	7-144	6-148	4-48	5.0	-197.52
C Collins	16-240	6-86	7-101	3-53	6.7	- 95.28
M J Grassick	12-151	3-45	6-64	3-42	7.9	- 49.75
P J Flynn	10-184	1-42	3-58	6-84	5.4	-138.73
A P O'Brien	8-103	1-33	2-30	5-40	7.8	- 52.77
Noel Meade	8-231	3-75	3-87	2-69	3.5	-177.25
D Hanley	7-51	1-19	4-24	2-8	13.7	+ 7.50
B V Kelly	7-83	2-26	3-33	2-24	8.4	+ 14.00
Daniel J Murphy	7-91	2-30	3-37	2-24	7.7	- 24.50
F Flood	5-23	1-3	1-3	3-17	21.7	+ 21.25
J Burns	5-76	2-29	1-33	2-14	6.6	- 34.25
F Dunne	5-84	0-28	0-35	5-21	6.0	- 34.50
P Mullins	5-103	0-15	2-26	3-62	4.9	- 40.00

LEADING IRISH TRAINERS BY MONTH 1990-94

March/April

	Total W-R	2-y-o	3-y-o	4-y-o+	Per cent	£1 Level Stake
J S Bolger	77-316	19-41	41-194	17-81	24.4	+ 47.56
John M Oxx	34-186	0-1	33-167	1-18	18.3	- 16.61
D K Weld	33-326	4-25	25-215	4-86	10.1	-205.39
T Stack	18-161	0-9	8-102	10-50	11.2	- 46.29
C Collins	16-196	2-22	10-127	4-47	8.2	- 48.95
K Prendergast	16-227	3-27	9-147	4-53	7.0	-107.77
M Kauntze	13-87	0-4	11-67	2-16	14.9	+ 10.75
P J Flynn	10-77	0-0	5-37	5-40	13.0	- 16.75
Noel Meade	9-134	1-14	8-91	0-29	6.7	- 79.00
B V Kelly	6-46	0-0	3-25	3-21	13.0	+ 18.50
Daniel J Murphy	4-37	0-3	3-24	1-10	10.8	- 14.00
M Halford	4-60	0-4	4-44	0-12	6.7	- 30.50
E J O'Grady	4-69	0-1	3-40	1-28	5.8	- 55.85
Liam Browne	4-84	1-10	3-59	0-15	4.8	- 58.20
Pat O'Leary	3-30	0-2	2-19	1-9	10.0	- 3.00
J T Gorman	3-43	0-7	1-29	2-7	7.0	+ 11.00
P Prendergast	3-62	0-6	0-34	3-22	4.8	- 28.50

May

	Total W-R	2-y-o	3-y-o	4-y-o+	Per cent	£1 Level Stake
D K Weld	76-357	7-53	50-199	19-105	21.3	- 43.67
J S Bolger	56-348	17-72	22-174	17-102	16.1	-103.56
John M Oxx	42-183	1-6	37-162	4-15	23.0	- 19.05
T Stack	21-173	1-17	14-111	6-45	12.1	- 61.27
K Prendergast	18-251	4-47	12-159	2-45	7.2	-135.42
C Collins	16-146	8-30	6-76	2-40	11.0	- 71.24
M J Grassick	14-94	1-9	7-57	6-28	14.9	- 10.95
Noel Meade	13-139	1-14	7-85	5-40	9.4	- 60.99
M Kauntze	12-131	4-25	7-87	1-19	9.2	- 60.23
P J Flynn	11-130	0-1	3-57	8-72	8.5	- 63.96
Liam Browne	10-84	4-19	5-50	1-15	11.9	- 15.75
J J McLoughlin	8-66	1-6	5-36	2-24	12.1	- 11.75
A P O'Brien	7-52	2-5	1-23	4-24	13.5	- 8.60
Augustine Leahy	7-82	1-13	4-45	2-24	8.5	- 42.92
J C Harley	5-31	1-6	1-8	3-17	16.1	+ 9.60
P Prendergast	5-51	3-16	0-20	2-15	9.8	- 27.20
F Dunne	5-51	1-6	2-29	2-16	9.8	- 4.00
Daniel J Murphy	5-65	1-5	2-40	2-20	7.7	- 20.50
M A O'Toole	5-71	0-10	2-35	3-26	7.0	- 29.10
D Gillespie	5-86	3-20	1-51	1-15	5.8	- 51.25

June

	Total W-R	2-y-o	3-y-o	4-y-o+	Per cent	£1 Level Stake
J S Bolger	72-424	26-96	34-213	12-115	17.0	-104.55
D K Weld	65-397	13-76	35-224	17-97	16.4	-131.32
John M Oxx	55-240	2-16	52-201	1-23	22.9	+ 24.36
K Prendergast	30-318	5-62	22-196	3-60	9.4	-142.02
C Collins	19-130	7-27	8-68	4-35	14.6	- 12.62
T Stack	18-171	3-22	14-114	1-35	10.5	- 66.87
Noel Meade	16-136	3-24	8-73	5-39	11.8	- 35.33
A P O'Brien	15-77	0-8	10-31	5-38	19.5	+ 10.38
P J Flynn	12-114	1-14	4-46	7-54	10.5	- 60.57
D Gillespie	10-85	2-18	5-50	3-17	11.8	- 24.77
J J McLoughlin	8-77	0-11	6-39	2-27	10.4	- 35.18
M J Grassick	8-77	0-10	4-42	4-25	10.4	- 41.95
W P Mullins	7-57	0-8	3-16	4-33	12.3	- 15.25
E J O'Grady	7-60	2-12	3-33	2-15	11.7	- 6.00
P Mullins	7-64	0-1	0-22	7-41	10.9	+ 4.25
F Dunne	7-77	1-20	3-39	3-18	9.1	+ 7.00
M Kauntze	7-107	3-21	4-65	0-21	6.5	- 85.33
Edward Lynam	6-66	1-11	2-41	3-14	9.1	- 26.50
Charles O'Brien	5-23	0-5	4-15	1-3	21.7	- 2.90
P Prendergast	5-46	2-9	1-21	2-16	10.9	- 15.67
Liam Browne	5-106	3-36	2-56	0-14	4.7	- 66.00

July

	Total W-R	2-y-o	3-y-o	4-y-o+	Per cent	£1 Level Stake
D K Weld	105-499	27-125	48-247	30-127	21.0	- 75.05
J S Bolger	95-463	36-125	39-217	20-121	20.5	- 64.40
John M Oxx	60-261	8-33	49-209	3-19	23.0	- 48.67
K Prendergast	29-354	10-91	15-201	4-62	8.2	-152.42
Noel Meade	21-161	5-26	10-89	6-46	13.0	- 38.32
A P O'Brien	19-112	2-18	9-59	8-35	17.0	- 8.20
C Collins	17-147	3-28	7-84	7-35	11.6	- 34.00
P J Flynn	15-119	3-14	4-40	8-65	12.6	- 23.83
T Stack	15-148	2-24	9-92	4-32	10.1	- 72.30
M J Grassick	12-83	3-16	8-46	1-21	14.5	- 16.85
D Gillespie	12-116	1-31	10-65	1-20	10.3	- 32.37
M Kauntze	12-119	5-34	5-62	2-23	10.1	- 68.35
M A O'Toole	10-99	1-14	5-55	4-30	10.1	- 22.83
E J O'Grady	9-77	2-17	4-47	3-13	11.7	+ 5.75
J J McLoughlin	9-105	1-19	8-54	0-32	8.6	- 18.00
Liam Browne	8-91	6-36	2-42	0-13	8.8	- 45.77
B V Kelly	7-60	2-16	2-27	3-17	11.7	+ 24.00
P Prendergast	6-51	1-12	3-24	2-15	11.8	- 17.40
J G Coogan	6-65	3-25	2-33	1-7	9.2	- 33.25
F Dunne	6-88	0-25	2-34	4-29	6.8	- 53.17
M Cunningham	5-47	1-5	0-14	4-28	10.6	- 16.17
Edward Lynam	5-80	0-18	3-52	2-10	6.3	- 54.00

August

	Total W-R	2-y-o	3-y-o	4-y-o+	Per cent	£1 Level Stake
D K Weld	109-550	24-145	55-265	30-140	19.8	-174.72
J S Bolger	88-534	57-187	22-238	9-109	16.5	-132.89
John M Oxx	79-286	14-52	63-220	2-14	27.6	+ 15.01
K Prendergast	47-381	9-106	28-225	10-50	12.3	-115.04
T Stack	26-186	4-52	15-105	7-29	14.0	- 30.20
C Collins	21-166	3-45	14-90	4-31	12.7	- 76.15
M Kauntze	19-131	6-44	11-68	2-19	14.5	0.00
Noel Meade	14-131	4-33	6-73	4-25	10.7	- 50.67
A P O'Brien	13-90	1-13	7-47	5-30	14.4	- 24.62
J J McLoughlin	13-114	1-20	9-57	3-37	11.4	- 14.75
P J Flynn	13-119	2-22	4-42	7-55	10.9	- 43.50
M J Grassick	12-87	5-25	5-42	2-20	13.8	- 7.77
P Mullins	9-65	0-17	3-21	6-27	13.8	- 24.63
P Prendergast	9-74	1-20	4-26	4-28	12.2	- 27.07
D Gillespie	9-88	2-30	6-44	1-14	10.2	- 38.90
W P Mullins	8-52	0-8	3-11	5-33	15.4	- 1.00
Augustine Leahy	8-89	0-25	7-37	1-27	9.0	- 37.50
M A O'Toole	8-94	2-16	4-54	2-24	8.5	- 30.50
F Dunne	7-99	0-30	3-40	4-29	7.1	- 50.00
J Burns	6-42	1-13	4-20	1-9	14.3	+ 7.00
J M Canty	6-57	0-9	1-22	5-26	10.5	- 24.00
Liam Browne	6-112	4-65	1-35	1-12	5.4	- 79.27
E P Harty	5-32	1-9	3-11	1-12	15.6	+ 24.00
J E Mulhern	5-57	1-10	1-23	3-24	8.8	- 4.17
Daniel J Murphy	5-61	1-9	3-39	1-13	8.2	- 18.43

September

	Total W-R	2-y-o	3-y-o	4-y-o+	Per cent	£1 Level Stake
D K Weld	72-390	36-137	24-161	12-92	18.5	- 102.11
John M Oxx	57-285	19-93	38-177	0-15	20.0	- 3.89
J S Bolger	50-397	26-164	16-161	8-72	12.6	-126.14
K Prendergast	25-247	9-83	14-124	2-40	10.1	- 57.53
M Kauntze	18-102	9-41	7-48	2-13	17.6	- 5.08
T Stack	15-125	5-45	9-64	1-16	12.0	- 41.62
P J Flynn	13-158	1-42	7-64	5-52	8.2	- 56.52
Noel Meade	12-120	3-53	7-46	2-21	10.0	- 20.47
C Collins	11-132	4-42	6-64	1-26	8.3	- 59.00
D Gillespie	8-91	2-32	5-49	1-10	8.8	- 44.37
F Dunne	7-56	0-17	4-23	3-16	12.5	+ 1.75
M Halford	7-64	0-20	6-27	1-17	10.9	- 14.50
J J McLoughlin	6-123	3-34	0-63	3-26	4.9	- 82.00
P Prendergast	5-44	1-17	4-14	0-13	11.4	- 15.20
Augustine Leahy	5-65	0-28	4-23	1-14	7.7	- 29.17
Liam Browne	5-80	2-49	2-19	1-12	6.3	- 39.22

October/November

	Total W-R	2-y-o	3-y-o	4-y-o+	Per cent	£1 Level Stake
J S Bolger	82-482	46-236	27-176	9-70	17.0	- 79.87
John M Oxx	59-303	39-154	20-144	0-5	19.5	- 64.46
D K Weld	57-446	24-183	16-168	17-95	12.8	-127.53
K Prendergast	25-373	8-155	11-165	6-53	6.7	-186.02
P J Flynn	23-197	4-71	10-65	9-61	11.7	- 22.27
M Kauntze	10-133	5-66	4-58	1-9	7.5	- 70.45
T Stack	9-105	3-57	6-35	0-13	8.6	- 40.52
C Collins	8-175	3-65	2-74	3-36	4.6	-106.50
A P O'Brien	7-90	1-48	2-24	4-18	7.8	- 51.00
J J McLoughlin	7-122	2-43	4-46	1-33	5.7	- 49.25
D Hanley	6-48	1-19	5-26	0-3	12.5	- 20.65
M J Grassick	6-124	2-52	4-50	0-22	4.8	- 75.27
Noel Meade	6-160	0-68	3-71	3-21	3.8	-117.25
Liam Browne	5-97	4-62	1-22	0-13	5.2	- 50.00

LEADING IRISH TRAINERS BY TYPE OF RACE 1990-94

2-y-o Non-Handicaps

	W-R	Per cent	£1 Level Stake		W-R	Per cent	£1 Level Stake
J S Bolger	202-809	25.0	- 158.94	D K Weld	123-669	18.4	-263.98
John M Oxx	83-341	24.3	- 26.61	K Prendergast	42-493	8.5	-203.80
M Kauntze	28-212	13.2	- 82.64	C Collins	28-235	11.9	- 70.86
Liam Browne	23-252	9.1	- 91.64	T Stack	15-204	7.4	-109.27
Noel Meade	15-206	7.3	- 113.25	M J Grassick	12-123	9.8	- 53.02
J G Coogan	11-138	8.0	- 71.75	P J Flynn	9-140	6.4	- 79.83
D Gillespie	9-158	5.7	- 100.54	P Prendergast	7-95	7.4	- 74.49
J C Hayden	6-83	7.2	- 55.45	E J O'Grady	6-103	5.8	- 52.25

3-y-o Non-Handicaps

	W-R	Per cent	£1 Level Stake		W-R	Per cent	£1 Level Stake
John M Oxx	218-882	24.7	- 43.58	D K Weld	182-903	20.2	-204.05
J S Bolger	130-870	14.9	- 230.18	K Prendergast	59-658	9.0	-354.37
T Stack	51-392	13.0	- 129.70	C Collins	40-393	10.2	-175.01
Noel Meade	27-250	10.8	- 83.49	M Kauntze	26-235	11.1	- 89.08
M J Grassick	18-200	9.0	- 64.82	Liam Browne	14-189	7.4	- 98.97
A P O'Brien	13-101	12.9	- 34.27	P J Flynn	13-145	9.0	- 56.00
D Hanley	12-70	17.1	- 4.65	D Gillespie	12-153	7.8	- 83.10
F Dunne	10-110	9.1	- 38.25	Daniel J Murphy	9-98	9.2	- 26.93
Charles O'Brien	9-99	9.1	- 61.65	M Halford	7-109	6.4	- 62.25
P Mullins	6-75	8.0	- 33.33	P Aspell	6-76	7.9	- 17.75
P Prendergast	6-83	7.2	- 63.40	B V Kelly	6-91	6.6	- 52.92
Augustine Leahy	6-114	5.3	- 74.92	Edward Lynam	6-135	4.4	- 98.67
J G Coogan	5-84	6.0	- 45.15	M A O'Toole	5-104	4.8	- 74.10
J Burns	5-105	4.8	- 62.00				

4-y-o+ Non-Handicaps

	W-R	Per cent	£1 Level Stake		W-R	Per cent	£1 Level Stake
D K Weld	55-222	24.8	- 6.08	J S Bolger	30-213	14.1	- 97.36
T Stack	12-83	14.5	- 25.65	P J Flynn	12-92	13.0	- 35.62
Noel Meade	10-59	16.9	+ 7.78	M J Grassick	8-50	16.0	- 0.70
A P O'Brien	8-63	12.7	- 19.77	M Kauntze	5-40	12.5	- 13.97
John M Oxx	5-41	12.2	- 2.25	P Mullins	5-44	11.4	- 8.13
K Prendergast	5-55	9.1	- 39.87				

Apprentice Non-Handicaps

	W-R	Per cent	£1 Level Stake		W-R	Per cent	£1 Level Stake
John M Oxx	3-5	60.0	+ 4.32	D K Weld	3-26	11.5	- 3.00
P Mullins	2-5	40.0	+ 13.00				

Amateur Non-Handicaps

	W-R	Per cent	£1 Level Stake		W-R	Per cent	£1 Level Stake
D K Weld	12-61	19.7	- 13.50	J S Bolger	10-72	13.9	- 32.19
John M Oxx	8-25	32.0	+ 11.08	M Kauntze	6-18	33.3	+ 12.75
T Stack	6-27	22.2	- 1.35	C Collins	4-16	25.0	+ 9.73
P J Flynn	4-20	20.0	- 9.75	F Dunne	4-23	17.4	+ 24.00
Noel Meade	3-13	23.1	- 5.88				

2-y-o Handicaps

	W-R	Per cent	£1 Level Stake		W-R	Per cent	£1 Level Stake
J S Bolger	25-110	22.7	+ 28.97	D K Weld	12-75	16.0	- 20.87
K Prendergast	6-77	7.8	- 41.77	M A O'Toole	4-14	28.6	+ 29.25
M Kauntze	4-23	17.4	+ 2.75	J J McLoughlin	4-25	16.0	+ 11.00
W P Mullins	3-14	21.4	+ 12.00	P Prendergast	3-19	15.8	+ 15.00
T Stack	3-22	13.6	- 6.50	E J O'Grady	3-27	11.1	+ 6.00
A P O'Brien	2-17	11.8	+ 5.00	Augustine Leahy	2-23	8.7	- 7.00
C Collins	2-24	8.3	- 6.50	P J Flynn	2-24	8.3	- 7.50
Noel Meade	2-26	7.7	- 15.50				

3-y-o Handicaps

	W-R	Per cent	£1 Level Stake		W-R	Per cent	£1 Level Stake
J S Bolger	64-438	14.6	- 46.98	John M Oxx	62-355	17.5	- 0.02
D K Weld	61-484	12.6	- 172.94	K Prendergast	46-500	9.2	- 136.42
J J McLoughlin	27-201	13.4	- 19.43	P J Flynn	23-189	12.2	- 23.25
Noel Meade	21-251	8.4	- 93.40	T Stack	19-196	9.7	- 71.10
A P O'Brien	18-113	15.9	- 4.22	M Kauntze	16-193	8.3	- 57.83
D Gillespie	15-160	9.4	- 61.62	Augustine Leahy	12-88	13.6	- 22.42
C Collins	12-173	6.9	- 89.25	M J Grassick	9-113	8.0	- 54.00
M A O'Toole	9-115	7.8	- 38.50	E J O'Grady	9-140	6.4	- 73.43
W P Mullins	8-49	16.3	- 1.00	P Prendergast	7-59	11.9	- 4.62
B V Kelly	7-82	8.5	- 12.50	M Halford	7-106	6.6	- 61.00
Edward Lynam	7-146	4.8	- 74.00	J T Gorman	6-101	5.9	- 40.50
Daniel J Murphy	6-106	5.7	- 45.50	E P Harty	5-29	17.2	- 5.00

4-y-o+ Handicaps

	W-R	Per cent	£1 Level Stake		W-R	Per cent	£1 Level Stake
D K Weld	64-426	15.0	- 102.37	J S Bolger	49-371	13.2	- 10.80
P J Flynn	28-253	11.1	- 62.95	K Prendergast	22-254	8.7	- 64.50
C Collins	17-181	9.4	- 37.20	A P O'Brien	16-85	18.8	- 4.15
F Dunne	14-91	15.4	+ 18.83	T Stack	11-105	10.5	- 7.00
J M Canty	11-133	8.3	- 56.25	P Prendergast	9-81	11.1	+ 10.10
M Cunningham	8-67	11.9	- 22.92	W P Mullins	8-95	8.4	- 44.25
Noel Meade	8-132	6.1	- 81.54	E J O'Grady	7-48	14.6	+ 15.50
J C Harley	7-68	10.3	- 10.40	P Mullins	7-107	6.5	- 62.17
M A O'Toole	7-111	6.3	- 43.50	J J McLoughlin	7-143	4.9	- 74.50
D P Kelly	6-46	13.0	+ 20.50	B V Kelly	6-91	6.6	- 28.00
T M Walsh	5-35	14.3	+ 27.00	Edward Lynam	5-41	12.2	- 5.00
D G McArdle	5-49	10.2	+ 18.00	M Kauntze	5-72	6.9	- 35.67
T F Lacy	5-81	6.2	- 43.50				

Apprentice Handicaps

	W-R	Per cent	£1 Level Stake		W-R	Per cent	£1 Level Stake
J S Bolger	8-55	14.5	- 0.37	M J Grassick	5-40	12.5	+ 4.50
D Gillespie	4-31	12.9	- 7.60	P J Flynn	4-33	12.1	- 3.00
K Prendergast	4-76	5.3	- 44.42	D K Weld	4-86	4.7	- 64.00
John M Oxx	3-21	14.3	- 10.25	D T Hughes	3-23	13.0	+ 2.50
T F Lacy	3-26	11.5	- 6.00	J J McLoughlin	3-26	11.5	- 4.00
T Stack	3-26	11.5	- 9.50	C Collins	3-32	9.4	- 6.50

Amateur Handicaps

	W-R	Per cent	£1 Level Stake		W-R	Per cent	£1 Level Stake
K Prendergast	3-10	30.0	+ 4.13	W Fennin	2-5	40.0	+ 5.00
F Flood	2-6	33.3	+ 9.00	M Cunningham	2-7	28.6	+ 3.25
A P O'Brien	2-9	22.2	+ 1.90	Noel Meade	2-10	20.0	+ 1.50
D Gillespie	2-10	20.0	+ 5.10	P J Flynn	2-17	11.8	- 8.50
J S Bolger	2-19	10.5	- 9.00				

LEADING IRISH TRAINERS' FAVOURITES 1990-1994

	W-R	Per cent	£1 Level Stake	% of Runners that Started Favourite	% of Winners that Started Favourite
D K Weld	280-791	35.4	- 83.10	26.7	54.2
J S Bolger	251-609	41.2	- 27.12	20.5	48.3
John M Oxx	217-478	45.4	+ 64.56	27.4	56.2
K Prendergast	54-209	25.8	- 46.41	9.7	28.4
T Stack	38-101	37.6	+ 6.60	9.4	31.1
C Collins	37-100	37.0	+ 11.49	9.2	34.3
M Kauntze	35-103	34.0	- 18.52	12.7	38.5
P J Flynn	32-91	35.2	+ 13.35	10.0	33.0
A P O'Brien	29-70	41.4	+ 17.02	13.5	43.3
Noel Meade	24-85	28.2	- 22.86	8.7	26.4
M J Grassick	15-36	41.7	+ 4.46	5.7	25.9
P Prendergast	15-47	31.9	- 5.86	12.1	40.5
D Gillespie	14-45	31.1	- 7.37	7.1	29.8
J J McLoughlin	11-29	37.9	+ 3.32	4.3	21.2
M A O'Toole	9-37	24.3	- 12.43	7.5	27.3
Liam Browne	9-37	24.3	- 16.34	5.7	20.9
E J O'Grady	8-25	32.0	- 6.63	5.1	25.0
P Mullins	8-27	29.6	- 3.71	6.6	28.6
Augustine Leahy	8-30	26.7	- 2.92	6.1	27.6
J G Coogan	7-19	36.8	+ 2.60	5.2	31.8
Edward Lynam	7-28	25.0	+ 4.00	5.5	30.4
M Cunningham	6-9	66.7	+ 6.92	3.4	37.5
J M Canty	6-21	28.6	- 1.01	6.2	26.1
Charles O'Brien	6-26	23.1	- 11.55	16.0	40.0
E P Harty	5-9	55.6	+ 6.30	5.6	45.5
J C Hayden	5-15	33.3	- 0.95	4.2	26.3
M A McCullagh	4-5	80.0	+ 11.00	8.8	57.1
D Hanley	4-11	36.4	+ 6.35	6.5	18.2
W P Mullins	4-13	30.8	+ 2.00	4.1	15.4
M Halford	4-17	23.5	- 0.75	4.3	18.2
B V Kelly	4-19	21.1	- 2.75	4.9	16.7
T F Lacy	3-5	60.0	+ 3.75	1.4	23.1
W P Browne	3-9	33.3	- 3.33	11.8	75.0
J C Harley	3-10	30.0	- 0.75	5.1	21.4
J E Mulhern	3-17	17.6	- 6.00	6.3	20.0
K F O'Sullivan	2-2	100.0	+ 5.33	2.3	40.0
M Hourigan	2-3	66.7	+ 2.00	5.7	28.6
Anthony Mullins	2-3	66.7	+ 3.75	2.6	40.0
T A Regan	2-5	40.0	+ 2.25	3.7	40.0
F Flood	2-5	40.0	- 0.85	7.1	22.2
J E Kiely	2-5	40.0	- 0.25	12.8	100.0
P Hughes	2-7	28.6	- 2.08	7.8	40.0
T M Walsh	2-10	20.0	- 5.10	7.3	20.0
F Dunne	2-13	15.4	- 6.25	2.9	6.1
Daniel J Murphy	2-16	12.5	- 11.68	4.3	7.7
D T Hughes	2-21	9.5	- 12.50	8.4	15.4

TRAINER TIPS FOR 1995

J Berry	-	Runners in March
H R A Cecil	-	Runners at Royal Ascot
P Chapple-Hyam	-	Two-year-olds at Ayr and Newbury
R Charlton	-	Runners in June
L M Cumani	-	Runners at Brighton
J L Dunlop	-	Runners at Thirsk
J H M Gosden	-	Runners in September
B Hanbury	-	Runners at Hamilton
D R Loder	-	Two-year-olds at Beverley
Lord Huntingdon	-	Older horses in non-handicaps
Sir Mark Prescott	-	Runners at Carlisle
Favourites	-	All-aged handicaps at York

TRAINER INDEX

COURSE INDEX

Ring ASM Ltd for all
Sporting Life publications
(01536) 762860

NOTES

NOTES

NOTES

NOTES

NOTES

NOTES

Ring ASM Ltd for all
Sporting Life publications
(01536) 762 860

NOTES

NOTES

NOTES

NOTES

NOTES

NOTES

NOTES

NOTES

NOTES

Ring ASM Ltd for all
Sporting Life publications
(01536) 762860